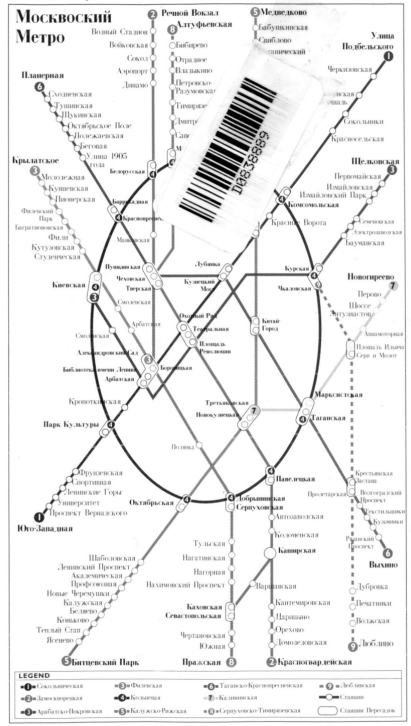

Москвоский Метро

Москвоский Метро

Речной Вокзал
Медведково

Планерная

Крылатское

Щёлковская

Новогиреево

Киевская

Улица Подбельского

Юго-Западная

Выхино

Битцевский Парк

Пражская

Красногвардейская

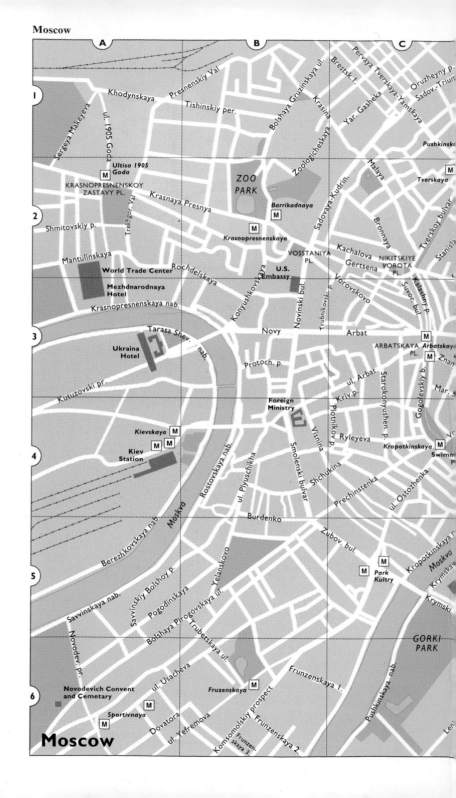

D   E   F

OTECHNAYA PL.
Garden Ring
Sadovaya-Sukh.
TO LENINGRADSKI STATION
Komsomolskaya
Kazan Station

Karetny Ryad
Trubnaya
Tsvetnoy bul.
Sukharevskaya
Sadovaya-Spasskaya
Novokirovskaya
Kalanchevskaya

ras. bul.
Petrovsky bul.
Tsvetnoy Bulvar
Ulanskiy p.
Krasny Vorota
Sad. Cher.

khovskaya
Petrovka
Neglinnaya
TRUBNAYA PL.
Rozh. bul.
Sret. bul.
Myasnitskaya
Christopud. bul.
Chernyshevskovo
Zemlyanoi Val

Pushkin.
Kuznetskiy Most
B. Lubyanka
Lubyan. M.
Myasnitskaya
Krivoko p.
Turgenevskaya
Chistye Prudy

erskaya
Bolshoy
Lubyanka
Maroseika
Pokrovskiy bul.
Kurskaya

Teatralnaya Pl.
Okhotny Ryad
Pl. Revolyutsii
Arkhipova
pr. Serova
Kursk Station

Belinskovo
Okhotny Ryad
GUM
Ilyinka
STARAYA PL.
Podkoloklny p.
Obukha

Mokhov.
RED SQUARE
St. Basil's
Varvarka
Kitai-Gorod
Yauz bul.

eksandrovski Sad
KREMLIN
Rossia Hotel
Serebryaniches. nab.
Bernikovsk. nab.

Biblioteka im.Lenina
skaya
Kremlevskaya nab.
Moskvoretskaya nab.
Ulyanovskaya
Zemlyanoi Val

nab. Morisa Tor.
Raushkaya nab.
Ustin pr.
nab. Maksima Gorkovo

Serafim.
Labaznaya
Osipenko
Kotelnicheskaya nab.

Balch.
Ovchinnikov nab.
Osipenko
TAGANSKAYA PL.

bersanev nab.
Kadas hevsk.nab.
Ordynka Bolshaya
Taganskaya

Bolotnaya nab.
Staromonetnyy per.
Tretyakovskaya
Ozerovskaya nab.
Marksistskaya

Yakiman. nab.
Polyanka Bol.
Novokuznetskaya
Taganskaya

Ostrovskovo A.N.
Zemlyachki
Tatarskaya
Gonch. pr.
Voronsovskaya

Polyanka
Novokiznetskaya
Bakhrushina

e Art Gallery
Central House rtists

Oktyabrskaya
Zatsep. Val
Shlyuzov. nab.

Lenin numont
Zhitnaya
Valovaya
Paveletskaya
Kozhevnicheskaya

tyabrskaya
Dobryninskaya
Serpukhovskaya
Paveletski Station
Krutitskaya nab.

Shabolovka
Mytnaya
Lyusinovskaya
Serpukhovsk. Bol.
Dublininskaya

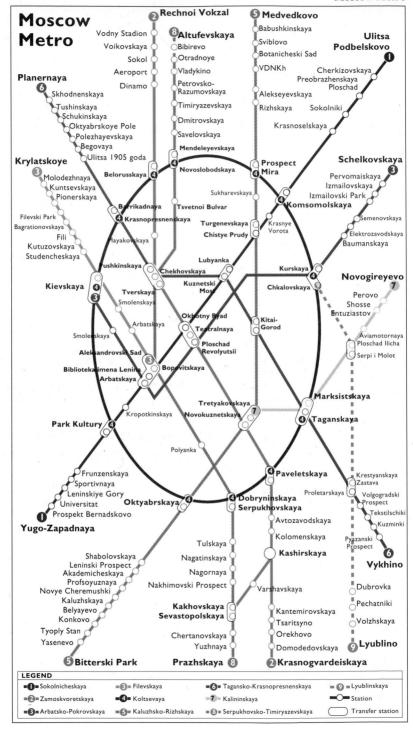

Moscow Metro

Planernaya ⑥
Krylatskoye ③
Kievskaya ④ ③
Park Kultury ④
Yugo-Zapadnaya ①

Vodny Stadion
Voikovskaya
Sokol
Aeroport
Dinamo
Skhodnenskaya
Tushinskaya
Schukinskaya
Oktyabrskoye Pole
Polezhayevskaya
Begovaya
Ulitsa 1905 goda
Molodezhnaya
Kuntsevskaya
Pionerskaya
Filevski Park
Bagrationovskaya
Fili
Kutuzovskaya
Studencheskaya

Belorusskaya ④
Barrikadnaya
Krasnopresnenskaya ④
Mayakovskaya
Pushkinskaya
Tverskaya
Smolenskaya
Arbatskaya
Smolenskaya
Aleksandrovski Sad
Biblioteka imena Lenina
Arbatskaya
Kropotkinskaya

Rechnoi Vokzal ②
Altufevskaya ⑧
Bibirevo
Otradnoye
Vladykino
Petrovsko-Razumovskaya
Timiryazevskaya
Dmitrovskaya
Savelovskaya
Mendeleyevskaya
Novoslobodskaya ④
Tsvetnoi Bulvar
Sukharevskaya
Turgenevskaya
Chistye Prudy
Lubyanka
Chekhovskaya
Kuznetski Most
Okhotny Ryad
Teatralnaya
Ploschad Revolyutsii
Borovitskaya
Tretyakovskaya ⑦
Novokuznetskaya
Polyanka

Medvedkovo ⑤
Babushkinskaya
Sviblovo
Botanicheski Sad
VDNKh
Alekseyevskaya
Rizhskaya
Krasnoselskaya
Prospect Mira ④
Komsomolskaya ④
Krasnye Vorota
Kurskaya ④
Chkalovskaya ⑨
Kitai-Gorod

Ulitsa Podbelskovo ①
Cherkizovskaya
Preobrazhenskaya Ploschad
Sokolniki
Schelkovskaya ③
Pervomaiskaya
Izmailovskaya
Izmailovski Park
Semenovskaya
Elektrozavodskaya
Baumanskaya
Novogireyevo ⑦
Perovo
Shosse Entuziastov
Aviamotornaya
Ploschad Ilicha
Serpi i Molot
Marksistskaya
Taganskaya ④

Frunzenskaya
Sportivnaya
Leninskiye Gory
Universitat
Prospekt Bernadskovo
Oktyabrskaya ④
Shabolovskaya
Leninski Prospect
Akademicheskaya
Profsoyuznaya
Novye Cheremushki
Kaluzhskaya
Belyayevo
Konkovo
Tyoply Stan
Yasenevo
Bitterski Park ⑤

Tulskaya
Nagatinskaya
Nagornaya
Nakhimovski Prospect
Kakhovskaya Sevastopolskaya
Chertanovskaya
Yuzhnaya
Prazhskaya ⑧

Dobryninskaya ④
Serpukhovskaya
Avtozavodskaya
Kolomenskaya
Kashirskaya
Varshavskaya
Kantemirovskaya
Tsaritsyno
Orekhovo
Domodedovskaya
Krasnogvardeiskaya ②

Paveletskaya ④
Proletarskaya
Krestyanskaya Zastava
Volgogradski Prospect
Tekstilshchiki
Kuzminki
Pyazanski Prospect
Vykhino ⑥
Dubrovka
Pechatniki
Volzhskaya
Lyublino ⑨

Let's Go

EASTERN EUROPE

is the best book for anyone traveling on a budget. Here's why:

▓ No other guidebook has as many budget listings.

In Eastern Europe we list over 6,000 budget travel bargains. We tell you the cheapest way to get around, and where to get an inexpensive and satisfying meal once you've arrived. We give hundreds of money-saving tips that anyone can use, plus invaluable advice on discounts and deals for students, children, families, and senior travelers.

▓ Let's Go researchers have to make it on their own.

Our Harvard-Radcliffe researcher-writers travel on budgets as tight as your own—no expense accounts, no free hotel rooms.

▓ Let's Go is completely revised each year.

We don't just update the prices, we go back to the place. If a charming café has become an overpriced tourist trap, we'll replace the listing with a new and better one.

▓ No other guidebook includes all this:

Honest, engaging coverage of both the cities and the countryside; up-to-the-minute prices, directions, addresses, phone numbers, and opening hours; in-depth essays on local culture, history, and politics; comprehensive listings on transportation between and within regions and cities; straight advice on work and study, budget accommodations, sights, nightlife, and food; detailed city and regional maps; and much more.

▓ Let's Go is for anyone who wants to see Eastern Europe on a budget.

Books by Let's Go, Inc.

EUROPE

Let's Go: Europe

Let's Go: Austria & Switzerland

Let's Go: Britain & Ireland

Let's Go: Eastern Europe

Let's Go: France

Let's Go: Germany

Let's Go: Greece & Turkey

Let's Go: Ireland

Let's Go: Italy

Let's Go: London

Let's Go: Paris

Let's Go: Rome

Let's Go: Spain & Portugal

NORTH & CENTRAL AMERICA

Let's Go: USA & Canada

Let's Go: Alaska & The Pacific Northwest

Let's Go: California

Let's Go: New York City

Let's Go: Washington, D.C.

Let's Go: Mexico

MIDDLE EAST & ASIA

Let's Go: Israel & Egypt

Let's Go: Thailand

Let's Go

The Budget Guide to

EASTERN EUROPE
1995

Luiza Chwiałkowska
Editor

Katarzyna Drozd
Associate Editor

Samuel P. Trumbull
Associate Editor

Jol Andrew Silversmith
Assistant Editor

Written by
Let's Go, Inc.
A subsidiary of
Harvard Student Agencies, Inc.

St. Martin's Press ▪ New York

HELPING LET'S GO

If you have suggestions or corrections, or just want to share your discoveries, drop us a line. We read every piece of correspondence, whether a 10-page e-mail letter, a velveteen Elvis postcard, or, as in one case, a collage. All suggestions are passed along to our researcher-writers. Please note that mail received after May 5, 1995 will probably be too late for the 1996 book, but will be retained for the following edition.
Address mail to:

> **Let's Go: Eastern Europe**
> **Let's Go, Inc.**
> **I Story Street**
> **Cambridge, MA 02138**
> **USA**

Or send e-mail (please include in the subject header the titles of the *Let's Go* guides you discuss in your message) to:
> **letsgo@delphi.com**

In addition to the invaluable travel advice our readers share with us, many are kind enough to offer their services as researchers or editors. Unfortunately, the charter of Let's Go, Inc. and Harvard Student Agencies, Inc. enables us to employ only currently enrolled Harvard-Radcliffe students.

Contents

Maps

■ About Let's Go

Back in 1960, a few students at Harvard University got together to produce a 20-page pamphlet offering a collection of tips on budget travel in Europe. For three years, Harvard Student Agencies, a student-run nonprofit corporation, had been doing a brisk business booking charter flights to Europe; this modest, mimeographed packet was offered to passengers as an extra. The following year, students traveling to Europe researched the first full-fledged edition of *Let's Go: Europe*, a pocket-sized book featuring advice on shoestring travel, irreverent write-ups of sights, and a decidedly youthful slant.

Throughout the 60s, the guides reflected the times: one section of the 1968 *Let's Go: Europe* talked about "Street Singing in Europe on No Dollars a Day." During the 70s, *Let's Go* gradually became a large-scale operation, adding regional European guides and expanding coverage into North Africa and Asia. The 80s saw the arrival of *Let's Go: USA & Canada* and *Let's Go: Mexico*, as well as regional North American guides; in the 90s we introduced five in-depth city guides to Paris, London, Rome, New York City, and Washington, DC. And as the budget travel world expands, so do we; the first edition of *Let's Go: Thailand* hit the shelves last year, and this year's edition adds coverage of Malaysia, Singapore, Tokyo, and Hong Kong.

This year we're proud to announce the birth of *Let's Go: Eastern Europe*—the most comprehensive guide to this renascent region, with more practical information and insider tips than any other. *Let's Go: Eastern Europe* brings our total number of titles, with their spirit of adventure and reputation for honesty, accuracy, and editorial integrity, to 21.

We've seen a lot in 35 years. *Let's Go: Europe* is now the world's #1 best selling international guide, translated into seven languages. And our guides are still researched, written, and produced entirely by students who know first-hand how to see the world on the cheap.

Every spring, we recruit over 100 researchers and 50 editors to write our books anew. Come summertime, after several months of training, researchers hit the road for seven weeks of exploration, from Bangkok to Budapest, Anchorage to Ankara. With pen and notebook in hand, a few changes of underwear stuffed in our backpacks, and a budget as tight as yours, we visit every *pensione*, *palapa*, pizzeria, café, club, campground, or castle we can find to make sure you'll get the most out of *your* trip.

We've put the best of our discoveries into the book you're now holding. A brand-new edition of each guide hits the shelves every year, only months after it is researched, so you know you're getting the most reliable, up-to-date, and comprehensive information available. The budget travel world is constantly changing, and where other guides quickly become obsolete, our annual research keeps you abreast of the very latest travel insights. And even as you read this, work on next year's editions is well underway.

At *Let's Go*, we think of budget travel not only as a means of cutting down on costs, but as a way of breaking down a few walls as well. Living cheap and simple on the road brings you closer to the real people and places you've been saving up to visit. This book will ease your anxieties and answer your questions about the basics—to help *you* get off the beaten track and explore. We encourage you to put *Let's Go* away now and then and strike out on your own. As any seasoned traveler will tell you, the best discoveries are often those you make yourself. If you find something worth sharing, drop us a line. We're at Let's Go, Inc., 1 Story Street, Cambridge, MA, 02138, USA (e-mail: letsgo@delphi.com).

Happy travels!

■ Acknowledgments

Pete Keith believed it could happen and Marc Zelanko made it so. Alexis Averbuck kept the hardware and the book alive. Matt Heid counted our pennies. Anne Chisholm was the wise grown-up we needed. Jed Willard, R.I. Wilson, and Brian Erskine wrote histories when they should have been sleeping. Liz Theran, Joann Chan, and Kardyhm Kelly performed elegant mega-edits. Glenn Davis spoke the right tongues. Tim Hiçylmaz, Attila Bódis, and Andrew Prihodko filled in the gaps. Declan Fox, Anna Dahlstein, and Tina Tseng patiently hit our misses. For proofing we owe Sucharita Mulpuru, Gunner Trumbull, Tim Perlstein, Mary Sadanaga, Jim Ebenhoh, Liz Squires, Tanya Bezreh, Amy Cooper, Emily Hobson, Amelia Kaplan, Brian Galle, Mike Cisneros, Olivia Gentile, Roy Prieb, & Alp "Young Turk" Aker. Special thanks to Jan Passoff in Moscow and to the Slovenian Tourist Office.

Thanx Sammy for grins, Kasia for being a pro & Jol for perfection; Brian for plaid & spaghetti *flambé;* the Freeze and McCorkell families for Canadian generosity; my family for endless help, and Zofia Kołecka for teaching all that was necessary.—**LCh**

Thanks to Liz Theran, Luiza Chwiałkowska, and Sam Trumbull for being such good friends; to my family for their moral support and help with the book; to Joan Caterino for her incredible hospitality. —**KD**

Luiza and Kasia, thank you for being there and making every minute great; to Glenn, Yale, Rachel, and those in the canoes and at supper, thanks for the friendship and the fun. And always; Gunnar, Nat, Lena, and my parents, thank you. —**SPT**

All who helped behind the scenes including: Aaron, Anna (remember Keszthely?), Brian, Dora, Josh, Liz S., Liz T., Squirt, Yuki, and, of course, the family.—**JAS**

STAFF

Editor	Luiza Chwiałkowska
Associate Editor	Katarzyna Drozd
Associate Editor	Samuel P. Trumbull
Assistant Editor	Jol Andrew Silversmith
Managing Editor	Marc David Zelanko
Publishing Director	Pete Keith
Production Manager	Alexis G. Averbuck
Production Assistant	Elizabeth J. Stein
Financial Manager	Matt Heid
Assistant General Manager	Anne E. Chisholm
Sales Group Manager	Sherice R. Guillory
Sales Department Coordinator	Andrea N. Taylor
Sales Group Representatives	Eli K. Aheto
	Timur Okay Harry Hiçyılmaz
	Arzhang Kamerei
	Hollister Jane Leopold
	David L. Yuan
President	Lucienne D. Lester
General Manager	Richard M. Olken

Researcher-Writers

Kelly Adams   *Bulgaria, Former Yugoslav Republic of Macedonia*
After a year in Sofia, Kelly knew where to go and how to bring it back beautifully. Only once did she get stuck in a sea of Bulgarian sheep. She thanks the Stanislavovs, S. Kuchukov, V. Zahavinov, V. Korshumov, friends at the U.S.Embassy in Sofia, and Steve.

Paul Berger   *Hungary*
Citing the Finno-Ugric connection, our East-Asiophile hoped that he would find a remote village in Hungary where people spoke a distant dialect of Japanese. The village was not to be found, but he did learn enough Hungarian to realize the difference between "Here's to your health," and "Here's to your ass." Paul thanks Zsolt Bujáki, Robert Brooker, Béla Tannhauser, and Budapest Tourinform.

Justyna Fife   *Poland*
A student of Slavic literatures, Justyna faced a huge country and covered every inch, devoting 115% to each town. Her perceptive prose wove together an intricate portrait of this complicated land. She thanks Darren Ranco.

Charlotte Kaiser   *Western Russia*
After distributing "humanitarian aid" (surplus Gulf War sunblock) to Russian villagers, she returned to Russia to teach startled comrades in her hotel kitchen that one can boil things other than potatoes. Her writing was cutting, brilliant, and legible.

Natasha Leland   *Western Russia*
Former editor of *Let's Go: London* and *Let's Go: Paris,* Natasha researched Orthodox Churches wearing Charlotte's green bedsheets (she forgot to bring a skirt), yes, she researched with style. Natasha's writing was cutting and brilliant.

Roderick MacFarquhar   *Volga-Don, Southern Russia*
Working for news bureaus and famous economists in Moscow wasn't exciting enough for Rory; instead, he spent his summer hunting for running water in Russia's opaque south. He shared living quarters with covert government officials and a Muscovite whose snore echoed across the Volga. And every word he wrote was perfect.

Mark Moody   *Belarus, Estonia, Kaliningrad, Latvia, Lithuania*
Mark has pluck. Former editor of *LG:USA*, Mark ran away to the Baltics on a Fulbright grant to study post-socialist mafia-ridden nightlife. We think he earned a PhD—and he's still alive "someplace in Latvia" or at least somewhere in cyberspace.

Şerban Nacu   *Croatia, Republic of Moldova, Romania, Slovenia*
A poet posing as a mathematician, Şerban brought literary sensitivity to the Balkans. He also somehow managed to send us his copy from Japan. He thanks: Kiki, Nana, Bebe Olteanu, Adi Şalic, Mike, Magda, Brane, and their friend from Jesenice.

Geneviève Roach   *Albania, Ukraine*
A veteran *Let's Go*-er and gifted linguist, Geneviève embarked on her trip with a backpack the size of a small dishtowel. Professional to the core, she sent back beautifully written and meticulously researched wisdom. These days, you can track her down somewhere in Vietnam; she's the one talking to herself in Albanian.

Raimond Tullius   *Czech Republic, Slovak Republic*
Love of history and beer have drawn this Canadian eastward many times. After teaching in rural Romania and backpacking across Hungary and Croatia, he came to the Czech Republic in search of a tall, cool one. Raimond thanks Daniel Polan.

Jonathan D. Caverly   *Vienna*

Michael O'Shea   *Berlin*

Stephanie Rosborough   *Trieste*

How To Use This Book

The guide is divided into two parts. The opening section, **Essentials,** will guide you through the quagmire of preparations, with tips on passport and visa acquisition, packing, planning itineraries across Eastern Europe, and the budget travel opportunities you'll find once you're there. It also addresses specific concerns, such as those of women, bisexuals, gays, lesbians, travelers with disabilities, senior citizens, and travelers with children.

The rest of the book covers 17 countries of Eastern Europe as well as Vienna, Berlin and Trieste, gateway cities for many east-bound travelers. Individual countries are listed alphabetically and include a historical, cultural, political, and linguistic introduction, as well as country-specific Essentials and Life and Times sections where you'll find such tidbits as visa requirements and the lowdown on transportation, accommodation services, and regional cuisine.

For each major city, the **Orientation and Practical Information** section gives you a clue about the city's layout, as well as how to get there, how to communicate with folks back home, how to use its transportation system, and where to seek help in medical emergencies and crisis situations. Then we shower you with information on **Accommodations, Camping, Food, Sights, Entertainment,** and **Nightlife.** Smaller towns are usually divided in half: first we describe the sights and entertainment hotspots, then we dig into the nitty-gritty: accommodations, food, and practical information.

Eastern Europe is busy reinventing itself everyday. We hope you'll let us know what has changed and what we have yet to discover.

A NOTE TO OUR READERS

The information for this book is gathered by *Let's Go*'s researchers during the late spring and summer months. Each listing is derived from the assigned researcher's opinion based upon his or her visit at a particular time. The opinions are expressed in a candid and forthright manner. Other travelers might disagree. Those traveling at a different time may have different experiences since prices, dates, hours, and conditions are always subject to change. You are urged to check beforehand to avoid inconvenience and surprises. Travel always involves a certain degree of risk, especially in low-cost areas. When traveling, especially on a budget, you should always take particular care to ensure your safety.

NORTH RUSSIAN PLAIN

Vologda

Izhevsk

0   200 miles
0   200 kilometers

Volga R.

Kazan

Yaroslavl

Volga R.

Nizhny Novgorod

N

Vladimir

Simbirsk

Tolyatti

Moscow

Samara

Ryazan

Tula

Penza

Smolensk

R U S S I A

Vol sk

Saratov

Bryansk

Voronezh

Homyel

Povorino

Kursk

KAZAKH-STAN

Bakhmach

Kiev

Kharkiv

Volgograd

Donets R.

Volga R.

CASPIAN DEPRESSION

Dnieper R.

Smila

Don R.

Astrakhan

UKRAINE

Dnipropetrovsk

Rostov na Donu

CASPIAN SEA

Kryvy Rih

Donetsk

Zaporizhya

Balta

Azov

Mariupol

Mykolayiv

Primorsko Akhtarsk

Odessa

Sea of Azov

Dzhankoy

Kerch

Stavropol

CRIMEA

Krasnodar

Sevastopol

Simferopol

Tuapse

Grozny

Yalta

Sochi

CAUCASUS MOUNTAINS

GEORGIA

BLACK SEA

Batum

Tbilisi

ARMENIA

Sinop

Yerevan

Istanbul

AZERBAIJAN

Bursa

Ankara

Kizilirmak R.

T U R K E Y

Eastern Europe

ESSENTIALS

PLANNING YOUR TRIP

Sometimes bureaucratic and Kafka-esque, sometimes utterly lawless, travel in Eastern Europe is never predictable. Start your travel planning well in advance: begin stalking consulates for visas the very moment you decide to go, contact the useful organizations we list, faithfully follow the news, plan out every detail of your itinerary. . . and be prepared to scrap the whole thing once you arrive. Things change quickly in Eastern Europe: exchange rates, telephone numbers, borders. . . the most important thing to plan for is flexibility.

What we have called "Eastern Europe" is not a single monolithic region but 17 very different countries. *Let's Go* can take you as far east as the Volga, Europe's longest river and doorstep to Asia; farther north than Anchorage, Alaska; south as far as the Greek border; and westward into the very heart of Europe. Whether you put it to work in historic cultural centers such as Prague, Budapest, or St. Petersburg, on an alpine hike in Slovenia, along a wilderness trip through the Carpathian mountains, or in beach towns along the Black Sea, Baltic or Adriatic, we urge you to unleash your curiosity and to follow your own spirit.

■■■ USEFUL ADDRESSES

The following organizations can help familiarize you with your destination countries before you get there and help you organize your travel plans.

TRAVEL ORGANIZATIONS

Campus Travel, 52 Grosvenor Gardens, London SW1W 0AG (tel. (0171) 730 88 32, fax 730 57 39). Offices across the U.K. Student and youth fares on travel by train, boat, and bus, as well as flexible airline tickets. Offers telephone booking service from **Europe** (tel. (0171) 730 34 02), **North America** (tel. (0171) 730 21 01), and **worldwide** (tel. (0171) 730 81 11). Supplies maps, guides, ID cards for youths, and special travel insurance for students and those under 35.

Council on International Educational Exchange (CIEE), 205 East 42nd St., New York NY 10017 (tel. (212) 661-1414). A private, non-profit organization, CIEE administers work, volunteer, academic and professional programs worldwide. Offers identity cards (including the ISIC and the GO 25) and a range of publications, among them *Student Travels* (free, postage US$1); for more info see it's entry under Alternatives to Tourism.

Council Charter, 205 East 42nd St., New York, NY 10017 (tel. (212) 661-0311 or (800) 800-8222). CIEE subsidiary. Offers a combination of inexpensive charter and scheduled airfares from a variety of U.S. gateways to most major European destinations. One-way fares and "open jaws" (which allow you to fly into one city and out of another) are available. Council Charter also offers a cancellation waiver which for US$30 allows passengers to cancel for any reason up to three hours prior to departure from the U.S. and receive a full refund.

Council Travel. CIEE subsidiary. Specializes in student and budget travel. Offers charter flight tickets, guidebooks, ISIC, ITIC, and GO 25 cards, hostelling cards, and travel gear. Forty-one U.S. offices, including: 729 Boylston St. #201, **Boston,** MA 02116 (tel. (617) 266-1926); 1153 N. Dearborn St., 2nd Fl., **Chicago,** IL 60610 (tel. (312) 951-0585); 6715 Hillcrest, **Dallas,** TX 75205 (tel. (214) 363-9941); 1093 Broxton Ave., Suite 220, **Los Angeles,** CA 90024 (tel. (310) 208-3551); 205 East 42nd St., **New York,** NY 10017 (tel. (212) 661-1450); 715 SW Morrison #600, **Portland,** OR 97205 (tel. (503) 228-1900); 530 Bush St., Ground Fl., **San Francisco,** CA 94108 (tel. (415) 421-3473); and 1314 North-

PRESENTING AN INDEPENDENT APPROACH TO TRAVEL.

If you have independent ideas about travel, we specialize in putting you exactly where you want to be. And with over 100 offices worldwide, we'll take care of you when you're there. So when it's time to plan your trip, call us at 1.800.777.0112.

New York: 212-477-7166
Washington DC: 202-887-0912
Philadelphia: 215-382-2928
Boston: 617-266-6014
Los Angeles: 213-934-8722
San Francisco: 415-391-8407

STA

STA TRAVEL

We've been there.

east 43rd St. #210, **Seattle,** WA 98105 (tel. (206) 632-2448). Also in San Diego, CA, Tempe, AZ, Washington, DC, Miami, FL, Ann Arbor, MI, Providence, RI, and Cambridge, MA. In **Europe,** 28A Poland St. (Oxford Circus), **London** W1V 3DB (tel. (0171) 437 77 67).

Federation of International Youth Travel Organizations (FITYO), Bredgade 25H, DK-1260, Copenhagen K, Denmark (tel. 33 33 96 00, fax 33 93 96 76). International organization promoting educational, cultural and social travel for young people. Members include language schools, educational travel companies, national tourist boards, accommodation centers and suppliers of travel services to youth and students. Sponsors the GO 25 Card, which offers various discounts and benefits worldwide. Like the ISIC, this card can be obtained from local student travel services, as well as from some hostel associations.

International Student Travel Confederation, Store Kongensgade 40H, 1264 Copenhagen K, Denmark (tel. 33 93 93 03, fax 33 93 73 77). Sells ISIC. Affiliated organizations include International Student Rail Association (ISRA), Student Air Travel Association (SATA), ISIS Travel Insurance, and the International Association for Educational and Work Exchange Programmes (IAEWEP).

Let's Go Travel, Harvard Student Agencies, Inc., 53-A Church St., Cambridge, MA 02138 (tel. (800) 5-LETS GO (553-8746) or (617) 495-9649). Offers railpasses, HI/AYH memberships, ISICs, International Teacher ID cards, GO 25 cards, guidebooks, maps, bargain flights, and a complete line of budget travel gear. All items available by mail; call or write for a catalog. Also see the insert in this book.

STA Travel, 5900 Wilshire Blvd. #2110, Los Angeles, CA 90036 (tel. (800) 777-0112 nationwide). Discount airfares for travelers under 26 and full-time students under 32, railpasses, accommodations, tours, insurance, and ISICs. 11 U.S. offices include: 297 Newbury St., **Boston,** MA 02116 (tel. (617) 266-6014); 48 E. 11th St., **New York,** NY 10003 (tel. (212) 477-7166); 51 Grant Ave., **San Francisco,** CA 94108 (tel. (415) 391-8407); and 2401 Pennsylvania Ave., **Washington,** DC 20037 (tel. (202) 887-0912). In the **U.K.,** 117 Euston Rd., **London** NW1 2SX (tel. (0171) 937 99 21l). In **Australia,** 222 Faraday St., **Melbourne,** VIC 3053 (tel. (03) 349 24 11). In **New Zealand,** 10 High St., **Auckland** (tel. (09) 398 99 95).

Travel CUTS (Canadian University Travel Services Limited), 187 College St., Toronto, Ont. M5T 1P7 (tel. (416) 798-CUTS (798-2887), fax 979-8167). Offices across Canada. In the **U.K.,** 295-A Regent St., London W1R 7YA (tel. (0171) 637 31 61). Discounted transatlantic and domestic flights; ISIC, GO 25, and HI hostel cards; and discount travel passes. Special student fares with valid ISIC. Offers free *Student Traveller* magazine, and info on Student Work Abroad Program (SWAP).

University and Student Travel (USTN). A national association of university travel agencies (in most cases located on campus in student unions). Offers ISICs, GO 25 Cards, youth hostel cards, STA and CIEE student tickets, USTN student discount airline tickets, Eurailpasses, student tours, etc. Member agencies across the U.S, including Berkeley Northside Travel, 1824 Euclid Ave., **Berkeley,** CA 94709 (tel. (510) 843-1000, fax 843-7537); James Travel Points, UMC/Rm. 162, Campus Box 207, **Boulder,** CO 80309 (tel. (303) 492-5154, fax 492-2183); Mid America Travel, 515 East Green St., **Champaign,** IL 61820 (tel. (217) 344-1600, fax 344-6171); and ASUCLA Travel Service, Ackerman Union, 308 Westwood Plaza, **Los Angeles,** CA 90024 (tel. (310) 825-9131, fax 206-3212).

Red Bear Tours, 320B Glenferrie Rd., Malvern, Melbourne, Victoria 3144, Australia (tel. (03) 824 71 83, fax 822 39 56; toll free (008) 33 70 31). For those departing from Australia, Red Bear also provide rail tickets across Russia and assorted tours. Their newsletter has the most recent information on their services.

USIT Ltd., Aston Quay, O'Connell Bridge, Dublin 2 (tel. (01) 679 88 33, fax 677 88 43). Sells ISIC, HI hostel cards and *Let's Go.* In addition to selling discounted student fares on scheduled flights, USIT books its own charter flights in the summer for some of the best flight deals going.

EMBASSIES AND CONSULATES

Albania: U.S. (Embassy): 1511 K St., NW, Suite 1010, Washington, DC 20005. Tel. (202) 223-4942.

ESSENTIALS

TOP 5 Ways to Save Money While Traveling

5. Ship yourself in a crate marked "Livestock." Remember to poke holes in the crate.

4. Board a train dressed as Elvis and sneer and say "The King rides for free."

3. Ask if you can walk through the Channel Tunnel.

2. Board the plane dressed as an airline pilot, nod to the flight attendants, and hide in the rest room until the plane lands.

1. Bring a balloon to the airline ticket counter, kneel, breathe in the helium, and ask for the kiddie fare.

But if you're serious about saving money while you're traveling abroad, just get an ISIC—the International Student Identity Card. Discounts for students on international airfares, hotels and motels, car rentals, international phone calls, financial services, and more.

International Student Identity Card
Carte internationale d'étudiant/Carnet internacional de estudiante

GRAHAM
DONNA
10/29/70   7/5/94
USA
U OREGON
STUDENT

For more information:

In the United States:

 Council on International Educational Exchange
205 East 42nd St.
New York, NY 10017
1-800-GET-AN-ID
Available at Council Travel offices (see inside front cover)

In Canada:

 Travel CUTS
243 College Street,
Toronto, Ontario M5T 2Y1
(416) 977-3703
Available at Travel CUTS offices nationwide

Belarus: U.S. (Embassy): 1619 New Hampshire Ave., NW, Washington, DC 20009. Tel. (202) 986-1604. Fax 986-1805. **(Consulate):** 708 Third Ave., Suite 1802, New York, NY 10017. Tel. (212) 682-5392. Fax 682 5491. **U.K. (Embassy):** 1 St. Stephan's Crescent, Bayswater, London W2 5QT. Tel. (0171) 221 39 41. Fax 221 39 46.
Bulgaria: U.S. (Embassy): 1621 22nd St., NW, Washington, DC 20008. Tel.(202) 387-7969. Fax (202) 234-7973. **Canada (Consulate):** 65 Overlea Blvd. #406, Toronto, ON M4H 1P1. Tel. (416) 696-2420 or 696-2778. Fax 696-8019. **U.K. (Embassy):** Sofia House, 19 Conduit St., London W1R 9TD. Tel. (0171) 491 44 99. Fax 491 70 68. **Australia (Consulate):** 1/4 Carlotta Rd., Double Bay, Sydney, NSW 2028. Tel. (02) 327 75 92 or 327 44 40. Fax 327 80 67.
Croatia: U.S. (Embassy): 2343 Massachusetts Ave., NW, Washington, DC 20008. Tel. (202) 588-5899. Fax 588-8938. **Canada (Embassy):** 116 Albert St., Suite 606, Ottawa, Ontario K1P 5G3. Tel. (613) 230-7351. Fax 230-7388. **(Office):** 918 Dundas St. E, Suite 302, Mississauga, Ontario L4Y 2B6. Tel. (416) 277-1198. Fax 277-5432. **U.K. (Embassy):** 18-21 Jermyn St., London SW1Y 6HP. Tel. (0171) 434 29 46. Fax 434 29 53. **Australia (Embassy):** O'Malley, Canberra ACT 2606. Tel. (06) 286 69 88 or 286 24 27. Fax 186 35 44 or 286 66 21. **(Consulate):** 9/24 Albert Rd., South Melbourne, Victoria 3205. Tel (03) 699 26 33. Fax 696 82 71. **(Consulate):** 78 Mill Point Rd., South Perth, Western Australia 6151. Tel (09) 474 16 20. Fax 474 16 21. **(Consulate):** 379 Kent St., Level 4, Sydney, NSW 200. Tel. (02) 299 88 99. Fax 299 88 55 or 299 88 89. **South Africa (Office):** P.O. Box 30, Cresta 2118. Tel. (11) 434 13 61. Fax 434 28 37.
Czech Republic: U.S. (Embassy): 3900 Spring of Freedom St., NW, Washington, DC 20008. Tel. (202) 363-6315. Fax 966-8540. **Canada (Embassy):** 541 Sussex Dr., Ottawa, Ont. K1N 6Z6. Tel (613) 562-3875. Fax 562-3878. **(Consulate):** 1305 Av. des Peins ouest, Montréal, Qué. H3G 1B2. Tel. (514) 849-4495. Fax 849-4117. **U.K. (Embassy):** 26 Kensington Palace Gardens, London W8 4QY. Tel. (0171) 243 11 15 or 243 79 01. Fax 727 96 54. **Australia (Embassy)** 38 Culgoa Circuit, O'Malley, Canberra, ACT 2606. Tel. (06) 290 13 86. Fax 290 00 06. **South Africa (Embassy):** 936 Pretorius St., Arcadia, Pretoria 0083, or P.O. Box 3326, 0001 Pretoria. Tel. (12) 342 34 77 or 43 36 01. Fax 43 20 33.
Estonia: U.S. (Embassy): 1030 15th St. NW, Suite #1000, Washington, DC 20005. Tel. (202) 789-0320. **(Consulate):** 630 5th Ave., Suite 2415, New York, NY 10111. Tel. (212) 247-7634. Fax 262-0893. **Canada (Consulate):** 958 Broadview Ave., Toronto, Ont. M4K 2R6. Tel. (416) 461-0764. **U.K. (Consulate):** 16 Hyde Park Gate, London SW7 5D6. Tel. (0171) 589 34 28.
Hungary: U.S. (Embassy): 3910 Shoemaker St., NW, Washington, DC 20008. Tel. (202) 362-6730. Fax 966-8135. **(Consulate):** 223 East 52nd St., New York, NY 10022. Tel. (212) 752-0661. Fax 755-5986. **(Consulate):** 11766 Wilshire Blvd.S 410, Los Angeles, CA 90025. Tel. (310) 473-9344. Fax 479-6443. **Canada (Embassy):** 7 Delaware Ave., Ottawa, Ontario K2P OZ2. Tel. (613) 232-1711. Fax 232-5620. **(Consulate):** 102 Bloor St. West Suite 1001, Toronto, Ontario M5S 1M8. Tel. (416) 923-8981. Fax 923-2732. **(Consulate):** 1200 McGill College Ave., S:2040 Montreal, Quebec H3B HG7. Tel. (514) 393-3302. Fax 393-8226. **U.K. (Embassy):** 35 Eaton Place, London SW 1X 8BY. Tel. (0171) 235 71 91. Fax 823 13 48. **Ireland (Embassy):** 2 Fitzwilliam Place, Dublin 2. Tel. (01) 661 29 02. Fax 661 29 05. **Australia (Embassy):** 17 Beale Crescent, Deakin ACT 2600. Tel. (06) 22 82 32 26. Fax 22 85 30 12. **(Consulate):** Edgecliff Centre 203-233, Suite 405, New South Head Road Edgecliff, NSW. 2027 SY. Tel. (02) 328 78 59. Fax 327 18 29. **South Africa (Consulate):** P.O. Box 27077, Sunnyside 0132, 959 Arcadia St., Arcadia. Tel. (012) 43 30 30. Fax 43 30 29.
Latvia: U.S. (Embassy): 4325 17th St., NW, Washington, DC 20011. Tel. (202) 726-8213. Fax 726-6785. **Canada (Consulate):** 230 Clemow Ave., Ottawa, Ont. K1S 2B6. Tel. (613) 238-6868. **U.K. (Embassy):** 72 Queensborough Terr., London W23SP. Tel. (0171) 727 16 98. **Australia (Consulate):** P.O. Box 23, Kew, Victoria, 3101, Melbourne. Tel. (03) 499 69 20.
Lithuania: U.S. (Embassy): 2622 16th St., NW, Washington, DC 20009. Tel. (202) 234-5860. Fax 328-0466. **(Consulate):** 420 5th Ave., NY 10018. Tel. (212) 354-7849. Fax 354-7911. **Canada (Honorary Consulate):** 235 Yorkland Blvd., Wil-

lowdale, Ont. M2J Tel. (416) 494-4099. Fax 494-4382. **U.K. (Embassy):** 17 Essex Villas, London W87BP. Tel. (0171) 937 15 88 or 938 24 81. **Australia (Honorary Consulate):** 26 Jalanga Crescent, Aranda ACT 2614. Tel./Fax (616) 253 20 63. **F.Y.R. of Macedonia: U.S. (Office):** 3050 K St. NW, Suite #210, Washington, DC 20007. Tel. (202) 337-3063. Fax 337-3093. **Moldova: U.S. (Embassy):** 1511 K St., NW, Suite 329, Washington, DC 20005. Tel. (202) 783-3012. Fax 783-3342. **Poland: U.S. (Embassy):** 2224 Wyoming Ave., NW, Washington, DC 20008. Tel. (202) 234-2501. Fax 328-2152. **(Consulate):** 233 Madison Ave,. New York, NY 10016. Tel (212) 889-8360. Fax 779-3062. **(Consulate):** 12400 Wilshire Blvd., Suite #555, Los Angeles, CA 90025. Tel. (310) 442-8500. Fax 442-8515. **(Consulate):** 1530 North Lake Shore Drive, Chicago, IL 60610. Tel. (312) 337-8166. Fax 337-7841. **Canada: (Embassy):** 443 Daly St., Ottawa 2, Ont., K1N 6H3. Tel. (613) 789-0468. Fax 232-3463. **(Consulate):** 1500 Pine Ave. West, Montreal, Quebec H3G 1B4. Tel. (514) 937-9481. Fax 937-7271. **(Consulate):** 2603 Lakeshore Blvd. West, Toronto, Ont., M8V 1G5. Tel (416) 252-4171. Fax 252-0509. **(Consulate):** 1177 West Hastings St., Suite #1600, Vancouver, BC V6E 2K3. Tel. (604) 688-3530 or 688-4730. Fax 688-3537. **U.K. (Embassy):** 47 Portland Place, London W1N 3AG. Tel. (0171) 580 43 29. Fax 323 40 18. **(Consulate):** 73 New Cavendish St., London W1N 7RB. Tel. (0171) 580 04 76. Fax 323 23 20. **(Consulate):** 2 Kinnear Rd, Edinburgh EH3 5PE. Tel. (031) 552 03 01. Fax 552 10 86. **Ireland (Embassy):** 5 Ailesbury Rd., Dublin 4. Tel. (01) 269 13 70. Fax 269 83 09. **Australia (Embassy):** 7 Turrana St, Yarralumla ACT 2600 Canberra. Tel. (06) 273 12 08 or 273 12 11. Fax 273 31 84. **(Consulate):** 10 Trelawney St., Woollahra NSW 2025, Sydney. Tel. (02) 327 98 17. Fax 327 85 66. **New Zealand (Embassy)** 17 Upland Rd., Kelburn, Wellington. Tel. (04) 71 24 56. Fax 71 24 55. **South Africa (Embassy):** 14 Arnos St., Colbyn, Pretoria 0083. Tel. (012) 43 26 21. Fax 346 13 66.
Romania: U.S. (Embassy): 1607 23rd St., NW, Washington, DC 20008. Tel. (202) 332-4846. Fax 232-4748. **Canada (Embassy):** 655 Rideau St., Ottawa, Ont. K1N 6A3. Tel. (613) 789-3709 or 789-5345. Fax 789-4365. **U.K. (Embassy):** 4 Palace Green, Kensington, London, W84 QD. Tel. (0171) 937 96 66. Fax 937 80 69. **Australia (Consulate):** 333 Old South Head Road Bondi, Sydney. Tel. (02) 36 50 15. Fax 30 57 14. **South Africa (Consulate):** 16 Breda St. Gardens, Capetown. Tel. (021) 461 48 60. Fax 461 24 85.
Russia: U.S. (Embassy): Consular Division, 1825 Phelps Place, NW, Washington, DC 20008. Tel. (202) 939-8907/11/13. **(Consulate):** 9 East 91st St., New York, NY, 10128. Tel. (212) 348-0926. Fax 831-9162. (Consulate): 2790 Green St., San Francisco, CA 94123. Tel. (415) 202-9800. **Canada (Embassy):** 285 Charlotte St., Ottawa, Ontario, K1N 8L5. Tel. (613) 235-4341. **U.K. (Embassy):** 13 Kensington Palace Gardens, London W8 4QX. Tel. (0171) 229 36 28. **Ireland (Embassy):** 186 Orwell Rd., Dublin 14. Tel. 492 35 25. **Australia (Embassy):** 78 Canberra Ave., Griffith ACT, 2603 Canberra. Tel. (06) 295 90 33. **New Zealand (Embassy):** 57 Messines Rd., KAR 0RI, Wellington. Tel. (04) 76 61 13.
Slovakia: U.S. (Embassy): 2201 Wisconsin Ave., NW, Washington, DC 20007. Tel. (202) 965-5161. Fax 965-5166. **Canada (Embassy):** 50 Rideau Terrace, Ottawa, Ontario K1M 2A1. Tel. (613) 749-4442. Fax 749-4989. **U.K. (Embassy):** 25 Kensington Place Gardens, London W8 4QY. Tel. (0171) 243 08 03. Fax 727 58 24. Australia (Embassy): 47 Culgoa Circuit, O'Malley, Canberra ACT 2606. Tel. (06) 290 15 16. Fax 290 17 55. **South Africa (Embassy):** Matroosberg Rd. 103, Waterkloof 0145, Pretoria. Tel. (012) 346 36 50. Fax 46 02 26.
Slovenia: U.S. (Embassy): 1525 New Hampshire Ave., NW, Washington, DC 20036. Tel. (202) 667-5363. Fax 667-4563. **(Consulate):** 600 3rd Ave., 24th Floor, New York, NY 10016. Tel. (212) 370-3006. Fax 370-3581. **(Honorary Consulate):** 1111 Chester Ave., Suite #520, Cleveland, OH 44114. Tel. (216) 589-9220. Fax 589-9210. **Canada (Embassy):** 150 Metcalfe St., Suite 2101, Ottawa, Ontario K2P 1P1. Tel. (613) 565-5781. Fax 565-5783. **U.K. (Embassy):** Suite One Cavendish Court 11-15, Wigmore St., London W1H 9LA. Tel. (0171) 495 77 75. Fax 495 77 76. **Australia (Embassy):** P.O. Box 284-60, Marcus Clarke St., Canberra ACT 2601. Tel. (06) 243 48 30. **(Honorary Consulate):** P.O. Box 118, Coo-

gee, Sydney NSW 2034. Tel. (02) 314 51 16. Fax 399 62 46. **New Zealand (Consulate):** Eastern Hutt Rd., Pomare, Lower Hutt, Wellington. Tel. (04) 567 00 27. Fax 567 00 24.
Ukraine: U.S. (Embassy): 3350 M St., NW, Washington, DC 20007. Tel. (202) 333-0606. Fax 333-7510. **(Consulate):** 240 East 49th St., New York, NY 10017. Tel. (212) 371-5690. Fax 371-5547. **(Consulate):** 10 E.Huron St., Chicago, IL 60611. Tel. (312) 642-4388. Fax 642-4385. **Canada (Embassy):** 331 Metcalfe St., Ottawa, Ont. K2P153. Tel. (613) 230-2961. Fax 230-2400. **U.K. (Embassy):** 78 Kensington Park Rd., London W112PL. Tel. (0171) 727 63 12. Fax 792 17 08.
Australia (Embassy): 4 Bloom St., Moonee Pons, 3039, Melbourne. Tel. (613) 326 01 35. Fax 326 01 39.

NATIONAL TOURIST OFFICES

Bulgaria: U.S.: Balkan Holidays: 41 E. 42nd St. #508, New York, NY 10017. Tel. (212) 573-5530. Fax 573-5538. **U.K.: Balkan Holidays:** Sofia House, 19 Conduit St., London, W1R 9TD.Tel. (0171) 491 44 99. Fax 491 70 68. **Ireland: Trade Representative:** 22 Burlington Rd., Dublin. Tel. (01) 68 40 10.
Czech Republic: ČEDOK (Private Tourist Agency): **U.S.:** 10 E. 40th St., New York, NY 10016. Tel. (212) 689-9720. Fax 481-0597. **U.K.:** 49 Southwark St., London SE1 1RU. Tel. (0171) 378 60 09. Fax 403 23 21.
Croatia: U.K.: POB 1401, 15 Cambridge, 210 Shepherds Bush Road, London W6 7ZU. Tel. (0171) 371 11 22. Fax 602 93 24.
Hungary: U.S.: IBUSZ, 1 Parker Plaza #1104, Fort Lee, NJ 07024. Tel. (201) 592-8585. Fax 592-8736. **U.K.:** Danube Travel, 6 Conduit St., London W1R 9TG. Tel. (0171) 493 02 63. Fax 493 69 63.
Poland: U.S.: 275 Madison Ave., Suite #1711, New York, NY 10016. Tel. (212) 338-9412. Fax 338-9283. Or, 333 N. Michigan Ave. #224, Chicago, IL, 60601. Tel. (312) 236-9013. Fax 236-1125.
Romania: U.S.: 342 Madison Ave., Suite # 210, New York, NY 10173. Tel. (212) 697-6971. Fax 697-6972. **U.K.:** 83 A Marylebone High St., London W1M 3DE. Tel. (0171) 222 36 92.
Russia: Intourist is in the process of regrouping and is no longer a national tourist office, however it may soon regain that function: **U.S.:** 630 Fifth Ave., Suite #603, New York, NY 10020. Tel. (212) 757-3884 or 757-3885; for reservations (800) 982-8416. Fax (212) 459-0031. **Canada:** 1801 McGill College Ave. #630, Montréal, Qué. H3A 2N4. Tel. (514) 849-6394. **U.K.:** 219 Marsh Wall, London E14 9FJ. Tel. (0171) 538 86 00.
Slovakia Travel Service: U.S.: 10 E. 40th St., Suite #3601, New York, NY 10016. Tel. (212) 213-3865 or 213-3862. Fax 213-4461 or 684-7648.
Slovenia: U.S.: 122 E. 42nd St., Suite 3006, New York, NY 10168-0072. Tel. (212) 682-5896. Fax 661-2469. **U.K.:** 57 Grosvenor St., London W1X 9PA. Tel. (0171) 499 74 88. Fax 355 48 28.

■■■ COMPUTER RESOURCES

Keeping up to date on events in Eastern Europe is an art. Though events in the former Yugoslavia and in Russia are energetically covered by the mainstream press, other Eastern European countries receive scant coverage unless Michael Jackson happens to be visiting. Luckily, the international computer network known as the **Internet** offers a vast amount of information to travelers, from daily news digests to ferry schedules. Some **commercial services** such as America On-Line, CompuServe, Delphi, and Prodigy offer sophisticated services such as the ability to make airline reservations on-line.

GETTING WIRED

Most universities and many businesses in the West, and increasing number in Eastern Europe, offer students and employees access to the Internet; ask your Computer Science department or resident **computer geek.** If you own a modem, you can also gain access through a commercial provider such as **Netcom On-Line Communica-**

tion Services, 4000 Moorpark Ave., Suite 200, San Jose, CA 95117 (tel. (800) 501-8649, fax (408) 241-9145, e-mail info@netcom.com). Individual accounts cost US$17.50-19.50 per month; Netcom has access numbers in more than 20 U.S. cities.

There are over 2000 forums on the Internet known as **"usenet newsgroups"** that address topics ranging from computers to comedians, accessible by users all over the world. Some of these newsgroups are devoted to information about Eastern Europe and allow the opportunity to converse with natives and people familiar with the region. New groups are always being created, and not all groups are available on all systems, so the list that follows may not be comprehensive. One of most common **news-reading programs** can be accessed on many systems by typing "rn" for "read news." Some systems and programs provide a tutorial; for others you should consult a system manager or knowledgable friend. Since most newsgroups are unmoderated and unsupervised, the quality of conversation and the reliability of information posted within them is not always sure.

BREAKING NEWS

The **RFE/RL Daily Report** is an invaluable on-line digest of daily events in Russia, Transcaucasia, Central Asia, and Central and Eastern Europe. The daily reports are compiled by correspondents for Radio Free Europe/Radio Liberty Research Institute, a U.S. Congress-funded organization. The daily report covers everything from privatization in Albania to election results in Belarus. You can access the newsgroup through "rn" at misc.news.east-europe.rferl or have it sent by e-mail.

Some computer systems also provide access to **"Clarinet"** groups which provide the latest news from Reuters, the Associated Press, and other news wires:

clari.world.europe.balkans (Albania, Bulgaria, Romania, Former Yugoslavia)
clari.world.europe.central (Czech Rep., Hungary, Poland, Slovakia)
clari.world.europe.eastern (Baltic States, Belarus, Moldova, Ukraine)
clari.world.europe.russia

DISCUSSION FORUMS

There are several "hierarchies" of newsgroups. One, the "soc" groups, is a spawning ground for discussion and arguments about social issues and current events.

soc.culture.baltics soc.culture.bosna-herzgvna
soc.culture.bulgaria soc.culture.croatia
soc.culture.czecho-slovak soc.culture.europe
soc.culture.magyar soc.culture.polish
soc.culture.romanian soc.culture.slovenia
soc.culture.soviet soc.culture.ukrainian
soc.culture.yugoslavia

The "alt" groups are a collection of newsgroups that are less formally organized than groups in the other hierarchies and may receive a more limited circulation:

alt.current-events.bosnia alt.current-events.russia
alt.current-events.ukraine alt.politics.europe.misc

The "rec" groups are oriented towards the arts, hobbies, and recreation:

rec.travel.air rec.travel.europe
rec.travel.marketplace rec.travel.misc

ELECTRONIC MAILING LISTS

Users who only have access to electronic mail can still participate in some discussions forums; the text of some newsgroups is also available on a daily basis by e-mail. Some discussion forums take place primarily through e-mail; you can subscribe or unsubscribe most mailing lists by sending a request to an e-mail address formed by putting "-request" after the list name in the right column but before the "@":

bit.listserv.bosnet	(Bosnia) bosnet@cu23.crl.aecl.ca
bit.listserv.e-europe	(business issues)
	europe@pucc.princeton.edu
bit.listserv.euearn-l	(Eastern Europe)
bit.listserv.hungary	hungary@gwuvm.gwu.edu
bit.listserv.mideur-l	(Middle Europe)
bit.listserv.slovak-l	slovak-l@ubvm.cc.buffalo.edu
bit.listserv.travel-l	travel-l@vm3090.ege.edu.tr
misc.news.east-europe.rferl	rferl-l@ubvm.cc.buffalo.edu
soc.culture.soviet	scs-l@indycms.iupui.edu

OTHER TOOLS

Internet Relay Chat, or "IRC" allows real-time (typed) conservation with users around the world. The number and nature of the "channels" available is more variable than for newsgroups, but you're quite likely to find discussions on travel and/or Eastern Europe, or you can start one of your own. Like newsgroups, IRC is virtually unsupervised. From most systems, type "irc" and then type "/help newuser".

Other services available on the Internet include **FTP** (file transfer protocol), **gopher**, and **World Wide Web** (WWW); each is a means by which to obtain files and other information stored in publicly-accessible areas of other computer systems. Thousands of such archives exist, including many with travel information, answers to frequently asked questions and statistics about Eastern Europe. A particularly useful archive is "rec-travel" at ftp.cc.umanitoba.ca; it includes travelogues, U.S. State Department Advisories, and a plethora of other useful information. Talk to your system manager or a knowledgable friend, or consult one of the many comprehensive guides to the Internet available in most bookstores.

Let's Go may be reached by e-mail at letsgo@delphi.com.

■■■ DOCUMENTS & FORMALITIES

Travel to most of Eastern Europe has become less bureaucratic than it once was. However, procuring the appropriate travel documents, especially from Russia and Ukraine, can be time consuming and expensive. Be sure to file all applications several weeks or months in advance of your planned departure date.

When you travel, always carry on your person two or more forms of identification, including at least one photo ID. A passport combined with a driver's license or birth certificate usually serves as adequate proof of your identity and citizenship. Many establishments, especially banks, require several IDs before cashing traveler's checks. Never carry all your forms of ID together, however; you risk being left entirely without ID or funds in case of theft or loss. Also, carry half a dozen extra passport-size photos that you can attach to the sundry IDs or railpasses you will eventually acquire. If you plan an extended stay, register your passport with the nearest embassy or consulate.

ENTRANCE REQUIREMENTS

Citizens of the U.S., Canada, the U.K., Ireland, Australia, New Zealand, and South Africa all need valid **passports** to enter any Eastern European country and to re-enter their own country. Some countries will not allow entrance if the holder's passport will expire in less than six months, and returning to the U.S. with an expired passport may result in a fine. Most countries in Eastern Europe require a **visa**; Ukraine and Russia require **invitations** from a sponsoring individual or organization.

When you enter a country, dress neatly and carry **proof of your financial independence,** such as a visa to the next country on your itinerary, an airplane ticket to depart, enough money to cover the cost of your living expenses, etc. Admission as a visitor does not include the right to work, which is authorized only by a work permit (see Alternatives to Tourism below). Entering certain countries to study requires a special visa, and immigration officers may also want to see proof of acceptance from a school, proof that the course of study will take up most of your time in the country, and as always, proof that you can support yourself.

PASSPORTS

Before you leave, photocopy the page of your passport that contains your photograph and identifying information, especially your passport number. Carry this photocopy in a safe place apart from your passport, and leave another copy at home. These measures will help prove your citizenship and facilitate the issuing of a new passport if you lose the original document. Consulates also recommend you carry an expired passport or an official copy of your birth certificate in a part of your baggage separate from other documents. You can request a duplicate birth certificate from the Bureau of Vital Records and Statistics in your state or province of birth.

If you do lose your passport, it may take weeks to process a replacement, and your new one may be valid only for a limited time. In addition, any visas stamped in your old passport will be irretrievably lost. If this happens, immediately notify the local police and the nearest embassy or consulate of your home government. To expedite its replacement, you will need to know all information previously recorded and show identification and proof of citizenship. Some consulates can issue new passports within two days if you can give them proof of citizenship. In an emergency, ask for immediate temporary traveling papers that will permit you to reenter your home country.

Your passport is a public document that belongs to your nation's government. You may have to surrender it to a foreign government official; however, if you don't get it back in a reasonable amount of time, inform the nearest mission of your home country.

Applying for a Passport

U.S. and Canada

U.S. citizens may apply for a passport, valid for 10 years (five years if under 18) at any federal or state **courthouse** or **post office** authorized to accept passport applications, or at a **U.S. Passport Agency,** located in Boston, Chicago, Honolulu, Houston, Los Angeles, Miami, New Orleans, New York, Philadelphia, San Francisco, Seattle, Stamford, or Washington, DC. Refer to the "U.S. Government, State Department" section of the telephone directory or call your local post office for addresses. Parents must apply in person for children under age 13. You must apply in person if this is your first passport, you're under age 18, or if your current passport is more than 12 years old or was issued before your 18th birthday. It will cost US$65 (under 18, US$40). You can **renew** your passport by mail or in person for US$55. Processing usually takes three to four weeks. Passport agencies offer **rush service** if you have proof that you're departing within five working days (e.g. an airplane ticket). For more info, contact the U.S. Passport Information's **24-hr. recorded message** (tel. (202) 647-0518). If your passport is lost or stolen in the U.S., report it in writing to Passport Services, U.S. Department of State, 1111 19th St., NW, Washington, DC 20522-1705, or to the nearest passport agency.

Canadian application forms in English and French are available at all passport offices, post offices, and most travel agencies. Citizens may apply in person at any one of 28 regional Passport Offices across Canada. Travel agents can direct the applicant to the nearest location. Canadian citizens residing abroad should contact the nearest Canadian embassy or consulate. You can apply by mail by sending a completed application form with appropriate documentation and the CDN$35 fee to Passport Office, Foreign Affairs, Ottawa, Ont., K1A OG3. Processing takes approximately five business days for in-person applications and three weeks for mailed ones. A passport is valid for five years and is not renewable. Keep in mind that some countries require a child to carry his or her own passport whether traveling with a parent or not. If a passport is lost abroad, Canadians must be able to prove citizenship with another document. For additional info, call (800) 567-6868 (24 hrs.; from Canada only). In Metro Toronto call 973-3251. Montrealers should dial 283-2152. Refer to the booklet *Bon Voyage, But...* for further help and a list of Canadian embassies and consulates abroad. It is available free of charge from any passport office or from Info-Export (BPTE), External Affairs, Ottawa, Ont., K1A OG2.

U.K., Ireland, Australia, New Zealand, and South Africa

British citizens, British Dependent Territories citizens, and British Overseas citizens may apply for a **full passport.** Residents of the U.K., the Channel Islands and the Isle of Man also have the option of applying for a more restricted **British Visitor's Passport.** For a full passport, valid for 10 years (five years if under 16), apply in person or by mail to a passport office, located in London, Liverpool, Newport, Peterborough, Glasgow, or Belfast. The fee is UK£18. Children under 16 may be included on a parent's passport. Processing by mail usually takes four to six weeks. The London office offers same-day walk-in rush service; arrive early. A Visitor's Passport, valid for one year in some Western European countries and Bermuda only, is available from main post offices in England, Scotland and Wales, and from passport offices in Northern Ireland, the Channel Islands and the Isle of Man. The fee is UK£12.

Irish citizens can apply for a passport by mail to either the Department of Foreign Affairs, Passport Office, Setanta Centre, Molesworth St., Dublin 2 (tel. (01) 671 16 33), or the Passport Office, 1A South Mall, Cork (tel. (021) 27 25 25). You can obtain an application form at a local Garda station or request one from a passport office. Passports cost IR£45 and are valid for 10 years. Citizens under 18 or over 65 can request a three-year passport that costs IR£10.

Australian citizens must apply for a passport in person at a post office, a passport office, or an Australian diplomatic mission overseas. An appointment may be necessary. Passport offices are located in Adelaide, Brisbane, Canberra, Darwin, Hobart, Melbourne, Newcastle, Perth, and Sydney. A parent may file an application for a child who is under 18 and unmarried. Application fees are adjusted every three months.

Applicants for **New Zealand passports** must contact their local Link Centre, travel agent, or New Zealand Representative for an application form, which they must complete and mail to the New Zealand Passport Office, Documents of National Identity Division, Department of Internal Affairs, Box 10-526, Wellington (tel. (04) 474 81 00). The application fee is NZ$80 for an application submitted in New Zealand and NZ$130 for one submitted overseas (if under age 16, NZ$40 and NZ$65, respectively). Standard processing time is 10 working days from receipt of completed application. Overseas citizens should send the passport application to the nearest embassy, high commission, or consulate that is authorized to issue passports.

South African citizens can apply for a passport at any Home Affairs Office. Two photos, either a birth certificate or an identity book, and the SAR38 fee must accompany a completed application. For further information, contact the nearest Department of Home Affairs Office.

VISAS

A visa is an endorsement that a foreign government stamps into a passport; it allows the bearer to stay in that country for a specified purpose and period of time. Most visas cost US$10-50 and allow you to spend about a month in a country, within six months to a year from the date of issue. Eastern European countries' visa requirements have been eroding steadily since 1989 but vary greatly for citizens of different countries. We list specific visa requirements in the Getting There section of each country introduction. Check the country's visa requirements and restrictions as close to your departure date as possible.

Certain countries in Eastern Europe require travelers to register with the local police or with a special office upon arrival, and to have their visas stamped. Other countries require travelers to keep a statistical card on which they must keep track of where they spend each and every night while in the country.

Russia and Ukraine will only issue visas to travelers possessing invitations from friends, relatives, or a sponsoring organization in the country. If you don't have someone to invite you, there are several organizations in the West that can arrange the appropriate paper work for a fee. We list these in the Getting There section of each country. Visas to Russia and Ukraine must also list all the cities and towns on your itinerary. Although this rule is inconsistently enforced, local police and hotel managers can be nasty if the mood strikes them. Failing to produce the required documents when asked has ruined, and even ended many trips.

Some visas are incompatible: Greece won't let you in if you have a passport stamp from Northern Cyprus; Morocco and most Arab countries turn away those with Israeli stamps. You may ask that visa or entry stamps be placed on a removable page in your passport.

If you want to stay for longer, apply for a visa at the country's embassy or consulate in your home country well before your departure. Unless you are a student, extending your stay once you are abroad is more difficult. You must contact the country's immigration officials or local police well before your time is up, and show sound proof of financial resources (see Entrance Requirements).

For more information, send for *Foreign Visa Requirements* (US$0.50) from **Consumer Information Center,** Dept. 454V, Pueblo, CO 81009 (tel. (719) 948-3334), or contact **Center for International Business and Travel (CIBT),** 25 West 43rd St. #1420, New York, NY 10036 (tel. (800) 925-2428 or (212) 575-2811 from NYC). This organization secures visas for travel to and from all countries. The service charge varies; the average cost for a U.S. citizen is US$15-20 per visa.

HOSTEL MEMBERSHIP

Hostelling International (HI), 9 Guessens Rd., Welwyn Garden City, Hertfordshire AL8 6QW, England (tel. (0707) 33 24 87). A worldwide federation of youth hostels (more than 5000 total) and of individual national hostelling associations. All of the organizations listed below are HI national affiliates, and thus comply with any standards and regulations set by HI. Official youth hostels worldwide will normally display the HI logo (a blue triangle) alongside the symbol of one of the 70 national hostel associations.

A one-year HI membership permits you to stay at an increasing number of youth hostels all over Eastern Europe at unbeatable prices. And, despite the name, you need not be a youth; travelers over 25 pay only a slight surcharge for a bed. Save yourself potential trouble by procuring a membership card at home; some hostels don't sell them on the spot. For the most part, membership must be acquired through the HI affiliate in one's own country, not abroad. For more details on youth hostels, see Accommodations in each country's Essentials section.

One-year hostel membership cards are available from some travel agencies, including Council Travel, Let's Go Travel, and STA Travel (see Travel Organizations, above), and from the following organizations:

American Youth Hostels (HI-AYH), 733 15th St., NW, #840, Washington, DC, 20005 (tel. (202) 783-6161, fax 783-6171). Comprised of 39 local councils which, in addition to licensing hostels (150 in 36 states and the District of Columbia), provide local members and visitors with special programs, events, trips, and activities. HI-AYH membership cards cost US$25, renewals US$20 (under 18, US$10; over 54, US$15; family cards, US$35). Membership valid for one year from date of issue. Contact AYH for ISIC, student and charter flights, travel equipment, literature on budget travel, and information on summer positions as a group leader for domestic outings.

Hostelling International—Canada (HI-C), 400-205 Catherine St., Ottawa, Ont. K2P 1C3 (tel. (613) 237-7884, fax 237-7868). One-year membership fee CDN$26.75, under 18 CDN$12.84, two-year CDN$37.45.

Youth Hostels Association of England and Wales (YHA), Trevelyan House, 8 St. Stephen's Hill, St. Albans, Herts. AL1 2DY (tel. (0727) 85 52 15) or 14 Southampton St., Covent Garden, London WC2E 7HY (tel. (0171) 836 10 36). Enrollment fees are UK£9, under 18 UK£3, two-day introductory membership (over 18) UK£3, children 5-18 enrolled free when a parent joins.

An Óige (Irish Youth Hostel Association), 61 Mountjoy St., Dublin 7 (tel. (01) 830 45 55, fax 830 58 08). One-year membership is IR£7.50, under 18 IR£4, and family IR£15.

Youth Hostels Association of Northern Ireland (YHANI), 22-32 Donegall Rd., Belfast BT12 5JN, Northern Ireland (tel. (0232) 32 47 33, fax 43 96 99).

Scottish Youth Hostels Association (SYHA), 7 Glebe Crescent, Sterling FK8 2JA (tel. (0786) 45 11 81, fax 45 01 98). Membership UK£6, under 18 UK£2.50.

Australian Youth Hostels Association (AYHA), Level 3, 10 Mallett St., Camperdown, NSW, 2050 (tel. (02) 565 16 99, fax 565 13 25). Fee AUS$40, renewal AUS$24; under 18 fee and renewal both AUS$12.

Youth Hostels Association of New Zealand (YHANZ), P.O. Box 436, 173 Gloucester St., Christchurch 1 (tel. (03) 379 99 70, fax 365 44 76). Annual memberships: Senior (adult) NZ$34, Youth (15-17) NZ$12, under 15 free. Rates are lower for 2- and 3-year memberships. Life membership NZ$240. New Zealand memberships are not renewable overseas.

Hostel Association of South Africa, 606 Boston House, Strand St., Cape Town 8001 (tel. (21) 419 18 53).

Budget Accommodation Vol. 1: Europe and the Mediterranean (US$11, CDN$13, UK£7, AUS$15), lists up-to-date information on HI hostels; it's available from any hostel association.

HI has recently instituted an **International Booking Network** which allows you to make confirmed reservations at any of almost 200 hostels in the U.S. and abroad. To reserve space in high season, obtain an International Booking Voucher from any national youth hostel association (in your home country or the one you will visit) and send it to a participating hostel four to eight weeks in advance of your stay, along with US$2 in local currency. You can contact some hostels, indicated in the guide, by fax. If your plans are firm enough to allow it, pre-booking is wise. Reservations can be made for up to three consecutive nights and for groups of up to nine people, and changes can be made up to three or more days before the date of the reservation. Credit card (MC or Visa) guarantee required.

YOUTH, STUDENT, & TEACHER IDENTIFICATION

The **International Student Identity Card (ISIC)** is the most widely accepted form of student identification. Flashing this card can garner you discounts for sights, theaters, museums, accommodations, train, ferry, and airplane travel, and other services throughout Europe. Present the card wherever you go, and ask about discounts even when none are advertised. It also provides accident insurance of up to US$3000 as well as US$100 per day of in-hospital care for up to 60 days. In addition, cardholders have access to a toll-free Traveler's Assistance hotline whose multilingual staff can provide help in medical, legal, and financial emergencies overseas.

Many student travel offices issue ISICs, including Council Travel, Let's Go Travel, and STA Travel in the U.S.; Travel CUTS in Canada; and any of the organizations under the auspices of the International Student Travel Confederation (ISTC) around the world (see Travel Organizations, above). When you apply for the card, request a copy of the International Student Identity Card Handbook, which lists by country some of the available discounts. You can also write to CIEE for a copy (see Travel Organizations). The card is valid from September to December of the following year. The fee is US$16. Applicants must be at least 12 years old and must be a degree-seeking student of a secondary or post-secondary school. Because of the pro-liferation of phony ISICs, many airlines and some other services now require other proof of student identity: have a signed letter from the registrar attesting to your stu-dent status and stamped with the school seal, and carry your school ID card. The new, US$16 **International Teacher Identity Card (ITIC)** offers similar but limited discounts, as well as medical insurance coverage.

Federation of International Youth Travel Organisations (FIYTO) issues a dis-count card to travelers who are not students but are under 26. Also known as the **International Youth Discount Travel Card**, or the **GO 25 Card**, this one-year card offers many of the same benefits as the ISIC, and most organizations that sell the ISIC also sell the Go 25 Card. A brochure that lists discounts is free when you purchase the card. To apply, bring: (1) proof of birthdate (copy of birth certificate, passport, or valid driver's license); and (2) a passport-sized photo (with your name printed on the back). The fee is US$16, CDN$12, or UK£4. For information, contact CIEE in the U.S. or FIYTO in Denmark (addresses in Travel Organizations, above)

DRIVING PERMITS AND INSURANCE

You must have an **International Driving Permit** (IDP) to drive in Europe, though certain countries allow travelers to drive with a valid American or Canadian license for a limited number of months. A valid driver's license from your home country must always accompany the IDP. Call an automobile association to find out if your destination country requires the IDP. Even if it doesn't it may be a good idea to get one anyway, in case you're in a position (such as an accident or stranded in a smaller town) where the police may not read or speak English.

Your IDP must be issued in your own country before you depart. U.S. license holders can obtain an International Driving Permit (US$10), valid for one year, at any **American Automobile Association (AAA)** office or by writing to its main office, AAA Florida, Travel Agency Services Department, 1000 AAA Drive (mail stop 28), Heathrow, FL 32746-5080 (tel. (407) 444-4245, fax 444-7823). For further infor-mation, contact a local AAA office.

Canadian license holders can obtain an IDP (CDN$10) through any **Canadian Automobile Association (CAA)** branch office in Canada, or by writing to CAA Tor-onto, 60 Commerce Valley Dr. East, Markham, Ont., L3T 7P9 (tel. (416) 771-3170).

If you are renting a car in Europe chances are that your rental company will sup-ply insurance. Be sure, however, that if you are traveling through more than one country, your insurance is valid in all countries on your itinerary. For those using their own cars while traveling, the **green card,** or **International Insurance Certifi-cate,** to prove that you have liability insurance, is necessary. Contact any AAA or CAA office to find out which countries have special restrictions on green card auto insurance. European drivers should contact their car insurance companies to check the limitations of their policies for international driving. If you have a collision while in Europe, the accident will show up on your domestic records. Theft insurance is not paid by the rental agency in some countries; in any case, you will be required to pay for insurance when the agency does not.

■■■ MONEY

If you stay in hostels and prepare your own food, expect to spend anywhere from US$12-50 per day plus transportation, depending on the local cost of living and your needs. Don't sacrifice your health or safety for a cheaper tab. Also remember to check the financial pages of a large newspaper for up-to-the-minute exchange rates before embarking on your journey. Certain countries in Eastern Europe are experi-encing high levels of inflation and currency depreciation.

CURRENCY AND EXCHANGE

Banks in Europe often use a three-letter code based on the name of the country and the name of the currency. We list this code at the beginning of each country section, with the abbreviation we use for that country's currency and the September, 1994 exchange rate for U.S. dollars (US$), Canadian dollars (CDN$), British pounds (UK£), Irish pounds (IR£), Australian dollars (AUS$), New Zealand dollars (NZ$) and South African Rand (SAR).

It is more expensive to buy foreign currency than to buy domestic; i.e., Hungarian Forints will be less costly in Hungary than in the U.S. However, converting some money before you go—if that currency is available abroad—will allow you to breeze through the airport while others languish in exchange lines, and is a good practice in case you find yourself stuck with no money after banking hours or on a holiday. It's generally wise to bring at least enough foreign currency to last for the first 24-72 hours of a trip, depending on the day of week you will be arriving. Also, observe commission rates closely, and check newspapers to get the standard rate of exchange. Bank rates are generally the best. Of course, services vary; sometimes the tourist office or exchange kiosks may have the best rates.

Since you lose money with every transaction, convert in large sums (unless the currency is rapidly depreciating), but not more of any one currency than you will need. Save transaction receipts; some countries require them to reconvert local currency. Certain countries, such as the Slovak Republic, will not allow foreigners to reconvert the local currency back to dollars or pounds. Get around this by converting in small sums, or by finding a trustworthy local willing to take your left over currency to the bank on your behalf. Exchanging some of your old currency before moving on to a new country, is, although a little more costly, good insurance against arriving after hours in a bankless town.

American Express offices usually charge no commission, but often have slightly worse rates than other exchanges. Carry some bills or checks in small denominations, especially for those moments when you are forced to exchange money at train stations or, worse yet, at luxury hotels or restaurants. In general, you should carry a range of denominations since, in some countries, charges are levied per check cashed.

Australian and New Zealand dollars are impossible to exchange in many East European countries. U.S. dollars are generally preferred, though certain establishments will only accept German Deutschmarks. Western currency will often be the preferred payment in Eastern European hotels; find out which hotels and restaurants require hard currency before going there, and don't use Western money when you don't need to. Don't throw dollars around visibly to gain preferential treatment, however; besides being offensive, it'll make you an instant target for theft. Some restaurant owners, proprietors, or even taxi drivers may pick up on the fact that you're a foreigner and try to force you to pay in hard currency when it's not necessary. Stick to your guns or go somewhere else.

TRAVELER'S CHECKS

Traveler's Checks are the safest way to hold money; if they get lost or stolen, travelers get reimbursed by the checks' issuers. Though many establishments in Eastern Europe do not yet accept traveler's checks, there is usually a place in town that will cash them for the local currency; this is infinitely safer than carrying large amounts of western currency. Checks should be ordered well in advance, especially if large sums are being requested. Keep check receipts and a record of which checks you've cashed in a separate place from the checks themselves. Leave a photocopy of check serial numbers with someone at home as back-up in case you lose your copy. Never countersign checks until you're prepared to cash them. Be sure to keep cash on hand, particularly in less touristy regions; many establishments may not accept traveler's checks. Finally, be sure to bring your passport with you any time you plan to use the checks.

American Express: Call (800) 221-7282 in U.S. and Canada, (0800) 52 13 13 in the U.K., (008) 25 19 02 in Australia, and (0800) 44 10 68 in New Zealand. Elsewhere, call U.S. collect (801) 964-6665. AmEx traveler's checks are now available in 9

Don't forget to write.

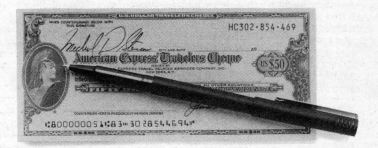

Now that you've said, "Let's go," it's time to say "Let's get American Express® Travelers Cheques." If they are lost or stolen, you can get a fast and full refund virtually anywhere you travel. So before you leave be sure and write.

currencies: British, Canadian, Dutch, French, German, Japanese, Saudi Arabian, Swiss, and U.S. They are the most widely recognized worldwide and easiest to replace if lost or stolen. Checks can be purchased for a small fee at American Express Travel Service Offices, banks and American Automobile Association offices. Cardmembers can also purchase checks at American Express Dispensers at Travel Service Offices, at airports, and by ordering them via phone (tel. (800) ORDER-TC (673-3782)). AmEx offices cash their checks commission-free (except where prohibited by national governments) and sell checks which can be signed by either of 2 people traveling together. AAA members can obtain AmEx traveler's checks commission-free at AAA offices. Request AmEx's booklet "Traveler's Companion," listing travel office addresses and stolen check hotlines for each European country.

Barclays Bank: Call (800) 221-2426 in the U.S. and Canada. Sells Visa traveler's checks in U.S. and Canadian dollars, British pounds, and German marks; a 1-3% commission is charged depending on the bank at which the checks are purchased. When the checks are issued, you will receive the number to call from outside the U.S. for lost or stolen checks. Branches throughout Britain. Barclays branches cash any Visa brand checks for free.

Citicorp: Call (800) 645-6556 in the U.S. and Canada, (0171) 982 40 40 in the U.K. Elsewhere, call U.S. collect at (813) 623-1709. Sells both Citicorp and Citicorp Visa traveler's checks in U.S. and Australian dollars, Japanese yen, German marks, and British pounds. Commission 1-2% on check purchases. Citicorp's World Courier Service guarantees hand-delivery of traveler's checks anywhere in the world.

MasterCard International: Call (800) 223-9920 in U.S. and Canada; elsewhere call U.S. collect (609) 987-7300; from abroad, call (733) 50 29 95 in the U.K. collect. Offers checks in British, German, Canadian, Australian, Hong Kong, Japanese, French, Swiss, Dutch, Spanish, and U.S. currencies. Commission 1-2% for purchases. Try buying the checks at a Thomas Cook office (see below) for potentially lower commissions.

Thomas Cook: Call (800) 223-7373 for refunds and (800) 223-4030 for orders in the U.S. Elsewhere call U.S. collect (212) 974-5696. Distributes traveler's checks with both the MasterCard and Thomas Cook names printed on them. Checks available in U.S. dollars as well as 10 other currencies. 0-2% commission on purchase. Rates often better than those for MasterCard International.

Visa: Call (800) 227-6811 in the U.S. and Canada, (0171) 937 80 91 in the U.K., elsewhere call U.S. collect (212) 858-8500. Any kind of Visa traveler's checks (Barclays or Citicorp) can be reported lost at the general Visa number.

CREDIT CARDS AND CASH CARDS

Credit cards are not always useful to the budget traveler, but they can prove invaluable in a financial emergency. For the most part, only expensive, western-oriented establishments in Eastern Europe take them, but some banks will allow you to withdraw money from ATM machines with a credit card. Visa and MasterCard are the most common, followed by American Express and Diner's Club. The British "Barclaycard" is equivalent to Visa and Mastercard is better-known in Europe as "Euro-Card" or "Access." You can often reduce conversion fees by charging a purchase instead of changing traveler's checks. With credit cards such as American Express, Visa, and MasterCard, associated banks will give you an instant cash advance in the local currency as large as your remaining credit line, but in most cases, you will pay devastating rates of interest for such an advance.

American Express (tel. (800) CASH-NOW (528-4800)) has a hefty annual fee (US$55) but offers a number of services. AmEx cardholders can cash personal checks at AmEx offices abroad. Global Assist, a 24-hr. hotline offering information and legal assistance in emergencies, is also available (tel. (800) 554-2639 in U.S. and Canada; from abroad call U.S. collect (202) 783-7474). Cardholders can also take advantage of the American Express Travel Service; benefits include assistance in changing airline, hotel, and car rental reservations, sending mailgrams and international cables, and holding your mail at one of the more than 1500 AmEx offices around the world. **MasterCard** (tel. (800) 999-0454) and **Visa** (tel. (800) 336-8472) credit cards are sold by individual banks, and each bank offers different services in conjunction with the card.

Automatic Teller Machines (ATMs; operated by bank and credit cards) in Eastern Europe are rare, but some banks in larger cities are connected to an international money network, usually **CIRRUS** (U.S. tel. (800) 4-CIRRUS (424-7787)) or **PLUS** (U.S. tel. (800) 843-7587). Cirrus now has international cash machines in 43 countries and territories. It charges US$5 to withdraw non-domestically. However, depending on the amount of the withdrawal, the fee might be worth it because ATMs offer advantageous exchange rates. PLUS is not as extensive as Cirrus, but can also be accessed in some foreign countries. Soon, traveler's checks will be available from ATM machines through a new **American Express** service (tel. (800) 528-4800). Call to find out if this service is available near you.

Depending on your home bank's system, you will probably be able to access your own personal bank account whenever you're in need of funds. Do this whenever possible, because ATM machines get the wholesale exchange rate which is generally 5% better than the retail rate most banks use; the service fee will depend on your bank. An important note: European ATMs may not have letters on their keypads, so be sure you memorize your PIN by its numbers before you take off.

SENDING MONEY ABROAD

The easiest way to get money from home is to bring an **American Express card;** AmEx allows green-card holders to draw cash from their checking accounts at any of its major offices and many of its representatives' offices, up to US$1000 every 21 days (no service charge, no interest). AmEx also offers the **American Express Moneygram Service** through which money can be sent from the U.S. to Europe. Fees are commensurate with the amount of money being sent and the particular service requested: ten-minute delivery, overnight, or three to five days. For details about your particular country, call (800) 543-4080 in the U.S. or (800) 933-3278 in Canada.

Western Union (tel. (800) 325-6000 in the U.S., Mexico, and Canada and (448) 17 41 36 39 or (0800) 83 38 33 in Europe) cables money. Again, fees for sending money depend not on where the money's going, but on how much is being sent. Rates are US$29 to send US$250, US$40 to send US$500, and US$50 to send US$1000.

Another option is to **cable money** from bank to bank. Find a local bank big enough to have an international department; bring the address of the receiving bank and the destination account number. Both sender and receiver must usually have accounts at the respective institutions. Transfer can take up to a few days; the fee is usually a flat US$20-30. Outside an AmEx office, avoid trying to cash checks in foreign currencies; they take weeks and a US$30 fee to clear.

If you're an American and suddenly find yourself in big trouble, you can have money sent to you via the State Department's **Citizens Emergency Center** (tel. (202) 647-5225, after business hours 647-7000). The State Department, 2201 C St., NW, Washington, DC 20520, will cable a modest amount of money to foreign consular offices, which will then disburse it accordingly. Those wishing to send money abroad through the State Department can drop it off at the department itself or cable money to the department through Western Union. Similar contingencies are available to citizens of other countries. In an emergency, contact the nearest consulate and they will contact your home country for a transfer of funds.

▓▓▓ PACKING

PACK LIGHT! (and pack *brown*.) Eschew colorful luggage that screams "rich-Western-tourist" for boring brown or drab grey to keep muggers away. Before you leave, pack your bag, strap it on, and imagine yourself walking uphill on hot asphalt for the next three hours. At the slightest sign of heaviness, unpack something. A good rule is to set out what you think you'll need, then take half of it and more money. *The Packing Book* (US$7.95), by Judith Gilford, teaches you how to overcome the "overpacking syndrome," provides various checklists and suggested ward-robes, addresses safety concerns, imparts packing techniques, and more. Order from Ten Speed Press (tel. (800) 841-2665).

If you plan to cover a lot of ground by foot, a sturdy **backpack** is hard to beat. Internal frames stand up to airline baggage handlers and can often be converted to shoulder bags; external frames distribute weight more evenly. Good packs usually cost at least US$100, but if you know how to travel simply, adequate gear can often be found for much less at army surplus stores. A plastic bag packed inside your luggage will be useful for dirty laundry, while a small **daypack** is indispensable on plane flights, and for carrying your camera, lunch, and *Let's Go*. Keep your valuables in a **moneybelt** or **neck pouch** under your clothing (see Safety and Security, below).

Comfortable **shoes** are crucial. Do not bring your flashiest Nikes to Eastern Europe, especially to the former Soviet Union. They will brand you as a tourist and a target for theft (and will make it difficult for you to pass as a local in hotels and museums that charge higher rates for foreigners). Opt for nondescript brown leather, instead. In sunny climates, sandals or other light shoes serve well. For heavy-duty hiking, sturdy lace-up walking boots are necessary. Make sure they have good ventilation. A double pair of socks—light absorbent cotton inside and thick wool outside—will cushion feet, keep them dry, and help prevent blisters. Bring a pair of light flip-flops for protection against the fungal floors of some hostel showers.

In wet regions, **raingear** is essential. A waterproof jacket plus a backpack rain cover will take care of you and your pack at a moment's notice. Carry extra toiletries—especially aspirin, razor blades, and tampons—and toilet paper, *lots* of toilet paper. Eastern European trains are grimier than those in the West and the toilet facilities are unreliable. Even if you don't normally use it, bring a bottle of astringent and some cottonballs to rescue your skin on longer train journeys, especially in summer, or be prepared to arrive heavily pimple-faced. In summer, trains are not air-conditioned, and on-board soft drinks are overpriced. Bring a full, sturdy plastic water-bottle. Also consider taking a pocketknife (with all the gizmos), needle and thread, safety pins, masking tape, a flashlight, cutlery (for use in hostels), detergent soap, an alarm clock, a bath towel, bags that seal shut (for damp clothing, soaps or messy foods), and a padlock.

Bringing along a camera, while it allows you to immortalize those raucous soldiers you met on the train, can invite a lot of extra worry. If you do, pack some rolls of **film** as well, since it can be quite expensive in well-touristed areas.

Across Eastern Europe, **electricity** is 220 volts AC, enough to fry any 110V North American appliance. Visit a hardware store for an adapter (which changes the shape of the plug) and a converter (which changes the voltage). Do not make the mistake of using only an adapter, or you'll melt your radio. Also remember that the frequency is usually different (50 instead of 60Hz); its OK if your shaver runs slightly slower, but many motorized appliances will be unhappy at best.

■■■ ALTERNATIVES TO TOURISM

STUDY

Since the end of the Cold War, the number of foreign study programs offered in Eastern Europe has increased dramatically. But programs vary tremendously in expense, academic quality, living conditions, degree of contact with local students, and exposure to the local culture and language. Most American undergraduates enroll in programs sponsored by U.S. universities, but depending on your interests and language skills you might wish to consider direct enrollment in an Eastern European institution. Many colleges staff offices to provide advice and information on study abroad, from the choice of programs to financial aid. Take advantage of these counselors and put in some hours in their libraries. Ask for the names of recent participants in the programs, and get in touch.

Selected Organizations and Publishers

CIEE (Council on International Educational Exchange) (see Travel Organizations as well as Work and Volunteering, both below) is involved with the administration of education exchange programs, and also provides general information on academic, work, volunteer, and professional opportunities abroad (see below). The free brochures *Basic Facts on Study Abroad,* and *International Workcamps* are useful and available at Council Charter locations. Also available: *Work, Study, Travel Abroad: The Whole World Handbook* (US$13.95, postage US$1.50); *Going Places: The High School Student's Guide to Study, Travel, and Adventure Abroad* (US$13.95, postage US$1.50); and *Smart Vacations: The Traveler's Guide to Learning Adventures Abroad* (US$14.95, postage US$1.50).

The Institute of International Education Books (IIE Books), 809 United Nations Plaza, New York, NY 10017-3580 (tel. (212) 984-5412, fax 984-5358) puts out several annually updated, extensive reference books on study abroad. *Academic Year Abroad* (US$42.95) and *Vacation Study Abroad* (US$36.95) detail over 3600 programs offered by U.S. colleges and universities overseas. IIE Books also offers the free pamphlet *Basic Facts on Foreign Study* and sells other useful reference books. They distribute several books published by the Central Bureau for Educational Visits and Exchanges (see separate listing under Work), including *Study Holidays, Working Holidays,* and *Home From Home,* but they charge a good deal more for them (US$22.95 each). IIE Books also operates the International Education Center at their UN Plaza address (open Tues.-Fri. 11am-4pm). If you order books directly from IIE, postage is US$4 per book.

Unipub Co., 4611-F Assembly Dr., Lanham, MD 20706-4391 (tel. (800) 274-4888, fax (301) 459-0056). distributes UNESCO publications including *Study Abroad,* a guide to international scholarships and courses for students of all ages (US$24.95 plus postage and handling).

Selected Programs

American Field Service Intercultural Programs (AFS), 220 East 42nd Street, 3rd Floor, New York, NY 10017. Call (800) 237-4636 or speak to Rory Vibar at the

Program Information Office (tel. (212) 949-4242). Founded in 1947, the AFS provides summer, semester, and year-long homestay exchange programs for high school students. Short-term adult programs are also offered. Financial aid available. Exchanges in Eastern Europe to: Czech Republic, Hungary, Latvia, Russia, and Slovakia.

American Institute for Foreign Study/American Council for International Studies. College Division: 102 Greenwich Avenue, Greenwich CT 06830 (tel. (800) 727-2437). High school traveling programs: call (800) 888-ACIS. AIFS/ACIS organizes academic year, semester, summer, and academic quarter study abroad programs in Eastern Europe in St. Petersburg. Also organizes multi-country traveling courses. All programs include tuition, accommodation in student residences, most meals, insurance, one-way air fare (round-trip for summer programs), and the services of an on-site Resident Director. Programs are open to interested adults. Minority and merit scholarships available.

Beaver College Center for Education Abroad, 450 S. Easton Road, Glenside, PA 19038-3295 (tel. (800) 755-5607), runs an Eastern European program in Hungary. Write to request their hefty catalog.

Eurocentres, 101 N. Union St., Suite 300, Alexandria, VA 22314 (tel. (800) 648-4809 or (703) 684-1494, fax (703) 684-1495) or Eurocentres, Head Office, Seestrasse 247, CH-8038 Zurich, Switzerland. Eurocentres coordinates language programs and homestays for college students and adults in Eastern Europe in Russian in Moscow. College credit is available. Minimum age is 18. Program fees range from about US$900-1160, airfare not included, and lengths from three to four weeks. Some financial aid is available. You can also pick up one of their confusing introductory brochures at Council Travel/CIEE offices.

Language Immersion Institute, JFT 916, The College at New Paltz, New Paltz, NY 12561 (tel. (914) 257-3500), provides language instruction at all levels in Czech, Hungarian, Polish, Russian, and Ukrainian. They emphasize rapid acquisition and conduct weekend immersion courses (ooh, Hungarian in 48 hours!) which are held in New Paltz; they also conduct two-week summer courses and some overseas courses. Program fees are about US$250 for a weekend or US$650 per week for the longer courses.

Open Door Student Exchange, 839 Stewart Avenue Suite D, Garden City, New York, NY 11530 (tel. (516) 486-7330) is a high school exchange program with stays in countries in Eastern Europe and the CIS.

School for International Training (SIT), College Semester Abroad Admissions, Kipling Road, P.O. Box 676, Brattleboro, VT 05302 (tel. (800) 336-1616 or (802) 258-3279). Runs 16-credit, semester long academic programs in Eastern Europe in the Czech Republic and Russia that feature cross-cultural orientation, intensive language study, interdisciplinary academic seminars, homestay, field study and independent study projects. Semester programs cost US$8500-9300, including tuition, room and board, round-trip international airfare, insurance, and all other program-related expenses. U.S. Federal financial aid applies and aid from your home institution may apply; additionally, SIT offers limited scholarships.

Youth for Understanding International Exchange (YFU), 3501 Newark St., Washington DC 20016 (tel. (800) TEENAGE or (202) 966-6800, fax (202) 895-1104), places U.S. high school students worldwide for homestays of a summer, a semester, or a year. YFU also offers a Community College program in which international students from 18-29 years of age spend one year with an American family and attend a community college.

WORK

The good news is that there's no better way to submerge yourself in a foreign culture than to become part of its economy. The bad news is that in many countries in Eastern Europe it's difficult to find a temporary unskilled job; even the most menial labor may be taking needed employment away from a local citizen. Possible (relatively) unskilled jobs include ones in agriculture, as an au pair, in summer camps, as a freelance teacher of English, or at tourist sites. But they will rarely be glamorous and may not even pay for your plane ticket over. Also consider the potential health risks of certain types of employment (see Health).

On the flip side, many foreign companies are infiltrating Eastern Europe and often require office workers who speak English and are familiar with Western business practices. Before leaving, find out which companies in your country have offices in Eastern Europe and get the name of a contact person in the country that interests you. Pester him or her with phone calls, letters and resumes. Once abroad, your best bet is to be brazen and contact the local offices of any foreign company that you come across, and to look for ads in local newspapers. International aid and economic development agencies and intergovernmental bodies also hire motivated English-speakers who are familiar with the region. If you speak an Eastern European language, translation jobs are easy to find. Another possibility is to try your luck with the local English-language newspaper (though expect to be underpaid).

Officially, if you can hold a job at all you usually can do so only with a work permit, applied for by your prospective employer (or by you, with supporting papers from the employer). Often an employer must demonstrate that a potential employee has skills that locals lack. The catch-22 is that commonly you must physically enter the country in order to have immigration officials validate your work permit papers and note your status in your passport. This means that if you can't set up a job from afar (which requires contacts and time) and have the work permit sent to you, you must enter the country to look for a job, find an employer, and have them start the permit process, then leave the country until the permit is sent to you, and finally reenter the country and start work. Further restrictions may exist, such as that foreigners can only work for foreign or part-foreign enterprises. Contact an embassy or consulate for more information.

In practice, it may not be so complicated—but Eastern Europe oscillates between the intensely bureaucratic and the seemingly lawless. Friends in Europe may be able to help expedite work permits or arrange work-for-accommodations swaps. Many permitless agricultural workers go untroubled by local authorities, who recognize the need for seasonal help. The best tips on jobs for foreigners often come from other travelers, so be alert and inquisitive. (Also be aware of your rights as an employee; should a crafty national try to refuse payment at the end of the season, it'll help to have a written confirmation of your agreement.) Some youth hostels may feed and house travelers willing to stay a while and help run the place.

Teaching English has long been the traditional job for foreign visitors to Eastern Europe. These days, so many foreigners are descending on Prague, Budapest, and Warsaw that finding a position in these cities is difficult. Increasingly, you will need a Teacher of English as a Foreign Language (TEFL) certification to get a job. You can take a 3-week course at your local U.S. Literacy Council (US$40) to get it. Work in rural areas is easier to find. Students can check with their universities' foreign language departments, which may have official or unofficial connections to job openings abroad. Post a sign in markets or learning centers stating that you are a native speaker, and scan the classifieds of local newspapers, where residents often advertise for language instruction. Various organizations in the U.S. will place you in a (low-paying) teaching job. Professional English-teaching positions are harder to get; many schools require at least a bachelor's degree and training in teaching English as a foreign language. The books listed below provide more detailed information and references for employers, of English teachers and otherwise, in Eastern Europe:

Addison Wesley, Jacob Way, Reading, MA 01867 (tel. (800) 358-4566), publishes *International Jobs: Where They Are, How to Get Them,* by Eric Kocher. Request it from your local bookstore or write to Addison-Wesley's Order Department. The new edition costs US$14.95.

Central Bureau for Educational Visits and Exchanges, Seymour Mews House, Seymour Mews, London W1H 9PE, England (tel. (0171) 486 51 01, fax 935 57 41), publishes several useful books. *Working Holidays* is an annual guide to short-term paid and voluntary work opportunities in Britain and around the world and *Teach Abroad* is a guide to organizations who recruit qualified teachers to recruit overseas, either on a paid or voluntary basis. Other books published by the Bureau are *A Year Between, Home From Home,* and *Study Holidays.* All books are £8.99 including postage.

CIEE (Council on International Educational Exchange) (see Travel Organizations, Study, and Volunteering) publishes a booklet *Work Abroad.* However, none of its work permit programs are currently available for Eastern European countries.

InterExchange, 161 Sixth Avenue, New York, NY 10013 (tel. (212) 924-0446), provides information on international work programs and au pair positions in Eastern Europe in the Czech Republic, Hungary, and Poland.

International Schools Services, P.O. Box 5910, Princeton, NJ 08543 (tel. (609) 452-0990), publishes a free newsletter, *NewsLinks,* which provides information mostly for teachers and school administrators. Call or write to get on the mailing list. ISS's Educational Staffing Department, which coordinates placement of teachers in international and American schools, publishes the free brochure *Your Brochure to Teaching and Administrative Opportunities Abroad*

Office of Overseas Schools, A-OS, Room 245, SA-29, Department of State, Washington DC 20522 (tel. (703) 875-7800), maintains a list of elementary and secondary schools abroad and agencies which arrange placement for Americans to teach abroad.

Peterson's Guides, 202 Carnegie Center, Princeton, NJ 08543 (tel. (800) 338-3282 or (609) 243-9111). The *ISS Directory of Overseas Schools* (US$34.95) is published by International School Services but distributed by Peterson's. The useful annual *Directory of Overseas Summer Jobs* (US$14.95) and *Work Your Way Around the World* (US$17.95), are published by Vacation Work Publications but distributed by Peterson's. These books can be requested from a good bookstore or ordered directly from Peterson's (postage US$5.75 for the first book and US$1 for each additional one).

Surrey Books, 230 E. Ohio St., Chicago, IL 60611 (tel. (800) 326-4430) publishes *How to Get a Job in Europe: The Insider's Guide.* The currently available edition, published in 1991, is wildly inaccurate for Eastern Europe, but a new edition is due in February 1995.

Vacation Work Publications, 9 Park End St., Oxford, OX1 1HJ, England (tel. (0865) 24 19 78, fax 79 08 85) publishes a number of directories with job listings for summer and year-long employment around the world and several guides for the budget traveler. Some are distributed in the U.S. by Peterson's Guides; others available in the U.S. include: *The Au Pair and Nanny's Guide to Working Abroad, Working in Ski Resorts—Europe and North America,* and *Teaching English Abroad.*

World Trade Academy Press, 50 East 42nd St., New York, NY 10017 (tel. (212) 697-4999), publishes *Looking for Employment in Foreign Countries* (US$16.50) which gives information on federal, commercial, and volunteer jobs abroad and advice on resumes and interviews.

VOLUNTEERING

Like paid jobs, volunteer jobs are not necessarily as readily available in Eastern Europe as in the West; nevertheless, they do exist. You may receive room and board in exchange for your labor, and the work can be fascinating. Opportunities include community service, workcamp projects and office work for international organizations. Keep in mind: the organizations that arrange placement sometimes charge high application fees in addition to the workcamps' charges for room and board. You can sometimes avoid this extra fee by contacting the individual workcamps directly; check with the organization. English-language newspapers and some international aid agencies also love unpaid interns. Listings in Vacation Work's *International Directory of Voluntary Work* (£8.95; see ordering information under Work, above) can be helpful.

Archaeological Institute of America publishes the *Archaeological Field Work Opportunities Bulletin.* The Institute does not distribute the bulletin, but they may have further information about work opportunities; write to the Archaeological Institute of America, 675 Commonwealth Avenue, Boston, MA 02215 (tel. (617) 353-9361, fax 353-6550). The Bulletin can be purchased from Kendall/Hunt Publishing, 4500 Westmark Drive, Dubuque, Iowa 52002 (tel. (800) 228-0810).

Central Bureau for Educational Visits and Exchanges, (see Work above) also publishes *Volunteer Work* is a guide to organizations recruiting individuals, usually those with skills and experience, for long-term voluntary service worldwide.

Council on International Educational Exchange (CIEE) (see Travel Organizations and Study and Work) publishes *Volunteer! The Comprehensive Guide to Voluntary Service in the U.S. and Abroad* (US$9, US$1.50 postage). Available from Council Travel offices and CIEE. CIEE's International Voluntary Service Department arranges placement in workcamps for two to four weeks on environmental or community service projects in the Czech Republic, Lithuania, Poland, Slovenia, and Ukraine. Registration fee for the placement service is US$165.

International Association for the Exchange of Students for Technical Experience (IAESTE) Training Program, c/o AIPT, #250, 10400 Little Patuxent Parkway, Columbia, MD 21044 (tel. (410) 997-2200), is an internship exchange for science, architecture, engineering, agriculture, and math students who have completed at least two years at an accredited four-year institution. There is a nonrefundable US$75 application fee; apply by December 10 for a summer placement (year-long placements are rare).

Service Civil International-Voluntary Service (SCI-VS), Route 2, Box 560B, Crozet, VA 22932 (tel. (804) 823-1826), arranges placement in workcamps in Europe and the U.S. for people over 18 or 16, depending on the camp. Registration fees range up to US$200 (CIS). Established after WWI as a means to promote peace and international understanding.

Volunteers for Peace Inc. (VFP), 43 Tiffany Rd., Belmont, VT 05730 (tel. (802) 259-2759, fax 259-2922; ask for Peter Coldwell), has been coordinating workcamps since 1981. VFP publishes the *International Workcamp Directory,* which is updated every year and can be ordered directly from them for US$10 (including postage, and deductible from future program fees). You can also receive their free newsletter. The directory covers 40 countries, and placement is quick – reservations are generally confirmed within three days. Programs in Eastern Europe in: Belarus, Bulgaria, Czech Republic, Hungary, Poland, Romania, Russia, Slovakia, Slovenia, and Ukraine. Most volunteers register between mid-April and mid-May. Work together with 10-15 volunteers from around the world on environmental projects, construction or renovation of buildings or historical monuments, creating playschemes for children, painting houses, schools, or murals, and much more. Most workcamps' fees are US$150, and some are open to 16-18-year-olds for a slightly higher fee (US$175).

U.S. Peace Corps, Room 9320, Washington, DC 20526 (tel. (800) 424-8580) offers volunteering opportunities all over the world in education, health, and agriculture; joining means filling a two-year commitment. Programs in Eastern Europe in: Albania, Belarus, Bulgaria, Czech Republic, Estonia, Hungary, Latvia, Lithuania, Moldova, Poland, Romania, Russia, Slovakia, and Ukraine. Applicants of all ages and experiences are encouraged, but you must be a U.S. citizen.

WorldTeach, Harvard Institute for International Development, 1 Eliot St., Cambridge, MA 02138 (tel. (617) 495-5527), runs volunteer teaching programs in Poland and Russia.

YMCA International Camp Counselor Abroad Program, 71 West 23rd St., Suite 1904, New York, NY 10010 (tel. (212) 727-8800, fax 727-8814), provides placement in YMCA camps abroad. Applicants must be over 20, U.S. citizens, and have worked in a YMCA camp before.

■■■ BOOKS, GUIDES, MAPS, ETC.

You might supplement your *Let's Go* library with publications that serve more specific purposes. **Handy Dictionaries** (US$7-9) in over 90 languages and language tapes can be obtained through Hippocrene Books, Inc. 171 Madison Ave., New York, NY 10016 (orders: tel. (718) 454-2366, fax 454-1391). Request their free catalog, which lists maps and travel reference books too. Hard-to-find **maps** are stocked by Wide World Books and Maps, 1911 N. 45th St., Seattle, WA 98103 (tel. (206) 634-3453).

The inspired *People to People* guides by Jim Haynes list names, addresses and mini-biographies of people in all sorts of places across Eastern Europe who speak English and want to meet you. "They're waiting for you. And they're nice." Write to Zephyr Press, 13 Robinson Street, Somerville, MA 02145 USA (tel. (617) 628-9726, fax 776-8246) or Canongate Press, 14 Frederick Street, Edinburgh, EH2 2HB, Scotland (tel. (31) 220 38 00).

Peruse Mona Winks: Self-Guided Tours of Europe's Top Museums (U.S.$17) or take Europe 101: Art and History for the Traveler (US$16) with "Professor" Rick Steves, a veteran traveler who offers great advice on the dos and don'ts of budget travel in *Europe Through the Back Door* (US$18) and *Russia and the Baltics Through the Back Door* (US$5.95) written by veteran *Let's Go* editor Ian Watson. All three can be obtained from John Muir Publications, P.O. Box 613, Santa Fe, NM 87504 (tel. (505) 982-4078 or (800) 888-7504).

For the inside story on *Hiking in Poland & the Ukraine* (US$17), write to Hunter Publishing, 300 Raritan Center Parkway, Edison, NJ 08818 (tel. (908) 225-1900, fax 417-0482) for their catalog. *The Passport*, a booklet listing hints about every aspect of traveling and studying abroad is distributed free of charge to universities; call The College Connection at (800) 952-7277. Travel gear as well as maps, guidebooks, railpasses, timetables, and youth hostel memberships can also be purchased from the Forsyth Travel Library, P.O. Box 2975, Shawnee Mission, KS 662011 (tel. (800) 367-7984, fax (913) 384-3553). MC, Visa, Discover, no COD.

■■■ HEALTH

PREPARING FOR A HEALTHY TRIP

Common sense is the simplest prescription for good health while you travel: eat well, drink enough, get enough sleep, and don't overexert yourself. If you're going to do a lot of walking, take some quick-energy foods to keep your strength up. You'll need plenty of protein (for sustained energy) and fluids (to prevent dehydration and constipation, two of the most common health problems for travelers). Carry a water bottle and drink frequently. If you are prone to sunburn, use a potent sunscreen, cover up with long sleeves and a hat, and drink plenty of fluids. Remember to treat your most valuable resource well: lavish your feet with attention. Make sure your shoes are appropriate for extended walking, change your socks often, and pad hotspots with **moleskin** before they become painful blisters. For minor health problems, a compact **first-aid kit** should suffice. Bring any **medication** you may need, as well as a copy of the prescription and/or a statement from your doctor, especially if you will be bringing insulin, syringes, or any prescribed narcotics into European countries. Carry separate batches, stored in different parts of your luggage, in case of loss or theft.If you wear **glasses** or **contact lenses,** take an extra prescription with you and arrange for someone at home to send you a replacement pair in an emergency. If you wear contacts, bring glasses and extra solutions, enzyme tablets, and eyedrops; the price for these can be exorbitant if they're available at all.

Any traveler with a medical condition that cannot be easily recognized (i.e. diabetes, epilepsy, heart conditions, allergies to antibiotics) may want to obtain the internationally recognized **Medic Alert Identification Tag,** which indicates the bearer's condition and the number of Medic Alert's 24-hour hotline. Contact Medic Alert Foundation (tel. (800) 432-5378). The **American Diabetes Association**, (tel. (800) 232-3472) provides diabetic ID cards with messages in 18 languages.

Reliable **contraception** may be difficult to come by. Women on the pill should bring enough to allow for possible loss or extended stays. Stock up on your favorite brand of **condoms** before you go; availability and quality vary across Eastern Europe. Attitudes towards and availability of **abortions** vary from country to country. Contact your embassy or consulate for a list of doctors who perform abortions.

The **International Association for Medical Assistance to Travelers (IAMAT)** provides brochures on health for travelers, an ID card, a chart detailing advisable immunizations for 200 countries and territories, and a worldwide directory of English-speaking physicians. Membership is free (donations are welcome) and doctors are on call 24 hours a day for IAMAT members. Contact chapters in the **U.S.,** 417 Center St., Lewiston, NY, 14092 (tel. (716) 754-4883), in **Canada,** 1287 St. Clair Ave. West, Toronto, M6E 1B8 (tel. (416) 652-0137), or **New Zealand,** P.O. Box 5049, 438 Pananui Rd., Christchurch 5 (tel. (03) 352 90 53, fax 352 46 30).

STAYING HEALTHY

In summer, protect yourself against **heatstroke**. In the early stages, sweating stops, body temperature rises, and an intense headache develops, followed by confusion: you may find yourself levitating above your hotel bed. To treat heatstroke, cool off immediately with fruit juice or salted water, wet towels, and shade. Rush the victim to the hospital. Extreme cold is no less dangerous. The signs of **hypothermia** are uncontrollable shivering, poor coordination, and exhaustion, followed by slurred speech, hallucinations, and amnesia. Do not let victims fall asleep—unconsciousness can lead to death. To avoid hypothermia, keep dry, wear wool, dress in layers, and wear a hat. **Frostbite** turns skin white, waxy, and cold. *Never* rub frostbite—the skin is easily damaged. See a doctor as soon as possible. Travelers in **high altitudes** should allow a couple of days to adjust to lower oxygen levels before engaging in strenuous activity, particularly long hikes. Those new to high altitudes may feel drowsy; alcoholic beverages will have stronger effects.

Food poisoning can spoil any trip. Some of the cheapest and most convenient eating options are also most prone: street vendors, tap water, and carrying perishable food for hours in a hot backpack. **Diarrhea** has unmistakable symptoms but also, thankfully, some means of relief, such as the over-the-counter remedy Immodium. Since dehydration is the most common side effect of diarrhea, those suffering should drink plenty of fruit juice and water. The simplest anti-dehydration formula is still the most effective: 8 oz. of water with a ½ tsp. of sugar or honey and a pinch of salt. Down several of these a day, rest, and let the disease run its course. If it does not subside within a few days, see a doctor immediately. Traveler's diarrhea may be the symptom of dysentery, giardia, or other parasitic conditions which can haunt your gastro-intestinal tract for years after your trip is over (see below).

Women traveling in unsanitary conditions are vulnerable to **urinary tract and bladder infections**, common and severely uncomfortable bacterial diseases which cause a burning sensation and pain during urination. Drink tons of juice rich in vitamin C, plenty of water, and urinate frequently. If symptoms persist, see a doctor.

HEALTH ADVISORIES

The Centers for Disease Control and Prevention (CDC) warn that travelers to Eastern Europe must (1) protect themselves from insects, (2) ensure the quality of their food and drinking water, and (3) be knowledgeable about potential diseases in the region. You should also confirm that your normal **"childhood" vaccines** are up-to-date, including for measles, mumps, rubella, tetanus, pertussis, and polio. Pregnant travelers or travelers with children should contact the CDC for additional information; call the **CDC International Traveler's Hotline** at (404) 332-4559.

Diseases Transmitted by Insects When hiking, camping, or working in or around forest regions, you should remain in well-screened areas, use mosquito nets, and wear clothes that cover most of the body. And always use insect repellent. **Tick-borne Encephalitis** is a viral infection of the central nervous system transmitted by tick bites or by eating unpasteurized dairy products. Symptoms range from none at all to the abrupt onset of headache, fever, and flu-like symptoms to complications involving the swelling of the brain. There is no specific drug to treat Tick-borne Encephalitis. A vaccine is available in Europe but the CDC does not recommend it for most travelers. If unimmunized, travelers should protect themselves from ticks and check for ticks daily. **Lyme disease** is a bacterial infection caused by the bite of certain, very small infected ticks. The illness is characterized by a circular rash of two inches or more with a bull's eye appearance, and is often accompanied by "flu-like" symptoms. If untreated Lyme disease can cause further problems involving the heart, joints, and nervous system. It can be treated with antibiotics.

Diseases Transmitted by Food and Water Food and waterborne diseases are the number one cause of illness to travelers in Eastern Europe. Viruses and bacteria can cause diarrhea and vomiting (typhoid fever, cholera, and parasites), liver damage (hepatitis) and muscle paralysis (polio).

Hepatitis A is a viral infection of the liver transmitted by the fecal oral route; direct person-to-person contact; contaminated water, ice or shellfish; or from fruits or uncooked vegetables contaminated through handling. Symptoms include fatigue, fever, loss of appetite, dark urine, jaundice, vomiting, aches and pains, and light stools. No specific therapy is available. Experts recommend killing the virus in food or water by boiling or cooking to 85 degrees centigrade for one minute. The CDC recommends that travelers who may be at risk receive an injection of immune serum globulin (IG) prepared by procedures that conform to U.S. standards.

Cholera is an intestinal infection caused by a bacterium from contaminated water or food that causes voluminous diarrhea, dehydration, vomiting, and muscle cramps. The CDC reports that risk of infection for westerners is low if they follow the usual tourist itineraries and stay in standard accommodations. Otherwise, eat only thoroughly cooked food, peel your own fruit, and drink either boiled water, bottled carbonated water, or bottled carbonated soft drinks. A vaccine is only recommended if you have stomach ulcers, use anti-acid therapy, or will be living in unsanitary conditions in areas of high cholera activity. Cholera may be treated by simple fluid and electrolyte-replacement therapy, but treatment must be immediate.

Parasitic infections result from eating or drinking contaminated food or water, from direct contact with soil or water containing parasites or their larva, or from insect bites. Symptoms include swollen lymph nodes, rashes or itchy skin, digestive problems such as abdominal pain or diarrhea, eye problems, and anemia. Again, travelers should eat only thoroughly cooked food, drink safe water, wear shoes, and avoid contact with insects, particularly mosquitoes, biting flies, gnats, and midges.

Diseases Transmitted by Intimate Contact Human immunodeficiency virus (HIV) which causes acquired immunodeficiency syndrome or **AIDS** is found in Eastern Europe but its magnitude and transmission modes in the region are not well-defined. HIV is transmitted through the exchange of body fluids with an infected individual, or through the transfusion of unscreened blood. Remember that there is no assurance that someone is not infected: HIV tests only show antibodies after a six-month lapse. Do not have sex without using a condom or share intravenous needles. The U.S. Center for Disease Control's **AIDS Hotline** can refer you to organizations with information on European countries (tel. (800) 342-2437). Travelers who are HIV-positive or have AIDS should inquire about country-specific immigration restrictions; **U.S. State Department** (tel. (202) 647-1488, fax 647-3000).

Hepatitis B is a viral infection of the liver transmitted the same way as HIV. An effective vaccination is available; the CDC recommends that travelers to high-risk areas whose activities may result in blood exposure or sexual contact with the local population, who will reside in rural areas or have daily physical contact with the local population for long periods of time (six months or more) or who is likely to seek either medical, dental, or other treatment in local facilities during their stay be vaccinated. Vaccination should ideally begin six months before travel.

Travelers should also take precautions to protect themselves against infection by other **sexually transmitted diseases (STDs)** by *always* using latex condoms.

Other Diseases in Eastern Europe For most countries in Eastern Europe there is a risk of **rabies**, a viral infection that affects the central nervous system and is transmitted by all warm-blooded animal bites, especially by dogs and foxes. Do not handle any animals; any animal bite should be promptly cleaned with large amounts of soap and (clean) water and receive medical attention. Vaccination is recommended for those visiting for more than 30 days, visiting areas where rabies is known to exist, and for spelunkers. The CDC also warns travelers that since 1990 outbreaks of **diphtheria**, an acute contagious bacterial disease marked by fever and by the coating of the air passages with a membrane that interferes with breathing, have been reported in **Moscow** and **St. Petersburg,** Russia and **Kiev,** Ukraine. Proof of immunity is not required, but the Advisory Committee on Immunization Practices recommends diphtheria immunization for anyone traveling to these cities.

■■■ INSURANCE

Beware of unnecessary coverage—your current policies might well extend to many travel-related accidents. **Medical insurance** (especially university policies) often cover costs incurred abroad. Canadians are protected by their home province's health insurance plan: check with the provincial Ministry of Health or Health Plan Headquarters. Australians should consult Medicare's brochure "Health Care for Australians Travelling Overseas" to find out the extent of coverage and how to obtain benefits. Contact the Commonwealth Department of Health, Housing and Community Services, GPO Box 9848 in your capital city. Take out travel insurance to cover those eventualities not covered by reciprocal agreements such as ambulance coverage and medical evacuation. Your **homeowners' insurance** (or your family's coverage) often covers theft during travel. Homeowners are generally covered against loss of travel documents (passport, plane ticket, railpass, etc.) up to US$500.

ISIC provides US$3000 worth of accident and illness insurance and US$100 per day up to 60 days of hospitalization. **CIEE** offers the Trip-Safe plan, with options that cover medical treatment and hospitalization, accidents, baggage loss, and charter flights missed due to illness; **STA** offers a pricier, more comprehensive plan. **American Express** cardholders receive car-rental and flight insurance on purchases made with the card. (For addresses, see Travel Organizations and Money, above.)

Insurance companies usually require a copy of police reports for thefts, or evidence of having paid medical expenses (doctor's statements, receipts) before they will honor a claim, and may have time limits on filing. Always carry policy numbers and proof of insurance. Check with each insurance carrier for specific restrictions.

Globalcare Travel Insurance, 220 Broadway, Lynnfield, MA, 01940 (tel. (800) 821-2488, fax (617) 592-7720). Complete medical, legal, emergency, and travel-related services. On-the-spot payments and special student programs.

Travel Assistance International, Worldwide Assistance Services, Inc., 1133 15th St., NW, Washington DC 20005-2710 (tel. (800) 821-2828, fax (202) 331-1530). Provides on-the-spot medical coverage (US$15,000-90,000) and unlimited medical evacuation insurance, 24-hr. emergency multilingual assistance hotline and worldwide local presence. Trip cancellation/interruption, baggage and accidental death and dismemberment insurance are also offered.

Travel Insured International, Inc., 52-S Oakland Avenue, P.O. Box 280568, East Hartford, CT 06128-0568 (tel. (800) 243-3174, fax (203) 528-8005). Insure against accident, baggage loss, sickness, trip cancellation/interruption, travel delay, and default. Covers emergency medical evacuation and automatic flight insurance.

■■■ SAFETY AND SECURITY

A perception exists in Eastern Europe that Westerners are uniformly rich and stupid. Therefore, anyone recognizable as a foreigner and especially a Westerner is immediately subject to risk of **theft**. Laws are minimally observed of late, and the best way to protect yourself is to act as understated as possible. Con-artists abound, in official postions as well as unofficial ones; keep your guard up every minute of every day.

Though it is a good idea to blend in as much as possible while traveling anywhere in Europe, travel in Eastern Europe calls for special effort. Westerners are walking bags of hard currency as far as thieves are concerned, and crime is on the upswing in economically depressed areas. Even the savviest of travelers have been mugged and robbed on recent trips to the former Soviet Union, in particular.

Muggings are more often impromptu than planned; walking with nervous, over-the-shoulder glances can be a tip that you have something valuable to protect. Carry all your valuables (including your passport, railpass, traveler's checks, and airline ticket) either in a money belt or neckpouch stashed securely inside your clothing. This will protect you from skilled thieves who use razors to slash open backpacks and fanny packs (particular favorites of skilled bag-snatchers), and they should be kept on your person at all times, including trips to the shower if you are staying in the dorm-style rooms of most hostels. Making photocopies of important documents will allow you to recover them in case they are lost or filched. Carry one copy separate from the documents and leave another copy at home. A simple, but effective, theft deterrent is a small padlock readily available in luggage stores that is small enough to ensure your backpack or daypack remains shut as you walk about.

When exploring new **cities,** extra vigilance may be wise, but don't let fear inhibit your ability to experience another culture. When walking at night, turn day-time precautions into mandates. Stay near crowded, well-lit places and do not attempt to cross through parks, parking lots, or any other large, deserted areas. Among the more colorful aspects of many large cities are the **con artists.** Be aware of certain classics: sob stories that require money, rolls of bills "found" on the street, ice-cream or mustard spilled (or saliva spit) onto your shoulder distracting you for enough time to snatch your bag. Always carry a shoulder bag so that the strap passes over your head and runs diagonally across your torso. Hustlers often work in groups, and children are among the most effective. A firm "no" should communicate that you are no dupe. Contact the police if a hustler acts particularly insistent or aggressive.

Trains are notoriously easy spots for thieving. Professionals wait for tourists to fall asleep and then carry off everything they can. When traveling in pairs, sleep in alternating shifts; when alone use good judgment in selecting a train compartment:

never stay in an empty one, and try to get a top bunk. When sleeping, wrap the straps of your luggage securely about you. Travelers taking the Moscow-St.Petersburg train route in Russia should be especially vigilant. The U.S. Embassy confirms that "a powerful odorless gas, derived from ether, has been used by criminals to drug passengers to prevent their waking during a robbery." Travelers are advised to secure their door with heavy wire while they sleep.

Sleeping in your **automobile** is one of the most dangerous ways to get your rest. Park in a well-lit area as close to a police station or 24-hr. service station as possible. **Sleeping outside** is often illegal and exposes you to ever more hazards—camping is recommendable only in official, supervised, campsites.

A good self-defense course will give you more concrete ways to react to different types of aggression, but it might cost you more money than your trip. **Model Mugging** (East Coast tel. (617) 232-7900, Midwest tel. (312) 338-4545, West Coast tel. (415) 592-7300), a U.S. national organization with offices in several major cities, teaches a comprehensive course on self-defense (US$400-500; women's and men's courses offered). The **U.S. Department of State's** (tel. (202) 783-3238) pamphlet *A Safe Trip Abroad* (US$1) summarizes safety information for travelers. For official Dept. of State **travel advisories** on European countries, call their 24-hour hotline at (202) 647-5225. **Travel Assistance International** provides its members with a 24-hr. hotline for emergencies and referrals (see Insurance below.)

■■■ SPECIFIC CONCERNS

WOMEN AND TRAVEL

Women exploring any area on their own inevitably face additional safety concerns. Always trust your instincts: if you'd feel better somewhere else, move on. Always carry extra money for a phone call, bus, or taxi. Consider staying in hostels which offer single rooms that lock from the inside or in religious organizations that offer rooms for women only; avoid any hostel with "communal" showers. Stick to centrally-located accommodations and avoid late-night treks or metro rides. Hitching is never safe for lone women, or even for two women traveling together. Choose train compartments occupied by other women or couples; ask the conductor to put together a women-only compartment if he doesn't offer to do so first.

Single women almost never go to restaurants and may be significantly harassed if they do, even at midday. Small cafés and cafeterias are much safer options; even hotel restaurants may be dangerous. In crowds, you may be pinched or squeezed by oversexed slimeballs; wearing a wedding band may help prevent such incidents. The look on the face is the key to avoiding unwanted attention. Feigned deafness, sitting motionless and staring at the ground will do a world of good that no reaction will ever achieve. If need be, turn to an older woman for help in an uncomfortable situation; her stern rebukes will usually be enough to embarrass the most persistent jerks. Looking like a native often involves wearing a generous amount of make-up and very rarely shorts or T-shirts. It's a good idea to observe the way local women dress and to invest in the newest "in" thing, even if you wouldn't dream of wearing it at home. The best way to repulse amorous Eastern European men is to don a *babushka* style kerchief, tied under the chin.

Don't hesitate to seek out a police officer or a passerby if you are being harassed. Memorize the emergency numbers in the countries you visit. Carry a whistle or an airhorn on your keychain, and don't hesitate to use it in an emergency. A **model mugging** course will not only prepare you for a potential mugging, but will also raise your level of awareness of your surroundings as well as your confidence (see Safety and Security, below). Women also face additional health concerns when traveling (see Health, above). All of these warnings and suggestions should not discourage women from traveling alone. Don't take unnecessary risks, but don't lose your spirit of adventure either.

For general information, contact the **National Organization for Women (NOW)**, which boasts branches across the country that can refer women travelers to rape crisis centers, and counselling services, and provide lists of feminist events in the area. Main offices include: 22 W. 21st St., 7th Fl., **New York,** NY 10010 (tel. (212) 807-0721); 425 13th St., NW, **Washington,** DC 20004 (tel. (202) 234-4558); and 3543 18th St., **San Francisco,** CA 94110 (tel. (415) 861-8880). The following publications also offer tips for women travelers as well as travelogue-type perspectives by women about their experiences:

> **Handbook for Women Travelers** by Maggie and Gemma Moss (UK£9). Encyclopedic and well-written. From Piaktus Books, 5 Windmill St., London W1P 1HF (tel. (0171) 631 07 10).
> **Index/Directory of Women's Media.** Lists women's publishers, bookstores, theaters, and news organizations. Published by the Women's Institute for the Freedom of the Press, 3306 Ross Place, NW, Washington, DC 20008 (tel. (202) 966-7793).
> **A Journey of One's Own** by Thalia Zepatos (Eight Mountain Press, US$15). The latest on the market, interesting and full of good advice, plus a specific and manageable bibliography of books and resources.
> **Women Going Places** (US$14). From Inland Book Company, P.O. Box 12061, East Haven, CT 06512 (tel. (203) 467-4257). A women's travel and resource guide emphasizing women-owned enterprises. Geared toward lesbians, but offers advice appropriate for all women.
> **Women Travel: Adventures, Advice & Experience** by Miranda Davies and Natania Jansz (Penguin, US$13). Has info on specific foreign countries, plus a decent bibliography and resource index.
> **Wander Women,** 136 N. Grand Ave. #237, West Covina, CA 91791 (tel. (818) 966-8857) is a travel and adventure networking organization for women over 40. Publishes the quarterly newsletter *Journal 'n' Footnotes*. US$29 annual membership fee.

OLDER TRAVELERS AND SENIOR CITIZENS

Proof of senior citizen status is required for many of the services listed below.

> **AARP (American Association of Retired Persons),** 601 E St., NW, Washington, DC 20049 (tel. (202) 434-2277 or (800) 927-0111). U.S. residents over 50 and their spouses receive benefits which include the AARP Travel Experience from American Express (tel. (800) 927-0111), the AARP Motoring Plan from Amoco (tel. (800) 334-3300), and discounts on lodging, car rental, and sight-seeing. US$8 annual fee per couple.
> **Elderhostel,** 75 Federal St., 3rd Fl., Boston, MA 02110-1941 (tel. (617) 426-8056). You must be 60 or over, and may bring a spouse. Programs at colleges and universities in over 47 countries focus on varied subjects and generally last one week.
> **National Council of Senior Citizens,** 1331 F St., NW, Washington, DC 20004 (tel. (202) 347-8800). For US$12 a year, US$30 for three years, or US$150 for a lifetime, an individual or couple can receive hotel and auto rental discounts, a senior citizen newspaper, use of a discount travel agency, supplemental Medicare insurance (if you're over 65), and a mail-order prescription drug service.
> **Gateway Books,** 2023 Clemens Road, Oakland, CA 94602 (tel. (510) 530-0299, fax 530-0497). Publishes **Get Up and Go: A Guide for the Mature Traveler** (US$11) and **Adventures Abroad** (US$13) which offer general hints for the budget-conscious senior considering a long stay or retiring abroad. For credit card orders call (800) 669-0773.
> **Pilot Books,** 103 Cooper St., Babylon, NY 11702 (tel. (516) 422-2225). Publishes **The International Health Guide for Senior Citizens** (US$5, postage US$1) and **The Senior Citizens' Guide to Budget Travel in Europe** (US$6 postage US$1).
> **Unbelievably Good Deals and Great Adventures That You Absolutely Can't Get Unless You're Over 50** by Joan Heilman (Contemporary Books, US$8). After you finish reading the title page, check inside for some great tips on senior discounts and the like.

TRAVELERS WITH CHILDREN
Virtually all museums and tourist attractions also have a children's rate. Be sure to make sure your child carries some sort of ID in case of an emergency. By airplane, children under two generally fly free on domestic flights and for 10% of the adult fare on international flights (this does not, however, necessarily include a seat). Children 2 to 12 usually fly half price.

Backpacking with Babies and Small Children (US$11). From Wilderness Press, 2440 Bancroft Way, Berkeley, CA 94704 (tel. (800) 443-7227 or (510) 843-8080). *Take Your Kids to Europe* by Cynthia W. Harriman (US$14). A budget travel guide geared towards families. Even includes cartoon illustrations. Published by Mason-Grant Publications, P.O. Box 6547, Portsmouth, NH 03802 (tel. (603) 436-1608, fax 427-0015). *Travel with Children* by Maureen Wheeler (US$11, postage US$1.50 in the U.S.). Published by Lonely Planet Publications, Embarcadero West, 155 Philbert St., Suite 251, Oakland, CA 94607 (tel. (510) 893-8555 or (800) 275-8555, fax (510) 893-8563). Also P.O. Box 617, Hawthorn, Victoria 3122, Australia.

TRAVELERS WITH DISABILITIES
Countries vary in their general accessibility to travelers with disabilities. Some national and regional tourist boards provide directories on the accessibility of various accommodations and transportation services. If these services are not available, contact institutions of interest directly. Those with disabilities should also inform airlines and hotels of their disabilities when making arrangements for travel; some time may be needed to prepare special accommodations.

Rail is probably the most convenient form of travel. Contact your destination's station in advance for specific information, or call **Rail Europe** in the U.S. at (800) 345-1990 (fax (914) 682-2821). Most countries require a six-month quarantine for all animals, including guide dogs. To obtain an import license, owners must supply current certification of the animal's rabies, distemper and contagious hepatitis inoculations, and a veterinarian's letter attesting to its health. They should inquire as to the specific quarantine policies of each destination country.

The following organizations provide information or publications that might be of assistance:

American Foundation for the Blind, 15 W. 16th St., New York, NY 10011 (tel. (212) 620-2147). Provides ID cards (US$10); write for an application, or call the Product Center at (800) 829-0500. Also call this number to order AFB catalogs in braille, print, or on cassette or disk.
Directions Unlimited, 720 North Bedford Rd., Bedford Hills, NY 10507 (tel. (800) 533-5343 or (914) 241-1700, fax (914) 241-0243). Specializes in arranging individual and group vacations, tours, and cruises for those with disabilities.
Facts on File, 460 Park Ave. S., New York, NY 10016 (tel. (800) 829-0500 or (212) 683-2244 in Alaska and Hawaii). Publishers of *Access to the World* (US$16.95), a guide to accessible accommodations and sights. Available in bookstores or by mail order.
Flying Wheels Travel Service, P.O. Box 382, 143 W. Bridge St., Owatonne, MN 55060 (tel. (800) 535-6790, fax (507) 451-1685). Arranges international trips for groups or individuals in wheelchairs or with other sorts of limited mobility.
Graphic Language Press, P.O. Box 270, Cardiff by the Sea, CA 92007 (tel. (619) 944-9594). Publishes *Wheelchair Through Europe* (US$12.95, postage paid), which provides comprehensive advice for the wheelchair-bound traveler, including planning advice and specifics on wheelchair-related resources in various cities throughout Europe.
Guided Tour, Inc. Elkins Park House #114B, 7900 Old York Road, Elkins Park, PA 19117-2339 (tel. (215) 635-2637 or (800) 738-5841). Year-round travel programs (domestic and international) for persons with developmental and physical challenges as well as those geared to the needs of persons requiring renal dialysis. Call or write for a free brochure.

Mobility International, USA (MIUSA), P.O. Box 10767, Eugene, OR 97440 (tel. (503) 343-1284 (voice and TDD), fax 343-6812). International headquarters in Britain, 228 Borough High St., London SE1 1JX (tel. (0171) 403 56 88). Contacts in 30 countries. Information on travel programs, international workcamps, accommodations, access guides, and organized tours. Membership costs US$20 per year, newsletter US$10. Sells updated and expanded *A World of Options: A Guide to International Educational Exchange, Community Service, and Travel for Persons with Disabilities* (US$14, nonmembers US$16, postpaid).

Moss Rehabilitation Hospital Travel Information Service, 1200 W. Tabor Rd., Philadelphia, PA 19141 (tel. (215) 456-9603). A telephone information resource center concerned with international travel accessibility and other related concerns. Nominal fee charged for packet of information on tourist sights, accommodations, and transportation. Will refer callers to other agencies if they cannot provide information.

Society for the Advancement of Travel for the Handicapped, 347 Fifth Ave. #610, New York, NY 10016 (tel. (212) 447-7284), fax 725-8253). Publishes quarterly travel newsletter SATH News and information booklets (free for members, US$3 each for nonmembers). Advice on trip-planning for people with disabilities. Annual membership is US$45, students and seniors US$25.

Twin Peaks Press, P.O. Box 129, Vancouver, WA 98666-0129 (tel. (206) 694-2462, fax 696-3210). Publishes *Travel for the Disabled,* (US$20) which lists tips and resources for disabled travelers. Also available are the *Directory for Travel Agencies of the Disabled* (US$20), *Directory of Accessible Van Rentals* (US$10), and *Wheelchair Vagabond* (US$15). Postage US$2 first book, US$1 each additional.

BISEXUAL, GAY, AND LESBIAN TRAVELERS

Attitudes toward bisexual, gay, and lesbian travelers are, naturally, particular to each country and to the cities within it. Listed below are contact organizations and publishers which offer materials addressing those concerns. Homosexuality is against the law in several Eastern European countries.

Ferrari Publications, P.O. Box 37887, Phoenix, AZ 85069 (tel. (602) 863-2408). Publishes *Ferrari's Places of Interest* (US$16), *Ferrari's Places for Men* (US$15), *Ferrari's Places for Women* (US$13), and *Inn Places: USA and Worldwide Gay Accommodations* (US$15). Available in bookstores or by mail order (postage US$3.50 for the first item, US$0.50 for each additional).

Gay's the Word, 66 Marchmont St., London WC1N 1AB, England (tel. (0171) 278 76 54). Tube: Russel Sq. Open Mon.-Fri. 11am-7pm, Sat. 10am-6pm, Sun. and holidays 2-6pm. A gay and lesbian bookshop which also sells videos, jewelry and postcards. Mail order service available. No catalogue of listings, but they will provide you with a list of titles germane to a given subject.

Giovanni's Room, 345 S. 12th St., Philadelphia, PA 19107 (tel. (215) 923-2960, fax 923-0813). International feminist, lesbian, and gay bookstore with mail-order service which carries many of the publications listed here. Call or write for a free catalogue.

Inland Book Company, P.O. Box 120261, East Haven, CT 06512 (tel. (203) 467-4257). Publishes *Women Going Places* (US$14), an international travel and resource guide emphasizing women-owned enterprises, geared toward lesbians, but offering advice appropriate for all women. Available in bookstores. Sells directly only to distributors.

Renaissance House, P.O. Box 533, Village Station, New York, NY 10014 (tel. (212) 674-0120, fax 420-1126). A comprehensive gay bookstore which carries many of the titles listed in this section. Send self-addressed stamped envelope for a free catalogue.

Spartacus International Gay Guide, (US$30). Published by Bruno Gmünder, Postfach 301345, D-1000 Berlin 30, Germany (tel. (30) 25 49 82 00). Lists of bars, restaurants, hotels, and bookstores around the world catering to gay men. Also lists hotlines for gay men in various countries. Available in the U.S. from Giovanni's Room and Renaissance House.

KOSHER AND VEGETARIAN TRAVELERS

Before you head off, contact national tourist offices. They often publish lists of kosher and vegetarian restaurants in their respective countries.

> **The European Vegetarian Guide: Restaurants and Hotels** is available from the Vegetarian Times (tel. (800) 435-9610, orders only).
> **The International Vegetarian Travel Guide** (UK£3) was last published in 1991, but copies are still available from the **Vegetarian Society of the UK**, Parkdale, Dunham Rd., Altringham, Cheshire WA14 4QG (tel. (61) 928 07 93). VSUK also publishes other titles; call or send a self-addressed, stamped envelope for a listing.
> **The Jewish Travel Guide** (US$12, postage US$1.75) lists synagogues, kosher restaurants, and Jewish institutions in over 80 countries. Available in the U.K. from **Jewish Chronicle Publications,** 25 Furnival St., London EC4A 1JT (tel. (0171) 405 92 52, fax 831 51 88), and in the U.S. from **Sepher-Hermon Press,** 1265 46th St., Brooklyn, NY 11219 (tel. (718) 972-9010).

MINORITY TRAVELERS

The most ill-regarded minority in Eastern Europe are Gypsies *(Romany)*. Other minority travelers, especially those of African or Asian descent, will usually meet more curiosity than hostility, especially outside of big cities. Travelers of Arab ethnicity may be treated more suspiciously. Skinheads are on the rise in Eastern Europe and minority travelers should regard them with caution. In Slovenia and Croatia, dark skinned travelers should make an effort not to be taken for Bosnian Muslims. This is one of the few occasions to play up your Westernness.

■■■ GETTING THERE

Finding a cheap airfare to Eastern Europe in the airline industry's computerized jungle will be easier if you understand the airlines' systems better than they think you do. Call every toll-free number and ask about discounts. Have a knowledgeable travel agent guide you; better yet, have several knowledgeable travel agents guide you. Remember that travel agents may not want to do the legwork to find the cheapest fares (for which they receive the lowest commissions). Students and people under 26 should never need to pay full price for a ticket. Seniors can also get great deals; many airlines offer senior traveler clubs or airline passes and discounts for their companions as well. Sunday newspapers have travel sections that list bargain fares from the local airport. Australians should consult the Saturday travel section of the *Sydney Morning Herald*, as well as the ethnic press, where special deals may be advertised. Outsmart airline reps with the phone-book-sized *Official Airline Guide* (at large libraries), a monthly guide listing every scheduled flight in the world (with prices). *The Airline Passenger's Guerrilla Handbook* (US$15; last published in 1990) is a more renegade resource.

Most airfares peak between mid-June and early September. Midweek (Mon.-Thurs.) flights run about US$30 cheaper each way than on weekends. Traveling from hubs such as New York, Atlanta, Dallas, Chicago, Los Angeles, San Francisco, Vancouver, Toronto, Mirabel, Qué., Sydney, Melbourne, Brisbane, Auckland, or Wellington to London, Frankfurt, Paris, Brussels, Luxembourg, Rome or Amsterdam will win a more competitive fare than from smaller cities. Return-date flexibility is usually not an option for the budget traveler; except on youth fares purchased through the airlines, traveling with an "open return" ticket can be pricier than fixing a return date and paying to change it. Be wary of one-way tickets, too: the flight to Europe may be economical, but the return fares are outrageous. Whenever flying internationally, pick up your ticket well in advance of the departure date and arrive at the airport at least two hours before your flight.

COMMERCIAL AIRLINES

Even if you pay an airline's lowest published fare, you may waste hundreds of dollars. The commercial airlines' lowest regular offer is the **APEX** (Advance Purchase

Excursion Fare); specials advertised in newspapers may be cheaper, but have more restrictions and fewer available seats. APEX fares provide you with confirmed reservations and allow "open-jaw" tickets (landing in and returning from different cities). Reservations usually must be made at least 21 days in advance, with 7- to 14-day minimum and 60- to 90-day maximum stay limits, and hefty cancellation and change penalties. Payment must be made within 72 hours of departure. For summer travel, book APEX fares early; by May it will be hard to get the departure date you want.

Most airlines no longer offer standby fares, once a staple of the budget traveler. Standby in the United States has given way to the **3-day-advance-purchase youth fare,** a cousin of the one-day variety prevalent in Europe. It's available only to those under 25 (sometimes 24) and only within three days of departure, a gamble that can backfire. Return dates are open, but you must come back within a year, and again, can book your return seat no more than three days ahead. Youth fares in summer aren't really cheaper than APEX, but off-season prices drop deliciously.

Look into flights to less-popular destinations or on smaller carriers. **Icelandair** (tel. (800) 223-5500) has last-minute offers and a stand-by fare from New York to Luxembourg (April-June 15 and Sept.-Oct. US$398; June 15-Aug. US$598) for travelers under 25 years of age. Reservations must be made within three days of departure.

EASTERN EUROPEAN AIRLINES

The safety and service of airlines in Eastern Europe varies wildly. Some airlines have completely modernized since 1989 and operate according to Western standards; others have seen safety and service deteriorate. Be careful when choosing a carrier. In April 1994 the International Airline Passenger Association advised travelers to avoid air travel in the former Soviet Union because of declining safety standards. The following accident records have been reported by the Associated Press.

Albanian Airlines, a 1992 joint venture with Tyrolean, the Austrian regional carrier, served Vienna, Munich, Zurich and Skopje, Macedonia, without any major accidents. Albanian shut down at the beginning of August 1994 because of financial losses. Albania is still served by a number of West European airlines.

Belarus: Belavia flies to Shannon Airport, Ireland with connections to New York on Aeroflot and Aer Lingus.

Bulgaria: Balkan Airlines serves 55 cities in 46 countries with a fleet of planes built in Russia, Western Europe and the United States. The state-owned carrier plans a partial privatization in an effort to become profitable. Service is improving, but can still be spartan. There have been no serious accidents since 1988, when a Soviet-built Yak-40 crashed during takeoff from Sofia on a domestic flight, killing 25 passengers.

Croatian Airlines was founded in 1989 and uses Western-built planes. The carrier flies to major European cities. Service is comparable to established Western carriers. The airline is turning a profit, and there have been no accidents.

Czech Republic: CSA was once the national airline of Czechoslovakia, but now operates in the Czech Republic since the split up. The Czech state has repurchased the 40 percent of CSA sold to Air France in 1992. Its reputation for safety and maintenance is among the best in Eastern Europe, and there have been no recent serious accidents. Of its 28 planes, 11 are western.

Estonian Air, established in 1991, flies to domestic and European destinations including Copenhagen, Hamburg, Amsterdam, Helsinki, Kiev, Minsk, Moscow, Stockholm, Vilnius, and Tampere, Finland.

Hungary: MALEV has modernized its fleet since 1989, and offers flights to most European cities as well as several U.S. destinations. Its safety record is considered good and there have been no recent accidents. Of its 27 planes, 6 are Western.

Latvia: Latavio flies to Stockholm, Amsterdam, Warsaw, and Moscow, among other international destinations.

Lithuania: Lietuvos Avalinijos flies to Berlin, Frankfurt, and Copenhagen, among other international destinations.

Macedonia: Eight carriers have been founded in Macedonia since independence in 1991, but poor safety standards and a lack of equipment have resulted in 207 fatalities in a rash of accidents. The worst crash was in November 1993, when a Soviet-made Yak-42, chartered by Avioimpex, overshot a runway in Eastern Macedonia and hit a mountain, killing 116.

Poland: LOT is the national airline, with service to major cities across the world. After selling off its tired planes to Ukraine and China, LOT acquired the one of the world's newest Boeing fleets. Of its 22 planes, 18 are Western.

Romania: TAROM serves most major European cities and some U.S. destinations. TAROM has benefitted from JAT's woes (see Yugoslavia, below) by picking up Balkan business that normally went through Belgrade and has recently begun to turn a profit. Its safety record is good with no accidents involving passenger deaths since 1978.

Russia: Aeroflot. In July 1994 the U.S. State Department warned U.S. citizens to avoid flying on domestic Russian airlines because of safety concerns, following similar warnings by the U.K. and Canada.

Slovak Republic: Air Tatra, created after Slovakia split from the Czech Republic in 1993, went out of business in 1994 for lack of passengers.

Slovenia: Adria Airways, formed in 1961, is making a profit with its nine-plane fleet. Service is on par with Western carriers. In 1981, a jetliner crashed into mountains while attempting to land in Ajaccio, Corsica, killing more than 100 passengers and crew. There have been no serious accidents since then.

Air Ukraine International flies from a number of European capitals as well as Chicago, New York, and Washington, DC to Kiev and Lviv (Ivano-Frankivsk).

Yugoslavia: JAT airlines has withered as the country broke up. The Belgrade-based carrier ranked 33rd in the world in 1989 and carried 5 million passengers. Now, because of sanctions against Yugoslavia due to the Bosnian war, JAT is restricted to domestic flights in Serbia and Montenegro. Service has deteriorated, but there have been no reports of major accidents.

STUDENT TRAVEL AGENCIES

Students and people under 26 with proper ID qualify for reduced airfares. These are rarely available from airlines or travel agents, but instead from student travel agencies like **Let's Go Travel, STA, Travel CUTS, USTN** and CIEE's **Council Travel** (see Travel Organizations, above). These agencies negotiate special reduced-rate bulk purchases with the airlines, then resell them to the youth market; in 1994, peak season round-trip rates from the East Coast of North America to even the off-beat corners of Europe rarely topped US$700 (though flights to Russia were higher), and off-season fares were considerably lower. Round-trip fares from Australia or New Zealand through STA or Flight Centres International cost between AUS$1600 (low season) and AUS$2500 (high season). Return-date change fees also tend to be low (around US$50 through Council or Let's Go Travel). Most of their flights are on major airlines, though in peak season some seats may be on less reliable chartered aircraft. Student travel agencies can also help non-students and people over 26, but probably won't be able to get the same low fares.

CHARTER FLIGHTS AND CONSOLIDATORS

Ticket consolidators resell unsold tickets on commercial and charter airlines. Look for their tiny ads in weekend papers (in the U.S., the *Sunday New York Times* is best), and start calling them all. There is rarely a maximum age; tickets are also heavily discounted, and may offer extra flexibility or bypass advance purchase requirements, since you aren't tangled in airline bureaucracy. But unlike tickets bought through an airline, you won't be able to use your tickets on another flight if you miss yours, and you will have to go back to the consolidator to get a refund, rather than the airline. Phone around and pay with a credit card so you can stop payment if you never receive your tickets. Don't be tempted solely by the low prices; find out everything you can about the agency you're considering, and get a copy of their refund policy in writing. Ask also about accommodations and car rental discounts; some consolidators have fingers in many pies. Insist on a **receipt** that gives full details about the tickets, refunds, and restrictions, and if they don't want to give you one or just generally seem clueless or shady, use a different company. A 10% fee will usually be deducted from any refunds.

The theory behind a **charter** is that a tour operator contracts with an airline (usually one specializing in charters) to fly extra loads of passengers to peak-season destinations. Charter flights fly less frequently than major airlines and have more restrictions, particularly on refunds. They are also almost always fully booked, and schedules and itineraries may change or be cancelled at the last moment (as late as 48 hours before the trip, and without a full refund); you'll be much better off purchasing a ticket on a regularly scheduled airline. As always, pay with a credit card if you can; consider travelers insurance against trip interruption.

It's best to buy from a major organization that has experience in placing individuals on charter flights. One of the most reputable is the CIEE-affiliated **Council Charter**, 205 E. 42nd St., New York, NY 10017 (tel. (800) 800-8222); their flights can also be booked through Council Travel offices. Also try **Interworld** (tel. (800) 331-4456; in Florida, (305) 443-4929); **Rebel** (tel. (800) 227-3235); and **Travac** (tel. (800) 872-8800). Don't be afraid to call every number and hunt for the best deal.

If budget travel inspires your utmost bravery and patience, **Airhitch**, 2641 Broadway, New York, NY 10025 (tel. (212) 864-2000) and 1415 Third St., Santa Monica, CA 90410 (tel. (310) 394-0550), will add a certain thrill to the prospects of how you will get to Europe and where exactly you will end up. Complete flexibility on both sides of the Atlantic is necessary; flights cost US$169 each way when departing from the East Coast, US$269 from the West Coast, and US$229 from most places between. The snag is that you must choose a five-day period in which to travel and draw up a list of preferred destinations. There are several offices in Europe so you can wait to register for your return; the main one is in Paris (tel. (1) 44 75 39 90). Airhitch only guarantees that you'll end up in Europe; check all flight times and departure/arrival sites directly with the airline carrier; read all the fine print, and compare it to what people tell you. The Better Business Bureau of New York City has received complaints about this company; be warned that it is difficult to receive refunds, and that clients' vouchers will not be honored when an airline fails to receive payment from Airhitch in time.

Eleventh-hour **discount clubs** and **fare brokers** offer members savings on European travel, including charter flights and tour packages. Research your options carefully. **Last Minute Travel Club**, 1249 Boylston St., Boston, MA 02215 (tel. (800) 527-8646 or (617) 267-9800), and **Discount Travel International** (tel. (212) 362-3636) are among the few travel clubs that don't charge a membership fee. Others include **Moment's Notice** (tel. (212) 486-0503; US$25 annual fee), **Traveler's Advantage** (tel. (800) 835-8747; US$49 annual fee), and **Worldwide Discount Travel Club** (tel. (305) 534-2082; US$50 annual fee). For a ticketing fee of 5-12%, depending on the number of travelers and the itinerary, **Travel Avenue** (tel. (800) 333-3335) will search for the lowest international airfare available and then take 7% off the base price. Study these organizations' contracts closely; you don't want to end up with an unwanted overnight layover.

COURIER FLIGHTS AND FREIGHTERS

Those who travel light should consider flying to Europe as a **courier.** The company hiring you will use your checked luggage space for freight; you're only allowed to bring carry-ons. Restrictions to watch for: you must be at least 18, most flights are round-trip only with fixed-length stays (usually short); you may not be able to travel with a companion (single tickets only); and most flights are from New York (including a scenic visit to the courier office in the 'burbs). Round-trip fares to Western Europe from the U.S. range from US$200-350 (during the off-season) to US$400-550 (during the summer). **NOW Voyager,** 74 Varick St., New York, NY 10013 (tel. (212) 431-1616), acts as an agent for many courier flights worldwide from New York, with some flights available from Houston. They offer special last-minute deals to such cities as London, Paris, Rome, and Frankfurt for as little as US$300 round-trip plus a US$50 registration fee. Other agents to try are **Able Travel** (tel. (212) 779-

8530), **Halbart Express,** 147-05 176th St., Jamaica, NY 11434 (tel. (718) 656-8279), **Courier Travel Service,** 530 Central Avenue, Cedarhurst, NY 11516 (tel. (516) 374-2299), and **Discount Travel International** (NY tel. (212) 362-3636, Miami tel. (305) 538-1616).

You can also go directly through courier companies in New York, or check your bookstore or library for handbooks such as *The Insider's Guide to Air Courier Bargains* (US$15). *The Courier Air Travel Handbook* (US$10.70) explains the procedure for traveling as an air courier and contains names, phone numbers, and contact points of courier companies. It can be ordered directly from Thunderbird Press, 5930-10 W. Greenway Rd., Suite 112, Glendale, AZ 85306 (tel. (800) 345-0096). **Travel Unlimited,** P.O. Box 1058, Allston, MA 02134-1058, publishes a comprehensive, monthly newsletter that details all possible options for courier travel (often 50% off discount commercial fares). A one-year subscription is US$25 (outside of the U.S. US$35).

If you really have travel time to spare, **Ford's Travel Guides,** 19448 Londelius St., Northridge, CA 91324 (tel. (818) 701-7414) lists **freighter companies** that will take trans-Atlantic passengers. Ask for their *Freighter Travel Guide and Waterways of the World* (US$15, plus US$2.50 postage if mailed outside the U.S.).

ONCE THERE

■■■ GETTING AROUND

BY TRAIN
Many train stations have different counters for domestic and international tickets, seat reservations, and information; check before lining up. On major lines, reservations are always advisable, and often required, even with a railpass; make them at least a few hours in advance at the train station (usually less than US$3). In the former Soviet Union, you may need to purchase tickets days in advance, before they sell out.

Railpasses
Buying a railpass is both a popular and sensible option for those whose itineraries include a large chunk of Western Europe. You may find it tough to make your railpass pay for itself in Eastern Europe, where train fares are reasonable. Ideally conceived, a railpass allows you to jump on any train in Europe, go wherever you want whenever you want, and change your plans at will. The handbook that comes with your railpass tells you everything you need to know and includes a timetable for major routes, a map, and details on ferry discounts. In practice, of course, it's not so simple. You still must stand in line to pay for seat reservations, supplements, and couchette reservations, as well as to have your pass validated when you first use it. More importantly, railpasses don't always pay off. Find a travel agent with a copy of the **Eurailtariff** manual to weigh the wisdom of purchasing them. Add up the second-class fares for your planned routes and deduct 5% (listed prices automatically include commission) for comparison.

Eurailpass covers only Hungary in Eastern Europe, while the European **East Pass** covers Poland, the Czech Republic, the Slovak Republic, and Hungary. You'll almost certainly find it easiest to buy a pass before you arrive in Europe; contact Council Travel, Travel CUTS, or Let's Go Travel (see Travel Organizations, above), other travel agents or **Rail Europe,** 226 Westchester Ave., White Plains, NY 10604 (tel. (800) 4-EURAIL (438-7245) in the U.S., and (800) 361-RAIL (361-7245), fax (416) 602-4198 in Canada) provides extensive information on pass options and publishes the *Europe on Track* booklet.

If you plan to focus your travels in one country, consider a national railpass. Some of these passes can be bought only in Europe, some only outside of Europe, and for some it doesn't matter; check with a railpass agent or with national tourist offices.

Discount rail tickets

For travelers under 26, **BIJ** tickets (Billets Internationals de Jeunesse, sold under the names **Wasteels, Eurotrain,** and **Route 26**) are a great alternative to railpasses. Available for international trips across Eastern and Western Europe, they knock 30-45% off regular second-class fares. Tickets are all good for 60 days after purchase and allow an unlimited number of free stopovers along the normal direct route of the train journey. Issued for a specific international route between two designated points in different countries, they must be used in the direction and order of the designated route without side- or back-tracking. You can buy BIJ tickets at Wasteels or Eurotrain offices (usually in or near train stations). For international journeys departing from the U.K., France, and Germany, tickets can be issued in the U.S. by **Wasteels Travel,** 7041 Grand National Dr. #207, Orlando, FL 32819 (tel. (407) 351-2537, fax 363-1041); for departure from other countries, tickets can be purchased through many European agents or directly at the ticket counter in some nations.

Useful Resources

The ultimate reference is the ***Thomas Cook European Timetable*** (US$25; US$34 includes a map of Europe highlighting all train and ferry routes; plus US$4 for postage). The timetable, updated monthly, covers all major and many minor train routes in Europe. In the U.S., order it from **Forsyth Travel Library,** P.O. Box 2975, Shawnee Mission, KS 66201 (tel. (800) 367-7984 or (913) 384-3440), which provides other useful travel books as well. **Hunter Publishing,** 300 Raritan Center Parkway, Edison, NJ 08818 (tel. (908) 225-1900, fax 417-0482) provides a comprehensive catalog of handy rail atlases, travel maps, and guidebooks that include ***Eastern Europe by Rail*** and other country-specific materials. The ***Eurail Guide*** (US$15, postage US$3), available in bookstores, lists train schedules and brief cultural information for almost every country on earth. Requests can also be directed to **Eurail Guide Annual,** 27540 Pacific Coast Highway, Malibu, CA 90265 (tel. (310) 457-7286). Rick Steves's free ***Europe Through the Back Door*** travel newsletter and catalog, 109 Fourth Ave. N., P.O. Box 2009, Edmonds, WA 98020 (tel. (206) 771-8303, fax 771-0833) provides comprehensive information on railpasses (both Eurail and national/regional passes).

BY BUS

Though European trains and railpasses are extremely popular, long-distance bus networks may be more extensive, efficient, and often more comfortable than train services. All over Eastern Europe, short-haul buses reach rural areas inaccessible by train. In the Balkans, air-conditioned buses run by private companies are a godsend.

BY CAR AND VAN

Cars offer great speed, great freedom, access to the countryside, and an escape from the town-to-town mentality of trains. Unfortunately, they also insulate you from the *esprit de corps* rail travelers enjoy. Although a single traveler won't save by renting a car, four usually will.

The availability of **rental cars** varies across Eastern Europe. One option is to rent a car in a Western European country and drive it eastward if the rental agreement allows. Often, a car rented in Austria can be taken across the border into Czech Republic, Slovakia, Slovenia, and Hungary. Rates go up, however, and a loss/damage waiver becomes mandatory. Car rental agencies in the Balkans often require you to rent a driver along with the car. The former Soviet Union is generally off-limits to cars rented in the West.

You can rent a car from either a U.S.-based firm (Avis, Budget, or Hertz) with its own European offices, from a European-based company with local representatives

Railways of
Eastern Europe

(National and American International represent Europcar and Ansa, respectively), or from a tour operator (Europe by Car, Auto Europe, Foremost, Kemwel, and Wheels International), which will arrange a rental for you from a European company at its own rates. Not surprisingly, the multinationals offer greater flexibility, but the tour operators often strike good deals and may have lower rates. Rentals vary considerably by company, season, and pick-up point; expect to pay at least US$140 a week, plus tax, for a teensy car. Reserve well before leaving for Europe and pay in advance if you can; rates within Europe are harsh. Always check if prices quoted include tax and collision insurance; some credit card companies will cover this automatically. Ask about student and other discounts and be flexible in your itinerary. Ask your airline about special packages; sometimes you can get up to a week of free rental. Minimum age restrictions vary by country; rarely, if ever, is it below 21. Try **Auto Europe,** 10 Sharp's Wharf, P.O. Box 1097, Camden ME 04843 (tel. (800) 223-5555); **Avis Rent a Car** (tel. (800) 331-1084); **Budget Rent a Car** (tel. (800) 472-3325); **Europe by Car,** Rockefeller Plaza, New York, NY 10021 (tel. (800) 223-1516 or (212) 581-3040); **Europcar,** 145 Avenue Malekoff, 75016 Paris (tel. (1) 45 00 08 06); **Foremost Euro-Car** (tel. (800) 272-3299; in Canada (800) 253-3876); **Hertz Rent a Car** (tel. (800) 654-3001); **The Kemwel Group** (tel. (800) 678-0678); **Maiellano Tours,** 441 Lexington Ave., New York, NY 10051 (tel. (212) 687-7725); or **Payless Car Rental** (tel. (800) PAY-LESS (729-5377)).

If you're brave or know what you're doing, **buying** a used car or van in Europe and selling it just before you leave can provide the cheapest wheels on the Continent. Check with consulates for different countries' import-export laws concerning used vehicles, registration, and safety and emission standards. David Shore and Patty Campbell's annually updated *Europe By Van And Motorhome* (US$14, US$1 postage, US$8 overseas airmail) guides you through the entire process, from buy-back agreements to insurance and dealer listings. To order, write to 1842 Santa Margarita Dr., Fallbrook, CA 92028 (tel. (800) 659-5222 or (619) 723-6184). *How to Buy and Sell a Used Car in Europe* (US$6 plus US$0.75 postage, from Gil Friedman, P.O. Box 1063,

Arcata, CA 95521, tel. (707) 822-5001), also contains practical information on the process of avoiding rental and lease hassles with a bit of wangling.

Driving a camper-van or motorhome gives the advantages of car rental without the hassle of finding lodgings or cramming six friends into a Renault. You'll need those friends to split the gasoline bills, however, although many European vehicles use diesel or propane, which are cheaper. The car rental firms listed above have more information. *Moto-Europa,* by Eric Bredesen (US$20 plus US$3 shipping to North America, US$7 overseas), available from Seren Publishing, P.O. Box 1212 Dubuque, IA 52004 (tel. (800) EUROPA-8 (387-6728)) is a new comprehensive guide to all of these moto-options. From itinerary suggestions to a motorists' phrasebook, the guide provides all sorts of useful tips on the whole undertaking, whatever the chosen mode of transport. More general information is available from the **American Automobile Association** (AAA), Travel Agency Services Dept., 1000 AAA Dr., Heathrow, FL 32746-5080 (tel. (800) 222-4357 or (417) 444-7380); the **American Automobile Touring Alliance,** Bayside Plaza, 188 The Embarcadero, San Francisco, CA 94105 (tel. (415) 771-3170); and, the **Canadian Automobile Association (CAA),** 60 Commerce Valley Dr. East, Markham, Ont. L3T 7P9.

Before setting off, be sure you know the laws of the country in which you're driving. Scandinavians and Western Europeans use unleaded gas almost exclusively, but it's essentially nonexistent in Eastern Europe. At most agencies in Europe, all that's required to rent a car is a U.S. license and proof that you've had it for a year (but make sure to double-check that the country doesn't require an IDP; remember that it's usually a good idea to carry one anyway). See the International Driving Permits section, above, for more details on the IDP and how to get one.

BY AIRPLANE

Unless you're under 25, flying across Eastern Europe on regularly scheduled flights will eat your budget. If you are 24 or under, special fares on most European airlines requiring ticket purchase either the day before or the day of departure are a lovely exception to this rule. These are often cheaper than the corresponding regular train fare, though not always as cheap as student rail tickets or railpasses. Student travel agencies also sell cheap tickets. Consult budget travel agents and local newspapers and magazines. The **Air Travel Advisory Bureau,** 41-45 Goswell Road, London EC1V 7DN England (tel. (0171) 636 5000), can put you in touch with discount flights to worldwide destinations, for free.

BY BOAT

> *"Sometimes, yes, boats go to Yalta. . . but not today."*
> —ferry ticket clerk in Odessa

Ferries serving Eastern Europe divide into two major groups. **Riverboats** acquaint you with many towns and enclaves that trains can only wink at. The legendary waterways of Eastern Europe—the Danube, the Volga, the Dnieper—offer a bewitching alternative to land travel. However, the further east you go, the more often your travel plans can be interrupted by fuel shortages. Most riverboats are palatial and well-equipped; the cheapest fare still gives you full use of the boat—including reclining chairs and couchettes allow you to sleep the trip away in the sun or shade. Schedule information is scarce, inquire in the area of your trip.

Ferries in the **North Sea** and **Baltic Sea** are prized by Scandinavians for their duty-free candy and alcohol shops; they also offer student and youth discounts, are universally reliable, and go everywhere (in summer, you can go from St. Petersburg to Iceland or Scotland without once using land transport). Those content with deck passage rarely need to book ahead. You should check in at least two hours early for a prime spot and allow plenty of time for late trains and getting to the port. It's a good idea to bring your own food and avoid the astronomically priced cafeteria cuisine. Fares jump sharply in July and August. Always ask for discounts; ISIC holders can often get student fares and Eurail passholders get many reductions and free trips (check the brochure that comes with your railpass). You'll occasionally have to pay a small port tax (under US$10). Advance planning and reserved ticket purchases through a travel agency can spare you several tedious days of waiting in dreary ports for the next sailing. The best American source for information on Scandinavian ferries and visa-free cruises to Russia is **EuroCruises,** 303 W. 13th St., New York, NY 10014 (tel. (212) 691-2099 or (800) 688-3876).

BY BICYCLE

Today, biking is one of the key elements of the classic budget Eurovoyage. Everyone else in the youth hostel is doing it, and with the proliferation of mountain bikes, you can do some serious natural sight-seeing. Be aware that touring involves pedaling both yourself and whatever you store in the panniers (bags which strap to your bike). Take some reasonably challenging day-long rides at home to prepare yourself before you leave. Have your bike tuned up by a reputable shop. Wear visible clothing, drink plenty of water (even if you're not thirsty), and ride on the same side as the traffic. Learn the international signals for turns and use them. Learn how to fix a modern derailleur-equipped mount and change a tire, and practice on your own bike before you have to do it overseas. A few simple tools and a good bike manual will be invaluable. For information about touring routes, consult national tourist offices or any of the numerous books available. **The Mountaineers Books,** 1011 Klickitat Way #107, Seattle, WA 98134 (tel. (800 553-4453) offers several nation-specific tour books (especially for Germany, Ireland, France and the U.K.), as well as *Europe By Bike,* by Karen and Terry Whitehill (US$14.95), a great source of specific area tours in 11 countries. Send for a catalog. *Cycling Europe: Budget Bike Touring in the Old World,* by N. Slavinski (US$12.95) may also be a helpful addition to your library. **Michelin road maps** are also clear and detailed guides.

Most airlines will count your bike as your second free piece of luggage (you're usually allowed two pieces of checked baggage and a carry-on). As an extra piece, it will cost about US$85 each way. Policies on charters and budget flights vary; check with the airline. The safest way to send your bike is in a box, with the handlebars, pedals, and front wheel detached. Within Europe, most ferries let you take your

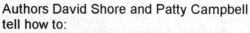

bike for free. You can always ship your bike on trains, though the cost varies from a small fixed fee to a substantial fraction of the ticket price.

Riding a bike with a frame pack strapped on it or on your back is about as safe as pedaling blindfolded over a sheet of ice; panniers are essential. The first thing to buy, however, is a suitable **bike helmet.** At about US$50-100, they're a much better buy than head injury or death. To lessen the odds of theft, buy a U-shaped **Citadel** or **Kryptonite** lock. These are expensive (about US$20-55), but the companies insure their locks against theft of your bike for one to two years. **Bike Nashbar,** 4112 Simon Rd., Youngstown, OH 44512 (tel. (800) 627-4227), has excellent prices on equipment.

BY HITCHHIKING

Let's Go strongly urges you to seriously consider the risks before you choose to hitch. We do not recommend hitching as a safe means of transportation and none of the information presented here is intended to do so.

No one should hitch without careful consideration of the risks involved. Not everyone can be an airplane pilot, but almost any bozo can drive a car. Hitching means entrusting your life to a random person who happens to stop beside you on the road and risking theft, assault, sexual harassment, and unsafe driving. In spite of this, there are gains to hitching. Favorable hitching experiences allow hitchers to meet local people and get where they're going where public transportation is sketchy. If you do decide to hitch, consider where you are. Hitching remains common in Eastern Europe, though Westerners are a definite target for theft. In Russia, the Baltics, and some other Eastern European countries, there is no clear difference between hitchhiking and hailing a taxi. The choice, however, remains yours.

Depending on the circumstances and the norms of the country, men and women traveling in groups and men traveling alone might consider hitching (called "autostop" in much of Europe) to locations beyond the scope of bus or train routes. If you're a woman traveling alone, don't hitch. It's just too dangerous. A man and a woman are a safer combination, two men will have a harder time finding a ride, and three will go nowhere.

Where you stand is also vital. Experienced hitchers pick a spot outside of built-up areas, where drivers can stop, return to the road without causing an accident, and have time to look over potential passengers as they approach. Hitching (or even standing) on super-highways is generally illegal: you may only thumb at rest stops, or at the entrance ramps to highways. In the Practical Information section of some cities, we list the tram or bus lines that will take travelers to strategic points for hitching out.

Finally, success will depend on what you look like. Successful hitchers travel light and stack their belongings in a compact but visible cluster. Most Europeans signal with an open hand, rather than a thumb; many write their destination on a sign in large, bold letters and draw a smiley-face under it. Drivers prefer hitchers who are neat and wholesome. No one stops for anyone wearing sunglasses.

Safety issues are always imperative, even when traveling with another person. Experienced hitchers avoid getting in the back of a two-door car, and never let go of a backpack. Hitchhiking at night can be particularly dangerous; hitchers stand in a well-lit place and expect drivers to be leery of nocturnal thumbers. They don't get into a car that they can't get out of again in a hurry. If they ever feel threatened, they insist on being let off, regardless of where they are. If the driver refuses to stop, some try acting as if they're going to open the car door or vomit on the upholstery.

Europe: A Manual for Hitchhikers gives directions for hitching out of hundreds of cities, rates rest areas and entrance ramps, and deciphers national highway and license plate systems. It's available from Vacation Work Publications (see Work section for complete address).

Fortunately, when you travel on Rail Europe, there are some sights you'll miss.

No goofy hats. No big sunglasses. No plaid shirts with striped shorts. Instead, on Rail Europe, you'll experience Europe the way Europeans do. You'll enjoy scenic countryside no one else can show you. And meet unique and interesting people. In short, you'll explore Europe the way it was meant to be explored. When it comes to visiting 33 European countries, get real. Go Rail Europe. Because traveling any other way could end up showing you some pretty dreadful sights. To learn more, call your travel agent or 1-800-4-EURAIL. (1-800-438-7245)

Rail Europe

Europe. To the trained eye.

BY WALKING AND HIKING

Eastern Europe's grandest scenery can often be seen only by foot. *Let's Go* describes many daytrips for those who want to hoof it, but native inhabitants (Europeans are fervent, almost obsessive hikers), hostel proprietors, and fellow travelers are the best source of tips.

■■■ ACCOMMODATIONS

If you arrive in a town without a reservation, your first stop should be the local tourist office. These offices distribute extensive accommodations listings free of charge and will also reserve a room for a small fee (though some favor their friends' establishments). As a rule, expect all prices to rise each January.

ROOMS IN PRIVATE HOMES

Throughout Eastern Europe, it is commonplace for locals with rooms to rent to approach you in ports or train stations. This may seem dangerous, but it is an accepted custom and is often a more attractive option for individual travelers than a night in an overpriced 1970s-revival hotel. Some parts of Eastern Europe, the former Soviet Union especially, are not prepared for solo travelers; the tourism industry in many places is still recovering from an era when all travel was done by organized groups. In small villages in the Balkans, travelers find a roof for the night simply by walking the streets and knocking on doors, or by asking locals for tips. The conditions are sometimes far superior to those at local hotels. However, there is no guarantee of these hawkers' trustworthiness or of the quality of their establishments. Carry your own baggage, ask for their identification, check the bathroom facilities, and have them write down the offered price.

HOSTELS

Especially in summer, much of Eastern Europe is overrun by young, budget-conscious travelers. Hostels are the hub of this gigantic subculture, providing innumerable opportunities to meet students from all over the world, find new traveling partners, trade stories, and learn about places to visit. At US$7-20 per night, prices are extraordinarily low; only camping is cheaper. Guests tend to be in their teens and twenties, but most hostels welcome travelers of all ages. In the average hostel, you and anywhere from 1 to 50 roommates will sleep in a gender-segregated room full of bunk beds, with common bathrooms and a lounge down the hall. The hostel warden may be a laid-back student, a hippie dropout, or a crotchety disciplinarian. Most hostels have well-equipped kitchens; some serve hot meals.

The basic disadvantage of hostels is their regimentation. Most have an early curfew—fine if you're climbing a mountain the next morning, but a distinct cramp in your style if you plan to rage in town. There is also usually a lockout from morning to mid-afternoon. Conditions are generally spartan and cramped, with little privacy, and you may run into more screaming pre-teen tour groups than you care to remember. Hostel quality also varies dramatically. Some are set in strikingly beautiful castles, others in run-down barracks far from the town center. Rural hostels are generally more appealing than those in large cities. Hostels usually prohibit sleeping bags for sanitary reasons and provide blankets and sheets instead. Some require **sleepsacks;** make your own by folding a sheet and sewing it shut on two sides. If you're lazy or less domestic, you can order one (about US$14) from Let's Go Travel or a youth hostel federation. Large hostels are reluctant to take advance telephone reservations because of the high no-show rate; citing an exact train arrival time or promising to call again and confirm can sometimes help.

Depending on where you're going in Eastern Europe, it may pay off to join the official youth hostel association in your home country; all national hostel associations are part of **Hostelling International (HI).** (For HI headquarters or national member association addresses, see Documents and Formalities, above.) In Eastern Europe, most hostels are not HI members, though membership increases every year. HI-member hostels are most common in Central Eastern Europe. If you haven't become a member in advance, show up at an HI hostel and ask for a blank membership card with space for six validation stamps. Each night you'll pay a nonmember supplement (equal to one-sixth the membership fee) and earn one Guest Stamp; get six stamps and you're a member. Most student travel agencies sell HI cards on the spot; otherwise, contact one of the national hostel organizations listed below. Ask about the *Budget Accommodation: Volume I: Europe and the Mediterranean* (US$11). **Privately owned hostels** are found in major tourist centers and throughout some countries. No membership is required, and you won't always have to contend with early curfews or daytime lockouts, but their quality varies widely.

HOTELS

In **hotels** couples can usually get by fairly well (rooms with a double bed are generally cheaper than those with two twin beds), as can groups of three or four. Always specify that you want the cheapest room available; some managers assume that Westerner expect rooms with phone, fridge and TV—and that they're willing to pay for the privilege. Inexpensive East European hotels may come as a rude shock to pampered North American travelers. You'll share a bathroom down the hall; one of your own is a rarity and costs extra when provided. Hot showers may also cost more, *if* they're available. Also check to make sure that toilets flush. Some hotels offer "full pension" (all meals) and "half pension" (breakfast and lunch). Unmarried couples will generally have no trouble getting a room together, although couples under age 21 may occasionally encounter resistance.

CAMPING

Camping in Europe can rock or suck. **Organized campgrounds** exist in many Eastern European city, most accessible by foot, car, or public transportation. Showers, bathrooms, and a small restaurant or store are common; some sites have more elaborate facilities. Prices range from US$1-10 per person with an additional charge for a tent. Money and time expended in getting to the campsite may eat away at your budget and your patience, but camping will bring you into the vacation subculture of young Eastern Europeans since it is often the only affordable accommodation for locals. Many campgrounds also offer cabins or bungalows for a slightly higher fee.

Europa Camping and Caravanning, an annually updated catalog of campsites in Europe, is available through Recreational Equipment, Inc., REI, P.O. Box 1700, Sumner, WA 98352-0001 (tel. (800) 426-4840) for US$20. Finally, the Automobile Association, Norfolk House, Basingstoke, Hampshire RG24 9NY, England (tel. (0256) 201 23), publishes *Camping and Caravanning in Europe* (UK£7.99). An **International Camping Carnet** (membership card) is required by some European campgrounds but can usually be bought on the spot. The card entitles you to a discount at some campgrounds, and often may be substituted for your passport as a security deposit. In the U.S., it's available for US$30 through Family Campers and RVers, 4804 Transit Rd., Bldg. #2, Depew, NY 14043 (tel. (716) 668-6242; carnet price includes a FCRV membership fee).

Prospective campers will need to invest a lot of money in good camping equipment and a lot of energy carrying it on their shoulders. Use the reputable mail-order firms to gauge prices; order from them if you can't do as well locally. In the fall, the previous year's merchandise may be reduced by as much as 50%. **Campmor,** 28 Park Way, Upper Saddle River, NJ 07458-0700 (tel. (800) 526-4784), has name-brand equipment at low prices. **Cabela's,** 812 13th Ave., Sidney, NE 69160 (tel. (800) 237-4444), also offers great prices. **REI** (listed above) stocks a wide range of the latest gear and holds great seasonal sales. And 24 hrs. per day, 365 days per year, **L.L. Bean,** Freeport, ME 04033 (tel. (800) 341-4341), supplies its own equipment and national-brand merchandise.

Most of the better **sleeping bags**—down (lightweight and warm) or synthetic (cheaper, heavier, more durable, and warmer when wet)—have ratings for specific minimum temperatures. The lower the mercury, the higher the price. Estimate the most severe conditions you may encounter, subtract a few degrees, and then buy a bag. Expect to pay at least US$65 for a synthetic bag and up to US$270-550 for a down bag suitable for use in sub-freezing temperatures. **Sleeping bag pads** range from US$15-30, while **air mattresses** go for about US$30-60. The best **tents** are free-standing, with their own frames and suspension systems. They set up quickly and require no staking. Remember to use the tent's protective rain fly and seal the seams to protect against water seepage. Backpackers and cyclists will require especially small, lightweight models, costing US$145 and up. **Sierra Design**, 2039 4th St., Berkeley, CA 94710, sells a two-person tent that weighs less than 1.76kg (4lbs.).

Other camping basics include a battery-operated **lantern** (*never* gas) and a simple plastic **groundcloth** to protect the tent floor. When camping in autumn, winter, or spring, bring along a "space blanket," a lightweight silvery sheet that helps you retain your body heat. Large, collapsible **water sacks** will significantly improve your lot in primitive campgrounds and weigh practically nothing when empty. **Camp-stoves** come in all sizes, weights, and fuel types, but none are truly cheap (US$30-120) or light. Consider GAZ, a form of bottled propane gas that is easy to use and widely available in Europe and remember waterproof matches. A canteen, Swiss army knife, and insect repellent are small, essential items. For further information about camping equipment and other camping concerns, contact **Wilderness Press**, 2440 Bancroft Way, Berkeley, CA 94704-1676 (tel. (800) 443-7227 or (510) 843-8080), which publishes useful books such as *Backpacking Basics* (US$11, including postage) and *Backpacking with Babies and Small Children* (US$11).

THE GREAT OUTDOORS

The first thing to preserve in the wilderness is yourself—health, safety, and food should be your primary concerns. See the Health section for information about basic medical concerns and first-aid. One comprehensive guide to outdoor survival is *How to Stay Alive in the Woods*, by Bradford Angier (Macmillan, US$8). Many rivers, streams, and lakes are contaminated with bacteria such as giardia, which causes gas, cramps, loss of appetite, and violent diarrhea. To protect yourself from the effects of this microscopic trip-wrecker, always boil your water vigorously for at least five minutes before drinking it, or use a purifying iodine solution. Filters do not remove all bacteria. *Never go camping or hiking by yourself for any significant time or distance*. If you're going into an area that is not well-traveled or well-marked, let someone know where you're hiking and how long you intend to be out. If you fail to return on schedule, searchers will at least know where to look for you.

The second thing to protect while you are outdoors is the wilderness. Pitch your tent on high, dry ground, don't cut vegetation, and don't clear campsites. If there are no toilet facilities, bury human waste at least four inches deep and 100 feet or more from any water supplies and campsites. Use only biosafe soap or detergents in streams or lakes. Always pack up your trash in a plastic bag and carry it with you until you reach the next trash can.

ALTERNATIVE ACCOMMODATIONS

In university and college towns, **student dormitories** may be open to travelers when school is not in session. Prices are usually comparable to those of youth hostels, and you usually won't have to share a room with strangers or endure stringent curfew and eviction regulations. Also, some **monasteries** and **convents** will open their doors. A letter of introduction from a clergy member could facilitate matters.

Host networks can help you find accommodations with families throughout Europe. **Servas** is an organization devoted to promoting world peace and understanding among people of different cultures. Traveling members may stay free for two nights in other members' homes in over 100 countries. You are asked to contact hosts in advance, and you must be willing to fit into the household routine. Membership is US$55, and for a US$25 deposit you will receive up to five host lists, which provide a short self-description of each host member. Write to U.S. Servas, Inc., 11 John St., #407, New York, NY 10038-4009 (tel. (212) 267-0252, fax 267-0292).

Sleeping in European train stations is a time-honored tradition. While it's free and often tolerated by authorities, it's neither comfortable nor safe. Don't spend the night in an urban park unless you place a low value on your life.

■■■ KEEPING IN TOUCH

MAIL

Mail can be sent internationally through **Poste Restante** (the international phrase for General Delivery) to any city or town; it's well worth using and much more reliable than you might think. Mark the envelope "HOLD" and address it, for example, "Kimberly McCORKELL, Poste Restante, City, Country." The last name should be capitalized and underlined. The mail will go to a special desk in the central post office, unless you specify a post office by street address or postal code. You should put a "1" after the city name to ensure mail goes to the central post office. As a rule, it is best to use the largest post office in the area; when possible, it is safer, quicker, and more reliable to send mail express or registered. Letters are often opened by criminals in search of valuables; *never* send cash.

When picking up your mail, bring your passport or other ID. If the clerk insists that there is nothing for you, try checking under your first name as well. In a few countries you will have to pay a minimal fee (perhaps US$0.50) per item received. *Let's Go* lists post offices in the Practical Information section for each city and most towns.

The cheapest letters you can send are aerograms, which provide a limited amount of writing space and fold over into envelopes (no enclosures allowed). It helps to mark air mail in the appropriate language if possible though *par avion* is universally understood.

Sending mail c/o **American Express** offices is quite reliable; they will hold your mail for free if you have AmEx traveler's checks (or, as AmEx calls them, "Cheques") or the card. Even if you use another brand of traveler's checks, you can use this service by buying some AmEx checks. Mail will automatically be held 30 days; to have it held longer, write "Hold for x days" on the envelope. Again the sender should capitalize and underline your last name, marking the envelope "Client Letter Service." Check the Practical Information section of the countries you plan to visit; we list AmEx office locations for most large cities. A complete list is available for free from AmEx (tel. (800) 528-4800) in the booklet *Traveler's Companion*.

Allow at least 2 weeks for airmail from Eastern Europe to reach the U.S., and more for Australia, New Zealand, and South Africa. Mail to and from parts of Eastern Europe can require up to 4 or 6 weeks. From Russia to anywhere can take a year.

Surface mail is by far the cheapest and slowest way to send mail. It takes one to three months to cross the Atlantic, appropriate for sending large quantities of items you won't need to see for a while. It is vital, therefore to distinguish your airmail from surface mail by explicitly labeling air mail in the appropriate language. When ordering books and materials from another country, include one or two **International Reply Coupons (IRC),** available at the post office, with your request. IRCs provide the recipient of your order with postage to cover delivery.

TELEPHONES

In Essentials and country listings, the **country code** is not included with phone numbers; please consult the beginning of each country's chapter, where the country code is listed with exchange rates. In the Practical Information section for large cities, **city codes** are listed under Telephones; and, in smaller cities and regions, the codes are listed in parentheses with the phone numbers.

Some countries in Eastern Europe do not have an international dialing code; you must go through the operator. In some other countries you must wait for a tone after the international dialing code. For more information, see each country's Practical Information section.

You can sometimes make direct international calls from a pay phone, but you may need to feed money in as you speak. In some countries, pay phones are card-operated; some even accept major credit cards. The best places to call from are phone booths and post offices since phones in cafés, hotels, and restaurants tend to carry surcharges of 30% or more.

English-speaking operators are often available for both local and international assistance. Operators in most European countries will place **collect calls** for you. It's cheaper to find a pay phone and deposit just enough money to be able to say "Call me" and give your number (though some pay phones in Europe can't receive calls).

A **calling card** is another alternative; your local long-distance phone company will have a number for you to dial while in Europe (either toll-free or charged as a local call) to connect instantly to an operator in your home country. The calls (plus a small surcharge) are then billed either collect or to a calling card. Some companies will be able to connect you to numbers only in your home country; others will be able to provide other European or worldwide connections. For more information, call **AT&T** about its **USADirect** and **World Connect** services (tel. (800) 331-1140, from abroad (412) 553-7458); **Sprint Express** (tel. (800) 877-4646); or **MCI World Phone** and **World Reach** (tel. (800) 996-7535). Similar services are available for Canada (Bell Canada **Canada Direct**, tel. (800) 561-8868), Australia (Telecom Australia **Australia Direct),** New Zealand (Telecom New Zealand **NZ Direct),** South Africa (Telkom South Africa **SA Direct),** Ireland (Telecom Eireann **Ireland Direct,** tel. (800) 25 25 25**),** and the U.K. (British Telecom **BT Direct,** tel. (800) 34 51 44).

Phone rates tend to be highest in the morning, low in the evening, and lowest on Sunday and at night (AT&T's and MCI's phone rates remain constant). Also, remember **time differences** when you call. Estonia, Latvia, Lithuania, western Russia, Romania, and Bulgaria are 2 hours ahead of Greenwich Mean Time (GMT)—7 hours ahead of Eastern Standard Time. Moscow is 3 hours ahead. Everywhere else in this book is 1 hour ahead of GMT. Some countries ignore daylight savings time, and fall and spring switchover times vary between those countries that do use it.

FAXES, E-MAIL, AND MORE

In Eastern Europe, domestic and international telegrams can be faster and cheaper than using the phone. Fill out a form at any post or telephone office; cables to North America arrive in two days. Major cities also have bureaus where you can pay to send and receive **faxes.** If you're spending a year abroad and want to keep in touch with friends or colleagues in a college or research institution, **electronic mail** ("e-mail") is an attractive option. It takes a minimum of computer knowledge a little prearranged planning, and it beams messages anywhere for no per-message charges. In some cities bureaus may offer access to e-mail for sending individual messages. Between May 2 and Octoberfest, EurAide (P.O. Box 2375, Naperville, IL 60567; tel. (708) 420-2343) offers **Overseas Access,** a service most useful to travelers without a set itinerary. The cost is US$15 per week or US$40 per month for an electronic message box, plus a US$15 registration fee. To reach you, people call the "home base" in Munich and leave a message; you receive it by calling Munich whenever you wish. For an additional US$20 per month, EurAide will forward mail sent to Munich to any addresses you specify..

■■■ CUSTOMS

Upon entering a country as well as returning home, you must declare all articles you acquired abroad and must pay a duty on the value of those articles that exceed the allowance established by your country's customs service. Holding onto receipts for purchases made abroad will help establish values when you return. It is wise to make a list, including serial numbers, of any valuables that you carry with you from home; if you register this list with customs before your departure and have an official stamp it, you will avoid import duty charges and ensure an easy passage upon your return. Be especially careful to document items manufactured abroad. In some Eastern European countries, it is illegal to take anything out of the country that was manufactured there before the year 1945.

Goods and gifts purchased at duty-free shops abroad are not exempt from duty or sales tax at your point of return; you must declare these items, as well. "Duty-free" merely means that you need not pay a tax in the country of purchase.

United States citizens returning home may bring US$400 worth of accompanying goods duty-free and must pay a 10% tax on the next US$1000. You must declare all purchases, so have sales slips ready. Goods are considered duty-free if they are for personal or household use (this includes gifts) and cannot include more than 100 cigars, 200 cigarettes (Cuban tobacco products may only be included if purchased in Cuba), and 1l of wine or liquor. You must be over 21 to bring liquor into the U.S. To be eligible for the duty-free allowance, you must have remained abroad for at least 48 hours and cannot have used this exemption or any part of it within the preceding 30 days.

You can mail unsolicited gifts duty-free if they are worth less than US$100, though you may not mail alcohol, tobacco, or perfume. Officials occasionally spot check parcels, so mark the price and nature of the gift and the words "Unsolicited Gift" on the package. If your package exceeds the duty-free limit, the U.S. Postal Service will collect customs duties and handling charges in the form of "postage due" stamps. Duty on gifts or other packages mailed from abroad cannot be prepaid. If you mail home personal goods of U.S. origin, you can avoid duty charges by marking the package "American goods returned." For more information, consult the brochure *Know Before You Go*, available from the U.S. Customs Service, P.O. Box 7407, Washington, DC 20044 (tel. (202) 927-6724). Foreign nationals living in the U.S. are subject to different regulations; refer to the leaflet *Customs Hints for Visitors (Nonresidents)*.

Canadian citizens who remain abroad for at least one week may bring back up to CDN$300 worth of goods duty-free once every calendar year; goods that exceed the allowance will be taxed at 12%. You are permitted to ship goods home under this exemption as long as you declare them when you arrive. Citizens over the legal age (which varies by province) may import in-person (not through the mail) up to 200 cigarettes, 50 cigars, 400g loose tobacco, 1.14l wine or alcohol, and 355ml beer; the value of these products is included in the CDN$300 allowance. For more information, contact Canadian Customs, 2265 St. Laurent Blvd., Ottawa, Ont. K1G 4K3 (tel. (613) 993-0534). Or, from within Canada, tel. (800) 461-9999.

British citizens or visitors arriving in the U.K. from outside the European Union must declare any goods in excess of the following allowances: 1) 200 cigarettes, 100 cigarillos, 50 cigars or 250g tobacco; 2) 2l still table wine; 3) 1l liquor, 2l fortified or sparkling wine, or an additional 2l still wine; 4) 60ml perfume; 5) 250ml toilet water; 6) UK£136 worth of all other goods including gifts and souvenirs. You must be over 17 to import liquor or tobacco. These allowances also apply to duty-free purchases within the EU, except for the last category, other goods, which then has an allowance of UK£71. Goods obtained duty- and tax-paid for personal use (regulated according to set guide levels) within the EU do not require any further customs duty. For more information about U.K. customs, contact Her Majesty's Customs and Excise, Custom House, Heathrow Airport North, Hounslow, Middlesex TW6 2LA (tel. (0181) 910 37 44, fax 910 37 65). HM Customs & Excise Notice 1 explains the allowances for people travelling to the U.K. both from within and without the European Union.

Irish citizens must declare everything in excess of the following allowances for goods obtained outside the EU or duty and tax free in the EU: 1) 200 cigarettes, 100 cigarillos, 50 cigars, or 250g tobacco; 2) 1l liquor or 2l wine; 3) 2l still wine; 4) 50g perfume; 5) 250ml toilet water; 6) IR£34 of other goods per adult traveler (IR£17 per traveler under age 15). A maximum of 25l beer may be imported as a part of, but not in addition to, the adult allowance. Goods obtained duty and tax paid in another

EU country, within certain limits set out for personal use, will not be subject to additional customs duty. Travelers under 17 are not entitled to any allowance for tobacco or alcoholic products. For more information, contact The Revenue Commissioners, Dublin Castle (tel. (01) 679 27 77, fax 671 20 21) or The Collector of Customs and Excise, The Custom House, Dublin 1.

Australian citizens may import AUS$400 (under 18 AUS$200) of goods duty-free, in addition to the allowance of 250 cigarettes, 250g tobacco, and 1l alcohol. You must be over 18 to import either. There is no limit to the amount of Australian and/or foreign cash that may be brought into or taken out of the country. However, amounts of AUS$5000 or more, or the equivalent in foreign currency, must be reported. For information, contact the Australian Customs Service, 5 Constitution Ave., Canberra, ACT 2601 (tel. (06) 275 62 55, fax 275 69 89).

New Zealand citizens may bring home up to NZ$700 worth of goods duty-free if they are intended for personal use or are unsolicited gifts. The concession is 200 cigarettes (1 carton) or 250g tobacco or 50 cigars or a combination of all three not to exceed 250g. You may also bring in 4.5l of beer or wine and 1.125l of liquor. Only travelers over 17 may bring tobacco or alcoholic beverages into the country. For more information, consult the *New Zealand Customs Guide for Travelers,* available from customs offices, or contact New Zealand Customs, 50 Anzac Avenue, Box 29, Auckland (tel. (09) 377 35 20, fax 309 29 78).

South African citizens may import duty-free: 400 cigarettes, 50 cigars, 250g tobacco, 2l wine, 1l of spirits, 250ml toilet water, and 50ml perfume, and other items up to a value of SAR500. Golf clubs and firearms do not fall within the duty-free allowances for travelers who have been absent from the republic for less than six months, and goods acquired abroad and sent to the republic as unaccompanied baggage do not qualify for any allowances. You may not export or import South African bank notes in excess of SAR500. Persons who require specific information or advice concerning customs and excise duties can address their inquiries to: The Commissioner for Customs and Excise, Private Bag X47, Pretoria, 0001. This agency distributes the pamphlet *South African Customs Information,* for visitors and residents who travel abroad. South Africans residing in the U.S. should contact: South African Mission, 3201 New Mexico Ave. #380, NW, Washington, DC 20016 (tel. (202) 364-8320 or 364-8321, fax 364-6008)

■■■ WEIGHTS AND MEASURES

1 centimeter (cm) = 0.39 inches

1 meter (m) = 3.28 feet

1 kilometer (km) = 0.62 miles

1 gram (g) = 0.04 ounces

1 kilogram (kg) = 2.2 pounds

1 liter = 0.26 gallons

1 Imperial gallon (U.K.) = 1.2 gallons

1 inch = 2.54cm

1 foot = 0.31m

1 mile = 1.61km

1 ounce = 28g

1 pound = 0.45kg

1 gallon = 3.76l

1 gallon = .83 Imperial Gallons

To convert from °C to °F, multiply by 1.8 and add 32.
To convert from °F to °C, subtract 32 and multiply by 5/9.

°C	35	30	25	20	15	10	5	0	-5	-10
°F	95	86	75	68	59	50	41	32	23	14

Castles and Monasteries

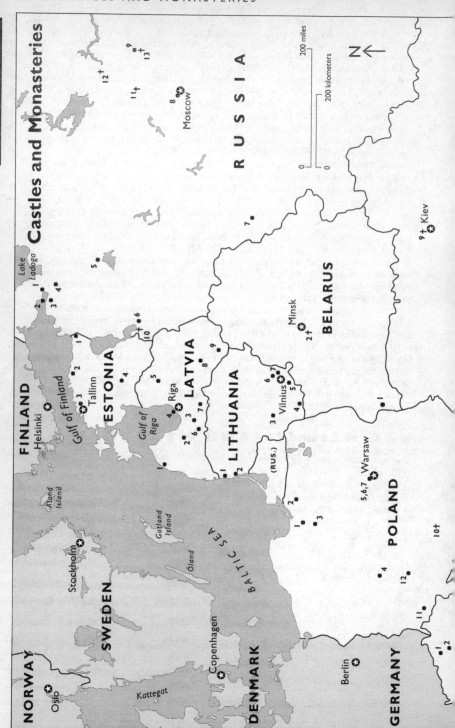

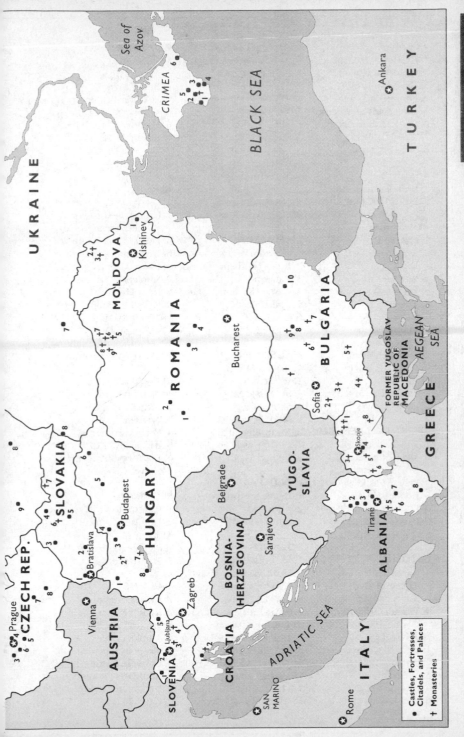

• Castles, Fortresses,
  Citadels, and Palaces
† Monasteries

ESSENTIALS

LIST OF CASTLES AND MONASTERIES

ALBANIA
1. Citadel of Rodafat
2. Citadel of Lezha
3. Citadel of Kruja
4. Fortress in Tiranë
5. Shen Maria in Ardenica
6. Shenmri in Apollonia
7. Citadel of Berati
8. Shen Prodhrom

BELARUS
1. Brest Fortress
2. Bernardine Conven

BULGARIA
1. Cherepish
2. Zemen
3. Rila
4. Rozhen
5. Bachkovo
6. Troyan
7. Shipka
8. Tsarevets Citadel
9. Preobrazhenski M.
10. Shumen Citadel

CROATIA
1. Trsat Castle in Rijeka
2. Franciscan M.

THE CZECH REPUBLIC
1. Kalich Castle
2. Melnik Castle
3. Křivoklat Castle
4. Prague Castle
5. Konopiště Castle
6. Karlštejn Castle
7. Pernštejn Castle
8. Špilberk Castle in Brno

ESTONIA
1. Narva Castle
2. Palmse Moisad
3. Kuressaare Castle
4. Viljandi Castle ruins

HUNGARY
1. Esterházy Palace
2. Pannonhalma Abbey
3. Öregvár Castle
4. Esztergom Palace
5. Eger Castle

6. Rákoczi Castle
7. Abbey Church (Tihany)
8. Festetics Palace

LATVIA
1. Ventspils Castle
2. Jaunspils Castle
3. Jelgava Castle
4. Castle of Riga
5. Cēsis
6. Tērvete
7. Bauska Castle
8. Krustpils Castle
9. Daugavpils Castle

LITHUANIA
1. Museum of Amber
2. Ruins of Klaipeda Castle
3. Raudondvaris Castle
4. Castle Hill at Merkiné
5. Trakai Castle
6. Kernavé Castle ruins
7. Castle Hill (Gediminas)

MACEDONIA
1. Joakim Osogovski M.
2. Psača M.
3. Sv. Nikita M.
4. Skopje Castle
5. Markov M.
6. Jovan Biorski M.
7. Prilep Castle
8. Veljusa M.

MOLDOVA
1. Bendery Fortress
2. Rezina M.
3. Butucheny M.

POLAND
1. Malbork Castle
2. Lidzbark Warmiński C.
3. Kwidzyń Castle
4. Rogalin Castle
5. Royal Castle in Warsaw
6. Wilanów Palace
7. Łazienkowski Palace
8. Łańcut Palace
9. Wawel in Kraków
10. Jasna Góra
11. Książ Castle
12. Oleśnica Castle

ROMANIA
1. Hunedoara
2. Alba Iulia
3. Bran Castle
4. Peles Castle (Sinaia)
5. Voroneț M.
6. Humor M.
7. Arbore M.
8. Suceviṭa M.
9. Moldoviṭa M.

RUSSIA
1. Peter and Paul Fortress
2. Kronstadt Fortress
3. Petrrodvorets
4. Pushkin and Pavlovsk
5. Novgorod Kremlin
6. Pskov Kremlin
7. Smolensk Fortress
8. Kremlin (Moscow)
9. Suzdal Kremlin
10. Pechory M.
11. Donilovsky M.
12. M. of Transfiguration
13. M. of St. Euthymius

SLOVAKIA
1. Bratislava Castle
2. Nitra "Town Castle"
3. Trenčin
4. Oravski Podzámk
5. Banska Bystrica
6. Klaštor p. Znievom
7. Červený Klaštor

SLOVENIA
1. Bled Castle
2. Ljubljana CAstle
3. Stična M.
4. Pleterje M.
5. Ptuj Castle

UKRAINE
1. Khersnes ruins
2. Khan's Palace
3. Livadia Palace
4. Alupka Palace
5. Neapolis ruins
6. Genoese Castle
7. Kamenets-Podolsky C.
8. Uzhgorod Castle
9. Caves M.

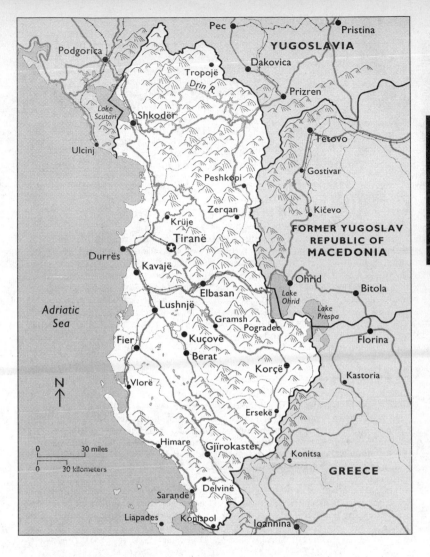

ALBANIA (SHQIPËRI)

US$1	= 85lek		100lek =	US$1.18
CDN$1	= 62lek		100lek =	CDN$1.61
UK£1	= 133lek		100lek =	UK£0.75
IR£1	= 131lek		100lek =	IR£0.77
AUS$1	= 63lek		100lek =	AUS$1.58
NZ$1	= 46lek		100lek =	NZ$2.17
SAR1	= 24lek		100lek =	SAR4.18
DM1	= 55lek		100lek =	DM1.81
Country Code: 355				

International Dialing Prefix: 00

Proud. Fierce. Defiant. Isolated on the frontier of Europe, Albania has played a part in every upsurge of the struggle between East and West. Over the centuries the nation has had barely a moment's rest between the attacks of its bordering countries, yet every time it has resisted with a fury that frightened far stronger powers. "Albanians have always had a taste for killing or getting themselves killed," snorts a frustrated enemy general in Ismail Kadarë's novel *The General of the Dead Army*. "They have killed each other when they haven't had anyone else to fight."

Today, Albania is working peacefully to preserve its tiny, ancient society in a shrinking world. Much of the countryside still provides a living picture of the primitive environment from which the modern nation has sprung. But economic reforms are succeeding, productivity is growing and the country is joining the modern age.

ALBANIA ESSENTIALS

A visa is not required of citizens of the United States, Australia, Canada, Ireland, New Zealand, or the U.K. South Africans require a visa valid for three months. The application requires a letter of invitation, costs US$10 and takes 25 days to process. See Essentials: Embassies and Consulates, page 3. Travelers of all nationalities may or may not need to pay a US$20 "entrance fee" at the door, depending on whether the border guards feel like charging it or not. An "exit fee" of US$10 may also be required. The following fee "rules" are arbitrarily applied: 1) Only Americans must pay, 2) Only Americans needn't pay, 3) You only have to pay if you're German, Italian, or Greek, 4) You pay if you're female, 5) You pay if you're male 6) You don't pay if you bribe the guard, 7) You don't pay if you proposition the guard. Welcome to Albania.

GETTING THERE

The most convenient way to reach Albania is by **plane.** The capital city, Tiranë, can be reached by **Balkan Airlines** via Sofia, **Swissair** via Zürich, **Alitalia** via Rome, **Olympic Airways** via Athens, or **Malev** via Budapest. **Delta** also offers connecting flights to Zurich, Rome, and other European capitals, where travelers change planes to continue their journey to Tiranë. In the summer of 1994, fares were around US$900; they usually go down by US$100-200 in the off-season months. Travelers under 25 can take advantage of the cheaper youth tickets (around US$700 in the summer of 1994). Unfortunately, these can be purchased only 72hrs. in advance; if you choose this option in high season, you risk having to change your entire itinerary at the very last minute. If you wish to visit other Eastern European countries before heading home from Albania, you can take **Malev** to Budapest (US$88); **Albtransport** to Rome (US$307 round trip); **Adria Airways** to Ljubljana (US$232 one way); **Albanian Airlines** to Warsaw (US$364 round trip), Skopje (US$100 one way), and Athens (students US$134 one way); and **Ada Air** to Bari (US$287 one way).

Ferry tickets are easiest to get in Tiranë at **Skanderbeg Travel, American Express,** or at **Albanian Travel and Tours,** which also has an office in Durrës. Ferries go from Durrës to: Bari (2 per week, 7hrs., 108,000 lire); Brindisi (2 per week, 7hrs., 108,000 lire); Koper, Slovenia (2 per week, 24hrs., US$115); and Ortona (2 per week, 28hrs., 106,000 lire).

Buses run to a few locations outside Albania. These are of a better quality than the domestic buses but are not 100% reliable. The kiosks just outside Skanderbeg Sq. in Tiranë, on Blvd. Deshmoret e Kombit to the north, are the source for tickets. **Albes-Turist** (tel. 421 66) sends buses to Istanbul (US$40) and Sofia (US$25) among other places, while **Agencja Turistike "Arte"** sends daily buses to various destinations in Kosovo. **Travel Agency Memedheu** runs a daily bus to İstanbul at 11am (US$41).

GETTING AROUND ALBANIA

Albanian cities are small enough to make walking a sufficient intra-city transport. Between cities, **buses** are the least offensive choice. The bus is usually owned by the driver and was bought off the "used" rack at some Greek, Italian, German, or Czech flea market; the upholstery may be ripped and buses are far from air-conditioned, but passengers find ways to compensate for the discomfort. If there's no cassette player to play loud rock music on, men in the back may very well start singing or chanting. A bus ride is a good time to strike up a conversation with the people next to you; you may have an offer to spend the night at their house by the end of the ride. The people next to you *will* talk to you; when they do, just smile and whip out the language section below.

There are a few main routes: the northern one runs to **Shkodër**; the southeast to **Elbasan, Pogradec,** and **Korçe**; the southwest to **Luzhnje, Fier, Gjirokastër,** and **Sarandë.** Buses also run between **Luzhnje** and **Berat.** You can get almost anywhere in the country for less than 500lek; the bus conductor (the driver's friend, cousin, or brother) will come around to collect the fare and give you a ticket, which you must keep until the end of the ride (the police often come to check). There are quite a few roadblocks throughout the country—attempts by the police to pretend that they still have some say in what goes on along the roads. At some point during the longer voyages, the bus will pull into a rest stop, and the driver will announce *"Pushim!"* There's time to grab lunch or a bottle of beer, as the driver probably will. There are no precise schedules for the buses, although approximations are possible: the main crop of buses leaves Tiranë between 7-7:30am; return buses on the south-west route and the Durrës route leave about once an hour; return buses pass through Pogradec at about 2-3pm. A bus will often stop for you whenever you ask it to, whether to pick you up or drop you off.

Trains are slower and less comfortable, but are slightly cheaper. The center of the train system is **Durrës.** The trains run to **Tiranë, Vlore, Fier, Pogradec,** and **Ballsh.** They claim to maintain a real schedule. There are no international passenger trains.

Car rental is one way to see the countryside without restricting yourself to train or bus "schedules." Either through one of the agencies in Tiranë or Durrës or simply by approaching a taxi in the street, it may be possible to argue the price down to a third of what was originally suggested. More agencies are beginning to appear as the demand increases. A good way to get a lower price is to ask if anyone knows a friend who might be willing to be your driver. At this point it is not possible to rent an insured car without a driver. Driving on Albanian roads without insurance is not recommended; the small country had 400 traffic fatalities last year.

Naturally, the frequency of auto accidents makes **hitchhiking** a particularly dangerous. *Let's Go* does not recommend hitchhiking as a safe means of transportation. However, it is not illegal and those who do it hold out one hand and wave, sometimes with the number of fingers extended being the number of passengers requesting a ride. Riders are usually expected to pay. Because of the mountainous terrain, **go-carts** are popular among travelers under 10 years old.

TOURIST SERVICES AND MONEY

Tourist offices are usually open from 9am to 7pm, with a long afternoon break (typically 1-4pm). **Skanderberg Travel** in Tiranë, one of the first private travel agencies in Albania, is the closest thing to a tourist office in the country; the staff speaks Italian, French, and German, and offers brochures in English. They also arrange private accommodations, organize tours, sell ferry tickets, and rent cars. Most travel agencies that sell bus tickets to destinations outside Albania (Albes-Turist, Agencja Turistike "Arta," Travel Agency Memedheu) speak English. Also, American Express in Tiranë performs all the tasks of a tourist agency, from finding private rooms to renting cars and organizing tours.

The **monetary unit** is the *lek,* worth 100 *qindarkas,* and hovers at an exchange rate around 100 to the U.S. dollar. Don't bother to change very much at a time: the dollar is in such common usage that it is almost the second currency of the nation. Exchange is legal pretty much anywhere and with whomever is willing.

COMMUNICATION AND LANGUAGE

Postal service within Albania is fairly reliable but slow; mailing letters abroad is even slower. A much faster way of communicating with the outside world is by telephone; however, AT&T USADirect and similar services are not yet available. International calls can be made via a local operator. Public telephones can be found at all post offices.

Years of Italian television account for the popularity of the language in the capital, but a surprisingly large number of Tiranans speak excellent English. French has also been taught in many schools for years, and German and Russian are spoken by a few learned Albanians. Greek is common in the south, along with some Turkish. Outside Tiranë, you'll be hard pressed to find anyone who speaks anything but Albanian. Learning a few sentences is not difficult and will make your stay a great deal more successful.

The **Albanian language** (called *Shqip* by Albanians) is a descendant of the extinct Illyrian tongue, and the only surviving member of its branch of the Indo-European language family. Over the centuries of foreign rule, it adopted many words from the Latin, Greek, Turkish, Italian, and Slavic languages. Two main dialects can be distinguished in present-day Albania: *Geg* (or *Gheg*) in the North and *Tosk* in the South. **Pronunciation** is phonetic, although there are some differences between *Geg Tosk*. There are seven **vowels**: *i* (ee), *e* (eh), *a* (ah), *o* (oh), *u* (oo), *ë* (e as in "chooses"), and *y* (ü as in German "über"). A final *ë* is not pronounced. **Consonants** are pronounced as in English, except for: *ç* (ch as in "chimi<u>cha</u>nga"), *dh* (th as in "<u>this</u>"), *gj* (j as in "jinx"), *j* (y as in "<u>y</u>en"), *q* (ch as in "<u>chee</u>sy"), *x* (dz as in "a<u>dze</u>"), and *xh* (j as in "judge").

Some necessary **verbs** are: (*unë*) *dua* (I want); (*unë*) *kam* [*nevojë për*] (I have [need for]); *mund* (I may); and *duhet* (I must). Add *te* plus another verb to form a clause, such as with: *flas* (I speak); *punoj* (I work); *kuptoj* (I understand); *udhetoj* (I travel); *studioj* (I study); *shkoj* (I go); *shikoj* (I see); *pije* (I drink); *ngrene* (I eat); *rri* (I stay); *bëj* (I do); *vizitoj* (I visit); *paguaj* (I pay). For example, *Dua te paguaj* (I want to pay) or *Duhet te shkoj* (I must go). "To be" is as follows: *unë jam* (I am); *ti je* (you (sing.) are); *ai/ajo është* (he/she is); *ne jemi* (we are); *ju jeni* (you are); *ata janë* (they are).

Nouns: *dhomë* (room); *shtëpi* (house); *rruga* (street); *ujë* (water); *ditë* (day); *natë* (night); *mengjez* (morning); *male* (mountains); *liçen* (lake); *banjë* (bathroom); *dush* (shower); *qytet* (city). **Adjectives:** *e lodhur* (tired); *e mirë* (good); *e bukur* (beautiful); *me te lirë* (cheapest); *te huajt* (foreign); *hapur* (open); *mbyll* (closed); *pak* (a little); *afër* (near); *larg* (far); *e madh* (big); *e vogël* (small). **Questions:** *ç'farë* (what); *në ç'farë orë* (what time); *sa* (how many/how much); *si* (how). **Miscellaneous:** *shummë* (very/a lot); *këtu* (here); *atje* (there); *nuk* or *s'* (not); *në* (in); *me* (with); *pa* (without); *për* (for); *qe* (which/that/who); *a* (placed at the beginning of a sentence to mark a question); *nga* (from); *s'ka* (there aren't any).

Yes	*po*	POH
No	*jo*	YOH
Today	*Sot*	SOHT
Tomorrow	*Nesër*	NEH-sihr
Hello	*Tungjatjeta*	toon-jat-YEHT-ah
Good morning	*Mirëmëngjes*	meer-mihn-JEHS
Good afternoon	*Mirëdita*	meer-DEE tah
Good evening	*Mirëmbrëma*	meerm-brih-MAH
Good night	*Natën e mirë*	NAH-tihn eh meer
Goodbye	*Mirupafshim*	mee-roo-pahf-SHIHM
Excuse me	*Mëfalni*	muh-FAHL-nee

Please	*Ju lutem*	yoo LOO-tehm
Thank you	*Faleminderit*	FAH-leh-meen-DEH-reet
When?	*Kur*	KOOR
Where is...?	*Ku është...?*	KOO uhsht
Help!	*Ndihmë*	n-DEE-mih
How much does it cost?	*Sa kushton/sa bën*	sah koosh-TOHN/sah bihn
Which way is the...?	*Ku është rruga për në...?*	koo uhsht ROO-gah pihr nih
My name is ...	*Unë quhem*	oon CHOO-hihm
Do you speak English?	*A flisni anglisht?*	ah FLEES-nee ahn- GLEESHT
I don't understand	*Unë nuk kuptoj*	oon nook KOOP-toy
Leave me alone; get lost!	*Ik*	eek

1—një (nyuh); 2—dy (dew); 3—tre (treh); 4—katër (KAHT-ihr); 5—pesë (pehs); 6—gjashtë (JAHS-t); 7—shtatë (sh-TAHT); 8—tetë (teht); 9—nënd (nihnd); 10—dhjetë (d-YEHT); 20—njëzet (NYUH-zeht); 30—tredhjetë (TREE-dyeht); 40—dyzet (DEW-zeht); 50—pesëdhjetë (PEH-sihd-YEHT); 60—gjashtëdhjëtë (JAH-shtihd-YEHT); 70—shtatëdhjetë (SHTAH-tihd-YEHT); 80—tetëdhjetë (TEH-tihd-YEHT); 90—nënddhjetë (nihn-dihd-YEHT); 100—njëqind (NYUH-cheend); 1000—njëmijë (NYUH-mee).

HEALTH AND SAFETY

In Albania, there are very few rules. In some ways, this makes things much easier — you don't have to worry about silly laws that are obscure to the foreigner. But there is very little official legislation of any sort to protect you. For instance, littering is perfectly acceptable. The no-smoking section is unheard of. And traffic rules are more guidelines than anything else.

Fortunately, Albanian hospitality is more than legendary. In the past, if a man's guest was harmed in any way, it was the host's duty to avenge the harm, at the cost of his own life if necessary. A foreigner (especially outside Tiranë) will be treated very well, although people's curiosity may be a little overbearing. As long as you don't do anything to grossly test their hospitality, you should be fine.

Women traveling alone are rare. Natives tend to be very protective, escorting you from place to place, and you may often encounter an attitude of "Don't worry your pretty little head about it." Curiously, although Albanian men in general are fairly polite, they are prone to catcalls in the afternoon and especially in the early evening. Later in the day, there are many more men than women on the streets, and women almost never go into a café or restaurant alone. However, even there you will likely encounter only surprise, not hostility. A good rule of thumb is to avoid cafés where loud music is playing; the crowd there has probably had more *raki* (the local drink) and less *kakao*. Going out alone at night is not advised, of course.

Most city dwellers do not drink or cook with the tap water, although it is safe for washing. Bottled water is easily available for about 85 lek per 1.5 liters. Medicine is somewhat primitive and folk remedies are still common outside of Tiranë. There are now pharmacies in many cities, although they are not very well stocked.

According to anthropological sources, **magic** is most active in the springtime, especially in the North. Keep on the lookout for the local *shpriga* (witch) and avoid leaving hair or nail clippings, the traditional stuff of spells, in obvious places.

ACCOMMODATIONS AND CAMPING

Tourist agencies outside the country will still sometimes try to fool you: "Hotels are of a modest standard" or "Suitable for a brief visit." Let's face it: many Albanian **hotels** define the expression "big dump." Albturist constructed one large hotel in each town especially for tour groups. These are now open to independent travelers but often lack running water, modern toilets, or even heat. Carpets are usually faded and tattered, beds sagging and uncomfortable. A few private hotels have been built in the last few years, however. These range from gorgeous and friendly to cramped but still friendly, and the facilities are generally a bit better than their state-run counterparts. With the larger hotels now being privatized, many will be refurbished in the next few years. Rooms run from US$15-35 per person. As of yet, there are no **hostels** in Albania except those directly connected with missionary groups; unless you're an affiliate, you can't stay there.

A few travel agencies in Tiranë now find **private rooms** for those who inquire. Although hot water, or water at all, is usually not guaranteed, the stay is much more pleasant than in a large hotel. There are no longer any restrictions on renting rooms and many people whom you meet will offer a night in their home for US$5-20. Whether you find your lodging through an agency or through luck, you will probably be given the largest bed in the house, possibly in a room with a few other people, and be fed dinner, coffee, and *raki*.

As of yet, there are no camping facilities in Albania, nor do any seem to be planned. Free camping is not illegal, and there are areas where it would be possible—but consider the safety risks.

LIFE AND TIMES

HISTORY

Archeological and anthropological studies indicate that Albanians are the direct descendants of the ancient **Illyrian tribes** who inhabited the western part of the Balkans in the 12th and 11th centuries BC. The Illyrians were known to be a sociable and hospitable people; experienced warriors, but also skillful miners, boat builders and sailors. In the 8th century BC, the **Greeks** started founding colonies on Illyrian soil, the most prominent of which were Epidamnus (modern Durrës) and Apollonia (near modern Vlorë). At the same time, Illyrian tribes began to form alliances with one another, thus forming more complex organizations and later, kingdoms.

From the 4th century BC onward, the Illyrians faced not only the expansionist Macedonia of Philip II and Alexander the Great, but also the increasingly powerful Romans, who set out to conquer the lands east of the Adriatic. In 229 BC, the **Roman Empire** succeeded in defeating Illyria and made it their province (Illyricum) for the next six centuries. The ancient Greek colony of **Apollonia** soon became the cultural center of the province; its celebrated school of philosophy attracted many scholars. Throughout this period, the Illyrians adopted many Latin words in their vocabulary, but they managed to resist complete assimilation into Roman culture. Before the advent of the Romans, the Illyrians worshipped their own gods, believed in an afterlife and buried their dead along with arms and other personal belongings. In the 1st century AD, the Romans introduced Christianity in the conquered province of Illyricum and, after a period of stagnation, the Christian community began to grow steadily, leading to the establishment of a bishopric in **Dyrrhachium** (the Greek Epidamnus or modern Durrës).

In 395 AD, the Roman Empire divided into east and west, and the lands of the Illyrians were partitioned. The territories of modern Albania became part of the **Byzantine Empire.** The Illyrian lands were invaded year after year by barbarian tribes of Visigoths, Huns, and Ostrogoths, until the **Slavs** started settling here in the 6th to 8th centuries. The northern Illyrian tribes were assimilated into what is now Slovenia, Croatia, Bosnia, and Herzegovina, while the southern tribes resisted assimilation and preserved their native tongue. Under the impact of Roman, Byzantine, and Slavic cultures, the name Illyria gradually gave way to the name of the **Albanoi** tribe, which then became **Arbëri** and, finally, Albania. Later on, around the 17th century, Albanians started calling themselves *shqiptarë*, meaning "sons of eagles," and their country *Shqipëria*, "the land of the eagle."

In 1054, when the Christian church split between the East and Rome, the country experienced its first religious fragmentation: southern Albania looked to the patriarch of Constantinople, while northern Albania remained under the jurisdiction of the Roman pope. Greek and Latin were the official languages of culture and literature, supported by the state and church; Albanian was not recognized as an official language.

The Byzantine Empire proved too weak to protect Albania from successive invasions by Bulgarians, Normans, Serbs, and Venetians. In 1347, the country was occupied by the **Serbs**, and only a few decades later, in 1388, invaded by the Ottoman Turks. Albania's greatest national hero, **Gjergj Kastrioti-Skanderbeg**, rose to power in the Turkish army and then recaptured his homeland in the 15th century. He repelled 25 attacks against Albania led by Turkish sultans and princes. After his death, however, Albanian resistance collapsed, and in 1506 the Turks reoccupied the country, cutting it off from West European civilization for more than four centuries. By the end of the 16th century, around two-thirds of the population had converted to Islam to escape persecutions by the Turks. Under Ottoman rule, Albania was built on a feudal system of landed estates (*timars*), awarded to military rulers for their services to the **Ottoman Empire.** As the empire began to decline, the power of these military lords, or *pashas,* increased. Some even attempted to create their own separate states within the empire, but were overthrown by the sultan. Turkey eventually abolished the *timar* system, and power passed from feudal lords to tribal chieftains called *bajraktars,* who presided over patriarchal societies, participated in blood feuds, and had their own code of revenge.

In response to the oppressive character of the Ottoman rule, Albanians founded the **Albanian League** in 1878; its goal was to unify all Albanian territories into one autonomous state, and to develop Albanian language, literature, and education. By the time the Turks managed to suppress the League, it had already become a symbol of the country's national awakening and its drive toward independence. When the Balkan states declared war on Turkey in October 1912, the Albanians proclaimed themselves independent in an attempt to preserve their country from Slavic invaders (Nov. 28). After the defeat of Turkey, the **conference of the Great Powers**—Britain, Germany, Russia, Austria-Hungary, France, and Italy—convened in London and agreed to recognize an independent state of Albania; however, when creating the state, they ignored ethnic divisions and gave Kosovo to Serbia, part of Çameria in the south to Greece, and parts of Greek Epirus to Albania.

During World War I, Albania was invaded by its neighbors, who planned to partition it among themselves. U.S. President Woodrow Wilson vetoed this partition at the **Paris Peace Conference,** however, and Albania regained its independent status. In the early 1920s, the country was divided between two opposing factions: the conservative *bajraktars,* led by the chieftain Zog, and liberal intellectuals and politicians, led by **Bishop Noli.** The liberal faction won—Noli was elected prime minister in 1924 and proceeded to democratize Albania. This period of Westernization lasted only a few months; **Zog** succeeded in overthrowing Noli and usurped leadership of the country. The renegade dictator crowned himself king in 1928.

King Zog's reign collapsed under Italian, Greek and Nazi occupations during World War II. But when Albania finally liberated itself from foreign powers, it once again fell under the heavy yoke of dictatorship, this time by the supremely self-aggrandizing Communist **Enver Hoxha**, who had led the resistance struggle of the Communist forces during the war. Hoxha proceeded to nationalize industry and collectivize agriculture, and tried to bring down the institution of the blood feud and revenge killings. Until his death in 1985, he and his Party of Labor formed and then rejected relationships with Yugoslavia, the Soviet Union and Red China, until finally closing Albania's doors to foreigners entirely. Travel abroad was forbidden to all but those on official business; religion was banned, and all Christian and Muslim houses of worship were closed. In the meantime, Hoxha's portrait was found in every home, and children wrote poems for him.

Hoxha's successor, **Ramiz Alia,** had to face a rising wave of opposition after the fall of Communism throughout Eastern Europe in 1989. Seeking to preserve the regime, Alia granted Albanians the right to travel abroad, restored religious freedom,

ALBANIA

and endorsed the creation of independent political parties. Finally, after numerous concessions made to the opposition, the regime collapsed—the March 1992 elections were a victory for the Democratic Party heading the anticommunist position. Alia was succeeded by **Sali Berisha,** the first democratic president of Albania since Bishop Noli.

ALBANIA TODAY

Albania is Europe's only predominantly Muslim country, a legacy of five centuries of Ottoman rule. Approximately 70 percent of the people are Muslim, 20 percent Eastern Orthodox, and 10 percent Roman Catholic. The Roman Catholics cluster in the northern part of the country, while Orthodox Christians live in the south, around towns such as Gjirokastër, Korçë, and Vlorë. The Muslims dominate the center. Albania also has several significant ethnic minorities: the largest group is Greek (in the south), followed by Gypsies, Vlachs, Macedonians, Armenians, Turks, Serbs, and Montenegrans (in the north of the country). Despite such a diverse religious and ethnic background, Albania is relatively free of inter-group conflicts.

The presence of a Greek minority in Southern Albania, however, which Greek nationalists refer to as "Northern Epirus," feeds ongoing tensions between Athens and Tiranë. Hundreds of thousands of illegal Albanian migrants into Greece have aggravated the situation and Albania has spurred further Greek anger by being one of the first countries to recognize an independent Macedonia. When Greece cut Macedonia off from the port of Thessaloniki, Albania offered Durrës. Albania's close relations with Turkey feed Greek fears of growing Muslim influence in the region. Serbia continues to deny Albania any influence over the ethnic Albanians in Kosovo, and Greek refusal to back NATO's decision to lift the siege of Sarajevo inflated Albanian fears of a future Greek-Serbian military alliance.

Increasing foreign contact is quickly Westernizing the cities. Conditions are improving rapidly and dramatically. Although travel is no longer difficult, there is still not enough of a stable infrastructure to make tourism popular. Thus the gorgeous landscapes and rugged stone cities of Albania remain largely unspoiled.

FOOD AND DRINK

Local shortages don't tend to be a problem for foreigners since more and more food is imported. Although Albania was dependent on food aid from the European Union in recent years, land reform has increased domestic production and the country is expected to export food by 1996. During the summer, fresh produce is sold on the streets and by roadsides for a reasonable cost. Restaurants now often have extensive menus—that is, if they have menus. A meal will run about 500-700 lekë.

Albanian cuisine revolves around meat and potatoes *(mish and patate)* which usually can be ordered with vegetables *(me garniturë),* probably salted and oiled, for an additional 100-200 lekë. There are definite Greek influences, and feta cheese is predominant. *Kos,* Albanian yogurt, can be served at just about any meal. In the northern mountains, try *oriz më tamel,* a delicious sheep's-milk rice pudding. Follow the customs of your native companions—for instance, in the north it is considered a sign of dissatisfaction if you wipe your plate with bread at the end of your meal.

The table wines supplied with every meal are a little rough, but generally cheap and cheerful. The local firewater is *raki,* made from grapes or other fruit; it stars in some of Albania's most powerful folk songs. *Raki* is drunk in small sips, never a whole glass at a time.

CUSTOMS AND ETIQUETTE

Albanian etiquette is rooted in traditions of hospitality, still influenced by the ancient law of *Kanun*—the legendary code of the medieval lawgiver Lek Dukagjini. They will even override obligations for revenge, so that a house will shelter and feed a man who has killed one of its members. (The *Kanun* is now available in English translation, with prescriptions on all aspects of life from vendetta etiquette to the ritual of the first haircut.) Assuming things don't get so dramatic, you will still be served coffee and *raki* and offered a smoke whenever you enter a home. It is polite to accept it, but nowadays no offense will be taken if a cigarette is refused. It is customary to take off your shoes upon crossing the threshold of a house.

For women, dress is more conservative in Albania than elsewhere in Europe, and although shorts and jeans are known, especially in Tiranë, they are quite uncommon. Men are usually clean-shaven, and long hair on male travelers will probably cause some stares.

Physical affection between members of the same sex is quite common, and young women may often feel as if their grandmothers have been conspiring with Albanian females, as their cheeks are pinched for the fiftieth time. A two-sided kiss, which seems to have evolved from the forehead tap observed in the north, is the normal greeting and farewell between members of the same sex. A man and a woman will usually just shake hands. Physical affection between members of the opposite sex is rather scandalous.

■ Tiranë

A century of miserable neglect, frenetic modernization, and political upheavals have left Tiranë exhausted; in some ways the entire city looks like a construction zone, with open manholes, crumbling exteriors, broken glass, and unidentifiable objects scattered over the muddy streets. It can be shocking at first sight. The government had a hard time maintaining any coherent central structure after the fall of communism, and the electric and plumbing systems have become shaky, although the situation is improving. Electrical grids only cover a block or two, so, even if you have no power, your neighbor might. Power outages are worst in winter. Currently tap water is available during three periods of the day, but the situation is variable. The water shortage is most dire from mid-July to mid-August. Trash is being collected once again, foreign capital is beginning to fund the reconstruction of some buildings, and drivers are beginning to course through the streets a little less wildly.

Like the first new blades of grass sprouting from a plowed field, scores of tiny new kiosks have pushed their way up through the rubble of Tiranë's overturned earth. Most are not specialty shops; they sell everything from ballpoint pens to bananas and shoes. Along with the kiosks, plastic-walled cafés are springing up everywhere—consisting of half a dozen flimsy chairs and tables, a cappuccino machine, a few bottles of liquor, and a jolly crowd of Tiranans discussing the world and patting each other on the back as they watch motorcycles and buses careen through the dust and sunlight.

Most of Tiranë's museums are closed for renovation. However, it's probably worth spending a night or two in the capital hanging out in the cafés, taking an evening *volta* (stroll), and watching a show; it's a good way to accustom yourself to Albania before venturing out into the countryside. The city is changing rapidly—in 1920, when it was made the capital, there were only a few huts divided by cobbled paths here; before the beginning of this decade, the city sported no more than a few dozen private cars as such bourgeois trappings were illegal under communism. Tiranë is where you go on your way to see the rest of the country, so you might as well enjoy yourself while you're there.

ORIENTATION AND PRACTICAL INFORMATION

Although there are now two maps (*harta e qytetit*) of Tiranë available, Albanians are not big on grids, street names, or street numbers. A street may be marked or not, the buildings numbered in no particular order, and the name on the street is only sometimes the same as the one on the map. Ask anyone *"Ju lutem, ku është?"* (yoo-

LOO-tehm, koo UHSHT? "Please, where is?") and you'll probably be conducted there.

The bus from the airport drops you off in the center of town, **Skanderbeg Square.** Through the square runs the main street of Tiranë, **Bulevardi Deshmoret e Kombit,** dividing briefly to pass around **Skanderbeg's statue.** Skanderbeg, if he began to move, would proceed north up the boulevard to the train station. Behind him, the boulevard stretches south to the **university,** past Hotel Dajti, the Cultural Center (formerly the Enver Hoxha museum), and the Prime Minister's office on the left. To the west (left if you're facing the same direction as the statue) are **Rr. Durrësit,** running north-west past the **Historical Museum** (the building with the murals), and **Rr. Kavajës** running west past the **National Bank.** Durrësit divides in two at the **Hambo restaurant;** the right branch becomes **Rr. Mine Peza.** Durrësit is known on maps as Rr. Kongresi i Permetit; Kavajës is Rr. Konferenca e Pezes. **Hotel Tirana** marks the northeast corner of the square and the **mosque** the southeast corner. Between them, the building with all the pillars is the **opera house.** If you must have a **map,** one is sold at kiosks and the other is found in the back of the yellow information booklet sold at newsstands and at the American Express office for 250 lekë. Although drivers are beginning to obey traffic rules, bicycles and motorcycles do not. Stay out of the way of anything that moves faster than you do, even while walking on footbridges.

Tourist Offices: Skanderbeg Travel, Rr. Durrësit (tel./fax 003 55); they do not always have maps available. Italian, French, and German spoken; brochures also in English. Arranges accommodation in Hotel Dajti, Hotel Arberia, Hotel Tirana (when it reopens), and in private rooms (3 beds US$40, 4 beds US$50, 5 beds US$60). Car and driver rental, guided excursions (day trips and regional voyages), and ferry tickets also available. Advance notice for car rental preferred. Open Mon.-Sat. 8am-1pm and 4:30-7:30pm. American Express also acts as a tourist agency (see below).

Embassies: U.S., Rr. Elbasanit (tel. 328 75 or 335 20). Walk towards the university on Blvd. Deshmoret e Kombit, turn left after the Prime Minister's office, right at the television stations and then immediately left. The embassy is ahead of you toward the right, in bright yellow ochre. Open Mon.-Fri. 8am-4:30pm, services for Americans open Mon.-Fri. 1-4pm. You will have passed the embassy of **Italy** on your way; all the others are on Rr. Kravajës (Rr. Konferenca e Prezes on maps).

Currency Exchange: The private exchangers who lurk in front of the bank usually have the best rates and are recognizable by the calculators they hold. The national bank itself, in the southwestern corner of the square, accepts traveler's checks but has limited, unmarked hours and a reputation for uncooperativeness. The lobby of Hotel Dajti has a full exchange counter open daily 6:30am-10pm but is happy to change dollars whenever you desire. American Express only changes dollars and their own traveler's checks. Major currencies are exchanged at the airport, along with some traveler's checks.

American Express: The office is on Rr. e Durrësit, on the left heading away from the square (tel. 279 08). Provides cash advances, emergency cash, and officially holds mail for members only; mail for non-cardholders is not officially refused. Also sells ferry tickets, rents cars and drivers, arranges private accommodations (US$30-60), and organizes group and individual tours. It sells an excellent **information book** (250 lekë).

Post Office: Behind the National Bank. Open daily 7am-9pm; some services only until 6pm.

Telephones: International calls are possible from the **Post Office, Hotel Dajti** (open 24 hrs.), the Italian telephone trailer to the right of the national bank (open daily 2-9pm), or the **Telekomi office** across from Hotel Arborea (open daily 10am-1pm and 2-9pm). Calls to the U.S. 230 lekë per minute. **City Code:** 42.

Flights: Rinas Airport is 26km from town. Get your passport checked and go through the metal detector—then you are free to wait for the small blue bus which merrily shuttles passengers to Skanderbeg Sq. for 35 lekë, if running every few hours can really be called shuttling. The bus leaves Tiranë from in front of the

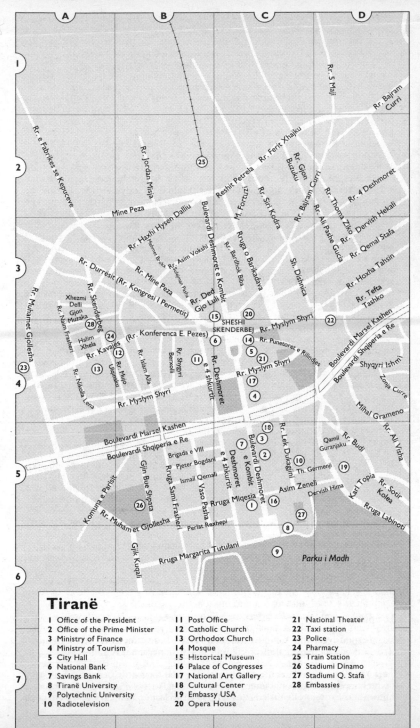

Tiranë

1 Office of the President
2 Office of the Prime Minister
3 Ministry of Finance
4 Ministry of Tourism
5 City Hall
6 National Bank
7 Savings Bank
8 Tiranë University
9 Polytechnic University
10 Radiotelevision
11 Post Office
12 Catholic Church
13 Orthodox Church
14 Mosque
15 Historical Museum
16 Palace of Congresses
17 National Art Gallery
18 Cultural Center
19 Embassy USA
20 Opera House
21 National Theater
22 Taxi station
23 Police
24 Pharmacy
25 Train Station
26 Stadiumi Dinamo
27 Stadiumi Q. Stafa
28 Embassies

ALBANIA

airline agency, to the right of HambO, 5-6 times daily. The schedule is posted in the window 50m beyond Albanian Airlines office. At the other end, you can relax in the café outside the airport until the bus comes. Pay the driver when you get off and count your change. If you're in a hurry, a taxi runs US$5-10. Keep your eye out during the trip for the **Coca-Cola plant**—it's hard to miss.

Trains: When Albania opened its first external rail line in 1986, it finally became possible to send freight, if not ride internationally—to Yugoslavia. Oh well. Currently there are no **international** passenger trains out of Albania. **Domestic** trains leave Tiranë from the north end of Blvd. Deshmoret e Kombit. Schedules are posted on the wall next to the track. The ticket windows are on the right. To: Durrës (7 daily, 36 lek), Vlorë (2 daily), and Fier (2 daily).

Buses: Buses leave from three locations in the city. The **Kavajë-Fier-Gjirokastër-Sarandë** route and the **Elbasan-Pogradecc-Korçë** route begin behind the football stadium in the southwest of the city. From Skanderbeg Sq., walk south on Deshmoret e Kombit and turn right at the "river." Follow the river for a few minutes and turn left when the "Shqipëria Sot" building is on your right. Ask for the *stacioni i autobuzit*. Most buses leave around 7am, or whenever they fill up. The prices may differ on the way back, but are generally low. To: Gjirokastër (300 lekë) and Pogradec (100 lekë). Buses to **Durrës** leave in front of the train station several times per day, about one per hour in the morning and tapering off towards the evening (50 lekë). Buses to **Krujë, Shkodër,** and points north leave from the Pallati Sportit "Asllan Rusi" on Rr. Durrësit (Kongresi i Permetit). All buses have signs in their windows stating their main destinations, although there may be many other stops.

Public Transportation: At birth, the Albanian is apparently endowed with a superhuman knowledge of where city buses go, where they stop, and how much to pay, despite the complete lack of signs, marked routes, or even maps. Luckily for the foreigner, Tiranë is small enough that walking is not a problem.

Taxis: The best place to get one is in Skanderbeg Sq. The low cost makes trips outside Tiranë reasonable. Taxis also hang out in front of Hotel Dajti. As is true for all Albanian cars and buses, you may feel better if you close your eyes and begin to pray upon entering the vehicle. Negotiate a price first. Dollars happily accepted.

Car Rental: Most car rentals include a driver; it is a reasonable option for groups of 2-4 people. Go to Skanderbeg Travel or American Express (see above). It is possible to rent a car individually only without insurance. You should *not* drive in Albania without insurance. Such rentals are available at: **Hertz** on Deshmoret (tel. 23 768), and **Vesa,** Rr. Qamil Guranjaku 9 (tel. 274 03).

Luggage Storage: The staff at Hotel Dajti will guard your luggage as long as their shifts last but can't guarantee anything after that. Changing of the guard at 2pm.

Ticket Agencies: Tickets for **sporting events** can be had at the kiosk Billetari Sporti on the other side of the square from the statue (open Mon.-Fri. 7am-1pm, Sat. 7am-noon, Sun. 7-10am). The ticket window for the **Opera House** (tel. 274 95) is on the left of the façade (open Mon.-Fri. 9am-noon and 5-6:55pm, Sat.-Sun. 9am-noon).

24-Hr. Pharmacy: With the Hotel Arborea on your left, turn right on the next street (tel. 222 41).

Hospital: Qendra Spitalore Universitare, at Rr. Bajram Curri (tel. 326 31 or 321 21).

ACCOMMODATIONS

Private rooms and room-finding services are sure to become more common as the influx of foreigners into Albania continues to increase. Any time you meet an Albanian, it is always worth finding out find out whether he or she knows anyone willing to let a room. **American Express** and **Skanderbeg Travel** already make such arrangements in an organized fashion, but at a cost. Hotels are very uncomfortable, and very expensive. Make sure any room you take has a water reservoir or you'll be stuck depending on the vagaries of the miserable Tiranë water system.

Hotel Krujë, on Mine Peza 1½ blocks past the market. Small, decent rooms with better atmosphere than anywhere else in the city. Feels like staying in your aunt's house, in the rooms of your cousins who have grown up and left but whose beds are still there. Boisterous, friendly café/bar/restaurant downstairs. Doubles US$20. Triples US$30.

Motel Armstrong, Rr. Labinoti—J. De Rada 83, off Rr. Myslym Shyri across from the Parliament (tel. 257 33). A family has converted its home into a boarding-house by buying a reservoir, hanging up a sign with a florid picture of Louis Armstrong, and learning fluent English. Two doubles with bath each US$50. One three-bed, two-room "apartment" with bath US$70.

Hotel Dajti, Blvd. Deshmoret e Kombit (tel. 321 72, 333 26, 254 06, or 263 85). On the left as you walk towards the university, behind a verdant grove you'll find the "best hotel in Albania": reservoir and water heater in every room, elevator, magnificent lobby, currency exchange, duty-free shop, telephones, TVs which might even work, and English spoken fluently by everyone. It's definitely beyond a *Let's Go* budget, but darn it, if you can't go without hot water, this is the *only* option. Businessmen claim it's the only hotel in Albania. Unfortunately, it's about to undergo renovations. Reception open 24 hrs. Check-in by noon; check-out is officially noon of the next day, but they're flexible. Singles 3500 lekë, with shower 4000 lekë. Doubles with bath 6000 lekë.

Hotel Tirana, the 15-story tall building in the middle of the square, will re-open when the Dajti is undergoes renovation; the hotels are run by the same Italian out-fit, so they'll never be closed simultaneously.

Hotel Klodiana, Rr. Shyqyri Bërxollis, Zagjía 57, Nr. 1. No phone yet. Turn right on Myslym Shyri just before Hotel Dajti. Shyqyri Bërxollis is a small side street to the right. Two tiny doubles with bath in a pretty, white, stuccoed upstairs apart-ment. Enkeleda Mullaj is the English-speaker of the family, and her mom smiles a lot. Doubles US$40.

Hotel Arberia, Blvd. Deshmoret e Kombit, towards the train station (tel./fax 428 13). It has water, although the taps leak, and the beds are clean if unstable. Not beautiful but livable. One of those vexing places where the natives get better prices. Reception open 24 hrs. Check-out 10am. Singles 1750 lekë, with bath 2300 lekë. Doubles 2300 lekë, with bath 3500 lekë.

Hotel Drini, Rr. Myslym Slugi (tel. 227 41). No reservations necessary because very few people stay here any more. There is no reservoir, so its taps are dependent on the flow of Tiranë water (currently 6-8am, 1-3pm, and 7-8:30pm). The rooms appear rather sad and abandoned. But it has the friendliest staff you're likely to meet, with a genuine concern for your welfare. US$17.

Hotel Arbana, Blvd. Shqiperia e Re, to the east just before the "river" is freed from its concrete bed. There might have been running water here once. The (stand-up) toilets may have worked once. There probably never was a shower or sink. Check-in noon. Check-out 10am. 1500 lekë per person, 700 lekë per person in groups.

FOOD

Food shortages no longer seem to be a problem in Tiranë as the country gets back on its feet. There are now quite a number of restaurants serving the general popu-lace as well as those in the enormous old hotels. Many fruits and vegetables are sold on the streets in the summer; these are generally safe, but be sure to wash and peel them—their storage conditions have not been sanitary. A daily market appears between Mine Peza and Durrësit; it is especially active on Sunday morning. Any-where you see *"Buke,"* bread is being sold. Many bakeries operate through a small hole in the wall. Read the prices outside, hand your money through the window and you'll be handed back your bread. Just to the left of the Historical Museum on Rr. Ded Gjon Luli are a couple of Tiranë's newest and swankiest joints, but between the city's four Chinese restaurants and a few local hangouts you should be able to find a better buy. If shelves do seem bare, consult the Greek supermarket **Ilios** on the right side of Deshmoret e Kombit heading towards the train station; it's always well-stocked (open Mon.-Sat. 8am-2pm, 5pm-8pm).

Restorant Simpatia, Rr. Durrësit. Family-run-and-owned; good basic chow. Entrees 150-550 lekë. Open daily 7am-11pm.

Restorant Rogova, Rr. Myslym Shyri; take a right just before Hotel Dajti. A very typical Albanian restaurant "where the Chinese Specialists used to eat." Entrees 25-420 lekë. Open daily 7am-10pm.

Restorant Drini, next to Hotel Drini. The shish kebab makes it worth the sad view. Wonderfully friendly service. Entrees 300-400 lekë. Open daily 6am-9pm.

Restorant Dajti, in the Hotel Dajti. The view from the terrace is absolutely unique: the flying-saucer-like Cultural Center on your right, a tropical garden in front of you, and Mt. Dajti in the distance. Oh, and the food's famous. Some vegetarian fare. Entrees start at 250 lekë and soar to 2800 lekë. Open daily 6-9:30am, 12:30-3:30pm, and 6:30-10:30pm.

HambO, Rr. Durrësit and Mine Peza. Like McDonald's, only in Albanian. Fries 100 lekë. Beer 100 lekë. Cheeseburger 140 lekë. Open daily 7am-midnight.

La Perla, reached by following signs from the west side of Skanderbeg Sq. (tel. 429 51). The almost decent Italian place where all the important people used to eat before Piazza hit town. Open Mon.-Sat. 8am-1pm and 4:30-8pm, Sun. 8am-1pm.

Restorant Piazza, Rr. Ded Gjon Luli (tel. 427 06). Whip out the credit card and pretend you too are important. Très posh. Antipasto 300-700 lekë. Primi piatti 150-500 lekë. Secondi piatti 600-700 lekë. Fish 2800 lekë per kilogram.

China Restaurant Hong Kong, Rr. Komuna e Parisit Nr. 1; head west along the river. Perfectly civilized and pleasantly warm; a nice retreat from Tiranë streets. Food is hot and well-flavored but somehow not fabulous. Smallish entrees 190-780 lekë. Soups 180-190 lekë. Open daily noon-3pm and 6-9pm.

SIGHTS AND ENTERTAINMENT

Unfortunately, most of Tiranë's excellent museums are closed, either for refurbishing or simply because there are not enough resources to support them. Instead, take a morning stroll to get an idea of what Tiranë has to offer. Tiranë centers around **Skanderbeg Square.** This is an entirely Communist square, from the **mural** in mosaic on the side of the Historical Museum, portraying the valiant struggle of the Albanian people (entitled, shockingly, "Albania") to the prominent platform where **Enver Hoxha's statue** used to stand, daring anyone to defy it—until in 1991 they did. If the **Historical Museum** ever reopens, the collection will probably be worth seeing; it was formerly reputed to be the best quick introduction to Albanian history available.

Walking up and back **Rr. Kavajës** is a good way to see the bustling commercial side of Tiranë. You can catch a film at the **Kinema Republika,** on the left as you walk away from the square. Heading down Deshmoret e Kombit to the south, you pass government ministries in the Italian yellow ochre buildings on either side. Further on, the **National Art Gallery** is still sometimes open although now hidden just to the left of Hotel Dajti (open Tues.-Sun. 9am-8pm). The **Hotel Dajti** itself is an excellent place to take a breather from a sultry Tiranë midday.

Continuing on Deshmoret e Kombit, the immense **Cultural Center** emerges—a 20th-century pyramid originally built to deify Enver Hoxha. It now holds occasional temporary exhibitions from various industrial or political groups but is worth a visit to the inside even if nothing is on display, if only to glimpse the weird genius of the structure (open daily 8am-8pm). At the end of the boulevard, the **Archaeological Museum** will still sometimes open its doors if you can find the guide. It is occasionally on display for researchers. The **university** surrounds the end of the boulevard. Behind it, the **Big Park** (*Parku i Madh*) provides a welcome rush of untamed greenery. Boats are sometimes available to rent for a paddle around the **lake.** The park formerly contained a **zoo,** which may reopen any day now.

Back in the square, you can visit the **souvenir shops** on Rr. Ded Gjon Luli to the left of the Historical Museum, and on Deshmoret e Kombit across from Hotel Arborea. Then while away the afternoon at one of Tiranë's many **cafés.** Most evenings, the **Opera House** puts on a show and **soccer** (football) games are popular weekend entertainment.

■ NEAR TIRANË

An easy daytrip from Tiranë is Gjergj Kastrioti-Skanderbeg's mighty fortress at **Krujë**. The bus stops quite close to the castle; now is a good time to ask, "*Në çfarë orë kthehet autobuzi*" (nuh chfahr or KTHEH-het ow-toe-BOOZ-ee, "What time does the bus return?") Hikers can get off at the bottom of the mountain and wind their way up the serpentine, imagining what the poor Turks must have gone through in their four attempts to capture this fort (Ismaíl Kadarë has already imagined it for you in his novel *The Castle*). Watch out for falling rocks.

Between the bus station and the citadel, a dozen or so shops form the "bazaar," a good place to hunt for souvenirs. The restored art of the castle represents hero-worship in its highest form; a museum contains the original sword and helmet of Albania's most respected citizen, as well as busts of all his associates, a library of more than 1000 books about him, and larger-than-life sculptures and paintings. Numerous romantic paintings portray Skanderbeg with a fiercely-wielded scimitar bludgeoning his way through a thickly packed Turkish army. One of the busts is of his warrior sister. (Open Tues.-Wed. and Fri.-Sun. 9am-1pm and 4-7pm, Thurs. 9am-1pm; admission 100 lekë.) Within the citadel walls, one building has been converted into an example of a traditional Albanian house, including Turkish baths, a working mill, spinning wheel and a *raki* still. This is a must for anyone with even a vague interest in Albanian culture. (Open Mon. and Wed.-Sat. 9am-1pm and 3-6pm, Sun. 9am-3pm; admission 100 lekë.) Ask to see it even if it isn't officially open. Watch out for the sheep and their, ahem, dung. Buses to Krujë leave from the Pallati Sportit in Tiranë. It's sometimes possible to get a ride home on one of the private minibuses.

Another excursion from Tiranë is a trip up **Mt. Dajti**, the range's highest peak. You'll have to rent a car, but it shouldn't cost over US$20. Although the television station lays claim to the highest point, there's nothing to block the view from one of the many lookout points.

■ ■ ■ DURRËS

Although it's the most accessible **beach** to Tiranë, Durrës isn't really worth more than a day's visit. From the train station, the Adriatik Hotel bus runs to the beach at 7, 8, 8:30, and 9am—although it's worth walking the 3 km for the view of the shining turquoise Adriatic. From the train station on foot, walk to the left of the station and cross the tracks. Continue along the beach road; the farther you go, the better the beach. Once on the beach, watch out—this is a popular location for testing out new cars. If you have the time, seek out the **Roman amphitheater excavations** and the **palace of King Zog.** The excavations are free and open to the public, but Zog's pad is guarded by an armed soldier. Still, skulking around the grounds affords a good view of the palace, the Adriatic, and the town.

A short walk to the right of the port will bring you to the train station which sends **trains** to Tiranë (7 per day, 36 lekë). Buy tickets at the small unmarked "window" (really more of a hole in a box) to the right of the waiting room, behind the kiosks, between Kafe Bulini and Genti Maritime Agency. Trains also run to: Pogradec (2 per day, 103 lekë), Vlore (2 per day, 86 lekë), Shkodër (2 per day, 80 lekë), and Elbasan (1 per day, 65 lekë). **Buses** to Durrës from Tiranë stop at the beach and in front of the train station; you can catch a ride back from the beach on a bus on its return from Sarandë (35 lekë). **Exchange currency** at the Hotel Adriatiku.

If you're arriving by ferry and want to spend the night, the only real option is the **hotel privat Teli** on Rr. Nako Spiru L. Nr. 1 (tel. (0035552) 241 49); it would probably seem like paradise itself if not for the fact that its beautiful new singles are US$40, with shower US$50; doubles US$50, with bath US$70; triples US$75. Any restaurant marked "*Peshk*" is bound to be a good source for fresh fish.

ALBANIA

■■■ LAKE OCHRID

A 4-hr. trip from Tiranë by bus will take you over some of the most spectacular mountain scenery in Europe, through Elbasan's vast, horrifying metal refinery, and agricultural villages that seem to preserve a centuries-old lifestyle, up a winding serpentine strewn with poppies and mustard, and finally to the fabulous panorama of Lake Ochrid, as seen from the thousand-meter high Macedonian border. Visitors stay in the sleepy town of Pogradec, once a tourist center which has only recently begun to resume its former activity. Bring a bathing suit.

The key to visiting Lake Ochrid is choosing the right time. Among crowds and on a hot summer day, the fresh mountain air and the smooth lake with its leaping fish are inviting and refreshing; under cloudy skies the town of Pogradec is dismal and the metal refinery looms larger than it ought to. Check the Albanian television station's weather report which comes on at 8:30pm every evening, although it often isn't very accurate. Tourist season begins in mid-June, peaks in mid-July, and trails off in mid-September. The **beach** is open right up to the Macedonian border, a few miles away. It gets sandier and less pebbly as you walk east. Although there is no official agency for renting **rowboats,** the shore is lined with boats that private owners are often willing to rent. In bad weather, the lake can be dangerously windy; remember that it's 310m to the bottom. At night, those feeling frisky from the high altitude (650m) can try the **DiskoKlub** on the left side of Reshit Çollaku, heading away from the hotel towards the refinery.

While on top of the mountain, buses stop for a few seconds near a **border crossing** to Macedonia (where the lake's known as *Ohrid).*

Traveling to Pogradec by **train** is not recommended; half of the reason to go is to enjoy the mountain view. Plus, the train stops 4km away from town, right next to the refinery (a paltry service station compared to the monster in Elbasan). Instead, take the **bus** from Tiranë (4hrs.), Elbasan (2hrs.), or Korçë (1½hrs.). Pogradec isn't marked on buses, but every bus that goes to Korçë can easily stop in Pogradec if you so request. You will be dropped off somewhere along the main drag, Bulevard Reshit Çollaku, which follows the south side of the lake. With the lake on your left, the hotel, the only tall building in town, is on the left side of the street and the PTT **(post office)** building is on the right (open daily 6:30am-10pm). A hundred meters later, the road divides in two. The small street that runs between the two branches hides the **police station** and the town's only **pharmacy** (open daily 8am-9pm). There's no official place to **exchange currency** but many people are happy to change dollars to lekë at whatever the day's rate happens to be.

There is really only one place to stay in Pogradec, the **Hotel Guri i Kuq** ("red stone," tel. 414). Fortunately, it's only a bit shabby and the view of the lake more than makes up for the lack of hot water. (Singles with bath 1840 lekë, doubles with bath 2300 lekë, half-price for one person. Apartment 2530 lekë.)

The specialty of Lake Ochrid is *koran,* a type of trout. Keep an eye out for it here, because the only place it's found outside of Albania is in Siberia. If you have cooking implements, you can buy *koran* from local fisherman along the road to the refinery, but if not, **Restorant Borana** on the left fork of the main street serves fish specialties for 350-700 lekë along with regular entrees for 15-360 lekë (open daily 8am-4pm and 5-11pm). The locals hang out on the other branch of the main street at **Restorant Palma** where entrees go for 200-400 lekë and *raki* can be had for 50 lekë a glass. No wonder there was an uprising of drunk peasants in 1992. (Open daily 8am-10pm.) Both have an English-speaking staff and something resembling a non-smoking section.

■■■ GJIROKASTËR

The severe incline of crooked, cobbled streets, the breathtaking spectacle of majestic mountains, and the stern stone citadel staring coldly down at the ripples of red roofs have inspired legends, mysteries, and fine literature. Battered by world wars and shuffled among invading powers, Gjirokastër is said to be the quintessential Albanian city—fierce, cold, and a little hapless.

Two enormous mountains stand starkly before the city. According to legend, there were once two brothers who lived near here, one of whom wielded a mace, and the other, a sword. Their mother caught them ripping each other to shreds in a fight over a girl. Angered, she turned them into mountains and the girl into a river. To this day, the lines of the sword wounds and the holes of the mace wounds are still visible on the sides of the mountains.

Wandering is certainly the best way to see Gjirokastër. Give yourself time—the city isn't as small as it looks, and the thin mountain air and steep streets take a lot out of you. From the top of the hill you can get a pretty good idea of the town's layout, which is utterly confounding on the ground. The high school is on the left, the only yellow building with a red roof. Across from it is the **Ethnographic Museum,** which is open during the daytime if you knock. Foreign investment is funding recent renovations (admission US$1). You can also see the **lookout point** where yet another statue of Enver Hoxha used to stand.

The **castle** and resident **Museum of Arms** is the real center of town. Its looming, dark chambers full of iron cannons and gold-inlaid firearms awe and terrify. The courtyard also affords a number of excellent prospects of the town (open Mon. 8am-2pm, Tues.-Sun. 8am-2pm and 4:30-6:30pm).

Exchange currency at the Banka e Komerseve, near the Enver Hoxha platform (open Mon.-Fri. 9am-1pm). A **Greek consulate** is just up the street from the hotels, under the flag. From Gjirokastër to Tiranë, **buses** leave about once per hour in the morning. On the way back is a spring where people stop to fill their bottles. The water is pure and delicious. Buses leave from the Express Oil station at the bottom of the mountain. Buses to the oft-praised pebbly beaches of **Sarandë** leave at around 2pm from across the street (under the *Vend Qendrim Autobuzi* sign). A stop at **Tepelen** is also possible on the way to Tiranë.

There are no street names in Gjirokastër. Following the main road from the base of the mountain brings you to the city's main street, where the hotels are located (20-min. walk or taxi US$2). **Hotel Sopoti** offers sad little doubles with sinks and stoves (400-600 lekë). **Hotel Argjiro** is about to be renovated away from its swaying iron beds and creaking doors (doubles US$20, triples US$30). **Hotel Çaiupi** (tel. 726 26 26) has a pleasant lobby, even if it is crawling with Greek soldiers. All bathrooms have old-fashioned toilets; no showers are available (US$45, doubles US$20 per person). For **private rooms,** Emir Aslani can put you up in his home (3 kids included) or in touch with someone else looking for lodgers (tel. 726 24 66, fax 726 39 77; French and German spoken; US$10). **Restaurants** are hard to find, but **Çaiupi's** should have reopened and the main road has **snack stands** and **produce stands.**

ALBANIA

BELARUS (БЕЛАРУСЬ)

US$1	= 23,500BR (Belarusian Rubles)	10000BR =	**US$0.42**
CDN$1	= 17,200BR	10000BR =	**CDN$0.58**
UK£1	= 36,900BR	10000BR =	**UK£0.27**
IR£1	= 36,200BR	10000BR =	**IR£0.28**
AUS$1	= 17,500BR	10000BR =	**AUS$0.57**
NZ$1	= 12,800BR	10000BR =	**NZ$0.78**
SAR1	= 6600BR	10000BR =	**SAR1.51**
DM1	= 15,300BR	10000BR =	**DM0.65**
Country Code: 7		**International Dialing Prefix: 00**	

Rampant inflation means that the BR is virtually guaranteed to lose much of its value in the near future. During an 11-day period in the summer of 1994, the BR exchange rate shifted from 20,000 to the dollar to 23,500 to the dollar.

Belarus still seems confused about the meaning of the word "independence." Felix Dzerzhinski, founder of the KGB, is still a national hero; busts of Lenin persist everywhere; streets are still named in honor of Marx, the October Revolution, and the Red Army. It's tempting to write off Belarus as a sort of Communist theme park, a bold step back into Brezhnev-era stagnation. But Belarus is far from stagnant;

beneath the veneer Soviet orthodoxy, the country is grappling with all the contradictions of a nascent republic. After three years, there's still no national anthem, and the national symbol, a knight on a rearing horse, looks suspiciously like the label from a Holstein beer can. While talk-show hosts speak Belarusian, the audience and the guests pipe up in Russian.

Even the countryside feels like a patchwork. The natural setting is wildly diverse: Belarus contains both the largest swath of swampland in Europe and the biggest surviving primeval forest on the continent, home to thousands of European bison. Minsk is glaringly Soviet while Brest is now a Polish-style free-market. Catholic-Baroque Hrodna evokes memories of Vilnius, while the lower tenth of the country has been evacuated in the wake of Chernobyl's radioactive fallout, leaving an eerie barren stretch of villages along the Ukraine border. To find the real Belarus, you have to visit all of these places; venture out to the smaller towns like Polack if you can, and take in all the complexities of life in a republic struggling to find its identity.

BELARUS ESSENTIALS

Belarusian visas vary dramatically in price. What may cost you US$30 at the Belarus embassy in Rīga or New York (plus a week or two of waiting) will cost US$62 if you get it via same-day service. See Essentials: Embassies and Consulates, page 3. Seemingly just to frustrate the traveler, transit visas at the border are usually available for only US$10-30—but if your train leaves while you're still outside getting your visa, that's your problem alone; at some Belarusian embassies and consulates, such as the ones in Daugavpils, Latvia and Kiev, Ukraine, same-day transit visas are only US$12. Shop around if you can.

GETTING THERE AND GETTING AROUND

Buy all tickets to destinations outside Belarus at a city's Advance Booking Office; tickets for same-day trains within Belarus can be purchased at the station. Don't be upset if a scowling clerk refuses to sell you a ticket from Minsk to Pinsk via Slutsk (or to wherever) just because you're a foreigner. Get in another line, and eventually some cashier will sell you a ticket. The difference in price (a US$0.50 ticket at the station runs US$25-30 through Belintourist) makes it worth the wait and effort.

TOURIST SERVICES

Bureaucracy is often at its worst in Belarus. Undaunted by the fall of the Soviet Union, Soviet logic continues to flourish in the administration of hotels, railway regulations, and all sorts of nooks and crannies of the Belarusian infrastructure. One consequence is that **Belintourist,** the state-run agency that has a monopoly on tourism in Belarus, is still the only authorized channel through which foreigners can buy rail and bus tickets. Tourists are also required to book hotel rooms, excursions, and clear their itineraries with Belintourist, just like when Brezhnev's eyebrows were still bushy. Outside of Minsk, hotel administrators may protest that Americans aren't allowed to stay overnight in their town; try howling about how the Soviet Union and its travel restrictions are gone, and you may get a room eventually. The good news is that most of the time you can avoid dealing with this dollar-hungry institution. Since foreigners were not allowed to travel outside of Minsk and Brest before independence, there aren't any interfering Belintourist offices in the other cities of Belarus. Of course, you'll then be without a safety net, even such as it is.

MONEY

Be sure to carry a supply of hard currency for use in Belarus since many institutions in Minsk, Brest, and other large cities will accept only stable currencies. Dollars, Deutschemarks, and Russian Rubles are the preferred mediums of exchange; you will have a great deal of trouble changing "minor" currencies such as the British Pound, to say nothing of Canadian or Australian dollars and other currencies.

> Belarusian Rubles (BR), popularly called "rabbits" (зайчыкі), are likely to be replaced by the Russian Ruble sometime in 1995, as Belarus begins a headlong plunge back into the shadow of Moscow (at least money-wise).

COMMUNICATION
Postal rates in Belarus are identical to those in Russia, but since the Belarusian Ruble is worth only a fraction of the Russian Ruble, mail is a real bargain. In 1994, public phones throughout Belarus were free for local calls (if you could find one that worked). Long-distance phone calls usually must be made at a telephone office or from your hotel. To reach the **BT Direct operator** (U.K.), dial 88 00 44. Rates for international calls are absurdly low; you can call the U.S. for 17,800BR (US$0.80) per minute. One English-language paper, the monthly *Minsk Economic Times,* is available but almost unbelievably scarce.

LANGUAGE
Belarusians speak mostly Russian and only rarely Belarusian. (See page 509 for Russian phrases and alphabet.) In western cities such as Hrodna and Brest, Polish and German are also fairly common. Don't worry too much about learning Belarusian phrases if you'll just be staying in big cities such as Minsk and Brest—most townies won't know them either. In this book, names have been written in the Belarusian form, since most street signs are slowly being converted from Russian. There are no Belarusian-English dictionaries available yet in Belarus, but multitudes of Belarusian-Russian dictionaries can be bought for around 190BR, a testimony to the many linguistic problems Belarusians are experiencing, now that they have the freedom to use their national language.

HEALTH AND SAFETY
Belarus was more affected by the Chernobyl accident than any other country in the world, including Ukraine. With the faulty reactor situated just 12km south of the Belarusian border, and the weather patterns prevailing for the first six days after the explosion, much of the radioactive material was blown north into Belarus and deposited into the soil of the southeastern quarter of the nation. An area of approximately 1200 sq. km just north of Chernobyl has been totally evacuated on account of the extremely high concentrations of Strontium-90, Plutonium-239/240, and Cesium-137. Don't panic—the radiation danger to visitors is practically non-existent, and none of the Belarusian cities covered in *Let's Go* are within regions affected by the radiation. Nonetheless, stay cautious.

ACCOMMODATIONS AND CAMPING
See Tourist Services, above, for more information on how Belintourist will be your personal vacation manager whether you like it or not. Belarus still requires that your visa be registered at a hotel every night during your stay. At the border, a customs officer may just ask to see proof of where you slept every night, and might levy "fines" if you don't keep all those little slips of paper from your hotels.

LIFE AND TIMES

HISTORY
Belarus has virtually no history as a sovereign state; for centuries the area was subdivided among warring powers and lumped together with other regions in a shifting mosaic of political boundaries. Modern Belarus is a strange political hybrid, patched

together from scraps of long-dead empires. Belarusians, in search of a national identity, are seeking for a common denominator—but it sure ain't history.

Belarus was one of the first areas settled by the Slavs, who came here in the 6th century. By the mid-9th century, the region became part of **Kievan Rus,** the first East Slavic state. Slavic tribes lived semi-nomadic lives, farming burned-over forests, hunting for fur, and trading up and down the Dnieper river. By the late 12th century, many towns in present-day Belarus had already been established.

In 1240, marauding Mongols swept in and overthrew Kievan Rus, incorporating much of Belarus into the **empire of the Golden Horde.** Over the next 150 years, the grand **duchy of Lithuania** swelled to include a large portion of Belarus; after Lithuania united with Poland in 1386, Polish cultural and political influences were added to the melting pot of Belarusian identity. The Belarusian aristocracy was mainly Roman Catholic and Polish-speaking, while peasants remained Orthodox. A series of agricultural reforms in the mid-16th century made farming more productive and efficient and expanded the powers of the nobility. Under this codified feudal system, Belarusian peasants were stripped of their liberties and made serfs on large estates. Although Belarusians rose up against their Polish landlords in the 1600s, the feudal system remained largely intact into the 20th century.

Successive partitions of Poland had put all of Belarus under **Russian rule** by the beginning of the 19th century. Small timber and glass industries grew up in Belarusian towns, but many areas—especially the remote Pripet Marshes—remained economically stagnant. The emancipation of the serfs in the 1860s gave Belarusian industry a shot in the arm. But the regional economy was still so bad that between 1896 and 1915, over 600,000 people left Belarus—for Siberia, of all places. The area witnessed heavy fighting between German and Russian troops during World War I; in early 1918, Russia ceded part of Belarus to Germany, only to get it back a few months later at the end of the war.

Meanwhile, Belarus was stumbling toward statehood. The **Russian Revolution of 1905** triggered peasant revolts in the region, and in 1918 Belarus declared itself a democratic republic. But the Bolsheviks muscled in as soon as Germany pulled out of Belarus, while Polish troops marched in from the west. In 1921, Russia and Poland divided the region among themselves, and the Russian portion metamorphosed into the **Belarusian Soviet Socialist Republic.** Moscow tacked on bits and pieces of nearby regions to the Belarusian S.S.R., meanwhile establishing new industries in Belarusian cities and purging the republic of dissidents and intellectuals.

World War II brought more turmoil to Belarus and shifted its political boundaries once again. Soviet troops invaded Poland from the east, occupying the region up to the Bug River and taking back some of the land ceded to Poland in 1921. German armies overran the Belarusian S.S.R. in 1941, despite the brave resistance of a Belarusian garrison at Brest.

When the Soviets retook Belarus after the war, they forcibly deported the region's Polish population to Poland. Wartime damage was rapidly repaired, and major cities were further industrialized, sapping rural areas of their population. By 1973, Minsk's population had reached the one million mark. In 1986, the explosion of the nuclear plant at Chernobyl spewed radioactive material across the southernmost part of the republic; the Belarusian zone nearest Chernobyl was immediately evacuated, but other dangerously contaminated regions in the republic were not evacuated until 1990.

While nearby Baltic republics struggled to break away from Moscow in the late 1980s, Belarus moved sluggishly. National separatism grew slowly under *glasnost* and *perestroika,* and Belarus finally declared independence on August 25, 1991 amid political turmoil in Moscow. The fledgling republic joined the Commonwealth of Independent states—a weak organization of former Soviet Republics—but faced a difficult transition to capitalism and true independence.

BELARUS TODAY

Belarus is still trying to define its relationship with Russia. A closer alliance between the republics seems likely; newly-elected President Lukashenko campaigned on a platform of forging stronger ties with Russia and eliminating the national currency to return to the Russian ruble. But national opinion is far from unified. Right-wing extremists are demanding a restoration of the Soviet Union, while Belarusian students recently demonstrated in front of the parliament in opposition to a Russian alliance. Belarus economic transition has been rocky; former Communists in the legislature have stalled free-market reforms. As industrial production drops, Belarus remains dependent on Russia for 90% of its oil and gas supplies. Experts estimate that as many as 70,000 Belarusians may be unemployed. Meanwhile, Chernobyl's tragic legacy has not disappeared. The disaster contaminated as much as 40% of Belarus with radioactive cesium, triggering a rash of thyroid cancers among children. Belarus future seems shaky; only time can heal the wounds of this much-scarred nation.

■ Minsk (Мінск)

Minsk is a baffling city. Although it may be the capital of the Commonwealth of Independent States (CIS), Lenin's statue still stands in Independence Square. Red Army Street and Communism Street still intersect, and statues of Felix Dzerzhinski, the Belarusian who founded the KGB, line the avenues bearing his name. Flattened in World War II, the entire city was redesigned and rebuilt as a showpiece of Soviet style. Every monumental building, every park, and every alleyway exude Central Planning. Still groaning under the weight of stifling Soviet bureaucracy, the new laws of the CIS and of independent Belarus are piled on top of old ones, making Western triplicate forms look like an exercise in simplicity. Some signs in Belarusian have been erected, and some streets have had their names changed, but no one in the city seems to speak the language; asking for directions can be a nightmare if and when you get the old Russian names instead. Like something out of an anarchist's daydream, Brezhnev-era Minsk has suddenly arrived in the 1990s, and it isn't quite sure what to make of it.

ORIENTATION AND PRACTICAL INFORMATION

Minsk was constructed on a grand scale. With nothing to hinder their ideas, Stalin's architects laid out wide avenues and city blocks of vast proportion. The main area of the city is contained between northeastern **Victory Square** (Плошча Перамогі in Belarusian; formerly Ploschad Pobedy in Russian), and southwestern **Independence Square** (Плошча Незалежнасці; Ploschad Lenina in the good old days). However, the distance between these two points is almost 3km. **Praspect Frantsishka Skaryny** (Праспект Францішка Скарыны; formerly pr. Lenina) runs between the two squares. Halfway up Skaryny, Praspect Masherava (Праспект Машэрава; formerly bul. Lenina) runs northwest to southeast between Nyamiga (Нямига) and Ulyanaiskaya (Ульянаўская) to mark the other extremes of the city center. The rail station sits behind **In-Front-of-the-Station Square** (Прывакзальная Плошча), a block south of Lenin—er, we mean, Independence—Square.

Be sure to pick up the brand-new *Minsk in Your Pocket*, the latest addition to the brilliant city-guide series that started in Vilnius. The city and metro maps alone are well worth the price (US$1 in BR). The I'm-going-out-of-my-mind-living-in-Minsk humor is an added bonus. By the way, **jaywalking** carries a 3000BR fine in Minsk.

Tourist Office: Belintourist, pr. Masherava 19 (пр. Машэрава) (tel. 25 16 34), next to the Hotel Yubileyni. Intourist still holds the reins of power in Minsk.; "Bel" is

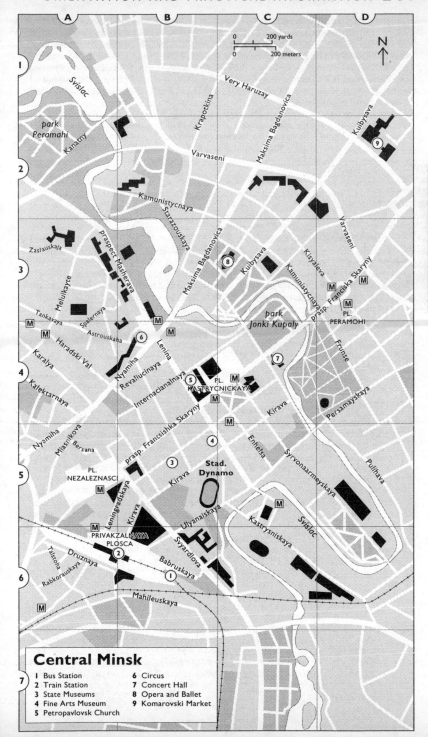

BELARUS

Central Minsk

1 Bus Station
2 Train Station
3 State Museums
4 Fine Arts Museum
5 Petropavlovsk Church
6 Circus
7 Concert Hall
8 Opera and Ballet
9 Komarovski Market

just painted on in front of "Intourist" on the old signs. The good news is that you can safely ignore them. They'll try to tell you that you have to pay US$60 for a round-trip to Vicebsk, that there are no trains or buses between cities outside of Minsk, and that you'll have to keep coming back to Minsk in order to travel to different cities elsewhere in Belarus. Wrong, wrong, and wrong. But they are the closest thing in Minsk to a tourist office, and they can help with rooms, maps, and just about anything you need. Just take what they say with a grain of salt. Open daily 9am-1pm and 2-6pm.

Currency Exchange: Follow the Абмен Валюты (**Abmen Valyuty**) signs. The exchange office on the second floor of the GUM department store may offer the best rates around. Consider patronizing the sweatsuit-clad gentlemen muttering better exchange rates to the people waiting in line, but also consider the risks. There are exchange bureaus in every hotel lobby. Get a Visa cash advance in the Hotel Belarus lobby.

Embassies: U.S., vul. Staravilenskaya 46 (вул. Старавіленская) (tel. 31 50 00; after hours 76 01 35); **U.K.,** vul. Zakharava 26 (вул. Захарава) (tel. 33 07 52); **Latvia,** in the Hotel Belarus, room 1907 (tel. 39 16 12); **Ukraine,** vul. Kirava 17 (вул. Кірава) (tel. 27 23 54); **Russia,** vul. Staravilenskaya 48 (tel. 50 36 66); **Poland,** vul. Rumyantsava 6 (вул. Румянцава) (tel. 33 11 14). To extend your Visa go to the **Ministry of Foreign Affairs,** vul. Lenina 19 (tel. 27 51 54), with US$30, a good reason, and some miscellaneous papers to back it up. Open Mon.-Fri. 10am-1pm and 2-5pm.

Post Office: The central Паштамт (*Pashtamt*), vul. F. Skaryny 10 (tel. 27 85 12), is across from the Hotel Minsk. To send or receive packages, go through the side entrance on vul. Svyardlova and up to the second floor. International postcard: 600BR. Open Mon.-Fri. 8am-8pm, Sat.-Sun. 10am-5pm. **Postal Code:** 220030.

Telephones and Telegraph: In the same building as the central post office, in the hall to the left immediately upon entering. Book a call to the U.S. for 17,800BR per min., 35,600BR per min. to be put through without waiting. Open daily 7:30am-11pm. **City Code:** 0172.

Faxes: In the main hall of the post office, at booth 11 (tel. 26 02 22; fax 26 05 30). Open Mon.-Fri. 8am-8pm.

Trains: Buying a train ticket in Minsk can be hellish. Foreigners are required to buy tickets (in dollars) at the *Belintourist* office. If you think you can pass for a nonforeigner, buy tickets to destinations outside Belarus (or within Belarus more than a day in advance) at the **Advance-Booking Office,** pr. F. Skaryny 18 (tel. 051; open Mon.-Sat. 9am-1pm and 2-6pm). To buy same-day tickets for destinations within Belarus, head down to the station and stand in line on the second floor (open 24 hrs.). The cashiers will probably send you back to Belintourist. If you pretend not to understand that you aren't allowed to buy a ticket from them, they may just sell you one to get rid of you. Prices quoted below are from Belintourist; for comparison, a ticket to Vicebsk is US$22 from Belintourist but 13,300BR ($0.57) at the station. Trains to: Moscow (20 per day, 12hrs.; US$30); Kiev (3 per day, 11hrs.; US$34); Kishinev (1 per day, 29hrs.; US$64); Vilnius (5 per day, 5hrs; US$25); Brest (12 per day, 5½hrs.; US$21). Tickets to Warsaw are available only at the advance-booking office, only more than one day ahead, and only for dollars or Deutschemarks (4 per day, 9hrs.; US$42).

Buses: There are two stations in Minsk. The **Central Station,** just east of the train station at vul. Babruskaya 12 (вул. Бабруйская), handles buses to all points west of Minsk except Warsaw. The **Eastern Station** is almost 9km out of the center, at vul. Vaneyeba 34 (вул. Ванэева). Not surprisingly, there's no direct bus between the stations. Furthermore, foreigners are technically not allowed to buy bus tickets at all. Considering that they often are much slower than trains, that's not such a tragic loss. **Information:** tel. 29 44 44.

Public Transportation: There is a Metro that runs under vul. F. Skaryny. A second line is currently being built perpendicular to this one. Because of inflation, cashiers limit sales of metro tokens (100BR) to four at a time. Buses and trams also dart around the city. There is a detailed map of their routes on one page of the *Plan Goroda Minsk,* a Russian-language map available in Kiosks (700BR). Buy monthly passes, good for all forms of city transport, in the main lobby of the central post office (14,000BR).

Car Rental: Avis has an office in the Hotel Belarus (tel. and fax 39 16 13). Toyotas, Volvos, and Fords; the cheapest class is US$47 per day, plus US$0.47 per km. For unlimited kilometrage, pay US$102 per day. Open daily 8am-6pm.

Taxi: Free-enterprise "competition" in Minsk consists of one company driving Volgas and Ladas for different rates (tel. 061 or 70 90 11). Fares subject to discussion; don't pay more than US$2 for a trip between the two main squares.

Pharmacy: Apotheke, vul. Yakuba Kolasa 49 (вул. Якуба Коласа). Western pharmaceuticals for more-than-Western prices, and only for Western currencies. Open Mon.-Sat. 10am-7pm.

Emergencies: Fire: tel. 01; **Police:** tel. 02; **Ambulance:** tel. 03.

ACCOMMODATIONS

Because Intourist's philosophy of tourism ("Westerners pay according to *our* needs.") still predominates in Minsk, hotels are universally expensive. Hostels as such don't exist here, despite an eight-page list of hostels in the phone book (such as the poetic "October Revolution Tractor Plant no. 9 Tool-Makers' Association Hostel of Comrades"—yes, seriously). But don't give up hope. You can try the three hostels run by the **Pedagogical Institute for Foreign Languages,** which sometimes accept foreign students for a night or two at the same 3000BR rate that Belarusian students pay. None are particularly close to the center of town. **Hostels** are located at: vul. Rumyantseva 12 (вул. Румянцева) (tel. 33 91 61); vul. Slesarnaya 35 (вул. Слесарная) (tel. 36 49 22); and vul. Varvasheni 80 (вул. Варвашені) (tel. 34 34 26).

Gastsinitsa Minsk (Гасцініца Мінск), vul. F. Skaryny 11 (tel. 20 01 32). Right in the center of town, just 1km from the train station. Try to get one of the more recently renovated rooms in the wing farthest from the front desk. Rooms with TV, phone, fridge, and showers that actually have water pressure. Singles US$36. Doubles US$40. AmEx accepted.

Gastsinitsa Belarus (Гасцініца Беларусь), vul. Starazoskaya 15 (вул. Старазоўская) (tel. 39 17 05), on the north side of the river 3km out of town, opposite the Hotels Jubileyni and Planeta. Rooms on floors 4-5 of this 23-story monster have been "renovated" to Western prices. Don't be taken in by the newer furniture. Rooms with private bath, TV, sauna. Singles US$36, "renovated" US$50. Doubles US$40, "renovated" US$60. Visa and AmEx accepted.

Gastsinitsa Jubileyni (Гасцініца Юбілейны), pr. Masherava 19 (tel. 26 90 24). In a higher price bracket than the above hotels for no apparent reason except that it once was an official Intourist hotel. Rooms with TV, phone, bath, etc. The Belintourist office is in the building next door. Singles US$53. Doubles US$63. Visa and AmEx accepted.

Gastsinitsa Planeta (Гасцініца Планэта), pr. Masherava 31 (tel. 23 85 87). Paired with the Hotel Jubileyni in the old Intourist price-bracket, but farther out from the city and without bathtubs—there's just a shower nozzle in a corner of the tiled bathrooms. Singles US$53. Doubles US$63. Visa and AmEx accepted.

FOOD

Sem Pyatnid (Сем Пятнід), vul. F. Skaryny 19 (tel. 27 69 01). Popular among the local Mercedes-and-cellular-phone crowd, this is an excellent Polish restaurant decorated in bright, art-gallery red, black, and yellow. Very crowded in the evenings, so go for lunch. Start your meal with a *solyanka* (солянка) chock full of raisins, peanuts, and green onions (12,000BR); add *zharkoe s chernochlivom* (жаркое с черночливом), a rich dish of pork with prunes (32,000BR); and finish with coffee (8000BR). Tack on salads, dessert, and an appetizer, and you still won't go over US$3.50. Open daily noon-5pm and 7pm-4am.

Café Uzbekistan (Кафе Ухбекистан), vul. Kirava 25 (вул. Кірава), at the corner with vul. Lenina. Exotic dishes chock full of *cardamom*, a welcome change from boiled potatoes and pork, in a tiny cooperative restaurant. Spicy, excellent *shurpa* (шурпа; "soup") warms you on those cold and rainy days (15,400BR). *Plov no uzbeski* (плов но узбески) is a rice dish with lamb chunks (31,000BR). Menu changes daily. Open Mon.-Sat. noon-9pm.

Molochnoe Café (Молочное Кафе), vul. Yanki Kupaly 17 (вул. Янкі Купалы), near the river. Your basic, cheap eatery for locals. Two large *blinichki* (блиничкий; "pancakes stuffed with meat or cheese") 3000BR. Stuff yourself silly for under a buck. Open Mon.-Fri. 10am-3pm and 4-10pm, Sat.-Sun. 10am-8pm.

Restarant Maraviya (Рэстаран Маравія), vul. Zakharava 31 (вул. Захарава) (tel. 36 74 55), 0.5km east of Victory Square just past the British Embassy. A cozy semi-underground place with Pilsner Urqell on tap (1 liter 24,000BR). The Minsk Jazz Quartet performs here on weekend nights. Main courses are a bit expensive by Minsk standards (20,000-46,000BR), but they're worth the extra money and the walk. Open daily 11am-11pm.

Restarant Yubileyni (Рэстаран Маравія), pr. Masherava 19, on the second floor of the hotel. Decorated in inimitable Intourist fashion, including tacky tapestries of Belarusian peasants. Fairly predictable hotel fare; the menu is actually a list of what the chef would *like* to make, so ask the administrator what she recommends or has available instead. A full meal including soup, a liter of juice, and a chicken dish runs about 50,000BR. Open daily noon-11pm.

SIGHTS

A Western journalist once suggested that Belarus should be developed as a sort of "Communism theme park," with Minsk as its hub *à la* Cinderella's castle. If arguing with (Bel)Intourist and standing in lines at the train station hasn't left you feeling like you're in a Soviet time warp, take a walk around the city. Minsk is probably most noteworthy for its utter Sovietness, a state of mind which exudes from the architecture, emanates from the people, radiates from every bust and statue and street name, and is especially in evidence at the city's museums.

Minsk was named one of the 13 **"Hero Cities"** of the Soviet Union because it was decimated in World War II. Over 80% of the buildings and nearly 60% of the population, including almost all of the 300,000 Jews who lived there, were obliterated between 1941 and 1944. Needless to say, there's not much of medieval Minsk left to look at. The reconstructed **Old Town** on the north bank of the Svislac, west of vul. Nyamiga, is a nice area for a mid-afternoon stroll through souvenir shops and beer gardens. However, very few of the buildings in these blocks are of any authentic age. For a genuine example of old Belarusian architecture, wander far out pr. Masherava, past the Planeta, and go down the hill in back of the large Soviet **war memorial;** you'll find yourself in a rare area of pre-war Minsk. In the square east of the Nyamiga Metro stop (Ploschad Svobody) a dazzling 18th-century **orthodox cathedral** and a 17th-century **Bernadine monastery** are being restored.

The **Belarusian Exhibition of Economic Achievements,** vul. Yank Kupaly 27 (вул. Янкі Купалы), is the place where all those tales of touring Tractor Factories come alive. Yes, it's a monumental collection of tractors, dump trucks, plowers, harvesters, and other exciting farm implements. Avoid the tour guides, who will ramble on at length about Five-year Plans (open Wed.-Sun. 10am-5pm; admission 600BR). The **Museum of the Great Patriotic War,** vul. F. Skaryny 25-a (tel. 27 11 66), features 28 rooms of maps, guns, tanks, documents, and other displays, including a hall devoted to the Nazi death camps. More than 20% of the Belarusian population was killed during World War II, and this museum gives a grim, detailed picture of the war in Belarus (open Tues.-Sun. 10am-6pm. Admission 3000BR. If you call ahead, a tour can be arranged in English for US$5.)

The **History and Culture National Museum,** vul. K. Marksa 12, explores the history of everything Belarusian. Discover arrowheads, farm implements, 19th-century folk costumes, and whole halls devoted to the glory of the Belarusian SSR. If you had doubts that Belarus was a valid country with a true culture, this is the place to visit. Exhibits are labeled only in Russian (open Tues.-Sun. 11am-7pm; admission 2700BR). The **Museum of the First Congress of the Russian Social-Democratic Labor Party,** vul. F. Skaryny 31-a, remembers that Tsarist Russia's first Marxist party was founded in 1898 in this tiny wooden house by the Svislac River (open Sat.-Thurs. 11am-5pm; admission 1100BR).

ENTERTAINMENT AND NIGHTLIFE

Minsk has excellent cultural opportunities, provided by a major philharmonic **orchestra,** an impressive **opera** company, and a world-renowned **ballet.** Theater groups of all kinds add to the list of performances. The central **ticket office** for all performances is at vul. F. Skaryny 13 (tel. 34 07 21), not far north of the Hotel Minsk. Tickets to all shows range from 50,000-250,000BR. You may have trouble getting tickets for same-day performances of popular shows, but there is always something available from the scalpers in front of the office (open daily 9am-6pm).

Nightlife in Minsk is a lively blend of Western diplomats, Georgian businessmen, and local gentlemen who own luxury cars with no plates. To see this mix at its best, go to **Xantia,** vul. Syrvonaarmeyskaya 3 (вул. Сырвонаармейская) in the old Officers' Club (tel. 26 06 02), where the self-styled elite of Minsk dance the night away in a marble hall full of new BMWs. (Cover US$15. Open daily 7pm-4am.) The **Paradise** disco, vul. Mawdrava 13 in the Kino "Moskva," has plenty of dancing spread out over two floors, with an erotic floor show to boot. (Cover US$10. Open Thurs.-Sat. 11pm-6am.)

■■■ BREST (БРЭСТ)

Made famous by the 1918 Treaty of Brest-Litovsk, whereby Lenin and his associates ceded Poland, the Baltics, Belarus, and most of Ukraine to the Germans in order to get out of World War I, Brest-Litovsk remained a Polish city between the wars despite the later nullification of many parts of the agreement. World War II thrust Brest into the spotlight a second time, as the massive Brest Fortress held fast for over a month against the Germans. Today the city is a massive rail junction; nearly all train traffic from Western Europe passes through here to the CIS. Despite the transportation hustle and bustle, Brest is a pleasant, green city of parks, well worth a brief stop to refresh yourself in the last dot of Polish-style Westernism before Moscow. Stroll around the Brest Fortress (a park as big as the city center), savor a meal at the best restaurant south of Tallinn, and relax.

ORIENTATION AND PRACTICAL INFORMATION

There is an excellent map of Brest available at some kiosks in the city, the *Brest i Okrstnosti* (Брест и Окрстности) (1500BR). The text is in Russian, not Belarusian, but it's enough to get around. If you're too broke to buy it, don't worry: you can't get lost since the city is only about 2 sq. km. The **Mukhavets** and **Bug rivers** mark off the southern and western boundaries. At their confluence lie the islands which support the Brest Fortress stands. The Bug also marks the Polish border. From the rail station, vul. Lenina (вул. Леніна) leads south to the Mukhavets. Vul. Maskaiskaya (вул. Маскаўская) parallels the river at the end of Lenina leading from the Hotel Intourist to the Fortress. Halfway down from the station, **vul. Gogalya** (вул. Гоголя) is the main east-west thoroughfare. Just north of Gogalya (Гоголя), pl. Lenina still glorifies the man with pedestrian streets to the west and vul. Pushkinskaya (вул. Пушкінская) to the east.

Tourist Office: The Belintourist office in the Hotel Intourist, vul. Maskaiskaya 15 (tel. 510 71), is the only show in town. Not a lot of maps or information, but they do try. English, German, and Polish spoken. **Tours** of the Brest Fortress can be arranged in English for US$5 per person if you can get at least three people together. Open Mon.-Fri. 9am-6pm, Sat. 10am-5pm.

Currency Exchange: Enough Western currency flows into Brest from Poland that rates are universally much worse than in Minsk, or anywhere else in Belarus. **Five Stars,** a private currency-change operation at vul. Pushkinskaya 10, on the corner with vul. Kamsomolskaya (вул. Камсамольская), offers what are probably the best rates in town. Open Mon.-Sat. 7:30am-7:30pm, Sun. am-5pm. There's also an exchange bureau at the **Hotel Intourist** with horrid rates, but it is open 24 hrs.

Post Office: On the vul. Pushkinskaya side of Ploshcha Lenina. Open Mon.-Fri. 8:30am-2:30pm and 3:30-8pm, Sat. 8:30am-5pm, Sun. 8:30am-3pm.

Telephones and Telegraph: In the same building as the post office with the same hours. **City Code:** 01622.

Trains: Busy, busy, busy (tel. 005; open 24 hrs.). The Stalin-era passenger station, just north of vul. Ardzhanikidze (вул. Арджанікідзе), gleams a shining white welcome to the former Soviet Union, while the more dignified station built by the Poles is slowly being restored. Trains to just about anywhere, including: Prague (2 per day, 18hrs.; DM240); Warsaw (13 per day, 2½hrs., US$11); Rīga (1 per day, 20hrs., 135,000BR); Beijing (3 per week, 173hrs, US$350 plus 139,000BR in first-class); and Minsk (so many that one left while you read this, 5hrs.; 14,000BR).

Buses: Station at the corner of vul. Kubyshava (вул. Куйбышава) and vul. Mitskevicha (вул. Мішкевіча), near the central market (tel. 551 36; tickets sold daily 6am-11pm, station open 24 hrs.). A more active station than those in the rest of Belarus. Buses to: Hrodna (2 per day, 7.5hrs.; 29,800BR); Kiev (1 per day, 14hrs.; 130,000BR); Lviv (2 per day, 8hrs.; 98,000BR); Warsaw (4 per day, 6hrs.; 102,000BR).

Luggage Storage: Lockers in the bus station, in the hall opposite the ticket windows (2500BR; open 24 hrs.).

Emergencies: Fire: tel. 01. **Police:** tel. 02. **Ambulance:** tel. 03.

ACCOMMODATIONS

Brest is already well-accommodated to Western tourism, probably due to its legacy as the main entry point for rail traffic from Europe.

Gastsinitsa Vesta (Гасцініца Веста), vul. Krupskai 16 (вул. Крупскай) (tel. 371 69), 1km from the train station, in the green, park-like area west of Ploshcha Lenina. The best hotel in Brest for the money, the Vesta boasts a fridge, TV, and new furniture in every completely renovated room. Consistently hot water is the crowning achievement. Singles 120,000BR. Doubles 180,000BR. If you explain that you have a late-night train, you'll only be charged for a half-day.

Gastsinitsa Bug, vul. Lenina 2 (tel. 454 24), just across the bridge from the train station. Take a step back into severe Sovietism; the English sign says "Hotel Bug," and the rooms live up to the advertisement; but at least they don't have outrageous rates for foreigners. Singles 37,000BR. Doubles 74,000BR.

Gastsinitsa Intourist, vul. Maskaiskaya 15 (вул. Маскаўская) (tel. 520 83). The only place where foreigners were allowed to stay in Soviet times still seems to get most of the German and Polish businessmen that swarm around Brest. Rooms have TV and private bath, but you've got to be made of money to pay the rates they charge. Singles DM100. Doubles DM180.

FOOD

Brest is rightly famed among Westerners living in Belarus as having the **single best restaurant** in the country. Diplomats in Minsk drive to Brest on weekends just to dine there. Businessmen from Rīga to Kaliningrad to Vicebsk talk nostalgically about the meals they have eaten there. Ask around and you'll hear all about it. Open just over a year, it is the:

Restaurant India, vul. Gogalya at vul. K. Marksa. Revive your deadened palate on authentic, spicy Indian food. This could be the best restaurant west of Moscow; the chef, maitre d', and waiters were hired from Delhi to open this place by a businessman who missed Indian food. Sumptuous *shorba-e-noor* (lentil soup) US$1.50. Creamy *gosht korma* (lamb in sauce) US$5. Piping hot Indian bread US$0.75. Sure, the prices are Western, but splurge away! Dollars or Deutsche-marks only. Open daily noon-midnight.

Pizzeria (Піццерия), vul. K. Marksa at vul. Pushkinskaya. Masters of the potato-salad genre, this is actually intended to be a pizza place; come here for the smoke-free atmosphere if nothing else. The *kaprichchiya* (каприччыя) is a concoction of ham, garlic, mushrooms, and an olive (6000BR). Six-inch pizzas 2500-8500BR. Open daily 11am-4pm and 5pm-midnight.

Restaurant Brest (Рестаран Брэст), vul. Pushkinskaya 20, a block west of the market. A faded establishment of the Soviet era, this two-story dining and dancing hall is still a popular place for a night out on the town. Entrees 2500-41,000BR (at the high end, veal with caviar). This is one of the few elite places in Belarus where you can get a Belarusian beer (2400BR). Open Wed.-Mon. noon-5pm and 6pm-midnight, Tues. noon-5pm and 6-9pm.

Pinguin, vul. Maskaiskaya 11, a block or two west of the Hotel Intourist. Ice cream 2000BR. You knew there had to be one here, didn't you? Darn pinguins breed like rabbits... Open daily 10am-10pm.

SIGHTS

The **Brest Fortress** (Крэпасць Брэст-Літоўск; Krepasts Brest-Litoisk) dominates three square km around the Bug and Mukhavets rivers, smack-dab on the Polish border at the west end of town. What are now rolling grass-covered hills and tree-strewn streets used to be the best-equipped fortress in Tsarist Russia. After the experience of Napoleon's attack on Russia in 1812, several cities in Poland, Lithuania, and Belarus were heavily fortified to protect against any future aggression. The massive works at Brest-Litovsk were intended to be the central defensive point. No fortress had existed here before, and from 1838-41, the entire city was moved east to open up the site where the fort was built. Fifty-foot-thick brick walls, moats, rivers, and encasements made this a formidable battlement. But in the Treaty of Brest-Litovsk in 1918, Lenin ceded Brest to the Germans. The Poles held it between the wars, but another Russian-German agreement, this time the Molotrov-Ribbentrop pact of 1939, brought Brest-Litovsk back into the Russian fold. Embarrassed by the associations of the old name, Stalin ordered the city to be called simply Brest, just in time for Hitler's armies to attack the Soviet Union on June 22, 1941.

For the first time since it was built one century earlier, the fortress came under fire. While the Germans swept forward to Minsk and beyond, the garrison of Brest stood firm for six weeks. Nearly the entire fortress was reduced to rubble before the Russian Alamo finally surrendered. The selfless courage of its defenders earned Brest the honor of being one of the 13 "Hero Cities" of the Soviet Union. What remains of the fortress has been turned into a sometimes-dramatic, sometimes-dogmatic, testimonial to the heroes of Brest.

From the **Principal Entrance** (Галоўны ўваход) at the end of vul. Maskaiskaya, where patriotic Red Army songs and the sounds of gunfire emanate eerily from cavernous openings above your head, roads lead to different areas of the park. To the right lies the **Eastern Fort** (Усходні Форт), a football-field-sized complex where tenacious Russians completely cut off from their comrades held their ground for three weeks. To the north lies the **Northern Gate** (Паўночная Брама), the only remaining fully intact gate. To gain a sense of the fortress' former magnitude, try and remember that the whole place used to look like this.

To the right of the main gate, the first thing you will see is an immense boulder towering over the central island of the fortress. A chiseled-chin Soviet soldier's head is carved into it, making it not unlike a **Soviet Mount Rushmore.** Around the base of the monolith are **memorials** to the defenders, and an eternal flame to all 13 of the "Hero Cities." Ethereal, mournful music rises from under the slabs. In front of the sculpture are the foundations of the **White Palace** (Белы Палац), where the 1918 treaty was signed. To the right of this sculpture, the **Museum of the Defense of the Brest Hero-Fortress** (Музей Абароны Брэсцкая Крэпасці-Героя) is in the reconstructed guards' barracks. A ten-room, detailed history of the fort, it recounts the siege during World War II and the perfection of Communism as demonstrated by this heroic defense (nevermind that they ultimately lost). A tacked-on display about the Molotrov-Ribbentrop Pact has been added to explain just how Soviet soldiers happened to be here, when World War II started (open daily 9am-6pm; admission 400BR). Through the ruined gate to the left of the boulder is the **Museum of Brest Archaeology** (Музей Археалагічны Брэсце), a glass-enclosed fieldhouse full of coins, keys, pots, combs, and the 13th-century wooden foundations of early Brest exposed in a giant loamy pit (open Wed.-Mon.10am-6pm; admission 3000BR).

■■■ HRODNA (ГРОДНА)

If you're traveling from Warsaw to Vilnius, you're going to pass through Hrodna. Even if you just have a transit visa, you can get off the train and spend a pleasant afternoon wandering the streets of this multi-cultural border town, which at various times in its history has been Polish, Lithuanian, Russian, and Belarusian. Culturally, Hrodna is much closer to Warsaw and Vilnius than to Moscow or even Minsk. Catholic cathedrals loom over winding, twisting, streets of Baroque buildings and the pink, yellow, and tan tones prominent in the old towns of Poland and Lithuania are present here. Fully 70% of the people in the city speak Polish or Lithuanian as their first language; Russian comes next, and Belarusian is a distant third which is not surprising, considering that until 1939, the year Hitler and Stalin carved up Poland, Hrodna had been the Polish city of Grodno for more than 500 years.

Orientation and Practical Information   The layout of Hrodna is a bit confusing, but essentially the Old Town is contained between the railroad tracks in the east, the river to the south, and a series of wooded hills on the west; the railway station marks the northern boundary. The main north-south streets are, from east to west, vul. Saciyalistychnaya (вул. Сацыялістычная), vul. Krupskay (вул. Крупскай), and vul. Savetskaya (вул. Савецкая). Running perpendicular to these, the important roads are vul. K. Marksa (вул. К. Маркса) and vul. Kirava (вул. Кірава). If you know Russian, German, or Polish, you can get loads of information on the city from the **Belintourist** office, vul. Azheshka 41 (вул. Ажэшка), on the way into town from the train station (open Mon.-Fri. 8:30am-5pm). The **post and telephone office** dials and stamps from vul. K. Marksa 35. (Post open Mon.-Sat. 9:30am-7pm, Sun. 10am-3pm. Telephones open daily 8am-8pm). The **telephone city code** is 0152.

   Trains are the only realistic way to reach Hrodna. The brand-spanking-new station (tel. 005; open 24 hrs.) looks a lot like the Honolulu Airport, and is just about as busy—until 1994, every train from Western Europe to the Baltics or St. Petersburg came through Hrodna, and even now only the daily Tallinn-Warsaw express avoids the Belarusian visa fees by changing trains at the Polish-Lithuanian border. Trains run to: Minsk (4 per day, 6hrs.; 24,000BR); Vilnius (8 per day, 3hrs.; 37,000BR); Rīga (1 per day, 12hrs.; 76,000BR); Warsaw (6 per day, 5hrs.; US$14 and 2200BR).

   The **bus** station (tel. 004) is about 1.5km south of the train station on pr. Kasmanaitai (пр. Касманаўтаў), over the railroad bridge from the end of vul. Kirava. Don't waste your time going there—the only buses operating in this time of economic trouble run to small villages near Hrodna; there's not even a daily bus to Minsk. **Store luggage** in lockers in the lower half of the train station (2500BR, or two 15-kopeck Soviet coins, probably worth more than the BR).

Accommodations and Food   With all the trains going through Hrodna, there's not much reason to stay the night. If you're stuck, try the **Gastsinitsa Nyoman** (Гасцініца Нёман), vul. Krupskai 8 (tel. 45 42 47), at the southern point of the city. Only some of the rooms are open to foreigners, but if you plead in Russian, you may be able to convince the administrator that you're a Latvian-American, or something else not quite totally "foreign." (Singles 100,000BR. Doubles 180,000BR.)

   Grab a mid-day bite in the **Café** at vul. K. Marksa 10, just up the street from St. Anthony's. Wonderful, creamy, shop-made ice cream beats Pinguin by a mile (1000BR). Coffee for those in need costs 900BR (open daily 10am-6pm). To stock up for an overnight train ride, the **Hrodna Market** (Цэнтральны Рынак; *Tsentralny Rynak*) is on a hilltop 0.5km south of the bus station, along vul. Paligrafistai (вул. Паліграфістаў). (Open Mon.-Fri. 9am-6pm, Sat.-Sun. 8am-4pm.)

Sights and Entertainment   Leaving the train station, head to the Hrodna **Zoo,** immediately to the right as you exit the station. This is the best zoo in Belarus, complete with tigers, bears, zebras, and an elephant (oh my!). At just 1000BR to get in, why not? (Open May-Sept. daily 10am-6pm.) After watching the frisky fish in the zoo aquarium, follow vul. Azheshka south into the city. Along the way, notice the impressive **Russian Orthodox cathedral,** built in the 1870s for the Tsar's garrison here. And yes, that is a **Soviet Ty-124** airplane grounded in the park just a bit farther down.

Where vul. Azheshka (вул. Ажэшка) intersects vul. Satsiyalistychnaya (вул. Сацыялістычная), take Satsiyalistychnaya uphill to the left—but only after a short detour to look at the Lenin statue in the square just to the north. Turning right onto vul. K. Marksa will lead you into the central plaza of the city, which is dominated by the silver **St. Anthony's Cathedral,** an awe-inspiring 17th-century church that managed to stay open throughout the Soviet era. The magnificent altar with its many intricate figures is actually carved wood polished to look like stone.

Following vul. Krupskai south leads to a valley, between two buildings of vastly different eras but similar purpose: the 1970s **drama theater** on the right hill is a strangely pleasing complement to the 16th-century cathedral on the opposite summit. Performances are given in the theater year-round; the cashier's office is at the building's rear (tickets 4000-9000BR). At the foot of Krupskai sits a fine example of what to do with war-surplus **tanks.** Vul. Savetskaya, which leads north from the tank monument, is a **shopping** street full of souvenir shops, fancy stores with Adidas shoes, and outdoor artists selling paintings, jewelry, and other goodies; following it about 1km will bring you back to vul. Azheshka, just west of Lenin. Say "hi."

■■■ POLACK (ПОЛАЦК)

Probably the most ethnically Belarusian city in Belarus, Polack was at one time the center of the Russian state, and recently celebrated its 1000th anniversary. But its prominence as a river port faded long ago; today it is a quiet city of about 30,000, where you'll likely be misunderstood if you ask for the *gostinitsa* (гостиница—Russian) instead of the *gastsinitsa* (гасцініца—Belarusian).

Orientation and Practical Information No maps of Polack are available, but the layout is simple enough. Ploshcha Frantsysk Skaryna (Плошча Францыск Скарына) is the central square in town, with restaurants and the hotel. Vul. Golalya (вул. Голалля) runs north from the square to the train station, past the market. Pr. K. Marksa (пр. К. Маркса) runs east-west through the square; vul. Lenina (вул. Леніна) runs parallel to Marksa one block down along the Dzvina river. Getting into and out of Polack is easy enough. **Trains** stop at the **Vakzal** ("train station"; tel. 005) at the north end of vul. Gogalya, just past the most impressive of the many Lenin statues in town. Avoid cashier #1, who will demand Intourist prices (and dollars) from hapless foreigners. Trains creak their way to Vicebsk (4 per day, 2hrs.; 7400BR); Minsk (1 per day, 7½hrs., 12,000BR); Rīga (2 per day, 7hrs.; 30,000BR); and Warsaw (2 per week, 14hrs.; US$18—no BR accepted). If you feel like playing by the rules, the **Advance Booking Office** is three blocks down vul. Gogalya at vul. Kamunistychnaya 18 (бул. Камыністычная) (open daily 9am-6pm; station open 24 hrs., tickets sold daily 5am-10pm). The **Autavakzal** (Аўтавакзал; "bus station") is just to the right of the train station (tel. 004; open 5am-10pm). They're not quite Greyhound, but the Hungarian-built Ikarus buses do manage to make their way to Gomel (1 per day, 12hrs.; 22,750BR); Grodno (4 per week, 11hrs.; 29,675 BR); Minsk (4 per day, 7hrs.; 12,150BR); and Vicebsk (dozens per day, 2hrs.; 5050BR). **Exchange money** into near-worthless BRs at Natsiyanalny Bank Belarus (Напынальны Банк Беларусь), pr. K. Marksa 24, which has the only (legal) *abmen valyuty* in Polack. (Open Mon.-Fri. 9:30am-1pm). Otherwise, brave the black-leather-jacket crowd at the entrance to the market, who will be more than happy to beat the bank's rates. The **post office** (Пошта; *Poshta*), pr. K. Marksa 32 (open 8:30am-2pm and 3-7:30pm) also contains the city telephone office (open daily 9am-8pm). The **telephone city code** is 02144.

Accommodations and Food The **Gastsinitsa Dzvina** (Гасцініца Дзвіна), pr. K. Marksa 13 (tel. 422 35), right on the corner of Ploshcha Frantsysk Skaryna, is the only hotel in Polack. They're not really used to foreigners; you may have to argue to remind the hotel administrator that the old Soviet travel restrictions no longer apply. Roomy, airy singles (29,000BR) and doubles (42,000BR) have private baths and—sometimes—a TV. The **Yunatstva Café** (Юнацтва Кафе), at the corner of K. Marksa and Gogalya across from the hotel, is a cafeteria serving decent, if greasy, portions of beefsteaks, *borscht,* and other Slavic delights. A full meal will run about 5000BR (open daily 8am-3pm and 4-8pm). In the same building, **Café Morozhenoe** (Кафе Мороженое) takes the place of the strangely absent Pinguin (open daily 10am-10pm). Eating in Polack is probably best done by picking up a feast from the **Polack Market,** which stretches east from the corner of vul. Gogalya and vul. F. Skaryny. The food selection can be sparse, but there are some excellent *shashlik* stalls to browse among (8000BR). If you get tired of looking at the food, wander to the far end of the market where the **Polack Car Swap** takes place every weekend. How about a new BMW for US$350 cash? Papers? Well, no, we kind of lost the registration papers. Yeah, the plates are German, so what? No. Man, I swear the car's legal.

Sights The most enjoyable way to spend a day in Polack is to wander west along vul. K. Marksa, starting in fountain-decorated **Ploshcha Frantsysk Skaryna,** named for the first Belarusian book-printer. About halfway down, you'll pass a Lenin statue in the "Lenin as simple worker" motif; farther down, the street widens into a plaza, at the center of which is a **monument** to a battle against Napoleon. From this plaza, vul. Zamkovaya (вул. Замковая) snakes its way steeply uphill behind a shopping center, reaching the top near the crown jewel of Polack, the **Church of St. Sophia.** This amazing double-spired Baroque cathedral dominates the landscape for miles around from its position on the cliffs overlooking the Dzvina. Built from the 11th to the 18th centuries, it was originally a Polish Catholic church, but eventually became an Orthodox cathedral. Today it houses the **City Museum** of Polack (open Fri.-Wed. 10am-5pm). From the church, a sandy path leads west across a narrow wooden footbridge to a neighborhood of traditional Belarusian houses from the closing decades of the last century.

Vul. Lenina is **"museum row"** in Polack. Starting from the end nearest the Cathedral, the **Museum of General Knowledge** exudes a heady, musty smell at vul. Lenina 5, near the corner with vul. Frunze. It's full of old bones, stone tools, World War II uniforms, and dust (open Sat.-Thurs. 10am-5pm; admission 600BR). East along Lenina is the **Museum of Belarusian Book-Printing,** with displays on the life of Francisk Skariny, the first man to publish books in the Belarusian language (open Sat.-Mon. and Wed.-Thurs. 10am-5pm; admission 600BR). Next door is the only functioning church in town, until recently a concert hall. Note the brand-new icons. Peter the Great lived in a house at vul. Lenina 33 in 1705—for three days.

■■■ VICEBSK (ВІЦЕБСК)

Situated 180km northeast of Minsk on the steep banks of the Dzvina (Dvina to upriver Russians, Daugava to the Latvians downstream), Vicebsk was virtually flattened in World War II during intense battles across the river in winter 1943-44. Although it is over 1000 years old, the city now has little to show for its age, and best serves as a base for exploring the small towns in the north of Belarus. About the only way to spend time in Vicebsk is to walk around the city. The bus and train stations sit at the west end of vul. Kirava, which runs about 1km across the river and ends in front of the Hotel Vicebsk, where Kirava becomes pr. Frunze. One block farther east Frunze crosses vul. Lenina, the main north-south artery. Maskoiski Praspekt runs east-west 1km south of Frunze, marking the southern boundary of the central city.

Directly in front of the Hotel Vicebsk, on the site of what used to be a massive Russian Orthodox cathedral, a **church** has recently been constructed in the traditional wooden style next to the impressive ruins. Farther south, almost to Maskoiski praspekt, there stands an absolutely immense **memorial** to the fierce battles fought here in World War II, complete with reflecting ponds, eternal flame, and an excellent view of the river valley. Vicebsk is in the grip of a massive financial crunch, and the **theater** and both **museums** are closed on a more-or-less permanent basis. This may change; try contacting the **Intourist** office, located in the Hotel Vetraz (tel. 91 22 74) for information on the region surrounding the city.

Trains run to Minsk (8 per day, 5hrs.; 12,500BR); Brest (2 per day, 10hrs.; 24,000BR); Polack (8 per day, 2hrs.; 8000BR); St. Petersburg (13 per day, 13hrs.; 40,000BR). The station is at the west end of vul. Kirava (tel. 643 33; open 24 hrs). **Buses** depart from the Autavakzal, just a few meters north of the train station, to Minsk (2 per day, 6 hrs.; 13,930BR) and Polack (5 per day, 2hrs.; 5050BR). Other buses run to just about every hamlet in the Vicebsk *voblasts* (administrative region; tel. 650 32; open daily 7am-7pm). If you need a **taxi**, call tel. 650 01. Rates are extremely negotiable; a ride across town runs about 10,000BR. **Exchange currency** at Ashchadny Bank Belarus (Ашчадны Банк Беларус), vul. Lenina 30 east of the Hotel Vicebsk (open Mon.-Fri. 8:30am-7pm, Sat. 8:30am-5pm). The central **Post, Telephone, and Telegraph Office,** Maskoiski Praspekt 10 (open daily 8am-11pm), isn't really so central. The **telephone city code** is 0212.

Before the breakup of the Soviet Union, there were five hotels in Vicebsk. Today there are only two, although two others seem set to reopen as heavily refurbished, Western-priced facilities. For now, the **Gastsinitsa Vitsebsk** (Гасцініца Віцебск), vul. Zamkavaya 5/2-a (tel. 37 28 35), at the corner with pr. Frunze on the east river bank, is probably the best deal. Warm, comfy rooms have hot water, TV, radio, and phone; ask for a room on the 11th floor with a view of the river, it's beautiful at night. (Singles 167,000BR. Doubles 252,000BR. Visa accepted.) The other option is the much-less-central **Gastsnitsa Vetraz** (Гасцініца Ветраз), 3km south of town at pr. Charnyakhoiskava 25/1 (tel. 91 22 74), the old Intourist haunt. The rooms are no better (and possibly worse) than those at the Vitsebsk, with the same amenities. (Singles 201,000BR. Doubles 301,000BR.)

It's decidely difficult to find a worthwhile restaurant in Vicebsk. The hotel restaurant at the **Vitsebsk** (Біцебск) is an inexpensive and filling option—if you can stomach the unbearably loud music, *Saturday Night Fever* lighting, and Vegas-style girlie shows. This place gets packed on weekend nights (open daily noon-11pm). The best atmosphere in town is probably at the **Café Teatralnoe** (Кафе Театральное) vul. Zamkavaya 2 (вул. Замкавая), an artsy underground place next to the immense, pink collonaded theater across from the Vicebsk. This is the hangout for foreign students at the Medical College (many more than you might expect). Live music and dancing take place daily from 8pm. A full dinner of soup, salad, beer, and entree costs about 25,000BR (open daily 11am-5pm and 6-11pm).

BELARUS

BULGARIA (БЪЛГАРИЯ)

US$1	= 55Lv (leva, or BGL)	10Lv =	**US$0.18**
CDN$1	= 39Lv	10Lv =	**CDN$0.25**
UK£1	= 82Lv	10Lv =	**UK£0.12**
IR£1	= 80.5Lv	10Lv =	**IR£0.12**
AUS$1	= 40.4Lv	10Lv =	**AUS$0.25**
NZ$1	= 32.45Lv	10Lv =	**NZ$0.31**
SAR1	= 15.2Lv	10Lv =	**SAR0.66**
DM1	= 35.7Lv	10Lv =	**DM0.28**
Country Code: 359		**International Dialing Prefix: 00 (EU)**	

Pristine Black Sea beaches, resplendent monasteries and stunning ski slopes have made Bulgaria Eastern Europe's coveted vacation spot for years. While the West groggily wakes up to Bulgaria's possibilites, visitors can still lose themselves in the country's natural and artistic grandeur for a pittance. And there has never been a better time to visit; Bulgarians are now eager to show off the country that almost won the 1994 World Cup

Nearly half of the country is covered in mountains. The Stara Planina mountain range bisects Bulgaria horizontally from Sofia to Varna, sloping down toward the Danube in the north. The Rila and Pirin Mountains are south of Sofia, and the

Rhodopi Mountains center around the resort of Pamporovo, south of Plovdiv. Between the Rhodopis and the Stara Planina hides the famous Valley of Roses.

BULGARIA ESSENTIALS

As of June 1994, U.S. citizens could visit Bulgaria **visa**-free for up to 30 days; but Australian, British, Canadian, Irish, South African, and New Zealander citizens need either a 1-month tourist visa (US$34) or a 30-hour transit visa (US$24). Even in European capitals, visas usually take a week or more to process, so try to get one in your home country. Citizens of Australia, Canada, Ireland, New Zealand, South Africa and the U.K. can obtain 30-day single-entry tourist visas from their local consulate (US$34 for normal delivery, US$64 for express). See Essentials: Embassies and Consulates, page 3. A stay of more than 30 days will require a visit to the **Foreign Passports Agency** (Задгранични Паспорти) on 48 bul. Knyaginya Maria Luiza (Княгиня Мария Луиза). From Pl. Sveta Nedelya, walk past the central department store four blocks; it's on the right. (Open Mon.-Fri. 8:45am-12:30pm and 1:30-5:15pm. Duty officer available Sat. 9am-2pm.) You'll need your passport, the statistical card given to you upon entry to the country, and around US$30 in leva. Expect long lines and red tape. It's better to take care of this before you leave home.

GETTING THERE

For more information, contact the private agency **Balkan Holidays,** 41 East 42nd St., #508, New York, NY, 10017 (tel. (800) 852-0944 or (212) 573-5530, fax (212) 573-5538). The war in the former Yugoslavia has cut Bulgaria off from its main train link to Western Europe. Competition from **Balkan Air**—the Bulgarian national airline— Lufthansa, and British Airways have made **air travel** the best option for traveling to Bulgaria. Balkan Air now flies direct to Sofia from New York; ask for direct fares from other cities.

GETTING AROUND BULGARIA

Public transportation in Bulgaria costs about 15Lv per 100km. The **train** system is quite comprehensive, but very slow, crowded, and aged. Direct trains run between Sofia and all major towns. Trains come in three varieties: express (експрес), fast (бързи), and slow (пътнически). Couchettes are an option (usually 15Lv); purchase spots in advance. To buy an international ticket, you must go to the appropriate office, usually in the town center; look for **Rila Travel** (РИЛА). In Sofia, Rila is at ul. General Gurko 5 (tel. 87 07 77) and at NDK, the Palace of Culture (tel. 59 31 06). Rila no longer gives any ISIC discounts. You can only buy domestic tickets at train stations, except for the Sofia Central Railway Station (Централна Гара-София) where there is an international ticket counter. Buying a ticket on the train doubles the cost. Stations are poorly marked, and signs are often only in Cyrillic. Try to find out the exact time you are due at your destination or take along a current map that shows your route. If you miss your stop on a main express line, get off at the next stop and try to get the express in the opposite direction (which should be coming in 15-30min). Otherwise you could blow the entire day trying to get back. Express trains usually have cafés serving snacks, unidentifiable meats, and alcohol to make the ride more bearable. Bring a bottle of water along, just in case. Be prepared for smoke-filled corridors, unaesthetic bathrooms, breathtaking views of the Bulgarian countryside, and friendly fellow travellers. Some useful words are: влак *(vlak,* "train"); автобус *(avtobus,* "bus"); гара *(gara,* "station"); перон *(peron,* "platform"); коловоз *(kolovoz,* "track"); билет *(bilet,* "ticket"); заминаваши *(zaminavashti,* "departure"); пристигаши *(pristigashti,* "arrival"); пушачи *(pushachi,* "smoking"); непушачи *(nepushachi,* "non-smoking"); and спален вагон *(spalen vagon,* "sleeping car").

Rising train ticket prices have made travel by **bus** an attractive option. Their prices often beat the trains and you can save up to three hours on travel time from the capital to the Black Sea coast. Tourist offices such as **Balkantourist** have comfortable express buses which are an excellent option for long distances. An even better option are private bus companies such as **Group Travel, Ltd.** These companies offer big, modern buses equipped with air conditioning, bathrooms, and VCRs. You can buy your seat ahead of time from the agency office (the recommended procedure) or pay as you board. Buses stop in many towns en route and you can get snacks at each stop. You can eat on the buses, but there are no trash bins. Take your litter with you. Some buses have set departure times, while others, especially on busy routes, leave whenever they are full. Private companies also have great package deals on international travel. Representatives usually speak some English. The main drawback to bus travel is, once again, the smoke. Windows are often sealed shut and you'll get off the bus smelling like a tobacco factory.

The once-cheap **Balkan Air** shuttle fares have swollen enormously over the past year (Sofia to Varna or Burgas: US$65 one-way). There are no youth discounts on Balkan Air within Bulgaria. Unless you are in a big hurry to get to the coast, take the bus or train.

Renting a car is a great way to see many of the off-the-beaten-track places in Bulgaria. Like air travel, however, this option may be prohibitively expensive. Major car rental companies such as Hertz and EuroDollar are represented in the big hotels but you'll pay as much as US$80 per day for a Russian Lada or Moskvich. To drive in Bulgaria you will need your driver's licence and an International Driving Permit. Be prepared for tremendously high speeds and questionable maneuvers. Read the information about driving regulations and road markings first. Driving in Bulgaria can be a very rewarding experience and you probably won't die.

Taxis are usually a good deal in cities and larger towns. Eschew the private taxis (private cars which have been turned into taxis for the day or week) in favor of the cab companies. Taxi drivers, in theory, meter their fares. In practice the fare structure depends on the company, the honesty of the driver, and the age of the meter. Many drivers will try not to meter their fares to the major hotels, the train stations, and especially the airports. Always refuse to pay in dollars and insist that you want the ride metered *("sus apparata")*. The exception is at Sofia airport. Taxi drivers will wait for you at the door, asking for US$20 to take you to the center. Do not pay more than US$10. In Sofia fares are about 5-6Lv per kilometer with a 10% increase after 10pm. You can request a taxi by phone in Sofia by calling 142 or 68 01 01.

Hitchhiking, once popular and reliable in Bulgaria, is now a growing risk with worsening economic conditions, particularly for Westerners who are targets for theft. *Let's Go* does not recommend hitchhiking as a safe means of transportation. There have also been reports about attacks on drivers from hitchhikers recently. Consequently, male hitchhikers will have little luck finding a ride. Transportation is so cheap that having to wait and possibly getting stuck under the scorching Balkan sun makes hitchhiking simply not worth it.

TOURIST SERVICES

Balkantourist, the former national tourist bureau, maintains offices throughout the country, although many of these have been privatized and turned into mom-and-pop type travel agencies which offer the same services as their state-owned predecessors. The staff changes money, and books hotel rooms and private accommodations. Hotels throughout the country often maintain tourist offices which can be of great help. They usually speak English.

Businesses open around 8-9am. Banking hours are usually 8:30am-4pm, but some banks close around 2pm. Tourist bureaus, post offices, and shops remain open until 6 or 8pm; in more touristy areas and bigger cities shops may close as late as 10pm, but they're often shut on Sundays. In government offices and state agencies, expect an hour lunch break around 1pm. Private shops, restaurants, cafés, and bars have extended hours and are usually open on weekends. "Non-stop" signs in English indicate that the place is open 24 hrs. National holidays are: January 1-2 (New Year's

Day), March 3 (Liberation from the Ottoman Yoke), a few days around Orthodox Easter, May 24 (Saints Cyril and Methodius's Day), and 3-4 days around Christmas.

MONEY

One **lev** (Lv; plural: leva), the standard monetary unit, is divided into 100 stotinki (st). We list most prices in U.S. dollars (US$). Inflation has made stotinki obsolete, except for the old 50st. coin *(not* the new) which is worth its weight in gold since it is the only coin that can be used in public telephones. Hoard them. New leva bills are now being introduced. Take a look at the old ones while you can—they still have the hammer and sickle. The official rate of US$1 to approximately 55Lv closely coincides with the rates offered by private banks and numerous private exchange bureaus. The advantage of the latter is that they tend to have extended hours (24-hr. ones have a "Change Non-Stop" sign in English) but they may not be able to buy all currencies (especially NZ$). The private exchange bureaus often take most major credit cards and **American Express** traveler's checks. Hotels have less favorable rates and people who approach you on the street to change money usually do not have the best intentions. Do not be tempted by the high rates they offer; they will often hand you a wad of blank paper surrounded by a 100Lv note. Because of money reform in the early 1970s, any Bulgarian bill dated before 1974 is worthless—check carefully. Change bureaus will be checking just as carefully; counterfeiting is rampant in Bulgaria. Any well-worn or ripped Western currencies will not be accepted.

You can cash American Express Traveler's Cheques in dollars or leva at major banks such as the **First Private Bank** which has branches throughout the country, or at the **Bulgaria Foreign Trade Bank** on **Ploshtad Sveta Nedelya** (**St. Nedelya's Square**, площад Света Неделя) opposite the Sheraton in Sofia (commission: US$10 for every US$1000 regardless of the number of checks). There are American Express Travel Service offices in Sofia at 1 Lesvki Street a across from the former Georgi Dimitrov Mausoleum and in Varna at 33 Slivnitza Blvd. Both offices will hold mail. The former American Express office at 1 Vitosha Blvd. reports that it still has old client mail—pick it up, already. Credit cards are still not widely accepted except in the larger hotels and more expensive resorts. Do not be misled by credit card advertisements in store windows; many of these are attempts by shopkeepers who have never seen a credit card to make their stores look more "Western." In most hotels both U.S. dollars and leva are accepted. In all other transactions use leva.

COMMUNICATION

Making international **telephone** calls from Bulgaria requires tremendous patience. To reach the new **AT&T USADirect operator,** dial 00 18 00 00 10. To call collect dial 0123 for an international operator or have the telephone office or hotel receptionist order the call for you. You can usually make international calls at any post office. All lines go through Sofia, though, so getting a call through often takes a while. Calls to the U.S. average about US$1.50 per minute, but you can expect to pay as much as US$4 per minute from hotel phones. **Betkom** direct dial telephones with digital display screens are found at most major hotels and resort areas. They service only Europe and the Middle East and require a special calling card sold from a kiosk near the phone. In an emergency (such as visa complications or urgent phone calls) go to the consular section of your embassy.

Faxes are now widely used in Bulgaria. You can send a fax from almost every post office for the price of a phone call. You may also be able to receive faxes at the post office. Check when you get into a new town. Many hotels now have business centers which will let you use their faxes, typewriters, and telephones for a steep fee. **E-mail** can be sent from the business center at the Sheraton in Sofia on Pl. Sveta Nedelya for about US$5 per minute. Some universities also have access to the Internet.

Photocopies can usually be made at the post office for about 4Lv per page. Many private companies offer photocopy services. Look for the phrase Копирни услуги *(kopirni uslugi)* or Ксерокс *(Xerox).* Across from the Sheraton in Sofia there is a

Rank Xerox Copy Center which offers color copies and professional binding services. **Postage** (including packages) is very cheap: 6-15Lv depending on the destination. **DHL** and **Federal Express** services are now available in larger cities.

Foreign language newspapers can be found in many of the large hotels. You can get the *International Herald Tribune* and *USA Today* at the Sheraton and at the **Central Department Store** (TSUM) in Sofia. Odds are that you will not be able to find any Russian newspapers. Bulgarian **television** picks up the international francophone channel and a Russian channel. CNN can be seen in the lobbies of many major hotels. The **BBC** and **VOA Europe** can be heard throughout the day on Bulgarian radio. The Bulgarian newspaper Стандарт (*Standart*) has a summary of the daily news in English on the last page.

LANGUAGE

Bulgarian is a South-slavic language of the Indo-European language family. Quite a few words in Bulgarian are borrowed from Turkish and Greek, but by and large, Bulgarian is most similar to Russian. The Bulgarian alphabet and phonetic pronunciations is as follows:

Аа - a	Жж - zh	Мм - m	Тт - t	Шш - sh
Бб - b	Зз - z	Нн - n	Уу - u	Щщ - sht
Вв - v	Ии - i	Оо - o	Фф - f	Ъъ - u
Гг - g	Йй - ii	Пп - p	Хх - h	Юю - yu
Дд - d	Кк - k	Рр - r	Цц - ts	Яя - ya
Ее - e	Лл - l	Сс - s	Чч - ch	

The Bulgarian transliteration is much the same as the Russian except that x is *h*, ш is *sht*, and ъ is sometimes transliterated as *â* (pronounced as in English b*u*g). Key phrases include колко (KOL-ko, "how much"), поща (PO-shta, "post office"), частна квартира (CHAHST-na kvar-TEE-ra, "private room"), говорите-ли английски? (Go-VO-rite-li ang-LIY-ski?, "Do you speak English?), тоалетна (toaletna, "toilet," "Ж" for women, "М" for men), Отворено/затворено (otvoreno/zatvoreno, "open/closed"), and the all-purpose Добре (dobreh; "good" or "OK," used in almost every sentence).

Yes	Да	dah
No	Не	neh
Hello	Добър ден	DOH-bur den
Good morning	Добро утро	doh-Braw OO-troh
Good night	Добър вечер	doh-BER VEH-cher
Goodbye	Довиждане	doh-VEEZH-dan-eh
Excuse me	Извинете	izvenete
Please	Моля	MOE-lya
Thank you	Благодаря	blahg-oh-dahr-YAH
When?	Кога	ko-GA
Where?	Къде	kuh-DEH
Help!	Помощ!	Pomosht
How much does it cost?	Колко струва?	KOHL-ko STROO-va
How do I get to...?	Къде се намира..?	kuh-DEH seh nah-MEE-rah...?
My name is ...	Аз се казвам..	ahz seh KAHZ-vahm...
I don't understand	Аз не разбирам	az ne raz-BI-ram
Leave me alone; get lost!	Престани!	preh-STAH-nee!

1—едно (ed-noh); 2—две (dvey); 3—три (tree); 4—четири (cheh-teh-rey); 5—пет (pet); 6—шест (shest); 7—седем (seh-dehm); 8—осем (oh-sehm); 9—девет (deh-veht); **10**—десет (deh-seht); **20**—двадесет (dvah-deh-seht); **30**—тридесет (tree-deh-seht); **40**—четиридесет (cheh-ti h-rey-deh-seht); **50**—петдесет (peht-deh-seht); **60**—шестдесет (shest-deh-seht); **70**—седемдесет (seh-dehm-deh-seht); **80**—осемдесет (oh-sehm-deh-seht); **90**—деветдесет (deh-veht-deh-seht); **100**—сто (stoh); **1000**—хиляда (heel-yah-dah).

Russian is widely understood, but it is best to ask permission before using it. Many Bulgarians are learning English and it is widely spoken in travel agencies and tourist areas. In the countryside, however, you'll be on your own. Take some time on the plane or train ride over to learn the alphabet. There are hundreds of cognates with English and the Bulgarians will be impressed that you are trying to speak their language. Bulgarian-English phrasebooks are sold at book-stands and bookstores for about 30Lv. If you need an English speaker in one of the major towns during the school year (Sept. 15-June 30), ask for help at the language school (езикова гимназия; *yezikova gimnaziya),* or at any of the universities. Many older Bulgarians speak French, and German is popular in the resort towns along the Black Sea. Since Bulgarian head movements for "yes" and "no" are the reverse of the West's, try to confirm everything with *da* (yes) or *ne* (no). Also be aware that many street names will be changed as the country decommunizes, but many old signs have not yet been replaced. Use both the old and new street names, and, once there, try to find the most recent map that you can. In smaller towns, new maps may not yet be available and residents may have no idea what the new name of a street or square is; confusion often abounds.

HEALTH AND SAFETY

Don't find out about the state of public **bathrooms** the hard way; some of which consist of nothing more than a hole in the ground, so pack a small bar of soap and some toilet paper. Public bathrooms often require a 1 or 2Lv note as a toilet paper charge. Have small bills ready.

Look for **pharmacies** under the sign аптека *(apteka).* Small towns usually have two or three. They often have late hours and are sometimes non-stop. Pharmacists should be able to recommend medications and direct you to a doctor, hospital or clinic. Basic medicines in Bulgaria have unfamiliar names; all cost under 100Lv. *Analgin* is aspirin and *analgin chinin* is cold and flu medicine. Band-aids are *sitoplast;* cotton wool is *pamuk.* More and more Western medications are popping up in Bulgarian pharmacies, but renew prescriptions before arrival. Condoms *("priservatif")* can be bought in pharmacies: 3Lv for Bulgarian and 8Lv for imported brands. Bulgaria's Black Sea coast is a thriving pick-up scene. Safe sex isn't universal, and one should be especially careful to minimize the risk of contracting AIDS or other sexually transmitted diseases. Women should bring a sufficient supply of tampons and sanitary pads. While a selection of toiletries and cosmetics are now available, they will be unfamiliar brands. Contact lens wearers should bring all necessary supplies.

The climate in Bulgaria is mild: the average winter day is around 0°C (32°F) while summer days max out at around 30°C (86°F) with low humidity. Winters are cold and long in the mountains, and while there are days of extreme Balkan heat, the summers are very pleasant. Spring is usually very rainy, but the past few years have witnessed a drought. After 40 years of Communist misuse and neglect, Sofia and other large cities in Bulgaria are polluted. Central heating in buildings is fired by sulphurous brown coal. Sofia itself is situated in a valley and on still days the smog hovers above the city. Usually, though, the air is brisk and fresh in Bulgaria. If the conditions of the cities get you down, spend a day hiking in any of the mountain ranges, which have been left mostly untouched through the ages.

While Sofia is still safer than most Western capitals, there is a sense of lawlessness that can be experienced only in other former Soviet bloc countries, or perhaps Dodge City of the Old West. The locals generally don't trust the police and when there are laws, there is no one to enforce them. The end of central government control and intervention has put goods on the shelves, but left consumers vulnerable to scams and defective products. Do not buy bottles of alcohol from street vendors—there have been cases of poisoning and contamination. Anything you buy on the street is likely to be counterfeit and/or contraband. Remember, if the price is too good to be true even by Bulgarian standards, you're probably being swindled. Sofia streets can be deadly. Pedestrians, it seems, do not have the right of way. Driving is erratic and speeds are high. The sidewalks aren't completely safe either—they're where the Bulgarians park.

Safety concerns are of special importance in a country where hard currency is desired above all. Avoid speculators. If you take a taxi, choose your driver carefully. Similarly, avoid walking alone after dark, even if you're sure of where you're going. There is a general lack of tolerance towards homosexuals in the country, though the chances of being attacked are minimal. Discretion will make life easier.

ACCOMMODATIONS AND CAMPING

When you cross the border you will be given a yellow **statistical card** to document where you stay each night. The establishments in which you stay will add stamps to the card, which is collected when you leave the country. If you lose it, you may have difficulty getting a hotel room. Years ago, tourists were fined if they didn't have a stamp for each night they had spent in Bulgaria; now, border officials tend to be much less strict, so any card with at least a couple of stamps on it may suffice. If you are staying with friends your entire visit, you'll have to register with the **Bulgarian Registration Office.** See the consular section of your embassy for details.

Private rooms are arranged through Balkantourist or other tourist offices for US$8-13 a night, and can be an excellent opportunity to get to know a Bulgarian family. Be sure to ask for a central location and try to find out if any family members speak English. Bulgarian **hotels** are classed by stars; rooms in one-star hotels are almost identical to those in two- and three-star hotels but have no private bathrooms; they average about US$8 for singles and US$17 for doubles. Foreigners are always charged higher prices than Bulgarians, payable in hard currency or leva. While some discounts were available through Balkantourist as of June 1994, Bulgaria no longer offers any ISIC discounts in hotels. The majority of Bulgarian **youth hostels** are located in the countryside and are popular with student groups; in Sofia try to make reservations through **ORBITA,** 48 Hristo Botev (Христо Ботев; tel. 80 01 02, fax 88 58 14) or **Pirin Tours,** bul. Stamboliiski 30 (бул. Стамболийски) (tel. 87 06 87). Many youth hostels give HI discounts and almost all provide bedding. ORBITA and Pirin Tours may also be able to arrange university housing. You can deal with both agencies in English. Outside major towns, **campgrounds** give you a chance to meet Eastern European backpackers (US$3-5 per person). Spartan wooden bungalows await at nearly every site but are often full, and many have closed as their land is being given back to its original owners as part of the restitution program currently under way in the country. Freelance camping is popular, but you risk a fine (and your safety). Camping in reserve areas is strictly prohibited; watch for the signs.

LIFE AND TIMES

HISTORY

The ancient **Thracian tribes** occupied Bulgaria from at least 3500 BC. Skilled warriors and artisans, the Thracians left behind over 1000 ruins in Bulgaria as well as vast collections of gold and silver artifacts. Influenced and colonized by the **Greeks** from the 8th century BC, southern and eastern Thrace served as crossroads and battlegrounds for Greek-Persian trade and warfare until the **Macedonian conquest** of 343-342 BC. Lysimachus of Thrace, a general of Alexander the Great, ruled what is now Bulgaria from 323-281 BC. His death ushered in two centuries of chaos seasoned with Celtic invasions. By 46 AD Thrace had fallen to the **Romans;** the area between the Danube and the Balkan range became the province of Moesia, and what is now southern Bulgaria was called Thracia. Remains of Roman villas have been dug up near the village of Madara near Shoumen. Moesia and Thrace were among the biggest and richest of Roman provinces. They lay on the route to the Orient and exported cereal, timber, crafts, ore, slaves, and gladiators (Spartacus was a Thracian by origin). As the Roman Empire began to crumble in the 3rd century, Visigoths and the occasional Ostrogoth began to threaten the Danube and Black Sea borders. The dam broke in the 370s, and Visigoths, Huns, and bad Samaritans swept in, followed by **Slav tribes** moving southward from the banks of the Pripet (today's Belarus and Ukraine). As the Goths moved out, the Slavs moved in, settling what is now Bulgaria and dodging Byzantine armies for three centuries.

Meanwhile, the Huns had retreated to the steppes of what is now eastern Ukraine. There, near the Lower Don Valley, they mixed with the locals and established the original **Bulgar** state. The state reached its height in the 7th century, when the Bulgars settled the upper Volga and lower Danube valleys before being destroyed by the Khazars in the 8th century. The Danube valley settlement would prove to be the genesis of modern Bulgaria. Acting in alliance with the resident Slavs, the **proto-Bulgarian tribes** of the Danube set up a fortified camp and began raiding the Byzantine Empire to the south. The **Byzantines**, who had held Bulgaria south of the Danube since driving out the Visigoths in the 5th century, were not pleased with this new development. A retaliatory campaign by the Emperor Constans IV Pagonatus surprised the Proto-Bulgarian camp by attacking from land and sea. The Emperor, however, left suddenly for Constantinople under the pretext of needing curative baths. His departure caused confusion and Byzantine withdrawal. The proto-Bulgarians attacked the departing Byzantines and continued their raids south. Threatened by Arab attacks from the east, the Byzantines surrendered in 681, and a new Slav-Bulgar state was born, the first Slavic nation. Though the majority of the population were Slavs, the aristocracy were Bulgars and the state called itself **Bulgaria;** at its head was the Khan Asparoukh. The members of the ruling aristocracy, the tribal *Knyazes* (princes), participated in central government meetings called *boils.*

The 8th and 9th centuries saw the growth and consolidation of the Bulgarian state. Brothers Cyril and Methodius created the first Bulgarian alphabet, called *glagolitsa*, in the 8th century; their disciple Kliment Ohridski was the author of the modern-day **Cyrillic** alphabet. The Slavs and Bulgarians followed two different pagan religions until Tsar Boris I (852-889) tired of Bulgarians being considered barbarians by the neighboring empires and accepted **Orthodox Christianity** in 865. The Bulgarian Church was then set up under Tsar **Simeon the Great** (893-927). The adoption of a common religion brought the seven founding tribes closer together; while an independent church helped to ward off the ambitions of the Constantinople Patriarchate and the *Curia Romana.*

Under Simeon, the **First Greater Bulgarian Empire** reached the zenith of its power and military might. His ambition was to unite all the Southern Slavs under Bulgarian rule, overthrow the Byzantines in the Balkans, and finally capture Constantinople. Supported by his knights, Simeon took on all of Bulgaria's neighbors: Byzantines, Magyars, Serbs, and Croats. His forces penetrated as far south as the isthmus of Corinth. To progress further, Simeon and his boyars needed a fleet from the Arabs in North Africa. But the envoys to the African khalif were captured and the Serbs suddenly turned coat, foiling Simeon's ambitious plans. The Serbs were promptly defeated and made into a Bulgarian province but Simeon died in 927, still dreaming of his invasion of Constantinople.

Simeon was succeeded by his incompetent brother Peter, under whose leadership the country declined. Eastern Bulgaria was captured by the Byzantine Emperor John I Tzimisces during the Russian Wars of 969-976 (the Bulgarians were allied with the Varangians of Russia who were actually Swedish Vikings. Seriously). Tzimices successor, Basil II "Bulgar-Slayer," took western Bulgaria (modern Serbia and

Macedonia) in 1014. To ensure Bulgar submission, Basil blinded his 14,000 prisoners, leaving one man out of every hundred with one eye to guide the others home.

Bulgaria became a Byzantine province in 1018, but after over 100 years of effective Byzantine rule, the **Second Greater Bulgarian Empire** (1187-1242) arose under Ivan and Peter Asen, who aided the Third Crusade in exchange for papal blessing. Taking advantage of the Fourth Crusade's sack of Constantinople in 1204, Bulgaria expanded its borders from the Black Sea to the Aegean and the Adriatic Seas, with its capital at **Veliko Turnovo**. Towns and roads, fortresses and royal palaces, and churches and monasteries were erected. Each feudal lord was anxious to ensure his physical and eternal security by building fortress and churches. On Tsarevets Hill in Veliko Turnovo stood the Royal Palace, and above it the Patriarchate building. Among the lavishly decorated churches then built were the monasteries of Rila and Bachkovo and the fabulous churches in Nesebur.

Unable to subdue either the Byzantine Empire in Asia Minor or the Latin Empire in Greece, Bulgaria fell prey to **Mongol** hordes in 1242. After losses to the expanding Serbian and Hungarian Kingdoms, the fragmented Bulgarians were not prepared to face a new threat from the east. The **Ottoman Turks** moved across the Dardanelles into the Balkan Peninsula in 1352, destroying the Bulgarian capital in 1393. In 1396 the last Bulgarian stronghold in **Vidin** fell, leaving Bulgaria as a nation of oppressed peasants for the next five centuries. Over time, the **haidouk** resistance movement emerged to take vengeance on the Turks for violated honor and plundered property. They operated in detachments under the command of *voevodes*, some of whom were women. Many folk songs glorify their exploits and fearlessness in the face of death. As churches were turned into mosques, monasteries became repositories of Bulgarian culture. Many of Bulgaria's 150 monasteries had been destroyed during the conquest but were rebuilt during the 15th and 16th centuries. Liturgical books were transcribed in Bulgarian; the Bulgarian language and literature endured. A national liberation ideology was born in 1762 with the publishing of the **Slav-Bulgarian History** by Paissi of Hilendar, from Bansko. Meanwhile, Bulgarian towns grew during the 18th century and an urban bourgeoisie developed trade.

At the beginning of the 19th century, many Bulgarians took part in the liberation struggle which first broke out in Serbia, and then in Greece in the 1820s. Cultural development continued apace; the **Bulgarian National Revival** had the character of the West European Renaissance, laying the groundwork for capitalism, rationalism, etc. The 1800s saw the flourishing of Bulgarian national crafts: painting and woodworking. The Schools of Painting, of Bansko, of Tryavna and others left behind fabulous iconostases in churches and monasteries. Wood carving was a major factor in the decoration of wealthy houses; many are preserved in museum towns such as Koprivshtitsa. The first secular school was opened in **Gabrovo** in 1835. Despite this flowering of culture, Bulgarians main goal remained liberation from foreign occupation. In 1839, the Sultan issued the **Hatisherif** decree providing for land reform and religious tolerance—but no legislation to guarantee private land ownership. As the Bulgarian countryside languished under the feudal system, peasant uprisings washed over the country. These were violently suppressed by the Turks, resulting in tens of thousands of deaths.

Georgi Rakovski, Bulgaria's first revolutionary, was born in Kotel in 1821. Rakovski drew up the first program for national revolution and set up the first **Bulgarian Legion** of trained youth in Belgrade in 1861. **Vasil Levski,** born in Karlovo in 1837, organized revolutionary committees, believing that any revolution must be independent rather than dependent on outside help. **Hristo Botev** was another revolutionary strategist, born in Kalofer in 1847, as well as a journalist and a poet. The masses were ready for revolution but lacked arms, organization, and a common ideology. Levski was hung by the Ottoman authorities in 1873, but his legacy, the **Internal Revolutionary Organization,** continued to prepare for an armed uprising. Encouraged by a recent revolt in Bosnia-Hercegovina, the **April Uprising** triggered revolts across Bulgaria in 1875-76, each viciously snuffed by the Turks.

Bulgarians then pinned their hopes of liberation on **Russia.** In fall 1878, after Turkey had defeated Serbian and Montenegran forces, Russia intervened to preserve it's Slavic allies in the Balkans. Tsar Alexander II sent an ultimatum to the Sultan demanding a halt to hostilities against Serbia and Montenegro, followed by a declaration of war on April 24, 1877. Romania joined the Russians in the hope of securing their own independence. The decisive battle was fought at the **Shipka Pass,** defended by a mixed Russo-Bulgarian force which included the Bulgarian volunteer corps. The Slavic force numbered 7000 men, who managed to defeat Suleiman Pasha's 30,000-strong army. The Western detachment of the Russo-Bulgarian force then advanced south toward **Pleven,** where the army of Osman Pasha had fortified itself. The Russians, now reinforced by Romanian troops, made three attempts to capture Pleven as more Ottoman forces approached from the south and the east. It finally fell on December 10, 1877. A truce was signed on January 31, 1878, granting Bulgaria a huge portion of the Balkans. In the **Treaty of San-Stefano,** Northern Dobroudja was ceded to Romania in compensation for Southern Bessarabia (Moldova) which was returned to Russia. In an effort to preserve a Turkish bulwark against Russian expansion, the western powers declared at the **Berlin Congress** of 1878 that southern Bulgaria would remain within the sphere of the Ottoman Empire.

The **First Balkan War** broke out in 1912 as every power in the Balkans fought over Macedonia, which was still occupied by Turkey. Turkey was quickly defeated, but no one could agree on how to divide the spoils. Bulgarian troops turned on their Serbain and Greek allies, causing the **Second Balkan War.** The Bulgarians were soon defeated, losing Dobroudja to the Romanians in the process. Frustrated by these losses, The Bulgarian government, led by German-born king Alexander of Battenberg, sided with the Central Powers (Germany, Austria-Hungary, and Turkey) against Serbia and Russia during **World War I,** a course supported neither by the people nor the military. Troops mutinied, leading to an early armistice and further losses of Bulgarian territory

Bulgarian claims on Macedonia led the country to side with Germany again during **World War II.** After ceding Dobroudja to Romania yet again and joining the 1941 Nazi invasion of Yugoslavia, Bulgaria for a long time resisted German pressure to declare war on the USSR, citing pan-Slavic affection. Bulgaria also protected its Jewish population. An underground anti-German movement emerged in 1942, as Agrarian and Social Democrats, leftist intellectuals, military reserve officers called *Zveno* (Link), and the underground Communist Party joined in the the **Fatherland Front.** In August 1944, the Soviet army advanced across Bulgaria and, for a brief time, the country was at war with both Allied and Axis powers. Bulgaria quickly declared neutrality, disarmed the resident German troops, then fought alongside the Soviet army until war's end. On September 9, 1944, Fatherland Front partisans took Sofia. Bulgaria was declared a republic two years later. The country retained Dobroudja this time but later ceded territory to Yugoslavia and Greece.

The late 1940s saw the collectivization of agriculture and the beginnings of industrialization. Under Communist leader **Georgi Dimitrov,** good economic and political relations with the Soviet Union allowed Bulgaria to specialize in light manufacturing and serve as the **breadbasket** of the Eastern bloc.

Todor Zhivkov became Bulgaria's leader in 1954 and endured until 1989, making him the longest-lasting Communist leader in Eastern Europe. Stability, restraint and fanatical alignment with the Soviet Union were the traits of his leadership; at one point he proposed that the Soviet Union annex Bulgaria to make it the sixteenth Soviet republic. Under Zhivkov, Bulgaria's international image was epitomized by a security service that used poisoned umbrella tips to assassinate its dissidents, by rumored ties to the attempted assassination of the Pope, and by world-champion female bodybuilders.

BULGARIA

BULGARIA TODAY

On November 10, 1989, the Bulgarian Communist Party retired Todor Zhivkov, by then an unpopular and much-ridiculed leader, and held elections after changing its name to the **Socialist Party** (BSP). Despite the initial victories of the Socialist Party, Bulgaria succeeded in establishing a non-Communist government in November, 1991. The country's first open presidential elections, held in January 1992, re-elected philosopher **Zhelu Zhelev** as president and poet **Blaga Dimitrova** as vice-president. The following year, however, Dimitrova resigned in protest of economic and social policies supported by the government. In the most recent elections, the Turks, who make up approximately 10% of the Bulgarian population, have exercised a disproportionate influence on the country's politics through their party, the Movement for Rights and Freedoms. Meanwhile, Bulgaria's other major ethnic group, the Gypsies, remain politically unconsolidated and on the fringes of mainstream society.

Personal freedoms in Bulgaria have bounded ahead, yet many Bulgarians are starting to feel the stranglehold of financial limitations and skyrocketing inflation, brought about by the difficult economic transition to a market economy. Economic transition has also resulted in the creation of social classes in a formerly classless society. As in the rest of Eastern Europe, crime is on the rise and travelers are increasingly at risk. For tourists, some of the onerous regulations, such as visa requirements, have been relaxed, while others, such as the statistical card issued at the border, remain.

FOOD AND DRINK

Food from kiosks is cheap (35-50Lv for a sandwich or burger and a Coke), and restaurants average 100Lv per meal. Kiosks sell *kebabcheta* (small hamburgers, 10Lv), salami sandwiches (7Lv), pizzas (12Lv), and *banitsa* (cheese-filled breads, 5Lv). Fruits and vegetables are usually sold in vegetable shops (зеленчуков магазин, *zelenchukov magazin)*, in markets (пазар, *pazar)* or directly on the streets from stalls. 24-hr. mini-markets sell cheese, bread, milk, and snack foods. In the summer Bulgaria is blessed with delicious fruits and vegetables. Try *shopska salata,* an addictive salad of tomatoes, peppers, and cucumbers covered with feta cheese. *Kiopolou* and *imam bayaldu* are eggplant dishes. A *gjuvetch* is a mixed vegetable stew with onion, eggplant, peppers, beans, potatoes, parsley, and peas. Also try *tarator*—a cold soup made with yogurt, cucumber, and garlic. There is a heavy emphasis on meat in the Bulgarian menu. Try *kuverma*—a meat dish with cheese melted over the top, or the Bulgarian version of the Greek *moussaka.* For the more adventurous there is *shkembe chorba*—a tripe soup which is said to cure hangovers. There are also lots of organ-based dishes like *mozik* (brain) or *ezik* (tongue). The Bulgarians are known for their cheese and yogurt. Try *sirene*—a feta cheese, and *kashkaval*—a hard yellow cheese. You can get desserts like baklava and *sladoled* (ice cream) in sweetshops called Sladkarnitsi (сладкарнии).

Bulgarian coffee is served Turkish style and cappuccino is widely available. Well-stirred *airan,* Bulgarian yogurt with a little water and a few ice cubes, can bring you back to life on a hot summer day. Another popular summer drink is *ais-nektar* (a thick fruit juice with a scoop of ice cream). *Boza* is a milky-brown wheat drink sold in glass bottles—it's taste is, well, interesting. The water is probably purer than the stuff you're used to drinking back home. Bulgaria exports mineral water and the locals swear by its healing qualities. The fountains and taps scattered throughout the cities and countryside will save your life on more than one day under the Balkan sun. Bring a water bottle and a hearty spirit.

Delicious red and white wines are produced in various regions of the country. Even the most expensive bottles are less than US$1. If you find yourself in a village restaurant, ask for some of the homemade stuff—you'll never want to go home. Bulgarians begin their meals with salads and *rakiya*—a grape brandy. Be careful; it has quite a kick. The traditional toast is *"Na Zdrave"* (to your health). Beer, both domestic and imported, is also widely available. Cans are more expensive than bottles, but both are usually under US$1.50. Good Bulgarian labels are *Astika* and *Zagorka*.

Tipping is not obligatory, but 10% doesn't hurt. The word for bill is сметката (smit-KAH-tah). Remember—in Bulgarian restaurants and *mehani* (taverns) there is usually a small charge to use the restrooms. Many restaurants are now serving Bulgarian specialties; try 'em all, but eat carefully. Don't drink the unpasteurized milk unless it's been very well heated. Eschew sour yogurt and resist rare hamburgers. *Priaten appetit!*

CUSTOMS AND ETIQUETTE

Bulgarians shake their heads to indicate "yes" and "no" in the opposite directions from Westerners. It is easier to just hold your head still while saying yes (да, *da*) or no (не, *neh*). Only bring odd numbers of flowers when visiting Bulgarian families. It is customary to share tables in restaurants and taverns. In churches, it is respectful to buy a candle or two from the souvenir stand out front. Light the candle and place it near the others already in the church. Candles placed high are in remembrance of the living, while those placed low are in remembrance of the dead. The photo-copied pictures of people you may see tacked on trees, doors, and basically everywhere else are not "wanted" or "missing" signs but death notices.

ENTERTAINMENT

During the Communist era, the performing arts were heavily subsidized and everyone could afford a night out to see a play or opera. Today, the subsidies are gone and the best performers and groups spend much of their time abroad. Still, most cities in Bulgaria have their own symphony, ballet, theater, and opera. Prices are cheap (the most expensive ticket is 50Lv) and the standards are quite high, especially in the capital. Jazz and blues clubs are now popping up in the major cities. Country music is gaining popularity. To try out Bulgarian folk music before you arrive, you can buy *"Le Mystère des Voix Bulgares"* in the international music section of any record store back home. For the most part circuses and zoos have fallen into disrepair. There are many movie theaters (кино or kino) in Bulgaria. American films are usually shown. They have the original English dialogue and Bulgarian subtitles. Tickets for films can be purchased ahead of time and seats are usually reserved. Prices range from 15-30Lv.

Best buys when shopping are **Bulgarian handicrafts,** including embroidered blouses and tablecloths, rose oil sold in small wooden cannisters, artwork, metal work, crafted jewelry, ceramics, antiques and rugs. In winter you can often find babushkas selling hand-made wool sweaters for a few dollars. There's also a lot of Soviet kitsch flowing over the border. Whatever you set out to buy, bring a plastic bag with you. Bags are still hard to come by in Bulgaria.

■ Sofia (СОФИЯ)

If Prague is the new Paris, then Sofia is the new Prague. Affordable and undiscovered, feeding on cool jazz and cheap, delicious wine, Sofia offers an unequaled night on the town for pennies. With the overthrow of the Communists, youth has come to dominate business and control the tempo of life in the city. Western visitors are few, but it's only a matter of time.

The center of town, with its grid of enormously wide *bulevards* paved with yellow bricks, may make you feel like you've arrived in the Land of Oz. Five thousand years ago the first settlers in Sofia were probably attracted to the warm mineral springs in its heart and environs that still exist today. Located at the crossroads between Europe and Asia, the city has changed hands countless times and has been known also as Serdika, Sredetz, and Triaditza. The city has survived Thracian, Roman, Byzantine, Ottoman, and most recently Communist conquerors. Today, Western influences abound and often seem out of place. Sofia is for the most part a new city—a carnival of beastly socialist structures where only a few medieval churches and two mosques survive—but its older architecture, often a cross between German Baroque and Russian Imperial styles, reflects Bulgaria's role as a bridge between Turkey and Western Europe.

True to its motto, "Ever growing, never aging," Sofia is expanding—continually pulling suburbs and small villages into its orbit. Outside the center, the Emerald City ends and Sofia rapidly turns into an aesthetic nightmare of run-down neighborhoods and shoddy new high-rises. Leave these behind for the serenity of the national park located on the massif of Vitosha. Even when the smog is unbearable, the air on the mountain will be crisp and refreshing.

ORIENTATION AND PRACTICAL INFORMATION

Sofia's 1.2 million inhabitants occupy the center of the Balkan peninsula, 500km southeast of Belgrade. International trains run to Belgrade, Thessaloniki, Athens, İstanbul, and Bucharest. **Ploshad Sveta Nedelya** (St. Nedelya Square, площад Света Неделя), once named for Lenin, is the center of Sofia. Most of the sights are within walking distance of the city center and easily found with the aid of a map. The central district is ringed by a road that changes names as it circles the city. Incoming roads intersect this ring; the most important starts life as bul. Vitosha (Витоша) and runs north through Pl. Sveta Nedelya, where it changes its name to bul. Knyaginya Maria Luiza (Княгиня Мария Луиза) and bends around to reach the train station at the northern end of the city. Perpendicular to bul. Knyaginya Maria Luiza, bul. Stamboliiski (Стамболийски) and bul. Dondukov (Дондуков) are two other major thoroughfares. Residents orient themselves by the **radio tower** on Mt. Vitosha. Maps are sold at tourist offices and at stalls on the street (30Lv). Useful English-language **Sofia city guides** (published every month) are available at major hotels for about US$1.

Tourist Offices: Balkantourist, bul. Stamboliiski 27 (tel. (02) 88 55 43, fax 83 30 58). From Pl. Sveta Nedelya, walk up Stamboliiski three blocks and it's on your left. English-speaking staff books accommodations in hotels and private houses, exchanges money, and sells out-of-date maps. No bus or train reservations. Open Mon.-Fri. 8:30am-5pm, Sat.-Sun. 9am-8pm. The office at bul. Vitosha 1 (tel. 97 51 92, fax 80 01 34) will give you cash advances from all credit cards except American Express. Offers hotel reservations, rental cars, and bus tickets. It is the former American Express office and is still collecting customer mail. Excellent English spoken. Open Mon.-Fri. 8am-8pm, Sat. 8:30am-1:30pm. **Pirin Tours (HI),** bul. Stamboliiski 30 (tel. 87 06 87, fax 65 00 52), across from Balkantourist, helps arrange transportation and accommodations and provides youth hostel information, homestays, and university housing. Open Mon.-Fri. 9am-5:30pm.

American Express is located at **Megatours,** 1 Levski St. (tel. 88 04 19, fax 87 25 67) across from Dimitrov's Mausoleum on Pl. Aleksander Batenberg (Александър Батенберг). Your home away from home, the office cashes traveler's cheques, distributes replacement cards, collects mail, and issues airplane tickets. Flawless English. Open Mon.-Fri. 9am-6:30pm, Sat. 9am-noon.

Budget Travel: ORBITA Travel, Hristo Botev 48 (tel. 80 01 02 or 87 91 28, fax 88 58 14). From Pl. Sveta Nedelya, walk up Stamboliiski, and make a left on Hristo Botev. Can make hotel reservations and will help you find university, hotel, and hostel accommodations. English spoken. Hotel discounts for students. Makes international and domestic train reservations. Open Mon.-Fri. 9am-5:30pm. **Branch office** in the ORBITA Hotel (tel. 65 74 47).

Embassies: U.S., ul. Suborna 1a (tel. 88 48 01, 88 48 02, 88 48 03, 88 48 04, or 88 48 05), three blocks from Pl. Sveta Nedelya behind the Sheraton Hotel. Consular section at ul. Kapitan Andreev 1 (tel. 65 94 59), behind the Economic Tehnikum, near Hotel Hemus. Americans are recommended to register with the consular section when they arrive in Bulgaria. Open Mon.-Fri. 9am-4:30pm for American citizens. The United States Information Service has an **American Center** at bul.

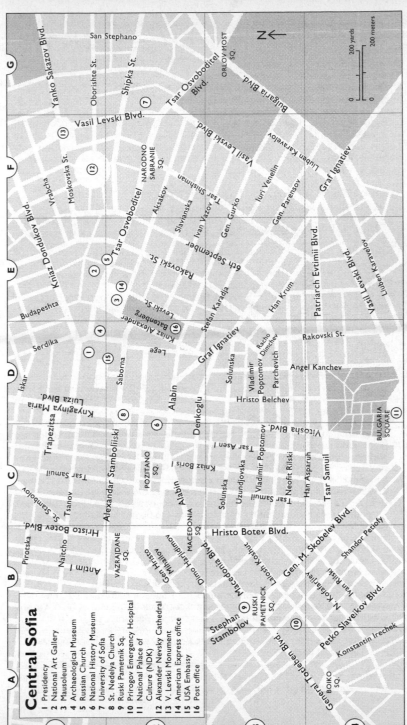

BULGARIA

Central Sofia

1 Presidency
2 National Art Gallery
3 Mausoleum
4 Archaeological Museum
5 Russian Church
6 National History Museum
7 University of Sofia
8 St. Nedelya Church
9 Ruski Pametnik Sq.
10 Prirogov Emergency Hospital
11 National Palace of
   Culture (NDK)
12 Alexander Nevsky Cathedral
13 V. Levski Monument
14 American Express office
15 USA Embassy
16 Post office

San Stephano

Yanko Sakazov Blvd.
Oborishte St.
Shipka St.
Tsar Osvoboditel Blvd.
ORLOV MOST SQ.
Bulgaria Blvd.

Vasil Levski Blvd.
Vrabcha
Moskovska St.
NARODNO SABRANIE SQ.
Tsar Osvoboditel Blvd.
Vasil Levski Blvd.
Liuben Karavelov
Graf Ignatiev

Kniaz Dondukov Blvd.
Aksakov
Tsar Shishman
Slavianska
Ivan Vazov
Gen. Gurko
Iuri Venelin
Gen. Parensov
Patriarch Evtimii Blvd.
Vasil Levski Blvd.
Lluben Karavelov

Budapeshta
Tsar Osvoboditel
Rakovski St.
6th September
Stefan Karadja
Han Krum
Rakovski St.

Iskar
Serdika
Knjaz Alexander Batenberg
Levski St.
Lege
Graf Ignatiev
Solunska
Vladimir Poptomov
Racho Dimchev
Parchevich
Angel Kanchev

Knyaginya Maria Luiza Blvd.
Saborna
Alabin
Denkoglu
Hristo Belchev

Trapezitsa
Alexandar Stamboliiski
POZITANO SQ.
Alabin
Kniaz Boris I
Uzundjovska
Vladimir Poptomov
Tsar Asen I
Vitosha Blvd.
BULGARIA SQUARE

Tsar Samuil
Tsanov
Hristo Botev Blvd.
MACEDONIA SQ.
Solunska
Tsar Samuil
Neofit Rilski
Han Asparuh
Tsar Samuil
Gen. M. Skobelev Blvd.
Shandor Petofy

Pirotska
Naitcho
Antim I
VAZRAJDANE SQ.
Gen Hristo
Dimo Hadjimov
RUSKI PAMETNICK SQ.
Laroth Kostur
N. Koflarievi
Ivan Rilski
Petko Slaveikov Blvd.
Konstantin Irechek

Stephan Stambolov
General Totleben Blvd.
BOIKO SQ.

Pirotska
St. Stambolov
Tsar Samuil
Hristo Botev Blvd.

N ←
200 yards
200 meters
0

Vitosha 18. Library and exhibits. Call the embassy for more information. Open Mon.-Fri. 10am-4pm. **U.K.,** bul. Vasil Levksi 65 *(not* Vasil Levski Street; tel. 88 53 61), three blocks northwest of the Palace of Culture. Open Mon.-Thurs. 8:30am-12:30pm and 1:30-5pm, Fri. 8:30am-1pm. Neither embassy holds mail. Citizens of **Canada, Australia,** and **New Zealand** should contact the British embassy. **Romania,** ul. Sitniakovo 4 (tel. 70 70 46). **Greece,** bul. Evlogi Georgiev 103 (tel. 44 37 65 or 46 42 80). **Turkey,** bul. Vasil Levski 80 (tel. 87 23 06), open Mon.-Fri. 9am-6pm).

Currency Exchange: At **Balkantourist** offices and all large hotels. Generally open daily 8am-10pm. They usually provide better rates than private exchange offices like **Lindor,** bul. Vitosha 31 (tel. 88 14 92), **Inter,** bul. Vasil Levski 72 (tel. 81 57 40), and **7M** (branches throughout Sofia). All take major credit cards and traveler's checks. Traveler's checks may be cashed at the **First Private Bank** at ul. Suborna 2a (tel. 46 51 28), open Mon.-Fri. 9am-12:30pm, and the **Bulgarian Foreign Trade Bank,** Pl. Sveta Nedelya 7 (tel. 84 91, fax 88 46 36 or 88 53 70), across from the Sheraton. Open Mon.-Fri. 8:30am-12:30pm and 2-4pm.

Post Office: ul. General Gurko 2, at the park east of Pl. Sveta Nedelya. **Poste Restante** generally open 7am-8:30pm. Many hotels also provide postal services. **DHL,** bul. Tsar Osvoboditel 8 (tel. 88 23 09 or 87 79 27, fax 793 33). Document to U.S.—US$35.

Telephones: Across from the post office. Expect long lines; open 7:30am-1am. To avoid the lines, call from the Sheraton Hotel's lobby phones, but expect to pay nearly four times as much. For local calls, use 50st coins. Local phone numbers have between four and seven digits. **City Code:** 02.

Faxes: Can be sent from the **telephone office** across from the post office between 8am-9:30pm. Faxes received at tel. 87 33 78 (office open Mon.-Fri. 7:30am-8pm, Sat. 8am-2pm). Faxes can also be sent at the **Sheraton Business Center.**

Photocopies: Services at the **post office** 3.5Lv per page. Open Mon.-Fri. 8am-noon and 12:30-4:30pm. Also try **Rank Xerox Copy Center** across from the Sheraton. 2Lv per page. Color copies, printing, binding services. Open Mon.-Fri. 8am-8pm, Sat 8am-6pm, Sun. 9am-5pm.

Film and Photo Developing: Agfa and **Kodak** centers are on nearly every major street. Try the **Fuji Film** place at bul. Vitosha 42. 6.5Lv per picture for 24 hr. developing, 7.5Lv per picture for 1 hr. service. Open Mon.-Fri. 8am-8pm, Sat. and Sun. 10am-3pm.

Flights: Airport Sofia (tel. 793 21). Call 72 06 72 or 79 80 35 for international departure information; 79 32 11 for international arrivals; 72 24 14 for domestic flight information. Municipal buses #84 and 284 run regularly. **Bulgarian Balkan Airlines** has an office at Pl. Narodno Subranie 12 (tel. 88 06 63). Round-trip fares to Varna or Burgas: US$130; Moscow: US$284; Warsaw: US$194; Prague: US$284; London: US$512; Athens: US$120; and İstanbul: $US142. Open Mon.-Fri. 7:30am-7:30pm, Sat. 8am-2pm. Also try the ticket office at the Palace of Culture (NDK) (tel. 65 95 57 or 65 95 17) or the branch at 19 Legue St. (tel. 88 41 92). Always ask for **youth fares** if you're under 26; the savings can be more than 50%.

Trains: Sofia's central train station is north of the center on bul. Knyaginya Maria Luiza. Trams #1, 7, and 15 travel to pl. Sveta Nedelya. The windows at the station sell domestic tickets only. For information, international tickets, and couchette reservations, visit the **Rila Travel office** at ul. General Gurko 5 (tel. 87 07 77), open Mon.-Fri.7am-7pm, Sat. 8am-1pm. One-way fares to Athens: US$63; Thessaloniski: US$31; Bucharest: US$15; Budapest: US$40; and İstanbul: US$32. No ISIC discounts. Also try the ticket office under the Palace of Culture (NDK; tel. 65 95 57 or 65 95 17); they also sell domestic tickets. Walk to the end of Blvd. Vitosha until you get to a huge building which looks like a spaceship.

There have been reports of travelers being drugged with sleep-inducing gas on the Sofia-Istanbul line.

Buses: The terminal at bul. Gen. H. Mihailov 23 (tel. 52 50 04) handles tickets for international routes. No ISIC discounts. **Group Travel,** a private bus company will take you practically anywhere you want to go in Bulgaria and Eastern Europe, from ul. Rakovski 85 (tel. 83 14 54, fax 83 24 26). From the Sheraton, walk up bul. Knjaz Dondukov and make a left on Rakovski. Round-trip fares to the Black Sea Coast: US$5; Budapest: US$23; Warsaw: US$36; and Prague: US$29. Children under 10 receive a 30% discount. Children under 6 ride free. All Group Travel buses and other private buses leave from the **Novotel Europa,** directly across from the central train station.

Public Transportation: The system of trams, trolley buses, and buses is gleefully cheap (3Lv per ticket, 10Lv for an all-day ticket). Buy tickets at kiosks or from the driver and punch 'em in the small machines between the bus windows. The operating hours are officially 4am-1am, but many routes stop before midnight. It may be tempting not to punch your ticket—but if you get caught you'll be fined 50Lv and thrown off the train or bus.

Hitchhiking: *Let's Go* does not recommend hitchhiking as a safe means of transportation. Hitching in the Sofia area is getting increasingly dangerous. Those hitching to Rila Monastery take tram #5 to highway E79. Those headed to Koprivshtitsa take tram #3 from Sofia. They leave early to return the same day.

Laundromats: There aren't any per se in Bulgaria. The larger hotels are often unwilling to wash non-guests' clothing, even for hard currency. Don't despair; the hot Balkan sun dries hand-washed clothes pretty quickly. If you're staying in a private room, arrange it with your hosts for a minimal charge. A good **dry cleaner** is Svezhest (Свежест) at Vasil Kolarov 19. From pl. Sveta Nedelya, walk up Vitosha and make a left on Vasil Kolarov. Open Mon.-Fri. 7am-7pm.

Pharmacy: Pl. Sveta Nedelya 5, (tel. 81 50 89), open 24 hrs. Night pharmacies throughout the city are generally open 10pm-7am. Try **1st Private Pharmacy** at the intersection of Neofit Rilski and Tsar Asen. Also try **Megapharma** at bul. Vitosha 69, on the corner of bul. Vitosha and Patriarch Evtimii across from NDK. Open daily 8am-11pm. Pharmacists can usually recommend good doctors.

Medical Assistance: In an emergency, contact a hotel receptionist. Emergency aid for foreigners, offered by state-owned hospitals, is free of charge. If you are mobile go to **Pirogov emergency hospital,** bul. Totleben 21 across from the Rodina Hotel (tel. 53 31; open 24 hrs). An English-speaking **dentist** with modern equipment is Dr. Anton Filchev (tel. 66 29 84 or 516 92 34). He will give you directions to his office. For more information about medical care in Bulgaria, ask for a handout when you register at your embassy.

Emergencies: Police: tel. 166. **Ambulance:** tel. 150. **Fire:** tel. 160.

ACCOMMODATIONS

Balkantourist and ORBITA (see above) arrange all types of private rooms for US$8-15 per night. So do our friends at the train station (but remember that these "cheap private room" pushers may not stamp your statistical card). If you arrive in Sofia after Balkantourist closes, you're on your own. **Private accommodations** are the smartest option in Sofia. For a minimal extra charge you may get tea, coffee, breakfast, and laundry facilities. The hotels are not always worth their prices and the cheapest ones can be unsafe. Apart from the Balkantourist office at bul. Stamboliiski 27, you may also find private lodgings at **Markela,** bul. Knyaginya Maria Luiza 17, across from the Central Department Store (tel. 81 52 99). Average cost: US$6-7.50 per person; full apartments for US$13-14.50 per night. They will stamp your statistical card and give you the keys to your apartment along with directions. Markela can also change money and give you information about private lodging in other Bulgarian cities (open Mon.-Sat. 10am-7pm). After hours you may call Hristo or Daniella (tel. 54 69 69 or 62 35 02). They speak English.

Hotel Baldjieva (Балджиева), 23 Tsar Asen St., (tel. 97 29 14). A private hotel in the city center right off Vitosha Blvd. Clean, small rooms with shared bath. Hotel offers direct-dial phones, mini-bar, laundry and dry-cleaning. Pay in dollars or leva. Singles US$18. Doubles US$32. No credit cards accepted.

Hotel Nicky, ul. Neofit Rilski 16, off Bl. Vitosha (tel. 51 19 15). Private showers and beautiful restored Bulgarian architecture. Billiard room, café/bar, and restaurant. Pay in dollars or leva. Singles US$20. Doubles US$40. Ask for the 10% student discount. No credit cards accepted.

Orbita Hotel, bul. James Bourchier 76. (tel. 65 74 47 or 88 10 19). Take tram #9 south past the Palace of Culture to the intersection with bul. Anton Ivanov and look behind the Hotel Vitosha. A 2-star Communist behemoth which offers clean, plain rooms with private bath. A rocking disco awaits you downstairs. All rooms with refrigerators, some with TVs. Singles US$26. Doubles US$34. No credit cards accepted, but discounts can be had through Balkantourist

Hotel Hemus (Хемус), bul. Cherni Vruh 31 (Черни Връх; tel. 66 13 19 or 639 51). A 3-star hotel past the Palace of Culture at the southern extreme of downtown. Take tram #1, 7, or 15 to Palace of Culture, then head for the high-rise up bul. Cherni Vruh. Lots o' groups. Rooms have baths with shower, phones, and capital views of the city. Friendly English-speaking receptionists. Singles US$40. Doubles US$60 (US$25 and US$40 through Balkantourist). MC and Visa accepted.

Slavianska Beseda (Славянска Беседа), Slavianska St. 3 (tel. 87 21 23, fax 87 56 38). In the center near the post office. Depressing halls lead to clean rooms with showers and tubs. Pay in dollars or leva. Singles US$30. Doubles US$40. Credit cards soon to be accepted. Ask for a student discount.

Hotel Sevastopol (Севастопол), on ul. Rakovski (Раковски) near ul. General Gurko (tel. 87 59 41). Take the boulevard on the left of the Sheraton five blocks, then turn right onto ul. Rakovski. Centrally located on a noisy street; it sort of looks like a jail. Shun the communal showers—some doors don't lock and there's no hot water anyway. A **casino** and **nightclub** await you downstairs. Singles US$7. Doubles US$9. You get what you pay for. No credit cards accepted.

Hotel Edelweis, Maria Luiza 79. Centrally located, a few blocks from the train station. Pungent rooms, communal showers and bathrooms. Pay in leva only. Singles US$5.50, doubles US$8. No credit cards accepted

Instead of staying in the expensive, sometimes filthy, hotels in the center of Sofia, many travelers choose to stay in one of the suburbs. The small town **Dragalevtzi** (Драгалевци) offers many clean, private hotels for US$6-15 per person. Take tram #9 to the last stop, then pick up bus #64. Get off in the main square of Dragalevtzi.

Hotel Orhidea (Орхидея), ul. Angel Bukopeshtliev 9 (Ангел Букорешлиев; tel. 67 27 39). Clean rooms, hot water, shared baths. All rooms have TV. Coffee and tea served. Singles US$9. Doubles US$6-10 per person.

Hotel Darling (Дарлинг), 14 Iabalkova gradina St. (Ябълкова градина; tel. 67 19 86). Right next to hotel Orhidea. TV in all rooms. Café downstairs. Home cooking. Doubles US$11.

FOOD

From fast food to Bulgarian specialties, inexpensive meals are easy to find in Sofia. Tipping is not expected. If there are no empty tables, it is customary to sit with others. Make some new friends.

Pizza Palace (Пица), bul. Vitosha 34 (tel. 81 08 69). Delicious, medium-sized pizzas for US$2-4. Menu in English. Also sells *USA Today* and the *International Herald Tribune.* Open daily 11am-2am.

Palace of Culture Café, on the 8th floor of NDK. Coffee, sandwiches, and desserts with the best view in Sofia. Bring a camera. Open daily 9am-10pm.

Havana (Хавана), bul. Vitosha 27 (tel. 87 69 19). Havana is a restaurant, a café, and a cocktail bar—all with Cuban decor. Spicy food, Latino music, and a young crowd; open daily 11am-11pm. For a really hopping time, go next door to the bingo hall.

Budapest (Будапеша), ul. Rakovski 145 (tel. 87 27 50). Hungarian cuisine like goulash and schwitzel. Full meals US$5. Bring your Bulgarian grandparents to help you read the menu. Open Mon.-Fri. 10am-11pm, Sat. 10am-midnight.

Amerikana (Американа), on the first floor of the Central Department Store (store tel. 87 96 21). Balkanized versions of American fast food (full meals US$2-3). McDonald's need not fear. Open Mon.-Fri. 8am-9pm.

Chez Louis (Шер Луи), also at the Central Department Store, fifth floor (store tel. 87 96 21). Wide selection of pizza, pasta, burgers, and milk shakes. Open Mon.-Fri. 8am-9pm)

Café Luciano (Лучано), ul. Rakovski, two blocks from hotel Sevastopol and various other locations in Sofia. A chain of pastry cafés worth visiting each time you pass a new one. Amazing tortes, whole cakes for US$3.75. Open Mon.-Fri. 7:30am-11pm, Sat. and Sun. 9am-11pm.

Mussi Fast Food (Мусси), bul. Vitosha 59. Hamburgers, kebabs, broasted chicken, and fresh fries—all under US$1. Open daily 7:30am-11pm.

Eddy's Tex-Mex Diner, bul. Vitosha 4 (tel. 87 67 83). Interpreted Mexican dishes including margaritas and burritos. Nightly jazz or country music. The hippest place in town. Major credit cards accepted. When famous bands play there is a 50Lv cover. Entrees US$3-4. Open 10am-when the last customer leaves. Dinner served until 11pm.

Wiener Café, Sheraton Hotel, first floor, on pl. Sveta Nedelya. Sandwiches served from 10am-2pm. Otherwise, a full selection of tortes, ice cream, and alcohol. Fresh made banana bread loaves to go or enjoy in the courtyard. Menu in English. Open daily 10am-11pm.

Venezia Pizzeria (Венеция), 12 Benkovski St. (tel. 87 63 64). Head up Dondukov from pl. Sveta Nedelya, and turn right on Benkovski at the "Pizzeria" sign. Brick oven pizzas, ravioli, and lasagne. Famous throughout Sofia. Menu in English. Open daily noon-midnight.

Ramanyana, 32 Hristro Belchev St. (ул. Христо Белчев; tel. 80 53 03, fax 80 52 84), one street over from Vitosha Blvd. between NDK and the Sheraton. Sofia's first Indian restaurant. The chefs offer real *samosa* (85Lv), spicy shrimp, chicken and lamb dishes, and lots of veggie specials. Entrees US$1-4. Menu in English. Outdoor seating area and air conditioning to cool you down while eating the extra hot curry dishes. Open daily noon-midnight.

SIGHTS

Sofia's two most venerable churches, the late Roman **St. George's Rotunda** and the early Byzantine **St. Sofia,** date from the 4th and 6th centuries, respectively. St. George's hides in the courtyard of the Sheraton Hotel, while St. Sofia, the city's namesake, stands several blocks behind the Party house. Across the square from St. Sofia looms the massive, gold-domed **St. Alexander Nevsky Cathedral,** erected in the early 20th century in memory of the 200,000 Russians who died in the 1877-78 Russo-Turkish War. The **crypt** houses a monstrous collection of painted icons and religious artifacts from the past 1000 years. (Cathedral open Sun.-Fri. 8am-6pm, Sat. 8-10am and 4-8pm. Crypt open Wed.-Mon. 10am-6pm.) In an underpass at pl. Sveta Nedelya is the tiny 14th-century **Church of Saint Petka Samardzhiiska,** which contains some eye-grabbing frescoes; despite its size, this is one of Sofia's finest churches. (Open daily 8am-6pm. Donations encouraged.)

Along the way to the central train station from the Central Department Store, you'll see **Banya Bashi Mosque.** Built in the 16th century and named after the mineral baths nearby, the mosque has one minaret and is once again used as a place of worship. Across the street, and behind what used to be the covered market, you'll find the **Central Synagogue** at Exarch Yosif St. 16. It opened for services in 1909. The foundations of the building were built with stones from the old Jewish cemetery in Sofia. At Bl. Tsar Osvoboditel 3, there is a beautiful **Russian Church** named for St. Nicholas. It has five onion domes and was built in 1913. Between the Central Department Store and the Sheraton, you'll see the old **Communist Party Head-quarters.** There used to be a red star atop the high metal pole on the building's roof. Walk along the yellow brick road and you can still see where a group of protestors set the building ablaze during the turbulent 1989-90 transition.

The former **Georgi Dimitrov Mausoleum,** on pl. Aleksander Batenberg (Александр Батенберг), is a memorial to Stalin's former right-hand man, long-hated and now officially vilified. While debate still rages over the fate of the building, Bulgarians have put it to practical use as a public bathroom. Practice your Bulgarian by

BULGARIA

reading the graffiti. Continue up the yellow brick road and make a left on Dondukov and you'll see the **National Opera House**. The official address is 59 Dondukov, but the main entrance is on the side street Vrabcha. It was built in 1950 and has 1270 seats. The **Ivan Vazov National Theatre** is at 5 Levski St. It was built in 1907 in neo-Classical style; most of it was destroyed by fire in 1923 but restored in 1927.

The **University of Sofia,** named for Kliment of Ohrid (Софийски Университет Св. Климент Охридски"), is at bul. Tsar Osvoboditel 15, on the corner with bul. Vasil Levski. It was designed by the French architect Breancon and was built between 1920-34. The library is in the courtyard. Walk around and meet some students; most of them speak English. The **Vasil Levski Stadium** is on Bul. Bulgaria near the park. Sofia's favorite soccer team "Levski" plays here. The **Palace of Culture (NDK)** is located at the end of Vitosha Blvd. The building contains restaurants, theaters, and movie halls and has boldly gone where no man has gone before. There is a great view of Sofia from the top.

The labels in the **National Museum of History,** bul. Vitosha 2 off pl. Sveta Nedelya, are in Bulgarian only, but the magnificent Thracian treasures need no commentary (open Wed.-Fri. 9-11:15am and 1-5:15pm, Sat.-Sun. 9-11:15am and 3-5:15pm; admission 5 Lv, students 3Lv). The **Archeological Museum,** at the southwestern end of pl. Aleksandr Batenberg, houses items from the Thracian, Greek, Roman, and Turkish settlements in Bulgaria (open Tues.-Sun. 10am-noon and 2-6pm). Traditional Bulgaria is preserved at the **National Ethnographic Museum** (open Mon.-Fri. 10am-3:30pm; admission 20 Lv). The **National Museum of Fine Arts** is also located on the square (open Tues.-Sun. 10am-6pm). Bulgarian impressionism and modern art can be found at the **Sofia Municipal Art Gallery,** ul. General Gurko 1, near ul. Sofiiska Komuna (open Wed.-Sun. 10:30am-6:30pm; free).

ENTERTAINMENT AND NIGHTLIFE

The **nightlife** in Sofia gets wilder every year. Outdoor cafés and bars share **Bul. Vitosha** with musicians, gypsies and dancing bears. At **Frankie's Jazz Club/Piano Bar,** right off bul. Vitosha across from the American Center, there is a 40Lv cover for the best jazz east of New Orleans (open 10am-2am). Smartly-dressed Sofians go to the cafés around the park outside **NDK** to see and be seen. Euro-techno pop brings down the house at the **Orbilux** disco at the Orbita hotel, bul. James Boucher 76 (tel. 66 89 97). Music starts around 10pm. The **disco** underneath the Palace of Culture rocks until 4am (small cover). More bars and dance floors await at the **Angel Club** at 9 Narodni Sabranie, near Balkan Airlines and the Hotel Sofia. Small cover.

The opera and theatre seasons run September-June. Good seats at the **Opera House** are under US$1 (tel. 87 70 11; box office open daily 9:30am-7pm). There are no performances on Mondays. You can get tickets for the **Ivan Vazov National Theatre** at 5 Levski St. (tel. 88 28 84) for 15-30Lv. Movie theaters are plentiful and films are usually in English. Two good theaters are at bul. Vitosha 62 (tel. 88 58 78) and the **Serdica** at 1 Vasil Levski Sq. (tel. 43 17 97).

SHOPPING

The main shopping district is along bul. Vitosha. You'll find familiar names here, such as Benetton and Levi's. The **Central Department Store (TSUM)** has five floors of clothing, electronics, and household wares. On the first floor there's a newsstand with European newspapers, a kodak film developer, a change bureau, and a pharmacy (open Mon.-Fri. 8am-11pm, Sat. 9am-5pm). There is a clothing bazaar under the Palace of Culture, mostly of imports from Turkey and Greece (open Mon.-Fri. 9am-9pm).

There is a **grocery store** in the basement of the Central Department Store (open Mon. 9am-8:45pm, Tue.-Fri. 8am-8:45pm, Sat. 9:30am-4:45pm). Along Vitosha Blvd. there are 24-hr. markets. There is also an **open market** on Georgi Kirkov St. From pl. Sveta Nedelya walk along Maria Luiza a few blocks, then make a left. The market goes on for several city blocks. You can't miss it. Bring plastic bags for fresh fruit and vegetables. (Open daily in the morning, but it is especially hopping on weekends.)

Souvenirs can be bought at the Society of Master Craftsmen, bul. Vitosha 14 (tel. 87 01 47; open Mon.-Sat. 9am-7pm) or at the "Naroden Magazin" on ul. Levski 1, next to the American Express office (open Mon. 10am-6pm, Tue.-Fri. 10am-7pm, Sat. 10am-2pm). There is also a souvenir stand on the first floor of the Central Department Store. Lots of **antique stores** haunt Sofia. Most can be found on Rakovski and Tsar Osvoboditel streets. Best buy: a larger-than-life size bust of Stalin.

There are two **artist parks** in Sofia which are not to be missed. The first is in front of **Nevski Cathedral.** Here you can find antiques, Soviet paraphernalia, and hand-made crafts. If you walk diagonally across Nevski Cathedral to the other side of the square, the market continues with lots of Bulgarian grandmothers offering **traditional Bulgarian embroidery.** The second artists park is in the underpass between the Sheraton Hotel and the Central Department Store. Here artists of varying talent display their works and guinea pigs tell your fortune for 10Lv. Not to be missed (both parks open daily).

■ NEAR SOFIA: RILA MONASTERY (РИЛСКИЯ МАНАСТИР)

By the 10th century, Bulgaria's towns had become too worldly for poor Ivan of Rila. His quest for an impenetrable peace brought the monk into a dense forest 120km south of Sofia where he founded **Rila Monastery,** now the largest and most spectacular monastery in the country. Repeatedly plundered and ravaged by the Byzantines and Ottomans (bullet holes are still visible in the main gates), Rila nonetheless managed to shelter Bulgaria's arts of icon painting and manuscript copying during the foreign occupations. Much of the monastery was lost to fire in 1833, but was immediately rebuilt as we see it today.

Rila's cold, uninviting exterior is deceptive; inside you will be astounded by the vibrant blues and reds of the **murals** created by the best National Revival artists of the famed Samokov and Bansko schools of painting. The 1200 **frescoes** on the central **chapel** and surrounding walls form an outdoor art **gallery.** Try to make one of the services at 7am or 4:30pm (monastery open 6am-dusk). The monastery also houses three **museums** with ornate religious objects and items from Bulgaria's past such as coins, weapons, jewelry, and embroidery. (Admission 20Lv. Tours in various languages can be arranged through the museum.) In the hills surrounding the monastery there are excellent opportunities for both short and long **hikes.** Inquire at Pirin Tours in Sofia or at any of the souvenir shops in the monastery complex for more information. There are maps and suggested hiking routes posted outside the monastery.

To reach the monastery from Sofia, take the lone direct **bus** at 6:30am from the Ovcha Kupel (Овча Купел) station in Sofia (accessible by tram #5). The bus returns from the monastery at 10:30am and, in the summer only, again at 5:30pm. Another route to the monastery is by way of one of the many daily **trains** to Blagoevgrad. From Blagoevgrad there are hourly buses to Rila town and seven buses daily from Rila town to the monastery. If you don't want to schlep to Rila by public transportation, Balkantourist and Group Travel have day excursions to the monastery. Remember to bring a sweater—Rila is always chilly, even on the most sizzling summer days in Sofia. A **post office** is open Mon.-Fri. 8:30am-4:30pm. The **telephone city code** is 97054. **Exchange money** at the Bank for Agricultural Credit has a change bureau and capricious hours. There are several **souvenir shops** open during monastery hours, offering traditional Bulgarian crafts, icons, maps and guidebooks.

For a memorable night, secure a **room in the monastery** itself. Inquire in room 169, next to the museum. For US$6.50 per person, you get a small heated room with toilet but no shower facilities and no hot water. Hordes of tourists make it difficult to recreate the life of a hermit, but you can try. Just outside the back gate of the monastery and above the restaurant there is a small **hostel.** Go to the administration office, open 24 hrs. The bathrooms and showers are shared and the rooms have 8-10 beds (US$4.50 per person, no lockout). If you're hungry, buy a piping hot loaf of the most delicious bread in Bulgaria, baked by toiling monks and sold for only 10Lv in the **monastery bakery**.

About a 30-minute walk up the road behind the the monastery you'll find the three-star **Hotel Rilets** (Рилец; tel. 21 06; singles US$24, doubles US$36). This Balkantourist hotel takes Visa but charges an 8% surcharge. It has a restaurant and a night club; in the winter it rents ski gear. The **Hotel Tsarev Vran,** just beyond the monastery hostel, is due to open in late summer 1994. Prices are bound to be high. On the way to Rila monastery there is the impressive youth hostel **Hizha Eleshnitsa** (Хижа Елешница; tel. 26 22). Each room has a toilet and a sink; showers are shared. It is open year-round but in the summer there is also a café, billiard and ping-pong room, and a restaurant. Everything is clean and the managers can provide information about hikes in the Rila mountains. (US$1.80 per person with HI card, US$2.70 without. No lock out. Make reservations directly from Sofia.) **Restaurant Rila,** just outside the western gate of the monastery, serves up a beautiful view of the mountains and monastery and delicious local trout (US$2-4). Menu in English.

■■■ KOPRIVSHTITSA (КОПРИВЩИЦА)

Wood-and-stone cottages and a proud history of revolution make Koprivshtitsa one of Bulgaria's most enchanting villages. In 1876, Todor Kableshkov drafted his momentous "letter of blood" here, announcing the April uprising against Ottoman rule—the most passionately glorified event in Bulgarian history. The Turks savagely crushed the insurgency, but their brutality sparked the Russo-Turkish War of 1877-78, which led to Bulgarian independence. After the botched uprising in 1876, the Ottomans traveled throughout Bulgaria, systematically destroying villages and towns, but the shrewd citizens of Koprivshtitsa bribed the Ottomans into sparing their village. Hence, today Koprivshtitsa flaunts brilliant examples of National Revival architecture.

Every five years, the tranquility of this Sredna Gora valley hamlet is shattered by the **Koprivshtitsa Folk Festival,** Bulgaria's answer to Woodstock. Book rooms early if you plan to attend; the next one is set for August 1996.

Old Bulgaria is preserved in two distinct types of **museum cottages:** the first are sturdy, half-timbered, early 19th-century houses with open porches, high stone walls, and sparse ornamentation; the more common type features enclosed verandas and delicate woodwork. Many of the homes of the leaders of the 1876 April Uprising have been turned into museums. Buy a map and a guidebook in one of the little **souvenir shops** just off the main square. The most important sites are the **Oslekov House,** which once belonged to a merchant who died in the uprising, and the **Lyutov House,** known for its murals. Other museums include the houses of Dimcho Debelyanov, Todor Kableshkov, Georgi Benkovski, and Lyuben Karavelov. (Houses and museums are usually open 8am-noon and 1:30-5:30pm. Many are closed on Monday or Tuesday. A single ticket, 20Lv at the museum ticket office in the central square, provides entrance to all sites.)

Koprivshtitsa is a tiny town where the streets have no names. There is a **post office** behind the bus station (open Mon.-Fri. 7:30am-noon and 1:30-4:30pm). You can make **telephone** calls here daily 7:30am-8:30pm. Across the tiny bridge opposite the bus station you'll find a bank which **exchanges money** (open Mon.-Fri. 9am-5pm). Otherwise, change money at Hotel Koprivshtitsa. **Trains** from Sofia to Varna stop at Koprivshtitsa station (the stop after Anton), 8km away from the town (10 per day, 2hr., 30Lv). A bus awaits to take you into town (10min.). The **bus** station in Koprivshtitsa is a short walk from the main square. Tickets back from the bus station can be bought from the driver. There is a **pharmacy** next to the Diado Liben restaurant (open Mon.-Fri. 8:30am-12:30pm and 2-6pm).

Koprivshtitsa is an easy day trip from Sofia, but staying in one of the fairy tale houses is also possible. All your accommodation needs can be met at the reception desk of the **Hotel Koprivshtitsa** (Хотел Копривщица; tel. 21 82). Cross the second stone bridge from the center and ascend the steps. They can arrange **private rooms** for US$5 per person or book rooms in the hotel itself for US$6 per person, breakfast included. All rooms have private baths, but you'll get hot water only on weekends. Some devious maps show a nonexistent campground. The **Restaurant Diado Liben** (ресторант Дядо Либен) in the blue house across the river from the center serves grilled specialties including *sirene po trakiski* (сирене по тракийски; cheese with sausage) and *diado liben* (Дядо Либен; a pork and vegetable dish, 70Lv). An excellent **cafeteria** is in the restaurant complex in the town center. Above the cafeteria is a **disco** which rocks little Koprivshtitsa every night.

■ ■ ■ PLOVDIV (ПЛОВДИВ)

At first glance, most of Bulgaria's second-largest city seems to be the country's worst sprawl of gray apartment complexes and exhaust-ridden boulevards. Hold your disappointment until you stroll into the rambling stairway-streets of the **Old Town** via the **Trimontsium** (Трихълмието). In the Old Town, National Revival houses hang their beamed, protruding upper stories over the cobblestones, windows stare down into alleyways at impossible angles, and churches and mosques hide in secluded corners. Plovdiv was founded by the Thracians around 600 BC on the trade route between Europe and the Middle East, and was an important commercial and administrative center for the Macedonians, Romans, Byzantines, and Ottomans. The city now rivals Sofia as a tourist and cultural center. Twice a year the Bulgarian business world focuses on Plovdiv when the city hosts trade fairs in May and September.

ORIENTATION AND PRACTICAL INFORMATION

The main street in Plovdiv is Knyaz Aleksander (Княз Александър), a pedestrian walkway which ends in the main square Centralen (пл. Централен).

Tourist Offices: The English-speaking staff at the **Puldin Tours** office, bul. Bulgaria 106 (tel. 55 38 48), proffers a city map and guides to Plovdiv history (45Lv), arranges private accommodations (singles US$10, doubles US$15), and changes traveler's checks (US$5 commission). From the train station, take the trolley #102 to bul. Bulgaria (the ninth stop) near Plovdiv's fairgrounds. Walk back one block—it's on your right. Open Mon.-Fri. 9am-8pm; winter Mon.-Fri. 8am-6pm. There is a **Pirin Tourist** at 20 Petko Petkov St. (ул. Петко Петков; tel. 22 63 11), a few blocks from the Hotel Feniks.

Currency Exchange: Numerous bureaus line Knyaz Aleksander (Княз Александър).

Post Office: At the main square Centralen (пл. Централен), open Mon.-Sat. 8am-5pm).

Telephones: International calls may be made from the post office daily 6am-11pm. **City Code:** 032.

Faxes: May be sent and received at the post office (fax 492 00 44).

Photocopies and Film and Photo Developing: A **Fuji film** developer with photocopy services can be found across from Hotel Bulgaria on the central square (open Mon.-Fri. 9am-7:30pm, Sat. 9am-5pm).

Trains: Most trains from Sofia to İstanbul stop in Plovdiv, as do most Sofia-Burgas trains. Sofia-Plovdiv service runs about every 2 hours (2½hr., US$1). The **Rila** bureau is at ul. Liljiana Dimitrova (Лиляна Димитрова), just past the church.

Buses: Buses from Sofia to Plovdiv leave from the Novotel Europa about every 40 minutes (1hr, 8Lv). Return buses depart Plovdiv from the bus station Jug (Автогара юг). The private company **Traffic Express** (Трафик Експрес) sells tickets at bul. Hristo Botev 45, at the Jug station (tel. 26 57 87, fax 26 51 51). They also sell tickets for the Black Sea Coast, Athens, İstanbul, and capitals in Eastern Europe. **International buses** also leave from Park-Hotel Saint-Petersburg (Парк-хотел Санкт-Петербург) or bus station Rodopi (автогара "Родопи").

Public Transportation: The fare for buses and trolleys is 3Lv.

Taxis: Taxis can be hailed by calling 56 60 60.

Pharmacy: The private pharmacy **Fleming** (Флеминг) is on the pedestrian walkway (tel. 26 00 57); open daily 9am-9pm.

BULGARIA

ACCOMMODATIONS

Unless you like East European tractor demonstrations, it's best to avoid Plovdiv during the biannual trade fairs (beginning on the first Mon. of May in spring, May 1 in 1995, and the last Mon. of Sept. in fall, Sept. 4 in 1995) when accommodation prices swell by up to 500%. If you strike out with Pirin Tours, there is a **private room agency** (Квартирна Агенция) called **Prima Vista** right off of the central square, one block from Hotel Bulgaria (tel. 27 27 78, fax 27 20 54). It offers private lodging and hotel reservations (open Mon.-Fri. 10am-noon and 2-8pm, Sat. 10am-5pm).

Hostel Touristicheski Dom (Туристически Дом) on P.R. Slaveykov St. (Славейков) in the old town (tel. 26 92 99). English is not spoken, so it may be better to book through Orbita in Sofia if you plan to stay here. Shared rooms go for US$7 per person. Café inside.

Hotel Leipzig (Хотел Лайпциг), bul. Ruski 70 (Руски), is just three blocks from the rail station and 10 minutes from the town center (tel. 23 22 50, fax 45 31 60). Though located in a noisy area, the hotel has excellent prices and clean rooms. Singles US$18. Doubles US$34.

Hotel Feniks (Феникс) Kapitan Raicho 79 (Капитан Райчо; tel. 22 47 29 and 23 69 60). From pl. Centralen, walk across bl. Vzrazhdane to Kapitan Raicho. Private hotel in a huge apartment complex. Rooms have satellite TV and access to kitchen and laundry facilities. US$15-20 per room (usually 2-3 people per room).

Hotel Bulgaria ul. Patriarch Evtimii 13 (Патриарх Евтимий), right on pl. Centralen (пл. Централен; tel. 22 60 64, fax 22 62 64) is a pricier option. Singles US$36. Doubles US$50.

If you prefer to camp or stay in small bungalows, **Trakia Camping,** on the old highway to Sofia, is open year-round. The bar doubles as a reception desk. Disco every night. Bungalows for 2-3 people go for US$7 a night. (Take the #23 bus from the train station.)

FOOD

Taverna Puldin (Пълдин), ul. Knjaz Tseritelev 3 (Княз Церетелев), in the heart of the Old Town, built right into the Roman walls (tel. 23 17 20). Take ul. Maksim Gorky (Максим Горки) to its fourth right through the Turkish gate; it's your second right. Full meal US$6-9. Open daily 10am-midnight.

Restaurant Alafrangite (Алафрангите), ul. Kiril Nektariev 17 (Кирил Нектариев), in an eye-catching National Revival house in the Old Town that once appeared in a *National Geographic* article (tel. 26 95 95). From behind the Dzhumaya Mosque follow ul. Maksim Gorky; make the 3rd right. Their specialty is *vreteno,* a pork or veal steak with a cheese and mushroom filling. Entrees average US$3. Open daily 11:30am-midnight.

The Union Club (Юнион Клуб), ul. Hiney 6 (Хайне; tel. 27 05 51), is a new restaurant in the Old Town run by a master chef. Beautiful outdoor garden, credit cards accepted. Open daily 9am-until last customer leaves.

Trakiski Stan (Тракейски Стан) ul. Puldin 5, (tel. 22 45 10). Bulgarian Folk music fills this tavern most evenings. Enjoy the shade of the grapevines in the courtyard and feast on their special vegetable dish called, you guessed it, *Trakiski Stan.*

Grill Land, across from the Plovdiv post office. A new spotless fast food joint. Breezy balconies overlook the central square. They serve syrupy pastries, pizza, beer, and fries. Their clean bathrooms are a godsend. Open daily 7am-11pm.

SIGHTS AND ENTERTAINMENT

Start at the **Dzhumaya Mosque** (Джумая джамия) on ul. Knyaz Aleksandr I (Княз Александър I), and wander up ul. Suborna (Съборна). Turn to find the 2nd-century **Amphitheater of Philippopolis**, at the entrance to the tunnel that runs under the old town. Try to see a performance in the amphitheater (such as June's **Theater Festivities** or the summer run of the National Opera. Tickets can be bought for about 50Lv at the box office, ul. Gurko 19 (ул. Гурко; tel. 22 55 53). Also ask at the Puldin Tours office about the **Plovdiv Chamber Music Festival** (June-July).

Back on Suborna, continue a bit farther to the **National Ethnographic Museum** (Етнографски Музей) that contains a well-presented collection of artifacts from the same period (open Tues.-Thurs. and Sat.-Sun. 9am-noon and 2-5pm, Fri. 2-5pm). Colorful Baroque houses are down the hill, through the Roman gate. The **Georgiadi House** (къша Д. Георгиади) displays exhibits from the War of Liberation.

On a cool evening, head to the fountainside café in the **Public Garden** (formerly the Garden of King Boris), within walking distance from the Old Town. Multicolored strobes illuminate the fountain—the most popular hangout in town—and you can rent rowboats to splash your way around the small lake. One of the many **movie theatres** on Knyaz Aleksandr I is bound to be showing a film in English. From Mon.-Sat. **Strymna St.** (ул. Стрьмна) becomes an **artist park;** watch craftspeople make pottery, calligraphy and textiles and have your portrait drawn by one of the many artists in front of the Dzhumaya Mosque. For **nightlife,** stroll around the Old Town. Pop in when you hear laughter and music—home cooking and *rakiya* await.

■ NEAR PLOVDIV: BACHKOVO MONASTERY

About 28km south of Plovdiv lies the 11th-century **Bachkovo monastery,** the second largest in the country after Rila, where visitors can spend the night for under US$1. The monastery was built in 1083 by the Georgian brothers Gregory and Abbassy Balcuriani. Mostly destroyed by the Turks in the early 16th century, it was rebuilt in the late 16th and early 17th centuries. The cemetery chapel is the only building remaining from the 11th century. Most of the fabulous murals are from the National Revival period. Take a bus from the main station in Plovdiv to Asenovgrad, where you can catch a bus to the monastery. Inquire about the spartan **accommodations** at the administrative office on the second floor; ask for Brother Gurman (tel. (03327) 277). Keep in mind that the monastery will be booked solid around traditional holidays: Aug. 15th; Orthodox Easter, the 25th day after Easter on the Gregorian calendar; and Christmas. There are several gift shops (invest in some incense at 3Lv a pack), cafés, and stands selling grilled meats surrounding the monastery.

PIRIN MOUNTAIN REGION

Peroun, the god of thunder, is said to preside over the secluded marble peaks in southwestern Bulgaria named in his honor by ancient Slav tribes. At his feet, relentless Pleistocene glaciers chiselled hundreds of clear alpine lakes out of rock laced with edelweiss and white firs. Bulgaria's highest peaks and least touristed paths make the Pirin mountains a rewarding skiing and hiking destination.

■ ■ ■ BLAGOEVGRAD(БЛАГОЕВГРАД)

Legend has it that hundreds of years ago a pale, sickly horse wandered off from a farm. After searching many months, the owner found that the horse had been turned into a hearty black stallion by the curative waters of the Bistrica river and the fresh air from the Rila peaks. The owner decided to found a settlement at the site which later became known as Blagoevgrad. To the modern eye, perhaps it would have been better if he had not found the horse; most of today's Bagoevgrad is industrial and dreary. But the preserved old town of Varosha and the American University of Bulgaria make the city a worthwhile stopover en route to the ski slopes.

You can cover the major points of interest in Blagoevgrad in half an hour or so; if you arrive during the school year, it's more fun to spend time making friends with the students at the **American University of Bulgaria (AUBG),** most of whom speak flawless English. The AUBG is the first U.S. college in Eastern Europe. The useful **information office** (tel. 254 21) is on the first floor (open Mon.-Fri. 8am-5pm). The lobby holds the school's **bookstore** where you can buy condoms, phone cards, and books in English (open Mon.-Fri. 9am-1pm and 2-6pm). In the **university café** across the corridor you can enjoy the coldest glass of Kool-aid in town and watch MTV or CNN via satellite (open Mon.-Fri. 7:30am-5pm). The world renowned music and dance ensemble *Pirin* has its home in the same building as the Chinese restaurant. They tour abroad regularly but check the box office to see if they are in town.

Walking across the bridge from Macedonia Square, tranquil **Varosha** (old town) lies to the left. In Varosha, stroll through the grounds of the 1884 **Mitropolitska Church** (Митрополинка Църква). (Services daily at 8am and 5pm. Check to see when the church's choir is giving its next performance.) Next to Varosha is the **Regional Museum of History,** housing a gun and sword collection (open Tues.-Sun. 9am-noon and 2-5:30pm; admission US$1, free on Thursdays). At night, party with students at the **Central Disco** (Дискотека Централ), next to the First Private Bank and across from the university (open every night from about 9pm). Also next to the First Private Bank is a **fitness center** (tel. 647 69) that allows you to use the facilities for 50Lv per day. Trainer, weights, Stairmaster, and showers (open daily 8am-10pm).

Arriving by bus from Sofia (10-12 per day, 60Lv) or from the Rila monastery via the town of Rila (20Lv) walk back 50m or so from the drop-off point. Turn right at the traffic lights and walk up bul. Kiril and Methodius (Кирил и Методий), the city's main street. The railway station is the crimson building behind you at the end of the boulevard. Walk straight for 5-6 blocks until you reach a small square of white stone. To the left is the **American University of Bulgaria (AUBG).** Most important sites in Blagoevgrad are clustered around this bright city square. The staff of the **Tourist Service** office (tel. 232 18), next door to the Alan Mak Hotel, are very knowledge-able about bus and train schedules to Sofia, Bansko, and Melnik (open Mon.-Fri. 8am-noon and 1:30-5:30pm). Or simply call the bus station (tel. 237 50) or train station (tel. 236 95) for the latest schedules.

The **Alfatour Room Bureau** (Алфатур Квартирно Бюро; tel. 223 92, 235 98, or 628 41) can arrange rooms in private houses. The agency also offers **translation, bus ticket,** and **photocopy** services. Walk through the garden past the Alan Mak hotel and turn left at the pedestrian walkway of Krali Marko (Крали Марко). If you arrive after hours, call Mrs. Chumeva (tel. 624 95). The bureau is next to the Bank for Agri-cultural Credit where you can **exchange money** (open Mon.-Fri. 8am-noon and 1-6pm) and cash traveler's checks at the First Private Bank on the right side of Pl. G. Izmirliev-Makedoncheto (tel./fax 264 59; open Mon.-Fri. 8:15-noon and 1-4:15pm, Sat. 9am-noon). The central **post office** is located on Pl. Hristo Botev (open Mon-Sat. 7am-8pm, Sun. 7am-2pm). **Telephones** are available at the post office (open daily 7am-9pm); you can send and receive **faxes** as well (fax 255 82; open daily 7am-8:30pm). On na. Macedonia (Македония) there is a **photo developing** store that sells Agfa film (open daily 9am-9pm). A private **pharmacy,** Panacea, is at 9 Hristo Smirn-enski (Христо Смирненски) St. near the Hotel Volga (tel. 639 81; open daily 8am-9pm). They can recommend doctors.

Try to secure a private room with **Alfatour.** Another option is the **Hotel Bor** (Xotel Bor), a long trudge away in southeastern Blagoevgrad (tel. 224 91). The hotel is a two-star facility and features a restaurant, tavern, and disco. The path through the park to the hotel isn't lit at night. (Singles US$24. Doubles US$30.) The three-star **Alan Mak** offers clean singles for US$30. The food in Blagoevgrad is varied and inex-pensive; the locals joke that there are more cafés than people. Believe it or not, the best Chinese restaurant in Bulgaria is the newly-opened **Great Wall Restaurant,** in the building next to the American University (tel./fax 649 44). They don't always have everything listed on the extensive menu but what is available is tasty. Try the chicken with peanuts or the noodle soup. Entrees are about US$2; the menu is in English (open daily noon-midnight). For a more Bulgarian experience, try the 24-hr. **Bar-Restaurant Evropa** (Бар-Ресторант Европа), located on the back of a block of apartments along the main commercial street. It's tricky to find; ask for directions. It's worth the effort—a full lunch here will cost about US$1. Try the *pasta Bachi-novo* (паста Бачиново), a local dessert specialty.

■■■ BANSKO (БАНСКО)

At the base of the Pirin mountains, sleepy **Bansko** is a gateway to 87 steep peaks and 150 lakes scattered across a sea of forget-me-nots and alpine poppies. An artisan center during the National Revival period (18th-19th centuries), the town spawned the iconoclast **Bansko school of painting;** well-preserved examples of skilled National Revival architecture still crowd the town's narrow lanes. Recently Bansko has become popular with young Bulgarians who can't afford more expensive Westerner-oriented ski resorts. The accommodations and ski facilities here are just as good and the home-cooking private restaurants even better than those at any of the fancier ski havens. Highest peak: **Vihren** (2914m).

The Bansko school of painting is highlighted at the **Icon Exhibit** (икона узложба) just off Pl. Vuzrazhdane (open Tues.-Sat. 9am-5pm). The **Neofit Rilski House** (Меофит Рилски) on Pirin Street is open Tues.-Sun. 9am-5pm. The pride of Bansko is the Holy Trinity **Church** (Света Троица) and its clock tower, right on Pl. Vuzrazhdane. Here you'll see excellent examples of the Bansko School and traditional woodworking (open daily 8am-noon and 2-6pm). At night, try one of the **discos** in many of the big hotels or breeze into a warm *mehana* for some folk music and *rakiya*.

Bansko is located 150km from Sofia and has a population of 12,000. The bus station is on Patriarh Evtimii. Follow the signs to the Pirin Hotel at 68 Tsar Simeon St.; at the hotel, you can pick up a current map of the city. There are five daily **buses** from Sofia to Bansko, departing from the Ovcha Kupel station (85Lv). You can also reach Bansko by bus from Blagoevgrad (9 daily) and Plovdiv and Petrich (1 each daily). **Group Travel** runs buses to Bansko in the summer months. Private buses depart Pirin for the ski lifts (US$13). **Balkan Holidays** and a **Hertz** regional office are located at 6 Demokratsia Square (tel. 50 30, fax 50 31; variable summer hours). The **post office** is right across from the Pirin Hotel (open daily 7am-9:30pm). You can also make **telephone** calls and send **faxes** here. The **telephone city code** is 07443. **Exchange currency** at the TSB Bank on Demokratsia Square (tel. 50 91, fax 50 90; open Mon.-Fri. 8am-4pm, Sat. 9am-1pm). Just across from the bank is the **pharmacy.** Inquire there for information about doctors and dentists (tel. 23 43; open Mon.-Fri. 24 hrs., Sat. and Sun. 7:30am-noon and 3:30-8pm). There is a small grocery **market** offering bread, meats, and alcohol in the main square (open Mon.-Sat. 9am-1pm and 1:30-7:30pm).

The best bet for **private rooms** is the **tourist bureau** in the Hotel Alpin (Алпин) on 6 Neofit Rilski St. (Неофит Рилски; tel. 51 00, fax 51 01). Run by the hotel reservation desk, they can usually secure travelers a place to stay even after regular working hours. Since private rooms tend to be more expensive in Bansko than elsewhere in Bulgaria (US$15), hotels are a viable option. The **Edelweis Youth Hostel (HI)** (Туристически Дом Еделвайс), 12 Nikola Vaptsorov (Ванщаров; tel. 22 71) offers clean rooms with bedding and sinks but shared showers. (Reception open 6am-noon and 1:30-11pm. Lockout at 11pm. HI members US$3.60, non-members US$5.) **Hotel Strazhite** (Стражите), bul. Pirin (tel.44 52), is a short walk from the town center, offering big, clean rooms with baths; fringe benefits include a bar, a a restaurant, and nightclub with nightly live entertainment. Ask at reception if you can be booked at the **Hadjirovskov Houses Complex** (Комплекс Хаджирускови Къши). The prices are the same, but you get a night in a restored National Revival house. (Singles US$14. Doubles US$16. Apartment with refrigerator and TV US$17.) The **Hotel Alpin** (Алпин) is at 6 Neofit Rilski St. (Неофит Рилски; tel. 30 54, fax 51 01). All rooms have shower, telephone, and satellite TV. Homestyle cooking in the café. (Singles US$17. Doubles US$24.)

A wonderful *mehana* (a Bulgarian old-style **tavern**) is right off Vuzrazhdane Square across from the Icon Exhibit. Feast on Bansko specialties like *kavarma*, a meat, rice and cabbage dish or *banski staretz*, a homemade sausage. Meals under US$2 (open 24 hrs.). At night, explore the pathways between houses around Demokratsiya Square. You'll find that many enterprising families have turned their houses into small **cafés.** Nothing will beat the cooking, prices or Bansko hospitality.

■■■ MELNIK(МЕЛНИК)

Deep in a sandstone gorge cut into pinnacles by wind and water, tiny Melnik quietly and tirelessly produces its delicious wine. Like the generations before them, the town's 450 residents leave their stone white homes every day to tend to the ancestral vineyards. The ground floors of the town's exquisitely preserved National Revival houses are built high, with the upper floors overhanging the lower ones. Their basements hold the cellars where the famous Melnik wine is aged and shared with visitors for pennies.

Cross the stream and make the mandatory stop at the **wine store**. Best buy: Cabernet Souvignon Melnik 1987, US$0.54 per bottle. Sample a few wines in the huge oak casks. Further on the left is the **Art Center.** The owner is a Sofia native who left the big city to get away from it all. He sells film, folk art, and compact discs of Bulgarian folk music (usually open daily 10am-6pm). Ask to be let into one of the **wine making caves** built into the sandstone hills. Also worth seeing are the ruins of the 13th-century **Boyar's House** on the hill at the end of the town and the affiliated **museum** (open daily 9am-noon and 2-6pm). At night go on a **wine tasting** tour in the various *mekhani* and listen to the sad Pirin folk songs that fill the small private taverns. Remains of the 13th-century **monastery** of St. Nikola and a richly decorated **church** are found on the hill south of Melnik. Slav, the Bulgarian despot, built his fortress southwest of the monastery; the fortress walls are 3m thick.

Melnik is built along two sides of a small stream: there are no streets. The bus will drop you off at the bottom of the town. As you walk up, first stop by the small **tourist bureau/souvenir shop** on your right. They'll be able to give you information about the town and can arrange private rooms (US$2.70; open daily 8am-6pm). There is one daily **bus** from Sofia to Melnik from the central bus station (70Lv). An alternative route is to catch a bus to Sandanski (Сандански) and then hop one of the five daily buses to Melnik (20Lv; buy ticket from the driver). Continue up the right side of the stream and you'll pass a **mini-market** (мини маркет) that sells coffee, wine, meats, and snack foods. Across the river and up the cobblestone alleyway you'll find the **post office,** with **telephones** available during regular hours (open Mon.-Fri. 8am-noon and 1:30-4pm). Next door, you'll find the **pharmacy** (tel. 21 43, after hours tel. 388; open Wed.-Mon. 8am-noon and 2-6pm).

If you can't find a room through the tourist bureau, walk around the town and you'll see signs advertising **private rooms.** The **Tourist Hostel** (tel. 218) offers small rooms with shared baths. (Reception open 8am-8pm. No curfew. US$4.90 per person.) **Lumparova House** (Лумпарова къша; tel. 216) has beautiful views, furry bed covers, and private baths in a traditional Bulgarian home. (US$15 per person. Accepts both dollars and leva.) **Hotel Melnik** is the largest hotel in town, just completely remodelled. All rooms feature wall-to-wall carpet, balconies, refrigerators, and TVs. Guests can satisfy most of their immediate needs at the restaurant, casino, and exchange bureau. (Singles US$ 25. Doubles US$50.) There are several **cafés** and **restaurants** in Melnik. The best strategy is to walk around and listen for loud music coming from the windows. Make sure to ask for the homemade wines. The natives always keep the best for themselves and bottle the rest. In all the restaurants you'll find traditional Bulgarian fare at low prices.

A quick bus ride or an hour's hike from Melnik, the **Rozhen Monastery** (Роженският Манастир) dates from the 14th century, with a major restoration in the 16th century. Check out the carved lecterns and calligraphy among the murals.

VALLEY OF ROSES (РОЗОВА ДОЛИНА)

More expensive by weight than gold and used in the most luxuriant of perfumes, over 70% of the world's **rose oil** is produced in Bulgaria. Workers trudge out into the famed fields of the **Valley of the Roses** in the heart of the country to pick rose petals, one by one, in late May and early June of every year. To make a single gram of attar of roses (rose oil), 2000 petals are needed (and all must be picked before sunrise to capture the precious fragrance). Each June, the valley stops to take a deep breath and puts on an extravagant rose festival.

■■■ KARLOVO (КАРЛОВО)AND KAZANLAK (КАЗАНЛЪК)

Karlovo (Карлово), huddled at the foot of the Stara Planina, two and a half hours east of Sofia along the Sofia-Varna train line, and **Kazanlak,** about 50km east of Karlovo, make the most of the marketability of this annual ritual. Notable for little besides Stalinist blocks and seas of sheep throughout most of the year, the two towns wage a modern day War of the Roses in trying to outdo each other's pageantry during the annual week-long **Rose Festival** (Празник на Розата), held to end the first weekend in June). The festival features performances by traditional Bulgarian song-and-dance troupes and comedians, as well as soccer matches, bazaars, and the like.

During the festival, check out the ethnographic **Rose Museum** (Музей на Розата) in Kazanlak by jumping on bus #2 from the central square; ask the driver to stop at the museum (open daily 8:30am-5pm; admission for students 20Lv). The **Kazanlak Tomb,** in Tyulberto Park, is actually a *copy* of the tomb which dates back to the late 4th century BC (open daily 8am-noon and 1:30-6pm; students 25Lv). A local tale has it that young men drinking water from the fountain off the city's central square are destined to marry a local maiden.

For a grand view of the festivities in Karlovo, book a room in the **Rozova Dolina Hotel** (tel. 33 80, fax 68 90; singles US$17, doubles US$25). Its best to book early with a travel agent as there will be lots o' tourists. Karlovo's **Roza Tours** office occupies the hotel lobby. **Trains** connect Karlovo with Kazanlak several times a day (1½hr., US$0.50). In Kazanlak, snag the best hotel deal in town at the **Hotel Roza,** ul. Rozova Dolina 2, facing the central square (tel. 24 605, fax 40 029; singles US$28, doubles US$40. Make reservations for the festival). Or try the **Campground Kazanlushka Roza** (Къмпинг "Казанлъшка роза") 4km north of Kazanlak (open May-Sept.). Escape the overbearing, gray socialist blocks in the **women's monastery** (Женския Манастир), at Tsar Osvoboditel #9 (tel. 222 16), which rents rooms to both men and women for donations only. The nuns lead an isolated existence, so be prepared to *talk* (reception open daily until 6:30pm). For budget dining in Kazanlak search out the restaurant **Starata Kushta** (Старата Къща) on ul. Dr. Baev 19 (tel. 21 231). Heading into the central square, take your second left onto ul. Gen. M. Skobelev and then the first right on ul. Gen. Gurke. Meals cost less than US$1 (open daily 10am-until the last customer leaves).

In Kazanlak, the **tourist office** (tel. 251 52 or 210 87) is located on the 1st floor of Hotel Kazanlak, on the central square (open Mon.-Fri. 8:30-11:30am and 2-5pm). Many private **bus** lines to nearby towns and cities such as Karlovo, Gabrovo, and Stara Zagora start from the bus and railway station just south of the center of town; buses to further points depart from the parking lot in front of the Hotel Kazanlak.

Ten km south of Kazanlak (US$6 by taxi) is **Lake Koprinka** (Копринка), formerly Georgi Dimitrov, a scenic, brownish lake on whose bottom lies the remains of the Thracian city Sevtopolis. To reach the legendary **Shipka Pass** (see below) take bus #6 from the city center.

■■■ SHIPKA (ШИПКА)

At the northern extreme of the Valley of Roses looms the legendary **Shipka Pass** (Шипченски Проход), site of the bloody and pivotal battle which decided the outcome of the Russo-Turkish War of 1877-78 that liberated Bulgaria from the Ottoman Empire. In honor of the Russian soldiers who lost their lives in the battle at Shipka, the Bulgarians built a breathtaking rose-colored 17th-century Russian style **memo-**

BULGARIA

rial church in the town of Shipka, just below the Shipka Pass. You can hear its seventeen bells throughout the Rose Valley (open daily 8:30am-5pm; admission 20Lv, English-speaking guide 50Lv).

An hour hike up the mountain will bring you to the Shipka Pass and the **Monument to Liberty,** a stone structure which doubles as a museum (open daily 8:30am-5pm; admission 20Lv). Once you've scaled the 894 steps leading up to the monument, you'll be treated to unmatched views of the Rose Valley. There's a spaceship-like structure visible to the east. That's not the *Death Star,* that's the former Communist party museum, built on the site of the first meeting of the Bulgarian Communist party. Word has it that it's being turned into a luxury hotel. Bring a sweater and a plastic bag for the wild strawberries.

If you decide to stay the night near the monument, you have two options. The private **Hotel St. Nicholas** (Свети Никола; tel. 27 65, fax 266 11) has simple rooms, private baths, and great views for US$6 per person, breakfast included. The owners run a home-style restaurant (open daily 7am-2am). If the hotel is full, try the Balkantourist **Hotel Shipka** (tel. 291 19, fax in Varna (52) 25 11 01). Singles with shared baths cost US$9, doubles US$12. They also have a restaurant and bar. You'll find lots of little **grills** and **souvenir stands** at the foot of the steps leading to the monument.

Take **bus #6** from Kazanlak to get to Shipka town. From there you can **hike** to the Shipka Pass, or take one of the three daily buses to Gabrovo, which will let you off just below the Monument to Freedom. Bus #6 to Shipka town will drop you off in front of **Hotel Shipka** (different from the hotel above; tel. 27 89), a hiker/student-oriented hotel which offers clean rooms and shared baths at rock-bottom prices. The manager, Ivan, speaks perfect English and can tell you the best way to hike to the Monument. Under the hotel there is a **grocery store** and across from the hotel there is a small **restaurant** offering hamburgers and salads (full meals US$2). The **telephone city code** is 94324.

■■■ GABROVO (ГАБРОВО)

It is said that Gabrovians cut the tails off their cats in order to save heat when letting the cat indoors. Located between Shipka and Veliko Turnovo and populated by people known for being misers, **Gabrovo** is Bulgaria's capital of satire. On weekends residents "party" in low voices and slippers so they can hear the bands from neighboring towns and don't have to hire their own. They put green-tinted glasses on their donkeys so that they (the donkeys) will eat rotten hay. They keep the lights on in the chicken coops so that the chickens, thinking it day, will continually lay eggs.

The humor of Gabrovo is captured in the **Gabrovo House of Humor and Satire** (Дом на Хумора и Сатирата) on satirical posters, sculptures, cartoons, books, and films, 68 Bryansica St. (tel. 272 29, fax 269 89) Every odd year (but what year isn't odd around here?), the museum hosts the **International Biennial of Humor and Satire in the Arts,** an international competition of satirical art held under the motto "The World Lasts Because it Laughs." In 1995, the competition will begin on May 12. In the souvenir shop, be sure to pick up a book of Gabrovian jokes and a traditional Gabrovo handicraft—like a spoon with a hole in it (keeps your guests from taking all the sugar) or a coffee mug cut in half (ditto for coffee. Open Tues.-Sun. 9am-1pm and 2-6pm. English-speaking, wise-cracking guides are available. Admission 50Lv.)

To reach Gabrovo, take one of the many **buses** from Kazanlak or Veliko Turnovo. You can also take a **train** west from Veliko Turnovo's Gorna Oryahoritsa station. The newly-privatized **Balkan Hotel,** in the center at 12 Emil Manov (tel. in Varna (52) 24 69 77, fax 25 11 01) offers singles for US$16 and doubles for US$22. On the outskirts of town is the **Hotel Loven dom** (Ловен Дом) at bl. Humus 2 (tel. 450 90). Take trolleybus #32; US$10 per person. Both hotels have **restaurants.** The House of Humor has a café, nightclub, and **variety theatre.** The **telephone city code** is 066.

■ NEAR GABROVO

ETURA (ЕТЪРА)

Etura is a living museum established in the 1960s to preserve arts and crafts skills from the National Revival period. You and your hippy friends can watch the manual production of flour, sheets, gold jewelry, and wool carpets and, if you wish, purchase your own. Years ago, Balkantourist used to arrange **internships** with the master craftsmen. Today, if you are interested in honing your skills as a cobbler, blacksmith, or tanner, you'll have to arrange it with one of the craftsmen themselves. About 50km southwest of Veliko Turnovo, it's a bit out of the way, but well worth a half-day's visit; take the train west from Gorna Oryahovitsa train station and get off in Gabrovo. Etura is just on the outskirts of town. This outdoor museum also contains a **herbal pharmacy** and two **bakeries** selling candy and delicious bagel-like breads. (Tickets for the complex are 50Lv. You can hire a guide for 50Lv.)

The **telephone city code** is 062. If you decide to spend the night, go to the **Hotel/Restaurant Etura** (tel. 420 26). Located at the foot of the museum, the hotel has a homey interior and offers singles with private baths for US$22, doubles US$33. The restaurant specializes in homemade bread made with buffalo cheese (open 7:30am-3pm and 5-11pm).

TRYAVNA (ТРЯВНА)

Master craftsmanship of the 17th-century Tryavna School of Woodworking and Icon Painting has been preserved in the town of **Tryavna**, a few minutes by bus from Gabrovo. Wealthy Bulgarians used to outdo each other in the ornate designs of their carved ceilings and woodworking. See the exhibits in the **Daskalovata House** (Даскаловата Къща), 27 P. R. Slaveykov St. (open summer daily 9am-6pm, winter daily 8am-noon and 1-5pm). At the entrance of the Old Town, don't miss the 12th-century **Church of the Arch Angel Mihail** (Църква на Свети Архангел Михаил) and its icon museum, ul. Angel Kanchev 9 (Ангел Кънчев; open daily 7am-noon, 3-6pm).

Tryavna is generally not tourist-friendly. **Accommodations** are hard to come by, and English language **maps** and change bureaus are practically nonexistent. The **telephone city code** is 0677. The best way to get to Tryavna is to take one of the hourly **buses** from Gabrovo or the **train** from Veliko Turnovo (6 daily, 20Lv). If you spend the night, an acceptable option is the **Hotel/Restaurant Tryavna,** in the town center (tel. 34 48, fax 25 27; singles US$9, doubles US$14). The surprisingly good **restaurant** is open Mon.-Sun. noon-2pm and 6:30pm-midnight. There's a **movie theater** next to the hotel and many private **cafés** and **sweetshops** throughout the town, if you choose to shun hotel food.

NORTHERN BULGARIA

■ ■ ■ VELIKO TURNOVO
(ВЕЛИКО ТЪРНОВО)

Perched on the steep hills above the twisting Yantra River, **Veliko Turnovo** has been watching over Bulgaria for five thousand years. Its citizens led the national uprising against Byzantine rule in 1185; its fortress walls and battle towers have stood since the 12th to 14th centuries, when the warrior city was the capital of Bulgaria's Second Kingdom, an empire that defied Rome and Constantinople, and extended from the Black Sea to the Adriatic. After the overthrow of the Turks, the country's first constitution was signed here and named for the city. Lined with outdoor cafés and workshops, the lantern-lit streets of today's Veliko Turnovo wind from church to church through Bulgaria's biggest treasure trove of ruins.

ORIENTATION AND PRACTICAL INFORMATION

Veliko Turnovo is difficult to navigate; buy a new map and orient yourself by the fortress.

Tourist Office: Yantra Tourist, the privatized version of Balkantourist, is located next to the Hotel Etur (tel. 202 36 or 281 65). They have useful brochures and 50Lv maps of the city. Open Mon.-Fri. 8am-noon and 1-5:30pm.
Telephone City Code: 062.
Trains: Veliko Turnovo is about 8km off the main international train route. Trains stop in **Gorna Oryahovitza** (Горна Оряховица). There is continual bus service between Gorna Orechovitza and Veliko Turnovo (bus #10 or 14, 4Lv). There are six direct trains from Sofia to Veliko Turnovo's smaller train station as well; take bus #4 to get to the center.
Buses: The station is located on Nicola Gabrovski St. (Никола Габровски). Take bus #7 or 10 five stops to the center. **Private buses** will pick you up and drop you off in the center in front of the hotel Etur. There is a **Group Travel** bus company office there (tel. 282 92), open Mon.-Fri. 8:30am-12:30pm and 2-6pm). Group Travel buses to Gorna Orechovitza will drop you off at the Hotel Pachovetz (Хотел Паховец; tel. 301 50).
Public Transportation: The standard bus fare in Veliko Turnovo is 4Lv.
24-Hour Pharmacy: There is a 24-hr. pharmacy at ul. Vasil Levski 23 (Левски; tel. 302 68).
Emergency: tel. 150.

ACCOMMODATIONS

First, try to snag a **private room** arranged by **Yantra Tourist.** If that fails, there are plenty of affordable accommodations in and around the town.

Orbita Hotel, 15 Hristo Botev (Христо Ботев), fourth floor, just off the main square (tel. 220 41). It offers clean rooms with shared baths at amazingly cheap rates— US$2.60 per person.
Hotel Trapezitsa (Хотел Трапезица) houses an excellent **youth hostel** at ul. Stefan Stambolov 79 (Стефан Стамболов; tel. 220 61). All rooms have private bathrooms. Singles US$10, US$7 with ISIC. Doubles US$19, students US$16.
Hotel Etur, Ivalo St. 1, just off Stamboliiski in the center (tel. 218 38, fax 218 07), has great views and breakfast is included. US$12, US$19 with bath. Accepts Visa.
Hostel Momina Krepost (Момина Крепост), at the Ksilifor Itija (tel. 234 10, fax 234 41), is a picture-perfect hostel 4km from the city center; take bus #7 or 11 to the end of their routes, then walk about 2km up the hill. Singles with bath US$10. Doubles US$20. The complex contains a **restaurant** (open daily at 7:30am) and a **disco** which rocks nightly from 9pm until the early morning hours.
Hotel Stadium, ul. Todor Balina 24 (Тодор Балина) is just west of the center; take bus #7 or 11 (tel. 203 24, fax 223 92). Singles with shower US$9. Doubles US$17, with bath US$19.
Motel Sveta Gora (tel. 204 72, fax 302 85) provides cheap lodging about 2km west of town; take bus #14. Singles with shower US$11. Doubles US$15. Bungalows and camping are no longer available.
Private Hotel Vachev, Bacho Kiro 1 (Бачо Киро) is in the center (tel. 312 38). Located in a block of apartments, it offers rooms with TVs and refrigerators for US$20 (single or double).

FOOD

There's a *pazar* (market) at ul. Vasil Levski and ul. Dimitur Ivanov. Along **rakovska** are several taverns with homemade Bulgarian specialities. Many are closed Sundays.

Panorama Complex (Комплекс Панорама), offers window seats next door to Hotel Trapezitsa. A place for a superb meal complete with quick, friendly service and a fantastic view. Full meals under US$3. Open daily 6am-midnight.

Mehana Hadji Mincho (Механа Хаджи Минчо) is located in the small square across from the Hotel Trapezitsa. This is a fine place to sample *shishlik* (lamb kebab), *tarator* (cucumber yogurt and garlic soup), and live Bulgarian music. Have someone translate the history of the famous citizen of Veliko Turnovo, Hodji Mincho, written on the walls of the tavern. Full meal US$2.50. Open daily 6am-11:30pm).

Restaurant Etur (Етър), upstairs from the Hotel Trapezitsa, offers lots of organ-based dishes and salads. The place lacks personality, but there's live music every night (open daily 8am-until the last customer leaves). Also next to the hotel is a slick new **snack bar** which serves up desserts and amazing views of the Tsarquets Fortress. Open daily 8am-midnight.

Samovadska Krachma (Самовадска Къчма), ul. Rakovska 31 (Раковска) offers cheap traditional Bulgarian dishes (open Mon.-Sat. 10:30am-midnight).

SIGHTS AND ENTERTAINMENT

The ruins of the **Fortress Tsarevets** (Царевец), which once housed the royal palace and a cathedral, stretch across the top of an entire overgrown hill (open daily 8am-7pm; admission 50Lv). You can explore the battle towers and the newly-restored **Ascension Church**, which has some amazing murals, or stand on the rock from which traitors were hurled to their death. A ticket kiosk at the bottom of the hill sells brochures. The 1185 insurrection leading to the Second Bulgarian Kingdom was planned in **Church of St. Dimitri.** As you wander to or from the fortress, stop at the **Archeological Museum,** off ul. Ivan Vazov (Иван Вазов), which contains wonderful Thracian pottery, a fine collection of medieval crafts from the Turnovo ruins, and copies of the most famous Bulgarian religious frescoes (open Tues.-Sun. 9am-noon and 1-6pm; admission 50Lv). The light-blue building next to the Archeological Museum is the **Museum of the National Revival** (Музей на Възраждането). Come learn about Bulgaria's great cultural and religious resurgence of the 19th century, not to mention all the architecture you've seen (open daily 7am-noon and 1-5pm; winter daily 7am-noon and 1-6pm). You can see 20th-century depictions of Veliko Turnovo over the ages at the municipal **art museum,** situated on the peninsula within the river's bend. This is a great place from which to take a picture of the city (open daily 10am-6pm; admission 10Lv, students 5Lv, free for all on Thursdays).

On summer evenings there is sometimes a **sound and light show** held above Tsaravets Hill. Financial constraints have prevented the city from putting on nightly performance; check with Hotel Inter off Stamboliiski St. for performance dates. Rakovska St. is great for souvenir shopping. Many master craftspeople have shops on the lower floors of their homes. See them making colorful Bulgarian-style pottery and jewelry. At night the complex Poltava (Полтава) right on the main square has a **disco, movie theater,** and **casino.**

■ NEAR VELIKO TURNOVO: ARBANASI (АРБАНАСИ)

The 15th-century town of **Arbanasi** lies 4km from Veliko Turnovo. Its beautiful hilltop mansions built by wealthy Bulgarian traders have been turned into museums. The restored white houses resemble fortresses on the outside, but inside have murals dripping with color and intricately-carved wooden ceilings and furnishings. Todor Zhirkov, Bulgaria's long-time Communist leader, liked Arbanasi so much he had a residence built here. It has now been turned into a luxury resort.

The town is too small for street names. Your first stop should be the ticket kiosk. For 50Lv you can get tickets to the **Hadji Iliya House** (Хаджи Илиевата Къща), the **Constantziliev House** (Константилиевата Къща), and two **churches**—the Church of the Nativity of Christ (Рождество Христово) and the Church of Angels Gabriel and Michael (Арахангели Гавраил и Михаил). The houses are grand examples of 16th-century Bulgarian architecture. The Church of the Nativity of Christ was built in 1632-49 and contains original frescoes. Hire an English-speaking guide (100Lv) to supply the details (open daily 9am-noon and 1-5:30pm).

From Veliko Turnovo, take the Arbanasi bus (8 daily, 10Lv) leaving from the *pazar* (пазар) on Vasil Levski St. It will let you off in the center of Arbanasi. If you'd like to stay the night in quiet Arbanasi, go to the **Lambrinova House** (Ламбринова Къша) on the main street next to the **Paika Tavern** (Механа Паяка; tel. 351 53 or 342 57 and ask for Ivanka Nedelcheva). This private hotel is probably the best deal in the Veliko Turnovo area. Stay in an old Arbanasi house with beautifully hand-carved furniture and traditional Bulgarian decor for US$8 per person. The rooms have shared baths and eating facilities. Make reservations 2-3 days in advance. There are several **taverns** lining the main drag in Arbanasi; all offer fresh trout. Don't miss the impromptu **bazaar** lining the main street. Handmade wool sweaters and traditional embroidery are a bargain-hunter's dream come true.

■■■ RUSE (РУСЕ)

Eclectic and splendid, **Ruse** has always looked westward. For centuries, foreigners have drifted down the Danube into the city, bringing with them their strange and beautiful tastes in music, art, and architecture. Clever Ruse made the most of all the attention. Not only did the city adopt the Baroque, Renaissance, and Art Deco styles of its wordly guests, but it held dances, concerts, and performances for which it collected fees from Europe's *gliteratti* that were used to support underground revolutionary activity against Turkish oppression. Ruse is still known for its outstanding musical traditions which have made it the setting of Bulgaria's biggest symphonic music festival—the **March Musical Days** (Мартенски Музикални Дни).

A Thracian tribe first settled Ruse in the 6th-5th centuries BC. Later it was a Roman town known as *Seksaginta Prista* or "The Town of Sixty Ships." Even under the Ottoman occupation, Western European influences continued to float down the Danube to Ruse, then known as *Ruschuk*. The Danubian city saw the construction of the first railway line in Bulgaria (1864), the opening of the first bookstore (1867), the first movies (1897), and the first newspaper printed in Bulgarian. Built in the 1950s, the largest steel bridge in Europe stretches from Ruse across the Danube into Romania, a 2.8km long monument to socialist "friendship."

Today, one may come to the conclusion that Ruse has seen better days. International monitoring of the Danube, due to the war in the former Yugoslavia, has cut off the city from its traditional links to Western Europe. In addition, Ruse has become quite polluted due to huge industrial projects around the city and emissions from the chemical plant in the Romanian city of Giurgiu, just across the river.

ORIENTATION AND PRACTICAL INFORMATION

Tourist Office: Dunav Tours (Дунав Турс), 13 Rakovska (Раковска) right off pl. Svoboda (Свобода) should be your first stop (tel. 22 42 68 or 22 52 50, fax 27 71 77). Friendly and fluent in English, they can arrange **private accommodations** for a US$5 fee, provide maps and brochures, sell **tickets** to the opera, theatre, and anything else that may be going on in Ruse during your stay. You can hire a guide for US$4 per hour.

Currency Exchange: First Private Bank is located on the corner of ul. Alexandrovska (Александровска) and Ferdinandova (open Mon.-Fri. 8:15-11:30am and 1-3:30pm, Sat. 8:30am-1:30pm). They will cash **American Express** traveler's checks and change money. If you don't like their rates, go to any of the numerous **private change bureaus** on Alexandrovska.

Post Office: The central office is a little ways off pl. Svoboda (open Mon.-Fri. 7am-7pm, Sat. 7:30am-6pm, Sun. 8am-noon). **DHL** is located off the main square at ul. Petko Petkov 8 (Петко Петков; tel. 27 11 18; open Mon.-Fri. 9am-5:30pm). A letter to the USA costs US$36, to the United Kingdom US$30.

Telephones: At the central post office (open daily 7am-10pm). You can also send and receives **faxes** (fax 23 36 00). **City Code:** 082.

Photocopies: There is a **Xerox** copy center at 25 Knyazheska (tel./fax 22 23 20; open Mon.-Fri. 8am-8pm, Sat. 9:30am-4:30pm).

Film and Photo Developing: There is a **Fuji Film** on Alexandrovska, right off the square (open daily 9am-7:30pm).

Trains: Ruse can be reached by train from Bucharest (1 per day, 618Lv), Sofia (4 per day, 143Lv), Varna (2 per day, 84Lv), or Veliko Turnovo. The station is about 2km south of the city center. The **Rila** bureau is on the right side of the central post office at ul. Knyazheska 33 (Княжеска; tel. 22 39 20; open Mon.-Fri. 8am-noon and 1-6pm, Sat. 8am-2pm).

Buses: Ruse can be reached by bus from Sofia, Varna, or Veliko Turnovo. The station is adjacent to the train station. Only **private buses** go to Sofia. **Group Travel** has two offices in Ruse, one at the reception desk of the Dunav Hotel on the central square (tel. 22 65 18, ext. 120), the other at the bus station (hotel office open Mon.-Fri. 7:30am-noon and 1-4:30pm). Off hours, you can buy tickets from the hotel desk. Group Travel runs four daily trips to Sofia (175Lv one way). Some buses leave from the hotel, some from the bus station; check at an office.

Hydrofoil: There is service once per day to the Romanian city of Giurgiv, 500Lv. The station is on the Danube, a 5-minute walk from the Hotel Riga. Ferry service is expected to resume to Western European cities once military conflict in the former Yugoslavia ends.

Public Transportation: Buses and trolley buses cost 4Lv.

Taxis: Service is widely available.

Pharmacy: A pharmacy and clinic is located across from Hotel Helios on Nickolaevska 2 (Николаевска; open Mon.-Sat. 8am-7:30pm).

ACCOMMODATIONS

Private rooms are generally your best option; secure them at Dunav Tours. If none are available or you're otherwise inclined, try the options below.

Hotel Helios (Хелиос), Nikolaevska 1 (tel. 22 56 61); from Pl. Svoboda, walk past the post office on Alexandrovska to the end, walk diagonally through the park, and make a left on Nikolaevska. Try here if Dunav Tours is closed; they offer non-descript singles with laughably-small private baths for US$20. Doubles US$30.

Hotel Balkan (Хотел Балкан) is located on Alexandrovska, the primary street (tel. 27 91 89). The building is old and beautiful but in desperate need of renovation. Odoriferous singles with shared bath US$10. Doubles US$16.

Hostel Prista (Хижа Приста), located next to the campground, is a better bet (tel. 23 41 67). The hostel has an office in town at Knyazheska 1 so you can make reservations in advance (tel. 22 47 05; open Mon.-Fri. 9am-noon and 1-6pm). It's right on the Danube with great views and canoe rentals. Clean rooms with big beds. Ask for an HI discount. Lockout 11:30pm. US$4 per person.

Hotel/Restaurant Petrov (Петров) is located farther down the hill to the river (tel./fax 22 24 01). A small, private hotel, it has motor boat rentals, a restaurant, and great views. US$10 per room (singles or doubles).

Camping: Campground Ribarska Koliba (Рибарска Колиба) is 8km west of the city center (tel. 22 40 68). Hop on bus #6 or 16 from the city center. Ask to be let off at "Camping." Spartan but clean bungalows for US$3 per bed. Open April-Oct.

FOOD

Life in Ruse centers around **Ulitsa Alexandrovska** which is lined with shops, cafés, and restaurants, and extends from both sides of **Svoboda Square**. For a solid, inexpensive meal, stop at any of the restaurants along the main street. At one end of Alexandrovska is the **Asko-Denitsa** (Аско Деница) Department Store, a Bulgarian-German joint venture. At the other end is the Asko-Denitsa grocery store, the closest thing Bulgaria has to a Western-style **supermarket** (both open Mon.-Fri. 10am-7pm, Sat. 9am-2pm).

Restaurant Potsdam (Ресторант Потсдам), ul. Alexandrovska 79, to the east of the main square. Full meal US$3. Open daily 8am-midnight.

Restaurant Alibi (Алиби), Alexandrovska 128. The vegetarian in you will be pleased; it serves many salads, plus omelettes and desserts. Full meals US$3.

Dallas Dinner, Alexandrovska 43, is a new Tex-Mex place with western decor and country music. Pepper steaks, salsa, ribs, and a wide variety of beer. Enjoy a cold brewski at one of their outdoor picnic tables while listening to Kenny Rogers and watching the locals go about their business. Open daily 7am-11pm.

Sladkarnitsa Bosfor (Сладкарница Босфор), again on Alexandrovska, is across from the Asko-Dentista Department Store. Have some *boza* (pungent wheat drink) and Viennese pastries at this great bakery. Open daily 6am-10pm.

Panorama Café, at the top of the **Riga Hotel** on the Danube, serves up delicious mixed drinks and great views of the city. Open daily 6pm-3am.

Restaurant Ribarska Koliba, next to the campground of the same name, is a Ruse institution (tel. 22 43 57). A seafood place known for its fish soup (рибска чорба, 18Lv), it features bamboo ceilings and a wine cellar. Open 11am-until the last customer leaves.

Leventa (Левента) is Ruse's most renowned restaurant. Bus #17 takes you to the tallest TV tower in the Balkans, where Leventa sports 11 halls, each decorated in a different style. Try the **café-bar** on top of the tower for a fab view and delicious *torta zapaw* (chocolate cake). Reservations suggested. Nightly entertainment. Café open daily 4-11:30pm. Restaurant open daily 11:30am-midnight.

SIGHTS AND ENTERTAINMENT

At Pl. Svoboda you will find a beautiful Italian-style monument and a magnificent theater building reminiscent of Vienna. Unique to Ruse, however, is former Communist party headquarters, aptly named *Koraba* ("the ship") behind the statue on pl. Svoboda. To the left is the **Opera House** and next to it the **Holy Trinity Church** (Света Троица). Erected in 1632 during the Ottoman occupation, the church was prohibited from rising higher than any Turkish mosque in the city (main building open Sat.-Sun. 6am-8:30pm). Ruse is also home to one of the few Catholic churches in Bulgaria—**St. Paul's Church** (Свети Павел), currently under reconstruction.

In the evening, Ruse's most popular park, **Mladezhki Park** (Младежки Парк) on the eastern side of the city, is a nice place for a stroll. At night, try one of the **movie theaters** on Aneksandrovska or the lovely **discos** in the Riga and Dunav hotels. Dunav Tours can arrange for a guide to show you the city. You can also buy opera and **theatre** tickets through them at the ridiculously low price of US$0.50. If you are in Ruse in March, don't forget the festivities of the **March Music Days;** tickets through Dunav Tours are just US$1.

A day trip from Ruse will take you to the **Rock Monasteries of Ivanovo,** 18km from the city center. Medieval chapels and monastic cells await carved into mountain sides; they contain unique frescoes from the 13th and 14th centuries which are on UNESCO's list of world cultural heritage. You can't get here by public transportation; an organized trip is run by Dunav Tours (US$20 including lunch and guide).

■■■ SHOUMEN (ШУМЕН)

The only reasons to venture to tired and dusty **Shoumen** are its brewery and proximity to Bulgaria's most treasured archaeological sites at **Preslav, Pliska,** and **Madora.** The **Tombul Mosque,** just minutes from the Shoumen Hotel, was built in 1744. It features a beautiful gray stone courtyard which will make you forget that you are in the industrial heartland of Bulgaria (open daily 9:15am-4:15pm). Shoumen's history reaches back to the early 10th century; it is apparently named for Bulgarian King Simeon (864-927 AD).Three buses per day run from the train station to the **Shoumen Fortress** (Шуменска Крепост), built by the Thracians in the 5th century BC and later used by the Romans and Byzantines (open Mon.-Fri. 8am-6pm, Sat.-Sun. 8am-2pm). After dark, dance the night away under the stars in the open air **disco** "La Strada" next to the bus station. Or choose the more refined "Terminator 2" disco at the Shoumen Hotel.

The **tourist office** is located next to the Shoumen Hotel (tel. 553 13, fax 525 91). They can arrange **private accommodations** for US$6 and also provide maps of the city. The **post office** is on Slavyanska St. (ул. Славянска), the main drag in Shoumen (open Mon.-Fri. 8am-noon and 1-5pm). **Telephones** are available at the post office (daily 7am-10:45 pm); the **city code** is 054. **Faxes** can be received at the post office (fax 500 22). Shoumen is linked to Sofia and Varna by **bus** and **train**. The stations are directly across from each other; take bus #1 to the city center. **Group Travel** offers private buses to all of Bulgaria. They have an office is on Pl. Oborishte across from the Shoumen Hotel (tel. 330 79; open Mon.-Fri. 9am-5:30pm) and a kiosk at the bus station (tel. 627 17); buses leave from both locations.

If you plan ahead and arrange a voucher with Balkantourist in Sofia, you can stay at the classy **Hotel Shoumen** (tel. 591 41, fax 581 34; singles US$20, doubles US$26, breakfast included). Otherwise head for the well-hidden **Orbita Hotel** at Kyuoshk-ovete Park (tel. 563 74). Take bus #6 or 10 from the center. They offer singles with private bath for 160Lv, but you'll probably need reservations and patience to deal with the potential odors from the small petting zoo next door.

Along Slavyanska you'll find lots of places to eat and relax. Try **Café Mural** (Мирал), offering Turkish coffee and sweets in the courtyard and computer poker games inside. The Shoumen Hotel Restaurant has a menu in English and offers specialities like "Irish Magic," a pork filet in a pancake for 190Lv (open daily 6am-1am). The best restaurant in town is probably the **Popsneytanova House** (Попшейтанова Кыща), on Pl. Oborishte next to the Shoumen Hotel (tel. 574 02). A touristy, Bulgarian folk tavern, it has live music nightly and specialities like *starata kushta* (старата кыща), a filet with cheeses, mushrooms, and tomatoes for 90Lv. For a real treat, drop by the restaurant of the **Shoumen Brewery** just across from the Orbita Hotel where they make the famous Shoumen beer (Шуменско Пиво). Ask for a "*shoumensko special*"—you'll get a huge draft beer for 12Lv (open daily 11am-11pm).

■ NEAR SHOUMEN

Pliska (Плиска), the first Bulgarian capital (681-893), lies 23km northeast of Shoumen. **Buses** run from Shoumen to Pliska hourly (13Lv). A huge archaeological **excavation** has unearthed parts of palaces and fortifications. The dig is about 3km from the village but public transportation is non-existent. If you ask around one of the locals is bound to give you a ride, if you don't want to make the hike. The Pliska Motel is closed, no matter what locals say.

Preslav (Преслав), 18km from Shoumen, became the **second Bulgarian capital** in 893. **Buses** run from Shoumen to Preslav hourly (13Lv). Go first to the **Archaeological Museum** (tel. (054) 32 43) where you can hire a guide to take you to the ruins which consist of the **Golden Temple** (built in 908) and the ruins of the **Palace of Tsar Simeon** (museum open daily 9am-4pm; admission 50Lv). If you decide to stay the night, your only option is the **Hotel Preslav** (tel. (054) 25 08). Clean, comfortable singles US$10. Doubles and apartments US$20. The hotel also has a currency exchange and a restaurant with a beautiful courtyard.

Madara (Мадара) is 16km east of Shoumen, and believe it or not was *not* the third Bulgarian capital. However, it is the home of the famous **stone relief** "Madara Horseman." On a vertical cliff, 25m above the ground, the life-size relief features a horse with rider, a lion, and a dog. The artist is unknown, but the work was done in the 8th century and supposedly symbolizes the victories of the Bulgarian ruler Han Tervel over his enemies. Take a bus from Shoumen, and hike about 30min. from the village center. The Tourist Office in Shoumen can provide you with more information.

■■■ PLEVEN (ПЛЕВЕН)

A medium-sized city 175km northeast of Sofia, Pleven is a living monument to the Russian-Turkish War of 1877-1878. There are more than 150 monuments of different sizes and forms to the Battle of Pleven (1877) which was a turning point in the fight for Bulgarian liberation from the Turks.

BULGARIA

Orientation and Practical Information   From Sofia, take one of the two daily **buses** (111Lv) or eight **trains** (109Lv). If your bus stops in **Yablenitsa** (Яблаиица) on the way to Pleven, be sure to pick up some of the town's famed *Halva* (Халва; a huge container of the sesame dessert costs US$2 at any of the kiosks along the road). **Balkan Tourist,** at the southernmost point of the main square at 3 San Stefano St. (tel. 237 56), has maps of the city and arranges private rooms. **Exchange money** and deal in American Express travelers checks at the **Bulgarian Post Bank** in the main square (open Mon.-Fri. 8:30am-noon and 1:30-3:30pm). En route to Balkan Tourist is the **post office** (open Mon.-Fri. 8am-noon, 1-5pm) where international **telephone** calls and **faxes** (fax 475 05) can be made 7am-10pm every day. The **telephone city code** is 064. **Group Travel** runs two buses to and from Pleven. There's no office yet, so buy the ticket from the driver. The bus and train stations are located next to each other, a short walk from the main square **Svobodata** (Площад на Свободата). In the official-looking building across from the Mausoleum (4th floor, room 401), the U.S. Peace Corps has a **business center** where you can watch **CNN** (open Mon.-Fri. 9am-5pm).

Accommodations and Food   Private rooms from Balkantourist are the cheapest option (US$6). Otherwise, you'll have to choose between two overpriced Stalinist blocks. One is the musty two-star **Rostov na Don** (*Rostov na Don;* tel. 238 92). Singles US$17, doubles US$28; most credit cards are accepted. Downstairs are a bar, restaurant, change bureau, and disco. The other hotel in town is the classier but just as musty **Hotel Pleven**, near the bus/train station (tel. 301 81, fax 383 13; singles US$25, doubles $36).

A memorable meal can be had at **Mehana Staria Oreh** (Механа Стария Орех; "Old Walnut Tavern") in the main square. Grab a seat in the garden next to the mural showing a priest eyeing a barmaid in a miniskirt. The specialty is the "Old Walnut"—a pork filet stuffed with mushrooms and cheese and shaped into a walnut, a bargain at US$1.40 (tel. 335 06; open daily 11am-10:30pm). The most famous (and touristed) restaurant in Pleven is **Peshterata** (Пещерата), 3km from town in **Kailika Pork** (Кайлъка; tel. 225 72). The restaurant is usually packed with wedding parties, but they'll make room for you. Enjoy traditional Bulgarian specialties in the restaurant built into a sandstone cave. The menu is in English. Take a taxi, or trolleybus #1, 3, or 7 from the center (open 24 hrs.).

Sights   The granddaddy of sights in Pleven is the **Panorama** which depicts the third Russo-Turkish Battle of Pleven and the liberation of Bulgaria. The four halls of murals show the history of the Bulgarian liberation. Be sure to hire a guide—it makes all the difference (US$4). From the city center take bus #1, 9, or 12 to the next to last stop, then hike up the hill (open Tues.-Sun. 9am-5:30pm; students 25Lv, free on Thurs.). The **Mausoleum** of Russian and Romanian Soldiers, built in 1902-04, is across from the post office. Inside are frescoes, ancient icons, and a vault holding the remains of many soldiers. Call ahead (tel. 235 69) to arrange a tour in English for 30Lv (open Tues.-Sun. 8am-6pm; museum free). Further down on the main square is the former **Turkish bath,** an orange and white structure with key-hole shaped doors and windows which is occasionally used as an art gallery.

The **Museum of the Liberation of Pleven** (Музей на освобождението Плевен 1877) is actually a small ethnographic museum. In December 1877, the Turkish General Osman Pasha handed over his sword to the "Tsar Liberator" the Russian Alexander II after the Turkish defeat at Pleven; the Tsar then gave the sword back out of respect for the general (open Tues.-Sun. 8am-noon and 2-6pm; admission 15Lv). Next door is the **Church of St. Nicholas,** which doubles as an icon museum. Service at 8am and 5pm daily. The church was built in 1834, two meters under sea level in compliance with a requirement that no church be higher than the local mosques. The holes in the walls and ceiling hold more than 600 clay pots built to enhance the acoustics of the structure. The huge **historical museum** is minutes by foot from the center (tel. 235 69 or 235 02). If you don't feel like walking take trolley #5 or 9

(3Lv). (Museum open Tues.-Sat. 8am-noon and 12:30-5:30pm. Admission 40Lv. An English-speaking guide costs US$5.) Across the street is the **City Art Gallery** on Skobolev Square #1 (tel. 300 30; open Mon.-Sat. 9am-5:30pm; free).

■■■ VIDIN (ВИДИН)

Baba Vida fortress (Баба Вида), the only intact medieval fortress in Bulgaria, stands on the site of ancient Roman ruins in Vidin, only 30km from Serbia. According to legend, the fortress, complete with a moat and towers, was built by the vain daughter of a powerful Bulgarian tsar. After refusing the eligible Slavic bachelors who came to court her, the princess died a lonely old maid behind the fortress walls (open Mon.-Fri. 8am-noon and 2pm-5:30pm, Sat.-Sun. 9am-noon and 2pm-5:30pm; admission 20Lv). The huge onion domes towering over the town square belong to the **church of St. Dimitir** which holds services every morning at 8am. A National Revival building at the west end of the main square houses the **archaeological museum** (open Tues.-Sun. 9am-noon and 2-6pm) and the **history museum** (open Tues.-Sat. 9am-noon and 1:30-5:30pm). On the Danube across from the Hotel Bonina is the **Art Gallery** (open Tues.-Fri. 8:30am-12:30pm and 2-7pm, Sat. 8:30am-12:30pm). After you've explored the museums and ruins, grab an ice cream and stroll along the Danube. Across the river in **Kalafat** Romanians are doing the same thing.

The **main square** is two blocks behind the post office. At 2 Dondukov (Дондуков) is a run down and less than helpful **Balkan Tourist** office (tel. 228 00 or 249 76; open Mon.-Fri. 8am-noon and 1-5pm). **Exchange money** at the First Private Bank, through the gate from the 7th-century **Stambul Kapiy** (Стамбул Капия; Istanbul Gate) at the northern side of the main square (open Mon.-Fri. 9-11:30am and 2-4:30pm). Across from the train station is the **post office** (open Mon.-Fri. 7:30am-noon and 2pm-5:30pm). You can make international **telephone** calls from 7am-9:30pm daily and send **faxes** Mon.-Fri. 7:30am-noon and 1-6:30pm. Five **trains** run between Vidin and Sofia daily (US$3). **Group Travel,** across from the train station (tel. 279 87), sends two **buses** per day to Sofia (US$4). State buses no longer run but the bus station next door houses the town's only **private room agency.** Look for the sign "Частни Квартири" in the small **pharmacy.** Both the bus and train stations have **luggage storage** (Гардероб).

The **Hostel Bononia** (Туристически Дом Бонония; tel. 228 13), off the main square on Isicra 3 (Искра), has newly-furnished rooms with TV and refrigerator. Lockout coincides with the early morning closing of the **disco** downstairs; check for times. (Singles US$14, US$8 with HI card. Doubles US$21, US$14 with HI card.) Built into the back of the Stambul Gate, the **Bar/Restaurant Lago Di Garda** (tel. 201 46) is a cool and cave-like Italian restaurant serving salads and pork filet stuffed with cheese, mushrooms, and ham, covered in tomato sauce (US$1.85; open daily 9am-until the last customer leaves). **Venetzianski Sklad** (Бенешиански Склад, "Venetian Warehouse"), next to Baba Vida (tel. 222 98), is a restaurant, bar, and nightclub in an underground weapons warehouse built by Romans in the 4th century (open daily 7pm-dawn). **Sgt. Pepper's Lonely Heart's Club,** Stefan Karadja St. 13 (Стефан Караджа, tel. 346 42), is a tiny bar that plays only Fab Four music (open daily 10am-until the last Beatlemaniac leaves).

BLACK SEA COAST

The Black Sea is a sentimental journey through the sweet stuff of every Bulgarian's life: bare-bottomed childhood vacations, summer jobs flipping *kebabche,* first loves and second loves and... The many campgrounds and "international youth centers" have long been popular with young party-bound Eastern Europeans; for years the coast was the only place Bulgarians could come in contact with the West. Today, ancient ruins, modern resorts, fishing villages, sandy beaches, and every sport from para-sailing to horseback riding remain within the budget traveler's reach. **Varna** and **Burgas** are the principal transportation centers. From there you'll have to decide whether to go north or south. Go north if you like rocky cliffs and small villages; go south for seaside campgrounds and untouched beaches.

The sad cement empire of resorts built by Balkantourist to lure the hard currency of western vacationers isn't quite up to western standards but; still, it's too expensive for many locals. The hotels are somewhat-pricey tourist ghettos crammed with flabby, middle-aged East Europeans and Germans. The facilities are showing their age and security tends to be lax. Still, the sporting facilities and nightlife of resorts like **Sunny Beach, Albena,** and **Golden Sands** can't be beat. To meet Bulgarian vacationers, head to the bungalows and campgrounds instead. A good vacation strategy is to do what the Bulgarians do: rent a **private room** (US$4-6) or **bungalow** (US$3-10) in one of the small fishing hamlets or campgrounds that dot the coast and then commute by bus or hike along the beach to jet ski, sunbathe, and party.

The coast is tourist-heavy in July and August; crowds and the high prices they inspire can be avoided by vacationing in May or September. **Train** travel from Sofia is cheap (US$4) but excruciatingly crowded and slow; **buses** are quicker (5-6hrs.), more comfortable, and cost about the same. Along the coast, frequent but crowded buses run between most points of interest. The resorts run **minivans** from the major villages and cities (US$0.50). Due to low demand there was no hydrofoil service operating along the coast in June, 1994. Street names are often—thankfully—written in the Latin script, and many signs are even in English and German.

Love is free and rampant on Bulgaria's biggest pick-up scene; unfortunately, birth-control and disease-protection is not. Pack your own along with sunscreen and bug spray—the mosquitoes can be merciless.

■■■ VARNA (ВАРНА)

Varna has been crawling with sunburned Greek sailors since 600 BC, when it was a young port city known as Odessos. By the time the Romans arrived in the 2nd century AD, Varna was busy trading and doing all the things that cosmopolitan cultural centers do. These days, Bulgaria's third-largest city and "sea capital" harbors an alluring old town, seaside gardens, and a beach ideal for Rollerblading. Every August, Varna chills out during its **International Jazz Festival.**

ORIENTATION AND PRACTICAL INFORMATION

Although Varna is a sprawling city, the major points of interest are close together and the Latin script on the street signs makes the city easier to navigate.

Tourist Office: Balkantourist has been transformed into several small travel agencies in Varna. One of the best is **Varnenski Bryag Co.** (Варненски Бряг; tel. 22 55 24, fax 25 30 83). The English-speaking clerks have maps for sale, transportation information, and can arrange **private accommodations** for US$5-6 per night depending on the location of the room. Open summer daily 8am-9pm, winter Mon.-Sat. 8am-6pm. To get there from the train station, go through the underpass and walk straight up the street onto which it opens, ul. Tsar Simeon I, until you come to the large Independence Sq. (пл. Независимост). The bureau is on the 2nd side street to your right, at ul. Musala 3. They have another, less helpful branch right across from the train station at Slaveykov Sq. 6 (пл. Славейков; tel. 22 22 06), open summer Mon.-Sun. 8am-6pm.

Currency Exchange: Try First Private Bank at blvd. Slivnitsa 16 (пл. Сливница; tel./fax 23 90 25), open Mon.-Fri. 9:30am-2pm and 3-5pm; on Sat. they have a small branch open at the train station. There are also private **change bureaus** lurking in every corner of the city.

American Express: There is a branch at Megatours, Slivnitsa 33, right off the main drag, Knyaz Boris I (tel. 22 00 47 or 22 00 58, fax 22 00 61). They will hold client mail, sell traveler's checks for a 1% fee, and give cash advances for 4.5%. Open

The Black
Sea Coast

BULGARIA

Black Sea

COASTAL TOWNS

1 Periprava	17 Eforie Sud 🏖🏕	33 Bålgarevo	49 Nesebâr 🏖🏕
2 C.A. Rosetti	18 Vasile Roaită	34 Tuzlata 🏖🏕	50 Ravda
3 Sulina 🏖	19 Costineşti	35 Balčik 🏕	51 Pomorie 🏕
4 Dunevăţo de Jos 🏕	20 Neptun 🏖	36 Albena 🏖🏕	52 Saratovo
5 Babadag 🏕	21 Jupiter 🏖🏕	37 Kranevo 🏕	53 Burgas 🏖
6 Jurilovca	22 Venus 🏖🏕	38 Zlatni pjasăci 🏖🏕	54 Krajmarie 🏕
7 Sinoie	23 Saturn 🏖	39 Družba 🏖🏕	55 Černomorec 🏕
8 Istria	24 Mangalia	40 Varna 🏖	56 Sozopol 🏖🏕
9 Săcele	25 Jama Veche	41 Galata 🏕	57 Primorsko 🏖🏕
10 Corbu	26 Durankulak	42 Kamčija 🏖🏕	58 Kiten 🏕
11 Mamaia-Sat 🏕	27 Krapec 🏕	43 Novo Orjahovo 🏕	59 Lozenec 🏕
12 Mamaia Băi 🏖	28 Šabla 🏕	44 Škorpilovci 🏕	60 Mičurin 🏕
13 Constanţa 🏖	29 Tjulenovo	45 Bjala 🏕	61 Varvata
14 Cumpăna	30 Kamen brjag	46 Obzor 🏖🏕	62 Ahtopol 🏕
15 Agigea 🏖	31 Sveti Nikola	47 Emona 🏕	63 Sinemorec 🏕
16 Eforie Nord 🏖	32 Rusalka 🏖	48 Slančev brjag 🏕	64 Rezovo 🏕

🏖 Towns with beach   🏕 Towns with campsite nearby

Mon.-Fri. 9am-6pm, Sat. 9am-noon. This may be the only place on the Black Sea Coast that honors the American Express card.

Post Office: Behind the Cathedral. Open Mon.-Fri. 7am-7pm, Sat. 7:30am-7pm, Sun. 8am-noon.

Telephones: In the post office; open daily 7am-10pm. **City Code:** 052.

Faxes: Can be sent and received at the post office (fax 440 30), open Mon.-Fri. 7am-8:30pm, Sat. 8am-2pm.

Photocopies: You can not only make copies but also rent rooms (US$6) at a shop at Sheypovo 4 (Шейпово), right off Knyaz Boris I (tel. 23 31 75), open Mon.-Fri. 8:30am-5:30pm.

Film and Photo Developing: Try the one-hour studio at Knyaz Boris I 34. Open summer daily 9am-10pm, winter daily 9am-7pm.

Flights: If you're heading to or from the airport, take bus #50 to/from the Cathedral (tel. 442 32).

Trains: Varna's train station, the **Gare Centrale,** is located near the port on ul. Devnya (Девня). Six trains daily travel to Sofia (US$4.80). There is a helpful **Rila** international trains bureau at ul. Shipka 3 (Шипка; tel. 22 62 73), a side street off ul. Knyaz Boris I. Open Mon.-Fri. 8am-4:30pm.

Buses: Group Travel buses stop just across the street from the train station. Five daily buses to Sofia (US$4.35) and connections along the coast. The main office is located on Varna's main pedestrian walkway at ul. Knyaz Boris 6 (Княз Борис I; tel. 25 67 34), open daily 8:30am-7pm. Bus #41 (5Lv) will take you from the train station to the bus station.

Hydrofoil: Service may be available in 1995. Check at the port next to train station.

Public Transportation: The Cathedral is a major stopping point for shuttle buses between the main resorts; look for the name of your resort on the front of the bus or minivan (tickets US$0.50). Take bus #1 or trolley #82 or 86 from the train station to the Cathedral.

Taxis: A central congregation point is outside the train station.

Luggage Storage: Drop your bags at the **Garderob** (Гардероб) at the train station (5Lv per bag per day), open daily 6am-10:30pm.

Pharmacy: A well stocked pharmacy is located at Knyaz Boris I 29 (tel. 22 22 87), open Mon.-Sat. 7:30am-8pm.

ACCOMMODATIONS

There may be more **private room bureaus** in Varna than there are private rooms. At least it may seem that way in the peak season, when many agencies are reluctant to rent rooms for a single night stay. If you are traveling in July or August, it's best to reserve a room ahead of time. If you strike out at **Varnenski Bryag,** try the agency right in the train station. They have no phone and their hours are scheduled around major train arrivals. They charge US$6 per night and will accompany you via public transportation to your room (open Mon.-Fri. 6am-10pm, Sat. 8am-10pm, Sun. 6-10pm). There are several private room bureaus on Knyaz Boris i. Look for the sign *"Chastni Kvartiri"* (Частни Квартири). Prices range from US$4-6 per night, and most of them double as change bureaus. Remember that the train station is closed every night from 11:30pm-4:30am, so napping there is not even an option. In summer, if everything is booked, travelers often crash in the park next to the train station.

Orbita Hotel, Tsar Osvoboditel 25 (tel. 22 51 62, fax 25 92 88), and **Hotel Odessa,** Blvd. Slivnitsa 1 (tel. 22 83 81, fax 25 30 88), are major landmarks but demonstrate why Varna is not known as a cornucopia of budget hotels; singles are overpriced at $45 and $35, respectively.

Hotel Idilia (Идилия), 3 Bratya Skorpil (Братя Шкорпил), is a better bet, a short walk from the center (tel. 23 20 92). This private hotel has clean rooms with private baths for US$16.50 per person.

Hotel Orel (Орел), 131 Blvd. Primorski (Приморски), along the seaside gardens. Huge rooms with shared baths for US$20 per person, breakfast included (tel. 22 42 30, fax 25 92 95). There's a 24-hr. café and a packaged goods place downstairs, so you'll never be out of luck when the craving for an *Astika* beer strikes.

Hotel Musala, ul. Musala 3 (Мусала), next door to the tourist bureau, is unattractive but cheap (tel. 22 39 25). Showers off the hall. Singles with basin US$12. Doubles with basin US$18. If you're traveling alone, the management might want to put someone in your extra bed.

FOOD

The pedestrian boulevards Knyaz Boris I and Slivnitsa swarm with cafés, kiosks, and vendors selling everything from foot-long hot dogs (US$0.33) to roasted nuts, fruit, corn-on-the-cob, cotton candy, and lots of ice cream. Varna is a great place to pick up a bottle of locally-produced *Albena* champagne (US$1 per bottle).

The Dragon (Дракона), on Bld. Slivnitsa across from the AmEx office (tel./fax 25 04 42), is a new chinese restaurant. It's a bit pricey by Bulgarian standards, but you can find lots of duck dishes and vegetarian specialties for under US$2. They take Visa and AmEx. Menu in English. Ask for chopsticks.

Restaurant Musala (Мусала), on the main square is a bright, airy, and efficient. Try the ghoulash (42Lv) on a brisk Varna evening (open daily 10:30am-11pm).

Orbita Hotel Restaurant, Tsar Osvoboditel 25, is a great place to have an omelette or any of a number of imaginative organ-based dishes with the many Eastern European youth groups that frequent the place. Prices are cheap, portions are large, and the amount of beer served tends to overcome all language barriers. Open daily 7am-11pm. After closing time, everyone heads to the disco next door to conduct some international relations.

SIGHTS AND ENTERTAINMENT

As you stroll along Varna's **Seaside Gardens,** have a look inside the **Marine Museum** (Военно-морски Музей; tel. 22 26 55), which presents the history of navigation on the Black Sea and the Danube River open 10am-5:30pm; admission 50Lv, additional charge for permission to take photos). Also check out the **Aquarium** (Аквариум; open Mon. noon-5pm, Tues.-Sat. 9am-7pm; admission 20Lv). The **Dolphinarium,** in the northern part of the park (tel. 88 14 92), has two 30-minute shows. Take bus #8, 9, or 14 (Tues.-Sun. at 11am and 3pm). Hidden among the many fountains, trees, and old men charging a few Leva to weigh you on their bathroom scales in the seaside gardens, you'll find an absolutely gorgeous, vine-covered **open-air theatre,** the home of international ballet competitions and festivals every year (tel. 22 83 85). Theatre performances take place May-October. You can buy tickets (150Lv) at the gate or at the ticket office near the Cherno More hotel (Хотел Черно Море).

In the old part of the city, known as the Greek neighborhood (Гръцка Махала), you can see the impressive **Roman baths** (Римски Терми; open summer Mon.-Sat. 10am-5pm, open winter Tues.-Sat. 10am-5pm; admission 30Lv). The second-largest cathedral in the country, **Sv. Bogoroditsa,** is in the center of the city, across from the post office. Built in 1882-86 in honor of the Russian soldiers who fought for the liberation of Bulgaria, it has services daily at 8am and 5pm. On 1 ul. L. Karavelov (Л. Каравелов) near the cathedral you can have a look at the exquisite **art gallery** (tel. 24 31 23). Chamber concerts are held here; inquire at the tourist bureau for a schedule (open Tues.-Sun. 10am-7pm; the sign "free day Monday" means it's closed then.)

The **History Museum** at 41 Primorski Polk (Приморски Полк) presents the cultural history of Varna (open Tues.-Sun. 10am-6pm). There's yet another **Ethnographic Museum** (Етнографски Музей) at 22 ul. Panagyurishte (ул. Панагюрище) housed in a traditional National Revival-era structure (tel. 22 00 98; open Tues.-Sun. 10am-5pm; admission 40Lv). You can't miss the imposing red **Opera House** on the main square (tel. 22 33 88). The schedule is reduced in summer months. Inquire at the ticket office in front; to make reservations call 22 30 89. Performances start at 7:30pm; tickets are 50Lv.

Varna's **beach** can be reached through the Seaside Gardens. There is a nominal 10Lv charge to get through the many gates. Trying to sneak in is not worth the hassle of the beach bouncers who take their jobs very seriously. On the beautiful, sandy family-dominated beaches you can rent umbrellas for 10Lv and store your stuff for

20Lv. For more serious sunbathing and lots of watersports, head to one of the nearby resorts. **Nightlife** centers around Pl. Nezavisimost and along ul. Knyaz Boris I. A very popular hangout for younger crowds is the festival complex (Фестивалния Комплекс) which houses a movie theater and a disco. The disco at the Orbita Hotel is popular with Eastern European backpackers (open nightly 11pm-sunrise). In the summer a good number of discos and bars open up by the beach.

■■■ NEAR VARNA

ALADZHA MONASTERY AND EVKSINOGRAD

Known as the *"skalen"* (rock) monastery, **Aladzha Monastery** (Аладжа Манастир) was carved out of the side of a nearby mountain (open Tues.-Sun. 10am-5pm; admission 5Lv). Bus #29 from the Cathedral in Varna will drop you off at the foot of a hill a few minutes trek from the monastery. On your way back down, have a snack at the small café that serves crab cocktail and fried fish. Also at the bottom of the hill is **Lovna Sreshta** (Ловна Среща), where you can dine on wild boar (US$2.80), stewed pheasant (US$3.40), or frogs' legs (US$2.20; tel. 85 51 90). During the summer they have a nightly outdoor folk show featuring the *"Nestinari dancers"*—women who walk barefoot on hot coals (open daily 11am-2am).

Also close to Varna is the former royal and later high Communist officials' residence, **Evksinograd** (tel. 86 12 41). Reached by bus #9, it might blow your mind with its meticulously kept park. It's best to call ahead to reserve a place (tours start on the hour; admission 40Lv). While there, pick up a bottle of wine or brandy produced at the famous Evksinograd **winery.**

GOLDEN SANDS (ЗЛАТНИ ПЯСЬЗИ)

The beaches here are truly exquisite, but in July and August you'll have to fight for a spot on the Golden Sands, 17km north of Varna. A monstrous complex of 74 hotels, numerous cottages and campgrounds, 30 restaurants, 30 discos, 70 stores, and more, it was built in the architectural style only Stalin could love, but still attracts hordes of tourists—you'll either love it or hate it. To get there from Varna, hop on **bus #9,** which leaves every half hour and stops near the center (by the cathedral) and by the Cherno More Hotel (15Lv each way). You can also take any of the private minivans leaving from the cathedral. Your first stop should be the 24-hr. **reception** and accommodation office (tel. 85 56 81, fax 85 55 87) that will provide you with an invaluable map of the resort and can arrange pricey **hotel rooms** (singles $46) or more affordable **bungalows** (US$10) in the camping areas.

Admission to the resort and its beaches is free. To use the many facilities, you pay as you go. The resort features a **post office** where you can also make international **telephone** calls and send **faxes;** a 24-hr. **polyclinic** which gives injections for unspecified purposes for US$2.50; **laundry** facilities; and **photocopy** services. You can play **tennis** (US$4.80 per hour); **windsurf** (US$4.80 per hour); **waterski** (US$3.81 per 5min.); **bowl** (US$1.85 per hour); work out in the state-of-the-art **fitness center** (US$4.40 per hour); play **miniature golf;** or take **Bulgarian language lessons.** At night, grasp your map of the resort and experience some of the varied nightlife. Hear folk music at the **Gypsy Hideaway** (Цигански Табор), try some *souvlaki* at **Dionysos,** a Greek tavern; don some *Lederhosen* at **DAB,** a **German Beer Hall;** or try some warm beer at the **Golden Lion,** an English pub. Later, spin the roulette wheel at the **Shipka Casino,** or dance to the fierce rhythms at the **Astoria Disco.** All this, and no danger from predatory animals (or so the brochures reassure).

ALBENA

Brand new and slicker than slickers, Albena is strikingly unique in appearance and atmosphere. The seaside string of 36 modern family-oriented hotels is located 14km north of Golden Sands. Rent-a-cops and a steep parking tax keep mobile day-trippers to a minimum, so Albena is usually less crowded than the larger resorts. The facilities include **horseback riding, waterskiing, windsurfing, fishing, bowling,** and **mineral baths.** Every year international **chess** and **volleyball tournaments** are held here. The resort has 7km of beach, 27 restaurants, 32 bars, and five discos and nightclubs from which to choose. The neon-pink eyesore at the entrance of the resort is the **Variete Casino Albena** featuring international and Bulgarian performers nightly.

Regular buses and minivans serve Albena from the Cathedral in Varna. Stop by the **accommodations office** to pick up a map or arrange a deluxe bungalow in the campground (singles US$18, breakfast included) or a lower priced hotel room inevitably perched high atop the resort, about 10min. from the sea (US$20, breakfast included). The **telephone city code** is 5722. For reservations and information dial 29 20, fax 22 03. The resort has the normal conveniences such as a **post office, business center, polyclinic** and **pharmacy, markets, souvenir shops,** and a **cinema.** You can watch CNN in the information office 9am-9pm.

■■■ DOBROUDJA (ДОБРУДЖА)

Dobroudja, the northernmost part of the Bulgarian coast, belonged to Romania between the two world wars. Today some villagers still remember the "Romanian Occupation" and can still speak the Romanian language they were forced to learn in school. You'll see the Romanian influence in the many Gypsies that wander the streets with violins and dancing bears.

BALCHIK (БАЛЧИК)

Balchik looks almost too beautiful to be true with its white houses and orange roofs carved into the rocky cliffs. Winding roads and crooked stairways will patiently lead you to the village's sun-kissed beaches. This small, sleepy fishing village is a perfect base for a northern Black Sea vacation. Here, you'll have most of the conveniences of a town but without the high prices and crowds. The Romanian Queen Maria had her summer residence built here after World War I. You can tour the **Palace** and **Botanical Gardens** and marvel at the confusion of architectural styles that pervades the complex. The main building even has a **minaret**—which local lore says was built by the queen in honor of her Turkish lover. The botanical gardens boast a breathtaking **rose garden** and plenty more thorns in the largest **cactus collection** in the Balkans. Walk south along the beach 2km from the port or take one of the little trains that leave hourly from the center. (Open daily 9am-8:30pm; 5Lv. Palace open daily during the summer 8am-8pm, in winter daily 8am-5pm. Admission 50Lv.)

To get to Balchik from Varna, take any of the northern-bound buses from Varna's Central Bus Station. The sign on the front of the bus should read "Balchik" ("Балчик"). You can also hop on a bus from the Albena resort. In the summer these buses run hourly. The **telephone city code** is 0579. There is no private accommodation agency in Balchik and Balkantourist has closed up shop. To find a room, go first to **Hotel Esperanza** (Хотел Есперанса) on the main drag, Cherno Moré St. 16 (ул. Черно Море; tel. 57 48). This is a small private hotel with high ceilings, spacious rooms, shared baths, and a monarchist motif (US$5.55 per person). You can negotiate for homemade meals and room service. The proprietress also runs a pseudo-private room bureau; if the hotel is booked, she'll try to find another place for you to stay.

You can also try the hotel **Dionysopolsis** (Хотел Дионисополис) on the beach at Primorska 1 (Приморска; tel./fax 21 75). The hotel has seen better days, but is perfectly acceptable. All rooms have private baths. (Singles US$5.15. Doubles US$6.50.) The hotel also houses a restaurant, panorama bar, and disco. About 15 restaurants set up shop during the summer months along the beach. Prices are cheap (full meals US$3). Also on Primorska St. along the beach is the **Mehana "Bachus"** (tel. 20 65) serving Greek delights and fish dishes (entrees about 83Lv; open daily 7pm-midnight). Live bands play nightly next door at the **disco** club Saturn. The best meal in Balchik can be found at the **Restaurant Emona** (Емона) at 14 Emona St., high atop the mountain overlooking the harbor (tel. 22 69). You can't miss it—it's shaped like a big ocean liner. From the beach, work up an appetite by climbing the ivy-covered stairs up the hill to the restaurant. Delicious fish and chicken dishes and an unrivaled view of the harbor await. The menu is in English. The owner is one of the many local monarchists and doesn't believe the queen really had a Turkish lover... (open daily 10am-midnight).

TOPOLA (ТОПОЛА)

In the little village of Topola 6km north of Balchik you'll find the **White Sand Tourist Complex** (Белият Бряг), a campground run by the Bulgarian Union of Motorists. From Varna, take the bus to Balchik. From June trough October, the complex, known as "Camping Say-Bey-A" (Къмпинг СБА) has a **minivan** going hourly from the bus station in Balchik to the campground (6Lv). The bus will take you down a winding road with beautiful views of the sea and pink sandstone cliffs. The complex has two **hotels** (US$10 per person, breakfast included) and 100 **bungalows,** all with private baths (US$5 per person, breakfast included). You can put up a **tent** for US$2. The complex also has three **restaurants,** three **discos,** a **post office,** a 24-hr. **nurse,** and **laundry** facilities. When you are finished frolicking in the sea and have had your fill of rented waterbikes, boats, tennis, and miniature golf, soak your aching body in one of the resort's four **mineral baths**—rumored to be great for arthritis and anything else that ails you. The complex's main **office** is in Dobrich (tel./fax 300 31; open Mon.-Fri. 8am-noon and 1-5pm). There's a 24-hr. operator to answer questions and take reservations. The **telephone city code** is 058.

KAVARNA (КАВАРНА)

At first glance, tiny **Kavarna** looks sick and tired of it all. The tall Stalinist structures are now crumbling and in the off-season the beach town is deserted. But because few tourists make it up here, Kavarna is a good place to find lonely beaches and affordable lodging. The northbound buses will drop you off at the bus station. Make your way to the town's central square, which contains a **post and telephone office** and a place to **exchange currency,** the First Private Bank. Look for the **tourist office** Coop Tourist (Кооп Турист; tel. 23 31, fax 50 44). The friendly staff will provide you with maps, arrange **private accommodations** (US$10 per person including all meals), and set up cheap **outings** to the Cape (US$4.80), fishing expeditions (US$2.50 per hour), and horse and buggy picnics (US$4.80). They can also pick you up in Varna for $10 and hire out English-speaking guides (open Mon.-Fri. 7:30am-noon, 1:30-8pm, Sat. 7:30am-noon, Sun. noon-8pm). The **telephone city code** is 0570. An unhelpful **Balkantourist** dinosaur is located here in the **Hotel Dobrotitsa** (Хотел Добротица), but the hotel itself is an affordable and comfortable option (hotel tel./fax 21 91). Clean singles with bath will set you back US$9.25, doubles are US$14.80. The hotel can change money and hosts a hopping disco every night beginning around midnight. The **beach** is about 3km from the town center. On the beach you can rent **boats** or **jet skis,** or go **horseback riding.** Grab a bite in one of the beach side **cafés.**

An archaeological site with ruins of medieval **fortress** walls, **Cape Kaliakra** (Нос Калиакра) is a nice daytrip from Kavarna. You can spy on the dolphins in the waters below from the rocky cape that juts far into the Black Sea. Legend has it that when the Turks came to conquer Kaliakra, forty Bulgarian maidens braided their long hair to each others and, in sisterly solidarity, jumped off the high cliff into the turbulent sea in order to avoid being the love slaves of the Ottomans. Today, Kaliakra is a major tourist attraction featuring a **museum** built inside a grotto (open daily 10am-4pm; admission 50Lv) and an open-air **restaurant** (open daily 9am-midnight). Excursions to Kaliakra can be arranged through Coop Tourist.

SHABLA (ШАБЛА)

In the evening, take a romantic stroll along **Shabla's** secluded beach to the oldest **lighthouse** on Bulgaria's coast. The village is 21km north of Cape Kaliakra and 23km south of the Romanian border; its main attraction is the incredibly affordable and varied lodging available at the peaceful **Dobroudja** (Добруджа) complex.

BULGARIA

Dobroudja, actually 7km from the village center, offers deluxe beachfront **villas** which include bath and kitchen for US$3.70 per person. They also offer cheaper **bungalows** and **tent** sites, but you'll have to share a bath. The campsite has a **post office, change bureau, cinema,** and several **cafés.** In the summer, **restaurants** pop up around the lighthouse. If your taste is slightly more cosmopolitan, you can stay in Shabla itself at the **Hotel Dobroudja** (tel. 24 43). A deal at US$2 for a single, the hotel can also provide you with maps and make restaurant and travel suggestions. **Buses** run regularly between Varna, Albena, and Shabla and between the Shabla bus station and the campsite.

■■■ VARNA TO BURGAS

OBSOR (ОБЗОР)

Obsor—the beach town Greek colonists named Helliopolis, the city of sunshine— is 48km south of Varna. About six **buses** per day run between Varna and Burgas and Obsor's little bus station. At the bus station, next to the public bathrooms, you'll find a **private accommodation** agency (Квартирно Бюро; tel. 23 03). They only speak Bulgarian but rent **rooms** for US$2.20 per person plus taxes (open daily 8am-7pm). They may refuse to serve foreigners and send you to the very helpful but easy to miss **Balkantourist** on 3rd of March St. 36 (Трети Март; tel. 23 06). It's in an old building on a corner just off the beach street. The one-woman staff will arrange rooms for US$3.33 or book you at nearby **Campground Prostor** (Простор) for US$4.60 per bungalow (open Mon.-Sat. 8am-7pm; if you arrive off-hours, she'll have left her address and phone number on the door). The **telephone city code** is 995507.

Other affordable options include **Hotel Ticha** (Хотел Тича) on the beach street Cherno Morska (ул. Черноморска; tel. 21 87). For US$6 per person, you'll get a huge room with a balcony overlooking the clean, sandy beach (restaurant is open daily 7:30am-midnight). Also try **Hotel Amore** (Хотел Аморе) farther up at Cherno Mor-ska 12 (tel. 22 52). The private hotel rents out **motorboats** and can arrange **water-skiing** excursions. US$12 gets you a big room and all meals. For **nightlife** head south to the restless Sunny Beach resort.

SUNNY BEACH (СЛЪНЧЕВ БРЯГ)

The largest, hottest, and hairiest resort on the coast is **Sunny Beach,** the dizzy home of 108 hotels, 130 restaurants, clubs, discos, and cafés, and 8km of dune-covered, golden beaches. Get here by way of the many private **minivans** that travel between Varna's bus station and the bus station in Burgas. For your navigational sanity, stop by the **accommodation complex** across the street from the huge **Hotel Cuban** (Кубан; tel. 21 06, fax 29 21). You can get a map of the facilities, a description of din-ing and entertainment options, and reservations in the houses and campgrounds. **Prices** are similar to those in Albena and Golden Sands. The **beach** is free and fea-tures watersports, swimming pools, and rides for the kiddies. Every other June, the resort hosts the **Golden Orpheus International Festival of Pop Songs** which attracts performers from all over the world. The next festival will be held in June 1996. Every September the resort hosts an international competition for child per-formers. **Volleyball** and **chess tournaments** are also held regularly.

The resort features arguably the best **artist park** in Bulgaria. Have your portrait drawn by a professional for US$10-20. There is also a fruit and vegetable **market** and lots of kiosks selling every finger food imaginable. The **Restaurant Fregata** is shaped like a pirate ship and serves excellent fish dishes and goblets of "Pirate Blood Wine." Belly dancers shake up the **Oasis Restaurant** while the beach warriors who feed at **Hanska Shatra** (Khan's tent) prefer the huge wooden tables and battle murals on the walls. Almost all of the restaurants have floor shows and full meals usually come in at around US$5. For serious partying that goes well into the morn-ing hours, try the **Bar Variety** or the **Casino.**

Sunny Beach's biggest attraction, however, is probably its proximity to little **Nesebur,** the jewel of Bulgaria's Black Sea coast.

■■■ NESEBUR (НЕСЕБЪР)

A sweet alternative to generic coastal tourist ghettos is **Nesebur** (Несебър), a museum town atop the peninsula at the southern end of Sunny Beach. It is difficult to turn a corner in Nesebur without stumbling across a medieval church or Thracian, Byzantine, or Roman ruin. The **old town,** founded by the Thracians who called it Messembria, is connected to the **new town** by a narrow, 400m-long isthmus. There are 10 major churches left in the old town and 100 National Revival houses. A 6th-century **Metropolitan Church** survives in the old center of Nesebur. The 11th-century **Church of St.Stephen** is plastered in 16th-century frescoes. The **Church of Jesus Pancrator** (The Almighty) dates from the 13th century and in the summer, doubles as an art gallery featuring works for sale by local artists. The **Ethnographic Museum** is on Yana Laskova (Яна Ласкова; open 9am-noon and 2-6pm). Artists sell their wares along the alleys and in front of all churches and ruins (pen and ink drawings of Nesebur's Old Town go for US$3-10).

At the beginning of the old town is the **Tourist Bureau Messembria** (tel. 28 55, fax 60 11) which sells **Group Travel** tickets for a daily bus to Sofia (US$5; open daily 8am-8pm, winter Mon.-Fri. 8am-noon and 1-5pm). **Buses** from Burgas run every hour, and from Sunny Beach every 15 minutes. All buses cross the land bridge connecting old and new Nesebur, passing two old windmills on the way. The station is across from the tourist office. **Exchange money** at the **TS Bank** at the beginning of Messembria St. (ул. Месембриа; open Mon.-Sat. 8:30am-1:30pm and 2-8pm, Sun. 9am-1pm). Other change bureaus are in every nook and cranny. The **post office** is in the main square Messembria (open Mon.-Fri. 7:30am-5pm; **telephones** open daily 7:30am-9:45pm). Artists and artisans gather around the monuments and churches to sell their wares. A **farmer's market** sets up at the harbor next to the bus station.

The tourist office rents **private rooms** in the old and new town (US$8) and in the old town's only hotel **Messembria** (singles US$14). In high season it may be difficult to find a room for less than a three-night stay. If you have your heart set on staying in beautiful Nesebur, do as the Bulgarians do and knock on doors in the new town. Many families have rooms to let (US$3-5).

Along the harbor you can munch on fresh calamari and trout served with french fries and *shopska* salad for US$3 at any of the street **kiosks.** Or you can order steaming-hot seafood from the kiosks and add fresh vegetables from the **farmers' market** next door. **Restaurant Ronko** (Ронко), 14A Messembria Ave. (tel. 4121), will take you to cheery ol'England with its roast beef, Yorkshire pudding, and kidney pie (entrees US$4). Top it all off with some homemade apple pie à la mode (US$1). Menu in English (open 11am-11pm; closed in winter). The **Captain's Table** (Капитанска Среща) on ul. Chaika (Чайка), serves up the best seafood in Nesebur (tel. 34 29). The 200 year-old building and the "fish on a tile" specialty (130Lv) make the touristy atmosphere forgivable (open May-Nov. daily 11am-11:30pm).

■■■ BURGAS (БУРГАС)

Generally untouristed, Burgas is the ugly but convenient transportation link to villages and beaches of the southern coast. The town's **seaside gardens** are quieter and better manicured than those in Varna and kids of all ages enjoy the giant **water slide** (open daily 9am-10pm; 5Lv). For more intellectual pursuits, look at the **Archeological Museum** at 21 Bogorodi St. (open Mon.-Fri. 9am-noon and 2-5pm). The bells of the **Armenian Church** awaken the main square every morning; on weekends, nervous brides and grooms line up to be married in the "ritual hall" next door.

The bus and train stations are located next to each other at Station Square (*Garov pl.,* Гаров). **Store luggage** at one of the two **Garderobs** (Гардероб) for 5-6Lv per bag per day. Insurance is available. **Buses** (6 per day, 2½hr.; 120Lv) connect Burgas with Varna's main bus station. You can also catch one of the many **minivans** to the camp groups and resorts to the north and south. **Group Travel** has an office on the main pedestrian walkway Bogorodi (Богороди) #42 (open daily 7am-6pm). Buses to Sofia (2-3 per day, 235Lv) leave from right near the bus/train station on **#1 K. Fominov St.** (К. Фоминов ул.). There are eight trains per day to Sofia (175Lv).

Messembria Tourist Bureau, ul. Aleksandrovska #2 (Александровска; tel. 472 75), has lots of private rooms available (US$4). The staff speaks English, has old maps in English, and sells bus tickets to Sofia (140Lv) and İstanbul (one per night, US$18). The bureau is located at the corner of the pedestrian street which opens up to the train/bus station. Just across from the train station, another **tourist bureau** (tel. 427 27) offers rooms for US$5, sells Group Travel bus tickets, and offers copy and fax services (open Mon.-Fri. 8:30am-8:15pm). **Exchange money** at the **Bank for Agricultural Credit** branch right inside the train station (open 8:30am-noon and 12:45-7:15pm). No banks in Burgas have weekend hours, but all change bureaus take American Express Traveler's Cheques. The **post office** is two blocks to the left of the train station along bul. Vazov, at ul. Tsar Petur I (Цар Петър I; open Mon.-Fri. 7:30am-7pm, Sat. 8am-noon and 1-5pm, Sun. 8am-1pm). International **telephone** calls can only be placed from the new post office at #70 Bul. Osvobozhdenie (Освобождение). The **telephone city code** is 056.

Private rooms are plentiful (see tourist offices, above) and the cheapest housing option (US$4-5). **Kraimone Campground,** 10km from Burgas on the hourly #17 bus, offers motel rooms; wide, clean beaches (entrance 3Lv); and tennis and various water sports. (Doubles US$10, bungalows US$8.) In town, even the cheapest hotels are overpriced. **Hotel Park** (Хотел Парк) at the northern end of the Burgas Seaside Gardens (tel. 227 87, fax 297 32) offers rooms in a dormitory for touring college students. Take bus #4 (singles US$22, doubles US$28). The slick **Hotel Primoretz,** also by the gardens, offers singles for US$36, breakfast included. The complex contains a restaurant, cafe, and disco.

Avoid **tap water** in Burgas; its metal content burns tender Western stomachs. Most restaurants are on the main pedestrian streets—**Bogorodi** (formerly Lenin St.) and **Aleksandrovska.** From the bus station you will pass a new Chinese restaurant, **The Garden** (Градината), at #16 Alexsandrovska (tel. 419 96). Feast on curry dishes (US$2.50) and chop suey (US$1). The menu is in English (open daily 11am-midnight). Bogorodi St. wades in **hamburger joints** and **ice cream stands.** The **ART café,** in the light blue "CDC" building, offers a variety of soups and vegetarian dishes in a garden lined with unusual murals (meals US$4-5). **Starata Gemiya** (Старата Гемия) is on the beach behind the Hotel Primorets in the Maritime Park (tel. 457 08). Known locally as "Fregata", it specializes in seafood. A full meal will cost you US$3 (open daily 9am-midnight). The open-air **Black Sea Nightclub** smolders next door to the seaside gardens (open 24 hrs; live performances every night at 1, 3, and 4:30am).

■■■ SOUTH OF BURGAS

Enchanting bays and beaches line the coast between Burgas and **Ahtopol** (Ахтопол). Tourists thin out toward the Turkish border. There are about 15 campgrounds, and many small and inexpensive private hotels are now appearing.

SOZOPOL (СОЗОПОЛ)

Sozopol (Созопол), 34km south of Burgas (buses hourly 5am-8pm, 30Lv one way), is Bulgaria's oldest Black Sea town, settled in 610 BC and later known as Apollonia. Less touristed than Nesebur, the **Old Town** sits on a rocky peninsula with a Mediterranean mystique; old women still sell beautiful handmade lace on the street.

The bus from Burgas lets you off near the **Sozopol Tourist Office** (tel. 17 84) where you may have trouble finding help in English. **Helio Tours,** the former Balkantourist, is located on Ropotamo ul. in a large white building (tel. 251). Its English-

BULGARIA

speaking staff can arrange private accommodations for US$6 and can book you at and arrange transport to the nearby **Camping Kavacite, Camping Gradina,** and **Camping Cherno Moretz** (US$5-6 per person for beachside bungalows with bath; open daily 8am-10pm). The **post office** (open Mon.-Fri. 7:30am-noon and 1-4pm) and **telephones** (open daily 7:45am-8:45pm) are in the Old Town on beautiful Apollonia St. You can send and receive **faxes** here (fax 306; open Mon.-Fri. 7:30am-noon and 1:30-5pm). The **city code** is 05514.

Hotel Radik (Хотел Радик), ul. Republikanska 4 (Републиканска; tel. 17 06), has a gorgeous panoramic view of the harbor. Rooms are small but comfortable (US$5 per bed). Across the street, **Hotel Alpha-Vita** (tel. 18 52) offers similar accommodations at the same price. The **Marine Club** (Военно-Морски клуб), in the center of the new town, offers singles for US$6 but is often packed and reserves the right to put another person in the bed next to yours. Apollonia St. is the site of an **artists' park** and home to many **kiosks** offering fresh fried fish and calamari. **Pizzeria John** (Джон), 16 Apollonia St., offers piping-hot brick oven pizzas for US$2 (open daily 10am-midnight). **Restaurant Palace** (Палас) serves up Greek dishes nightly (open 6pm-midnight). In the parking lot along the harbor, try the definitely-not-wheel-chair-accessible **Restaurant Druzhba** (Дружба), an actual fishing trawler converted into a café. For a delicious meal and a romantic view of the sea, walk to the northern end of the Old Town to the ivy-covered **Restaurant Vyaturna Melnitsa** (Вятърна Мелница) on ul. Morski Skali (Морски Скали; tel. 844). The menu is in English. Meals hover around US$3 (open daily 8am-1am).

ROPOTAMO RIVER NATURAL PRESERVE

Fifty kilometers south of Burgas, the Ropotamo River is home to legions of snakes and water lilies. For US$12, you can join the hour-long **cruise** and **picnic** offered by **Ropotamo Tours** (June-Oct. 8am-8:30pm). While on the cruise, you might be lucky enough to catch sight of one of the many red deer, wild boar, or jackals living in the natural preserve. Buses from Burgas pass by the Ropotamo stop hourly (50Lv).

PRIMORSKO (ПРИМОРСКО)

When young Bulgarians think of Primorsko, they think of the **International Youth Center,** formerly named for Communist leader Georgi Dimitrov, where the best Komsomols and Pioneers from all over Eastern Europe were once sent to strengthen international comradeship and have a dip in the sea. Today the center is a rocking, inexpensive resort crawling with young, scantily-clad East Europeans; it's the mother of Bulgarian pick-up places. At the meticulously manicured **beach** you can rent all types of **boats;** in the oak forest surrounding the complex, you have a choice of **tennis, volleyball, basketball,** and **handball** courts. The resort runs special **buses** from the bus station in Burgas June-October (50Lv). Go first to the **tourist office** (tel. 21 01) in the **Hotel Druzhba** (Хотел Дружба) to pick up a map of the complex and to book a room in one of the many **hotels** (doubles US$20) or rent one of the seven varieties of **bungalows** ($US4-10 per person). The complex has a **post office, medical center, open-air theater, cinema,** and **mini-casino.**

To get to the hamlet of Primorsko, take a southern bound coastal bus that will let you off on the main street **Cherno More** (Черно Море). The **post office** and **telephones** are right at the bus stop. The somewhat hidden **Balkantourist** across the street (tel. 21 82) books **private accommodations** and spaces at nearby **campgrounds Yug** and **Kiten** (open daily 8am-noon and 1-10pm). In high season, Cherno More Street is a teeming **artist park,** and **cafés** and kiosks abound.

Croatia

CROATIA (HRVATSKA)

US$1	= 6.01K (Kuna)		1K =	US$0.17
CDN$1	= 4.39K		1K =	CDN$0.23
UK£1	= 9.42K		1K =	UK£0.11
IR£1	= 9.24K		1K =	IR£0.11
AUS$1	= 4.47K		1K =	AUS$0.22
NZ$1	= 3.26K		1K =	NZ$0.31
SAR1	= 1.69K		1K =	SAR0.59
DM1	= 3.90K		1K =	DM0.26

Country Code: 385   **International Dialing Prefix: 00**

History, not geography, has determined the strange, forked shape of Croatia. The northeastern, inland section of the country, partly occupied by Serbia, lies in the valleys of the Drava and Sava Rivers. The capital, Zagreb, sits on the Sava River between the two prongs of the fork. In the southwest, Croatia's rugged, stunning coast and islands dominate the Adriatic's western shore, stretching from Slovenia to Montenegro. The Istrian peninsula, in the northwest, belonged to Venice centuries ago and to Italy between the World Wars; it still contains a small Italian minority. After World War II, a massive influx of Serbs, encouraged by the Croat communist dictator Tito, altered Croatia's demography. Farther south, the Dinaric Alps rise from the waters of the sea; many say that it is one of the most beautiful coasts in the world. The water is warm and the scenery incredible, but the war in Bosnia-Herzegovina has hurt tourism and caused a decline in the standard of hospitality. Good beaches, especially sandy ones, are scarce. Even so, the coast used to be a favorite European vacation spot, packed during the summer.

CROATIA ESSENTIALS

Citizens of the U.K. and Ireland do not need visas to enter Croatia. Citizens of Australia, Canada, New Zealand, South Africa, and the U.S. do need visas. See Essentials: Embassies and Consulates, page 3. Single-entry visas (valid for 1 year) and multiple-entry visas both cost US$10. Visas require a valid passport, one photograph, and a payment by personal check or money order only (cash is not accepted). If applying by mail, applicants must send an additional US$9 to cover return postage. Single-entry visas take either two days (regular service) or one day (rush service); multiple-entry visas take six weeks to process, and a letter indicating valid reasons for your need for this type of visa must be submitted along with the application. It is also possible to procure single-entry visas at the border for no additional fee, but to save time travelers are advised to obtain one before leaving home. While in Croatia, visas can be renewed at any local police station.

GETTING THERE
Croatia Airlines flies to Zagreb from several Western cities, including London, Paris, Frankfurt, Toronto, Chicago and New York (information and reservation tel. (041) 45 12 44; fax 45 14 15). They also operate flights within Croatia, but fares are several times more expensive than the equivalent bus or train fares (i. e. plane from Zagreb to Split US$70; bus US$14; inexpensive bus US$10).

If arriving by **train**, the main entry point is Zagreb. Trains come from Ljubljana, Vienna, and Budapest, and depart for many additional destinations in northern Croatia. The rail route to Split and southern Croatia is currently under Serbian control; there are no trains traversing the route at press time. Schedules are posted all around the stations. *"Odlazak"* means departures, *"dolazak"* means arrivals.

GETTING AROUND CROATIA
If you plan to make **trains** your main means of transportation, consider buying a **K-15 ticket**: they offer low fares on trips of at least 100km, allowing at most three stops in a 10-day period (other restrictions apply; ask about them before you purchase the ticket). If you do not speak Croatian, it may be impossible to get station bureaucrats to issue the ticket. One possible route for a K-15 ticket could be Rijeka-Zagreb-Hungarian border.

Buses are slow, poorly ventilated, and can be hellishly crowded. On the other hand, they often have more convenient schedules than trains, and sometimes are the only option. From Zagreb, buses run to Rijeka, Split, and Dubrovnik. To get to Istra, travel from Koper or Portorož in Slovenia to Poreč, Pula,or Rijeka. You can buy a ticket on the bus, but it's better to get one at the station. In theory, if you have heavy luggage (such as a big backpack) it must be stowed separately for an additional fee. Consider acting brash and taking it on the bus with you, which is what everybody else seems to do, but you may be in trouble if the bus gets crowded. During the school vacations in July and August, both trains and buses tend to be very crowded. Most train and bus stations have a *garderoba* (luggage storage). You may be asked to show your passport when you deposit your luggage. Pay when you pick up your luggage (US$0.50-1 per day). Watch for closing times.

Ferry service is run by **Jadrolinija**. Boats sail on the route Rijeka-Split-Dubrovnik, stopping at some of the islands on the way. There are also ferries from Split to Ancona, Italy, and from Dubrovnik to Bari, Italy. Ferries are unquestionably more comfortable than buses, though they may be even slower. They're also inexpensive, but a basic fare only guarantees you a place on the deck; most trips are at night, and you'll want a bed. Buy your ticket in advance to get a lower price (Rijeka-Split basic fare 80K, couchettes an additional 60K). The cheap beds sell out fast; if you delay, you may have to pay twice as much. Sometimes the travel agency will only sell you a basic ticket; if that is the case, *run* to get a bed on board. There are also airplane-style reclining seats, quite comfortable compared to the ordinary ones. In theory, there is an extra charge for them, but locals rarely bother to pay it. There is usually a restaurant, though not of high quality (breakfast US$3-4, dinner about US$9). If it's not crowded and you are not a light sleeper, you can try to sleep in the bar, or at least watch TV. People will likely smoke like chimneys, and nobody will care if you suffocate. There are also usually phones—this might be a good time to call home to let everyone know that you are safe, sound, and at sea.

TOURIST SERVICES

Most major cities and tourist sites have tourist offices, some run by the local communities, some by the government. There are also private agencies; the two biggest chains are **Kompas** and **Atlas** (associated with American Express). *Turist biro* (tourist offices) exchange money, offer directions, and help find private rooms. Beware, however, of the chaos that reigns everywhere due to the war. Double-check schedules and important information. Do not rely on second-hand information; your best bet is to go directly to the primary source. Don't believe everything that Croatian travel agents tell you—their professional ethics sometimes run low; when asked about departures and schedules, some may be inclined to bend the truth simply to keep you waiting (and eating) in certain cafés.

Offices tend to keep long hours, usually weekdays 8am-6pm, and Saturdays 8:30am-1:30pm. Many stores stay open weekdays until 8pm with shorter hours on weekends, but the warmer regions of the country may have a break from noon to 6pm, with stores reopening in the evening for several hours. Generally, only restaurants are open between noon Saturday and 8am Monday 8am; if you arrive in a town on a weekend, you may have difficulty finding a room. However, some tourist offices do open on Sundays.

MONEY

Currency exchange services are available at most tourist offices, bus and train stations, hotels, and banks. Traveler's checks can be exchanged only at a few banks; the AmEx offices do not accept them. In 1994, Croatia introduced its new currency, the *kuna*, replacing the inflation-plagued Croatian *dinar* (1 kuna = 1000 dinars). Dinars are no longer valid. In theory, kunas are convertible, but it may be impossible to exchange them abroad.

COMMUNICATION

To use a **telephone**, you will need to buy *zhetons* (tokens, good for a 3min. local call, 1K) or a *telekarta* (phone card; the cheapest is 28K) at a post office. Calls to the U.S. are very expensive (about 16K per min.). To reach the **AT&T USADirect operator**, dial 99 38 00 11; to reach the **BT Direct operator** (U.K.), dial 99 38 00 44. Technically, these calls are free, but some phones may require a card or token. You can also make telephone calls from **post offices;** pay after you talk.

LANGUAGE

The Croats are a Slavic people; they speak almost the same language as the Serbs, but write in Latin characters (whereas the Serbs use the Cyrillic alphabet). If you speak Russian or any other Slavic language, you will be able to understand many words. In Zagreb almost everyone seems to speak English, but on the coast the most popular foreign language seems to be Italian or German. Almost everyone involved in the tourist industry speaks German, though some will admit to speaking "a little" English. Tourist offices usually can work in English, but if you rent a private room, a few German phrases might be of great help in communicating with the owners. Most young people speak English.

Street names, especially those named after Communist officials, are starting to change—*Tito* is now taboo. Street names on signs often differ from names on maps by "-va" or "-a" because of grammatical declensions.

Yes	*da*	dah
No	*ne*	neh
Hello	*dobar dan*	DOB-ar dahn
Good morning	*dobro jutro*	DOB-roh Yoo-troh
Good night	*laku noć*	LAH-koo noch
Goodbye	*zbogom*	ZBOG-ohm
Excuse me	*oprostite*	op-ROHST-eet-eh
Please/You're welcome	*molim*	MOH-lihm
Thank you	*hvala vam*	FAH-lah vahm
Do you speak English?	*Govorte li engleski?*	GOV-oh-ree-teh lee EN-gles-kee
How much is this?	*Koliko to košta?*	KOHL-ee-koh TOH kosh-ta
How do I get to...?	*Koji je put za...*	KO-yee yej POOT zah
My name is ...	*Ja se zovem...*	YAH seh ZO-vem
I don't understand	*Ne razumjem*	neh ra-ZOOM-yem

1—jedan (YEH-dahn); 2—dva (DVAH); 3—tri (TREE); 4—četiri (CHEH-tee-ree); 5—pet (PEHT); 6—šest (SHEHST); 7—sedam (SEH-dahm); 8—osam (OH-sahm); 9—devet (DEH-veht); 10—deset (DEH-seht); 20—dvadeset (DVAH-deh-seht); 30—trideset (TREE-deh-seht); 40—četrdeset (chet-er-DEH-seht); 50—pedeset (peh-DEH-seht); 60—šezdeset (shehz-DEH-seht); 70—sedamdeset (seh-dahm-DEH-seht); 80—osamdeset (oh-sahm-DEH-seht); 90—devedeset (deh-veh-DEH-seht); 100—sto (STOH); 1000—hiljada (HEEL-yah-dah).

HEALTH AND SAFETY

The climate in Croatia is generally mild, continental around Zagreb and mediterranean along the coast. It can get hot on summer afternoons; if you are in Split, you can at least rest in the shade of palm trees.

As of June 1994 there was no fighting on Croatian territory, but Serbian paramilitary groups were stationed in the northeast near the Serbian border (the *Krajina* region) and had cut the railway line to Split in the southwest. Those regions should be categorically avoided. Zagreb, the Istra peninsula on the Adriatic sea, and the coast near Zadar are relatively safe. However, one should always travel with caution. Cities such as Dubrovnik lie only a few miles from the Bosnian border—there is no predicting what might happen there. The islands in the Adriatic are also generally safe, but as that situation is changing, always check in advance, and heed U.S. State Department and other advisories.

ACCOMMODATIONS AND CAMPING

Most **hotels** are expensive, but the current situation makes many prices unpredictable. It is rumored that special deals are offered to attract tourists to the Southern Adriatic. So far, however, most places have stayed empty because of the war next door. Be aware that most places will charge travelers 20-50% more than they charge Croats. There is nothing you can do about this; such are the regulations.

Sobe (rooms to let, often advertised as *zimmer)* can be a delight, but prices are mounting. In summer 1994, rooms cost US$10-30 per person, showers included. Singles are expensive and scarce. The brochure *Private Accommodation Rates,* available at major tourist offices, lists virtually all offices that arrange **private rooms.** Official agencies often raise their prices by up to 50% if you stay less than two or three nights. In the most popular waterfront cities, crowds of room-letters greet travelers at transport terminals. Bargain them down; aim for a price 20% less than tourist offices charge. Check your luggage at the *garderoba* in stations and see the room first. Organized **campgrounds,** usually open from April/May to September/ October, speckle the country and are usually densely packed.

LIFE AND TIMES

HISTORY

Though Croatia has never been a major power, the people of Croatia have a long history and a distinct, well-defined identity. Croats were part of the great **Slavic migration** to central and eastern Europe in the 7th century. In the 8th and 9th centuries, missionaries from the medieval archbishoprics of Salzburg and Aquileia (near Venice) brought **Catholicism** to Croatia. The Croats resisted Charlemagne's attempts to gain control of the eastern shore of the Adriatic, maintaining their independence. Tomislav, the first king, earned papal recognition as ruler in 925; he and his able assistant Bishop Gregory **united the Croat people.** King Demetrius Zvonimir expelled the Byzantines and was crowned by Pope Gregory in 1076, decisively strengthening Croatia's orientation toward Catholic western Europe after the Great Schism of 1054. During the 11th century, Croatia often fought Venice for control of the ports on the Adriatic coast, while control the region between the Drava and Sava Rivers shifted frequently between Croatia and Hungary. In 1102, the Kingdom of Croatia-Slavonia entered as a junior partner into a dynastic **union with Hungary,** preserving much independence. Instability prevailed after 1241, when barbarian Mongol invaders, sweeping on horseback through eastern Europe, crushed Hungarian forces at the Sajo River. Local rulers became everywhere more powerful at the expense of the Hungarian king of Hungary-Croatia. From the late 14th to the late 15th centuries the united kingdom recovered, controlling the Adriatic coast for much of the 14th century before losing it again to Venice. The Croatian towns on the coast remained self-governing, regardless of control.

During this period, however, all other Balkan kingdoms fell desperately fighting the Turks, who had crossed into Europe at Gallipoli in 1354. Despite heroic resistance everywhere, influencing strongly the national consciousness of the Balkan states, the victorious Turks left a series of silent, corpse-strewn, blood-soaked fields, razed towns, and shattered kingdoms in their devastating wake. Serbia was the first to fall, in Kosovo in 1389; Bulgaria at Tirnovo in 1393; Wallachia in 1394; Greek Constantinople in 1453; the Kingdom of Bosnia in 1463; Albania in 1468; Herzegovina ("Independent State") in 1483; and Moldavia in 1512. Croatia became an embattled, divided border region after the Turks annihilated the Hungarian army at Mohàcs in 1526. After this unmitigated disaster, the **Austrian Hapsburgs** resisted the Turkish siege of Vienna in 1529 and took what little of Croatia, including Zagreb, and Hungary they were able to salvage.

The Reformation barely touched Croatia, as Turkish rule and the vigor of the Counter-Reformation in Austrian lands under Ferdinand II preserved Catholic unity. The defeat of the second Vienna siege in 1683 gave the Austrians momentum to drive the Turks from Croatia, Hungary and Transylvania by 1700. Croatia-Slavonia became part of the **Hungarian kingdom,** including Zagreb and Rijeka; most of the coast, including Istra, Zadar, and Dubrovnik, became part of the Austrian kingdom. The Austrian Emperor retained both crowns. Croatia enjoyed over a century of quiet, submerged existence as one of the Austrian Empire's dozen nationalities, though Napoleon added part of Croatia to French Illyria after thrashing the Austrians in his 1805 campaign.

From 1700, Hungarian nobles grew in power in their half of the Austrian Empire and achieved much autonomy, while Hungarian arrogance toward Croatian and other minorities under their rule built tension. When in 1848 Austrian revolutionaries seized Vienna and the Hungarian diet met at Bratislava and secured self-government under the Habsburg Emperor, the Croats convoked a diet in Zagreb and

CROATIA

demanded the same rights. The demands of the Croats and other minorities conflicted with the Hungarian national program. **Josip Jelačic,** chief of the Zagreb diet, ordered Croatia to break with Hungary, proclaimed loyalty to the Austrian Emperor Franz Josef, and led an army toward Budapest to "end the rebellion in Hungary." Though the Hungarians beat his army at Pákozd in 1848, when the Imperial general Windischgrätz later besieged the Austrian rebels in Vienna, the Croats under Jelačić successfully blocked aid to the rebels from Hungary. Though the struggle continued into 1849, Croat participation on the Imperial side helped defeat the Magyar cause. Following defeat by Prussia in 1866, the Austrians were forced to grant a constitution and much independence to Hungary. Initially the Hungarian government adopted a liberal attitude toward the Croat minority, but between 1875 and 1890 Tisza's Liberal Party campaigned to Magyarize Hungary, forcing minority children to learn Hungarian and making it the only official language.

During World War I, Croatian troops fought the Allies along with the rest of Austria-Hungary, but from November 1914, political exiles propounded the novel idea of political unity of the Serb, Croat, and Slovene nations. After the collapse of the Central Powers, Croatia broke with Hungary and the monarchy on October 29, 1918. Austria-Hungary sued the Allies for peace on November 3; on December 1 the Kingdom of the Serbs, Croats, and Slovenes (the original name for **Yugoslavia**) declared independence, with two rival governments: the National Council in Zagreb and the Serb royal government in Belgrade. Further complicating the situation, the Allies had concluded secret treaties with Italy during the war, and after negotiations, Italy was awarded Istra (Istria), Zadar (Zara), and several Adriatic islands. In 1919, Gabriel D'Annunzio marched with a thousand black-shirted followers into Rijeka (Fiume) and for a year embarrassed the Italian government with a comic regime, communicating with his followers from a balcony at open-air rallies involving a rhythmic series of platitudinous questions and answers. The Italians gave him the boot, but kept the port.

In Yugoslavia, Croats and Slovenes demanded a federal state, but the monarchy was Serb, and King Alexander failed to work for reconciliation, proclaiming a dictatorship in 1929. In 1934, Croat nationalists assassinated him during a visit to Marseille. In 1939, Croatia finally won **autonomous** administration and government. Neutral at the outbreak of World War II, Yugoslavia almost joined the Axis for protection, but British-assisted Greek triumphs over Italian invaders provoked a pro-Allied coup in Belgrade in 1941. Hitler, taking the whole series of events as a personal insult, immediately postponed preparations for attacking the Soviet Union and diverted forces to smash Yugoslavia. It didn't take long: German bombers reduced Belgrade to rubble, Hungary and Bulgaria pitched in, Italy annexed part of Slovenia and Split, the Germans made Croatia a puppet state, and Serbia became a German-occupied territory.

World War II caused an extraordinarily grim and complex situation in Yugoslavia, with savage fighting between Serbs and Croats. The Croatian puppet state created by Croat **fascists** (Ustašis) under Ante Pavelić collaborated with the Germans and planned to exterminate all Serbs on its territory; conversely, Croats tell horror stories about the Četniks, anti-Croat Serb royalist partisans. Partisan resistance in Yugoslavia had no equal in occupied Europe. Many Croats and Serbs fought in the **communist partisan ranks,** who were most effective and received assistance from the Allies; their leader was a Croat, **Josip Broz Tito,** the general secretary of the Yugoslav Communist Party. Yugoslavia owed its liberation from German and Ustaši rule more to its partisans than to Soviet forces, though so many Partisan groups contested control that Tito was unable to enter Zagreb until May 9, 1945, the day after the German capitulation.

Yugoslav Croatia recovered Istra, Rijeka, the Adriatic islands, and Zadar from Italy after the war. In 1945, Tito forcibly placed all industry and natural resources under state control. Under Tito's unchallenged rule, and aided by the lack of Soviet forces on its territory, Yugoslavia **broke from Stalinism** in 1948; the Soviet Union was totally unable to dictate to Yugoslavia. Tito decentralized the administration, proclaiming a federal republic in 1963. Ethnic rivalries were suppressed, and Yugoslavia became a relatively tolerant, prosperous communist country. Tito ruled until his death in 1980.

Yugoslavia, with its volatile ethnic mix, proved highly susceptible to quick disintegration and a descent into **violence** after communism's wholesale defeat and collapse in Europe. In response to the nationalist discourses of Slobodan Milošević, the ex-communist leader of Serbia, the people of Croatia approved a referendum for independence on May 19, 1991. Croatia declared its independence on June 25, 1991. Encouraged by Milošević, the Serbs on Croatian territory have tried to separate themselves from Croatia and unite with Serbia.

CROATIA TODAY

At press time, Serbs hold about a third of Croatia's territory (so-called *Krajina,* in the northeast), though international protests have prevented them from officially unifying this territory with Serbia. Both sides have agreed to a cease-fire that has been in effect for months, but the ultimate solution is not yet clear. The situation is further complicated by the conflict in Bosnia, where Croat/Bosnian Muslim and Serb forces continue to clash. Franjo Tudjman is the President of Croatia at press time. As Croatia copes with the effects of the war, a devastated economy, and thousands of refugees from Bosnia, the euphoria of independence is long gone. Police and soldiers roam the streets, and no one seems to clean the graffiti that covers every wall. War costs money, and popular discontent with deteriorating standards of living is increasing. It is unclear what the next elections, scheduled for 1996, will bring.

Croatia is trying to rapidly integrate into Western Europe, and most Croats are friendly to Westerners, even though many of them feel that the U.S. let them down by not recognizing their independence sooner (it took the U.S. two years to do so). The flavor of the day in Croatia is German, in gratitude for their support of Croatian independence. Serbs see in this policy a return to German expansionism.

FOOD AND DRINK

Croatian stores are generally not well stocked, but you can usually find decent food. Prices are high for Eastern Europe, near or at Western European levels. Some prices are on the products, some are listed on the walls. A quick and convenient option are the ubiquitous **kiosks** selling fast food or local specialties such as *burek,* a layered pie filled with *sirom* (cheese) or *meso* (meat). Many **restaurants** are closed due to the lack of tourists (most Croats eat at home). *Purica s mlincima* (turkey with pasta) is the national dish. Along the coast, try *lingje* (squid) or *prt* (smoked Dalmatian ham). *Sladoled* (ice cream) is always a welcome delight (expect 2-3K for a small scoop). Avoid the local orange juice.

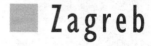

Zagreb

Brimming with Gothic churches, Baroque façades, and sparkling cafés, Zagreb is submerged in the atmosphere of Balkan idleness (some call it *laissez-faire).* The medieval city is beautifully preserved and the turn-of-the-century aura gives it a charm you will not find in more famous European capitals. Zagreb is the capital and most important city in Croatia; among its million inhabitants are 150,000 students. In 1994 Zagreb celebrated its 900th anniversary with a series of prime cultural events.

ORIENTATION AND PRACTICAL INFORMATION

Zagreb is 120km south of the Austrian border. **Trains** run here from Ljubljana, Vienna and Budapest, while **buses** connect it with most major cities in Croatia and

Slovenia. From the train station, walk forward along the parks then down on **Praška St.** to reach the main square, **Trg bana Jelačića** (formerly Trg Republike). The tourist office is in the southeast corner of the square. Up the hill from Trg Jelačića is the cathedral and the cobblestone streets of the old town. The bus station is 1km to the right of the train station (three stops on tram #2, 3 or 6).

Tourist Office: Tourist Information Center (TIC), Trg J.Jelačića 11 (tel. 27 25 30, fax 27 40 83). Open Mon.-Fri. 8am-8pm, Sat.-Sun. 9am-6pm.

Embassies: U.S., Hebrangova 2 (tel. 44 48 00, fax 27 40 83). Open daily 8am-4:45pm. The American cultural center is located in the same building, but the entrance is around the corner at Zrinjeva 13. Open Mon.-Fri. 9am-4pm and Thurs. until 6:30pm. **Canada,** Mihanovićeva 1, Esplanade (tel. 45 07 85, fax 45 09 13), by the train station. **U.K.,** Tratinska 5/II (tel. 34 03 11, fax 33 88 93). Open 8:30am-4:30pm. **Australia,** Mihanovićeva 1, Esplanade (tel. 45 16 63, fax 45 16 63). Open 8am-4pm.

Currency Exchange: at banks, hotels, travel agencies, train and bus stations.

American Express: Atlas, Zrinjeva 17 (tel. 42 76 23). Open Mon.-Fri. 8am-8pm, Sat. 8am-1pm. Mail held and lost cards replaced but *no business in traveler's checks.* The only place that accepts traveler's checks is **Zagrebačka Banka,** in Trg Jelačića next to the tourist office.

Post Offices: Branimirova 2, next to the train station (tel.27 15 93; open Mon.-Sat. 7am-8pm) and Junišićeva 13 (tel. 27 71 12), one block east of Trg Jelačića. **Postal code:** 41000.

Telephones: In post offices. **City Code:** 41.

Flights: The airport is 27km southeast of Zagreb near Velika Gorica. **Croatia Airlines** flies to many destinations in Europe and America; check at their office, at Teslina 5 (tel. 42 77 52, fax 42 79 35). Other airlines also fly to Zagreb.

Trains: Glavni Kolodvor, Tomislavova 12 (tel. 27 22 44). To: Ljubljana (2hrs, 40K), Budapest (7½hrs), Vienna, and most cities in northern Croatia. **Croatia Express**, in the station building, sells youth (BIJ-Wasteels) train tickets, but not to Ljubljana. No youth tickets on domestic routes.

Buses: Autobusni Kolodvor, Marina Drzica (tel. 51 50 37), in a modern building. Service to Ljubljana, Rijeka, and Split.

Public Transportation: Extensive tram system. Buy tickets from newsstands (one-way fare 4K).

Laundromat: At Hotel Intercontinental (tel. 45 34 11, ext. 1749), but through a separate entry. Expensive. Prices are not by pound, but by item (i.e. $1.75 per shirt). Open Mon.-Fri. 8am-4am.

Xerox: KOPIRADNA MB & Super Copia, Pertinska 32a (tel. 43 06 19). Copies 0.40K per page. Color copies also available. Open daily 8am-6pm.

24-Hour Pharmacy: Centralna Ljekarna (Central Pharmacy), Trg Jelačića 3 (tel. 27 63 05).

Medical Assistance: Dordićeva 26 (tel. 44 44 44).

Emergencies: Police: tel. 92. **Ambulance:** tel. 94.

ACCOMMODATIONS

The Omladinski Turistički Centar (HI), Petrinjska 77 (tel. 43 49 64, fax 43 49 62), is conveniently located two blocks away from the train station. The rooms are clean but small; the bathrooms are tiny. (Curfew 1am. Check-out 9am. Singles 127K, with shower 172K. Doubles 175K, with shower 235K. Bed in a six-person dorm-style room 73K.) **Private rooms** are almost as expensive as the hostel. The TIC can help you find one, or call **DI-PROM** (tel. 52 36 17): they speak English. (Singles DM40. Doubles DM20 per person. 50% surcharge for one-night stays.)

FOOD

There is a huge daily **market** on the terrace behind Trg Jelačića.

Mensa, Studentski Centar. The food is not great, but it's cheap (full meal under 10K; set meals 4K, or dine on more expensive but tasty food *a la carte).* All you need to do to start a conversation is to address one of your neighbors in English.

Zagreb

1 Train station
2 Post office
3 Tourist information
4 Studentski center
5 Hotel Inter Continental
6 St. Stephen's Cathedral
7 Dolac marketplace
8 St. Mark's Church
9 Jelačić Palace
10 Priest's tower observatory
11 Rauch Palace
12 Lotrešćak Tower
13 Funicular
14 St. Catherine's Church
15 Art museum
16 Rudolfova vojarna
17 National Theater
18 Arts and Crafts Museum
19 Mimara museum
20 Exhibition Pavilion
21 Bus station

CROATIA

N ←

300 yards
300 meters
0
0

Domjanićeva
KVATERNIKOV TRG
Crvenog Križa
Ljudevita Posavskog
Derenčinova
Šubićeva
Vojnovićeva
Stančićeva
Zvonimirova
Bauerova
Višeslavova
Hrvojeva
KREŠIMIROV TRG
Jelene
Držićeva
Autobusni Kolodvar
Branimirova
Vončarska
Petrova
Derenčinova
Martićeva
Vlaška
Račkoga
Držislavova TRG
HRVATSKIH VELIKANA
Mislavova
Domagojeva
Trpimirova
Bornina
Vončinina
Rubetićeva
Šalata
Novakova
Đorđićeva
Palmoticeva
Jurišićeva
Amruševa
Boškovićeva
Hatzova
Šenolna
Ribnjak
Cesarćeva
KAPTOL
Kaptol
Opatovina
Tkalčićeva
Radićeva
Demetrova
MARKOV TRG
GORNJI GRAD
Strossmayerov
Masarykova
TRG BANA JOSIPA JELAČIĆA
Bogovićeva
Berislavićeva
Teslina
Preradovićeva
Ilica
Petrinjska
STROSSMAYEROV TRG
Trenkova
TOMISLAVOV TRG
Gajeva
Haulikova
Glavni Kolodvor
Zerjavićeva
Mihanovićeva
Gundulićeva
Hebrangova
DONJI GRAD
Frankopanska
Vlaška
Vatšavska
TRG MARŠALA TITA
BOTANIČKI VRT
Dalmatinska
Medulićeva
ROOSEVELTOV TRG
Savska
Vodnikova
Crnatkova
BRITANSKI TRG
Kačićeva
Klaićeva
Kršnjavoga
Jukićeva
Brozova
Primorska
Prilaz Giure Deželića
Jagićeva
Aduliina
Kranjčevićeva
Krajiška
Republike Austrije
Zapadni Kolodvor

1
2
3
4
5
6
7
8
9
10
11
12
13
14
15
16
17
18
19
20
21

From the train station, walk west on Vodnikova then turn left on Savska and enter the Student Center on your left. You need food coupons to eat here; most students will be more than willing to trade them for kunas. Join the line (5-10 minutes), then grab your food, pick up your bill, and pay on your way out after your meal. They do not usually check IDs.

Kamenita Vrata, Kamenita 2, at the entrance to the Old Town. A small, cozy pizzeria with a pseudo-medieval interior. Pizzas 20-24K, soft drinks 7K. Open Mon.-Fri. 9am-11pm, Sat.-Sun. 10am-11pm.

Pod Gričkim Topom, on the stairway leading down from the Old Town to Ilica, by the funicular. An idyllic, stylish, and pricey terrace with a great view of the city. Features, among other dishes, pork, veal, and squid. Come here only if you feel like spending some bucks. Entrees 60-80K.

Gornji Grad, on Ćirilometodska in the Old Town. Classy with stained-glass windows. When you enter, the restaurant is on your right; on your left, a fast-food bar sells burgers and fries for 15K. Entrees in the restaurant 25-50K. Open Mon.-Sat. 8am-11pm, Sun. 8:30am-10pm.

Mosor, Jurišićeva 2, across from the TIC. A self-service place, once elegant, but increasingly dingy. Convenient location and moderate prices. Grab a *burek* if nothing else.

Medulić, Medulićeva 2 (tel. 42 64 47). Walk 10 minutes from Trg Jelačića down Ilica. Vegetarian and carnivorous menus in English. Veggie dishes are relatively cheap (around 30K). Relax and "enjoy" the sound of trams on Ilica three meters away; no soundproof windows here. Open daily 8am-11pm.

Centar, Jurišićeva 24, two blocks east of Trg Jelačića. It's small, so be careful not to miss it. Cakes, shakes, and the best ice cream in Zagreb.

SIGHTS

The immense **Trg Jelačića** is the beginning and end of many strolls through Zagreb. Directly behind the scrubby fountain is the **Neo-Gothic Zagreb Cathedral.** The Zagreb bishopric was established in 1094, and the first cathedral was finished in 1217. The original building was subjected to a Tartar invasion and several fires; the present building has little to do with the original. However, it still boasts 14th-century **frescoes** and an **altarpiece** attributed to **Dürer.** The buildings around the cathedral constitute **Kaptol,** the clerical half of medieval Zagreb. Walk up Kaptol St. from the cathedral; beyond the wall on the right is **Park Ribnjak.** Turn left by the small **Gothic church;** inside, a deep blue starry sky is painted on its ceiling. Across from the church is a small park, a perfect spot to rest in the warmth of the sun. Dogs occasionally drag noisy cans on the pebbles, waking up tired travelers from their rightful sleep after a night spent on the bus. If this happens, do not count on the dogs' owners to quiet their pets—they are far too busy chatting with one another in some faroff corner of the park, and are obviously used to the racket.

Gradec, now called **Gornji Grad,** was the craftsmen's half of Old Zagreb. Walk up Radićeva from the main square, then turn left through **Kamenita Vrata** (the old Stone Gate). Walk up Kamenita to the **Church of Sr. Marko;** it boasts a Gothic entrance, a technicolor tile roof, and several works by the former Yugoslavia's famous sculptor, **Ivan Meštrovič.** Down on Ćirilometodska is the Lotreščakova Tower, which you can climb for a fine Kodak moment of the city (open Mon.-Fri. 10am-6pm, Sun. 10am-2pm; admission 7K), and a small church of Byzantine rite. Down on the left end of Katarinin Trg is the Baroque **St. Catherine's Church,** which frequently hosts classical concerts.

The **Strossmayerovo promenade** at the foot of the hill seems to be the romantic spot in the city; it's full of couples embracing on benches or slowly walking hand in hand. If you make it this far, you can take the funicular down to Ilica, two blocks west of Trg Jelačića, or take a short walk down the stairs. **Donji Grad** (the Lower Town) contains several museums. Most of them are closed either for financial reasons or because of war-related security concerns. Some may re-open in the near future; check with the tourist office upon your arrival in Zagreb. If the **Mimara museum** is closed, at least enjoy its imposing façade at Trg Roosevelt 4. If it's open, it is one of the finest museums in Europe, even though there are rumors that some of the paintings on display are fake. Across from the museum and to the east is the National Theater; to the south, orient yourself by the ugly and modernistic Hotel Intercontinental. The **Botanical Garden,** to the southeast, is an oasis of color by the railway lines. Farther to the south is the river Sava.

There are several daytrips to be taken from Zagreb. North of the city is **Medvednica Mountain;** hike to the summit **Sljeme** (1035m) or take the cable car. Beyond the mountain, the valleys of **Hrvatsko Zagorje** are populated with medieval castles and churches. South of Zagreb, along the road to Zadar, are the beautiful **Plitvice lakes,** a natural park chosen by UNESCO as one of the wonders of the world. Unfortunately, it is now held by Serbs, so you might want to reconsider visiting it if you left your bulletproof vest at home. But who knows? By the time you come to Croatia, the war may have ended.

ENTERTAINMENT

Tkalčićeva, in the Old Town, bursts with cafés, street musicians, boutiques and small galleries. Dig the art in progress at the café **Grička Vještica,** Tkalciceva 57; it depicts legends from Zagreb's history. **The Saloon,** Tuškanac 1a (tel. 43 24 34), resounds with dance music and pick-up lines. Head west on Ilica from Trg Jelačića and turn right onto Dežmonova (open Tues.-Sun. 10pm-3am). **17 Ilica** is a popular pool hall. Zagreb is arguably the most fanatic of **basketball**-mad Croatian towns. **Cibona,** the local team, has twice been the champion of Europe, and only Croatia has been able to seriously challenge the American "Dream Teams." The season lasts from mid-October through May; tickets are available at the silver-tower stadium south of Savskaa (tram #4 from the train station, #14 or 17 from Trg Jelačića). Try to be in Zagreb during the last week of July for the **International Folklore Festival,** a premier gathering of European folk dance troupes and singing groups..

■■■ PULA

Although idle and provincial, Pula's amphitheater rivals the Colosseum, if not in size then in age; the Temple of Augustus, finished in 14 C.E., is almost intact. There are rocky, beaches nearby, and the city is an excellent base to explore the south of Istra. However, the streets could be cleaner, and the rampant confusion among tourist services is almost unequaled.

Orientation and Practical Information The Old Town is organized in concentric circles between Istarska and the sea; one way to enter the city is through the arch on the right, at the end of Giardini. For more information on the city, stop by one of the many **tourist offices. Adriatic Action Life,** Mate Balote 7 (tel. 334 86, fax 447 15), changes money, organizes trips, sells souvenirs, and has a rental car representative on the premises. **Atlas,** P. Drapšina 1 (tel. 237 32, fax 236 86), organizes daily excursions, arranges hotel and private accommodations, changes money, sells railway, boat and plane tickets, and offers **American Express** services. **Globtour Istra,** Giardini 10 (tel. 412 55, fax 418 58), specializes in finding private rooms, hotels, apartments, and bungalows. **Kompas Adria,** Zagrebačka 2 (tel. 424 11, fax 415 92), organizes tours and arranges accommodations. **Viatours,** Ul. Mate Balote 4 (tel. 420 33, fax 449 02), is conveniently located near the bus station. Its helpful and efficient staff change money and find private rooms. City maps are yours for 12K. Head down Ul. Balote Mate and turn left onto Istarska. To reach the **post office** (tel. 988); from the train station, head down Ul. Mate Balote and turn left onto Istarska; the office will be on your left. The **telephone city code** is 052.

Pula can be reached by **train** from Zagreb or Postojna, but the journey is roundabout (station tel. 54 17 33). **Buses** follow a more direct route, but they are unnervingly slow, and stop at just about every deserted hut along the road. Buses run from Pula to: Poreč (57km), Portorož (100km); Trieste (125km); Rijeka (105km, 2hrs, 33K); Zagreb; Split; Postojna; and Ljubljana. The bus station (tel. 221 32; 237 71) is located in a dark underpass between Ul. Mate Balote and Istarska Ul., close to downtown. Schedules are posted at the station, and the staff of the information booths usually speak some English, though they are often busy over the phone. You can also get here plane from Zagreb, Rijejka, and London—contact **Croatia Airlines** at Ulica Mate Balote 4 (tel. 233 22, fax 419 98) or at the **airport** (tel. 236 33, fax 425 18). In an **emergency,** contact the **police** (tel. 92 or 225 55) or the **fire department** (tel. 93) as appropriate.

Accommodations and Food Private rooms are not as good as in other Croatian cities, but they are cheaper. (Singles US$12-$15 in July-Aug. Doubles a slightly better deal.) Most travel agencies will find rooms, but keep in mind that amid confusion, agencies sometimes give out wrong or contradictory information about hotels, restaurants, or schedules. It is not unusual to find yourself at the wrong address when you rent a private room, or to receive an outdated schedule. Since hotels tend to be expensive and private rooms may be hard to find, especially in season, you may want to stay at one of the ten camping sites in the area: **Stoja** (tel. 241 44, fax 421 38), **Ribarska Koliba** (tel. 229 66, fax 421 38), and **Punitižela** (tel. 252 02 or 429 26; fax 429 26). As of June 1994, many restaurants were closed. **Delfin**, Kovačića 17 (tel. 222 89), is in the Old Town close to the sea. Highly recommended by the locals, it offers delicious fish and other seafood entrees. **Pizzeria "La Dolce Vita,"** Prvog maja ul. (tel. 435 97), is also located in the Old Town, just a few steps from Giardini. It's a bit dingy inside, but you can choose to eat your pizza (20-30K) at a table outside. With few customers, the owner keeps himself occupied by playing darts. Watch out.

Sights and Entertainment Some of the city's Roman monuments have been beautifully preserved. From the bus station, walk down to Giardini, and enter the city through the arch on your right at the end of Giardini. From here, it is only a short walk to the **Amphitheater,** built in the 1st century. Walk along Marsala Tita obala, and turn left to enter the large Trg Republike; children there loiter on the steps of the majestic **Temple of Augustus.** Other sights include the 6th-century **St. Nicholas' Orthodox Church,** the **Franciscan Church,** and the **Cathedral.** Among the many daytrips you can take from Pula, a worthwhile voyage is the island of **Brioni,** famous for its unspoiled wildlife. Ships sail to Brioni from the Pula harbor: check the schedules at any tourist office, then double-check them at another.

Verudela, 2 miles south of Pula, has rocky but relatively clean beaches. Take bus #2 or 4 from Giardini (direction: Verudela; 7K round-trip—buy the tickets at newsstands) to the last stop, then walk in the direction of the bus route, and turn right for the best beaches. Dip into the warm, salty waters of the Adriatic, and watch your belongings. The disco-club **Piramida** is considered the best in Pula. Take the same bus #2 or 4 toward Verudela, and get off at the Piramida stop; then look to your right. It should be very easy to spot the building—it really looks like a pyramid.

■■■ RIJEKA

Just east of Istra, Rijeka (Italian: Fiume) is the peninsula's connection to the rest of Croatia. It is also a major port, and the starting point of many ferry routes towards the Southern Adriatic and the islands. Before World War II, Rijeka was a border city, and the river divided it into two parts—Italian and Yugoslav. After the war, along with the whole Istran peninsula, the city became Yugoslav. The most interesting sights are in what used to be the Italian part, with examples of beautiful Venetian architecture. Rijeka is a town of ancient, rich tradition, and it has all the qualities of a good vacation town: quiet beaches and tourist facilities. Like in many other Croatian cities, however, hospitality has been dampened by apathy caused by the war.

Orientation and Practical Information If you have the time for some sightseeing, walk down Kresimirova Ul. past both the train and bus stations until you get to Trg Palmiro Togliatti. This is where the pedestrian street of **Korzo** (Corso) starts, with all its cafés, restaurants, shops, galleries and banks. Walk about a 100m down Korzo to get to Generalturist, the **tourist office,** which will be on your left (open Mon.-Fri. 8am-7pm, Sat. 9am-1pm). The general store **Robna Kuća** is a few meters ahead on the right (closes at 3pm). Next door is the **post office,** Kresimirova 7 (open daily 7am-9pm). The **telephone city code** is 051.

The city is connected by **train** with Ljubljana and Zagreb (7 per day), and by **bus** with Poreč and Pula (33K) in the west, Ljubljana and Postojna in the north, Zagreb in the east, and Split and Dubrovnik in the south. The bus and train stations are both close to downtown, between the port and Kresimirova Ulica. Schedules are posted outside the bus station, but they are not necessarily accurate; double-check departure times at the information booth. To get from the train station to the bus station, turn right onto Kresimirova and walk a few hundred meters—the bus station is on the same side of the street as the train station. If you are walking from the bus station to the train station, make sure to go past the first building (a cargo station) to the actual train station; it's easy to confuse the two.

Ferries arrive from any port on the Adriatic that you can think of (and a few you can't). The once impressive but now decaying headquarters of **Jadrolinija** are a few meters east of the bus station. The entrance to the travel bureau is from the waterfront, at Riva 16 (tel. 21 14 44, fax 21 31 16; open daily 7am-6pm). Jadrolinija runs ferries daily to Zadar, Split (12hrs.; 79K, couchette 140K), Hvar, and Korčula (three times per week they continue to Dubrovnik (22hrs.; 95K, couchette 240K)) from late May-late September, usually departing at 6pm. Breakfast on board is about 20K, dinner 50K. **Kvarner Express,** Trg Palmiro Togliatti, runs high-speed catamarans on the route Rijeka-Hvar-Supetar-Split about once a week (open Mon.-Fri. 8am-4pm, Sat. 8am-1pm). For flight info., contact **Croatia Airlines** in Rijeka (tel. 302 07).

Accommodations and Food Due to the lack of tourists, many hotels and restaurants are closed. Expensive **hotels** that cater to foreigners cluster at Opatija, a few miles from the city. A more affordable alternative are the **private rooms available** through the Generalturist office (see above). Though not as well supplied as their Slovenian counterparts, many shops are good sources of food—the **supermarket** on Korzo has its food section in the basement. There is an **outdoor market** between Kresimirova and the sea; turn right at the eastern end of Korzo; get there before 2pm when it closes, leaving a dirty mess behind. Most of the nearby *burek* kiosks are closed—it's the war. But you can always grab some ice cream on Korzo. For a bite of real food, try the **Galeb Express Restaurant** on the waterfront, two blocks east on Riva from the bus station.; it has a view of the port, and the prices are moderate (chicken and fries 35K).

Sights The historic downtown is squeezed between **Korzo** and **Ulica Žrtava fašizma.** There are sightseeing guide-panels in several places; follow the yellow **TM (Turist Magistrala)** signs for a tour of the city. With its stone pavement and Baroque buildings, Korzo is the most attractive street in town. Sip a soda in one if its cafés and watch passers-by while you wait for your ferry—this seems to be a favorite occupation of the locals. It's impossible to miss the symbol of the town: the beautifully ornamented **clock tower** stands across from the main post office. Walk a few more steps to the east, and then right: the **St. Nicholas Church** is still standing, untouched by the growing tensions between the Orthodox Serbs and the Catholic Croats. The oldest monument in Rijeka, the **Roman arch,** is also in the Old Town.

In the upper part of the city, near the police station, the **Church of San Vito** features a miraculous **crucifix.** According to the legend, a young man, angry about losing at dice, hit the crucifix with a hammer. The statue started to bleed, then the Earth ruptured and swallowed the sinner. Farther to the east is the river that used to divide Italy from Yugoslavia. If you have time, climb the hill to the tower where the Croatian flag is flapping in the wind.

CROATIA

■■■ SPLIT

Split is an architectural jewel, from its 3rd-century Roman ruins to the orange façades and white colonnades of Trg Republike. Many a tourist has climbed the green hills for a view of the city in its Mediterranean splendor. But the good days when the local soccer team, Hajduk, aced Europe's tournaments and people and lights filled the streets in the evenings are long gone. The city now must cope with a devastated economy, poverty, isolation, and the lack of tourists who used to be its main source of income.

Orientation and Practical Information Split is scenically located between the rocky hills of the Dinaric Alps in the north and the Adriatic sea in the south. The Marjan peninsula extends into the sea towards the west. Past the train station and post office, Domagojeva curves and changes its name to obala Hrvatskog Narodnog Preporoda; this is where the Old Town starts. Parallel to the main street runs the beautiful **promenade Riva.** lined with palm trees. At the west end of the boulevard is Trg. republike. Most travel agencies are located in this area. The main **tourist office** is at Hrvatskog Narodnog Preporoda 12 (tel. 241 42). **American Express** is at **Atlas**, Trg Braće Radić 7 (tel. 430 55; open Mon.-Fri 8am-1:30pm, 2pm-8am, Sat. 8am-1pm). Most agencies are closed on Sundays; one of the few that stay open is **Croatia Express** on Domagojeva near the train station (tel. 444 99; open daily 7am-9pm). The **British Consulate** is at Hrvatskog Narodnog Preporoda 20. Down Domagojeva obala past to the train station and to the right is the main **post office**. The **telephone city code** is 058.

    Ferries link Split daily with Rijeka and other major Croatian ports. Ferries from Rijeka usually arrive early in the morning (6am). The **Jadrolinija** office is right on the pier. When you get off the ferry, turn left and walk along the sea on Domagojeva obala. The Serbs are currently blocking the rail connections with almost all of the rest of Croatia, but several companies run **buses** run north to Zagreb (8-10hrs., 60-85K) and Rijeka, south to Dubrovnik, and even west to the heart of Bosnia—but you *don't* want to go there. **Eurosplit**, Domagojeva 7 (tel. 58 72 04), is one of the most expensive agencies, but has air-conditioned buses and offers seat reservations (a good idea for the crowded Zagreb route). The bus station is a few meters away from the ferry pier; it's open all day long and seems to be the only booming business in Split. Schedules are posted outside the station. **Croatia Airlines** also flies to Split (office tel. 36 25 67; *aerodrom* (airport) tel. 51 51 05 or 55 19 93, fax 55 13 89). Flights are expensive; one way fare from Zagreb to Split is about US$70. The port, train station, and bus station are all located on Domagojeva obala, within walking distance of downtown. If you do not intend to spend the night at Split but simply want to do a little sightseeing, you can **store luggage** at the bus station (office open 6am-8pm). The **public restrooms** at the train station are dirty but functional.

Accommodations To rent a **private room,** go to the tourist office (see above); unless you are very lucky, most travel agencies will tell you that they do not offer this kind of service. The other option is to deal directly with the owners—the lack of tourists brings many people, especially older women, to the bus station in search of lodgers. They quote prices in the range of DM20-40, but you can bargain.

    Most hotels are filled with refugees from Bosnia and do not admit tourists. **Hotel Park,** Setaliste 1 (in a quiet area close to the harbor) and **Hotel Bellevue,** Trg Republike (500m from the train and bus stations) both have vacant but expensive rooms (doubles DM100). The high prices are the product of the so-called war tourists, UN officials, and journalists—for them, Split is the perfect base from which to cover Bosnia, and they *can* afford to pay. If you are unsuccessful in hunting down a room, or if you cannot afford one, there is always the ferry to Rijeka or the bus to Zagreb.

Food As of June 1994, many restaurants were closed. The **Hotel Bellevue restaurant** was one of the few that remained open—and empty. The location is good, on

Trg Republike, but the food is on the expensive side: entrees start around 30K. A cheaper alternative is to buy your food in one of the many little **stores** in town, but none are very well supplied. There is a **supermarket** on Domagojeva, across from the bus station. Try to ignore the employees who follow you with their eyes the entire time you are in the store—they are just doing their job, watching out for potential delinquents who might want to take off with the store's already meager supplies. There is also a **marketplace** near Hrvatskog Narodnog Preporoda, to the right of the Old Town; everything is sold here, from bananas to used batteries. **Kiosks** by the bus station sell *bureks* and hamburgers. **Bars** and **cafés** abound and most of them are actually open; if you don't find anything more filling and healthy, you can always kill your hunger with coffee and Coca-Cola.

Sights The city center is an architect's delight. Significant ruins remain from **Emperor Diocletian's Palace**, dated 305 C.E. The city of Split grew out of these ruins in levels; one can easily see the additions made during the centuries. Medieval buildings were constructed on the ancient foundations, and modern buildings form yet another layer. It is a wonder that the ancient remains have managed to survive seventeen centuries, under the burden of buildings continuously piling up on top of them. The best place to enter the Old Town is from the right, through the market-place. The exterior wall is almost intact. A few steps inside is **Peristil**, with Corynthian columns, arches, and a **sphinx**, and a Christian church built on "pagan" foundations. Climb the **tower**, if it's open, and enjoy the view.

Walking down the narrow streets of the Old Town is a real pleasure; the town is a labyrinth, but it's relatively easy to find your way out. Near the Peristil, stairs lead to the lower level, from where an underpass takes you to the waterfront. Some of the subterranean galleries are part of a museum, but they are currently closed. In the middle of the Old Town is Narodni Trg; the ruins extend to the left to Marmontova street. Parallel to the street is the **Trg Republike,** with colonnades and rectangular façades. Before the war, the square was filled every night with light and music from the cafés. Farther to the left, the **Marjan peninsula** is a vast park centered around the hill; walk up to the Croatian flag on the top (20-30 minutes) for a magnificent view of the city and of the Adriatic.

Riva, the sea-front promenade, is the favorite hangout of the locals; it fills every afternoon with people (especially couples) of all ages. Tall palm trees shade the benches underneath from the ruthless rays of the southern sun. There are several **beaches** nearby, east of the harbor, but the water is very dirty; you are probably better off staying away from it, no matter how tempting a quick dip in the Adriatic on a hot afternoon may be. Cleaner beaches can be found on the Marjan peninsula, in the outskirts of the city. As always on the Adriatic, don't expect sand. Away from the center, the Mediterranean charm and lightness starts to fade, and is quickly replaced with communist-style concrete blocks. It is here that the effects of the war are most visible: uncollected garbage, graffiti, and an atmosphere of general decay. Venturing up those streets is an experience in itself; if you do travel into this part of the city, check out the **Prodajni centar koteks,** a modernistic ensemble of shops and performance halls (10-15 minutes from downtown).

■ NEAR SPLIT

The **islands** on the Adriatic are a great place to enjoy beaches and unspoiled nature. Ships run from the harbor, but schedules are chaotic, and different agencies will tell you different things. The port authorities don't seem to know anything, so save yourself the trouble of asking. Inquire at the main tourist office in Split.

Dubrovnik, "the pearl of the Adriatic," is only 4½hrs. away by bus. Though bombed by the Serbian navy, much of the city is intact, and rumors have it that prices are very low due to the lack of tourists. Be aware that although the city itself is considered generally safe, it *is* located only a few kilometers from the Bosnian border; going there might turn out to be a risky enterprise.

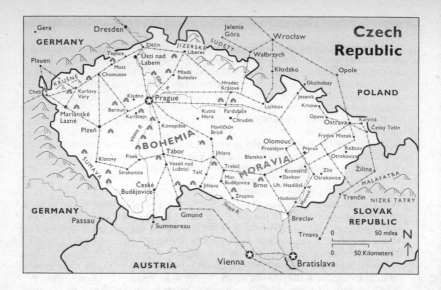

THE CZECH REPUBLIC

US$1	= 28.32kč (koruny, or CK)	10kč =	US$0.35
CDN$1	= 20.73kč	10kč =	CDN$0.48
UK£1	= 44.45kč	10kč =	UK£0.22
IR£1	= 43.61kč	10kč =	IR£0.23
AUS$1	= 21.10kč	10kč =	AUS$0.47
NZ$1	= 15.40kč	10kč =	NZ$0.65
SAR1	= 7.98kč	10kč =	SAR1.25
DM1	= 18.43kč	10kč =	DM0.54
Country Code: 42		International Dialing Prefix: 00	

On New Year's Day, 1993, after more than three quarters of a century of relatively unabrasive coexistence, the Czech and Slovak Republics, formerly known as Czechoslovakia, split, bloodlessly. The notion of self-determination is new to the Czech people; from the Holy Roman Empire to the Nazis and the Soviets, foreigners have driven their internal affairs; even the 1968 Prague Spring was frozen by the iron rumble of Soviet tanks. Today, the Czech Republic is facing yet another invasion: enamored Westerners are sweeping into the country to savor the historic towns, magnificent capital and the world's best beer.

CZECH REPUBLIC ESSENTIALS

American citizens may visit the Czech Republic visa-free for up to 30 days, citizens of the U.K. and Ireland for up to 90 days. Australians, Canadians, New Zealanders and South Africans require visas available from their Czech Embassy (See Essentials: Embassies and Consulates, page 3) and at three border crossings: Rozvadov, Dolni Dvoriste or Hate. Visas cost US$21 (single entry or transit; US$44 for Canadians) and US$49 (multiple entry), payable by cash or money order. They require two photos and two days to process. Canadian citizens must register with the police upon arrival in the Czech Republic and have their visa stamped.

GETTING THERE AND GETTING AROUND

Eastrail has been accepted in the Czech Republic since 1991, but **Eurail** is not yet valid here. Because rail travel remains such a bargain, however (about 30kč per 100km on a second-class *rychlík* train), railpasses are less of a necessity here than in Western Europe. The fastest trains are the *expresný*. The *rychlík* trains cost as much as the express, while the few *spešný* (semi-fast) trains cost less; avoid *osobný* (slow) trains. **ČSD**, the national transportation company, publishes the monster *Jízdní řád* (train schedule, 74kč), helpful if only for the two-page English explanation in front. *Odjezd* (departures) are printed in train stations on yellow posters, *prijezd* (arrivals) on white. **Čedok** gives ISIC holders up to 50% off international tickets bought at their offices. If heading to **Austria** or **Hungary,** it's generally less expensive to buy a Czech ticket to the border, then buy a separate ticket at the crossing to your destination once inside the other country. Seat reservations *(místenka,* 6kč) are required on almost all express and international trains and for all first class seating; snag them at the counter labeled by a boxed "R." A slip of paper with the destination, time, date, and a capital letter "R" expedites the transaction. Be sure to have valid transit visas if you plan to go through Slovakia—or route your trip through red-tape-free Vienna instead.

    Buses can be significantly faster and only slightly more expensive than trains, especially near Prague and for shorter distances. **ČSAD** runs national and international bus lines. From **Prague,** buses run a few times per week to Munich, Milan, and other international hubs; buses depart from **Brno** to **Linz,** in Austria. Consult the timetables posted at stations or buy your own bus schedule (25kč) from bookstores and newsstands.

    Because of the inherent risks, *Let's Go* does not recommend **hitchhiking** as a safe means of transportation. However, hitchhikers report that it still remains a popular option in the Czech Republic, especially during morning commuting hours (6-8am).

TOURIST SERVICES AND MONEY

The importance of **Čedok,** the official state tourist company and a relic of centralized Communist bureaucracy, has largely diminished since 1989. **CKM,** its junior affiliate, remains helpful for the student and budget traveler, serving as a clearinghouse for youth hostel beds and issuing ISIC and HI cards. The quality and trustworthiness of private tourist agencies varies; use your instincts. **Information offices** in major cities provide heaps of printed matter on sights and cultural events, as well as lists of hostels and hotels. City maps (*plán města*) are available for 28-60kč.

    There is no longer any mandatory foreign **currency exchange** requirement, but keep a few exchange receipts to change money back upon leaving. The **black market** for hard cash is still in operation, but graying around the temples; since the official exchange rate has almost reached street levels, it is hardly worth the risk. Bring some western currency in small denominations—it's still the preferred payment in larger hotels and private accommodations in larger cities. Banks are generally open from 8am to 4pm. Czech money is not valid in Slovakia.

COMMUNICATION

The Czech Republic's **postal system** has been converted to capitalist efficiency; letters reach the U.S. in under ten days. **International phone calls** are possible, though finding a gray and blue pay phone that works can be challenging. Look for a phone with a globe above it; most of the booths in post offices work. Buy the invaluable **phone cards** (100kč) at most newsstands, at the main post office, and at shops displaying the yellow and blue sign. Inserting the coin at the right time in Czech phones is an art. In the **gray phones,** place the change in the holding slot and dial; as soon as the other party answers, push in the coin. In the **orange boxes,** the coin will fall automatically when you connect. Local calls cost 2kč regardless of length. For inter-city calls, insert additional coins when the warning tone sounds. Use an international long-distance system to avoid the hefty charges of the Czech telephone bureaucracy—calls run 25kč per minute to Austria; 31kč per minute to the U.K., Italy, or France; 63kč per minute to the U.S., Canada, Australia, or Japan; and 94kč per minute to New Zealand. To reach the **AT&T USADirect operator** dial 00 42 00 01 01; to reach the **MCI WorldPhone operator** dial 00 42 00 01 12; to reach the **Canada Direct operator** dial 00 42 00 01 51; to reach the **BT Direct operator** (U.K.) dial 00 42 00 44 01.

LANGUAGE

Russian *was* every student's mandatory second language. These days, English will earn you more friends. A few German phrases go even further, especially in Prague. English-Czech dictionaries are indispensable; before you leave home, pick up a *Say it in Czech* phrasebook. A few handy phrases includes "*Zaplatíme*" (ZAH-plah-tyee-meh, "We're ready to pay"). Just this once, "*no*" (NOH) or "*ano*" (ah-NOH) means "yes," and "*ne*" (NEH) means "no."

Word or Phrase	Spelling	Pronunciation
Yes	*no* or *ano*	NOH or ah-NOH
No	*ne*	NEH
Hello	*Dobrý den*	doh-BREE den
Good morning	*Dobrý večer*	doh-BREE veh-CHER
Good night	*Dobrou noc*	doh-BROH NOTS
Goodbye	*Na shledanou*	nah SLEH-dah-noh-oo
Excuse me	*S dovolenim*	z-DOH-voh-leh-neem
Sorry	*Promiňte*	PROH-mihn-teh
Please/You're welcome	*Prosím*	PROH-seem
Thank you	*Děkuji*	DYEH-koo-yih
When?	*Kdy?*	k-DEE
Where?	*Kde?*	k-DEH
Help!	*Pomoc!*	poh-MOTS
How much does this cost?	*Kolik?*	KOH-lihk
How do I get to..?	*Jak se dostanu do...?*	YAHK seh dohs-TAH-noo doh
I don't understand	Nerozumím	neh-roh-zoo-MEEM

1—jedna (YEHD-nah); 2—dvě (dv-YEH); 3—tři (tr-ZHIH); 4—čtyři (choo-teer-ZHEE); 5—pět (p-YEHT); 6—šest (SHEHST); 7—sedm (SEH-duhm); 8—(osm (OSS-uhm); 9—devět (dehv-YEHT); 10—deset (dess-SEHT); 20—dvacet (dvah-TSEHT); 30—třicet (tr-zhih-TSEHT); 40—čtyřicet (choo-tihr-zhih-TSEHT); 50—padesát (pah-dess-AHT); 60—šedesát (sheh-dess-AHT); 70—sedmdesát (seh-duhm-dess-AHT); 80—osmdesát (oss-uhm-dess-AHT); 90—devadesát (deh-vah-dess-AHT); 100—sto (STOH); 1000—tisíc (tih-SEETS).

HEALTH AND SAFETY

Crime has climbed dramatically since the 1989 revolution; beware purse-snatchers and pickpockets prowling among the crowds in the Old Town Square, on the way to the Castle and on trams. There is a moral code: lost wallets and purses sometimes appear at embassies with only the cash missing. In **emergencies,** notify your embassy or consulate; local police may not be well versed in English. The **emergency phone number** throughout the country is **158.**

ACCOMMODATIONS AND CAMPING

Converted **university dorms** under the auspices of **CKM** are the cheapest option in July and August. Comfy two- to four-bed rooms go for 200-400kč per person. CKM also runs **Junior Hotels** (year-round hostels loosely affiliated with HI, which give discounts to both HI and ISIC cardholders) that are comfortable but often full. Private hostel operations have usurped CKM's monopoly on youth lodgings, but have not necessarily surpassed its reliability. Showers and bedding are usually included; occasionally breakfast is too, especially outside of Prague.

Across the country, **private homes** have become a legal and feasible lodging option. In Prague, hawkers offer expensive rooms (US$16-30, but don't agree to more than US$25), often including breakfast. Scan train stations for "hostel," "*Zimmer*," or "accommodations" ads. Quality varies widely; *don't* pay in advance. Make sure anything you accept is easily accessible by public transport; be prepared for a healthy commute to the center of town. Outside of Prague, **Čedok** handles private room booking, although private agencies are burgeoning around train and bus stations. If you're sticking to **hotels,** consider reserving ahead from June to September in Prague and Brno, even if pre-payment is required. Outside of the major cities it is easier to find a bed. Hotels come in flavors to suit a variety of tastes: A-star, A, B-star, B, and C. Many of the grungy C hotels are quickly disappearing. In the summer of 1994, singles in a B hotel averaged 650kč and doubles 900kč (within Prague, 950kč and 1400kč, respectively).

Inexpensive **campgrounds** are available throughout the country, ranging from 60-100kč per person (most sites are open only mid-May to September). The book *Ubytování ČSR,* in decodable Czech, comprehensively lists the hotels, inns, hostels, huts, and campgrounds in Bohemia and Moravia. Bookstores also sell a fine hiking map of the country, *Soubor Turistických Map,* with an English key.

LIFE AND TIMES

HISTORY

The area now known as the Czech Republic has been inhabited since the earliest human settlement of Europe. **Paleolithic** flake-tools are still found in Bohemian caves, though their users had become Mesolithic hunter-gatherers as early as 10,000 BC. A few millennia later, **Neolithic** farmers in Bohemia made a big splash in the European fashion scene; their Linear pottery decorations dominated central European art for 2000 years. The Unetice and Tumulus cultures crafted gold and **bronze** treasures to hide in tomb-mounds until the **Celts** arrived around 1300 BC, bringing improved trade, a warrior aristocracy, and a fetish for cremation. Little affected by the Iron Age civilizations flourishing to the south or by Scythian invaders from the east, Bohemia changed little until the **La Tène** Celts introduced iron weapons and urban civilization around 450 BC. **Germanic** settlers soon arrived from the north, while trade picked up with the Roman Empire to the south.

In the fifth century AD, as the Germans moved southward into the crumbling Empire, the Czech Republic's present inhabitants arrived. **West Slavs** settled the area: Sorbs (not Serbs) in the mountainous northwest, Moravians in the southeast, and Bohemians (Czechs) in the center. **Christianization** of the Bohemians and Sorbs began during the reign of Charlemagne. A Catholic bishopric was established in Prague in 973. The **Moravians** were enslaved by the invading Avars but freed by the Frankish merchant Samo in 626. Falling to Charlemagne in 805, the Moravians regained independence in 830 by converting to Greek Orthodoxy. Missionary activity by the Greeks commenced, but Moravia reverted to Catholicism in 880. After being destroyed by the Hungarians in 906, Moravia's luck declined; it was traded between Poland, the Empire, and Bohemia for hundreds of years, and ended up permanently joined to the last.

The **Bohemians** were united in the 9th century by the **Przemyslid Dynasty** of Prague, quickly becoming a strong, autonomous state. The most famous early Przemyslid was the Catholic Duke Wenceslas I (c.903-935), who was later canonized as **St. Wenceslas** of Christmas song fame and became the patron saint of Bohemia. During the Slavic Wars of 928-929, the Holy Roman Empire subjugated the **Sorbs** but had to sign a treaty with the Bohemians in order to fight of the Magyars of Hungary. Two more strikes in 950 and 975 and the Holy Roman Empire was out, though a surprise Polish invasion in 1003 caught Bohemia and Moravia off guard. Bohemia fell to the Empire the following year, and, after the defeat of Bretislav of Bohemia in

1041, became a German fief. In 1140, Bohemia became a hereditary kingdom under Vladislav II. The country gradually gained in power and prestige, reaching a peak under **Przemysl Ottokar II** (1253-1278), who conquered Austria and Slovenia before falling to Holy Roman Emperor Rudolf of Habsburg. Bohemia and Moravia remained in Przemyslid hands until the death of Wenceslas III in 1306, when they became Imperial estates.

Holy Roman Emperor **Charles IV** (1346-1378) made Bohemia the center of Imperial power. As his capital, Prague experienced a Golden Age. Charles built hundreds of buildings, including St. Vitus Cathedral and the Hradcany Castle. He established Prague as an Archbishopric and founded Charles University, the first university in Central Europe. Many Czechs regard him as their greatest "national hero" and look back on his reign with nostalgia. Charles improved the lot of both his Czech-speaking and his German-speaking subjects through governmental reforms, and while some Czechs and Germans claim Charles IV as their own, the fact is that this king was unfamiliar with ethnic nationalism, which was invented much later and, typically, superimposed on the past.

Charles's son Wenceslas "the Lazy" failed to live up to his father in any capacity. After being deposed as emperor and defeated by his Moravian cousin, Wenceslas watched as order disintegrated in Bohemia. During his reign, **Jan Hus** (1369-1415) spoke out against the evils of the Catholic Church hierarchy and the corruption of the Pope, for which he was burned to death as a heretic. Four years after his death, Hus' followers performed the first defenestration of Prague, which launched 15 years of **Hussite Wars.** After withstanding five imperial and crusader invasions and campaigning all the way to Danzig (Gdańsk) on the Baltic coast, the Hussites warred amongst themselves; the moderate side winning the Battle of Lipan in 1434. Catholic Church machinery failed to crush Hussitism, which survived in the form of the Community of the Bohemian and Moravian Brethren and was a significant precursor of the Protestant Reformation.

After a century of being periodically traded between Poland and the Empire, angry Bohemian Protestants held the second, and more famous, **Defenestration of Prague,** during which imperial deputies were thrown out windows. Such errant behavior launched the **Thirty Years War** (1618-1648). The early, Bohemian Phase (1618-1623) of the war saw an Imperial counter-attack and victory over the Bohemian nobles at the **Battle of White Mountain** in 1620. Executions, massive land-confiscations, forced Catholic conversion, and coerced German emigration followed, sowing the seeds of Czech-German dislike and linking Bohemia and Moravia to Habsburg Austria. The remainder of the war brought about the utter destruction of Bohemia, resulting in the deaths of over one-third of its inhabitants. While the Counter-Reformation inspired the building of magnificent Baroque churches, including Dienzenhofer's masterpieces in Prague and Karlovy Vary, the absorption of Czech territory into the **Austrian Empire** turned into three centuries of oppressive rule. The frightening bureaucratic/police state forced upon the Czechs directly inspired Franz Kafka's nightmare world. More than Kakfaesque, it was Kafka.

As the spirit of national invention swept Europe from west to east, Bohemia became the home of **Czech nationalism.** Josef Dobrovský and Josef Jungmann helped revive and standardize the Czech language in the late eighteenth century. In the Revolution of 1848, Czech nationalism not only clashed with the Habsburg conservatism that crushed the rebellion, but also encountered German nationalism that was becoming an increasingly powerful ideology in Bohemia's German-speaking community. Although the Czech leader and historian **František Palacký** and the Bohemian-German representative Löhner wanted to federalize Austria along ethnic lines, the Habsburg regime ignored their proposals and vainly tried to suppress nationalism with reactionary decrees. Karl Marx wrote rabid diatribes in response to the 1848 Czech national movement in which he denied the existence of the Czech nation. In 1848 there were no Marxists in Bohemia.

The anachronistic Habsburg Empire never got around to addressing the nationalities question. Unquenched nationalism congealed into extremist groups in the late nineteenth century, including Pan-Slavs, Young Czechs, and Pan-Germans. World War I did nothing to increase harmony among the nationalities of Austria's Empire. In the post-war confusion of 1918, **Edvard Beneš** and **Tomáš Masaryk** convinced the victorious Allies to legitimize a new state, uniting Bohemia, Moravia, and Slovakia (a Hungarian territory for 1000 years) into Czechoslovakia. Unique in Eastern Europe, Czechoslovakia remained a parliamentary democracy between the wars. The Great depression of the 1930s and the agitating German minority, however, created an instability exploited by Hitler in the 1938 **Munich Agreement.** France, Great Britain, and Italy agreed to the annexation the Sudetenland and other Czechoslovak territory by Germany, Hungary, and Poland in order to avoid another world war. Many Czechs, as well as many British and Americans, regarded this decision by the West as a betrayal (see the film *Night Train to Munich*). The Munich agreement failed to appease Hitler, who invaded the following year, brutally annexing Bohemia and Moravia as a "Protectorate" and turning Slovakia into an independent fascist state. Before World War II, Prague's thriving Jewish population earned it the nickname "The Jerusalem of Europe." Despite the protection of many valiant Czech Christians, most of Czechoslovakia's Jews were murdered by the Nazis and their allies during the five year occupation.

In 1945, Soviet troops swept through Czechoslovakia and the American army reached Plzeň. Czechoslovakia was formally reconstituted after the war, and the Communists won 38% of the vote in the 1946 elections, the highest percentage of any country in post-war Eastern Europe. Pressed by their Soviet backers, the unsatisfied Czech communists led by **Klement Gottwald** seized power in 1948. Czechoslovakia's industrial economy crumbled under Stalinism, and the country stagnated in the 50s as a depressed satellite state. In 1968, however, the new Communist Party secretary **Alexander Dubček** sought to implement "socialism with a human face," dramatically reforming the country's economy and easing political oppression during the **"Prague Spring."** Not pleased with the new developments, the USSR and its Warsaw Pact puppet states invaded Czechoslovakia to suppress Dubček's heretical counter-revolution. Under Soviet guidance, Gustáv Husák introduced an even more repressive and economically disastrous totalitarian system that lasted for twenty-one years.

After the demise of the Communist Parties in Hungary and Poland and after the fall of the Berlin Wall in 1989, the **Velvet Revolution** came to Czechoslovakia. Despite Communist crackdowns, Czechs increasingly demonstrated in Prague and other cities in November, and within a month, the Communist government had resigned and **Václav Havel** emerged as the main political leader. Known as an anti-Communist dissident, a playwright, and the founder of the human rights group Charter 77, Havel had been a political prisoner until six months before the Velvet Revolution. The transformation to constitutional democracy, economic market reforms, and the departure of Soviet troops were overseen by Havel and his Civic Forum Party, which had united with the Slovakian Public Against Violence Party in the free elections of June 1990. Havel attempted to preserve the Czech-Slovak union, but three years of debate and a popular vote resulted in the separation of the two nations on January 1, 1993.

THE CZECH REPUBLIC TODAY

Although Havel temporarily stepped down during the divorce with Slovakia, Czechs today have much respect for their playwright-president and for the most part are embracing the Westernization process that continues at a dizzying pace. The Czech Republic boasts Eastern Europe's most stable currency and the region's second-largest GDP per capita, after Slovenia. It may be only a matter of time before the Czech Republic joins the EU.

FOOD

The vintage Central European mix of Austrian, German, and Hungarian influences make food in the Czech Republic cosmopolitan in a charming 19th-century sort of way. The health-food craze has yet to hit: the four basic food groups here are sausages *(párek, klobosa)*, cheese *(sýr)*, ice cream *(zmrzlina)*, and beer *(pivo)*.

Restaurants *(Restaurace)* come in three categories, with Category I being often over-priced and pretentious and Category III being the most authentic and reasonably priced (main course under 70kč). The traditional Czech national meal is *vepřové, knedlíky,* and *zelí* (roast pork, dumplings, and Bohemian sauerkraut). *Guláš,* a variation on Hungarian pork or beef stew, is well-seasoned and made from a decent cut of meat. Also scrumptious are *Vídeňský řízek* (Wiener schnitzel) and its pork counterpart, *vepřový řízek. Svíčková na smetaně* is a Czech type of *Sauerbraten* (well-seasoned roast beef with gravy).

Other words worth recognizing on the *Hotová Jídla* (ready dishes) section of menus are: *hovězi* (beef), *sekaná pečeně* (meatloaf), and *klobása* (sausage). Meat can be *pečeně* (roasted), *vařené* (boiled) or *mleté* (ground). *Kuře* (chicken) is eaten less often here than in North America. *Ryby* (fish) include *kapr* (carp) and *pstruh* (trout). If you are in a hurry, you can grab a pair of *párky* (frankfurters) or some *sýr* (cheese) at either a *bufet, samoobsluha* (self-service), or *občerstveni,* all variations on the stand-up snack bar. If you love ice cream, learn to pronounce *zmrzlina.*

For desserts, sweets, or mere *kaffeeklatsch,* visit a *kavárna* (café) or a *cukrárna* (pastry shop). *Káva* (coffee) is often served Turkish-style with a layer of grounds at the bottom of the cup. *Koblihy* (doughnuts), *jablkový závin* (apple strudel), *koláč* (pie), and *palačinky* (pancakes) are favorites.

It is customary to round the bill up by a few crowns—often it will be done for you. At finer eateries, you should add a 10% tip as you pay; do not leave the tip on the table. Vegetarian restaurants have begun to sprout in larger cities. **Vegetarians** can also munch on *smaženy sýr* (fried cheese), a scrumptious Czech specialty sold at food stands, and produce from *ovoce zelenina* stores (green-grocers) or *potraviny* (general grocery stores). From Saturday noon to Sunday morning, all grocery stores and some restaurants close.

DRINK

One of the fines attributes of Czech cuisine is that it goes so well with beer *(pivo)*. The Czech Republic has been producing some of the best beers in the world for a millenium. It's therefore little surprise that the future American brewing giant Anheuser-Busch named its most popular (if rather pale, to say the least) beers after the Bohemian beer town of Budweis (today *České Budějovice).*

Most European and Czech beers are lagers, or bottom-fermented beers. Bohemia has a special place in the discovery and perfection of the lager. Although the great Viennese brewer Anton Dreher invented the lagering process of bottom fermentation in Vienna, he built a brewing empire with brasseries in Budapest, Trieste, and the sleepy Bohemian village of Michelob (today *Měcholupy,* in the heart of the Saaz hops-growing region.

The lager was perfected at Pilsen (today *Plzeň)* in the 1840s with the creation of crisp and hoppy lager. Known as *Plzeňský Prazdroj/Pilsner Urquell*, this original Pilsner beer is best enjoyed from a keg. Original Budweiser *Budvar* is also popular and duly famous. Many Czechs laud the tasty *Velkopopovický Kozel,* a type of bock beer. In Prague, the ubiquitous *Staropramen* is a respectable light *(světlé)* lager and *Měšťán* is an excellent dark *(tmavé)* lager. Another classic dark lager is *Purkmistr* from Domažlice in Western Bohemia. From the Saaz hops-growing region come the very good *Žatecký* and *Lounský ležak (Graf von Louny* in its export variety). *Egg- enberg* from South Bohemia is a refreshing brew. In Moravia, the rich *Staro Brno* is better than the mass-produced *Radegast.*

With such a variety of types of beer comes a great choice of where to drink. A **piv- nice** is a beer-hall typically rich in atmosphere and local company. Some *pivnice,* however, cater exclusively to tourists (and simply want your money). The **hostinec** (pub) must be approached with a bit more caution, as the proletarian imbibers and anxious owners sometimes force those who do not speak Czech to drink their beer outdoors—yet another sorrow to be drowned in quality *pivo.*

Produced chiefly in Moravia, Czech wines are surprisingly decent, despite their limited popularity outside the Czech Republic. The *Rulandské* (Ruländers) from Znojmo in Southern Moravia is good, but the *Müller-Thurgau* is more variable in terms of quality. Any Moravian *Welschriesling* is drinkable. People typically drink wine at the *vinárna* (wine bar), which usually has flasks of different types of wine "on tap." Wine bars also serve a variety of hard spirits, including the flavorful *Becherovka* (herbal bitter) and *slivovica* (plum brandy). One of the northernmost wine-producing regions in Europe is the town of Mělník, lying at the confluence of the Labe (Elbe) and Vltava (Moldau) rivers in Bohemia. Charles IV planted Burgundy wines in Mělník in the 14th century. Since then, Mělník has attracted visitors year-round, but particularly during its wine festival in the last week of September.

■ Prague (Praha)

According to legend, the Princess Libuše stood atop one of seven hills overlooking the River Vltava and declared, "I see a city whose glory will touch the stars; it shall be called Praha (threshold)." From its mythological inception to the present, benefactors have placed Prague on the cusp of the divine. Founded at the end of the 8th century, the city became the capital of the Holy Roman Empire six centuries later. Charles IV, King of Bohemia and Holy Roman Emperor, envisioned a royal seat worthy of his rank. He rebuilt 14th-century Prague into the "city of a hundred spires," with soaring cathedrals and lavish palaces, thus elevating the city to an imperial magnificence eclipsed only by Rome and Constantinople.

Prague's lively squares and avenues give the city a festive air, and its museums, concert halls, and ballet and opera performances are world-class. Artists and musicians have always been drawn here; Prague was the first to appreciate Mozart fully. The capital has waltzed through the 20th century as if charmed; it escaped the ravages suffered by other European cities during both World Wars. Since the Velvet Revolution of 1989, the city has exploded from relative obscurity and isolation behind the Iron Curtain into a tourist destination surpassing the great capitals of Western Europe. Prague allows a glimpse back into a quickly fading world that politics rendered almost inaccessible for decades.

Over 20,000 Yappies ("Young Americans in Prague") call the city home, and more than 750,000 visitors left envying them last year. While many locals can't keep up with the rising prices, Prague is still a fabulous bargain by Western standards. Just don't flaunt your affluence; struggling locals don't need to hear how inexpensive items might seem to you. Instead, immerse yourself as seamlessly as possible into the humbling magnificence of this millennium-old metropolis.

ORIENTATION AND PRACTICAL INFORMATION

Prague is a sumptuous blend of nature and architecture in the center of Czech Bohemia. The town is built on seven hills; seventeen bridges span the River **Vltava** ("Moldau" in German) on its course through the city. Direct rail and bus service links Prague with Vienna, Berlin, Munich, and Warsaw (see Transportation, page 166). All train and bus terminals are on or near the excellent Metro system, the nám. Republiky Metro B station (*E3*) is closest to the principal tourist offices and accommodations agencies. *Tabak* stands and bookstores vend indexed *plán města* **(maps)**. Prague's two **English-language newspapers,** *Prognosis* and *The Prague Post,* both provide numerous tips for visitors along with the usual news.

Prague will be in the process of carrying out a much-needed telephone-system overhaul through 1996; many of the numbers listed may change.

CZECH REPUBLIC

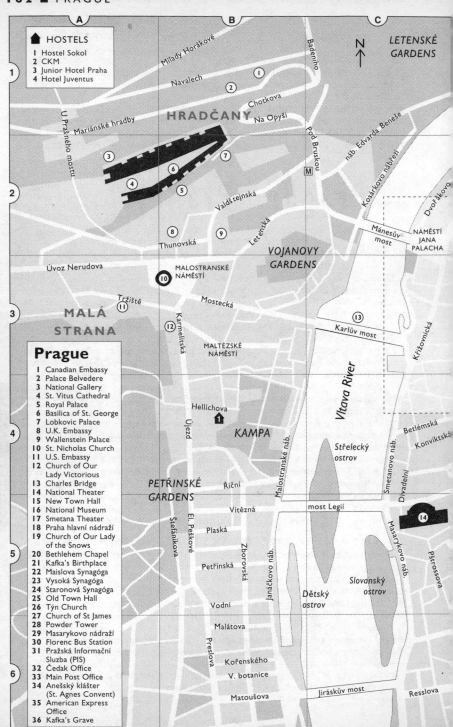

HOSTELS

1 Hostel Sokol
2 CKM
3 Junior Hotel Praha
4 Hotel Juventus

Prague

1 Canadian Embassy
2 Palace Belvedere
3 National Gallery
4 St. Vitus Cathedral
5 Royal Palace
6 Basilica of St. George
7 Lobkovic Palace
8 U.K. Embassy
9 Wallenstein Palace
10 St. Nicholas Church
11 U.S. Embassy
12 Church of Our
   Lady Victorious
13 Charles Bridge
14 National Theater
15 New Town Hall
16 National Museum
17 Smetana Theater
18 Praha hlavní nádraží
19 Church of Our Lady
   of the Snows
20 Bethlehem Chapel
21 Kafka's Birthplace
22 Maislova Synagóga
23 Vysoká Synagóga
24 Staronová Synagóga
25 Old Town Hall
26 Týn Church
27 Church of St James
28 Powder Tower
29 Masarykovo nádraží
30 Florenc Bus Station
31 Pražská Informační
   Sluzba (PIS)
32 Čedak Office
33 Main Post Office
34 Anešský klášter
   (St. Agnes Convent)
35 American Express
   Office
36 Kafka's Grave

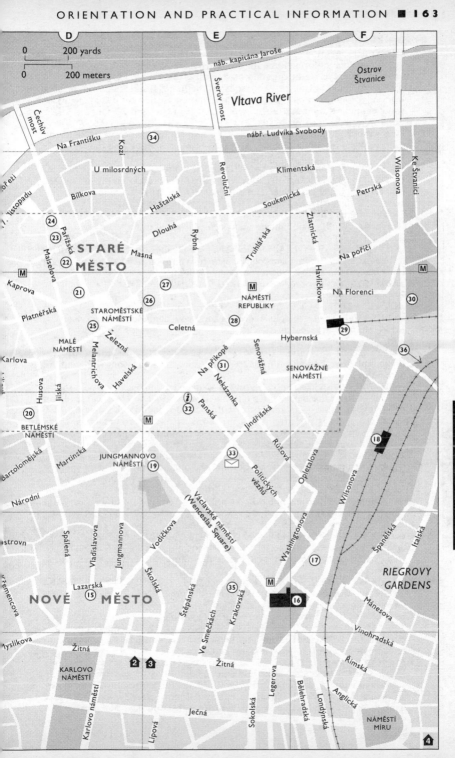

0   200 yards

0   200 meters

Vltava River

náb. kapitána Jaroše

Šverův most

Čechův most

Ostrov Štvanice

Na Františku

Kozí

(34)

náb. Ludvíka Svobody

U milosrdných

Bílkova

Haštalská

Revoluční

Klimentská

Soukenická

Petrská

Wilsonova

Ke Štvanici

Zlatnická

Na Poříčí

Dlouhá

Rybná

Truhlářská

(24)

(23)

Pařížská

Maiselova

STARÉ

MĚSTO

(22)

Masná

Kaprova

(21)

Platnéřská

STAROMĚSTSKÉ NÁMĚSTÍ

(25)

(27)

(26)

Železná

Celetná

M

NÁMĚSTÍ REPUBLIKY

(28)

Havlíčkova

Na Florenci

M

(30)

(29)

Hybernská

MALÉ NÁMĚSTÍ

Melantrichova

Havelská

Na příkopě

Senovážná

SENOVÁŽNÉ NÁMĚSTÍ

Karlova

Husova

Jilská

Nekázanka

(31)

(36)

(20)

BETLÉMSKÉ NÁMĚSTÍ

i

(32)

Panská

Jindřišská

M

Růžova

(18)

Bartolomějská

Martinská

JUNGMANNOVO NÁMĚSTÍ

(19)

(33)

Politických vězňů

Opletalova

Wilsonova

Národní

Václavské náměstí (Wenceslas Square)

strovn

Spálená

Vladislavova

Jungmannova

Vodičkova

Školská

Štěpánská

Washingtonova

(17)

Španělská

Italská

RIEGROVY GARDENS

Lazarská

(15)

NOVÉ   MĚSTO

Krakovská

(35)

M

(16)

Mánesova

Vinohradská

řemenova

yslíkova

Žitná

KARLOVO NÁMĚSTÍ

Karlovo náměstí

Lipová

(2)

(3)

Ve Smečkách

Žitná

Sokolská

Legerova

Bělehradská

Londýnská

Římská

Anglická

Ječná

NÁMĚSTÍ MÍRU

(4)

D   E   F

CZECH REPUBLIC

Organizations

Tourist Offices: Many state-owned tourist offices have been replaced by new private outfits. Small information outlets or kiosks are plentiful and easy to recognize by the small "i" or the question mark symbol ("?").
CKM (*DE6*), Žitná 12 (tel. 29 12 40), next to the Junior Hotel Praha. Offers information, accommodations, and transportation tickets. Beware of old maps that show extinct CKM branch offices. Open daily 9am-1pm and 2-7pm.
Čedok (*E3-4*), Na příkopě 18 (tel. 212 71 11, fax 29 07 98 or 24 22 77 18). No longer essential, but a convenient place for information on private accommodations and sightseeing in Prague. Also sells train, bus and plane tickets. Open Mon.-Fri. 9am-7pm, Sat. 8:30am-2pm.
Prague Information Service (Pražská Informační Služba), Staroměstske nám. 22 (tel. 224 45 23) Sells a massive variety of maps and booklets on Prague and the Czech Republic. English and German spoken. Open daily 9am-5pm.
Embassies: If you've been robbed, try your embassy or consulate first for advice on how and where to report the theft; police usually speak little English. All Western embassies will hold mail. Embassy and consular services are contained in the same building unless otherwise noted.
U.S. (*A3*), Tržiště 15, Praha 12548 (tel. 24 51 04 47, after hours 52 12 00). Metro A: "Malostranská." From Malostranské nám. turn into Karmelitská and then right on Tržiště. Open Mon.-Fri. 8am-1pm and 2-4:30pm.
Canada (*B1*), Mickiewiczova 6 (tel. 312 02 51). Open Mon.-Fri. 8:30am-noon and 2-4pm.
U.K. (*B2-3*), Thunovská 14 (tel. 24 51 04 39). Open Mon.-Fri. 8:30am-12:30pm and 1:30-5pm. Travelers from **Australia** and **New Zealand** should contact the British embassy in an emergency.
South Africa, Ruská 65 (tel. 67 31 11 14 or 67 31 25 75).
Hungary (*D5-6*), Badeního 1 (tel. 36 50 41). Same-day visas for citizens of **Australia** and **New Zealand** for US$20 plus 2 photos. Open Mon.-Wed. and Fri. 9am-noon.
Poland (*B2*), Valdštejnská 8 (tel. 53 69 51). **Consulate** (*E4-5*), Václavské nám. 49 (tel. 26 44 64). Same-day visas for citizens of **Australia** and **New Zealand** cost US$28 plus 2 photos; students US$21 with ISIC. Open Mon.-Fri. 9am-1pm.
Russia (*C1*), Pod kaštany 1 (tel. 38 19 45). **Consulate** (*C1*), around the corner at Korunovačni 34 (tel. 37 37 23). Visas US$25 (invitation required); citizens of **Australia** pay US$50. Open Mon., Wed., and Fri. 9:30am-1pm.
Slovakia, Pod Hradbami 1 (tel. 32 05 02). **Canadian** citizens pay US$43 for a visa.
Currency Exchange: Beware the **black market.** You may end up with counterfeit bills no one will accept. **Banks** offer better rates than the private *bureaux de change*. If you are having difficulty reconverting your crowns into your own currency, contact the **Komerčni bank,** Na příkopě 42 (tel. 24 02 11 11, fax. 24 24 30 20). Most banks are open from 8-11am and 4-6pm. On weekends and holidays, exchange counters in large hotels will convert money.
Čedok (*E3-4*) offers the best rates on cash, in spite of a 2% commission.
State bank (*E3-4*), Na příkopě 14, a stone's throw from Čedok (tel. 23 31 11 11), cashes US$ or DM traveler's checks. Open Mon.-Fri. 7:30am-noon and 1-3:30pm.
Živnostenská bank (*E3-4*), Na příkopě 2 (tel. 24 12 11 11, fax 24 12 55 55). Also gives cash advances on Visa and MasterCard. Commission 1% on cash, 2% on traveler's checks. Open Mon.-Fri. 8am-5pm.
Chequepoint offices are located in all of Prague's highly touristed areas. About 10% commission on top of a service charge—*egad!* The Chequepoints at the intersections of Václavské nám. and Vodičková and of Václavské nám. and 28 října are open 24 hrs. for travelers in a jam.
American Express: (*E5*) Václavské nám. 56 (tel. 24 22 77 86, fax 24 22 77 08). Metro A or C: "Muzeum." If the line extends out the door, just walk 5min. up Václavské nám. to the bank branches listed above. Address mail as follows: "Kimberly McCORKELL, American Express, Client Letter Service, Václavské nám. 56, 113 26 Praha 1, Česka Republika/Czech Republic." Mail held at U.S.

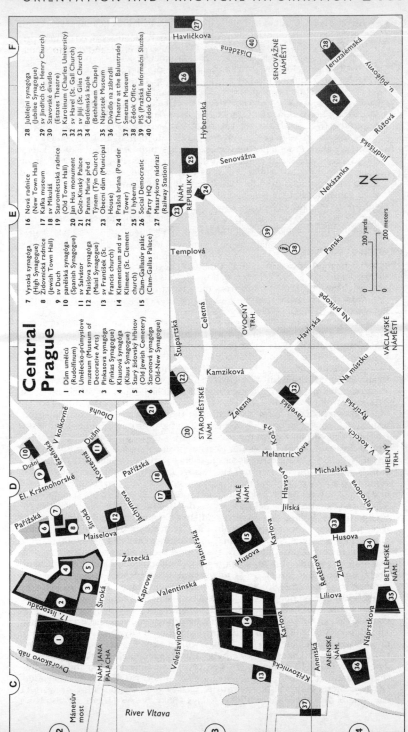

Central Prague

1 Dům umělců (Rudolfinum)
2 Umělecko-průmyslové muzeum (Museum of Decorative Arts)
3 Pinkasova synagóga (Pinkas Synagogue)
4 Klausova synagóga (Klaus Synagogue)
5 Starý židovský hřbitov (Old Jewish Cemetery)
6 Staronová synagóga (Old-New Synagogue)
7 Vysoká synagóga (High Synagogue)
8 Židovnická radnice (Jewish Town Hall)
9 sv Duch
10 paněiská synagóga (Spanish Synagogue)
11 sv Salvator
12 Maislova synagóga (Maisl Synagogue)
13 sv František (St. Francis church)
14 Klementinum and sv Kliment (St. Clement church)
15 Clam-Gallasův palác (Clam-Gallas Palace)
16 Nová radnice (New Town Hall)
17 Kafka museum
18 sv Mikuláš
19 Staroměstská radnice (Old Town Hall)
20 Jan Hus monument
21 Golz-Kinský Palace
22 Panna Marie před Týnem (Týn Church)
23 Obecní dům (Municipal House)
24 Prašná brána (Powder Tower)
25 U hyberňů
26 Social Democratic Party HQ
27 Masarykovo nádraží (Railway Station)
28 Jubilejní synagóga (Jubilee Synagogue)
29 sv Jindřich (St. Henry Church)
30 Stavovské divadlo (Estates Theatre)
31 Karolinum (Charles University)
32 sv Havel (St. Gall Church)
33 sv Jiljí (St. Giles Church)
34 Betlémská kaple (Bethlehem Chapel)
35 Náprstek Museum
36 Divadlo na zábradlí (Theatre at the Balustrade)
37 Smetana Museum
38 Čedok Office
39 PIS (Pražská Informační Služba)
40 Čedok Office

CZECH REPUBLIC

visitors' counter. Cardholders' personal checks cashed for kč only. MasterCard advances. Express cash machine. Open Mon.-Fri. 9am-6pm, Sat. 9am-noon. **Thomas Cook:** (*E5*), Václavské nám 47 (tel. 26 31 06 or 24 22 86 58, fax 26 56 95 or 26 09 90). Cash your Thomas Cook Eurocheques here. Popular for its flexible hours. Open Mon.-Fri. 9am-9pm, Sat. 9am-4pm and Sun. 10am-2pm. **ATMs:** Personal banking machines are popping up all over Prague. For the nearest one that features your network (i.e. **Cirrus, Plus,** etc.) consult one of the banks listed above. For **lost credit cards,** contact: **Visa** and **Diner's Club** (tel. 236 66 88), **MasterCard** (tel. 23 92 21 35), or **American Express** (above). **Post Office:** (*E4*), Jindřišská 14. (tel. 26 41 93) Metro A or B: "Můstek." Address *Poste Restante* as follows: Kimberly McCORKELL, Jindřišská 14, 110 00 Praha 1, Czech Republic. *Poste Restante* at window 28, stamps at windows 20-23, letters and parcels under 2kg at windows 10-12. Open 24 hrs. Parcels over 2kg can be mailed only at **Pošta-Celnice,** Plzeňská 139. Take tram #9 west. Airmail should arrive within 10 days from the U.S. Open Mon.-Tues. and Thurs.-Fri. 7am-3pm, Wed. 7am-6pm, and Sat. 8am-noon. **Telephones:** On many city streets, most train and metro stations, and post offices. Phone cards (100kč) are available at post offices and many newsstands; they provide about 2min. calling time to the U.S. **City Code: 02.**

Transportation

Flights: Ruzyně Airport (tel. 334 33 14), 20km northwest of city center. Take bus #119 from the "Dejvická" Metro A station. Various private companies offer rather expensive (around 100kč) buses from the airport to locations in downtown Prague. **ČSA** (Czech National Airlines; tel. 36 78 14, fax 24 81 04 26), is located on Revoluční north of nám. Republiky.

Trains: There are four train stations in Prague; always ask what your point of departure will be—the information may not be volunteered. Czech speakers can call **train information** (tel. 24 44 41 or 26 49 30).

Praha-Holešovice. Metro C "Nádraží Holešovice." The main international terminal—you'll probably arrive here or at Hlavní Nádraží.

Praha Hlavní Nádraží (or Wilsonovo Nádraží). Metro C: "Hlavní Nádraží." Some international and many domestic routes. To: Vienna (5 per day, 5hr.); Budapest (6 per day, 9hr.); Berlin (6 per day, 6hr.); and Warsaw (2 per day, 10hr.).

Masarykovo Nádraží (formerly Střední), at Hybernská and Havlíčkova. Metro B: "nám. Republiky." Serves only domestic routes, primarily in Central and Western Bohemia (Kolín, Chomutov, Žatec, Louny, Česká Třebova).

Praha-Smíchov, south across the river, opposite Vyšehrad. Metro B: "Smíchovské Nádraží." Serves nearby domestic routes, such as Karlštejn and Beroun.

Buses: ČSAD has three terminals (Autobusové nádraží). **Praha-Florenc** (*F2-3*) is central, on Křižíkova, behind the Masarykovo nádraží train station (tel. 22 86 42 or 22 26 29). Metro B or C: "Florenc." Staff speaks little English, but schedules are legible and extensive. Buy tickets at least a day in advance; they often sell out. To: Vienna (daily); Venice (4 per week); Milan (2 per week); and Munich (2 per week). Extensive service throughout the Czech Republic and Slovakia. Open Mon.-Fri. 6am-6:30pm, Sat. 6am-1pm, Sun. 8:30am-noon and 12:30-3:30pm.

Public Transportation: The **Metro, tram,** and **bus** systems serve the city well. Bus routes frequently shift for street repairs. **Tickets,** good for all forms of transportation, cost 6kč. Stock up at **newsstands** and **tabak** shops—the orange automat machines in Metro stations require exact change. **Punch your ticket** when boarding, and punch a new ticket when switching vehicles—except in the Metro, where your ticket is valid on all lines for 1hr. after punching, as long as you don't go above ground. If you lose it before exiting, you'll face a 200kč fine. The Metro's 3 main lines run daily 5am-midnight: on city maps, line A is green, line B is yellow, and line C is red. "Můstek" (lines A and B), "Muzeum" (lines A and C), and "Florenc" (lines B and C) are the primary junctions. **Night trams** #51-58 and **buses** #500-510 run midnight-5am (every 40min.); look for the dark blue signs at transport stops. The municipal transit authority (**DP** or Dopravní Podnik Hlavního Města Prahy) also sells **tourist passes** valid for the entire network (1 day 50kč, 2 days 85kč, 3 days 110kč, 4 days 135kč, 5 days 170kč). DP also has a

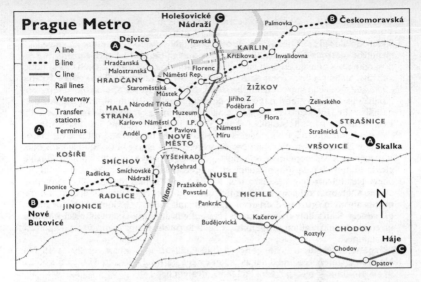

green incentive: buy a set of 25 "ekological" single-journey tickets valid only for the tram and the Metro for an amazing 115kč. **DP offices:** Jungmannovo nám. (tel. 24 22 51 35; Metro A and B: Můstek) and Palackého nám. (tel. 29 46 82; Metro B: Karlovo náměstí). Open daily 7am-9pm.

Taxis: tel. 35 03 20 or 35 04 91 or 202 95 19 or 203 94 19. Regular taxis cost 12kč per km; larger taxis in front of the airport and hotels charge 28kč per km. Ask for a price before entering the cab, and check to see that the meter starts at "0." On shorter trips, make sure the meter is running by saying *"Zapněte taxametr," ;* for longer trips set a price beforehand. If problems arise, ask the driver for a receipt before paying: *"Prosím, dejte, mi paragon."* Receipts usually state the distance traveled and the price paid. Downtown to airport costs about 500kč. Locals strongly distrust cab drivers and warn foreigners against using taxis.

Car Rental: Dollar Rent-a-Car in Ruzyně Airport has flexible hours. **Hertz** has 5 locations: Ruzyně Airport (tel./fax 312 07 17), open daily 8am-8pm; Karlovo nám. 28 (tel./fax 29 78 36), open daily 8am-8pm; Hotel Diplomat, Evropská 15 (tel. 24 39 41 55), open daily 8am-8pm; Hotel Forum at Kongresová 1 (tel. 61 19 12 13), open daily 8am-8pm; Hotel Atrium at Pobřezni 1 (tel. 24 84 20 47); open Mon.-Fri. 8:30am-5pm.

Hitchhiking: *Let's Go* does not recommend hitchhiking as a safe means of transportation. Hitchhiking in and around Prague has become increasingly dangerous; luckily, cheap but extensive train and bus service render it largely unnecessary. Those hitching east take tram #1, 9, or 16 to the last stop. To points south, they take Metro C to "Pražskeho povstání," then walk left 100m, crossing náměstí Hrdinů to 5 Kvétná (highway D1). To Munich, hitchers take tram #4 or 9 to the intersection of Plzeňská at Kukulova/Bucharova, then hitch south. Those going north take a tram or bus to "Kobyliské nám.," then bus #175 up Hornátecká.

Other Practical Information

Luggage Storage: There are lockers in every train and bus station (10kč). Those in the main train station are usually full, so try the 24-hr. baggage storage in the basement (25kč per day for first 15kg). Beware of nimble thieves who might relieve you of heavy baggage while you set your 4-digit locker code.

Laundromat: In some private flats, travelers ask to include their laundry with the family's. Often underwear comes back darned and ironed. Otherwise, go to **Laundry Kings** (*B1*) at Dejvická 16, one block from the "Hradčanská" Metro A stop. Cross the tram *and* railroad tracks, then turn left onto Dejvická. Self-service wash 50kč per load, dry 15kč per 8min. Soap 10-20kč. Full-service is 30kč more and takes up to 24 hr. Filled with similarly soiled and thirsty travelers; throw back a few cold ones while waiting (beer 11kč). Open daily 8am-10pm.

English Bookstores: The Globe Bookstore, Janovského 14. Metro C: "Vltavská." From the Metro, walk under the overpass on the right, then turn right onto Janovského. Lots of used English-language paperbacks (about 80kč each). Will trade and buy used books. Open daily 9am-5pm. **International Bookstore Praha** (*D2*), at Pařížská 25, across from the Intercontinental Hotel. Specializes in English-language art, literary, and reference books. Open daily 10am-8pm. At the **American Center** (*EF3*) on Hybernská 7a, you can peruse books and current periodicals. Metro B: "nám. Republiky." Open Mon.-Thurs. 11am-5pm, Fri. 11am-3pm.

Pharmacies (Lékarná): Pharmacies are plentiful in Prague and offer a variety of Western European products at very Western prices. Don't hesitate to ask for contraceptives (kontrcepční prostředky), bandages (náplast), or tampons (dámské vložky). There is a 24-hr. pharmacy at Na Příkopw 7 (tel. 22 00 81).

Police: Headquarters at Olšanská (tel. 21 21 11 11), open Mon.-Fri. 7:30am-2pm. Metro A: "Flora," then walk down Jičinská and turn right into Olšanska; the station is about 200m ahead on your right. Or take tram #9. Come here for a visa extension. **Canadian citizens** must register with the police at Olšanska 2 within three working days of arriving in the Czech Republic. Your compulsory visa must be stamped.

Emergencies: Medical Emergency Aid in English and German. tel. 29 93 81. **Na Homolce** (foreigners' medical assistance): tel. 52 92 21 46, after hours 52 92 21 91. **Ambulance:** tel. 155. **Fire:** tel. 150. **Police:** tel. 158.

ACCOMMODATIONS AND CAMPING

Prices in Prague are rising rapidly. The prices listed below are certain to increase (perhaps by 50-100kč). Luckily, beds are plentiful. A growing number of Prague residents rent **spare rooms** to travelers, either privately or through private agencies (see below). Other budget options are a bed in a **youth hostel,** a class B (2-star) or class C (1-star) **hotel** room, or a **campground.** In late June, universities empty for the summer and free up hundreds of sterile and boxy—albeit cheap—**dorm rooms.** If CKM is mobbed, head directly to the dorms.

Accommodations Agencies

Many of the hawkers who besiege visitors at the train station are actually agents for other people. The going rates hover around US$15-30 (500-1000kč), depending primarily on rooms' proximity to downtown. Try haggling. These are generally safe arrangements, but if you're wary of bargaining on the street, you can try private agencies. Make sure any room you accept is close to public transportation and that you understand what you are paying for; have the staff write it down. Payment is usually accepted in Czech, U.S., or German currency.

CKM (*DE6*), Žitná 12 (tel. 29 12 40). Metro C: "I.P. Pavlova," and then backtrack down Žitná. The definitive place to find youth-hostel-esque lodging. Expect to pay 220-400kč per person. Open daily 9am-1pm and 2-7pm.

Primo Agency (*D5-6*), Žitná 17 (tel./fax 24 91 03 40), down the street from CKM. Private rooms are 850kč per person, but groups can get lower rates by haggling. Hostel beds start at 295kč per person. Open daily 11am-8pm.

Hello Ltd. (*F3*), Senovážné nám 3 (formerly Gorkého nám. 3), between Na Příkopě and Hlavní Nádraží (tel./fax 24 27 27 61). Deutschmark fetishists. They offer private apartments (from DM30 per person) and rooms at youth hostels (from DM15 per person). Private rooms start at 370kč per person, although most cost 620kč, 740kč, or 860kč. Open daily 9am-10pm.

CK OK, Wilsonova (tel. 24 61 71 19, fax 54 90 21), on the top floor of the Hlavní Nádraží train station opposite the men's room. Offers lodging in private flats and pricey hotels. Most rooms are "in the city" but without private bathrooms. Singles start at 680kč. Doubles start at 425kč per person. Open daily 6am-10pm.

Pragotur (*E3*), U Obecního domu 2 (tel. 232 22 05 or 232 51 28, fax 24 81 16 51), a side street off nám. Republiky across from the Hotel Paříž. Metro B: "nám.

Republiky." Singles with shared bathrooms start at 605kč and doubles at 460kč per person downtown; they start at 385kč and 460kč on the periphery. Makes hotel and motel reservations. Open Mon.-Sat. 9am-6pm, Sun. 9am-3pm.

Vesta (*F4*), Wilsonova (tel. 236 81 90 or 236 81 92, fax 236 81 28 or 24 22 57 69), on the top floor of the Hlavní Nádraží train station. 58 hostel beds and private accommodation for 12 people are available. Private rooms (doubles only) start at 700kč per person. Hotel rooms start at 900kč for singles, 1200kč for doubles, and 1500kč for triples. Open Mon.-Sat. 8:30am-7:30pm, Sun. 8:30am-4:30pm.

Prague Suites (*D4*), Melantrichova 8 (tel./fax 24 22 99 61), two blocks north of the Václavské nám. and Na Příkopě intersection. Singles, doubles, and triples with shared bath all start at US$20 per person in central Prague, and at US$12 on the periphery. Open Mon.-Fri. 9am-6pm, Sat. 9am-2pm.

Wolff Travel, Na Příkopě 24 (tel. 26 15 05 or 24 22 79 89, fax 24 22 88 49). Singles in central Prague with shared bathroom 700kč, with private bath 800kč. Central doubles with a shared bath 1000kč, with private bath 1200kč. Also makes hotel reservations. Open Mon.-Fri. 9:30am-6:30pm, Sat. 10am-6pm, Sun. 10am-4pm.

Slunečko CK Travel Service, Ostrov Štvanice Hlávkův Most (tel. 37 16 92 or 26 42 08, fax 35 13 66) where Wilsonova crosses the Vltava River. Lots to choose from. Hostels start at US$8 per person. Private rooms start at US$12.50 per night and become more expensive as you approach central Prague. Bed-and-breakfasts begin at US$16.50 per person. Hotel rooms with private bathrooms start at US$27 per night. Open daily 10am-10pm.

Hostels (Studentska Kolej)

Next to the Olympic stadium in the Strahov neighborhood west of the river, an enormous cluster of dorms/hostels frees up for travelers from July to mid-September. Expect limited availability the rest of the year. These rooms may be the best bet for travelers who arrive in the middle of the night *sans* clue. But call ahead and inquire about vacancies before schlepping out there.

ESTEC Hostel , Vaníčkova 5 (formerly Spartakiádní 5), blok (building) 5 (tel. 52 73 44). Take bus #217 or 143 from the "Dejvická" Metro A stop or bus #176 from "Karlovo nám." Metro B to "Koleje Strahov." Reception open 24 hrs. Check-out 10am. No curfew. 500 beds July-mid-Sept.; 70 beds mid-Sept.-June. Recently renovated; you can smell the fresh paint. Singles 360kč. Doubles 240kč. Breakfast 50kč. English spoken. Lively bars and discos in the adjacent village of Communist-era blocks. Beer garden on premises. Student **grocery store** next door. (Open Mon.-Fri. 7am-7pm and Sat.-Sun. 7am-noon.)

Interjunior Travel: Juniorhostel Strahov, Vaníčkova 5 (formerly Spartakiádní 5) blok 7. (tel./fax 252 08 51.) Next to the ESTEC Hostel. Reception open daily 9:30am-1pm and 2-6pm. Check-out 10am. Doubles and triples 220kč per person. Breakfast 35kč. To reserve: Interjunior Travel, Vaníčkova 5, blok 7/136, 16000 Praha 6, Czech Republic. In summer, they also reserve doubles in ugly but functional buildings throughout Prague: Kolej Větrník (150kč per person); Komenského Kolej (370kč); Kolej Kajetánka (280kč); Kolej J. Dimitrova (300kč); and Kolej 17 Listopadu (280kč).

Oasa, Posepného nám (tel. 792 63 15). Take Metro C to "Roztyly" or bus #505 from "Muzeum" Metro station. Reception open 24 hrs. No curfew. 170kč per person. Showers, lockers, kitchen, sauna, and weight room.

Hostel Sokol (*B4*), Hellichova 1 (tel. 54 81 41, 561 85 64 or 24 51 06 07, ext. 397 or 020, fax 511 85 64). Metro A: "Malostranská." Take tram #12 or 22 to "Hellichova" and follow the signs. 5min. from the Charles Bridge. Offers clean and comfortable 10- to 15-bed rooms, co-ed by floor. Storage room for valuables. Reception open 6-10am and 3pm-12:30am. Curfew 12:30am; 18kč charge to be let in afterwards. 180kč per person. Breakfast 20kč. Open June-Sept.

Pension Unitas, Bartolomějská 9 (tel. 232 77 00, fax 232 77 09). A short walk through the Old Town from Metro B: "Národni." A Jesuit monastery where Beethoven once performed, transformed by Communists into a state prison in which Václav Havel was repeatedly jailed. Thoroughly renovated but you can still visit the "torture room." No alcohol. Reception open 24 hrs. Check-out 10am. Closed 1am-6am. Singles 920kč. Doubles 1100kč. Breakfast included.

TJ Slavoj, V náklích (tel. 46 00 70). Take tram #3 or 17 from the "Braník" Metro station. Lonely 10-minute walk from the tram stop; look for it in the daytime, especially if traveling alone. About 50 beds in a boathouse by the river. 3- to 5-bed rooms. No curfew. No lockout. Still a mere 170kč pr person. Hearty meals 40kč.

Domov Mládeže, Dykova 20 (tel. 25 06 88, fax 25 14 29). Take tram #16 from "Ječná" to the fourth stop, or Metro A to "nám. Míru," and then tram #16 to the second stop. At the streetcar stop, head right on Nitranská, and turn left on Dykova. Hall showers. 60 beds in the peaceful Vinohrady district. Reception open 24 hrs. No curfew. No lockout. 260kč per person. Breakfast 30kč.

Hostel Braník, Urbova 1233 (tel. 46 26 41 or 46 26 42, fax 46 26 43). Metro B: "Smíchovské nádraží," then take bus #196 or 198 to "Ve Studeném" and walk 100m up the hill. 180 beds in singles, doubles, triples, and quads. Reception open 24 hrs. No curfew. No lockout. 280kč per person. Breakfast included.

Pension Novodvorská, Novodvorská 151 (tel. 471 84 14). Take Metro B to "Smíchovské nádraží," and then bus #196 or 198 to "Sídl. Novodvorská." Many floors of student housing, often full. Reception open 24 hrs. 420kč per person.

TJ Sokol Karlin, Malého 1 (tel. 22 20 09), behind the Praha-Florenc bus station, arguably the sleaziest area of Prague. Hold your bag tightly and beware of pickpockets. Metro B or C: "Florenc." 5- to 12-bed rooms plus cots in a gymnasium. Not elegant, but there's usually room. A last resort. Reception open 6pm-midnight. Check-out 7am. Lockout 8am-6pm. 170kč per person; cots 110kč.

Hotels

With so many Western tourists infiltrating Prague, hotels are upgrading both service and appearance. Budget hotels are fading faster than you can say *demokracia*. The difference in price between B and C hotels is often dramatic, though quality levels are comparable. Beware that hotels may try to bill you for a more expensive room than the one you in which you stayed. Come armed with pen, paper, and receipts.

Hotel Madape, Malešická 74 (tel. 89 31 04, tel./fax 77 13 55). Take bus #234 from the "Želivského" Metro A station 5 stops to "Vackov." Beside the cemetery where Kafka is buried. B-category. Private baths. Often full. Some German spoken. Doubles off hospital-like corridors 610kč. Breakfast 100kč.

Hotel Kafka, Cimburkova 24 (tel. 27 31 01, tel./fax 27 29 84), in the Žižkov district near the television tower. Brand new hotel in a pleasant 19th-century neighborhood with nearby restaurants and *pivnice*. Reception open 24hrs. Singles 900kč. Doubles 1300kč. Breakfast 55kč.

Hotel Bílý Pev, Cimburkova 20 (tel. 27 11 26, fax 27 32 71), in the Žižkov district. Another freshly renovated hotel. Reception open 24hrs. Singles 1240kč. Doubles 2360kč. Breakfast included.

Hotel Ariston, Seifertova 65 (tel. 627 88 40 or 627 98 26, fax 22 30 08), in the Žižkov district. New and clean air-conditioned rooms. Restaurant and bar. Reception open 24hrs. Singles 1700kč. Doubles 2650kč. Breakfast included.

Betlem Club, Betlémské náměsti 9 (tel. 24 21 68 72, fax 24 21 80 54). Recently renovated Romanesque and Gothic parlors from the 13th century in central Prague, facing the church where Jan Hus preached his heretic message of reform. German spoken. Reception open 24hrs. Singles 1530kč. Doubles 2720kč.

Hotel Julián, Elišky Peškové 11 (tel. 53 51 37, fax 54 75 25), south of Malostranské nám. down Karmelitská and Újezd. In a beautiful neighborhood with many restaurants nearby. Renovated last year, but the building retains its Art Nouveau charm. Reception open 24hrs. Singles 1840kč. Doubles 2480kč. Breakfast included.

Junior Hotel Praha (*D5-6*), Žitná 10 (tel. 29 29 84), right next to CKM. Decor on the cutting edge of 1970s revival. Private showers and baths. Singles 1400kč. Doubles 1900kč. Breakfast included. Reserve in advance.

Camping

For a round-up of camping options, visit **Slunečko CK Travel** on the left-hand side of Hlávkův Most, where Wilsonova crosses the Vltava River (tel. 37 16 92; open daily 10am-10pm). Camping prices begin at US$6 per person.

Císařska Louka, on an island between Smíchov and Vyšehrad (tel. 54 50 64 or 54 09 25, fax 20 40 21 or 54 33 05). A tranquil setting along the banks of the Vltava River immortalized by Bedřich Smetana. Caravan parking, currency exchange, and tennis courts. US$6 per person. To reserve, write to: TJ Císařska Louka, Praha 5 - Smíchov, přístar č. 599, Česka Republika/Czech Republic.

Sokol Troja, Trojská 171 (tel. 84 28 33), is the largest of a cluster of campgrounds north of the center in the Troja district of Prague. Take bus #112 from the Metro C stop "Nádraží Holešovice" to "Kazanka," the fourth stop, and walk 100m. 100kč per person, 80kč per small tent, 180kč per bungalow bed. Reservations recommended.

Sokol Dolní Počernice, Dolní Počernice, Nad rybníkem (tel. 71 80 34). Take tram #9 to the end of the line, then hop on bus #109.

FOOD

Restaurants in Prague eat careless travelers alive. After hidden charges are added in, the bill can be nearly twice what you expected. *Anything* offered with your meal (even french fries) will cost extra, as will everything placed on your table, including bread and ketchup. Check the bill scrupulously. The further from the mobs of Old Town tourists, the less you'll spend. "*Hotová Jídla*" ("prepared meals") are least expensive. For a quick bite, the window stands selling tasty *párek v rohliku* (sausage in a roll) for 7-15kč are a bargain. Outlying Metro stops become impromptu marketplaces in summer; look for the daily **vegetable market** (*D3-4*) at the intersection of Havelská and Melantrichova in the Old Town.

Old Town (Staré Město)

Restaurace U Dvou Koček (*D4*), Uhelný trh. 10 (tel./fax 24 22 99 82). Menu rotates among paprikáš, guláš, and schnitzel, starting at 39kč. Beware the 25kč service charge. A ½-liter of Pilsner *Urquell* costs 15kč. Open daily 11am-11pm.

Restaurace U Medvíko (*D4*), Na Perštýně 7 (tel./fax 22 09 30). Offerings traditional Czech dishes such as guláš, fish, and schnitzel. Budweiser *Budvar* on tap sells for 15kč per ½ liter. God bless it. Open Mon.-Sat. 11:30am-11:30pm and Sun. 11:30am-10pm.

U Radnických Restaurace (*DE4*), Havelská 9, in the historic *Radnice* (old town hall, tel. 26 06 63). Duck, duchen, and fish dishes for under 50kč. A ½-liter of Prague's very own *Staropramen* lager will cost you a mere 15kč.

Bitburger Pils Snack Bar (*D3-4*), Husova 5 in the Betlém Palais. A great location in central Prague. A plate of spaghetti is 69kč. Duck dishes paddle around 120kč. Imported *Bitburger Pils* is on draft. Open Mon.-Fri. until 8pm.

Restaurant Canadian Lobster (*D3-4*), Husova 15. The changing daily seafood menu costs roughly 140kč. If you feel an uncontrollable urge to splurge, order one of the lobster dishes, starting at a mere 990kč. Cover charge 30kč. Hours change weekly.

Košer Restaurant Shalom (*D2-3*), Maiselova 18 (tel. 231 89 96). Right across the street from the Old Jewish Graveyard and the Staronová Synagogue in Josefov. Excellent lunches and dinners for about 540kč. Open daily noon-10pm.

Queenz Grill Bar (*DE4*), Havelská 12 (tel. 26 00 95, fax 73 90 26). For that taste of Cairo, Riyadh or New York City street stands, order a falafel, gyro, or kebab. Open Mon.-Sat. 10am-10pm and Sun. noon-10pm.

Pivnice Ve Skořepce (*D4*), Skořepka 1 (tel. 22 80 81). Take Metro B to "Národní třída," walk up Na Perštýné, and take the second right. Wood-paneling, Czech pork and sausage dishes (80-150kč); *pivo* in gorgeous one liter mugs. Cover charge 8kč. Open Mon.-Sat. 11:30am-11pm and Sun. 11:30am-10pm.

New Town (Nové Město)

Restaurace U Pravdů (*DE6*), Žitná 15 (tel. 29 95 92). Best schnitzel (*řízek*) in Prague. Wood and plaster decor, together with the chandelier and high ceiling take you back to a kinder, gentler time. The young staff are friendly and eager to practice their English and German. *Radegast* and *Staropramen* are on tap (12kč for a ½ liter). Open daily 11am-10pm.

Krab Haus (*D4*), Jungmannovo náměsti. Cheap and close to Wenceslas Square. Sandwiches and pastries start at under 10kč. Fine *Eggenberger* beer on tap. Open Mon.-Fri. 9am-8pm and Sat.-Sun. 10am-6pm.

Restaurace U Purkmistra (*E5*), Vodičkova 26. Outdoor seating. Authentic Czech dishes start at 30kč. Try *svíčková* (Sauerbraten). Open daily until 11pm.

Little Caesar's Pizza Station (*D4*), Národní across from Na Perštýne underneath the huge K-mart. Unlike the American pizza chain of the same name, this Little Caesar's has a "happy hour" between 3-5pm: buy a ½-liter of beer, get one free. *Velkopopovický Kozel* is on tap: light for 19kč and dark for 17kč. A cheese pizza costs 99kč and a combo slice is 39kč. Open daily until dusk.

Lucerna Barrandov (*E5*), Štěpánska 61 (tel. 232 22 16). In the Lucerna arcade off Štěpánska, just down from Wenceslas Square. Pork, potatoes, and cabbage at bargain prices. The self-serve stainless steel counters draw gray-haired Prague proletarians, nostalgic for the flavor of the former socialist regime. The meat you do not eat returns to the kitchen. *Eggenberger* on tap, a ½-liter for a mere 11kč. Open Mon.-Fri. 8am-8:30pm, Sat. 10am-8pm, and Sun. 10am-6pm.

Černý Pivovar (*D6*), Karlovo Náměstí 15 (tel. 294 45 23). Metro B: "Karlovo Náměstí." An enormous mural runs the length of the wall, depicting good comrades happily sweating in the brewery that runs the restaurant. Vegetarian and Czech entrees for under 30kč. One of the best beer bargains in Prague; a ½-liter of *Krušovice* costs 8kč. Open Mon.-Fri. 7:30am-8pm and Sat.-Sun. 9am-8pm.

Buffalo Bill's (*E4-5*), Vodičkova 9 (tel. 235 00 21). A Tex-Mex restaurant 10,500km northeast of the border. A dinner of fajitas, enchiladas, or quesadillas costs around 100kč. Open daily 11am-midnight.

U Benedikta (*E2*), Benediktská 11 (tel. 231 15 27). Take Metro B to "nám. Republiky," and walk down U Obecního domů and turn right on Rybná. Enjoy Czech and other European entrees (70-150kč) on the pleasant terrace. A ½-liter of Bernard Beer (*světlé* or *tmavé*) costs 16kč. Open daily 11:30am-11pm.

The John Bull Pub (*E3*), Senovážna 8 south of the Powder Tower. Generous quantities of first-rate Czech pub-fare, including *guláš*, roast beef and roast pork, at fair prices (about 46kč). Only Czech is spoken. John Bull Bitter and Pilsner *Urquell* are on draft at slightly above-average prices. Open Mon.-Sat. 11am-11pm.

U Tří Osmiček (*E3-4*) Nekázanka 20 south of Na Příkopě. A popular stand-up eatery offering Dutch *schnitzel* (22kč) and fried chicken (31kč). *Prosím*, in Czech only. Open Mon.-Fri. 9:30am-5:30pm.

České Kuře (*E2*), Soukenká 3 off Revoluční (tel./fax 231 72 51). Half a chewy Czech chicken for 45kč. Open Mon.-Fri. 9:30am-7pm.

Mister Pizza (*E2*), Revoluční 16. Life-giving pizza fixes for under 50kč, 24hrs. per day. The bar serves wine, beer, and a sea of hard liquors.

Snack Bar V Jonáš (*E2*), Revoluční 21, near Republiky nám. Chicken sautée, Kung Pao chicken, or "Chinese" chicken, each for less than 59kč. Wash these interesting attempts down with a ½-liter of Pilsner *Urquell* (15kč). Open Mon.-Fri. 9am-10pm and Sat.-Sun. 10am-10pm.

NONSTOP (*F3*), Masarykovo train station. Cheap, fast, and never quits. *Guláš* available around the clock for 22kč. Beer and juice for reasonable prices.

Malá Strana

Malostranská Hospoda (*B3*), Karmelitská 25 (tel. 53 20 76), two blocks south of Malostranské nám. Quality Bohemian pub fare, including sirloin, roast pork, and *guláš*, for less than 50kč. Draft *Staropramen* costs 13kč for a ½-liter. Open Mon.-Sat. 10am-midnight, Sun. 11am-midnight).

U Švejka (*B4*), Újezd 22 (tel. 52 56 20) a few blocks south of Malostranské nám. Good Bohemian cuisine, including roast pork and the house speciality "*Schweik-*

guláš." A ½-liter of Pilsner *Urquell* costs 19kč in the adjacent beer garden. Open daily 11am-midnight.

Bistro U Sv. Mikuláše (*B4*), Karmelitská 28, south of Malostranské nám. Quick, painless Czech fast food. Sandwiches under 20kč. Open Mon.-Sat. 8am-8pm, Sun. 9am-7pm.

U Vrtbovské Zahrady (*B4*), Karmelitská 23, south of Malostranské nám. A smorgasbord of inexpensive chow. Pizza under 40kč. Traditional Prague-style *guláš* 55kč. Open daily 10am-10pm.

Jo's Bar (*AB3*), Malostranské Náměstí 7. You can bet the ranch that everyone in here will speak English (and carry a camera, have 2.6 kids and an Oldsmobile). Burritos, quesadillas, and nachos 75-200kč. See Nightlife for more info.

Bistro v Soudním Dvoře (*B3*), Karmelitská 19 (tel. 53 00 54). From the "Malostranská" Metro A stop walk south along Karmelitská until you spot a free-standing chalk-board on the right. Bravely enter the alleyway, take your first left, and then make a right (2min. from Malostranské Náměstí). One-horse bistro home to many a quiet conversation. Few tourists; nothing resembling English. Meals around 60kč per person. Beer 9kč. Open daily 10am-6pm.

Café Bar Bílý Orel (White Eagle; *AB3*), Malostranské Naměstí, Minská 10 (tel. 53 17 37). Right by the streetcar stop. Stylish but touristy. Outdoor seating in the thick of Malá Strana's hustle and bustle—tourists everywhere, trams whizzing by, cars speeding in reverse, small children shouting imprecations. For those who like to eat *in* the city. Average entree under 100kč. Fearsomely overpriced *pivo.* Extensive breakfast menu. Kitchen closes at midnight. Open Mon.-Fri. 9am-4am.

Holešovice-Bubny (Metro: Vltavska)

Restaurace U Houbaře, Dukelských Hrdinů 30, north of nám Strossmayerovo. Authentic and satisfying Czech dishes. The Pilsner *Urquell* on tap is heavenly (½ liter for 15kč. Open daily 11am-10pm.

Caffé Dante, Dukelských Hrdinů 16 (tel. 87 01 93), north of nám Strossmayerovo. Pizzas under 50kč. Local youth love the spaghetti and ravioli. Pilsner *Urquell* on tap (½-liter for 25kč). Open Mon.-Fri. 8am-11pm and Sat.-Sun. 11am-11pm.

U Sv. Antonička, Dukelských Hrdinů at Plk. Sochora north of nám Strossmayerovo. Extremely popular and often full. Czech dishes, including roast pork, gulás, and prepared beef entrees. Only Czech spoken, so bring your courage and your phrasebook. Most meals under 40kč. *Velkopopovický Kozel* on tap at a bargain price. Open Mon.-Fri. 9am-11pm and Sat.-Sun. 10:30am-9pm.

Jídelna na Křižovatkou, Milady Horákové 8 (tel. 37 00 34), west of nám Strossmayerovo. Vlad Krejbich does a heck of a job keeping the neighborhood's beloved self-serve joint in order. Only Czech spoken. A meal including beer costs under 60kč. Open Mon.-Sat. 8:30am-8pm.

Žižkov (East of Wilsonova)

Hospůda U Trojky, Táboritská 12. A smoke-filled two-tier pub with wooden paneling, plaster, and high ceilings. Like the café from *Clockwork Orange* with a twist: phallus pretzel dispensers at every table (3kč each—the pretzels, not the phalluses). *Guláš* 36kč. A ½-liter of *Braník* beer costs a measly 8kč—so what if it's bland? Open daily 10am-10pm.

Rebecca, Táboritská at Jičínská (tel. 627 69 20). Roast beef dishes cost around 80kč. Plenty of over-priced booze and dull decor, but it's open 24hrs.

Cafés

Café Espresso Paulus (*AB3*), Malostranské náměstí on the square, right behind Dienzenhofer's famous Baroque St. Nicholas Church. Wonderful location; hip and happening. Coffee 15kč. Vodka 30kč. Open daily 10am-8pm.

Nebozízek (*B4-5*), Petřínské sady 411 (tel. 53 79 05). Pricey but worth the view. A funicular runs from Újezd street, between Všehrdova and Říční, to the midpoint of the Petřín summit. The lift stops only twice: at Nebozízek and at the miniature of the Eiffel Tower (see above). Open daily noon-6pm and 7-11pm.

Café Savoy (*B5*), Vítězná 1 (tel. 53 94 90). Raise your spirits (brandy 20kč) with a toast inside. The lofty ceiling features outrageously ornate restored paintings and intricate woodwork. Open daily noon-midnight.

U Zlatých Nůžek (*AB2*), Na Kampě 6, near the castle (tel. 24 51 01 10). Nonsmokers frequent this bastion of caffeination. Fresh baked goods complement over 50 teas and coffees. Open daily 10am-8pm.

Caffè Dante, Dukelských Hrdinů 16 (tel. 87 01 93), north of nám Strossmayerovo. A relatively new café, popular with Holešovice's youthful crowd. Coffee 12kč. Pizza under 50kč. Cover 5kč. Open Mon.-Fri. 8am-11pm, Sat.-Sun. 11am-11pm.

The Globe Coffeehouse, Janovského 14, inside Prague's newest and largest English-language bookstore. Peruse *Let's Go* as you sip a hot beverage and contemplate literary self-reference. Open daily 10am-midnight.

Caféfour (*E2*), Soukenická 2, off Revoluční, north of nám Republiky. A quiet, local café with flexible hours and reasonable prices. Coffee 9kč. Pizza 29kč. Chicken 55kč. Open daily 9am-11pm.

PLHA Café (*E2*), Revoluční at Klimentská, north of nám Republiky. Offers a great variety of wines, coffees, teas, and other beverages together with delicious palčinky, sweet koláč, and other baked goods. Open daily 9am-10pm.

Supermarkets

Krone department store (*E4*), on Wenceslas Square at the intersection with Jindřišska (tel. 26 94 35 or 24 23 04 77). Look for the snack bar on the first floor. Open Mon.-Wed. and Fri.-Sun. 8am-7pm, Thurs. 8am-9pm.

Kotva department store (*E3*), at the corner of Revoluční and Náměstí Republiky (tel. 24 21 54 62 or 235 00 02). Metro B: "nam. Republiky." Kotva is consistently well-stocked; the basement grocery store has everything you'll need. Open Mon.-Wed. and Fri.-Sun. 8am-7pm, Thurs. 8am-9pm.

Máj department store (*D4*), at the corner of Národní and Spálena (tel. 24 22 79 71 or 26 23 41). Metro B: "Národní třída." K-Mart bought out this formerly state-owned chain. Open Mon.-Wed. and Fri.-Sun. 8am-7pm, Thurs. 8am-9pm.

Potraviny (*D5*), Křemencova 16. A convenient food store in the Nové Město. Open daily until midnight.

Potraviny (*F2*), Zlatnická at Na Pořtěr, near Musarykovo train station. Run by a friendly fellow named Merxbauer, this corner store has a great selection of food and drink at decent prices. Open Mon.-Fri. 8am-9pm and Sat. 9am-9pm.

SIGHTS

At the top of the west bank of the Vltava lies **Hradčany** (*AB1*), Prague's castle and main landmark. Below the fortress are the lovely palaces and gardens of **Malá Strana** (Lesser Town; *A3*), originally built and populated by Prague's urban gentry. From Malá Strana, the pedestrian-only **Karlův Most** (Charles Bridge; *C3*) crosses the river and leads into **Staré Město** (Old Town; *E3*) at the center of which is the huge, architecturally resplendent plaza, **Staroměstské náměstí.** Gothic spires representing 600 years of construction rise from every corner in this area. North of Staroměstské náměstí is **Josefov,** the old Jewish quarter. The rich 19th-century façades of **Nové Město** (New Town; *D5*), established in 1348 by Charles IV, lie to the south. Most of Prague's architectural monuments are in the castle district and the Old Town—Nové Město is busier and more commercial.

Central Prague is shaped by three streets forming a leaning "*T.*" The long stem of the *T,* separating Old and New Towns, is **Václavské náměstí** (Wenceslas Square; actually a grand boulevard; *E4-05*). The **National Museum** glistens at the bottom of the *T* (*EF5*). Busy and pedestrian, **Na příkopě** (*E3-4*) forms the right arm and leads to **náměstí Republiky** (*E3*). On the left, 28. Října becomes **Národní** (*C5-D4*) after a block, leading to the **National Theater** (*C5*) on the river. A maze of small streets leads to Staroměstské nám. two blocks above the *T.* There are two prominent **St. Nicholas cathedrals,** in Malá Strana (*A3*) near the castle and in Staroměstské nám. (*D3*), and two **Powder Towers,** one in the castle (*AB2*) and another in nám. Republiky (*E3*).

Joggers will find that Prague has plentiful green space along **Petřín Hill** in Malá Strana. Miles of pathways traverse the Kinsky, Strahov, Lobkowitz, Schönborn, and Seminář **gardens,** but most are badly eroded. Many try the promenade on the banks of the Vitara (Moldau) south of **most Legií** along **Masarykoro nábřeží** in the New Town (Nové Město) during daylight hours. Use common sense and don't jog alone.

Wenceslas Square

"I've taken my grandchildren to the top of Wenceslas Square where St. Wenceslas looks over the entire square. I tell them to imagine all the things St. Wenceslas might have seen sitting there on his horse: the trading markets hundreds of years ago, Hitler's troops, the Soviet tanks, and our Velvet Revolution in 1989. I can still imagine these things; it's the boulevard where much of our history, good and bad, has passed."
—Bedřich Šimáček, driver of tram #22, quoted in the Prague Post

Václavské náměstí (Wenceslas Square; *E4-5*), the festive heart of Prague, was actually designed as a quiet promenade in the late 19th century. The statue of the king and saint **Wenceslas** (*EF5*), has presided over a century of turmoil and triumph, witnessing no less than five full revolutions from his southeast pedestal, in front of the National Museum. The present equestrian statue of Saint Václav was completed in 1912, though a Wenceslas monument of some sort has graced the square since 1680. The statue was the site for student Jan Palach's 1969 self-immolation protesting Soviet intervention in the Prague Spring; his self-sacrifice sparked a series of similar demonstrations around the country.

Wenceslas Square spreads from the former bridge (or "Můstek" as the Metro A and B stop is aptly named) through the Old Town all the way to the **National Museum** (*EF5*, tel. 24 23 04 85, open Wed.-Mon. 9am-5pm). The Wilsonova highway that eventually crosses the Vltava to Holešovice is a six-lane monstrosity originally named Vitězného února ("victorious February") in honor of the 1948 Soviet-backed Communist seizure of power. In 1989, it was renamed to pay tribute to President Woodrow Wilson, who helped forge the ultimately doomed inter-war Czechoslovak state. The **Radio Prague Building** (*EF5*), behind the National Museum, was the scene of a tense battle between Soviet tanks and Prague's citizens attempting to protect the studios by human barricade. The radio station succeeded in transmitting "free" and impartial updates for the first 14 hours of the invasion.

Stretching north from the Wenceslas monument, Art Nouveau houses peck out among the modernist offices at the sides of the Václavské náměstí. The premier example of Bohemian *Jugendstil* is the 1903 **Hotel Evropa** (E4), just before the intersection with Jindřišská on the right-hand side of the street. Most of the other Art Nouveau structures along the square were designed by Jan Kotěra, the noted disciple of Viennese architectural giant Otto Wagner.

From the northern end of the Václavské nám., take a quick detour to Jungmannovo nám. and the **Church of Our Lady of the Snows** (*Panna Marie Sněžná; E4*). Founded by King Charles IV in 1347, this edifice was intended to be the largest church in Prague; the Gothic walls are, indeed, higher than any other house of worship, but the rest of the structure is still unfinished—there was only enough cash to complete the choir. It still feels tiny, despite the Baroque altar and the magnificently vaulted ceiling (open daily 7am-6pm). Enter the **Františkánská zahrada** (*D4*) through the arch at the intersection of Jungmannova and Národní. These gardens, once the rose fields of Franciscan friars, offer quiet detachment amid the shrubbery just minutes from the bustle of Wenceslas Square (open daily 7am-9pm). Under the arcades halfway down Národní stands a **memorial** (*D4*) that honors hundreds of Prague's citizens beaten on November 17, 1989. Marching in a government-sanctioned protest, they were greeted by a line of shield-bearing, truncheon-armed police. After a stalemate, the "protectors of the people" bludgeoned the marchers, injuring hundreds. This event marked the inception of the Velvet Revolution, headquartered at the **Magic Lantern Theater** (*B4*), Národní 4. From within its bowels,

Václav Havel and other dissidents delivered their latest releases to the press and developed their peaceful program to topple the Soviet-backed regime.

Staroměstské náměstí

Na můstku and Melantrichova lead up from Wenceslas Square through a labyrinth of Old World alleyways into **Staroměstské náměstí** (*D3*), the "other" center of town. To gain permission to found the **Old Town Hall** (*Staroměstská radnice*; *D3*), the councillors of Prague traveled to Paris and presented their request to the, er, remote Czech King John of Luxembourg. Beside the Town Hall, **crosses** on the ground mark the spot where 27 Protestant leaders were executed on June 21, 1621 for a (failed) rebellion against the Catholic Habsburgs. The **Old Senate** (*D3*), with a magnificent coffered ceiling, boasts a Baroque stove with a figure of Justice and a sculpture of Christ. The inscription reads, "Judge justly—sons of Man." An extension of the town hall that once encroached upon the St. Nicholas Church was demolished by Nazi tanks on the very last day of World War II; only a patch of grass remains. Onlookers gather on the hour to see the town hall's fabulous **Astronomical Clock** (*orloj; D3*), with 12 peering apostles and a bell-ringing skeleton representing death. The clockmaker's eyes were reputedly put out by his patron so he could not craft another. A statue of martyred Czech theologian and leader **Jan Hus** occupies the place of honor in the center of the square; the monument was unveiled in 1915, on the 500th anniversary of his death.

Jan Palach Square (*D3*), next to the Staroměstská metro station, was known as Red Army Square before 1989. Palach was a philosophy student at **Charles University,** still located on this square. On the left corner of the philosophy department's façade is a copy of Palach's death mask, erected as a memorial after his self-immolation. Eight hundred thousand citizens followed his coffin from the Old Town Square to the Olšany Cemetery, where he is buried today.

Across from the Town Hall is **Týn Church** (*Panna Marie před Týnem*; *DE3*). The tower on the right represents Adam shielding Eve, the tower on the left, from the midday sun. Astronomer Tycho de Brahe, whose tables laid the foundation for Johannes Kepler's planetary discoveries, is buried inside. To the left of the church, the **House at Stone Bell** (Dům U kamenného zvonu; *DE3*) shows the Gothic core that lurks under many of Prague's Baroque façades. The **Goltz-Kinský Palace** (*DE3*) on the left is the finest of Prague's Rococo buildings. **St. Nicholas Church** (*Sv Mikuláš; DE3*), sits just across Staroměstské nám. The church was built in only three years by Kilian Ignaz Dienzenhofer; Dienzenhofer and his dad then built the **St. Nicholas Church** (*AB3*) in Malá Strana, right by the castle. Between Maiselova and Týn Church is **Franz Kafka's** former home (*DE3*), marked with a plaque. (Kafka fans can visit the writer's final resting place at the Jewish Graveyard right outside the "Želivského" Metro A stop.)

Malá Štupartská, behind Týn Church, supports **St. Jacob's Cathedral** (*Kostel sv Jakuba; DE3*), home to 21 altars and bloated with Baroque ornamentation. Note the decaying limb dangling from the wall next to the entrance. Legend holds that a 15th-century thief attempted to pilfer one of the gems from the **Virgin Mary of Suffering** statue, whereupon the figure came to life and seized the thief's arm at the elbow and wrenched it off. The monks took pity on the repentant, profusely bleeding soul by inviting him to join their order. He accepted and remained faithfully pious; the arm hung around as a constant reminder of the great potential for movie rights (open daily 6:45am-4:30pm).

Out of the way near the Florenc metro station stands the former **Communist Party Central Committee Headquarters** (*F2*). Alexander Dupček and leaders of the Prague Spring maintained offices here—until Soviet special forces surrounded the building and took them away in handcuffs to Moscow. The building now houses the Ministry of Transportation.

En route to Charles Bridge

Ditch the tourists by departing Staroměstské nám. down Gilská to arrive at Betlémské nám, a tranquil square that takes you back to medieval Prague. Imagine Jan Hus marching out of the **Bethlehem Chapel** *(kaple; D4)* after delivering a litany against the abuses and corruption of the Catholic Church. His burning at the stake by the Inquisition only made Jan a martyr; many Czechs still regard him as a hero.

Karlův most (Charles Bridge; *C3*) is to Prague like sex is to Madonna: central, essential and non-discriminating. Artisans and street musicians fill Europe's most festive bridge day and night above a bevy of swans. The musical tradition is ancient; Austrian minstrel Dan von der Kuper once wandered the planks of the Charles. At the center of the bridge, the eighth statue from the right is a monument to legendary hero **Jan Nepomucký** (John of Nepomuk), confessor to Queen Žofie. At the statue's base is a depiction of hapless Jan, being tossed over the side of the Charles for faithfully guarding his queen's confidences from a suspicious King Wenceslas IV. Torture by hot irons and other devices failed to loosen Jan's lips, so the King ordered him to be drowned in the Vltava. A halo of five gold stars supposedly appeared as Jan plunged into the icy water. The right-hand rail, from whence Jan was supposedly ejected, is now marked with a cross and five stars between the fifth and sixth statues. Place one finger on each star and make a wish; not only is your wish *guaranteed* to come true, but any wish made on this spot will at some point in the future whisk the wisher back to Prague.

A stone bridge on the site of Jan's murder was ravaged by flood waters in 1342, and King Charles IV decided to build a bridge of unprecedented proportions—520m by 10m. The foundation stone was laid at 5 hours and 31 minutes on the morning of July 9, 1357, the most significant astrological point for Leo, which symbolizes the Kingdom of Bohemia. The cosmological order is formed by the odd numbers, 1, 3, 5, 7, 9, 7, 5, 3, 1. Legend has it that the builder made a pact with the devil in order to complete the massive bridge. Satan was allotted the first soul to cross the completed bridge, but the builder's wife and newborn babe unwittingly traversed the finished structure first; the devil could not take the baby's pure soul, so he instead cast a spell over the bridge. In the evening, you may now hear the faint cry of an infant, the ghostly wails of a surrogate spirit child—or is it the plaintive whining of prepubescent hostel youth?

Climb the Gothic **defense tower** *(BC3)* on the Malá Strana side of the bridge for a superb view of the city (open daily 10am-5:30pm; admission 20kč, students 10kč). Head down the stairs on the left side of the bridge (as you face the castle district) to **Hroznová** *(BC3-4)*, where a mural honors John Lennon and the peace movement of the 1960s. **Slovanský ostrov** *(C4-5)*, **Dětský ostrov** *(B5-6)*, and **Střelecký ostrov** *(C5-6)* islands are accessible from Janáčkovo nábřeží and the **most Legií** bridge. From the Charles, you can see rowboat outlets renting the vessels necessary to explore these islands and the remainder of the **Vltava** (boat rental open daily 11am-9pm; 40kč per hour).

Josefov

Prague's historic Jewish neighborhood, Josefov *(D2)*, is located north of Staroměstí náměstí along Maiselova and several side streets. It's cultural wealth lies in five well-preserved synagogues. To gain access to all five and the historic Jewish cemetery, purchase an all-purpose ticket at the **State Jewish Museum** *(Státní Židovské Muzeum*, tel. 231 06 81, Táchymova 3); the desolate remains of this formerly vibrant community are reproduced in the scattered buildings (see Museums below; admission 80kč, students 30kč). At the ninety-degree bend in U starého hřbitova is the entrance to the **Old Jewish cemetery,** where members of Prague's Jewish community were buried from the14th-18th centuries. Randomly placed trees and the 12,000 tombstones create a truly melancholic atmosphere, in spite of the milling camera-laden tourists. At U starého hřbitova and Maiselova is the **Old-New Synagogue** *(Staronová synagogá)*, one of the few remaining early Gothic synagogues in Europe. Dating from 1270, it is the oldest synagogue in Europe still in use. En route to the Old-New Synagogue is the **Klausen Synagogue** (*Klausová synagogá*) which houses valuable Hebrew manuscripts within its 17th-century walls, as well as an incongruously merry relic; look for the cycle of paintings of the Prague Burial Society, depicted happily undertaking various duties of the order. The eclectic 1906 **Ceremonial Hall** currently holds exhibits from the Jewish museum.

Next to the Old-New Synagogue is the **High Synagogue** (*Vysoká synagoga*) from the 16th century. Today it holds several exhibits of ceremonial items and religious tapestries. The neighboring **Jewish Town Hall** (*Židovnická radnice*) was once the administrative control center of old *Josefstadt*, as Jews referred to Josefov in the early 19th century. Search out the Hebrew clock that runs counterclockwise in the pink Rococo exterior of the Town Hall. Walk down Maiselova and turn right on Široka until you reach the **Pinkas Synagogue** (*Pinkasova synagogá*) which displays a **memorial** to the Jews of Bohemia who perished in the Holocaust. A Torah from this synagogue is on permanent loan to Temple Beth Torah in Dix Hills, New York; many Central European synagogues have donated their scrolls to American and Israeli synagogues. Turning right onto Maiselova again, you can enter the ornate **Maisel Synagogue** (*Maisle synagogá*). At Jáchymova 3 are the rich collections of the **library of the State Jewish Museum** (open Tues., Thurs. 9am-noon and 2-5pm).

The Henry Parish

This former heart of Prague's German community (*Jundřich* or *Heinrich*) lies in the parish situated between Na příkopě and Wilsonova (*E4-5*). **St. Henry's Church** (*Sv. Jindřich* or *St. Heinrich*) dominates the southern part of Senovážné náměstí, known as Gorkého náměstí under the Communists and Heuwagsplatz in the 19th century. Although the church is undergoing renovations to improve its dilapidated appearance, it is open to all interested visitors on Fridays at 3pm and Sundays at 8am. The tower of St. Henry's may appear short and squat compared to the neighboring tower of St. Cunegunde, but the Gothic interior of St. Henry's is awe-inspiring. Down from St. Henry's on Jeruzalémská is the curiously striped **Jubilee Synagogue** (*Jubilejní synagoga*), built in the wild and eclectic style of the turn of this century. Unfortunately, it is closed to the public.

Turn right onto Opletalova and then left two blocks later onto Politických Vězňů (Political Prisoners). The distinctively 19th-century Kaisergelb building in front of you is the **State Opera** (Státni Opera), formerly the New German Theatre. The surrounding cement blocks and noisy highways stand in stark contrast to the gardens that once enveloped the theatre.

Bear right on Jindřišská until you reach Nekázanka on your left. The 19th-century façades of the tall buildings on Nekázanka were once tempered by neighborhood beer-halls and wine-cellars bearing names such as *Lippert, Gold Kreuzel*, and *Bodega*. Walking under the two bridges connecting the buildings on both sides of the street, you arrive at **Na příkopě**, formerly called Graben, which has remained a crucial business and commercial street. The **Slovan House** (Slovanský dům, the former Deutsche Casino) at Na příkopě 16 was the social, cultural, and commercial meeting-place of Prague's German-Jewish haute bourgeoisie.

Havířská leads to the **Estates Theater** (Stavovské divadlo), a glorious early-Classicist building constructed in the 1780s. Originally called the Nostitz Theater, the house hosted the world premiere of Mozart's **Don Giovanni** in 1787. Carl Maria von Weber was once the opera director here and Tyl's play **Fidlovačka** premiered here in 1834.

Malá Strana

The **Malá Strana** (Lesser Town; *A3*) is rich in palaces, ornate gardens, and grand Baroque churches. The fairest of them all is the 18th-century **St. Nicholas' Church** (sv Mikuláš; *AB3*), the highest achievement of Bohemian Baroque art. Mozart tickled the organ's ivories here; concerts of his work are held almost every night at 5pm. (Open daily 9am-5pm. Admission 20kč, students 10kč. Concerts 100kč.) Nearby on Karmelitská rises the more modest **Panna Marie Vítězné** (Church of Our Lady Victorious; *B3*). This holy edifice is the repository of the world-famous porcelain statue of the **Infant Jesus of Prague,** which reputedly bestows miracles on the faithful. The figurine has an elaborate wardrobe of over 380 outfits; every sunrise, the Infant is swaddled anew from the nuns of a nearby convent. The statue first arrived in town in the arms of a 17th-century Spanish noblewoman who married into the Bohemian royalty; mysteriously, the plague bypassed Prague shortly thereafter. In 1628, the Barefooted Carmelite nunnery gained custody of the Infant and allowed pilgrims to pray to the statue; the public has been infatuated with its magic ever since. Try asking the statue for a special favor yourself (church open 10am-7:30pm).

Designed by Kristof and Kilian Ignaz Dienzenhofer, the duo responsible for the Břevnov Monastery's undulating façade (see Outer Prague), the **St. Thomas Church** (*B2-3*) stands at Letenská off Malostranské náměstí, toward the Vltava. Rubens facsimiles await within, adjacent to the saintly reliquaries adorning the side altars (open daily 7am-6pm). A simple wooden gate just down the street at Letenská 10 opens onto the **Valdštejnská zahrada** (Wallenstein Garden; *B2*), one of Prague's best-kept secrets. This tranquil 17th-century Baroque garden is enclosed by old buildings that glow golden on sunny afternoons. General Albrecht Wallenstein, owner of the palace of the same name, held his parties here among Vredeman de Vries's classical bronze **statues**—when the works were plundered by Swedish troops in the waning hours of the Thirty Years War, Wallenstein replaced the original casts with facsimiles. **Frescoes** inside the arcaded loggia depict your favorite episodes from the Trojan War (open daily 9am-7pm). Across the street from the Malostranská metro stop, a marker in a small park, called the **Charousková Memorial** (*AB3*), is the sole memorial to the slain of 1968. It commemorates Marie Charousková, a graduate student who was machine-gunned by a Soviet soldier for refusing to remove a black ribbon protesting the invasion from her shirt.

Prague Castle

You can spend days wandering about the structures that comprise the **Pražský hrad** (Prague Castle; *AB2*), just to the north. Every style since Prague's founding contributes to the castle's splendor. Film director Miloš Forman thought that the aged passageways appeared more Viennese than Vienna—most of the movie *Amadeus* was filmed here. The fortress houses the **National Gallery of Bohemian Art** (see Museums below), but the primary attraction is the soaring **Katedrála sv Víta** (St. Vitus's Cathedral), completed in 1930 after 600 years of construction. You must pass through two castle courtyards and into a third in order to arrive at the Czech Republic's largest church, a curious blend of weathered Gothic and *faux*-weathered neo-Gothic. To the right of the high altar stands the **tomb of St. John of Nepomuk** (Jan Nepomucký), three meters of solid, glistening silver, weighing two tons. The enormous silver sepulchre is crowned by an angel holding a silver tongue in her hand; supposedly, this tongue was the only part of Jan Nepomucký still recognizable when his body was discovered by fishermen in the spring after his execution. The queen placed the tongue in the notorious cathedral confessional to commemorate its faithful silence; eventually, it was silvered and put on display.

Below the cathedral lies the ominous **Royal Crypt,** which houses the tombs of various Bohemian Kings; the four wives of Charles IV all share a tomb beside him. (Open daily 9am-5pm. Admission to choir and crypt 20kč, students 10kč. If you plan to visit the rest of the castle, a **combined ticket**—65kč, students 30kč—is a worthy investment.) The walls of the **St. Wenceslas Chapel** are lined with precious stones and a painting cycle that depicts the legend of the eponymous saint. The massive stained-glass windows date from 1930. A mammoth door leads from the chapel to a room where the coronation jewels of Bohemia are stored; you'll have to ask Mr. Havel for the keys.

Stroll across the third interior courtyard to enter the **Starý královský palác** (Old Royal Palace). Inside is the vast **Vladislav Hall,** with ample room for the jousting competitions that once took place here. Climb the 287 steps of the **Cathedral Tower** for a breathtaking view of the castle and the city (open daily 10am-4pm;

admission 15kč, students 8kč). In the nearby **Chancellery of Bohemia,** two Catholic Habsburg officials were lobbed out the window by fed-up Protestant noblemen in 1618 in the notorious **Defenestration of Prague.** Though a dungheap broke their fall, the die was cast, and war ravaged Europe for the next 30 years. Built in 1485 to enhance the castle's fortifications, the **Powder Tower** (*Mihulka*) houses a reconstructed alchemist's laboratory (admission 10kč, students 5kč).

The Romanesque **Basilica of St. George** (*Bazilika sv Jiří*) was erected in 921 just behind the Starý královský palác. Immediately on the right as you enter, note the wood and glass tomb enclosing St. Ludmila's skeleton. When the basilica was first under construction, the thigh bone vanished mysteriously. One week later, the architect was found dead; the two architects who were hired to complete the job both died within a year. Finally, the original architect's son discovered the thigh bone among his father's personal effects; he snuck into the convent, returned the skeletal link, and thereby ended the curse (basilica open daily 9am-4:45pm).

The **Lobkovic Palace,** at the bottom (northeast) of Jiřská, contains a replica of the coronation jewels of Bohemia and an exhibit recounting the history of the lands that today comprise the Czech Republic (admission 30kč, students 15kč; not included in the combined admission ticket). Halfway up is a tiny street carved into the fortified wall—Kafka held an office on this **Golden Lane** (*Zlatá ulička*), where the court alchemists supposedly toiled (all palace-related buildings open Tues.-Sun. 9am-5pm; Oct.-March Tues.-Sun. 9am-4pm).

Exiting the castle grounds across the **Powder Bridge** (*Prašný most*), you'll see the entrance to the serene **Royal Garden** (*Královská zahrada*), sculpted in 1534 to include the glorious and newly renovated Renaissance palace **Belvedér.** Devastated by Swedes and Saxons during the Thirty Years War, today the garden houses an **Orangery** and **Fig Garden** (open Tues.-Sun. 10am-5:45pm; admission 5kč, students 2kč). If, instead, you exit the castle through the main gate and walk straight for 200 yards, the lovely **Loreto** will be on your right. An aggrandized replica of Jesus' birthplace and a diamond mine of a treasury imperiously anchor the complex, constructed by the ubiquitous Dienzenhofer family of architects (open Tues.-Sun. 9am-4:30pm; admission 30kč, students 20kč). For more information on the entire castle complex, seek out the **Informační středisko** behind the cathedral.

Outer Prague

A model of the **Eiffel Tower** tops the **Petřínské sady** gardens (*A4*) on the hills just to the south of the castle (open May daily 9am-10pm, July-Aug. daily 9am-11pm; admission 20kč, students 5kč). The funicular to the top (4kč—look for *lanová dráby* signs) leaves from just above the intersection of Vítézná and Újezd. The neo-Gothic building next to the tower is a wacky little castle offering juvenile bliss—a **hall of mirrors** awaits inside this **Bludiště** (open daily April-Oct. 9am-6pm; admission 10kč, students 5kč). Just east of the park lies **Strahov Stadium,** the world's largest, enclosing the space of 10 soccer fields.

Take tram #22 west of the castle to "Břevnovský klášter," and you'll find yourself staring down the **Břevnov Monastery,** Bohemia's oldest Benedictine order. The monastery was founded in 993 by King Boleslav II and St. Adalbert; both were independently guided by a divine dream to create a monastery atop a bubbling stream. **St. Margaret's Cathedral** (*Kostel sv Markéty*), a Benedictine chapel, waits inside the complex. Beneath the altar rests the tomb of St. Vintíř, who vowed to forego all forms of meat. On one particular diplomatic excursion, St. Vintíř met and dined with a German king, a fanatical hunter; the main course was an enormous pheasant slain that morning by the monarch's own hand. The saint prayed for delivery from the myriad *faux pas* possibilities, whereupon the main course sprang to life and flew out the window.

Only the green bell tower and red tile roof of the monastery building are all that remain of the original Romanesque construction; the complex was redesigned in High Baroque by the Dienzenhofer father and son team. During the Soviet occupation, the monastery was allegedly used to store truckloads of secret police files. See if you can graft yourself onto a guided tour of the grounds, the crypt, and the prelature (tours daily 10am-6pm; 50kč).

Bus #112 winds from the "Nádraží Holešovice" Metro C station to "Troja," the site of French architect J.B. Mathey's masterful **château.** The pleasure palace, overlooking the Vltava from north of the U-shaped bend, includes a terraced garden, an oval staircase, and a collection of 19th-century Czech paintings. Drop by the tourist office to pick up a copy of the schedule of **free concerts** in the Château's great hall (chateau open daily 9am-5pm).

A half-hour walk south of Nové Město is the quiet fortress **Vyšehrad,** the Czech Republic's most revered landmark. On the mount above the river, the fortress encompasses a neo-Gothic church, a Romanesque rotunda, and the **Vyšehrad Cemetery** (home to the remains of Smetana and Dvořák). Take Metro C to "Vyšehrad." Even the subway stop has a movie-sweep vista of Prague (complex open 24 hrs.).

For a magnificent view of the Old Town and castle from the east, stroll up forested **Pohled z Vítkova** (Vítkov Hill), topped by the world's largest equestrian monument. One-eyed Hussite leader Jan Žižka scans the terrain for Crusaders, whom he stomped out on this spot in 1420. Take Metro B to "Křižíkova," walk down Thámova, through the tunnel, and up the hill (open 24 hrs.; free).

Although less a pilgrimage destination than the Old Jewish Cemetery, the **New Jewish Cemetery,** far to the southeast, is one of the largest burial grounds in central Europe. Kafka is interred here; obtain a map of the enormous complex from the attendant before you start hunting for the tombstone. The cemetery's main entrance is at the "Želivského" Metro A stop (open daily 8am-6pm).

MUSEUMS

National Museum (*EF5*), Václavské nám. 68 (tel. 24 23 04 85). Metro A or C: "Muzeum." Vast collection including meteorites, enormous minerals, fossils; and a skeleton horse and rider. Soviet soldiers mistook the landmark for a government building and fired on it; traces of the damage are still visible. Open Mon. and Wed.-Fri. 9am-5pm and Sat.-Sun. 10am-6pm. Admission 20kč, students 10kč.

National Gallery: collections are housed in nine different historical buildings. The **National Gallery of European Art** is in the **Šternberk Palace** (*AB2*), Hradčanské nám. 15 (tel. 24 51 05 94), just outside the front gate of the Prague Castle. It includes works by Rubens, Breughel, Dürer, Picasso, and your favorite Impressionists. The **National Gallery of Bohemian Art** (*AB2*), ranging from Gothic to Baroque, is housed in **St. George's Monastery,** Jírské nám. 33 (tel. 24 51 06 95), inside the castle. It showcases works by Czech artists including Master Theodorik, court painter for Charles IV. More Bohemian creations are exhibited at the **Anežský areal.** (*D2*), at the corner of Anežka and Řásnovka; the structure was for centuries the Cloister of St. Agnes. All collections open Tues.-Sun. 10am-6pm. Admission to each gallery 40kč, students 10kč.

Betramka Mozart Museum (*A6*), Mozartova 169 (tel. 54 38 93). Take Metro B to "Anděl," make a left on Pleňská, and turn left on Mozartova. In the Villa Bertramka, where Mozart lived (and reputedly wrote *Don Giovanni*) in 1787. Open daily 9:30am-6pm. Admission 50kč, students 30kč. Garden concerts in July and Aug. on Fri. at 7:30pm; call ahead for tickets.

The Prague Municipal Museum (Muzeum Hlavního Města Prahy; *EF2-3*), Na poříčí 52 (tel. 24 22 31 79). Metro B or C: "Florenc." Holds the original calendar board from the Town Hall's Astronomical Clock and a 1:480 scale model of old Prague, meticulously precise to the last window pane on over 2000 houses and all of Prague's great monuments. See what your hostel looked like in 1834. Other exhibits from the same collection reside in the **House at Stone Bell,** in Staroměstské nám. just to the left of Týn Church. Both buildings open Tues.-Sun. 10am-6pm. Admission 10kč, students 5kč.

State Jewish Museum (Státní Židovské Muzeum; *D2*), Jáchymova 3 (tel. 231 06 81). Metro A: "Staroměstská." Includes access to the five fascinating synagogues (see Josefov) and to the museum building itself. Among the features is a collection of children's drawings from the Nazi camp of Terezín. Open Mon.-Fri. and Sun. 9:30am-5pm. Admission 80kč, students 30kč.

Museum of National Literature (*AB2*), Strahovské nádvoři 18 (tel. 24 51 11 37). Walk from the castle's main gate and bear left. The star attraction here is the **Strahov library**, with its magnificent **Theological and Philosophical Halls.** The frescoed, vaulted ceilings of the two Baroque reading rooms were intended to spur enlightened monks to the loftiest peaks of erudition; great pagan thinkers of antiquity oversee their progress from the ceiling in the Philosophical Hall. Open daily 9am-noon and 1-5pm. Admission 20kč, students 5kč.

Military Museum (*AB2*), Hradčanské nám. 12, in the **Schwarzenberg Palace**, just outside the castle's main gate. Tools of Bohemian warfare throughout the ages. Open Tues.-Sun. 10am-6pm. Admission 20kč, students 10kč.

Museum of Decorative Arts (*D2-3*), 17. Listopadu 2, (tel. 24 81 12 41). Metro A: "Staroměstská"; right behind the Old Jewish Cemetery. Displays exquisite ceramics and richly carved and bejeweled furnishings from Renaissance and Baroque palaces. The second floor houses one of the world's largest glasswork collections. Open Tues.-Sun. 10am-6pm. Admission 20kč, students 10kč.

Planetarium, Královská abora 233 (tel. 37 43 52). Among the world's most advanced and sophisticated planetaria. Consult their busy program for events.

ENTERTAINMENT

For a listing of current concerts and performances, consult the **Prague Post,** the **Prague News, Prognosis, Prager Zeitung,** or **Český Böhmen Expres.** Most shows begin at 7pm; unsold tickets are sometimes available a half-hour before showtime. From mid-May to early June, the **Prague Spring Festival** draws musicians from around the world. Tickets (270-540kč) can be bought at **Bohemia Ticket International** (*E3-4*), Na příkopě 16, next to Čedok (tel. 22 87 38; open Mon.-Fri. 9am-6pm, Sat. 9am-3pm, Sun. 9am-2pm).

National Theater (Národní Divadlo; *C5*), Národní třida 2-4 (tel. 24 91 34 37). The "Golden Shrine" features dramatic, operatic, and ballet ensembles. Tickets 100-1000kč. Box office open Mon.-Fri. 10am-8pm, Sat.-Sun. 3-8pm.

Estates Theater (Stavovské divadlo; *DE4*), Ovocný trh 6, Metro A or B: "Mustek," (tel. 24 21 50 01). Reconstructed in 1992, the former Nostitz theater premiered Mozart's *Don Giovanni* in 1787 and continues to hold Mozart festivals. Provides earphones for simultaneous English translation. Box office, in the Kolowrat Palace around the corner, open Tues.-Sat. 10am-6pm, Sun.-Mon. noon-6pm.

State Opera (Státní Opera; *F4-5*), Wilsonova třida, between the "Muzeum" Metro A or C stop and south of Hlavní nádraži (tel. 26 53 53). Though not as famous as the National or the Estates Theater, the State Opera retains an impressive program. Box office open Mon.-Fri. 10am-6pm, Sat.-Sun. noon-6pm.

The Magic Lantern (Laterna Magica; *CD4-5*), Národní třida 4 (tel. 24 21 26 91). The theatre which served as the headquarters of Václav Havel's Velvet Revolution now shows a unique integration of film, drama, and dance. Tourists welcomed with open arms. Performances Mon.-Fri. at 8pm, Sat. 5pm and 8pm. Box office open Mon.-Sat. 3-6pm. Tickets 300-450kč. Often sells out.

Old Town Theater (Divadlo na Starém Městě; *E2*), Dlouhá 39 (tel. 231 45 34). Relive your childhood at this theater that caters to the very young.

Vinohrady Theater (Divadlo na Vinohradech; *F6*) nám Míru 7 (tel. 25 24 52). Classical theater fare in a striking turn-of the century Art Nouveau building.

Říše Loutek (National Marionette Theatre; *D3*), Žatecká in the Old Town (tel. 232 34 29). Marionette theater is a two-century-old Prague tradition. Box office open Mon. and Tues. 2-8pm.

NIGHTLIFE

Nightlife in Prague is fluid—sometimes a dark, quiet brew, sometimes a charged molten metal—but always slipping through your fingers like beads of quicksilver. Hotspots appear and evaporate overnight. **Václavské náměstí** (*E4-5*) quakes with numerous dance floors, but the best way to enjoy Prague at night is to find a *pivnice* (beer-hall) or a *vinárna* (wine hall).

Pivnice and vinárna (Beer-Halls and Wine-Halls)

V Masné *(E2)*, Masná 17. Go up Rybná from nám Republiky and turn left onto masná. Authentic Czech *pivnice* with Budweiser *Budvar* (the real thing) on tap, happily removed from tourists and high prices. Open daily 10am-10pm.

Bar Minor *(E3)*, Senovážné náměstí 28. Hippest of hang-outs. Enjoy wine and mingle with the Czech *nouveau-riches*, if you dare. Open daily 11am-11pm.

U sv. Tomáše *(B2-3)*, Letenská 12. Live Czech folk music that starts daily at 7:45pm. Average prices for beer. Open daily 11:30am-midnight.

U Pravdů *(DE6)*, Žitná 15 (tel/fax. 29 95 92). Wood panelling, high ceilings, smoke, and beer. *Staropramen* and *Radegast* on tap (a ½-liter for a mere 12kč). Open daily 11am-10pm.

Pivnice U Zlatého Tygra *(D3-4)*, Husova 17. Veteran *pivnice* whose patrons included Czech dissident author Bohumil Hrabal. Open daily 3-11pm.

Krušovická Pivnice *(DE3)*, Široká 20, two blocks from Staroměstské nám. off Pařížská. Traditional Czech *pivnice*, serving light, dark, and half-and-half. Beer 13kč. Open Mon.-Sat. 11am-midnight.

Pivnice Ve Skořepce *(D4)*, Skořepka 1 (tel. 22 80 81). Monstrous jugs of beer and wood-paneled chambers. Open Mon.-Fri. 11am-10pm, Sat. 11am-8pm.

U Švejka *(B4-5)*, Újezd 22 in Malá Strama (tel. 52 56 20). An impressive beer garden with die-hard *pivo*-loving patrons. A ½-liter of draft Pilsner *Urquell* costs 19kč. Open daily 11am-midnight.

In Vino Veritas *(D3)*, Havelská 12 in the fruit and vegetable market area. Find your truth in this pleasant *vinárna's* wide selection of wine. Great location in the Old Town. Open daily until 10pm.

Clubs and Bars

Highlander-Blue Note *(C-D4)*, Národní tř. 28 (tel. 24 21 35 55), down Národní from Metro station "Můstek." Possibly the most popular jazz club in Prague. Live music starts at 9pm. Open Mon.-Sat. 11am-2am and Sun. 11am-midnight.

Agharta *(E5)*, Krakovská 5, just down Krakovská from Wenceslas Square. Jazz club and café featuring live ensembles. Open daily 9pm-midnight.

Agnes Bar Club *(E3)*, Hybernská 1, just down the street from nám Republiky. A motley of music and plenty of drinks, from potent spirits to 10kč coffee. Open daily until 6am.

Rock Club Bunkr *(F2)*, Lodecká 2 (tel. 231 31 23). From the "nám. Republiky" Metro B stop, walk down Na Poříčí and left on Zlatnická. Hot Czech and American rock-n-roll bands in an erstwhile Communist-regime nuclear bunker. Cover usually 50kč. Open daily 7pm-5am. Café upstairs open daily 11am-3am.

Repre Club *(E3)*, downstairs in the Obecní Dům, nám. Republiky 5. Huge nightclub in the basement of the beautiful Art Nouveau Municipal House. It may be the prettiest building you'll ever get wasted in, but it's closing soon for repairs. Live music until midnight, DJ after that. Cover 50kč. Open daily 9pm-5am.

Radost FX *(F6)*, Bělehradská 120 (tel. 25 12 10), below Café FX. An alternative dance club, becoming swiftly mainstream and *hating* every ounce of extra popularity. Replete with a "virtual reality light show" and driving techno beat. Cover 50kč. Open daily 9pm-6am.

Jo's Bar *(AB3)*, Malostranské nám. 7, right in the shadow of St. Nicholas Church in Malostranské nám. You'll lose your Czech here, but you'll get friendly service and Mexican food. Nachos 70kč, beer 30kč. Kitchen open Sun.-Thurs. until 11pm, Fri.-Sat. until midnight. Open Mon.-Sat. 11am-2am, Sun. 11am-1am)

Reduta *(CD4-5)*, Národní 20 (tel. 24 91 22 46). Live jazz nightly and a clientele of artists drowning in tourists. Cover 80kč (open Mon.-Sat. 9pm-2am).

Rock Café *(CD4-5)*, right next to Reduta (tel. 24 91 44 16). MTV pumped in on satellite, and the occasional rockumentary. Sadly, *This Is Spinal Tap* doesn't survive the translation into Czech (open Mon.-Fri. 10am-3am, Sat. noon-3am).

■ NEAR PRAGUE

The Central Bohemian hills around Prague contain 14 castles, some built as early as the 13th century. A 45-minute train ride southwest from Prague (8kč) brings you to

Karlštejn, a walled and turreted fortress built by Charles IV to house his crown jewels and holy relics. The **Chapel of the Holy Cross** is decorated with more than 2000 inlaid precious stones and 128 apocalyptic paintings by medieval artist Master Theodorik. Trains cart gawkers hourly from Praha-Smíchov station. Metro B: "Smíchovské nádraži." (Open Tues.-Sun. 9am-4pm. Admission with foreign-language guide 90kč, students 40kč; in Czech 10kč, students 5kč.) A **campground** (tel. (0311) 942 63) is located on the left bank of the River Berounka (open 24hrs.).

Animal-rights activists might wish to avoid mighty **Konopiště,** south of Prague in **Benešov** (bus from Praha-Florenc station, 1½hr.), a Renaissance palace with a luxurious interior preserved from the days when Archduke Franz Ferdinand bagged game here—more than 300,000 animals. Fittingly, the **Weapons Hall** contains one of the finest collections of 16th- to 18th-century European arms.

Ninety minutes east of Prague by bus is the former mining town **Kutná Hora.** Soon after a lucky miner struck a silver vein here in the 13th century, a royal mint— **Vlašský dvůr**—was established to produce the Prague *groschen* (silver coin). The unenthralling coin museum has commentary written entirely in Czech, but up the stairs from the courtyard is a magnificent **Gothic Hall** with frescoes and lovely carved wooden triptychs. The most convincing evidence of the wealth that once flowed through the town is the fantastic, begargoyled **Cathedral of St. Barbara,** built to rival St. Vitus in Prague. Buses leave nearly hourly from Prague's Metro A: želivského, platform #2 and from Praha-Florenc station.

At the end of the 18th century, Austrian Empress Maria Theresa had a **fortress** built at the confluence of the *Labe* (Elbe) and *Ohře* (Eger) known as **Terezín** or Theresienstadt. Little did she know the miseries to which this fortress would bear witness. The Nazis established a **concentration camp** here in 1940 in which 32,000 prisoners were held, often en route to death camps. Among the inmates were Jews, Poles, Germans, British POWs, and Communists. Nearby the Nazis constructed **Terezín ghetto,** a sham "model village" to satisfy the International Red Cross (all Terezín residents were murdered after the Red Cross visit). After the Red Army captured the camp in May, 1945, the Czech regime used Terezín as an internment camp for Sudeten and Bohemian Germans. The fortress is now a monument and museum (tel. (0416) 922 25 or 924 42, fax 922 45). Buses leave the Jewish Town Hall, Maiselova 18, twice per week (every Sunday and Thursday at 10am and return at 3pm) and daily from the Florenc bus station (Buses #17 and 20). The ride takes about an hour (fortress open daily 8am-4:30pm; museum open daily 9am-6pm).

NORTHERN BOHEMIA

Although Northern Bohemia is often characterized too simply as "industrial," the region features Teplice, one of Bohemia's most famous spas, and its fascinating capital, Liberec.

■■■ LIBEREC

In the 19th century, Liberec was known as Reichenberg and was one of the most rapidly industrializing regions of Austria-Hungary. As a discussion in any pub will reveal, Liberec has been the site of considerable ethnic conflict in subsequent years. Regarding themselves as second-class citizens, the Sudeten Germans of Reichenberg protested their forced inclusion in Czechoslovakia in 1918. Twenty years later, Hitler garnered a measure of support among this disgruntled population and annexed Liberec and the surrounding Sudetenland, expelling the Czech inhabitants in the process. In 1945, the newly reconstituted Czechoslovakia expelled the majority of Sudeten Germans and repopulated Liberec. Today Liberec is a Czech city with only a small German-speaking minority.

ORIENTATION AND PRACTICAL INFORMATION

Tourist Office: Tourist Information, nám. Benešovo 14 (tel./fax 298 54) in the main square. The helpful staff speaks English and sells several **maps,** guidebooks, and pamphlets on Liberec and Northern Bohemia. Open Mon.-Fri. 9am-5pm. **ČEDOK,** Soukenné nám. 8 (tel. 210 47). Full range of travel agency services; information on Liberec and environs. Open Mon.-Fri. 9am-4pm, Sat. 9am-noon.
Currency Exchange: Komerční Banka, Felberová and Moskerská. The Czech Republic's largest private bank. Open Mon.-Fri. 8am-11:30am and 1-3:30pm. **Česká Banka,** Soukenné nám. on the square. Smaller than Komerční Banka, but with more flexible hours. Open Mon.-Fri. 8am-4pm. **Inform,** Moskevská 11. This little *bureau de change* has the most flexible hours in Liberec. Open Mon.-Fri. 7:30am-7pm and Sat. 9am-3pm.
Post Office: Nám. Benešovo 30 (tel. 232 00).
Telephones: At the post office. **City Code:** 048.
Trains: The train station, *Žel. Stanice Liberec,* is located at the very end of 1. máje, which connects it to Soukenné nám.
Buses: The bus station, *Autobus. nádraží,* is located on Na rybničku, just off 1. máje between the train station and Soukenné nám.
Bookstore: J. Fryč, Pražka 14 south of nám. The largest selection of new books in Liberec, and an enrapturing antiquariat collection of old Czech, German, and Austro-Hungarian volumes. Open Mon.-Fri. 7am-7pm, Sat.-Sun. 8am-6pm.
Pharmacy: Nám. Benešovo 11 (tel. 223 18), on the main square. The most flexible pharmacy hours in Liberec. Open Mon.-Fri. 7:30am-7pm, Sat. 7:30am-1pm.
Police: Pastyřska 3 or Fügnerova 1 (tel. 201 29) off Soukenné nam.

ACCOMMODATIONS

Well-priced and well-located rooms are available through **Tourist Information,** nám. Benešovo 14 (tel./fax 298 54). Expect to pay 250-300kč per person (open Mon.-Fri. 9am-5pm). **ČEDOK,** Soukenné nám. 8 (tel. 210 47), finds rooms for 300-400kč per person, breakfast included (open Mon.-Fri. 9am-4pm, Sat. 9am-noon).

Hotel Česká Beseda, Na rybničku 143 (tel. 231 61) near the bus station. Centrally located. Reception open 10am-10pm. Rooms start at 390kč per person. Shared showers and toilets.
Pension Rosa, Sportovní 354 (tel./fax 346 18). Reception open 24hrs. Not as centrally located as other hotels but not exorbitantly priced: 390kč per person, breakfast included.
Dum Rekreace Liberec, Šaldovo nám. 1345 (tel. 42 19 32, fax 42 18 15). A 3-min. walk from the main square, nám. Benešovo. Features a bar, TV room, and a sauna. Reception open 24 hrs. 665kč per person.

FOOD

Radničkní Sklep, in the town hall *(radnice)* on nám. Benešovo (tel. 237 33). Authentic Czech cuisine served in an atmospheric neo-Gothic subterranean chamber. Budweiser *budvar* on tap. Offers *guláš* and *schnitzel,* among other Bohemian dishes. Open daily 11am-10pm.
Restaurace Černy Kun, Nerudovo nám. north of Benešovo nám. Czech meat dishes including *guláš* and *svíčková* under 30kč. Open Mon.-Fri. 9am-11pm, Sat. 11am-11pm, Sun. 3-11pm.
Restaurant Hotel Eden, Chrastavská 13 (tel. 248 19 or 275 21, fax 292 08). Chinese food Czech-style and chop suey 80-90kč. A ½-liter of *Radegast* is 14kč. Visa accepted. Flexible hours.
Cukrárna, 5. května 15 between nám. Benešovo and nám. Šaldovo. A popular shop selling all sorts of pastries, sweets, and baked goods. Very tasty. Open Mon.-Fri. 8am-6pm, Sat. 9am-6pm, Sun. 1-6pm.
Pivnice Šavlovna, (tel. 460 30 891), on the Máli námeští. Many locals and a few tourists down buckets of *Velkopopvicky Kozel.* Open Mon.-Thurs. until 11pm, Fri.-Sat. until midnight, and Sun. until 10pm.

SIGHTS

The thriving businesses and imposing 19th-century architecture of the **Old Town** (*Staré Město*) surround náměstí Benešovo, named after Czechoslovakia's most important interwar political figure. In 1888, the Liberec city council commissioned Viennese architect F. V. Neumann to build a new **City Hall** (*radnice*). The larger 19th-century neo-Gothic *Rathaus* in Vienna inspired Neumann's design. While the 65m-high tower is not open to the public, the foyer of the building welcomes visitors who admire the intricate stained-glass windows.

Walk down Železná until you reach **Sokolovské náměstí,** another square surrounded by 19th-century buildings, that are far more run-down than those on nám. Benešovo. The gray neo-Gothic **Church of St. Antonius** (*Arciděkansky Chrám sv. Antonina*) is yet another product of the last two decades of the 19th century. The timbered houses on Větrná visible from Sokolovské náměstí are the oldest buildings in Liberec. Known as the **Wallenstein Houses** (*Valdštejnské domky*), the plaster and timber constructions from 1670 feel somewhat out of place in the uniformly 1800s city. At the end of Větrná is **Malé náměstí,** the small square with a petite Baroque church. Unfortunately, the interior is not open to further exploration.

To the east of nám Benešovo, down Felberova, is the **Castle** (*Zámek*). Originally built in 1582, the castle building has been renovated so many times that virtually nothing of the original remains. The most recent renovations ended in 1994 and made good use of J. J. Kunze's neoclassical refurbishing of the castle's exterior in the late 19th century. It's an attractive but not memorable building. Today the castle houses a restaurant and exhibits glassware manufactured in Northern Bohemia.

Full of pedestrians, **5. května** is a pleasant capitalist promenade along which opens into **Nerudovo náměstí,** a square with a beer garden on each side. At this point 5. května becomes Masarykova and the towering **Museum of Northern Bohemia** (*Severočeské muzeum*) Maraykova 11 (tel. 237 50 06), emerges on the left. Another neo-Renaissance edifice from the late-19th century, its tower was meant to be a foil to that of the town hall. The museum features the largest collection of Oriental tapestries in the Czech Republic and details Northern Bohemia's history, ethnography, and archaeology; there are also collections of porcelain, glassware, and renowned Liberec textiles (open Wed.-Sun. 9am-5pm, Tues. noon-5pm).

Virtually all of the wooded hills that surround Liberec are worth exploring, if you enjoy hiking and you have a good map of the surroundings of the city (available at Tourist Information). Mount Ještěd (*Jeschken*), is southwest of the Old Town. To reach the foot of the mountain walk down Ještědská or pick up tramway #3 along the way. Ještědská begins on the other side of the train station, relative to 1. majé and the Old Town. Where Ještědská ends and a large parking lot emerges, find the Stanice Horské služby, where you can take a chair lift to the top of Mount Ještěd. At the top of the mountain, soak up the view of Liberec and the valleys of Northern Bohemia. At the top, you can rest your aching feet at the **hotel** and **café,** or layer on some new blisters at the **nightclub** (open daily 8am-midnight). Enjoy the fresh breeze from the surrounding forest and the oxygen-deficient air; you are over 1km above sea level.

ENTERTAINMENT AND NIGHTLIFE

Pivnice Parlament, in the town hall (*Radnice*) on Benešovo nám. A neo-Gothic beer-hall serving Budweiser *Budvar,* pumped in fresh. Open daily 1-10pm.

Pivnice Černy Kun, Nerudovo nám. north of Benešovo nám. A huge beer garden serving *Velkopopovicky Kozel* to throngs of local carousers. Open Mon.-Fri. 9am-11pm, Sat. 11am-11pm, Sun. 3-11pm.

Azyl Snack Bar, Lazebnicky Vrch off Pražká. Enjoy pints of the local *Vratislav* beer (from the nearby village Maffersdorf where Ferdinand Porsche was born, today part of Liberec) on a terrace overlooking the south. Open daily 10am-3am.

Club Fair Play, on Revoluční between Soukenné nám. and Rumunska. Thump with the locals to the latest techno and rap efforts. Open Mon.-Thurs. 11am-midnight, Fri.-Sat. 11am-4am.

■ NEAR LIBEREC: JABLONEC NAD NISON

From Soukenné nám in Liberec take tram #11 to make the 15km journey to Jablonec nad Nison. Long famous for its jewelry, the tradition continues today both in Jablonec and in Neugablonz in Bavaria, where exiled Sudeten Germans founded a twin city. The **Museum of Jewelry and Glassware** *(Muzeum skla a bižutérie)*, Jiráskova 4 (tel. 225 22 or 226 50), chronicles the development of glassware and jewelry production in the city. Jablonec also features a turn-of-the-century *Jugendstil* **Theater** *(Divadlo)*. The modernist **Town Hall** *(Radnice)* dates from the early 1930s.

■■■ TEPLICE

Ancient Celts and Romans were the first to enjoy the curative springs of Teplice. The name *"Teplice"* has its origins in an ancient Slavonic word that means "warm springs." In its 19th-century heyday, Teplice was a favorite schmoozing ground for Europe's intellectual elite. Arthur Schopenhauer pondered pessimism while soaking his tender tootsies in Teplice, and Johann Wolfgang von Goethe came to gather steam for his next masterful literary work. Also attracted by Teplice's charming and mysterious curative powers were composers, including Frederyk Chopin, Bedřich Smetana, Richard Wagner, Franz Liszt, and Ludwig van Beethoven. World War I ruined things for the resort town; brown-coal industries began to sully this part of Bohemia and lessened its appeal. Today, a sign outside Teplice's main train station warns *"Pozor! Smog!"* ("Danger! Smog!"). Traces of 19th-century glory are rare, but the town's abundant squares and gardens do allow the long, contemplative promenades of yore.

ORIENTATION AND PRACTICAL INFORMATION

Tourist Office: ČEDOK, Masarykova 48 (tel. 299 73, fax 296 01). The friendly staff does not speak English, but can handle German. They sell **maps** of Teplice and the environs, as well as provide transportation, communication, and accommodation information. Open Mon., Wed., and Fri. 8am-4pm, Tues. and Thurs. 9am-4pm, Sat. 9am-noon.

Currency Exchange: Try **Komerční Banka,** the largest bank in the Czech Republic, at Mírové náměstí 2970, to the south of náměstí Svobody (tel. 31 33, fax 283 89). Open Mon.-Fri. 8am-4pm with a 1hr. *siesta* for lunch

Post Office: *(Česká Pošta)* Nádražní náměstí 12 next to the main train station. The downtown office is on náměstí Svobody.

Telephone City Code: 0417.

Trains: The station is called *"Teplice v Čechách"* to distinguish it from other localities also named *"Teplice."* It is on Nádražni náměstí, north of downtown Teplice. For Czech-language ČD train information, tel. 290 71.

Buses: The *autobusové nádraží* is located next to the train station on Nádražní náměstí. For Czech-language ČAD bus information, tel. 236 66.

Pharmacies: There is a 24-hr. pharmacy *(Lékárna nepřetržita služba)* at Duchcovská 2602 (tel. 273 53) located to the west of downtown Teplice.

Police: tel. 158.

ACCOMMODATIONS

Although the number of spa-goers to Teplice has declined, few efforts are being made to attract budget travelers. There are no private room agencies in Teplice and the refurbished 19th-century grand hotels are unabashedly expensive. The few new *penzions* are the only realistic option for budget travelers.

ČEDOK, Masarykova 48 (tel. 299 73, fax 296 01), does not offer private rooms, but makes reservations at hotels and at spa houses *(Kurhaus* in central Teplice, Šanov, and Dubí. 500-1000kč per person.)

Hotel Neptun, Sládkova 1 (tel. 279 80, fax 279 78), near the wooded main square in Šanov, Sady Čs. Armády. All rooms have radios, TVs, minibars, and telephones.

Reception open 24hrs. Doubles range from 1000-1230kč and the 6-person suite goes for 2583kč. Add 215kč per person for bedding.

Gizela Penzion, Vrchlického 17 (tel./fax 288 67) is between the train station and the gardens in Šanov. Located among handsome 19th-century villas in a quiet, yet central neighborhood. Reception open 24hrs. Singles and quads go for 342kč per person, breakfast included.

Penzion Šárka, Kmochova Cesta 3 (tel. 412 31), is located east of Sady Čs. Armády in Šanov. Off the beaten track but reasonably priced. Multi-person rooms but no singles. In winter, 250kč per person; in summer 350-400kč per person.

FOOD

Except for a few tourist lures, most restaurants in Teplice are moderately priced (entrees under 70kč); many can be found on Masarykova, the main business street.

Restaurant Hotel de Saxe, Masarykova 35 (tel. 438 45, fax 438 43), between the train station and náměstí Svobody. A restored 19th-century rendezvous of Europe's wise and wealthy. *Guláš, svíčková,* pork dishes, and Chinese entrees for 40-90kč. Pilsner Urquell on tap, pricey, but good. Open daily 6am-11pm.

Restaurant Slávie, Dubská 2 north of náměstí Svobody. Czech pork and beef entrees under 30kč. Popular with local folk; often full. Open daily 10am-10pm.

Centr Grill, Masarykova 13 on the main drag. A popular stand-up joint with dishes under 40kč. Open Mon.-Fri. 8am-6pm and Sat. 8am-1pm.

Gastronom Restaurace, Masarykovo 8. Features a broad selection of Czech dishes including roast beef, roast pork, and sausages. Most entrees under 40kč. Open Mon.-Fri. 9am-10pm and Sat.-Sun. 10am-10pm.

Pizza, Musarykova 38. Simple name, simple food, simple hours. Slice of pizza 15kč. Hamburger 16kč. Open 24hrs.

SIGHTS

Most of Teplice can be seen in about half a day. The main commercial street, **Masarykova,** touches the southernmost tip of Nádražní náměstí (the train and bus stations) and meanders west towards central Teplice. At its end, Masarykova is replaced by four streets. Take the narrowest of these, U Krupské, to reach **náměstí Benešovo,** a large square surrounded by fairly average and nondescript 19th-century buildings. Take advantage of the **public toilets** here; they are the only ones in downtown Teplice. From náměstí Benešovo, a small street called U radnice carries visitors to **náměstí Svobody.** A truly hideous collection of socialist-realist architecture overwhelms the Baroque statue and fountain dedicated to the **Virgin Mary** (*Krašna p. Marie*) and the **Old Town Hall** (*Stará radnice*) that dates from 1807. Depart from náměstí Svobody on Dlouhá. The park on the left with the long grass and old benches is **Mirové náměstí.**

Dlouhá ends at the refreshingly beautiful **Zámecké náměstí,** where fine 18th- and 19th-century buildings offer the best glimpse of the town's days of glory. Although blackened by the sooty air, the **Statue of the Trinity** (*Morovy sloup Nejsvětější trojice*) remains the monumental work that its creator Mathias Braun envisioned in 1718. The main attraction of the square, is the **Château of Clary-Aldringen** (*Zámek*). Until the tidal wave of Communist nationalization of property in the late 1940s, this cheery yellow castle was the property of the noble family Clary-Aldringen. The attractive **Castle Gardens** (*Zámecká zahrada*) and ponds located behind the stately edifice are open to the public. Also on Zámecké náměstí is the castle church of **Holy Cross** (*Sv. Kříže*), which is closed to visitors. Fortunately, the impressive neighboring **Church of John the Baptist** (*Děkansky kostel sv. Jana Křtitele*) is open to those who wish to admire exquisite Baroque interior.

Lázenská connects Zámecké náměstí to the **Spa Gardens** (*Lázeňsky Sad*), crossed by pleasant promenades. Once you have leisurely traversed the gardens, continue your therapeutic walk along Lipová, which is bordered by a park on one side and villas on the other. At the end of Lipová is **Sady Čs. Armády,** the ensemble of gardens and trees that forms the heart of the Šanov neighborhood. Boathouses and aristocratic residences abound as they do in downtown Teplice. Walk up

Vrchlického (formerly *Gizela)* that is lined on both sides with handsome villas. Vrchlického ends at the junction of Masarykova and Nádražní náměstí, adjacent to the train station. Although it may sound unusual, the train station itself is an interesting sight because of its architectural contradictions. The whole building exudes grandeur and glory, meant to satisfy the artistic cravings of wealthy 19th-century aristocrats—with the notable exception of the windows. Notice their idealized depictions of factory-workers, laborers, farmers, and soldiers who were idolized by the Communist regime. The contrast between the painfully ornate Victorian ceiling and the socialist-realist kitsch of the windows is interesting, if not laughable.

ENTERTAINMENT
Forget techno. Most people come to Teplice for some peace and quiet, contemplation, or a cure. Come and be soothed at **Vinárina Hotel de Saxe,** Masarykova 35 (tel. 438 45, fax 438 43), a nice wine-bar in a restored 19th-century hotel. (Open Tues.-Sat. 8pm-3am.) At **Kaffee Klub Kevin,** on Masarykova across from Českobratrská (tel. 152), a testosterone-heavy clientele enjoys hard drinks over a game of pool. (Open daily 8am-2am.)

WESTERN BOHEMIA

With its great diversity in attractions, Western Bohemia is the Czech Republic's most popular destination after Prague. Medieval Cheb is not only one of the country's architectural gems, but the center of the spa region that includes the much celebrated Carlsbad. Also in Western Bohemia is Plzen, the home of the original Pilsner beer.

■■■ CHEB

Of all cities in Bohemia, Cheb ranks second only to Prague in terms of historical richness and architectural beauty. Cheb's ruined castle was one of the most important fortifications in the realm of Friedrich Barbarossa. It was in Cheb that Albrecht of Wallenstein was murdered, altering the course of the destructive Thirty Years War. The evils of nationalism increasingly influenced Cheb's development until heated disputes between Czechs and Sudeten Germans culminated in its occupation by the Nazis and the post-war expulsion of the Sudeten German community.

Despite the hardships of history, Cheb remains lively and beautiful. Often referred to in English by its German name, Eger, Cheb was the capital of the once-autonomous **Egerland** region, where influences from Bohemia, Bavaria, and Saxony met and intermingled. The rich museums of Cheb attest to this colorful crossing of principalities, duchies, and kingdoms.

ORIENTATION AND PRACTICAL INFORMATION
Rail lines from the three famous spa towns of West Bohemia (Karlovy Varg, Mariánské Lázně, and Františkovy Lázně) converge here. Cheb also lies on the main train route that connects Prague with Paris, Frankfurt, and Nürnberg.

> **Tourist Office: Čedok,** Májova 31 (tel. 339 51, fax 306 50), at Svobody, that connects the train station to the Old Town. The helpful English-speaking staff offer **maps** and information on Cheb and West Bohemia. Open Mon.-Fri. 8:30am-5pm, Sat. 8am-11pm
>
> **Currency Exchange: Česká Spořitelna,** Májova at Svobody opposite ČEDOK. Open Mon.-Fri. 8am-4:30pm. **Komerční Banka,** Obrněné Brigady 20, two blocks west of Svobody, features a *"Bankomat"* (ATM) on the Cirrus network that accepts Mastercard. Bank open Mon.-Fri. 7:30-11:30am and 1-4:30pm. **Kreditní Banka,** 26. Dubna 12 near Komerční Banka, is open Mon.-Fri. 8-11am and noon-5pm, Sat. 8-11am.

Post Office: Náměstí Jiřiho z Poděbrad, the main historic square. Another *Česka Pošta* is next to the train station. **Postal Code:** 0166.
Trains: The station is southeast of the Old Town at the end of Třida Svobody.
Buses: The *Autobu. nádraží* is next door to the train station, in the same building. The friendly staff speak only Czech.

ACCOMMODATIONS

There is no private room office in Cheb, although *penzions* have popped up, especially in surrounding villages. The central hotels usually have vacancies at reasonable prices. **ČEDOK** can direct you to an available hotel or pension.

Hotel Hradní Dvůr, Dlouhá 12 (tel. 224 44 or 220 06), one block from náměstí Jiřího z Poděbrad in the atmospheric Old Town. Very friendly English-speaking reception open 24 hours. Singles, doubles, triples, and quads start at 400kč per person. Showers cost 60kč per use. Restaurant and wine-bar.
Hotel Slávie, Svobody 32 (tel. 332 16), on the main pedestrian street. Fine location in historic Old Cheb. Some German but no English spoken. Reception open 24hrs. Every room priced differently, but expect to pay 515-715kč per person. Many restaurants, bakeries, and grocery stores nearby.
Hotel Hvězda, nám. Jiřiho z Poděbrad (tel. 225 49, fax 225 46), in the heart of the Old Town. Reception open 24hrs. Every room has a different price. Expect to pay about 500kč per person. Selected doubles which shower and toilet 1200kč, breakfast included.
Penzion Soukromé Ubytování M.Š., Valdštejnova 21 (tel. 330 88), one block west of Svobody. Close to the train station. 2 doubles 400-500kč per person. Call in advance to reserve a room.

FOOD

The mainstay of restaurants in Cheb are tourists, tourists, and more tourists.

Restaurace Roland, on náměstí Jiříno z Poděbrad. A great deal for the main square. Roast pork or *schnitzel* under 70kč. Open daily 10am-10pm.
Staročeská Kestaurace, náměstí Jiřsho z Poděbrad (tel. 234 98). Simple and sophisticated Bohemian dishes from 40-100kč. Deininger and Waldstein beers on tap. Open daily 11am-10pm.
Restaurant Hradní Dyůr, Dlouhá 12 (tel. 224 44). Stews and beef lunches under 50kč. Fancy pork dinners under 70kč. Beer 12kč. Open Mon.-Fri. until 8pm.
Cukrárna Kapucín, corner of Olouhá and Židorska. The best pastry shop in Cheb, with seating room and wonderful coffee (5kč). Gourmet pastries and treats 5-10kč. Open Mon.-Fri. 7am-6pm, Sat. 8am-1pm, Sun. 1-6pm.
Restaurant Metropolitan, náměstí Jiřího z Poděbrad. *Guláš,* roast pork, spaghetti, steak 70-125kč. Beer 20kč. Open daily 10am-10:30pm.
Jídelna Hvězda, náměstí Jiřiho z Poděbrad next to Hotel Hvězda. A self-serve eatery with snow-white trays. *Svíčkova (Sauerbraten)* and potatoes is the specialty. Bottled *Staropramen* beer from Prague. Full meals about 70kč. Open Mon.-Fri. 8am-3pm, Sat. 8am-1pm.
Restaurant Boccaccio, Májova 26, west of ČEDOK. Steak, *schnitzel,* and fish specialties. For Italian fare, go to Italy. Entrees 59-100kč. Open daily 10am-10pm.

SIGHTS

Pedestrians adore the Old Town's narrow medieval streets that remain relatively free of cars. Although Cheb is not a large city by today's standards (population under 50,000), the impressive castle, the large churches, and the expansive Old Town attest to the strategic importance of this city in previous centuries.

Lined with restaurants, outdoor terraces, bakeries, meat markets, and fruit stands, **Svoboda** is the commercial street of Cheb. It leads from the main train station to the very heart of historic Cheb, **náměstí Jiřího z Poděbrad**, the former marketplace. The square is surrounded by a fascinating collection of Gothic, Renaissance, and Baroque burghers' houses. Two fountains grace the square, one dedicated to Hercules and the other to Saint Roland. A collection of 11 small half-timbered buildings known collectively as the **Špalíček-Stöckl** merits particular attention. These unusual buildings date from the late Middle Ages, when they functioned as shops and storage houses. Today the Špalíček-Stöckl is to Cheb as the Eiffel Tower is to Paris—the symbol of the city.

The yellow and square Baroque tower of the **New City Hall** *(Nová radnice)* overlooks the square from the southeast. Today the city hall houses a wine bar *(vinárna)* and an **Art Gallery** *(Galerie výtvarného umění)* that houses the works of 20th-century Czech painters and sculptors little known outside the Czech Republic (open daily 9am-5pm). Across the square is the fading red **Grüner House** *(Grüneruv Dům)*, named after one of Cheb's wealthy burghers; today it houses a good bookstore. Farther down the side of the square is the intricate 19th-century **post office.** The richly decorated basement chambers house an atmospheric restaurant; the rest of the building still functions as a post office. The Gothic building behind Špalíček-Stöckl contains the **City Museum** *(Chebské Muzeum;* open Tues.-Sun. 9am-noon and 1-5pm; admission 5kč, toilets 2kč). The museum houses exhibits on the history and archaeology of the Cheb region and on General Albrecht of Wallenstein, a military figure of the Thirty Years War. The general was murdered in this very same building over 350 years ago, much to the surprise of Europe. Across from the City Museum and Špalíček-Stöckl is the **Gabler House** *(Gableruv Dům)* with interesting Gothic features (such as its triangular top) reminiscent of contemporary buildings in Hanseatic cities on the North and Baltic Seas.

The alley by the City Museum and Gabler House leads to the **Church of St. Nicholas** *(Kostel sv. Mikuláše)*, one of the finest Romanesque structures in Bohemia. The view of the church from Kasární náměstí and from across the Ohře River is quite impressive. The church is noted for its great stature and elegant proportions, both on the inside and the outside. Although American bombers damaged the church in April 1945, it has been faithfully rebuilt. The towering Gothic statue ensembles, the paintings of Master Lukas, and the late Romanesque West Portal retain their full glory. An outline of the church's history is available for 3kč. North of St. Nicholas is the much smaller Gothic church of **St. Bartholomew** *(Kostel sv. Bartoloměje)* that features an exhibition of Gothic sculpture. Retreating back towards the former marketplace, one passes **St. Wecelas** *(Kostel sv. Václava)*, a diminutive Baroque church in which elderly men and women gather in circular formations to sing religious songs. From the steeply inclined Janské náměstí, take Růžová to Růžový Kop. from where the entrance to the castle can be seen.

The **Imperial Castle of Barbarossa** *(Chebský hrad;* open Tues.-Sun. 9am-noon and 1-4pm; admission 10kč, students 2kč) is rich in both historical and architectural merit. Walking along the romantic ruins of the fortifications not only provides an opportunity to admire the castle, but also offers several fine views of Cheb and the Ohře River valley. For the best views, climb the 20m-high **Black Tower** *(Černá věž)*, from where a panorama of Cheb's Old Town and of the castle complex unfolds. The **Romanesque Chapel** *(Hradní Kaple)* is a rare gem among Bohemian religious buildings. The stony, cold, and barren interior of this 800-year-old building is refreshingly different from churches of later epochs, which become increasingly (and often overbearingly) ornate. The chapel has two levels, each harking back to times when art, worship, and life itself appeared simpler, though not necessarily gentler.

Exit the castle and return to Růžový Kop, from where you can stroll down **Dlouha,** one of the impressive streets of Cheb's Old Town. Three blocks on your right is the **Square of the Franciscans,** named after the cloister *(Františkánský klášter)* that borders on the square. The tall, gray, Gothic building is striking, but sadly closed to public inspection. Across the square is the white Baroque Church of **St. Clara** *(Kostel sv. Kláry)*, a masterpiece by Bohemian architect Kristof Dienzenhofer (and also closed to visitors). Next to St. Clara is the contemporary **Balthasar Neumann House** *(Dům Balthasara Neumanna)*, the community center of the local German-speaking inhabitants.

ENTERTAINMENT

South of the Square of the Franciscans is the local **Theater** *(Divadlo)*, housing the busy Theater Company of Western Bohemia. Farther south is the City Garden (Městské Sady), a sizeable expanse of tall trees, grass, and benches—ideal for a rest after penetrating the charms of Cheb.

Vinárna Rudniční Sklípek, náměstí Jiřího z Poděbrad (tel. 220 42), on the main square in a chamber of the City Hall. Hard-liquor-induced disco action. The hard-liquored power élite loves it. Open daily 8am-4am.

F Bar, náměstí Jiřího z Poděbrad. Decorated with half-timbered plaster, this new bar sells all sorts of hard drinks to a non-proletarian crowd. Open daily 10am-2am.

Blanik, Svobody at Karlova. A joint restaurant and pub offering the local *Chodovar* beer on tap. Enjoy a game of billiards over a few drafts. Open daily noon-1am.

Rock Café Disco Elektra, Svobody at Žižkova (tel. 337 06), across from the train station. The name says it all. Open daily 10am-4pm.

■■■ CARLSBAD (KARLOVY VARY)

The *"Karl"* in Karlovy Vary is the much beloved Charles *(Karel* or *Karl)* IV who beautified Prague in the 14th century. On a routine deer hunt in the forests of Western Bohemia, the Holy Roman Emperor and King of Bohemia stumbled upon a natural fountain spewing hot water high into the air. Charles was so impressed that he built a hunting lodge on the site; named after His Highness, it was known as Carlsbad in English and as Karlsbad in German. In 1370, 12 years after Charles's fateful discovery, Karlovy Vary acquired the privileges of a Royal City. Over the next six centuries, the spa developed into one of "the salons of Europe" visited by such diverse personalities as Sigmund Freud, Karl Marx, Otto von Bismarck, Peter the Great, Adam Mickiewicz, and Johann Sebastian Bach. It was during this period that present-day Karlovy Vary was built, largely by the Viennese architects Ferdinand Fellner and Hermann Helmer who were prolific throughout Austria-Hungary.

The impressive natural springs of the Karlovy Vary continue to be the city's most important attraction. Of the 85 thermal springs in the area, 12 have been designated as curative. Drinking these therapeutic waters is reputed to do everything from curing rheumatism to increasing potency. Perhaps the most beneficial of Karlovy Vary's springs is a herbal liqueur called **Becherovka.** Developed in the 1700s by David Becher, this fine alcoholic beverage is the careful synthesis of selected herbs and just the right amount of sugar. Whether you come to Karlovy Vary for the warm mineral-rich spring water, *Becherovka,* or a revealing picture of a luxurious 19th-century spa town, you will find all of them eagerly awaiting your indulgence.

ORIENTATION AND PRACTICAL INFORMATION

To the north of the center of the spa lie the **train station, bus station,** and main commercial streets (Masaryka and Dr. David Bechera).

Tourist Offices: ČEDOK, Moskevská 2 (tel. 222 92 or 222 26, fax 278 35). The friendly staff distributes small but free town **maps** and sells more sophisticated maps, pamphlets, and publications. (Open Mon.-Fri. 8am-noon and 1-5pm and Sat. 8am-noon.) There is a second office at Karla IV 1 (tel. 261 10 or 267 05). **Cestovní Kancelář Therma,** Varšavska 2 (tel. 280 89, fax 287 19). Young staff have helpful brochures, **maps,** and advice. (Open Mon.-Fri. 9am-11am and noon-4pm.)

Currency Exchange: Česká Spořitelná, Masaryka 14. Visa and American Express traveler's checks welcomed. The *bankomat* (ATM) accepts only Czech cards. (Open Mon.-Fri. 8am-5pm, Sat. 8am-noon.) **Čekobanka,** Masaryka 21. A little window on one of the commercial streets. English spoken, but beware the rates. Visa and American Express traveler's checks accepted. (Open daily 9am-9pm.)

Post Office: The *Česká Pošta* is located at the corner of Masaryká and Zahradní, near the bridge over the Teplá River to Hotel Thermal. Open Mon.-Fri. 7:30am-7pm and Sat.-Sun. 8am-1pm. **Postal Code:** 17.

Trains: The station is located well to the north of downtown Karlovy Vary, across the Ohře River. It is easier to cross the river on the Nabřeží Osvobozeni Bridge; the Chebský Most Bridge leads to a busy freeway. The station bathrooms are free. **Buses:** The station is one block east down Varšarská from Nabřeží Osvobozeni. **Car Rental:** An agency working in cooperation with ČEDOK offers rentals. Visit a ČEDOK office for more information. **Pharmacy:** A pharmacy with flexible hours is located at Dr. David Bechers 3. Open Mon.-Fri. 7:30am-1pm and 1:30-6pm, Sat. 8am-1pm.

ACCOMMODATIONS

Karlovy Vary has no shortage of accommodations agencies, hotels, and pensions, but prices vary greatly. The spa town welcomed Western tourists long before the revolution of 1989 and has since developed a network of expensive hotels, but there are also several options for the budget traveler.

Accommodations Agencies

ČEDOK, Moskerská 2 (tel. 222 92 or 222 26, fax 278 35). The main office arranges private rooms for individuals and groups. Expect to pay at least 369kč per person. Open Mon.-Fri. 8am-noon and 1-5pm, Sat. 8am-noon.

Cestovní Kancelář Therma, Varšavská 2 (tel. 280 89, fax 287 19). Offers several rooming options, but you must pay in Deutschmarks (DM). The English -speaking staff is friendly and helpful. Expect to pay DM15-20 per person depending on your room's location in the city. Open Mon.-Fri. 9am-11am and noon-4pm.

W Cestoní Kancelář, náměstí Republiky 5 (tel. 277 68, fax 277 68), west of the bus station. Although the business card is trilingual (Czech, German, English) the staff speaks only Czech. Private rooms cost about 400kč per person. Open Mon.-Fri. 10am-5pm.

ACCO-M, Jaltská 1 (tel. 23 75 68), off Dr. David Bechera. Private rooms (without breakfast and private toilet only) at reasonable prices. Centrally located rooms run 330kč per person, 250kč per person on the periphery. Open Mon.-Fri. 9:30am-6:30pm, Sat. 10am-2pm.

Hotels and Pensions

Hotel Adria, Západní 1 (tel. 237 65), near the bus station. A good value and a decent location. Very friendly and helpful reception open 24hrs. Singles 554kč. Doubles 820kč. Triples 1230kč. Prices slightly lower in the winter.

Hotel Turist, Dr. David Bechera 18 (tel. 268 37), not far from the bus station. Another good deal, with plenty of singles, doubles and triples. Reception open 24 hours. Expect to pay 400kč per person.

Penzion Kosmos, Zahradní 39 (tel. 231 68), near the prim and proper Dvořák Gardens *(Dvořákovy Sady)*. Scores big on location. English-speaking reception open until midnight. Singles 400kč. Doubles 700kč. Communal toilets and showers.

Penzion Ahlan, Sadová 53 (tel. 242 94), down the street from the Dvořák Gardens *(Dvořákovy Sady)* and the Park Colonnade. Spacious rooms in an impressive 19th-century building across from the Russian Orthodox Church. Friendly Czech-speaking reception open 24hrs. One single 650kč. Doubles 900kč.

Romania Penzion, Zahradní 49 (tel. 228 22), near the pretty Dvořák Gardens (Dvořákovy Sady). Friendly German-speaking reception open 24hrs. Check-out noon. Singles and doubles for 630kč per person. Breakfast included.

Penzion Suprahan, Vřídelní 27 (tel. 271 17), near Mill Colonnade. Reception inconveniently located above a music store. Dorm beds 600kč. Singles 990kč.

FOOD

Česka Restaurace, Jaltská 19. Popular with the locals, and with good reason. Roast beef, *schnitzel,* and steak entrees 60-100kč. Delicious and refreshing *Velko-popovicky Kozel* (dark and light) is on tap for 13kč per pint. Try the *řízek (schnitzel)* with *bramborak* (refried mashed potatoes). Open daily 10am-11pm.

Bar B&B, Nová Louka 25, near the Grand Hotel Pupp and the City Museum. A variety of fish, *schnitzel,* and roast dishes for 60-110kč. Open Mon.-Sat. noon-3pm and 5pm-midnight.

Café Radio Restaurant, Stará Louka 38. Centrally located and affordable. Calzones, spaghetti, *schnitzel,* and pizza 60-80kč. Open daily 11am-11pm.
Občerstvení, Stará Louka 58. It's sausage time, for a mere 12kč per *klobasa.* Draft Pilsner *Urquell* 13kč per ½-liter. Stand-up or sit-down. Open daily 9am-5pm.

SIGHTS

Between Masaryka and the Teplá River are the **Smetana Gardens** *(Smetanovy sady),* notable for their spa house and an arrangement of plants that spell out the date. Mararyka and Nabřeží Osvobozeni fuse into **Zahradní** (literally "Garden Street"), with lovely *fin-de-siècle* apartments on one side and the gray Hotel Thermal on the other. This building is an unfortunately vulgar product of the pre-1989 regime, but has a large capacity for spa visitors. Faithful to its name, Zahradní connects the Smetana Gardens to the **Dvořák Gardens** *(Dvořákovy sady)* in which stands a monument to the brilliant Czech composer. Dvořák was a frequent visitor to Karlovy Vary, where he met his fellow composer Johannes Brahms and premiered his "New World" Symphony.

Along the southern rim of the Dvořák Gardens stands the very Victorian **Park Colonnade,** where you can sip the curative waters of Karlovy Vary's 12th spring, the Park spring *(Sadový pramen).* The pedestrian promenade **Mlýnske nábřeží** meanders alongside the Teplá, past 19th-century apartment buildings. After the neo-Gothic building that houses Bath III *(Lázně III),* the pavillion of **Freedom Spring** *(Pramen Svobody)* emerges, deep in the heart of the spa complex. Buy one of the special porcelain drinking cups that everyone seems to be carrying (most gift shops sell them for 40-200kč depending on quality) and sample the precious liquids.

Next door is the impressive and imposing **Mill Colonnade** *(Mlýnská kolonáda),* built in the late 19th century by Czech architect Josef Zítek in a refined neo-Renaissance style. Six different springs surface in Mill Colonnade; this is the place to bring yourself to an enhanced state of being by curative waters. Farther along the spa area, the former **marketplace** *(Tržiště)* appears with the delicate white **Market Colonnade** *(Tržní kolonáda)* where two more springs bubble to the surface. On the square is a Baroque monument to the Holy Trinity, under the watchful gaze of the interesting geometric design of the **Castle Tower** *(Zámecká věž).*

Across the Teplá River is the **Church of Mary Magdalene** *(Kostel sv. Maří Madaléncy)* built in Baroque style by the Bohemian master architect Kilian Ignaz Diezenhofer. This church, unlike so many in the republic, is open to visitors. For those who want to consume more water, visit the **Sprudel Colonnade** (formerly the Yuri Gagarin Colonnade). Although the colonnade was built in miserably out–of-place style by the former Communist regime, it still merits a visit because of the **Sprudel Fountain** *(Vřídlo)* that can shoot over thirty liters of 72°C water several meters into the air in a single second. The symbolism of this wonder of Mother Nature is as impressive today as it was for King Charles IV six hundred years ago.

Follow Stará Louka (literally "Old Meadow") until you reach Mariánská; at the dead end is a funicular railway that rises to the **Diana Watchtower** (every 15min. daily 10am-6pm; 25kč one way, 35kč round-trip). If you want to horde your crowns or simply enjoy the forested hill's pathways, you can hike to Diana. Stará Louka comes to a grand end at the **Grandhotel Pupp.** Founded in 1774 by Johann Georg Pupp, the Grandhotel was the largest hotel in 19th-century Bohemia. The intricate façade that you see today is the work of the Viennese architects Helmer and Fellner. The building's interior features luxurious suites, a concert hall, and multiple ballrooms. Cross the next available bridge to reach Nová Louka ("New Meadow"), featuring the **Carlsbad Museum** *(Karlovarské Muzeum at Nová Louka 23;* tel. 26 25 23). Recently refurbished, the museum has several well-organized accounts of the town's past and present, the local Becherovka liquor industry, the manufacture of porcelain in Carlsbad, as well as geological and zoological exhibits (open Wed.-Sat. 9am-noon and 1-5pm; admission 16kč, students 8kč). Nová Louka ends with the local **Theater** *(Divaldo),* another creation of Helmer and Fellner. Theater Square is a pleasant resting point, with convenient access to the Sprudel Colonnade and the Church of Mary Magdalene.

ENTERTAINMENT

Tom Bar, Jaltská 7. Booze, loud music, and a happy Czech DJ. What more could you want? Open daily 4pm-6am.

Bar B&B, Nová Louka 25. A newly done-up bar for tourists and local folks, but not cheap. Open Mon.-Sat. 5pm-midnight.

Česká Restaurace, Jaltská 19. Down a few wonderfully chilled ½-liters of light or dark *Velkopopovicky Kozel* (13kč) with the locals in smoke-filled chambers with ceiling windows. Open daily 10am-11pm.

Denní Bar, I.P. Pavlova 8. Mellow music, *Becherovka,* and other spirits, hard and happy. Centrally located. Open daily 11am-11pm.

■■■ MARIÁNSKÉ LÁZNÉ

In 1779, as Dr. Josef Nehr was wandering through the thickly-wooded lands of the Tepl Monastery, he stumbled upon a compact area with well over a hundred gushing mineral springs. The enterprising Nehr erected a spa house on the site in 1808 and effectively founded today's Mariánské Lázně (Marienbad). Unlike its fellow spa towns to the north, Mariánské Lázně is not named after an emperor, but rather after the Virgin Mary, whose portrait was placed by the Tepl Monastery near one of Doctor Nehr's springs. Less than a century after Doctor Nehr had built his lone spa house, Mariánské Lázně became a bathing center of global repute, attracting over 30 thousand people per year. In the early 20th century, Mariánské Lázně earned the nickname of a "center of world politics," since its regular visitors included British King Edward VII, Austro-Hungarian Kaiser Franz Josef I, Mexican Emperor Maximilian, as well as numerous Prussian kings, Persian shahs, and Egyptian pashas. But the most famous visitor in its history was the Romantic playwright Johann Wolfgang von Goethe, after whom Mariánské Lázně's main square is named. It was in honor of the young and lovely Ulrike von Levetzow whom he met here, that Goethe wrote his renowned "Marienbader Elegie."

ORIENTATION AND PRACTICAL INFORMATION

Tourist Office: City Service, Hlavnítřída 626 (tel./fax 42 18). A small building on an island along Mariánské Lázně's main street. Friendly staff sells maps and guides of the city and Western Bohemia. Open Mon.-Fri. 8am-12:30pm and 1-5pm, Sat. 9am-12:30pm and 1-4pm, Sun. 10am-2pm.) **Activ Tour,** Nehrova 29 (tel./fax 732 46). An information outlet and travel agency run by an amicable couple. (Open daily 10am-noon and 1-5pm. **Fiesta Tour,** Nehrova 3 (tel./fax 33 85). Another travel information office offering maps, guidebooks, and services for groups. Open Mon.-Fri. 9am-11:30am and 2-5pm. **ČEDOK,** Třebízského 2 (tel. 22 54, fax 25 00). Come here for small, free maps of Mariánské Lázně, not for the unhelpful staff. Open Mon.-Fri. 8am-noon and 12:30-4:30pm, Sat. 8-11am.

Currency Exchange: Most banks in this tourist town charge an outrageous 5% commission. The bank inside the **post office** charges only 3% commission. The current facilities at **City Service,** Hlavní třída 626 (tel./fax 42 18), are convenient, but impose a 5% commission. Open Mon.-Fri. 8am-12:30pm and 1-5pm, Sat. 9am-12:30pm and 1-4pm, Sun. 10am-2pm.

Post Office: *Česká Pošta,* Poštovní 17, a 10-minute walk from the main colonnades and náměstí Goethovo. Open Mon.-Fri. 7am-8pm and Sat. 8am-3pm.

Telephone City Code: 165.

Trains: Nádraží ČD is located well to the south of the colonnades. Walk 25 minutes down Hlavní třída or take bus #5 or 3 from náměstí Goethovo.

Buses: Near the train station several bus stops constitute the town "bus station."

Public Toilets: Beware the ones at the train station; after a hunt for the key, you will be charged 2kč. The public WC at the Main Colonnade is free and open daily 9am-4pm, but ask the attendant for toilet paper.

Pharmacy: The *Lédárna* at Mírové náměstí 136 (tel./fax 25 26) is open Mon.-Fri. 7:30am-5:30pm.
Police: The *Městská Policie* are in the Town Hall *(Radnice)* building. One block from Hlavní along Ruska from its northern intersection with Hlavní.

ACCOMMODATIONS

Mariánské Lázně has an abundance of private rooms, inexpensive hotels, and exorbitant luxury hotels. The local ČEDOK office does not offer private rooms. Many hotels prefer payment in German marks.

City Service, Hlavní třída 626 (tel./fax 42 18). Arranges private and hotel rooms. Private rooms, depending on location, run around 400kč per person, breakfast included. Open Mon.-Fri. 8am-12:30pm and 1-5pm, Sat. 9am-12:30pm and 1-4pm, Sun. 10am-2pm.
Hotel Evropa, Třebízského 101 (tel. 20 63 or 50 64, fax 54 08). Centrally located. Friendly German-speaking reception open 24hrs. For a room without shower or toilet, expect to pay 550kč for a single, 850kč for a double, and 1100kč for a triple, plus a spa tax of 15kč per person. Breakfast 60kč.
Hotel Corso, Hlavní třída 41/16 (tel. 30 91 or 30 92, fax 30 93). Singles 400kč. Doubles 500kč, with shower 700kč. Groups over 15 get a 13%-33% discount. Breakfast 60kč. Reception open 24hrs.
Spa Hotel Pacifik, Mírové náměstí 84 (tel. 300 68, fax 26 45). Reception open 24hrs. Singles with sink DM29 (500kč). Doubles with sink DM48 (800kč). Payment in Deutschmarks preferred.
Hotel Atlantic, Hlavní 46 (tel. 59 11, fax 591 34). Singles with sink DM37 (612kč). Doubles with sink DM53 (877kč). Payment in Deutschmarks preferred. Reception open 24hrs.

FOOD

Like other spa towns of Western Bohemia, Mariánské Lázně is famous for a distinctive sweet treat known as *oblátky* or Oblaten, wafers layered with either vanilla, chocolate, or coffee fillings. Every flavor makes for a crisp and delicious snack. They can be found in most food shops in big square or circular boxes for 25-40kč. Also try the popular *Chodovar* beer, brewed in a nearby village.

Trio Občerstvení, Hlavní třída 30. A decent self-serve joint specializing in *svíčkova* (sauerbraten, 25kč). Cold orange juice too! Note the boar's head on the wall. Open Mon.-Fri. 6:30am-6pm, Sat. 7am-1pm and 2-6pm, Sun. 10am-1pm and 2-6pm.
Grill U Radnice, Ruska near Hlavní (tel. 37 64). Grilled chicken *(kuйře)* 80kč. Gobble every precious piece. Open daily 10am-8pm.
Pacifik, Mírové náměstí 84. Vegetarian dishes 20-40kč. Roast pork and *guláš* 50-65kč. Open daily 8am-10pm.
Corso Restaurant, Hlavní třída 41/16. Czech fowl dishes 70-90kč. Open daily 8am-3pm and 5:30-10pm.
Café Restaurant, Hlavní 50. *Schnitzel* and beef entrees 80-100kč. Imported Bitburger *Pils* on draft. Open daily 10am-midnight.

SIGHTS

Central Mariánské Lázně consists of one street *(Hlavntřída)*, two squares *(Goethovo náměstí* and *Mírové náměstí)*, and the Skalník Gardens. The area can easily be explored by foot and, depending on how much you want to spend sipping the spa's curative waters, can be seen in a matter of hours. **Goethovo náměstí** is old Marienbad's most impressive square. The well-kept gardens, lawns, and 19th-century lights vividly recreate the aura of the spa town's heyday. Among the beautiful spa houses is the **City Museum** *(Městské muzeum)*, Goethovo náměstí 11 (open daily 9am-4pm). Housed in Goethe and Ulrike's old love-nest, the museum exhibits a sizeable mineral collection. In front of the museum is a shiny new **Statue of Goethe,** replacing one torn down decades ago.

Across the gardens of Goethovo náměstí is the **Catholic Church** *(Kostel Nanebevzetí Panny Marie)*, a neo-Byzantine structure erected in 1848. From the stairs of the church there is a good view of the spa town. The huge Kaisergelb buildings on your left form the complex that houses the New Baths and the Casino. The large *fin-de-siècle* buildings contain a famous **Marble Room** *(Mramorový sál)*. The snow-white colonnade on the right is where people sample the waters of the **Rudolf Spring** *(Rudolfův Pramen)*. The changing gushes from the nearby modern **Music Fountain** *(Hrající fontána)* will undoubtedly seize your attention. At 11am and 1, 3 and 5pm the fountain's changing patterns are accompanied by music in an impressive but overrated spectacle. While others are entranced by its alleged magic, sneak over to the neo-Baroque **Main Colonnade**, reconstructed in 1975-81. The sulphuric delights of the Karolina and Rudolf Springs are available both hot and cold. To rinse your mouth out afterwards, fill your cup with water from a tap marked *Trinkwasser* ("drinking water"). The taps are open (so to speak) daily from 8am-noon and 4-6pm.

The park that descends from the Main Colonnade area is known as the **Skalník Gardens.** The gardens connect the Main Colonnade to Hlavní while offering plentiful opportunities for leisurely walks. The pathway system is rather chaotic, but you won't get lost because of the many orientation signs. At the northern entrance to the Main Colonnade is the **Fountain of the Cross** *(Křížový Pramen)*, housed in a neo-Classical pavillion. A sweet old lady sells porcelain drinking cups for 50-250kč, as well as flimsy but functional plastic cups for 2kč. Walk up the stair to Nehrova, which takes you to **Mírové náměstí,** which was partly under renovation in 1994. Admire the fancy spa houses and the closed-to-the-public **Evangelical Church.** Nehrova becomes Třebízského as the local **City Theater** *(Divadlo)* becomes visible. It's small, but it's the performances that matter.

Backtrack to **Hlavní třída,** the main street of Mariánské Lázně lined with restaurants and fancy hotels. The most expensive hotels have impressive restored 19th-century façades. Also, note the **Russian Orthodox Church** *(Pravoslamý hostel)*, built in 1900 for Russian aristocrats who visited Marienbad. Its porcelain icons and Byzantine atmosphere are worthy of exploration.

ENTERTAINMENT

Zahradní Pivnice Biergarten, Ruska at Hlavní. Follow the white footsteps to the magical beer garden. Refreshing draft Chodovar beer (13kč for a ½-liter).

Atlantic Disco, Hlavní 46 (tel. 59 11). Dancing and more dancing. Open daily 9:30pm-4am.

Café Bar Lisabon, Nehrova 4. Relatively new and well-stocked drinking establishment. Plenty of males *and* females. Open daily 8:30am-11pm.

Bar Brusel, Mírové náměstí 84. Spirits range from 15-35kč per shot. A glass of wine costs 16kč. Is this how you spell "Brussels" when drunk? Open daily 10am-10pm.

Modrá Cukrárna Kavárna Café, Hlavní 45 (tel. 26 57). A large café with white marble tables. Beer and many different types of coffee. Open Sun.-Wed. 9am-10pm, Thurs. 9am-7pm, Fri.-Sat. 9am-11pm.

■■■ FRANTIŠKOVY LÁZNĚ

Known simply as the "Fountain of Eger," the springs on this site were quite primitive until Austrian Emperor Franz I visited in 1803 and founded Franzenbad, today's Františkovy Lázně. Franz had the town tailored to his tastes; virtually every building in town is *Kaisergelb,* that shade of yellow with which Austrian emperors were so enamored. The character of Františkovy Lázně remains imperial. In the last few years, most of the buildings in the heart of the town have undergone renovations and the façades have been returned to their traditionally clean and cheery state.

In contrast to the busy shops, tall buildings, and sheer urbanity of Karlovy Vary, Františkovy Lázně resembles a gigantic park with the occasional pavillion bearing the healthful waters of its famous springs. The nine square blocks of 19th-century *Kaisergelb* edifices are engulfed in nature. The miles of promenades through gardens, forests, and grassy terrain, provide this spa with its unique charm. One-tenth the size of Karlovy Vary, it houses less than one-twentieth of Karlovy porcelain and glassware souvenir shops. Enjoy it while it remains, dare we say, undiscovered.

Orientation And Practical Information The train station, *Nádraží ČD*, is located at the end of Nádražní, which can be accessed from Kollárova, originating in the center of the town.There is no **bus station** in Františkovy Lázně, but the main stop, *Zastávka* (ČAD-sady) serves the locals just fine. The bus stop straddles both sides of **Americká** (formerly *Leninova*) northwest of the center. Buses depart for Prague, Aš, and Cheb (every ½hr. during the day).

For information on the town, stop by **ČEDOK**, at Národní třída 5 (tel. 94 22 09, tel./fax 94 22 10), has a professional and amicable staff who speak German but not English. They distribute a small but free map of Františkovy Lázně and sell more detailed maps of the town and surroundings. (Open Mon.-Fri. 8:30am-4:30pm, Sat. 9-11:30am.) **Exchange currency** at banks or at the many *bureaux de change*. The main Czech banks maintain a low profile here. The most convenient *bureau de change* is the **Směnárna Wechselstube** window at Národní 9 in central Františkovy Lázně (open daily 8:30am-8:30pm.). The main *lékárna* (**pharmacy**) is at the intersection of Tiráskova and Husova (tel. 94 24 65; open Mon.-Fri. 8:30am-noon and 1:30-4:30pm, Sat. 9-11am). The *Česka Pošta* (**post office**) is at Boženy Němcové 11, two blocks east of Národní třída along Poštovní. The **telephone city code** is 0166.

Accommodations As private pensions have emerged, the number of private rooms (around 300kč per person) that ČEDOK offers has diminished. Ask a local to recommend a pension; many of the new ones come and go without a trace. The least expensive pensions and rooms are a 15-20 minute walk from central Františkovy Lázně through parks. **Léčebný Dům ČKD,** Ruská 27 (tel. 942 70 12), has an English-speaking reception open until 10pm. (Doubles and triples with showers for 250kč per person.) **Pension Klíma,** Lesní 1 (tel. 94 28 90, tel./fax 94 26 91), is south of central Františkovy Lázně, 7min. by foot. All rooms are new and clean and have telephones. The reception is open until 10pm. (Singles with toilet 490kč. Doubles 850kč, with toilet 990kč. Add 255kč per person for bedding. Reservations welcomed.)

Food The vast majority of restaurants in town are reasonably priced. **Restaurant Pošta,** Národní 9, specializes in fish (around 80kč). When you order a whole fish, you get a *whole* fish. Traditional broiled pork and *schnitzel* dishes are also available for 50-60kč. (Open daily 8am-10pm.) **Bistro Hotel Palace,** on Ruská between Národní třída and Boženy Němcové, offers roast beef, *guláš,* or *svíčkova (Sauerbraten)* under 30kč. *Tak na jo!* It's very popular with the locals. (Open Mon.-Fri. 7am-6pm, Sat.-Sun. 10am-6pm.) **Grill U Františka,** Jiráskova 24, specializes in chicken *(kuře).* If you love or miss a good thigh, breast, or leg, come here. Entrees 50-60kč. (Open daily 10am-10pm.) **Restaurant Léčebný Dům ČKD, at** Ruská 12, attracts the ravenous with its *svíčkova (Sauerbraten)* and liver dishes, many under 40kč. (Open daily 7:30-9:30am, 11:30am-2pm, and 4:30-7:45pm.)

Sights and Entertainment Few cars or pedestrians interrupt a leisurely promenade down the grand streets and the gardens of Františkovy Lázně. Although most monuments and names from the Communist period have disappeared, the harmless **Peace Spring** *(Pramen Míru)* continues to cover the lot along Ruská opposite Národní třída. Next to this concrete creation is the petite, **Church of the Holy Cross** *(Kostel sv. Kříže).* The sparsely ornamented interior is one of the few examples of Empire-style religious architecture in Bohemia. Surrounding the cement fountain and imperial church are the **City Gardens** *(Sady Městské),* a perfect spot for extensive walks.

Národní Třída is lined with impressive and recently-restored *Kaisergelb* buildings. Among the most striking are the **Hotel Slovan** and, further down the street, the **Společenský dům** overlooking the complex of pavillions and colonnades that form the heart of Františkovy Lázně. In the square next to the Společenský dům, unimaginatively called nám. Míru ("peace"), is a statue of a naked infant holding a fish. The infant has been nicknamed *"František"* or "Franz" by the locals, in memory of the emperor who had founded the spa town. This not-so-innocent cherub is a symbol of fertility and, as such, has been touched many a time by those hoping to garner his favor. The nearby columned pavillion, with the date 1793 inscribed on its top, is the **Spring of Emperor Franz** *(Pramen František)* around which the present-day spa was built.

The neighboring **Colonnade of Summer** (Letní Kolonáda) was constructed between 1912-14. South of the colonnade is a vast park with several additional pavillions, each featuring the precious waters of a particular spring. The celebrated **Glauber Spring** *(Dvorana Glauberových pramenů)* occupies an impressive 1930s hall with ample seating for visitors who wish to admire the great gushing force with which Glauber emerges to the surface from the bowels of the Earth.

Ambling though the gardens, you may stumble upon **Isabelina promenada.** Turn right until you reach **Pohoreckého** and the legendary **Hotel Imperial,** a remnant of the pomp and glory that 19th-century visitors brought with them to the spa. The hotel is situated amidst yet another park, **Sady Bedřicha Smetany,** named after the famous Czech composer Smetana. On the left side of Pohoreckého stands the **City Museum** *(Městské muzeum),* Pohoreckého 8, encapsulating the history of the town and exhibiting glassware and porcelain (open Mon.-Fri. 9am-noon and 2-5pm, Sat.-Sun. 10am-4pm). At the corner of Pohoreckého and Ruská is the city's lone **Theater** *(Divadlo Boženy Nwmcové).* Down Kollárova is the **Russian Orthodox Church of St. Olga** *(Pravoslavný kostel sv. Olgy),* which met the religious needs of the once sizeable Russian aristocratic community and former guest Tsar Alexander.

After a long day of sightseeing, enjoy the centrally-located and well-stocked **Bar U Františka,** Jiráskova 24. (Open daily 10am-10pm.), or the small but jovial **Kavárna U Pošty** on Boženy Němcové 10. (Open daily 9am-10pm.)

■■■ PLZEŇ

Plzeň (Pilsen under Austria-Hungary) is a mecca for beer-lovers. The town that blessed the world with **Pilsner Urquell** savors its achievement at innumerable breweries, museums, pubs, and beer-gardens. Although residents of the city have been brewing since the 14th century, only in 1842 did local brewmasters unite to form the Burghers' Brewery of Pilsen and perfect the *lager* (bottom-fermenting beer).

The Pilsener **pivnice** (or beer-hall) has been a way of life in Plzeň for centuries. As the brewing industry flourished in the 19th century, so did the economic and cultural life of the city. Among those who came to enjoy a tall, cool one are the Czech engineer Emil Škoda, who founded the Škoda Industrial Works, which continues to manufacture automobiles today under the auspices of Volkswagen; the Czech playwright Josef Kajetán Tyl, who composed the Czech national anthem here in the 1850s; and the romantic composer Bedřich Smetana, who studied at the local university. Plzeň suffered British and American bombing raids 11 times in 1942, but was liberated by the U.S. Army from Nazi occupation in May 1945.

The Old Town boasts Bohemia's tallest Gothic Cathedral and a striking black Italianate Renaissance Town Hall. Throughout 1995, Plzeň will be celebrating its **700th anniversary.** In February, there will be a ball and a carnivalesque *Fasching*-type of celebration. The second week of March will be dedicated to honoring the composer Bedřich Smetana. In May the city will celebrate the 50th anniversary of the liberation by American troops. In June Plzeň will host the hottest Czech rock bands for a three-day **music festival** (no, it won't be called Plzeňstock). Naturally, the merriment will conclude with **"Beer Days"** from October 2-7, 1995.

ORIENTATION AND PRACTICAL INFORMATION

Tourist Offices: MIS (Městské informační středisko Plzeň), náměstí Republiky 41 (tel./fax 22 44 73), on the main square. The helpful and friendly staff speaks Czech, German, and English. **Maps,** brochures, and booklets on Plzeň are sold for average prices, as are postcards and souvenirs. Open daily 9am-5pm. **ČEDOK,** Prešovská 10 (tel. 366 48 or 374 19, fax 332 98). English-speaking staff offers complimentary **maps** of Plzeň and information on accommodations, tours, and transportation. Open Mon.-Fri. 9am-noon and 1-5pm, Sat. 9am-noon. **CK Rubys,** Rooseveltova 10 (tel. 22 59 61, fax 22 57 68). Amicable English-speaking employees offer **maps** and information. Open daily 9am-1pm and 3-6pm.

Currency Exchange: Komerční Banka, Goethova at Kopeckého. 2% commission on traveler's checks. (Open Mon.-Fri. 8am-noon and 1-5pm.) **Československá Obchodní Banka** on Kopeckého west of Františkanká (no street number). The 1% commission on traveler's checks (minimum 50kč) is accompanied by slightly poorer rates than at Komerční Banka. Do your math. Open Mon.-Fri. 8am-noon and 1:30-5pm. **Česká Spořitelna** on Kopeckého at Martinská. 15kčplus a 2% commission to cash each traveler's check. Open Mon. and Wed. 8am-5pm, Tues. and Thurs.-Fri. 8am-1pm. **ČEDOK,** Prešovská 10 (tel. 366 48 or 374 19, fax 332 98). Central location. Changes cash only—for a 2% commission. Open Mon.-Fri. 9am-noon and 1-5pm, Sat. 9am-noon.

Post Office: The *Česká Pošta* is at Solní 20 (tel. 22 00 24). Open 24hrs.

Telephone City Code: 019.

Trains: The *Plzeň Hlavní Nádraží* is located to the east of the Old Town along Americká in a yellow 19th-century building. Frequent service to Prague, as well as international routes to Paris, Munich, Dortmun, Frankfurt, and Nürnburg. Local trains to Cheb, Mariánské Lázně, Domažlice, Žatec, and Klatovy. For train information *(České dráhy informace)*, tel. 22 20 79.

Buses: The *Centrální Autobusové Nádraží* is located to the west of the Old Town at Husova 58, at the intersection with Skvrňanská. The Czech bus transportation service **ČSAD** (becoming ČAD) offers extensive service to surrounding towns and villages. For bus information *(ČSAD informace)*, tel. 22 37 04 or 22 40 19.

Public Transportation: Tramways, trolley buses, and buses provide a fine public transport system. Adult fares are 4kč (two of the 2kč tickets dispensed by orange vending machines). Stops near the train station tend to be confusing. Major trolley bus lines converge at Goethova and Americká or on Goethova itself. The main tramway lines stop at náměstí Republiky.

Car Rental: CS Czechocar Rent-a-Car operates through ČEDOK (see above).

Taxis: tel. 22 22 60, 22 77 00, or 22 68 38.

Bookstore: For a fascinating selection of old Czech, German, and Austro-Hungarian books, visit **Antiquariat Makovský,** Veleslavínova 25 (tel. 323 16). Open Mon.-Fri. 9am-6pm, Sat. 9am-noon.

Public Toilets: The modern building on the southern side of náměstí Republiky has new and fairly clean public facilities with toilet paper on demand for 2kč. The public toilets in the underground passage near the train station are often closed; if you must, use the poorly maintained rooms on the second floor of the train station (2kč).

Pharmacy: Lékárna U bílého jednorožce, náměstí Republiky 27 (tel. 22 00 46 or 367 41), is centrally located on the main square. Open Mon.-Fri. 7am-6pm, Sat. 7am-noon.

Police: In an **emergency** tel. 158. The *Městska Policie* have offices at Klatovská 45 (tel. 21 72) and Dominikánská 12 (tel. 334 29 or 22 36 19) among other locations.

ACCOMMODATIONS

Plzeň has many pensions, hotels, and private rooms at prices typical of the Czech Republic. The deeper into suburbia you penetrate, the less you spend.

Accommodations Agencies

ČEDOK, Prešovská 10 (see above). Friendly and English-speaking staff can help you find a private room, usually for about 300kč per person. Try to get one in Lobzy, as opposed to the distant and gray Northern suburbs.

CKM, Dominidánská 1 (tel. 363 93 or 375 85, fax 369 09). Patient and helpful Czech-speaking staff arranges private rooms for 250kč per person (300kč including breakfast) in distant suburbs. Open Mon.-Fri. 8am-6:30pm.

CK Rubys, Rooseveltora 10 (tel. 22 59 61, fax 22 57 68). Friendly English-speaking staff offers private rooms for as little as 410kč (DM24) if they are located well out of the center. Open daily 9am-1pm and 3-6pm.

Informance, at the front of the train station (tel. 22 32 85). Accommodations in pensions for DM25 per person. Pay in Deutschmarks only. Open Mon.-Fri. 9am-4pm.

DAEN, Bezručova 1 (tel. 22 03 17). Arranges accommodations in distant pensions for 425-510kč (DM25-30) per person. Open Mon.-Fri. 9am-noon and 1-6pm.

Pensions

Penzion J. Bárová, Solnjí 8 (tel. 366 52). An excellent new pension less than a block from the cathedral. Rooms have toilets, showers and radios. Reception open daily 9am-6pm. Singles 510kč. Doubles 850kč. Breakfast 85kč.

Penzion Müllerová, U svépomoci 23 (tel. 27 52 06). South of the Old Town in the Bory neighborhood. Rooms for 350kč (DM20) per person. Breakfast included.

Penzion Slavia, U borského parku 21 (tel. 27 17 70). Also in the Bory district, rooms with showers and toilets go for 370kč (DM22) per person.

Penzion Gigler, Raisova 39 (tel. 27 76 21). Another pension in Bory. Expect to pay 425kč (DM25) per person Breakfast included. Often full, so call ahead.

Privat Majak, Na výsluní 20 (tel. 414 35). Take trainway #1 southbound along Mikulášska, south of the train station. Then walk down Nepomucka until you reach the Bručna neighborhood. 25-300kč per person. Quite a trek, so call ahead.

FOOD

Na spilce, U Prazdroje, inside the Pilsner Urquell brewery complex. One of the largest restaurants in Europe serving one of the world's finest beers. Traditional Bohemian specialties 50-100kč. Open Mon.-Fri. 10am-11pm, Sat. 11am-10pm, and Sun. 11am-9pm.

U Kanónu, Rooseveltova 18. Wooden tables, smoke, and plenty of locals. Roast pork, *schnitzel,* and liver entrees 40-55kč. Open Mon.-Fri. 10am-11pm and Sat.-Sun. 10am-10pm.

Restaurant Evropa, Veleslavínova 22 (tel. 22 09 51, fax 22 99 82). Caters to tourists, but at reasonable prices. Vegetarian dishes 50-60kč. *Guláš* and roast pork dishes 60-80kč. Open Mon.-Fri. 11am-10pm.

U zlatého poháru, Rooseveltova 12 (tel. 367 97). Hearty Czech fare. Roast beef and roast pork, for 40-80č. Open Mon.-Fri. 11am-10pm.

U Žumbery, Bezručova 14 (tel. 22 24 36). A beer-hall serving decent *guláš* and roast pork dishes 25-50kč. Open Mon.-Sat. 9am-10pm and Sun. 9am-7pm.

U bílého Iva, Pražská 15 (tel. 22 69 98). Chicken medallions for 60kč, if you're tired of pork and beef. Open daily 10am-11pm.

Moravská vinárna, Bezručova 4. Enhance your roast pork or beef (40-60kč) with some wine, straight from the barrel. Very Moravian. Open Mon.-Sat. 10am-10pm and Sun. 11am-9pm.

U Šenku, Riegrova at Sedlačkova. A loud tavern serving heavy Czech food. *Guláš* for under 40kč and creative *schnitzel* dishes for 80kč. Pilsner *Urquell* and *Gambrinus* on tap for 14kč per pint. Open Mon.-Fri. 10am-10:30pm, Sat. 10am-9pm, and Sun. 11am-6pm.

SIGHTS

Lined with Gothic, Renaissance, Baroque, and Empire dwellings, náměstí Republiky is the core of Plzeň's Old Town. The former market square was one of the largest in Bohemia and continues to host the occasional festival or fair. The huge **Church of St. Bartholomew** *(kostel sv. Bartoloěje)* dominates the square with its 103-meter-high tower, the tallest in the Czech Republic. For the best possible panorama of Plzeň, climb the tower to its 60-meter-high observation deck (open daily 10am-6pm; admission 17kč). Although the exterior of St. Bartholomew has been refurbished several times since its foundation, the interior remains true to its late Gothic gran-

CZECH REPUBLIC

deur. At the main altar is the famous late 14th-century polychrome **Madonna of Pilsen,** which recalls Bohemia's glory days under Charles IV. Next to St. Bartholomew is the **Plague Column,** a Baroque monument with gold ornamentation. The black building with the golden clock near the column is Plzeň's **City Hall** *(Radnice),* a tasteful Renaissance creation erected by Giovanni de Statia in the 16th century. With its sgraffito, it looks like something out of Florence. Today the City Hall is connected on the inside to the neighboring **Kaiser House** *(císařský dům),* built in 1607 by J.M.Filipi for Austrian Emperor Rudolf II. Note the white statue of **Knight Žumbera,** decked out in armor and with a large lance.

From the northeast part of náměstí Republiky, the short street Pražská takes you to the former **Slaughter House** *(Masné Krámy),* an impressive late-Gothic building that is nowadays a division of the West Bohemian Gallery. Across the street is the **Water Tower** *(vodárenská věž),* built in 1532 as part of the city's medieval water works. Today the tower and the **Historic Underground Cellars** *(Plzeňské podzemí)* can be visited on a guided tour that starts inside Perlova 4, a building near the tower (open Tues.-Sun. 9am-4pm; admission 30kč for foreigners, 15kč for Czechs). The cellars were used primarily for the storage and the covert mass consumption of beer. The tour also features a collection of pottery and glass beer mugs. The tour ends at Veleslavínova, where one finds the **Brewery Museum** *(Pivovarské Muzeum;* tel. 330 34). Housed in a 15th-century malthouse that became a famous 19th-century beer-hall, the museum features an extensive collection of old documents and equipment used in the production of beer. The collection of 19th-century pub signs and memorabilia is most impressive (open Tues.-Sun. 10am-6pm; admission 30kč for foreigners, 15kč for foreign students).

Return down Veleslavínova to Rooseveltova (often misspelled Rooseweltova), which becomes Františkánská on the other side of the square. A gate to the **Franciscan Convent and Church** leads to one of the richest collections of sculpture in Plzeň. The complex suffered during the Thirty Years War, but the early Gothic interior of the Church is nonetheless well-preserved. The church also houses a fine Baroque main altar and the renowned **Black Madonna of Hájek,** an 18th-century sculpture placed in the Trinity Chapel. The neighboring **West Bohemian Sculpture Museum** (open daily 9am-5pm), which features a valuable and interesting collection of medieval works, stands on the site of old fortifications. Today people stroll and relax here in the shade of the trees, as traditional brass bands perform their repertoire of Bohemian polkas, waltzes, and folk tunes. At the eastern extremity of Kopeckého sady is the **Museum of Western Bohemia** *(Západočeské muzeum)* that houses natural, ethnographic, and archaeological collections. The exterior of the building is a fascinating and creative *fin-de-siècle* neo-Renaissance/Jugensdstil work, which is best viewed from the Americká Bridge. Moving west along the promenade, Kopeckého sady becomes Smetanovy sady, named after the Romantic Czech composer Bedřich Smetana whose statue decorates the park. At the corner of Smetanovy sady and Klatovská is the **J.K. Tyl Theater** *(Divadlo J.K.Yyla),* another *fin-de-siècle* neo-Renaissance construction. This site has been connected with Czech-language theater since 1818, when Czech playwright Josef Kajetán Tyl staged his works in the **House of the White Rose** (Dům U bílé růže). North of the theater along Sady Pětatřicátníků is the **Synagogue** *(Synagoga),* built in 1892 in a neo-Romanesque/moorish style. The twin-towered building is Bohemia's largest synagogue and remains an impressive monument to Plzeň's once-large Jewish community that fell victim to Nazi persecution.

Founded in 1842, the **Pilsner Urquell Burghers' Brewery** *(Měštanský Pivovar Plzeňský Prazdroj)* has become a center of the brewer's craft of global repute. The entrance to the complex is located 300m east of the Old Town, where Pražská becomes U Prazdroje. The entrance to the brewery area is marked by a huge neo-Renaissance gateway. Although you can explore the area on your own, a guided tour (Mon.-Fri. at 12:30pm from the gateway) takes you to the malting areas, the cellars, and includes a light-hearted, verging on foolish, film. Conducted in mixed and fragmented English and German, the 1-hour tour (including film) costs 30kč per person and unfortunately does *not* include a free sample of draft Pilsner *Urquell*. Nearby is the huge beer hall **Na spilce** where you can toss back a few delicious draft Urquells (see Food). Farther down U Prazdroje is the **Gambrinus Brewery,** closed to the public.

ENTERTAINMENT

Since Plzeň is a beer-town *par excellence*, entertain yourself with the local Pilsner *Urquell* and *Gambrinus* at a **pivnice** (beer-hall) or **zahradní** (beer garden). If you haven't acquired the taste for beer, Plzeň has several wine-pubs and ordinary bars.

Azyl, Veleslavínova 17. A new bar in the heart of the Old Town. Climb the ladder to reach the second story. Open Mon.-Sat. 10am-10pm, Sun. 3-10pm.

U Kanónu, Rooseveltova 18. Atmospheric beer-hall filled with both attractive young people and the middle-aged. *Helena miluji vás* (cheers). Draft Pilsner Urquell served at a brisk pace for 13kč per half-liter. Open Mon.-Fri. 10am-11pm, Sat.-Sun. 10am-10pm.

Na spilce, U Prazdroje, inside the Pilsner Urquell brewery complex. Room for thousands to quaff Pilsner *Urquell* in its birthplace. A huge beer-hall for carousing. Open Mon.-Fri. 10am-11pm, Sat. 11am-10pm, Sun. 11am-9pm.

Pivnice U Žumbery, Bezručova 14 (tel. 22 24 36). Drink your *Gambrinus* draft (13kč) in the beer-hall or in the outdoor beer garden. Never a quiet moment. Open Mon.-Sat. 9am-10pm, Sun. 9am-7pm.

Moravsdá vinárna, Bezručova 4, in the Old Town. Several wines are on tap in this quintessential Moravian wine-pub. Open Mon.-Sat. 10am-10pm, Sun. 11am-9pm.

SOUTHERN BOHEMIA

Bucolic and accessible, Southern Bohemia is a rustic region of scattered villages, unspoiled brooks and valleys, fish ponds, small lakes, and peat-bogs. Nature preserves have been set up for visitors and deer can be spotted by the road or railway. The rough and often ugly process of industrialization has barely affected the secluded region which remains a popular holiday destination for Czechs.

■■■ ČESKÉ BUDĚJOVICE

No quantity of beer will help you correctly pronounce České Budějovice (CHESS-kay BOOD-yay-yov-ee-tzeh); luckily for the paunchy world-wide, the town was known as **Budweis** in the 19th century when it inspired the name of the popular but pale North American *Budweiser*. The most famous beer brewed today in České Budějovice is the sweet and malty Budweiser *Budvar,* although the local Samson brewery is an older and equally celebrated institution that produces a fine lager.

Surrounded by the Vltava River, mill streams, and the Malše River, the Old Town is a fascinating amalgam of Gothic, Renaisssance, and Baroque houses scattered along winding medieval alleys and impeccably straight 18th-century streets. Emperors, kings, bishops, aristocrats, democrats, and Communists have been kind to České Budějovice, which has retained the historical chain of each era in its architectural and cultural *guláš*.

ORIENTATION AND PRACTICAL INFORMATION

Tourist Offices: CIS Travel Service, Lannova třída 6 (tel. 276 39 or 250 61, fax 250 61). On the main pedestrian street between the train station and the Old Town. English spoken. Helpful and friendly staff offer **maps** and pamphlets on České Budějovice and Southern Bohemia. Open Mon.-Fri. 8am-6pm, Sat. 8am-noon. **Turistické Informační Centrum Goetz & Hanzlik,** Náměstí Přemysla Otakara II 2 (tel. 594 80 or 532 51, fax 592 91). Located on the main square in the Old Town. One of the largest **map** selections in the Czech Republic. Open daily

9am-5:30pm. **CDM Cestovní Kancelář,** Lannova 63 at Nádražní. Conveniently located across the street from the main train station. Formerly a state-operated travel agency. Plenty of visitor information. Open Mon.-Fri. 9am-6pm. **Currency Exchange: CIS Travel Service,** Lannova Třída 6 (tel. 276 39 or 250 61, fax 250 61). Exchange cash for a mere 1.0-1.6% commission, with a minimum of 30kč. Open Mon.-Fri. 9am-6pm and Sat. 9am-noon. **Pošta Banka,** in the post office on Senovážné náměstí on the second floor. A high 5% commission. Open Mon.-Fri. 7am-6pm and Sat. 8am-2pm. **Komerční Banka,** Náražní 31 across the street from the main train station. Its *bankomat* (ATM) is linked to Cirrus, Mastercard and Eurocard. Open Mon.-Fri. 9am-6pm and Sat. 9am-noon. **Moravia Banka,** Kněžská 20 in the Old Town. This new local bank offers decent rates. Open Mon.-Fri. 8am-6pm.
Post Office: The *Česká Pošta* is on Senovážné náměstí south of Lannova. Open Mon.-Fri. 6am-8pm and Sat. 7am-4:30pm. There is another office north of the train station on Nádraní, between Lannova and Rudolfovská, with more limited hours.
Telephone City Code: 038.
Trains: The *Nádraší České Budějovice* is located at the junction of Lannova and Nádrašní, to the east of the Old Town, in a jolly yellow building. Trains to Prague (3hr.); Plzeň (2hrs. *rychlík* and 3½hrs. *osobný);* Brno (5hrs. via Veselí and Jihlava); and local South Bohemian towns (Český Krumlov, Tábor, Strakonice, and Jindřichův Hradec). International trains to Linz and Gműnd in Austria (via Velenice). For information, tel. 233 33.
Buses: The *Autobusové nádraží ČSAD* (tel. 255 55) is located south of the train station at the intersection of Žižková and Nádražní in a relatively new building. Bus service from České Budějovice to Czech destinations is generally no faster than trains; but it is a few cents cheaper and several degrees hotter in summer.
Taxis: tel. 233 17.
Public Toilets: At the bus and train stations, men pay 1kč for a *"pisoar"* and both sexes can enter a *"Kabina"* for 2kč. You must ask for toilet paper. Near the Old Town, there are public facilities near Restaurant Slavia at Jirsikova and Dukelská.
Pharmacy: At the corner of Lannova and Štínéko, between the Old Town and the main train station (open Mon.-Fri. 7am-6:30pm, Sat. 8am-noon).
Police: In an **emergency** tel. 158. The *Městská Policie* are in the Old Town at the corner of Radniční and Česká. and to the north at Pražská třída 5 (tel. 287 57).

ACCOMMODATIONS

CIS Travel Service, Lannova Tҏída 6 (tel. 276 39 or 250 61, fax 250 61)., arranges accommodations in pensions or in private rooms. Expect to pay 500k⁻ per person for a room in the center and 130-224k⁻ for one in the suburbs. (Open Mon.-Fri. 9am-6pm and Sat. 9am-noon.) Clubtour, Hroznová 9 (tel. 530 55, tel./fax 520 22). Private rooms range 350-500k⁻ per person, breakfast included (open Mon.-Fri. 9am-11:30am and noon-3pm).

AT Pension, Duelská 15 (tel. 731 25 29) has fabulous 2- and 3-bed rooms, some with private bath, in two buildings near the center along the peaceful Malše River. From the train station, walk down Žižkova, then left on U třlvů, and left on Dukelská. Reception open 24hrs. 400kč per person. Breakfast included.
Hotel Grand, Ndražní 27 (tel. 365 91, fax 525 68). Across the street from the train station. Reception open 24hrs. Singles with shower 580kč, with shower and toilet 640kč. Doubles with shower 835kč, and toilet 970kč. Breakfast included.
Hotel U Samsona, Karla EV 8-10. (tel. 598 85 or 586 25, fax 585 61). In a refurbished 19th-century brewery. All rooms have toilet and shower. Reception open 24hrs. Singles 990kč. Doubles 1260kč. Triples 1800kč. Breakfast included.

FOOD

No meal in České Budějovice goes unaccompanied by Budweiser *Budvar* or *Samson*. Relatively few restaurants are open Sundays.

Pivnice U Zlatého Soudku, Široká 29. The *řízek (schnitzel,* 40kč) is freshly cooked, not reheated. Refreshing draft *Samson* (dark or light) is a modest 9kč per ½-liter. Open Mon.-Sat. for lunch and dinner.

U Kneisslů, Česká at the corner of Panská. Decent Bohemian dishes under 30kč. Self-serve roast pork and *svíčkova (Sauerbraten).* Bottled *Platán* beer for 10kč. Open Mon.-Thurs. 9am-6pm and Fri. 9am-4pm.

U tří korun, Česká at the corner of Radniční. Traditional roast beef and roast pork dishes (45-80kč) in a dimly lit room. R. Draft *Budweiser Budvar* 14kč per ½-liter. Open Mon.-Sat. 10am-10pm.

Masné Krámy, Krajinská 13 (tel./fax 326 52). Daily specials (50kč) are a good deal, if you understand Czech. The entrees (posted in Czech and German) run 90-130kč. Draft *Budweiser Budvar* 15kč per half-liter. Open Sun.-Thurs. 10am-11pm and Fri.-Sat. 10am-midnight.

Pivnice U Švejka, Karla IV 8-10. Bohemian dishes for under 50kč in a 19th-century beer-hall. Large and raucous. *Samson* beer on tap. Open Mon.-Thurs. 10am-10pm, Fri.-Sat. 10am-11pm, Sun. 11am-10pm.

Restaurace Srdíčko, Lannova třída 23. Self-serve Czech food for under 40kč in a new blue building. Open Mon.-Fri. 9am-10pm and Sat. 9am-1pm.

Restaurace Krokodýl, Kněžská 25. An array of chicken and *Schnitzel* dishes between 60-70kč. Open Mon.-Fri. 11am-10pm and Sat. 11am-2pm.

SIGHTS

České Budějovice's Old Town rolls out from **náměstí Přemysla Otakara II,** lined with arcaded Baroque burghers' homes crawling with small businesses. The elegant **Samson Fountain** *(Samsonova Kašna)* in the center of the square is a remarkable Baroque work by the duo of Baugut and Dietrich. Note the pained expressions on the faces from which spew fountains of water. On the southwest side of the square is the famous **Town Hall** *(Radnice),* an exquisite Baroque edifice.

Nearby, the **Rabenstein Tower** *(Rabenštejnská věž)* stands alone by the peaceful mill stream. The narrow medieval alley Hradební or the route along the **Mill Stream** *(Mlýnská stoka;* tel. 525 08) provide an interesting walk through one of the oldest parts of town. From either street, turn right onto U Černé věže, which leads to the **Black Tower** *(Černá věž).* Though the Black Tower once functioned as a belfry and a watchtower for the neighboring church, today it serves only to exhaust tourists. You can climb the 72m-high tower (Tues.-Sun. 9am-5pm) for a mere 6kč. Next to the tower is the Baroque 17th-century **Church of St. Nicholas** *(Kostel sv. Mikuláše)* and farther along Kněžska is the Renaissance former **Church of St. Anne.**

The **Bishop's Residence** *(Sídlo biskupa),* down Karla IV, across the square, and south on Biskupská is in a plain and utilitarian former pianist college. When the Catholic Church made České Budějovice the seat of a bishopric in 1785, the townspeople did not construct a new ornate building as had so many European cities. Instead, the unusually pragmatic church fathers decided to house the bishop in the humble building we see today. The area surrounding the Old Town consists of pretty waterways and quiet green space. Stroll along the banks of the Malše on **Zátkovo nábřeži** and in the park that shadows **Dukelská.** The narrow street **Na Mlýnske stoce** follows the Mill Stream on the Old Town side; **Na Sadeck** (literally "by the gardens") is a pleasant wooded area along the Mill Stream.

The **Museum of Southern Bohemia** *(Jihočeské Muzeum,* tel. 574 81) at Dukelská 1, chronicles the ethnography, history, and archaeology of Southern Bohemia in a bright yellow neo-Renaissance example of the grand revival architecture of *fin-de-siècle* Austria (open Tues.-Sun. 9am-noon and 12:30-5pm; admission 18kč).

ENTERTAINMENT

Famous local beers flow freely in the **pivnice** (beer hall) of the Old Town. Winepubs and bars also exist, but are in the minority.

Masné Krámy, Krajinska 13 (tel./fax 326 52). A famous beer-hall with a large capacity. Draft *Budweiser Budvar* 15kč per ½-liter. Enjoy the beer and the Renaissance building. Open Sun.-Thurs. 10am-11pm and Fri.-Sat. 10am-midnight.

Split Diskoklub, Česká near Hroznová. A late-night spot for popular Czech musicians. You probably haven't heard of any of them, but the cover charges just might sound familiar. Open Sun.-Thurs. 8:30pm-3am and Fri.-Sat. 8pm-4am.
Pivnice U Zlatého Soudku, Široká 29. Atmospheric local pub. The draft *Samson* (dark and light) is refreshing at 9kč for a ½-liter. Open Mon.-Sat. until 10pm.
Pivnice U Švejka, Karla IV 8-10. This fascinating building housed the Burghers' Brewery in the 19th century. Popular beer-hall among the local folk. *Samson* on tap. Open Mon.-Thurs. 10am-10pm, Fri.-Sat. 10am-11pm, and Sun. 11am-10pm.
Vinárna Savoy, Stejskala 16. Late-night hang-out for wine-lovers. Liquor and draft Marovian wine. Open Tues.-Sat. 7pm-3am.

■ NEAR ČESKÉ BUDĚJOVICE:ČESKÝ KRUMLOV

Sixteen miles southwest of České Budějovice is Český Krumlov, the city that UNESCO has proclaimed Europe's second most historically valuable, surpassed only by Venice. Also known as **Krumau,** Krumlov has been the seat of several noble dynasties. Its immense **Castle** was the seat of the Vitkovci family and subsequently of the Rosenbergs, who moved to nearby Třeboň in 1602. The Schwarzenberg family later lived in the castle until their neo-Gothic *château* at Hluboká was built. The castle grounds are open year-round, but only for guided tours. The castle also houses a **chapel,** Eggenberg's **Gold Carriage,** and the **Masquerade Hall,** a lovely and festive chamber designed by the Třeboň painter J. Lederer. The winding Vltava (Moldau) River not only serves as a moat for the castle, but also surrounds Krumlov's **Old Town.** The meandering medieval alleys haven't changed in centuries.

The large late-Gothic **Church of St. Vitus** (*kostel sv. Vita*) overlooking the town has a rich interior dating from the early 15th century that features the works of medieval Bohemian masters. To reach the town center, **nám. Svornosti,** from the bus station, simply head towards the castle watchtower visible from the parking lot. Once there, you'll find numerous restaurants, including the one at the **Hotel Krumlov** at #14 (entrees 60-150kč; open daily 11am-10pm). For private rooms, try the **Tourist Service** office (tel. 46 05), inside the castle grounds at Zámek 57 (130-450kč; open daily 9am-6pm). **CTS Travel Service** has an office at Latrán 67 (tel. 28 21), but it's better to arrange a room through their office in České Budějovice. The **telephone city code** is 0337.

■■■ HLUBOKÁ

Although Hluboká markets itself as a cozy hamlet, it hides one of the most impressive **castles** in Bohemia. Irrepressible nostalgia among the European aristocracy of the 19th century found expression in lavish revivalist buildings. Like "Mad King" Ludwig II of Bavaria who built several monumental neo-Renaissance and neo-Baroque castles, the wealthy Austrian aristocrat Johann Schwarzenberg realized his neo-Gothic fantasies in Hluboká. Schwarzenberg's romantic château has been compared to Windsor Castle in England. Confiscated by Communists in the late 1940s, the building gradually dilapidated, but restoration is meeting with success. Sprawled along the Vltava (Moldau) River, Hluboká also has a wealth of natural resources at its doorstep for hunters, anglers, hikers, and cyclists.

ORIENTATION AND PRACTICAL INFORMATION

Hluboká is usually reached from České Budějovice (Budweis), only 10km away. Buses to and from České Budějovice can be hot and unpleasant. Moreover, they run very sporadically and take 25-30 minutes. The train takes only 10 minutes, but both of Hluboká's stations are located quite a distance from the village and *château*. Trains to and from České Budějovice run every hour or two. Although the town is impressive in its sprawl, mild breezes from nearby ponds make walking around Hluboká quite comfortable in the Bohemian summer.

Tourist Office: Informační Centrum, Masarykova 36 (tel. 96 53 29) across from the church. **Maps,** pamphlets, and fishing permits. Open Mon.-Sat. 10am-noon and 12:30-4:30pm, Sun. 9am-noon.

Currency Exchange: Investiční Banka, at Masarykova 42 is open Mon.-Fri. 8-11:30am and 1-4pm. **Poštovní Banka,** Masarykova 40, is next door. Open Mon.-Fri. 7:30am-5pm and Sat. 8-10am.

Post Office: at Masarykova 40. Open Mon.-Fri. 7:30am-5pm and Sat. 8-10am.

Telephone City Code: 038.

Trains: *Hluboká nad Vltavou* is 5km south of town, on the line that connects České Budějovice with Plzeň, Strakonice, and Protivín. Walk south along the road that hugs the Munický rybnik pond and turn right at the *"Nádraží"* sign. At a similar distance to the east of the town is the station *Hluboká Zámosti,* located on the line that connects České Budějovice with Prague, Tábor, and Veselí. From the town, cross the mighty Vltava River at Hamr and then follow the signs.

Buses: Hluboká is dotted with ČSAD stops. The most convenient is on the main road at Tyršova, one block south of Masarykova. Odd as it may seem, buses to and from České Budějovice stop on *both* sides of the street. To find out which side is best for you, consult and attempt to decipher the posted schedules (the stop is *"pod kostelem")* or ask a fellow traveler.

Public Toilets: Next to the church along Masarykova are public facilities in a squat white-washed building. Public toilets near the castle (across from the restaurant) charge 2kč for women, but men are free.

Pharmacy: at the corner of Masarykova and Husova. Open Mon., Wed., and Fri. 7:30am-2:45pm, Tues., Thurs. 7:30am-5:30pm.

Police: at the corner of Masarykova and 28. října. In an **emergency** tel. 158.

ACCOMMODATIONS

Along Masarykova, *Privat* or *Zimmer frei* signs advertise private rooms. Don't pay over 400kč per person. **Informační Centrum,** Masarykova 40 (tel. 96 53 29), finds private rooms (open Mon.-Sat. 10am-noon and 12:30-4:30pm, Sun. 9am-noon).

Parkhotel, at the end of Masarykova (tel. 96 52 81, fax 96 53 41). In a peaceful area. Doubles only, with toilet 700kč, with bath 800kč. Reception open 24hrs.

Hotel Bakalář, Masarykova 69 (tel./fax 96 55 16). Doubles 1012kč (DM60). Breakfast included. Reception open 24hrs.

FOOD

Zámecká Restaurace, on Tyršova, a couple of houses down from Masarykova. Good Bohemian dishes, especially the *guláš.* Excellent draft *Platan* beer goes for a mere 7kč per ½-liter, dark or light. Open daily 10am-10pm.

Restaurace Na Růžku, nám. ČSLA 25 (tel. 96 52 15 or 96 59 00). Notice the sign from the square next to the church. Czech fare and draft *Samson* beer. Open Mon.-Thurs. 10am-11pm, Fri.-Sat. 10am-1am, Sun. 9:30am-10pm.

Lok Ham Restaurant, Masarykova at Boženy Němcové. Local atmosphere and inexpensive Czech food. Ever-popular *Samson* beer on tap. Open Mon.-Thurs. 10am-10pm and Fri.-Sat. 11am-midnight.

Eleonora, on Bezručová east of Horní. Expensive Bohemian cuisine, but moderately-priced vegetarian entrees. Open daily 11am-1am.

SIGHTS

The Castle

From the main square in front of the church, signs direct visitors up a wooded hill to the **castle.** The trek up Bezručova Street takes only ten minutes. An impressive building called **Štekl,** designed in the same 19th-century neo-Gothic style as the castle, greets visitors. You can enter the park through a humble metal gate or rise farther above Štekl to enter the castle area. The **Castle Park** surrounds three sides of the *château* and features crimson rose beds and creative vine growths that provide shade in a "vine tunnel." The thick forest that covers the hill no doubt impressed the Schwarzenbergs as much as it does visitors today. At the tip of the park is the **Pod-**

skali Lookout, from where forests, fields, and the distant Bohemian Forest *(Šumava)* and the towers and rooftops of České Budějovice can be seen. The small park in front of the entrance to the courtyard is well-kept and offers excellent views of the *château* and its neo-Gothic towers. Enter the castle through the courtyard, not through the enclosed glass staircase. Just before the courtyard is a *Suvenýry* shop and the *Pokladna* where you can buy tickets for the guided tour of the castle's exquisite interior (open May-Sept. Tues.-Sun. 9am-5pm; admission 80kč for English or German tours, 30kč for Czech tours). The **courtyard** best conveys the neo-Gothic aura of Hluboká. The cold gray stone has been made to resemble a medieval knightly residence, albeit in the romanticized view of Johann Schwarzenberg. An enthusiastic hunter, he was fascinated by deer; the numerous deer heads carved in stone in the courtyard attest to this harmless obsession. If you happen to be thirsty or drowsy, look for the out-of-place automatic coffee dispenser, which spews brown liquid into plastic cups in the *ersatz* courtyard. Next to the entrance to the courtyard is the **South Bohemian Gallery of Mikuláš Aleš** *(Alšova jihočeská galerie),* which houses a fine collection of late-medieval Dutch works and modern Czech pieces (a visit to the gallery usually takes an hour; open daily 8am-5pm; admission 15kč).

The Town and Pond

Visible from a great distance, the **Town Church** *(kostel)* is a late-medieval creation, with its imposing tower and its dark gray walls. The interior is closed to the public. Across the street next to the *Informační Centrum* is the **Town Hall** *(Radnice)* whose strict façade contrasts with the bucolic buildings of Hluboká. The Rustic Baroque style flourished throughout the Habsburg empire in the early 19th century, reaching towns like Billéd and Sándorháza near Temesvár (today Timişoara in Romania). In Hluboká, the best examples of this style are on Tyršova, Horní, and Masarykova streets, with their white and yellow façades and triangular tops.

Five minutes south of the town along the **Munice Pond** *(Munický rybník)* pathway is a **Jewish Cemetery** *(Židovský hřbitov)* founded in 1724, and used by the local community until the Nazi period. The oldest tombstones have Hebrew inscriptions obscured by moss, while legible 19th-century memorials are in both Hebrew and German. On the southern edge of the pond is the 18th-century **Ohrada Hunting Castle** *(Lovecký zámek Ohrada).* Now a museum of hunting and forestry.

ENTERTAINMENT

Café Bar Adria, Masarykova at Zborovska. Shots (40mL) of booze run 14-50kč. Coffee 5kč. Open Mon.-Fri. 2-10pm, Sat. 2pm-midnight, Sun. 2-8pm.

Night Club Rosa, Masarykova at Zborovska (tel. 96 57 53). Local dance hall in the heart of town. Open daily 8pm-4am.

Vinárna Parkhotel, at the end of Masarykova (tel. 96 52 81). Wine-pub with occasional live entertainment. Open Tues.-Sat. 7pm-4am.

Lok Ham Pivnice, Masarykova at Boženy Němcové. Locals, smoke, and drowned sorrows. Inexpensive Czech food and *Samson* beer. Open Mon.-Thurs. 10am-10pm, Fri.-Sat. 11am-midnight.

MORAVIA

Moravia is the wine-making eastern half of the Czech Republic. The word "Český," grates on the ears in these parts; it describes both Bohemia as a historic territory and the Czechs as an ethnic community. Some Moravians go so far as to consider themselves ethnically Moravian, as opposed to Czech. Though some wanted the new Czech Republic to be called "Czechomoravia" *(Českomordvska),* there is no threat of Moravian separatism. The sub-regions of Moravia are equally finicky. The town of **Olomouc** proudly describes itself as the capital of the Hanák region; the Hanáks eagerly distinguish themselves from the Horňáks and the "Moravian Slovaks" to the east. Each group speaks a different dialect and has a unique style of dress.

■■■ BRNO

Midway on the rail line between Prague and Bratislava, Brno is the third-largest city in the Czech Republic and the political and cultural capital of Moravia. After the Thirty Years War, Habsburg Austria transformed Brno into a Baroque city as it replaced Olomouc as the new capital of Moravia. With the onset of industrialization, the new bourgeoisie was divided along the linguistic lines of Czech and German. (The latter called the city **Brünn.**) The two communities prospered in relative harmony here, in contrast to Bohemia, where ethnic tensions ran high. Even today, a Moravian dialect of Czech, replete with German phrases, flows from the tongues of Brno's inhabitants who proudly call their home **betelné štatl** ("the great city"). Among the town's famous sons were the Austrian monk-geneticist **Johann Gregor Mendel,** who revolutionized the study of biology, and Czech composer **Leoš Janáček,** who gave classical music a modern flavor. The local **Starobrno** brewery has produced one of the Czech Republic's finest beers since 1872.

ORIENTATION AND PRACTICAL INFORAMATION

Tourist Offices: ČEDOK, Nádražní 10/12 (tel. 42 21 15 61, fax 42 21 31 96), in front on the main train station. Eager and friendly staff offers several pamphlets, **maps,** and information on Brno and Southern Bohemia. Open Mon.-Fri. 8am-6pm and Sat. 9am-5pm. **Taxatour,** Nádražní 2 (tel. 717 22 30 or 258 90), inside the train station next to luggage storage. Although the staff members have difficulty communicating in English and in German, they sell **maps,** books, postcards, and magazines. Open 24 hrs. **CKM,** Ceská 11 (tel. 42 21 60 99, fax 42 21 26 90), one block north of Náměstí Svobody in the Old Town. **Maps** and brochures in abundance. Limited English spoken. Open Mon.-Fri. 9am-noon and 1-4:40pm. **CK Via Petrov,** Kozí 8 (tel. 42 21 40 21 or 42 21 00 12, fax 42 21 37 74). English-speaking staff offer **maps** and information pamphlets. Open Mon.-Fri. 9am-4pm.

Currency Exchange: The major Czech banks have offices in Brno that offer better rates and lower commission than shops, hotels, or exchange booths. **Kreditní Banka,** Masarykova 11/15, is on the main pedestrian street north of the main train station. Open Mon.-Fri. 8am-5pm. **Investiční Banka,** Josefká 15. Its new *bankomat* (ATM) accepts Mastercard and cards linked to the Cirrus network. Bank open Mon.-Fri. 7:30am-5pm and Fri 7:30am-noon. **Komerční Banka,** náměstí Svobody on the main square. Open Mon.-Fri. 8am-11am and 12:30-4:30pm. **Ceská Spořitelna,** Jánska 6. Open Mon.-Fri. 7:45am-6pm.

Post Office: The *Ceska Pošta,* Nádražní 2a (tel. 21 12), next to the train station, is open 24hrs. for most postal and telephone services. The post office in the Old Town is at Poštovská 1 (tel. 21 92), but open only typical Czech business hours.

Telephone City Code: 05.

Trains: The *Brno Hlavní Nádražní* is south of the Old Town where Masarykova ends at Nádražní. Frequent trains to Prague and local service to Znojmo, Jihlava, and Kroměříž. Two or 3 trains per day travel to Vienna, Berlin, Bratislava, Budapest, and Bucharest. For train information *(české drahy informace),* tel. 275 62.

Buses: The *Brno Ústř. Autobusové Nádražní* is south of the train station. Walk down Dornych, bear right on Platní, and turn right on Zvonařka that becomes Opuštěná. For bus information *(ČSAD informace),* tel. 33 72 26.

Public Transpotation: Tramways, trolley buses, and buses. Adult fare is 4kč and luggage costs 1kč a piece. Automats that dispense tickets don't always work; purchase tickets at a *tabak* or kiosk. Consider buying a day-pass that covers a specific 24hr. period for a mere 15kč at kiosks or ČEDOK.

Taxis: tel. 75 11 11, 245 04, 42 32 13 21, 256 06, or 272 65. The train station and major hotels have taxi stands.

Lost and Found: office at Malinovkého náměstí 3 (tel. 216 or 425).

Public Toilets: *free* on Malinovkého náměstí y during normal business hours. Otherwise, use the less clean facilities at the train station for a modest price.

CZECH REPUBLIC

Pharmacies: A 24hr. *Lékárna* is located at Koblížná 7 (tel. 222 75). There are other pharmacies located throughout the city.
Emergency: First Aid: tel. 155.
Police: In an **emergency** tel. 158. The passport and visa office is at Kounicova 46 (tel. 448). For traffic problems, visit Příční 31 (tel. 67 23 61).

ACCOMMODATIONS

Private accommodations are the way to go. Most affordable hotels in Brno are dilapidated 1960s edifices with unpleasant communal toilets and showers.

Accommodations Agencies

ČEDOK, Nádražní 10/12 (see above). Private rooms for 369kč per person. A few are located near the Old Town. Open Mon.-Fri. 8am-6pm and Sat. 9am-5pm.
CKM, Česka 11 (see above), one block north of náměstí Svobody in the Old Town. Reasonably priced private pads outside central Brno. Singles 315kč. Doubles 420kč. Open Mon.-Fri. 9am-noon and 1-4:30pm.
CK Via Petrou, Kozí 8 (see above). Helpfully arranges private accommodations at locations outside central Brno for 300kč per person. Open Mon.-Fri. 9am-4pm.
Taxatour, Nádražní 2 (see above). With patience, you can communicate a request for a private room for 350kč per person per night. Open 24hrs.

Hotels

Hotel Pegas, Jakubská 4 (tel./fax 42 21 12 32), near St. James Church. Wonderful new hotel in the heart of historic Brno above a hip local brew-pub. Shows familiarity with Western hygienic standards. Reception open 24hrs. Singles 880kč. Doubles 1400kč. Breakfast included.
Hotel Astoria, Novobranská 3 (tel. 225 41 or 275 26). Decor is vintage 1960s and the toilets sometimes communal. Reception open 24hrs. Singles 510kč. Doubles with shower 680kč, with a toilet and shower 1060kč. Breakfast included.
Hotel Avion, Česká 20 (tel. 42 21 50 16 or 42 32 13 03, fax 42 21 40 55) north of náměstí Svobody. In an avant-garde building designed by Bohuslav Fuchs in the 1920s. Communal toilets. Reception open 24hrs. Singles with shower 645kč.
Hotel U Svatého Jakuba, Jakubské náměstí 6 (tel. 42 21 07 95, fax 42 21 07 97). Sumptuous 1960s socialist decor. Communal toilets except in a few doubles. Singles with shower 795kč. Doubles with shower 1288kč. Reception open 24hrs.
Hotel Slovan, Masarykova 32 (tel. 41 32 12 07 or 41 21 20 20, fax 41 21 11 37), north of the Old Town. All rooms have private bath or shower and toilet. Reception open 24hrs. Singles 1290kč. Doubles 1690kč. Breakfast included.

FOOD

Restaurant Flora, Solniční 3a, near St. Thomas' Church in the former Pilsner Beer Hall. Roast beef, pork *medailonky* (lean pieces), and *schnitzel* entrees for 59-69kč. Draft *Gambrinus* 14kč per half-liter. Open Mon.-Sat. until 8pm.
Večerka, Kobližná at Poštovská. More a deluxe food shop with good hours than a real restaurant, Večerka offers fine meats, sweets, beers, juices, and Julius Meinl coffee. Open Mon. 2-9pm, Tues. 10am-9pm, and Sat. 11am-6pm.
Restaurace U Mioritů, Orlíat Minoritská. Traditional Moravian dishes 40-100kč. Pints of *Radegast* beer (15kč) served in the beer garden. Open Mon.-Fri. 10am-10pm and Sat. 10am-11pm.
Stopkova Plzeňska Pivnice, Česká 5. Founded in 1554, this beer hall serves traditional *svíčková* and roast pork (49kč.) Open Mon.-Sat. 11am-11pm.
Pivnice Pegas, Jakubská 4 (tel./fax 42 21 12 32). Moravian dishes in a pub atmosphere. The *guláš* accompanies the beer very, very well. Open daily 9am-midnight.
Pivnice Boby, Dominikánské náměstí, near the New City Hall. Typical Czech meals 70-120kč. Try the Olomouc-style pork strips *(medailonky,* 40kč) on the outdoor terrace by the Dominican Church. Open daily 11am-11pm.
Restaurace Petrov, Masarykova, one block north of the train station. Traditional and creative Czech entrees 40-1000kč. Open daily 10am-10pm.

Chicken Treat, across from the Main train station. All-chicken fast-food fare 30-80kč. Open Mon.-Fri. 8:30am-10pm and Sat.-Sun. 9am-9pm.

SIGHTS

When King of Bohemia **Charles IV** granted the city special privileges in the 14th century, Czechs lived near St. Peter's Cathedral, Germans inhabited the area around St. James's Church, the Jewish community encircled Capuchin Square and a once-flourishing Flemish population lived around the Dominican Church.

Masarykova, the main pedestrian shopping street begins in front of the **train station,** a huge and very yellow Art Nouveau building whose western tower was destroyed in World War II. **Kapucínské náměstí is** home to a humble **Capuchin Church** whose interior contains a fascinating **crypt** where local personalities are immortalized in glass-enclosed coffins. Most interesting are the rows of mummified Capuchin monks, some of whom appear to be smiling at you (as a result of the particular pattern of facial decay, or so they say). The corpses were not embalmed, but rather dried naturally by an innovative ventilation system designed by the monks themselves (open Tues.-Sat. 9am-noon and 2-4:30pm, Sun. 11-11:45am and 2-4:30pm; admission 10kč). Next door is **Dietrichstein Palace,** an attractive Baroque building in which the local Bishop resided. Today it houses the **Moravian Museum,** focusing on prehistory, geology, and the life of Great Moravia in the 8th century (open Tues.-Sun. 9am-6pm; admission to permanent exhibits 20kč, students 10kč).

By Dietrichstein Palace is **Zelnýtrh,** literally the vegetable market, and a Baroque **Fountain of Parnassus.** The tall, elegant tower and Renaissance cupola belongs to the **Old Town Hall,** dating from 1510. In the rear part is a wall in which an alderman was allegedly walled up alive because Emperor Sigismund's jester accused him of being a traitor. Towering above Zelnýtrh on Petrov Hill is the **Cathedral of Sts. Peter and Paul.** Although the cathedral was destroyed during the Swedish siege of Brno during the Thirty Years War, the building was re-Gothicized in the last two centuries and a Neo-Gothic high altar and 14th-century Madonna and Child remain.

Šilingrovo náměstí is lined with several impressive 19th-century buildings, on the site of an old medieval gate. Down the inclined Dominikánská Street is the **Residence of the Lords of Kunštát,** once prominent players in Moravian politics. The Renaissance building is connected to the **Schmetterhaus,** originally a market for Silesian cloth merchants. The *Schmetterhaus* was named after the noise *(schmetten)* that these traders allegedly made as they peddled their wares. At the end of the street is Dominikánské náměstí, the square of the **Dominican Church.** Although closed to the public, the Dominican church has pretty Baroque façade.

Next to the church is the two-story **New Town Hall,** whose Renaissance façade is the work of local architect Moritz Grimm. The courtyard is particularly impressive, as are the Renaissance steps that lead to an organ music-filled room. Directly across from the New Town Hall is a short alley that leads to **náměstí Svobody,** the main quarter of Brno. The partly gold column in the middle of the square was built in 1680 to commemorate the end of a plague.

North of náměstí Svobody along Rašínova is the great **Church of St. James.** Originally built for medieval Brno's Flemish and German communities, St. James has been refurbished several times. The interior of the church has a surprisingly open and free feel, in stark contrast to typically cluttered and constricted medieval interiors. The high altar and the impressive monument of de Souches, who defended Brno against Swedish invaders during the Thirty Years War, are particularly interesting. The strangely thin tower is nicknamed "the toothpick."

Down Joštova Street is the former **Seat of the Moravian Parliament,** one of the more peaceful diets of the Austrian monarchy. The Neo-Renaissance building is the work of Viennese architects Robert Raschka and Anton Hefft. Next door is the **Red Church,** a late 19th-century imitation of a medieval hall church by Heinrich Ferstel, who also built the unabashedly neo-Gothic *Votivkirche* in Vienna.

From Šilingrovo náměstí, a walk along **Pekařská** (literally Baker Street) leads to the heart of the "Old Brno" neighborhood, **Mendel Square** *(Mendlovo námwstí).*

The most striking building is the **Augustinian Monastery,** built in a High Gothic style. The church contains a famous Black Madonna and magnificent stained-glass windows but it is not open to the public. The monastery's most accomplished monk was **Johann Gregor Mendel,** immortalized as the founder of genetics. The **Mendelianum** and the adjacent courtyard feature several monuments to Mendel, including a statue, an Art Nouveau stone memorial, and the bee-house where Mendel conducted experiments. Demolished by Communists in the 1950s, the memorial has been faithfully restored. Next to the Mendelianum is the **Starobrno Brewery** and **beer-hall,** built in 1872 to replace the monastery brewery.

In the northeast, at Malinovského náměstí is the grand **Mahen Theater,** erected in the late 19th century by Helmer and Fellner. In contrast, the **Janáček Theater,** further north between Koliště and Rooseveltova, was the pride and joy of the 1960s Communist regime. A walk down Milady Horákové and a left on Černopolní will lead to the **Tugendhat Villa,** one of the most famous works by *Bauhaus* architect Ludwig Mies van der Rohe. The 1930s building is currently owned by the city of Brno, which can arrange visits for tourists. A left on Schodová takes you to **Lužánky Park,** the largest in Brno. The 200-year-old trees and the St. Ignatius Chapel once belonged to the Jesuits, but are now public domain.

Spielberg Castle (Hrad Špilberk)

Unfounded legends about torturing unfaithful wives with water and of chaining murderous criminals in rat-infested dungeons envelop the **Spielberg Castle.** Nevertheless, Spielberg was a prison until 1855 and hosted a fiery group of political activists, including Polish revolutionaries, Hungarian Jacobins, Italian nationalists, and Czech rebels. Afterwards, the fortress served as barracks for the Imperial and Royal Austrian Army. When the Nazis occupied Brno, they again turned the castle into a jail and imprisoned local Czech dissidents within. Although it is now a national monument, Spielberg retains the eerie and forbidding atmosphere. The upper story features several group cells, the prison kitchen, and the sinister "timber cells" reserved for the most demented criminals. There are more timber cells and the ruins of the telephone network installed by the Nazis on the lower story. A walk around the castle takes 20-40 minutes (open Tues.-Sun. 9am-6pm; admission 20kč, students 10kč).

ENTERTAINMENT

Even in the heart of wine-producing Moravia, wine pubs *(vinára)* are outdone by Brno's beer-halls.

Pivnice Minipivovar Pegas, Jakubská 4 (tel./fax 42 21 12 32). Founded in 1992, this microbrewery has acquired a loyal following among locals and visitors. The light and dark beers are brewed on the premises, and 0.4liter of either costs a mere 13kč. Inexpensive Moravian food also served. Open daily 9am-midnight.

Pivovarská Pivnice, Mendlovo náměstí, west of the Old Town. Located next door to the Starobrno brewery, this beer hall serves dark and light *Starobrno* drafts for 12kč. Open Mon.-Sat. 11am-10pm.

Černohorská pivnice, Kapucínské náměstí 1, near the Capuchin Church. Local males carouse and converse in the smoky beer-hall. The food isn't so great; the *guláš* is watery. The draft *Černá horá* beer is excellent and reasonably priced at 13kč for a ½-liter. Open Mon.-Fri. 8am-6pm, Sun. 8am-10pm.

Reduta Club, Kapcínské náměstí 9 (tel. 42 21 20 13), near the Capuchin Church. A former wine-pub transformed into a dance club. Open Mon.-Sat. 11am-2am.

Pavilon Disco Bar, Zelný trh. 20. Centrally located and popular beer terrace (open daily 9am-9pm) and dance club (9am-5am.)

Pivnice Boby, Dominikánské náměstí near the Dominican Church and the New Town Hall. Four Czech beers on tap: *Pilsner Urquell, Budweiser Budvar, Radegast,* and *Černá horá.* 17kč per ½-liter. Food served too. Open daily 11am-11pm.

Pivní Bar, Běhounská 10. A relatively new beer pub with inexpensive drafts. A ½-liter of *Černá horá* costs a mere 8kč. Open Mon.-Sat. noon-11pm.

Klub U Draka, Běhounská 10 (tel. 4221 3220). Choose from the huge selection of mixed drinks, wines, and beer. New and central. Open Mon.-Sat. 10am-11pm, Sun. 11am-11pm.

■ NEAR BRNO

MORAVIAN KRAS

Just 20km from Brno are the stalagmites and stalactites of the Moravian Kras (caves), home to four main networks of caverns open to visitors year-round. From Brno, take the bus to **Blansko** (7 per day May-Sept.; 1 hr.; 15kč), then hop on a bus to the caves. The 8 and 11am buses make a 4-hour tour that hits all of the major caverns. Runs at other times and in other seasons go only so far as the **Punkevní jeskyné** (4kč one way), a main cavern offering a 75-minute tour of the gaping **Macocha Abyss,** created when the cave roof fell in, as well as a boat ride on the subterranean Punkva River. Bring a sweater or jacket; it gets mighty chilly, even in summer. (Open Mon.-Fri. 7am-4:30pm, Sat.-Sun. 7:30am-4pm; Oct.-March Mon.-Fri. 7:30am-3pm, Sat.-Sun. 7:30am-4pm. Admission 20kč, students 10kč.)

TELČ

A stop on the bus line from České udějovice and Brno is the magnificently preserved Renaissance town of Telč (2 hrs. from either city; 42kč). Its pastel archways and stone watchtowers create a truly lovely square, **nám. Zachariáše z Hradce,** that is surprisingly free of tourists. The main attraction here is **Telč Castle,** erected in the late 14th and early 15th centuries (open Tues.-Sun. 8am-noon and 1-5pm, April and Sept.-Oct. 9am-noon and 1-4pm; admission 25kč, students 10kč). The castle complex, at the far end of the town square, houses a **museum** of Moravian and Telč history (same hours as above; admission 8kč, students 4kč) and a **gallery** of modern art by Jan Zrzavý, once held a "National Artist of Czechoslovakia." (Open Tues.-Fri. and Sun. 9am-noon and 1-4pm, Sat. 9am-4pm; April and Sept.-Oct. 9am-noon and 1-4pm. Admission 10kč, students 5kč.) To reach the town square from the bus stop, take a left from the parking lot; at the end of the street, turn left down Masarykova and look for the green, red, and yellow trail markers at Na parkane. Follow the cobblestones to the left, then cross the stone bridge on the right.

■ ■ ■ OLOMOUC

Off the beaten track, Olomouc is rich in history, architectural beauty, and the sneaky energy of a university town. The university was founded in 1573 and lost in the Thirty Years War along with 90% of the town's citizens. Under the patronage of Austria, the city was rebuilt in Baroque style and continued to be the seat of Europe's largest archbishopric. In 1767, 11-year-old Mozart composed his Sixth Symphony in the fortified city. The walls of Olomouc have also imprisoned revolutionaries, including Mikhail Bakunin and de Lafayette. In the chaos of the 1848 revolutions, Franz Josef ascended the Imperial throne of Austria during his "Olmütz Captivity."

ORIENTATION AND PRACTICAL INFORMATION

Tourist Offices: ČEDOK, Horní náměstí 2 (tel. 233 31 33, fax 522 44 31). Maps and information on Olomouc. Friendly staff. Open Mon.-Fri. 8am-5pm, Sat. 9am-noon. **CKM,** Denisova 4 (tel. 290 09, fax 522 39 39). More maps and information on Olomouc. More friendly staff. Open Mon.-Fri. 9am-5pm.

Budget Travel: Bohemian Fantasy, Riegrova 19 (tel. 522 25 57, fax 52 22 58 78). A new agency with a kinky name. Also friendly. Open Mon.-Fri. 8:30am-4:30pm.

Currency Exchange: Komerční Banka, Svobody 14 (tel. 522 44 05, fax 522 42 05). Large and central. Open Mon.-Thurs. 8am-noon and 1-5pm, Fri. 8am-noon and 1-4pm. **Investiční a Poštovní Banka,** Horní náměstí 27 on the main square near the City Hall. Open Mon.-Fri. 7am-7pm, Sat. 8am-noon. **Zemskí Banka,** Ostružnická 16. Open Mon.-Fri. 7:30am-noon and 1-4pm, Sat. 7:30-11am.

Post Office: The *Česká Pošta* is at Horní námwstí 27, next to the Town Hall. Open Mon.-Fri. 7am-7pm, Sat. 8am-noon. Another post office is next to the train station.
Telephone City Code: 068.
Trains: The *Olomouc Hlavní Nádraží* is a 10-minute walk from the Old Town, through a gray 1950s neighborhood, where Masarykova ends at Jeremenkova. For train information *(ČD informace)*, tel. 332 91.
Public Transportation: Tramways and streetcars. Tickets sold at kiosks and tabak stores. Adults 4kč. Route #4 connects the train station with the Old Town.
Public Toilets: Off the main square, Horní náměstí, along Riegrova. Men 1kč, women 2kč. Otherwise, try the train station.
Pharmacy: Lékárna Oúnz Olomouc, is near the train station at Masarykova 49. Open Mon.-Fri. 7:30am-6pm, Sat. 8am-noon.
Police: in an **emergency** tel. 158. The *České Republiky* are between the train station and the Old Town on náměstí Žižkovo.

ACCOMMODATIONS

Finding a reasonably priced private room in Olomouc can be a challenge. **CKM** (see above) is the least expensive agency. (English spoken. Doubles with toilet and shower 700kč.) **Bohemian Fantasy** (see above) offers accommodations from 600kč per person, with breakfast 700kč. **ČEDOK** (see above) is very expensive by comparison (accommodations from 1400kč per person).

Hotel U Dómy, Domská 4 (tel. 264 54). Opened in July 1994. Rooms with toilet, shower, kitchenette, satellite TV, and telephone. Reception open 24hrs. Beautiful quadruples for 1500kč. Singles, doubles, and triples are 1500kč, so check in as a group of four if possible. Clone yourself if necessary. Breakfast included.
Hotel Národní dům, 8. května 21 (tel. 522 48 07 or 522 48 06, fax 522 4808). Older but well-maintained. Singles with shower 765kč. Doubles with old toilet 1210kč, with new toilet 1520kč. No middle-aged toilets. A huge, ornate 19th-century apartment is 1770kč for two people. Reception open 24hrs.
Hotel Sigma, Jeremenkova 36 (tel. 269 41 or 271 53, fax 289 62). Across the street from the train station. All rooms have a toilet and shower. Reception open 24hrs. Singles 800kč. Doubles 900kč. Breakfast 80kč.
Hotel Palác, 1. máje 27 (tel./fax 232 84). Central location. Reception open 24hrs. Check-out noon. No singles. Doubles with bath and toilet 1300kč.

FOOD

Restaurace Huberta, 1. máje 3 (tel. 522 40 17). Daily Moravian specialties for 30-40kč. Try the *řízek brněnský* (Brno-style *schnitzel)* and the local Olomouc *Václav* beer on tap (10kč for ½-liter). Open Mon.-Sat. 10am-10pm.
Bistro Na Hradě, Univerzitní 18. Moravian pork and beef dishes under 50kč. Open Mon.-Fri. 10am-10pm, Sat. 11am-until the early morning hours.
Pivnice U Bakaláře, Zerotinovo náměstí 3. A friendly eatery serving Czech entrees (20-45kč) and copious quantities of beer. Open Mon.-Fri. 9am-8pm.
Lahůdka Občerstvení, Ostružnická 24. Self-serve Czech fare under 50kč. Two minutes from the main square, Horní náměstí. Open Mon.-Fri. 8am-6pm.
Vinárna MM, Riegrova 22 (tel. 522 87 33). Moravian food (entrees 20-70kč) and Moravian wine (1 liter 34kč). Open Mon.-Sat. 10am-10:30pm.
Apetit Občerstvení, Masarykova 42. A local self-serve joint near the train station. Czech dishes under 50kč. Bottled *Gambrinus.* Open Mon.-Fri. 6am-6pm, Sat. 7am-noon.
Neptun Rybí Restaurant, 1. máje, one block east of Dómska. Plentiful variations on the Moravian fish theme. Entrees 40-120kč. Accompany your fish with wine, beer, or liquor. Cover 6kč. Open Mon.-Fri. 11am-11pm.

SIGHTS

The treasures of Olomouc are concentrated in the Old Town, once a fortified stronghold of Moravian margraves and Austrian emperors. More peaceful than its namesake in Prague, **Wenceslas Square** *(Václavské náměstí)* is surrounded by elegant ecclesiastical edifices. Most striking is the **Cathedral of Saint Wenceslas**

(Chrám sv. Václava). Originally Gothic, Saint Wenceslas was redone in Baroque style in the 17th century, only to be enthusiastically re-Gothicized in the late 19th century. The church interior is in impeccable condition; the most valuable objects of artistic merit are located in the **crypt.** Old books, postcards, reliquaries, and medieval maps are also on display in the crypt-cum-museum. (Open Mon.-Fri. 9:30am-4pm; admission 5kč.) The **tower** commands a magnificent view of the Old Town. (Open Mon.-Fri. 9:30am-4pm; 5kč.)

Descend Dómská St. and climb up Wurmová to reach **Bishop's Square** *(Biskupské náměstí).* On the east side is the Renaissance-style **Archbishop's Palace** *(Arcibiskupský palác),* erected between 1665 and 1685 by Peter Schüller. While Austria was engulfed in the turmoil of the 1848 revolutions, Franz Josef ascended the Imperial throne in this building. The large military **Arsenal** *(Zbrojnice)* was built under Follow Křížkovského Street, lined with several buildings affiliated with Olomouc's **Palacký University,** founded in 1946. Křížkovského spills out onto **Square of the Republic** *(náměstí Republiky),* on which stands the **Olomouc Museum** *(Muzeum umění v Olomouci).* Among its exhibits are the clocks of Olomouc and the history of the city (open Tues.-Sun. 10am-4pm; admission 20kč, students 10kč).

The monumental Baroque Church across from the museum is **St. Mary's,** but it is often closed to the public. Along Univerzitní is a small but very pretty **Chapel** *(Kaple)* built early this century in neo-Baroque style. Its interior was undergoing reconstruction in the summer of 1994. Nearby Panská Street leads to the **Lower Square** *(Dolní náměstí),* surrounded by several historic buildings, most from the 19th century. The oldest building is the **Hauenschild Palace** *(Hauenschildův palác)* at the corner of the square and Lafayettova, built in 1580.

To the north is the **Upper Square** *(Horní náměstí),* dominated by the tower of the **City Hall** *(Radnice).* Originally Gothic, the building was even more intensely neo-Gothicized in 1904 and again in 1955. It's difficult to miss the huge **Trinity Monument** *(Sousoší Nejsvětější Trojice)* next to the City Hall. Soaring over 35m, this Baroque monument is one of the largest of its kind in Europe.

From the Upper Square the narrow 28. října leads to another ornate sculpture, behind which stands the **National House** *(Národní dům).* To the east are the squat towers of **St. Mauritius Church.** Although its external appearance is a crude patchwork of styles, its interior is one of the finest examples of Gothic architecture in Moravia. The purely Gothic sculptures date from 1399-1540, whereas the Renaissance chapel is a 16th-century work of Václav Edelmann. In 1745 the "Breslau Master" Michael Engler came to Olomouc and endowed St. Mauritius with the largest Baroque organ in Central Europe.

ENTERTAINMENT

Like all student towns, Olomouc has plenty of places in which to annihilate burdensome brain cells.

Pivnice U Bakaláře, Zerotinovo námwstí 3. A popular beer hall in the heart of the university district where students eat on the cheap. Open Mon.-Fri. 9am-8pm.

Hospoda U Musea, 1. máje 8 (tel. 522 34 01). A local pub serving Prague's *Staropramen* beer. Live music Thurs. nights. Open Mon.-Wed. 10am-11pm, Thurs.-Sat. noon-midnight.

Smíchovská Pivnice, Vodární 4. Established beer hall with a diverse clientele. *Staropramen* beer straight from the brewery in Prague's Smíchov neighborhood. Open Mon.-Fri. 9am-10, Sat. 10am-10pm.

Herni Bar, 1. máje 19, near Dómska. Very male bar with slot machines and dirt-cheap *Radegast* beer (8kč per half-liter). Open daily 5pm-5am.

Vinárna MM, Riegrova 22 (tel. 522 87 33). A mere 34kč for one precious liter of *vino.* Inexpensive Moravian meals too. Open Mon.-Sat. 10am-10:30pm.

ESTONIA (EESTI)

US$1	= 12.70EEK (Estonian Kroons) 7/22/94	10EEK =	US$0.79
CDN$1	= 9.39EEK	10EEK =	CDN$1.08
UK£1	= 19.93EEK	10EEK =	UK£0.50
IR£1	= 19.55EEK	10EEK =	IR£0.51
AUS$1	= 9.46EEK	10EEK =	AUS$1.06
NZ$1	= 6.90EEK	10EEK =	NZ$1.45
SAR1	= 3.58EEK	10EEK =	SAR2.79
DM1	= 8.26EEK	10EEK =	DM1.21
Country Code: 372		International Dialing Prefix: 810	

Fifty years ago, a massive social shift Russified Estonian culture and Sovietized Estonian supermarkets; today, Estonians are scratching their heads, trying to figure out how to reverse that enormous civil wallop. As Western ventures fill Tallinn with Volvos, cellular phones, and Mormons, it's increasingly evident that Estonians have already found their own unique solutions. This Baltic nation has thrown caution to the winds, discarding the prudent advice of the World Bank and an army of financial experts. As a result, the kroon has been steadily strengthening for the past year while countries like Kazakhstan that listened to the experts face rampant inflation.

Meanwhile, Estonian culture is experiencing a dramatic resurgence. Visitors are sure to come across boulders, lakes, and other natural objects connected with Estonia's national mythic hero Kalevipoeg, a sort of giant who fought bears, Germans, and other evil influences until he finally died saving the country from invasion. The legends differ in the Estonian islands, where Swedish influences persist and traditional folk costumes are still worn in the countryside: folktales here center around the giant (or troll, depending on who tells the story) Suur Tõll and his brother Leiger, mischievous but well-meaning nature spirits.

With a maximum span of under 300km, Estonia is the smallest of the Baltic nations. Tallinn, its cosmopolitan, fast-paced capital, is home to half a million people; Tartu, the hip Estonian Oxbridge, is a daytrip away. Farther afield, Pärnu and

Haapsalu shine as Baltic Coast resorts, doorways to the intoxicating islands of many vowels, Hiiumaa and Saaremaa.

ESTONIA ESSENTIALS

Citizens of the U.S., Canada, the U.K., and Australia can visit Estonia visa-free for up to 90 days. You're likely to meet a lot of Australians in Tallinn, since Estonia is one of the few East European nations that does not require visas of them. Bear in mind that since early 1993, the three Baltic states have been united in a common visa zone; a visa from any one of the three countries should be sufficient for travel to the other two. Latvian visas tend to be cheapest. Most Estonian consulates can issue a 30-day, single-entry tourist visa (US$10) or a 1-year, multiple-entry visa (US$50) to citizens of Ireland, New Zealand, and South Africa. It is possible to obtain a visa upon arriving in Estonia, but it is wiser to obtain one beforehand. See Essentials: Embassies and Consulates, page 3.

GETTING THERE

Several **cruise lines** reach Tallinn from Helsinki. **Merelle,** Kluuvik 6, 00100 Helsinki (tel. +358 (0) 65 87 33 or 65 10 11) sells tickets for the *MIS Tallink* (daily, 3½hrs.) and the *MIS Georg Ots* (daily from Helsinki 10am, from Tallinn 6pm; 3½hrs.). Both ships 120mk one-way. The **Estonian New Line** runs three hydrofoils, making five total round-trips per day in the summer (1½-2hrs.; one way 120mk, round-trip 230mk). Their cheapest fare, 100mk one-way, seats you on the ferry *Corbiere,* which leaves Helsinki daily at 8am and 8pm and arrives in Tallinn at 11:30am and 11:30pm respectively. Look for visa free tours at travel bureaus or the Helsinki office at Kalevank 1 (tel. +358 (0) 680 24 99, summer only). From Stockholm, **Estline,** Est-lineterminalen i Frihammnen, 11556 Stockholm (tel. +46 (8) 667 00 01), sails the *Nord Estonia* to Tallinn every other day at 5:30pm. (14½hrs.; 390kr).

Finnair flies daily to Tallinn (round-trip 475mk, under 25 standby 420mk) and **Estonian Airlines** flies daily from Helsinki (round-trip 435mk). **SAS** flies from Stockholm to Tallinn daily (round-trip 1600 Swedish kr).

GETTING AROUND ESTONIA

Buses and trains radiate to all points from Tallinn and Tartu. **Trains** never caught on in Estonia as they did in the rest of the Soviet Union; much of the railroad track that carried passengers when Estonia was independent between the World Wars was torn up over the years. Only three lines cross the Estonian border; two pass through Tartu from Moscow to Riga; the third goes through Narva to St. Petersburg. Major towns such as Pärnu and Haapsalu are all connected to Tallinn, but trains can be scarce. Prices are also on the rise, and Estonian rail tickets are now the most expensive in the former Soviet Union. **Buses** thoroughly link all towns, however, often more cheaply and efficiently than the trains. It's even possible to ride buses direct from the mainland to towns on the islands (via ferry), for less than the price of the ferry ride alone.

Flights within Estonia used to be ridiculously underpriced, but that era is over. During the winter of 1993-4, Estonian Airlines flew a Tallinn-Kuressaare route for 310EEK (60EEK for residents of Saaremaa); the service was heavily underwritten by the Estonian government because ferries sometimes required 14, 20, or even 36 hours to make the (normally) 1½-hour crossing on account of ice. Flights were suspended for the warm season, but are expected to resume in winter. For info, contact **Estonian Airlines** in Tallinn (tel. 44 63 82).

TOURIST SERVICES

Unlike most of the former Soviet Union, Estonia has grasped the importance of providing tourist services; most small towns now offer city maps, while larger towns

ESTONIA

and cites may have well-equipped tourist offices, loads of literature, and virtual armies of enthusiastic workers eager to help you find hotels, restaurants, free rides, or whatever you may need. There's such an abundance of information in Tallinn that you can usually get any info you need there, and never have to visit smaller tourist offices. But it's still a good idea to check in once you reach a smaller town.

As is the custom throughout the Baltics, St. John's Eve *(Jaaniõhtu)*, celebrated on the eve of the summer solstice, inspires bonfires, festivals of song, and open-air revelry. In Estonia, Saaremaa has the reputation for throwing the best bash. The main frolicking takes place on June 24, after which the whole country shuts down for a couple days to recover. Other important holidays include Independence Day (Feb. 24), Victory Day (June 23—how convenient), and the Day of Rebirth (Nov. 16).

MONEY

The unit of currency is the **Kroon** (EEK), divided into 100 **senti. Traveler's checks** are still hard to cash in Estonia; some of the larger banks *(pank)* can do it, but often charge an exorbitant 7% fee. **Credit cards** are still a rarity, but Visa, MasterCard, Diner's Club, and AmEx are all starting to put in appearances. You can get a cash advance from your Visa card in the lobby of the Hotel Viru in Tallinn. Bring cash, and there'll be smiles all around.

COMMUNICATIONS

A postcard or a letter to the U.S. costs 4EEK, a brilliant method of EEKing a little more money out of tourists. In summer 1994, public **telephones** were (usually) free outside of Tallinn, as they still had not been converted to take Estonian senti pieces. Within Tallinn, a few phones in the most obvious locations (the bus station, train station, airport, etc.) required a 20-senti coin for local calls. Theoretically, all phones nationwide will soon be converted to a **phonecard** system. AT&T, USADirect, and similar services are not yet available. Long-distance calls within Estonia, to points in Europe, or elsewhere can be made at the post offices. Calls to the Baltic states and Russia cost 5EEK per minute, while phoning the U.S. runs a steep 24EEK per minute. International calls can be ordered through the operator in the office, after which you'll have to wait 30-90 min. for the call to go through. In larger cities such as Tallinn, Tartu, and Kuressaare there are special orange direct-dial phones in post offices that use phonecards; dialing direct costs no more or less than ordering a call, but it can save you a long wait. Cards come in denominations of 16, 40, 95, and 190EEK. Instructions are provided in about a dozen different languages on these Finnish-made phones. City codes in Estonia are changing to accommodate new digital lines for faxes; where possible we have indicated the new codes as well as the old analog-line numbers. When calling Estonia from outside the former Soviet Union, drop the initial "2" from the city code; when calling Tallinn, use "2" instead of the city code.

English-language books and newspapers are relatively easy to find in Estonia, especially in Tallinn. The English-language weekly *Baltic Independent* has its offices in Tallinn; it's a good source for info on the latest in Tallinn and Tartu.

LANGUAGE

Estonians speak the best English in the Baltic states; most young people know at least a few phrases, though German is more common among the older set. Russian was theoretically taught in schools, but Estonians in secluded areas such as the islands of Hiiumaa and Vormsi are likely to have forgotten what they learned since few if any Russians live there. Despite what you may hear about radical Balts spitting at Russian speakers, no one actually seems to mind using Russian if there's no other way to communicate—but try English first. Estonian is one of those unusual (to Americans) Finno-Ugric languages, with 14 cases and all sorts of confounding letters. One popular Estonian rock group calls itself Jää-äär, meaning "on the edge of the ice." You're not going to master the language in a week, but basic phrases are easy enough.

Try familiarizing yourself with these words and phrases: *Kas Teie raagite inglis keelt?* (Kahs TEH-yeah REH-git-teh EEN-glis kehlt; "Do you speak English?"); *bussijaam* (BUSS-ee-yahm; "bus station"); *raudteejaam* (ROWD-tee-yahm; "train station"); *postkontor* (pohst-KON-tohr; "post office"; *avatud* (AH-vah-tuht; "open"); *suletud* (SUH-leh-tuht; "closed"). All of the "r"s in the Estonian language are trilled.

Yes	*ja*	yah
No	*ei*	rhymes with "hay"
Today	*täna*	TA-nuh
Tomorrow	*homme*	HOME-uh
Hello	*tere*	TEH-re
Good morning	*tere hommikust*	TEH-re ho-mih-KUHST
Good night	*head ööd*	hehaht(one syl.) euht
Goodbye	*head aega*	hehaht EYE-kah
Excuse me	*vabandage*	vah-pan-TAGE-euh
Sorry	*andke andeks*	ANT-keh an-TEKS
Please/Here you are	*palun*	PAH-luhn
Thank you	*aitäh*	EYE-tah
When?	*millal*	mih-LAL
Where is...?	*Kus on...*	Kuhs on
How much is it?	*Kui palju?*	Kwee PAL-you
How do I get to...?	*Mina sooviksin minna... se?*	MIH-nah soo-VIK-sin MIH-nah... seh
My name is...	*Minu nimi on...*	MIH-nuh nih-mih on...
Do you speak English?	*Kas te räägite inglise keelt?*	kass teh rah-KIHT-eh ihn-KLIS-eh keelt
I don't understand	*Ma ei saa aru.*	mah ay saw AH-rooh

1—üks (ewks); 2—kaks (kaks); 3—kolm (kohlm); 4—neli (NEH-lih); 5—viis (veese); 6—kuus (koose); 7—seitse (SATE-seh); 8—kaheksa (KAH-eks-ah); 9—üheksa (EUW-eks-ah); 10—kümme (KEUW-meh); 20—kakskümmend (kaks-KEUW-ment); 30—kolmkümmend (kohlm-KEUW-ment); 40—nelikümmend (neh-lih-KEUW-ment); 50—viiskümmend (veese-KEUW-ment); 60—kuuskümmend (koose-KEUW-ment); 70—seitsekümmend (sate-seh-KEUW-ment); 80—kaheksakümmend (kah-eks-ah-KEUW-ment); 90—üheksakümmend (euw-eks-ah-KEUW-ment); 100—sada (SAH-dah).

ACCOMMODATIONS AND CAMPING

The Baltic States: A Reference Book offers information ranging from maps and listings of hotels in every major town to a small "Who's Who" section for each country. Buy it for 200kr at Hotel Viru or in bookstores (where it'll be cheaper). Between the range of US$100-per-night ex-Intourist abodes and cheap, slightly drab hotels with no hot water, a few companies have set up youth hostels and started to arrange stays at private homes; contact the Tallinn tourist office. **FHS** (Hua Ai Trade Ltd.), Mere puiestee. 6, Tallinn (tel./fax (2) 44 11 87) and **CDS Reisid** (Baltic Bed and Breakfast), Raekoja plats 17, Tallinn (tel. (2) 44 52 62, fax 31 36 66), offer rooms in homes throughout the Baltic countries. FHS charges US$9-15 per person; CDS is computer-efficient, but charges US$25.

LIFE AND TIMES

HiSTORY

Estonia's history is a tale of invasions, foreign dominations, and more invasions—it's the basic recipe for Baltic Historical Stew—with a little Swedish culture and a dash

ESTONIA

of Danish influence thrown in for flavor. Ancient **Estonian tribes** were primitive farmers organized into loose patriarchal clans. Viking invasions in the 9th century set a pattern for foreign incursion that was to be repeated again and again. For several centuries, the ancient Estonians put up a good fight. Russia tried to colonize the region 13 times in the 11th and 12th centuries, but failed to subdue the resistant tribes. Meanwhile, Danish and Swedish missionaries were equally unsuccessful at Christianizing Estonian pagans.

The German **Brothers of the Sword** slowly marched across the region in the early 13th century, their ranks constantly replenished by new Teutonic crusaders from the west. Overwhelmed by the sheer number of German troops, and distracted by Russian incursions to the east, Estonia finally capitulated in 1217. When Denmark seized northern Estonia two years later, the last independent lands in Estonia fell to foreign blades; the conquest was complete. But, as before, the Estonians proved hard to pacify. Uprisings swelled to a crescendo in the mid-14th century until the Danish king threw up his hands in disgust and sold his Estonian lands to the Teutons. Germany ruled the region unopposed for the next century, gradually pressing their stubborn serfs into a Germanic religious and cultural mold.

When the Teutonic order crumbled in 1561, Sweden moved in to fill the vacuum, successfully beating out the Muscovite Tsar Ivan the Terrible. Ravaged by war, Estonia lay in anarchic ruins as German landlords continued to impose severe taxes on their Estonian serfs. Successive Swedish kings tried to protect Estonian peasants from greedy nobles; the Swedish interlude was a relatively respite for ordinary Estonians, as the worst abuses of the feudal system were curbed.

The German barons were understandably peeved, and when Russian armies came marching in from the east, the German nobility in Estonia readily betrayed their Swedish rulers. If Russian rule was good for the estate owners, it was bad for the peasants; serfs lost almost all their rights under Russian domination. Things improved, however, in the early 19th century, when the region's peasants won the right to own private property. Serfdom was soon abolished altogether; later laws of the 1860s banned forced labor and prohibited landowners from flogging their tenants. By the end of the 19th century, peasants controlled about 40% of the privately owned land in the country. But Moscow clamped down under Alexander III, prompting a nationalistic Estonian backlash led by **Konstantin Päts,** the editor of a radical newspaper.

The **Russian Revolution** of 1905 sparked rebellions in Estonia; after peasants and workers burned manor houses across the country, Russian authorities shot or hung hundreds of Estonians. The Revolution of 1917 intensified the Estonian struggle for independence. Invading German troops drove out the Russians in 1917, only to establish their own government in Estonia. After Germany began pulling out of the region in 1918, Estonia declared **independence,** but the declaration fell on deaf ears. The Red Army seized the war-torn nation easily; only with British and Finnish help did Estonians recapture their lands, again under Päts' leadership.

Finally, Estonians declared the right to self-rule. From 1919 to 1933, a **coalition government** ruled the country, successfully stamping out a Russian conspiracy. The decentralized government was unable to cope with economic depression and unemployment in the early 1930s, forcing president Päts to declare a state of emergency and rule as a benevolent dictator for three years. Constitutional reform in the late 1930s stabilized the situation, paving the way for democratic elections—which brought Päts back into power again.

In 1939, Moscow forced Estonia to accept a **mutual assistance treaty;** Soviet troops occupied the country a year later, and in August, 1940 Estonia was formally incorporated into the Soviet Union. Päts and other Estonian leaders were immediately arrested and deported; within a year, over 60,000 Estonians had been killed or deported, including some 10,000 persons who were rounded up and sent out of the country on the night of June 13-14, 1941. German troops drove out the Soviets several weeks later, and Estonia languished under **German occupation** for three years. As the Red Army slowly pushed out the Nazis in mid-1944, tens of thousands of Estonians fled to Germany or Sweden; thousands more died at sea while trying to escape their war-ravaged homeland.

The 1950s saw extreme repression and intense Russification under **Soviet rule;** 80,000 Estonians were deported to other parts of the Soviet Union in the first postwar decade; deportations and massive immigration reduced the proportion of ethnic Estonians within the population from 90% to 60%. Internal purges removed the few native Estonians holding seats in the Republic's Communist party. Even by the late 1980s, the ruling clique was primarily composed of immigrants. *Glastnost* and *perestroika* laid the foundation for an Estonian political renaissance. In 1988, a **Popular Front** emerged in opposition to the Communist government, pushing a resolution on independence through the Estonian legislature. Agitators for independence won a legislative majority in the 1990 elections; following the foiled Moscow coup of 1991, Estonia became truly autonomous.

ESTONIA TODAY

Despite warnings about the potential disaster of privatizing too rapidly, the rabidly free-market thirty-something Prime Minister Mart Laar and his cabinet of graduate-student ministers (average age: 31) shut down hundreds of businesses and privatized everything from oil companies to the national airline. Thousands are out of work and the government's popularity has plunged to under 15%, but their recovery plan is clearly working; Estonia is already within reach of Scandinavian standards of living while prices, to the joy of the budget traveler, remain clearly East European.

Estonia steadfastly refuses to accept the annexation by Russia of a region east of Narva and a province around Pechory; Russia guaranteed in the 1920 Treaty of Tartu to honor Estonian independence and her borders, but when Russia invaded in 1940 it added insult to injury by annexing 5% of its territory. In summer 1994, the Russian government had unilaterally demarcated the borders in these regions, but legal wrangling continues. However, the dispute presents no problems for travelers.

Matters of citizenship are another set of disputes in contemporary Estonia; nearly 35% of its residents are immigrants or the children of immigrants from the Soviet period; most are ethnic Russians. In an attempt to ensure Estonian cultural independence, a language law requires that to be a citizen one must have a conversational knowledge of Estonian. This law has prompted several thousand Russians in Estonia to opt for Russian citizenship, and has provided Russian President Boris Yeltsin with a (feeble) excuse to halt the withdrawal of Russian troops from Estonia. Yeltsin is not entirely unjustified in asserting that the law is an "obvious violation of the human rights of Russians." But it is also true that all Estonians were required to learn Russian under the Soviet government.

FOOD AND DRINK

It's hard to define exactly what is "Estonian Food"; go into any restaurant and you'll see the same assortment of drab carbonades, lifeless antrkots, greasy bullion, and cold fried potatoes that plague the rest of the former European USSR. If there is a difference in Estonia, it is that there is more fish on the menu. Trout is especially popular, and often the ham-stuffed soljanka you had in Riga and Moscow will undergo a sea-change here into a deliciously thick whitefish soup. Estonian beer is good stuff; the national brand *Saku* is downright excellent, especially the darker *Saku Tume*. Local brews like the *Saaremaa* beer available in Kuressaare can be volatile; keep an eye out for them. In Estonia, as in the rest of the Baltics, some restaurants and cafés take an hour break during the late afternoon or early evening. Most Estonian doorkeepers are friendly to Westerners, although you'll occasionally encounter a hardheaded Stalinist. Try smiling and speaking English, German, or French. If dining late, try to get in before 10pm. If possible, try making reservations around lunchtime.

ESTONIA

■ Tallinn

Just 80km from Helsinki, Tallinn already feels Scandinavian. It continues to slowly achieve a Western feel more solid than the ephemeral cellular phones and BMWs of Riga or Vilnius. Still, there is a discernible Soviet legacy. In the last 30 years, immigrants from Russia have more than doubled the city's population to half a million; ethnic Russians now number 40% of the city's inhabitants. Visitors will undoubtedly hear a great deal about the Estonian-language test being given to all Russians before they are granted citizenship; this requirement led Russian President Boris Yeltsin to balk at withdrawing the last Russian troops form Estonia in 1994, and could cause yet more trouble for this fledgling republic. Nonetheless, signs of Estonian-Russian friction are absent in Tallinn; clerks switch from Estonian to fluent Russian or even English without skipping a beat.

The heart of Tallinn, the most picturesque square kilometer in the Baltics, is still very much a stony and medieval Nordic Florence. The city is best enjoyed under the clear skies of summer's white nights, when the sun sets for only two hours and leaves the sky a glowing pink from evening until morning.

ORIENTATION AND PRACTICAL INFORMATION

Tallinn's **Vanalinn** (Old Town) is an egg-shaped maze ringed in by four main streets. **Põhja puiestee,** on the north, joins with Sadama to lead to the ferry terminal; **Mere puiestee** follows the eastern side, running south from Põhja to join **Pârnu maantee,** which itself circles around the southern edge of the Old Town and then runs off south; **Toom puiestee** completes the circle on the western side. **Narva maantee** will take you east from the junction of Mere and Pärnu toward the looming Hotel Viru, the central landmark in Tallinn. The Old Town peaks in the fortress-rock of Toompea, whose 13th-century streets are at the level of the church steeples in the **All-linn** (low town).

To reach the Old Town from the ferry terminal, walk 15 minutes along Sadama to Põhja, and then south on Pikk between stone towers. From the train station, cross Toom puiestee and go straight through the park along Nunne; the stairway up Patkuli trepp on your right leads directly to the Toompea. In the Old Town, **Pikk tee** (Long street) is the main artery, running from the seaward gates of the lower town to the one-time-only entrance to the Toompea through the Pikk Jalg tower. **Raekoja Plats,** the Town Hall square, is the scenic center of things in the lower town.

Tourist Office: Tallinna Turismiamet, Raekoja Plats 8 (tel. 44 88 86 or 66 69 59, fax 44 12 12), across from the Town Hall in Old Town. Shares space with **Danest Travel** (tel. 66 65 31) on the first floor. Get city maps (in English, 18EEK), hotel lists, and other useful brochures. The friendly English- and German-speaking staff will quote schedules and prices, while the Danest Travel agents can make bookings for ferries, planes, and other modes of transport. Information on package tours and other fun stuff also available. Open daily 10am-5pm.

Tours: Estonian Holidays (tel. 30 19 36 or 30 19 30) offers the bizzare Mystery Murder and Madness Tour, a 2-hr. walking tour of all the eerie spots in Tallinn.

Embassies: U.S., Kentmanni 20 (tel. 45 53 28 or 825 24 40 91; open Mon.-Fri. 8:30am-5:30pm). **U.K.,** also at Kentmanni 20 (tel. 31 20 21 or 825 24 02 04; open Mon.-Fri. 9:30am-12:30pm and 2-4:30pm). **Finland,** Liivalaia 12 (tel. 44 9522; open Mon.-Fri. 9am-2pm). **Russia,** Pikk 19 (tel. 44 30 14; open Mon.-Fri. 9am-noon). **Germany,** Raevela maantee 9 (tel. 45 56 06; open Mon.-Fri. 9am-noon). **Latvia,** Tönismägi 10 (tel. 68 16 68; open Mon.-Fri. 8am-1:30pm and 2:30-5pm).

Currency Exchange: Five **valuutavahetus** (currency exchanges) line the inside of the central post office, offering competitive rates that are among the best in Tallinn. In the Old Town, **AS-Tavid,** 31 Pikk, just up from Hell Hunt, has equally good rates. Open Mon.-Fri. 9am-6pm, Sat.-Sun. 10am-5pm.

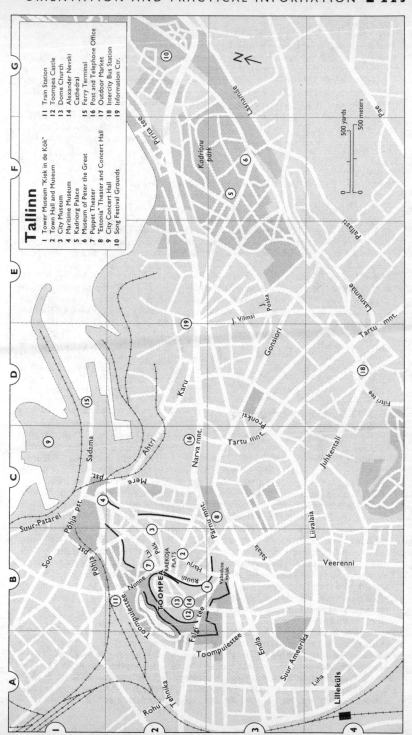

Tallinn

1 Tower Museum "Kiek in de Kök"
2 Town Hall and Museum
3 City Museum
4 Maritime Museum
5 Kadriorg Palace
6 Museum of Peter the Great
7 Puppet Theater
8 "Estonia" Theater and Concert Hall
9 City Concert Hall
10 Song Festival Grounds
11 Train Station
12 Toompea Castle
13 Dome Church
14 Alexander Nevski
   Cathedral
15 Ferry Terminal
16 Post and Telephone Office
17 Outdoor Market
18 Intercity Bus Station
19 Information Ctr.

500 yards
500 meters

ESTONIA

Post Office: The central *postkontor* is at Narva maantee 1, across from the Hotel Viru. Postal services on the second floor, including **Poste Restante**. Open Mon.-Fri. 8am-8pm, Sat. 9am-5pm. **Postal Code:** EE-0001.

Telephones and Telegraph Office: Central office on the first floor of post building at Narva maantee 1. Open daily 7am-10pm. Buy collector's edition phone cards (700EEK) and then call mom direct from the orange card-phones. Fax services here also (fax +372 (6) 31 30 88 from the U.S.—note the special city code). Local phones in Tallinn sometimes are free of charge, sometimes require a 20-senti coin, and (or also) sometimes just don't work. A phone-card system should be in place soon. It's possible to call Helsinki using Finnish marks in the special phones at the airport and the ferry terminal. The **telephone city code** is usually 249, but is 6 for new digital lines.

Flights: Estonian Air flies the Tampere, Finland-Tallinn route three times per week (840mk).

Ferries: The **Tallinna Reisisadam** (Tallinn Harbor) is a 15-min. walk from the city center, north on Mere puiestee. Bus #65 can take you there from Hotel Viru or the train station. **Estline** (tel. 31 36 36) runs ferries to Stockholm (every other day, 15hrs.; student deck fare 480EEK). **Tallink** (tel. 60 19 60) runs ferries to Helsinki (3-4 per day, 4hrs., 120mk). **Tallink** and **Estonian New Line** (tel. 42 83 82) both run **hydrofoils** to Helsinki in the summer (each 3 per day, 1½hrs.; 140mk). A ferry to Travemunde, Germany is in the works, to run twice weekly for about 720EEK. Ask at the tourist office for information.

Trains: The **Balti jaam** (Baltic station) at Toom puiestee 35 can be reached by tram #1 or 2 from the Hotel Viru (tel. 45 68 51 or 44 67 56; open daily 6:30am-11pm.). Almost unbelievably modern, with announcements in English and no shoving crowds of people. To: St. Petersburg (2 per day, 10hrs.; 108EEK, 66EEK in *platskartny* class); Minsk (1 per day, 23hrs.; 282EEK, 178EEK in *platskartny* class); Narva (5 per day, 4 hrs., 25EEK); and Tartu (5 per day, 3-4hrs.; 22EEK). Buy same-day international tickets at windows 4-6; if you're organized, buy them in advance upstairs at windows 7-12. Get domestic tickets (same-day only) at windows 13-18. The *Balti Ekspress* can whisk you away to Warsaw via Riga, Kaunas, and a train change at Šeštokai, Lithuania (1 per day, 21hrs., 851EEK, 551EEK in *platskartny* class). Buy tickets at window 7; 25% discount for students with ISIC. For train information, call 45 68 51 or 44 67 56 daily 6:30am-11pm.

Buses: The **Autobussijaam** (station) is on Masina, just south of Tartu maantee, and 1.5km southeast of the Old Town (tel. 31 32 22; open 4:30am-midnight). Tram #2 or 4 and bus #22 connect to the city center. To: Rīga (4 per day, 7hrs.; 71EEK); Kärdla on Hiiumaa Island (8 per day, 5hrs.; 39EEK); Kuressaare on Saaremaa Island (10 per day, 5-6hrs.; 52EEK); Tartu (25 per day, 2½hrs.; 38EEK); and Narva (3 per day, 4hrs.; 46EEK). Buy advance tickets at windows 1-2, same-day tickets at windows 4-6. Station open 4:30am-midnight. Call 31 32 22 for information.

Public Transportation: Buses, trams, and trolleybuses cover the entire Tallinn suburban area; each category has separate stops marked with ideograms. All run from 6am-midnight and require tickets which can be purchased only at newspaper kiosks (0.85EEK). Punch them once on board. You can get a comprehensive schedule (the *Tallinna Transporti Teatmik*) from some kiosks, but without a route map, it's not very helpful. A route map does exist, but only on a Russian-language map of Tallinn—hopefully this little tourism glitch will be cleared up soon.

Taxis: Around Hotel Viru, they'll likely overcharge you. Find a *Takso* stand, or call tel. 60 30 44 for the state-run agency. Rides around Tallinn, as far out as the bus station or the ferry terminal, should cost no more than US$6.

Luggage Storage: Rent lockers in the downstairs of the train station for 3EEK. Open 5:30am-11:30pm.

Pharmacy: RAE Apteek, 47 Pikk, has a good selection of Western medical supplies (mostly Scandinavian). Open Mon.-Fri. 9am-6pm. The pharmacy in the **Hotel Viru** is also well-stocked. **Raeapteek,** on the north side of Raekoja Plats, beats everybody when it comes to experience—it's been open since 1422.

Bookstores: Browse in the excellent **Homeros** at Mündi 5, just off Raekoja plats. They have a wide variety of works in English, German, and French. Open Mon.-Fri. 10am-7pm, Sat.-Sun. 11am-5pm. Buy your reference materials, including city guidebooks such as *Tallinn at Night* (10EEK), at **Kupar,** Harju 1, southeast of Raekoja plats. It also stocks navigation charts, maps, and travel books covering all of the Baltics. Open Mon.-Fri. 10am-6pm, Sat. 11am-3pm.

Laundry: At the corner of Herne and Magasini, a long block south of Liivalaia, the **Laundri** will do your wash for 8EEK per kilo, with one-day service.

Emergencies: Fire: tel. 01; **Police:** tel. 02; **Ambulance:** tel. 03.

ACCOMMODATIONS

While other prices skyrocket in rapidly-westernizing Tallinn, affordable rooms are still plentiful. Anticipated renovations of the Agnes and the Vitamin may change the picture somewhat by summer 1995, but the new **hostel** (in the process of opening in summer 1994) should even things out. HI-affiliated, the hostel is on the corner of Pârnu and Liivalaia, about 1km south of Old Town. All guests must register through the office of the **Karol** travel agency, nearby at Lembitu tn. 4/7 (tel. 45 49 00). Prices were not set at press time; expect to pay around 195EEK per person.

Not to be overlooked are the rooms available through the **bus station.** Inquire at the information desk in the main hall about a place to sleep; if there's room, you can grab a perfectly clean bed (communal bathrooms) for the amazingly low price of 40EEK a night. If you plan to come in after the bus station closes at midnight, you can even get a key. No reservations are accepted.

Agnes Youth Hostel (HI), Narva mnt. 7 (tel. 43 88 70), east of the Hotel Viru. Take tram #2 from the bus or train station. The hostel is in the courtyard. 34 bare-bones rooms with 2-4 beds each. Communal showers and bathrooms, complemented by a friendly Russian-speaking staff who also know some German and English. Knock on the door to get in after midnight. Beds 100EEK, students 90EEK. Open June 1-Aug. 24.

ETK Hotel Vitamin, Narva mnt. 7 (tel. 43 85 85), just a couple doors east of the Agnes. Same empty-feeling rooms with beds and a wardrobe, but the bathrooms are shared by fewer people. No English spoken. Singles 200EEK. Doubles 400EEK. The bar inside the hotel doesn't really merit a visit.

Family Hotel Service (Hua Ai Trade Ltd.), Mere puiestee 6 (tel. or fax 44 11 87), also near the Hotel Viru. Arranges private rooms with access to bathrooms and kitchen. Singles 100-190EEK. Doubles 180-290EEK. The more expensive rooms are in Old Town. It's best to call a couple of days ahead, but sometimes rooms can be arranged on the spur of the moment. Office open daily 10am-5pm.

CDS Reisid (Baltic Bed and Breakfast), Raekoja Plats 17 (tel. 44 52 62, fax 31 36 66), on the second floor. CDS sets up private rooms, breakfast included, with English-speaking hosts. They'll pick you up at the airport, train station, or wherever when you arrive in Tallinn. Singles 265EEK. Doubles 400EEK. Make reservations in advance. Office open Mon.-Fri. 10am-6pm, Sat.-Sun. 10am-3pm.

FOOD

Tallinn's Old Town and its surroundings are beginning to fill with small restaurants whose low prices and large portions guarantee budget travelers' satisfaction. On Uus 7, the **Roosakas Panter** (Pink Panther) 24-hr. store beckons the night owl. Tallinn also has quite a handful of Western-style **supermarkets,** where you can see ex-patriate Americans weep with joy at the chance to buy Hawaiian Punch, Lucky Charms, and Pop Tarts. The largest is **Kaubahall,** Aia tn. 7, a stone's throw from the Viru Gates into Old Town (open Mon.-Sat. 9am-8:30pm, Sun. 9am-3pm). The smaller **Kauplus Tallinn,** Narva maantee 2, across the street from the Hotel Vitamin, is open later and has better prices (open daily 9am-10pm).

Paks Margareeta (Fat Margaret's), Pikk 70, in the gate-tower housing the Maritime museum. A genuine American-style sub shop run by two gents from California. Getting a steady supply of roast beef in Tallinn can be problematic, but when they have it, the subs are heavenly. Small subs 12-15EEK, large 28-34EEK. After you eat, climb up to the observation deck atop the tower for a great view. Open daily 10am-6pm.

Sanjay's, Rataskaevu 5, on the second floor of a four-restaurant complex. A palate-pleasing mix of Indian and Chinese food is served amidst wingback chairs and white tablecloths. Spicy Singapore-style fried rice 34EEK, most other main dishes 50-70EEK. Visa, MC accepted. Open daily noon-11pm.

Foster's (The Tex-Mex Place), Tartu maantee 50, one tram stop west of the bus station. Hidden inside the Flexer Sports-club, this is the only Mexican food in the Baltics, so get it while you can. Burrito the size of your foot (unless you're Shaq) 35EEK; dripping chili cheeseburgers 25EEK. Fresh-baked pies differ from night to night (13EEK per slice). Open Mon.-Fri. 9am-9pm, Sat.-Sun. 10am-9pm.

Rüütli Baar, Kohtu 2, in a portico across from the Toomkirik. An oddly irreverent restaurant/bar with fake stained-glass windows and the steady drone of slot machines. Pan-fried trout with fries and veggies 19EE, *seljanka* (thick fish soup) 9EEK, and a Saku to wash it all down 12EEK . Open daily noon-11pm.

Baar Vegan, Uus 22, serves several vegetable and grain dishes from which you can compile a meal; each heaping ladleful costs 0.60-3EEK. Hot, clear soups 2EEK. Fruit and vegetable juices and literature on vegetarianism also available. Open daily 10am-6pm.

Eesli Tall, Dunkri 4 (tel. 44 80 33). The "Donkey Stable" is the best place in Tallinn for Balto-Russian cuisine; there's been a restaurant in these halls since the 1300s. It throngs with tourists in summer, so call ahead for dinner. Sup on meat and vegetarian dishes (20-50EEK) or tasty omelettes (9-20EEK) in a crazy post-modern interior: wooden planks in the ceiling are painted in floral patterns and futuristic landscapes. Open Sun.-Thurs. noon-midnight, Fri.-Sat. noon-1am.

Maiasmokk Kohvik, Pikk 16, where Pikk meets Pühavaimu. The first marzipan and chocolate producer in Estonia (est. 1864), they serve ice cream (8-15EEK), tea, coffee, chocolates, and pastries in the ground-floor café. The upstairs restaurant (separate entrance) is a good bet for lunch, with frothy soups (5-18EEK) and excellent salted or smoked trout sandwiches (7EEK—order a few, they're small). Café open Mon.-Sat. 8am-7pm, Sun. 10am-6pm; restaurant open daily 11am-10pm.

SIGHTS

You can get acquainted with the Old City by starting at Hotel Viru, walking down Narva maantee, and then continuing on along Viru past the 15th-century **Viru City Gate.** Along Uus, which runs north just inside the walls, there's a large sweater **market** during the summer; in winter it moves into the flower stalls that line Viru. Continue up Viru to **Raekoja Plats** (Town Hall Square) where handicrafts are sold on summer evenings and folk songs and dances are performed on a small outdoor stage. The **Raekoda** (Town Hall) was built between 1371-1404 and is guarded by **Vana Toomas** (Old Thomas), a cast-iron figurine of the legendary defender of Tallinn which dates from 1530. Thomas has done a good job so far; this is the oldest surviving town hall in Europe. Behind the Raekoda, at Raekoja 4/6, you'll find the **Raemuuseum** which served as the town jail the middle ages. Nowadays it houses an interesting exhibit on early Estonian photography and some contemporary Estonian sculpture (open Thurs.-Tues. 10:30-am-5:30pm; admission 3EEK). On the north side of the square, the claustrophobic Saia kang (Bread alley) twists its way out onto Pühavaimu, where the 14th-century **Pühavaimu kirik** (Holy Ghost Church) sports a 15th-century bell-tower and an intricate (but usually wrong) 17th-century wooden clock. Nearby is Hell Hunt (see below) if you're in the mood for a drop of ale.

For a view of the northern towers and bastion of the medieval city, from Viru go up Vene, take a right on Olevimägi, and then head up Uus. Along the way, you can bore yourself silly with rooms full of 19th-century knick-knacks at the **Tallinn City Museum** on Vene 17 (open Wed.-Fri. 10:30am-5:30pm, Sat.-Sun. 10:30am-4:30pm; admission 2EEK). In the large squat tower called **Paks Margareeta** (Fat Margaret), you'll find the **Meremuuseum** (Maritime museum), Pikk 70, which holds changing exhibits on Tallinn's history as a busy port (open Wed.-Sun. 10am-6pm; admission 5EEK). Be sure to grab lunch at the sub shop inside.

Going back down Pikk, you'll run into **Oleviste kirik** (St. Olav's Church), the tallest church in town, on your right. The murals inside the adjoining chapel illustrate the architect's death after he fell from the tower (open Sun. 10am-5pm; services Mon. and Thu. at 6:30pm). Go all the way down to the end of Pikk and hang a left on Rataskaevu to see **Niguliste kirik** (St. Nicholas' Church), frequent site of organ concerts, and its mighty spire. Inside is a fragment of Bernt Nothe's medieval masterpiece, *Danse Macabre* (open Wed. 2-9pm, Thurs.-Sun. 11am-6pm; admission 3EEK). At the base of the hill lie undisturbed World War II ruins, left as a reminder of the Russian bombing that gutted much of south Tallinn in 1944. Farther south along Rüütli, on your left you'll see the **Kiek in de Kök** (Peek in the Kitchen) tower; its name is an allusion to the fact that from it you could see into everyone's home in 16th-century Tallinn. The tower, still pockmarked with embedded cannonballs, was built in 1475 and has six floors of art and historical exhibits (open Tue.-Fri. 10:30am-5:30pm, Sat.-Sun. 11am-4:30pm; admission 3EEK). Straight ahead is the **Neitsitorni** (Virgin Tower), where you can drink *hõõgviin* (hot mulled wine) and hobnob with Bohemians. The doorman extorts a 3EEK entrance fee, and you'll get nailed with another 3EEK charge if you wander out onto the balcony.

Following the Lühike jalg uphill onto the Toompea from St. Nicholas' church will bring you out into Lossi Plats, a square dominated by the **Alexander Nevsky Cathedral,** begun under Tsar Alexander III and finished just a few years before the Bolshevik Revolution. A marble marker from 1910 recalls Peter the Great's victory over the Swedes in 1710. The exterior is under renovation, but the sumptuous interior is worth a look. (Open daily 8am-7pm.) The **Toompea Castle,** the present seat of the Estonian *Riigikogu* (parliament), rises directly before you here, but the door is barred to prying eyes. Directly behind it rises **Pikk Hermann,** the tallest of the towers in Tallinn, always topped by a fluttering Estonian flag. The recently opened **Eesti Kunstmuuseum** (Estonian Art Museum) on Kiriku plats across from the Toomkirik, higher up on the Toompea. It displays Estonian art from the 19th century to the 1940s, including a compelling exhibition of art-nouveau/avant-garde book printing from independent Estonia. (Open Wed.-Mon. 11am-6pm. 5EEK.) There are three excellent lookout points from the Toompea, all surrounded by artists selling watercolor versions of the views. The viewpoint at the north end of Kohtu, on the west side of Toompea, gives the best panorama of Old Town.

On the eastern side of Tallinn, reachable by tram #1 or 3: Kadriorg, is the seaside **Kadriorg Palace and Park.** The palace, erected from 1718-36 under Peter the Great, was home to the Imperial Family under the Tsars, and was the residence of the President of Estonia in the 1920s and 30s. Under the Soviets, it housed a collection of Estonian paintings and sculptures. It is now closed for renovations until mid-1995; whether it will again be a museum or a presidential palace is still up in the air. Also in the park is the wooden **Peter the Great Home Museum,** a cottage used by the great man while his palace was being built. (Open summer daily 9:30am-7:30pm; admission 5EEK.)

In **Rocca-Al-Mare,** a peninsula 12km west of Tallinn, the quaint **Estonian Open-Air Museum,** Vabaõhumuuseumi 12 (tel. 55 91 76), "contains" a collection of wooden mills and farmsteads from the 18th-20th centuries. Take bus #21 from the train station (30 min.) or a taxi (70EEK). (Open May-Oct. Wed.-Sun. 10am-6pm; admission 10EEK, students 6EEK).

ENTERTAINMENT AND NIGHTLIFE

In July, **Rock Summer** draws students and bands from around the world to Tallinn for a week-long music fest. In 1994, over 30 bands played; the $25 tickets allowed entry all week to hear the Pogues, Phil Collins, and Phish. For more info contact Makarov Music Management (tel. 23 84 03).

The verdict is in and it's not even close: when it comes to a night on the town, Tallinn clearly knocks out the rest of the former Soviet Union. While Minsk, Moscow, and Kiev suffer between the scylla of grim, vodka-doused cellars and the charibdys of slick, mafia-run nightclubs, Tallinn boasts a hefty pint of excellent drinking establishments.

ESTONIA

Hell Hunt (The Gentle Wolf), 39 Pikk. A rocking Irish Pub with Guinness and Killian's on tap. The pub in the back room serves up a mean cottage pie (30EEK); wash it down with Irish Coffee (21EEK) or make a sacrifice to the Tri-penile WolfGod with a shot of the special Hell Hunt home-brew, "Some Kind of Brandy" (25EEK). Never a cover charge, which is why you'll meet everyone here. Live music nightly, including local Irish bands. In summer, an outdoor beer garden dispenses suds across the street as long as it's light out. Open Sun.-Mon. 10am-1am, Tues.-Thurs. 10am-2am, Fri.-Sat. 10am-3am.

Eesli Tall Baar, Dunkri 4, in the cavernous cellar of the restaurant. Sailors, tourists, and intellectuals wander through a labyrinth of colored lights, archways, nooks, and crannies to imbibe and dance the night away. Saku Tume on draft 14EEK, imported beers 25-30EEK, and nightly live music. Open daily 4pm-4am.

George Brownes Irish Pub, Harju 6, 300 meters south of Raekoja Plats on the north edge of the Vabaduse väljak (Freedom Square). The posh lounge upstairs is out of the budget traveler's range, but the ground-level pub has live music in the evenings, several dartboards, and good bar snacks. Come during Happy Hour (Mon.-Thu. 5-7pm) to take advantage of two-for-one Guinness on tap (45EEK per pint). Open Mon.-Thurs. noon-11pm, Fri.-Sat. noon-midnight, Sun. noon-10pm.

Von Krahli Teater/Baar, Rataskaevu 10, on the western edge of the lower Old Town. The avant-garde theater showcases Baltic talent ranging through Lithuanian jazz, experimental dance, and cutting-edge music blending Gregorian chant with techno. The attached split-level bar has Saku (12EEK) and a dance floor that wiggles like nothing you've ever seen. Bar open daily 6pm-4am. Theater has shows at most nights at 8 or 10pm (tickets 15-20EEK).

Mündi Baar, Mündi 5, just off Raekoja Plats. A dark network of rooms in the cellar favored by locals. Have a Saku for less than at the supermarket (10EEK), and grab a corner table while your eyes adjust to the near-total lack of light. A good place to practice your Estonian. Open daily 2pm-3am.

■■■ TARTU

First mentioned in 1030 when a Kievan Prince burned the place down, Tartu is the oldest city in the Baltics. Since that inauspicious beginning, Tartu has been burned to the ground 55 times; very little remains of the medieval city. Tartu is most famous for its university (the oldest in Northern Europe) and its role in the Estonian and Latvian **National Awakenings.** As the only university town in the Russian province of Livonia, Tartu was the home of 19th-century Baltic nationalists who worked furiously to promote indigenous culture and to press for freedom from Moscow. As part of that struggle, the first **Estonian Song Festival** was hosted here in 1869; every five years since, thousands have convened to celebrate the occasion. The main festival has been held in Tallinn since 1894, but in 1994 30,000 people descended on Tartu. The summer traveler will see very little academia in action, but the 10,000 students at the University give the city an air of hipness unique in the Baltics which creates the perfect atmosphere for an afternoon or two of exploration.

ORIENTATION AND PRACTICAL INFORMATION

Tartu is a sprawling city, the second-largest in Estonia. Luckily, everything the traveler needs is located within a square kilometer bordered by the bus and train stations. The **Raekoja Plats** (town hall square) is at the center of the action, running west from the Emajõgi river towards the old castle hills. Rüütli heads north from the square; its end at Lai marks the boundary of the Old Town. Vabaduse Puistee follows the river southeast from the square to the bus station. In back of Town Hall, Lossi meanders uphill between the two peaks of the **Toomemägi** (Cathedral Hill). After passing under two bridges between the hills, Lossi dumps out into Vallikraavi, a crooked, cobblestoned road that together with von Baeri follows the path of the old moat circling the hills. The stretch of Vallikraavi that goes south meets up with Kuperjanovi, which in turn continues southwest to the train station.

Tourist Offices: There is an excellent office in Tartu, just off Raekoja Plats at Kûûtri 3 (tel. 321 41). An English- and German-speaking staff can answer questions, arrange hotel rooms, provide maps, and do just about anything else you need or want. The erratically-available and somewhat spotty *Tartu This Week* (5EEK) is a pale shadow of its brother guide to Tallinn. Open Mon.-Fri. 10am-6pm.

Tours: E-Tour, Gildi 5 (tel. 44 11 63), offers guided, 90-min. sightseeing tours of Tartu (30EEK).

Currency Exchange: Good rates are available at **ERA-Pank,** 11 Raekoja Plats. Open Mon-Thu. 9am-5pm, Fri. 9am-4pm). Beware—there are no 24-hr. offices.

Post Office: The *postkontor* is at Rüütli 15. Open Mon.-Fri. 9am-7pm, Sat.-Sun. 10am-3pm. **Postal Code:** EE-2400.

Telephone and Telegraph Office: Just north of the *Postkontor,* at the corner of Rüütli and Lai. Card-phones and a fax machine (fax 43 39 93). Open 24 hrs. Tartu is starting to reassign all of its telephone numbers, going from five to six digits. The current **telephone city code** is 234, but with the new numbers it will be 7.

Electronic Mail: In the University Computing Center (Arvutuskeskus), J. Liivi 2, just south of where Lossi meets Vallikraavi on the west side of the Toomemägi. Hours vary according to staff availability.

Flights: The airport, 8km south of the city, is inactive at present. Last year, the government ended airline subsidies, and all service here ended within months. Oops. Ask at the tourist office to see if flights to Tallinn will resume in winter 1994-5.

Trains: The *Vaksali* (station) is on Vaksali (original, eh?) at the intersection with Kuperjanovi, a good 1.5km southwest of city center. Information booth open daily 8am-1pm and 2-8pm. Trains clatter to: Riga (2 per day, 5hrs.; 72EEK); Moscow (1 per day, 18hrs.; 150EEK); and Tallinn (5 per day, 3hrs.; 40EEK). The *Baltic Express* also zips through Tartu daily en route to Warsaw (13hrs., 470EEK).

Buses: The *Bussijaam* (station) is on Vabaduse Puistee at the corner with Riia, about 0.3km southeast of Raekoja Plats along Vabaduse (tel. 47 53 55; open daily 4:45am-11:30pm). There are virtually no buses to destinations outside of Estonia. To: Narva (3 per day, 4hrs.; 36EEK); Pärnu (7 per day, 4hrs.; 38EEK); Tallinn (25 or more per day, 2-5hrs.—try to get an express bus; 38EEK); Valga (2 per day, 2hrs.; 17EEK). Every Monday, a private bus runs from Tartu to Berlin (28hrs. 900EEK, students 765EEK) via Riga (5hrs., 150EEK, students 125EEK); for info. tel. 47 22 46.

Public Transportation: Scarcely necessary; no buses run in the area between Raekoja Plats and the Toomemägi. Bus #12 for no apparent purpose runs from the bus station to the unused airport every half-hour daily 6am-7pm.

Taxis: Vast fleets wait outside the bus and train stations, charging 2EEK per km. A cross-town ride from the bus to the train stations runs about 15EEK.

Luggage Storage: Lockers (3EEK) on the main floor of the train station; buy tokens inside the room marked *"Vaksali Korraloaja"* in the main lobby.

Pharmacy: **Raekoja Apteek** (tel. 33 528) on the north side of Town Hall. Open Mon.-Fri. 8am-8pm, Sat. 9am-4pm.

Emergencies: Fire: tel. 01; **Police:** tel. 02; **Ambulance:** tel. 03.

ACCOMMODATIONS

There aren't many budget options left in Tartu in the aftermath of the 1994 Song Festvial (which prompted many hotels to renovate their rooms and their prices). The tourist office can help ferret out cheaper accomodations if those below are full.

Tartu Ülikool Üliopilaskonna Edustus (Tartu Students' Union), Narva Maantee 25 (tel. 353 31), right across the river from Raekoja Plats. It's best if you go early in the morning to the tourist office on Küütri; they get priority in reserving spaces for foreigners, and can arrange rooms for as little as 30EEK per night. If you arrive later, try going by between 2-4pm, when reception is officially open. Shared washrooms and somewhat spartan accommodation, but it's close and cheap.

Tartu Võõrastemaja, Soola 3 (tel. 320 91), behind the bus station. A hotel and a youth hostel. Soviet-stamped rooms with communal showers, but also a sauna (54EEK per hour). Singles 170EEK, doubles 230EEK. With an HI card, prices drop 50EEK.

ESTONIA

Hotel Salimo, Kopli 1 (tel. 47 08 88), 3km southeast of the train station off Võru; no buses even run close. Generic rooms with bare-bones furnishings and no-nonsense dingy white paint. Singles and doubles with private toilet and shower 75EEK.

FOOD AND ENTERTAINMENT

It's strange that in a university town there aren't more cheap, downscale restaurants. Try the bulletin boards just inside the entrance to the main university building (Ülikooli 20) for flyers on all the local events. Summer brings lots of folk music to Tartu, so be on the lookout for posters.

Restaurant-Bar Taverna, Raekoja Plats 20 (tel. 43 12 22), in the cellar of the out-of-place statue-cluttered Baroque building. Intended to be an upscale Italian restaurant, but also outstanding for its Estonian dishes. *Grillitud loomafilee* (grilled steak) 47EEK, *Milaano aedviljasupp* (Minestrone) 12EEK. Management can be picky about dress; don't wear shorts. Open daily noon-6pm, 6:30pm-midnight.

Püssirohukelder, Lossi 28 (tel. 341 24). This cavernous 18th-century gunpowder cellar in the side of the Toomemägi, now houses a two-level cellar bar and the jolliest restaurant in town. Make reservations for Wed., Fri., and Sat. nights, because the variety/erotic show (9-11pm) draws a full house. Clientele is slowly evolving into the Mercedes-and-Rolex crowd; you may feel out of place in a t-shirt, but they'll let you in. A full meal (soup, salad, main course, beer) runs 100EEK.

Kohvik Ülikooli, Ülikooli 20, in the university building. A good place to meet students and discuss the differences between Estonian and Finnish literature over a cup of coffee (2.40EEK) and cakes (1EEK). Open Mon.-Sat. 11am-9pm.

Pingviin, Vabaduse Puistee 2-a, at the base of Raekoja Plats. For some cosmic reason, this link in the chain spells its name differently than all the other. Oh, those wacky Estonians! Ice cream 5EEK. Open daily 8am-10pm.

SIGHTS

Raekoja Plats (Town Hall Square) is the center of Tartu. Appropriately, the Town Hall, a late 18th-century edifice now painted pink and white, dominates the square. The entire square dates to 1775, when the medieval market which previously stood on the site burned down in a gigantic fire—the most recent of the conflagrations that repeatedly razed the city. Nearly all of the buildings rest on wooden pylons, and some are slowly sinking into the marshy ground; 18 Raekoja Plats, once the house of Barclay de Tolly (a Scottish adventurer in the Russian army who became famous in the war against Napoleon) is the most dramatic example.

Ülikooli runs north-south behind the Town Hall; to the north, it passes **Tartu University** *(Tartu Ülikool).* The university was founded in 1632 as the University of Dorpat by King Gustavus II Adolphus of Sweden, making it the oldest university in northern Europe. The Great Northern War closed its doors in 1700, but when the dust finally settled 100 years later, Tsar Alexander I ordered it reopened, and the magnificent yellow collonaded building at Ülikooli 20 was constructed in 1803 to house it. The **Museum of Classical Art,** a small but charming gathering of Roman and Greek art, awaits inside (open Mon.-Fri. 11am-4:30pm; admission 5EEK). With the university's emphasis on science, and classes taught only in German and Russian, it is somewhat surprising that the **Estonian National Awakening** had its beginnings at the university. Nonetheless, in 1870 the **Eesti Üliopilaste Selts** (Estonian Student Association) was founded here, at the only university in Russia with the right to have fraternities. The nationalists who made up this fraternity became so central to the struggle for independence from Russia that when Estonia became free in 1919, the fraternity's colors (blue, white, black) became those of the national flag.

Farther up Ülikooli is the **Jaani-kirik** (St. John's Church), completed in 1323. Nearly unique in Gothic architecture were the thousands of terra-cotta figurines of saints, martyrs, and other figures which once adorned the outside walls, apparently depicting the Last Judgement. The Russian recapture of Tartu in 1944 nearly destroyed the church. Only a few hundred figures remain today, and the building itself is scarcely standing. Restoration was started in the 1980s, but funds have dried up, and the project is on hold for now. Across the street, the **Museum of the 19th-Century Tartu Citizen** has displays on town life in a particular era we'll leave for you to surmise (open Wed.-Sun. 11am-6pm; admission 6EEK).

The **Toomemägi** (Cathedral Hill) dominates Tartu from behind Town Hall. On the western hump are the majestic remainders of the 15th-century **Toomkirik** (Cathedral of St. Peter and Paul). Secularized into a granary during the late 1600s, the university took over the decaying cathedral in 1806 for a library. Today it houses the **Museum of Tartu University,** an in-depth series of displays with descriptions in Russian, Estonian, and German (open Wed.-Sun. 11am-5pm; admission 6EEK). Close by the church, the **Musumägi** (Kissing Hill) was once part of a prison tower, but is now a make-out spot. This is also the site of an ancient pagan **sacrificial stone,** where students now burn notes after exams. A **statue** of Karl Ernst von Baer tops this hill; the prominent embryologist also adorns the 2-kroon note.

The eastern hump of the Toomemägi can be reached by two bridges. The eastern bridge is the pink wooden **Angel's Bridge** *(Inglisild),* built in the 1830s. To the west, the **Devil's Bridge** *(Kuradisild)* is a less dramatic concrete span from 1913. Every year, a competition between the university choirs takes place on these bridges: men on the Devil's Bridge, women on the Angel's Bridge. Draw your own conclusions. On this part of Cathedral Hill is the **Observatory,** which was built in the early 19th century to house a 9-inch lens, in its time the largest in the world. The observatory now houses a museum and serves as a laboratory for the university (museum open Mon.-Fri. 11am-4pm; free). Nearby, down the hills, the **Estonian National Museum,** Veski 32, contains hordes of ethnographic materials and special displays on the National Awakening that started in Tartu (open Wed.-Sun. 11am-6pm; admission 7.50EEK).

■■■ PÄRNU

Pärnu is located 130km south of Tallinn on Estonia's west coast. The 19th-century heart of the city has been commercialized rapidly; staying on the main thorough-fare, Rüütli, will give you an incomplete picture of Pärnu. The best way to discover the charm of this coastal city is to walk on the wide, white sand of the Rand (beach) or through the immense parks immediately behind the beach. The beach pavilions and beautiful houses on the Esplanaadi (boulevard) were built in the late 19th century when Pärnu was famed throughout the Russian Empire for its therapeutic waters and mud baths.

Orientation and Practical Information Grab Pärnu maps and information at the closest thing to a **tourist office,** the Reiser Travel Agency, Rüütli 35 (tel. 445 00, fax 448 85). You can **exchange money** at the Hotel Pärnu; the rates aren't great (open 8am-midnight; see below). The **post and telephone office,** Akadeemia 7, is at the west end of Rüütli, less than 1km from the bus station *(postkontor* open Mon.-Fri. 8am-6pm, Sat.-Sun. 9am-3pm; *telefon/telegraaf* open daily 7am-10pm). The **postal code** is EE-3600; the **telephone city code** is 244. The **train** station *(Vak-sali)* is east of the city center, by the corner of Riia maantee and Raja (take buses #4 or 22 to and from the central post office). Passenger service south to Riga has stopped for the time being, and there never was a line going east, so you might as well catch one of the two daily trains north to Tallinn (3½hrs, 35EEK). Pärnu is best reached by **bus;** the station *(Pärnu Busijam)* is in the very center of town, a block down Ringi from the bus parking lot on your right (open daily 5am-9pm). Trains leave to: Riga (5 per day, 4hrs.; 41EEK); Tallinn (10 per day, 2-3 hrs.; 30EEK); Tartu (2 per day, 5hrs.; 40EEK); Kuressaare (4 per day, 3hrs.; 36EEK); and Haapsalu (2 per day, 3hrs., 24EEK). You can **store luggage** in the bus station, go through the door opposite the ticket office inscribed *Pakihoid* (3EEK). The Apteek at Rüütli 39 is the most western **pharmacy** in town (open Mon.-Sat. 9-am-7pm).

Accommodations The most centrally located rooms are at the **Hotell Pärnu,** Rüütli 44 (tel. 509 00, fax 509 05), right by the bus station. All rooms include TV and private bath. The "renovated" rooms feature new Danish furniture but not much else and aren't worth the extra money. (Singles 210EEK, renovated 510EEK. Doubles 290EEK, renovated 510EEK. Visa and AmEx accepted. Breakfast included.) The **Hotell** at Seedri 4 (tel. 430 98) near the beach is a small, plain place with hall showers and toilets, but with a fridge and a sink in every room (singles and doubles 120EEK). **Hotel Kajakas,** Seedri 2 (tel. 430 98), has a sauna but no hot water, and is otherwise identical to the hotel next door (singles and doubles 140EEK). If you've got the kroons, stay in the stunningly-renovated **Art Deco Rannahotell,** a luxury resort founded in 1938, on Ranna allee (tel. 453 12) a scant 100 yards from the ocean (doubles 1180EEK, breakfast included).

Food and Entertainment Just off the beach next to the mud baths, the high-ceilinged **Rannasalong** is a 1930s-era dance hall and restaurant that now also houses a restaurant and a movie house. A typical menu for the Baltics, but with Estonian spellings is served: *Seljanka* (7EEK), *Böfstrogaanof* (16EEK), and ice-cold *Saku* beer (6EEK; open daily noon-midnight). **Trahter Postipoiss,** Vee 12, has a courtyard café and restaurant in a 19th-century post office. Dine on excellent roast chicken (12EEK per quarter-chicken), and spicy soups (7-9EEK; open daily 11am-midnight). Batman's archnemesis, the **Pinguin,** plots apocalyptic revenge while serving up ice cream (5.50EEK) at Pühavaimu 13, just off Rüütli (open daily 10am-7pm). Other than the overpriced discos in the Hotell Pärnu and the Rannahotell, the only nightlife is the **Diskoklubs "Hamilton"** at Rüütli 1, just past the post office in the outdoor theater. Different DJs from all over Estonia spin tunes every night. (Cover 25EEK; open summer daily 9pm-5am.) Around Midsummer night *(Jâânipaev),* Pärnu hosts the week-long **FiESTa International Jazz Festival,** along with the **Baltoscandal,** a modernist extravaganza of Baltic and Scandinavian theater.

Sights Facing Hotell Pärnu at Rüütli 53, you'll find the **Museum of the City of Pärnu,** a quintessential municipal museum full of old clothes and arrowheads (open Wed.-Sun. 11am-6pm; admission 6EEK). The only other museum in town is the **Lydia Koidula Museum,** Jannseni 37, across the Pärnu river in the childhood home of the 19th-century poet who led a revival in Estonian-language verse and drama (open Wed.-Sun. 10am-4pm; admission 6EEK). South on Nikolai from Rüütli, you'll find the stern rust-red **Eliisabeti Kirik,** built in 1747. Farther west, at the corner of Uus and Vee a block north of Rüütli, the Russian Orthodox **Ekatarina Kirik** is a multi-spired, spiky, silver and white edifice of the 1760s. Rüütli ends at an **open-air theater** in the shadow of the ramparts constructed around a Swedish fortress of the late 1600s. The formidable **Tallinna Värav** (Tallinn Gate), the only gate into the city when the Swedes held it before the Great Northern War, pierces the ramparts at their widest point.

The broad, tree-lined street leading south from the Tallinn Gate takes you to a long pedestrian zone just behind the **beach.** Surrounding the boardwalk is the massive **Rannapark,** a great green area filling what was a vast empty space before its sudden leap to prominence when the therapeutic powers of its marshy mud were discovered in 1838. A small **amusement park,** including a ferris wheel (2EEK), lies just off the boardwalk (open summer daily 10am-8pm). The beach is the most inviting area of town; there are signs with disheartening notices such as "the water is too dirty for swimming" but no one seems to heed them. For **nude bathing,** wander up the beach to the right, well past the Rannasalong. Those famous **Mud Baths** that started Pärnu on the path to greatness still function in the neo-classical bath-house at the southern end of Supeluse puistee, where the pedestrian boardwalk ends. Pamper yourself silly with massage, sauna, mud baths, and therapeutic silt water (whatever that is.) (Open daily 9am-3pm; mud bath 70EEK).

■■■ HAAPSALU

Famed in the 19th century for its curative muds, Haapslu was once the seat of the Saare-Lääne (or Ösel-Wiek) Bishopric, which encompassed much of western Estonia and the islands. Under the Soviets, the city's main distinction was its airbase, but today Haapsalu is slowly regaining its reputation for a fine yachting harbor; already a resort feel is in the air. Ferries to the Estonian islands depart daily from 9km to the south, making Haapsalu a pleasant stopover en route to or from Tallinn.

Orientation and Practical Information Get the lowdown on Haapsalu maps, reservations on the Vormsi ferry, or tickets on the next flight from Tallinn-Oslo at the local **tourist/travel office,** Läänemaa Reisid/Westland Travel, Karja 2 (tel. 450 37, fax 457 72; open Mon.-Sat. 9am-5pm). The **post office** *(postkontor)* is appropriately located at Posti 1 (open Mon.-Fri. 7:30am-6pm, Sat. 8am-4pm). The **postal code** is EE-3170. The **telephone-telegraph office,** Kalda 2, just north of the post office, dot-dash-dash-dots to all corners of the world (open daily 7am-10pm). The **telephone city code** is 247. **Trains** are a rarity now in Haapsalu, though Tsar Nicholas II came here so often that he had a massive covered platform built so none of his party would get wet while disembarking from the train. The station still stands, apparently left to rot, on Raudtee at the southern end of town. One daily train still creeps to Tallinn (3 hrs., 25EEK). From the (functioning) station, walk east on Jaama past the market, and turn left on Posti at the traffic lights to reach central Haapsalu. **Buses** run frequently from the rail station to: Tallinn (17 per day, 2hrs.; 20EEK); Pärnu (2 per day, 2-3hrs.; 28EEK); Kärdla (2 per day, 3hrs.; 24EEK); and Virtsu (2 per day, 2hrs.; 23EEK). The nearby town of **Rohuküla,** 9km west of Haapsalu, offers ferries to Hiiumaa (hourly 10:30am-8:30pm, 1hr.; 20EEK) and Vormsi (Mon.-Fri. 3 per day, Sat.-Sun. 2 per day, 30 min.; 25EEK). Bus #1 runs to Rohuküla from the station in Haapsalu hourly. Keep in mind that it's significantly cheaper to take a bus from Haapsalu to Kärdla (Hiiumaa) or Sviby (Vormsi) than it is to ride the ferry alone and grab a bus once on the islands. For a **taxi** call tel. 453 30.

Accommodations Top dog in Haapsalu, especially during yachting season when everything else is likely full, is **Hotell Laine,** on the shores of the Väike-viik (tel. 441 91 or 442 91). It was the Sanatorium Laine in a previous life; it's amazing just how much a coat of paint can do to a place. No TV, but you can get a massage (100EEK per 90min.) or a pedicure at your leisure. (Singles 180EEK. Doubles 260EEK. Breakfast in the airy, cruise-ship-feel restaurant included, but the forgetful staff may not even charge you for the room.) Follow Posti north until it ends near the castle, go two blocks west on Ehte, then two blocks north on Sadama gatve; the entrance is at the rear of the building. If the Laine is full, try the **Haapsalu Hotell,** Posti 43 (tel. 448 47, fax 451 91), a completly renovated place that reeks of Western European involvement (and prices). The meticulously kept rooms include brand-new Scandinavian furniture, cable TV, and mini-bars with prices that'll make your eyes pop. (Singles 350EEK. Doubles 450EEK. Six-person suites with sofas are a good deal at 600EEK. Visa and AmEx accepted. Breakfast included.)

Food and Entertainment Sit down to dinner in the **Rootsituru Kohvik,** Karja 3 (tel. 450 58), a pink building on the corner with Ehte in the shadow of the castle. Be amazed as the Estonian chef proves that a standard ex-Soviet menu of *solyanka, borsch, karbonade, schnitzel,* and potatoes need not entail lukewarm, tasteless lumps. In fact, it's darn good—especially the mashed (!) potatoes. Try the *kala taignas,* a succulent salmon dish (36EEK; open daily 11am-10pm). Do your best to find a copy of the free broadside *Two Weeks in Haapsalu,* usually available at the Haapsalu Hotell, for information on events in town. The hot place at night is **Africa Discotheque,** Tallinna mnt. 1 (tel. 452 91), at the south end of Posti. Bigger and better than anything in Riga, Vilnius, or other nearby cities, the disco boasts tuxedoed staff, the bar has every kind of booze imaginable (except Southern Comfort), the

ESTONIA

men sport cellular phones and Rolexes, and there are eight women for every guy in the place. Go ahead, ask one to dance—that's what they're paid to do. The place if full of post-1989 *nouveaux riches,* so don't spit on the BMWs or Mercedes Benzes. (Cover Sun.-Thurs. 15EEK, Fri.-Sat. 25EEK Open Sun.-Thurs. noon-3am, Fri.-Sat. noon-5am.) The attached **Show-Bar** gyrates, thrusts, and strips nightly from 9pm; additional cover 100EEK.

Sights The center of Haapsalu is the 13th-century **Piiskopilinnus** (Bishop's Castle), finished in 1228. Enter it from Lossiplats, the square just east of the north end of Karja. Home to the Bishop of Saare-Lääne until he moved to Saaremaa in 1358, the castle is now mostly picturesque ruins surrounding the more impressive **cathedral.** The cathedral has a varied past, thrice destroyed and abandoned (most recently destroyed by a storm in 1726, it was left unrepaired until 1887). On the night of the August full moon, Haapsalu's **White Lady,** the ghost of a woman walled up in the cathedral for crossing its threshold in the 1280s—a time when only men were allowed inside—makes an apparitional appearance in one of the cathedral windows. The event is celebrated by a week-long **festival** including a play based on the story (castle grounds and cathedral open daily 7am-10pm).

If you've come to wallow in those famed mud baths, you're late; the last one dried up in 1953. But you can still wander along the blustery, sandy **Aafrikarand** (Africa Beach) northeast of the castle at the end of Rüütli. The old promenade runs 2km up to the yacht club, a wonderful walk on a sunny day.

■■■ KURESSAARE

A major resort between the World Wars, the island of Saaremaa was off-limits to out-siders during the Soviet occupation; consequently its largest city, Kuressaare, is reckoned to be more Estonian than Estonia itself. Despite a population of 16,000, Kuressaare is a sleepy but charming town; it was the seat of the Saare-Lääne bishop-ric from 1358 until the Bishop sold the island to the Danes in the 16th century. The Bishop's castle still dominates the town, but it is the pristine beaches and virgin woods of Saaremaa which define the feel of the city.

ORIENTATION AND PRACTICAL INFORMATION

Kuressaare rests on the south side of the Estonian island of Saaremaa, an easy three-hour bus ride from Tallinn. Kuressaare is a small place; you can walk from the Bishop's Castle on the west side of town to the modern bus station on the eastern border in less than 15 minutes. From the station, downtown is a short three blocks along Tallinna; at the center lies **Raekoja plats,** the narrow town square. Lossi con-tinues south from the square towards the castle. Maps of the town and the island are plentiful, there are at least two with English text; pick them up at the tourist office, the bus station, or from your hotel (10-15EEK).

Tourist Office: Baltic Tours, Tallinna 3 (tel. 554 80), on the Raekoja plats. Not exactly a tourist office, but they can help with ferry information, English-language **tours** around Kuressaare, hotels, etc. Open Mon.-Fri. 9am-1pm and 2-5pm.

Currency Exchange: Plenty of them around Kuressaare, including one inside the Baltic Tours office (see above).

Post Office: Torni 1, at the corner with Komandandi, one block north of Tallinna. Stamps, envelopes, and other postal paraphernalia. Open Mon.-Fri. 8am-6pm, Sat.-Sun. 10am-3pm. **Postal Code:** EE-3300.

Telephones and Telegraph: Shares quarters with the post office. Phone cards, etc. Open daily 7am-10pm. **Telephone City/Island Code:** 245; for digital lines (faxes, etc.) dial 5 instead.

Trains: This is an island, remember? No iron rails in these parts.

Buses: Autobussijaam, Pihtla tee 2 (info tel. 573 80, tickets 562 20), at the intersection with Tallinna. Frequent buses to the mainland: Tallinn (6 per day, 3-4hrs.; 52EEK); Pärnu (2 per day, 3hrs.; 36EEK); and Haapsalu (4 per day, 3hrs.; 34EEK).

Flights: Kuressaare Airport is 3km south of the city center on Roomassaare tee. During the winter of 1993-4, Estonian Airlines flew a Tallinn-Kuressaare route for 310EEK (60EEK for residents of Saaremaa) one way; flights were suspended for summer, but are expected to resume in winter. Contact Estonian Airlines in Tallinn (tel. (249) 44 63 82).

Ferries: If you're going to the Estonian mainland, it's easier (and cheaper) to take a direct bus (which will get first priority on the ferries). Most ferries to or from Saaremaa go through the port of **Kuivastu,** at the eastern end of Muhu Island 60km east of Kuressaare; crossings are to the town of **Virtsu** on the mainland (up to 30 per day, winter 10 or fewer per day, 20 min.; 5EEK). Call the terminals for information (tel. (245) 98 435 from Kuivastu, (247) 75 520 from Virtsu). Tiit Kruuse (tel. 956 89) runs a ferry on weekends to Hiiumaa from the northern Saaremaa port of **Orissaare,** 45km northeast of Kuressaaare (Sat.-Sun. only, 1 per day, 3hrs.; 55EEK; see Hiiumaa below). All buses to the mainland pass through Orissaare; buy tickets from the driver and remind him to stop there. Rumors hold that ferry service to Riga will resume in 1995 on a twice-weekly basis. Contact a travel agent to check on the status of this exciting crossing.

Public Transportation: In a city this small, buses are almost unecessary, but they do exist. The most important is #2, which runs roughly every 45 minutes from Raekoja plats to the airport (1.50EEK).

Taxis: There's a stand on the Raekoja plats, or you can call (tel. 549 39, 573 89, or 555 77). They're supposed to charge 2EEK per km outside of Kuressaare, a fairly economical rate for reaching other areas of the island; be sure to settle the fare before you go, however.

Bike Rentals: Steady Ltd., Vallimaa 5A (tel. 558 78), next door to the Mardi Öömaja. One-speeds 50EEK per day, including lock. Open daily 9am-6pm.

Pharmacy: Saaremaa Apteek, Lossi 1 (tel. 545 48), on the south end of the Raekoja plats. Not much Western stuff, but more than other places in town. Open Mon.-Fri. 8am-8pm, Sat. 9am-4pm, Sun. 9am-3pm.

Emergencies: Fire: tel. 01; **Police:** tel. 02; **Ambulance:** tel. 03.

ACCOMMODATIONS AND CAMPING

New pensions and small bed and breakfasts are sprouting up in Kuressaare all the time as the city regains its inter-war reputation as a resort town. Check in with a travel agent upon arrival to find out about the new crop, or try one of the following:

Panga Pansionaat, Tallinna 27 (tel. 579 89), around the back of the Kuressaare Maapank and sharing a phone line with them. Sparkling, airy rooms in a clean and modern place that feels like home. Floor showers or bath. It's a small pension, so make reservations if possible. Singles 190EEK. Doubles 380EEK. Large room-service breakfast included.

Mardi Öömaja, Vallimaa 5A (tel. 574 36), entrance at the rear of the large white building. Large but clean institutional-style rooms share toilet and shower (no hot water) with one other room. Reception on the second floor. Singles 100EEK. Doubles 200EEK. Triples 300EEK. Quints 500EEK. Got the pattern yet? The restaurant downstairs serves a Swedish-table breakfast for 30EEK.

Lossi Hotell, Lossi 27 (tel. 544 43, fax 560 84), in the park just meters from the Bishop's Castle. A wonderful wooden inn from the turn of the century, remodelled into a 15-room bed and breakfast. Floor toilets and showers. Singles 220EEK. Doubles 440EEK.

Camping: Kämping, in Mändjala (tel. 751 93), 8km outside of Kuressaare at the "Kämping" bus stop. Clean sandy beach, secluded pine woods. 98EEK per person in 4-bed rooms, breakfast included. Tent sites 10EEK. Open May 30-Sept. 1.

FOOD AND ENTERTAINMENT

Most restaurants in Kuressaare insist on calling themselves a *kohvik* (café), but there's plenty of food and beer at prices to make hardened travelers weep with joy.

ESTONIA

Kohvik Kursaal, Pargi 2, in the park north of the Bishop's castle. Definitely the best restaurant in town, located in a 1889 dance hall with high windows, ceiling fans, and the air of a bygone era. Main courses 7-19EEK, ice cream with brandy 5.40EEK. You won't find more tender beef anywhere in the Baltics. *Saku* 8EEK. Open daily noon-midnight.

Kodulinna Kohvik, Tallinna 11, downstairs off the Raekoja plats. The bar is pitch black, but grope your way into the restaurant for immense pancakes stuffed with rice and beef (4.90EEK), *schnitzel* (35EEK), soups (4.80EEK), or an ice-cold *Saku* (6.50EEK). Open daily 9am-3am.

Kohvik Veski, in the old windmill at Pärna 19, two blocks west of the Raekoja plats. Ludicrously Soviet "service," but convince them to give you a table—the food is excellent. Try making a reservation early in the day. While you sit in silent protest over the empty tables all around you, guzzle down some *Kuressaare* beer (on tap, 7EEK). Main dishes are 17-33EEK, including *eskallop*, a spicy fried pork cutlet (32EEK). When you're finished eating, try not to seethe about the 5EEK charge for "music" from the radio. Open daily noon-midnight.

Pinguin, east side of Raekoja plats. Yet another branch scoops up its flightless-waterfowl-inspired ice cream imitations (7EEK per scoop).

Disko Skada, in the Kino just north of Raekoja plats on Tallinna. The hot place on Saaremaa; stay long enough and you'll meet everyone from ages 13-35 in Kuressaare. Different DJ every night. 25EEK cover. Open nightly 10pm-whenever.

SIGHTS

The **Raekoja plats** (town hall square) is surrounded by interesting buildings from the 17th century, including the 1653 weighing-house, the first market in Kuressaare, and the 1670 **Raekoda,** a squarish building still serving its intended function as town hall. Just past the south end of the square stands a **monument** to the 1918-20 struggle for independence. Farther down Lossi, the simple **Nikolai Kirik** (St. Nicholas' church) was built in 1790 for the newly arrived Russian garrison.

Keep heading south and you'll soon see the **Kuressaare Linnus-Kindlus** (Episcopal Castle), the town's main attraction. First built in 1260 shortly after the Teutonic Order subdued the islanders, the present castle was constructed from 1336-80 as the island home of the Bishop of Saare-Lääne; he liked it so much that in 1358 he made it the administrative center of the bishopric. The castle traded hands a number of times during its history, starting when the Bishop sold it to the Danes in 1559. Later it became a Swedish, then a Russian stronghold. The Tsar finally retired the venerable fortress from military use in 1899. The castle houses the **Saaremaa Regional Museum,** a collection of stuffed wildlife, old bicycles, and trinkets from the 19th century and the 1918-20 War for Independence. The innumerable twisting and turning passages, stairwells, towers, and halls are enough to keep you busy all day; pick up a much-needed map (2EEK) at the entrance. (Castle and museum open Wed.-Sun. 11am-7pm. Last entry 5:30pm. Admission 18EEK, students 6EEK.)

After seeing the castle, stomp on over to the **Dinosauruste Minimaailm,** Pärgi 5A, a terrific collection of dinosaur bones, dioramas, models, and pictures sure to please the first-grader in all of us (open Wed.-Sun. 11am-6pm; admission 18EEK).

■ NEAR KURESSAARE: SAAREMAA ISLAND

Rent a bike and pedal south to the quiet, clean beaches of **Mändjala** and **Järve,** covering a stretch 8-12km from Kuressaare. Beaches dot the road south of here, such as the one at Tehumardi where a giant, ugly concrete sword marks the location of a 1944 battle. Farther on, 17km out of Kuressaare, the town of **Salme** makes a good lunch stop at the start of the **Sõrve Peninsula,** a 32km-long thumb of land pointing toward Latvia. About 2km out of Salme, take the major turnoff to the right (an unpaved road) and cut over to the western side of the peninsula, where the open Baltic makes for rocky beaches with good surf. At **Kaugatuma,** the locals make much of the "cliffs," but there is a good lookout from the lighthouse, and you can sunbathe alongside contended cows on the fossil-strewn beaches. Five kilometers farther down the road are the ruins of the World War II Lõpe-Kaimri trenches. Staying on the major gravel road, which now cuts inland, 12km of travel will bring you to the (real) cliffs at Ohessaare. At the very tip of the peninsula, the **Sõrve säär,** clear weather opens up a vista to Latvia, 25km south across the Baltic; see if someone will let you into the old lighthouse. Warning: the ride to the tip of the peninsula, especially on the one-speed bikes rented in Kuressaare, is likely to leave you with a really sore rump.

If you're left unsatisfied by the cliffs to the south, try out the 60m wonders at **Panga,** on the north coast of Saaremaa. Or just look at the picture on the back of the 100-EEK note. Buses to Panga leave from and return to Kuressaare just twice daily (2hrs., 10EEK), so be careful not to get stuck out there.

■ ■ ■ HIIUMAA

Originally settled by Swedish fisherfolk, Hiiumaa supported a large Swedish community right up until World War II, when the remaining 5000 were evacuated from the island to Sweden. Today Hiiumaa, Estonia's second-largest island, is a quiet, sparsely-populated wonder, with only 11,000 residents on its 1060 sq. km, most of whom live on the coast in small farming communities. Sealed off to outsiders (Russians, Estonians, and foreigners alike) for the fifty years of Soviet occupation, Hiiumaa has emerged as from a time capsule, virtually unchanged since the 1930s. Flat, woody terrain makes Hiiumaa ideal for biking, and inexpensive rental cars make it easy to take in all the island's sights, including scores of 19th-century windmills, the third-oldest lighthouse in the world, and a land bridge built by giants.

Orientation and Practical Information Hiiumaa is roughly cross-shaped, with the long end pointing west into the Baltic Sea. **Kärdla,** the only real city on the island (pop. 4000) is located on the north coast; **Käina,** with 200 residents, is the second-largest town, 16km away on the south coast. Roads (mostly paved) ring the island, but the interior is a woody wilderness unblemished by human habitation. The *Hiiumaa Reisijuht Guide* (10EEK), an excellent map of the island, is available at the **tourist office** on the north side of the Keskväljak in Kärdla (tel. 913 77). Run by Peace-corps volunteer Douglas Wells, this is one of the best-prepared tourist offices in the Baltics; ask any question and you'll almost certainly get an answer. Douglas helps arrange **car and bike rentals** (Russian mini-van 2EEK per km, quite a bargain for groups), and is a veritable font of information about **hiking** and wilderness possibilities (office open daily 9am-6pm).

Two **ferries** connect Hiiumaa to the outside world. From **Rohuküla,** just south of Haapsalu on the mainland, ferries make the 1-hour crossing to **Heltermaa** on the eastern tip of the island (Mon.-Fri. 9-10 per day, Sat.-Sun. 4-5 per day; winter 2 or fewer per day depending on the ice, that can make the journey take up to 36hrs.). Fares are low (10EEK), but it's easier to take a bus directly from Haapsalu to Kärdla or Käina (24EEK). For info on schedules, especially in winter, call the ferry ports (tel. 94 212 in Hiiumaa; 91 355 in Haapsalu). From the island of Saaremaa, a brand-new ferry service links tiny **Orissaare** to even tinier **Kassari.** For information, call the boat's captain, Tiit Kruuse (tel. (245) 956 89 on Saaremaa; see above). In Orissaare, get off the bus and walk straight down the road toward the large pink building; turn left at the post office and go to the farther docks. While you wait, a kohvik on the dock serves piping hot coffee (3EEK). The partially refitted fishing boat makes the crossing in three hours (departs Orissaare Sat.-Sun. at 9am, returns from Kassari at noon. One way 55EEK). Unfortunately, once you're in Kassari on the south coast of Hiiumaa, there's no bus to any other part of the island until 5 pm; it's a 5km walk to Käina, the nearest large settlement.

On Hiiumaa, it's theoretically possible to take local **buses** to any point of the island that has a house on it, since any mailbox is equivalent to a bus stop. But buses run to remote areas only once a day at best, and even between Käina and Kärdla, there can be 6-hour gaps in service. If you feel like getting somewhere anytime soon, state-run **taxis** (tel. 98 091) are a reasonable option (2EEK per km); the catch is that all are based in Kärdla, and you have to pay both directions of the driver's journey. To leave the island, go to the bus station in Kärdla, at the corner of Sadama and Kalda. Buses depart for Tallinn 4-6 times per day. **Exchange money** in Kärdla at the Kärdla Maapank, Põllu 3, just east of the Keskväljak (open Mon.-Fri. 9am-4pm); in Käina try the Hotell Liilia. The central Hiiumaa **post office** is in Kärdla, at Posti 7 about 200m north of the bus station (open Mon.-Fri. 8:30am-4:30pm, Sat. 9am-1pm). The **postal code** is EE-3200. The **Telephone and Telegraph Office** shares its quarters (open 24 hrs.). The **city/island telephone code** is 246.

Accommodations and Food There isn't a wide variety of places to stay on Hiiumaa, a legacy of its off-limits status to outsiders for 50 years. In Kärdla, **Est Dago Travel** runs the small **Võõrastemaja Kärdla,** Vabaduse 13 (tel. 914 45), left off Valli from the Keskväljak. No showers, and only cold water in the sinks, but there is a sauna next door (open 11am-7pm). They only have room for about 24 people, so arrive early (35EEK per person in doubles or quads). Another option is the **Hotell Sönajala,** Leigri väljak 3 (tel. 993 36), well south of the town center. Adjoining a tennis club, the rooms here are fairly plush and the sinks (but not the showers) have hot water. The staff speaks only Estonian, Swedish, and German. Walk south on Rookopli from the Keskväljak, turn right on Kõrgessaare maantee (the major intersection with a big stone head on the corner), and left onto Sönajala. The hotel will be in the complex on your right (20min.; singles 25EEK, doubles 50EEK). The third and final option is the **Best Western Hotell Liilia,** Hiiu maantee 22 (tel. 921 46, fax 925 46), on the central square in Käina. It's unclear why there's a Best Western in this neck of the woods, but the restaurant is pleasant, and Tiu, the woman who runs the bar, can tell you all the folk myths about the island. Besides, there's hot water, soft beds, and a mint on your pillow. (Singles 540EEK. Doubles 710EEK. Breakfast included.)

In the hamlet of **Kõrgessaare** (also called Viskoosa), about 17km west of Kärdla, a large granite-block building, first a 19th-century silk factory and later a vodka distillery, houses the best restaurant on the island. The **Viinaköök** (Vodka kitchen) has a hearty feel, a warm and woody interior, and specializes in serving up genuine Hiiumaa wild boar (45EEK). They isn't always a boar though; the salmon dishes are mouth-watering (20-30EEK; open Tue.-Sat. 11am-3am, Sun.-Mon. 11am-10pm). In Kärdla, grab an omelette (3EEK) for breakfast at **Priiankru,** Sadama 4, a pink wooden building at the corner with Posti (open daily 8am-midnight).

Sights Much of the island has been included in the **West-Estonian Islands Biosphere Reserve** on account of the immense variety of plants and waterfowl found here (more than two-thirds of all the plant species known in Estonia exist only on Hiiumaa). **Hiking** and **camping** are permitted and encouraged ways of viewing this cornucopia of wildlife, but be sure to pick up info on off-limits areas from the tourist office in Kärdla. The office also puts out *The Lighthouse Tour,* a guidebook to the sixteen major sights on Hiiumaa (16EEK). The highlight is the towering **Kõpu Lighthouse** on the western peninsula of the island. Constructed in the early 1500s by the Hanseatic League, a stairwell was an afterthought and was literally hacked out of the solid rock to provide access to the top. Over 100m high, the view from the top is an awe-inspiring panorama of the Baltic Sea, including all of Hiiumaa, and (on a sunny day) the island of Saaremaa to the south. Farther west of Kõpu, there is an abandoned Soviet **radar facility** at the tip of the island, at what used to be the northwesternmost point of the Soviet Union. On the south side of Hiiumaa, 1km from the town of Kassari, be sure to wander out onto the **Sääretirp,** a 1-3m-wide peninsula extending over 3km out into the sea, lined with wild strawberries and juniper bushes. Legend holds that this is the remains of a bridge built by the giant Leiger between Hiiumaa and Saaremaa so that his brother Suur Töll could come for a visit.

HUNGARY (MAGYARORSZÁG)

US$1	= 108.70forints (Ft, or HUF)		100Ft =	US$0.92
CAD$1	= 79.53Ft		100Ft =	CAD$1.26
UK£1	= 170.54Ft		100Ft =	UK£0.59
IR£1	= 167.34Ft		100Ft =	IR£0.60
AUS$1	= 80.97Ft		100Ft =	AUS$1.23
NZ$1	= 59.08Ft		100Ft =	NZ$1.69
SAR1	= 30.62Ft		100Ft =	SAR3.26
DM1	= 70.72FT		100Ft =	DM1.41
Country Code: 36			International Dialing Prefix: 00	

Forty-five years of isolation and relative powerlessness under Soviet rule are a mere blip in Hungary's prolific 1100-year history, and traces of socialism are evaporating with each passing iron-free day. Budapest dominates the country, though the capital by no means has a monopoly on cultural attractions. No provincial center is more than a three-hour train ride through corn and sunflower fields from Budapest. To the north lies the dramatic Danube Bend on the Slovak border and six low mountain ranges; to the east lies the Great Plain, long ago the home of the Hungarian woodsman, but now the range of the Magyar cowboy. In the west lies Transdanubia, once a Roman province, and subject to an ever-shifting set of influences ever since. To the southwest is Lake Balaton, the largest lake in Central Europe. Try not to forsake the beauty of the countryside for a whirlwind tour of the capital—you'll have skirted the heart of the country but will have missed its soul entirely.

HUNGARY

HUNGARY ESSENTIALS

Citizens of the United States, Canada, U.K., Ireland, and South Africa can travel to Hungary visa-free with a valid passport. Australians and New Zealanders must obtain 30-day tourist visas from their Hungarian Embassy (See Essentials: Embassies and Consulates, page 3) valid for 6 months after their date of issue, for US$15 (single entry), US$30 (double entry), US$60 (multiple entry) and US$15 (transit). Add US$5 for rush (on-the-spot) service. Obtaining a visa takes one day, requires a valid passport, 2 photographs (4 for multiple entry) and payment by cash or money order. You can apply for a visa extension at police stations in Hungary, but tourist visa holders cannot stay more than 90 days.

GETTING THERE AND GETTING AROUND

Hungary's national airline, **Málev,** began daily direct flights (9hrs.) from New York's Kennedy airport in May 1994. Budapest's **Ferihegy airport** handles all international traffic. Hungary's domestic transportation network radiates out from Budapest; most rail lines swerve through the capital. Use buses to travel among the outer provincial centers, or plan on returning to Budapest to make connections.

Hungarian **trains** *(vonat)* are reliable and inexpensive; Eurail and EastRail are valid here. Travelers under 26 are eligible for a 33% discount on domestic train fares. An **ISIC** commands discounts at IBUSZ, Express, and station ticket cowpunchers. (Book international tickets several days in advance.) The student discount on international trains is roughly 30% but sometimes you need to be persistent. Try flashing your ISIC and repeat "student," or the Hungarian, *"diák"* (pronounced DEE-ahk).

Személyvonat are excruciatingly slow; *gyorsvonat* trains (listed on schedules in red) cost the same and move at least twice as fast. All of the larger provincial towns are accessible by the blue express rail lines *(expressz)*. New air-conditioned Inter-City trains are the fastest way to travel. The express fare from Budapest to any of the provincial cities is between 400-900Ft one way, including a seat reservation (required on trains marked with "R" on schedules). Some basic vocabulary will help you navigate the rail system: *érkezés* (arrival), *indulás* (departure), *vágány* (track) and *állomás* or *pályaudvar* (station, abbreviated *pu.*). **International tickets** are no longer the bargain they once were. Budapest round-trip second-class to: Vienna (US$26); Prague (US$46); Warsaw (US$52), Munich (US$88). Berlin is 16hrs. away by train, Bucharest 19hrs. The platform for arrivals and departures is rarely indicated until the train approaches the station—there will be an announcement in Hungarian. If you don't understand, ask someone official at the very last moment—changes often occur up until then. Vendors sell drinks on long-distance and express trains.

The extensive **bus** system is cheap but crowded; it links many towns whose only rail connection is to Budapest. The **Erzsébet tér** bus station (*C4*) in Budapest posts schedules and fares. Inter-city bus tickets are purchased on the bus (get there early if you want a seat), while tickets for buses, trams, and the subway must be bought in advance from a newsstand (25Ft) and punched on board; they generally can't be bought from the driver and there is a 600-800Ft fine if you're caught ticketless. The Danube **hydrofoil** (via Bratislava) is the most enjoyable (and most expensive) way to go to Vienna. The trip between Vienna and Budapest costs about US$70, round-trip US$100; with ISIC, US$54, round-trip US$83 (payment in Austrian Schillings). Eurail pass holders receive a 50% discount. There is a US$10 charge for bicycles (one-way). Luggage is free up to 20kg; over that it is one dollar per kg. Some travelers **cross the Austrian border** by hitching on Highway E5, the main thoroughfare between Vienna and Budapest. *Let's Go* does not recommend hitchhiking as a safe method of transportation. Hitching, especially around Budapest, has become more dangerous in the past few years. It is a four-hour drive capital-to-capital. Avoid crossing the border on foot.

Over 600 street names in Budapest alone have changed since the 1989 revolution, so it's advisable to get the most recent maps available. To check if your map of

Budapest is useful, look at the avenue leading from Pest toward the City Park *(Városliget)* in the east: the modern name should be Andrássy út. Hungarian addresses usually involve one of the following: *utca,* abbreviated *u.* (street); *út* and the related *útja* (avenue); *tér* and the related *tere* (square, but may be a park, plaza, or boulevard); *híd* (bridge); and *körút,* abbreviated *krt.* (ring-boulevard). A single name such as Baross may be associated with several of these in completely separate parts of a city—i.e. Baross út, Baross u., Baross tér, etc. Numbers on either side of the street are not always in sync; some streets are numbered odd and even, some up one side and down the other, and some in consecutive primes.

Either IBUSZ or Tourinform can provide a brochure about **cycling** in Hungary that includes maps, suggested tours, sights, accommodations, bike rental locations, repair shops and recommended border-crossing points. Write to the tree-huggers at the **Hungarian Nature-Lovers' Federation** (MTSZ), 1065 Budapest, Bajcsy-Zsilinszky út 31 *(C3-4),* or the **Hungarian Cycling Federation,** 1146 Budapest, Szabó J. u. 3, for more information. Some rail stations rent bicycles to passengers.

TOURIST SERVICES

Perhaps the best word for foreigners in Hungary to know is **IBUSZ,** the Hungarian national travel bureau. Their offices throughout the country can make room arrangements, change money, sell train tickets, and charter tours. Snare the pamphlet *Tourist Information: Hungary* and the monthly entertainment guides *Programme in Hungary* and *Budapest Panorama* (all free and written in English). **Express,** the former national student travel bureau, handles youth hostels and changes money. Regional travel agencies are more helpful than IBUSZ and Express in the outlying areas. **Tourinform** is a fantastically helpful, non-profit information service with locations or licensed local agencies in all of Hungary's 19 counties. They have many free and helpful brochures and answer all your questions about Budapest and the rest of Hungary, often serving as interpreters.

General **business hours** in Hungary are Monday to Friday from 9am to 5pm (7am-7pm for food stores). Banks close around 3pm on Friday, but hours continue to expand. Larger shopping centers and food stores may sell food on Sundays; also try the numerous 24-hr. private food stores. Tourist bureaus usually open Monday-Saturday 8am-5pm in the summer (some are open until noon on Sun.); in the winter these hours shrink to Monday to Friday 10am to 4pm. Museums are usually open Tuesday to Sunday 10am to 6pm, with occasional free days on Tuesday. Students with an ISIC often get in for free or pay only half-price. Nothing is open on national holidays—including Christian festivals, May 1, and August 20. A national holiday on March 15 honors the 1848 revolt against the Habsburg Empire; October 23 commemorates the Hungarian uprising against the Soviets in 1956.

MONEY

The national currency is the *Forint* and is divided into 100 *fillérs.* The forint was depreciating in the summer of 1994 from an exchange rate of around 100Ft to US$1; it *may* be around 120-150Ft to US$1 in summer 1995. **Change money** only as you need it. Make sure to keep some Western cash to purchase visas, international train tickets and (less often) private accommodations. Hard currency may grease the wheels to lower prices and better service. **American Express** offices in Budapest, and IBUSZ offices around the country, convert traveler's checks to cash for a six percent commission. Cash advances on credit cards are available at a few locations in Budapest. All major credit cards are accepted at more expensive hotels and at many shops and restaurants; the smaller ones accept only American Express. The best exchange rates during summer 1994 could be found at branches of the OTP, IBUSZ, Mezőbank, agricultural banks, and MKB in Budapest. New Zealand dollars cannot be exchanged here, so pack another currency. At the few exchange offices with extended hours, the rates are generally poor. The maximum permissible commission for currency exchange (cash to cash) is one percent. Black market exchanges are both illegal and strikingly common, but the rates offered are rarely favorable enough (an extra 10%) to risk the large chance of being swindled. To make sure currency is not counterfeit, hold the note toward a light and find the metal strip. In banks outside of Budapest, there are no separate lines for currency exchange. Allow half an hour to exchange money, or go to IBUSZ for a marginally lower rate.

COMMUNICATION

Western newspapers and magazines are available in many Budapest newsstands and in large hotels. Hungary's English-language paper *Daily News* is published weekly. Used bookstores *(antikvárium)* often have English books at fire-sale prices. English-language radio and TV programming is found in the English language *Budapest Week,* which has excellent listings, survival tips, helpful hints, and articles about life in Hungary (published every Thursday, free at American Express offices and larger hotels; 62Ft). The weekly Hungarian-language flyer *Pestiest* lists all movies, concerts and performances in Budapest; pick up a free copy in restaurants, theaters, and clubs.

There are three **radio** stations that play Western programming in Hungary: Danubius, Juventus, and Radio Bridge, which broadcasts *Voice of America* news programs every hour. The frequencies vary from region to region, but in the Budapest area they are 103.3 FM, 89.5 FM, and 102.1 FM respectively.

Almost all telephone numbers in the countryside now have six digits and begin with "3." Hungary's pay **phones** require 10Ft per minute for local calls, 25Ft per minute for long-distance calls within Hungary. Wait for the tone and dial slowly. For long distance, dial 06 before the city code (two digits long, except for Budapest). **International calls** require red phones or new, digital-display blue ones, found at large post offices, on the street and in Metro stations. Though the blue phones are more handsome than their red brethren, they tend to cut you off after 3-9 minutes. At 160Ft per minute to the U.S., telephones suck money so fast you need a companion to feed them. Half of the public phones throughout the country require **telephone cards,** available at kiosks, train stations, and post offices. Direct calls can also be made from the telephone office in Budapest, with a three-minute minimum to the U.S. To call collect, dial 09 for the international operator. To reach the **AT&T USADirect operator,** put in a 5, 10 or 20Ft coin (which you'll get back), dial 00, wait for the second dial tone, then dial 80 00 11 11. To reach the **MCI WorldPhone operator,** dial 80 00 14 11; to reach the **Sprint Express operator,** dial 80 00 18 77; to reach the **Canada Direct operator,** dial 80 00 12 11; to reach the **BT Direct operator** (U.K.), dial 80 04 40 11; to reach the **Mercury Call UK operator,** dial 80 00 44 12; to reach the **Ireland Direct operator,** dial 80 00 35 31; to reach the **Australia Direct operator,** dial 80 00 61 11; to reach the **New Zealand Direct operator,** dial 80 00 64 11. Older six-digit Direct numbers may still be used until December 31, 1994. There is no charge to call the above Direct numbers.

The Hungarian **mail** system is perfectly reliable (airmail—*légiposta*—to the U.S. takes 5-10 days). Note that if you're mailing to a Hungarian citizen, the family name precedes the given name, as in "McCorkell Kimberly." Because Hungary's per capita telephone rate is the second-lowest in Europe (Albania wins/loses), it is very common to send telegrams, even across town. Ask for a telegram form *(táviratiűrlapot)* and fill it out before returning to the counter. Post offices are indicated by the sign **POSTA** and are generally open Mon.-Fri. 8am-7pm, Sat. 8am-1pm.

LANGUAGE

Hungarian belongs to the tongue-torturing Finno-Ugric family of languages that includes Finnish and Japanese. English is the country's very distant third language after Hungarian and German—much of western Hungary is set up for German speaking tourists. In eastern Hungary, however, even German may fail. *"Hallo"* is often used as an informal greeting or farewell. *"Szia!"* (sounds like "see ya!") is another greeting—it's common to hear long-parted friends cry, "Hello, see ya!" Those long-latent charades skills may yet come in handy; you'd be amazed what acting out your question can accomplish. Beware certain idiosyncracies, though; for example, if you want to visually express numbers, remember to start with the thumb for "one"—holding up your index finger means "wait."

A few starters for pronunciation: *c* is pronounced "ts" as in ca*ts; cs* is "ch" as in *ch*imichanga; *gy* is "dy" as in the French "*adieu*"; *ly* is "y" as in *y*am, *s* is "sh" as in *sh*ovel; *sz* is "s" as in Seattle; *zs* is "*jh*" as in pleasure, and *a* is "*a*" as in *a*lways. The first syllable usually gets the emphasis. Some useful phrases:, *kérek* (KEH-rek, "I'd like..."); *fizetni szeretnék* (VI-zet-ney SEH-ret-nayk, "I'd like to pay"); *beszél angolul/németül* (BES-el AWN-gohlul/NAY-met-yuhl, "Do you speak English/German?"); *viz* ("water"); *sör* (SHUR, "beer").

Word or Phrase	Spelling	Pronunciation
Yes	*Igen*	EE-gen
No	*Nem*	nem
Hello	*jó napot*	YOH naw-pot
Good morning	*jó reggelt*	YOH reh-gehlt
Good night	*jó éjszakást*	YOH ay-sokat
Good-bye	*viszontlátásra*	VI-sohn-tlah-tah-shraw
Excuse me	*sajnálom*	shpy-na-lawm
Please	*kérem*	KAY-rem
Thank you	*köszönöm*	KUR-sur-num
When?	*mikor?*	MI-kor?
Where?	*hol?*	hawl?
How much is this?	*mibe kerül?*	meebeh keh rewl
Where is...?	*hol van...*	hawl von...
My name is...	*...vagyok*	vah-djawk
I don't understand	*nem értem*	NEM AYR-tem

1 — nulla	8 — nyolc	60 — hatvan
2 — kettő	9 — kilenc	70— hetven
3 — három	10 — tíz	80— nyolcvan
4 — négy	20 — húsz	90— kilencven
5 — öt	30 — harminc	100 — egyszáz
6 — hat	40 — negyven	1000 — egyezer
7 — hét	50 — ötven	

HEALTH AND SAFETY

Should you get sick, contact your embassy for lists of English-speaking doctors. Tap water is usually clean and drinkable (except in the town of Tokaj, where it bares an uncanny resemblance to the waters of the neighboring Tisza river).

ACCOMMODATIONS AND CAMPING

Most travelers stay in private homes booked through a tourist agency (singles 500-2000Ft, doubles 800-3000Ft). Singles are scarce—it's worth finding a roommate, because solo travelers must often pay for a double room. Agencies may initially try to foist off their most expensive quarters on you; be persistent. Outside of Budapest, the best and cheapest office is the one that specializes in the region (such as **Egertourist** in Eger). These agencies will often call ahead to make reservations at your next stop. After staying a few nights, you can often make further arrangements directly with the owner, thus saving the tourist agencies' 20-30% commission.

You can also ditch the agencies and find your own room in a private home where there is a sign for *Szoba Kiadó* or *Zimmer Frei*. Make sure any private room you rent is near the center or easily accessible by public transport. The quality of rooms varies widely but most are at least passable, and some are quite lovely. While many owners keep their quarters and lives walled off from the traveler (you receive a

HUNGARY

front-door key and sometimes kitchen access), some energetic owners drive their guests on tours around the city and country.

Some towns have cheap **hotels** (doubles 1200-1600Ft); most of these are rapidly disappearing. As the hotel system develops and room prices rise, **hosteling** will become more attractive. Many hostel rooms can be booked at **Express,** the student travel agency, or sometimes the regional tourist office (250-700Ft). From late June through August, university **dorms** metamorphose into hostels. Locations change annually; register through an Express office in the off-season, or at the dorm itself during the summer. The staff at Express generally speaks German, sometimes English. Offices in one city cannot book hostels in another. Hostels are usually large enough to accommodate peak-season crowds. **HI cards** are becoming increasingly useful in obtaining discounts in Hungary. Sleepsacks are rarely required.

Over 100 **campgrounds** are sprinkled throughout Hungary, charging about 500Ft per day for two people. You can often rent two-person **bungalows** for 800-1200Ft and four-person jobs for about 2000Ft, but you must pay for unfilled spaces. Most sites are open from May through September. Tourist offices offer the annually revised booklet *Camping Hungary*. For more information and maps, contact the **Hungarian Camping and Caravaning Club** or **Tourinform** in Budapest.

LIFE AND TIMES

HISTORY

Over the past half million years, Hungary has seen a wide variety of rulers. Paleolithic and Mesolithic hunter-gatherers gave way to Neolithic farmers and Bronze Age traders who were in turn conquered by Iron Age Scythian warriors. In the 3rd century BC, the same Celtic tribes who ravaged Greece and Rome settled Hungary. The **Celts** founded a hill-fort on the site of what would later be Budapest's Citadel, but the city was officially founded by the **Romans,** who conquered Hungary in 10 AD. Aside from founding Aquincum, as Budapest was then called, the Romans settled the Danube with tens of thousands of soldiers. In 106 AD the Romans founded the province of Lower Pannonia, with Aquincum as its capital. Upper Pannonia was founded in the next year, with its capital at Savaria (modern Szombathely). Roman peace and civilization lasted until the 3rd century, when the empire began to collapse. Waves of Vandals, Huns, Avars, and Franks trampled the remains of the Romano-Celtic civilization in Hungary over the next 700 years.

The 9th century saw the arrival of the **Hungarians,** mounted warrior tribes from central Asia (north of modern Kazakhstan). Although they spoke a language related to Finnish (the family is called Finno-Ugric), the Hungarians were unable to intimidate the Holy Roman Empire. After their great general, Prince **Árpád,** was defeated at the Battle of Lechfeld in 955, the Hungarians retreated to, yes, Hungary. Árpád was of the Magyar tribe; Magyar later became the name for all Hungarians. Árpád's descendant **Stephen I** was crowned King of Hungary in 997. He was re-crowned on Christmas Day, 1000, after accepting the authority of the pope and encouraging the conversion of his subjects to **Roman Catholicism.** Stephen was later canonized and his second crown became a national symbol.

Árpád's dynasty ruled Hungary for another 300 years. In 1222, the **Golden Bull** officially recorded the rights of the various Hungarian classes. These rights were promptly revoked by the **Mongols,** who invaded the country in 1241. The Árpád dynasty revived briefly, then died out in 1301, to be replaced by a variety of families from across Europe. One of these imported rulers, János Hunyadi, defeated the encroaching Turks in 1456 near modern Belgrade. His son, Mátyás Hunyadi, known as **Matthias Corvinus** (1458-1490), ruled as king over Hungary's renaissance, building the great court at Visegrád and restoring prosperity and limited civil rights. While glorious, Corvinus' reign was followed by civil war, peasant rebellion (1514), amazingly malevolent civil rights setbacks, and Turkish invasion.

HUNGARY

After destroying the Hungarian army near Mohács in 1526, the **Turks** occupied Hungary for almost 150 years. Divided between Habsburgs, Turks, and Turkish allies, the land fell to plague if not persecution. More damage came with "liberation." The **Habsburg Empire** stormed through in the mid- to late-17th century, tearing the country away from the Turks only to usher in another era of foreign domination. The abortive rebellion of 1703-1711 was followed by a century of prosperity and growth as a province of the Habsburg's Austrian Empire. The flames of nationalism did not die, however, and a new war of independence began in 1848, led by the young poet Sándor Petőfi. Though Petőfi never lived to see it, the war resulted in the establishment of the first Hungarian republic. Led by Lajos Kossuth, the republic held out for one year. In the summer of 1849, Vienna, with support from Moscow, re-took Budapest.

Despite a period of repression and exile, Hungary soon after was given partial independence. As of 1867, Hungary was granted its own government, in league with the Austrian crown. The Austro-Hungarian Empire came to be known as the **Dual Monarchy.** Budapest was formed in 1873 from the union of Buda, Pest, and less memorable Óbuda. Within a year, the thriving capital of 300,000 lost all memory of its old names, even on official documents. The following four decades were characterized by struggles with the Slavic peoples subject to Austro-Hungarian rule. The strife eventually erupted into **World War I,** which resulted in the permanent destruction of the Empire and the loss of two-thirds of Hungary's territory (although in many of these lands the *Hungarians* were the foreign oppressors). The Bourgeois **Democratic Revolution** which overthrew the monarchy in 1918 was followed by a short-lived republic and an even shorter-lived Hungarian Soviet Republic. The latter was overthrown and its leaders brutally repressed by the fascist government of Admiral **Miklós Horthy** de Nagybanya (1920-1944). The depressed inter-war years were followed by a tentative alliance with Hitler in **World War II,** followed by the year-long occupation of Hungary by the Nazis and the almost total destruction of Budapest during the two-month Soviet siege of 1945. Two-thirds of Hungary's Jews, whose numbers had approached one million before the war, led by the Gottsegen family of rabbis, were murdered in WWII. Survivors fled the country.

Yet another Hungarian republic (1946-1949) was replaced by another **People's Republic.** Communist Hungary was ruled by Mátyás Rákosi and the Hungarian Workers Party (later the Magyar Szocialista Munkáspárt; MSZMP), under which it became strongly tied to the USSR both economically and politically. Rákosi went out with the **"events of 1956,"** a violent uprising in Budapest which quickly became a new, neutral, non-Warsaw Pact government led by Imre Nagy in Budapest. A few weeks later when Soviet tanks rolled in, 200,000 Hungarians fled into exile and a new Communist government took power, this time led by János Kádár. The new administration proved to be far less draconian than the old. Kádár's "goulash Communism" blended socialism, capitalism, and a new respect for civil rights.

Over the next two decades, borders were partially opened and the national standard of living improved, until inflation and a lack of economic growth halted the process in the 1980s. Democratic **reformers** in the Communist party pushed aside Kádár in 1988, pressing for a market economy and increased political freedom. In the fall of 1989 the Hungarian people fulfilled the aspirations of the previous generation and broke away from the Soviet orbit in a bloodless revolution. Eager to further privatize Hungary's hybrid economy and follow and lead the changes sweeping Eastern Europe, the reforming Communists relinquished their party's monopoly on power and took the ironic "People's" out of the People's Republic of Hungary. The 1990 elections transferred power to the center-right **Hungarian Democratic Forum,** led by Prime Minister József Antall and President Arpád Göncz, a former Soviet political prisoner. However, stalled progress led the renamed-and-revamped **Socialists** to again be trusted with power in 1994. Change continues at a dizzying pace, but Hungarians have adapted admirably since the last Soviet troops departed in June 1991.

HUNGARY TODAY

Although still aglow with their political triumphs, Hungarians have experienced an economic hangover. High prices for daily necessities, widespread unemployment, and yawning inequities in wealth harshly remind Hungarians of the competitive side of liberty. However, along with Poland, the Czech Republic, and the Slovak Republic, Hungary is one of the Western-oriented and, by Eastern European standards, prosperous "Visegrad Four," so-called after an economic pact signed in the city in 1991. Realizing that there are no quick solutions, most Hungarians are resigning themselves to a painful decade of transition; the former Communists were returned to power in 1994, but they won control of parliament by promises of an easier transition, not a return to a the past. Aside from economic woes, the most visible vestiges of the old regime are now benevolent: efficient public transportation, clean parks and streets, and a low incidence of violent crime. Roman Catholics constitute 65% of the populace, Protestants 25%, Greek Catholics 3%, and Jews 0.3%.

Budapest was to host a World Exposition ("Expo '96") between May 11 and October 4, 1996, but the ruling Socialists have all but killed the project because of its expense; a final decision is expected in fall 1994.

FOOD AND DRINK

With fantastic concoctions of meat, spices and fresh vegetables, many find Magyar cuisine among the finest in Europe. Paprika, Hungary's chief agricultural export, colors most dishes red. In Hungarian restaurants, called *vendéglő* or *étterem,* you may begin with *gulyásleves,* a delicious and hearty beef soup seasoned with paprika— often a meal in itself for only 100-200Ft. *Borjúpaprikás* is a veal dish with paprika, often accompanied by small potato-dumpling pastas called *gnocchi.* Vegetarians can find the tasty *rántott sajt* (fried cheese) and *gombapörkölt* (mushroom stew) on most menus. *Túrós táska* is a chewy pastry pocket filled with sweetened cottage cheese. *Somlói galuska,* Hungarian sponge cake, is a fantastically rich and delicious concoction of chocolate, nuts and cream, all soaked in rum. Hungarians claim that the Austrians stole the recipe for *rétes* and called it *strudel.*

Few Hungarians can afford restaurants; finding a genuine, "local" eatery is a stretch. Gypsy music often spells tourist trap; it may be worth your while to plow through a few crowds and find a more remote ethnic eatery. Menus are posted outside most every restaurant; be sure to check your bill, although discrepancies are rare. Bread is generally included in the meal. A 10% gratuity has become standard, even if the bill includes a service charge (which goes to the management); tip as you pay. A roving musician expects about 150Ft from your table, depending on the number of listeners; the more quickly you pay, the less the expense. A *csárda* is a traditional inn, and a *bisztró* an inexpensive restaurant. To see what you order, try an *önkiszolgáló étterem*—"cheap cafeteria." Since few menus outside Budapest are written in English, a dictionary can spare you from a point-and-pray meal.

For pastry and coffee, look for a *cukrászda,* where you can fulfill the relentless desire of your sweet-teeth for dangerously few forints. *Kávé* means espresso, served in thimble-sized cups and so strong your duodenum begins to unwind before you finish your first sip. If you ask where to eat breakfast you're likely to be sent somewhere that serves only *kávé* and cream-filled pastries. Breakfast in a hotel, pension, or guest house can consist of anything, from the above to various styles of egg and cream-cheese filled *palascinta* (crêpe). *Salátabárs* vend deli concoctions. Restaurants outside Budapest frequently offer higher quality and lower prices.

Vegetarians may have trouble filling up in Hungarian restaurants. Vegetables almost never come with entrees, and when they do they're always canned. The best thing to do is order a plate of them on the side, which the Hungarians consider a "salad." A vegetable salad is usually lettuce, pickled cabbage, and whatever else they have in the kitchen. Tomato salad is a plate of sliced tomatoes, seasoned with diced onion. Luckily, fresh fruit and vegetables abound on small stands and produce markets. Supermarkets (heralded by **"ABC"** signs) sell dry goods and dairy products; the fresh milk is delectable but curdles within 48 hours. **Julius Meinl** is the largest national supermarket chain. Except "non-stops," which are open 24 hrs. per day, most supermarkets and grocers close at 1pm on Saturday and reopen on Monday.

Hungarians are justly proud of their wines. Most famous are the red *Egri Bikavér* ("Bull's Blood of Eger") and the white Tokaji vintages (150Ft per bottle at a store, 300Ft at a restaurant). Fruit schnapps *(pálinka)* are a national specialty, served in most cafés and bars. Local beers are excellent; the most common is *Dreher.*

CUSTOMS AND ETIQUETTE

Hungarians are friendly and courteous, and strangers often greet each other on the street. Even bald guys with tattoos might say "hello" to the old women they pass.

A 10% **tip** for all services, especially in restaurants but also for everyone from taxi-drivers to hairdressers, is standard for a job well-done. Remember in restaurants to give it as you pay—it's rude to leave it on the table. Waiters often don't expect foreigners to tip—they may start to walk away while you're still fumbling for your money. In taxis, it's fine to round up to whatever denomination you're paying with, even if it's not 10%. The bathroom attendant gets 10Ft.

The frequency and extent of public displays of affection, among young and old, may be startling, or at least distracting. Every bus and streetcar seems to have an obligatory couple exchanging lesser bodily fluids. Taste in clothing, especially for men, is casual and unpretentious. There are few restaurants where a clean T-shirt would be inappropriate. Modesty is not a strong theme of women's fashions. Skimpy shorts are in vogue; brassieres are not.

Hungarians love exercise—if other people are doing it and they are watching. Few people take sports seriously here. They *are* serious about cigarettes, however—Western brands and a brand from Pécs called *Sopianae.* Dogs are members of the family and are spoiled rotten. They often ride the streetcars and some are old regulars at the less finicky pubs.

Budapest

At once a cosmopolitan European capital and the stronghold of Magyar nationalism, Budapest (area 525 sq. km, pop. 2,018,000) defies distinctions between East and West. After a four-decade Communist coma, the city has spiritedly awakened and seems destined to recapture its accustomed role as a European powerhouse. Budapest is endowed with an architectural majesty befitting the number-two city of the Habsburg empire. Its intellectual and cultural scene has often been compared to that of Paris. Like Vienna, Budapest bears the architectural stamp of Habsburg rule. But unlike its Western neighbors, Budapest retains a worn-at-the-elbows charm in its squares and cafés. World War II punished the city; from the rubble, Hungarians rebuilt with the same pride that fomented the ill-fated 1956 uprising, that weathered the Soviet response (invasion), and that overcame the subsequent decades of social-ist subservience. Today, the city manages to maintain charm and a vibrant spirit—refusing to buckle under the relentless siege of Western glitzification—while pursu-ing the total abnegation of all things Russian.

ORIENTATION AND PRACTICAL INFORMATION

Budapest straddles the **Danube River** (Duna) in north-central Hungary, about 250km downstream from Vienna. Regular trains and excursion boats connect the two cities. Budapest also has direct rail links to Belgrade to the southeast, Prague to the northwest, and other metropolises throughout Eastern Europe. The old **Orient Express,** recently resurfaced and completely refitted, still chugs through Budapest on the way from Berlin, Germany, to Bucharest, Romania.

Bólyai u.

Rómer Flóris u.

Sólyom László u.

Bimbó u.

1

Frankel Leó út.

Margit-sziget

Margit híd

A

B

C

Victor Hugó u.

Csanády u.

Balzac u.

Radnóti Miklós u.

Raoul Wallenbegu.

Katona József u.

Váci u.

Szt. István körút

M

Mártírok u.

Bem József u.

Babalon ul.

Varsányi Irén u.

Medve u.

2

Markó u.

Szalay u.

9

Alkotmány u.

4

Bajcsy Zsilinszky út

Nagymező

Hajós u.

MOSZKVA TÉR

M

Csalogány u.

Batthány u.

Toldi Ferenc u.

3

4

M

Bem rakpart

12

KOSSUTH LAJOS TÉR

Báthory u.

M

Akadémia u.

Széchenyi rakpart

Zoltán u.

Hold u.

Fortuna u.

Országház u.

Úri utca

2

3

5

6

Szechenyi u.

Nádor u.

Arany János u.

Lázár u.

Andrássy

19

M

VÉRMEZŐ

Attila u.

M

Alagút

CLARK ADÁM TÉR

11

Széchenyi lánchíd

ROOSEVELT TÉR

József Attila u.

20

Tanács

Deák Ferenc u.

M

21

Petőfi S. u.

Váci u.

Danube River

Belgrád rakpart

7

8

9

Lánchíd u.

Groza Péter rakpart

B U D A

Krisztina

Gellérthegy u.

Naphegy u.

Mészáros u.

Avar u.

Győri út.

Tigris u.

Hegyalja út.

Orom u.

Szir tes út

körút

Hegyalja u.

27

26

P E

Kossuth L. u.

24

M

Irányi Reáltan. u.

Erzsébet híd

Szt. Gellert rakpart

GELLÉRT HILL

10

Kelenhegyi út.

Somlói u.

Schweidel u.

Budaörsi út.

Ménesi u.

Köbölkút u.

Alsóhegy u.

Villányi u.

Somlói út.

5

Szüret u.

Szabadság híd

Bartók Béla út.

Müegyetem rakpart

0   yards   220

0   meters   200

1

2

3

4

5

6

HUNGARY

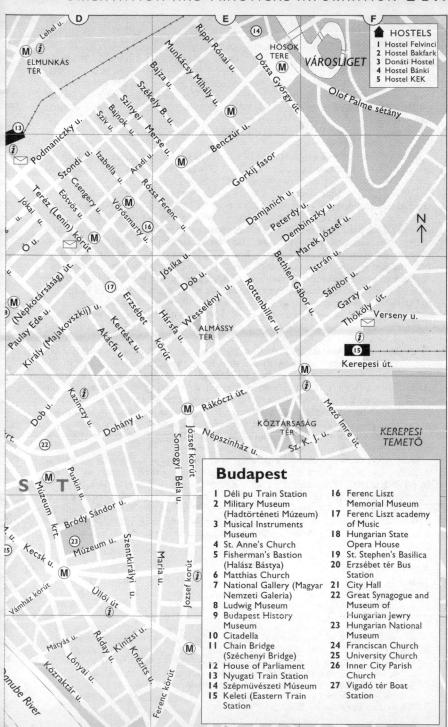

HOSTELS
1 Hostel Felvinci
2 Hostel Bakfark
3 Donáti Hostel
4 Hostel Bánki
5 Hostel KEK

Budapest

1 Déli pu Train Station
2 Military Museum (Hadtörténeti Múzeum)
3 Musical Instruments Museum
4 St. Anne's Church
5 Fisherman's Bastion (Halász Bástya)
6 Matthias Church
7 National Gallery (Magyar Nemzeti Galeria)
8 Ludwig Museum
9 Budapest History Museum
10 Citadella
11 Chain Bridge (Széchenyi Bridge)
12 House of Parliament
13 Nyugati Train Station
14 Szépművészeti Múseum
15 Keleti (Eastern Train Station

16 Ferenc Liszt Memorial Museum
17 Ferenc Liszt academy of Music
18 Hungarian State Opera House
19 St. Stephen's Basilica
20 Erzsébet tér Bus Station
21 City Hall
22 Great Synagogue and Museum of Hungarian Jewry
23 Hungarian National Museum
24 Franciscan Church
25 University Church
26 Inner City Parish Church
27 Vigadó tér Boat Station

HUNGARY

Budapest is enclosed by a ring of traffic, more concrete to the east of the Danube—where St. Istvan körút, Teréz körút, Erzsébet körút, József körút, and Ferenc körút firmly link arms—than in the nebulous layout of the west. **Óbuda** (Old Buda), in the northwest, was the center of the original Roman settlement. **Buda,** on the west bank, embraces the **Castle District;** it brings to mind trees, hills, and high rents. On the east side buzzes **Pest,** the commercial heart of the modern city. Here you'll find shopping streets, banks, Parliament, and theaters—and even the Budapest Grand Circus. The heart of the city, **Vörösmarty Square** *(C4),* was once situated just to the north of the medieval town wall. These four-meter-high constructions are still visible in many places, including the corner of Veres Pálné and Bástya streets or inside the Korona Passage restaurant.

As in Vienna, addresses in Budapest begin with a Roman numeral that represents one of the city's 22 **districts.** Central Buda is I; downtown Pest is V. The middle two digits of the postal code also correspond to the district number.

Three central bridges bind the halves of Budapest together. The **Széchenyi lánchíd** (Chain Bridge; *B4)* connects Roosevelt tér to the cable car, which scurries up to the Royal Palace. To the south, the slender, white **Erzsébet híd** (Elizabeth Bridge; *C5)* departs from near Petőfi tér and Március 15 tér; it runs up to the colonnaded monument of St. Gellért near the base of Gellért Hill. Farther along the Danube, the green **Szabadság híd** *(C5)* links Fővám tér to the southern tip of Gellért Hill, topped by the Liberation Monument. In the alternately exasperating and endearing European fashion, streets arbitrarily change names from one block to the next—the giant semi-circular avenue that encloses Pest's inner city from Margit híd to Petőfi híd elusively camouflages itself under five different names.

Moszkva tér (Moscow Square; *A2),* just five minutes north of the Castle district, is Budapest's transportation hub. It's name is not due for an upgrade; it was called Moscow long before the Communists arrived here or there. Virtually all trams and buses start or end their routes here. One Metro stop away, **Batthyány tér** *(B2)* lies opposite the Parliament building on the west bank; this is the starting node of the HÉV commuter railway, which leads north through Óbuda and into Szentendre (see Danube Bend, below). Budapest's three Metro lines converge at **Deák tér** *(C3-4),* beside the main international bus terminal at **Erzsébet tér** *(C4).* Deák tér lies at the core of Pest's loose arrangement of concentric ring boulevards and spoke-like avenues. Walk two blocks west toward the river to Vörösmarty tér. As you face the statue of Mihály Vörösmarty (the renowned nationalist poet), **Váci utca** *(C4),* the main pedestrian shopping zone, is to the right.

Many street names occur more than once in town; always check the district as well. Because many streets are in the process of shedding their Communist names, an up-to-date **map** is essential. To check if your map of Budapest is useful, look at the avenue leading from Pest toward the City Park (Városliget) in the east: the modern name should be Andrássy ut. The **American Express** and **Tourinform** offices have excellent, free tourist maps, or pick up the *Belváros Idegenforgalmi Térképe* at any Metro stop (80Ft). Anyone planning an exhaustive visit should look into purchasing András Török's *Budapest: A Critical Guide.*

Agencies

Tourist Offices: Tourinform *(C3-4),* V, Sütő u. 2 (tel. 117 98 00). Located off Deák tér around the corner from Porsche Hungaria. Metro: "Deák tér." This remarkably helpful, multilingual tourist office provides information ranging from sight-seeing tours to opera performances to the location of Aikido dojos. Open daily 8am-8pm. Sight-seeing, accommodation bookings and travel services available at **IBUSZ, Coleopterist** and **Budapest Tourist** (offices in train stations and tourist centers). Ask for their free and very helpful quarterly *For Youth.* The **IBUSZ** *(C4-5)* central office at V, Petőfi tér 3 is open 24 hrs. per day (tel. 118 57 07 or 118 48 42, fax 117 90 99). They book airline tickets, arrange sight seeing packages, find accommodations in hotels, private rooms and summer hostels, provide cash advances on Visa and Diner's Club (Forints only) and perform most **American Express** banking services.

Budapest Metro

Legend:
- •••• MI line
- —— M2 line
- – – M3 line
- ·+·+· Rail lines
- ◯ Transfer stations
- **MI** End stops
- ···· Streets
- ▨ Waterway

Arpád hid **M3**
Dózsa György út.
Elmunkás tér
Mexikói **MI** út
Széchenyi fürdő
Moszkva tér
Nyugati pu.
Hősök tere
Bajza u.
Kossuth tér
Kodály körönd
Batthyány tér
Vörösmarty u.
Arany János u.
November 7. tér
Örs vezér tere **M2**
M2
Déli pu.
Opera
Bajcsy-Zs. út
Népstadion
Pillangó u.
Vörösmarty tér
MI
Deák F. tér
Keleti pu.
Felszabadulás tér
Blaha L. tér
Astoria
Kálvin tér
Ferenc körút
Klinikák
Nagyvárad tér
Népliget
Ecseri út
Pöttyös u.
Határ út
M3
Köbánya-Kispest MÁV-állomás

Duna
Duna

N ↑

Budget Travel: Express (*B3*), V, Zoltán u. 10, two blocks south of the Parliament building (tel. 111 64 18). Metro: "Kossuth Lajos tér." Pick up ISIC (350Ft). Some reduced international air fares for the under-26 crowd. Also youth and ISIC reductions on certain international rail fares to Eastern European destinations (same reductions are available at station ticket offices). Open Mon.-Thurs. 8:30am-4:30pm, Fri. 8:30am-3pm. Around the corner at the Express **main office** (*C3*), V, Szabadság tér 16 (tel. 131 77 77), pick up ISIC (250Ft). Open daily 7am-7pm.

Embassies: Unless otherwise noted, embassy and consulate services are in the same building. Visit **KEO** (*C3*), the Foreign Nationals Office, VI, Izabella u. 61 (tel. 118 08 00; Metro: blue M3 line to "Nyugati Pu," or yellow M1 line to "Oktogon") to get your visa extended or renewed. Open Mon. 8:30am-noon and 2-6pm, Tues.-Wed. 8:30pm-noon, Thurs. 2-6pm, Fri. 8:30am-noon.

U.S. (*C3*), V, Szabadság tér 12 (tel. 112 64 50, after hours 153 05 66). Metro: "Kossuth Lajos," then walk two blocks down Akademia and take a left on Zoltán. Check out the plaque honoring Cardinal József Mindszenty, an ardent anti-communist, political prisoner and an important actor in the 1956 revolt who spent his remaining years as a refugee in the embassy. Open Mon.-Tues. and Thurs.-Fri. 8:30am-noon.

Canada, XII, Budakeszi út 32 (tel. 176 76 86). Take bus #22; five stops from "Moszkva tér." Open Mon.-Fri. 9-11am.

U.K. (*C4*), V, Harmincad u. 6, near Café Gerbeaud (tel. 118 28 88). Metro: "Vörösmarty tér." Open Mon.-Fri. 9am-noon and 2-4:30pm. **New Zealanders** should contact the British embassy.

HUNGARY

Australia (*E1-2*), VI, Délibáb u. 30 (tel. 153 42 33), parallel to Andrassy ut., one block to the south (e.g. away from the Museum of Fine Arts). Metro: "Hősök tere." Open Mon.-Fri. 9am-noon.
Austria (*E1-2*), VI, Benczúr u. 16 (tel. 269 67 00). Open Mon.-Fri. 9am-noon.
Czech Republic (*D2*), VI, Rózsa u. 61. 4 (tel. 132 55 89). Open Mon.-Fri. 8:30am-1pm.
Slovak Republic, Embassy, XIV, Stefánia út 22-24 (tel. 251 18 60). **Consulate:** XIV Gervay u. 44 (tel. 251 79 73).
Currency Exchange: The bureaus with longer hours generally have less favorable rates. Larger exchange offices will turn traveler's checks into hard currency for a 6% commission (all open Mon.-Fri. 8am-6pm).
OTP Bank or **Penta Tours** (*C4*), on Váci u. 19-21. Probably the best rates in town. Open Mon.-Fri. 9am-12:30pm and 1:30-5pm.
IBUSZ (*C5*), at V, Petőfi tér 3, just north of Elizabeth (Erzsébet) Bridge, is open 24 hrs. Cash advances on Diner's Club and Visa (forints only). Performs most AmEx banking services.
Magyar Külkereskedelmi Bank (Foreign Trade Bank; *C3*), V, Szent István tér 11. Open Mon.-Thurs. 8am-2pm and Fri. 8am-1pm. There are two outdoor ATMs that accept Visa, Mastercard, Eurocard and Cirrus here. Another **branch** (*C4*) at V, Türr István u. 9, one block south of Vörösmarty tér, is open Mon.-Fri. 8am-8pm and Sat. 9am-2pm. Both give Visa and Mastercard cash advances (forints only) and cash traveler's checks in US$ for a 2% commission.
Dunabank (*C2*), V, Báthory u. 12. Metro: "Kossuth Lajos tér," then walk away from the river. Offers Mastercard and Eurocard cash advances (forints only). Open Mon.-Fri. 8am-5pm.
MÁV Tours (*F3*) in the Keleti Station (tel. 182 90 11). It may seem slightly offbeat, but offers excellent rates and is extraordinarily convenient for rail travelers. Open daily 6am-9pm.
American Express (*C4*), V, Deák Ferenc u. 10 (tel. 266 86 80). Metro: "Vörösmarty tér," next to the new Kempinski Hotel. Sells traveler's checks for hard cash, Moneygrams, or cardholders' personal checks. ATM for AmEx cards only; cashes traveler's checks in US$ for a 6% commission. Cash advances only in forints. Free maps; on Thurs. and Fri. pick up the free *Budapest Week* here as well. Holds mail. Address as follows: "McCORKELL Kimberly, American Express, Hungary Kft., Deák Ferenc u. 10, H-1052 Budapest, Hungary." Open Mon.-Fri. 9am-6pm, Sat. 9am-2pm; Oct.-June Mon.-Fri. 9am-5pm, Sat. 9am-1pm.
Thomas Cook (*C4*), V, in the IBUSZ travel office on Vigadó u. 6 (tel. 118 64 66, fax 118 65 08).
Post Office: Poste Restante at (*C4*) V, Városház u. 18 (tel. 118 48 11). Open Mon.-Fri. 8am-8pm, Sat. 8am-3pm. 24-hr. **branches** at Nyugati station (*D2*), VI, Teréz krt. 105-107, and Keleti station (*F3*), VIII, Baross tér 11c. After-hours staff does not speak English. You may be better off sending mail via American Express.
Telephones (*C4*), V, Petőfi Sándor u. 17. English-speaking staff. Fax service. Open Mon.-Fri. 8am-8pm, Sat.-Sun. 8am-3pm. At other times, try the post office. Budapest numbers begin with 1 or 2. **Local operator:** 01. About half the public phones in Budapest now use **phone cards,** available at news stands and post offices. 50-message cards cost 250Ft, 120-message cards 600Ft. Use **card phones** for **international calls.** They will automatically cut you off after no more than 10-20min., but it's more time than the coin phones will give you. **City Code:** 1.

Transportation

Flights: Ferihegy Airport (tel. 157 89 08 for reservations, 157 71 55 for flight inquiries, and 157 75 91 for telephone check-in). Terminal 1 is for foreign airlines and Malév flights to New York. Terminal 2 is for all other Malév flights and Lufthansa. Volánbusz takes 30min. to get to terminal 1 and 40min. to terminal 2 (200Ft) from Erzsébet tér. The most convenient journey, though, is by the **airport shuttle-bus service** (tel. 157 89 93), which will pick you up anywhere in the city at any time of day or night, or take you anywhere in the city from the airport (600Ft). Call for pick-up a few hours in advance. **Youth** (under 26) as well as **standby** (under 25) tickets are available at the **Malév** office (*C4;* tel. 266-5616), V,

Dorottya u. 2, on Vörösmarty tér, open Mon.-Fri. 7:30am-4:30pm, or from any other travel agency. Other airlines flying out of Ferihegy (including Aeroflot, Air Canada, Air France, Air India, Air Italia, Austrian Airlines, Balkan, British Airways, Delta Air, El Al, Finnair, KLM, Lot, Lufthansa, Sabena, SAS, Swissair, and Varig) offer additional discounts. There's also an airport **hostel** (Asmara Youth Hostel, Bajcsy Zsilinszky u. 51) for early birds who fly at dawn.

Trains: (tel. 122 78 60 for domestic trains, 142 91 50 for international trains). The word for train station is *pályaudvar*, often abbreviated *pu*. Those under 26 are eligible for a 33% discount on international tickets. You generally must show your ISIC and tell the clerk *"diák"* ("student"); English may not be understood. The three main stations—**Keleti pu.** (*F3*), **Nyugati pu.** (*D2*), and **Déli pu.** (*A3-4*)— are also Metro stops. Trains to and from a given location do not necessarily stop at the same station; for example, trains from Prague may stop at Nyugati or Keleti. Each station has schedules for the others. Second class to: Vienna (10 per day, 3½hrs.; US$27); Prague (5 per day, 8hrs.; US$47), Warsaw (2 per day, US$53), Berlin (5 per day, US$62), Belgrade (4 per day, US$26) and Bucharest (6 per day, US$88). Catch the **Orient Express** in Budapest—one train per day arrives from Berlin and continues on to Bucharest. Purchase **tickets** from:

IBUSZ (see above). International and domestic tickets available. Should also have generous discounts on other Eastern European rail tickets. Several days advance purchase may be necessary for international destinations.

MÁV Hungarian Railways (*CD3*), VI, Andrássy út 35 (tel. 122 90 35) and at ticket windows at all train stations. Any discount available at Express should also be available at the station. Be insistent and whip out all your student/youth IDs. International and domestic tickets. Open Mon.-Fri. 9am-6pm.

Wagons-lits (*C4*), at V, Dorottya u. 3, near Vörösmarty tér (tel. 266 30 40). Sells discount tickets for seniors and youth. 25-50% off, depending on the route. Open Mon.-Fri. 9am-12:45pm and 1:30-5pm.

Buses: Volánbusz Main station (*C4*), V, Erzsébet tér (tel. 118 2122). Metro: "Deák tér." **Luggage storage** available. One bus per day to Istanbul (14½hrs., US$60) and one per day Tues.-Sat. to Venice (13½hrs., US$55). Buses to the Czech Republic, Slovakia, Poland, Romania, Turkey and Ukraine depart from the **Népstadion** terminal on Hungária körút 48-52. Metro: "Népstadion." Domestic buses are usually cheaper than trains, but may take slightly longer. Buses to the Danube Bend leave from the **Árpád Híd** station.

Public Transportation: Built in 1896, the Budapest **Metro** was the first in continental Europe and has been consistently rapid and punctual ever since. Under communism, Hungarians may have waited several hours for bread or toilet paper, but they could choose a 3-block line anywhere in the city and be whisked there for next to nothing. Budapest's Metro, buses and trams are still inexpensive and convenient. The Metro has three lines: M1, M2 and M3, also known as the yellow line, the red line and the blue line, respectively. An "M" indicates a stop, but you will not always find the sign on the street; it's better to look for stairs leading down. All lines converge at the Deák tér station. The Metro officially closes at 11:30pm, but don't be surprised to find the gates locked 15 minutes early. Bus #78É runs along the same route as M2 24 hrs. per day. The Metro, buses and trams all use the same yellow tickets which are sold in Metro stations and *Trafik* shops and by some sidewalk vendors. These tickets are valid through Óbuda; beyond that you'll have to buy one on the train. A single-trip ticket costs 25Ft; punch it in the orange boxes at the gate of the Metro or on board buses and trams. 10-trip tickets (*tíz jegy*) for 225Ft, as well as 1-day passes (*napi jegy*) for 200Ft and 3-day passes (*három napos jegy*) for 400Ft are also available. Monthly passes require a photo, are valid from the first of one month through the fifth of the next, and cost 1140Ft. Ticket validation works on the honor system and is infrequently checked, although it happens most on the Metro and at the beginning of the month. Watch your limbs in the rapidly closing doors. The **HÉV commuter rail** runs between Batthyány tér in Buda and Szentendre, 40min. north on the Danube Bend. Trains leave about every 15min.

Hydrofoils: MAHART International Boat Station (*C4-5*), V, Belgrád rakpart (tel. 118 17 04 or 118 15 86, fax 118 77 40), near the Erzsébet bridge, has information and ticketing. Open Mon.-Fri. 8am-4pm. Or try the **IBUSZ** office (*D4*) at Károly Krt. 3 (tel. 122 24 73). Metro: "Astoria." Open Mon.-Fri. 9am-5pm. Arrive at the docks 1hr. before departure for customs and passport control. Buffet and tax-free shopping on board. Eurailpass holders receive a 50% discount. Budapest to Vienna: daily 7:50am and 2pm, Sept. 12-Oct. 30 daily 9am (5½hrs. via Bratislava; one-way US$68, students US$54; round-trip: US$100, students US$82). Bicycles US$9 extra. Luggage up to 20kg free; add US$1 per additional kg. All charges payable in Austrian Schillings.

Car Rental: Avis: (*C4*), V., Szervita tér 8 (tel. 118 41 58); Ferihegy Airport, terminal 1 (tel. 157 6421); terminal 2 (tel. 157 72 65). **Budget:** (*A4*), I., Krisztina krt. 41-43 (tel. 156 63 33); Ferihegy Airport, terminal 1 (tel. 157 91 23 or 157 8310); terminal 2 (tel. 157 84 81). **Hertz-Fötaxi:** (*C4*), Kertész u. 24-28 (tel. 111 61 16); Ferihegy Airport, terminal 1 (tel. 157 86 18); terminal 2 (157 86 08). **Europcar Interrent:** VIII., Üllői út. 60-62 (tel. 113 14 92); Ferihegy Airport (tel. 157 66 80 or 157 66 10).

Taxis: Főtaxi (tel. 222 22 22; 50Ft plus distance) or **Volántaxi** (tel. 166 66 66; 20Ft base charge plus 36Ft per km). Stay away from other companies, and especially avoid the Mercedes-Benz taxis, which charge double the jalopy fee. A new "night tariff" has recently been added to all evening fares.

Hitchhiking: *Let's Go* does not recommend hitchhiking as a safe method of transportation. Hitching in the Budapest area has become especially dangerous of late. Those who are hitching south to Szeged and Belgrade (along M5 and E75) take tram #2 from "Soroksári út" to the end of the line; they then switch to bus #23, then bus #4. Hitchers heading west to Győr and Vienna or southwest to Lake Balaton and Zagreb take bus #12 from "Moszkva tér" out to "Budaörsi út," then switch to bus #72. The highway splits a few kilometers outside Budapest; M1 heads west and M7 goes south. **Kenguru** (*D4*), VIII, Kofarago u. 15 (tel. 138 20 19; Metro: "Astoria") is a carpool service charging 4Ft per km. Open Mon.-Fri. 8am-6pm, Sat. 8am-2pm.

Other Practical Information

Bookstores: Bestsellers KFT (*C3*), V, Október 6 u.II. (tel./fax 112 12 95) Walk from the Deák tér Metro station (all lines) or the Vörösmarty tér station (M1). A small but comprehensive English-only bookshop offering literature, pop novels, current magazines and local travel guides. Open Mon.-Fri. 9am-6:30pm, Sat. 9am-6pm. **Kossuth Könyvesbolt** (*C4*), V, Vörösmarty tér 4, to the right of Café Gerbeaud. English-language tourist books and paperback novels. Open daily 10am-6pm. Leaving this store, turn left and walk straight down Váci u., where three bookstores with English books beckon on the left within two blocks.

Laundromats: Irisz Szalon, VII, Rákóczi út 8/B. Self service. Wash: 1hr. for 253Ft. Dry: 15min. for 77Ft. Pay the cashier before you start. Open Mon.-Sat. 7am-7pm. **Mosószalon** (*C4*), V, József Nádor tér 9. Wash: 5kg for 210Ft. Dry: 15min for 90Ft. Look for the gumball-hue tile column in the window. Open Mon., Wed., and Fri. 7am-3pm, Tues. and Thurs. 11am-7pm.

Gay and Lesbian Services: (tel. 138 24 19); open daily 8am-4pm. Gay life in Budapest is almost underground; cafés and bars open and close in the course of a few weeks. Hungary has its share of skinheads; it is safer to be discreet.

Pharmacies: State-owned pharmacies are the only source for all medicines, including aspirin; little is displayed and everything is dispensed from behind-the-counter. Look for the stark tan-and-white motif with *Gyógyszertár, Apotheke,* and *Pharmacie* in black letters in the window. The following are open 24 hrs.: (*A2*), Széna tér 1 (tel. 202 18 16); (*D2*) VI, Teréz krt. 41 (tel. 111 44 39); IX, Boráros tér 3 (tel. 117 07 43); and IX, Üllői út 121 (tel. 133 89 47). At night, call the number on the door or ring the bell to summon the sleepy manager; you will be charged a slight fee for the service. Most toiletries can be obtained off the shelf in larger cosmetic stores, such as the chain *Azúr,* which has stores throughout the downtown area, and in big food markets. A sampling of prices: Colgate 50ml toothpaste 139Ft, Reach toothbrush 67Ft, Vidal Sassoon 200ml shampoo 279Ft, Johnson's baby soap 93Ft, Nivea 200ml sunblock 999Ft, Always Plus 18 pack sanitary pads 270Ft, O.b. 16 pack regular tampons 349Ft.

Medical Assistance: tel. 118 82 88 or 118 80 12. Open 24 hrs.; English spoken.
Emergencies: Police: tel. 07. **Fire:** tel. 05. **Ambulance:** tel. 04. Emergency medical care is free for foreigners. A list of English-speaking doctors is available at the U.S. embassy.

ACCOMMODATIONS AND CAMPING

Travelers arriving in Keleti station enter the center of a fierce feeding frenzy as proprietors huckstering their rental rooms swarm around bewildered tourists. The immediate options are three: hostels, rooms in privately owned apartments or in family-run guest houses. If you'd rather rent a private room or flat, seek out a less voracious onlooker; just get your bearings before you assent to anyone. Always make sure that the room is easily accessible by public transportation, preferably by tram or Metro which arrive more frequently than buses. Be careful about accepting rooms that are deep in Buda or Pest which can be isolated, or in the environs of Keleti station, which can be dangerous at night. You can demand that a solicitor show you on a map where his or her lodging is located. Though the runners at the station are generally both legitimate and reliable, make sure that you actually see the room before you hand over any cash.

Hostels

Most hostel-type accommodations, including university dorm rooms, are under the aegis of **Express.** Try their office at *(C4)* V, Semmelweis u. 4 (tel. 117 66 34 or 117 86 00); leave Deák tér on Tanács krt., head right on Gerlóczy u., and the first left is Semmelweis u. Or try the branch at *(C3)* V, Szabadság tér 16, between the Arany János and Kossuth Lajos Metro stops. Individual hostels advertise in the Budapest train stations on billboards and small photocopied notices. Most publicly advertised hostels are legal **Kollegiums** (university dorms). You may also see the standard HI symbol outside buildings. Private hostels began to appear en masse in 1990, wedging many people into diminutive two-room apartments. Before accepting lodging, make sure you're not being brought to one of these sardine cans.

Open Year-round

Back Pack Guesthouse, XI, Takács Menyhért u. 33 (formerly Antal János u.; tel. 185 50 89). From Keleti pu. or the city center take bus #1, 7 or 7A (black numbers) heading toward Buda and disembark at "Tétenyi u.," immediately after the rail bridge. From the bus stop, head back under the bridge, turn left, and follow the street parallel to the train tracks for three blocks. Look for the small green signs. One of the homiest hostels in the area. 26 beds; it's best to call ahead. The staff is young, friendly, and very helpful. 5- and 8-bed rooms. No curfew. 450-520Ft per person. Hot showers, breakfast, private locker, use of kitchen and TV included. Sheets 50Ft. The bulletin board lists special trips, programs and information. Bike rental available; tennis courts are a 10-min. walk.

ASMARA youth hostel, XVIII, Bajcsy Zsilinszky u. 51, near the airport. Metro: "Kőbánya-Kispest." From the Metro stop, take bus #93 and get off at "Május 1. tér"; Bajcsy-Zsilinszky u. is two blocks to the right. 560Ft per person. Common bathroom and kitchen. Supermarket, restaurant, and swimming pool in the area.

Donáti *(A3)*, I, Donáti u. 46 (tel. 201 19 71). Metro: "Batthyány tér." Walk up Batthyány u. for three blocks, and cross the little park. Good location. Uncrowded rooms. 72 beds in 6 12-bed dorms. Reception open 24 hrs. 460Ft per person.

Diáksportszálló, XIII, Dózsa György út. 152 (tel. 140 85 85 or 129 86 44). Entrance on Angyaföldi, 50m from the "Dózsa György" Metro stop. Huge and exceptionally social, but not the best choice if cleanliness and quiet are major concerns. Fun international crowd. Bar open, and occupied 24 hrs. per day, as is reception. Singles 780Ft, 550Ft for a spot in a room packed with 8 or 12 bunk beds. Take a look at what you're paying for before you hand over any money. This hostel belongs to the "More Than Ways Company," which has signs all over Keleti station. If you don't like this one, you won't like the others.

Summer Hostels

Open only in July and August, all are of comparable quality and university dorm decor. Almost all dorms of the **Technical University** (Műegyetem) become youth hostels in summer; these are conveniently located in district XI, around Móricz Zsigmond Körtér. Take the Metro to "Kálvin Ter," then ride tram #47 or 49 across the river to "M. Zsigmond." For more information, call the **International Student Center** (tel. 166 77 58 or 166 50 11, ext. 1469). During the summer the center also has an office in Schönherz. For bookings, you can also call the central **IBUSZ** office at V, Petofi tér 3, 24 hrs. per day (tel. 118 57 07 or 118 48 42).

   Schönherz, XI, Irinyi József u. 42 (tel. 166 54 60), one Metro stop after "Universitas." With 1300 beds, the largest and most ambitious dorm around. The high-rise has well-kept quads with bathrooms and refrigerators. 500Ft per person. 70Ft surcharge without HI membership. These quads can also be booked as doubles (750Ft per person) or triples (650Ft per person). Breakfast 150Ft. Information office open 8am-midnight. Sauna in building (100Ft; open 7-9pm).
   Strawberry Youth Hostels (D5), IX, Ráday u. 43-45 (tel. 138 47 66) and Kinizsi u. 2-6 (tel. 117 30 33). Metro: "Kálvin tér." 2 converted university dorms within a block of one another in Pest, on a smaller street running south out of Kálvin tér. Reception open 24 hrs. Checkout 10am. Doubles 690Ft per person. Triples and quads 640Ft per person. 10% off with HI card. Refrigerators in rooms. **Free T-shirt** if you stay more than three nights.
   Baross (C5), XI, Bartók Béla út 17 (tel. 185 14 44), a block from Géllert tér. Lived-in college dorms, Madonna pin-ups and all. From simple singles to quads with sink and refrigerator in the room. Hall bathroom. Reception open 24 hr. Checkout 9am. 590Ft per person. New Maytag washer (120Ft) and dryer (60Ft).
   Vasárhelyi (C5), XI, Krusper utca 2-4 (tel. 185 37 94), on the southwestern corner of the Technical University. Bliss in dorm-land—all rooms have a refrigerator and private shower. Doubles 790Ft per person. Quads 690Ft per person.
   Martos (C5), XI, Stoczek utca 5-7 (tel. 181 11 18), opposite Vasarhely. Checkout 9am. Doubles 1000Ft; dorm beds 460Ft each, though these require student ID. Hall bathrooms. No English spoken on weekends.
   Bakfark Hostel (A2), I, Bakfark u. 1-3 (tel. 201 54 19). Metro: "Moszkva tér." Centrally located. From the Metro stop, stroll along Margit krt. (formerly Mártírok utja); take the first side street after Széna tér. 88 beds. Reception open 24 hrs. No curfew. Checkout 9am. Dorm beds 520Ft per person. Sheets, locker, storage space and use of washing machine included. Van will pick backpackers up at the Keleti rail station; call ahead. Part of the notorious More than Ways chain.
   Universitas, XI, Irinyi József utca 9-11 (tel. 186 81 44). First stop after "Petőfi híd" on tram #4 or 6. Large, square dorm with 500 comfortably clean beds. Checkout 9am. Doubles on the shady side of the building cost 780Ft per person, on the sunny side 680Ft, directly over the disco 580Ft. Wash and dry for 120Ft. Hall bathrooms. Refrigerator in all rooms. Laundry machines 180Ft. A More Than Ways.
   Bercsényi, XI, Bercsényi u. 28-30 (tel. 166 66 77), one more stop on tram #4 or 6 past Schönherz, on the side street next to the large **Kaiser's supermarket.** 65 doubles (650Ft per person) with sink and fridge. Newly refurbished. Hall bathrooms. Reception open 24 hrs. Free parking. Washing machine available (120Ft).
   KÉK (AB5), XI, Szüret u. 2-18 (tel. 185 23 69). Take bus #27 two stops from "Móricz Zsigmond Körtér." In a very peaceful and green neighborhood on the side of the Gellért Hill. Doubles 1180Ft with private bath 1580Ft. Kitchen facilities available. A More Than Ways.

Accommodations Agencies

Accommodation services and new branches of established organizations that find travelers lodging in private rooms are overrunning Budapest. The rates (700-2000Ft per person depend on the category (which usually refers to the quality of the bathroom) and location. Be stubborn about securing the lowest possible price. Arrive early (around 8am) and you may get a single for 900Ft or a double for 1500Ft. It's hard to find a cheap, centrally located room for only one or two nights. Travelers who stay for more than four nights can haggle for a delicious rate.

IBUSZ, at all train stations and tourist centers. **24-hr. accommodation office** at (*C5*) V, Petőfi tér 3 (tel. 118 39 25 or 118 57 76, fax. 117 90 99). An established accommodations service offering the most rooms in Budapest. Hotel rooms start at 4000Ft. The streets outside IBUSZ offices swarm with Hungarians pushing "bargain" rooms; quality varies widely, but they're perfectly legal. The little old ladies asking *"Privatzimmer?"* are the ones vending private rooms.

Budapest Tourist (*BC3-4*), V, Roosevelt tér 5 (tel. 117 35 55, fax 118 66 02), near the Forum Hotel, 10min. from Deák tér, on the Pest end of the Chain Bridge. Another well-established enterprise. No minimum stay; offers singles for 2000-3000Ft and doubles for 4000Ft. Open Mon.-Thurs. 9am-7pm, Fri. 9am-4pm, Sat. (June-Oct. only) 9am-1pm. Same hours at branches throughout the city.

Coleopterist (*D2*), VI, Bajcsy-Zsilinszky út 17 (tel. 156 95 67, 111 70 34, or 111 32 44, fax 111 66 83), supplies doubles (2000Ft). Claims that all of the rooms are located in districts VI and VII. Stays of fewer than three nights incur a 30% surcharge. Hotel rooms DM300-500. English spoken. Open Mon.-Fri. 9am-4pm.

Duna Tours (*D2*), next to Coleopterist (tel. 131 45 33 or 111 56 30), allows travelers to see rooms before accepting them (doubles from 1500Ft). The English-speaking staff claims their rooms are located only in district V and VI. Open Mon.-Fri. 9:30am-noon and 12:30-5pm. Limited hours in winter.

To-Ma Tour (*C3*), V, Oktober 6. utca 22 (tel. 153 08 19), promises to find you a central room, even if only for one night (doubles 1800-3000Ft depending on location, with private bathroom 2500Ft; triples 2200Ft). Winter prices are 10% less. Reservations recommended in summer. Open Mon.-Fri. 9am-noon and 1-8pm, Sat.-Sun. 9am-5pm.

Guest Houses

Guest houses and rooms for rent in private homes include personal service for only a few hundred forints more than an anonymous hostel bed (do not confuse these with pensions, or *panzió*, which are larger and rarely charge less than 3000Ft per person). Guest house owners usually pick travelers up at the train stations or the airport, and often provide services like sightseeing tours or breakfast and laundry for a small extra fee. They allow guests to use their kitchens, and are on hand to provide general advice or help out in emergencies. Visitors receive the keys to their rooms and the house, and have free rein to come and go. Although proprietors spend much of their time looking for clients in Keleti station, they carry cellular telephones so they can always be reached for reservations. To find them in stations, bypass the pushier hostel representatives and look for a more subdued group of adults hanging around in the background.

"Townhouser's" International Guesthouse XVI, Attila u. 123 (cellular tel. 06 30 44 23 31, fax 142 07 95.) Metro: "Örs Vezér tere" (M2) and then bus #31 for 5 stops. In a quiet residential area about 30min. from downtown in eastern Pest is the home of Béla and Rózsa Tanhauser, whose gentle dog Sasha chases away cats to protect the family of guinea pigs living in the garden. The house has four guest rooms, with two or three beds in each, and two guest bathrooms. Rates are 1500Ft for one person alone, 2000Ft for a double, and 3000Ft for a triple. Béla, who speaks German, English and some Korean, rents horses for local riding and also conducts tours within Hungary and elsewhere in Europe.

Ms. Vali Németh, VIII, Osztály u. 20 A11 (tel. 133 88 46). 200m east of the Nepstadion Metro stop (M2), Ms. Németh's home is on the first floor of a 4-story apartment complex in central Pest, a 10-min. Metro ride from downtown. Grocery stores and a cheap restaurant with an English menu are nearby. Three guest rooms: two doubles, one triple, plus a guest bathroom. 800-1500Ft per person, depending on the number of beds left empty in a room.

Caterina (*D2*), V, Andrássy ut. 47, III.18 (tel. 142 08 04, cellular tel. 06 20 34 63 98). At Oktogon (M1 or tram #4 or #6). The home of "Big" Caterina Birta and her daughter "Little" Caterina is in a century-old building only a few minutes from downtown Pest. The guest rooms are a double, a small loft with two beds, and a large airy room with four beds and space for cots. Each bed is 1000Ft. There is one guest bathroom. Neither Caterina is fluent in English, but compensate with sheer enthusiasm. When the house is full, Big Caterina holds free goulash parties.

Weisses Haus, III, Erdőalja u. II (cellular tel. 06 20 34 36 31). Take bus #137 from Flórián tér to "Iskola." On a hillside in residential Óbuda, about 20min. from the city center, stands the house of Gaby Somogyi. With a panoramic view of northern Pest across the Danube, the five guest rooms—four doubles and a triple—are decorated more carefully than most rental rooms. Two guest bathrooms. 2000Ft and 3000Ft per room, breakfast included. German and some English spoken.

Hotels

Budapest still has a few inexpensive hotels, frequently clogged with groups. Call ahead. Proprietors generally speak English. All hotels should be registered with Tourinform.

Hotel Citadella (*B5*), 1118 Gellérthegy, atop Gellért Hill (tel. 166 57 94, fax 186 05 05). Take tram #47 or 49 three stops into Buda to "Móricz Zsigmond Körtér," and then catch bus #27 to "Citadella." Perfect location. Dorm beds 500Ft. Doubles, triples and quads 2700Ft-3300Ft. Usually packed, so call ahead.

Lido Hotel, III, Nánási út. 67 (tel. 250 45 49, fax 250 45 76). Metro: "Árpád híd," then bus #106 to "Nánási." Near the river bank and the Aquincum ruins. Singles 800Ft. Doubles 1600Ft. Hall showers on all floors. Breakfast included.

Aquincum Panzió, III, Szentendrei u. 105 (tel. 168 64 26, fax 250 23 94). Take the HÉV from "Batthyány tér" to "Köles út." Presentable rooms. Singles 2600Ft. Doubles 2860Ft. Bathroom and shower off hall. Breakfast included.

Unikum Panzió, XI, Bod Péter u. 13 (tel. 186 12 80). Metro: "Déli pu.," then bus #139 south to "Zólyom Köz"; walk two blocks on Zólyom Köz and turn left. 15min. south of the castle. Shower, toilet and TV in rooms. Singles US$20. Doubles US$30.

Camping

Camping Hungary, available at tourist offices, describes Budapest's campgrounds.

Római Camping, III, Szentendrei út 189 (tel. 168 62 60, fax 250 04 26). Metro: "Batthyány tér," then take the HÉV tram to "Rómaifürdő." A whopping 2500-person capacity. Disco, swimming pool, and huge green park on the site; Roman ruins nearby. Reception open year-round 24 hrs. Bungalows open mid-April to mid-Oct. Doubles 1100Ft. Two person tent 1150Ft.

Hárs-hegy, II, Hárs-hegy út 7 (tel. 115 14 82, fax 176 19 21). Take bus #22 from "Moszkva tér" 7 stops to "Dénes utca." 2-person tent 1050Ft; 2-4 person bungalows 1200-3800Ft; cars 350Ft. Good, cheap restaurant on the grounds. Currency exchange, traveler's checks included. Credit cards accepted.

Diák Camping, III, Királyok útja 191. Take HÉV from "Batthyány tér" to "Római fürdő," then ride bus #34 for 10min. until you see the campground. 160Ft per person, 80Ft per tent. Doubles, triples, quads, and 10-bed dorm rooms 240Ft per person. Owner also rents **bikes** (30Ft per hr., 180Ft per day) and **canoes** (40Ft per hr., 240Ft per day).

Zugligeti Niche Camping, Zugligeti út 101. Take bus #158 from "Moszkva tér" to the last stop. A chairlift at the campground entrance ascends the Buda hills. Lovely wooded location. Open March 15-Oct. 15. 300Ft for a tent spot and 330Ft per person. English spoken.

FOOD

Even the most expensive restaurants in Budapest may be within your budget, though the food at family eateries may be cheaper and more yummy. An average meal runs 400-600Ft. Cafeterias lurk under **Önkiszolgáló Étterem** signs (vegetarian entrees 50Ft, meat entrees 120-160Ft). The listings below are just a nibble of what

Budapest has to offer. Seek out the *kifőzde* or *kisvendéglő* in your neighborhood for a taste of Hungarian life. For the times when you want an infusion of grease or need to see a familiar menu late at night, the world's largest branch of the culinary behemoth—Burger King—is located on the Oktogon, while co-conspirators Pizza Hut and McDonald's lurk nearby. McWhatever is generally cheap (100-150Ft). A 10% tip has come to be expected in many establishments.

Travelers may also rely on markets and raisin-sized 24-hr. stores, labeled "Non-Stop," for staples. Take a gander at the **produce market** (*C D5*), IX, Vámház krt. 1-3 at Fővám tér (open Mon. 6am-3pm), the **ABC Food Hall** (*B2*), I, Batthyány tér 5-7 (open Sun. 7am-1pm) or the **Non-Stops** at (*C3*) V, Október 6. u. 5 and (*C4-5*) V, Régi Posta u., off Váci u. past McDonald's.

Restaurants

Central Pest

Vegetárium (*C5*), V, Cukor u. 3 (tel. 138 37 10). Metro: "Ferenciek tere." A block and a half from the Metro stop; walk up Ferenciek tere (formerly Károlyi M. u.) to Irány u. on the right; a quick left puts you on Cukor u. Vegetarian and macrobiotic dishes (tempura dinner 300Ft). A great place to detox after a week of meat. Classical guitar in the evening. Vigorously smoke-free environment. Menu in English. Open daily noon-10pm.

Alföldi Kisvendéglő (*D5*), V, Kecskeméti u. 4 (tel. 117 44 04). Metro: "Kálvin tér," 50m past the Best Western. Traditional Hungarian folk cuisine—even the booths are paprika-red. The sumptuous homemade rolls (24Ft) should be reason enough to come. Entrees 180-300Ft. Open daily 11am-midnight.

Claudia (*D5*), V, Bástya u., off of Kecskeméti u. (tel. 117 19 83). Metro: "Kálvin tér." Subterranean family restaurant with hearty, inexpensive food. Entrees 220-510Ft. Generous helpings of exotic specials are a highlight. Open daily 11am-11pm.

Golden Gastronomie (*C4*), V, Bécsi u. 8 (tel. 117 21 97), two doors down from American Express. The enticing deli fixings are provocatively displayed. You can sample the salads (60-85Ft per 100g) before making a choice and devour your selection under a cool artificial tree. English spoken. Open 24 hrs.

Apostolok (*C5*), V, Kígyó u. 4-6 (tel. 118 37 04). Visible from the "Ferenciek tér" Metro stop, on a pedestrian side-street toward the bridge. An eclectic, expensive evening of Gothic ambience and superb food in an old beer hall. Entrees 400-700Ft. Open daily 11am-11pm.

Szindbád (*C4*), V, Markó út 33 (tel. 132 29 66), at the corner of Bajcsy-Zsilinszky. 2 blocks from the "Nyugati tér" Metro stop. Impeccable elegance and stupendous desserts, but you pay for quality. Book two days ahead and look sharp. Open Mon.-Fri. 11:30am-3:30pm and 6:30pm-midnight, Sat.-Sun. 6pm-midnight.

Downtown Pest

Bohémtanya (*C3-4*), V, Paulay Ede u.6 (tel. 122 14 53) Walk from the "Deák tér" Metro station (all lines) or Bajcsy-Zsilinsky Metro station (M1). Packed at lunchtime for its large portions of delicious Hungarian food. Traditional brooding Hungarian atmosphere. Entrees from 230Ft. English menu and English-speaking staff. Open daily noon-11pm.

Picasso Point Kávéhaz (*C3*), VI, Hajós u.31 (tel. 132 47 50) Walk two blocks north of the "Arany János" Metro station (M3) and make a right onto Hajos U. A bohemian hang-out for students, intellectuals and foreigners. The English/Hungarian menu is an eclectic mix of traditional Hungarian and everything else - including chili, french onion soup and crêpes. Recently voted "Best Bar Food" in a *Budapest Weekly* survey. Live music. Open daily from noon to some vaguely defined point after 3am.

New York Bagels (*DE5*), IX, Ferenc körút 20 (tel. 215 78 80). A 200m walk toward the river from the "Ferenc körút" Metro stop, near the Petőfi Bridge. Eastern Europe's first and only bagel shop, with nine more branches throughout Hungary. Assorted bagels baked hourly, freshly made spreads, sandwiches, salads and the only chocolate chip cookies in Budapest. A bagel with lox, cream cheese and onions costs 379Ft. Counter service. Owned by a former *Let's Go* Researcher-Writer and a Wall Street escapee.

New York Bagels (the Sequel) (*C3*) VI, Bajcsy-Zsilinszky út 21, a block north of St. Stephen's Basilica (tel. 111 84 41, fax 131 83 02). The Budapest Bagel Baron strikes again. Same baked bliss in a more elaborate setting. Both stores accept delivery orders by phone and fax. Open daily 9am-midnight.

Marquis de Salade (*C3*), VI, Hajó u. 43 (no telephone). Two blocks north of the "Arany János" Metro station (M3) at the corner of Bajzy-Zilinsky ut. A self-service mix of salads and Middle Eastern food in a cozy storefront about the size of a large closet. The Azerbaijani owner speaks English and posts notes about her regulars on the walls. She has also been known to try new dishes on the spot at her patrons' urging. A plateful of anything offered costs 150Ft. Open Mon.-Fri. 9am-midnight, Sat.-Sun. noon-midnight.

Sancho (*D4*), VII, Dohány u. 20 (tel. 267 06 77). Walk up Károly Krt. from the "Astoria" Metro stop (M2). "American-Mexican" pub and restaurant serving tacos, burritos, chimichangas, and their ilk. Various popular local bands perform evenings. At "tequila time" (11pm) the waiter puts on a sombrero and carries around a tray of half-price shots. English menu, entrees from 350Ft. Open Mon.-Fri. 6pm-2am, Sat. 6pm-4am.

Fészek Müvész Klub Etterem (*E2-3*), VII, Kertész u. 36 (tel. 122 60 43). Metro to "Oktogon" (M1) or tram #4 0r #6 to Király u.; it's at the corner of Dob u. The name means "Nest Artist's Club Restaurant"; this was once the dining hall of a Golden Age private club for performing artists. Excellent Hungarian food and very low prices; the English menu is five pages single-spaced, and ranges from beef and fowl to venison and wild boar. Entrees from 270-600Ft. In warm weather, walk through to the leafy courtyard. Open daily noon-1am.

Sirály (*C4*), VI, Bajcsy-Zsilinszky út. 9 (tel. 122 88 64 or 122 88 80). Metro: "Deák tér." Well-prepared Hungarian food (entrees 250-400Ft) and imported beer. Just the place to partake of some potent paprika. Fast and friendly service. Menus and service in English. Open daily noon-midnight.

Megálló ("Bus stop"; *C5*), VII, Károly krt. 23, two doors to the left of the IBUSZ office. Metro: "Deák tér." Look beyond the ratty bearskin on the wall to the 130-item menu (available in English) which includes such temptations as "rumpsteak with gizzard in red wine." Dinner about 400Ft. Open daily 11am-11pm.

Bagolyvár (*F1*), XIV, Allatkerti Körut 2 (tel. 121 35 50). Metro: "Hősök tere." Directly behind the Museum of Fine Arts—a perfect place to deconstruct the chromatic schema presented on your supper plate. Exceptional Hungarian cuisine, yet remarkably affordable. Entrees 300-400Ft. Open daily noon-10pm. The Gundel Restaurant next door is Budapest's most famous—and most expensive.

Restaurant Hanna (*CD4*), VII, Dob u. 35 (tel. 142 10 72), a 10-min. walk from Deák tér. Wholesome kosher food in an Orthodox Jewish time-warp. Dress Conservatively. Open Mon.-Fri. and Sun. 11am-3pm.

Shalom Restaurant (*CD4*), VII, Klauzál tér 2, same directions as for Hanna above (tel. 122 14 64). Reform your palate at this elegant but inexpensive Kosher restaurant in the traditionally Jewish section of town. Entrees 300-400Ft. Open daily noon-11pm.

Buda

Remiz, II, Budakeszi út 5. (tel. 275 13 96). Take the #158 bus from Moszkva tér to "Szépilona" (about 10min.) and walk three stores beyond the stop. Traditional Hungarian cuisine in a cosmopolitan atmosphere. Frequented by Hungarian tennis-racket-wielding yuppies. Prices are average (entrees 380-880Ft) but it is just fancy enough for special occasions. Outdoor seating in warm weather, live music, menu in Hungarian, English, Italian and German. Call ahead for reservations. Open daily 9am-1am.

Söröző a Szent Jupáthoz (*A2*), II, Dékán u. 3 (tel. 115 18 98). 50m from the "Moszkva tér" Metro stop, with an entrance on Retek. Venture down the modest stairway, then right back up into a lively garden. Portions are gargantuan—be ready to roll yourself home. "Soup for Just Married Man" 139Ft. Entrees 300-900Ft. Open 24 hrs.

Marxim (*A2*), II, Kis Rókus u. 23 (tel. 115 50 36). Metro: "Moszkva tér." With your back to the Lego-esque castle, walk 200m along Margit körút and turn left. KGB pizza and Lenin salad are just a few of the revolutionary dishes served in structurally constrained, barbed-wire-laden booths. Food prepared by the staff according to their abilities, consumed by the patrons according to their needs. Join the locals in thumbing their nose at the erstwhile oppressive vanguard. Open Mon.-Fri. noon-1am, Sat. noon-2am, Sun. 6pm-1am.

Marcello's (*C5*), XI, Bartók Béla út 40 (tel. 166 62 31). May be the only pizzeria in Budapest to use tomato sauce rather than ketchup. Pizzas 160-340Ft; salad bar as well. Reservations suggested. Open Mon.-Sat. noon-10pm.

Cafés

The café in Budapest is like grandmother's house—more a living museum of a bygone era than just a place to be spoiled by scrumptious desserts and coffee. These amazing establishments were the pretentious haunts of Budapest's literary, intellectual, and cultural elite. If you lounge in the hallowed eateries long enough, you'll be smothered by the atmosphere. A leisurely repose at a Budapest café is a must for every visitor; best of all, the absurdly ornate pastries are inexpensive, even in the most genteel establishments. Order them at the counter and wait for them at your table.

Café New York (*C4*), VII, Erzsébet krt. 9-11 (tel. 122 38 49). Metro: "Blaha Lujza tér." Turn of the century "starving" *artistes* fed under its exquisite gilded ceilings. Cappuccino 100Ft. Ice cream and coffee delights 100-350Ft. Open daily 9am-midnight. Full, Hungarian-style meals are served in a separate section downstairs noon-midnight. Entrees from 700Ft.

Művész Kávéház (*D2*), VI, Andrássy út 29 (tel. 267 06 89). Diagonally across the street from the National Opera House; use Metro station "Opera" on M1. The highly-acclaimed café draws the pre- and post-Opera crowds with its Golden-period wood panelling and gilded ceilings. Pastries start at 60Ft. Under the same management as Lukács Cukrászda and Gerbeaud Cukrászda; the three are considered the most elegant in Budapest. Open daily 9am-midnight.

Lukács Cukrászda (*D2-3*), VI, Andrássy út 70. Metro: "Vörösmarty utca," near Hősök tere. One of the most stunning cafés in Budapest. Dieters will wish the heavenly cakes and tortes (30-50Ft) were more expensive. Seated service costs more. Open Mon.-Fri. 9am-8pm.

Gerbeaud Cukrászda (*C4*), V, Vörösmarty tér 7. Metro: "Vörösmarty tér." Formerly the meeting place of Budapest's literary elite, this café retains a stunning 19th-century elegance. You can write your own obscure novel by the time you're served. No menus in some sections. Pastries for about 90Ft. Open daily 7am-9pm.

Ruszwurm (*A-B3*), I, Szentháromság u. 7. Confecting since 1826 and strewn with period furniture. Stop by to relax after the majesty of Mátyás Cathedral down the street in the castle district. You won't be hurried on your way. Best ice cream in Budapest 20Ft per scoop. Cakes 50-70Ft. Open daily 10am-8pm.

Caffé Károlyi (*E6*), V, Károlyi u. 19 (tel. 267 02 06). South of the Ferenc krt. Metro stop (M3). Around the corner from a law school, this café with the look of a modern coffee shop is a favorite hangout for the young and the beautiful. Breakfast pastries from 30Ft. Cakes from 60Ft. Open 9am-1am.

Wiener Kaffeehaus (Bécsi Kávéház) (*C4*), V, Apáczai Csere János u. 12-14, inside the Forum Hotel on the Danube. Budapest's *crèmes de la cake* tantalize from glass cases. Give your life meaning for only 90Ft. Open daily 9am-9pm.

SIGHTS

Hungary celebrated its 1000-year anniversary in 1896. The various constructions for this Millenary Exhibition, still so prominent in the city, attest to the vast wealth and power of the Austro-Hungarian Empire at the turn of the century. Among the architectural marvels commissioned by the Habsburgs are the Parliament and the adjacent Supreme Court Buildings (now the Ethnographic Museum), Heroes' Square, Szabadság (Liberty) Bridge, Vajdahunyad Castle, and the first Metro station in continental Europe. The domes of both Parliament and St. Stephen's Basilica (completed several years later) are 96m high—vertical referents to the historic date.

Castle Hill

Budapest's **Castle District** (*AB3-4*) rests 100m above the Danube, atop the 2km mound called **Várhegy** (Castle Hill; *A3*). Cross the **Széchenyi lánchíd** (chain bridge; *B4*) and ride the *sikló* (cable car) to the top of the hill (daily 7:30am-10pm, 80Ft; closed the second and fourth Monday of the month). The upper lift station sits just inside the castle walls. Built in the 13th century, the castle was leveled in consecutive sieges by Mongols and Ottoman Turks. Christian Habsburg forces razed the rebuilt castle while ousting the Turks after a 145-year occupation. Reconstruction was completed just in time to be destroyed by the Germans in 1945. Determined Hungarians pasted the castle together once more, only to face the new Soviet menace; bullet holes in the palace façade recall the 1956 uprising. In the *post*-post-war period, sorely needed resources were channeled into its immediate reconstruction—evidence of its symbolic significance to the nation. During this rebuilding, extensive excavations revealed artifacts from the earliest castle on this site; they are now housed in the **Budapest History Museum** in the **Budavári palota** (Royal Palace; *B4*), The palace, just to the left of the cable car peak station, holds numerous other collections as well (see Museums below).

From the palace, stroll down Színház u. and Tárnok u. to reach **Trinity Square** (*A3*), site of the Disney-esque **Fisherman's Bastion** (*A3*). This arcaded stone wall supports a squat, fairy-tale tower with a magnificent view across the Duna. Behind the tower stands the neo-Gothic **Mátyás templom** (Matthias Church; *A3*), converted into a mosque literally overnight on September 2, 1541, when the Turks seized Buda; it remained a mosque for 145 years. These days, High Mass is celebrated Sundays at 10am with orchestra and choir (come early for a seat), and organ concerts lob melodies into the church's resplendent interior and into valley below on summer Fridays at 8pm (open daily 7am-7pm). Entrance into the church should get stricter as bombs placed by fringe groups from the former Yugoslav republics in the summer of 1994 destroyed valuable stained glass windows.

The holy edifice also conceals a **crypt** and a **treasury**; descend the stairway to the right of the altar. Besides the treasury's ecclesiastic relics, don't miss the stunning marble bust of Queen Elizabeth, next to the entrance to the **St. Stephen chapel.** The marble was hewn from the Italian Carrara mine, reputed to hold the world's finest carving stone from which Michelangelo's master sculptures were all crafted (treasury open daily 9am-5:30pm; admission 30Ft). A second side chapel contains the tomb of King Béla III and his wife, Anna Chatillon; this was the only sepulchre of the Árpád line of kings spared from Ottoman imperial looting. Outside the church is the grand **equestrian monument** of King Stephen, with his trademark double cross.

Next door sits the presumptuous **Budapest Hilton Hotel** (*A3*), which incorporates the remains of Castle Hill's oldest church, an abbey built in the 13th century. Intricate door-knockers and balconies adorn the Castle District's other historic buildings; ramble through **Úri utca** (Gentlemen's Street; *A3*) with its Baroque townhouses, or **Táncsics Mihály utca** (*A3*) in the old Jewish sector. You can enjoy a tremendous view of Buda from the Castle District's western walls. By **Vienna Gate** (*A3*) at the northern tip of the District, frequent minibuses run to Moszkva tér, though the walk down Várfok u. only takes about five minutes.

Elsewhere in Buda

The **Liberation Monument** crowns neighboring **Gellért Hill** (*B5*), just south of the Castle. This 100-foot bronze statue honors Soviet soldiers who died while "saving" Hungary from the Nazis. Hike up to the **Citadella** (*B5*) from beside Gellért Hotel at the base of the hill, or take bus #27 from "Móricz Zsigmond Körtér" to two bus stops beyond the hotel. The Habsburgs built the Citadella after the Revolution of 1848 to remind the populace just who held the reigns of power. The view from the top is especially spectacular at night, when the Duna and its bridges shimmer in black and gold.

Overlooking the Elizabeth bridge near the base of Gellért Hill is the statue of **St. Gellért,** complete with colonnaded backdrop and glistening waterfall. Bishop Gellért was sent by the Pope to the coronation of King Stephen, the first Christian Hungarian monarch, to assist in the conversion of the pagan Magyars. Many were not intrigued by his message; some disgruntled nonbelievers hurled the good bishop to his death from atop the hill that now bears his name.

Fresh forest air awaits in the suburban Buda Hills, far into the second and twelfth districts. Catch bus #56 from "Moszkva tér," north of the Castle, and ride up Szilagyi Erzsébet fasor and Hűvösvölgyi út to the end station. There you'll find the **Vadaskert** (Game Park), where boar roam while deer and antelope play—here, people speak optimistically and the skies are supposedly cloudless.

The fabulous **Pál-völgyi caves** hide east of the Vadaskert. Even if you've never spelunked before, you can enjoy the 15m-high caverns, remarkable stalactite formations, and such attractions as the Cave of the Stone Bat and the 25m-deep Radium Chamber. Be sure to wear your long johns, even in the summer—it's quite cool inside. Take the HÉV rail line from "Batthyány tér" two stops to "Szépvölgyi," and walk away from the river to Kolosy tér; then take bus #65 or 65a, across from the yellow church, five stops to "Pál-völgyi barlang." (Guided 45-min. tours leave May.-Sept. Tues.-Sun. on the hour 9am-4pm; Oct.-Dec. and Feb.-April Sat.-Sun. on the hour 9am-4pm. Admission 50Ft, students 30Ft.)

Between the caves and the Castle, the **Margit híd** (*B1*) spans the Duna to the lovely **Margitsziget** (*B1*). Off-limits to private cars, the island offers capacious thermal baths, luxurious garden pathways, and numerous shaded terraces. According to legend, the island is named after the daughter of King Béla IV; he vowed to rear young Margaret as a nun if the nation survived the Mongol invasion of 1241. The Mongols left Hungary decimated but not destroyed, and Margaret was confined to the island convent. Take bus #26 from "Szt. István krt." to the island

Pest

Cross the Danube to reach Pest, the throbbing commercial and administrative center of the capital. The **Inner City** (*C4*), is an old section rooted in the pedestrian zone of Váci u. and Vörösmarty tér. Pest's river bank sports a string of modern luxury hotels leading up to the magnificent neo-Gothic **Parliament** (*B2*) in Kossuth tér. Don't just marvel at one of Europe's most impressive structures from across the river; step out from the Metro stop "Kossuth tér" (arrange tours at IBUSZ and Budapest Tourist; 1200-1500Ft).

St. Stephen's Basilica (*C3*), just two blocks north of Deák tér, is by far the city's largest church, with room for 8500 worshippers under its massive dome. A very Christ-like depiction of St. Stephen (István) adorns the high altar. A 323-step climb up a spiral staircase to the Panorama tower yields a 360 degree view of the city from central Pest's tallest building (open daily 9am-6pm; admission 100Ft). St. Stephen's holy **right hand,** one of the nation's most revered religious relics, is displayed in the Basilica. (Open daily 8am-7pm. Free. Hand visible Mon.-Sat. 9am-5pm, Sun. 1-4pm; Oct.-March Mon.-Sat. 10am-4pm, Sun. 1-4pm.) On the other hand, you may want to visit the **Great Synagogue** (*D4*), on the corner of Dohány and Wesselényi streets, the largest active synagogue in Europe and the second largest in the world. The building was designed to hold almost 3000 worshippers, with men on the ground floor and women in the gallery. The **Holocaust Memorial** in the back garden is directly over mass graves dug during 1944-45. Inscribed on each leaf of the metal tree is the name of a victim. The harmonies of organ and mixed choir float through the entire structure during Friday evening services from 6-7pm. The synagogue is also open to visitors weekdays 10am-6pm (10am-3:30pm in winter) but the building has been under perpetual renovation since 1988 and much of the artwork is likely to be blocked from view. Next door, the **Jewish Museum** (*D4*) devotes one haunting room to photos and documents from the Holocaust (open April-Oct. Mon. and Thurs. 1-4pm, Tues.-Wed. and Fri. 10am-1pm).

Andrássy út (*CD2-3*), the nation's grandest boulevard, extends from the edge of the Belváros in downtown Pest and arrives in **Hősök tere** (Heroes' Square; *E1*), some 2km away. A stroll down Andrássy út from Hősök tere toward the inner city best evokes Budapest's golden age, somewhat tarnished by Soviet occupation. The most vivid reminder of this period is the **Hungarian National Opera House** (*Magyar Állami Operaház*; *D3*) at VI, Andrássy út 22. Laden with sculptures and paintings in the ornate Empire style in the 1880s, the building is even larger than it appears from the street—the gilded auditorium sits 1289 people. The Opera House is still one of the leading centers for the performing arts, and its audience is drawn from all over Europe by the absurdly low prices and top-quality operas, ballets and symphonies. Best tickets for National Ballet performances cost only 600Ft. The **box office** (tel. 153 01 70) is located in the left side of the building (open Tues.-Sat. 11am-1:45pm and 2:30pm-7pm, Sundays and holidays 10am-1pm and 4-7pm). Unclaimed tickets are sold at up to 50% discounts a half-hour before showtime. Tours of the Opera House are conducted in Hungarian, English, German, Italian and French (daily at 3 and 4pm; 300Ft, students 150Ft). The Metro station "Opera" on the yellow line is located directly in front of the building.

The grandest stretch of Andrássy út is between Hősök tere and the Oktogon. Metro line 1 runs directly underneath Andrássy. Hősök tere is dominated by the **Millennium monument** (*E1*), which showcases the nation's most prominent leaders and national heroes from 896 to 1896, when the structure was erected for the great 1000th Anniversary celebration. The seven fearsome horsemen led by Prince Árpád, represent the seven Magyar tribes who settled the Carpathian Basin. Overhead is the Archangel Gabriel, who, according to legend, offered Stephen the crown of Hungary in a dream. It was King (later Saint) Stephen who made Hungary an officially Christian state with his coronation on Christmas Day, 1000. Stephen (István) is the first of the figures on the colonnade.

Behind the monument, the **Városliget** (City Park; *F1*) contains a permanent circus, an amusement park, a zoo, a castle, and the impressive **Széchenyi Baths.** The **Vajdahunyad Castle** was also created for the Millenary Exhibition of 1896. Originally constructed of canvas and wood, the castle was redone with more durable materials in response to popular outcry. The façade, intended to chronicle 1000 years of architecture, is a stone collage of Romanesque, Gothic, Renaissance, and Baroque. The castle now houses the **Museum of Agriculture** (see Museums below). Rent a **rowboat** (June to mid-Sept. daily 9am-8pm; 150Ft per hr.) or **ice skates** (Nov.-March daily 9am-1pm and 4-8pm; 60Ft in morning, 100Ft in evening) on the lake next to the castle. Outside the Museum broods the hooded statue of **Anonymous,** the secretive scribe to whom we owe much of our knowledge of medieval Hungary, and, after Ibid., the most-quoted figure in history.

The ruins of the northern Budapest garrison town, **Aquincum,** continue to crumble in the outer regions of the third district. These are the most impressive vestiges of the Roman occupation, which spanned the first four centuries AD. The settlement's significance increased steadily over that time, eventually attaining the status of **colonia** and becoming the capital of Pannonia Inferior; Marcus Aurelius and Constantine were but two of the Emperors to bless the town with a visit. The **museum** on the grounds contains a model of the ancient city as well as musical instruments and other household items (open April-Sept. 9am-6pm, Oct. 9am-5pm; admission 20Ft). The remains of the **Roman military baths** are displayed to the south of the Roman encampment, beside the overpass at Flórián tér near the "Árpád híd" HÉV station. From the stop, just follow the main road away from the river.

MUSEUMS

Buda Castle (*B4*), I. Szentháromság tér 2. (tel. 175 75 33). Leveled by Soviet and Nazi combat at the end of World War II, the reconstructed palace now houses an assortment of fine museums. Wing A contains the **Museum of Contemporary**

History and the **Ludwig Museum,** a collection of international modern art. Open Tues.-Sun. 10am-6pm. Admission 100Ft, students 50Ft. Wings B-D hold the **Hungarian National Gallery,** a vast hoard containing the best in Hungarian painting and sculpture over a millennium. Open Tues.-Sun. 10am-6pm. Admission 60Ft, students 30Ft. One ticket is valid for all 3 wings. Wing E comprises the **Budapest History Museum,** which chronicles the development of Óbuda, Buda, and Pest over the years. Open Wed.-Mon. 10am-5pm. Admission 60Ft, students 30Ft.

Museum of Military History (*A3*), I, Tóth Árpád sétány 40, in the northwest corner of the Castle District. An intimidating collection of ancient and modern weapons, from the most functional to the most ornate. Some swords seem too splendid to sully with petty disembowelments. The upper floor presents the military history of World War II and a compelling day-by-day account of the 1956 uprising, from the student protests to the Soviet invasion. Don't miss the severed fist from the massive Stalin statue toppled in the uprising or the memorial to the revolutionaries caught Red-handed thereafter. Open Tues.-Sun. 10am-4pm, Sun. 10am-6pm. Admission 20Ft.

Museum of Fine Arts (Szépművészti Múzeum; *EF1*), XIV, Hősök tere (tel. 142 97 59). Simply spectacular. One of Europe's finest collections of artworks, from Duccio to Picasso. An immense Italian exhibit. Highlights include an entire room devoted to El Greco and an exhaustive display of Renaissance works. Cameos from all your favorite Impressionists, too. Open Tues.-Sun. 10am-6pm.

Museum of Ethnography (Néprajzi Múzeum; *BC2*), V, Kossuth Tér 12, across from the Parliament building (tel. 132 63 40). Outstanding exhibit of Hungarian folk culture, from the late 18th century to the First World War. It covers the whole cycle of peasant life and customs, from childhood to marriage (to taxes) to death. Though slightly skewed in presentation, the second floor houses an exceptional collection of cultural artifacts from Asian, African, and Aboriginal peoples. One of Budapest's best museums; located in the erstwhile home of the Hungarian Supreme Court. Open Tues.-Sun. 10am-5:30pm. Admission 50Ft, students free; everyone admitted free on Tues.

Hungarian National Museum (*D5*), VIII, Múzeum Krt. 14-16 (tel. 138 21 22). Includes a chronicle of Hungarian settlements, as well as the **Hungarian Crown Jewels,** supposedly the very crown and scepter used in the coronation of King Stephen on Christmas Day in 1000 AD. Don't miss Mihály Munkácsy's enormous "Golgotha" canvas in the room at the top of the stairs. Open Tues.-Sun. 10am-5pm. English guide book 75Ft. Admission 50Ft, students 20Ft.

Vásárhelyi Museum, III, Szentlélek tér 1 (tel. 250 15 40). Take the HÉV train from the "Batthyány tér" Metro to "Árpád híd." Room after room filled with the arresting work of Viktor Vásárhely, a pioneer of Op-Art. Open Tues.-Sun. 10am-6pm Admission 30Ft.

Museum of Agriculture, XIV, in the Vajdahunyad Castle. Offers exhibits like the "History of Pig Breeding." Also displays stuffed domestic animals and artificial fruit. Open Tues.-Sun. 10am-6pm. Admission 50Ft, free with ISIC and on Tues.

ENTERTAINMENT

Performances

Budapest offers a vast cultural program year-round. Pick up a copy of the English-language monthly *Programme in Hungary* or *Budapest Panorama*, both available free at tourist offices; they contain daily listings of all concerts, operas, and theater performances in the city. The "Style" section of the weekly English-language *Budapest Sun* is another excellent source for schedules of entertainment happenings.

The **Central Theater Booking Office** (*D3*), at VI, Andrassy u. 18, next to the Opera House (tel. 112 00 00), and the branch at Moszkva tér (tel. 135 91 36) both sell tickets without commission to almost every performance in the city (open Mon.-Thurs. 10am-1pm and 2-6pm, Fri. 10am-3pm). An extravaganza in the gilded, neo-Renaissance **State Opera House** (*D3*), VI, Andrássy út 22 (tel. 153 01 70; Metro: "Opera") can cost as little as 50Ft; the box-office sells any unclaimed tickets for amazing discounts (up to half-price) a half hour before showtime (ticket office open Tues.-Sun. 10am-7pm). The city's **Philharmonic Orchestra** is also world renowned; their concerts thunder through town almost every evening from September to June. The **National Philharmonic Ticket Office** (*C4*), Vörösmarty tér 1 (tel. 117 62 22) is next to the Opera House (open Mon.-Fri. 10am-6pm, Sat. 10am-2pm; tickets 600Ft).

When the weather turns warm, the Philharmonic takes a summer sabbatical, but the tide of culture never ebbs; **summer theaters** are located throughout the city. Classical music and opera are performed in the **Hilton Hotel Courtyard** (*A3*), I, Hess András tér 1-3 (tel. 175 10 00), next to the Matthias Church in the Castle District. The **Margitsziget Theater** (*B1*), XIII, on Margaret Island (tel. 111 24 96), features opera and Hungarian music concerts. Take tram #4 or 6 to "Margitsziget." Try **Zichy Mansion Courtyard,** III, Fö tér 1, for orchestral concerts. **Mátyás Church** (*A3*), Szentháromság tér, holds regular organ, orchestral and choral recitals at 8pm (tickets 100-320Ft). The **Pest Concert Hall** (Vigadó; *C4*), V, Vigadó tér 2, on the Danube bank near Vörösmarty tér (tel. 118 99 03), hosts operettas almost every other night (tickets 150-500Ft).

Folk-dancers stomp across the stage at the **Buda Park Theater,** XI, Kosztolányi Dezső tér (tel. 117 62 22). Brochures and concert tickets flood from the ticket office at Vörösmarty tér 1 (open Mon.-Fri. 11am-6pm; tickets 70-250Ft). For a psychedelic evening, try the laser shows at the **Planetarium** at Metro: "Népliget" (tel. 134 11 61). Performances—they even play Floyd on occasion (Tues.-Sat. at 6:30 and 9pm; admission 350Ft). The **Budapest Spring Festival,** in late March, provides an excellent chance to see the best in Hungarian art and music. The autumn **Budapest Arts Weeks** is another major festival.

Hungary has an outstanding cinematic tradition; most notable among its directors are Miklós Jancsó and István Szabó. Movie theaters abound in Budapest, screening the latest Hungarian and foreign films. The English-language *Budapest Sun* lists a surprising number of reasonably current movies in English; check the kiosks around town. If *szinkronizált* or *magyarul beszélő* appears next to the title, the movie has been dubbed. Tickets are largely a bargain, compared to the monstrous admission at American theaters (100-150Ft).

Bath Houses

To soak away weeks of city grime, crowded trains, and yammering camera-clickers, sink into a **thermal bath,** a constitutive part of the Budapest experience. The post-bath massages vary widely from a quick three-minute slap to a royal half-hour indulgence. Many baths are meeting places, though by no means exclusively, for Budapest's gay community.

Gellért (*C6*), XI, Kelenhegyi út. 4 (tel. 166 61 66). Take bus #7 to the Hotel Gellért at the base of Gellért Hill where women and men frolic nude in separate baths. Thermal bath 250Ft, mudpack 15Ft, massage 150Ft per 15min. Open Mon.-Fri. 6:30am-7pm, Sat.-Sun. 6:30am-1pm.

Király (*B3*), II, Fő u. 84 (tel. 115 30 00), take the M2 Metro until the first stop after the river at "Datthnay tér." Bathe in the splendor of Turkish cupolas and domes. Steam bath, 120Ft. Thermal bath, 120Ft. Massage 170Ft per 15min, 400Ft per 30min. Open Mon., Wed., and Fri., 6:30am-6pm to men only. Open exclusively to women on Tues. and Thurs. 6:30am-6pm, Sat. 6:30am-noon.

Széchenyi Fürdő (*F1*), XIV, Állatkerti u. 11 (tel. 121 03 10), beckons in the main city park (Városliget), near Heroes' Square. Metro: M1 (yellow) to "Hősők tere." Their thermal baths (120Ft) command a devoted following among the city's venerable gentry, while the large **outdoor swimming pool** (200Ft) delights their grandchildren. Bring your swimsuit. Massage 550Ftper 30min.

Rudas (*B5*), Döbrentei tér 9 (tel. 156 13 22). Take the #7 bus until the first stop after crossing into Buda. Located right on the river, under a dome built by Turks 400 years ago. The centuries haven't changed the dome, the bathing chamber, or

So, you're getting away from it all.

Just make sure you can get back.

AT&T Access Numbers
Dial the number of the country you're in to reach AT&T.

*AUSTRIA†††	022-903-011	*GREECE	00-800-1311	NORWAY	800-190-11
*BELGIUM	0-800-100-10	*HUNGARY	00◇-800-01111	POLAND†◆²	0◇010-480-0111
BULGARIA	00-1800-0010	*ICELAND	999-001	PORTUGAL†	05017-1-288
CANADA	1-800-575-2222	IRELAND	1-800-550-000	ROMANIA	01-800-4288
CROATIA†◆	99-38-0011	ISRAEL	177-100-2727	*RUSSIA† (MOSCOW)	155-5042
*CYPRUS	080-90010	*ITALY	172-1011	SLOVAKIA	00-420-00101
CZECH REPUBLIC	00-420-00101	KENYA†	0800-10	S. AFRICA	0-800-99-0123
*DENMARK	8001-0010	*LIECHTENSTEIN	155-00-11	SPAIN•	900-99-00-11
*EGYPT¹ (CAIRO)	510-0200	LITHUANIA◆	8◇196	*SWEDEN	020-795-611
*FINLAND	9800-100-10	LUXEMBOURG	0-800-0111	*SWITZERLAND	155-00-11
FRANCE	19◇-0011	F.Y.R. MACEDONIA	99-800-4288	*TURKEY	00-800-12277
*GAMBIA	00111	*MALTA	0800-890-110	UKRAINE†	8◇100-11
GERMANY	0130-0010	*NETHERLANDS	06-022-9111	UK	0500-89-0011

Countries in bold face permit country-to-country calling in addition to calls to the U.S. **World Connect℠** prices consist of **USADirect®** rates plus an additional charge based on the country you are calling. Collect calling available to the U.S. only. *Public phones require deposit of coin or phone card. ◇Await second dial tone. †May not be available from every phone. †††Public phones require local coin payment through the call duration. ◆Not available from public phones. • Calling available to most European countries. ¹Dial "02" first, outside Cairo. ²Dial 010-480-0111 from major Warsaw hotels. ©1994 AT&T.

Here's a travel tip that will make it easy to call back to the States. Dial the access number for the country you're visiting and connect right to AT&T. It's the quick way to get English-speaking AT&T operators and can minimize hotel telephone surcharges.

If all the countries you're visiting aren't listed above, call **1 800 241-5555** for a free wallet card with all AT&T access numbers. Easy international calling from AT&T. **TrueWorld Connections.**

AT&T

These people are only a third of the 150 students who bring you the *Let's Go* guides. With pen and notebook in hand, a few changes of underwear stuffed in our backpacks, and a budget as tight as yours, we visited every *penstone*, *palapa*, pizzeria, café, club, campground, or castle we could find to make sure you'll get the most out of *your* trip.

We've put the best of our discoveries into the book you're now holding. A brand-new edition of each guide hits the shelves every year, only months after it is researched, so you know you're getting the most reliable, up-to-date, and comprehensive information available.

But, as any seasoned traveler will tell you, the best discoveries are often those you make yourself. If you find something worth sharing, drop us a line. We're at Let's Go, Inc., 1 Story Street, Cambridge, MA 02138, USA (e-mail: letsgo@delphi.com).

HAPPY TRAVELS!

the *men only* rule. Vapor bath 120Ft. Therapeutic massage 200Ft per 15min., 400Ft per 30min. Mon.-Fri. 6am-7pm, Sat.-Sun. 6am-1pm.

NIGHTLIFE

After a few drinks, you'll forget you ever left home. Global village alternateens wearing familiar labels and grinding to a familiar beat make the club scene in Budapest, well, *familiar* to anyone who has ever partied in a western city. A virtually unenforced drinking age and cheap drinks may be the only cause for culture shock.

Tilos az Á ("A is Forbidden," as in "Trespassers W–"; *D5*), VIII, Mikszáth Kálmán tér 2 (tel. 118 06 84). Walk down Baross u. from the "Kálvin tér" Metro station for two blocks, then turn left. This cryptic Magyar name should strike a chord with hard-core Winnie the Pooh fans. Live music that ranges from jazz to funk to alternative and dancing until the wee hours. Cover 150-300Ft depending on the band. Open daily 8pm-4am.

Titanic *(D3)*, VII, Akácfa u. 56. Walk from the "Blaha Lujza tér" Metro station (M2). Live jazz in a labyrinthine basement for a mostly student crowd. 150Ft cover charge. Open Mon.-Thurs. 6pm-2am, Fri.-Sat. 6pm-5am. No icebergs.

Black and White Pizzeria *(D3-4)*, VII, Akácfa u. 13 (tel. 122-7645) Walk from the "Blaha Lujza tér" Metro station (M2). Live blues and jazz. Kitchen serves pizza, spaghetti and salads. Open Mon.-Sat. 11am-2am, Sun. 6pm-midnight.

Morrison's Music Pub *(D3)*, VI, Révay u. 25 (tel. 269 40 60), just to the left of the State Opera House. Metro: "Opera." Half pub, half hip dance club with cheap beer (80Ft). A young, international crowd. This may be the one place in Europe where Jim's *not* buried. Cover 100-200Ft. Functional English red telephone booth inside (although it's not connected to British Telecom). Open noon-4am.

Fregatt Pub *(C4)*, V, Molnár u. 26 (tel. 118 99 97), off Váci u. near the "Ferenciek tér" Metro station. Popular pub, usually filled with English-speaking twenty-somethings. Beer 110Ft. Shuts down at midnight.

Jazz Café *(BC2)*, V, Balassi Bálint u. 25 (tel. 132 43 77). Metro: "Kossuth tér," then walk across the square past the Parliament building. Live jazz under blue lights nightly at 8pm. Club closes at midnight.

Véndiák (Former Student), V, *(D5)* Egyetem tér (tel. 117 46 03). Metro: "Kálvin tér," then walk up Kecskeméti u. This late-night bar also has a lively dance floor. Popular with local students. Really picks up around 2am. Open 9pm-4am.

Táncház, an itinerant folk-dancing club, where you can stomp with Transylvanians. They invariably have a beginners' circle and an instructor. Locate them in *Pesti Mősor* (Budapest's weekly entertainment guide, in Hungarian) or ask at Tourinform.

DANUBE BEND

North of Budapest, the Danube sweeps south in a dramatic arc, called the Danube Bend *(Dunakanyar)*, as it flows east from Vienna along the Slovak border. Roman ruins from first-century settlements cover the countryside, and medieval palaces and fortresses glower upon the river in **Esztergom** and **Visegrád.** An artist colony thrives today amidst the museums and churches of **Szentendre.** Within 45km of Budapest, the region offers a variety of daytrips and overnights from the capital.

Hourly **buses** from Budapest's Árpád Híd Metro station link these three towns with the capital. If you are traveling directly to Esztergom, take the bus through Dorog; this 70-minute shortcut subtracts about a half-hour from the route that winds along the river through Visegrád (139Ft), stretches between the 3 cities cost 74Ft each). The suburban **railway** (HÉV) to Szentendre (every 15min., 40min.; 64Ft) starts from Batthyány tér in Budapest (M: Batthyány tér). The river boats from Budapest are a pleasurable, if painstaking, way to visit the region. **Boats** cast off from Budapest's Vigadó tér dock four times per day and steam upriver to Visegrád (3hrs., 180Ft) and Esztergom (5hrs., 120Ft), making short stops along the way. Not all boats stop at Szentendre (1hr., 75Ft). **Dunatours,** V, Bajcsy-Zsilinszky út. 17 (tel. 131 45 33), in Budapest, books private rooms in Szentendre (open Mon.-Thurs. 9:30am-noon and 12:30-5pm, Fri. 9:30am-noon and 12:30-4pm).

■■■ SZENTENDRE

Szentendre, named for Szent Endre (Saint Andrew) is both blessed and cursed by its proximity to Budapest. Only 20km away and connected by the convenient HÉV commuter rail line and frequent bus service, Szentendre is the most popular day-trip from the capital. Despite an active artistic community, superior galleries and art museums, and a near-overload of folk crafts, Szentendre lacks much of the easy charm and sense of history of towns outside Budapest's shadow. Thousands of visitors come to Szentendre every day in a tidal wave of humanity that floods the town in the morning and recedes at night; to residents—who eagerly await the chance to separate tourists from their money—it's like shooting fish in a barrel.

Orientation and Practical Information Szentendre sits on the west bank of the Danube, centered around the triangular Fő tér. Major streets leading from the square are Dumsta Jenő u., which runs south, and Bogányi u., which branches off to the northeast. **Tourinform,** at Dumsta Jenő u. 22 (tel. 31 79 65 or 31 79 66) has several English-speakers on its staff, and provides maps, brochures, and advice (open daily 10am-4pm). The main **post office** is at Kossuth Lajos u. 23, just north of the HÉV station. OTP Bank, at Dumsta Jenő u. 6, is excruciatingly slow but compensates by offering the best **currency exchange** rate (open Mon. 8am-5pm, Tues.-Thurs. 8am-3pm, Fri. 8am-noon). **IBUSZ,** at Bogdányi u. 4 (tel. 31 03 33), offers nearly as good a rate (open Mon.-Fri. 8:30am-3:30pm). The **HÉV commuter rail, train,** and **bus** station is south of the old town; to get to Fő tér, use the underpass and head up Kossuth. HÉV makes the trip between Budapest and Szentendre every 10-20min. (45min., 45Ft). Buses run from Budapest's Árpád bridge station every 10-40min. (30min., depending on traffic, 70Ft). At least once per hour buses continue to Visegrád (45min.) and Esztergom (90min.). The MAHART **hydrofoil** pier is northeast of Fő tér; walk inland one block to Bogdányi u. (3 per day to Budapest, 60min.; 160Ft). You can rent a **bike** at IBUSZ for 800Ft per day. Warning: there is **no luggage storage** available in Szentendre.The **telephone city code** is 26.

Accommodations and Food IBUSZ (see above) can arrange **private accommodations** (doubles 1200Ft, triples 1300Ft). **Dunatours,** Bogdányi u. 1 (tel. 31 13 11), is a little less sharp with English, but can find doubles starting at 1300Ft (open daily 9am-6pm). **Tourinform** (see above) can make reservations for rooms ranging from 1500-3000Ft per night. **Ilona Panzió,** near the center of town at Rákóczi Ferenc u. 11 (tel. 31 35 99), rents doubles with private baths for 2000Ft, breakfast included. **Róz Panzió,** just south of the HÉV station at Pannoni u. 6-8 (tel. 31 37 37), rents doubles for 2800-3800Ft, triples for 3100-4100Ft, breakfast included. **Pap-sziget Camping** (tel. 31 06 97), 1km north of the center of town on Pap-sziget island, rents doubles in motel rooms for 990-1190Ft, and triples in luxury bungalows for 1990Ft. The minimum charge for a campsite (space for two) is 830Ft.

Both Bogdányi u. and Duna-korzó near Fő tér are lined with pricey restaurants all serving nearly the same Hungarian fare. **Korona Vendéglő** on Fő tér has seating on the main square, perfect for people-watching (entrees 340-590Ft; open 11am-11pm). **Valvarház Étterem,** a few blocks south at Kucsera Ferenc u. 11 (tel. 31 57 71), has inexpensive lunch menus, and other entrees for 250-450Ft (open Sun.-Thurs. noon-11pm, Fri.-Sat. noon-midnight). The **Dixie Fried Chicken** at Dumsta Jenő u. 16 is a fast food joint with a Hungarian salad bar (heavy on sauces, light on fresh veggies) and frozen yogurt. There is a **non-stop grocery** at Dumsta Jenő u. 5.

Sights and Entertainment On Szentendre's **Templomdomb** (Church Hill) above Fő tér is the **Roman Catholic parish church,** Szentendre's first stone church, built in the 13th century. Parts of the structure added in the 14th century are still visible, but most of the building was redone in Baroque style in the 18th century. Facing the church is the **Czóbel Museum,** which exhibits works of Hungary's foremost impressionist, Béla Czóbel (open Tues.-Sun. 10am-4pm; admission 30Ft). To the north across Alkotmány u. is the red-and-yellow Baroque **Serbian Orthodox Church,** built in the 18th century. Inside, the ceiling frescoes have been worn away by age and neglect, but the iconostasis behind the altar holds dozens of vibrant gilt-framed paintings. The church is not open to visitors on a regular schedule, but the grounds house a **Museum of Serbian Religious Art** from the 18th century. The pieces were collected from abandoned churches when the area's Serbs returned home after the Ottoman Turkish threat had passed (open Wed.-Sun. 10am-6pm; admission 30Ft).

The most impressive of Szentendre's museums is the **Kovács Margit Múzeum,** at Vastagh György u. 1. It exhibits brilliant ceramic sculptures and tiles by the 20th-century Hungarian artist Margit Kovács (including the renowned Pound Cake Madonna). Much of her early work is cutesy and borders on the saccharine, but her later sculptures are subtle and haunting. (Open daily 10am-6pm. Admission 100Ft, students 25Ft. When the museum is full, visitors are asked to wait outside until others leave.) Connoisseurs should head for the **Wine Museum** *(Bormúzeum)* in the extensive wine cellar beneath the overpriced Labirintus Étterem restaurant Bogdányi u. 10. The exhibit itself is underwhelming, but the cellar offers **wine tastings** of the products of Hungary's 20 different winegrowing regions, from the famous *Tokaji* and *Egri Bikavér* (Bull's Blood) to ones that even Hungarians haven't heard of. If you're an aficionado, this may be your best chance to sample the fruit of all of Hungary's vines at once. Just make sure you can still get out of the cellar. (Open daily 11am-10pm. Admission 100Ft. Wine tasting 350Ft.)

In July and August, Szentendre frolics away the evenings with **Szentendrei Nyár** (Szentendre Summer), a festival of jazz, classical music, drama, and folk dancing. Tourinform distributes free programs and sells tickets.

■■■ VISEGRÁD

Ninety minutes north of Budapest between the Pilis and Börsöny mountains, Visegrád got its start as the high-water mark of the Roman Empire. After suffering one too many Mongol invasions, King Béla IV built a **citadel** on the hilltop in 1259. A second castle built at the foot of the hill later became the royal **palace** and seat of the royal court, as Visegrád and Buda alternated as the capital of Hungary for nearly two centuries. In the late 1400s during the reign of King Matthias, the palace was rebuilt by Italian masters into a huge, multi-level structure incorporating both late Gothic and Renaissance styles. Today, visitors come by bus or boat through Esztergom or Szentendre, to walk among the partially reconstructed ruins of the palace and castle and hike the hillsides above the Danube.

Orientation and Practical Information   The village of Visegrád stands along Route 11 on the east bank of the Danube. The two major streets are Fő utca, which runs parallel to the river, and Nagy Lajos utca, which goes up the hill. Buses on Route 11 stop in front of the ferry *(komp)* pier, which is opposite Nagy Lajos u., and in front of the MAHART pier, about a kilometer north.

The tourist information office is **Visegrád Tours,** Rév u. 13 (tel. 39 81 60; open daily 10am-8pm, Sept.-May 10am-6pm), between the ferry and Nagy Lajos u. The staff can handle English, German, Italian, and Russian, and provides free pamphlets and maps. **Buses** to Esztergom (45min.) and to Budapest (90min.) pass through Visegrád at least once per hour. **MAHART boats** run twice per day to: Esztergom (2 per day, 2hrs.); Szentendre (1 per day, 75min.); and to Budapest via Szentendre (3 per day, 2½hrs.). **City Bus Visegrád** is a private company that runs red minibuses up to the citadel and back for 800Ft one way, regardless of the number of passengers.

There's usually one waiting at the ferry pier across from Rév u. every hour on the hour. The **telephone city code** is 26.

Accommodations and Food   Visegrád is usually visited as a day trip, but accommodations are easy to find; Fő utca is lined with panzió and private homes displaying *Zimmer Frei* signs. **Visegrád Tours** (see above) can arrange doubles in private accommodations for 1200-2000Ft per night. **Haus Honti,** Fő u. 66 (tel. 39 81 20), is a comfortable panzió with five rooms (doubles 1500Ft, singles 1200Ft per night; breakfast 150Ft). The **Elte Guest House,** Fő u. 117 (tel. 39 81 65), has doubles for 1780Ft and triples for 2500Ft per night. All rooms include refrigerators, private baths, and balconies. **Camping Visegrád,** Fő u. 70 (tel. 39 81 02), has entrances both on Fő u. and on Route 11 (campsite use 55Ft per tent and 165Ft per person; open May 1-Oct. 11). Visegrád has mainly touristy restaurants. The biggest and most touristy of all is the **Sirály Restaurant,** Rév u. 7 (tel. 39 83 76), which has a menu in six languages. Entrees are traditional Hungarian fare and cost 350-550Ft (open 10am-10pm). More intimate and less glitzy is **Diófa Restaurant,** Fő u. 48 (tel. 31 81 31), which serves Swedish and Hungarian dishes for 230-450Ft. The **snack bar** next to the Citadel parking lot is open during visiting hours and is better than many of its ilk. There is a **grocery** on Rév u. across from Visegrád Tours.

Sights   **Salamon-Torony,** or "Solomon's Tower" (named for a king imprisoned here in the 11th century), is the hexagonal monolith standing at the foot of the hill. Formerly part of a fortress that regulated river traffic, it now houses the **King Matthias Museum,** which contains fountains and wall reliefs and other relics taken from the grounds of the palace, including the red marble **Lion Fountain,** one of the symbols of Visegrád. Be thorough—winding staircases and narrow passageways make it easy to miss a room (open May-Sept. daily 9am-5pm; admission 50Ft).

Now partially reconstructed, the **Royal Palace,** above the western end of Fő u., was abandoned for centuries and used as a source of building stones. Scattered replicas of arcades and fountains lend a sense of the palace's original grandeur to the labyrinth of stairways and open courtyards that were once rooms (open April-Oct. Tues.-Sun. 9am-5pm; admission 50Ft, students free). Some creative anachronism takes place on the palace grounds one weekend in early July each year during the **International Palace Games.** Costumed actors recreate medieval fights, contests, and coronations (call the managing office at 39 81 28 for dates and details).

High above the Danube, the **Citadel** holds exhibits on folkcraft, hunting, and local history, but the real attraction is the castle itself and the view it commands of the river and surrounding hills (open April-Nov. daily 8:30am-6pm; admission 50Ft, students 30Ft). You can reach the Citadel on foot or by bus—look for signs that say *"Fellegvár."* There are several hiking paths that take about 30 minutes. The easiest starts at the end of Kalvaria u.; the path that leads from behind Solomon's Tower is considerably more challenging. Some of the southbound buses on Route 11 turn left and head up Nagy Lajos u. They stop in front of the ferry pier (15min., 28Ft).

■■■ ESZTERGOM

Approached from the south, Esztergom emerges as a single blue-green dome atop a plateau. The hill and the cathedral sitting upon it have marked Esztergom for a thousand years. The present-day center of Hungarian Catholicism, Esztergom witnessed the birth and coronation of St. István (Stephen), Hungary's first Catholic king. While the nation's capital, Esztergom endured invasions by the Mongols, Turks, and Austrian Habsburgs. At the western edge of the Danube bend, Esztergom is 20km beyond Visegrád, and a stone's throw across the river from Slovakia.

ORIENTATION AND PRACTICAL INFORMATION

Shaped like an hourglass, Esztergom runs north-south on the eastern bank of the Danube. **Várhegy**—Castle Hill—stands over the river in the northwest section.

Directly to its south, separated by the Kis-Duna River is park-like **Primas Sziget,** or Primate Island. The center of town is a crossroads called Rákóczi tér, where the travel agencies and other services are clustered.

Tourist Office: Gran Tours, Széchenyi tér 25 (tel. 31 37 56), at the edge of Rákóczi tér, provides maps, English information, and current copies of *Time* and *Newsweek* for 200Ft. Open Mon.-Fri. 8am-3:30pm; in summer also Sat. 8am-noon.

Currency Exchange: The branch of **OTP** on Rákóczi tér gives the best exchange rate in town, but if you're pressed for time, check around the corner with **IBUSZ** at Lőrinc u. 1 (tel. 31 25 52). Open Mon.-Thurs. 8am-4pm, Fri. 8am-3pm.

Post Office: On the southern end of Széchenyi tér at Arany János u. 2.

Telephone City Code: 33.

Trains: The train station is at the southern edge of town. Get to Rákóczi tér by walking up Baross Gábor út, making a right onto Kiss János altábornagy út, and keeping straight as it becomes Kossuth Lajos utca. Eleven trains per day leave Esztergom for Budapest (1½hrs., 300Ft), but buses are generally more convenient.

Buses: The bus terminal is a few blocks south of the square—take Simor János utca straight up. Two or three buses per hour leave for Budapest via Dorog (80min., 200Ft). Buses that go through Visegrád (30min., 90Ft) and Szentendre (70min., 200Ft) before reaching Budapest (100min., 250Ft) leave each hour at 50 minutes past the hour, and sometimes more frequently.

Ferries: Twice a day, **MAHART** boats leave from the pier at the end of bőzhajó u. on Primate Island and stop at Visegrád (80min., 160Ft) and Szentendre (3½hrs., 180Ft) on the way to Budapest (4¾hrs., 200Ft).

Hydrofoil: Once a day on weekends, a hydrofoil leaves from the same pier and scoots directly to Budapest (70min., 600Ft).

ACCOMMODATIONS

IBUSZ (see above) can arrange private rooms (doubles) starting at 1000Ft per night.
Gran Tours (see above) averages about 1500Ft per night.

Platán Panzió, Kis-Duna Sétány 11 (tel. 31 13 55), between Rákóczi tér and Primate Island, is one of several pensions in the center of town. Doubles start at 3000Ft for one night, 2500Ft per night for longer stays, breakfast included.

Martos Flóra Kollégium, Szent Istvan tér 16 (tel. 31 28 13), just northeast of the cathedral. 400Ft per night in a 4-bed dorm room (open weekends during the school year and daily from late June-early Sept.).

Gran Camping, Nagy-Duna Sétány (tel. 31 13 27), is in the middle of Primate Island, within walking distance of all the sights. The pension charges 4000Ft for a double. The student hostel charges 320Ft per person in a 6-bed room (all these prices go up July-Aug.). Campsite use runs 270Ft per tent and 300Ft per person.

Vadvirág Camping, 11-es Fő út (tel. 31 22 34), is east of town on route 11. Triples in the motel cost 1200Ft, and 4-person bungalows cost 2000Ft. Campsite use is 210Ft per tent and 180Ft per person. From the bus terminal, take the bus for Visegrád, which leaves at 50 minutes past each hour, and sometimes more often.

FOOD

A **Julius Meinl supermarket** is located at Rákóczi tér, and a small non-stop **ABC** grocery lies across the street from it. The bus terminal is surrounded by various seedy **non-stop büfé,** as well as a non-stop **ABC.**

Alabárdos Restaurant, next door to the panzió at Bajcsy-Zsilinsky út 49 (tel. 31 26 40), serves excellent Hungarian specialties (entrees 350-580Ft). Menu in German, English, and Italian. Open daily noon-11pm.

Halász Csárda (tel. 31 10 52), at the Primate Island end of Bottyán Bridge, serves the catch of the day straight from the Danube for 195-590Ft, and other entrees for 295-580Ft. English menu. Open daily noon-10pm.

Alpesi Vendéglő, Babits Mihaly u. 4 (tel. 31 24 56). A friendly neighborhood eatery four blocks east of the bus terminal (entrees 180-420Ft). Open daily 10am-10pm.

Csülök Csárda, Batthány Lájos u. 9 (tel. 31 24 20), serves traditional fare next to the southern foot of Castle Hill (entrees 300-480Ft). Open daily 11am-11pm.
Belvárosi Kávéház, at Rákóczi tér, is the best place for dessert, coffee, and people-watching. Open Mon.-Sat. 8am-midnight, Sun. 8am-11pm.

SIGHTS AND ENTERTAINMENT

If you can't find the **Esztergom Cathedral,** you're either too close or in the wrong town; take a step back and look up. The main approach is on the east side, although there are shortcuts up the southeast side of the hill. A basilica was originally built here in 1010, but the present neo-Classical behemoth—the biggest church in Hungary and one of the biggest in Europe—was consecrated in 1856 (Franz Liszt composed and conducted the consecration mass). Inside, the cathedral is impressive mainly for its size—the immense domed hall and its bold designs are rather plain. At the main altar is a colossal copy of Titian's *Assumption.* On a smaller scale, the red marble **Bakócz chapel** on the south side of the cathedral is a masterwork of Renaissance Tuscan stone-carving. It once stood in another position on the hill—during construction of the present cathedral, it was dismantled into 1600 pieces and reassembled as part of the new building. To catch all the details, go all the way into the chapel before looking around. Climb to the 71.5m-high **cupola** for a view of Slovakia (10Ft), or descend into the Egyptian-style **crypt** to walk among the ranks of Hungary's archbishops.

Fight your way through the hordes of old ladies to enter the **Cathedral Treasury** through the passage on the north side of the main altar. The most extensive ecclesiastical collection in Hungary, the treasury contains case after case of gold, silver, and precious stones worked into chalices, monstrances, and vestments that go back 1000 years. The jewel-studded cross labelled #3 in the case facing the entrance to the main collection is the **Coronation Oath Cross,** on which all of Hungary's rulers pledged their oath from the 13th century until 1916 (open daily 9am-4:30pm; admission 60Ft, students 30Ft).

Next to the cathedral is the restored 12th-century **Esztergom Palace,** built in Gothic style by French architects commissioned by King Béla III. It is now the **Vármúzeum** (Castle Museum), which illustrates the history of the castle and the town from Roman times. Room #5 is said to be the oldest room of any residential building in Hungary, and original frescoes are visible throughout the palace. (open Tues.-Sun. 9am-4:30pm, winter 10am-3:30pm; admission 50Ft, students 25Ft). For an extra 10Ft, you can go up to the roof to survey the kingdom, including a panoramic view of the cathedral, the river, and the town.

At the foot of the hill, the **Keresztény Múzeum** (Christian Museum), at Berenyi Zsigmond u. 2, houses the country's most exceptional collection of Hungarian and Italian Renaissance religious artwork. Strap slippers on over your shoes and pad through altar panels, portraits, and gory pictures of martyrs. The Holy Sepulchre of Garamszentbenedek (1430) is a cross between a cart and a cathedral that depicts the Apostles and Roman soldiers guarding Christ's tomb (open Tues.-Sun. 10am-6pm; admission 60Ft, students 30Ft).

The **Duna Múzeum** (Water Affairs Museum), Kölcsey Ferenc út 2, is a fun little collection illustrating the history of water management in Hungary. There's no English, but there are a lot of dioramas, models, and engineering tools, including a working 1895 clockwork calculating machine that multiplies and divides (open Wed.-Mon. 1-5pm; admission 20Ft, students free).

Simor János u., north of the bus terminal, is an open-air food and clothing **market** with a country-town atmosphere (open daily 6am-5pm). On summer evenings, **organ concerts** are held in the cathedral, and the **Castle Theater** troupe performs dramas and musicals. **Gran Tours** sells tickets and has free English- and German-language programs of all events in the area.

NORTHERN HUNGARY

Hungary's northern upland is a series of six low mountain ranges running northeast from the Danube Bend along the Slovak border. The towns of the north are known for their skill at satisfying two of life's vital needs: recreation and alcohol. The **Bükk** and **Aggtelek National Parks** beckon hikers and explorers with their scenic trails and karst cave systems, while the dry volcanic soil of the hillsides yields the grapes for the famed white *Tokaj* and red *Egri Bikavér* wines.

■ ■ ■ EGER

In 1552, Captain Dobó István and his tiny army, holed up in Eger Castle, held off the invading Ottomans for an entire month. Credit for their fortitude is given to the potent *Egri Bikavér* ("Bull's Blood of Eger" wine) they quaffed before battle; today Dobó's name and likeness appear throughout the city, and the sweet red Bikaver still flows copiously and cheaply. Eger flourished in the 17th and 18th centuries, and ubiquitous Baroque architecture has set the town's character since. Eger's wealth of historical sights, pedestrian streets, cheap lodgings and tiny, atmospheric wine cellars are two hours northeast of Budapest by train. Eger is also a launch site for exploring the Baradla caves in Aggtelek and the Bükk and Mátra mountains, the loftiest in the country.

Orientation and Practical Information The center of Eger is Dobó tér, dotted with monuments to the hero, and just southwest of the castle and hill where he made his celebrated stand. Several blocks of pedestrian streets, where most services can be found, radiate from the square. The main **bus station** is five minutes west of Dobó tér. The main **train station** is about a 20-minute walk south of the center; to get to Dobó tér, take a bus to the bus terminal (#10, 11 or 14) or walk: make a right onto Deák Ferenc u., make a right and then a quick left onto Széchenyi u at the Cathedral, and then a right onto Ersek u., which leads into the square.

The upbeat **Tourinform** office is at Dobó tér 2 (tel. 32 18 07). They have stacks of brochures, pamphlet and maps (the good one costs 50Ft) and information about all the accommodations in town, and will research anything they don't already know (but sorry, not the average wing speed of an African swallow; open Mon.-Fri. 9am-6pm, Sat. 9am-2pm, in summer also Sun. 10am-1pm). **Exchange currency** at the branch of OTP Bank, Széchenyi u.2 (open Mon., Tues. and Thurs. 7:45am-3:15pm, Wed. 7:45am-5:15pm, Fri. 7:45am-2:30pm). The main **post office** is at Széchenyi u.22 (open Mon.-Fri. 8am-8pm, Sat. 8am-2pm, Sun. 8am-noon). The **telephone city code** is 36.

Trains from Budapest's Keleti station go directly to Eger three times a day, or make a tight connection in Füzesabony. Trains split in Hatvan (about a third of the way) so make sure you're in the right car. From Eger, there are three direct trains to Budapest (2hrs., 487Ft), and about 13 to Füzesabony (20min.) where there are connections to Budapest and Miskolc (90min., 230Ft). Seven local trains a day go to scenic Szilvasvárad (70min. 102Ft) passing through partially-scenic Bélapátfalva (where an octopusine cement factory strangles the green hills—45min, 76Ft). Fifteen **buses** a day take the highway to Budapest (2½hrs., 462Ft) and several others take local routes. Buses for Bélapátfalva (50min, 92Ft) and Szilvásvárad (90min, 108Ft) leave twice an hour on weekdays, hourly on weekends. One bus a day leaves to the caves at Aggtelek at 8:40am and makes the return trip at 3pm (times are subject to change, 3hrs., 390Ft one way).

Accommodations and Food Eger Tourist, Bajcsy-Zsilinszky u.9 (tel. 31 17 24) can arrange doubles in private homes in the center of town for 1040Ft, with private bath 1560Ft. 2-3-person apartments cost 2470Ft (open Mon.-Fri. 8:30am-7:30pm, Sat. 9am-1pm; Sept.-May Mon.-Fri. 9am-5pm, Sat. 9am-1pm). **IBUSZ** in the

HUNGARY

courtyard called Bajcsy-Zsilinszky tömb-belső next door (tel. 31 26 52) has doubles from 1000Ft. **Express,** Széchenyi u. 28 (tel. 31 07 57), relays info about summer rooms in university dorms (open Mon.-Fri. 8am-4pm). Eger Tourist operates a very basic **Tourist Motel,** Mekchey u. 2 (tel. 31 00 14). Doubles are 1200Ft, with private bath and breakfast 2300Ft. **Hotel Romantik,** Csik S. u. 26 (tel. 31 04 56), is a small pension with doubles equipped with TV and refrigerator for 2400-4000Ft. **Hotel Unicornis,** Dr. Mibay u. 2 (tel. 31 28 86), is a one-horn hotel; doubles cost 1400Ft, with private bath 1800Ft; breakfast included. Hostel facilities in the hotel run 250Ft per night in a room with 8, 12, or 13 beds; guests are obliged to eat one meal at the hotel (200-300Ft). The **Eszterházi Károly Kollégiuma,** Lányka u. 2 (tel. 41 20 66), east of the castle, charges 300-400Ft per night in a room with 3-4 beds (open July1-Sept. 5). Eger Tourist also operates **Autós Caravan Camping** (a.k.a. Eger Camping), Rákóczi u. 79 (tel. 31 05 58), north of the center. Motel doubles cost 1250Ft, as do doubles in cottages. Campsite use runs 280Ft per tent and 220Ft per person. Walk there in 20 minutes, or take bus #5, 10, 11, or 12. Twenty minutes southwest of the center, near the Valley of the Beautiful Women, is **Tulipán Camping,** Szépasszony Völgy 7 (tel. 31 05 80), where a place for two people and a tent costs 500Ft.

For quick and inexpensive gourmet food, go to the **MBM Bajor Söház,** Bajcsy-Zsilinsky u. 19 (tel. 31 63 12), next to Dobó tér, a Bavarian beer house that serves Hungarian specialties English menu; entrees run 229-459Ft (open daily 10am-10pm, Nov.-March Mon.-Sat. 10am-10pm). **The Belvárosi Étterem,** Bajcsy-Zsilinszky u. 8 (tel. 31 18 72), across the street, is a *csárda* that attracts a mix of tourists and locals. The *halászlé* (spicy fish soup) consists of an excellent paprika with some soup trickled around it. Entrees 200-750Ft (open daily 11am-11pm). **Gyros Étterem,** Széchenyi u. 10, serves identifiable gyros, souvlaki, and Greek salads. Pita gyros sandwiches 120Ft, entrees 235-480Ft (open daily 9am-10pm). **Kazamata** hibernates in a concrete cave in the shadow of the cathedral at Pyrker tér 3 (tel 31 15 38). Stuffed-meat pancakes are 90Ft, entrees 220-280Ft (open daily noon-7pm; Tue., Wed., Fri., and Sat. nights, it becomes a **disco** from 9pm).

Sights and Entertainment Eger can be thoroughly explored in a morning, but with good company or just plain determination, you can spend an entire afternoon and evening in the wine cellars of **Szépasszonyvölgy,** the Valley of the Beautiful Women. The valley is lined with the doors of hundreds of tiny pub-like cellars dug into the hills. Most consist of little more than 20m of tunnel and a few tables and benches, but each has its own personality: some cellars are subdued, and in others rowdy Hungarians and Gypsies hold candlelit sing-alongs. Eger is the red wine capital of Hungary, and the most popular libations are *Medina* and the sweeter *Bikavér* (order white at your own risk). There are various explanations for how the name *Bikavér* ("Bull's Blood") got its name. The most patriotic claim is that when the Ottomans saw the red-stained beards of Dobó's men, they assumed the Magyars drank bull's blood for strength before battle. Others say that the name was chosen in derision of the Turks, whose Muslim faith allowed them to drink anything—even bull's blood, according to the Hungarians—except alcohol. Some claim that at one point the wine was actually fortified with blood.

One-deciliter glasses are 30Ft, and little glasses for tasting are free. People force small coins into the spongy fungus on the cellar walls—if your coin sticks, you'll come back to that spot one day. Most cellars open at 1pm and begin to close around 8pm, or whenever their owners have had enough; the best time to go is late afternoon. Locals say the wine in the valley is watered down—you'll have to judge for yourself. Get there by walking west from Deák u. down Király u., which eventually becomes Szépasszonyvölgy u. and leads into the valley.

The yellow **cathedral** on Eszterházy tér is a good place to start a walking tour. The second-biggest church in Hungary, it was build in 1836 by Joseph Hild, who also built Hungary's largest—the Esztergom cathedral. Unlike the one in Esztergom, however, the interior is airy and spacious without being overwhelming. Distinguishing the real marble from the painted illusions is a challenge. Thirty-minute Baroque **organ concerts** are held here (Mon.-Sat. 11:30am and Sun. 12:30pm; 60Ft).

Opposite the cathedral is the 18th-century rococo **Lyceum.** The fresco in the magnificent library on the first floor depicts an ant's-eye view of the Council of Trent, which spawned the edicts of the Counter-Reformation (a slim lightning bolt at one end is blasting a pile of heretical books). Upstairs, a small **astronomical museum** houses 18th-century telescopes and instruments of the buildings's old observatory. A marble-line depression in the floor represents the meridian; when the sun strikes the center line through a tiny aperture in the southern wall, it is astronomical noon. Further up is an observation deck with great views. Another two floors higher is a periscope, which projects a live picture of the surrounding town onto a table in a perilously stifling room (open Mon.-Fri. 9:30am-1:30pm, Sat.-Sun. 9:30am-12:30pm; admission 60Ft, students 15Ft—buy tickets from the desk to the left of the entrance).

On the southern side of Dobó tér stands the luxuriously Baroque **Minorite Church,** built in 1773. It overlooks a statue of Captain Dobó and two co-defenders, including a woman poised to hurl a rock upon an unfortunate Turk. Hungarians revere medieval **Eger Castle;** it was here that Dobó István and his 2000 men repelled the unified Ottoman army, halting their advance for another 44 years. The castle's innards include subterranean barracks, catacombs, a crypt, and a wine cellar. An 80Ft ticket (students 40Ft), buys admission to a **picture gallery** showing Hungarian paintings from as early as the 15th century; the **Dobó Istvan Castle museum,** which displays excavated artifacts, armor, and an impressive array of sharp, spiky, and pointy weapons; and in summer, a **prison museum** where the collection of torture-chamber equipment will inspire sadists and masochists alike. A separate tour of the tunnels built into the casemates leaves from the cashier's window; the Hungarian-language tour costs 80Ft (students 40Ft) and tours in other languages, including English, can be arranged for 130Ft per person (students 90Ft).

Capture another Kodak moment from the 40m tall **Turkish minaret,** the Ottoman Empire's northernmost phallic symbol. Ascend the huge stone, uh, pencil (open daily 10am-6pm; admission 20Ft), but beware: the steep spiral staircase is not much wider than the average 20th-century person. The 18th-century **Serbian Orthodox church** on Vitkovics u. (at the northern end of the town center, parallel to Széchenyi u.) displays a magnificent altar and beautiful murals (open daily 10am-4pm; free).

Country women hawk produce and flowers in the cavernous **indoor market** at Kapona tér (open Mon.-Fri. 6am-6pm, Sat. 6am-1pm, Sun. 6am-10am). Upstairs are several tiny *büfé* selling pre-prepared food for paltry sums, daily until 7:30pm. Eger revels in its Baroque heritage during the **Baroque Festival** held throughout July. Nightly performances of operas and operettas and medieval and Renaissance court music are held in the courtyard of the Franciscan church, the cathedral, and in Dobó tér. An international folk-dance festival called **Eger Vintage Days** is held daily throughout September. See the Tourinform office for schedules and tickets.

■ NEAR EGER: AGGTELEK

The Baradla caves are a 24km-long system of limestone tunnels that wind between Hungary and Slovakia. Each chamber is a forest of dripping stalactites and stalagmites and fantastically shaped stone formations. The area also has excellent hiking.

Cave tours begin from two sites in Hungary—**Aggtelek** and **Jósvafő**—but they are more regular at Aggtelek, which is also easier to reach. The cave is open daily 8am-6pm, but visitors can only enter as part of a tour group (partly because they don't want anyone popping up in Slovakia). A large chamber with perfect acoustics has been converted into an auditorium, and the tours pause here for a light-and-sound show. The tunnels along the tour are all well lit, but the guide turns the lights off as you pass them in order to discourage stragglers. (Hour-long tours are scheduled to leave at 10am, 1pm, 3pm, and 5pm, but others are added on busy days. Admission 180Ft, students 90Ft.)

The one **bus** from Eger leaves at 8:40am, and arrives in Aggtelek around 11am (390Ft) in the front of the Cseppkő Hotel, 200m uphill from the cave entrance. The bus back to Eger leaves around 3pm; the bus to Miskolc leaves at 5:30pm. **Baradla Camping,** at the mouth of the cave (tel. (48) 31 27 00), has 8-bed dormitory rooms for 250Ft per person, as well as bungalows and campsites. There are several tiny *büfé* in the area, or you can try the restaurant in the **Cseppkő Hotel,** whose menu switches at random between English and German (entrees 200-500Ft).

■■■ TOKAJ

King Louis XIV called Tokaj wine (pronounced TOE-kai) "the wine of kings and the king of wines." Tokaj itself is just one of the 28 small towns and villages that take advantage of the volcanic soil and sunny climate at the feet of the Zemplén Mountains to produce unique white wines, but it lends its name to the entire class. Modern Tokaj is a dusty little town surrounded by vineyards and hills, where storks nest on chimneys and horse-drawn hay-wagons are a common sight.

Orientation and Practical Information   Tokaj runs north-south along the confluence of the Tisza and the Bodrog Rivers, and can be crossed on foot in about 15 minutes. The main street, Bajcsy-Zsilinszky Endre utca, becomes Rákóczi Ferenc utca. There is no tourist information office, nor travel agency of any sort in town; the hotel and some pensions distribute brochure that include street maps. The **post office,** Rákóczi Ferenc u. 24, is open Mon.-Fri. 8am-5pm, Sat. 8am-noon. **Exchange currency** at OTP Bank, at Rákóczi u. 35, open Mon.-Thurs. 8am-3:30pm, Fri. 8am-2:30pm. The **telephone city code** is 47. Nine trains per day run to Miskolc (1hr.). Fifteen per day run to Nyíregyháza (two directly, 2hrs., 264Ft), where there are regular connections to Debrecen. The station is a 15-minute walk southwest of town; walk east along the railroad embankment until you come to the underpass, then north on Bajcsy-Zsilinszky u. There is not much bus service to other towns.

Accommodations and Food   There is no tourist office to arrange private accommodations, but *Zimmer Frei* and *Szoba Kiadó* signs abound—your best bet is to walk along Rákóczi u. and choose one you like. The concrete and plexiglass-bubbled **Hotel Tokaj,** Rákóczi u. 5 (tel. 36 27 41), has comfortable singles for 2300Ft and doubles for 2600Ft. **Makk-Marci Panzió,** Liget Köz 1 (tel. 35 23 66), facing Rákóczi u., charges 1320Ft for one person, 2090Ft for two, 3190Ft for three, and 3190Ft for four. There are only five rooms, so reservations are a good idea. If you feel tougher than the mosquitoes that control the banks of the Tisza, **Tisza Camping** (tel. 35 20 12), across the river on Tiszapart, has bungalow doubles for 600Ft, triples for 1020Ft, and quads for 1200Ft. Campsite use costs 100Ft per person and 100Ft per tent. Just to the north, the slightly prettier **Pelsőczi Camping,** Tarcali u. 2 (tel. 35 26 26), charges 150Ft per person and 150Ft per tent.

At **Tiszavirag Halászcsarda,** Bajcsy-Zsilinsky u. 23 (tel. 35 26 32), burly waiters sling recent inhabitants of the Tisza. Fish dishes, including the fish soup *halászlé,* run 95-340Ft, other entrees 260-560Ft (open 9am-11pm). The **Pizzeria** in the Makk-Marci Panzió also serves cheap hamburgers and pasta, but don't expect to recognize the pizza (65-160Ft; open 10am-10pm). The **Róna Étterem,** Bethen Gábor u. 24, makes a half-hearted attempt at elegance, but serves acceptable food (entrees 250-400Ft; open 10am-10pm).

Sights and Entertainment   In Tokaj, wine is the word. There are nearly as many signs on the streets heralding private wine cellars—*Bor Pince* in Hungarian, or *Wein Kellar* in German—as there are signs for private accommodations.

Tokaj's main products are *Furmint,* a basic dry white wine, and *Hárslevelű,* which is slightly more complex. *Szamorodni* is an aperatif that ages in barrels for a year and a half. *Aszú* is *Furmint* sweetened with "noble rot" grapes (which ripen and dry out more quickly than the others in the same bunch) and aged for three years. The sweetness is measured in 3, 4, 5 or 6 *puttony,* or units of *Aszú* grapes added. *Fordítás* is another sweet wine, made from the byproduct of *Aszú,* and aged three years. Experts doing wine-tasting sample them in order from driest to sweetest. The wine barrels that line cellars are sealed with glass stoppers. If the barrel is empty, the stopper is pushed tightly into the hole. If it contains wine, the stopper is turned over and placed lightly over the hole to allow oxidation to occur.

The owners of the **private cellars** throughout the town are generally pleased to let visitors sample their wares (for a fee)—walk on in, or ring the bell if it looks shut. Serious **wine-tasting** takes place at **Rákóczi Pince,** Kossuth tér (tel. 35 20 09). This 1½km-long system of 24 tunnels was dug from volcanic rock in 1502, and served as the Imperial wine cellar for two centuries until the end of World War I. Hour-long **group tours** of the cellar, along with wine-tasting sessions, are held at 10am, 11am, and on the hour from 2-6pm. **Individual sessions** can be arranged at other times if there are no other guests. The walls of the tunnels are coated with 500 years' worth of dripping spongy fungus—it turns from cotton-ball white to sooty black in the presence of humans—which serves to keep the cellar at a constant 10°C and 80% humidity. A jacket helps down there, even in summer. Sessions are 150Ft for the tour and a single glass of wine, and 395Ft for 6 glasses. German-, English-, and occasionally French-speaking guides are available (open daily 9am-7pm).

The **Tokaji Museum,** Bethen Gábor u. 7. tells the history of the town through exhibits of the tools and equipment of wine production, and the glass bottles and porcelain decanters used for storing and serving wine over the last three centuries (open Tues.-Sun. 9am-5pm; admission 44Ft, students 20Ft).

The **Tokaji Galléria,** Rákóczi u. 23, in an old red-and-yellow Serbian Orthodox Church, houses exhibitions of local artists (open Tues.-Sun. 10am-noon and 1-5pm). The century-old **Great Synagogue,** guarded by a family of storks one block behind the gallery on Serház u., survived World War II by serving duty as a German barracks. It is newly yellow outside, but undergoing major renovations inside.

THE GREAT PLAIN

Romanticized in tales of cowboys as well as mirages rising off its flat soil, the Great Plain, or *Nagyalföld,* is an enormous grassland stretching southeast of Budapest and covering nearly one-half of Hungary's territory. Also called the *puszta,* or "ravaged land," the Great Plain was once a "Great Forest" until the occupying Turks chopped down all the trees. While much of the plain's eastern area is pasture and the south is mostly farmlands, a train ride through endless fields of sunflowers will bring you to the small, sophisticated cities of **Debrecen** and **Szeged.**

■■■ DEBRECEN

Debrecen is one of the few cities in the world with neither natural waterways nor defensive physical features; it began as the bread basket of the Great Plains, and later became a wealthy business center. Debrecen was once the "Calvinist Rome," the center of Protestantism during the Reformation in the 16th century. Even today more than 80% of its people are Protestant, making Debrecen the only city in Hungary where Catholics are the minority. Eighteenth century and more modern buildings alternate along Debrecen's broad streets, and the city's position near the Romanian border draws a haggling mix of Eastern Europeans.

Orientation and Practical Information The center of the city is **Kálvin tér;** nearly everything of interest to tourists is within walking distance. Running south from the square is the broad Piac utca, which ends with Petőfi tér and the train station. Three kilometers to the north is the recreational area and nature preserve **Nagyerdei Park.** Tram #1 (the only tram in town) runs from Petőfi tér

278 ■ THE GREAT PLAIN

through Kálvin tér, into the park, and then back. It is the most convenient way to get from the train to the town center, but be warned that ticket checks are frequent and merciless, and they don't fall for the "but-I'm-just-an-ignorant-tourist" bit. Get the 30Ft ticket from the kiosk in front of the station, or expect to pay the 350Ft fine at least once during your visit. The **bus station** is west of the center, on Külsö Vásártér. Walk east on Szédonyi u. to reach Piac U.

Tourinform, Piac u. 20 (tel. 41 22 50), has excellent English-speakers on staff to provide advice about anything, and gives away and sells several different maps of the city (open daily 8am-8pm, Sept.-May Mon.-Fri 8:30am-4:30pm). The main **post office** is west of Kálvin tér at Hatvan u. 7 (open Mon.-Fri. 7am-8pm, Sat. 8am-2pm, Sun. 8am-noon). The **telephone city code** is 52. The **Csökonai Konyvesbolt** bookstore at Piac U. 45 has a small and eclectic English selection spanning Shakespeare, Kipling, Tolkien, and Updike. The **Kossuth Lajos** University bookstore, at the edge of Nagyerdei Park at Egyetem Tér 1, has a larger stock. **Bus** service connecting Debrecen with other cities is sparse. There are four InterCity **trains** from Debrecen to Budapest each day (2hrs. 20min., 1080Ft). Fourteen less direct trains make the trip in 3hrs. (950Ft). There are five trains a day to Hortobágy (a village with a national park and a plains cowboy tradition; 1hr., 126Ft). There are two direct trains to Tokaj (2hrs., 264Ft) and two with a change in Nyiregyháza (2½hrs., 264Ft). Three trains per day run to Mihályfalva in Romania (2½hrs., US$27.50 or DM17).

Accommodations and Camping   **Majdútourist,** Kálvin tér 24 (tel. 31 96 16) can arrange singles in private accommodations for 500-800Ft, and doubles for 800-1500Ft (open Mon.-Fri. 8am-5pm, Sat 8am-12:30pm). **IBUSZ,** now at Piac u. 11-13 (tel. 41 55 55) but expected to move to larger quarters at Hatvan u. 1 by the summer of 1995, has doubles starting at 830Ft (open Mon.-Thurs. 8am-4pm, Fri. 8am-3pm). **Motel Sport,** in Nagyerdei Park at Oláh Gábor u. 5 (tel. 41 96 55) has doubles with shared bathrooms for 1500Ft. **Ludas Matyi Panzió,** one block east of Piac u. at Batthyány u. 26 (tel. 34 98 48), has singles with private bath for 1500Ft and doubles with private bath for 2400Ft. A night in an 8-bed dorm-style room costs 400Ft. The spanking-new dormitory *(újkollégium)* at **Kossuth Lajos University,** Egyetem tér 1 (tel. 31 66 66), has comfortable triples with shared bathrooms for 1600Ft (open July-August). The **Benczúr Kollégium,** in Nagyerdei Park at Pallagi út 11 (tel. 31 69 33), is a little run-down but is being renovated. Doubles cost 505Ft, and a bed in an 8- or 10-bed room costs 150Ft. **Termál Camping,** also in the park at Nagyerdei Krt 102 (tel. 41 24 56), has 4-person bungalows for 1800-2800Ft, and charges 250Ft per tent and 200Ft per person for campsite use.

Food   The best kitchen in town is in the wandering cellar of **Csokonai Söröző,** Kossuth u.21 (tel. 36 80 83), where over-attentive waiters smother their customers, and then allow them to roll dice for a free meal. The menu includes English translations and photographs of the food, and has entrées for 165-490Ft (open daily noon-11pm). **Gamrinus,** down a long courtyard at Piac u. 28b (tel. 32 66 92) serves good food in large portions, although the service is easily distracted. There is violin and cimbola music from 8pm, and the two old musicians sit in a corner arguing until showtime. Menu in English and German. Entrees 220-500Ft (open daily 11am-11pm). The doorway to **Serpince A Flaskához,** Miklós u.2 (tel. 41 25 82), is set in a giant wooden flask. Traditional Hungarian food, heavy on Debrecen specialties. The English menu is a very abridged version of the original. Entrees 190-360Ft (open daily 11:30am-midnight). The **Önkiszológáló Étterem,** next to the Arany Bika Motel at Piac u. 9, is an inexpensive cafeteria that fills up at lunch time. Entrees from 60Ft (open Mon.-Fri. 7am-6pm, Sat. 7am-3pm). **McDonald's** is at Piac u.53, at the corner of Arany Janos u. (open 8am-11pm).

Sights and Entertainment   Looming over the north end of Kálvin tér is the twin-spired **Nagy templom** (Great Church). Built in 1863, this is the largest Protestant church in Hungary. The T-shaped interior can hold 3000 people, and the huge organ threatening to crush the pulpit is the only major adornment. (Open to visitors Sun 11am-4pm, Mon.-Fri. 9am-noon, 2-4pm, Sat. 9am-noon. Admission 12Ft, students 6Ft. For an extra 40Ft you can climb to the top of the bell tower for a view of the city.) The **Reformed College,** Kálvin tér 16, was established in 1538 as a center for Protestant education. The present building, built in 1819, has housed the government of Hungary twice in 1839 during the War of Independence, and in 1944 during World War II. Today it holds Calvinist schools as well as a collection of religious art and an exhibit on the history of Protestantism in Debrecen. Explanations in Hungarian and German only. The 650,000-volume library is the second oldest in Hungary, and includes 16th-century bibles on display (open Tues.-Sat. 9am-5pm, Sun 9am-1pm; admission 50Ft, students 25Ft).

Two blocks east in Déri tér stands the **Déri Museum,** a collection that touches on everything from local history to Japanese lacquerware. See it for its exhibit on folkcraft since the 16th century, and its marvelous collection of gold and silver work (don't lean on the cases—the alarm system is *very* sensitive). Upstairs in the separate **Munkácsy Gallery** are three murals of Christ's trial and crucifixion by Mihály Munkácsy. Munkácsy painted himself into *Ecce Homo* as the old man in the crowd, next to the arch. (Museum open Tues.-Sun 10am-6pm. Admission 50Ft, students 25Ft. Admission to the Munkácsy gallery 40Ft, students 25Ft.)

The works of renowned sculptor Medgyessy Ferenc (1881-1958) are exhibited in the **Medgyessy Múzeum** at Péterfia u. 28. In the courtyard stands the sculpture of nursing mother and child that appears on the 1000Ft note. A report card the artist received in 1895 shows him getting the equivalent of Ds in everything but Natural History and Gym. When queried, the guides explain that Medgyessy is beloved by Hungarians for his unique expression of traditional Hungarian themes, and because he once had an exhibition in Paris that really impressed the French.

The morning **flea market** on Vágó hid utca east of the city center may be more impressive for its vendors—from Romania, the Ukraine, Poland, Serbia, and China—than for the rather cheap wares they peddle. Take bus #30 four stops east of the tram station. Speaking of fleas, farmers and dealers haggle over livestock at the **animal market** on the end of Diószegi u. Monday morning it's pigs, Tuesday it's horses and Wednesdays it's cattle. Take the #30 bus seven stops from the station.

Programs in Debrecen is a series of summer events which range from equestrian exhibitions to musical performances to air shows, and culminate in the huge **Flower Carnival** parade on August 10 every year. In early September, the music festival called **Jazz days** features well-known musicians and bands. See Tourinform for schedules and tickets for both events. The Debrecen summer school at Kossuth Lajos University offers one of Europe's cheapest and most popular **Hungarian language programs.** Five hundred students from 35 countries study in 4-week courses (tuition US$450) or 2-week courses (tuition US$225). Contact Debreceni Nyári Egyetem, Egyetem Tér 1, M-4010 Debrecen (tel./fax 32 91 17). See Alternatives to Tourism in the General Introduction for more info on study programs in Hungary.

■■■ SZEGED

The cultural center of the southern Great Plain, Szeged straddles the Tisza River about 10km north of the Yugoslav border. Its easy-going charm belies its status as the nation's only planned city; after an 1879 flood practically wiped out the town, streets were laid out in straight lines and orderly curves, and row after row of colorful neo-Renaissance and art nouveau buildings were intentionally created to complement each other in shape and style. Szeged is known both for its university culture and for its food—it is the home of the famous Pick salami, as well as the source of sweet paprika, and the best place for *halászlé*, a spicy fish soup.

ORIENTATION AND PRACTICAL INFORMATION

Szeged is split in two by the Tisza River. The downtown area, with most of the shops, businesses, and sights, is on the western bank. **Újszeged,** or "New Szeged," on the eastern bank, is mostly parks and residences. As in Budapest, curved körút connect the streets that radiate from the center. The inner road, **Tisza Lajos** krt., is a half-circle that starts and ends at the river, while the outer road—named at different segments for the European cities that helped rebuild Szeged after the flood—is a nearly complete circle that crosses the river from the downtown's northeast section. Most **travel bureaus** are in the center of town, on or near Klauzál tér.

Tourist Office: Tourinform, Victor Hugo u. 1 (tel. 31 17 11 or 31 19 66), has free maps and hires English-speaking staff in summer. Open Mon.-Fri. 8am-6pm, Sat. 10am-2pm. **Szeged Tourist,** at Klauzál tér 7 (tel. 32 18 00) has English speakers year-round; open Mon.-Fri. 8:30am-1pm and 1:30-5pm, Sat. 9am-1pm.
Currency Exchange: OTP Bank at Klauzál tér 5 is open Mon.- Fri. 8am-3pm.
Post Office: Széchenyi tér 1, on the corner of Híd u., open Mon.-Fri. 8am-8pm.
Telephone City Code: 62.
Trains: InterCity (express) to Budapest runs four times per day (2hrs. 10min., 710Ft, including reservation). Other trains, which leave about once an hour, take 2½-3hrs. and cost 600Ft. There are five trains per day to Debrecen, with a change in Cegléd (3-4hrs., 798Ft) and 15 trains to Kecskemét (1hr., 264Ft). One pre-dawn train runs to Belgrade (4½hrs., 2061Ft) and four to Subotica (1½hrs., 280Ft).
Buses: The bus terminal is in Mars tér just west of Londoni körút, a 10-minute walk west of the center. To: Budapest (6 per day, 3½hrs.; 650Ft); Debrecen (2 per day, 5½hrs.; 850Ft); Kecskemét (8 per day, 2hrs.; 350Ft), and Pécs (6 per day, 4½hrs.; 720Ft).
Public Transportation: The tram station is south of the center; tram #1 runs from the station past the square (get off in front of the post office in Széchenyi tér, a block beyond Klauzál tér). Tickets cost 30Ft at the kiosk outside the train station.

ACCOMMODATIONS

Szeged Tourist (see above) has the cheapest private accommodations, starting at 500Ft for singles and 1000Ft for doubles. **IBUSZ,** across the square at Klauzál tér 2 (tel.47 11 77; open Mon.-Fri. 8am-4pm), has doubles for 1200Ft.

Hotel Petro, Kállay u. 6-10 (tel. 43 14 28), in Újszeged near the river, has doubles with private bath for 2300Ft, and triples with shared bath for 1650Ft.
Fortuna Panzió, Pécskai u. 8 (tel. 43 15 85), one block west, has seven doubles with private baths for 2200Ft.
Pölös Panzió, Pacsirta u. 17/a (tel. 31 38 61), one block west of Páriszi körút, has nine rooms and charges 1500Ft for one person, 2800Ft for two together.
Apáthy István Kollégium, Apáthy István u. 1 (tel. 32 31 55), conveniently placed next to Dóm tér, the comfortable *kollégium* does care with triples that include private bathrooms. Singles and doubles 1400Ft, triples 1800Ft. Open July-Aug.
Eötvös Loránd Kollégium, Tisza Krt. 103 (tel. 31 06 41), just down the road from Hösök Kapuja, has singles for 477Ft and doubles for 901Ft.
Károlyi Mihály Kollégium, Kossuth Lajos sugarút 72b (tel. 32 53 22), is out of the city center, but is easily reached by tram #1 (10 stops from the train station). Triples 850Ft with shared bath. Sheets 50Ft. Reserve in advance.
Béke Kollégium, Béke u. 11-13, has doubles for 600Ft, triples for 750Ft and quads for 1000F. Open late June-early Sept.
Napfény, Dorozsmai u. 4 (tel. 42 18 00), is a hotel and campground complex west of the downtown area. Take tram #1 to the last stop, then cross the overpass behind you and walk to the right. Hotel rooms with private baths and breakfast: singles 2390Ft, doubles 2890Ft, triples 3690Ft, 2-room apartment 4890Ft. Bungalows: doubles 1800Ft, triples 2700Ft, quads 2500-3600Ft. A motel in the complex has doubles for 900Ft. Campsites cost 150Ft per tent and 150Ft per person. The hotel is open year round; the others only May-Sept.

FOOD

For those late-night cravings and supplies on weekends, there is a **non-stop ABC market** at 17 Mars tér, near the corner of Londoni krt. and Mikszáth Kálmán u.

Roosevelt téri Halászcsárda, Roosevelt tér 14 (tel. 48 01 17), is *the* place to sample the spicy fish soup that Szeged is famous for; try any of the *"hallé"* dishes (they're only spicy if you add the green paprika served on the side). The kitchen serves the catch of (practically) the day and other entrees for 230-490Ft. Ask for the English menu. Open daily 11am-10pm.

Alabárdos, Oskola u. 11 (tel. 31 29 14), protects its status as Szeged's upscale dining experience with attitude and a smug no-shorts dress code. Entrees 800-1000Ft; open Mon.-Sat. 11:30am-2pm and 6pm-midnight.

Boszorkány Konhya ("The Witch's Kitchen"), Híd u. 8, just off Széchenyi tér, is a cafeteria that serves entrees for 120-160Ft. Open daily 6:30am-9pm.

Numero Uno Pizzeria Étterem, Széchenyi tér 5 (tel. 31 37 45), has a Hungarian-style daily lunch menu for 120Ft, pasta dishes for 130-320Ft, pizza for 375-750Ft, and "American Specialities" like chili and steak for 180-490Ft. Open daily 11am-midnight.

Restaurant Piccolo Mondo, Deák Ferenc u. 24-6 (tel. 31 27 34), is right around the corner from the Mora Ferenc Múzeum. Hungarian entrees, pizza, and spaghetti 130-390Ft.

Kisvirag Cukrasda, in Klauzál tér, is the busiest place in town, serving excellent pastries (50Ft) and a dollop of ice cream (15Ft per scoop; open daily 8am-10pm).

Burger King, at Dugonics tér in the Nagyáruház shopping center, courts the MTV set with neon decor and strategically placed TVs (open Mon.-Thurs. 8am-11pm, Fri.-Sat. 8am-midnight, Sun. 10am-11pm).

McDonald's lurks at the corner of Kölcsey u. and Kárász u. Open 7am-midnight.

SIGHTS AND ENTERTAINMENT

An easy walking tour of Szeged can be done in an afternoon. Begin in park-like Széchenyi tér, a block north of Klauzál tér. The yellow **Old Town Hall** on the square's western edge was restored in its present eclectic style—with red and green majolika ceramic tiles for shingles—after the 1879 deluge destroyed most of the city. The bridge connecting it to the drab building next door (which, appropriately, once held the tax office) was built for Habsburg Emperor Ferenc József's inspection tour of the reconstruction, to prevent His Excellency from having to go all the way downstairs just to go upstairs again in the next building.

Walk east to the river, where the **Móra Ferenc Múzeum** stands in a huge neo-Classical building at Roosevelt tér 1-3. This collection boasts an exhibit of folk art from the 18th century to the present (keep an eye out for the waffle irons that look like giant salad tongs) and a fascinating display on the long-vanished Avar tribe that occupied the Carpathian basin from the 6th to the 9th centuries. Exhibits include detailed explanations in English, a true rarity outside Budapest (open Tues.-Sun. 10am-5pm; admission 40Ft, students 20Ft).

Head south on Oskola u. to **Dóm tér,** where the red brick **Votive Church** pierces the city's skyline with its twin 91m towers. Built by survivors of the great flood, the neo-Romanesque structure has too many tiny steeples and arches to be graceful. One of the largest churches in Hungary, it has an organ sporting over 10,000 pipes (open daily 9am-6pm, except during services including Sun. 10-11am). Standing alongside the church is the 12th-century **Demetrius Tower,** Szeged's oldest monument. Smaller and brighter than the Votive Church is the Baroque **Serbian Orthodox Church** across the street, built in 1778. Inside, the iconostasis holds 60 gilt-framed paintings, and the ceiling fresco of God creating the Earth swims in a sea of stars. (open whenever there's someone around to collect the 40Ft admission fee). Just southwest of Dóm tér, in Aradi Vértanuk tér, stands **Hősök Kapuja** (Hero's Gate), a fascist-looking arch erected in 1936 in honor of Horthy's White Guards, who brutally cleansed the nation of "Reds." The arch is guarded by likenesses of the soldiers it was meant to honor, and the soldiers in turn are protected by metal scaffolding to keep people from toppling them.

At the corner of Hajnóczi u. and Jósika u. stands the eclectic **Great Synagogue,** built in 1903. Second in size only to the synagogue in Budapest, the structure's Moorish altar and gardens, Romanesque columns, Gothic domes, and Baroque facades combine to make this the most beautiful Jewish temple in Hungary. The cupola is decorated with designs symbolizing Infinity and Faith, and seems to grow deeper the longer you look up into it. The walls of the vestibule are lined with the names of the 3100 members of the congregation who did not return from the concentration camps. English-speaking guides explain every detail of the building, which is now used mainly for concerts and memorials (open May-Sept. 9am-noon and 2-5pm; admission 50Ft, students 25Ft). The pachyderm-grey building next door is the neo-classical **Old Synagogue,** which is used mostly for storage, and which is disintegrating at roughly the same speed as renovation progresses.

Szeged's black market thrives in the **open-air market** at the intersection of Cserepes sor and Petőfi Sándor sugárút. Tram #4 stops directly in front. The **Szeged Open-Air Theater Festival,** running from mid-July to mid-August, is the country's largest outdoor theatrical festival. Traveling troupes perform folk dances, operas, and musicals in the amphitheater in Dóm tér, incorporating the Votive Church into their backdrop. Tickets are available at Deák Ferenc u. 28-30 (tel. 47 14 66).

TRANSDANUBIA

Transdanubia is the western half of Hungary, comprised of everything "across the Danube river" and running to the country's western border. Originally Pannonia, the Roman Empire's northernmost province, Transdanubia was later bloodied by battles that determined the fate of the Ottoman Empire's drive for control of Europe; most of Hungary fell to the Turks after the Battle of **Mohács** in 1526, but the carnage at **Szigetvar** in 1566 ended the eastern push to Vienna.

Gothic and Romanesque architecture, erased from most of Hungary by the Ottomans, survived in Western Transdanubia under Habsburg rule. Towns such as **Sopron** and **Veszprem** (listed under the Lake Balaton region) still resemble medieval Austrian cities more than Eastern European towns. The most prosperous part of the country, Transdanubia supports both industry and agriculture, and is regularly swamped by Germans and Austrians who pop over the border for vacations and bargain shopping. You may have to hunt to find English-speakers, but German will get you nearly as far as Hungarian.

■■■ PÉCS

Pécs (pronounced PAYTCH) has always been home to students and artists. There are five universities and colleges in Pécs; of a total population of 175,000, between eight and ten thousand are students. Several galleries house well-known collections, and Pécs's ballet and opera companies are acclaimed in Hungary. The city holds an international folk festival called **Pécsi Napolk** ("Pécs Days") each September.

The town was a civil administration center called Sopianae under the Romans, who left it with one of the oldest traditions of Christianity in Hungary. During the Middle Ages, Pécs was a bishopric whose city walls encircled an area larger than modern-day Vienna. The town was taken by the Turks in 1543 and served as an Ottoman cultural center for the next 143 years. The 19th century saw another spurt of development, and today cathedral towers, Ottoman minarets, and Mediterranean-style red-tiled roofs climb the hillside together.

ORIENTATION AND PRACTICAL INFORMATION

Pécs lies on the knees of the Mecsek mountain range; conveniently, north and south correspond to up and down the hillside. Tourists bustle through the historical **Inner City** district, a rectangle bounded to the north by Aradi vértanúk útja and Kalvaria utca, and to the south by Rákóczi út. The **ancient city walls** ran along these borders—and still do at many points around the city. The middle of the Inner City is Széchenyi tér (square), where Hunyadi Janos utca, Király utca, Irgalmasok utcaja,

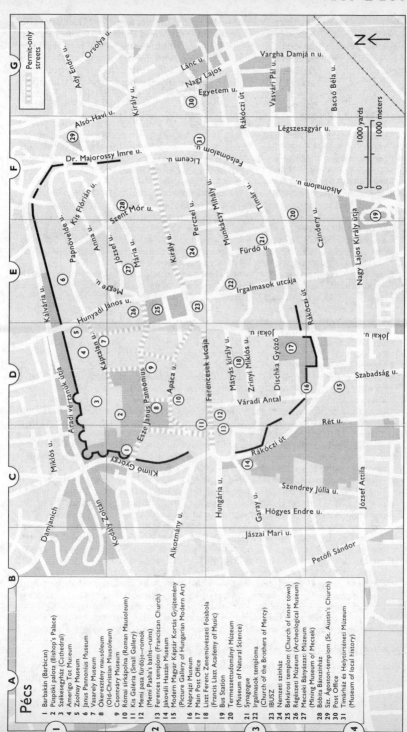

N←

Permit-only streets

Pécs

1 Barbakán (Barbican)
2 Püspöki palota (Bishop's Palace)
3 Székesegyház (Cathedral)
4 Amerigo Tot Museum
5 Zsolnay Museum
6 Janus Pannonius Museum
7 Vasarely Museum
8 Ókeresztény mausoleum (Old-Christian Mausoleum)
9 Csontváry Museum
10 Római sírkápolna (Roman Mausoleum)
11 Kis Galéria (Small Gallery)
12 Memi pasa fürdője—romok (Memi Pasha's baths—ruins)
13 Ferences templom (Franciscan Church)
14 Jakováli Hászán Museum
15 Modern Magyar Képtár Kortás Gyüjtemény (Picture Gallery of Hungarian Modern Art)
16 Néprajzi Museum
17 Main Post Office
18 Liszt Ferenc Zenemûvészeti Föisbola (Francis Liszt Academy of Music)
19 Bus Station
20 Természettudományi Múzeum (Museum of Natural Science)
21 Synagogue
22 Irgalmasok temploma (Church of the Brothers of Mercy)
23 IBUSZ
24 Nemzeti színház
25 Belvárosi templom (Church of inner town)
26 Régészeti Múzeum (Archeological Museum)
27 Mecseki Bányászati Múzeum (Mining Museum of Mecsek)
28 Bóbita Bábszínház
29 Szt. Ágoston-templom (St. Austin's Church)
30 Post Office
31 Tímárház és Helytörténeti Múzeum (Museum of local history)

HUNGARY

and Janus Pannonius utca converge, and where most of the tourist offices are located. The Inner City is small enough for pack-toters to visit on foot; it takes less than 20 minutes to cross from north to south (and a bit more to get back uphill). There are clearly marked street maps standing in each square.

Tourist Office: What little tourist information is available is geared towards speakers of German; your best bet is to drop by **Tourinform**, Széchenyi tér 9 (tel. 31 21 76). Its the only office for all of Baranya county—see them for information regarding local entertainment and travel in nearby regions, including Szigetvar. They sell two tourist **maps** of Pécs for 100Ft and 180Ft, as well as a slightly dated but informative guide to the city that discusses its history building by building; for 100Ft, how can you go wrong? Every Saturday in summer, they hold a sightseeing **tour** for foreigners; they will also arrange group tours for English speakers only (10am, 150Ft, English and German spoken). Open Mon.-Fri. 9am-7pm, Sat. 9am-4pm.; Sept.-May Mon.-Fri. 9am-5pm, Sat. 9am-4pm.

Budget Travel: Mecsek Tours, Széchenyi tér 1 (tel. 41 33 00). This travel agency sells the same map and guidebook at the same price as Tourinform. It also sells telephone cards and bus tickets, changes money, arranges tours, and will provide a private tour guide speaking any language for five hours for 1780Ft. Pick up a free copy of *Pécsi Tükör*, which lists cultural events, performances and movies (in Hungarian). English, German, French, and Croatian spoken. Open Mon.-Fri. 9am-5pm, Sat. 9am-1pm; Sept.-May Mon.-Sat. 8am-3:30pm.

Currency Exchange: The best rates can be found at the **Magyar Külkereskedelmi Bank (MKB)** on the edge of Széchenyi tér at Király u. 47 (tel. 42 54 04.) An outdoor **ATM** accepts Eurocard, MC, and Cirrus. On Saturdays, try **Mecsek Tours**, also in the square. The black market money changers who frequent Kossuth tér, the Új Centrum department store parking lot and Széchenyi tér are known for giving unsuspecting tourists old Croatian currency.

Post Office: Jókai Mór utca 10 (tel. 41 44 22). Sorry, no phone cards here—get them at a travel agency. Open Mon.-Fri. 8am-8pm, Sat. 8am-2pm, Sun. 8am-noon.

Telephone City Code: 72.

Trains: Pécs station (tel. 31 24 43) is located just beyond the bottom of the city's historic district, a 10-minute bus ride (#30 or 34) from the center of town. **Inter-City** (express) trains (tel. 41 50 03) make the two-and-a-half hour run both to and from Budapest four times a day (693Ft plus 130Ft reservation fee, 30% discount for ISIC holders.) Purchase tickets at the MÁV travel office in the station or at Rákóczi ut 39/c. Four trains per day leave for various towns around Lake Balaton. Several regular trains per day chug from Budapest-Déli station (3hrs., 632Ft).

Buses: Landholders in Baranya county have historically tried to put the greatest length of railway track possible on their land; the resulting tangle has made travelling between towns by bus far more convenient. The **Pécs Central Bus Station** (tel. 41 52 15 or 41 56 65) is located within walking distance from the center of town, at the intersection of Nagy Lajos Király útja and Alsómalom utca. The bus and train stations are about 800m apart at the bottom of the town's historic district; the bus station is closer to the center. Buses leave for the neighboring spa town Harkány and the lake resort Orfü every half hour. The bus for Szigetvár leaves 10 times per day on weekdays, seven times on weekends (40min., 100Ft.)

Bookstores: The **International English Center** at Mária u. 9 (tel. 31 20 10) has a bookstore that sells new and used books and an ESL section, and gets *USA Today*, the *Wall Street Journal*, and the *Guardian* only a day late. Open daily 8am-8pm. The Center also has a library, a café open daily 8am-midnight, and conference rooms. The powers that be also plan to open a restaurant by 1995. **Corvina International Bookstore**, Széchenyi tér 8, carries English, French and German travel guides and literature. Open Mon.-Fri. 9am-5pm, Sat 9am-noon.

ACCOMMODATIONS AND CAMPING

Private accommodations are usually arranged through the tourist offices in Széchenyi tér. For stays of less than three nights, a 30% fee is added to the first night's price.

Accommodations Agencies

Mecsek Tours, just across from IBUSZ at Széchenyi tér 1 (tel. 41 33 00, fax 41 20 44), has staff that speaks more English. Singles 650Ft. Doubles 950Ft. The agency also runs a campground (listed below). Reject the 180Ft map from Mecsek Tourist in favor of the 20Ft model from IBUSZ.

IBUSZ, Széchenyi tér 8 (tel. 31 21 76), has singles for 700Ft and doubles for 900Ft. Open Mon.-Thurs. 8am-noon and 12:30-4pm, Fri. 8am-noon and 12:30-3pm, Sat. 8am-noon.

Tourinform, Széchenyi tér 9 (tel. 41 33 15, fax 41 26 32) offers doubles for 1200Ft. Open Mon.-Fri. 8am-6pm; Oct.-May Mon.-Fri. 8am-4pm.

MÁV travel office, in the railway station (tel. 32 45 23), 10 minutes from the city center by bus, rents beds in its tourist hostel for 500Ft per night. Doubles 1100Ft. English spoken. Open Mon.-Thurs. 9am-4:30pm, Fri. 9am-4pm; Sept.-May Mon.-Thurs. 8am-4:30pm, Fri. 8am-3:30pm.

AIESEC Center, at the Economics University (tel. 31 14 33, ext. 273; open Mon.-Fri. 9am-4pm) can arrange student accommodations. Go directly to **hostels** (July-Aug. only) to pay less. Office open Mon.-Thurs. 8am-4pm, Fri. 8:15am-2pm.

Dormitories and Camping

Student dormitory, Rákóczi út 52, across from the Konzum department store (tel. 31 59 57) is bare but liveable. Doubles, triples and quads all 400Ft per person.

Janus Pannonius University Dormitory, at Szántó Kovács u. 1 (tel. 32 42 34); take bus #27 from Konzum Aruház. The best and the farthest away.

Szent Mór Kollégium, 48-es tér 4 (tel. 31 11 99), has doubles (800Ft) and triples (1150Ft) in a gorgeous old building.

Kollégium, Rókus u. 2 (tel. 32 42 77, ext. 174). Sunny quads with bunkbeds go for 400Ft per person and doubles for 450Ft apiece (550Ft with bath). Take bus #30 to the fourth stop after Széchenyi tér.

Camping: Mandulás Camping, Angyán János u. 2 (tel. 31 59 81), Early in the day or outside of peak season, just take bus #34 directly to the hills above the city, where tent sites (500Ft for 2 people), 3-bed bungalows (1600Ft) and doubles (2000Ft) in a 1-star hotel are located at the entrance to hiking trails into the Mecsek Hills. Call the campsite for same-day reservations. For advance reservations, call Mescek Tours (see above). Camp open mid-April to mid-Oct.

FOOD

A **Pizza Hut** and a **McDonald's** are expected to open in September 1994.

Liceum Söröző, in a cellar off Király utca 35 (formerly Kossuth Lajos; tel. 32 72 84), opposite the Liceum church. Low prices with a choice selection of beers makes this a favorite with the student community—don't even think about passing up the brew. Entrees from 250Ft. English menu. Open Tues.-Sun. 11am-10pm.

DÓM Vendéglő Restaurant, Király u. 3 (tel. 31 07 32), through the courtyard, last door on your right. Looks a bit crusty outside, but the interior is an impressive two-level wooden reproduction of a church, complete with stained-glass windows. Traditional Hungarian cuisine. Entrees 350-500Ft; menu in German. Open daily 11am-11pm.

Caflisch Cukrászda Café, at Kossuth Lajos u. 32, may be the best café in town. Sit inside to devour delightful Hungarian sweets, or sit outside and watch tourists watch you. Pastries from 60Ft. Open Sun.-Thurs. 8am-10pm, Fri.-Sat. 8am-11pm.

Salibár, Bártok Béla u. 34 (tel. 33 38 50), offers mostly vegetarian fare, including salads and rice, along with noodle and turkey dishes at unaccountably low prices. Ask for the English menu—it's kicking around somewhere. Entrees 120-260Ft. Open daily 11:30am-10pm.

Fregatt Arizona Pub, Király u. 21 (tel. 41 04 86). American Southwestern-style steaks and salads, with entrees from 430Ft. Canned country music and English menu. Open daily 11am-midnight.

HUNGARY

SIGHTS AND ENTERTAINMENT

Remnants of the Ottoman occupation are more visible in Pécs than in other Hungarian cities. The main square, **Széchenyi tér,** is dominated by the nation's largest **mosque,** dating from the 16th century. Today it serves as the Inner City Parish Church—the stone window grilles alone betray its former faith. An impressive **synagogue** *(Kossuth tér)* recalls a once-thriving Jewish community (open May-Oct. Sun.-Fri. 9:30am-1pm and 1:30-5pm; admission 35Ft, students 25Ft, including highly educational booklet). West of Széchenyi lies the distinctive four-towered **Cathedral,** whose earliest parts date back to the 4th century; it was restored in Romanesque style from 1881-92 (open Mon.-Sat. 9am-1pm and 2-5pm, Sun. 1-5pm; admission 40Ft, students 20Ft). Cycles of neglect and regeneration, traced in the building's different styles, mirror the city's schizophrenic history.

The **Archeological Museum,** behind the Inner City Parish Church, at Széchenyi tér 12, traces the history of the city. Eight more museums and galleries, some quite exceptional, are all clustered along Káptalan u. and can be seen on a leisurely but nonetheless rewarding afternoon stroll. The museums are all distinctive (all open Tues.-Sun. 10am-6pm; admission free for students). The **Zsolnay Porcelain Museum** houses some exquisite creations, while the **Victor Vasarely Museum** showcases arresting works by the famous Hungarian op-artist. Not to be missed is the **Csontváry Museum,** housing the works of Tivadar Csontváry Kosztka (1853-1919), Hungary's two-eared answer to Van Gogh. Snag a view of Pécs from the **TV tower** that looms above it; it also has a restaurant (take bus #35; admission 50Ft).

Pécs' **ballet** and **opera** companies perform locally between October and May, and touring companies and local groups hold concerts and plays often enough that some sort of artistic performance occurs in Pécs or its vicinity nearly every day of the year. There are also several **movie** theaters that show reasonably current foreign films. The best way to find out what's going on is to pick up an English-language schedule of regional events at Tourinform and a copy of *Pécsi Tükör* (in Hungarian, but the movie listings are self-explanatory) at Mecsek Tours. Pécs holds a regional **international folk festival** each autumn.

Clubs and **discos** come and go in a matter of months here, so ask at Tourinform for hotspots. Recent developments include the **Hard Rák Café,** Ipar u. 7, at the corner of Bajcsy-Zsilinsky u. south of the Inner City. If you pass the red brick slag heap, go back—it's inside (or you can just stand out in the bypass and listen for it). This club plays rock, alternative and hard core. "No soft music." Don't get run over by the bands arriving by VW bus (150Ft cover charge Thurs.-Sat. when live bands play; open daily 7pm-past 3am). At **Gyár** ("The Factory"), Czinderi u. 3-5 (Czinderi isn't marked—find it between Bajcsy-Zsilinsky u. and Alsómalom u.), the tables are old tires from earth-moving equipment. It's a hard core and alternative rock dance club, with live bands on weekends (open daily 6pm-dawn, but don't expect too much action in early evening).

■ NEAR PÉCS

NAGYHARSÁNY PARK

From Pécs, consider a daytrip to the incredible **sculpture park** in Nagyharsány, near the Croatian border 37km to the south. Located by a former quarry, the park contains pieces by artists from around the world. Facing the quarry, follow the path on the right for a climb to even better views of the town and the fruited plains below. First take a train to Villány (several per day; 1hr.; round-trip 220Ft); from the station, turn left and follow the main road (towards Siklós) about 4km. There is a map across from the ABC supermarket 1km along, or just ask for the *szoborpark*.

SZIGETVÁR CASTLE

In 1566, Miklós Zrínyi and his 2500 men were besieged in **Szigetvár Castle** by 50,000 Turkish troops under Suleiman Sultan. After a month-long struggle, with their drinking water exhausted and the inner fortification in flames, Zrínyi's men launched a desperate attack against their aggressors. They were wiped out before they broke free, but they managed to kill an estimated one-quarter of the Turkish troops in the process, and the Sultan himself died of natural causes during the battle. Demoralized and reluctant to face the oncoming winter, the Turks abandoned their real goal of invading Vienna and advanced no further. This heroic act is still Szigetvár's claim to fame. Tourists come to walk through the remains of the **castle** (open 24 hrs.) and visit the **Zrínyi Milkós Museum** inside, which chronicles the siege (open summer Wed.-Sun. 9am-4pm, winter 10am-3pm). Visitors usually make it a day-trip from Pécs or Kaposvár and stay for a few hours. Foreign tourists without a Hungarian's sense of history may find little that appeals to them here—the castle ruins are remnants of a structure built well after the battle, and consist mostly of red brick walls with a pleasant park inside. Szigetvár itself is a tiny town facing tough economic times and has little to offer by way of culture or entertainment.

The **bus** and **train stations** are next to each other at the southern end of town; buses come and go to Pécs about 10 times per day, and to Kaposvár four times per day. Visitors make the walk north to the castle in about 15 minutes. On the way, stop off at the **Mecsek Tourist Office** in the Oroszlán Hotel at Zrínyi tér 2 (tel. 31 01 16; open Mon.-Fri. 7:30am-4pm) for information and free photocopied maps of the town. The **telephone city code** is 73.

There are no good, cheap accommodations in Szigetvár. Mecsek Tourist operates a tourist hostel *(tourista szálló)* called the **Kazamata Hotel** inside the castle walls from April-Oct., but it's rather shabby and would likely appeal only to troglodytes. Tunnel-like rooms with rows of cots about a foot apart are built into the castle walls. The town's camping facilities closed down last year. If you're stuck, the **Oroszlán Hotel** has doubles without bath for 1700Ft. For coffee, try the **Kerek Erdö Café** on Katona u. The most popular restaurant in town is a pizzeria imaginatively called **Pizzeria** at Jozseph Attila u. 41. The menu has English and German. As you walk there, take a look at the partially-constructed new civic center on the left, which distinctly resembles two snails mating.

■■■ KAPOSVÁR

Midway between Pécs and Lake Balaton, Kaposvár (KAP-oash-var) is a popular destination among Europeans for daytrips and short stays from both regions. It's the seat of Somogy county, which includes the southern shore of Balaton, but it shares little in common with the lakeside towns; Kaposvár is surrounded by rolling hills and fields, and carefully nurtures its artistic and theatrical heritage.

Orientation and Practical Information The **train station** and **bus station** are less than two blocks apart and five minutes south of the downtown area. The most convenient connection with Balaton is the railway: daily 10 trains come and go to Fonyód (50min., 162Ft) and six to and from Siófok (3hrs., 238Ft). Buses run back and forth to Pécs (2 hrs., 236Ft) 13 times per day on weekdays and 11 times on weekends. Two blocks north is Fő utca, a pedestrian street lined with shops, restaurants and cafés that is the center of town. To reach it from the station, walk up Teleki utca to Kossuth tér. **Tourinform** (tel. 32 04 04), at Fő utca 8, is one of the few places in town where English is spoken. Drop by for maps, the town's tourist brochure, and lists of new restaurants and cultural events (open Mon.-Fri. 8am-12:30pm and 1-5pm, Sat. 8am-noon, and in the summer Sun. 8am-noon). **Change money** at Konzumbank RT or Takarébank on Teleki u. or Magyar Hitelbank, Magyar Nemzeti Bank or Országos Takarépénztar at Széchenyi tér. The main **post office** is at Bajcsy-Zsilinsky u. 15 (open Mon.-Fri. 8am-9pm, Sat 8am-2pm, Sun 8am-noon). The **telephone city code** is 82. City bus tickets can be bought for 27Ft at the bus station or for 40Ft from the driver.

Accommodations and Food   **IBUSZ,** at Teleki u. 1-3 (tel. 31 54 77), has doubles in private apartments downtown for 800-1000Ft per night (open Mon.-Thurs. 8am-4:30pm, Fri. 8am-3pm). **Siotour,** Fő u. 1 (tel. 31 15 09), has doubles for about 900Ft per night and rents flats throughout the city for four or more nights at 1500Ft per night (open Mon.-Fri. 8am-5:30pm, Sat. 8am-noon; Sept.-May Mon.-Fri. 8am-4:30pm, Sat. 8am-noon). **Flamingo Panzió,** Furedi u. 53 (tel. 41 67 28), has singles for 1200Ft, doubles for 1500Ft, and triples for 1900Ft. **Fehér Ház,** Arany Janos u. 97 (tel. 31 45 22 or 42 05 75), has doubles for 2250Ft, as does the **Asztalos Tiborné Panzió** at Tallián u. 53 (tel. 41 91 68). **Nyári Szalló** in the Kaffka Margit Kollegium at Bajcsy-Zilinsky u. 6 (tel. 31 90 11) has dorm beds for 300Ft from July-Aug. The **MÁV Nevelötthon Szállója** at Somssich u. 15 (tel. 32 03 16) has dorm rooms mid-June to late Aug. and mid.-Dec. to early Jan. for 500Ft. **Deseda Camping** (tel. 31 38 54 or 31 20 20) is a mediocre campground located 8km from the center of town (250Ft per person). At the **Ipar Kisvendéglo,** Teleki u. 8, entrees are lively and relatively cheap (200-400Ft); portions are substantial (open Mon.-Sat. 9am-8pm, Sun. 9am-4pm). **Bianco Nero,** Kossuth Tér, across from the Hotel Kapos, is a café with a salad bar (open daily 9am-8pm). If you don't mind ordering Greek food from a Hungarian menu, try **Görög Taverna,** Fő u. 14. (open Mon.-Sat. noon-midnight, Sun. 4pm-midnight).

Sights and Entertainment   At Fő u. 10, almost next door to the Tourinform office, is the **Somogy Megyei Museum.** This eclectic collection represents almost every aspect of the country's cultural life, ranging from prehistoric fossils and archaeological finds from the Bronze Age to regional folk handicrafts. The museum features exhibits on life in Kaposvár during Hungary's Golden Age at the turn of the century up through the nation's early motion-picture industry. Several rooms feature large temporary exhibitions by local painters and sculptors. Most of the exhibits are self-explanatory, but there is no written English material, and the guides speak only Hungarian and German (open Tues.-Sat. 11am-5pm; admission 40Ft, students 20Ft). If you feel like getting out to the country lanes above the town, head for the **Rippl-Rónai Villa** in Rómahegy (Rome Hill). One of Kaposvár's most famous sons, József Rippl-Rónai (1861-1927) was a French-trained post-Impressionist painter. The 19th-century house and studio in which he spent his final years have been made into a museum for his collection and many of his personal belongings. Although much of Rippl-Rónai's work is dark and brooding, the overall effect of the museum is one of tenderness and respect for the man. Take #15 city bus from the platform just south of the bus station, and ride about 12 minutes to the last stop; walk about 300m farther, keeping to the paved road. Ignore the map and don't bother looking for signs (open Tues.-Sun. 10am-6pm, Nov.-March 10am-4pm; admission 30Ft, students 20Ft). Kaposvár is home to the **Csiky Gergely Színház** (theater) at Rákóczi tér 2 (tel. 32 08 33) and its acting company, which is one of the most respected provincial groups in the country. There are several other cultural centers offering performances throughout the city. Unfortunately, nearly all of them, including the Csiky Geregely, are closed during the summer. Ask the Tourinform office for schedules.

■■■ SZÉKESFEHÉRVÁR

Székesfehérvár (pronounced SAY-kesh-fe-hare-var) is a modern industrial city wrapped protectively around a thousand-year-old core. The first capital of the unified Hungary, its Basilica was built in the early 11th century and was the site of all State events for hundreds of years. The Turks occupied the town between 1543 and 1614 and left it in ruins, but much of the architecture from the following century remains intact, and ongoing archaeological exploration is still unearthing artifacts from the earlier period. Though the old town's winding streets, pastel-colored 18th century buildings, and Baroque church steeples rest within the concrete embrace of uninspired Socialist architecture, Székesfehérvár is a pleasant place to explore. Convenient transportation links make it an easy trip from Budapest, and the old town has sights that take at least a full day to visit.

ORIENTATION AND PRACTICAL INFORMATION

Though Székesfehérvár is inconveniently spread out, almost everything of interest is compressed neatly into the old town. The pedestrian street **Fő utca** runs north-south through its middle. At its center, **Városház tér** and **Koronázó tér** are next to each other, branching off Fő u. to the west and east, respectively. (Under the naming system used until recently, they were both called Szabadság tér.) Most of Koronázó tér is under archaeological excavation. Székesfehérvár is a major transportation link for Transdanubia. Trains generally run more frequently than buses, but the central location of the bus terminal often makes buses more convenient.

Tourist Office: Tourinform at Városház tér 1 (tel. 34 05 30) shares space with **Panda Tours.** See them for a free map of the city and general information and advice. Open Mon.-Fri. 9am-5pm.

Currency Exchange: IBUSZ, at Holy Endre u. 2 (tel. 31 44 41), has nearly the same rates as most banks. Open Mon.-Thurs. 8am-4pm, Fri. 8am-3pm.

Telephone City Code: 22

Post Office: Kossuth u. 16 (tel. 31 22 68). Open Mon.-Fri. 8am-8pm, Sat. 8am-2pm, Sun 8am-noon.

Trains: The **train station** is 15min. south on foot, at Béke tér (tel. 31 22 93). To reach the center, walk north up Prohaszka Ottokár út and Várkörút, and make a left onto Koronázó tér opposite Rákóczi u. To: **Budapest** (33 per day, 50-60min.; 196Ft), **Balatonfüred** (13 per day, 60min.; 196Ft), **Siófok** (19 per day, 40-60min.; 126Ft); **Veszprém** (11 per day, 40-60min.; 126Ft)and **Pécs** (1 per day, 3hrs.; 598Ft).

Buses: Station is at Piac tér, a 5-min. walk west from Fő u. (tel. 31 10 57). To: Budapest (12 per day, 75min.; 256Ft), Balatonfüred (6 per day, 90min.; 236Ft), Siófok (6 per day, 60min.; 164Ft), Veszprém (22 per day, 60min.; 164Ft) and Pécs (3 per day, 4hrs.; 646Ft).

ACCOMMODATIONS AND CAMPING

Albatours, Városház tér 1 (tel. 31 24 94), has doubles in private accommodations for 800Ft per night, and rents flats for three and four people at 540Ft per person (open Mon.-Fri. 8am-4:30pm). **IBUSZ,** at Ady Endre u. 2 (see above) has doubles for 900-1000Ft per night.

Hotel Rév Szálló, József Attila u. 42 (tel. 32 70 15), at the corner of Bodai út has doubles with TVs and refrigerators for 1350Ft, and stripped-down triples for 1240Ft. All rooms have shared baths.

Hotel Hungalu Szálló, at Kórféum Lakótelep 14 and 14A (tel. 31 22 73), on the eastern edge of the city, has singles for 975-1300Ft, doubles for 1500-2000Ft, and apartments for 2000Ft. Take bus #14, 17, 20 or 22 to "Könnyűfémmű."

József Attila Kollégium, Széchenyi István u. 13 (tel. 31 31 55), has dorm rooms June-Aug. for 250Ft per bed.

Camping: Campground Székesfehérvári Kemping, Bregyó-köz 1 (tel. 31 34 33), charges 100Ft for a tent and 100Ft per person. It also has beds in 30-person bungalows for 260Ft a night. Open May-Sept.

FOOD

Ősfehérvár Étterem, Koronázó tér 2 (tel. 31 40 56), is a local favorite. It has a menu in German, French, and Russian, and a photocopied list of daily specials in Hungarian that includes low-priced set menus. Outdoor tables are right over the Basilica excavation work. Entrees 140-550Ft. Open daily 11am-10pm.

Főnix Étterem es Salátabár, in the courtyard at Tavirola u. 15 (tel. 31 79 70). The downstairs has sandwiches and a salad bar, open noon-midnight. The upstairs is an eclectic restaurant that incorporates Indian and French elements into Hungarian cooking. English menu; entrees 290-550Ft. Open 8am-midnight.

HUNGARY

Korzó Söröző, Fő u. 2 (tel. 32 64 72), has a limited menu in English, and the kitchen serves acceptable pub food for 150-290Ft. In warm weather, seating is outside on the main street. Open 7am-9:30pm.

McDonald's, Piac tér 1, across from the bus terminal (tel. 31 05 82). If you want greasy American food instead of greasy Hungarian food. Open 7am-1am.

SIGHTS AND ENTERTAINMENT

The best place to start a walking tour of Székesferhérvár is in the center of the old town, in Városház tér. The **fountain** in the middle represents the royal orb, which, along with the crown and sceptre, is one of the three symbols of the Hungarian king's authority. The writing around the middle is Latin for "All the civil liberties of Széksfehérvár were granted by King Stephen." The lime-green building to the west is the **town hall,** built in Baroque style in 1698 and enlarged in 1936-7.

Directly to the east, on Koronázó tér, is the **Garden of Ruins.** This courtyard contains the remains of Hungary's first **basilica** built 1016-1038 by St. Stephen, the country's first Christian king, while Székesfehérvár was the capital of the country. Throughout the late Middle Ages, this was the center for all State events: 37 kings were crowned here, and 17 were buried here. Unfortunately, all that's left is some fascinating rubble. When the Turks took the city in 1543, they used the basilica as a gunpowder storehouse; in 1601 an accidental explosion blew the building to smithereens. The excavation that has turned most of Koronázó tér into a sand pit is currently unearthing parts of the basilica that fared a little better. Scattered throughout the garden and displayed near the walls are fragments of **stonework** and sculpture. Archaeologists now generally concur that the **sarcophagus** on the right as you enter once contained the remains of St. Stephen himself (open April-Oct. Tues.-Sun. 9am-6pm; admission 50Ft, students free).

The long yellow building on Koronázó tér is the **Bishop's Palace,** built from 1790-1801 soon after the city became a Bishopric. The structure is made largely of stones from the old Basilica. It is still the Bishop's residence today, but tourists can occasionally wheedle a glimpse of the 40,000 volume library. The twin-spired building to the south of the square on Arany János u. is **St. Stephen's Cathedral.** (Don't confuse this with the **Church of St. János of Nepomuk,** which is also yellow and also has two towers, but is smaller and north of Varosház tér on Fő u.) It was built between 1759-1778 on the site of the tomb of Grand Duke Géza, the father of King Stephen and the founder of Székesfehérvár. Unless mass is in session, visitors can go no farther inside than the glass doors in the vestibule, but from there they can see the airy hall with its Baroque frescoes. The white paving stones on the street in front outline the foundations of the 10th-century church thought to have contained Géza's tomb. The small white building on the north side is **St. Anna's Chapel,** which was built in 1470 and used as a mosque during the Turkish occupation. On the eastern side of the cathedral is **Hősök tere** (Hero's Square), dedicated to the heroes of World War I.

Off Jókai u. is a courtyard with a small wrought iron sign that says **Törökudvar** (Turkish Yard). From the street it looks like a small vacant lot gone to weed, but it is the site of a 16th-century Turkish bath now under excavation. Stonework and brick arches are becoming visible as work progresses. The county-run **Szent István Király Múzeum,** or the **King St. Stephen Museum,** occupies several buildings throughout town, and constitutes the second largest collection in Hungary, after the National museum in Budapest. The main building is the **Permanent Exhibition of Archeology,** at Fő u. 6 (tel. 31 55 83). This collection spans the history of Fejér county form the first settlement of Transdanubia to the 1600s. The county has a particularly large collection of Roman artifacts, which come from the old settlement at nearby Gorsium. There is even a small exhibition on the Turkish bath now in ruins on Jókai u. English explanations (open Tues.-Sun. 10am-6pm; admission 50Ft, students free).

Budenz-ház, Arany János u. 12 (tel. 31 30 27), is home to the collection of the Ybl family which includes 19th- and 20th-century Hungarian art, and 18th- and 19th-century furniture. The house itself was built in 1781 but has a foundation that dates to the Middle Ages. It is named after the linguist József Budenz, who lived there 1858-1860 (open Tues.-Sun. 10am-6pm; admission 40Ft, students free). The **Fekete Sas Patikamúzeum,** or the Black Eagle Pharmacy at Fő u. 5 (tel. 31 5 5 83), was built by Jesuits in 1758, and remained a functioning pharmacy until 1971. It is now a very small museum, with all the original woodwork intact (open Tues.-Sun. 10am-6pm; free, but donations are encouraged). **Rotating art exhibitions** are shown in the branch of the King St. Stephen museum at Országzászlo tér 3 (tel. 31 17 34; open Tues.-Sun. 10am-6pm; admission 40Ft, students free).

If you've ever wondered what a stroll through Disneyland on qualudes would be like but were afraid to try, head for **Bory Castle** on the northeastern edge of the city at Bory tér (*Let's Go* does not recommend the use of Disneyland as a safe means of entertainment). One man's expressions of architectural and artistic whimsy, this ferro-concrete and brick masterpiece (or folly) could be the playground for the ulti-mate game of hide-and-seek. Architect and sculptor Jenő Bory (1879-1959) built it by hand over 40 summers as a memorial to his wife. The towers, gardens, crooked paths, winding staircases, incongruous statuary of historical figures and small stone chambers crowded with works of art were all made for exploring. On workdays it is nearly deserted (open Mon.-Fri. 9am-5pm, Sat.-Sun 10am-noon and 3-5pm; admis-sion 50Ft, students 30Ft) Take bus #26a from the terminal at Piac tér, or #32 from the train station to the corner of Kassai u. and Vagújihey u. (it's poorly marked; the stop is next to the white storefront with turquoise trim; tickets cost 45Ft on the bus and 30Ft at the terminal). Then walk north on Vagújihey u. to Bory tér.

Touring groups put on music and theater performances at **Vörösmarty Theater** on Fő u., or at the **open-air theater** in Pelikán udvar nearly every night. Get tickets and schedules at the box office at Fő u. 3 (tel. 31 45 91; open Mon.-Fri. 9am-6pm).

■ ■ ■ S Z O M B A T H E L Y

Szombathely (pronounced SOM-bat-hey) is a big town that acts small. It's the seat of Vas county and a crossroads that links Transdanubia to Austria, but on weekends and evenings the tree-shaded Fő tér in the center of the city fills with clusters of peo-ple gathering to relax and enjoy each other's company. Szombathely got its start in the first century as the Roman colony Claudia Savaria, and Roman ruins and artifacts are scattered throughout the town. Today, 18th-century buildings stand shoulder to shoulder with more modern ones, but the town never for a second loses its sense of the past or its Baroque atmosphere.

ORIENTATION AND PRACTICAL INFORMATION

The inner city of Szombathely can be crossed on foot in 20 minutes. The town focuses on several squares, the largest being Fő tér, its psychological center. The three main travel agencies are located around Mártirok tere, a few blocks north. The train station is northeast of the inner city; to reach Mártirok tere, take Széll Kálmán u. straight down. The bus station is in the northwest part of the inner city; reach Mártirok tere by following Petőfi Sándor u. east, and Király u. south.

> **Tourist Office:** For English information and maps, your best bet is Tourinform-licensed **Savaria Tourist,** Mártirok tere 1 (tel. 31 22 64). Open Mon.-Fri. 8am-5:30pm, Sat. 8am-noon.
> **Currency Exchange:** Across the street from the tourist office, at 10 Király u., is an **OTP Bank** that gives slightly better exchange rates than the travel agencies.
> **Post Office:** Kossuth Lajos u. 18 (tel. 31 15 84). Open Mon.-Fri. 8am-8pm, Sat. 8am-2pm, Sun. 8am-noon.
> **Telephone City Code:** 94.
> **Trains:** Information: tel. 31 20 50. Trains run frequently to and from Budapest and major destinations in Transdanubia. To: Budapest (8 per day, 3½hrs.; 680Ft); Veszprém (12 per day, 2½hrs.; 418Ft); Sopron (11 per day, 70min.; 196Ft); Győr

(3 per day, 2-2¾hrs.; 358Ft). Also trains to nearby Kőszeg every half-hour (30min., 72Ft).
Buses: Information: tel. 31 20 54. To: Budapest (1 per day, 3½hrs.; 850Ft); Veszprém (2 per day, 2hrs.; 460Ft); Sopron (6 per day, 2hrs.; 290Ft); Győr (4 per day, 2hrs.; 390Ft); Keszthely (3 per day, 3hrs.; 340Ft).

ACCOMMODATIONS AND CAMPING

For centrally located private rooms, try **Savaria Tourist** (see above), with doubles for 850-1100Ft in the homes of people who could be your grandparents' neighbors if this were Ft. Lauderdale. **IBUSZ,** Széll Kálmán u. 3-4 (tel. 31 41 41), has doubles for 1300Ft (open Mon.-Fri. 8am-4pm). **Express,** Király u. 12 (tel. 31 12 30) finds hostel beds, most open June 15-Sept. (open Mon.-Fri. 8am-5pm, Sat. 8am-noon).

Hotel Liget, Szent István Park 15 (tel. 31 41 68), a tourist hotel on the west side of town, has doubles with private baths for 2400Ft and doubles with TVs for 2900Ft.
Péterfy Kollégium, just west of the inner city at Magyar László u. 2 (tel. 31 26 53), charges 330Ft per person in a 2-bed or 7-bed room.
Orlay Hostel, central at Nagy Kar u. 1-3 (tel. 31 23 75), charges 300Ft per person in an 8-bed room and also accepts guests on weekends during the school year.
405 Kollégium, Holy tér 2 (tel. 31 21 98), is next to the bus terminal and charges 350Ft per person in a room with 4 beds.
Camping: Tópart Camping, Kondics u. 4 (tel. 31 47 66), has 4-person bungalows for 1800Ft and 5-person bungalows for 2200Ft. For campsites, it charges 60Ft per tent and 100Ft per person. Open May 1-Sept. 30.

FOOD

Gyöngyös Étterem, Széll Kálmán u. 8 (tel. 31 26 65), is reliable and popular among residents. Entrees are 210-450Ft, and there is also a cheaper daily set menu. Open 10am-10pm.
Ferences Söröző, Aréna u. 1, a pub with a low vaulted ceiling underneath the cloister of a Franciscan church. Entrees 145-400Ft. Open 11am-11pm.
Pannonia Étterem, Fő tér 29 (tel. 31 14 69), is centrally located and is attached to a pub. Weekend clientele is Austrian-tourist-heavy. Open daily 11am-11pm.
Saláta bár is the name of two different restaurants offering similar light meals and snacks, about 2 blocks apart. The one in the alley Belsikátor off Fő tér is open Mon.-Fri. 9am-5pm, Sat. 8am-8pm. The one at Hollán Ernő u. 3 is open Mon.-Fri. 9am-7pm, Sat. 9am-1pm.

SIGHTS AND ENTERTAINMENT

The **Szombathely Cathedral** at Templom tér was built in 1797 in Copf style—a cross between the Baroque and neo-Classical—and was once adorned with well-known frescoes and gilt ornaments. An Allied bombing raid in 1945 all but flattened the building, however, and so far the efforts at reconstruction have yielded disappointing results, with bare ceilings and no pews. Directly behind the cathedral and entered from its north side is the **Garden of Ruin,** the center of the original Roman colony from the first century. The ruins from several different periods have been excavated, and visitors can walk among town walls, road, a bathhouse, parts of a palace, official buildings, and some wonderful floor mosaics, one of which is thought to have been part of the Caesar's audience hall. An English-speaking guide can explain everything in copious detail (open daily 10am-5pm, Nov.-March daily 10am-4pm; admission 40Ft, students 20Ft).

The **Smidt Museum,** at Hollán Ernő u. 2, is the personal collection of Dr. Lajos Smidt, who collected just about everything he could get his hands on. The result is like a garage sale gone berserk—each case is packed to capacity with weapons, watches, currency, clothing, tableware, Roman artifacts, military paraphernalia, and some things that are just plain junk. It's not particularly educational, but the sheer mass of stuff makes it worth dropping by (open Tues.-Sun. 10am-5pm; admission 60Ft, students 30Ft).

The **Iseum,** at Rákóczi Ferenc u. 2, is the reconstructed remains of the Temple of Isis built by Roman legionnaires in the 2nd century. Touted as "one of Szombathely's best known monuments," it looks more like the wreck of an urban municipal building than a Roman temple. The Communists rebuilt all the missing parts using concrete, and the building stands in a weed-strewn lot flanked by an office block. The shed-like structure at the northern edge of the lot houses an exhibit about the temple (open daily 9am-4pm). Across the street at Rákóczi Ferenc u. 3 is the former **synagogue,** a double-spired, Moorish structure dating from the late 19th century. The façade has not been changed, but the interior has been completely remodelled into a modern concert hall. A memorial outside is dedicated to the 4228 Jews deported to Auschwitz from that spot during the Holocaust.

The **Savaria Museum,** Kisfalvaly Sándor u. 9 (tel. 31 25 54), unearths the roots of Vas county. The first floor has natural history exhibits and archaeological artifacts from the Roman settlement and afterwards. The basement level holds collections of medieval artifacts and Roman stonework, and the ground floor houses a rotating exhibit. Some of the guides speak English (open Tues.-Fri. 10am-6pm, Sat.-Sun. 10am-4pm; admission 60Ft, students 30Ft).

West of the inner city, at the end of Árpád u., is the **Vas County Village Museum,** a re-creation of a local farming village composed of actual 150-200 year old farmhouses transplanted here from throughout the region. The three rooms of each home are decorated with authentic furnishings—the "owner's" clothes are even laid out in them. A blacksmith occasionally works at the village forge, and all maintenance is done using traditional techniques (which are rapidly dwindling—a century ago, a thatched roof could last 60 years, but no one nowadays can figure out how to make them last more than 20). The English-speaking guide can explain everything, but is usually off on Saturday. A visit here is worth the 25-minute walk from Fő tér (open April-early Oct. Tues.-Sun. 10am-6pm; admission 60Ft, students 20Ft).

Weekends and evenings, there's usually something interesting going on in **Fő tér**—either concerts or performance or just good people-watching opportunities.

■ NEAR SZOMBATHELY: KŐSZEG

Surrounded by thriving farms and roadside shrines, the tiny town of Kőszeg is treasured for its medieval cityscape; **St. James' Church** is one of the country's most significant Gothic treasures. You can get there from Szombathely by **train** (nearly every half hour, 30 min.; 72Ft) or **bus** (6 per day, 45 min.; 92Ft) or from Sopron by bus (3 per day, 90 min.; 172Ft). The Szombathely line bus from Sopron stops first at the train station and then closer to the center. Step off and turn right on Kossuth Lajos u.; one block up is **Várkör** (Castle Ring), the ovoid main street. From the train station, cross the little bridge and bear right up Rákóczi u. about 1km into the center. The **telephone city code** is 94. **Savaria Tourist** on Várkör 69 (tel. 36 02 38), offers doubles in private homes for 1100Ft (only German spoken). Next door, at the corner of Városház u., is an **Express** office (tel. 36 02 47) with hotel rooms (doubles 1300Ft, with bathroom 1800Ft; 10% off with HI card, open May-Oct.). Twenty meters farther, **IBUSZ,** Városhaz 3 (tel. 36 03 76), has doubles from 900Ft. (All tourist offices open Mon.-Fri. roughly 8am-4pm, Sat. 8am-noon.) There is also a **campground** in town near the beach on route #87. The **castle** (tel. 36 02 27) at Rajnis u. 9 in Jurisics tér, has tourist dorm rooms for 280Ft per person. **Írottkő Restaurant,** Fő tér 4, offers tasty victuals (entrees 180-430Ft; open daily 7am-10pm), and the more authentic **Kulacs Restaurant,** Várkör 12, one block from Írottkő, is better yet (entrees 140-440Ft; open daily 9am-10pm).

■ ■ ■ GYŐR

Though usually associated with heavy industries such as the Rába truck factory, Győr (pronounced "jyur") is not without charm. Some of the finest 17th- and 18th-century buildings in all of Hungary crowd the inner city, and the occasional horse-drawn cart still plods through rush-hour traffic. The rivers that eventually flow into the Danube meet here, adding to Győr's air of timelessness. On the Vienna-Budapest rail line, nearly midway between the two cities, Győr is also the base for day-trips to the thousand-year-old abbey at Pannonhalma.

ORIENTATION AND PRACTICAL INFORMATION

Győr is built around the confluence of the Rába and Mosoni-Duna rivers. Four bridges cross the water in this area, and there is a small island near the mouth of the Rába. The oldest part of the city is between the east bank if the Rába and the south bank of the Mosoni-Duna, and can be crossed on foot in 25 minutes. The **train station** is just to the south of the inner city. The **bus station** is on the south side of the tracks across from the train station; the two are connected by the same underpass that links the railway platforms.

Tourist Office: One block up from the train station, **Ciklámen Tourist,** Aradi Vér-tanúk u. 22 (tel. 31 76 01 or 31 15 57). English-speakers on staff; free brochures and maps with old street names. New maps sold for 180Ft (you can buy cheaper maps in any bookstore along Baross Gábor út or Arany János u). Open Mon.-Thurs. 8am-4:30pm, Fri. 8am-3:30pm, Sat. 8am-12:30pm. A few blocks east, **IBUSZ,** Szent István út 29 (tel. 31 17 00 or 31 12 24), is bigger and has a helpful info desk. Open Mon.-Tues. and Thurs. 8am-3:30pm, Wed. and Fri. 8am-3pm.

Currency Exchange: OTP Bank offers the best exchange rates in town, but com-pensates with an excruciatingly slow-moving line. **IBUSZ** around the corner gives only a few hundredths of a cent less.

Post Office: The main post office at Bajcsy-Zsilinszky út 46, across from the ugly Kisfaludy Theater, is open Mon.-Fri. 8am-8pm.

Telephone City Code: 96.

Trains: Győr is 2-2½hrs. from Budapest (1-2 per day, 418Ft). To: Vienna (6 per day, 2hrs.; US$18); Veszprém (6 per day, 2½hrs.; 23Ft); Szombathely (4 per day, 2-3hrs.; 358Ft); Sopron (7 per day, 1-1½hrs.; 264Ft).

Buses: To: Budapest (hourly, 2½hrs.; 393Ft.); Veszprém (8 per day, 2hrs.; 290Ft); Sopron (hourly, 1½hrs.; 342Ft). There are 6 buses per day to the abbey at Pannon-halma; the trip takes 30min. and costs 92Ft.

ACCOMMODATIONS AND CAMPING

In July and August, accommodations in downtown Győr fill up, and rooms are scarce without advance reservations. **Ciklámen Tourist** (see above) has singles in **private accommodations** starting at 600Ft, and doubles for 1000Ft. **IBUSZ** (see above) has singles for 880Ft, and doubles for 990Ft. **Express,** Bajcsy-Zsilinszky út 41 (tel. 32 88 33), can help make hostel reservations (open Mon.-Fri. 8am-3:45pm).

Hotel Szárnyaskerék, Révai Miklós u. 5 (tel. 31 46 29), right outside the exit of the train station, is gloomy but clean. The sometimes-unfriendly staff speaks English. Doubles with shared bath 1320Ft, with private bath 2200Ft.

Teátrum Panzió, Schweidel u. 7 (tel. 31 06 40), and **Duna Panzió,** Vörösmarty u. 5 (tel. 32 90 84), are both downtown and have the same owner. Comfortable dou-bles with bathroom, TV, and refrigerator are 3000Ft. Flash your *Let's Go* and get 10% off the price of your room.

2sz. Fiú Kollégium (No.2 Boy's Dormitory), Damjanich u. 58 (tel. 31 10 08), just north of the Mosoni-Duna River, charges 400Ft per night in rooms with 3-4 beds. Open weekends throughout the year, and mid-June-Aug.

Széchenyi Istvan Főiskola Kollégiuma, Hédevári út 3 (tel. 42 97 22 or 42 93 48), also north of the river, has beds in triples for 300Ft per night, 250Ft for students. Open July-Aug. 15.

Camping: Kiskút-ligeti Camping, Kiskútliget (tel. 31 89 86), has a motel open year-round, with triples for 1800Ft. Camping and bungalows are open April 15-Oct. 15; 4-person bungalows 1200Ft; campsites 250Ft per tent, 200Ft per person.

FOOD

There is a tiny **non-stop market** in the train station, near the stairs to the underpass.

Piero, Munkácsy Mihály u. 6 (tel. 32 03 14), just south of the Petőfi Bridge, is an excellent French restaurant, slightly more upscale than the run-of-the-mill *étterem.* Entrees 365-595Ft, and the foot-and-a-half tall menu is in Hungarian, English, German, Italian, and of course, French. Open daily noon-midnight.

Sárkányluk (Dragon's Hole), Arany János u. 27 (tel. 31 71 16), is a popular little bistro whose seven tables fill up at regular mealtimes. Enthusiastic teenage waitstaff. Entrees 190-400Ft; open Mon.-Sat. 11am-9pm, Sun. 11am-3pm.

Komédiás, Czuczor Gergely u. 30 (tel. 31 90 50), is a cozy, family-run restaurant with wonderful food, including imaginative cold dishes. The ground floor looks like a post-modern coffee shop. English menu. Entrees 180-500Ft. Open Mon.-Sat. 11am-midnight, Sun. 7pm-midnight. **Biergarten** around back (beer 90Ft).

Vaskakas Tavern (Iron Rooster), Bécsi Kapu tér 7, is in a huge, dark dungeon built into the castle wall. Deserted during the day, but packed with Austrian tourists at night. Entrees 150-500Ft. Open Mon.-Sat. 11am-4am, Sun. 11am-midnight.

Pizza Hut, at Baross Gábor út 11 (tel. 31 06 95). The soundtrack is a tape of a Los Angeles radio station, complete with commercials, which can serve either as an antidote for homesickness or as a reminder of why you left California in the first place. Open Sun.-Thurs. 11am-11pm, Fri.-Sat. 11am-midnight.

McDonald's is down the street at Baross Gábor út 21. Open Mon.-Thurs. 7am-10pm, Fri.-Sat. 7am-midnight, Sun. 8am-10pm.

SIGHTS AND ENTERTAINMENT

Most historical sights in Győr are within a rough triangle between Bécsi Kapu tér (formerly Köztársaság tér), Káptalandomb (Chapter Hill), and Széchenyi tér. A few blocks apart from each other, all can be seen in a hectic afternoon or an easy day.

Bécsi Kapu tér is the site of the very yellow **Carmelite church** and the remains of a medieval **castle** built to defend against the Turks. A small branch of the **János Xanthus Memorial Museum,** built into the castle casemate at Bécsi Kapu tér 5, is a lapidarium containing Roman stone carvings and monuments. The collection is small and spread out, but the labyrinthine tunnel is cool on hot days and fun to walk through (open Tues.-Sun. 10am-6pm; admission 20Ft, students 10Ft). To the east of the square, at Kiraly u. 4, is the reddish house where Napoleon Bonaparte spent his one night in Hungary. It is now an art gallery and music school called Napoleon Ház.

At the top of Káptalandomb is the **Episcopal Cathedral,** originally built in 1030. Parts have been continuously added since then, so that from the outside it is a not-particularly-coherent hybrid of Romanesque, neo-Classical, and Gothic styles. The Baroque splendor inside is far more impressive, with dozens of golden cherubim and magnificent frescoes that make it one of the loveliest churches in Hungary. The miraculous **Weeping Madonna of Győr,** in the altar in the north nave, was brought from Ireland in the 1650s by a priest fleeing the regime of Oliver Cromwell. On St. Patrick's Day 1697, the painting spontaneously wept "blood and tears" for three hours, ostensibly in compassion for persecuted Irish Catholics. The **Herm of King St. Ladislas,** a masterwork of Gothic goldsmithery in the Hédeváry chapel on the south side of the cathedral, is a wide-eyed bust of one of Hungary's first saint-kings.

The **Diocesan Treasury,** at Káptalandomb 26, has an extensive assortment of the usual wonderfully ornate gold and silver religious accoutrements reaching back to the 14th century, but the real eye-catcher is an impressive collection of 15th- and 16th-century illuminated texts. The exhibits are marked in Hungarian, German, and English (open Tues.-Sun. 10am-5pm; admission 30Ft, students 15Ft). On the way to Széchenyi tér, walk through Gutenberg tér to pass the religious monument **Ark of the Covenant,** erected in 1731. There are various stories about its origin, but all agree that the king built it with funds appropriated from his mercenaries in order to keep them in line.

The **János Xanthus Memorial Museum,** Széchenyi tér 5, is worthwhile if you've never been to a town- or county-run museum in Hungary before. Otherwise, it comes across as a lot of dry and very familiar historical and archeological exhibits. All but forgotten and leaning unmarked against a corridor wall is the iron rooster weathervane that has served alternatively as Győr's symbol of Turkish oppression and Hungarian sovereignty. The Turks erected it on the town's highest tower when they invaded Győr, and bragged that they would hold the town as long as the cock remained silent and the half moon at its base never changed phase. When the Hungarians laid siege to the city and retook it four years later, they began their attack under a full moon, and a Hungarian soldier crowed like a cock at the defenders. English speakers get thick stacks of laminated fact sheets to guide them through the collection (open Tues.-Sun. 10am-6pm; admission 50Ft).

The **Imre Patkó Collection,** in the **Iron Log House** at Széchenyi tér 4 (so named for the stump outside, into which traveling 17th-century craftsmen would drive a nail when they spent the night—although the log is more likely a later advertising gimmick), contains two floors of the works of fine Hungarian modern artists, and a small room of foreign masters like Picasso and Chagall. The loft holds a collection of Asian and African works that Patkó amassed in his travels (open Tues.-Sun. 10am-6pm; admission 20Ft, students 10Ft). The **Margit Kovács Museum** at Rózsa Ferenc u. 1, one block north of the square, is one of Győr's hidden treasures, displaying the artist's distinctive ceramic sculptures and tiles (open Tues.-Sun.10am-6pm, Nov.-March 10am-5pm; admission 20Ft, students 10Ft).

The marketplace on the river transmogrifies into a **bazaar** on Wed., Fri., and Sat. mornings. Győr frolics away the June and July with **Győri Nyár,** a festival of daily concerts, theater, and ballet. Buy tickets at the box office on Baross Gábor út, or at the performance venue. Schedules are available at Ciklámen Tourist and IBUSZ.

■ NEAR GYŐR: PANNONHALMA ABBEY

Surrounded by shining fields and rolling hills, 18km southeast of Győr, is the hilltop **Archabbey of Pannonhalma** (tel. (96) 37 01 91). Established by the Benedictines in 996, the abbey has seen 10 centuries of destruction and rebuilding, and now boasts a 13th-century Romanesque and Gothic basilica, a library of 360,000 volumes, a small art gallery, and one of the finest boys' schools in Hungary. The 1055 royal charter establishing the Benedictine abbey at Tihany, which is the oldest document bearing Hungarian words, is also kept here. (Abbey open to visitors 8:30am to 4pm; admission 100Ft, students 50Ft. Join an hourly tour group at the Pax Tourist office at the entrance; Hungarian, German, English, French, and Italian-speaking guides usually available for the mandatory 60-minute tour.)

Renovations are under way for the abbey's 1000th anniversary in 1996, and have recently uncovered 12th-century frescoes underneath a 14th-century wall in the cloister outside. In the 19th-century library, look up at the skylights—mirrors are mounted underneath to direct as much sunlight as possible into the room. If you walk back and forth in front of the painting "The Body of Christ" in the gallery, the body seems to rotate so that the feet always point toward the viewer.

Pannonhalma is an easy morning's day trip from Győr (6 buses per day, 45min.; 92Ft), but do it in the morning—there is no bus back between 1 and 5:30pm. Buses leave from the Győr bus terminal and stop in front of the abbey gate.

■ ■ ■ TATA

Two hours from Budapest on the Budapest-Vienna rail line, the quiet vacation town of Tata stretches out around lakes, canals, and a 14th-century castle. A popular place for sunbathing, boating, and fishing, Tata's small area and low proportion of foreign tourists make it less pretentious than the Lake Balaton towns. Most of the sights and stores are along the northwestern shore of **Öreg-tó,** the "Old Lake." A few blocks to the east is the smaller **Cseke-tó,** surrounded by **Angol Park.**

Orientation and Practical Information   Drop by the **Komturist** office at Ady Endre u. 9 (tel. 38 18 05, 38 06 94) for information and a 55Ft map; they also arrange doubles in private accommodations for about 1200Ft (open Mon.-Fri. 8:30am-4:30pm, Sat. 8am-4:30pm; Sept.-May Mon.-Fri. 8am-4pm). The other option is **Cooptourist,** Tóparti Sétány 18 (tel. 38 16 02), which subscribes to the "you're in Hungary now—speak German" school of thought. Both agencies can arrange doubles in lakeside pensions for 2000-2500Ft; one of the most comfortable of these is **Mónika Panzió,** on Tóparti Sétány (tel. 38 32 08; for more information on lodgings, see Accommodations, below). The **telephone city code** is 34.

Eighteen **trains** per day go through Tata on their way to Budapest (1½-2hrs., 300Ft). You probably won't see the town name on the station, but Tata is the one with the slightly dilapidated yellow building. To get in from the train station takes about 15 minutes on foot. Walk south on Bacsó Béla utca, and make a right on Somogyi Béla utca. You'll end up in Országgyűlés tér, with its squat wooden clocktower, which is the center of town by default. About 15 **buses** per day leave for Esztergom (fewer on weekends). Buses go through the terminal about two blocks west of the castle and also stop in front of the Komturist building (not the agency office) at Ady Endre u. 24. **Bike rental, boat rental,** and **horseback riding** are available at various spots around town. Ask at Komturist for their locations.

Accommodations and Food   Hotel Malom, at Erzsébet tér 8 (tel. 38 35 30), has stark but clean doubles with shared baths for 1200Ft, and triples with shared baths for 1800Ft. **Öreg-tó Camping,** Fáklya u. 1 (tel. 38 34 93), has 4-person bungalows for 1800Ft, and charges 250Ft per tent and 300Ft per person for campsite use (open May 1-Oct. 1). The **Hotel Kristály Étterem** (not the attached söröző) at Ady Endre u. 22 (tel. 38 35 77), is the most elegant restaurant in town. Menu in German and English; entrees 220-550Ft (open 11am-2pm and 6-10pm). Across the street, **Bella Italia,** Ady Endre u. 33 (tel. 38 08 13), does a commendable job simulating Italian food. Keep a close eye on the bill—things you didn't order may turn up. Pasta and pizza 150-300Ft, other entrees 300-600Ft (open 8am-2am).

Sights and Entertainment   Öregvár, the Old Castle, is reflected in the still waters of the northern tip of the lake. Originally built in the late 1300s, what remains now is from an 18th-century restoration. The **museum** inside is the town's main tourist destination. The ground floor houses Roman and medieval archaeological finds, and the first floor holds a few artifacts from the castle itself, but breeze through these and head for the second floor, where the best stuff—the work of 18th-century master craftsmen in wood, metals, and porcelain—is kept (open Tues.-Sun. 10am-6pm; admission 50Ft, students 25Ft). The **German Minority Museum,** Alkotmány u. 2, is a restored mill housing three floors of exhibits of the life of ethnic Germans. The dioramas are decent, but look for the clothing and old photographs. Explanations in—you guessed it—German (open Sat.-Sun. 10am-4pm, Tues.-Fri. noon-4pm; free, but donations encouraged).

The big yellow building between Kastély tér and Hősök tere is the **old Esterházy mansion,** built in Baroque style in 1765. It is now used as a very yellow hospital. The converted synagogue at Hősök tere houses the **Greek-Roman Statuary Museum,** a collection of the copies of ancient statues and friezes that once stood along the paths that lined Angol Park. If you're looking for a good dare, take the stairs near the entrance up to the unlit mezzanine and wander through the frozen crowds waiting there (open Tues.-Sun. 10am-6pm; free). The **Great Church** dwarfs everything else on Kossuth tér. Commissioned by the Esterházys and finished in 1787, the façade is all Baroque, but the plainness of the interior is anticlimactic. **Angol Park,** around Cseke-tó, was Hungary's first English-style park. Quiet, tree-covered paths meander around the lake, and fishermen scowl at anyone walking too loudly. The Hungarian Olympic team trains at the sports facility along the south side of the park.

HUNGARY

■■■ SOPRON

Sopron, six kilometers from the Austrian border, is Hungary's most loyal town. In 1920, while the border was being determined under the Trianon Treaty, the people of Sopron put their nationality to a vote—and overwhelmingly chose to be Hungarian. This fidelity notwithstanding, Sopron is deluged daily by Austrians drawn by low prices for medical care and sausage—especially sausage.

More than any other place in Hungary, Sopron has the look and feel of a medieval Central European town. Neither the invading Mongols nor the Turks were able to reach the town center, so buildings dating to the 14th century are common, and many structures have foundations laid by the Romans. The old town of Sopron is full of winding cobblestone streets and hidden squares; you can't throw a rock without breaking a stained-glass window in a church, synagogue, or museum. So don't.

ORIENTATION AND PRACTICAL INFORMATION

The historic town center, where almost everything of interest to tourists is located, is a horse-shoe 1km long, bounded by Ógabona tér and Várkerület. The bus terminal is two blocks to the northwest, and the train station is a 10-minute walk south on Mátyás Király út.

> **Tourist Offices: Ciklámen Tourist,** Ógabona tér 8 (tel. 31 20 40), is Tourinform-licensed. Open Mon.-Fri. 8am-4:30pm, Sat. 8am-1pm.
>
> **Post Office:** Széchenyi tér 7-8, at the southern edge of the old town. Open Mon.-Fri. 8am-6pm.
>
> **Currency Exchange:** Skip the tourist attractions and smaller agencies in favor of **Magyar Külkereskedelmi Bank** on Várkerület 16, or **Budapest Bank** at Színház u. 5. Both are open Mon.-Fri. 8am-1pm.
>
> **Telephone City Code:** 99.
>
> **Trains:** About 15 trains per day run to Vienna's Südbanhof (1hr., 131 shillings). Seven trains per day run to Budapest (3-4hrs., 682Ft) seven more to Győr (1hr., 264Ft), and 10 chug to Szombathely (90 min., 196Ft).
>
> **Buses:** To: Budapest (5 per day, 4hrs.; 677Ft); Győr (about once per hour, 2hrs.; 350Ft); Szombathely (3 per day, 2hrs.; 290Ft); Fertőd (about every 30min., 50 min.; 100Ft); and Kőszeg (4 per day, 90min.; 250Ft).

ACCOMMODATIONS AND CAMPING

IBUSZ, Várkerület 41 (tel. 31 24 55), has doubles in private homes starting at 1300Ft (open Mon.-Fri. 8am-1pm, 1:30pm-4pm, Sat 8am-12:30pm). **Ciklámen Tourist** (see above) has one single for 1050Ft and doubles for 1400Ft. **Express,** Mátyás Király u. 7 (tel. 31 20 24), can help with hostel accommodations (open Mon.-Fri. 8am-3:30pm, Sat 8am-noon).

> **Hotel Locomotiv,** appropriately near the train station at Lővér Krt. 1 (tel. 31 41 80), has doubles for 2400Ft per night.
>
> **Talizmán Panzió,** Táncsics u. 15 (tel. 31 16 20), has doubles for 1200Ft, with bath 1500Ft. Show 'em your *Let's Go* and get a 200Ft room discount.
>
> **Galéria Szálló,** about a kilometer west of the inner city at Baross Gábor u. 4-6 (tel. 31 11 50), is open all year, and charges 600Ft per night, 400Ft for students.
>
> **Középiskolai Fiú Kollégium,** in the city center at Erzsébet u. 9 (tel. 31 12 60), and its sister dorm, **Középiskolai Leány Kollégium,** just west of the city center at Ferency János u. 60 (tel. 31 43 66), charge 380Ft per person in 4-bed rooms, available weekends during the school year and daily June 20-Aug. 20.
>
> **Camping: Lővér Campground** at the south end of town on Kőszegi u. (tel. 31 17 15) has 4-person bungalows for 3000Ft, 3-person bungalows for 1200Ft, and 2-person bungalows for 700-800Ft. For campsites, it charges 200Ft per tent and 180Ft per person. Open April 15-Oct. 15.

FOOD

There is a little non-stop **grocery store** on the corner of Móricz Zsigmond u. and Magyar u., and a larger **Julius Meinl grocery** at Várkerület 100-102. Go to **Deák Étterem** at Erzsébet u. 20 on Deák tér (tel. 31 16 86) to meet the English club, which comes in for a chat and a beer every Tuesday evening from Sept.-June. Decipher your meal from the rich, non-English menu in the huge green garden. (Entrees 150-480Ft; open Mon.-Sat. 10am-midnight, Sun 10am-10pm.) **Rondella Étterem,** Szent György u. 14, has excellent steaks for 320-560Ft, pizza and spaghetti for 130-280Ft, and plenty of young Austrians (not for sale; open 11am-11pm). **Cézár Pince,** Hátsókapu 2 (tel. 31 13 37), is a wine cellar that serves great light meals and snacks, including sausage platters and cheese platters for 90-190Ft.

SIGHTS AND ENTERTAINMENT

Most of Sopron's historic sights lie within the horseshoe-shaped old town—including four churches, two medieval synagogues and 10 museums—and are concentrated in Fő tér. Monday is a bad day in Sopron—most of the museums are closed. The **Fire Tower,** on the north side of the square, is a 17th-century Baroque spire atop a 16th-century tower sitting on a 12th-century base that straddles a Roman gate. Its clock is the source of the chimes heard throughout town, and visitors can climb to the balcony for a view of Sopron's steeples and tilted roofs and the surrounding hills (open Tues.-Sun. 10am-6pm; admission 40Ft, students 20Ft).

Across the square is the **Bencés Templom** (Goat Church), which was built in the 13th century with funds from a happy herder whose goats found gold. Goats frolic on the heraldic design above the main entrance. The small **Franciscan Monastery** next door dates from the late 13th century. Visitors can enter its Chapter's Hall, a room of textbook Gothic architecture enriched by 10 sculptures of human sins, and taped Gregorian muzak chants (church and Chapter's Hall open daily 10am-noon, 2pm-5pm; free, but donations are encouraged).

At Fő tér 6 is the Gothic **Fabricius House,** which is divided into three separate exhibits: the first and second floors hold a rather dry **historical/archaeological collection** called "3000 Years Along the Amber Route." Above that are **re-creations of domestic life** in Sopron in the 17th and 18th centuries. Pushy old women demand your native language as you enter each room, and thrust upon you a photocopied guide describing each article of the gorgeous antique furnishings. In the vaulted cellar—which was originally a Gothic chapel, and is now the coolest place in town on a hot day—is a **Roman Lapidarium,** which houses stonework and monuments dating to Sopron's start as the colony Scarbantia. The huge trio of Jupiter, Juno, and Minerva that once sat in the forum now adorn the hall (all exhibits open Tues.-Sun. 10am-6pm; admission for each is 40Ft, students 20Ft—buy tickets for each exhibit separately from the cashier as you enter the house).

Just to the right, at Fő tér 8, is the **Storno House,** the best museum in town. The Stornos were 19th-century Swiss-Italian restorers of monuments and cathedrals; their taste in churches is often less than impressive, but their home and personal collection of furniture and artwork spanning the Renaissance to the 19th century are exquisite. When you buy your ticket, the cashier hands you a chit with a number on it and sends you up the first floor, where there is a dry and poorly marked historical exhibit. Don't worry, that isn't the collection; the number on your chit is the time your guided tour on the second floor starts. The guide says almost nothing—instead, she carries around a tape recorder with narration in Hungarian or German and points out each item as it's mentioned, like a stewardess doing a pre-flight safety instruction. English-speakers get a photocopied fact sheet. The tour lasts 40 minutes (open Tues.-Sun. 10am-6pm; admission 60Ft, students 40Ft).

Across the square at Fő tér 2 is the **Angel Pharmacy Museum.** Once a working pharmacy, it now traces the history of the profession from the 15th to the 20th centuries (open Tues.-Sun. 9:30am-noon and 12:30-2pm; admission 20Ft, students 10Ft). Down Új u., once known as Zsidó utca—"Jewish street"—are two rare 14th-century synagogues which evoke the life of the local Jewish community, expelled in

1526. The **Old Synagogue**, at #22, was first built around 1300. It has been reconstructed to show the separate rooms for each gender, the stone Torah niche, the wooden pulpit, and (in a small building in the courtyard) the deep well used as the ritual bath (open Wed.-Mon. 9am-5pm; admission 40Ft, students 20Ft). The **new synagogue**, at #11, is new only because it was built 50 years later. After centuries of ignominy, it was rediscovered in 1957, and is now being restored.

Just north of the old town at Bécsi út. 5 is the **Bakery Museum,** which illustrates the history of professional baking from the 15th to the 20th centuries, but is really the restored home and shop of a successful 19th-century baker (open Wed., Fri., Sun. 10am-2pm and Tues., Thurs., Sat. 2-6pm; admission 40Ft, students 20Ft). Ten minutes south of the old town at the corner of Deák tér and Csatkai Endre u. is the **Liszt Ferenc Múzeum** (Franz Liszt museum) which houses a collection of folklore and folk craft that has nothing to do with the composer (open Tues.-Sun. 10am-6pm; admission 40Ft, students 20Ft).

During the **Sopron Festival Weeks** (June-July), the town hosts opera, ballet, and concerts, some set in the **Fertőrákos Quarry** caverns, 10km away. (1 bus per hr. from main bus terminal. Admission to quarry 10Ft for students. Concerts 300-400Ft. Buy tickets for all events from the Festival Bureau on Széchenyi tér. across from the post office; open Mon.-Fri. 10am-1pm and 2-5pm, Sat. 10am-1pm.)

■ NEAR SOPRON: FERTŐD

Twenty-seven kilometers east of Sopron, in tiny **Fertőd,** stands the magnificent Rococo **Eszterházy Palace,** Bartók Béla u. 2 (tel. (99) 37 04 71), nicknamed the "Hungarian Versailles" and easily the finest in Hungary. Miklós Eszterházy, known as Miklós the Sumptuous before he squandered his family's vast fortune, ordered the palace built in 1766 to hold his multi-day orgiastic feasts (open Tues.-Sun. 8am-noon, 1-5pm). Josef Haydn wrote and conducted here, and stellar **concerts** still resound within. **Buses** leave hourly for Fertőd from stage five in the station on Lackner Kristóf in Sopron (45min., 105Ft). Fertőd has dorm beds and a few doubles, but groups often fill them. Book with Ciklámen Tourist in Sopron.

LAKE BALATON

Shallow Balaton is the largest lake (600 sq. km) and one of the most coveted vacation spots in Central Europe. Villas first sprouted along its shores during the Roman Empire. When a railroad linked Lake Balaton to its surroundings in the 1860s, it mushroomed into a favored summer playground. Today, the region's rich scenery and comparatively low prices draw mobs of German, Austrian, and Hungarian vacationers. Once schools let out, the lakeside becomes raucous and crowded with young people, but at other times you will meet mostly retirees, their grandchildren, and leviathans in skimpy swimsuits that would put the fear of God into anyone.

Storms can roll in over Lake Balaton in less than 15 minutes, raising dangerous whitecaps on the otherwise placid lake. One minute the shore looks like a colony of sleeping elephant seals; the next, thunder crashes, wattles waggle, offspring are scooped up, and everyone runs for cover. Amber lights on top of taller hotels and the Meteorological Research Center at the Siófok harbor give weather warnings; 30 revolutions per minute means stay within 500m of shore; 60 revolutions per minute means swimmers must be within 100m, and all boats must be tied on shore.

Long and narrow, Lake Balaton is easily accessible from Budapest through **Balatonfüred** on the northern shore or **Siófok** on the southern shore (5 trains per day, 350-450Ft). These two centers sate vacationers with discos and bars but leave little for rainy days. Buses run from Balatonfüred to the quieter **Tihany** (1 per hr. from 6am-10pm, 44Ft), while ferries link the three towns. **MAHART ferries** are the most convenient and enjoyable way to travel to nearby towns on the lake; students save half off all fares (1 per hr. from Siófok mid-April to mid-Oct.; to Balatonfüred 1hr., to Tihany 80 min.; 156Ft, students 78Ft). Tourist agencies book private rooms at the bus and train stations, and *Zimmer Frei* (room for rent) signs line the streets.

■ ■ ■ SIÓFOK

The largest town on Lake Balaton, Siófok's (pronounced SHEE-oh-fok) **lakeside** is a tourist mecca for surf-starved Germans and Austrians. Extensive rail and bus service make it the gateway to Balaton for most people coming in from Budapest. Siófok is flashy and well-developed and focuses most of its energies on accommodating foreign tourists, stomping out any signs of indigenous culture along the way. The soul of the town is buried behind *Zimmer Frei* signs and *biergartens* with Hamill organ and accordion players. Be warned: in cooler months, especially October to April, the tourists disappear, and many enterprises close down.

Orientation and Practical Information Siófok runs east-west, huddled up against the southern shore of Balaton. The train and bus stations are adjacent to each other in roughly the center of town. The main drag, **Fő utca**, is just south of the railway line. A canal that connects the lake to the Danube cuts the town in half; the "Gold Coast" on the eastern side is the home of the older, larger hotels. The "Silver Coast" on the west has the newer, less expensive ones. **Tourinform** is located at Fő utca 41 (tel. 31 01 17) in the base of the wooden water tower. English, German, French, and Italian spoken. Pick up a map of town here (open Mon.-Sat. 8am-8pm, Sun. 8am-1pm; Sept.-June Mon.-Fri. 9am-4pm, Sat. 9am-noon). **IBUSZ** is a block further down at Fő utca 174 (tel. 31 11 07, 31 14 81, or 31 10 66; open Mon.-Sat. 8am-6pm, Sun. 9am-1pm; Sept.-May Mon.-Fri. 8am-4pm). The main **post office** at Fő utca 186 (tel. 31 02 10) is open Mon.-Fri. 8am-6pm, Sat. 8am-1pm. There is a **telephone and fax office** in a cluster of booths just east of the canal on Fő u. (open daily 8:30am-1:30pm and 3-9pm). The **telephone city code** is 84.

A **"fast bus"** *(Gyorsjárat)* leaves for Pécs three times a day (3hrs., 460Ft) from the bus terminal. **Express trains** that stop in Székesfehérvár on their way to either Déli station or Keleti station depart Siófok station (tel. 31 00 61) seven times a day. Many **local trains** make the same trip; since most of the local stops are south of Siófok, they do not take much longer to go north to Budapest. Two trains to Dresden, one to Zagreb, one to Rijeka, and one to Venice also depart from Siófok each day. **MAHART ferry** boats leave almost hourly to nearby Tihany from the docks next to the verdant **Jókai Park,** just 10min. from the train station (10min., 60Ft). To get to the harbor, which is about 15km west of Siófok, catch the bus marked "Szántód-Köröshegy" from the bus terminal; it runs about once per hour (52Ft).

Accommodations and Food For private accommodations, try any of the myriad travel agencies around town. If you prefer to search on your own, Erkel Ferenc u. to the west of the canal and Szent László u. to the east are residential streets close to the water where nearly every house displays a *Panzió* or *Zimmer Frei* sign. **Tourinform** (see above) doesn't charge a commission and will mediate in the negotiation of rates. The average price for a double in the center of town is 1300Ft, 2500 in high season. **IBUSZ** (see above) has singles for 600Ft and doubles for about 1400Ft; the price nearly doubles in high season. **Azúr Hotel,** Vitorlás u.11 (tel. 31 20 33), off Erkel Ferenc u. to the west of the canal, has bright singles with bathrooms for 1100Ft (2035Ft in high season) and doubles for 2200Ft (4020Ft). **Hotel Korona,** Erkel Ferenc u. 53 (tel. 31 04 71), has singles for 1600-3000Ft and doubles for 3000-6000Ft, breakfast included. **Tuja Panzió,** Szent László u. 74 (tel. 31 49 96), lets you pitch tents in the backyard for 400Ft per person. The panzió, meanwhile, has doubles for 1200Ft per person. **Aranypart Camping** (tel. 31 18 01), 5km east of the center of town, is open April-Sept. Two people can occupy a site near the water for 630Ft.

HUNGARY

Öskü
Várpalota
Berhida
Balatonkenese TO POLGÁRDI
Balatonfőkajár
Lepsény
Enying
Mezőkomárom
Balatonfűzfő
Balatonszabadi
Balaton-
almádi
Balatonvilágos
Sió
Adánd
Vörösberény
Alsóörs
Siófok
Som
Veszprém
Felsőörs
Csopak
Balatonfüred
BALATONSZÉPLAK
Ságvár
Zamárdi
Balatonendréd
Szentgál
Tihany
BALATONSZÉPLAK
Balatonföldvár
Kőröshegy
Nagyvázsony
Pécsely
Aszófő
Örvényes
Tihany-rév
Szántódi-rév
Nagycsepely
Úrkút
Balaton-
udvari
Kiliántelep
Balatonszárszó
Balaton-
őszöd
Balatonszepezd
Balatonszemes
Boglárlelle
Látrány
Szentgál
Köveskál
Balaton-
akali
Zánka
Révfülöp
Balatonboglár
Ordacsehi
Lengyeltóti
Halimba
Nyírád
Balatonhenye
Kővágóörs
BALATONBOGLÁR
Fonyód
Kapolcs
Badacsony
Tihany
Bozót-es
Taliándörögd
Sáska
Eger-víz.
Badacsony-
tördemic
Tapolca
Viszló-o.
Balatonmáriafürdő
Balatonújlak
Kéthely
Szigliget
Balatongyörök
Zalaszántó
Sümeg
Balatonederics
Gyenesdiás
Vonyarcvashegy
Balatonberény
Balatonkeresztúr
Hollád
Somogyszentpál
Keszthely
Balatonszentgyörgy
Zala
Lake Balaton
N ←

Architectural sights

4 miles
4 kilometers
0
0

Csárdás Restaurant, Fő u. 105 (tel. 31 06 42), offers traditional Hungarian dishes and live gypsy music. Entrees 300-500Ft (open daily 11am-11pm). **The Manhattan,** at Szőcs Menyhert u. 4, is a salad bar that also serves sandwiches. **McDonald's** has just extended its ever-widening reach with a branch at the corner of Tanácsház u. and Vak Bottyán u., on the west side of the canal. If the Big Macs aren't fresh enough for you, do-it-yourself with ingredients from the 24-hr. **ABC market** at Fő u. 85, east of the train station.

Sights and Entertainment All other attractions are but shadows in comparison with **the Strand,** which is not a beach but a series of park-like lawns running to the concrete shoreline. There are public and private sections, with some private spots charging as much as 100Ft per person depending on the location and the whim of the owner. Most sections have pedalboat and sailboard rentals. **Nightclubs** of varying degrees of seediness line the lakefront, while amphibious lounge lizards revel on the **Disco Boat** from Jul. 9-Aug. 21. For 300Ft, you too can frolic to ABBA and the Bee Gees as this funky craft takes you to Xanadu and beyond. This bell-bottomed boat leaves the harbor at 9:30pm. Another boat, with a live band playing pop music, runs from July-Aug. 21 and leaves the docks at 7pm and 9pm for a 1½ hour cruise (300Ft). Bring your Dramamine.

Siófok is also the hometown of composer Imre Kálmán. In his honor, an **operetta** is performed every night in the Cultural Center at Fő tér 2, near the Water Tower. During the high season every year, the town hosts an **International Folk Dance Festival** in which groups from all over the world give street dancing exhibitions, hold performances, and give dancing lessons for four days.

■■■ KESZTHELY

An attractive town with a large student population, good museums, and a location from which both the north and south shores of Lake Balaton are visible, Keszthely (pronounced KESS-tay) is well worth at least a day's stopover. Keszthely's main attraction is Helikon Kastélymúzeum, the **Festetics Palace,** which represents nothing less than every child's dreamhouse.

Orientation and Practical Information The lake's largest port, Keszthely runs mostly north-south along Balaton's northwest corner. The **train station** and **bus terminal** are adjacent to each other, about half a kilometer from the water. The town's main street, Kossuth Lajos utca, runs from south to north, with the **Festetics Palace** at its head. After Fő tér, it becomes a pedestrian street; most shops and services are clustered around this area. To reach Kossuth Lajos u. from the train station, walk straight up Mátirok utca. Turn right to head for Fő tér. **Tourinform** is at Kossuth Lajos 28 (tel. 31 41 44), just north of Fő tér (open July-Aug. Mon.-Fri. 9am-6pm, Sat.-Sun. 9am-1pm; Sept.-June Mon.-Sat. 9am-5pm). **IBUSZ** (tel. 31 29 51) is at Széchenyi u. 1-3 (open Mon.-Sat. 8am-6pm, Sun. 9am-1pm; Sept.-May Mon.-Thurs. 8am-4pm, Fri. 8am-3pm). The **post office** is located at Kossuth Lajos u. 48 (tel. 31 42 32), two blocks south of Fő tér (open Mon.-Fri. 8am-7pm, Sat. 8am-noon). The **telephone city code** is 83.

The most convenient way to reach Keszthely from Budapest is by train through Siófok. Five **express trains** run between Keszthely and Budapest each day (3hrs., 600Ft). **Buses** are better for local travel. Fifteen of them scoot to Veszprem each day (2hrs., 300Ft). Eight buses a day leave for Balatonfüred (2 hrs., 290Ft), and five go to Pécs (3hrs., 350Ft). These buses rarely leave from the terminal; instead, they use stops on the street in the center of town at either Fő tér or Georgikan utca. Get a bus schedule at Tourinform or at the Zala Volán travel agency located at Kossuth u. 43 (open Mon.-Sat. 9am-5pm). Each departure is marked with an "F" or a "G" to indicate which stop it uses. In summer, **ferries** run to and from Keszthely. Once per day there is a boat to Balatonboglár on the southern shore of the lake (2hrs., 40min., 260Ft) and another to Badacsony on the northern shore (2hrs., 200Ft).

Accommodations and Food Tourinform (see above) will find apartments with room for four people for 3000Ft per night. **IBUSZ** (see above) has doubles in private homes for 1320-1500Ft. **Zalatour,** Fő tér 1 (tel. 31 43 01), has doubles for 800Ft (open Mon.-Sat. 8am-9pm, Sun. 8am-noon). If those don't pan out, you can try any other agency in the area—almost all of them can help wary Teva-clad youths seeking shelter. If you'd rather look on your own, homes with *Zimmer Frei* signs are most common near the Strand, especially on Erzsébet Királyné u. The **Forras Panzió,** Romai út 1 (tel. 31 14 18), is social and popular with students—and has singles for 1300Ft and doubles for 2340Ft to boot. **Mr. Athla Lukic's** cozy **panzió** at Jókai Mór u. 16 (tel. 31 12 32) has doubles for 3000Ft; *Let's Go* readers receive a 20% discount. The **Vajda J. Középiskola Kollégiuma,** Gagarin u. 4 (tel.31 13 61), is a hostel that charges 350Ft for a bed in a dormitory room (open June-Aug.). **Sport Camping,** on Csárda u. (tel. 31 28 42), is a five-minute walk south from the train station and across the tracks; it has 2-person bungalows with bathroom for 1500Ft, without bathroom for 700Ft. These folks charge 150Ft per tent, and 140Ft per person (open May-Sept.).

The **Park Vendéglő,** Vörösmarty u. 1/a (tel. 31 16 54), has an English menu (entrees 280-550Ft). Readers of *Let's Go* get a 10% discount or a free glass of wine (open daily 11am-11pm). **Béke Vendéglő** (tel. 31 24 47) has a large, shady courtyard and live gypsy music in the evenings. Entrees 140-460Ft (open daily 8am-10pm). **Sramli** (tel. 31 46 33) is at Pethő u. 14 right off the pedestrian street. Entrees 240-550Ft (open daily 10am-10pm). **Reform,** at Rákóczi tér 3, is a vegetarian restaurant where, for 55Ft per 100 grams, you can take whatever you want—they'll make more (open daily 11am-9pm).

Sights Keszthely's pride is the Helikon Kastélymúzeum, the **Festetics Palace.** Built by one of the most powerful Austro-Hungarian families, the storybook palace does Baroque architecture proud. Of the 360 rooms, tourists can only visit the central wing, but it's enough. Check out the 90,000-volume **Helikon Library,** an arms collection that spans a thousand years, and rooms full of artwork and period furniture. Concerts are often held in the mirrored ballroom during summer. Check your bag at the door and pad through the collection wearing tie-on shoe covers (open Tues.-Sun. 9am-6pm; admission 250Ft, students 70Ft, Hungarians even less). The surrounding English-style park is a vast and well-kept strolling ground. To find the palace, follow Kossuth Lajos u. north until it becomes Kastély u. You can't miss it—it's the only one on the block.

The **Balaton Museum,** Kossuth Lajos u. 75, at the corner of Mártírok u., displays Balaton's indigenous wildlife and an ethnographic regional history (open Tues.-Sun. 10am-5pm; admission 50Ft, students 30Ft). The **Georgikon Major Múzeum** at Bercsényi u. 67 is an extremely amusing apotheosis of György Festetics, who founded Europe's oldest agricultural university here in 1797. Exhibits detail the history of agriculture throughout Europe (open April-Oct. Tues.-Sat. 10am-5pm, Sun. 10am-6pm; admission 30Ft, students free).

■ NEAR KESZTHELY: HÉVÍZ

Hévíz, just 8km northwest of Keszthely, is home to the world's second largest **hot-water lake.** With a surface area of 47,000 square meters and a temperature of 32-33°C in summer and 24-26°C in winter (about 91°F and 77°F, respectively), this gigantic hot tub is renowned for its medicinal mud at the bottom and its red water lilies floating up top (open daily 9am-5pm; admission 180Ft for 3 hours). **Buses** leave from Fő tér hourly from 5:30-10:30pm (20 min., 36Ft).

■■■ BALATONFÜRED

Most Hungarians you ask will urge you to visit Balatonfüred, because it's the place most of them would like to be. It is the oldest spa town on Lake Balaton, and summer homes here are a hot commodity. Balatonfüred is known for its mild climate, clean air, vineyards, and medicinal springs, and has been the site of a health resort for over 200 years. The largest town on the northern shore, it has a more dignified atmosphere than Siófok, with many historical buildings, and the State Hospital of Cardiology situated to take advantage of the hot springs. Leafy residential streets invite relaxed walks through town and pensive promenades along the water. One reason a stately stroll (or shuffle) is so prevalent in Balatonfüred is that many of the strollers are heart patients. On nice days, György tér is populated largely by those who can't go any further. Prices—especially for rooms—are high here, but Balatonfüred is still a refreshing destination for a day trip and makes an excellent base for exploring neighboring Tihany, only 20 minutes away.

Orientation and Practical Information The train line runs through the middle of town, and almost everything of interest to tourists lies between it and the water. The main street is **Jókai Mór utca,** which runs northwest to southeast. From the train or bus station, walk east on Horváth Mihály utca. The promenade, called **Tagore sétány,** runs along the water for half a kilometer, and is lined with shops and stalls and restaurants. **IBUSZ,** Petőfi Sándor u. 4/a (tel. 34 20 28), has maps and English info (open Mon.-Fri. 8am-6pm, Sat.-Sun. 8am-noon; Sept.-May Mon.-Fri. 8am-4pm). The **post office** is at Zsigmond u. 14 (tel. 34 21 15; open Mon.-Fri. 8am-6pm, Sat. 8am-noon). The **telephone city code** is 86. Most **buses** and **trains** on the north side of the lake go through Balatonfüred. Seven express trains a day leave for Budapest's Déli Station (2½hrs., 418Ft). Buses to the Tihany peninsula run hourly from the bus terminal (20min., 52Ft), but also stop at the corner of Széchenyi u. and Jókai Mór u. and along Széchenyi u. Buses to Veszprém leave at least once per hour from the terminal (35min., 70Ft). In summer, the **ferry** to Tihany runs from the Balatonfüred pier every 20 minutes (20min., 100Ft). Also in summer, **bicycle** and 50cc **scooter** rentals appear in parking lots near the water. Mountain bikes cost 150Ft per hour, scooters 500Ft per hour. Helmets are not mandatory within the town limits (but wear one anyway).

Accommodations and Food Private accommodations here are more expensive than in Budapest, and at the moment there is no hostel in town. Try **Cooptourist** first, at Jókai Mór u. 23 (tel. 34 26 77). They don't speak English, but they've got doubles for 1000-1500Ft (open Mon.-Fri. 9am-noon and 1-6pm, Sat. 9am-4pm; Sept.-May Mon.-Fri. 9am-noon and 1-6pm, Sat. 9am-noon). **Balatontourist** is located at Blaha Lujza u. 5 (tel. 34 28 22) and has doubles for 1400-1600Ft (open Mon.-Sat. 8:30am-6:30pm, Sun. 9am-12:30pm). Ask the folks at Balatontourist if 400Ft dorm rooms are available at **Ferenc Széchenyi College** on Iskola u. Renovations may be completed by now. **IBUSZ** (see above) has doubles from 1900Ft and rents villas for about 6800Ft per night. **Ficc-Rally Camping** at Széchenyi u. 24 (tel. 34 38 23) has 3-person bungalows for 4200Ft and 5-person bungalows for 7200Ft. It also rents space near the water for tents, cars, and campers at 60 square meters (1290Ft).

Hotel Blaha Lujza Restaurant and Bar, Blaha Lujza u. 4 (tel. 34 26 03), is centrally located and a class act. If you look like you really need it, the staff will scrape up an English menu for you. Entrees 290-450Ft (open Sun.-Thurs. 11am-10pm, Fri.-Sat. 11am-11pm). **Napsugár Vendéglő** ("Sunshine Restaurant"), Garai út 30 (tel. 342866), is in a residential neighborhood and has a veranda with a view of the lake. Entrees 320-620Ft (open daily 11am-midnight). For a pure tourist experience, try **Baricska Csárda** at Baricska dülő (tel. 34 31 05), the private lane leading up from the Shell station on Széchenyi u. Traditional Hungarian fare with a nightly Gypsy dance show at 8pm. Entrees 480-880Ft (open daily 11am-11pm).

Sights The **Jókai Mór Villa,** at Jókai Mór u. 1, was home to the prolific 19th-century writer/Parliamentarian Jókai Mór and his actress wife, Róza Laborfalvi. The house is now a museum containing their personal belongings for inquiring minds that want to know, as well as a varied collection amassed by the couple themselves (open April-Oct. Tues.-Sun. 10am-6pm; admission 40Ft, students 10Ft). The Kossuth Lajos **spring** runs from a fountain in a pavilion in György tér. This was the first of six thermal springs discovered in the area. The water is drinkable, although it tastes slightly citric from the carbonic acid it contains, and is ever-so-slightly radioactive. Yummy. The **State Hospital of Cardiology** next door at György tér 2, makes full use of their resource; patients bathe in it to cure cardio-vascular ills and drink it for diabetes and liver and digestive problems. It seems to do the trick—the **Sanatarium** (the yellow building at the top of the square) has a collection of memorial plaques from prominent people cured by the spring's magical waters. **The Strand** can be entered through the eastern end of Tagore Sétány. Unlike at Siófok, there is actually a strip of sand about 5 meters wide before the water, favored by couples pushing the limits of foreplay (admission 70Ft). If you rent a bike, try heading up to Siske, a neighborhood of traditional white-walled, thatched cottages ascending a terraced slope—virtually a world away from the crowded scene of the Strand. You can see the lake from here, but none of the tourist attractions. Go up Jókai Mór to Aracsi út and then turn left up the hillside on Siske u.

■■■ TIHANY

High on its peninsular hilltop, Tihany (pronounced TEE-hawn) is the most luscious spot on Lake Balaton. The discos of the lowlands give way to the town's venerable Baroque church and the inland lakes and hiking trails that lace the surrounding hills. The price of paradise is predictably high, and Tihany's isolation means fewer hedonistic diversions.

The two **ferry** landings, Tihany and, to the southwest, Tihanyi-rév, are easy to confuse. The village is at the top of the hill, marked by the twin-towered **church**. The **view** from atop the village is the best anywhere on the lake. Take the **bus** (departing frequently from both ferry wharves, or stay on the bus from Balatonfüred) up to town, or **hike** up the winding paths toward the church. Lording over the peninsula, the magnificent 1754 **Abbey Church** has Baroque altars, pulpit, and organ (open daily 10am-5pm; admission 20Ft, students 10Ft). Buried in the **crypt** is Andrew I, one of Hungary's first kings and the only king of the Árpád line who lies in his original resting place. His grant establishing the first church on the site in 1055 is one of the oldest extant Hungarian-language texts (before, they had all been in Latin). Inquire about occasional organ concerts during the summer. Next door, an 18th-century monastery has been reincarnated as the **Tihany Museum,** with psychedelic dreamscapes, colorized etchings, and Roman inscriptions displayed in a cool, subterranean *lapidarium* (room with stone carvings; open March-Oct. Tues.-Sun. 10am-6pm; admission 30Ft). Far from the madding crowd is the bizarre **garage-gallery** of "painter artist, writer, professor" Gergely Koós-Hutás, at Fürdőtelep 43, a five-minute climb from the wharf. Works include massive canvases of a didactic Lenin and several of the artist in front of famous edifices around the world, such as Grauman's Chinese Restaurant in Hollywood. Signed photos are a steal at 20Ft.

Balatontourist, the **post office,** and the church all huddle next to the bus stop. The **telephone city code** is 86. Balatontourist, Kossuth u. 20 (tel. 34 85 19), arranges private rooms in the village. Doubles 1570Ft; private apartments with kitchen, bath, and two double rooms 3500-4000Ft (open summer Mon.-Sat. 8am-6:30pm, Sun. 8am-1pm). Set up your own room at the numerous houses posting *Zimmer* signs. A room close to the lake (4000-5000Ft) is not worth the price, since the village is but a hop, skip, and jump away. The promenade behind the church also leads to the **beach** (follow the "strand" signs). For an indoor panorama, choose **Echo Rest,** the round building at the end of the promenade (250-550Ft; open daily 10am-11pm). Next to the abbey, **Rege Presso** (Panorama Teraze) has a more restricted view, but the most succulent pastries on the peninsula (50-60Ft; open daily 9am-7pm). The beach is open daily 7am to 7pm (admission 50Ft), though the side gate remains unlocked after hours.

■■■ VESZPRÉM

Sixteen kilometers north of Balaton, Veszprém is a lake town without the lake. Tourists are lured from the water for a day by Veszprém's wealth of Baroque architecture and art. The town got its start in the Middle Ages as a long, narrow castle built on a sheer promontory of dolomite 30 meters high. The castle itself was blown up by the Habsburgs in 1702, leaving only the walls and a few medieval buildings; the present-day Castle Hill harkens back to a frenzy of development in the 18th century. Today, visitors to the castle district come to walk the single windy street, to enter its several impressive churches and chapels, and to view the panorama of surrounding towns, fields, and mountains from the cliff wall.

Orientation and Practical Information The center of Veszprém is the pedestrian street Kossuth Lajos utca. **Castle Hill** is a ten minute walk northeast. For tourist information, **maps,** and **private accommodations,** try **Balatontourist** at Kossuth Lajos 21 (tel. 42 96 30; open June-Aug. Mon.-Fri. 8:30am-5pm, Sat. 9am-noon; Sept-May Mon.-Fri. 8:30am-4pm, Sat 9am-noon). **IBUSZ** is on the ground floor of Kossuth Lajos 6 (tel. 42 42 00; open Mon.-Thurs. 7:30am-4pm, Fri. 8am-3pm). Both have doubles starting at 1000Ft. **Express** is at Kossuth Lajos 6 (tel. 42 45 08). They charge commission for setting up reservations in campgrounds and hostels, including the ones listed below (open Mon.-Fri. 9am-5pm, Sat 9am-1pm). The main **post office** is at Kossuth Lajos 19 (tel. 42 44 55; open Mon.-Fri. 8am-8pm, Sat. 9am-1pm). The **telephone city code** is 88. There are several banks that **exchange currency** and **travel agencies** along this stretch. From the bus station, walk a block south to the pedestrian underpass. From the train station, take bus #11 or 14v to the Hotel Veszprém. **Trains** head to Budapest: (7 per day, 2 hrs.; 230Ft); Székesfehérvár, on the same line (126Ft); and Győr (5 per day, 2 hrs.; 230Ft). **Buses** travel to: Budapest (26 per day, 2¼hrs.; 426Ft); Székesfehérvár on the way to Budapest (55 min., 198Ft); Keszthely (10 per day, 90 min.; 250Ft); and Győr (16 per day, 1hr. 40 min.; 292Ft). Buses to Balatonfüred leave every 20 minutes (30 min., 90Ft).

Accommodations and Food Hotel **Veszprém** is about as central as you can get, at Budapest u. 6 (tel. 42 48 76). Doubles with shared baths are 1300Ft, with private bath 2000Ft; breakfast included (prices go up in summer). The **Éllő György Panziója,** Yosef Attila u. 25 (tel. 32 00 97) and the **Diana Panzió** across the street at József Attila u. 22 (tel. 42 10 61), both have doubles for 3500Ft. The **University of Veszprém Youth Hostel,** a 10-min. walk south of Castle Hill at Egyetem u. 10 (tel. 42 90 10) has beds in dorm rooms for 330-430Ft. (June 15-Aug.). The **Erdei Motel and Camping,** Kittenberger u. 14 (tel. 42 67 51), has 2-person bungalows for 500Ft, and charges 250Ft per person and 700Ft per tent for campsite use (open May-Sept. 15). The **Skorpió Grill,** Virág Benedek u. 1B (tel. 42 03 19), is part restaurant and part pub. Entrees 220-550Ft, menu in German, English, and Italian (open 11am-11pm). **Óváros Restaurant,** Óváros tér 14 (tel. 32 67 90), is near the entrance to the castle. Entrees 190-370Ft (open 11am-11pm). **Cserhát,** Kossuth Lajos u. 6 (tel. 42 54 11), is self-service and the cheapest eatery in town. You get what you pay for—don't take your food to the outdoor tables if you're a fussy eater.

Sights Enter the historic district through the **Castle Gate,** which was built in 1936 to honor soldiers who died in World War I. To the southwest is the **Fire Tower,** the source of Veszprém's hourly chimes. Climb to the top for a great view of the town and the surrounding mountains; looking down at the sudden drop of the hillside at the tower's base makes it seem much taller than its 48 meters. Enter through the courtyard at Vár u. 17 (open 9am-6pm; admission 40Ft, students 25Ft). At Vár u. 21 is the late Baroque **House of the Aged Priests.** It was built in 1778 as the Piarist secondary school, but later became an old folk's home for clergymen. Now it's used for offices. The **Piarist Church** at number 14 is more gallery than church. In summer it houses exhibitions of religious art (admission 10Ft). The Bishop's Palace, built 1776, is the E-shaped building at number 16.

The **Dubinczay-ház**, at #29, was built in 1751 by the Canon Istvan Dubinczay. Over the doorway is written his motto, *"Non est mortale quod opto"* — "That which I wish for is not mortal." The house is now used as a gallery for modern art exhibits (open daily 10am-6pm). Further up the road is the **Franciscan Church**, built in 1730. The painting at the main altar depicts St. Stephen offering the crown of Hungary to the Virgin Mary. The church is closed to tourists, but you can peer through the glass doors in the vestibule. Across the street is the 13th-century **Gizella Chapel**, which has experienced partial destruction and several well-meaning restorations, but still contains 700-year-old frescoes of six of the 12 apostles (admission 10Ft, students 5Ft). A bit further up is **St. Michael's Cathedral**, which tradition holds was commissioned by Queen Gizella, the wife of St. Stephen, Hungary's first Christian king. The oldest remaining section is the **Gothic Crypt**, built in the 14th century. Most of the building was renovated in rather uninspiring Neo-Roman style in 1910 (open Tues.-Sun. 9am-7pm).

Just past the cathedral is a small glass-walled dome protecting the ruins of the 11th-century **St. George's Chapel**. The little building started out round, but was rebuilt as an octogon in the 13th century. What's left is mostly the foundation and some stonework (open daily 9am-5pm; admission 10Ft, students 5Ft). On the opposite side of Vár u. is the **Diocesan Museum of Veszprém**, which has an exhibition of religious art that includes paintings, sculpture, and vestments (open May-Oct. daily 9am-5pm; admission 20Ft, students 10Ft). For an impressive view of the buildings of Castle Hill crowded at the edge of the cliff wall, take the stairs behind the cathedral and walk north along Benedek-hegy, a narrow arm of the hill that shoots north, slightly lower than the rest, cutting the community below in half.

Ten minutes north of Castle Hill at Erzsébet Sétány 7 is the **Laczkó Dezső Museum**. The collection illustrates the history of the area, ranging from Bronze-age artifacts to folk costumes to warfare to agriculture (open Tues.-Sun. 10am-6pm; admission 40Ft, students 20Ft). Next door is **Bakonyi Ház**, a reproduction of a typical three-room peasant's house. The rooms are furnished with hand-crafted antiques, and the guide takes down nearly every item for visitors one at a time. If you try to escape, she will thrust an 18th-century bible or antique wine jug at you. Act suitably impressed (open Tues.-Sun. 10am-6pm; admission 30Ft, students 10Ft.).

LATVIA (LATVIJA)

US$1	= 0.54 Lati	1 Lat =	US$1.85
CDN$1	= 0.40 Lati	1 Lat =	CDN$2.53
UK£1	= 0.85 Lati	1 Lat =	UK£1.18
IR£1	= 0.83 Lati	1 Lat =	IR£1.20
AUS$1	= 0.40 Lati	1 Lat =	AUS$2.48
NZ$1	= 0.29 Lati	1 Lat =	NZ$3.40
SAR1	= 0.15 Lati	1 Lat =	SAR6.57
DM1	= 0.35 Lati	1 Lat =	DM2.84
Country Code: 371		International Dialing Prefix: 810	

Latvia (pop. 2.6 million) is situated on the Baltic coast between Lithuania and Estonia. The little nation is no exception to the region's history of foreign domination; since the 13th century, Latvia has suffered under Germans, Swedes, Poles, and Russians. The fifty-year occupation of Latvia by the Soviet Union has left deep marks, as massive influxes of Russian workers reduced Latvians to a near-minority in their own country. But Latvia has managed to retain its national identity, as reflected in music, art, and folk culture. Once again independent, Latvia is quickly becoming a player in world business markets. With a population of nearly a million, Rīga is the largest and most exciting city in the Baltics, a resplendent mix of medieval Hanseatic influences and 19th-century *art nouveau*.

Visiting Rīga alone won't give you the full picture of Latvia. In a country full of storks and tranquil farmsteads, Rīga is the nation's head, but the heart of Latvia is the countryside. Try to go to the woodsy river-valley of the Gauja in Vidzeme, overflowing with castles, legends, and hiking trails; Rūndāles Pils, a palatial reminder of 18th-century Latvian grandeur in Zemgale; Daugavpils, in lake-strewn Catholic Latgale; or wander the pine roads of Kurzeme, whose Duke Jacob once held colonies in Africa.

LATVIA ESSENTIALS

Citizens of the U.K. can visit Latvia visa-free for up to 90 days. Citizens of the U.S., Canada, Ireland, Australia, New Zealand, and South Africa require a visa (free to Americans and Canadians), which can be obtained at the airport or on the border. Keep in mind that since early 1993, the three Baltic states have formed a common visa zone, meaning that a visa from any one of the three countries is sufficient for travel to the other two. Latvian visas are the cheapest of the three. If you want to go to the Baltics for a long time, you should also plan to get a Latvian visa; negotiations currently underway should make it possible for U.S. citizens to obtain 12-month, multiple-entry visas for Latvia by summer 1995. See Essentials: Embassies and Consulates, page 3.

GETTING THERE AND GETTING AROUND

Latvia is well-connected by **train** to Moscow, St. Petersburg, Vilnius, Tallinn, and even Berlin. **Buses** also have an efficient long-distance network running to Estonia and Lithuania, though with less routes to other countries. **Ferries** run to Rīga from Stockholm and Kiel, though it is cheaper from Stockholm to go to Tallinn and take a train; from Kiel, it's often better to go to Klaipåda and catch a bus. The least expensive way to reach Rīga if you're already in the Baltics is definitely by train or bus; if you travel by train, be sure to secure a *coupé* or a first-class compartment. **Flights** to Latvia use the overworked Rīga Airport, whose only runway was short enough to cause safety concern when President Clinton visited in July 1994. Latavio, the Latvian national airline, has good connections to Stockholm, Amsterdam, Warsaw, and Moscow. Lufthansa flies from Berlin and Frankfurt, ČSA from Prague, Hamburg Airlines from Hamburg, Baltic International from Belfast and New York, and LOT from Warsaw and Vilnius. Note that timetables for buses and trains in the Baltics may run horizontally instead of vertically.

Buses and trains run everywhere in Latvia; getting from town to town is rarely a problem. You can buy complete schedules *(Saraksts)* of the diesel-train, bus, ferry, and electric-train systems radiating from Rīga at bookstores for 40 santīmu. The electric suburban train system centered in Rīga actually covers nearly half the country, stretching between the Lithuanian and Estonian borders. To cross Latvia by train from Liepaja to Daugavpils (via Rīga) takes about nine hours. Buses are generally faster but more expensive. In the vast eastern region of Latgale, the virtual lack of trains leaves buses the only option.

TOURIST SERVICES

Tourist offices are uncommon in Latvia. Rīga has *Riga this Week,* an unhelpful English/German compendium of casino ads published every 5-8 months. Matthias Lûfkes, creator of the *Vilnius in Your Pocket* series, has been talking about doing a Rīga guide; keep your eyes open for it. A city map of Rīga is sold at newsstands (85LVR), and the excellent, encyclopedic *The Baltic States: A Reference Book* can be bought at many main hotels and hard-currency shops. When in Rīga, take full advantage of the **Tourist Club of Latvia,** Skārņu iela 22 (tel. (2) 22 17 31, fax 22 76 80), right behind St. Peter's Church; immense amounts of information on travel to Russia, Ukraine, Belarus, Lithuania, Latvia, Germany, and other destinations are available from the manager, Marģers Laiviņš. Unfortunately, he only speaks German, Latvian, and Russian, but other office staff know some English (open daily 9am-5pm). The **Latvijas Universitāte Tūrists Klubs,** in the main University building at Raiņa bulv. 19, room 107 (tel. (2) 22 52 98, fax (8) 82 01 13), is another great source for info on Latvia, especially on hiking and bicycling options. (open daily 9am-6pm). **Latvia Tours,** shares an office with **American Express** on Grēcinieku iela 22/24 (tel. (2) 21 36 52, fax 21 36 66). As in the rest of the Baltics, stores sometimes close for an hour or two between noon and 3pm, and restaurants may take a break between 5 and 7pm.

Major holidays in Latvia include the National Day (Nov. 18), celebrating the anniversary of Latvia's independence (1918), but the most important date is June 23, the Midsummer's Eve Festival called *Ligo* or *Jāni* (St. John's Day). Rīga is a ghost town during the weekend around Ligo, when everyone retreats to the countryside for dancing, singing, bonfires, and other invigorating pagan traditions.

MONEY

The Latvian **Lats** (100 santīmu = 1 Lats) has an almost unreal value; at press time, one Lats was worth significantly more than a unit of any other currency in the world, attesting to the amount of business being transacted in Latvia. Fortunately, this economic precociousness means that traveler's checks can be cashed in Rīga. Credit card debits were unavailable in summer 1994, but should be accessible in the larger banks by summer 1995. Visa, MasterCard, and AmEx are all commonly accepted in Rīga; outside the capital, Visa is your best bet.

COMMUNICATIONS

The phone system in Latvia is currently a mess, but a recent deal with a Finnish company may result in Latvia soon being the first country in the world with an entirely digital phone network. These extensive renovations mean that public phones throughout Latvia are expect to be replaced by cardphones in late 1994 or 1995, but the conversion may not proceed on schedule. In summer 1994, local phones in Latvia required special *žetoni,* purchasable at kiosks and post offices for 1 santīms each (good for a 3min. local call). Long-distance calls within Latvia can be made from some of the old gray public phones with the double-grooved *žetoni* sold at post offices (6 santīmi each, good for anywhere from 30sec.-2min.). For international calls to the West, the only options at present are at the post office or from your hotel room. To do it yourself, dial 8-194 and talk to the operator in Latvian or Russian; you'll be asked for where you want to call, the number, your number, your name, and when you want to talk (or you may just be told to wait). Direct-dial lines to Sweden and the U.K. should have been installed by fall 1994, with more to follow. AT&T USADirect and similar services are not yet available. International calls within the former Soviet Union can be placed directly by dialing 8, followed by the old Soviet city code (usually the same as the current code). In general, try to avoid making international calls from Latvia; phone rates climbed in August, 1994 to an astounding 1.85 Lati per minute to the US (roughly US$3.50 per min.). It's cheaper for mom and dad to call *you*

LANGUAGE

In Latvia, even more than in Lithuania or Estonia, life proceeds in a bilingual fashion. In Rīga, nearly 65% of the people are Russians speaking little (if any) Latvian. Cities such as Daugavpils, in eastern Latvia, have populations over 95% Latvian. A language law requires that signs, menus, and other public writings be in Latvian; this can seem obnoxious when you struggle to order from a Latvian menu only to discover your waiter speaks only Russian and Polish. If you know Russian, use it in Rīga and other large cities, where it will get you around with a minimum of hassle. Latvians may very well speak Russian, albeit reluctantly. Most young Latvians study English or German, but probably aren't fluent. In smaller towns where only Latvian is usually spoken, some Latvian phrases may bring old women to beam and laden you with flowers, fruit, and warmth.

An aromatic blend of German, Russian, and Swedish influences, the Latvian language is a member of the Baltic language group along with Lithuanian. A short course in Latvian would include several essential words and phrases. *Alus* (beer) is a crucial word in any language. Some key places are the *autoosta* (bus station); *stacija* (train station); *lidosta* (airport); *viesnīca* (hotel); and *pasts* (post office). For longer conversations, learn: *Vai jūs runājiet Angliski?* "Do you speak English?" Other good things to know: *Mani sauc ir...* "My name is..."; *Vai tu grībi dējot?*

Yes	*jā*	yah
No	*nē*	ney
Today	*šodien*	SHOW-deeyen
Tomorrow	*rīt*	REET
Hello/Good day	*labdien*	LAHB-dyen
Good morning	*labrīt*	LAHB-reet
Good night	*labvakar*	LAHB-vah-kahr
Goodbye	*atā*	ah-tah
Excuse me	*atvainojiet*	AHT-vye-no-yet
I'm sorry	*atvainojos*	AHT-vye-no-yohs
Please	*lūdzu*	LOOD-zuh
Thank you	*paldies*	PAHL-dee-yes
When?	*kad?*	KAHD
Where is...?	*Kur ir...*	kuhr ihr
Do you speak English?	*Vai jūs runājiet angliski?*	vye yoos RUH-nah-yee-eht AHN-glee-ski?
How much is it?	*Cik maksā?*	sikh MAHK-sah
How do I get to...?	*Es gribu iet uz...*	ehs GREE-boo EE-yet ooze
My name is ...	*Mani suac ir...*	MAH-nih sowts ihr
I don't understand	*Es nesaprotu*	ehs NEH-sah-proh-too
Help!	*palīdzājiet!*	PAH-leedz-ah-yee-eht!
Get lost!	*atstājiet!*	AHT-stah-yee-eht

1—viens (vee-YENZ); 2—divi (DIH-vih); 3—trīs (TREESE); 4—četri (CHEH-trih); 5—pieci (PYET-sih); 6—seši (SEH-shih); 7—septiņi (SEHP-tih-nyih); 8—astoņi (AHS-toh-nyih); 9—deviņi (DEH-vih-nyih); 10—desmit (DEZ-miht); 20—divdesmit (DIHV-dez-miht); 30—trīsdesmit (TREEZ-dez-miht); 40—četrdesmit (CHEH-truh-dez-iht); 50—piecdesmit (PYETZ-dez-miht); 60—sešdesmit (SEHZH-dez-miht); 70—septiņdesmit (SEHP-tinh-dez-miht); 80—astoņdesmit (AHS-tohnh-dez-miht); 90—deviņdesmit (DEH-vihnh-dez-miht); 100—simts (SIHMTS)

ACCOMMODATIONS AND CAMPING

Tourservice (Latvian Travel Company) at Elizabetes iela 27 (tel. 32 60 09, fax 16 11 83) has listings of budget accommodations and makes travel arrangements (open Mon.-Fri. 10am-6pm, Sat. 10am-2pm). **Patricia**, Elizabetes 22-4a (tel. 28 48 68, fax 28 66 50), provides info in English and arranges homestays (average US$10 per night) as well as apartment rentals (US$30-40 per night; open Mon.-Fri. 9am-7pm).

LIFE AND TIMES

HISTORY

In **ancient times,** Latvia was inhabited by the tribe known as the Balts. According to the Roman historian Tacitus, the Latvian people traded precious **amber** to the Roman Empire—thus the region has been rather romantically dubbed "Amber Coast." In the 9th century, fierce Viking ships swept down from the northwest to conquer the Balts, while Slavic invaders chewed away at the region's eastern frontier. In the 12th and 13th centuries, German warriors known as the **Brothers of the Sword** subdued the area with the blessing of the Pope, beginning a long period of German hegemony. Missionaries rapidly Christianized the region, though the indigenous religions are still around today. The ethnic Latvian leaders melted into countryside while rural Latvians labored as serfs on German feudal estates. The Teutonic conquerors squeezed taxes, tithes, and forced labor from their Latvian peons; only the city of Rīga remained temporarily free.

In the 16th and 17th centuries, Latvia was divided and subdivided into tiny fragments torn apart by a hungry pack of imperialist nations. Lithuania grabbed everything north of the Daugava River; peculiarly, the southern half of the country (which borders Lithuania) remained semi-autonomous for a time. Sweden first seized Rīga, then took the entire northern region. Russian tsars battled Sweden and Poland for the entire region; finally Peter the Great captured Rīga from the Swedes in 1710, and by the end of the 18th century, Russia ruled all of Latvia.

Latvian peasants gained some degree of freedom after the **Napoleonic Wars,** under emperor Alexander I. But serfs still could not purchase lands from their German landlords, and peasant unrest spread. When serfs were liberated throughout the Russian empire in 1861, Latvian peasants finally won the right to buy the lands their forefathers had farmed for centuries. Meanwhile, however, ethnic Latvians had become restless under constant foreign domination; calls for independence were increasingly vocal.

Reacting to the Bolshevik coup of November 1917, the **Latvian People's Council** proclaimed independence on November 18, 1918. The new autonomous government in Rīga was led by Kārlis Ulmanis. But true autonomy was a distant dream indeed; instead, over the next few years, Latvia was overrun by a perplexing diversity of battling armies. German armies, allied with White Russians, fought against a loose coalition of Latvians, British, French, Estonians, and eventually Lithuanians; the Red Army represented a third faction.

When the fighting ended in early 1920, the Latvians themselves were in control. **Democratic coalitions** ruled the country for over a decade, with Ulmanis serving four terms as prime minister. However, proposed constitutional reforms threw liberals and ethnic minorities into an uproar, and the burgeoning Nazi movement spread like a cancer among the minority German population. In 1934, Ulmanis dissolved all political parties and established a ruling dictatorship.

World War II turned Latvia upside down once again. Soviet troops invaded in June 1940 and soon incorporated it into the Soviet Union. Within a year, the Soviets had deported 35,000 Latvians, primarily intellectuals. Germany invaded the region (yes, again) in 1941; by 1945, the Red Army had driven the Nazis out.

Latvia was one of the wealthiest and most industrialized regions of the Soviet Union. But under **Soviet rule,** Latvia was torn by radical economic restructuring, extreme political repression, and a thorough Russification of its national culture. In 1949, in an attempt to communize agriculture, the Soviets deported huge numbers of Latvians; by the end of the Communist era, at least 100,000 had been driven from their homes. Meanwhile, immigrants from the rest of the Soviet Union poured into Latvia. Within four decades, ethnic Latvians accounted for only half the population, as compared to three quarters before the war.

Under *glasnost* and *perestroika,* Latvians began to take advantage of their newfound freedoms. Mass protests in 1987 demanded more regulations to protect the environment, and the Latvian Popular Front was created a year later to oppose the Soviet establishment. Fueled by growing unrest, the opposition thoroughly trounced the Soviets in the 1990 elections. On May 4 of that year, the new legislature declared Latvia independent once again, but continued Soviet intervention sparked violent clashes in Rīga in 1991. Finally, following the foiled Moscow coup in August, the Latvian legislature reasserted its independence; this time (Latvians hope) for good.

LATVIA TODAY

Latvia's transition to capitalism has been rocky. Industrial production has plummeted, and the standard of living continues to fall. Latvia still depends on Russia for fuel and as a major market for its washing machines, refrigerators, motor scooters, radios, textiles, and shoes. However, the Latvian government has tightened its belt; fiscal austerity has been relatively successful at reducing inflation. In March, 1993, the government introduced a permanent currency called the lat to replace the old Latvian ruble.

Latvia's first free elections in June, 1993, handed conservative deputies a majority in the Saeima (parliament). Not all Latvians may vote, however; suffrage is limited to those who have been citizens since 1940 and their descendants. About 34% of all Latvians, mainly Slavs, are disenfranchised. Relations with Russia remain tense as Latvia demands a full withdrawal of Russian troops while Russia drags its heels and accuses Latvia of discriminating against the Russian-speaking minority.

ARTS AND CULTURE

Folklore is even still very much a part of Latvian culture. In the National Awakening of the 19th century, Andrējs Pumpurs wrote the national epic, *Lāčplēsis the Bear-Slayer,* based on Latvian folktales. Lāčplēsis kills a bear, battles German oppression, and conquers the German Black Knight—all only to fall into the Daugava River. Someday, legend says, he shall return to free Latvia (they didn't wait for him, though).

Krišjānis Barons, another 19th-century folklorist, collected and published over 20,000 Latvian *dainas*—pithy, poetic folksongs still widely known by many. Work songs, seasonal celebration melodies, rounds, and dancing songs remain popular. Much Latvian folk music is characterized by asymmetric meters, mixed measures, a narrow range, and harmonizing but melodically independent voices. (Translation: they might sound a bit peculiar to western ears—sort of dense and resonant.) Folk dances have survived the cultural tides of time, group and round dances retaining prominence. Early folk dances evolved as semi-religious rituals performed during the solstice to protect the community from evil spirits.

FOOD AND DRINK

Latvian food is heavy and filling, operating on the theory that "you have to be thick to survive the winter." Simple and tasty on the whole, national specialties include smoked *sprats* (once the fame of Rīga), the essential holiday dish of *zirņi* (gray peas with onions and smoked fat), *maizes zupa* (bread soup usually made from cornbread and full of currants, cream, and other goodies), and the warming *Rīgas balzams* (a sweet black liquor great on ice cream or in coffee). Dark rye bread is an essential staple of the Latvian table, and homemade bread and pastries are deliciously worth asking for. Try the *speka rauói,* a warm pastry, or *biezpienmaize,* bread with sweet curds. The beer in Latvia is excellent, plentiful, and inexpensive; standouts include the Aldaris brewery's *Porteris* and *Luxus* labels.

■ Rīga

The largest city in the Baltics, cultured, cosmopolitan Rīga has a s sordid history of conquest that left Swedes, Germans, Poles, and Russians in charge of the capital ever since the early 1200s; only in the 20th century have Latvians come to rule their own roost. Just as the famed *art-nouveau* architecture of the city reflects vanished German influences, the metropolitan population (nearly two-thirds of which is Russian) is an inescapable legacy of the Soviet-era. Tensions between disenfranchised Russians, *nouveau-riche* "businessmen" flashing cellular phones, and returning Latvians who fled in the '40s after Stalin's annexation of the country make Rīga a hotbed of post-Soviet politics. But in the shade of the Old City's many beer gardens, grievances dissipate in the foam of some of the best beer on the continent.

ORIENTATION AND PRACTICAL INFORMATION

Rīga's city-center consists of an expanding series of concentric half-circles focused on **Vecrīga** (Old Rīga), along the banks of the Daugava River. Vecrīga is bordered by **Kr. Valdemāra iela** in the north and **Marijas iela** in the south, while the *Pilsētas*

LATVIA

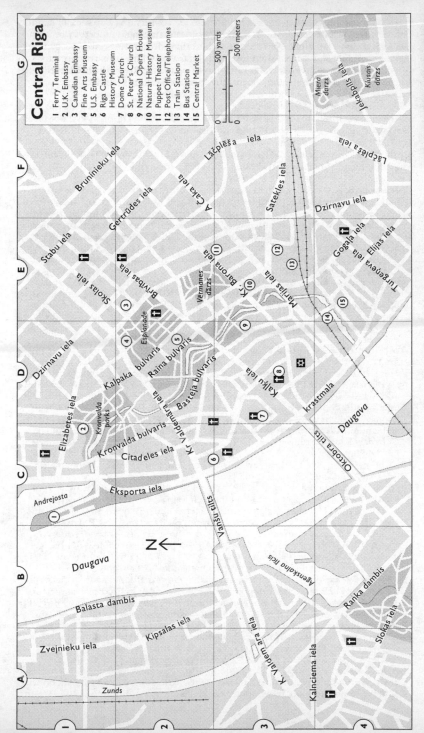

Central Riga

1 Ferry Terminal
2 U.K. Embassy
3 Canadian Embassy
4 Fine Arts Museum
5 U.S. Embassy
6 Riga Castle
History Museum
7 Dome Church
8 St. Peter's Church
9 National Opera House
10 Natural History Museum
11 Puppet Theater
12 Post Office/Telephones
13 Train Station
14 Bus Station
15 Central Market

500 yards
500 meters

kanāls (the old city moat) marks off the first circle—about a 15-min.. walk in diameter. Beyond the canal, a ring of parks and boulevards laid out in the 19th century make up the second circle; **Elizabetes iela,** one km from the river, bounds this newer region. Beyond sprawls the noisy, dirty metropolis. Vecrīga has two sections, divided by a street called **Kaļķu iela** (Chalk street) in the old town, **Brīvības bulvāris** (Freedom boulevard) in the new city, and **Brīvības iela** out past Elizabetes. The **train and bus stations** sit on the southeastern edge of the city center.

Excellent city **maps** of Rīga are available at kiosks and bookstores everywhere for about 0.57 Lati; these are invaluable for public transportation information if nothing else. Unfortunately, no good city guide to Rīga exists. The erratic *Rīga This Week* (actually published only twice in 1994) provides some basic info, but isn't really worth the 1 Lati cover price. The free *Rīga by Night* is harder to find but offers schedules of concerts and the addresses of every casino in the city.

Tourist Office: Would you believe Rīga's got one!? Naturally, it's smack out in the middle of nowhere, at Elizabetes iela 6 (tel. 32 60 09, fax 32 33 21). Brochures and prices on ferries, hotels, restaurants, trains, planes, and automobiles. Open Mon.-Sat. 9am-8pm. You could also try pestering the people at Latvia Tours (see below). The best bet for Baltics omniscience is the **Tourist Club of Latvia,** Skārņu iela 22 (tel. 22 17 31, fax 22 76 80), right behind St. Peter's Church. They can arrange for Russian visas at US$30 (given 10-day notice), bypassing the need to stand in endless lines. Unfortunately, only staffer Aira Andriksone speaks English; the rest, however, know Latvian, Russian, German, and French. Open daily 9am-5pm. The **Latvijas Universitāte Tūrists Klubs,** in the main University building at Raiņa bulv. 19, room 107 (tel. 225 98, fax (8) 82 01 13), is another good bet, perhaps better if you need an English-speaker. The enthusiastic staff here plans out weeks of hiking and canoeing options in Latvia and can help with bus connections to Prague. Open daily 9am-6pm.

American Express: Latvia Tours, Grēcinieku iela 22/24 (tel. 22 18 96), is the AmEx rep in Latvia, *but they don't cash traveler's checks.* Open Mon.-Fri. 9am-5pm. To cash those little purple bug-bears, go to **Deutsch-Lettische Bank,** Jēkaba iela 3/5 (tel. 22 24 05), just off Doma Laukums; ask for Raith Erickson or Michael Heukels. Open Mon.-Fri. 9am-5pm.

Embassies: U.S., Raiņa bulv. 7 (tel. 21 00 05 or 22 03 67), open Mon.-Fri. 9am-noon and 2-5pm. **U.K.,** Elizabetes iela 2 (tel. 32 07 37), open Mon.-Fri. 9am-1pm and 2-5pm. **Australians** and **New Zealanders** should call the U.K. Consulate. **Canada,** Doma Laukums 4 (tel. 33 33 55), open Mon.-Fri. 10am-1pm. **Denmark,** Pils laukums 11 (tel. 22 62 10). **Finland,** Teātra 9 (tel. 21 60 52). **Sweden,** Lāčplēša 13 (tel. 28 62 76). **Belarus,** Elizabetes iela 25 (tel. 33 32 44), open Mon.-Fri. 10am-2pm and 3-5pm. **Estonia,** Skolas iela 13 (tel. 22 68 45), open Mon.-Fri. 10am-1pm. **Lithuania,** Elizabetes iela 2 (tel. 32 15 19), open Mon.-Fri. 10am-1pm. **Russia,** Antonijas iela 2, consular entrance, on Kalpaka (tel. 22 06 93), open Mon.-Fri. 10am-1pm. **Ukraine,** Kalpaka bulv. 3 (tel. 33 20 46), open Mon.-Fri. 10am-1pm. The embassies of **Israel, Spain, Taiwan, Switzerland,** and **Poland** are all at Elizabetes iela 2, convenient for one-stop shopping. To **extend your visa,** report to the Foreign Ministry *(Ārlietu Ministrija),* Elizabetes iela 57; but get there early. One-day service is the norm, but it's best to go well before your visa has actually expired. Free for Americans. Open Mon.-Fri. 9am-noon.

Currency Exchange: At any of the innumerable *Valutos Maiņa* kiosks or shops in the city. A 24-hr. exchange with good rates operates on Aspazijas bulv., at the corner with Smilšu iela, near the German embassy. Always ask for an official (stamped) receipt so that the money-changers pay some taxes on the transaction.

Post Office: Stacijas Laukums 1, near the railway station. Open Mon.-Fri. 8am-8pm, Sat. 8am-6pm, Sun. 10am-4pm. **Poste Restante:** LV-1050. **Postal Code:** LV-1000.

Telephones and Telegraph Office: Central office, Brīvības bulv. 21, open 24 hrs.; smaller office in the main post office by the railway station. **City Code:** 2 (8 for digital lines).

Courier Services: DHL, Avotu iela 9 (tel. 21 09 73, fax (8) 82 82 33), 0.5km north of the railway station on Marijas (later Čaka) iela.

Electronic Mail: At the Economics Faculty of the University of Latvia, Aspazijas bulv. 5, in the yellowish "Computerland" building. Go through the entry hall, cross the courtyard, and turn right once inside. Open daily (usually) 9am-5pm.

Flights: Lidosta Rīga (Rīga Airport), 8km southwest of the Old Town. Take bus #22 from the Arhitektu iela stop, on the east side of the main university building, and punch three tickets. **Flight info:** tel. 20 70 09. Baltic International (tel. 22 50 21) flies to New York via Belfast daily (US$848 round-trip) and to Tallinn daily (US$53 one-way). Latavio, the Latvian successor to Aeroflot, flies to Stockholm, Warsaw, and Vienna (US$122 one-way).

Trains: Rīgas Centrālā Stacija is on Stacijas Laukums, just east of the Old Town and north of the canal (tel. 007 for information, but don't ask for Mr. Bond). Really 2 stations, the long-distance trains are in the larger building to the left. Departures (*Atiešanas*) listed on the board at right as you enter. To: Daugavpils (3 per day, 4hrs.; 1.35 Lati); Tallinn (2 per day, 8hrs.; 4.54 Lati); Moscow (2 per day, 17½hrs.; 8.14 Lati); St. Petersburg (1 per day, 15hrs.; 6.59 Lati); Kaliningrad (3 per week, 12hrs.; 5.12 Lati); Vilnius (2 per day, 8hrs.; 5.77 Lati); and Berlin (1 per day (via Vilnius, Warsaw, and a tiny corner of Belarus, so get necessary visas), 35hrs.; 48 Lati). Suburban trains, which can actually run as far as the Estonian border at Valga (Lugaži), are in the smaller building. To: Cēsis (6 per day, 2hrs.; 0.55 Lati); Saulkrasti (every half-hour, 1hr.; 0.30 Lati). Buy tickets for suburban trains in the suburban hall. For long-distance trains, purchase same-day tickets in the long-distance hall; advance tickets are in the advance-booking office off the right side of the suburban hall. Tickets to destinations outside the former Soviet Union must be purchased at the 3 windows at the end of the tunnel under the long-distance tracks in the long-distance hall. Both stations open 24hrs.

Buses: Autoosta, 200m south of the train station along Marijas iela, across the canal from the Central Market. To: Vilnius (2 per day, 5½hrs.; 2.70 Lati); Tallinn (4 per day, 6hrs.; 2.80 Lati); Pârnu (4 per day, 3½hrs.; 1.90 Lati); Klaipåda (4 per day, 2-4hrs., 1.02 Lati); Kuldiga (7 per day, 4hrs., 0.90 Lati). Information desk (tel. 21 36 11) open daily 7am-8pm. Station open daily 5am-midnight. **Latvia Tours** (see above) runs an express Rīga-Prague bus every Wed. at 9am (27hrs., US$55).

Ferries: The **Sea Terminal** (*Osta;* tel. 32 98 82) is 1km north of the Rīga Castle along Eksporta iela. Ever since the Travemünde ferry was cancelled, Rīga has been poorly served by sea. **Mercuri** runs a ferry to and from Kiel, Germany, departing Rīga Tues. at 4pm, arriving in Kiel Thurs. at 8pm. The least expensive fare is DM360 one-way (4-person cabin with hall shower and toilet). **Baltic Line** sails the *M/S Ilich,* departing Rīga Thurs. at 6pm, arriving in Stockholm Fri. at 10am. A very limited number of 2-person cabins with hall shower/toilet go for 40 Lati per person one-way, but tend to book up even 3 months ahead. The next cheapest fare is 65 Lati. It's less expensive to take a train to Tallinn and catch the every-other-day ferry from there.

Public Transportation: Buses, trams, and trolleybuses all require 6-santīmi tickets that can be purchased at kiosks, post offices, and (sometimes) on board. Punch tickets once on board. The city has 3 travel zones, requiring 1 ticket per zone of travel. Most trips will require 1 ticket; only the airport is in zone 3. The system runs daily 5am-midnight, though some sections start late and stop early. Buy a copy of the city map put out by Jāṇa Sēta (0.30 Lati), which shows all the routes and stops.

Taxis: For state-run taxis, tel. 33 40 41. Private taxis outnumber the state taxis; they show a green light in the windshield. Haggle for a good price (no more than 3 Lati to go cross-town at night).

Car Rental: Avis, in the Rīga Airport (tel. 20 73 53), has the cheapest rentals in Latvia: US$45 per day, with 100km included (US$0.35 per extra km). Minimum age 22, no entry to the CIS allowed. Open daily 9am-6pm.

Bookstore: Aperto Libro, Kr. Baronas iela 31, including an attached café where you can sip cappucino and peruse your brand-new *Moby Dick.* Open Mon.-Sat. 10am-7pm.

Luggage Storage: In the bus station, put your bags on guarded racks (0.20 Lati per bag), open daily 7am-8pm. At the train station, lockers (0.30 Lati) are available in the tunnel under the long-distance tracks, open 24 hrs.

Laundromat: Yessiree—a real laundromat in the Baltics! **Miele,** Elizabetes iela 85a (tel. 21 76 96), about 2 blocks from the train station in the courtyard through the archway. Washers 1.76 Lati; dryers 0.60 Lati. Groaning German machines that take 2hrs. to wash a load (let alone drying), so plan ahead. Open daily 8am-8pm.
Pharmacy: Grindex, corner of Audēju and Valņu, just north of the central department store. Some Western goods and the products of the premiere pharmaceutical research company in the Soviet Union, including herbal balms. Open Mon., Sat. 9am-5pm, Tues.-Fri. 8am-8pm.
Emergencies: Fire: tel. 01; **Police:** tel. 02; **Ambulance:** tel. 03.

ACCOMMODATIONS

One of the things to love about Rīga is that the old Intourist haunts have dusted off their counters, and easily-fooled Western businessmen now shell out US$100 per night for their rooms. But if you don't desperately need CNN and MTV, you can still bunk down for as little as US$5 a night. Alternatives include cheery hostels and networks of private rooms.

Rīga Hostel, Kalnciema iela 10/12 (tel. 22 64 63, fax 22 47 85), in Āgenkalns, on the opposite side of the river from Vecrīga. Take tram #4 or 5; 5 stops from Grecinieku iela on the south end of the Latvian Rifleman's Square, then walk back along Kalnciema. On the 3rd floor of a music and ballet school. Spartan but large rooms share clean hall showers with plenty of hot water. English spoken. No curfew. Singles 5 Lati. Doubles 10 Lati. The hostel is perennially uncertain about its future, and may not exist in 1995. If it does, it will be open June-Sept.
Viktorija, A. Čaka iela 55 (tel. 27 23 05), 8 blocks from the railway station on Marijas iela (which becomes Čaka), or 2 stops on trolleybus #11 or 18. Convenient to the Bimini nightclub; the lobby (but not the rooms) has been remodeled. Singles 8 Lati, with private bath, TV, and refrigerator 13 Lati. Doubles 10 Lati, with private bath, TV, and refrigerator 18 Lati.
Latvijas Universitāte Tūrists Klubs, Raiņa bulv. 19, room 107 (tel. 22 52 98), can set you up in student dorms for 4-8 Lati per person in 3 locations around the city, one of which only functions during the summer. Devoid of character, the rooms share hall showers and toilets; the more expensive spots are more central.
Tourist Club of Latvia, Skārņu iela 22 (tel. 22 17 31), has 4 rooms above their offices right in Vecrīga. Spacious and clean, with TV, radio, and washbasin. The hall showers and toilets are immaculate. Rooms go for US$30-50 depending on size (2 beds in each room). In summer, be sure to call ahead.
Avrora, Marijas iela 5 (tel. 22 44 79), across from the railway station. An unreformed Soviet hotel, but it's the cheapest in town that will accept Westerners. The somewhat musty rooms boast shaving basins and probably-broken cheap plastic radios. Hall showers and toilets. Singles 2.72 Lati. Doubles 5.44 Lati.
Sport, Gogol iela 5 (tel. 22 67 80), near the Stalinist Academy of Sciences, 200m behind the railway station. Almost a twin of the Avrora. The slightly bigger rooms don't overlook a busy street, but there's no hot water, and the desk staff only speaks Russian. Singles 3 Lati. Doubles 6 Lati.
Patricia, Elizabetes iela 22-4a (tel. 28 48 68), 2 blocks from the train station, has an English- and German-speaking staff that can arrange homestays in Vecrīga for US$15 per person. June-July it's best to call ahead. Office open daily 8am-8pm.

FOOD

Wander into the wrong restaurant in Rīga and you could suffer bland (but cheap) Soviet-style *karbonades, kotletes,* and *bifšteks.* On the other hand, you might stumble into an establishment featuring roast suckling pig (120 Lati) and a clientele bristling with cellular phones. Between the extremes, options for a good meal abound in Vecrīga, most of the time letting you get away for under US$5. A few 24-hr. stores are cropping up in Rīga. The most central is **Interpegro** across from the railway station, at the corner of Marijas and Raiņa bulvāris; the food's not cheap, but you can charge it on your Visa card. The first floor of the **Universālveikals Centrs,** Audēju iela 16, is a prime place to stock up on pre-packaged goods. The **Central Market** *(Centrālais Tirgus),* in the 5 immense zeppelin hangars hanging out behind the bus station, is the largest market in Europe and an experience not to be missed. Take a warm July-afternoon stroll through the odiferous *Gaļa Paviljons* (meat hall) to learn why refrigeration is a good thing (open Tues.-Sun. 7am-6pm, Mon. 7am-3pm).

Fredis Café, Audēju iela 5, near the Pēterbaznīcas. Subs (0.80-1.30 Lati), spaghetti with mushrooms (2 Lati), and french onion soup (0.70 Lati) make this the premier choice for fast and tasty dining in Rīga. Not listed on the English menu, the raspberry-coated chocolate cake is heavenly (0.25 Lati). *Hasta la Vista* is a chicken sub inspired by Arnie (0.80 Lati); you'll be baak. Open daily 9am-midnight.

Pie Kristapa, Jauniela 25/29 (tel. 22 75 30), on the main street south from Doma Laukums. An incredible beer hall downstairs serves hearty portions of simply delicious Latvian cuisine and home-brewed beer in giant 2-liter ceramic jugs (0.95 Lati). Be sure to try the Latvian national dish, *zirņi* (gray peas with onions and smoked fat; 1.30 Lati). The restaurant may have moved by the time you arrive, so call first. Open daily noon-6pm and 7pm-midnight.

Pie Kaleja, Kalēju 50, was one of the better state-run cafeterias of the Soviet era, and has been smoothly making the transition to a good café/restaurant. Popular among university students, most entrees are 1.25-1.60 Lati and salads are 0.20-0.30 Lati. Try the Latvian bread soup (*maizes zupa ar putukrēj*), a cornbread-based soup with currants and cream (0.35 Lati). Open Mon.-Fri. 8am-8pm, Sat.-Sun. noon-7pm.

Zilais putns, Tirgoņu iela 4. The "bluebird" has good thin-crust pizza downstairs or outside (the chicken and onion pie for 2.20 Lati is one of the best); upstairs awaits the best pasta in Rīga. While enjoying a great view of the Doma Laukums, try the *Pasta con mare* (seafood pasta), a shrimp, oyster, and squid-stuffed masterpiece (3 Lati). The upstairs restaurant is usually packed in the evenings, but empty at lunch; downstairs is vice-versa. Open daily noon-11pm.

Rozamunde, Mazā Smilšu 8, a great pub 1 block off the Filharmonija Laukums. Run by the Rīga Jazz Company, professional musicians play nightly 8am-10pm in a cozy atmosphere where you can fill up on lamb curry (3.50 Lati) or an exceptional soljanka (1.30 Lati). Paulaner beer on tap (1 Lati). Open daily 11am-11pm.

Šanhaja, Grēcinieku iela 26, just behind the Occupation Museum. The restaurant in the back half is somewhat expensive, but the bistro in front dishes up large plates of *šīniešu nūdeles* (pork-fried noodles, 1.25 Lati), and spicy *krabju zupa* (shrimp soup, 0.50 Lati). Open daily noon-10pm.

Hotel Latvija, Elizabetes 55, on the corner with Brīvības past the Freedom Monument. The "express bar" on the 1st floor serves up yummy omelettes (0.70-1.50 Lati) perfect for Sunday brunch. The surprisingly delicious banana omelette is only 0.80 Lati. Plans are afoot to dynamite this ugly, unsafe hotel (the fire escapes were welded shut 10 years ago to cut maintenance costs), so it may be gone when you arrive. Otherwise, it's open daily 10am-9pm (be careful, though...).

Pica Lulū, Kr. Valdemāra iela 145/2 (tel. 36 12 34), 2.5km from Vecrīga (they couldn't find a building in the center with the electricity to handle a pizza oven). Honest-to-god American pizza, courtesy of 2 Canadians; large pizza loaded with goodies 5 Lati, slices 0.60 Lati. They'll deliver anywhere in Rīga for a 20% surcharge. Take trolleybus #3 from the corner of Merķeļa and Marijas, near the railway station. Open daily 9am-11pm.

U.S. Embassy canteen. One of the most jealously-guarded secrets in the Baltics is that this is open to U.S. citizens and their guests. Don't tell. Latvian-influenced versions of fried chicken with potatoes or spaghetti and ice cream run about 1.50-2 Lati; it's also the only place in Rīga with clam chowda'. Open Mon.-Fri. noon-2pm.

Lubavitch Soup Kitchen, Mazā Pietavas behind the synagogue. Slated to open soon, it will be the one place in town to eat kosher and say *kiddush*.

SIGHTS

To reach **Vecrīga** (the Old Town) from the bus station, go under the bridge on your left and cross the street to Vaļņu iela. From the train station, walk down Marijas iela toward the river for 3-4 minutes, then turn right on Vaļņu. Go down Vaļņu, take a left on Audēju iela, and you'll come to the **Pētera baznīca** (St. Peter's Church) a few blocks down on your right. First built in 1209, the present building dates from 1408. For an amazing view of Rīga's rooftops, scale the tower—which before World War II was the tallest wooden structure in the world. At a height of 72m (now the top level), you can see the Baltic Sea. Inside the church are exhibitions on the fire that destroyed the original tower in 1941 (open Tues.-Sun. 10am-7pm, winter Tues.-Sun 10am-4:30pm; admission 0.75 Lati). Just behind the church, at Skārņu iela 10, is the oldest stone building in Rīga; the 1208 **Juras Kirik** (St. George's Church), was originally the chapel for the German Knights of the Sword sent by the Pope to convert Latvia to Christianity. By the mid-16th century the secularized church was carved up into three warehouses by German merchants. It is now home to the magnificent **Museum of Applied Arts**, showcasing Latvian ceramics, pottery, jewelry, bookmaking, and tapestries (open Tues.-Sun. 10am-6pm; admission 0.50 Lati).

Further to the right on Skārņu, at the corner with Jāņa iela, stands the **Sv. Jāņa baznīca** (St. John's Church), originally a small 13th-century chapel sporadically added onto until the 1830s in a swirl of architectural styles from Gothic to Baroque to neo-Classical. On the wall facing St. Peter's, notice the cross-shaped window covered with a grill that imprisoned two monks in the 1300s (open daily 10am-1pm). Through a tiny alleyway at the left of St. John's is the **Jāņa Sēta** (St. John's Courtyard), the oldest area of Rīga, where the first city castle stood. Part of the old city wall is preserved here, and in the summer there's an excellent beer garden. South of St. Peter's is the **Latvian Riflemen Square** *(Latviešu Strēlnieku Laukums)*, the site of Rīga's town hall before it burned to the ground in 1941. Dedicated in Soviet times to the Latvian Red Riflemen (Lenin's bodyguards after the Revolution), the square has since been renamed for the Latvian Riflemen, the first non-Russian military unit formed in World War I. The museum and statue may be torn down to rebuild the old town hall, but for now you can tour the **Latvian Occupation Museum,** an absorbing display demonstrating Stalin's flimsy pretext for annexing Latvia in 1940, subsequent mass deportations to Siberia, the horrors of the Nazi occupation, and then the return of the despised Red Army in 1944-5 (open Tues.-Sun. 11am-5pm; free).

After the Occupation Museum, go north along Kaļķu iela until you come to another large square, the **Filharmonija Laukums.** At the far end of the square is a jeepers-creepers bright yellow building, Rīga's famous **Cat House** (with a space), whose felines hiss at the old German merchant guild houses across the street. Legend has it that because the house's owner was not accepted into the guilds, Zirgu iela (which passes between the two guild houses) leads directly into the vast, irregular, cobblestoned expanse of **Doma Laukums** (Dom Square), which appeared on Rīga's map in 1936 so that Latvia's President Ulmanis could have crowds hear him speak from the balcony of the Stock Exchange. Looming over one end of the square is the **Rīgas Doms** (Rīga cathedral), the largest church in the Baltics, first consecrated in 1226 and since modified by various and sundry architects. Notice the impressive German pipe organ that dates from 1844; boasting 6786 pipes, it's among the biggest (and best) in the world. (Church open Mon. and Fri. 10am-2pm, Tues.-Thurs. and Sat. 1-4pm; 0.30 Lati). Behind the Dom, at Palasta iela 4, is the Rīga **History and Maritime Museum,** a thorough exploration of Rīga's complex Germano-Russo-Swedish-Latvian history (phew!) and auxiliary displays on the Latvian naval tradition. If you like this place, there's a branch museum in the town of Ainaži, on the coast by the Estonian border (open Wed.-Sun. 11am-5pm; admission 0.35 Lati).

Upon leaving the church, go back to the square and walk north along Jēkaba iela. Take your first left, Mazā Pils iela. Halfway down are the **Three Brothers** (Trīs brāli), the three oldest houses in Rīga. **Rīga Pils** (Rīga Castle) awaits you at the end of the street; nowadays, it houses three museums. The **Museum of Latvian History** and the **Museum of Foreign Art** contain reproductions of Classical sculptures, Latvian paintings, works of German and Dutch masters, and exhibits on the decorative arts (open Tues.-Sun. 11am-5pm; admission to each 0.40 Lati). The **Rainis Museum of Literature** honors the memory of Latvia's greatest poet and nationalist, Jānis Rainis,

his wife (also a poet) Aspazija, and other Latvian literary figures (open Mon.-Tues., Thurs.-Sat. 11am-5pm, Wed. 1-7pm; admission 0.30 Lati). North of the castle, a graceful sculpture garden teems with works by 20th-century sculptors.
   If you go back to Jēkaba iela and continue north, you'll pass **St. Jacob's church,** a small 13th-century Gothic church built outside the original city walls. Opposite, at Jēkaba 11, is Latvia's **Parliament** *(Saeima)*. A focus of Latvian nationalism during the struggle for independence, the barricades of 1991-92 were entirely removed in early 1993. The small street across Jēkaba from the Parliament, **Trokšņu iela** (Noisy Street), was named so because it ran just inside the city walls, where soldiers were constantly clattering about. A block down this narrow passageway is the **Swedish Gate,** built into the city walls in 1698 when Sweden ruled Latvia. Through the gate, Torņa iela leads to the **Pulvertornis** (Powder Tower), one of Rīga's oldest landmarks and the only city tower left. Nine cannonballs are still lodged in its 14th-century walls; it's not clear why they're on the side facing *into* the city. Inside, visit the **Latvian Museum of War,** with exhibits on Latvian resistance to the Soviet occupation; the Latvians hated communism so much that 200,000 Latvians enlisted in the German army during World War II (although appeals to their German heritage were also a factor), and guerilla bands continued fighting until the mid-1950s. If you saw the Occupation Museum, you'll understand why (open Tues.-Sun. 11am-6pm; admission 0.30 Lati).
   Beyond the Powder Tower, a belt of parks swaddles the city in green where the old city defenses were torn down in the 19th century. The **Bastejkalns** is nearest to the War Museum, with ruins of the old walls atop the hill. Across and around the city canal, which used to be a defensive moat, five red stone slabs stand as **memorials** to the dead of Jan. 20, 1991, when Soviet special-forces troops stormed the Interior Ministry on Raiņa bulvāris across the park. The dead included a schoolboy and two cameramen recording the events. At the far north end of the park, on Kr. Valdemāra iela, is the **National Theater** where Latvia first declared its independence on Nov. 18, 1918. To the south of the Bastejklans, Kaļķu iela widens to become Brīvības bulvāris, where the beloved **Latvian Freedom Monument** *(Brīvības Piemineklis)* was dedicated in 1935 while Latvia was an independent republic. Remarkably, the Soviets left this standing, but Intourist craftily explained that the surmounting figure represented Mother Russia supporting the three Baltic States (it actually shows Liberty raising up the three regions of Latvia —Vidzeme, Latgale, and Kurzeme). A few blocks up Brīvības, in the Esplanāde, the **Orthodox Metropolitan Cathedral** rises over the greenery; it's still being restored after having served as a planetarium during the Soviet occupation. Across the Esplanāde, near the corner of Kr. Valdemāra and Elizabetes, you'll find the **State Museum of Latvian Art,** Rīga's foremost art museum, that boasts 19th- and 20th-century works by such artists as Kazaks, Tone, and the colorful Rēriks (open Wed.-Mon. 11am-6pm, winter Wed.-Mon. 11am-5pm; admission 0.50 Lati).
   Outside the city center are several other sights worth soaking up. On Zaķusalas island, in the middle of the Daugava River, the Rīga **TV Tower** (tel. 20 09 43) has a viewing platform and café looming 98m over the city, offering excellent panoramas of Old Rīga. Trolleybus #20 goes to the tower. To the north, **Mežaparks,** at the end of tram line #11, is a six-square-km woodland park home to the city **zoo,** an open-air **concert shell,** and innumerable great jogging paths. On the south end of this expanse are the three main cemeteries of Rīga, monumental areas that symbolize Latvian nationhood. The **Brāļu Kapi** (Brothers' Cemetery) is dedicated to the soldiers who fell in the two World Wars and the struggle for independence from 1918-20. Smaller **Rainis Kapi** is the resting spot of poet Janis Rainis s well as other Latvian nationalists, literary figures, and—more controversially—important communist stooges of the last 50 years. **Meža Kapi** (Forest Cemetery) is a peaceful area filled with intriguing stones designed to reflect the personality of the men and women they commemorate. All three cemeteries can be reached by taking tram #11 to "Braļu Kapi" (eleven stops from the starting point, behind the Computerland building at Kr. Baronas and Aspazijas near the railway station). The **Open-Air Ethno-**

graphic Museum *(Etnogrāfiskais Brīvdabas Muzejs)*, on the shores of the *Juglas Ezers* (Lake Jugla), has collected nearly a hundred 18th- and 19th-century buildings from all regions of Latvia, including churches, complete farmsteads, and a windmill. On the first weekend of June, the annual crafts fair here brings hundreds of artists together. To get to the museum, take tram #6 to the end of the line, then walk 0.5km further across the bridge, and turn right onto Brīvdabas iela (open May-Oct. daily 10am-5pm).

ENTERTAINMENT AND NIGHTLIFE

Nightlife in Rīga is better than in any of the other Baltic cities. A prime evening plan is a three-point hop around the city: from dinner to a beer garden and on to a dance club around midnight. The largest groups lemming their way from the food in Fredis to the beer gardens in Doma Laukums, then to boogie in Bimini, but there are plenty of other ways to while away the long, light summer nights.

Beer Gardens

The undisputed king of beer gardens is the **Carlsberg** garden that fills **Doma Laukums** year-round (though crowds are thin in February). **Filharmonija Laukums,** just a block away, is another popular spot, with more local beers. But **Jāņa Sēta,** in the small courtyard behind St. John's church, is a local jewel, great for afternoon coffee or evening suds. The *alus* stops flowing at midnight in all three of these spots, but at **Ala** (the "cave") on Vecpilsētas iela near Fredis, to the left of the Okinawa Bar, live bands keep the place going until 4am. Their *karsts vīns un viskijs* (hot wine and whiskey; 0.50 Lati) is great when it gets chilly.

Dancing

Bimini, A. Čaka iela 67/69, is top rhino among nightspots in Rīga, boasting a consistently packed dance floor, karaoke, and Monday night jazz. Even if you don't dance, come to watch mafiosi, backpackers, prostitutes, and diplomats rub shoulders. Cover after 8pm 2.50 Lati, Fri.-Sat. 3 Lati. Open daily noon-6am.

Klubs Hellfire, Trijadibas iela 5, advertises itself as an "American Night Music Club." You may be surprised by this rendition of America; at least the music is better than the average East European Pet Shop Boys/Rap amalgam. Cover 2 Lati. Open Thurs.-Sun. 7pm-5am.

The Studentu Klubs, Raiņa bulv. 23, is an erratically-open disco run by the University's Music Academy; look for signs on the door. Always packed with students when it's on. Cover 0.50 Lati. Usually open Thurs.-Sat. 9pm-5am.

Club Next (Kabata II), Krāmu iela 4, is a genuine punk club with unbelievably cheap beer (0.15 Lati), a low cover (1 Lati), and scads of people in a crowded, thrashing, smoke-filled basement. Open Wed.-Thurs. and Sat. 5-10pm.

Performances

Like Cinderella, most of Rīga tries to head home around midnight; hey—if the shoe fits, wear it. Birthplace of Mikhail Baryshnikov, Rīga is home to the **Latvian National Opera** and the excellent **Rīga Ballet,** but with the Opera house under reconstruction until at least until the next millenium, both companies are currently performing in the **Kongress zāle***, in the Kronvalda parks on the corner of Kr. Valdemāra and Kalpaka. Posters throughout the city announce upcoming events, or tel. 61 57 73. Tickets are all under 2 Lati, some as low as 0.35 Lati. **Organ concerts** *(ērģeļmūzikas koncerti)* at the Dom cathedral are worth experiencing; the organ is the third-largest in existence. Tickets can be purchased at Doma Laukums 1, opposite the main entrance at the *koncertzales kase* (open noon-3pm and 4-7pm). The **Latvian Symphony Orchestra** has frequent concerts in the Large and Small guilds off Filharmonija Laukums, while ensembles and artists from abroad perform in the **Vāgnera zāle,** on R. Vāgnera iela. The ticket office, which sells tickets for nearly all concerts in Rīga, is on the first floor of the Large Guild, at Amatu iela 6 (tel. 22 36 18).

■ NEAR RĪGA

The most popular daytrips from Rīga are to the beaches of Jūrmala or the forests and valleys of the Gauja National Park (see Jūrmala and Sigulda for information). Sun-lovers who don't care for the crowds of Jūrmala should head to **Saulkrasti,** about one hour north of Rīga on the suburban trains (0.35 Lati). The beaches here are wider, less-peopled, and get direct sun later into the evening. Also nearby is the memorial at **Salaspils,** where the Nazis had the Kurtenhof concentration camp during World War II. Suburban trains run to the nearby stop at **Dārziņi** (on the line to Ogre), where a path leads one km to the camp and museum (open daily 10am-5pm; free). The memorial to the 100,000 victims of Kurtenhof was built in the 1960s; as you enter, the inscription overhead reads "behind this gate the earth moans."

■ ■ ■ JŪRMALA

Only 20km west of Rīga, the sandy beaches of Jūrmala beckon on hot summer days. Ever since the late 19th century, Rīgans have been spending their summers on this narrow spit of sand between the Gulf of Rīga and the Lielupe River; in 1959, 14 towns were conglomerated into the city-resort of Jūrmala (seashore = *Jūrmala*). To get there, take one of the frequent trains (every 15-20min. 4am-11pm) from the rail station in Rīga. A handful of towns dot the coast—coming from Rīga, Priedaine is the first stop in Jūrmala, but there are no beaches here. Stay on the train; you'll pass over the Lielupe River and quickly through the towns of Lielupe, Bulduri, Dzintari, Majori, Dubulti, Jaundubulti, Pumpuri, Melluži, Asari, Vaivari, and Sloka before heading back inland to Kudra and Ķemeri.

Lielupe (from Rīga 30min., 0.23 Lati), the first township with beach access, also has docks on the Lielupe River where you can **rent sailboats, sailboards,** and other water toys during the summer. The docks are off of Vikīngu iela, the first major street on the right leading away from the station (you can see the docks as you cross the river on the train). Sailboards go for a hefty 2 Lati per hour; sailboats are more, depending on size, usually around 5 Lati per hour. On the side facing the Gulf, Lielupe's sand dunes are the most dramatic in Latvia.

The towns between **Bulduri** and **Dubulti** are the most popular spots for sunning and swimming. The water in the Gulf is reputed to be polluted, and since 1987 all swimming has been strictly prohibited; but in the past few years, taking a dip has made an unsanctioned comeback. The beaches are wide and seem clean, backed by pine trees and dotted with volleyball courts; grab a spot of sand and relax.

Majori (4th stop after crossing the river, 40min., 0.28 Lati) is the largest town on Jūrmala. With a lively shopping area, good cafés, and turn-of-the-century wooden beach homes, it's one of the most enjoyable spots on coast. Walk down the short road immediately across the street behind the station, take your first right, and you'll be on Jomas iela, Majori's pedestrian street, lined with shops, cafés, restaurants, and bars. Every street to the left off Jomas leads to the beaches along the Gulf of Rīga. On one of these side streets, at Pliekšāna iela 7, is the **Jānis Rainis Memorial Museum,** in the villa where he died in 1929. Displays of the great poet's works, books, and photos fill the house (open Wed.-Sun. 10am-5pm; admission 0.20 Lati). **Café Omega,** behind the tourist office at Jomas 42, serves tasty warm sandwiches. Vegetarians can ask for meatless ones (open Mon.-Fri. 3-10pm, Sat.-Sun. noon-10pm).

If you go all the way to the end of Jūrmala at **Ķemeri,** you'll reach what was once the prime health resort of the Russian Empire, where therapeutic mud baths, sulphur water, and other "cures" have been at work since the mid-18th century. The impressive white **Sanatorium,** built to look like an art-deco ocean liner, is still surrounded by beautiful gardens, though lack of guests has forced it to close its doors in recent years. The gardens are open (and free); wander about, sip some of the refreshing (?) waters, pick mushrooms, and enjoy the clean air of the countryside.

LATVIA

■ ■ ■ SIGULDA

Sigulda lies just 60km from Rīga, at the entrance to the Gauja National Park and the 920 sq. km of woods, bluffs, brooks, and ancient oaks lining the hilly Gauja river valley, locally called the "Switzerland of Latvia." Only three of the seven regions of the park are open to visitors; the rest are nature reserves off limits since the 1930s. Around Sigulda, numerous castles, caves, and woodsy walks make a playground in summer or winter.

From the bus and train stations, walk up Raiņa iela to reach the center of town. The road bends around the large **Siguldas baznīca** (Sigulda Church), built in the 1220s and reconstructed in 1701. The name of the street here changes to Gaujas iela. Pils iela, behind the church, leads off to the ruins of the **Siguldas pilsdrupas** (Sigulda castle), built by the German Knights of the Sword in the early 13th century, and destroyed during the Great Northern War. The view from the ruins peers across the river to the **castle of the Rīga Archbishop;** in 1207 the Pope had divided control of Livonia between the Archbishop and the crusading Knights, but control of the important trading town of Sigulda was a source of conflict for centuries thereafter. If you follow the paved path that runs parallel to the road from the intersection of Cēsu and Gaujas, opposite the church, you'll reach the cable car which will whisk you over the river in a memorable crossing of the Gauja gorge (10min., 0.25 Lati).

On the opposite bank, off to the right of the cable car terminal, the **Krimuldas pilsdrupas** (Krimulda Castle) sits in ruined isolation, destroyed in the Polish-Swedish war of 1601. Behind the castle, footpaths lead off through the woods, with occasional views of the river valley. Follow these paths down the hill to the gravel road that runs alongside Turaidas iela, and after about 0.5km, you'll come to a group of caves. **Gūtmaņa ala** (Gūtmanis's Cave) is the largest in Latvia, a sandstone grotto covered with chiseled inscriptions and coats of arms from the 16th century to the 1940s. The spring which issues from the cave is said to have magical powers; the water is certainly cleaner than in Rīga. According to legend, the beautiful Maija was courted by everyone in Latvia, but actually loved a castle gardener named Viktors. Tricked into coming to the cave by a Polish officer, she offered him a magic scarf if he would let her go.

The road continues another half km to a set of wooden steps that lead up a steep hill to the **Turaidas Castle** (Turaidas Pils), the local residence of the Archbishop of Rīga. Restored in the 1950s, the main tower houses the **Sigulda History Museum,** offering marvelous views of the river valley from 30 meters up. Tickets to the complex are sold at the gate to the left after you climb the stairs (open daily 9:30am-6pm, winter Tues.-Sun. 10am-5pm; admission 0.40 Lati). Near the castle, the wooden **Turaida Church** dates from 1750. To the left of the church, in the shade of two lime trees said to have been planted by Viktors, is the **Grave of Maija**, with the inscription to the "Rose of Turaida." Behind the church, a sculpture park covers **Daiņa kalns,** dedicated to Krišjānis Barons, the 19th-century folklorist who collected and preserved over 20,000 Latvian *dainas* (pithy, poetic folksongs).

Hiking options around Sigulda are numerous. One excellent walk heads two km south from a path off Turaidas iela that follows the Gauja River to the steep **Piķenes Slopes,** where two more caves merit a look: the deep **Velna ala** (Devil's cave), and the **Mazā velnala** (Little Devil's cave). The nearby spring is believed to be a literal **Font of Wisdom,** and mothers traditionally bathe their babies here to imbue them with intellect. Another good hike follows paths from the Sigulda castle downhill to the Gauja, then upstream for a km or so until you cross the Vējupīte creek; another 100m upstream on the Vējupīte, stairs lead up to the **Paradīzes kalns** (Paradise hill, also called Painters' Hill), where 19th-century Latvian painters like Jānis Rozentāls made the superb view of the valley famous.

Sigulda was the site of the training facility for the Soviet Olympic **bobsled** team, and the Olympic-size run sits on Ausekļa iela, 500m west of the train station. In the winter, you can take a run down the track yourself in a rubber sled (0.50 Lati) or in a real bobsled piloted by members of the Latvian team (1 Lat). Ice is maintained on the track into the spring, sometimes even as late as mid-June, as in 1994 (open Mon.-Sat. noon-5pm).

Comprehensive **maps** of Sigulda (0.50 Lati) are available at kiosks in the train station, or in Rīga. The multitudinous **trains** from Rīga run on the suburban rail system (15 per day, 1hr.; 0.45 Lati), stopping at the train station in the center of town; less-common buses (8-10 per day, 1½hrs., 0.36 Lati) go to the *autoosta* one block north of the railway station on Raiņa iela.

■■■ CĒSIS

Once the headquarters of the mighty Livonian Order (a federation of German knights who controlled Latvia and Estonia in the 13th-16th centuries), Cēsis has since declined in its glory despite a 1930s heyday as a resort center. In the center of the Gauja National Park, it serves as an excellent base for hikes south along the Gauja River or a pleasant daytrip from Rīga. In late July every year, the massive **Cēsis Beer Festival** takes place at the local brewery, the oldest in the Baltics.

Orientation and Practical Information From the bus and train stations, Raunas iela darts straight into the center of town to empty into **Vienības Laukums** (Unity Square). The streets heading downhill at the south end of the square (Rīgas and Vaļņu) lead into the older section of town, where they meet at **Līvu Laukums,** the original 13th-century heart of the city. Lenču iela, which runs away from Vienības Laukums on the opposite side from Raunas, takes you to the main sight in town, the old castle. Cēsis is easily reached by train, since the station (*Stacijas Cēsis*) is a stop on the suburban system of Rīga commuter trains. On the main line from Rīga into Estonia, trains bound for Tallinn, St. Petersburg, and other locations all stop here, making Cēsis ideal for a daytrip *en route* to Tartu or some other point north. Tickets can be hard to get in Cēsis; it's best to purchase them at the Rīga station before coming. Six **trains** per day come from Rīga (2hrs., 0.55 Lati). The **bus** station is in front of the train station. Service from Rīga runs about 12 times per day (2-2½hrs., 0.48 Lati). There is a brand-new **map** of Cēsis available in Rīga (0.50 Lati), but it can be hard to find in Cēsis itself; try at the history museum in the Castle. **Public transportation** in Cēsis consists of two buses; #9 runs west to the Gauja river, which may be its only use to casual travelers. The **post and telephone office** is on the Raunas iela corner of Vienības Laukums (postal services Mon.-Fri. 8am-6pm, Sat. 8am-1pm; telephone office open daily 7am-11pm). The **telephone city code** is 241.

Accommodations and Food You can stay overnight in Cēsis, but there's not much point. The only choice in town is the **Dan Lat Hotel,** on the north side of the Vienības Laukums (tel. 223 92). This Soviet-style hotel has been renovated by a Danish-Latvian joint venture, but the biggest change is the prices (singles 11 Lati, doubles 20 Lati). **Saieta Nams,** at the south end of Rīgas iela on Līvu Laukums, is a small but excellent cellar restaurant where food is actually cooked to order. The *pankukas* (pancakes, 0.35 Lati) are superb. Full meals of entree, salad, desert, and beverage average 2 Lati. During the summer, seating outside in their beer garden is possible and worthwhile (open daily 11am-5pm and 6pm-midnight).

Sights Cēsis was taken by the Livonian Order in 1209 after a battle reputed to have spawned the Latvian flag; the Latvian leader was wounded and laid down to die on a white sheet, staining it a deep crimson on two sides, but leaving the middle section white. The castle that the German knights built to dominate the region was begun in the same year, and was a mighty fortress with 4m-thick walls by the time it was finished in the 1280s. By the late 16th century, the Order was no longer a real power; when Russia's Ivan the Terrible laid seige to the fortress in 1577, the garrison filled the cellars with gunpowder and blew the castle (and themselves) up rather than surrender. Today the castle remnants are preserved thanks to the 19th-century baron who built the adjoining "new castle" and laid out a park around the older ruins, including a large reflecting pond. The park is a fun place to wander around; ask one of the museum attendants to show you the town Lenin, now lying down under a giant wooden crate that looks a lot like a coffin. The two castles make up the **Cēsis History Museum** *(Cēsis Vēstures Muzejs),* a well-presented collection of regional ephemera and the obligatory old coins, arrowheads, and jewelry (open Tues.-Sun. 10am-5pm; admission 0.20 Lati). Be sure to find your way up to the tower of the new castle to garner great views of the area.

Virtually next door to the castle is the **Cēsis Beer Brewery** *(Cēsu Alus Darī tava),* the brewery for the excellent Cēsis beer, in operation since the 1870s. The beer garden out back is a great place to quench your thirst before and after a castle visit. Tours are sometimes possible; ask at the entrance. The brewery is west on Lenču iela from the castle, visible from the parking lot in front. If you follow Torņa iela out of the parking lot right next to the castle, you'll be heading into Cēsis's picturesque Old Town. The main sight of the narrow cobbled streets is the immense gothic **Jāņa baznīca** (St. John's church), built in 1280-87.

The Gauja River flows on the east side of town, and a number of good hiking trails lead along the many cliffs that line this stretch of river. A three km journey along Gaujas iela, which leads from Līvu Laukums, will bring you to the base of these trails; bus #9, which you can catch in front of the hotel on Vienības Laukums, will also bring you out here. The best cliffs are to the south.

■■■ DAUGAVPILS

Founded in 1275 as an eastern stronghold for the German Teutonic Order, what was then called **Dūnaburg** languished unnoticed until 1577, when Ivan the Terrible swept through during the 25-year Livonian War, effectively ending German rule. For the next 50 years, Poles, Lithuanians, Russian, Germans and Swedes battled over eastern Latvia *(Latgale);* in the end the Poles emerged victorious; the town was rechristened Dvinsk, and Latgale grew up Catholic. Devastated by heavy fighting in World War I, the city lost 80% of its population; it did not reach the same population again until 1979. During World War II, the city was again flattened; Soviet rule repopulated it with settlers from Ukraine, Belarus, and Russia to counter the traditional Polish-Latvian mix. Today little more than a tenth of the people living here are Latvians.

ORIENTATION AND PRACTICAL INFORMATION

Daugavpils is an eminently walkable city, carved in twain by two hills and the railroad tracks between them. From the train station, pedestrian **Rigas iela** leads to the heart of the commercial section of town, **Centrs.** North of the station, tram #1 loops through Old Town before circling around in back of the station to Jaunbūve, the residential half of the city. An excellent map of Daugavpils was released in the summer of 1994, the first since before World War II; it should be available at most kiosks (0.57 Lati).

> **Consulates: Belarus:** Pilsētas Valde, room 216, entrance from Krišjāna Valdemāra iela at Teatra iela (tel. 223 38). Open Mon.-Tues., Thurs.-Fri. 10am-4pm. Belarusian visas are only US$12 here, compared to US$62 in Rīga, with same-day service.
> **Currency Exchange:** The best rates in town are at the 24-hr. exchange booth inside the railway station, where you can unload everything from dollars to those pesky *zloty* you've been hauling around.
> **Post Office:** Cietokšņa iela 28, one block east and three blocks south of the Viesnīca Latvija (tel. 223 55). Open Mon.-Fri. 8am-8:30pm, Sat.-Sun. 8am-4pm. **Postal Code:** LV-5407.
> **Telephones and Telegraph Office:** Inside the post office at Cietokšņa iela 24. Open daily 7:30am-11pm. **City Code:** 254.
> **Flights:** There is an airport in Daugavpils—the city was long a massive Soviet air base. But with the departure of the Russians, the immense airport hosts only a few tiny prop-driven planes that hop to and from Rīga on an irregular basis. The

ticket office is in the Vienības Nams, entrance from Saules iela, in the currency exchange office. Open daily 10am-1pm and 2-5pm.

Trains: Dzelzceļa stacija, located at the end of Rīgas iela, on the eastern edge of the commercial half of the city. There is a left-luggage office downstairs (0.20 Lati). Train information: tel. 005. To: Rīga (3 per day, 3-6 hrs;, 1.20 Lati); Vilnius (4 per day, 4 hrs.; 1.56 Lati); St. Petersburg (6 per day, 11-12 hrs.; 5-7.50 Lati).

Buses: Daugavpils Autoosta is at Viestura iela 26 (tel. 243 47; info 004). Open daily 5am-midnight, cashiers 5am-7pm. To: Aglona (2 per day, 90min.; 0.53 Lati); Warsaw (1 per day, 16hrs.; 10 Lati); and Vilnius (1 per day, 3hrs.; 2 Lati).

Public Transportation: There are trams and buses, but ignore the buses. Tram #1 runs from the railway station past the market and the Viesnīca Latvija to Jaunbūve. Tram #3 runs from the fortress past the market and the Latvija to Jaunbūve. Buy tickets (0.04 Lati) on the tram.

Taxis: State taxi service (tel. 254 50).

Pharmacy: Aptieka #1, Rīgas iela 54, at Viesta iela (tel. 264 61). Open Mon.-Fri. 8am-6pm, Sat.-Sun. 10am-6pm.

Emergencies: Fire: tel. 01; **Police:** tel. 02; **Ambulance:** tel. 03.

ACCOMMODATIONS

Even with only two hotels in town, there is an overabundance of rooms in Daugavpils, except in mid-August during the massive religious festival in nearby Aglona.

Viesnīca Latvija, Ģimnāzijas iela 46 (tel. 290 03). From the train station, walk a half km on Rīgas iela until this Soviet monstrosity rears its glass-and-concrete head. Checkout 2pm. Singles 4.50 Lati; with toilet, shower, TV, phone, and balcony, 9.30 Lati. Doubles 8.22 Lati, with the extras 17.12 Lati. Prices halved for Latvians.

Viesnīca Celtnieks, Strādnieku iela at Jelgavas iela, near the stadium (tel. 325 10). Definitely the better buy in town. Spacious rooms built to host visiting teams. 1.80 Lati per person if you opt for the hall showers and toilets, 2.50 Lati per person for private facilities. You can use the incredible saunas for 1.50 Lati per hour.

FOOD

If the restaurant selection in Daugavpils leaves you unimpressed, you're not alone. Fortunately there are other options. The **Tirgus** (town market) is on Parādes iela, just behind the Viesnīca Latvija, with outdoor produce stalls and indoor meat and fish sections (open daily 7am-4pm). The bread shop **Svaiga Maizes,** on the Cietokšņa iela side of the Viesnīca Latvija complex, has amazing breakfast rolls, danishes, and other sweet breads for just 0.09 Lats (open daily 8am-8pm). There is one **24-hr. store** in Daugavpils, the **Interpegro** at 22 Rīgas iela.

Kafejnīca "Vecais Draugs," Vienības iela 17. Nothing special; in fact, the place is pretty darn Soviet. The meat and cheese salads (0.20 Lati) and soups (0.30 Lati) are tolerable, and it is centrally located. Open daily 11am-2:30pm and 3:30-11pm.

Mārtiņš, on Muzeja iela at Imantas iela, near the river. Easily the best restaurant in Daugavpils, even with the Russian-dubbed movies blaring from the TV. The menu is in Latvian but the waitstaff only speaks Russian. *Medus karbonade* (honey-dipped carbonade) 1.50 Lati, other main courses 0.50-1.75 Lati. Open daily noon-5pm and 6pm-midnight.

SIGHTS AND ENTERTAINMENT

The **"four churches"** district, in the eastern half of Daugavpils, has always been the city's draw for tourists. Take tram #3 to the "Lokomotīve" stop, just past the bridge over the railway tracks. Large **Borisa-Gļeba katedrāle** loom visibly on the hill at the end of Varšavas iela. Inside, thousands of icons clutter every available surface; a local belief held that every member of the congregation had to have a different patron saint. The red-brick **Luterāņu baznīca** a block away along 18. Novembra iela was part of the train-engineers' technical school in Daugavpils until a fire in 1987 prompted the cash-strapped city government to return it to the congregation.

Repairs are still underway. Just a block further east, down Andreja Pumpura iela, the stunningly Baroque **Jaunavas Marijas katoļu baznīca** stands witness to long-standing Polish influence in the region and serves as the center for the 13% of Daugavpilsians who are Polishy. North along Andreja Pumpura iela is the **Viecticlbnieku baznīca** (church of the Old Believers), home to a long-persecuted Russian sect that fled in large numbers to Latvia during the reign of Peter the Great. A fifth church, in the center of town, is **Sv. Pētera baznīca** on Rīgas iela near the Viesnīcca Latvija. It was built in the 1840s to imitate St. Peter's Church in Rome.

The other big sight in Daugavpils these days is the immense **Fortress** *(Cietoksnis)* abandoned by the Soviet air force in 1992. The Teutonic Order had a stockade on the same site as long ago as 1288, later replaced by a larger fort built by Ivan the Terrible in 1577. The current ring of bricks and earthen mounds only dates to the early 19th century; the base was used as Stalag-340 by the Nazis in World War II. Now, the immense network of military buildings has been totally stripped, while the families that remained behind in Latvia still live in the other half of the complex. A lone guard ostensibly keeps nosy visitors out of the central courtyards, but with nothing in particular to protect, he may be just as likely to give you a tour. Take tram #3 north from the central market to the end, and walk under the railroad trestle.

Aside from a few *diskotekas*, there isn't much to recommend Daugavpils' **nightlife.** The disco in the **Vienības nams** seems to attract most everyone under 25 (open Sat.-Sun. 8pm-midnight; admission 0.50 Lati). Next-door to the Viesnīca Celtnieks, the **Rock Club Hammer Smashed Face** has a thrashier atmosphere (if you couldn't have guessed), murals inspired by old Ozzy Ozbourne album-covers, occasional live bands, and a 1 Lati cover charge (open Mon.-Sat. 8pm-1am). For something more subdued, there are occasional concerts, ballets, jazz sets, and other performances at the **Pilsūtas Valde,** mostly by itinerant organizations like the Latvian State Philharmonic, but also by St. Petersburg groups that layover in Daugavpils en route to Berlin (tickets 0.30-1.50 Lati).

■ NEAR DAUGAVPILS

Forty kilometers north of Daugavpils, the town of **Aglona** is a site of Catholic pilgrimage on August 15 every year (Ascension Day); thousands walk from all over Latvia (many carrying elaborate carved wooden crosses) to celebrate at its 17th-century cathedral. In 1993, Pope John Paul II put in an appearance. Buses run to Aglona from Daugavpils twice daily, but don't get caught here overnight; there's not a rentable room in the city

■■■ BAUSKA

The city of Bauska was founded in 1443 when the Teutonic Order built a stronghold on the hills at the confluence of the Mūsa and Memele rivers, where they become the Lielupe. The town never amounted to much, and the castle itself was blown up by the Russians in 1706 during the Great Northern War. The town is easily explored, but you'll quickly discover that the castle is the only thing worth seeing. From the bus station, follow Zalā iela to Uzvāras iela for a total of about one km, and you'll be right at the castle. Restoration began a few years ago and is proceeding rapidly, but you'll question the wisdom of using white bricks seemingly from Brezhnev-era housing projects to restore a hewn-stone castle. Climb the central tower inside for a view of the countryside (castle open daily 10am-6pm; admission 0.30 Lati).

The **bus station** *(Autoosta)* is where you'll come into town—no trains run to this area of Latvia. Buses go from here to Rīga 17 times per day (1½hrs., 0.75 Lati), the last departing at 7:20pm. The **post and telephone office** is right behind the station, next to the hotel (postal services Mon.-Fri. 8am-6pm, Sat. 8am-1pm; telephones open daily 7am-11pm). The **telephone city code** is 239. There is one hotel in Bauska, the **Viesnīca Bauska,** Slimnīcas iela 7 (tel. 247 05), just behind the bus station. It tends to be booked full during the annual **Old Music Festival** in late July, but empty the rest of the year. These are your run-of-the-mill rooms in the ex-Soviet Union, cut from a mold just like a Motel 6 in the States (singles and doubles with private bath 5 Lati). The best restaurant in Bauska is the **Restorāns Pils Kalns,** at the foot of the castle hill. Blackjack tables and disco lamps make this place seem cheesier than it really is. *Karbonade* and some kind of soup with beer is the standard meal (around 3 Lati; open daily noon-midnight).

■■■ RUNDĀLES PILS

Now that you've seen all that Bauska has to offer, hop a bus out to the grand edifice at **Rundāle Pils** (Rundāles Palace). Built for the power-hungry Baltic German nobleman Baron Ernst Johann von Bühren (Bīrons to the Latvians), this magnificent palace was designed by the same famous Italian architect who designed the Winter Palace in St. Petersburg, Francesco Rastrelli. When construction began in 1736, Curonia (the western and southern parts of modern Latvia) was a semi-independent duchy under Polish and Russian influence. With the death of Peter the Great in 1730, his niece Anna inherited the throne of Russia, and her marriage to the Duke of Courland thrust the area into the spotlight. The Duke's untimely demise left Anna free to promote her lover, Bīrons, to Duke of Courland, and she loaned him Rastrelli to design the palace.

Rundāles Pils was built in one year, and by 1738 the interior was almost finished. About that time, Bīrons decided that he should have a *second* palace in Jelgava, the capital of Curonia, so he ordered Rastrelli to begin work there instead of finishing the palace at Rundāles. Tsarina Anna's death in 1740 brought Bīrons's enemies to power and he was exiled to Siberia for 22 years, leaving both palaces unfinished. In 1763, however, Catherine the Great—another German—ascended the throne, and Bīrons was allowed to return to finish his palace. Over the next four years, Rundāles was completed in Rococo style, an odd contrast to the already-completed Baroque areas of the palace. Bīrons managed to hold onto the palace until 1795, when Russia annexed Courland and he was forced to flee to Germany. Easy come, easy go.

Used variously as a grain storehouse, stable, primary school, and hospital by the Soviets (some at the same time), the palace was in a horrendous state by the early 1970s, when restoration began. To get an idea of how it looked before work started, walk around to the back side of the palace and compare after seeing the inside. On the first floor, there is also a multi-room display on the original construction of the palace and its restoration. With 138 rooms to refurbish, only one wing has been finished, but it includes the most opulent rooms of the palace, ballroom, and the Duke's bedchambers. Upstairs, the opulent Gold Room *(Zelta Zāle)* is the marble and gold leaf throne room, with dramatic murals on the ceiling. The White Room *(Balta Zāle)* beyond was the ballroom; ornate plasterwork cherubim depict the four seasons and the four elemental forces (earth, air, fire, and water). Be sure to notice the smiling cherub shooting a happy deer while jolly friends look on, but don't tell the SPCA. The duke's chambers are immense, straddling the center of the palace and overlooking the vast gardens in back. The kitchen has also been redone and now houses an overpriced café; its immense fireplaces heated the ballroom above all year round and cooked an estimated 1200 eggs and one steer every day.

The palace is open Wed.-Sun. 10am-6pm, winter 10am-5pm. Admission is 0.25 Lati. An extremely detailed book describes all of the rooms in the palace and is available in English, German, Latvian, and Russian. To get there, take one of the many daily buses from Bauska towards Jelgava (0.15 Lati) and ask the driver to drop you at Pilsrundāle. You'll have a 1.3km walk from the road to the palace.

LITHUANIA (LIETUVA)

US$1 = 4.00LT (Lits)	1LT =	US$0.25
CDN$1= 2.93LT	1LT =	CDN$0.34
UK£1 = 6.28LT	1LT =	UK£0.16
IR£1 = 6.16LT	1LT =	IR£0.16
AUS$1 = 2.98LT	1LT =	AUS$0.34
NZ$1 = 2.17LT	1LT =	NZ$0.46
SAR1 = 1.13LT	1LT =	SAR0.89
DM1 = 2.60LT	1LT =	DM0.38
Country Code: 370	International Dialing Prefix: 810	

You're not likely to associate Lithuania with the word "empire"—the Roman, Ottoman, and British empires will come to mind much more readily—but in fact, Lithuania, now long forgotten by most of the world, was once the superpower of Eastern
Europe. The grand duchy of Lithuania, which included Belarus, western Ukraine,
and modern-day Lithuania, was one of the most influential powers in the entire
region during the 14th through 16th centuries. Today, Lithuania (pop. 3.5 million) is
struggling to chart a new political and economic course in the vacuum of Soviet
collapse.

Visitors to Lithuania will be pleasantly surprised by its scenery and historical attractions. Vilnius is one of the most habitable capital cities in the Baltic Republics, graced by green parks, relaxed cafés, and a low, unassuming skyline. Ruined medieval castles and fortifications stand as mute reminders of Lithuania's glorious past; not far away are the sophisticated, modern, cosmopolitan cities of Kaunas and Klaipėda. The best beaches in the Baltics await at Palanga, which is also home to lovely botanical gardens and relaxing mineral springs. The Curonian Spit offers more sun and fun, featuring dunes of fine white sand framed by dense forests.

LITHUANIA ESSENTIALS

Citizens of the U.S. and the U.K. can visit Lithuania visa-free for up to 90 days. Keep in mind that since early 1993, the three Baltic states have formed a common visa zone; a visa from any one of the three countries should be sufficient for travel to the other two. Latvian visas tend to be the cheapest of the three. See Essentials: Embassies and Consulates, page 3.

GETTING THERE

Klaipėda, Kaunas, and Vilnius are easily reached by train or bus from Latvia, Poland, and Russia. If traveling from Poland, note that all trains to Vilnius go through Belarus, requiring a transit visa (US$30). Only a few rail options circumvent a Belorussian interlude by a complicated pre-World War II rail route across the Polish-Lithuanian border, requiring a change of trains because of the different rail gauges in Poland and the former Soviet Union. The *Baltic Express* plies the rails from Warsaw to Tallinn and back daily, departing Warsaw at 2:30pm, passing through Kaunas, Lithuania at midnight, and arriving in Tallinn the next day at 1:10pm. There is also one overnight train running between Warsaw and Šeštokai, Lithuania (the end of the wide Polish-gauge line); it arrives at 6:30pm, two hours before a Šeštokai-Kaunas-Vilnius train departs. Buses from Poland to Lithuania do not go through Belarus.

GETTING AROUND LITHUANIA

Buses, though slightly more expensive, are better for travel within Lithuania; the trains are slow, noisy, and often horridly crowded. Two major train lines cross Lithuania: one runs north-south from Latvia through Šiauliai and Kaunas to Poland; the other runs east-west from Belarus through Vilnius and Kaunas to Kaliningrad, or on a branch line from Vilnius through Šiauliai to Klaipėda. Buses, however, radiate from all the cities of Lithuania, and unlike in Latvia, Belarus, and other post-Soviet countries, bus services in Lithuania have yet to be seriously pruned, leaving seeming millions of buses zipping around the byroads of the nation.

TOURIST SERVICES

There may eventually be tourist offices in Lithuania; in the meantime, read the excellent English-language *Vilnius in Your Pocket,* an exhaustive compendium about the capital city produced by enterprising German journalist Matthias Lûfkens. It's thoroughly updated every two months and is available at newsstands in Vilnius (3 Lits). Also check out its sister guides *Kaunas in Your Pocket* and *Klaipėda in Your Pocket,* currently published only annually, but just as comprehensive. Be sure to take advantage of Lithuanian Youth Hostels (LJNN), an organization of eight hostels across Lithuania. HI membership is nominally required, but an LJNN guest card (US$3 at any of the hostels) will suffice. The head office is in Vilnius, Kauno 1A-407 (tel. (22) 26 26 60, fax 26 06 31; open daily 8am-6pm). Grab a copy of their *Hostel Guide,* a handy little booklet with info. on bike and car rentals, advance booking, and city maps showing how to reach the various hostels.

St. John's Eve (Rasos), celebrated as elsewhere in the Baltics on the eve of the summer solstice (the night of June 23), is a beer-drinking, folk-dancing, song-singing, countryside party. The highlight of the evening is wandering into the woods to search for *fern flowers,* a Lithuanian herb best shown to you by someone of the opposite sex, if you know what we mean. Other big holidays also commemorated on street signs are: Vasario 16 (Feb. 16; Independence Day, 1918); Kovo 11 (Mar. 11; Independence Restoration Day, 1990); Day of Mourning and Hope (June 14); and Mindaugas's Day (July 6, 1253, the day the first King of Lithuania was crowned).

As in the rest of the Baltics, a bathroom door bedecked with a triangle whose point faces down indicates "men;" with the point facing up, it symbolizes "women."

MONEY

The unit of currency is the **Lit** (LT); 1 Lit = 100 centų. Since March 1994, the Lit has been tied to the U.S. dollar (US$1 = 4.00 Lits). Lithuania is well ahead of its Baltic neighbors in introducing the use of credit cards, and traveler's checks can be cashed at most banks (usually for a 2-3% fee); Thomas Cook seems to be the company of choice. Cash advances on a VISA card can usually be obtained with a minimum of hassle in some of these banks; Lietuvos Akcinis Inovacinis Bankas also accept MasterCard.

COMMUNICATION

Local phones in Lithuania are mostly free (and mostly broken), though in some locations in Kaunas and Vilnius the phones have been mysteriously maintained to require old Soviet 15-kopeck coins, which nearby kiosk vendors conveniently have on hand for 0.15 Lits. Long-distance calls can be made from some of the old grey public phones with the wide-grooved gold žetoni sold at post offices (0.24 Lits). For **international calls,** it is often best to use the Norwegian card phones which have been installed at some locations, such as the main phone offices and railway terminals of the larger cities; cards are sold at the phone offices in denominations of 15, 17.70, 32, 96, and 196 Lits. Rates for international calls: U.S. 10.50 Lits per minute; Latvia and Estonia 0.95 Lits per minute; Europe 5.80 Lits per minute. You can also book international calls through the operator at the central phone office (pay when finished), but you'll have to wait 20-45 minutes for the call to go through.

Direct dialing has arrived in Lithuania, though only to some countries. Dial 8, wait for the second tone, and dial 10 followed by the country code and number. Calls to cities within the former Soviet Union can be placed directly by dialing 8, followed by the old Soviet city code. For countries to which direct dialing is not available, dial 8, wait for the second tone, and dial 195 (English-speaking operators available). To reach the **AT&T USADirect operator,** instead dial 196; to reach the **Sprint Express** operator, dial 197.

English-language books are cheaper in Lithuania than in any of the other Baltic States, though not as plentiful; a shop in Vilnius, and a few random books in Klaipėda and Kaunas are about all you can expect. Vilnius, like Tallinn and Rīga, has it's own English-language weekly, *Lithuanian Weekly,* which covers Lithuanian events in fair depth for 2 Lits per copy. Unfortunately, it is increasingly hard to find, has never been available outside Vilnius, and may not exist at all by the time you get to Lithuania. The Tallinn-based *Baltic Independent* and Rīga's *Baltic Observer* are both available in Vilnius, Kaunas, and Klaipėda. In Vilnius, pick up Voice of America Radio at 105.6 FM, broadcasting 24 hrs.

LANGUAGE

Lithuanians pride themselves on the fact that their national language is the most archaic among the spoken Indo-European tongues, more closely related to Latin and Sanskrit than to modern languages. One of only two surviving languages in the Baltic branch (Latvian is the other), it has a rolling, hearty sound full of wonderful letters like ų, ė, į, ž, and ū. All of the "r"s in the Lithuanian language are trilled. Nearly all Lithuanians speak Russian, the legacy of the Soviet occupation, but attempts to use your freshman-year college Russian will be better received after trying to communicate in English or German first. A few Lithuanian words tossed in will secure instant goodwill.

For shopping, you may want to know the words *atidarytas* (ah-tee-DAR-ee-tass; "open") and *uždarytas* (oozh-DAR-ee-tass; "closed"). "Hotel" is *viešbutis (vee-esh-BOO-tee)*, and "market" is *turgus (tuhr-GUHSS)*. If you can, try and tune in everyone's favorite radio program in Lithuania, *Sister Barbara's English Lesson;* Sister Barbara, a Lithuanian-American from New Orleans, comes on daily to teach Lithuanians important phrases in English like "Is this cheese hot?"

Yes	*taip*	TAYE-p
No	*ne*	neh
Today	*Šiandien*	shee-YAN-dyen
Tomorrow	*rytoj*	REE-toy
Hello/Good day	*laba diena*	LAH-bah DEE-yen-ah
Good morning	*labas rytas*	LAH-bass REE-tass
Good night	*labanakt*	lah-bah-NAKT
Goodbye	*viso gero*	VEE-soh GEH-roh
Excuse me/I'm sorry	*atsiprašau*	AHT-sih-prah-SHAU
Please/You're welcome	*prašau*	prah-SHAU
Thank you	*Ačiu*	AH-chyoo
When?	*kada*	KAH-da
Where is...?	*Kur yra...*	Koor EE-rah
How much does it cost?	*Kiek kainuoja?*	KEE-yek KYE-new-oh-yah
How do I get to...?	*Noręčiau nueiti į*	nor-RAY-chee-yow new-ih-tih ee...
My name is ...	*Mano vardas...*	MAH-noh VAR-dass...
Do you speak English?	*Ar kalbate angliškai?*	AHR AHN-gleesh-kye
I don't understand	*Aš nesuprantu*	AHSH neh-soo-PRAHN-too

1—vienas (vee-AYN-ahss); 2—du (doo); 3—trys (treese); 4—keturi (keh-TUH-ree); 5—penki (PEHN-kee); 6—šeši (SHEH-shih); 7—septyni (sehp-TEE-nih); 8—aštuoni (ahsh-too-OH-nih); 9—devyni (deh-VEE-nih); 10—dešimt (deh-SHIMT); 20—dvidešimt (dvih-deh-SHIMT); 30—trisdešimt (triz-deh-SHIMT); 40—keturiasdešimt (keh-too-ree-AHZ-deh-SHIMT); 50—penkiasdešimt (pen-kee-AHZ-deh-SHIMT); 60—šešiasdešimt (sheh-shee-AHZ-deh-SHIMT); 70—septyniasdešimt (sehp-tee-nee-AHZ-deh-SHIMT); 80—astuoniasdešimt (ahs-too-oh-nee-AHZ-deh-SHIMT); 90—devyniasdešimt (deh-vee-nee-AHZ-deh-SHIMT); 100—šimtas (SHIHM-tahss)

LIFE AND TIMES

HISTORY

Lithuania has played a grand role in the pageant of Eastern European history. Its ancient inhabitants were the only **Baltic tribes** who succeeded in creating their own political state in premodern times. Whereas Teutonic armies conquered the other Baltic peoples, the Lithuanians managed to fend off the invaders, shielded by dense forests and protected by natural moats of swampy marshland. In the mid-13th century, the German menace prompted various Lithuanian tribes to unite under a single leader, Mindaugas. Crowned king of Lithuania by the Pope in 1253, Mindaugas soon rejected Christianity altogether, sliding back into his old pagan ways; the country would not be Christianized for more than a century.

The 14th-century ruler Gediminas consolidated the **Lithuanian empire,** subjugating East Slavs and other peoples under a generally tolerant rule. Political anarchy broke out after Gediminas, Lear-like "in the infirmity of his age," unwisely divided his empire among his seven sons. The eldest of the seven, Jogaila, finally defeated assorted brothers, uncles, and cousins—only to face a German invasion from the west. Jogaila chose to ally Lithuania with Poland, assuming the Polish throne as king and marrying the 12-year-old Polish queen Jadwiga in 1385. By 1410, Jogaila had effectively crushed the marauding German armies. The new Polish alliance brought Roman Catholicism to Lithuania, and Jogaila rewarded newly baptized nobles with feudal estates. The Lithuanian empire reached its zenith in the mid-15th century, stretching from the Baltic Sea to the Black Sea, and sprawling east to within 100 miles of Moscow.

For the next two centuries, Lithuania successfully fended off Muscovite incursions on its eastern frontier. Meanwhile, political and cultural ties with Poland strengthened, although peasants retained their ancient language. But Lithuania's fortunes declined in the **18th century.** Gradually, bits and pieces of the empire slipped away to be engulfed by the swelling Russian state. Lithuanians repeatedly rose up against Russian rule during the early 19th century; each revolt was met with harsh repression and intensified **Russification.** The tsars closed the 250-year-old University of Vilnius, abolished the Lithuanian legal code, and banned the Lithuanian language in public places. But the Russian Revolution of 1905 thawed the freeze on Lithuanian liberties, prompting new demands for independence.

World War I ignited a new power struggle in the region. German armies entered Lithuania in 1915, almost exactly 500 years after their last defeat. A Lithuanian congress made the rather futile gesture of declaring its independence, but Germany continued to occupy the region until 1918. No sooner had the invaders departed than the Soviets moved in, hot on the Teutons' heels. Lithuania finally managed to evict the Reds in mid-1919, inaugurating a brief period of independence.

The **interlude** was a troubled one. A fragile parliamentary democracy floundered, collapsing in a 1926 coup d'état. Under the dictatorship of Antanas Smetona, all opposition parties were banned. Meanwhile, border disputes spread like wildfire. Poland had taken Vilnius from the Red Army in 1919, and now refused to give it back. Over the next few years, the Poles and the Soviets battled each other for the city as Lithuania stood by helplessly. The Nazis, intent on building a German empire, gazed covetously on the Lithuanian city of Klaipéda. In 1939, Germany overpowered Lithuania and seized the valuable Baltic port.

The façade of autonomy crumbled in **1939,** when Moscow forced Lithuania to admit Soviet troops; in return, Lithuania got back Vilnius and about one-third of the territory that Poland had seized in 1920. A year later, Lithuania was entirely sucked up into the vast Soviet Union, ostensibly by a "unanimous" vote of the parliament. **Sovietization** entailed a total restructuring of Lithuania's government, economy, culture, and social structure. On the night of June 13-14, 1941, the Soviet government began pulling Lithuanians from their homes; the mass campaign of deportations eventually displaced 35,000 Lithuanians of all social classes.

The invasion of the Nazis in **1941** triggered a Lithuanian revolt against Soviet rule. The rebels wanted complete independence; when Germany made it clear it wanted to use the Lithuanians as a administrative tool, the provisional government called it quits. In three years of German occupation, 250,000 Lithuanians died; the Lithuanian Jewish community was virtually wiped out.

When the Red Army expelled the Nazis in 1944, they initiated a period of extreme repression and Russification. But the iron fist of Soviet rule did not go unopposed; Lithuanian **guerrilla fighters,** at times 40,000 strong, badgered the Soviets into the early 1950s. Moscow's grip had relaxed by the early 1960s, and Antanas Snieckus, party secretary since 1936, slowly transformed the republic's government into a nativized political machine. Unlike Latvia, Lithuania resisted an influx of Russian immigrants; ethnic Lithuanians still compose 80% of the population.

The orthodox backlash of the 1970s and early 80s failed to quell **Lithuanian nationalism;** during this period, the republic produced more per capita *samizdat* (dissident underground publications) than any other in the Soviet Union. *Glasnost* and *perestroika* spawned a Lithuanian mass reform movement, imaginatively dubbed Sąjūdis ("Movement"). In March 1990, Lithuania shocked the world by declaring itself independent from the Soviet Union. The international community reacted uneasily, and Moscow immediately began reprisals, starting with a rather ineffective shutoff of all oil and gas supplies. In January 1991 Moscow launched an assault on Vilnius's radio and TV center, leaving 14 people dead. Only in the wake of the failed Soviet *putsch* of August 1991 did Lithuania achieve a true measure of independence, finally realizing the goal that had seemed so improbable for 51 years.

LITHUANIA TODAY

Despite an early start—Lithuania began dismantling the Soviet economic system even before achieving independence from Moscow—Lithuania's economic reforms have run aground on rocky shores. Privatization has ground to a halt under new, restrictive government regulations. Lithuania is still heavily dependent on Russia for fuel, and trade with the West has increased only slightly. In the face of declining industrial production and high consumer prices, the standard of living continues to slide; in 1993, more than two-thirds of the average salary was gobbled up by food expenses. In June 1993, the government introduced a new national currency, the litas, in an attempt to tighten monetary policy.

Fickle Lithuanian voters have since thrown out the right-wing pro-independence legislators, replacing them with former Communists, now reorganized into the Lithuanian Democratic Labor Party (LDLP). In a surprising reversal of fortune, the conservative Sąjūdis movement now languishes in defeat, although former members have recently regrouped under the new Homeland Union, which promises to become a formidable conservative force in Lithuania. Despite internal divisions, all Lithuanians found cause to rejoice on August 31, 1993, when the last Russian soldiers finally left Lithuanian soil.

ARTS AND CULTURE

Lithuanians remain closely connected to their national culture and heritage. A well-developed network of museums, theaters, public libraries, and amateur cultural centers bring the arts to the general public. As in other countries of the region, folk traditions remain an important influence on modern arts. Lithuanian folklore provides a strong cultural tie; legends, fairy tales, and proverbs handed down from generation to generation preserve one of the oldest folk traditions in Europe. Folk art pieces—woodcarvings, ceramics, leatherwork, and textiles—are characterized by geometric or floral patterns and subdued coloring. A rich Lithuanian musical heritage comes alive every summer, when dances and singing festivals spring up in towns and villages across the country.

Early Lithuanian literature was primarily religious in subject matter. The early 19th century saw a new literary movement focusing on Romantic themes and the early history of Lithuania. Kristijonas Donelaitis' poem *Metai* (1818; "The Four Seasons") depicted scenes from village life throughout the year. In the wake of the French Revolution, Western influences triggered a renaissance in Lithuanian literature. Many writers violated the ban on publishing Lithuanian works in Latin letters (as opposed to Cyrilic), seeking to overthrow Russia's political control and Poland's cultural hegemony. After independence in 1918, this nationalistic trend intensified, but Lithuanian writers were again gagged and shackled by Soviet rule following World War II. The visual arts in Lithuanian have been strongly influenced by the Vilnius drawing school since its founding in 1866. Refined displays of technique and uses of natural color have won accolades for Lithuanian artists in the international art world.

FOOD AND DRINK

Lithuanian cuisine has miraculously survived Soviet-restaurant-blight; go into any restaurant and you'll see some evidence of an indigenous Lithuanian style of cookery. *Cepelinai* are a heavy, potato-dough missiles stuffed with meat, cheese, and mushrooms, most prominent in western Lithuania. *Šaltibarščiai* is a beet and cucumber soup not unlike cold *borscht* that is prevalent in the eastern half of the country. Lithuanian beer is passable, though there is no national-level brew to recommend. Of the local brews, *Žalsvytis,* produced in Kaunas, is probably among the best.

■ Vilnius

Sprawling, multilingual, and defiant, the capital city of Lithuania has stood at the crossroads of foreign influences for centuries without losing its preeminence as Lithuania's cultural and social center. Called *Wilno* by Poles, Vilnius has also had a major role in Polish cultural development, reflected by the fact that the city was long part of Poland until 1939. The multinational flavor of the city today embraces ethnic Poles, Belarussians, and Russians. Religiously, it is firmly Catholic, with a magnificent church on every corner in the Old Town. This was not always the case; Lithuania, in 1382, was the last nation in Europe to embrace Christianity, and from the 18th century to World War II, half-Jewish Vilnius was known as the "Jerusalem of Europe" and the world's center of Yiddish cultural and literary life. Today, Vilnius is the greenest of the Baltic capitals, an open city of parks, courtyards, and cafés, with a provincial feel heightened by low-rise architecture and gregarious residents.

ORIENTATION AND PRACTICAL INFORMATION

Vilnius's **Senamiestis** (Old Town) is a maze of winding cobblestone streets. From the train or bus stations, walk east on Geležinkelio gatvė and turn left at its end; ahead are the southern gates of the Old Town. From these gates, Aušros vartų gatvė leads north, changing its name first to Didžioji, and then to Pilies where it becomes a pedestrian mall. At the north end, Cathedral Square and the Castle Hill loom over the banks of the river Neris. Gedimino pr., the main commercial artery of Vilnius, leads west from the square.

Tourist Office: Vilnius *still* doesn't have a tourist office. For help, try the **Lithuanian Youth Hostels'** main office, Kauno 1A-407 (tel. 26 26 60), open daily 8am-6pm, or the service desks of the **Hotel Astorija,** Didžioji 35/2 in Old Town, and the **Hotel Lietuva,** Ukmergės gatvė 20, north of the river. The first thing you should do when you get into town besides change money is buy a copy of *Vilnius in Your Pocket* (3 Lits); with this excellent (and hilarious) guide in hand, you don't *need* a tourist office.

Embassies: U.S., Akmenų 6 (tel. 22 30 31, fax 22 27 79), open Mon.-Fri. 9am-5:30pm. **U.K.,** Antakalnio 2 (tel. 22 20 70, fax 35 75 79), open Mon.-Fri. 9am-5pm. **Poland,** Aušros Vartų 7 (tel. 22 44 44), in the courtyard through the high gate, open Mon.-Fri. 9am-1pm. **Russia,** Latvių 53/54 (tel. 35 78 68), open Mon.-Fri. 10am-1pm. **Latvia,** Tumo-Vaižganto 2 (tel. 22 05 22, fax 22 24 00), open Mon.-Fri. 10am-noon and 2-4pm. **Belarus,** Klimo 8 (tel. 65 08 71), open Mon.-Fri. 9am-noon. **Extending your Visa:** Go to the **Board of Immigration** *(Imigracijos Taryba),* Verkių 3 (tel. 75 64 53), about 2km north of Old Town, with 40 Lits and an entertaining story. Open Mon.-Fri. 9am-noon.

Currency Exchange: Central Currency Exchange Office, inside the central post office, Gedimino pr. 7 (tel. 22 28 15), offers the best rates in town on currencies other than the U.S. dollar and the Deutschemark, including those hard-to-get-rid-of Polish zloty. Open Mon.-Fri. 8am-8pm, Sat.-Sun. 11am-7pm.

Post Office: Gedimino pr. 7 (tel. 61 66 14), one long block west of Cathedral Square. Postcards to the U.S. 0.80 Lits. Open Mon.-Fri. 8am-8pm, Sat.-Sun. 11am-7pm. **Postal Code:** LT-2001. **DHL,** Vytauto 6/4 (tel. 35 51 44), open Mon.-Fri. 9am-5pm. **UPS,** Vasario 16 gatvė 2a (tel. 61 08 83, fax 22 61 11), open Mon.-Fri. 9am-5pm.

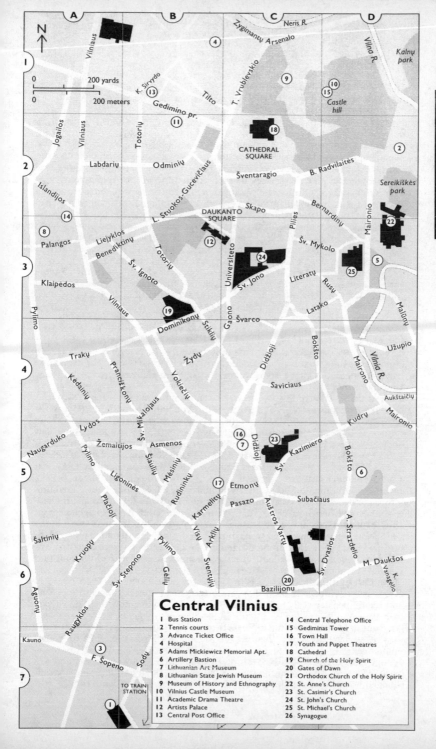

Central Vilnius

1 Bus Station
2 Tennis courts
3 Advance Ticket Office
4 Hospital
5 Adams Mickiewicz Memorial Apt.
6 Artillery Bastion
7 Lithuanian Art Museum
8 Lithuanian State Jewish Museum
9 Museum of History and Ethnography
10 Vilnius Castle Museum
11 Academic Drama Theatre
12 Artists Palace
13 Central Post Office

14 Central Telephone Office
15 Gediminas Tower
16 Town Hall
17 Youth and Puppet Theatres
18 Cathedral
19 Church of the Holy Spirit
20 Gates of Dawn
21 Orthodox Church of the Holy Spirit
22 St. Anne's Church
23 St. Casimir's Church
24 St. John's Church
25 St. Michael's Church
26 Synagogue

LITHUANIA

Telephones and Telegraph Office: Place calls abroad at the **Central Telegraph Office,** Vilniaus 33/2 (tel. 61 99 50); the entrance is on Islandijos gatvė. Special Norwegian phones here take phone-cards (17.70 Lits), and allow direct dialing to the West. **Directory Information:** tel. 09. **City Code:** 22 (2 if calling from the West).

Faxes: Fax Center, Universiteto 14/2 (tel. 62 66 49, fax 22 34 51), in a purple building near Cathedral Square. Receives for 1.08 Lits per page. Transmits to U.S. for 32.05 Lits per page; Europe 17.89 Lits per page; CIS 5.50 Lits per page. **Photocopies** 0.30 Lits per page. Open 24 hrs.

Flights: The Vilnius *Aerouostas* (airport) is 13km south of town; take bus #1 from the train station. For flight information, tel. 63 02 01 or 63 55 60. Daily flights to: Warsaw (LOT, tel. 63 01 95); Moscow and Frankfurt (Lithuanian Airlines, tel. 75 25 88); and Copenhagen (SAS, tel. 66 02 02).

Trains: Geležinkelio Stotis, Geležinkelio16, a big pink building approximately 500m south of the Old Town (tel. 63 00 88 or 63 00 86). The system for buying tickets in Vilnius is still immensely complicated. Tickets for local trains are sold in a separate hall, to the left of the main (pink) building. To: Trakai (8 per day, 30min.; 0.60 Lits); Druskininkai (4 per day, 3hrs.; 3.60 Lits). Tickets for long-distance Lithuanian destinations (plus Daugavplis, Latvia) are sold at windows 1-4 in the main station. To: Klaipėda (2 per day, 9hrs.; 10.50 Lits); Kaunas (16 per day, 2-3hrs.; 2.90 Lits); Daugavpils (4 per day, 4hrs.; 14 Lits). To get same-day tickets for trains within the former Soviet Union, go to the hall to the right of the main lobby; to purchase tickets in advance, tel. 62 69 56 or go to the **Advance Reservation Office,** Šopeno 3 (tel. 62 30 44); walk one block straight out of the station and turn left. To: Moscow (4 per day, 18hrs.; 120 Lits); Kaliningrad (4 per day, 7.5hrs.; 38 Lits); Rīga (2 per day, 8hrs.; 56 Lits); Minsk (4 per day, 5.5hrs.; 20 Lits). If you want to leave the former Soviet Union (now why would you *possibly* want to do that?), go out to the **Lithuanian Railways** office at the Hotel Lietuva, Ukmergės gatvė 20 (tel. 35 62 25). To: Warsaw via Belarus (get that visa!; 3 per day, 12hrs.; 85 Lits). You can also get other advance-reservation tickets here. Station open 24 hrs. Reservation Office open Mon.-Sat. 8am-8pm, Sun. 9am-5pm. Lithuanian Railways Office open Mon.-Fri. 10am-1pm and 2-6pm, Sat.-Sun. 10am-1pm and 2-4pm.

Buses: At the **Autobusų Stotis,** Sodų 22, 50m from the railway station. Two halls here: the *Priemiestinė Salė,* on the left side as you enter, is for buses to local destinations; the *Tarpmiestinė Salė* covers longer-distance buses. Windows 13-15 are for tickets to destinations outside the former Soviet Union. To: Rīga (3 per day, 6hrs.; 19 Lits); Minsk (6 per day, 5hrs.; 9.40 Lits); Tallinn (1 per day via Rīga, 12hrs.; 38 Lits); Klaipėda (10 per day, 5hrs.; 14 Lits); Kaliningrad (2 per day, 8hrs.; 32 Lits); Warsaw (2 per day, 11hrs.; 55 Lits). "Latvija" microbuses race to Kaunas a full 30 minutes faster than regular buses (20 or more per day, 90min.; 5 Lits). There is an information booth in the long-distance hall (open daily 7am-8pm). Information: tel. 26 24 82; Domestic Advance Booking: tel. 26 29 77; International Advance Booking: tel. 63 52 77. Station open daily 7:30am-11:30pm.

Public Transportation: A good system; it doesn't run (but isn't necessary) in the Old Town. Rides on buses and trolleybuses all cost 0.30 Lits; monthly pass 12 Lits. Buy tickets at kiosks. Don't forget to punch the tickets once you're on board. System runs roughly 6am-midnight. There is a comprehensive map of the transport grid in *Vilnius in Your Pocket.*

Car Rental: Avis, in the Hotel Turistas, Ukmergės gatvė 14 (tel. 73 32 26, fax 35 31 61). Least expensive rental is a Toyota Corolla (US$37 per day, plus US$0.37 per km; US$83 per day with 150km free; US$104 per day for unlimited km). Open daily 9am-5pm.

Bike Rental: Lithuanian Youth Hostels rents bikes for US$2 per day with a $50 deposit. Contact the main office, Kauno 1A-407 (tel. 26 26 60), open daily 8am-6pm.

Luggage Storage: At the **bus station,** on racks attended by old women (*free!*), open daily 6am-11pm, or in the tunnels underneath the train station, where middle-aged women assume the watch (1 Lit per bag), open daily 6am-11pm.

Bookstores: There's a good English-language bookstore in Vilnius, the **Penki Kontinentai,** Vilniaus 39/6, near the central telegraph office. These are the cheapest English books in the Baltics, so stock up (open Mon.-Fri. 10am-7pm). For maps, try the **Knygnas Vilnius,** Gedimino pr. 13, close to the central post office. Open Mon.-Fri. 10am-2pm and 3-7pm.

Taxis: For the state taxi service, tel. 22 88 88. Set rate of 1 Lit plus 1 Lit per km (rate doubles after 10pm). Private taxis show a green light in the windshield; debate the fare before you go.

Pharmacy: Apotheke, Didžioji 13 (tel. 22 42 32), a German company with lots of Western goods, right in Old Town. Open Mon.-Fri. 9am-7pm, Sat. 10am-6pm.

Emergencies: Fire: tel. 01; **Police:** tel. 02; **Ambulance:** tel. 03.

ACCOMMODATIONS

There's a room crunch in Vilnius, but the new **International Youth Hostel** should open soon in Old Town (hopefully by summer 1995). In the meantime, there are plenty of budget options, but they all have a nasty habit of filling up.

Lithuanian Youth Hostels (LJNN/HI), main office at Kauno 1A -407 (tel. 26 26 60, fax 26 06 31; open daily 8am-6pm), just a block from the train station. The **Filaretų Hostel,** Filaretų 17 (tel. 69 66 27), is in a peaceful neighborhood on the outskirts of Old Town, best reached by bus #34 from the station (7 stops). Communal showers, clean but lacking hot water. Lockout midnight. 20 Lits with HI card or LJNN guest card. Hot breakfast served 9-10am in the sunny dining room.

Hotel Vilnius, Gedimino pr. 20/1 (tel. 62 36 65). This centrally located, unremodeled, state-run hotel can't keep doing business at its prices much longer, and is in fact up for sale. Rooms include sink, TV, and telephone; floor showers. Singles 70 Lits. Doubles 140 Lits. Double room with private bath 240 Lits.

Hotel Turistas, Ukmergės gatvė 14 (tel. 73 31 06), across the river. A Lithuanian-Swiss joint venture has remodeled the rooms, apparently using a Motel 6 manual. TV, private bath/shower, and telephone. Singles 160 Lits. Doubles 200 Lits. Breakfast included. Visa, AmEx accepted.

Litinterp, main office at Bernardinų 7-2 (tel. 22 32 91, fax 22 35 59), south of Cathedral Square. Arranges homestays with English-speakers and/or private apartments in Old Town. Reservations preferred. Singles 75 Lits. Doubles 125 Lits.

Viešbutis "Hotel," reception at Kauno 8, near the train station, open daily 7am-9pm. The "hotel" itself is on Gedimino pr., near Cathedral Square. This somehow seems a bit of an odd operation, but the rooms are clean enough, in a small, privatized Soviet hotel. Washbasins in room, floor showers, and toilets. 20 Lits per person in 2-bed rooms.

Pažanga, Saulėtekio 39a (tel. 76 38 96). Way out from the center, the dorms of Vilniaus Universitētas have 20 spacious, cinder-block rooms to let. Some have TV or radio; all have a shower and toilet shared with the neighboring room. Kitchen on the floor. 20 Lits per person. Reservations required.

FOOD

Supermarkets have been in Vilnius for some time. The best chain is probably the French **Iki** stores, stocking loads of Western goods in four locations around the city. The closest to Old Town is at Žirmūnų gatvė 68, 1.5km north on the other side of the Neris. Bus #5 or 7, or trolleybus #10, 13, or 17 will get you there (open Mon.-Fri. 9am-7:30pm, Sat. 9am-4pm). For a market experience of a different stripe, head out to the **Gariūnai Market** on the road to Trakai, where you can buy *everything:* possibly stolen Mercedes, Chernobyl-influenced veggies, western CDs, toothpaste, smoked eel, and so on (open Tues.-Sun. 7am-noon).

Vilnius has a handful of marvelous restaurants with excellent food and contrasting atmospheres. Order appetizers, ice cream, and an extra entree with you meal; often it still won't cost more than US$3-4.

Ritos Sléptuvė, A. Goštauto gatvė 8, entrance on Mečetės gatvė, west of Old Town along the Neris. "Rita's Hideaway" is the place to go if you've only got one night in Vilnius. Swift service, funky decor, and best of all, "no training-gear allowed" — a subtle ban on the local mafia's supposed uniforms. Chicago-style 12" pizza (12 Lits), great chili (6.50 Lits), heaping plates of fresh pasta (5-10 Lits), and bottomless cups of coffee (3 Lits). Check out the carvings on the tables, especially in the third booth on the right. Visa accepted. Open daily 10am-2am.

Stikliai, a four-restaurant, virtual monopoly on the corner of Gaono and Stklių, is a block south of the university. In addition to the restaurant below, there is a new **Stikliai** ice cream parlor, a wine bar is due to open soon, and they're remodeling a restaurant on Gedimino pr.

Stikliai Restaurant, Gaono 7 (tel. 22 23 18), opened in 1987 as the best restaurant in the Baltics; it's still excellent, but a light lunch special will set you back at least 40 Lits. Open daily noon-midnight.

Stikliai Aludė (Beer Bar), around the corner at Stiklių 7, is less pricey, just as good, and has a warmer atmosphere to boot. Plus—they've got excellent Lithuanian beers like Biržai (5 Lits). Open daily 11am-1am.

Café Stikliai, Stiklių 18, is a bright and shining example of how to make decent spaghetti (5 Lits), small pizzas (4-7 Lits), and darn good cappuccino (2.50 Lits). Open Mon.-Fri. 9am-11pm, Sat. noon-10pm, Sun. 10am-10pm.

Viola, Kalvarių 3, across from St. Raphael's Church. A lively Armenian restaurant with good service and a warm, inviting atmosphere. Try the *šašlik,* a spice-coated confection of lamb shish-kebab (3.90 Lits), along with some Armenian cheese (2.20 Lits) and an Armenian meat salad (2 Lits). Entrees 2-6 Lits. Menu in Russian and Lithuanian. Nightly live band plays a *bit* too loud sometimes. Open daily 1pm-midnight.

Deli-France, Aušros vartų 17-4a, a cozy little place for fast, fruit-filled crepes (2.80 Lits) or smallish, tasty subs (5.00 Lits). Open Mon.-Fri. 8am-7pm, Sat.-Sun. 10am-5pm.

Literatų Svetainė, Gedimino pr. 1 on the edge of Cathedral Square. You'll come back again and again to this cozy restaurant, full of dark wood and velvet; the atmosphere is romantic and the service attentive. English menu, plus imported beer. Entrees 3-6 Lits. Open daily noon-11pm.

Kavinė Romeda, Totorių 15, at the corner with Odminių, a block south of Gedimino. An intimate, brick-walled café in one half, and a beer bar in the other. Strong, dark coffee, rich cakes, and small salads. A coffee with a good half-dozen cakes is 1.50 Lits. Open daily 10am-8pm.

Blyninė, Pilies 8. Look for two bronze arms holding a plate of pancakes above the door. Not an IHOP, but you can get great *blynai* (Lithuanian pancakes) with meat or cheese fillings smothered in cream, butter, jelly, and other heart-stopping sauces. (0.60-1.30 Lits). Open Mon.-Fri. 11am-8pm, Sat.-Sun. 9am-7pm.

Vilnius University cafeteria, through the iron gates on the side of the *Istorijos Fakultetas,* on Universiteto gatvė. No prizes for gourmet cooking here, but you can get palatable soup, two salads, coffee, and a main dish for under 4 Lits. Open Mon.-Fri. noon-4pm.

SIGHTS

From the railway station, the **Aušros Vartai** (Gates of Dawn), the largest such gates in the Baltics, welcome you into Vilnius' Old Town. Built in the 16th century, the gates are the only surviving entrance from the old city wall. They feature griffins and the crest of Lithuania on their outer facade. Go through the gates, enter the first door on your right, and walk up the steps to the **Chapel of Our Lady of Vilnius,** a 17th-century shrine built around an icon variously said to have been captured in Ukraine by Grand Duke Vytautas, or to be a portrait of a 16th-century Lithuanian princess. A point of pilgrimage for East European Catholics, the icon is usually surrounded by the fervent. Going back down to the street and entering the doorway at the end of the building, you'll reach the **Church of St. Theresa,** whose 1630s interior is a vivid example of early Baroque art. On your way out, notice the worn crucifix by the door; the devout kiss its feet upon entering and leaving the church. A few steps farther down, a gateway leads to the front courtyard of the pink, 17th-century **Church of the Holy Ghost,** seat of the Russian Orthodox Archbishop of Lithuania. Once again a functioning monastery, the church is also the final resting place for Saints Antonius, Ivan, and Eustachius, martyred in 1371. The amazingly well-preserved bodies are in a tomb under the altar, normally clothed in red, but dressed up in white for Christmas and black at Lent. Across the street, the somewhat dilapidated **Basilian Gates,** bedecked with a photo of the Pope, lead up a narrow cobbled street to a much-reduced monastery, now also home to the Polish Embassy.

Beyond the gates, Aušros vartų turns into Didžioji gatvė (Great Street), and the magnificent crown-topped **St. Casimir's Church,** named after the country's patron saint, soon appears. The oldest Baroque church in Vilnius, it was built by the Jesuits in 1604 to model the Il Jesu church in Rome. In 1832 the church became Russian Orthodox, gaining an onion dome. In World War I the Germans made it Lutheran; when they came back during World War II they tore down the onion dome. The Soviets then turned it into a museum of Atheism in 1966. It was finally restored as a Catholic church in 1989. After this landmark, Didžioji broadens into **Town Hall Square** (Rotušės aikštė). The ancient marketplace of Vilnius, the square is now dominated by the 18th-century **Town Hall,** a columned edifice home to the **Lithuanian Art Museum** *(Lietuvos Dailės Muziejus),* with a collection rich in late 19th- and 20th-century Lithuanian paintings (open Tue.-Sun. noon-6pm; admission 0.40 Lits, free on Wed.). Behind it stands the **Contemporary Art Center** *(Čiuolaukinio Meno Centras),* with a large display hall on the second floor to accommodate traveling exhibitions (open Tues.-Sun. noon-6pm; admission 0.30 Lits). Next door, the **Dailės centrinis salonas,** Vokiečių gatvė 2, is an art salon always full of intriguing modern works by Lithuanian artists, as well as more traditional metalwork and jewelry (open Mon.-Fri. 11am-7pm).

As Didžioji continues north, you'll pass **St. Nicholas' Church** *(Šv. Mikalojaus),* the oldest church in Lithuania, built in 1320 for Hanseatic merchants living in the city. Shortly after it, Didžioji widens into a triangular square where it merges into **Pilies gatvė,** a pedestrian street lined with souvenir stands and cafés. At the corner of Pilies and Šv. Jono is the main entrance to the **University of Vilnius.** Founded in 1579, the Jesuit-run university was one of the major players in the Counter-Reformation. Closed by the Tsars in 1832, it reopened its doors in 1944; today 16,000 students study here. The main courtyard is one of 12 in the University complex, a labyrinth of faculties that fills the block between Pilies and Universiteto. On the east side of the courtyard is **St. John's Church,** completed in 1387; a museum of science under the Soviets, it is slowly being restored for worship. Go through the arches opposite from St. John's Church and you'll see the remarkable **Astronomical Observatory,** a 17th-century building with zodiacal signs on the frieze atop the facade, once rivalled in importance only by Greenwich and the Sorbonne. The university library, on Universiteto, was once among the largest in Europe, and is still a contender with over 5 million volumes.

Continue north on Pilies (or Universiteto) and you'll come out onto **Cathedral Square** (Katedros aikštė), pictured on the back of the 50-Lit note. A church has stood here since 1387, when Grand Duke Jogaila converted his country to Catholicism to win the Polish throne. The present cathedral dates to the late 18th century; built in a style reminiscent of Greek temples (perhaps a reminder that this was also the site of the principal temple to the Lithuanian god of Thunder before 1387). The contorted figures on the southern wall depict Lithuanian Grand Dukes in religious fervor. Inside, peek into the early Baroque **Chapel of St. Casimir,** a colored-marble cakework which houses a royal mausoleum. Back out in the square, the octagonal clock tower, built in 1522 atop one of the wall-towers of the lower fortress, is one of the best places to meet people in the city. Behind the cathedral, walk up the long cobbled path of the Castle Hill and climb to the top of **Gedimino Tower** for an excellent view of Vilnius' spires and a modest historical museum (open Wed.-Mon. 10am-6pm, winter 11am-5pm; admission 1 Lit).

When you come down off the hill, meander through the park to the south until you reach Mairionio gatvė, which will lead you south to Vilnius' Gothic treasure, **St. Anne's Church and Bernadine Monastery.** St. Anne's is a red-brick confection built at the height of the Gothic style, so beautiful that Napoleon is said to have exclaimed that he wanted to carry it back to France in his hand. Tough. The Bernadine monastery in back was built as part of the city walls in 1520; today it partly houses the Art Academy and Design School of the University of Vilnius. Across the street, **St. Michael's** is a Renaissance church built in 1625 to house a family mausoleum; it now shelters a bland Soviet-style **Museum of Architecture** (open Wed.-Sun. 11am-5pm; admission 1 Lit). Another museum in the area is the **Adam Mickiewicz Memorial Apartment** at Bernadinų 11, on the road back toward Pilies gatvė. The famous Lithuanian-Polish poet lived here in 1822 (open Fri. 2-6pmand Sat. 10am-2pm; free). Go south on Mairionio from St. Michael's to the very un-Russian **Russian Orthodox Church of the Holy Mother of God,** a 19th-century restoration of a 16th-century church which was originally incorporated into the city walls. Continue on Maironio, and follow the steps uphill to Bokšto gatvė, where there is a nice view of **Užupio** (literally, "across the river"), the oldest area of Vilnius outside the medieval city walls. The **Bastion Museum** is a restored section of the 17th-century fortifications that once surrounded Vilnius, full of cannons, armor, and rusty swords (open Wed.-Sun. 10am-6pm; admission 1 Lit). One of the very few remaining stretches of the old city wall is south of here; if you follow it all the way around, you'll come back to the Außros Vartai.

Once a Jewish cultural center on a par with Warsaw and New York, Vilnius had a population of 100,000 Jews (in a city of 230,000) at the outbreak of World War II. Ruthless Nazi persecution left only 6000 survivors by the time the Red Army recaptured the city in late 1944. Of 96 **synagogues** in pre-war Vilnius, only one remains, at Pylimo 39, 1/2km west of the Außros Vartai. The Nazis used it to store medical supplies; it's now undergoing its first exhaustive restoration. The old **Jewish Quarter** of the city filled the streets west of Didžioji; its approximate boundaries are traced by Didžioji, Rūdininkų, Pylimo, Trakų, and Dominikonų, a large wedge stretching from the University to the old city walls. Plaques memorializing this lost community have started to appear; they are especially noticeable around the Stikliai restaurants. Some of the street names here remind you of the past as well; Žydų (Jew) street runs south of Stiklių from the restaurants. The new **Jewish State Museum,** in two buildings, offers testimonial to the vitality of Yiddish culture in Lithuania, and homage to the victims of the Holocaust. An exhibition on Jewish life is at Pylimo 4, with rotating exhibits and a permanent display of items salvaged from the disappeared synagogues (open Sun.-Fri. 10am-5pm; donation requested). The **Holocaust Museum,** at Pamėnkalnio gatvė 12, presents a chilling display which illustrates the immensity of destruction of the Vilnius Jewish community, including meticulous SS records of daily executions (open Sun.-Fri. 10-am-5pm; donation requested).

If you're interested in the Soviet History of Lithuania, be sure to visit the **KGB Museum (Museum of the Lithuanian Genocide),** Gedimino 40, in the old KGB prison. The tour guides were once prisoners in these very cells. The prison is a fascinating and appalling place rife with torture and execution chambers; be sure to notice the mounds of documents partially destroyed by the KGB before they left in 1991 (open Tues.-Sun. 10am-1pm and 2-5pm; donation requested). Across the Neris River, at Studentų 8 just off riverside Upės gatvė, is the **Lithuanian State Museum** (*Lietuvos Valstybės Muziejus),* with exhibits on the January 1991 crackdown in Vilnius and the deportations to Siberia of the 1940s and 50s (open Wed.-Sun. 11am-6pm; 1 Lit). Wander by the **Parliament** at the west end of Gediminio pr., just before the Neris. In January 1991 the world watched as plucky Lithuanians raised barricades to protect their President and Parliament from the Soviet army. President Landsbergis later said that all of the deputies expected to become martyrs on the night of January 13, but the main attack instead came at the **TV tower,** where 14 unarmed civilians were killed as the Red Army stormed the state TV station and put it off the air. Crosses and memorials surround the spot today. The tower is visible from the city center, especially if you climb the Castle Hill; to reach the tower take trolleybus #11 going west from the "Planeta" stop on the south end of the Kalvarių Bridge (14 stops).

Rising above the east side of the Old Town is the high **Hill of Three Crosses,** visible throughout Vilnius. White crosses were originally erected in the 18th century on this spot to commemorate seven Franciscan friars who were crucified on the hill by pagan Lithuanians in the 13th century. During Lithuania's first period of independence, a white stone memorial of three crosses was erected on the hilltop. Torn down by the Soviets in the 1950s, the present monument is a copy that was unveiled in 1989. One final must-see is the high Baroque **St. Peter and Paul Church,** built around 1688. Located on Antakalnio, on the circle with the British and Danish embassies, it's a 10-minute walk from Cathedral Square, or take trolleybus #12 or 13 three stops east to "Meno mokykla" from the "Planeta" stop at the foot of the Kalvarių Bridge. Look up at the ceiling, where over two thousand carved figures dance, sing, and levitate. The church's founder is buried in the wall next to the door; his tombstone reads in Latin *Hic jacet peccator*—"here lies the sinner."

■ NEAR VILNIUS

TRAKAI

Don't miss the opportunity to visit the peaceful lakeside village of Trakai, 30km west from Vilnius. The capital of the Grand Duchy of Lithuania in the 14 and 15th centuries, modern Trakai is an island- and lake-strewn idyll full of intricate wooden cottages, castles, and picturesque ruins. From the bus station, take a right and walk down Vytauto gatvė about 1km to the intersection with a large wooden religious carving in the center; here Vytauto changes its name to Karaimų.

Off to the right down Kęstučio gatvė are the untouched ruins of the first castle, built from 1362-82 by Grand Duke Kęstutis. This castle was repeatedly besieged by German knights, and was captured twice, prompting Grand Duke Vytautas to build a new castle on the largest island of Lake Galvė in 1406. **Trakai Castle,** the picture-perfect result, is a *piece de resistance.* The castle is accessible by a footbridge another half-kilometer down Karamių. Restored thoroughly from 1952-80, the rooms of the 30m-high watchtower are stocked with historical displays of the importance of the castle (explanatory material in Lithuanian only). Other rooms of the castle house the **City and Castle History Museum,** which includes information on the restoration of Trakai, and a massive collections of china, wax seals, and furniture made from deer and elk parts. Be sure to hike around the outside of the castle for views of the lake (open Tue.-Sun. 10am-6pm; admission 4 Lits, students 2 Lits, photo permission 1 Lit). Rent a **rowboat** on the lake shores for 2 Lits per hour, or board one of the **yachts** for a tour of the many islands (fees negotiable; try for about 20 Lits).

Karamių gatvė is the cottage-lined residential district of the smallest ethnic group in Lithuania, the religious sect of the **Karaites,** a fundamentalist Jewish sect adhering only to the Laws of Moses. Upon returning from campaigns in Crimea, Grand Duke Vytautas brought a few hundred of this Turkic-speaking group back to serve as his royal guard. Today 150 Karaites live in Trakai; their **Kenessa** (prayer-house) is at Karamių 30. A small **museum** at Karamių 22 displays and explains (though only in Russian and Lithuanian) the life of the sect in Lithuania (open when the curator feels like being there; free).

Four **trains** per day go to Trakai from Vilnius (40 min., 0.80 Lits), and there are about 15 **buses** per day (50 min., 1.10 Lits). The train station in Trakai is on Vilniaus gatvė, about 0.5km south of the bus station; follow the crowd into town.

KERNAVĖ

A small town (200 people) on the Neris River about 30km northwest of Vilnius, Kernavė is considered to have been the first capital of Lithuania. This was the site of the 1253 coronation of Mindaugas, who united the Lithuanian tribes to oppose German invaders bent on converting the pagan Lithuanians to Christianity. Forgetting his original purpose, Mindaugas himself converted in 1263 and was promptly assassinated; the Lithuanian tribes quickly disunited, and Kernavė became just another town.

Today the remains of Mindaugas' 10-year reign consist of a 12th-century **fortress,** an odd gathering of four massive man-made hills that command a breathtaking view of the river. If you've got the time, this is a great place for a picnic. A **museum** of items found in excavations of the fortress does a lot to explain the importance of the hills (open Mon.-Fri. noon-4pm; admission2 Lits). The fortress, the museum, and some accompanying archaeological excavations are all behind the large neo-Gothic **church** at the end of the town's main street. **Buses** to Kernavė come from Vilnius (#65 or 67) about four times per day (1.10 Lits), and return just as often.

■■■ ŠIAULIAI

Šiauliai first entered into history because of a critical battle fought here in 1236. The German **Knights of the Sword,** returning north following a campaign to Christianize the Lithuanians, were caught unawares at sunrise and massacred in a battle that ended to German influence in the area until 1398. The city that grew up on the site later took its name from the Lithuanian word for "sun" *(saulė)*, on account of the time of day when the battle was fought. Burned to the ground by Napoleon in 1812, the city recovered only in time to be incinerated again in 1875, and then again during World War I. This is the wrong place to ask for a light.

The main attraction of Šiauliai today is the bizarre **Hill of Crosses** *(Kryziu Kalns),* 10km northwest of the city. It is thought that the tradition of placing crosses on this hill began as early as the 14th century. During the 19th century, the pace picked up after the peasant uprisings of 1831 and 1863 as Lithuanian nationalists commemorated the dead and deported with crosses. During the Soviet era, more crosses appeared for those exiled to Siberia or killed in Stalin's death camps. Determined to wipe out such an obvious symbol of Christianity, and of Lithuanian nationalism, the Soviets had the hill completely bulldozed three times. Each time, the crosses were stealthily replaced. Since independence, there has been an eruption of crosses to commemorate all those who were victims of the Soviet regime.

Even for the non-religious, the hill is a compelling sight. Thousands and thousands of crosses—elaborately carved monuments, simple plastic and metal crosses, silver crucifixes, and stone crosses—make the hill from a distance look like a sort of Catholic pin-cushion. It is a traditional custom for visitors to add a cross to the hill in memory of the victims of the Soviets. Take one of the 15 or so daily buses running north along highway 216 (0.4 Lits). Any bus to Joniškis, Meškuičiai, Rīga, or Tallinn will do—be sure to tell the driver to stop for you at Kryziu Kalns, since it is not a regular stop. Then walk down the marked road about 2km. Don't try and take one of the many buses to Kryžkalnis; it's an entirely different spot, about 30km south of Šiauliai! In town, at the corner of Aušros and Tilžės, the immense Renaissance/ Baroque Church of **St. Peter and Paul** *(Šv Petro ir Povilo bažnyčia)* looms over the city from atop a hill, thrusting its 17th-century steeple, the tallest in Lithuania, 70 meters skyward.

Ťiauliai is a simple city to master. The train station is at the southern point of the city. From here, Draugystės prospektas runs north to Vilniaus gatvė; the city hotel stands at the intersection. Vilniaus is a pedestrian street over 1km long, running west to the town market. About halfway down, Vilniaus is crossed by TilŤès gatvė which runs south to the bus station and north one block to Aušros alėja, which goes parallel to Vilniaus. Stoties gatvė runs slightly over 0.5km from the bus depot to the train station. **Exchange money** at the booth inside the station (open daily 10am-7pm). The **post and telephone office** is at Aušros alėja 42 (open Mon.-Fri. 8am-8pm, Sat.-Sun.10am-5pm).**Trains** run from the Gelenžinkelio Stotis at Dubijos gatvė 44 (tel. 005), to: Rīga (6 per day, 4 hrs.; 11Lits); Vilnius (7 per day, 4hrs.; 7.10Lits); and Kaunas (3 per day, 2hrs.; 5.50Lits). **Buses** zip off from the Autobusų Stotis, Tilžės gatvė 109 (tel. 004), to: Klaipėda (26 per day, 4hrs.; 6.15Lits), Kaunas (20 per day,

3hrs.; 6.40Lits), and Rīga (13 per day, 3½hrs.; 6.60Lits). You can **store luggage** in the lockers in the train station (0.30Lits). The **telephone city code** is 214. The **Viešbutis Šiauliai**, Draugystės prospektas 25 (tel. 373 33), is a typical medium-sized-town Soviet hotel of 14 stories. (Single and doubles with TV and shared bath 75 Lits, with private bath 100Lits. Breakfast included.) Another housing option is **Janina** (actually the name of the hotel administrator; tel. 314 83) who can arrange a private house for 3-4 people (40Lits per person, breakfast included). At mealtime, head to the **Kaštonas Kavinė**, Aušros alėja 52-c, a hip café good for coffee with amaretto (2.50Lits), or a heart-stopping lunch of *Šemaičių blynai*—immense meat-stuffed pancakes slathered in butter and onions (2.50 Lits; open daily 10am-11pm). For those in a hurry, the **Restorans Dubysa**, Stoties gatvė 2 near the bus and train stations, has a cafeteria downstairs (open daily 8am-6pm) and a restaurant upstairs where you can get average karbonades and the like (entrees 2-4Lits; open daily noon-11pm).

■■■ KAUNAS

Over 90% Lithuanian, many claim that Kaunas is the true heart of Lithuania. The "provisional capital" during Lithuania's first period of independence (1918-1940), Kaunas matured from a German-oriented trading hub into a clean, modern city of pedestrian design and graceful architecture that still charms with a provincial spirit. Easily visited in a day from Vilnius, the cosmopolitan air of this university city refreshes and renews.

ORIENTATION AND PRACTICAL INFORMATION

Large sections of central Kaunas are blocked off to traffic, making Kaunas a pedestrian-oriented city. Think of Kaunas as an isosceles triangle pointing west, with the **Old Town** *(Senamiestis)* at the western point, the bus and train stations at the southeastern tip, and the hilly suburbs of Žaliakalnis in the north. The cosmopolitan, commercial **New Town** *(Naujamiestis)* fills the middle. From the bus or train stations, Vytauto pr. leads north to Laisvės aleja, a 2km-long pedestrian mall that bolts due west, lined with all the shops, restaurants, cafés, and bars of modern Kaunas. When the street bears left, it joins also-pedestrian Vilniaus gatvė at the entrance to Old Town, leading 1km west to **Town Hall Square** *(Rotušes aikštė)*.

Tourist Office: Make a mental note to name your first-born after Matthias Lûfkens, who once again astounds and informs with *Kaunas in Your Pocket*, the portable tourist-office available at fine kiosks everywhere (3 Lits).

Currency Exchange: Look for the *Valiutos Keitykla* signs up and down Laisvės and Vilniaus. Remember that the Lit is pegged to the US$ at a 4:1 exchange rate.

Post Office: Kaunas' central post office stamps it up at Laisvės aleja 102 (tel. 22 62 20), open Mon.-Sat. 8am-7pm. **Postal Code:** LT-3000.

Telephone and Telegraph Office: In the hall to the left as you enter the central post office. Card-phones in the rear of the hall; phones using *žetoni* are in the main lobby. Open daily 8am-10pm. **City Code:** 27.

Trains: The station is at M. K. Čiurlionio 16 (tel. 22 10 93), 1.5km southeast of the New Town. Trains chug to: Kaliningrad (5 per day, 6hrs.; 20 Lits); Rīga (2 per day, 7hrs.; 25 Lits); Klaipėda (1 per day, 7hrs.; 9.60 Lits); and Vilnius (10 per day, 2hrs.; 3.20 Lits). The Tallinn-Warsaw *Baltic Express* passes through Kaunas northbound at 11:55pm, southbound at 5:53am. Station open 24 hrs. The **Advance Booking Office** is at Šv. Gertrūdos 7 (tel. 29 24 08), where Laisvės merges into Vilniaus on the edge of Old Town. Open Mon.-Sat. 9am-2pm and 3-7pm. Trolleybus #7, 5, or 3 will whisk you 3 stops to "Gedimino," 1 block south of the start of Laisvės aleja.

Buses: Autobusų Stotis at Vytauto pr. 24/26 (tel. 22 41 92), near the train station. To: Šiauliai (10 per day, 3hrs.; 7 Lits); Ignalina (4 per day, 4hrs.; 7.90 Lits); Klaipėda (15 per day, 4½hrs.; 10 Lits); and Minsk (2 per day, 7hrs.; 13.50 Lits). Innumerable buses and microbuses to Vilnius depart roughly every half-hour (1½-2 hrs., 4-5 Lits). Station open 7am-10pm.

Hydrofoils: In summer, the *Raketa* hydrofoils link Kaunas to Nida on the Curonian Spit via the Neumanas River (1 per day, 4hrs.; 25 Lits). On Sat. and Sun., the boats continue to Klaipėda (29 Lits). Departures at 8am from the ferry terminal at Raudondvario plentas 107 (tel. 26 13 48), in the trans-Neris town of Vilijampolė. Trolleybus #7 from the rail/bus stations, or #4, 10, or 11 from the stop at the west end of Laisvės aleja; get off at "Kedainių," the third stop across the river.

Public Transport: The trolleybus system in Kaunas is fairly efficient; tickets (0.15 Lits) are available at kiosks. Memorize magic #7, which is the trolleybus that can take you from the train/bus stations to the ferry terminal, via the Old and New Towns.

Taxis: State Taxi Company (tel. 23 66 66 or 23 77 77). Official rate is 1 Lit/km. **Private Taxi Company** (tel. 23 98 80). Rates may depend on how rich you look.

Luggage Storage: There are lockers (0.30 Lits) in a tunnel under the train station, open 24 hrs.

Bookstore: Buy maps and guidebooks to Kaunas in the bookstore at Laisvės aleja 81, the largest in Kaunas. Get your Polish-language versions of *Let's Go* here! Open Tues.-Sat. 10am-2pm and 3-7pm, Sun.-Mon. 10am-5pm.

Pharmacy: Apatheka, Vilniaus gatvė 39. There's no well-stocked Western-style pharmacy in Kaunas yet, but this is the best of the old state-run shops. Open Mon.-Fri. 8am-8pm.

Emergencies: Fire: tel. 01; **Police:** tel. 02; **Ambulance:** tel. 03.

ACCOMMODATIONS

Kaunas doesn't have a lot of choices for the overnight visitor; there are only ten hotels in the city, three of which won't take Westerners; of the rest, only two have spaces for under 120 Lits per person. Thankfully, there's the **Youth Hostel,** Prancūzų gatvė 59 (tel. 74 89 72), 1km uphill behind the train station, in a residential area. Inside the **Viešbutis Republika,** you can get a large bedroom, bathroom with shower, kitchen with stove and fridge, and balcony all to yourself for just 40 Lits per night. No hot water, but just heat some on the stove. There's a **café/bar** on the 11th floor, open all night. The **Baltija Hotel,** Vytauto pr. 71 (tel. 29 32 02), is more convenient to town, though it's tiny, spartan rooms don't even boast a shower—just a cold-water spigot in a corner of the bathroom. (Singles 60 Lits. Doubles 120 Lits. Convince them you're Latvian and get in for 25 Lits.)

FOOD

Dining in Kaunas offers no frills, and fewer thrills. New restaurants, including Chinese, are due to open by Summer 1995; check out the exhaustive listings in *Kaunas in Your Pocket* to see what's around.

Metropolis, Laisvės 68. Test your patience with Soviet-style dining at what was a premier establishment before World War II. The grand red hall may be empty, but the waiter may still try to put additional diners at your table just to make his life easier. Meat-and-potatoes-and-beets entrees (4-7.50 Lits), plus nightly live music after 9pm. Open daily noon-5pm and 6pm-midnight.

Tulpe, Laisvės 49, was once the literary hangout of Kaunas, but today the interior is just *too* retro. Good service, tasty pita-pizzas (2.50-3.80 Lits), and great ice cream (2-4 Lits) at lunch are somehow replaced by ogresses, bland *karbonades,* and a barrage of decibel-shattering synthesizer music at night. Open Mon.-Thurs. noon-11:30pm, Fri.-Sat. noon-1am, Sun. noon-7pm. 1 Lit cover after 6pm.

Gildija, Rotušea aikštė 2 on Town Hall Square, is the best restaurant for the money in Kaunas. The wood-beamed, red-tabled Gothic dining hall seats only 24, but it always seems to be empty anyway. The sausage platter (6.50 Lits) is spicy and filling, but the soups (2-3 Lits) are nothing to write about. Open daily noon-10pm.

Medžiotojų Užeiga (Hunter's Inn), Rotušea aikštė 10 in Old Town, was a favorite haunt of Mickiewicz. Enjoy the darkness. Full meal 8 Lits. Open daily 11am-9pm.

Pinguin. The ice cream mogul haunts Kaunas at two spots on Laisvės; the proof is left as an exercise for the student.

SIGHTS

Begin your tour of Kaunas by walking around the massive, majestic **St. Michael the Archangel Church** that commands the eastern end of Laisvės aleja. Built in the 1890s for the Russian garrison that came with the nine forts e built by the Tsar around Kaunas, the sumptuous Neo-Byzantine interior is a feast for the eyes, though the exterior is currently undergoing much-needed renovation. In the southern shadow of the church is the **Mykolo Žilinsko Dailės Galerija** (M. Žilinskis Art Gallery), with rotating exhibitions of modern art on the first floor and an eclectic collection of mummies, ceramics, and 19th-century paintings including works by Cezanne, Renoir, and Manet on the upper levels (open Tues.-Sun. noon-6pm; admission 2 Lits).

Walk down Laisvės for two blocks, turn right on S. Daukanto gatvė, and after one block you'll exit into **Unity Square** (Vienybės aikštė), depicted in etched glory on the back of the 20-Lit note. On the south side are **Vytautas Magnus University** and the older **Kaunas Technological Univeristy;** together they account for a student population of more than 16,000. Across the street is an outdoor shrine to Lithuanian statehood; busts of famous Lithuanians flank a corridor leading from the **Freedom Monument** to an eternal flame for those who died to win that freedom in 1918-20. When Lithuania was annexed by the Soviet Union, these symbols of nationhood disappeared, only to re-emerge from their hiding place in St. Michael's Church in 1989.

Surrounding this plaza are several museums. The **Vytautas the Great War Museum** *(Vytauto Didžiojo Karo Muziejus)* isn't really as bellicose as it sounds, with exhibits on the history of Kaunas and Lithuania, including the aircraft in which two Lithuanian-Americans, Darius and Girėnas, tried to fly from New York to Kaunas non-stop in 1933 (they crashed in Germany—check out the back of the 10-Lit bill; open Wed.-Sun. 11am-5pm; admission 2 Lits, free on Wed.). Go through the arcade with the cannons on your right as you leave the museum, out onto V. Putvinskio gatvė, to find the **M.K. Čiurlionis Museum,** honoring the works of the prolific avant-garde artist who sought to combine painting and music into a single artistic medium. Special listening rooms allow you to hear his works after viewing them (open Tues.-Sun. noon-6pm; admission 2.50 Lits, free Wed.). Across the street, at V. Putvinskio 64, you'll find the hellish **Devil Museum of Kaunas,** more properly known as the A. Žmuidzinavičiaus Museum, that houses a collection of nearly 2000 devils, most of them Lithuanian folk carvings, but also includes examples from Africa, Siberia, the Urals, and South America. Don't miss the widely-famed sculpture that shows Devil Hitler and Devil Stalin chasing each other across bone-covered Lithuania (open Tues.-Sun. 11am-5pm; admission 1.50 Lits). On a high hill in back of the Devil Museum is **Christ's Resurrection Church,** an architecturally-famous modernist church begun in 1932 but left unfinished on account of Stalin's meddling paws. Pictured on one of Lithuania's recent postage stamps, it has been undergoing restoration since it was returned to use in 1988.

Where Laisvės ends, Kaunas's Old Town begins; follow Vilniaus gatvė through an underpass and you'll be inside the medieval city walls. Two blocks farther, take a left on L. Zamenhofo gatvė to reach the absorbing **Museum of Folk Instruments,** Kurpių 12, a collection of hand-carved fiddles, accordions, and strange Lithuanian sound-makers such as dried, inflated sheep's bladders on a string (open Wed.-Sun. 11am-6pm; donation requested). Three blocks later, you'll come to the **Kaunas Basilica,** the largest Gothic building in Lithuania, constructed on order of Vytautas the Great in 1410. The interior is pristine, dynamic late Baroque, with a wooden altar exceedingly similar to the one in St. Anthony's Cathedral in Hrodna, Belarus. On the south wall is the **Tomb of Maironis,** a priest from Kaunas whose poetry played a central role in Lithuania's 19th-century National Awakening. Just to the west of the cathedral is **Town Hall Square** (Rotušes aikštė), crowned by the wedding-cake **Town Hall,** a multi-leveled, multi-styled concoction constructed in chunks from 1542-1771. At one time an official residence of the Tsar, it is now a municipal wedding palace and unenthralling **ceramics museum** (open Mon.-Sat. 11am; 6pm; free). Behind the town hall is a lackluster **postal museum** run by the

Kaunas post office (open Tues.-Sat. 10am-6pm). Wander up Karaliaus dvaro off the north end of the square, and you'll arrive at the **Santakos Parkas,** a tree-dotted chunk of land where the Neris and Neumanas rivers meet, the site of Kaunas's 11th-century **castle** part of which has been reconstructed as a small museum.

Follow Aleksoto towards the river from the southeast corner of the Town Hall Square, and you'll see the marvelous **Perkūnas House,** a late gothic brick masterpiece highly reminiscent of **St. Anne's Church** in Vilnius. Built for Hanseatic merchants in the early 15th century, it was discovered during 19th-century renovations that this had previously been the site of a temple to the Lithuanian thunder god, Perkūnas. Kitty-corner to this electrifying edifice is the **Vytautas Church,** also built in the early 1400s. Next to the church, a decrepit Stalin-era bridge (note the hammer and sickle) creaks across the Neumanas River; a funicular railway (0.15 Lits) leads up the steep hill to an unrivaled panorama of Kaunas.

There's one last jewel in Kaunas; the **Pažaislis Monastery and Church,** a vibrant Baroque ensemble with rich frescoes on the right bank of the Neumanas, 10km east of central Kaunas. The church was commissioned by the Chancellor of Lithuania, Kristunas Pacas, and was dedicated in 1674 after 60 years of labor and 2 million ducats. Used as a KGB-run "psychiatric hospital" in Stalin's era, the monastery has been under restoration since the 1960s, and was returned to the Catholic Church in 1990 (open Mon.-Sat. 10am-5pm, Sun. 10am-6pm). Take trolleybus #5 from the train station to the end of the line; then walk down the road for 1km. The church is just past a small beach.

Across the Neris river from the castle lies the town of **Vilijampolė,** which gained infamy during World War II as the Jewish Ghetto of Kaunas, vividly immortalized in Avraham Tory's *Kovno Ghetto Diary,* a detailed account of Nazi terror used after the war to convict many of the perpetrators. The ghetto was originally in the area north of Jurbarko, east of Panerių, and south of Demokratų, though its size was cruelly reduced as more and more Jews arrived from Poland. The **Ninth Fort,** Žemaičių plentas 73, a few kilometers north of the ghetto, was one of the nine massive forts constructed in the 1880s around Kaunas as the first line of defense against the German Empire. During World War II, it became a Nazi concentration camp, and was later used by Stalin's KGB. The museum concentrates on the Nazi atrocities, but also includes newer exhibits on the mass deportations of Lithuanians in the 1940s and 50s, and the guerilla resistance which continued until 1952. Take bus #45 from the railway station to the "IX Fortas" stop (open Wed.-Sun. 10am-6pm; admission 2 Lits., free on Wed.).

ENTERTAINMENT

The scene in Kaunas is good, probably due to the large student population. At night, head to the Town Hall Square where several outdoor bars offer live music in the evenings.

Kipšas, V. Putvinskio 64, is a hip café inside the Devil Museum, popular with the university crowd for its spicy dishes (3-5 Lits) and rich coffee (2.50 Lits). Open Tue.-Sun. 11am-5pm.

Skliautai, Rotušea aikštė 26, has a mannequin hanging outside. Attracts local artists and some great jazz from the likes of Vilnius saxophonist Petras Vyšniauskas. Open daily 11am-midnight.

Vilija, across the Neris in Vilijampolė (take that #7 trolleybus!), is the reputed local *mafija* hangout. Nightly erotic show, plus dancing to live bands (including *Boney M.*). A cellular phone and no neck is *de rigeur.* 20 Lit cover. Open daily noon-3am.

■■■ KLAIPĖDA

The third-largest city in Lithuania is rather cosmopolitan—it's one of the few places in Lithuania where you can dance 'til 3am. Klaipėda is the capital of "Lithuania

Minor," the western coast of the country that was, until very recently, German territory. First settled when the Livonian Order erected a castle here in 1252, Klaipėda was originally called Memel. After World War I, the French army occupied the city and part of the nearby Curonian Spit, but in 1923 Lithuanian troops gave the French the boot and changed the city's name to Klaipėda. With a German population of well over 85%, Klaipėda and the Curonian Spit were the object of Hitler's last land grab before World War II, in March 1939. Razed during the war, Klaipėda has been heavily rebuilt, and the population today is almost 90% Lithuanian, but the millions of nostalgia-tripping German tourists may confuse you.

ORIENTATION AND PRACTICAL INFORMATION

Klaipėda sits on the Lithuanian mainland, protected from the open Baltic by the Curonian Spit (Kuršių Nerija), a narrow belt of dramatic dunes just a short ferry ride across the Kuršių marios (Curonian Lagoon; see below). The Danė River divides the city into the **Senamiestis** (Old City), south of the river, and the **Naujamiestis** (New City) north of the river. Herkus Manto gatvė is the main north-south artery, though it changes its name to Tiltų as it crosses the Old City, and then is Taikos thereafter. Liepų gatvė (also called Naujoji sodo) is the main east-west street in the New City; Turgaus gatvė in the Old City leads directly to Teatro aikštė.

Tourist Office: No tourist office yet, so bless Matthias Lûfkens yet again for his "in Your Pocket" series; the bilingual (English and German) *Klaipėda in Your Pocket* includes city maps and information on nearby Palanga and Nida as well. Worth every centas of the 3-Lits cover price.

Currency Exchange: In kiosks surrounding the train station and the bus station, or in one of the multitudinous banks in the city. **Akcinis Inovacinis Bankas,** Pilies 12, behind the Teatro aikštė, will cash Thomas Cook travelers checks.

Post Office: Central post office at Liepų 16 (tel. 159 31), in an impressive neo-Gothic brick fantasy from 1890, one of the few buildings left undamaged by World War II. Open Mon.-Fri. 9am-7pm, Sat.-Sun. 9am-5pm. **Postal Code:** LT-5800. **DHL** and **UPS,** share quarters at H. Manto 2 (DHL tel. 165 10; UPS tel. 180 74). Both open Mon.-Fri. 10am-6pm.

Telephone and Telegraph Office: Inside the central post office (how original!). **Directory Information:** tel. 09. Open daily 8am-11pm. **City Code:** 261.

Trains: The extremely unbusy *Gelenžinkelio Stotis* (railway station), Priestočio 7 (information tel. 146 14, reservations 963 56), has a few trains running to Vilnius (3 per day, 5-9hrs.; 12.40 Lits); all go via Šiauliai (2-4hrs.; 7.10 Lits).

Buses: Autobusų Stotis at Butkų Juzės 9 (information tel. 148 63, reservations 114 34), within sight of the entrance to the train station. Buses lope to: Kaliningrad (2 per day via Sovietsk, *not* the Curonian Spit, 5hrs.; 12 Lits); Liepaja (3 per day, 3½hrs.; 5.40 Lits); Vilnius (13 per day, 7½hrs.; 14 Lits); and Palanga (20 per day, 30min.; 1.80 Lits). Station open 24 hrs.

Ferries: International ferries link Klaipėda to Kiel, Germany (4 per week, 30hrs.) and Åhus, Sweden (1 per week, 17hrs.). Fares on these cargo ships depend on time of year and amount of cargo, among other factors . Contact the Krantas travel agency, Perkėlos 10 in Klaipėda (tel. 561 16, fax 166 18), for info. On summer weekends, **hydrofoils** link Klaipėda via the Courland lagoon and the Neumanas River (1per day Sat.-Sun. at 2:30pm). Departures from the old ferry terminal at Žvejų 8 (tel. 122 24), in the Old City. To: Nida (5 Lits), Juodkrante (4 Lits), and Kaunas (29 Lits); tickets available 90 minutes before departure.

Flights: The *aerouostas* (airport) in Klaipėda, Liepos pl. 1 (tel. 520 66), is not a happening place, but **Air Lithuania,** with a ticket office at Daukanto 23-2 (tel. 106 65, fax 106 83), offers five weekly flights to Kaunas, just in case you're too impatient to take a bus.

Taxis: Call the state company (tel. 000) and pander to Soviet-style centralization, or phone a private company (tel. 007) and support burgeoning Lithuanian businessmen. Hail one on the street to directly promote free-enterprise competition.

Luggage Storage: The secure left-luggage lockers at the far end of the hall in the train station (0.30 Lits) are better than the luggage racks at the bus station in the rear of the hall (1 Lit), open 5:30am-11:30pm.

Laundry: No, not a laundromat, but **Cheminis valymas,** H. Manto gatvė 36, will do your wash in a day for 8 Lits per kg. Open Mon.-Fri. 10am-6pm, Sat. 10am-4pm.

Pharmacy: Apotheka, Turgaus 22, at the corner with Tiltų gatvė. Lots of Western products here. Open Mon.-Fri. 8am-8pm, Sat. 11am-5pm.

Timeline: tel. 004.

Emergencies: Fire: tel. 01; **Police:** tel. 02; **Ambulance:** tel. 03.

ACCOMMODATIONS

With the youth hostels of Palanga and the Curonian Spit both within spitting distance, staying the night in the mostly dismal hotels of Klaipėda isn't really worthwhile. Nonetheless, Klaipėda has a few cozy hotels. You guess which is which.

Hotel Vėtrungė, Taikos 28 (tel. 548 01), 1.5km away from the Old City, serviced by buses #8 and 10. Rooms come with bath, shower, telephone, and a cheap plastic radio. Singles and doubles 48 Lits.

Hotel Viktorija, S. Ťimkaus gatvė 2 (tel. 136 70), one block west of H. Manto gatvė, in the New City. A cheap plastic radio and a telephone in every tiny, drab room. Share your (cold) shower with the rest of the floor. 33 Lits per person.

Hotel Baltija, Janonio 4 (tel. 149 67), at the corner with H. Manto gatvė. With communal showers and toilets, and not even a cheap plastic radio in the rooms, its location close to the train and bus stations is its only grace. Oh—it is cheap, too. Singles 26 Lits. Doubles 35 Lits.

FOOD

If you're not in the mood to sit down for your meal, wander into the Market Square (Turgaus aikštė), where Tiltų changes its name to Taikos, at the south end of the Old City. A bonanza of food stalls and fruit awaits.

Astra, Pilies 14, a bit south of Teatro aikštė along Sukilėlių gatvė, is a small, candlelit cellar restaurant under the now-defunct Astra Hotel. Close to the Smltynė ferry, this is a great place for Lithuanian fare. *Cepelinai* (potato cakes filled with meat, cheese, and mushrooms; 10.50 Lits) are extremely filling and deserve to be washed down with a couple excellent dark *Utenos* beers (2.50 Lits). Menu changed daily; most entrees 8.50-13.50 Lits. Open daily noon-8pm.

Café Juoda-Balta, H. Manto 15, true to its name has a black and white interior with mirrors and red, green, and cool blue lighting, as well as some excellent food. The flaming ice cream (6 Lits) is a liquor-coated, burning mountain perfect for an afternoon's indulgence. Open daily 11am-midnight.

Prūsija, S. Šimkaus 6, near the Hotel Viktorija. MTV blares at near-painful levels in contrast to the softer, less modern decor. Insist on speaking softly and the waiter might turn it down in frustration just to hear your order. Main courses 7-9 Lits. Lithuanian beer 3 Lits. Open daily 10am-4pm and 5pm-midnight.

Restaurant Klaipėda, Naujoji sodo 1, in the Hotel Klaipėda. A huge hall that cannot disguise its Intourist-inspired past is nevertheless sunny, clean, and offers friendly service and a huge menu that is usually all available. Entrees run 8-24 Lits. Avoid dining after 7pm to escape the deafening synthesizer music. Open Wed.-Mon. noon-4pm and 6:30pm-1am, Tues. noon-4pm and 6:30-10pm.

SIGHTS

Since Klaipėda was pretty much obliterated by the Red Army during World War II, the **beach** at nearby Smiltynė is the main appeal of the town. But there are a few cultural things to do and see, mainly in the Old City. **Teatro aikštė** (Theater Square) is the center of old Klaipėda. Originally cleared for a new town market in the 18th century, the classical **Klaipeda Theater** now dominates it from the north end. Built in 1857, the theater is famous as one of Wagner's favorite haunts, and infamous for the *anschluss* (annexation) speech Hitler gave from its balcony in 1939. In front of the theater, obscured in summer by seething multitudes of Lithuanians selling amber jewelry, old coins, and Soviet military relics, is the **Simon Dach Fountain,** at the center of which is the symbol of Klaipėda, a statue of Ânnchen von Tharau. The Memel-born Dach wrote a famous German song for the wedding of young Anna, expressing his love for her. You may wonder how the groom felt about Dach calling Anna "my soul, my flesh, and my blood" at his (the groom's) wedding. The original statue disappeared in World War II; the copy standing today was erected by German expatriates in 1989.

There are a few museums in Klaipėda, including the **History Museum of Lithuania Minor,** a collection of clothing, maps, rusty swords, coins and buttons from the Iron Age to the present. The city's **Lenin statue** hides in the museum's backyard; before 1991 it stood on the square next to the Hotel Klaipėda (open Wed.-Sun. 11am-7pm; admission 1 Lit). In the New City, next to the main post office, the **Clock Museum** (*Laikrodžiu Muziejus*), Liepų 12, is a ticking mansion filled with every conceivable contraption to tell time, from Egyptian sun-dials to Chinese candle clocks and modern quartz watch-pens. None of the clocks are synchronized, and the constant chiming of random hours of the day is sure to leave you disoriented. (open Tue.-Sun. noon-6pm; admission 1 Lit).

Be sure to wander through **Aukštoji gatvė** in the Old City, one of the best-preserved areas of old Klaipėda. Craftsmen's quarters from the 18th and 19th centuries have been restored for use as craft shops, cafés, and boutiques. The **Old Post Office,** Aukštoji 13, can serve your postcard needs with a special cancellation. The old **castle ruins** (really half a moat and some grassy knolls with rocks) are just behind the old ferry terminal, worth a glance as you board for Smiltynė.

ENTERTAINMENT

Klaipėda's nightlife makes Lithuania's other cities pale by comparison, and is one of the city's prime attractions. Dozens of tiny beer bars speckle the Old City; some are well-marked, others appear to be just random doorways in buildings. All serve good, strong Lithuanian beer and loads of salted, smoked, and dried fish as finger food.

Žvejų, Žvejų 3, on the riverfront in the Old City, is one of the best of these pubs. Cold Utenos on tap (2.20 Lits), and lots of salted herring. What do you expect from a pub called "The Fishery"? Open daily 10am-10pm.

Pas Alberta, at the corner of Sukilėliu and Daržu at the south end of the Old City, is a place for a real night out. The most popular place in town, despite the hefty cover charge and the leather-jacket, crew-cut, gold-chain, BMW mentality of the male customers. Dancing every night to the DJ's favorite Pet Shop Boys album. Cover charge 12 Lits. Open daily noon-6pmand 8pm-2:30am.

■ NEAR KLAIPĖDA: SMILTYNĖ

The main attraction of Smiltynė is its **Sea Museum and Aquarium,** housed in an 1860s German fortress that protected the entrance to Klaipėda. The aquarium suffers from a lack of funds, but there are still plenty of penguins, sea lions, seals, and fish to keep you entertained. The **Dolphinarium** should be finished by late 1994, launching a new series of dolphin shows for 1995. Meanwhile, the central basin, originally planned to replicate conditions in the Caspian Sea, lingers in limbo as independent Lithuania realizes that it has no connection to that body of water (open daily 2-6pm, winter Wed.-Sun. 11am-5pm; admission 3 Lits).

From the food-stall-lined ferry landing, a mainly pedestrian road leads 1.5km north along the east side of the Spit towards **Kopgalis** (literally, "the head"), where the Curonian Lagoon meets the Baltic Sea. Marked paths also lead west through forests about 0.5km to the **beaches,** though by walking north a kilometer or so before crossing over you can virtually ensure having some sand to yourself. Once at the beach, pay attention to signs announcing gender-restricted areas for **nude bathing**— - *moteru* is for women only, *vyru* for men. Lining the road north are several museums and displays. First is the **Kuršiu Nerija Nature Museum,** a small two-floor cottage with some fascinating displays on the natural and human history of the Curonian Spit, including dioramas showing the locations of villages buried by the shifting dues (open daily 11am-6pm; free). The **Veteran Fishing Boats,** four forlorn ships on concrete pillars, and the **Ethnographic Coastal Fishermen's Village,** a reconstruction of a 17th-century village on the Spit, are farther north.

A seven-minute ferry ride across the Kuršių marios, the dunes, pine forests, and beaches of Smiltynė are the real reason to come to Klaipėda. **Ferries** drift off from the old ferry terminal in Klaipėda (daily, every hour 7-9am and every 30min. 10am-11pm, less frequently in winter). Larger ferries for cars run from the new terminal at Nemuno 8 (tel. 397 96) south of the city (daily ever hour 7:30am-8:30pm; 0.40 Lits per person, automobiles 10 Lits). From the ferry landing, 7 buses a day plus multitudinous **route-taxis** *(maršrutinis taxis)* head south down the Curonian Spit. Only a few go all the way to Nida, but all go as far as Juodkrantė (bus 2 Lits, route-taxi 5 Lits). The last transport south is a bus at 9pm, after which you'll have to shell out 25 Lits for a normal taxi to Juodkrantė.

■■■ PALANGA

The major port of Lithuania until the Swedes destroyed the harbor in 1701, Palanga was more recently famed as one of the prime beach resorts of the former Soviet Union. Palanga entices visitors with 22km of fine sandy beaches, extensive and beautiful botanical gardens, mineral springs, and a relaxing small-town feel untainted by Soviet block-house architecture. Despite a permanent population of just 22,000, in summers past Palanga swam with more than 150,000 people, but tourist traffic has dropped by more than 80% since the demise of the union. Take advantage of the lull to plop down on the best beach in the Baltics and soak up the heady scent of pine on a sea breeze.

Orientation and Practical Information Palanga's layout is simple to master. The bus station and post office mark the approximate center of town along the main north-south boulevard, Vytauto gatvė. Approximately 200m south of the station, Basanavičiaus gatvė runs 1km west to the beach, lined with shops, restaurants, and vendors of all kinds, ending at the pier. The entrance to the huge Botanical Park, which marks the southern end of the city, is another kilometer south along Vytauto. There is a small **tourist office** on the outside of the bus station that primarily seems to sell postcards and maps, but can suggest good restaurants and help arrange accommodations (open daily 9am-7pm during tourist season). Exchange money at the booth inside the post office (open Mon.-Sat. 9-14 and 15-19, Sun. 9-15). The **post office** is at Aušros alėja 42, across from the bus station (open Mon.-Sat. 9am-2pm and 3-7pm, Sun. 9am-3pm). International **telephone** calls can be made from the new building behind the post office (open daily 8am-11pm). The **telephone city code** is 236. **Buses** run from the buzzing *Autobusų Stotis,* on Kretingos gatvė at Vytauto (tel. 004). Every bus going south or east from Palanga stops in Klaipėda (more than 30 per day, 30min.; 1.35 Lits). Other buses run to: Kaunas (9 per day, 4-5hrs.; 11 Lits); Liepaja (3 per day, 3hrs.; 13 Lits); Šiauliai (3 per day, 3½hrs.; 7.40 Lits); and Kaliningrad (2 per day via Sovietsk, 5-6hrs.; 21 Lits). Ticket office open daily 6:30am-10pm.

Accommodations The **Youth Hostel,** S. Nėries gatvė 23 (tel. 570 76), is the obvious place to stay in Palanga. A sunny and restful one-time resthome with 10 rooms of 2-3 beds; the communal kitchen and toilets are in a detached building. From the bus station, walk on the path behind the post office to S. Nėries gatvė; the hostel is set back on the left side of the road. (16 Lits per person. Reservations *highly* recommended.) There are no showers at the hostel, but you can get hot showers (1.50 Lits) at the Palanga **City Health Palace** *(Palangos Miesto Sveikatos Rūmai),* S. Nėries gatvė 44, at the end of the street before the beach. Massages (10 Lits per hour), mud-treatments (20 Lits), and swimming in a heated pool (4 Lits;

open daily 9:40am-7:40pm). Other housing options in Palanga include the dozens of **resthomes** that are struggling to privatize. Many are not accustomed to foreigners, and may take some convincing before they let you stay (often for less than US$3 a night). Ask at the tourist office at the bus station for recommendations if the hostel is full.

Food For a resort town, breakfast can be pretty hard to find, and the town is mostly dead until 11am. If you're hungry (or just awake) before then, the **Gaisra Kavine,** Vytauto gatvė 102 north of the bus station, is your best bet. Scrounge a decent morning meal out of yogurt, coffee, cakes, pastries, beer, vodka, and mixed drinks. The inside is dark and oppressive, but the tables outside are right in the morning sun (open daily 8:30am-11pm). **Eglė Šalčių Karalienė** (Queen of Grass Snakes), Basanavičiaus gatvė 6, is a tiny, cozy restaurant named for a Lithuanian girl who became Queen of the Grass Snakes after marrying a snake who climbed into her clothes while she swam. We won't talk about the symbolism; just be careful at the beach. Most of the tempting fish entrees are in the 15-25 Lit range; the *kepsnys Baravykas* (fried salmon) is excellent at 15 Lits (open daily 11am-11pm).

Sights Palanga is a pleasant city for strolling around, with no musty, arrowhead-and-rusty-teapot-stuffed city museum to detract from having a good time. The best way to spend a day here is at the **beach,** which runs unhindered from Girkeliai, 5km south of town, all the way to the Latvian border, 18km north. At the end of Basan-avičiaus gatvė, a fountain-bedecked plaza opens onto the boardwalk which runs just behind the dunes for the length of the town. Cafés and beer gardens make this a great place to sip away the late evening hours; during the daylight, hike up into the dunes and pick a spot to sun. The beach may look surprisingly deserted at first, because the fierce winds off the Baltic make it more enjoyable to lie in the wind-breaks among the dunes, out of sight of the sea. **Nude bathing** is allowed—women control a section of beach starting about 200m north of the pier, but shy men have no place to call their own.

On a cold day, or when evening comes, wander through the **Botanical Gardens** at the south end of Palanga. In the early 19th century, the Polish Count Tyskiewicz bought the entire town, recognizing its growing popularity as a beach resort. Once he owned the town, he levelled half of it to lay out the magnificent 495-acre park that surrounds his palace, bringing in a French landscape architect put out of work by the recent Revolution to design it for him. Well-marked paths and flowering trails make for romantic strolls around sunset. Towards the center of the park, view-strewn **Birutės kalnas** (Birutė's Hill) was the site of a pagan shrine in the olden days; a late-19th-century chapel surmounts it now. Just east of the hill, Count Tyskiewicz's **palace** now contains the glittering **Amber Museum,** a gargantuan collection of more than 35,000 pieces of amber, including a veritable graveyard of 15,000 pieces containing insects. The definitive history of amber is also contained here, including displays on mining and processing, and large collections of modern and ancient jew-elry and carvings. This is probably the best museum in Lithuania, so don't miss it (open Tue.-Sun. 11am-7pm; admission 3 Lits).

■■■ CURONIAN SPIT (NERINGA)

Superlatives fail to do the Curonian Spit justice. Sixty-meter-high dunes of fine white sand, deep forests of pine and birch, and wide beaches facing the Baltic are the per-fect getaway. Declared a National Park in 1976, development has been halted on the entire Lithuanian portion of the Spit, a 100-km needle of land never more than 3km wide that runs south from Klaipėda to Kaliningrad. The Lithuanian portion stretches 50km to the Russian border just below Nida; you can wander along sculpture-lined trails, rent a sailboat on the Kuršių marios, or lie in the sun and sand of this paradise.

Getting to Neringa is easy; frequent **ferries** from Klaipėda float to Smiltynė, at its northern terminus. Another option is to go by **hydrofoil** from Kaunas to Nida. A paved road runs south from Smiltynė, passing through the four towns of Juodkrantė, **Pervalka, Preila,** and Nida; a toll point at the entrance to the Park restricts traffic in Neringa with a fee of 4.50 Lits per car and 0.80 Lits for pedestrians or bicyclists. **Public transportation** on the Spit consists of the various buses and route-taxis *maršrutinis taxis)* that ply the road from Smiltynė. From the ferry landing, 7 buses per day plus multitudinous route-taxis head south down the Curonian Spit. Only a few go all the way to Nida, but all go as far as Juodkrantė (bus 2 Lits, route-taxis 5 Lits). The last transport south is a bus at 9pm. Be warned also that catching these buses or taxis at points *en route* is difficult as they often fill up; you may have to wait through 6-7 buses before one has room.

JUODKRANTĖ

Twenty km south of Smiltynė, Juodkrantė is the second-largest settlement of Neringa, but still ranks as a small town by any measure. Established around a tavern from the mid-1600s, the town that the Germans called Schwarzort (meaning "black shore") was rechristened as Juodkrantė ("black shore" in Lithuanian) when the territory became part of Lithuania. Amber was extracted by the ton from a harbor at the north end of town as recently as World War I, but the supply is depleted now, leaving a quiet grouping of summer cottages among the pine-covered dunes.

The forests around Juodkrantė are the thickest on the Spit, thanks to the reforestation efforts of a local postmaster. Most of Neringa was denuded of trees in the 18th century by shipbuilders; over the next 100 years, the suddenly shifting sands buried a dozen towns. In 1882 a startled postmaster (how can you deliver the mail if you can't find the town?) started planting trees to restrain the dunes. One excellent way to explore the forests here is by hiking up the **Raganų kalnas** (Witches' Hill), where carved wooden sculptures of wood spirits, monsters, and local personalities line the trails to the top. Entrance to the trail is on a marked side road south of the main section of town. Dozens of other good trails lead across the Spit towards fabulous beaches on the Baltic side. Ask at the hostel which trails are best; Neringa's mother knows them all like the back of her hand (see below).

Juodkranė is spread out into three distinct clumps, with the bus stop in the center one. **Buses** and **route-taxis** come by north- and south-bound roads roughly every 20 minutes during the day, but be aware that the schedule posted here is not exact; arrive to catch a bus at least 15 minutes early, and flag your arms wildly when you see it coming. Immediately in back of the bus stop, a **ferry** dock allows connections on the summer "Raketa" **hydrofoils** that run from Kaunas to Klaipėda (1 per day Sat.-Sun.). North from the bus stop is the **Gintaro įlanka** (Amber Bay); south leads towards the center of town.

Juodkrantė has an excellent **Youth Hostel.** Neringa, Juodkrantė's charming kindergarten teacher, has set up 12 beds in an unused classroom at the primary school. Blocks, finger-paint, and a piano make this a great place to spend the night, and the little-people-sized toilets and shower make you feel like a grown-up at last. Walk south from the bus stop and turn right onto Ievos Kalno gatvė. Reception is at #18, apt. 6 (tel. 533 14). 16 Lits per person. For an extra 8 Lits, the school cook will make you a *massive* breakfast that will leave you full for the rest of the day.) Food is hard to come by in Juodkrantė, so stock up before you arrive. The **Parduotuve** just south of the bus stop stocks some groceries, and a small **café** in the town center, farther south than the hostel, serves cheap but desultory food until 9pm.

NIDA

Buried three times by shifting dunes, Nida took 300 years to settle on a location, but it seems to have done pretty well in the end. The most famous town on the whole of the Curonian Spit, Nida was an artist's haven in late 19th-century Germany. When Nida became Lithuanian after World War I, most of the artsy folk left, but a new literary crowd, led by Thomas Mann, rediscovered Nida's beauty in the 1930s. Even the Communists recognized the magic of Nida, reserving nearly the whole town as a capital-P Party resort.

All the **wooden houses** in Nida are classified as historical monuments; many are still roofed with thatch. The most interesting examples of this old fishermen's architecture line Pamario on the approach to the brick Gothic church, finished in 1888. The old **cemetery** of Nida is in the woods near here, a strange, hilly place full of wooden markers. Farther out of the center, just past the junction of Skruzdynės gatvė with Pamario, the **Thomas Mann House** marks where the famous German lived from 1930-33. It is now a museum devoted to the author, with his books, photos, and writing desk (open Tues.-Sun. 10am-5pm; admission 2 Lits).

A walk down Naglių or Lotmißkio south from the town center leads through the old artists' colony of Nida, a collection of well-kept wooden cottages now interspersed with cafés and souvenir shops. On the docks at the end of the streets, you can rent **paddleboats** and **sailboats** (4 Lits per hour). A path leads along the beach from here up to the top of the 52m-high **Parnidžio kopa,** one of the largest and most magnificent dunes on the Spit. From the top, sand stretches out below in near-desert majesty, and views of Nida, the Baltic, and Neringa open up all around. The Russian border is just 500m or so beyond this dune, but there are no controls on this side of the Spit. *Let's Go* does not advocate thumbing your nose at petty Russian authority by crossing the border and yelling *"Nyah!"* (or even *"Nyet!"*) at the top of your lungs, but feel free to do it anyhow. Just remember that we warned you if you end up in Siberia.

Central Nida is defined by north-south Naglių gatvė, which changes its name to Pamario at the north end of town, and the major cross-street, Taikos gatvė, which runs uphill to the southwest from the harbor. The central town square is about a block north of their intersection. Kuverto gatvė runs inland from Pamario, 100m north of the name change. **Exchanging money** in Nida can be a problem on weekends, since neither of its two banks is open. You can get a Visa cash advance at the Vilniaus Bankas office inside the Jūrate Resthome, Pamario 3 (open Mon.-Fri. 9am-6pm). The post and telephone office is at Taikos 13 (postal section open Mon.-Sat. 10am-1pm and 2-6pm; telephone section open daily 8am-2pm and 3pm-midnight). The **telephone city code** is 259. **Buses** from the north end of the Spit deposit you at the town bus stop on Naglių gatvė, just east of the central square. Seven buses and roughly 30 route-taxis per day head north to Klaipėda, Smiltynė (8 Lits), and points on the Spit. Currently, no buses run south to the Russian portion of the Spit. You can catch the "Raketa" **hydrofoils** to Kaunas at the harbor (1 per day in summer at 3:30pm, 4hrs., 24 Lits); on Saturday and Sunday at noon the hydrofoil also runs to Klaipėda (1hr., 5 Lits). Tickets sold 90min. before departure.

Off-limits to foreigners under the Soviet occupation, German tour groups now routinely book entire hotels in Nida for the entire summer, leaving few choices for travelers without reservations. **Auksinės Kopos,** Kuverto gatvė 17 (tel. 522 12), is a remodeled Soviet-era resthome primarily frequented by Lithuanians, with private baths and a fridge. (Singles 35 Lits. Doubles 58 Lits. Luxury suites featuring a TV 75 Lits. Breakfast included.) **Jūrate Resthome,** Pamario gatvė 3 (tel. 523 00), overlooks a park 250m north of the harbor. The largest resthome in Nida with ten buildings (the best of which are permanently booked by German tour groups). Large, clean rooms have a shared bath and a hall TV. (Singles DM30. Doubles DM45. Breakfast included.)

Meals are available in the resthomes, but if you have the itch to head out, you could try **Peteris,** Taikos 13, sharing an address with the post office. Fish is the specialty here, ranging from eel to perch and salmon. Most entrees cost 15-30 Lits (open daily noon-midnight). There are some food shops near the central square, though none has any real variety and what they do have is expensive; bring in your own supplies if you can. One thing you shouldn't miss is smoked fish, a Nida specialty. **Rū0kyta Žuvis** is one outlet for this delicacy, on the right side of the disco set back from the central square. One giant fish (enough to stuff two hungry soles) is 5 Lits (open "days"). The **Disco Baras,** in the large grey "Agila" building on central square, is the only point for nightlife in town, regularly filled to bursting with "Spiting" teenagers. (No cover. Open daily noon-3am.)

LITHUANIA

FORMER YUGOSLAV REPUBLIC OF MACEDONIA
(Македонија)

US$1	= 42dn (denars)	10dn =	US$0.24
CDN$1	= 32dn	10dn =	CDN$0.31
UK£1	= 67dn	10dn =	UK£0.15
IR£1	= 66dn	10dn =	IR£0.15
AUS$1	= 33dn	10dn =	AUS$0.30
NZ$1	= 23dn	10dn =	NZ$0.44
SAR1	= 12dn	10dn =	SAR0.84
DM1	= 27dn	10dn =	DM0.36
Country Code: 389		**International Dialing Prefix: 900**	

The best way to enjoy Macedonia is to breeze through Skopje with its *Battlestar Galactica* architecture, steer clear of the contested Serbian border, and head straight to the divine, ancient shores of Lake Ohrid, a UNESCO-protected world cultural and heritage site since 1980.

> For the sake of brevity, *Let's Go* uses the name "Macedonia" throughout this chapter to refer to the Former Yugoslav Republic of Macedonia. *Let's Go* does not endorse any perceived claims of the former Yugoslav Republic to the Greek territory of the same name.

F.Y.R. MACEDONIA ESSENTIALS

As of July 1994, American and British citizens could visit Macedonia **visa**-free for up to three months. Citizens of Australia, Canada, Ireland, New Zealand, and South Africa need visas. All visas must be procured at the border and are free of charge, since the Republic of Macedonia has not yet established consular offices abroad.

GETTING THERE

You can reach F.Y.R. Macedonia by **air, bus,** or **train.** *Adria* (Slovenian) and *PALAIR* (Macedonian) both fly to the capital, Skopje. Many people prefer to travel over land to and from Sofia (Bulgaria) or Thessaloniki (Greece) to gain access to a broader range of international flights. Smog causes frequent closures of the airport in Skopje.

GETTING AROUND F.Y.R. MACEDONIA

The **train** system is not extensive. Luckily, private **bus** companies have introduced good service and air conditioning to public transportation in Macedonia. You can buy train and bus **tickets** at the respective stations in Skopje and smaller towns. Helpful words include билет *(bilet,* ticket), воз *(voz,* train), железница *(zhelezhnitsa,* railway), автобус *(autobus,* bus), станица *(stanitsa,* station), повратен билет *(povraten bilet,* return ticket), линија *(linia,* track), перон *(peron,* platform), информации *(informatsii,* information), тргување *(trugvane,* departures), пристигнување *(pristignuvane,* arrivals). **Hitchhiking** in Macedonia is becoming increasingly dangerous, especially for foreigners. *Let's Go* does not recommend hitchhiking as a safe means of transportation.

As the country decommunizes, many street names are being changed, but the old street signs often remain. When asking for directions, use both the new and old names. Try to get a new map as soon as possible; many are now available in English.

TOURIST SERVICES

The Macedonian government still operates **tourist bureaus** throughout the country which give out maps, often rent **private rooms,** and sell train and airline tickets. Look for the **(i)** signs. **Shops** are generally open from 8am-8pm. Weekend hours vary from shop to shop. Some **banks,** especially in tourist areas, are open seven days per week. Expect an hour lunch break around noon at most offices and shops.

MONEY

The monetary unit is the **Denar** which comes in bills of 10, 20, 50, 100, and 500 denars, and in coins of 0.5, one, two, and five denars. *Let's Go* lists most prices in U.S. dollars (US$). The official rate of approximately US$1 to 42dn closely coincides with the rates offered by private banks and numerous private change bureaus. Hotels have worse rates, and changing money on the street in not only unwise but illegal. Most hard currency prices in F.Y.R. Macedonia are given in deutschmarks; often banks and exchange offices will only have deutschmarks and denars in stock. Change your dollars and pounds before you arrive: they will be worthless outside the capital. You can cash **American Express** traveler's checks at most banks. The country does not yet accept **credit cards.** Even major hotels accept only cash.

COMMUNICATION

Though Macedonia now has **AT&T USADirect** service (tel. (99) 800 42 88), the **phone system** in the country is still poor by Western standards and you may have difficulty placing calls. **Betkom** direct dial telephones are nowhere to be found. To get an international line, dial 99. Calls to the U.S. average US$2 per minute. Service is generally efficient at local post offices. To make local calls from public phones, you must buy a token called a **zheton** (жетон) for 4dn at a post office. Some kiosks also sell them. When calling home, remember: F.Y.R. Macedonia is in the same **time zone** as Western Europe (GMT plus 1, EST plus 6), one hour behind Bulgaria and Greece.

Faxes can be sent at most telephone centers; prices are comparable to phone calls. **Photocopy** centers abound. Look for the sign "Фотокопир." Prices average 10dn per copy. Some businesses in Skopje have access to **e-mail.** If you are desperate to log on, check at the American Center in Skopje. Some of the large hotels televise CNN in their lobbies. *Newsweek* and *Time* are widely sold at city kiosks. The **Voice of America** (VOA) and **BBC** can be heard on Macedonian radio. American movies with Macedonian subtitles are shown frequently on Macedonian TV.

LANGUAGE

Key phrases include: здраво (Zdra-vo, "hello," "goodbye," "good luck"), , "goodbye"), пошта (POSH-ta, "post office") соби (SO-bee, "private rooms"), добро (DO-bro, "OK"), зборувате ли англиски (ZBOR-oo-va-te LEE-an-GLEE-ski, "do you speak English?"). Macedonian and Bulgarian are mutually intelligible. Russian is still widely understood, as is Serbian, but it would be wise to ask before using either. English is quickly becoming the second language of choice in Macedonia, and many young people in urban areas are fluent. Macedonian-English phrasebooks (разговорник, *razgovornik)* are sold at bookstores and kiosks throughout the country for US$4. As in Bulgaria, the head movements for "yes" and "no" are reversed from in the West, so it's a good idea to confirm everything with *Da* (yes) or *Ne* (no).

Yes	Да	Dah
No	Не	Neh
Hello	Добар ден	DAW-bahr den
Good morning	Добро утро	DAW-broh OOT-raw
Good night	Добро вечер	DAW-broh VYEH-cher
Goodbye	Довидување	daw-ve-DYOU-va-ne
Excuse me	Дозволете	dohz-voh-leh-teh
Please	Повелете	poh-VEL-et-ey
Thank you	Фала	FAH-lah
When?	Кога	koh-GAG
Where?	Каде	kah-DEY
Help!	Помош	PAW-mosh
How much does it cost?	Колку чини	KOL-ku CHI-nee
How do I get to...?	Каде е..?	kah-DEY ay..?
My name is ...	Се викам...	Say VEE-kahm...
I don't understand	Не разбирам	Neh rahz-BEE-rahm
Leave me alone; get lost!	Оставете ме на мира!	Ohs-TAH-veh-teh mey nah MEE-rah!

1—еден (Eh-den); 2—два (dvah); 3—три (tree); 4—четири(cheh-TIH-ree); 5—пет (peht); 6—шест (shest); 7—седум (SEH-doom); 8—осум (AW-soom); 9—девет (DEH-veht); 10—десет (DEH-seht); 20—двaесет (DVAH-eh-seht); 30—триесет (TREE-eh-seht); 40—четириесет (cheh-TIH-ree-eh-seht); 50—педесет (PEH-deh-seht); 60—шеесет (SHEH-eh-seht); 70—седумдесет (SEH-doom-deh-seht); 80—осумдесет (W-soom-deh-seht); 90—деведесет (DEH-veh-deh-seht); 100—сто (stoh); 1000—иљада (il-YAH-dah).

HEALTH AND SAFETY

Pack a small bar of soap and some toilet paper for the public bathrooms. It is often necessary to pay 10dn for access to restaurant bathrooms. It's also wise to travel with a water bottle, flip-flops, and a lot of patience. Basic medicines are widely available in Macedonian pharmacies (апека, *apteka*). *Analgin Cafetin* is aspirin and *Arbid* is cold medicine. Bandages are *Flexogal*. Condoms are sold in the kiosks all over town and sometimes in pharmacies. They are10dn each and come only in neon green, purple, and red. If you are particular about quality and brands, bring your own medications and supplies, especially for feminine hygiene products.

There is a general lack of tolerance toward homosexuals in Macedonia. Life here will be made easier if you do not express your views or preferences openly.

Visitors should avoid traveling near the border with Serbia; relations between the two countries are tense and shots have been fired by border patrols.

The climate in Macedonia is generally mild: the average temperature in Skopje is 13.5°C, 55°F. Mountain areas receive snow from early fall to late spring. Fog is often a problem in the capital in January and February, causing frequent flight delays and cancellations. The summers in Skopje are often stifling while the winters can be very cold—especially when the heat is turned off for eight hours nightly.

ACCOMMODATIONS AND CAMPING

You will receive a white **statistical card** at the border which you will use as a passport-equivalent within the country when the hotel or hostel takes your passport at check-in: all businesses that offer accommodations are required by law to **register your passport** with the police. Don't worry: when you settle up with the hotel proprietor at the end of your stay, you'll get your passport back. If you are staying with friends, they officially must do this as well, although this law is often ignored.

Private rooms outside the tourist areas of Lakes Ohrid and Prespa are expensive (US$20) and difficult to find. Check with the local tourist office. In the resort towns, you'll be met at the bus and train stations by hordes of locals offering rooms. Prices are usually given in deutschmarks and improve with haggling. **Hotels** in Macedonia are exorbitantly expensive (US$60-80 per person in summer). Service is better and prices more reasonable at new private hotels (US$17 per person in summer.) Most **youth hostels** are located outside urban centers and are popular with student groups; you can make reservations for hostels throughout the country through the hostel in Skopje. Many **campgrounds** are in a state of disarray. Call before heading out to these campsites. **Freelance camping** is very popular, but you risk a fine and it's not a safe option. Camping in reserve areas is prohibited.

LIFE AND TIMES

HISTORY

The **Greek Migrations** of 1200-1000 BC forced the Myceneans out of the Peloponnese and settled what is now the Republic of Macedonia with iron-wielding **Dorians**. While their cousins to the south prospered, the northern Dorians were attacked by Hallstatt Celts in the 8th century BC and Central Asian Scythians in the 7th century BC. The flourishing Greek culture to the south only seeped into the fringes of the area, then known as **Paeonia**. King Philip II of Macedonia (situated to the south of the modern Republic) joined Paeonia with his kingdom in 358 BC and incorporated it into a developing Empire which under his son, Alexander the Great, would stretch from Albania to the Indus. Following Alexander's death, his empire was divided. Macedonia fell to the general Cassander, whose kingdom was lost to invading La Tène Celts and the acquisitive **Antigonid** family after his death in the early 3rd century.

Macedonia, including eastern Paeonia, was ruled by the Antigonids from 279 to 168 BC. Alliances with Carthage and Egypt led to losses to Rome in the 1st and 2nd **Macedonian Wars,** while the 3rd Macedonian War (171-168 BC) found Paeonia split from its southern neighbors. It remained an independent territory for 20 years before being incorporated into the larger **Roman** province of Macedon (the territory would not be independent again for 2140 years). Under Roman rule, Paeonia enjoyed over five centuries of cattle grazing and quiet *pax.*

Change arrived in the 390s AD with the rampaging Visigoths, who tore through the area on their way to Italy and Spain, opening up Paeonia to settlement by **Balkan Slavs,** who arrived steadily over the next 300 years. These Slavs, the ancestors of the Republic's modern inhabitants, were soon re-incorporated into the Byzantine Empire. The **Byzantines** and **Bulgarians** periodically warred over the territory from the 7th to the 14th centuries, both empires treating the people as spoils and inserting their own nobles as feudal overlords. Serbian rule from 1330 ended with the Battle of Kossovo in 1389, and over the next 70 years the territory was completely absorbed into the Ottoman Empire.

In the 19th century, after over four centuries of Ottoman rule, the Balkan Slavs began agitating for independence. With Russian backing, the Slavs went to war in the late 1870s. After the fall of Plevin to Slavic forces, the Ottomans signed a truce on January 31, 1878, but Macedonia remained in Turkish hands. Every power in the Balkans fought over Macedonia in the **First Balkan War,** which broke out in 1912. Turkey was quickly defeated but no one could agree on how to divide the spoils. Bulgarian troops turned on their Serbian and Greek allies, causing the **Second Balkan War.** The Bulgarians were soon defeated and the area which would later be the Republic was awarded to Serbia.

World War I found Serbia (and Skopje) on the winning side, and the province's borders were stretched eastward to its present size at the expense of Bulgaria. The nations of the northeast Balkan Peninsula were united as **Yugoslavia,** which remained intact, albeit shaken by internal disputes, until **World War II.** After years of Nazi occupation, Yugoslavia reformed under the non-Warsaw Pact Communism of **Tito.** His personal rule held the country together until his death on May 4, 1980, at the age of 88, which was followed by a decade of furious politics and gradual breakup. On September 8, 1991, 96% of the population in Macedonia voted for independence.

MACEDONIA TODAY

Macedonia declared independence on September 17, 1991 and became the only former Yugoslav Republic to leave the federation peacefully; it was admitted to the United Nations in April, 1993. There are half a million more sheep in Macedonia than there are people. If only the people got along as well as the sheep. Today there are rising ethnic tensions among Slavic Macedonians, Albanians, Serbs and Bulgars. Mosques mingle with Orthodox churches and nationalist propaganda is prevalent. 500 U.S. soldiers work as part of a 1,200-member United Nations observer force trying to keep the peace. Serbia has ambitions in the area and its soldiers have dug trenches several hundred meters across the Macedonian border.

Already the poorest of Yugoslavia's republics, its situation has worsened as a result of the UN-enforced embargo against its traditional market of Yugoslavia. Greece has also imposed a trade blockade in an effort to pressure Macedonia to change its name, currency, and a phrase of its constitution, all of which, according to Athens, imply pretensions to the Greek province of the same name.

FOOD AND DRINK

Food is not cheap in Macedonia. Kiosks sell grilled meats (скара, *skara*), especially small hamburgers (кебабри, US$1), and *burek* (бурек, delicious, warm filo-dough pastry stuffed with either veggies, feta cheese, or meat, US$1). Fruits and vegetables can be bought at outdoor markets or *pazar* (пазар). The standard salad is *shopska,* which consists of cucumber, tomato, onion, and grated feta cheese. The expensive national dish is the *Letnitsa* trout, found only in Lake Ohrid. *Eyeyar* and *Rindzur*

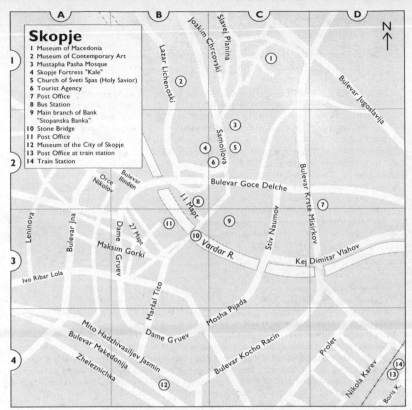

Skopje

1 Museum of Macedonia
2 Museum of Contemporary Art
3 Mustapha Pasha Mosque
4 Skopje Fortress "Kale"
5 Church of Sveti Spas (Holy Savior)
6 Tourist Agency
7 Post Office
8 Bus Station
9 Main branch of Bank
   "Stopanska Banka"
10 Stone Bridge
11 Post Office
12 Museum of the City of Skopje
13 Post Office at train station
14 Train Station

F.Y.R. MACEDONIA

are tomato-based pasta dishes. Bean soup (боп, *bop*) and *goulash* are also popular. Wash it all down with some delicious Macedonian wine (вино, *vino*) or *rakiya*, a grape or plum brandy. The water is safe to drink, and there are fountains throughout the cities and in tourist sites. Tipping is not customary, but always appreciated. When restaurants are crowded, share a table with the locals and practice your Macedonian.

■ Skopje (Скопје)

The rolling hills, fields of sunflowers, and orange-roofed suburbs that surround Skopje lend the city an air of serenity almost unbefitting an object of such controversy. Skopje itself is clean and modern. In 1962, 90% of the city's structures were destroyed in a disastrous earthquake. After this tragedy, international aid poured in to rebuild the city. Skopje now calls itself the "city of international solidarity," though "city of Socialist Realist concrete" would perhaps be more appropriate. Thankfully, some ancient structures were spared and the Old Bazaar area remains intact. Skopje has always been a meeting place for Eastern and Western cultures; today many Albanians, Gypsies, and Slavic peoples still call the city home.

ORIENTATION AND PRACTICAL INFORMATION

Skopje is a city of a half-million people situated on the Vardar River. Several bridges, the most famous being an old stone pedestrian bridge, connect the Old and New sections of the city. **Maps** of Skopje are sold at the tourist office and at some kiosks. While some street signs are in Latin script, most are printed in Cyrillic.

Tourist Office: Turistička Agencija, around the corner from the bus station across from the old Turkish Baths at the beginning of the Old Bazaar (tel. 11 68 54, fax 61 34 47). Look for the "i" signs. Cheery English-speakers provide maps of the city, bus and train tickets, accommodations for US$20 including breakfast, and English-Bulgarian phrasebooks. Open Mon.-Sat. 8am-8pm, Sun. 9am-2pm.

Embassies: The **U.S.** Liaison Office is located in a new, yellow building in the New Town's main square (tel. 11 72 11 or 11 70 32). Open Mon.-Fri. 8am-4:15pm. The **American Cultural Center,** Gradski zd., block 4 (tel. 11 66 23, fax 11 84 31), has an air-conditioned library replete with English-language newspapers, journals, and books. Open Mon.-Fri. 10am-4pm. **U.K.,** 26 Veljko Vlohivič, fourth floor (tel. 11 67 72). U.S., British, and German flags out front. Citizens of **Canada, Australia,** and **New Zealand** should contact the U.K. office in Skopje.

Currency Exchange: Stopanska Banka, in the shopping mall in the main square of the New Town (tel. 11 53 22, fax 11 45 03), exchanges money and cashes American Express traveler's checks. Open Mon.-Fri. 7am-7pm, Sat. 7am-1pm.

Post Office: In the train station. **Post Restante** is at window #18; bring your passport to pick up mail. Open Mon.-Sat. 7am-8pm. **DHL** is located near the Continental Hotel (tel. 11 67 03 or 23 81 11). **Postal code:** 91000.

Telephones: Next to the post office in the train station. Open Mon.-Sat. 7am-8pm. On Sundays use the telephone office in the bus station. For local calls, use the 4dn *zheton,* available at the post office or kiosks. **City Code:** 91.

Faxes: Can be sent and received at the post office—fax 16 25 24.

Flights: Skopje Airport, 23km from downtown, is near the village of Petroveč (tel. 23 51 56). *Adria* (Slovenian) and *PALAIR* (Macedonian) both serve Skopje. The tourist office has flight schedules and offers tickets and youth discounts.

Trains: The train station (Железничка) is right on the river (tel. 23 42 55). International tickets sold upstairs, domestic downstairs. To: Bitola (6 per day, US$3.50); Belgrade (5 per day, US$17.80); Thessaloniki (2 per day, US$22.60); Athens (2 per day, US$69); Budapest (1 per day, US$71); and Vienna (1 per day, US$93).

Buses: The bus station (Аутобуска Станица) is at the entrance to the Old Town (tel. 23 62 53). From the train station walk three blocks to the river, keeping the mountains on your left, then cross the third bridge. Buy domestic tickets at the station, international tickets at private bus kiosks around the station. To: Sofia (1 per day, US$9.50); Ohrid (7 per day, US$5.50); Bitola (10 per day, US$5); Tirana (1 per day, US$33).

Public transportation: Buy tokens for city buses from kiosks (15dn) or from the driver (30dn). Then stamp the token with the machine inside the bus.

Taxis: Taxis are relatively safe and reliable, and charge 12-15dn per km.

Luggage Storage: Garderoba (гардероба) in the bus station.

Laundromats: Do not exist in Macedonia. Bring a sink plug.

Pharmacy: A pharmacy in the shopping mall on the main square (tel. 23 77 47) sells sunblock and other useful items. Open Mon.-Fri. 7am-8pm, Sat. 8am-2pm.

Medical Assistance: Contact your hotel receptionist. The **General Hospital** is at 53 October 11th St. (tel. 22 11 33 or 21 12 30).

Emergencies: Police: 92. **Ambulance:** 94.

ACCOMMODATIONS

Accommodations are difficult to find and woefully overpriced in Skopje. Low-end hotel rooms run around US$70 per person. The tourist office offers **private rooms** for US$20, breakfast included.

Youth Hostel Skopje, Prolet 25 (Пролет; tel. 11 55 19 or 10 48 49, fax 23 50 29). From the train station, walk toward the river and take the second left onto Prolet to the big building with psychedelic murals. Friendly, English-speaking reception.

Beds in clean, 10-bed rooms for US$10.50 with HI membership, US$14.30 without. Half of the hostel functions as a **hotel**. Double rooms with private bath are US$32 with HI card. All prices include breakfast. The complex also includes a **travel agency** and **restaurant.** Get information about the nightlife in Skopje or update your HI membership here. Open year-round.

Student Dormitory K.J. Pitu (Пито), Ribar 58 (Рибар; tel. 11 60 27) is in the southwestern part of the city. Spartan rooms with communal showers US$7.70, with full board US$17.70. Open July 1-August 25.

Hotel Lackey (Хотел Лаки), 79 ul. Leninova (Ленинова; tel. 23 55 97 or 20 59 75), is in the southwest and one of Skopje's first **private hotels.** Apartment-style rooms (but with shared bath and TV room) US$16.70 per person. Sociable young people work in the restaurant downstairs and the variety of international guests who somehow make their way here take the pain out of the high prices.

FOOD

Goulashes, stuffed peppers, and grilled meats are peddled in the **Old Bazaar.**

Gostinitsa Tourist (Гостиница Турист), on the small square (tel. 22 90 07). For US$1.90 you can feast on a boiled head of lamb (eyeballs and brain included), or choose more mundane salads (US$1) and grills (US$3). Open daily 7am-until the last customer leaves.

Tree Yavora (Три Јавора), on the far end of the Old Bazaar at #77 Bit Pazarska (Бит Пазарска; (tel. 22 76 26). Delicious pizzas (US$3.60) and Greek salads (US$1.90) go well with the specialty of the house: *Izvara* (Извара), a tangy cheese spread served with freshly baked loaves of bread (US$1.60). Open Mon.-Sat. 9am-2am.

Dal Metu Bu (Дал Мету Бу), Across the river in the New Town (tel. 112 48 32). Imaginative pizzas, like the Indiana (tomato, cheese, chicken and curry sauce, US$3.50), and beef stroganoff (US$6.90) served in the huge and bright joint frequented by U.S. Marines. Open Mon.-Sat. 9am-11pm, Sun. 6-11:30pm.

SIGHTS AND ENTERTAINMENT

Most of Skopje's historical sights are an easy walk from the bus station: as you exit onto the main street, trot uphill 100m to find the 15th-century **Daut-pašin Amam** (Turkish bath; tel. 23 39 04), now an art gallery containing medieval icons, copies of frescoes, and models of medieval monasteries in Macedonia (open Sun.-Mon. 10am-3pm, Tues.-Sat. 8am-7pm). Entering the **Old Bazaar** from the baths, bear left up the main street to the **Church of Sveti Spas** (Свети Спас). Inside stands a masterful walnut iconostasis that required seven years to carve. Much of the church's interior is below ground level; churches were once prohibited from being higher than mosques. In the courtyard is the sarcophagus of revered revolutionary Goce Delčeu, who died in 1903. (The church is open Tues.-Sun. 7am-7pm.)

Farther up the hill, the **Mustafa Pašina džamija** (Mastafa Pasha Mosque) and the elegant **Kuršumli hon** (Turkish Inn) recall five centuries of Ottoman occupation. The inn is located in the former ironmongers' section of the bazaar, and has served various functions (inn, prison, museum) in the course of its history. Across from the inn gleams the recently renovated **Museum of Macedonia**, with archaeological, historical, and ethnological exhibits (open Tues.-Sun. 9am-5pm). The **Old Railway Station,** a monument to the disastrous earthquake of 1963, houses the **Skopje City Museum** (open Tues.-Sat. 9:30am-5pm, Sun. 9:30am-3pm). The 6th-century **stone bridge** connecting the Old and New sections of Skopje was one of the few structures to survive the earthquake. Until recently, each street of the **Old Bazaar** represented a particular handicraft: tanners, goldsmiths, and potters competed with one another in their isolated zones. Though the bazaar is now touristy, the narrow lanes are still a fascinating place in which to get lost.

Party-hungry Skopjans gather at bars in the central mall to bar- and disco-hop until the wee hours. Popular open-air discos **Tequila, Havana,** and **Met** are in the park on Ilindenska (Илинденска). No cover (open at midnight). A younger set frequents the **Copacabana** disco in the space-age City Cultural Center (music starts at 8pm).

F.Y.R. MACEDONIA

Eight kilometers northwest of Skopje is the archaeological site **Skupi.** In 518, the Roman town of Skupi was destroyed by an earthquake and the refugees from the town moved on to found Skopje. No public transportation runs to the site; to visit it, make arrangements for a tour at the City Museum or tourist office.

■■■ BITOLA (БИТОЛА)

Between the Baba and Nidže Mountains, **Bitola** lies 180km south of Skopje. Macedonia's second-largest city, an easy daytrip from Skopje or Ohrid, is of interest principally for its archaeological ruins. Once a major stop on the Roman road *Via Egnatia* that connected the Adriatic and the Aegean coastal towns, Bitola today seems to be caught between the times. Ancient mosques mingle with shiny, black glass banking buildings; ABBA-filled discos surround centuries-old ruins.

Ruins of the ancient city of **Heraclea Lyncestis** (4th-century BC to 6th century AD) lie near the center of town. The foundations of many ancient buildings, including Roman theatre and baths, and numerous marble sculptures have been unearthed since the 1950s. Heraclea was an episcopal seat at the beginning of the millennium; two basilicas and the episcopal palace have survived, their resplendent floor mosaics intact. From the train/bus station, walk to the main road and make a left; it's a 10-minute walk (open dawn-dusk; admission US$2.40). The **Archaeological Museum** is opposite an odd-looking white fountain at the start of ul. Gotse Delchev (tel. 353 87) and often attracts interesting exhibitions (open Tues.-Sun. 10am-noon and 5-9pm; admission 30dn). A few blocks to the right of the old covered market is the century-old **Old Bazaar.** The **Clock Tower** dates back to the 17th century. The **Deboj** and **Ajdar-Qadi Mosques** are still active, and the 1830 **St. Dimitrija Cathedral** is one of the largest Orthodox churches in the Balkans.

There is a **cinema** in the House of Culture, across from the Epinal Hotel in the main square. An olympic-size **swimming pool** beckons in the park near the bus station (50dn). At night, hike up the hill called **Tumba Café** (Тумба Кафе) to dance until dawn at the open-air **Koloseum Disco/restaurant.** Arrange a ride back down the hill as the path isn't marked or lit (open late May-late Sept. 11pm-dawn).

Putnik Tours, 77 Gotse Delchev, has old maps of the city (open Mon.-Sat. 8am-5pm). From Skopje, there are 10 daily **buses** (one way US$5) and six **trains** (one way US$3.50). From Ohrid there are 10 daily buses (1½hrs., one way US$5). The train and bus stations are located across from each other, a 10-minute walk from the town center. Neither has luggage storage. To get to the center, follow the main road opposite the train station, and make a right to **ul. Gotse Delchev** (Гоце Делчев), formerly Marshal Tito. This main drag is lined with **exchange bureaus.** The Stopanska Bank is farther up, to the right at Radoslavevik 17 (Радославьевик; open Mon.-Fri. 7am-7pm). Around the corner at Ruzveltova 1 (Рузвелтова) is the **post office** (open Mon.-Fri. 7am-7pm). Make international **phone** calls or send **faxes** (fax 333 61) here daily 7am-8pm.

A reason to keep Bitola to a day trip is its dearth of accommodations. The only hotel currently open is **Epinal,** Ruzveltova 55 (tel. 247 77, fax 247 78), on the main square. Unremarkable singles are a whopping US$33. Doubles US$60. There is no private room bureau. Bitola does offer many epicurean options, especially along the main pedestrian walkway. On Gotse Delchev, try **Korzo** (Корзо), a huge indoor-outdoor complex set far back off the square among trees and a small man-made moat. Savor famous Ohrid trout for US$10 or try any of the grills (US$5). The fatty and entrail-filled soups are not tempting. **Fontana Beni** (Фонтана Бени), known as *Kayh Kuburot* (Кај Кубурот) is in the *Bezisten,* the yellow building between the mosques in the city center (tel. 246 55); it was a covered marketplace between the 16th and 19th centuries. The specialty of the house is *bistrichka zhelka,* a pork filet stuffed with cheese, veggies, and meats and shaped like a squirrel (US$6; open daily 7am-10pm).

■■■ LAKE OHRID (ОХРИД)

Four million years ago, a few restless tectonic plates lambadad, and a world treasure was born. The 349 square kilometers of Lake Ohrid's crystal clear water fill a breathtaking, mountain-ringed basin, 693 meters above sea level. Roughly one third of the lake belongs to Albania. One of the world's oldest lakes, it is suspected that Ohrid dates from the same period as Tanganyika in Africa and Titicaca in South America. Like the world's deepest lake, Lake Baikal in Siberia, Ohrid was formed by a rare vertical sinking of land; the two are home to similar flora and fauna, not found elsewhere on earth.

The azure waters of Ohrid are surrounded by tranquil beaches, inexpensive accommodations, and storied Byzantine churches. Under the Romans, the lakeside town of Ohrid became an important stop on the *Via Egnatia*, the road to Constantinople. Slavs settled the area in the 6th century and renamed it as they saw it: *vo hrid* (on a hill). Clement, a disciple of the missionary brothers Cyril and Methodious of Salonica, came to Ohrid in 886 and set up a university at Sveti Pantelejmon in 893, nearly 200 years before the University of Bologna first sent out acceptance slips. The 3500 alumni of this school spread the Slavonic script and culture across the Slavic lands as far as Kiev.

The *letnica* trout, found only in Lake Ohrid, commands high prices in restaurants throughout Macedonia. The lake is also famous for the *Ohridski biser* (Охридски Бисер; pearl), that can be picked up at any of the many bazaars and jewelry shops in Ohrid Town. On rainy days, you can lose yourself in the narrow, winding streets of the Old Town, still unsullied by cars. Once in a while, you'll run into a horse and buggy plodding its way up a steep hill, or the blood of a slaughtered pig mixing with the rain and trickling down the cobblestone streets.

Orientation and Practical Information   To get to the center from the bus station, make a right onto Partizanska. The stunning orange-roofed white houses on the hill are the Old Town. At the foot of the hill is the pedestrian walkway, **Sveti Kliment Ohridski,** (Климент Охридски) Ohrid's main street. **Tourist bureau Bilyana** (Билјана) is next to the Ohrid bus station at Parizanska 3 (Партизанска; tel. 224 94, fax 241 14). The friendly, English-speaking staff find **private rooms** (US$10 per person) and provide new town **maps** (open daily 7am-9pm; winter Mon.-Fri. 7am-9pm, Sat. 7am-2pm). The **post office** is off the main street and contains an exchange bureau (open Mon.-Sat. 7am-9pm). The **postal code** is 96000. **Telephones** are in the post office (open daily 7am-9pm). You can also send and receive **faxes** (fax 322 15) during the same hours. The **telephone city code** is 096. **Buses** connect Ohrid with Skopje (7 per day, US$5.50). The quickest route (3½ hrs.) is via Kičevo; the longer western route (4½ hrs.) winds its way through picturesque mountains, but seems to take forever and is not recommended. **Exchange money** at the Stopanska Banka at 110 Kliment Ohridski (tel. 314 00); they also cash AmEx traveler's checks. Bring lots of deutschmarks; you'll have trouble getting rid of other currencies, even U.S. dollars (open Mon.-Sat. 8am-8pm, Sun. 7am-1pm). **Store luggage** at the bus station. Toward the lake at 8 Tsar Samuil (Цар Самоил) is a surprisingly Western **pharmacy** (tel./fax 216 33) that sells sunblock, antioxidents, and garlic tablets; it also functions as a private **polyclinic** and has a **dentist** on duty (open daily 8am-10pm; call for off-hours treatment). Also on the main drag is the **drugstore** Letnitsa (Драгстор Летница). All the kiosks in town sell *Time* and *Newsweek*.

Accommodations and Camping   Travelers getting off the bus in Ohrid are bombarded by offers of **private rooms.** The rates are good (US$5.30-6.66), almost evil, but lower-end offers usually don't include the US$2 fee for registration with the authorities. Find out where the room is located and what exactly is included; then bargain the price down. The shy can shun the madness at the **tourist bureau** (rooms US$10). The town's two **youth hostels** are out of the way and overpriced. **Hostel Magnus** (Магнус; tel. 216 71, fax 322 14) works as a hotel. (No lockout. Singles US$16 per person, US$21.33 without HI card. All meals included. Open year-round; 20% off-season discount.) **Hostel Mladost** (Младост; tel. 216 26) is a campground with bungalows. (No lockout. Rooms US$9.14 per person. All meals included. Open July1-Aug. 25.) The hostels are next to each other and share the same facilities: a private beach, basketball court, beach volleyball, restaurants, cafés, and a disco. Take any Ohrid Struga (Струга) bus, leaving every 30 minutes from the bus station (30dn). Tell the driver to stop at Mladost.

Food　A **mini-market** sells beer, soda, snacks, and big tubs of ice cream on Sveti Kliment Ohridski (open daily 7am-11pm). You can savor rare Lake Ohrid trout (US$6) at **Restaurant Letnica,** across from the bus station. Cheerful waitresses keep the self-serve section spotless and efficient (open daily 6am-10pm). **Pizzeria Costa Nostra,** on the other side of Letnica, offers 24 different kinds of pizza, including *Costa Nostra,* a concoction of sauce, ham, cheese, mushrooms, bacon, eggs, mayonnaise, cream cheese, olives, and sausage (large 180dn). For less daring palates, they also serve lasagna and cheese pizza (open 9am-2am.) Locals drink and enjoy live folk music at the beautifully restored **Restaurant Antico** at Tsar Samuil 36. It resembles a stone castle. Menu in English (open daily 10am-midnight).

Sights and Entertainment　**Sveta Sofija,** Ohrid's oldest church, dates from the 9th century; facing the lake, make a right onto Tsar Samuil and follow the signs (open Tues.-Sun. 9am-1pm and 4-8pm). Performances of the **Festival Ohridsko Leto** (July-Aug.) and the **Balkan Folklore Festival** (mid-July) are held with the church as a backdrop. Up the hill from Sv. Sofija along Ilindenska is the fabulous church of **Sveti Kliment;** its 600-year-old frescoes are in superb condition. You can buy posters of these at the tourist bureau. Across from the church is the **Icon Gallery,** with works spanning seven centuries, including depictions of Stoic saints enduring torture by horrid beasties (open Tues.-Sun. 9am-1pm and 4-8pm). Again from Sveti Sofija, mount the steps behind the stage to Kosta Racin and walk along the lip of the cliff to the 13th-century **Church of Sveti Jovan,** almost too perfect to be real. Sunsets viewed from the hill are sure to please.

There are several **souvenir shops** along the main street, and many artists with card tables display hand-made jewelry made with the famed Ohrid pearls. The pedestrian walkway leads into a **flea market** where you can buy a cheap pair of flip-flops (good for Lake Ohrid's often-rocky bottom). Farther down is an overflowing **farmer's market.** The rocky shore near Ohrid leaves something to be desired. The best **beach** in the area is **Gradište** (Градиште). It has sandy man-made beaches, crystal-clear water, and hot nightlife.

The exquisitely adorned 10th-century monastery of **Sveti Naum** (Свети Наум) is 28km south along the lake from Ohrid. Take any bus to Gradište (Градиште; 9 per day, 60dn). Tell the driver you want to get off at Sveti Naum. Try to make a Sunday morning service, or arrive on the night of July 2, the eve of the saint's carnival.

■ NEAR LAKE OHRID

About 40km from Ohrid Town is a smaller lake and the resort town **Prespa.** Take any of the 12 daily buses to Bitola (битола) and get off in **Resen** (Ресен). From Resen, take one of the hourly buses to Prespa. Among the expensive resort hotels in Prespa is the **youth hostel Pretor (HI;** tel. 500 27). Reception speaks some English. No lockout. Wooden bungalows with outside bath US$8 per person, all meals included. There's a 20% surcharge for non-HI members (open July 1-Aug. 25).

The museum town of **Struga** (Струга) lies 15km northeast of Ohrid town on Ohrid Lake. Every year in the second half of August the picturesque town hosts the **Struga Poetry Evenings:** poets from around the world gather here to read their works from the bridge under which the River Crni Drim flows out of Lake Ohrid. Buses from Ohrid to Struga run every 20min. (35dn).

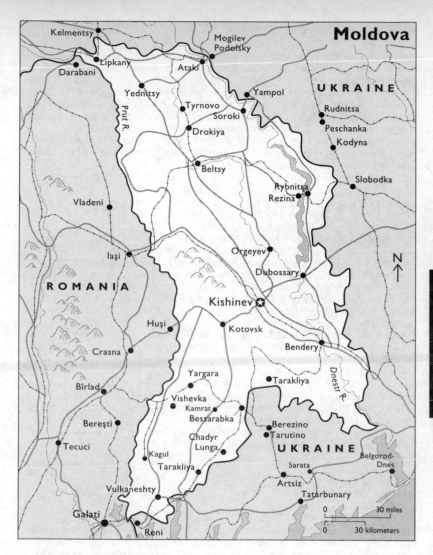

MOLDOVA

US$1   = 4.05 lei (or leu)
CDN$1 = 2.97 lei
UK£1 = 6.36 lei
IR£1   = 6.24 lei
AUS$1 = 3.02 lei
NZ$1 = 2.20 lei
SAR1 = 1.14 lei
DM1   = 2.64 lei
Country Code: 373

1 lei =   US$0.25
1 lei = CDN$0.34
1 lei =   UK£0.16
1 lei =   IR£0.16
1 lei = AUS$0.33
1 lei =   NZ$0.45
1 lei =   SAR0.87
1 lei =   DM0.38
International Dialing Prefix: 00

Moldova is a bit like chocolate cake—everybody wants a bite. The "last bastion of healthy communist order" survives in the breakaway "Dniester Republic" on the Russian-controlled left bank of the Dniester River. The south, dominated by the *Gagauz* (Christian Turks) has also effectively seceded. Seventy percent of Moldova's land and people are on the right bank of the Dniester River and they are mostly ethnic Romanians. Yet, the Republic of Moldova is one of few European countries to define itself as a multi-ethnic entity and not as a one-nation state.

Western tourists are rare in Moldova, and Moldovans are shy towards foreigners. Most people will be surprised by your presence—some will be eager to talk and a few may try to rip you off.

MOLDOVA ESSENTIALS

Citizens of Australia, Canada, Ireland, New Zealand, South Africa, the U.K., and the U.S. need visas to enter Moldova. Single-entry visas (valid 1 month) are US$40 (U.S. citizens pay US$30), multiple-entry visas are US$80-270 (valid 1-12 months; U.S. citizens pay US$80-180), and transit visas are US$25 (or US$50 for a double) Regular service takes five days. Rush service is also available and requires an additional US$20. For those who need visas, invitations are a must. For more information, contact the appropriate diplomatic office in your country of residence—see Essentials: Embassies and Consulates, page 3.

Trains connect Chişinău to Iaşi and Bucureşti in Romania, Kiev and Odessa in Ukraine, and many other former USSR cities (many via Kiev). Buses run in many directions, including İstanbul (via Romania).

The **monetary unit,** the **lei,** is worth 100 *bani* (often called by its diminutive form, *bănuţi or bănişori).* Do not confuse the Moldovan lei with the Romanian currency of the same name. 1000 Romanian lei = 2.21 Moldovan lei.

AT&T USADirect and similar **telephone** services are not yet available. In terms of **tongues,** Almost everybody speaks Romanian and Russian; some, but not many, speak English. Most signs are bilingual (Romanian-Russian). Some Russians may refuse to answer if addressed in Romanian.

LIFE AND TIMES

HISTORY

The borders of present-day Moldova overlap (approximately) those of the region known historically as Bessarabia. The Volokh, ancestors of ethnic Moldovans, migrated east to the region from the Carpathian Mountains; there they formed an independent principality in 1359. Soon after, Bessarabia was annexed by its neighbor to the west (also known, confusingly, as Moldova). In the second half of the 15th century, Stefan the Great expanded Moldova's frontiers, pushing back Poles to the north and Turks to the south, and defeating Vlad the Impaler (a.k.a. Dracula), ruler of Wallachia. The Turks got their revenge, though, extracting tribute from Stefan's son, Bogdan the One-Eyed.

For the next three centuries, Moldova was torn apart by greedy neighbors—Russia, Transylvania, Poland, Wallachia, and Turkey. Russia seized Bessarabia from the Turks over and over again, only to lose its grip within a few years. Finally, in 1812, Turkey handed the region over to Russia. The Christian Bessarabian peasants were faced with a tough choice: submit to serfdom under Russian rule, or flee west to pagan Turkish lands? Many chose heresy over slavery and fled west across the Prut river—only to be executed by the Turks as suspected carriers of the plague.

Bessarabia's new rulers attempted to Russify the region's civil and religious institutions, but most peasants remained illiterate and culturally more similar to Romania.

Despite tensions between Moldovans and their Russian rulers, Bessarabia prospered under Moscow's authority; Bessarabia's agricultural produce found a hungry market in the Russian empire. The birth of Romania as a nearby autonomous kingdom (1881) fueled a smoldering Moldovan nationalist sentiment in Bessarabia. A quarter-century later, resentment erupted in a full-fledged nationalist movement following the Russian Revolution of 1905.

Although Moldovans fought alongside Russians in World War I, separatist sentiment remained strong; in early 1917, Bessarabia declared itself an independent Moldovan republic. The Bolsheviks reacted by invading the region, but Moldovan forces were able to drive them out with Romanian help. Alarmed by the power of the German-sponsored government in nearby Ukraine, the new Moldovan state decided to unite itself with Romania in 1920. Frustrated, the Soviets decided to create their own pseudo-Moldova; in 1924, Moscow set up another tiny "Moldovan" state on Ukranian territory, right across the Dniester river from the "real" Moldova. Meanwhile, Moldova languished under Romanian control; Moldova's export crops and railroad infrastructure were all geared toward Russia, not Romania, and the region's economy stagnated.

In 1939, the Soviets invaded once again. They united "traditional" Moldova (central Bessarabia) with the miniscule Communist "Moldova" (in the Ukraine); the final conglomerate included territory on both sides of the Dniester river. The Red Army expropriated Moldovan lands and expelled the German population. During most of World War II, Romania occupied the region as Germany's ally. Romania killed or deported many Bessarabian Jews, resettling the region with Romanian peasants.

By 1944, the Soviets had retaken the region. Moscow reintegrated the war-torn area into the Soviet empire as the Moldovan Soviet Socialist Republic. Under Communist rule, the Moldovan S.S.R. was radically collectivized and industrialized. Any kind of autonomous "Moldovan" culture or society was stamped out, and the republic was thoroughly Russified. In the late 1980s, a new spirit of openness allowed open public debate to resume in Moldova. On August 27, 1991, amid political chaos in Moscow, the republic declared independence.

MOLDOVA TODAY

Unlike the Baltic States, Moldova has taken a benevolent stand with respect to its ethnic minorities and permits citizenship for all residents. "Moldovan" was declared the official language, but minority languages are fully tolerated.

Romanians call the republic of Moldova *Basarabia* to distinguish it from Romanian Moldova. Even now, 65% of the population is Romanian, despite the severe denationalization campaign led by Moscow: a separate Moldovan language was created as Romanian was rewritten using the Cyrillic characters, and Romanian history was taboo. Along with Gorbachev's reforms came a powerful nationalistic movement; they succeeded in gathering 600,000 people at a meeting in the capital, Kishinev (Chişinău), and forced the Communist leaders to return to the Latin alphabet and select the same national flag and hymn as Romania. National symbols replaced Communist ones.

The "Dniester Republic," backed by Russian ultra-nationalists, declared independence from Kishinev in September 1990, spurred by the prospect of Moldovan union with Romania. It is the last remaining region in Eastern Europe favoring Soviet-style socialism and a return to Russian control. Dneister commandos played an enthusiastic role in the rebellion in Moscow in October 1993. Although armed conflicts around the city of Tiraspol claimed several lives, things have quietened since Moldova joined the CIS and promised it would not unite with Romania.

The incumbent former-Communist government claims to lead politics of independence from both Romania and Russia; however, they decided to join the CIS—reentering, many fear, the Russian sphere of influence. Economic reforms have still to come and things haven't changed a lot since the days of the Soviet Union. Reading the Russia Essentials may help you here.

■ Kishinev (Chişinău)

The capital of Moldova, Chişinău has 700,000 inhabitants, and it looks the way you would expect: like a Soviet provincial city. It is built in a rectangular grid, with large distances and concrete monsters on a Stalinist scale; yet, there are glimpses of its better past in the many Neoclassical mansions along the main street. As a sign that "the times they are-a-changing," a statue of Romanian prince and national hero Ştefan cel Mare has replaced one of Lenin, and the main street is now called Bd. Ştefan, instead of prospekt Lenina. Most streets have changed their names from Soviet to Romanian figures; apart from that, there are not many signs of incoming capitalism or freedom. It seems the shadow of Lenin is still floating above the town.

ORIENTATION AND PRACTICAL INFORMATION

There is a daily train covering Bucureşti-Iaşi-Chişinău; trains from Sofia to Moscow also pass on this route. The trip Iaşi-Chişinău takes about 6hrs., of which only about 2hrs. are spent in motion; the rest is taken by the tantalizingly slow border controls and changing of train wheels (since Russian rail tracks are of a larger gauge than other European ones); if you haven't seen it before, it's cool. Trains typically leave Iaşi around 2am; prepare for a sleepless night (even though you get a couchette, the border controls will wake you up). Border guards are rather suspicious and will probably open your luggage. All in all, not a very pleasant trip, but it can be interesting. There are also buses between Iaşi and Chişinău, leaving at more convenient hours, but they have other drawbacks. Inquire at the bus station.

From the train station, walk up the park in front, then turn right, walk up to hotel Cosmos, then turn left on **Bd. Negruzzi;** after a few hundred yards, it turns right slightly and becomes **Bd. Ştefan cel Mare.** This seemingly endless boulevard spans the city from southeast to northwest; most interesting sights are clustered around it. Most of the trolleys near the train station travel along it.

Tourist Office: Moldovatur (formerly Intourist), at Hotel Naţional, Bd. Ştefan cel Mare 4 (tel. 26 65 64 or 26 25 98). From the hotel lobby, go right, climb the stairway to the second floor, enter the dark corridor, and knock on and enter the last door on the left (marked *Ghizi Interpreţi*). Friendly staff speaks major European languages and can answer questions. Hotel reservations, car rentals (see below), and maps (older ones are useless due to street names changes; open 9am-5pm).

Budget Travel: Sputnik, Str. Malina Mare 7, two blocks west of Hotel Cosmos.

Embassies: U.S., Str. Alexe Mateevici 4 (formerly Livezilor, tel. 23 34 76; fax 23 30 44), near the university. Take trolley #9 or 10 from the center.

Currency Exchange: This is one of the few businesses booming in Chişinău. There are exchange booths everywhere; rates vary. Everybody accepts Deutschmarks and U.S. dollars. Romanian lei can be exchanged, but at disadvantageous rates compared to western currencies. Exchanging traveler's checks is difficult. Black market sharks are common, but take care: it's better to have receipts for all currency exchanged to tame nasty customs officials (who make you declare all the money you're carrying when you enter the country).

Telephones: On Bd. Ştefan cel Mare, two blocks up from Hotel Naţional (open Mon.-Sat. 8am-10pm). The **telephone city code** varies depending on where you're calling from. Calling internationally, dial 3732; from Romania, it's like a domestic call: dial 022.

Flights: The airport is 12km from downtown (tel. 52 54 12); take bus #65 from the railway station. The **Air Moldova** agency is on Bd. Negruzzi 8, near Hotel Naţional (for domestic flights tel. 26 40 09, for international flights tel. 26 13 98). Flights to Vienna, Frankfurt, and İstanbul.

Trains: The station is rather disorderly (tel. 25 27 35). You can buy international tickets at the Intourist booth on the 2nd floor, but they'll overcharge you (i.e. Chişinău-Iaşi US$7 one way); it's much cheaper to buy a round-trip ticket in

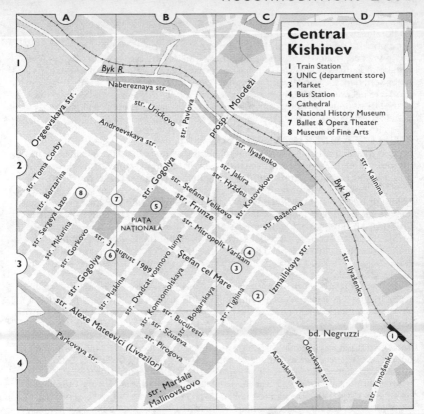

Central Kishinev

1 Train Station
2 UNIC (department store)
3 Market
4 Bus Station
5 Cathedral
6 National History Museum
7 Ballet & Opera Theater
8 Museum of Fine Arts

MOLDOVA

Romania (Iași-Chișinău US$4 round-trip). However, you will have to specify in advance which train you'll be taking back. To enter the quai, you'll have to show your ticket or pay a 25bani entry fee.

Buses: The main bus station is at Str. Mitropolit Varlaam 58, one block to the right of the main street (tel. 22 26 11).

Public Transportation: Extensive trolley system; buy tickets (15 bani each) on the bus, from the driver, or in the stations. Once on board, validate your ticket; if it's too crowded, ask your neighbor to do it. Posters warn that fines for not having a ticket are up to 15% of the "minimum salary"—hopefully not an American one!

Car Rental: At the tourist office; driver included and mandatory. US$0.35 per km.

ACCOMMODATIONS

Coopertiva Adresa, Bd. Negruzzi 1 across from hotel Cosmos (tel. 26 64 14) rents **private rooms** for 9lei per person (open Mon.-Sat. 9am-9pm, Sun. 9am-6pm). Though not as cheap, hotels remain affordable. **Hotel Cosmos** (tel. 26 44 57) charges 75lei for singles and 85lei for doubles. One block up, **Hotel Național** (formerly an Intourist facility) charges 84lei for singles and 130lei for doubles (discounts for Romanian and CIS citizens). Besides being cheaper, Cosmos is the hang-out of many Americans. The rooms are similar, typical of cozy Soviet hotels with slightly dingy bathrooms.

FOOD

Finding good and cheap food can be a problem. Try the **marketplace** right of the main street. One of the best restaurants in town is **Belluno,** on the main street, serving so-called Moldo-Italian cuisine; meals can easily reach US$15 here. You can also try hotel restaurants, or the so-called national restaurants—but they might be a disappointment. **Restaurant Butoiaş** ("Little Barrel") is located at the northern end of the town; take trolley #11 to the last stop and look for the big barrel on the left. The restaurant is inside the barrel and has ambiance, but unfortunately it doesn't have too much food: the choices are often soup, pork, or chicken. But for only US$3 you can have decent chicken, bread, and mineral water *"Răcoarea Codrilor"* ("Coolness of the woods"), synthetically produced at a Chişinău experimental plant (open noon-4pm and 6pm-midnight).

SIGHTS AND ENTERTAINMENT

It's easy to tour most of the monuments in Chişinău; just wall up Bd. Ştefan cel Mare. In front of Hotel Cosmos, the first statue you will see represents **Kotovski:** a sort of Robin Hood for Soviet apparatchiks, a bandit for Romanians. In the 1920s, he attacked Romania in flash raids from across the Nistru. Not as dramatic as Lenin's accomplishments, but unlike Lenin, Kotovski's statue is still up. Further up on the left rise the deep blue towers of the **Cioflea church,** perhaps the most beautiful in Chişinău. All along the main boulevard, Stalinist blocks and neo-Classical buildings compete for attention. A few blocks up on the left are the Corinthian columns and orange façade of the **National Theatre.** Near it, two gentle lions guard the **Organ Hall;** check the board for concert schedules. A flag crowns the small tower of the nearby **City Hall.**

On the right of **Piaţa Naţională** (the main square) is a triumphal arch, raised in 1846; behind it lie a **park** and the temple-like **cathedral,** badly in need of restoration. On the upper left corner of the square is the statue of the legendary **Ştefan cel Mare** (Stephen the Great). The statue was made in 1928, moved to-and-fro during World War II to avoid the Bolsheviks until it finally fell into their hands in 1945. Its inscriptions were then modified. In 1972, it was moved to a hidden place inside the park, but the 1990 national revival finally brought it back to its initial place. The park also contains an alley with statues from the classics of Romanian literature.

Several other monuments lie around the city. The **National History Museum** is on str. 31 august 1989 (parallel to the main street), near Piaţa Naţională. The history section has several interesting exhibits such as of 16th-century books, but explanations are only in Romanian and Russian. The religious painting exhibition is definitely worth seeing; it has a beautiful 17th-century Last Judgment, among others. In the basement, the Treasury features old coins, medals, watches, and jewelry (open Tues.-Sun. 10am-6pm; admission 50bani, students 20 bani; separate admission to the treasury). In front of the museum, the statue of a she-wolf feeding the two founders of Rome, Remus and Romulus, stands as a reminder of Moldova's Latin ancestors.

About five blocks left of the main street is the central park, with a lake. Nearby is the **university;** students hang out here, and many speak English. If you're in the mood for something a little different, try shopping at one of the **department stores. UNIC** (formerly GUM) is on Bd. Ştefan cel Mare, one block up from Hotel Naţional. **Lumea Copiilor** (Children's World) is four blocks up from UNIC. Neither is anywhere close to western standards. For souvenirs, try **Samovar** or **Fondul Artei Plastice,** on opposite sides of the street close to Hotel Naţional. The latter also has several cool temporary exhibitions.

POLAND (POLSKA)

US$1 = 23,200zł (złoty, or PLZ)	1000zł =	US$0.43
CDN$1= 17,000zł	1000zł =	CDN$0.59
UK£1 = 36,500zł	1000zł =	UK£0.27
IR£1 = 25,800zł	1000zł =	IR£0.28
AUS$1 = 17,300zł	1000zł =	AUS$0.58
NZ$1 = 12,600zł	1000zł =	NZ$0.79
SAR1 = 6550zł	1000zł =	SAR1.53
DM1 = 15,130zł	1000zł =	DM0.66
Country Code: 48	International Dialing Prefix: 00	

From the amber-strewn shores of the Baltic in the north to the snow-capped peaks of the Tatra range in the south, Poland is shaking off the remnants of half a century of Communism and is reclaiming its heritage as one of the world's oldest democracies. Struggle has been a way of life for Poles who have enjoyed only 26 years of freedom in this century; they have drawn their strength from the Catholic Church and a rich intellectual tradition. Memories of World War II linger, but a new, headstrong generation is emerging, determined to rebuild the country in its own image.

POLAND ESSENTIALS

Citizens of the U.S. and Ireland do not require a visa to visit Poland for up to 90 days, nor do citizens of the U.K. for stays of up to 6 months. Citizens of Australia, Canada, New Zealand, and South Africa need visas. Single-entry visas (valid for 3 months) cost US$32 (students US$24; Canadians US$50, Can. students US$38); two-entry visas cost US$60 (students US$45; Canadians US$95, Can. students US$72), three-entry visas cost US$88 (students US$65; Canadians US$140, Can. students US$105); four-entry visas cost US$116 (students US$87; Canadians US$186, Can. students US$139); and multiple-entry visas cost US$135 (students US$101; Canadians US$210, Can. students US$153). Transit visas (valid 48hrs.) cost US$16 (students US$12; Canadians US$25, Can. students US$19). A visa application requires a valid passport, two photographs, and payment by money order, traveler's check, certified check, cashier's check, or cash. It is also possible to apply by mail. Regular service takes up to 14 days; rush service (24 hrs.) costs US$17 extra. For more information, contact the Polish Embassies and Consulates listed on page 3.

GETTING THERE

By Ferry

Polferries runs ships from Ystad, **Sweden** or Copenhagen, **Denmark** to **Świnouj-ście** in northeast Poland; and from Öxelösund, **Sweden** or Helsinki, **Finland** to **Gdańsk**. The owner, **Polish Baltic Shipping Co.**, is at ul. Portowa 41, PL 78-100 Kołobrzeg (tel. (965) 252 11, fax (965) 266 12). To make reservations or purchase tickets in advance, contact Polferries's agents abroad:

Sweden: Pol-Line AB, Färjeterminalen, Ystad (tel. (0411) 160 10, fax 169 22) or Oxelösunds Färjeterminal, Oxelösund (tel. (0155) 781 00, fax 331 00).
Finland: Puolan Laivamtkat, Lutherinkatu 12, Helsinki (tel. (044) 54 48, fax 58 48).
Denmark: Vindrose Rejser, Nordre Toldbod 12A, Copenhagen (tel. (045) 33 11 46 45, fax 33 11 95 78).
Germany: Darpol GmbH, Kaiser-Fridrich-St. 19, Berlin, Charlottenburg (tel. (030) 342 00 74, fax 342 24 72).
Great Britain: Gdynia America Shipping lines Ltd., 238 City Road, London (tel. (0171) 251 33 89, fax 250 36 25).
Austria: Universal Reisen G.m.b.H, at Schubertring 9, Vienna (tel. (01) 73 63 48 or 73 63 49).
France: Office du Tourisme Polonais at 49 Avenue de l'Opera, Paris (tel. (00331) 47 42 07 72, fax 49 24 94 36).

By Train or Bus

Poland is a tiresome train trip from Berlin (3hrs.), Prague or Budapest. The Lithuanian road border is open; bus and train travel to Lviv in Ukraine is quick if you can snag a visa and a seat, and trains run to St. Petersburg and Moscow from Warsaw. To Slovakia, cross by bus or foot through the Tatra Mountains from Zakopane or by train from Kraków to Prešov and Košice. There are six road crossings to Slovakia in the Podhale region—Chyżne, Piwniczna, Łysa Polana, Chochołów, Niedzica, Konieczna—and one train crossing, in Muszyna. Chyżne is mobbed in summer; 6000 cars and buses line up on an average day. Chyżne and Konieczna are open 24 hrs.; Chochołów and Niedzica are restricted to Poles and Slovaks.

GETTING AROUND POLAND

By Train

PKP trains scurry to most towns; although prices have dramatically increased, Westerners will hardly notice. International train tickets can only be purchased with złoty. ISIC cardholders get 25% off international fares through ALMATUR, but only for the Polish portion of the trip. ALMATUR sells **Interrail** passes and, for those under 26, **Wasteels** discount tickets and **Eurotrain passes** that offer 40% discounts on trains between European cities. Discount tickets for those under 26 are also sold at major train stations and ORBIS offices.

Train stations have large boards with alphabetical listings of towns, and posters with chronological listings of trains. *Odjazdy* (departures) are in yellow; *przyjazdy* (arrivals) in white. *Ekspresowy* (express) trains are listed in red with an "Ex" in front of the train number. *Pośpieszny* (direct trains, listed in red without the "Ex"), chug along almost as fast. *Osobowy* trains (listed in black) are the slowest and cheapest— about 35% less. Once you know which train you want, note the *peron* (platform) number, write down the destination, type of train, date, and time; then hand the information to the clerk. All *ekspresowy* and some *pośpieszny* trains require seat reservations; if you see a boxed R on the schedule, ask the clerk for a *miejscówka* (30,000zł). A *bilet* (BEE-let, ticket) in *pierwsza klasa* (1st class) is 50% more and worth it for overnights—the seats fold back all the way. Buy your ticket aboard the train for a small surcharge, but find the *konduktor* (conductor) before he finds you or risk an outrageous 900,000zł fine. Train tickets are only valid on the day of issue.

By Bus, Plane, and Thumb

PKS buses are cheapest and fastest for short excursions. Purchase advance tickets at the bus station. In the countryside, PKS markers (like yellow Mercedes-Benz symbols) indicate bus stops, but drivers will often halt wherever you flag them down. The domestic airline, **LOT**, gives students under 26 a 25% discount.

Although legal throughout the country, **hitching** is becoming increasingly dangerous for foreigners; *Let's Go* does not recommend hitchhiking as a safe means of transportation. Hand-waving, not an outstretched thumb, is the accepted sign. The Polish government-sponsored *Autostop Hitchhike Book*, sold by PTTK for 40,000zł (valid May-Sept.), includes an insurance policy, an ID card, a tourist information book, and vouchers that qualify drivers for prizes and compensation.

Urban Transportation

City public transportation (*komunikacja miejska*) is cheap and efficient. Buy tickets from any Ruch kiosk, and punch your ticket (*bilet*) on board. Technically, only Polish students can ride for the lower *ulgowy* fare; if caught by the conductor, you will be fined 250,000zł. In most cities, trams stop running as early as 10pm.

Taxis will probably rip you off. Search out official vehicles with the city coat-of-arms on the door. It is generally cheaper to use one of the Radio Taxi services available in most cities—919 is the country-wide telephone number, but local newspapers publish the telephone numbers of various taxi companies. When you get in the taxi, always check if the meter is turned on. You will be asked to pay for the driver's return trip if you travel outside the city. At night, taxi-drivers use a different meter; it should say "2" on the left side and increases fares by 50%. It is not safe to accept rides from private car owners, even though they might cost less.

TOURIST SERVICES

ORBIS is the Polish state travel bureau, with offices in most major hotels and elsewhere in major cities. They sell international (*międzynarodowe*) and domestic (*krajowe*) train tickets and international bus tickets. **ALMATUR,** the Polish student travel organization, sells ISIC and Eurotrain passes, and can help find university dorm rooms in summer. Both provide maps and brochures, as do **PTTK** and **IT** (Tourist Information) bureaus, on the main street of every town. Since 1989, **private tourist agencies** have mushroomed all over Poland; their prices are often more competitive than those of ORBIS, but watch out for scams.

Shopping hours vary; supermarkets and department stores are usually open from 9am to 8pm, small shops from 11am to 7pm, and grocery stores from 6am to 6pm or 7pm. Privatization has brightened shops, filled shelves, and banished sourpuss clerks. Foreign-made goods (at very western prices) often outnumber local products in stores. **Outdoor markets** swarm at the feet of larger suburban apartment blocks; you can haggle for everything from Russian watches to Harvard t-shirts.

Legal **holidays** include New Year's Day, Easter Monday, Labor Day (May 1), Constitution Day (May 3), Corpus Christi (variable; a Thursday in May or June), Ascension Day (Aug. 15), All Saints' Day (Nov. 1), National Independence Day (Nov. 11), and Christmas (Dec. 25-26). **Museum hours** are Tues.-Sun. 10am-4pm. Museums ordinarily close the day after a holiday as well.

MONEY

The Polish **złoty** (zwoh-tee) is convertible but not widely traded in the West. Change back your currency before leaving. For cash, *kantor* offices (private exchange counters) offer marginally better rates than banks or hotels. **Bank PKO S.A.** exchanges traveler's checks and gives VISA/MC cash advances at branch offices all over Poland. **Banking hours** are Mon.-Fri. 8am-4pm, though some banks stay open until 6pm. Exchange windows generally operate from 9am to 6pm, and stay open 24 hrs. in some ORBIS hotels and in airports, train stations, border crossings. The **black market** is extinct. Major **credit cards** are accepted at most hotels, restaurants and LOT offices in major cities.

Polish banknotes confuse foreigners and locals alike. The smallest include 50 and 100 złoty, which are to be substituted with coins. The 1000-zł bill resembles the 100,000-zł bill. Scheduled for January 1, 1995, **currency reform** will remove four zeros from every Polish bill—one new złoty will be worth 10,000 old PZL.

COMMUNICATION

Mail to and from Poland is becoming increasingly efficient, though still plagued by theft. Airmail *(lotnicza)* letters usually take 7-10 days to the U.S. For **Poste Restante,** put a "1" after the city name to make sure it goes to the main post office (pick-up costs 3000zł). Pay **phones** now use tokens *(żetony),* which come in two denominations ("A" for local calls, 1200zł, and "C" for inter-city calls, 11,800zł). PPTT **phone cards** are available for local and international calls, and come in several denominations (100 units 117,700zł). Special phones have card slots and instructions in English. Both tokens and phone cards are available at the *poczta* (post office). To reach the **AT&T USADirect operator** dial 01 04 80 01 11 (from outside Warsaw dial a 0 and wait for a tone first); **MCI WorldPhone,** dial 01 04 80 02 22; **Sprint Express,** dial 01 04 80 01 15; **Canada Direct,** dial 01 04 80 01 18; **BT Direct** (U.K.), dial 044 00 99 48. To make a **collect call,** write the name of the city or country and the number plus *"Rozmowa 'R'* on a slip of paper, hand it to a post office clerk, and be patient. Direct calls to most Western European countries and the U.S. can be made from private phones—dial 0 plus the country code and the number you are calling.

LANGUAGE

Polish belongs to the West Slavic group of languages (along with Czech and Slovak), and has regional dialects that correspond to the old tribal Małopolska (Little Poland), Pomorze (Pomerania), and Mazowsze (Mazovia). The Kashubs of Pomerania in the north and *Górale* (highlanders) of Podhale in the south have distinctive dialects that some linguists classify as separate languages. Try English before Russian, but German is more common. Students may know French as well. Spelling is fully phonetic and not as painful as it looks.

Yes	*Tak*	tak
No	*Nie*	nyeh
Hello	*Cześć*	tcheshch
Good morning	*Dzień dobry*	jane DOH-brih
Good night	*Dobranoc*	doh-BRAH-notz
Goodbye	*Do widzenia*	doh vee-DZEN-ya
Excuse me	*Przepraszam*	psheh-PRAH-sham

POLAND

Please/You're welcome	*Proszę*	PROH-sheh
Thank you	*Dziękuję*	jeng-KOO-yeh
When?	*Kiedy?*	KYEH-dih ?
Where?	*Gdzie?*	g-jeh ?
Help!	*Na pomoc!*	nah POH-motz !
How much is this?	*Ile to kosztuje?*	EE-leh toh kosh-TOO-yeh ?
How do I get to...?	*Ktorędy do...?*	ktoo-REN-dih doh... ?
My name is ...	*Nazywam się..*	nah-ZIH-vam sheh...
I don't understand	*Nie rozumiem*	nyeh roh-ZOO-myem
Leave me alone; get lost!	*Odczep się!*	OHD-chep sheh!

1—jeden (YEH-den); 2—dwa (dvah); 3—trzy (tshih); 4—cztery (cht-EHR-ih); 5—pięć (pyench); 6—sześć (sheshch); 7—siedem (SHEH-dem); 8—osiem (OH-shem); 9—dziewięć (JYEH-vyench); 10—dziesięć (JYEH-shench);20—dwadzieścia (dvah-JYEH-shchah; 30—trzydzieści (tshih-JYEH-shchih); 40—czterdzieści (chtehr-JYEH-shchih); 50—pięćdziesiąt (pyen-JYEH-shont); 60—sześćdziesiąt (sheshch-JYEH-shont); 70—siedemdziesiąt (sheh-dem-JYEH-shont); 80—osiemdziesiăt (oh-shem-JYEH-shont)90—dziewięćdziesiąt (jyeh-vyen-JYEH-shont); 100—sto (stoh); 1000—tysiąc (TIH-shontz).

ACCOMMODATIONS AND CAMPING

Grandmotherly private room owners smother travelers at the train station or outside the tourist office. Private rooms are usually safe, clean, and convenient, but sometimes far from city centers. Expect to pay about US$15 per person.

PTSM is the national hostel organization. **HI youth hostels** *(schroniska młodzieżowe)* are generally crowded, spartan, and quite uncomfortable, but they're everywhere and average US$3 per night (less for "juniors" under 18 or 26, more for nonmembers). Hot water is chancy. **University dorms** transform into sparse but cheap tourist housing in July and August. Ask at ALMATUR; the Warsaw office can arrange stays in all major cities. **PTTK** runs a number of hotels called **Domy Turysty,** where you can stay in multi-bed rooms for US$2-5. Many towns have a **Biuro Zakwaterowań,** which arranges stays in private homes. Rooms come in three categories: Category I are most centrally located and have hot water. Category II rooms are less centrally located, and category III rooms almost never have hot water.

Campsites average US$2 per person, US$4 with car. **Bungalows** are often available; a bed costs about US$5. *Polska Mapa Campingów* (Polish Campground Map) lists all campgrounds. ALMATUR also runs a number of campgrounds in summer; ask for a list at one of their offices.

HEALTH AND SAFETY

Public restrooms are marked by a triangle for men and a circle for women (3000zł). They can be nasty; don't get discouraged. Soap, towel, and toilet paper cost extra.

Polish **pharmacies** are well-stocked with over-priced western medicines and hygiene products. Western-style medical clinics are opening up around the country. Avoid drinking tap water; instead try the local bottled mineral water.

Criminals sniff out hard currency for a living; carry only a bare minimum of cash. As unemployment grows, drunks and con-artists multiply. Many cities in Poland are plagued by organized crime. In the summer of 1994, the Old Town in Warsaw became the target of mafia attacks, though restaurateurs shut down their establishments in protest. If the need arises, dial 997 for **police,** 998 for the **fire department,** and 999 for an **ambulance.**

POLAND

LIFE AND TIMES

HISTORY

The territory of present-day Poland was settled around the 7th century by Slavic tribes. The Slavs were then divided into three main branches: the Eastern Slavs were the ancestors of the Russians; the Southern Slavs became the Bulgarians, Serbs, Croats, and Slovenes; and the **Western Slavs** became the Poles, Czechs, and Slovaks. Poland is named after the *Polanie*, who lived in the lowlands of present-day Poland in the 9th century. The tribe's name, in turn, is derived from the Slavic word *pole* meaning "field"—the *Polanie* were skilled farmers.

Prince Svatopulok introduced both Latin and Greek Christianity in the 9th century, but not until 966 did **Prince Mieszko I,** of the **Piast dynasty,** officially convert to Catholicism. By 1000, the Catholic Church was firmly established in the new state, with seats at Gniezno, Poznań, Wrocław, Kraków, and Kołobrzeg. In 1025, Mieszko's oldest son, **Bolesław Chrobry,** was the first ruler to be formerly called king. In those early years, the kingdom of Poland was known as *Polonia.* Under Bolesław Chrobry (the Brave), Poland fought Bohemia, the German Empire, and Kievan Rus with success. In the 11th century, Poland's territory coincided remarkably with its present boundaries; King Kazimierz moved the capital south to Kraków. By the early 12th century, Polish kings had centralized the administration and strengthened their hold on the land.

Despite this promising start, the decision of 1138 to establish the "seniorate" and divide the country into duchies disastrously reversed this positive trend; by the 13th century, political fragmentation caused weakness and infighting. Coastal Pomerania broke away and was lost for several centuries; Mongols attacked in 1241, beating a combined Polish-German army at Lignice. Polish princes invited German settlers into Pomerania and Silesia, offering land for development and planning cities. The mix of the German and Polish peoples was peaceful, but the areas became heavily Germanized. The **Teutonic Knights** returned from the Fourth Crusade and, growing bored, accepted an invitation from Mazovia, one of Poland's nine fragmented duchies, to help defeat the pagan Baltic peoples living northeast of Poland. However, they broke the pact made with **Conrad of Mazovia** and proceeded to conquer East Prussia, thus cutting of Poland's access to the Baltic. Przemysław II, Duke of Great Poland, tried to restore unity with a coronation at Gniezno in 1295, but was murdered the following year. Polish territory shrank; the situation grew so bad that a Bohemian Czech king ruled briefly.

Poland was reunited in the 14th century, under **King Kazimierz Wielki** (Casimir the Great), one of the greatest rulers of medieval Europe. The country experienced a period of unprecedented religious and political tolerance, and became a refuge for the Jews expelled from Western Europe. Tens of thousands of Jews emigrated to Poland, which was then the only European country where different religious creeds could coexist without bloodshed. Thanks to Kazimierz, Poland developed into a truly cosmopolitan empire: Poles, Germans, Ruthenians, Flemings, Jews, Armenians, and Tatars lived peacefully side by side. Kazimierz rebuilt the country's defenses, made strategic peace pacts, and expanded the territories under Polish rule. Poland was largely spared the ravages of the Black Death, which killed about one person in three in the rest of Europe. Scholars codified Polish law in 1347, and a university was founded at Kraków in 1364, making Kraków the cultural center of Poland.

Kazimierz's daughter, **Princess Jadwiga,** was obliged to give up her Habsburg fiancé to marry the Lithuanian duke **Władysław Jagiełło.** A political alliance more than a union of love, the marriage was designed to bring together the two kingdoms of Poland and Lithuania. Lithuania was then a country of staggering size; having moved into the power vacuum left by the Mongols, it included much of present-day Lithuania, Belarus, Ukraine, and a large chunk of Russia. The alliance of two powerful kingdoms allowed Jagiełło to crush the Teutonic Knights in the **battle of Grun-**

LET'S GO® TRAVEL

CATALOG

1995

WE GIVE YOU THE WORLD... AT A DISCOUNT

Discounted Flights, Eurail Passes, Travel Gear, Let's Go™ Series Guides, Hostel Memberships... and more

Let's Go Travel

a division of

Harvard Student Agencies, Inc.

Bargains to every corner of the world!

Travel Gear

A Let's Go T-Shirt...$10
100% combed cotton. Let's Go logo on front left chest. Four color printing on back. L and XL. Way cool.

B Let's Go Supreme..........$175
Innovative hideaway suspension with parallel stay internal frame turns backpack into carry-on suitcase. Includes lumbar support pad, torso, and waist adjustment, leather trim, and detachable daypack. Waterproof Cordura nylon, lifetime gurantee, 4400 cu. in. Navy, Green, or Black.

C Let's Go Backpack/Suitcase......................$130
Hideaway suspension turns backpack into carry-on suitcase. Internal frame. Detachable daypack makes 3 bags in 1. Waterproof Cordura nylon, lifetime guarantee, 3750 cu. in. Navy, Green, or Black.

D Let's Go Backcountry I..$210
Full size, slim profile expedition pack designed for the serious trekker. New Airflex suspension. X-frame pack with advanced composite tube suspension. Velcro height adjustment, side compression straps. Detachable hood converts into a fanny pack. Waterproof Cordura nylon, lifetime guarantee, main compartment 3375 cu. in., extends to 4875 cu. in.

E Let's Go Backcountry II............................$240
Backcountry I's Big Brother. Magnum Helix Airflex Suspension. Deluxe bi-lam contoured shoulder harness. Adjustable sterm strap. Adjustable bi-lam Cordura waist belt. 5350 cubic inches. 7130 cubic inches extended. Not pictured.

800-5-LETSGO

Discounted Flights

Call Let's Go now for inexpensive airfare to points across the country and around the world.
EUROPE • SOUTH AMERICA • ASIA • THE CARRIBEAN • AUSTRALIA •
AFRICA

Eurail Passes

Eurailpass (First Class)

15 days....................................$498
1 month (30 days)....................$798
2 months (60 days).................$1098

*Unlimited rail travel anywhere
on Europe's 100,000 mile rail network.
Accepted in 17 countries.*

Eurail Flexipass (First Class)

*A number of individual travel days
to be used at your convenience
within a two-month period.*

Any 5 days in 2 months.............$348
Any 10 days in 2 months...........$560
Any 15 days in 2 months...........$740

Eurail Youthpass (Second Class)

15 days....................................$398
1 month (30 days)....................$578
2 months (60 days)..................$768

*All the benefits of the Eurail Pass
at a lower price. For those passengers
under 26 on their first day of travel.*

Eurail Youth Flexipass (Second Class)

*Eurail Flexipass at a reduced rate
for passengers under 26
on their first day of travel.*

Any 5 days in 2 months.............$255
Any 10 days in 2 months...........$398
Any 15 days in 2 months...........$540

Europass (First & Second Class)

First Class starting at................$280
Second Class starting at............$198
For more details.....................CALL

*Discounted fares for those passengers
travelling in France, Germany, Italy,
Spain and Switzerland.*

Hostelling Essentials

F **Undercover Neckpouch............$9.95**
Ripstop nylon with soft Cambrelle back. Three
pockets. 6 x 7". Lifetime guarantee. Black or Tan.

G **Undercover Waistpouch.........$9.95**
Ripstop nylon with soft Cambrelle back. Two
pockets. 5 x 12" with adjustable waistband.
Lifetime guarantee. Black or Tan.

H **Sleepsack...............................$13.95**
Required at all hostels. 18" pillow pocket.
Washable poly/cotton. Durable. Compact.

I **Hostelling International Card**
Required by most international hostels. For U.S.
residents only. Adults, $25. Under 18, $10.

J **Int'l Youth Hostel Guide.......$10.95**
Indispensable guide to prices, locations, and
reservations for over 4000 hostels in Europe
and the Mediterranean.

K **ISIC, ITIC, IYTC..........$16, $16, $17**
ID cards for students, teachers and those people
under 26. Each offers many travel discounts.

800-5-LETSGO

Order Form

Please print or type — Incomplete applications will not be processed

Last Name	First Name	Date of Birth

Street *(We cannot ship to P.O. boxes)*

City	State	Zip

Country	Citizenship	Date of Travel

( ) -

Phone · School (if applicable)

Item Code	Description, Size & Color	Quantity	Unit Price	Total Price
			SUBTOTAL:	

Domestic Shipping & Handling		Shipping and Handling (see box at left):	
Order Total:	Add:	Add $10 for RUSH, $20 for overnite:	
Up to $30.00	$4.00	MA Residents add 5% tax on books and gear:	
$30.01 to $100.00	$6.00		
Over $100.00	$7.00	GRAND TOTAL:	
Call for int'l or off-shore delivery			

MasterCard / VISA Order

CARDHOLDER NAME _____

CARD NUMBER _____

EXPIRATION DATE _____

Enclose check or money order payable to:
Harvard Student Agencies, Inc.
53A Church Street
Cambridge, MA 02138

Allow 2-3 weeks for delivery. Rush orders guaranteed within one week of our receipt. Overnight orders sent via FedEx the same afternoon.

Missing a Let's Go Book from your collection?
Add one to any $50 order at 50% off the cover price!

Let's Go Travel
1-800-5-LETSGO

(617) 495-9649   Fax: (617) 496-8015
53A Church Street
Cambridge MA 02138

wald in 1410, dispensing with the common enemy, opening access to the Baltic, and making Poland-Lithuania one of the greatest powers in Europe. Under Kazimierz IV, Prussia was forcibly subordinated to Poland. By 1500, Poland-Lithuania seemed invincible in Eastern Europe.

All Protestant confessions made inroads into Poland during the Reformation; tolerance was reaffirmed in the mid-16th century, though the Jesuits were powerful and Catholicism remained the religion of the vast majority. Still, there was no religious warfare like that which killed hundreds of thousands in the rest of Europe. Under **King Zygmunt I Stary** (the Old), the Renaissance sped to Poland through his marriage to Bona, of the powerful Italian family of Sforzas. The queen had a great impact on the development of Polish art and architecture; years after her death, nobles still built castles modeled on Wawel Castle in Kraków, whose reconstruction she had supervised. Under the reign of **Zygmunt II August,** Bona's son, the Kraków school of painting developed along Flemish lines, brilliant Copernicus created a planetary theory, and the poet Kochanowski and the scholars of jurisprudence Włodowic and Ostorok lectured and worked at Kraków. Zygmunt August died in 1572 without leaving an heir; the marriage of his sister, Anna, to the Hungarian magnate Stefan Batory, made the latter King of Poland and marked the end of the **Jagiełło dynasty.**

After the death of Zygmunt August, the *szlachta* (nobles) in the *Sejm* (Parliament) decided upon an elected kingship, which gave them the power to surveil royal policy, the right to approve taxes, declarations of war, treaties, and the right to resist the king's decisions. Elections became a major political event, and too often an excuse for the highest ranking members of the *szlachta* to indulge in political intrigues and feuds, letting fiery temperaments get the better of reason. In the early 17th century, one of the elected kings, **Zygmunt III Waza** of the Swedish Waza line, moved the capital farther away from the border, from Kraków to Warszawa. The citizens of Warszawa erected a huge column, graced with Zygmunt's statue, to commemorate this event; Krakovians, on the other hand, never forgave the king for depriving their city of royal status. The rule of the Wazas ended abruptly in the 17th century, in bloody wars against the Swedish invader ("the Swedish Deluge"). The most noteworthy of the elected kings was **Jan III Sobieski,** known for crushing the Turks and lifting the siege of Vienna in 1683. In so doing, he exhausted Poland and left it weaker against Prussia, Sweden, and Russia. Sobieski was the last Polish king whose courage and adherence to traditional values earned him the love and respect of his people; after his death, Poland entered an unstable period, marked by increasing Russian influence in internal affairs and culminating in the three partitions. The infamous Russian-sponsored Parliament of 1717 limited Polish armed forces to a paltry 24,000. The Saxon kings ruling after Sobieski were Russian tools.

The First Partition of Poland (1772) gave almost 30% of Poland's eastern territories to Russia; Austria received Małopolska (Little Poland), and Prussia obtained Royal Prussia, comprising the region of Warmia and part of Wielkopolska (Greater Poland), but without the cities of Gdańsk and Toruń. As a result of the **Second Partition** (1793), Russia took the remaining Ruthenian lands, and Prussia received the rest of Greater Poland and part of Mazovia. The popular insurrection, led by **Tadeusz Kościuszko** in 1794, was defeated by the much stronger Russian forces. Finally, in the **Third Partition** (1795), Russia took all the territories east of the Niemen and Bug Rivers, Austria received Galicia, and Prussia took Gdańsk, Poznań, and Warsaw. Reduced to a harmless puppet throughout his reign, **Stanisław August Poniatowski,** the last Polish king, abdicated in 1795, and Poland was effectively eradicated from the map for the next 123 years..

Napoleon's campaigns briefly restored a Polish state; many Poles fought enthusiastically for his cause. After his defeat, however, the Congress of Vienna transferred much of Poland from Prussia to Russia. But while the 19th century was, for most of Europe, an age of Empire, Expansion, Improvement, and Big Progress, for Poland it was an ordeal. Russia forestalled development of modern institutions in the 1820s; bloody rebellions in 1830 and 1848 were crushed. After industrialization, Poland quietly became the most developed and prosperous part of the Russian Empire. Russification and germanization was enforced in the areas controlled by Russia and Prussia. Austria gave the Poles more autonomy, and the University of Kraków continued to flourish, but Galicia remained a backward area.

Poland did not regain its **independence** until 1918, under extremely chaotic conditions. True to one of President Wilson's basic war aims, the Allies gave Poznań and West Prussia to Poland, with access to the port of Gdańsk (Danzig); but war with Soviet Russia, Ukrainian nationalists, and Lithuania raged in the east. The Bolshevik victory in Russia had spawned monstrous invasion forces in Europe and Asia aiming to spread communism; but the Poles and French whipped Kamienev's Red Army in front of Warsaw and chased its shattered remnants back to the Soviet Union. The Allied Powers approved Polish occupation of the western Ukraine to keep Bolshevik forces out of the area. Polish forces also drove the Lithuanians from their capital, Vilnius, and annexed about a third of the country. From the 1920s until 1935, Poland was governed by the autocratic **Piłsudski,** with only a formal preservation of the parliamentary authority. One of the post-World War I Prime Ministers was, surprisingly, **Ignacy Paderewski,** better known as one of the most famous concert pianists of his time. During the war, he had toured America using his name on Poland's behalf in an attempt to raise funds for the concept of Polish freedom. A great pianist and a successful fund-raiser, he proved to be a disastrous choice for the position of Prime Minister, and resigned after only a year in office.

In the interwar period, Poland had defensive treaties with France and a non-aggression pact with Germany. On August 23, 1939, Hitler and Stalin signed a non-agression pact, known as the **Ribbentrop-Molotov pact,** and sometimes referred to as the "Fourth Partition of Poland." World War II broke out on September 1, 1939: Poland fought courageously, lasting an entire month against the raging Nazi war machine despite the Soviet attacks from the east. For six long years, Poland was the site of massive destruction, unspeakable atrocities, death camps, and Nazi terror. Over 6 million of its inhabitants died, including 3 million Polish Jews. "Liberated" by the Soviet Union, which obstructed the return of the Polish government and installed communist proxies after the war, Poland spent 45 miserable years bound to Russia in the Soviet bloc.

In 1979, **Karol Wojtyła** became the first Polish Pope, John Paul II; this ultimately brought the Poles together and triggered the events of 1980. That year, *Solidarność* was born, the first independent workers' union in Eastern Europe, led by the charismatic **Lech Wałęsa,** a former electrician at the Gdańsk shipyards. Later, *Solidarność* was to be one of the most important factors in bringing down Communism in Eastern Europe, but in 1980-82 it was still an isolated movement which could not hope to overthrow even the local government. Its actions resulted in the declaration of martial law in 1981; **General Jaruzelski,** then head of the Polish government, allegedly imposed it solely as a means of protecting the Polish nation from a Soviet invasion. Wałęsa was jailed and released only when *Solidarność* was dissolved by the government in 1982. But although officially disbanded and outlawed by Jaruzelski, the organization continued its fight for labor's rights underground.

The first and most gracious of the 1989 Eastern European shakedowns unfolded in Poland with a diplomacy more typical of chess games than revolutions. After over 20 years of anti-government union strikes, economic distress, and political imprisonments, Wojciech Jaruzelski's communists were forced by the Polish people to meet with Lech Wałęsa and other Solidarity leaders during several weeks of "round-table" discussions. In return for Solidarity's pledge to end the strikes, the government agreed to legalize the union, amend the constitution, and hold free elections. Solidarity members swept into all but one of the contested seats, and the editor of its newspaper, **Tadeusz Mazowiecki,** was sworn in as Eastern Europe's first noncommunist Prime Minister in 40 years.

POLAND TODAY

The largest and most populous of Eastern European nations is gritting its teeth in a determined attempt to rejoin the modern world. In 1990, the Solidarity government opted to take the bitter dose of capitalism in one gulp. To woo Western investment, the government eliminated subsidies, froze wages, and devalued the currency, throwing the already antiquated economy into recession and producing the first unemployment in 45 years. Consumer goods now fill the shelves, and budding capitalists truck in supplies to sell at sidewalk bazaars, though few people have any free cash to spend. Although prices have continued to increase, Poland is still a bargain for Westerners. For the locals, however, availability of consumer goods on the market does not compensate for the rise in prices and in unemployment. More and more families are finding it hard to make ends meet, and are beginning to oppose the reforms implemented by the Solidarity government, in fact, the growing dissatisfaction of the population is the main factor behind the victory of the left in the elections of 1993.

FOOD AND DRINK

Foreign monks, merchants, invaders, and dynastic unions have all flavored Polish cuisine. Since the Middle Ages, the city of Toruń has been known for its *pierniki* (honey-spice cakes). In the early 16th-century, Queen Bona Sforza brought seeds, spices, and expert cooks from her native Italy. Polish cuisine was refined in the 17th century through closer relations with France. Today, Polish cuisine is a blend of hearty dishes drawing from French, Italian, Jewish, Bohemian, and Greek traditions. And while traditional Polish food is often loaded with cholesterol through its extensive use of eggs, butter, and sour cream, it is less starchy than that of the Czech Republic or Slovakia, and less fiery than that of Hungary or Bulgaria.

Rules of *Polska gościnność* (Polish hospitality) require hosts to offer their guests more than they can possibly eat, or face eternal damnation. A heavy *śniadanie* (breakfast) of bread, cheese, cold cuts and eggs is usually consumed between 5-8am; cereal is not very popular, although carried by most food stores. *Drugie śniadanie* ("second breakfast"), an American-style bag lunch, is gobbled up around 9-11am. *Obiad* (dinner), invariably prefaced by soup, is served in the late afternoon. Unlike the Americans who eat their salads before the main course, or the French who eat it afterwards, the Poles consume salads *with* the main course.

Eating out is affordable in Poland; more expensive does not always mean better. A *restauracja* (restaurant) or *kawiarnia* (café) has waiters; a *bar* is self-service; a *bar mleczny* (milk bar) is usually super-cheap. A 10-15% **tip** is expected in restaurants and cafés. The following glossary can help decipher consonant-heavy menus:

Barszcz (barshch): ubiquitous beet broth, served both hot and cold.
Bigos (BEE-gohs): "hunter's stew." Sauerkraut cooked with beef, sausage, and sometimes onions or mushroom. Served with rye bread or potatoes.
Chłodnik (HWOH-dneek): cold savory soups; usually a shocking-pink beet soup with buttermilk, and eyeball-like hard-boiled eggs floating about.
Czernina (tcher-nEE-nah): duck soup.
Flaczki (FLAH-tchkee): face it, it's tripe.
Gołąbki (gow-OHMP-kee): "little pigeons." Cabbage rolls stuffed with meat and rice (or mushrooms, cheese, eggs, and sauerkraut).
Grochówka (groh-HOOF-hak): thick and creamy pea soup.
Kapuśniak (kah-POOSH-nyak): sauerkraut soup.
Kartoflanka (kahr-toh-FLAHN-kah): potato soup.
Kisiel (KEE-shell): jelly/pudding with a taste and texture all its own.
Kopytka (koh-PIHT-kah): "little hooves." Polish *gnocchi*. Potato dumplings, topped with buttered bread crumbs. Often served in place of regular potatoes.
Kotlet schabowy (KOHT-let s-hah-bOH-vih): pork chops; you won't escape them.
Krupnik (KROOP-neek): barley soup.
Naleśniki (nah-lesh-nEE-kee): pancakes, filled with fruit, cheese, jam, or cream.
Pierogi (pyeh-ROH-ghee): Dumplings with various fillings (fruit, meat, cheese, potato, cabbage, mushroom) and toppings (butter, sour cream, sweet cream, fruit syrup, bacon bits, browned onions). Blueberry are best.

POLAND

Zapiekanka (zah-pyeh-KAHN-kah): Pizza gone astray. Mushrooms, melted cheese, and ketchup on French bread. Sold at hot dog and hamburger stands.
Zupa owocowa (ZOO-pah oh-voh-tzOH-vah): fruit soup.
Żur/Żurek (zhoor/ZHOO-rehk): creamy soup made with barley flour and loaded with crumbs, eggs, and sausage.

Food is the stuff of Polish rituals—*Wigilia* (Christmas Eve Supper) begins with sharing the *opłatek* (wafer), and is followed by a dozen or so meatless dishes, each with its own religious significance. At Easter, *święconka*—a beribboned basket of bread, sausage, and eggs—is carried to Church to be blessed. Newlyweds are greeted with bread (so they'll never be hungry) and salt (to preserve the union).

Wines are imported and often expensive. Bulgarian *Sofia* is relatively cheap and not too bad. Polish beer is dubious, but try *Żywiec* or *Okocim* (if you want it cold, say so). Vodka, the national specialty, flows in many flavors and brands: *Wyborowa*, *Żytnia* and *Polonez* are a few. The herbal vodka *Żubrówka* comes with a blade of grass from the region where the bison *(żubr)* roam. Two of the oldest Polish drinks, *miód* and *krupnik,* were best loved by the *szlachta* (gentry) of the past.

CUSTOMS AND ETIQUETTE

In general, don't do anything your mother wouldn't recommend. You can be seriously **fined** for (among other things) jaywalking, putting your shoes on a train seat, riding a tram or bus without a validated ticket, or playing cards in a public place—don't pull out your deck in bars, cafés, or even train stations. When arriving as a guest, be sure to bring your host an odd number of flowers.

There are several telephone numbers that you can dial from any place in Poland in case of an emergency: **police** tel. 997, **fire** tel. 998, **ambulance** tel. 999.

■ Warsaw (Warszawa)

Contemnire procellas (to defy the storms) is Warsaw's motto. At least two-thirds of the city's population perished during World War II and by 1945, 85% of the capital's structures had fallen. Over 50 years after the German invasion, the colorful narrow buildings of the *Stare Miasto* (old town) have been painstakingly restored. Buildings that never existed rose above the rubble, built after plans found in old archives.

International businesspeople inject an air of purposefulness into the city's smog, and glass office buildings scrape the grey sky. Downtown boulevards brim with galleries, *salons de parfum,* and BMWs while elsewhere, entire families cram into decrepit apartment blocks and drive tiny Fiats. When they can, Varsovians escape to private suburban gardens *(działki)* but outsiders must content themselves with strolls along the knotted paths of swan-filled Łazienki Park, in the city's southeast.

ORIENTATION AND PRACTICAL INFORMATION

The country's principal air and rail hub, Warsaw lies in east-central Poland, about 150km from the Belorusian border. The *Śródmieście* (city center) and most major points of interest lie on the west bank of the **Wisła River,** which bisects the city. To the right of the main train station **Warszawa Centralna, ul. Marszałkowska** intersects **Aleje Jerozolimskie,** forming the center of the modern downtown. Beyond, Aleje Jerozolimskie extends toward the river to cross the boutique-lined boulevard, **Nowy Świat.** A right on Nowy Świat leads down embassy row to Łazienki and Wilanów palaces; a left leads north to the old town. A good **map** with bus and tram lines is *essential;* purchase one at the *Ruch* (news and tobacco) stand on any street corner, in large hotels or bookstores, in the airport, or in bus and train stations.

Central Warsaw

1 Barbican (Barbakan)
2 Warsaw Historical Museum
3 St. John's Cathedral
4 Royal Castle
5 Statue of King Zygmunt III
6 St. Anne's Church
7 Krasiński Palace
8 John Paul II Collection
9 The Grand Theater and Opera House
10 Caricature Museum
11 Tomb of the Unknown Soldier
12 Warsaw University
13 Church of the Holy Cross (Św. Krzyża)
14 Ethnographic Museum
15 Chopin Museum
16 Palace of Culture and Science
17 National Museum
18 Warsaw Operetta
19 Parliament (Sejm)
20 Medical Academy
21 Politechnical University
22 Chopin Monument
23 Łazienki Palace
24 Orbis
25 Orbis
26 Almatur
27 Central Railway Station
28 Śródmieście Railway Station
29 Powiśle Railway Station
30 American Express
31 US Embassy
32 Canadian Embassy
33 British Embassy
34 LOT Polish Airlines

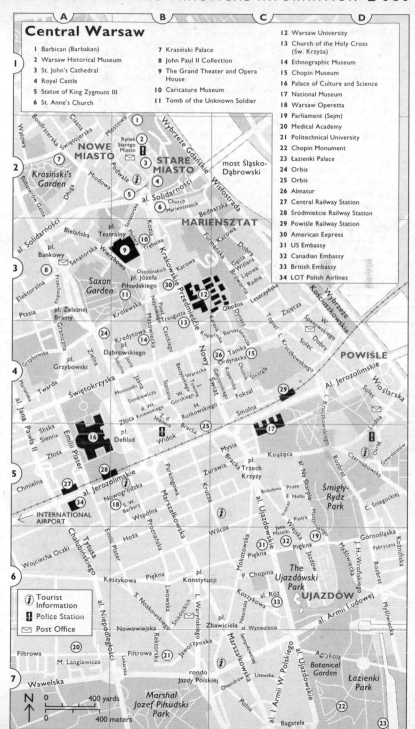

POLAND

(i) Tourist Information
⊟ Police Station
✉ Post Office

Tourist Offices: Tourist information tel. 635 18 81, Mon.-Fri. 9am-6pm, Sat.-Sun. 11am-6pm. Information on current cultural events tel. 29 84 89, Mon.-Fri. 10am-9pm, Sat.-Sun. 10am-6pm, or get a copy of the monthly *Warszawski Informator Kuturalny*, sold in kiosks (11,000zł). Though written in Polish, it's filled with decipherable addresses and schedules of upcoming events. The *Warsaw Voice*, a weekly local newspaper geared to the city's growing international population. The monthly *Warsaw: What, Where, When?*, available at major hotels and tourist offices, is another indispensable guide.

ORBIS, ul. Bracka 16 (tel. 27 01 72). Entrance on al. Jerozolimskie near Nowy Świat, at the back of the department store "Smyk." Train, plane, and bus tickets. Open Mon.-Fri. 8am-7pm, Sat. 8am-3pm. **UPS** window open Mon.-Fri. 8am-4pm. A mega office branch at ul. Marszałkowska 142 (tel. 27 67 66, fax 27 11 23), is open Mon.-Sat. 9am-6pm. Both branches change money, transact Visa/MC cash advances, and cash traveler's checks for a 5% commission.

Centrum Informacji Turystycznej (Tourist Information Center), pl. Zamkowy 1/3 in the Old Town (tel. 635 18 81). Efficient English-speaking staff provides **maps,** guidebooks, listings of hotels and restaurants, currency exchange, and hotel reservations. Open Mon.-Fri. 9am-6pm, Sat. 10am-6pm, Sun. 11am-6pm.

Budget Travel: Several tourist offices in Warsaw cater specifically to budget travelers, but the best is the student office ALMATUR.

ALMATUR, ul. Kopernika 23 (tel. 26 35 12 or 26 26 39), off Nowy Świat. Good place for travel information and English speakers. Sells ISICs, travel insurance (US$8), international bus tickets, plane tickets at a student discount, and changes reservations of plane tickets purchased at Council Travel offices. Hotel vouchers to ALMATUR hotels in all major Polish cities (with student ID US$10/person or US$18 for two; under 35 US$12 per person or US$20 for two). Open Mon.-Fri. 9am-6pm, Sat. 10am-2pm. **Room 19,** ul. Krakowskie Przedmieście 24 (tel. 26 75 41), is ALMATUR's train ticket department. Go through the main university entrance, and it's the first building on the right. Interrail and Eurotrain tickets available. Open Mon.-Fri. 9am-4pm. **ALMATUR's head office,** ul. Kopernika 15 (tel. 26 23 56 or 26 35 07, fax 26 35 07), organizes sailing, kayaking, cycling, horsebackriding, and cross-country skiing trips.

PTSM, ul. Chocimska 28, room #427 (tel. 49 83 54), near pl. Unii Lubelskiej. The Polish youth hostel federation. Listings of all Polish youth hostels. Membership cards (100,000zł, college students 70,000zł). Open Mon.-Fri. 9am-3pm. Their **branch office** is at ul. Szpitalna 5 (tel. 27 78 43), behind the department stores "Domy Centrum." Open Wed. and Fri. 1-5pm.

PTTK, Podwale Śródmieście 23 (tel. 635 27 25), in the Old Town. Info on its budget hotels *(Domy Turysty)* across Poland, camping, kayaking, and hiking. Open Mon.-Fri. 11am-5pm. The other branch is right in the Old Town, at Rynek 23 (tel. 31 05 44); in addition to the services offered by the first office, it sells hitchhikers' guides (40,000zł). Open Mon.-Fri. 10am-4pm.

Embassies: Most embassies are clustered around Al. Ujazdowskie, the so-called "embassy row," in the center of Warsaw.

U.S., al. Ujazdowskie 29/31 (tel. 628 30 41); entrance around the corner at ul. Piękna 12. Open Mon.-Fri. 9am-noon.

Canada, ul. Matejki 1/5 (tel. 29 80 51). Open Mon.-Fri. 8:30am-1pm and 2-5pm.

U.K., al. Róż 1 (tel. 628 10 01). Consular office at Wawelska 14 (tel. 25 80 31). Open Mon.-Fri. 9am-noon.

Australia, ul. Estońska 3/5 (tel. 617 60 81).

New Zealand citizens should contact the British embassy.

Belarus, ul. Ateńska 67 (tel. 617 39 54).

Czech Republic, ul. Koszykowa 18 (tel. 628 72 21). Open Mon.-Fri. 9am-1pm.

Finland, ul. Chopina 4/8 (tel. 29 40 91).

Germany, ul. Dabrowiecka 6 (tel. 617 30 11).

Lithuania, al. Ujazdowskie 13 (tel. 625 34 10).

Norway, ul. Chopina 2a (tel. 621 42 31).

Russia, ul. Belwederska 49, building C (tel. 621 34 53). Open Wed. and Fri. 8am-1pm.

Slovakia, ul. Litewska 6. (tel. 41 01 12).

Ukraine, ul. Szuka 7 (tel. 29 64 49).

Currency Exchange: For **cash:** all hotels, banks, and tourist offices as well as private *kantor* counters (with slightly better rates) throughout the city. 24-hr. exchange places at: *Dworzec Centralny* (Central Railway Station), al. Jerozolimskie 54 (tel. 25 50 50); at the International Airport in the departures area, ul. Żwirki i Wigury (tel. 46 96 24 or 46 96 94); and at Hotel Vera, ul. Bitwy Warszawskiej 1920 16 (tel. 22 74 21). For **traveler's checks: Bank PKO S.A.** (tel. 637 10 00), in the blue skyscraper at pl. Bankowy 2. Travelers checks cashed for 0.5-1.5% commission; Visa/MC cash advances. Other Warsaw branches: ul. Mazowiecka 14 (tel. 661 25 79), ul. Traugutta 7/9 (tel. 26 92 11), ul. Grójecka 1/3 in the Hotel Sobieski (tel. 658 83 52), and in the Marriott Hotel at al. Jerozolimskie 65/79, 3rd fl. (tel. 30 04 64 or 630 53 03). All branches open Mon.-Fri. 8am-6pm.

ORBIS offices: hefty 5% commission for cashing travelers checks, and a 1% commission for Visa/MC cash advances. The ORBIS *kantor* at ul. Marszałkowska 142 (tel. 27 67 66) is open Mon.-Fri. 8:30am-6pm, Sat. 8:30am-2pm.

Bank PKO Rotunda in a round building opposite the tall Hotel Forum, ul. Marszałkowska 100 (tel. 26 00 61). VISA traveler's checks cashed without commission. Open Mon.-Fri. 7am-8pm.

Bank Inicjatyw Gospodarczych, ul. Kopernika 36/40 (tel. 657 51 85). Visa cash advances without commission. Open Mon.-Fri. 8:30am-3:30pm.

Prosper Bank S.A., ul. Krakowskie Przedmieście 55 (tel. 26 20 21; 635 88 93, fax 635 34 90). Representative of Western Union in Poland—fastest way to have money sent to you from anywhere in the world (Western Union Money Transfer Info tel. 31 70 08). Open Mon.-Fri. 8am-6pm.

American Express: ul. Krakowskie Przedmieście 11 (tel. 635 20 02). Full service. Express cash machine, open 24 hrs. Postal code: 00-950. Open Mon.-Fri. 9am-5pm, Sat. 10am-2pm.

Post Office: Main post office at ul. Świętokrzyska 31/33 (tel. 26 60 01 or 26 04 11). **Poste Restante** at counter #12. **Fax** bureau (130,000zł/page to U.S., fax number 30 00 21). **Postal Code:** 00-001. Open 24 hrs.

Courier Services: UPS, ul. 17-go Stycznia 39 (tel. 606 63 50, fax 606 82 50), open Mon.-Fri. 8am-4:30pm. **DHL,** al. Jerozolimskie 30 (tel. 26 32 92), open Mon.-Fri. 8am-4pm for pick-up and delivery.

Telephones: at the post office. Long lines during the day. **City Code:** 022 for six-digit numbers, 02 for seven-digit numbers.

Photocopies: Copy General, al. Jerozolimskie 63 (tel. 628 62 52, fax 625 47 32); entrance on ul. Emilii Plater. Self-service. 800zł per page. Open 24 hrs.

Flights: All flights use the new **Port Lotniczy Warszawa-Okęcie** on ul. Żwirki i Wigury, commonly referred to as Terminal 1. To the city center, take bus #175 (after 11pm, bus #611). Bus tickets at the *Ruch* kiosk in the departure hall or at the *kantor* outside (6000zł). The Airport City Bus (35,000zł) is a faster way to the center (runs 5:35am-11:37pm, every 20min. on weekdays and every 30min. on weekends; stops at major hotels in Warsaw: Novotel, Jan III Sobieski, Marriott, Forum, Metropol, Europejski. Bristol, Victoria. Buy tickets at the ORBIS desk at the airport, the LOT office in the Marriott Hotel, or from the driver.)

Airline Offices: the main **LOT** office is in the Marriott Hotel, al. Jerozolimskie 65/79 (tel. 952 or 953). **British Airways,** ul. Krucza 49 (tel. 628 94 31 or 638 39 91). **Delta Air Lines,** ul. Królewska 11 (tel. 26 02 57, 27 92 00, or 27 21 24).

Trains: Most trains use *Warszawa Centralna,* the well-organized central train station. Platforms *(perony)* are on the underground level, most services on the ground floor, main ticket windows 1 floor up, and international windows on top floor. To: Berlin (6 per day, 8hr.; 654,000zł); Budapest (2 per day, 10hr., 1,382,000zł); Prague (3 per day, 12hr., 822,000zł); Moscow (4 per day, 27hr., 1,130,000zł); St. Petersburg (1 per day, 24hr., 1,114,000zł); Minsk (5 per day, 12hr., 630,000zł); Kiev (2 per day, 22hr., 820,000zł); Vilnius (1 per day, 12hr., 570,000zł); Vienna (2 per day, 9hr., 1,400,000zł plus 332,0000zł for couchette); Gdańsk (12 per day, 4hr., 153,000zł); Kraków (16 per day, 2½hr., 135,000zł); Zakopane (4 per day, 8½hr., 171,000zł). In the main hall: **post office** open daily 8am-8pm; **self-service photo booth** (4 medium or 16 tiny pictures for a

110,000zł token bought in the nearby kiosk); domestic train tickets windows; **Wasteels** ticket window, between the information window and the post office (open Mon.-Fri. 7am-9pm, Sat.-Sun. 9am-5pm. After hours, go the international tickets window, located on the first floor).

Warning: Theft is on the increase on overnight trains from Warsaw to Berlin and Prague. Travelers should protect their safety and property.

Buses: Main bus station is **PKS Warszawa Zachodnia** (tel. 23 64 94; 23 64 95) next to the Warszawa Zachodnia train station at al. Jerozolimskie 144. From the main train station, take bus M or #127 headed west. Bus station open daily 5am-11pm. Check with the International Bus Information window for connections to Western Europe (open Mon.-Fri. 8am-4pm). To: Minsk (3 per day, 11hrs.; 315,000zł); Vilnius (2 per day, 12 hrs.; 326,000zł), Riga (1 per day, 14hrs.; 643,000zł). Also on the premises: **Café Bogota** (pastries 3000zł, open daily 7am-10pm); **Bar Non Stop** (hamburgers 15,000zł; fries 9000zł), open daily 5am-11pm); currency exchange *kantor,* open Mon.-Fri. 9am–6pm, Sat. 10am-3pm.

Public Transportation: Bus and tram lines are marked on the standard city map. Day trams and buses (including express lines) cost 6000zł, students 3000zł. Night buses 18,000zł. Large baggage 6000zł per piece. Buy tickets at a *Ruch* stand or street vendor; there are no conductors on buses or trams. Punch both ends of the ticket in the machines on board or face a 250,000zł fine.

Taxis: Stands marked by blue and white signs. For cheap 24-hr. taxi service, tel. 96 22 or 96 24. Avoid cabs in front of hotels, at the airport, at the *Warszawa Centralna* station, and the Marszałkowska-al. Jerozolimskie rotary; you'll be overcharged. Taxi meters usually start at 30,000zł. Night rates are about 20% higher.

Hitchhiking: *Let's Go* does not recommend hitchhiking as a safe means of transportation. Hitchers pick up *Książeczka autostopu* (The Hitchhiker's Book), at the PTTK office, Rynek Starego Miasta 23 (tel. 31 05 44), open Mon.-Fri. 10am-4pm.

Luggage Storage: At the bus station, open 7am-8pm (20,600zł per piece per day). At the main train station, the *przechowalnia bagażu* on the level below the main hall stores for a max. 15 days. Lockers come in three sizes and operate on tokens: "A" (30,000zł per day), "B" (50,000zł per day) and "C" (100,000zł per day).

Bookstores: Klub Międzynarodowej Prasy i Książki, ul. Marszałkowska 116/122, has a good selection of English-language magazines. Open Mon.-Fri. 9am-8pm, Sat. 9am-4pm. **Bookland,** next to the British Institute at al. Jerozolimskie 61 (tel. 625 41 46), sells Penguin and Random House paperbacks. Open Mon.-Fri. 10am-4pm, Sat. 10am-2pm. The *kiosk* at Hotel Bristol, ul. Krakowskie Przedmieście 42/44 (tel. 625 25 25), has the latest copy of the *Wall Street Journal.* Open Mon.-Fri. 7am-11pm, Sat.-Sun. 8am-11pm. International books and press are also available at *kiosk* in the Marriott Hotel (tel. 630 50 61); open daily 7am-11pm.

Laundromat: ul. Karmelicka 17 (tel. 31 73 17). Take bus #180 north from ul. Marszałkowska, or bus #33 from ul. Jana Pawła II towards Żoliborz and get off at ul. Anielewicza. Open Mon.-Fri. 9am-7pm, Sat. 9am-1pm; reservations recommended. Wash and dry 86,000zł/kg. Bring your own detergent. **Alba,** ul. Chmielna 26, provides 24-hr. dry-cleaning (tel. 27 45 10). Shirt 49,000zł, pants 59,000zł, jacket 79,000zł. Add 50% for express, 6-hour service. Open Mon.-Fri. 8am-7pm, Sat. 9am-1pm.

24-Hr. Pharmacies: Apteka Grabowski at the central train station and **Apteka** at ul. Grójecka 76 (tel. 22 28 91).

Medical Assistance: The **Health Info Line** provides information about health services (tel. 26 27 61 or 26 83 00); open Mon.-Sat. 7:30am-7:30pm, Sun. 8am-3pm. **Medical Info Line,** ul. Smolna 34/22 (tel. 27 89 62). Directs you to private doctors and dentists. Open Mon.-Fri 8am-8pm, Sat. 8am-3pm. **24-hr. service** and **ambulance** at ul. Hoża 56 (tel. 999 or 628 24 24). Doctors' services also available 24 hrs. at **Capricorn,** ul. Podwale 11 (tel. 31 89 69 or 31 76 07). Hospitals that treat foreigners: **Marriott Hotel Medical Center,** al. Jerozolimskie 65/79 (tel. 21 06 46 or 630 51 15), or the **European School of Oncology,** ul. Mochnackiego 10 (tel. 22 24 14 or 659 88 51, fax 22 14 53); hours depend on what you want done—try calling Mon.-Sat. between 8am-6pm. **Dentists:** Private dentists are at

Prywatna Poradnia Stomatologiczna, ul. Rakowiecka 33/27 (tel. 49 45 20), open Mon.-Fri. 9am-8pm. **24-hr. dental service** available at ul. Ludna 10 (tel. 635 01 02 or 625 01 05) and at **"Curatum,"** ul. Walecznych 2 (tel. 617 61 76). **Useful Numbers: 24-Hr. Psychological Help Line:** tel. 628 36 36. **Women's Hotline:** tel. 635 47 91, open Mon.-Fri. 4-8pm. **Drugs Hotline:** tel. 313 01, open Mon.-Fri. 5-7pm. **AIDS Hotline:** tel. 628 03 36, open Mon.-Fri. 10am-10pm. **Emergencies:** Emergency room in the Hospital Szpital Śródmiejski in the center, ul. Solec 93 (tel. 625 22 31 or 625 33 27). **Police Headquarters:** tel. 26 24 24.

ACCOMMODATIONS AND CAMPING

Syrena at ul. Krucza 17 (tel. 628 75 40) pins down rooms in private homes; arrive early. From the train station, turn left toward downtown at al. Jerozolimskie, continue to ul. Krucza and take a right. (Singles 220,000zł. Doubles 340,000zł. Open Mon.-Sat. 8am-7pm, Sun. 8am-5pm.) **Romeo i Julia,** ul. Emilii Plater 15/30 (tel. 29 29 93), directly opposite the central train station, also finds rooms. (Singles 300,000zł; doubles 430,000zł. Breakfast 10,000zł. Open Mon.-Fri. 10am-7pm.) **Informacja noclegowa** (tel. 643 95 92 Mon.-Fri. 10am-5pm and tel. 671 58 25 Mon.-Fri. 5-10pm, Sat.-Sun.11am-5pm) is a phone service which directs people to hotels. **Centrum Informacji Turystycznej** (see above) also finds rooms in hotels.

Hotel Bursa Artystów, ul. Miodowa 24a (tel. 635 79 05 or 635 41 74), just before the entrance to the Old Town. The art school dorm becomes a hostel in summer. Doubles 440,000zł. Triples 660,000zł. Open July1-Aug.30.

Schronisko Młodzieżowe (HI), ul. Smolna 30, top floor (tel. 27 89 52), across from the National Museum. Take bus #158 or 175, or tram #22 from al. Jerozolimskie. Clean but basic rooms, 80,000-91,000zł, with HI 64,000zł. Sheets 15,000zł. Full by the end of the evening. Lockout (including reception) 10am-5pm. Curfew 11pm. Showers, kitchen, baggage room. English spoken.

Schronisko Młodzieżowe (Summer Youth Hostel), ul. Międzyparkowa 4/6 (tel. 31 17 66). Close to the river, between two parks. Take tram #2, 18 or 19 northbound from ul. Marszałkowska and get off at ul. Andersa after the stadium on your right. Foreigners: 75,000zł; 65,000zł with ID. Sheets 18,000zł. Open April 15-Oct.15.

Schronisko Młodzieżowe (HI), ul. Karolkowa 53a (tel. 32 88 29). Take tram #22 west from al. Jerozolimskie or train station. Get off at "Okopowa." Left on al. Solidarności (Gen. K. Świerczewskiego on old maps), and then right onto ul. Karolkowa. Pretty but out of the way. Lockout 10am-5pm. Curfew 11pm. 4- to 7-bed rooms. Foreigners: 75,000zł, with ID 70,000zł. Doubles 280,000zł. Triples 120,000zł/person. Sheets 10,000zł. Kitchen. Baggage room 5000zł. No showers.

Hotel Harenda (PTTK), also known as **Dom Turysty,** ul. Krakowskie Przedmieście 4/6 (tel. 26 26 25). From train station, take bus #175 to "Uniwersytet." Walk *back* to the end of the block; take the first left on Oboźna. Very near tourist zone. Clean, modern showers. Singles 450,000zł, with bath 600,000zł. Doubles 600,000zł, with bath 850,000zł. Triples without bath 630,000zł. Quads without bath 660,000zł. Mini-bar open daily 8am-10pm.

Dom Nauczyciela (Teacher's House), Wybrzeże Kościuszkowskie 31/33 (tel. 625 05 71), opposite the Ateneum theater. From Świętojerska, take bus #150 or 155 to *Pomnik Syreny* stop. Overlooks a park, the river, a highway, and an electric plant. Well-kept rooms. Singles 300,000zł, with bath 490,000zł. Doubles 480,000zł, with bath 660,000zł. Triples 750,000zł, with bath 1,350,000zł.

Hotel-Uniwersytet Warszawski, ul. Belwederska 26/30 (tel. 41 13 08). Take bus #131 or 180 from Marszałkowska to *Spacerowa* stop. An international tourist crowd beds down south of the Park Łazienkowski. Singles 417,300zł. Doubles 631,300zł (without baths). Breakfast included.

Dom Chłopa, pl. Powstańców Warszawy 2 (tel. 27 92 51), between the Pałac Kultury and Nowy Świat. A real hotel, attracting an older clientele, but young Poles crowd the pool hall. Reception open 24hrs. Singles with sink 400,000zł. Doubles with bath 900,000zł. Café and restaurant on the premises, open daily 9am-10pm and 7am-2am, respectively.

Dom Literata, ul. Krakowskie Przedmieście 2/8 (tel. 635 39 20 or 635 04 04). Prime location, at the entrance to the Old Town, over a posh café full of writers and artists. Singles 300,000zł. Doubles 400,000zł. No baths in rooms.

Hotel Instytutu Fizyki PAN (Institute of Physics of the Polish Academy of Sciences), al. Lotników 32. A 30-minute ride by bus # 174 from Al. Jana Pawła II. Singles 300,000zł. Doubles 400,000zł. Breakfast included. Showers in rooms.

Hotel Pałacyk, ul. Koszykowa 80 (tel. 628 41 31 or 621 91 94). A 10-minute walk from the central train station along ul. Chałubińskiego; turn left onto ul. Koszykowa; or take tram #15 or 19 to *Plac Politechniki* and walk north on ul. Noakowskiego until you see the sign *Pałacyk* on your left. Singles with bath 353,000zł. Doubles with bath 600,000zł. Triples with bath 900,000zł.

Hotel MDM, pl. Konstytucji 1 (tel. 628 25 26). A grand, graying edifice brooding over a noisy, commercial stretch of Marszałkowska south of the centrum. Singles 500,000zł, with bath 650,000zł. Doubles with bath 900,000-1,100,000zł. Triples with bath 1,300,000zł. Breakfast included. 20% discount for students with valid ID. The **restaurant Ugarit** (tel. 62 52 48 or 625 39 27), serves Syrian and Polish entrees for 70,000-120,000zł. Open 24 hrs.

Harctur, ul. Niemcewicza 17 (tel. 659 00 11). Take bus #521 or tram #7 from main train station toward Airport *Okęcie,* and get off at pl. Narutowicza. Gray building that once housed scouts. Doubles 514,000zł, with bath 685,000zł. Triples wih sink 610,000zł. Quads with sink 728,000zł.

Camping Gromada, ul. Żwirki i Wigury 32 (tel. 25 43 91). Take bus #175 (direction *Port Lotniczy*) 1 stop past *Pomnik Lotnika.* 75,000zł/person, 55,000zł/tent per day. 2-person bungalows 150,000zł, 4-person 300,000zł. Open May 1-Sept. 30.

Camping Wisła, ul. Bitwy Warszawskiej 1920r 15/17 (tel. 23 37 48). Next to the main bus station; take bus #127 or 517 from main train station toward *Ursus.* 20,000zł per tent, 40,000zł per person per day. Fits 100 tents. 2-, 3-, 4-bed cabins fit a total of 120 people, 75,000zł per person. Open April 15-October 15.

Camping Turysta, ul. Grochowska 1 (tel. 610 63 66). Far from the center, on the other side of the Wisła River. Take bus #610 from main train station to the *Praga Południe* district; get off at the big intersection of ul. Ostrobramska and ul. Grochowska. No tents. 2-, 3-, 4-, and 5-person bungalows: 80,000zł per person, with bath 90,000zł. Open year-round.

FOOD

You can blow your budget on roast duck or grilled salmon at any of Warsaw's best restaurants bunched around the **Rynek Starego Miasta,** the market square of the Old Town, but proletarian cafeterias are infinitely cheaper and more colorful. *Górale* (highlanders) sell *oscypek,* a firm, goat's milk cheese in the underground passageway to the central train station. During the day, stop by a *sklep spożywczy* (grocery store) and test your food vocabulary. There is a **24-Hr. Grocery Store** at the central train station on the lowest level, as well as **Bestpol,** ul. Grójecka 47 (tel. 28 67 21) and ul. Nowogrodzka 56 (tel. 71 48 84).

Polish Cuisine

Bar Uniwersytecki, Krakowskie Przedmieście 16/18. Next to the university under the yellow awning. One of the last bastions of cheap food in big helpings. Rice with apples 6850zł. Homemade soups 7000-11050zł. Pancakes with apples 6600zł. Omelettes 7200zł. Open Mon.-Fri. 7am-8pm, Sat.-Sun. 9am-5pm.

Zapiecek, ul. Piwna 34/36 (tel. 31 56 93), on the corner of ul. Piwna and Zapiecek in the Old Town. Candle-lit intimacy with a German bent. Barszcz 20,000zł. Viennese veal 65,000zł. Open daily 11am-11pm.

Pod Herbami Restaurant, ul. Piwna 21/23 (tel. 31 64 47). Pleasant, pseudo-medieval tavern full of local folk. Grilled salmon 130,000zł. Open Sun.-Thurs. 11am-11pm, Fri.-Sat. 11am-1am.

Ekologiczna "Nove Miasto" Restaurant, Rynek Nowego Miasta 13/15 (tel. 31 43 79). Warsaw's first natural food restaurant. Organically grown vegetarian entrees 69,000-98,000zł. Whole grain desserts, health food soups, a variety of crêpes, and a whole salad theater: *Juliet in a New Dress, Ophelia, Hamlet, King Lear, As You*

Like It, The Taming of the Shrew and more. Polish beer and German wine. Outdoor seating available. Live music nightly. Credit cards accepted. Wheelchair accessible. Open daily 10am-midnight.

Hetmańska Restaurant, ul. Przyczółkowa 394 (tel. 642 54 11). Eclectic menu: traditional Polish food (cheese *naleśniki* 20,000zł) alongside Chinese entrees (40,000zł) and pizzas (29,000-35,000zł). Open daily 9am-10pm.

Restauracja "Pod Wierzbami" (Under the Willows), is the only place in Żelazowa Wola where you can get a solid meal (tel. 222 43). One of those no-frills places with basic but tasty Polish dishes: beefsteaks 70,000zł; fried chicken 58,000zł; and cabbage *pierogi* 25,000zł. Open daily 9am-11pm

Italian Cuisine

Pizzeria Bambola, al. Jerozolimskie 11a (tel. 29 80 08). 28 kinds of pizza 35,000-89,000zł, including the delicious Pizza Bambola with ham and shrimp. Lasagna 60,000zł. Open Mon. 11am-midnight, Tues.-Sat. 10am-midnight, Sun. noon-midnight. Other branches of Bambola: ul. Nowy Świat 426 (tel. 26 46 77), ul. Wspólna 27 (tel. 628 31 83), ul. Puławska 16 (tel. 49 44 42).

Pizzeria Pama, ul. Zgoda 6 (tel. 26 80 30). 45 different kinds of pizzas includes a *UFO pizza* with ham, mushrooms, tuna, and salami for 95,000zł. Price range 40,000-199,000zł. Open daily 10am-9pm.

Pizzeria Pod Wieżą (Under the Tower), ul. Krakowskie Przedmieście 68 (tel. 38 62 75). Pizzas 38,000-75,000zł. Outdoor seating. (Open daily 11am-11pm.) Climb the tower for a panoramic view of Warsaw for a mere 10,000zł (open Mon.-Fri. 10am-6pm, Sat. 10am-3pm). Both the tower and the pizzeria belong to the Catholic Student Center of St. Anne's church—all profits go to charities.

Pizzeria Giovanni, ul. Krakowskie Przedmieście 37 (tel. 26 27 88). 25 kinds of pizzas 45,000-85,000zł. Delicious shrimp salad 45,000zł. Smiling service; home delivery available. Open daily 11am-11pm.

Ethnic Restaurants

Hoang Kim Restaurant, ul. Freta 18/20 (tel. 635 79 59). 90 Chinese and Vietnamese dishes in an Asian setting. Lunch starts at 45,000zł. Fried shrimp 169,000zł. 10% off if you choose the take-out option. Credit cards accepted. Open daily 11am-11pm.

El Popo, ul. Senatorska 27 (tel. 27 23 40). Yucca trees, colorful parrots, and desert brown hues make it a real Mexican *casa*. Start with nachos con guacamole (52,400zł) or ceviche (36,400zł), and follow them up with tamales (162,6000zł) or fajitas (190,500zł). Margaritas 97,600zł. Live music from Spain and South and Central America. Open daily noon-midnight.

Insam, ul. Senatorska 27 (tel. 27 97 07). Next to the Mexican El Popo. Brings a taste of Korea to Poland for around 80,000zł an entree. Open daily 11am-11pm.

Parnas, ul. Krakowskie Przedmieście 4/6 (tel. 26 41 79), in the same building as the Harenda, opposite the monument to Kopernik. The best Greek place in town. Classic avgolemono soup 35,000zł. Souvlaki 140,000zł. Mousaka 90,000zł. Credit cards accepted. Open 1pm-midnight. The café upstairs is open 10am-10pm.

Le Petit Trianon, ul. Piwna 42 (tel. 31 73 13), in the Old Town. Polish and French cuisine in an intimate setting. A handful of tables in a room laden with roses and gold-framed mirrors. French specialties: onion soup 55,000zł; escargots 160,000zł; Burgundy beef 140,000zł; chocolate crêpes 90,000zł. Reservations a must. Open Tues.-Sun. 1pm-midnight.

Restaurant Maharaja, ul. Szeroki Dunaj 13 (tel. 635 25 01). The Hindu heaven, hidden in a corner of the Old Town. Follow the curry smell down the steep stairs. Tandoori chicken 94,000zł; naan bread 35,000zł. Open daily noon-midnight. Their second location is at ul. Marszalkowska 34/50 (tel. 621 13 92).

Restaurant Pod Samsonem, ul. Freta 3/5 (tel. 31 17 88). Cheap eats on the way from the Old Town to the New, opposite Maria Skłodowska-Curie's museum. The Jewish-Polish cuisine is supposed to make you big and strong like Samson. Jewish cymes salad 15,000zł. Pork chop 70,000zł. Open daily 10am-10pm.

POLAND

Bar Krokiecik, ul. Zgoda 1 (tel. 27 30 37). Hungarian soups 28,000zł; croquets 15,000-20,000zł; pancakes with strawberries and whipped cream 19,000zł. Open Mon.-Sat. 9am-8pm.

Cafés

Blikle, ul. Nowy Świat 35 (tel. 26 66 19, or 26 64 50). Best pastries in the city, by the same Swiss family since the 1870s. Delectables from 3000zł. Open Mon.-Fri. 10am-7pm, Sat. 10am-3pm.

Café Blikle, ul. Nowy Swiat 33. New and chic. Enjoy tortes (33,000-53,000zł) and espresso (23,000zł) while listening to jazz music. Open Sun.-Thurs. 7:30am-11pm, Fri.-Sat. 7:30am-midnight.

Café Nowy Świat, ul. Nowy Świat 61 (tel. 26 58 03). Incredible chandeliers and antique flavor. Breakfast includes omelettes for 35,000zł and cheese-and-raisin pancakes for 33,000zł, while the lunch menu offers lasagna for 72,000zł and Hawaiian toast for 45,000zł. Open Mon.-Sat. 7am-10pm, Sun. 9am-10pm.

Hotel Bristol Café, ul. Krakowskie Przedmieście 42/44 (tel. 625 25 25). Attracts *crème de la crème* of Polish filmmakers and actors. Great place to relax and sip *Baronesse*—a strawberry and sherry milkshake for 95,000zł—a prologue to a stylishly filling *Notre Dame* sandwich with salmon and cream cheese (95,000zł). Smoked chicken salad 90,000zł. Cappuccino 32,000zł. Open daily 9am-9pm.

Kawiarnia Bazyliszek, Rynek Starego Miasta 3/9 (tel. 31 18 41). A relaxing outdoor café amid the restored splendor of Warsaw's Old Town. Tortes 20,000zł. Coffee 15,000zł. Open daily 9am-9pm.

Gwiazdeczka, ul. Piwna 40, in the Old Town (tel. 31 94 63). Lovers meet under the Renaissance arches of its open-air garden. Principally a café, but also serves alcohol. Open daily 9am-10pm.

Lody W. Hoduń, ul. Nowomiejska 11/13, in the Old Town. Ice cream in waffle cones 3500zł a scoop. Open daily 10am-7pm.

Fast Food

Avoided by some, cherished by many, fast food places have overrun Warsaw. Besides the American-style burger and pizza joints, salad bars are slowly settling in and threatening the market for cholesterol.

Salad Bar, ul. Chmielna 13 (tel. 27 25 47). Small self-service place between ul. Marszałkowska and ul. Nowy Świat. Salads 12,000zł. Open Mon.-Thurs. 11am-7pm, Fri. 10am-7pm, Sat. 10am-3pm.

McDonald's has four locations in Warsaw: **Sezam** at ul. Marszałkowska 124/136 (tel. 27 57 77), next to the grocery store Sezam; **Ikea** at Al. Jerozolimskie 56c (tel. 630 222 31); **Smyk** at ul. Krucza 30 (tel. 27 90 37); and **Randall** in the underground passage at the Al. Jana Pawła II intersection (tel. 25 58 02). Big Mac 33,000zł. All locations open daily 6:30am-11pm.

Burger King: at Krakowskie Przedmieście 4/6 (tel. 26 28 99); on pl. Zbawiciela next to the movie theater Luna (tel. 625 36 85); on pl. Konstytucji, next to the movie theater Polonia (tel. 625 40 58); and on al. Solidarności (tel. 635 31 12). Open daily 8am-10pm.

Domino's Pizza: ul. Krakowskie Przedmiescie 4/6 (shares the space with Burger King), and ul. Grójecka 120. (Open Mon.-Thurs. 8am-10pm, Fri. 8am-2am, Sat.-Sun. 8am-midnight.) For free home delivery, call 27 76 63 or 22 30 41. (Your order has to be at least 85,000zł to be delivered.)

Pizza Hut, Taco Bell and Kentucky Fried Chicken all have their headquarters at ul. Widok 24, behind the department stores Wars and Sawa. They stuff East Europeans with taco supremes for 23,000zł; chili fries for 21,000zł; slices of vegetarian pizza for 23,000zł; chicken, fries, and coleslaw combo for 36,000zł. Open daily 10am-midnight. Shared office at ul. Widok 26 (tel. 625 02 05) lists other locations.

SIGHTS

Razed beyond recognition during World War II, Warsaw was rebuilt from ruins and rubble by defiant survivors. To those left homeless by the war, even cookie-cutter concrete blocks were beautiful.

Stare Miasto (Old Town)

Warsaw's postwar reconstruction shows its finest face in the narrow, cobbled streets and colorful façades of the **Stare Miasto** (Old Town). At right side of the entrance to Stare Miasto stands the impressive **Zamek Królewski** (Royal Castle), an early-Baroque structure with Gothic fragments and a Rococo façade. In the Middle Ages it was the residence of the Dukes of Mazovia, and in the late 16th century it replaced Kraków's *Wawel* as the official royal residence. Burned down in September 1939 and plundered by the Nazis, who shipped all the major works of art abroad, the castle was to become a symbol of Polish patriotism. Many inhabitants of Warsaw risked their lives hiding the priceless works in the hope that they would return to the castle after the horrors of the war were over. When Poland regained its independence in 1945, original plans of the castle and some of the works of art that had once adorned its interiors were retrieved from the hiding places and the Castle was rebuilt (see Museums).

On the square in front of the castle stands **Kolumna Zygmunta III Wazy** (the column of King Zygmunt III Waza). Constructed in 1644 in honor of the king who transferred the capital from Kraków to Warsaw, it stood here for three hundred years before it was destroyed in World War II.

As you leave the Column behind you and proceed past the Royal Castle to turn left onto ul. Świętojańska, where the *kasa* to the Castle is located, you will see the **Katedra Św. Jana** (Cathedral of St. John), the oldest church building in Warsaw, from the turn of the 13th and 14th centuries. Almost completely destroyed during the Warsaw Uprising of 1944, it was rebuilt after the war in Vistulian Gothic style. Within its walls the historic case against the Order of Teutonic Knights, who had broken the pact made with Conrad of Mazovia, was brought by Poland in 1339. The cathedral and its crypts are open to the public; the crypts contain the graves of the dukes of Mazovia, and of such famous Poles as the writer Henryk Sienkiewicz, winner of a Nobel Prize for his novel *Quo Vadis,* and Gabriel Narutowicz, first president of an independent Poland. One of the side altars contains the sarcophagus of Cardinal Stefan Wyszyński.

Ulica Świętojańska takes you straight to the pristinely restored Renaissance and Baroque houses of the **Rynek Starego Miasta** (Old Town Market Square). On the southeast side of the Rynek, at no.3/9, the **House "Pod Bazyliszkiem"** (Under the Basilisk) immortalizes the Old Town monster whose stare was supposed to bring instant death to those unfortunate enough to cross his path. Although most of the houses surrounding the Rynek were razed to their foundations during the Warsaw Uprising, a few managed to survive World War II—like the **house at no. 31,** which dates back to the 14th century. The Rynek oozes with cafés, kitschy art, and tourists.

Most of the buildings on the north side of the Rynek make up the **Muzeum Historyczne miasta Warszawy** (the Historical Museum of Warsaw), with the entrance at no. 28. The museum chronicles the city's past from the Middle Ages through World War II, and the amazing post-war restoration. Next door, at no. 20, the **Muzeum Literatury im. Adama Mickiewicza** (Museum of Literature) is dedicated to Adam Mickiewicz, one of Poland's greatest poets.

In the northeast corner of the Rynek starts ul. Krzywe Koło (Crooked Wheel). If you turn left from Krzywe Koło onto Kamienne Schodki (Stone Steps), the **steps** of this picturesque street will carry you straight to the banks of the Wisła River. Ul. Krzywe Koło leads to the **Barbakan** (Barbican), a rare example of 16th-century Polish fortifications. The **Little Insurgent Monument** located here honors the heroism of the youngest soldiers of the Warsaw Uprising. Ulica Krzywe Koło is lined with stands set up by local artists, displaying paintings, handicraft, and strings of amber. Around the Barbakan, you can see the reconstructed remains of the walls that used to surround the entire Old Town; they are decorated by a statue of the **Warszawska Syrenka** (Warsaw mermaid), the symbol of Warsaw. Legend has it that a fisherman named Wars caught a beautiful mermaid in his nets while fishing in the Wisła River. The mermaid begged Wars to free her, pledging in exchange her protection of a new city that he and his wife would establish on the spot where he stood. Wars let

POLAND

her go and returned home to his wife, Sawa, and they founded a city on the banks of the Wisła River, which grew and prospered under the mermaid's care. It was called Warszawa, in memory of its founders, Wars and Sawa, and the mermaid was immortalized in the monument and by her inclusion in the city's coat-of-arms.

Nowe Miasto (New Town)

As you pass through the Barbican Gate, you find yourself on ul. Freta, at the edge of the **Nowe Miasto** (New Town). In spite of its name, this is actually the second-oldest district in the city. Also destroyed during World War II, it is now restored to its 18th- and 19th-century glory.

Among the houses lining ul. Freta on the right stands the former home of the Skłodowski family. Here, at ul. Freta 16, the great physicist and chemist **Maria Skłodowska-Curie**, winner of two Nobel prizes, was born in 1867. In 1967, on the 100th anniversary of Maria's birthday, the house was converted into a museum dedicated to the life and work of the revolutionary scientist. The exhibition chronicles Maria's life in Poland, emigration to France, and marriage to scientist Pierre Curie, with whom she discovered radium, polonium, and marital bliss.

Ulica Freta leads to the the **Rynek Nowego Miasta** (New Town Market Square), the site of **Kościół Sakramentek** (Church of the Blessed Sacrament). The church was founded in 1688 to commemorate the 1683 victory of King Jan Sobieski over the Turks in Vienna.

Trakt Królewski (Royal Route)

The 4km-long **Trakt Królewski**, the city's most attractive thoroughfare, begins on Plac Zamkowy (Castle Square) in the Stare Miasto and continues all along ul. **Krakowskie Przedmieście**. The street is named for Kraków, because it leads south toward the former capital of Poland. It is lined with fine palaces, churches, and convents built when the royal family moved to Warsaw.

On your left, as you leave the Castle Square, stands the **Kościół Św. Anny** (St. Anne's church), the oldest parts of which date from the 15th century. Farther down the street is the building in which Maria Skłodowska-Curie carried out her first experiments, and the **Adam Mickiewicz Monument** gazes toward Piłsudski Square and the Saxon Gardens containing the **Tomb of the Unknown Soldier.** Urns holding earth from the graves of Polish soldiers murdered in Katyń, and from the battlefields marked by Polish blood, were laid here after World War II. A ceremonial changing of the guard takes place in front of the Tomb every Sunday at noon.

Krakowskie Przedmieście is also known as the neighborhood where Fryderyk Chopin spent his childhood and youth. He gave his first public concert in the **Koniecpolski-Radziwiłł Palace** guarded by four stone lions at no. 46/48. He played the organs in **Kościół Wizytek** (Church of the Visitation Nuns), one block down the street, and composed in the **Czapski-Krasiński Palace,** which now houses the Academy of Fine Arts and the **Salonik Chopinów** (The Chopins' Drawing Room). The *Salonik* was Chopin's last Warsaw home until he left for France in 1830. Today it is a division of the public **Fryderyk Chopin Museum.** The main part of the museum is located in the Ostrogskis Castle at Okólnik 1—a few blocks down the street from the Academy, turn left onto ul. Ordynacka and follow it to Okólnik. Chopin died abroad at the age of 39, but his heart returned to Poland; it lies in an urn in the left nave of **Kościół Św. Krzyża** (Holy Cross Church).

Before you reach the Holy Cross church, you will pass a complex of rebuilt palaces on your left, now belonging to the **University of Warsaw,** founded in 1816. **Kazimierzowski Palace** at the end of the alley leading from the main entrance to the University, now houses the Rector's Offices, but was once the seat of the School of Knighthood. Among its students was the famous Tadeusz Kościuszko, Polish general and patriot, who fought in the American Revolutionary War and later led an unsuccessful revolt against Russia.

The **Mikołaj Kopernik Monument** and the **Staszic Palace,** now the seat of the Polish Academy of Sciences, mark the end of ul. Krakowskie Przedmieście. The

Royal Route continues as **ul. Nowy Świat** (New World), lined with cafés, boutiques, and street vendors. The name of the street dates back to the mid-17th century, when a new settlement was started here, composed mainly of lower-class people. It was not until the 18th century that aristocracy started moving into this area, embellishing it with their ornate manors and residences. Eventually, Nowy Świat became the main street of Warsaw. Today, there are wider and busier streets in the city, but none quite as charming in aspect.

Ulica Nowy Świat crosses the main artery of **Aleje Jerozolimskie** (Jerusalem Avenue). In the 18th century, it was just a dirt road leading to a Jewish settlement called New Jerusalem – hence the name of the street. On the left corner of ul. Nowy Świat and al. Jerozolimskie stands a massive gray building that was the seat of the Polish Communist Party until 1989; today, it houses the Warsaw Stock Market Exchange. After crossing al. Jerozolimskie, ul. Nowy Świat leads directly to **Plac Trzech Krzyży** (Three Crosses Square), with **Kościół Św. Aleksandra** (St. Alexander Church) in the middle. On the opposite side of the square, the Royal Route changes names one last time to **Aleje Ujazdowskie**, the direct extension of ul. Nowy Świat. This avenue is lined with embassies, including those of the United States, Switzerland, and Great Britain. To the left is the Ujazdowski Park and the **Ujazdowski Castle**, a former residence of the Waza royal family, recently reconstructed in early-Baroque style.

The Royal Route terminates with the **Botanical Gardens** on the left side of al. Ujazdowskie, and with the **Łazienkowski Park**, summer residence of the last Polish king, Stanisław August Poniatowski. Al. Ujazdowskie then becomes ul. Belwederska. The route, leading all the way from the Royal Castle to Łazienki and Belweder, thus connects two of the royal residences in Warsaw—the main one in the Old Town's Royal Castle and the summer Palace-on-Water in Łazienki.

Łazienki

With its swans and majestic peacocks, the Łazienki park is an appropriate setting for the striking Neoclassical **Pałac Łazienkowski,** also called **Pałac na Wodzie** (Place on the Water), containing galleries of 17th- and 18th-century art. It was designed by the architect Dominik Merlini, and built in 1775-1795 for King Stanisław August Poniatowski. (Open Tues.-Sun. 9:30am-4pm barring rain. Admission 20,000zł, students 12,000zł. Guided tour in Polish 80,000zł, in English 300,000zł.)

Also in the park, **Stara Pomarańczarnia** (the Old Orangery; 1786-88) was used not only as a greenhouse for orange trees, but also as a theater and servants' quarters. The **Teatr Stanisławowski** celebrated its grand opening on September 6, 1788. In 1791, Stanisław August donated the theater to Wojciech Bogusławski, an accomplished actor, director, and playwright considered by many the "father of Polish theater." Bogusławski accepted the gift and opened the theater to the general public. (Open Tues.-Sun. 9:30am-4pm. 10,000zł, students 5000zł. Guided tour in Polish 30,000zł, in English 100,000zł.) The west wing of the Old Orangery contains the **Galeria Rzeźby Polskie**j (Gallery of Polish Sculpture); 140 sculptures illustrate the evolution of Polish sculpture from the end of the 16th century through 1939. (Open Tues.-Sun. 9:30am-4pm. Admission 10,000zł, students 5000zł. Guided tour in Polish 50,000zł, in English 200,000zł.) **Pałac Myślewicki** (Myślewicki Palace), yet another example of Neoclassical architecture, was also designed by Dominik Merlini, whose skills were obviously very much in demand in the late 1770s. Built around the same time that the construction of the Palace on the Water was undertaken, it was given by King Stanisław August to Prince Józef Poniatowski. (Open Tues.-Sun. 9:30am-4pm. Admission 12,000zł, students 6000zł. Guided tour in Polish 80,000zł, in English 300,000zł.)

It's not just the monuments and museums that attract tourists to Łazienki; the serene surroundings, the greenery, and the many species of trees make it an oasis of peace in the busy city of Warsaw. Leave contemporary Warsaw behind for a while, stroll down the shadowed, pebbled alleys of the park, and relax to the soothing sound of Chopin's music, played by Polish and foreign pianists at **Pomnik Chopina** (Chopin Monument) every Sunday from spring to autumn.

POLAND

Commercial District and the Warsaw Ghetto

Warsaw's commercial district lies southwest of the Old Town along ul. Marszałkowska. Here, at al. Jerozolimskie 3, is the **Muzeum Narodowe** (National Museum), with stellar though sporadically gruesome collections of 8th- to 12th-century Coptic and medieval art.

The best panorama of Warsaw is from atop the 70-story, 242-m "Stalin Gothic" **Pałac Kultury i Nauki** (Palace of Culture and Science) on ul. Marszałkowska, as this is the only location from which the hulking beast itself is not visible. The Palace has over 3000 offices, exhibition and conference facilities, three theaters, two museums – **Museum Ewolucji** (Museum of Evolution) and **Muzeum Techniki** (Museum of Technology)—a swimming pool with a diving tower 10m high, and several movie theaters. Because of its size and central location, the Palace often plays host to fairs, like the biggest Computer Fair east of the Elbe River, or the International Book Fair, an annual meeting of book publishers and book buyers organized in May.

Below, Plac Zwycięstwa (Victory Square) in front of the Palace is the site of the dubious **Cricoland**, a miniature amusement park. (Its various contraptions look none too safe—venture in at your own risk.) Next to Cricoland buzzes one of the capital's many post-communist bazaars. Shopping and commerce have flooded the streets since the inception of crash capitalism in January 1990; Polish, Russian, and Ukrainian street vendors, forced out of the main streets of Marszałkowska and Świętokrzyska by the city's mayor, have moved to this square. Everything from kitchen sinks to kiwi fruit goes for what the market will bear. **Bazar Różyckiego** is across the river on ul. Targowa (open daily, tram #7 from al. Jerozolimskie); another bazaar unfolds every weekend across the river in the Praga district, on and around the **Stadion Dziesięciolecia** (bus #158 from in front of the Hotel Forum). Watch your wallet at the bazaars.

Still referred to as "the Ghetto," the modern Muranów neighborhood of Warsaw holds few vestiges of what was once a community numbering 400,000. The beautifully reconstructed **Nożyk Synagogue** at ul. Twarda 6 lies just north of the Pałac Kultury. Farther north, at ul. Tłomackiego 3/5, off al. Solidarności (former al. Świerczewskiego), stands **Muzeum Żydowskiego Instytutu Historycznego** (Museum of the Jewish Historical Institute). On ul. Zamenhofa, look for the **Ghetto Uprising Monument**. The **Jewish Cemetery** on ul. Okopowa stretches for miles, a forest-covered treasure of gravestone art (open Mon.-Thurs. 9am-3pm, Fri. 9am-1pm). At Umschlagplatz, a huge monument marks the spot where 300,000 Jews were rounded up to be sent to death camps. Farther north, in the Żoliborz section, Father Jerzy Popiełuszko delivered outspoken anti-government sermons at the **św. Stanisława Kostki Church** until his brutal murder by the secret police in 1984. Today his grave is a shrine to both the Church and Solidarity. Take tram #6, 15, 31, or 36 to Plac Wilsona; the church is on ul. Kozietulskiego.

Wilanów

Up to the 17th century, Wilanów was a village named Milanowo. After his coronation in 1677, King Jan III Sobieski bought the village and had the existing mansion rebuilt into a Baroque-style palace. The decoration of the palace was the domain of Sobieski's wife, Marysieńka. The name given to the new royal residence, Villa Nova, was translated into Polish "Wilanów." The palace was successively owned by the aristocratic families of the Sieniawskis, Lubomirskis, Czartoryskis, Potockis, and Branickis. One of the Potockis, Stanisław Kostka Potocki, played a crucial role in the palace's history—in 1805, he opened it to visitors, thus founding one of the first public museums in Poland. Since then, the **Wilanów Palace** has functioned both as a museum and as a residence for the highest ranking guests of the Polish state – among many others, Reza Pahlavi of Iran, Hajle Sellasje of Ethiopia, and the French general and president, Charles de Gaulle, stayed here during their official visits in Poland. To get there, take bus #180 or express bus B from ul. Marszałkowska. (Open Wed.-Mon. 9:30am-2:45pm. Admission 28,000zł, students 18,000zł. Guides in

English, German, French, Italian or Russian available if at least 10 people sign up, in which case everyone has to contribute 16,000zł in addition to the admission fee.) Also worth seeing are the Oranżeria (Orangery) and the Kuchnia Pałacowa (Old Palace Kitchen). The **Oranżeria** illustrates the role of local craftsmanship in Wilanów, while the **Kuchnia Pałacowa** hosts various temporary exhibitions (i.e., "The Far East in Wilanów's art collections"). Both museums are open Wed.-Mon. 9:30am-3:30pm (admission 4000zł, students 2000zł.) A stroll through the romantic **park,** a mosaic of colorful flower beds and meticulously manicured trees, is definitely worthwhile (open Wed.-Mon. 9:30am-3:30pm; admission 10,000zł, students 5000zł). The pavilion next to the palace houses the **Muzeum Plakatu** (Poster Museum; tel. 42 26 06). Founded in 1968, it was the first institution of its kind in the world; it boasts an impressive collection of around 50,000 posters from the last hundred years or so (open Tues.-Sun. 10am-4pm; admission 10,000zł, students 5000zł).

MUSEUMS

Muzeum Narodowe (National Museum), al. Jerozolimskie 3 (tel. 621 10 31). Largest museum in Poland. Founded in 1862 as a Museum of Fine Arts, converted into a national museum in 1915. Impressive illustration of the evolution of Polish art over the centuries. Also houses a Gallery of Medieval Art and a Gallery of European Art, which includes Italian works from the 14th-18th centuries, German art from the 15th-16th centuries, and Dutch and Flemish paintings from the 17th centuries. Open Tues. and Sun. 10am-5pm, Wed., Fri. and Sat. 10am-4pm, Thurs. noon-6pm. Admission 12,000zł, students 7000zł, Thurs. free.

Muzeum Wojska Polskiego (Polish Military Museum), al. Jerozolimskie 3 (tel. 29 52 71; 628 58 43). Polish weaponry from the Middle Ages to the present. Detailed history of Poland's fight for independence against the Soviets and the Nazis during World War II. Open Wed.-Sun. 10am-4pm. Admission 15,000zł, students 10,000zł, Fri. free. Guided tour an additional 150,000zł. Library and reading room open Wed.-Fri. noon-3pm.

Muzeum Etnograficzne (Ethnographical Museum), ul. Kredytowa 1 (tel. 27 76 41). Wide display of Polish folk costumes, customs, traditions, and handicraft. Open Tues., Thurs.-Fri. 9am-4pm, Wed. 11am-6pm. Sat.-Sun. 10am-5pm. Admission 10,000zł, students 5000zł. Wed. free. Guided tour 50,0000zł.

Muzeum Archeologiczne (State Archeological Museum), "ARSENAŁ," ul. Długa 52 (tel. 31 32 21; 31 15 37). Among the many artifacts that tell the ancient history of Poland, 1500 silver and gold Roman coins, and the armor of the first leaders of Poland—the Piasts. Open Mon.-Fri. 9am-6pm, Sun. 10am-4pm. Closed on Saturdays and on the third Sunday of each month. 15,000zł, students 8000zł, Sun. free.

Muzeum Historyczne miasta Warszawy (Warsaw Historical Museum), Rynek Starego Miasta 28 (tel. 635 16 25). Chronicles the city's resilient past. The main exhibition—"Seven Centuries in the Life of Warsaw"—illustrates the city's history, the evolution of styles in architecture, furniture, jewelry, and clothing, from the 13th century to the present. Open Tues. and Thurs. noon-7pm, Wed., Fri., Sat. 10am-3:30pm, and Sun. 10:30am-4:30pm. Admission 20,000zł, students 5000zł, Sun. free.

Zamek Królewski (Royal Castle), Plac Zamkowy 4 (tel. 31 91 99, ext. 170). Residence of the Polish kings after the capital of Poland was moved from Kraków to Warsaw by King Zygmunt III Waza. Completely destroyed during World War II, it was reconstructed by the inhabitants of Warsaw. **Royal Suites** open to guided tours only; individual sight-seeing possible in other parts of the Castle. Open Tues.-Sun. 10am-6pm. Royal suite: admission 50,000zł, students 25,000zł. Other interiors: admission 30,000zł, students 15,000zł; Thurs. free, but you have to pick up your free passes at the *kasa*. Exhibitions (i.e. history of Polish numismatics) 15,000zł, students 10,000zł. Tours in English, German, French, Russian, Italian, Spanish, and Portuguese 160,000zł. The *kasa*, where you can purchase tickets and reserve guides, is located across from the Castle, at ul. Świętojańska 2 (tel. 635 39 95). Open Tues.-Sun. 10am-6:45pm. Guides can be reserved only Tues.-Fri. 10am-2pm.

Muzeum Marii Skłodowskiej-Curie (Maria Skłodowska-Curie Museum), ul. Freta 16 (tel. 31 80 92). In the house that belonged to the Skłodowski family. Founded

in 1967, on the 100th anniversary of Maria's birthday. Describes the life and work of the scientist, winner of two Nobel Prizes, in 1903 and 1911. Open Tues.-Sat. 10am-4:30pm, Sun. 10am-2:30pm. Admission 10,000zł, students 4000zł.
Łazienki Królewskie (Royal Łazienki), ul. Agrykoli 1 (tel. 621 62 41, ext. 233, 234; reservations 621 82 12). Branch of the National Museum; summer residence of the last Polish king, Stanisław August Poniatowski, and one of the finest 18th-century palace complexes of its kind in Europe (see Sights).
Muzeum Fryderyka Chopina (Chopin Museum), has three divisions. The main one is at ul. Okólnik 1 in the **Zamek Ostrogskich** (tel. 27 54 71, ext. 34 or 35). The life and works of Chopin, both in Poland and abroad, after his emigration. Portraits, manuscripts, letters, keepsakes, and a piano belonging to the great composer, which he used during the last two years of his life. Open Mon., Wed., Fri. 10am-5pm, Thurs. noon-6pm, Sat.-Sun. 10am-2pm. Admission 20,000zl, students 10,000zl. The Ostrogski Castle is also the seat of the Fryderyk Chopin Society, which organizes Chopin recitals, chamber concerts and exhibitions, and courses in Chopin's music interpretation. The other division of the museum is located at ul. Krakowskie Przedmiescie 5, and is called **Salonik Chopinów** (The Chopins' Drawing Room), open year-round Mon.-Fri. 10am-2pm. Finally, there is the museum in Żelazowa **Wola**—for a detailed description, see page 398.
Muzeum w Wilanowie (Wilanów Palace), ul. Wiertnicza 1 (tel. 42 81 01). See page 394, above.

ENTERTAINMENT

Much of Warsaw's social life revolves around its *winiarnie* (wine cellars) and *kawiarnie* (cafés). The most popular outdoor cafés are those on the Rynek Starego Miasta and along Nowy Świat. In addition to the cafés, discos, jazz clubs, and pubs add flavor to the Warsaw night life.

Student Clubs

Café Lapidarium, ul. Nowomiejska 6 (tel. 635 68 28 or 31 85 36). Open-air garden, full of the young and famous. Rock concerts Wed.-Sun. 7pm on the Big Stage, 10pm on the Small Stage. Tickets 50,000zł. Munch on delicious crêpes while listening to the music: strawberry crêpes 22,000zł; crêpes with cottage cheese and chives 15,000zł. Foster's on tap 40,000zł. The owners also operate a ship **Barka na Wiśle,** down the hill from the Old Town on ul. Mostowa, where live music vibrates Fri.-Sun. 7pm-2am.
Jazz Club Akwarium, ul. Emilii Plater 49 (tel. 20 50 72). Top spot in the city for live jazz. Funky African masks on the first floor. Drinks and food served: steamed vegetables 45,000zł; broccoli in butter 55,000zł. Concerts daily. Various artists—stop by or call for their program. Shows start at 8:30pm.
Park, al. Niepodległóśći 196 (tel. 25 71 99; 25 91 65). International disco; one of the more popular student hangouts in Warsaw. Cover 60,000zł, students and women 30,000zł. 50% off with ISIC. Beer starts at 15,000zł. Entrees 30,000-60,000zł. Open Fri.-Sat. 9pm-4am.
Hybrydy, ul. Złota 7/9 (tel. 27 37 63), near the commercial district. A major-rager for footloose students. Look for ads in local papers. Rock and pop concerts mainly on Tues. and Wed. Rap and funk Fri.-Sat. 7pm-4am. Cover: Fri. 50,000zł, Sat. 40,000zł, women 10,000zł. Also open on Sun. 10am-2pm—60s music, 15,000zł. Informal dress.
Klub Stodoła, ul. Batorego 10 (tel. 25 86 25; 28 60 31). Local rock bands perform Sun. and Tues. 7pm (no charge). Discos: Fri. 8pm-4am, Sat. 8pm-4am—rock 'n' roll, reggae, hip-hop, techno. Cover: Fri. 50,000zł, students 30,000zł; Sat. 70,000zł, students 40,000zł.
Riviera-Remont, ul. Waryńskiego 12 (tel. 25 74 97). Tuesdays 9pm-2am: reggae party, free of charge. Wed. 9pm-2am: rap, acid jazz, reggae. Grilled dishes and snacks. Men 30,000zł.
Klub Medyka, ul. Oczki 5/7 (tel. 628 33 76, ext. 12). Disco: Fri.-Sat. 8pm-4am; cover 60,000zł, students 20,000zł, the first 100 women pay no cover. Sundays 6pm-10:30pm, Latino music, 20,000zł.

Club Giovanni, ul. Krakowskie Przedmieście 24 (tel. 26 92 39). On the premises of the Warsaw University, to the right and down the steps as you enter through the main gate. Student hangout. Vegetarian pizza 85,000zł; 45,000zł for half; 22,000zł for a quarter. Open Mon.-Fri. 10am-2am, Sat.-Sun. noon-10pm.

Concerts and Theater

Classical concerts fill the Gallery of Sculptures in the **Pomarańczarnia** near the Pałac Łazienkowski on Sundays at 5pm in June and July. Enquire about concerts at **Warszawskie Towarzystwo Muzyczne** (Warsaw Music Society), located at ul. Morskie Oko 2 (tel. 49 68 58). Tickets are available Mon.-Fri. 9am-3pm and before concerts. Also, the **Pomnik Chopina** (Chopin Monument) nearby in the Park Łazienkowski hosts free Sunday performances by some of Poland's most distinguished classical artists. (May-Oct. noon and 4pm.) **Teatr Wielki,** Plac Teatralny 1 (tel. 26 30 01), Warsaw's main opera and ballet hall, offers performances almost daily. **Filharmonia Narodowa** (National Philharmonic Orchestra) gives regular concerts in its hall at ul. Jasna 5 (tel. 26 72 81), but is closed during the summer. For information and tickets, visit the **ZASP** *kasy teatralne* (tel. 21 94 54; 21 93 83), al. Jerozolimskie 25 (open Mon.-Fri. 11am-6pm, Sat. 11am-2pm). Classical music is also played in the Sala Koncertowa (concert hall) of the Royal Castle, at pl. Zamkowy 4 (tel. 635 41 95). Tickets sold Tues.-Sun. 10am-3pm.

The best place to go for live jazz is the **Akwarium** at ul. Emilii Plater 49 (tel. 20 50 72), open Mon.-Thurs. 11am-11pm, Fri.-Sun. 11am-3am. **Sala Kongresowa** (tel. 20 49 80, or 693 61 40), at the Palace of Culture and Science, hosts "serious" jazz and rock concerts. Herbie Hancock and Bob Dylan performed there recently. The entrance to the Sala Kongresowa is from ul. Emilii Plater.

Pubs

The Irish Pub, ul. Miodowa 3 (tel. 26 25 33). Promotes folk and country music. concerts start at 7:30pm, free of charge. Not surprisingly, Irish music prevails. Guinness or Kilkenny are the obvious favorites here, at 35,000-70,000zł.

Harenda Pub, at the Harenda Hotel, ul. Krakowskie Przedmieście 4/6 (tel. 262 90 00). A slightly older crowd. Wooden benches make for a rustic but cozy decor. Beefsteaks 70,000zł. Open daily 8am-3am.

Pub Falcon That's It, ul. Marszałkowska 55/73 (tel. 621 96 75). Free rock 'n' roll and funk concerts at 7pm on random evenings. Greek salad 50,000zł, tuna salad 45,000zł.

John Bull Pub, ul. Jezuicka 4 (tel. 31 37 62, ext. 14). The first English pub in Warsaw. Open daily noon-midnight.

Pod Baryłką (Under the Barrel), Mariensztat Square. 34 kinds of Polish beer, pizza and sandwiches. Open daily 11am-11pm.

Sports

Fitness Clubs: *Studio "Na Trakcie,"* pl. Zamkowy 10 (tel. 31 71 85), has step and aerobics classes daily 9am-10pm. *Ośrodek Rekreacji Solec,* ul. Solec 71 (tel. 21 68 63), features a weightroom, sauna, and a variety of aerobics classes. *Ośrodek Rozbrat,* ul. Rozbrat 26 (tel. 628 94 81), prides itself on its aerobics, yoga, and karate classes.

Horseback Riding: *Arkan,* ul. Stefana Batorego 37/128 (tel. 25 36 14). *Pa-ta-taj,* at ul. Krótka 9 in Kanie, near Warsaw (tel. 58 58 35). *Hubert,* ul. Statkowskiego 52 (tel. 42 15 10).

Outdoor Swimming Pools: *Basen Warszawianka,* ul. Merliniego 9 (tel. 44 62 07), open daily 9am-6:45pm. 35,000zl. Solarium, beach chairs 30,000zł per day. *Basen Wisła,* ul. Wał Miedzeszyński 407 (tel. 17 24 94), open daily 9am-7pm. 35,000zł. Beach chairs 20,000zł per day. Pool tables 15,000zł per hour. *Skra,* ul. Wawelska 5 (tel. 25 36 21), open daily 9am-7pm. 30,000zł. Beach chairs 15,000zł per day. Tennis courts 15,000zł per hour.

Skating: *Stegny,* ul. Inspektorowa 1 (tel. 42 27 68). *Torwar,* ul. Łazienkowska 6a (tel. 21 44 71), is open year-round.

Kayaking, Sculling, Sailing: Clubs along Wał Miedzeszyński on the Wisła: *AZS*, ul. Wał Miedzeszyński 399 and 373 (tel. 17 74 92 and 17 84 99 respectively); *Warszawski Klub Wodniaków PTTK*, ul. Wał Miedzeszyński 295 (tel. 17 89 76); *Yacht Klub Polski*, ul. Wał Miedzeszyński 337 (tel. 17 75 01). The *PTTK Sailing Center* has its office at ul. Solec 8 (tel. 21 56 20).

■ NEAR WARSAW: ŻELAZOWA WOLA

Żelazowa Wola, the birthplace of Fryderyk Chopin, is 50km from Warsaw. It can be reached by bus or train, but should be planned as an entire daytrip (unless you have a car). Take the bus to Sochaczew from the main PKS bus station, or a train from the central train station going in the same direction. In Sochaczew, change to local bus #6, which will take you directly to Żelazowa Wola.

The unpretentious little **cottage**, surrounded by a beautiful, romantic park, is a division of the Fryderyk Chopin Museum. At one time, Żelazowa Wola was the site of a large manor-house that belonged to the Skarbek family. The composer's father, a Frenchman named Nicolas Chopin, worked as a French tutor in the house of Count Skarbek. Here, he met and married Justyna Krzyżanowska, a distant cousin of the count. They had four children—three daughters and a son, Fryderyk, who was born on February 22, 1810. The Chopin family did not stay at Żelazowa Wola for very long; they moved to Warsaw in October 1810, shortly after Justyna had given birth to Fryderyk. The relations between the Chopin and the Skarbek families remained cordial and young Chopin often came back to Żelazowa Wola for his vacations.

The alcove in which Fryderyk was born is always adorned with fresh flowers. The interiors, although lacking the original furniture that had belonged to the Chopin family, are maintained in the style of the era. Among the various mementos on display, are the composer's birth certificate and the first *polonaise* he had written at the age of seven. Every Sunday at 11am and 3pm, locals and tourists gather here to listen to the weekly **concerts**; Chopin's soulful music resonates throughout the park, captivating the hearts of the listeners, as it did some 160 years ago. The **museum** (tel. 223 00) is open Tues.-Sun. 9am-5:30pm (May 1-Sept. 30), and 10am-4pm during the remaining part of the year. (Tickets to the house and park 40,000zł, students 15,000zł. Park only 10,000zł, students 5000zł. Tape-recorded tours in English, German, French, Italian 50,000zł. Concerts 100,000zł.)

THE BALTIC COAST AND LAKE REGIONS

Northern Poland includes the Baltic Coast, the ancient regions of Pomerania (Pomorze), Mazuria (Mazury), and Podlasie. **Pomerania** means "along the sea," and indeed it stretches along swamps and dunes of the Baltic coast. The main urban centers of this region are the port of **Szczecin** (Stettin) on the lower Odra River in the West, and **Gdańsk** (Danzig) and **Gdynia** in the East. The landscape between Szczecin and Gdynia is desolate, but beautiful and far from monotonous—the dunes, coastal lakes, lagoons, and small fishing ports form a captivating *mise-en-scène*.

West of Pomerania, **Masuria** is a region of woods and lakes; its nickname, "the land of a thousand lakes," is by no means an exaggeration—in fact, Masuria and the Suwałki region in the far Northwest count about 4000 lakes. This is where the largest and the deepest of the Polish lakes are located. **Śniardwy** and **Mamry** are each over 100 square kilometers (39 square miles) in area; **Hańcza** reaches 108m (354 feet) in depth. The lakes of Masuria and Suwalki are connected by canals, rivers, and streams, creating excellent conditions for kayaking and sailing. The main urban centers are **Olsztyn** and **Augustów,** the last outposts of civilization for tourists venturing out into the wild and beautiful lake regions.

The **Podlasie** region is especially known for the **Puszcza Białowieska** (the Białowieża Forest). Once the favorite hunting ground of Poland's kings, the forest is

Baltic Coast of Poland

POLAND

RUSSIA

Baltic Sea

Camping Sites ▲

TO YSTAD
AND RONNE

TO COPENHAGEN
AND TRAVEMÜNDE

TO YSTAD   TO OXELÖSUND   TO HELSINKI

GERMANY

Zatoka
Gdańska

Zalew
Szczeciński

Odra R.

Wisła R.

Pasłęka R.

Zalew Wiślany

Mierzeja Wiślana

Zat. Pucka

N

20 miles

20 kilometers

Frombork
Elbląg
Pasłęk
Morąg
Ostróda
Iława
Brodnica
Malbork
Dzierzgoń
Kwidzyn
Grudziądz
Chełmno
Wąbrzeźno
Toruń
Świecie
Gdańsk
Gdynia
Hel
Jastarnia
Tczew
Pelplin
Skórcz
Starogard Gd.
Kościerzyna
Przywidz
Kartuzy
Wejherowo
Władysławowo
Lębork
Łeba
Rowy
Ustka
Jarosławiec
Dąbki
Darłowo
Sławno
Koszalin
Słupsk
Kępice
Miastko
Bytów
Czersk
Chojnice
Tuchola
Sępólno Kraj.
Wiecbork
Złotów
Wyrzysk
Margonin
Bydgoszcz
Piła
Wałcz
Jastrowie
Szczecinek
Czaplinek
Drawno
Białogard
Łobez
Kołobrzeg
Mrzeżyno
Rewal
Pobierowo
Dziwnówek
Dziwnów
Świnoujście
Police
Szczecin
Stargard Szcz.
Goleniów

J. Narie
J. Jeziorak
Zarnowieckie
J. Łebsko
J. Gardno
J. Wicko
J. Bukowo
J. Jamno
J. Raduńskie
J. Wdzydze
Bobięcińskie
J. Wierzchowo
J. Wielimie
Charzykowskie
J. Piłe
J. Betyn
J. Lubie
J. Drawsko
Mielno
Ustronie Morskie

0
0

now a national park, and the habitat of a huge variety of wildlife, but the undisputed king of the forest is the European bison. The entire region has been christened "Poland's green lungs," and is given maximum environmental protection. The main urban center of the region is **Białystok,** to the north of the forest preserve.

■■■ SZCZECIN

Szczecin (SHCHEH-cheen) is situated near the Polish-German border at the mouth of the Odra River, about 65km from the Baltic Sea coast. Settled in the 8th century and chartered in 1278, the city has changed hands repeatedly due to the strategic value of its ports. Now a major industrial center and international port, it is filled with the blue and white uniforms of sailors disembarking from their ships. Along with Świnoujście, Szczecin is a good starting point for tourists coming to Poland from Germany, Sweden or Denmark.

ORIENTATION AND PRACTICAL INFORMATION

The most convenient way to reach Szczecin is by train—there are lines linking Szczecin with major cities in both Poland and Germany. The Szczecin Główny railway station is very conveniently located—near the river in the center of the city, within walking distance of most hotels and sights.

Tourist Offices: ORBIS, pl. Zwycięstwa 1 (tel. 431 06), has the same address as the Hotel Policyjny, but is located on the other side of the square. Open Mon.-Fri. 9am-5pm and Sat. 9am-1pm. **COIT (Centralny Ośrodek Informacji Turystycznej),** ul. Wyszyńskiego 26 (tel. 34 04 40), sells maps and brochures. Their pride is a book on the history of Szczecin in cartoons, illustrated by Henryk Sawka, a comic strip artist. English spoken. Open Mon.-Fri. 9am-5pm.

Budget Travel: ALMATUR, ul. Bohaterów Warszawy 83 (tel. 34 63 56), arranges accommodations in summer hostels.

American Express: At Hotel Radisson, pl. Rodła 10 (tel. 59 51 58). Cash your traveler's checks here, 24 hrs. per day, 7 days a week. 5% commission.

Post Office: ul. Bogurodzicy 1 (tel. 34 61 24). Open Mon.-Sat. 8am-8pm. **Postal Code:** 70-405.

Telephones: at the post office, open 24 hrs. **City Code:** 0-91

Trains: The train station is at the end of ul. 3-go Maja; take tram #3 to the center, or walk 10 minutes. To: Gdańsk (3 per day, 5hrs.; 153,000zł), Poznań (5 per day, 3hrs.; 109,500zł), Berlin (2 per day, 2½hrs.; 360,000zł). The railway recently introduced **antique trains**—*pociągi turystyczne "Retro"*—they travel to four tourist locations around the city on weekends (including the lakes, Drawno and Wirów, 100km). Schedules posted at train station and ORBIS offices (59,000-138,000zł round-trip; trains leave around 8am and return 2-4pm).

Buses: The bus station is at pl. Tobrucki, two minutes away from the train station to the northeast.

Hydrofoil: The hydrofoil that used to connect Szczecin and Świnoujście started operating again in June 1994; at press time, there were two trips per day (130,000zł one way; 1hr. to Świnoujście).

ACCOMMODATIONS

For a complete list of summer youth hostels, call **ALMATUR** (tel. 34 63 56) or stop by their office at ul. Bohaterów Warszawy 83.

Youth Hostel, ul. Monte Cassino 19a (tel. 22 47 41). Take tram #3 from the train station or the center to ul. Kołłątaja; then go one stop on bus #67 in the direction of ul. Karola Miarki. Junior with hostel ID 65,000zł; senior with ID 75,000zł; all others 90,000zł. Sheets 25,000zł. Lock-out 10am-5pm. Open year-round.

Hotel Policyjny, pl. Zwycięstwa 1 (tel. 51 31 91). Better quality rooms. This ex-police barrack merely displays a sign "Hotel," in black Gothic-style letters, above the oak-shadowed entrance. Singles 214,000zł. Doubles 235,000zł, with bath 353,000zł. Triples 288,000zł. Quints 321,000zł.

Hotel Garnizonowy, ul. Potulicka 113 (tel. 74 26 85; 79 53 43). Slightly rougher conditions for less $$$. Singles 160,000zł. Doubles 300,000zł. Triples 390,000zł. They also mix and match travelers in 8-bed rooms for 85,600zł per person.
Hotel Pomorski, Brama Portowa 4 (tel. 33 61 51). Very good location, across from the hotels Policyjny and Garnizonowy. Singles with bath 440,000zł. Doubles without bath 450,000zł.
Youth Hostel, ul Grodzka 22 (tel. 33 29 24), at Szkoła Podstawowa no.63 (elementary school). 10 minutes away from the Szczecin Castle. Operates June 24-Aug.26.
"Foundation in Support of Local Democracy" Hostel, ul. Marii Skłodowskiej-Curie 4 (tel. 704 72). In a white school building called "Zachodniopomorska Szkoła Samorządu Terytorialnego." Take tram #9 to "Traugutta," continue two blocks, turn left, and walk to the end of the street. The service and facilities are worth the long trek. Singles 180,000zł. Doubles 36,000zł, with bath 500,000zł.

FOOD

Pod Muzami, pl. Żołnierza Polskiego 2 (tel. 34 72 09). Connected to the expensive Hotel Victoria. Heavily carpeted atmosphere with brass chandeliers. Standard Polish fare for about 80,000zł. A live band plays nearly every night at 9pm; cover charge 50,000zł. Open Sun.-Thurs. noon-4pm, Fri. and Sat. noon-5am.
Café Vega (tel. 48 99 85), at entrance H of the Palace of Pomeranian Princes. Quick and convenient, with an English menu. Eclectic entrees, ranging from breakfast meals and pizza to Chinese dishes. Their tastes in art and design are eclectic too: white furniture and blue tablecloths accompanied by Ukrainian watercolors on the walls. Entrees 35,000-50,000zł.
Mic Mac Fast Food, ul. Niepodległości 13, at the Brama Portowa. A sparkling Polish McDonald's clone—good food in a spotless neo-Greek interior. Regular burgers 25,000zł. Veggie burgers 16,500zl. Veggie and chicken salads 29,500zł. Open 24 hrs.
Kamiro Bar, at train station. Pork chops, *bigos*, or shish kebabs for 30,000zł. No chairs. Open 24 hrs. with breaks (7-8am, 7-8pm, and 2:30-4am).
Całusek ("The Little Kiss") and **Kogucik** ("The Little Rooster") are kiosks around the Brama Portowa, where you can get a taste of the more affordable "people's food." Both serve burgers, hot dogs, fried chicken and shish kebabs for around 15,000zł. **Całusek** is open daily 11am-7pm and **Kogucik** is open 10am-7pm.
Marwit kiosk, ul. Niepodległości 3, across the street from Całusek and Kogucik. Stop by for a glass of deliciously healthy carrot (6300zł) or beet juice (3400zł). A taste of the "old Poland."

SIGHTS

A few original structures remain, but much of the city's beauty lies in its restorations. A relic of the Prussian settlement, the Baroque **Brama Portowa** (Port Gate) marks the downtown area. Originally called the Brandenburg and later the Berlin Gate, it was built in 1725 and spared during the removal of the city fortifications in 1875 because of its architectural value. It features Odra's god, Viadus, leaning against the jug from which flow the waters of the river, female figures blowing trumpets, a Latin inscription commemorating Frederic Wilhelm I, King of Prussia, and a panoramic view of 18th-century Szczecin.

A block away on ul. Wyszyńskiego, the 13th-century **Katedra Św. Jana** (Cathedral of St. James the Apostle) looms over the town. Destroyed during World War II, it was carefully restored to its original Gothic shape; however, restoration has yet to replace its windows. The history of the cathedral was written down by organist Karol Loewe, and is now displayed in a show-case in the vestibule for all visitors to read.

On ul. Korsarzy, the giant, newly restored **Zamek Książąt Pomerańskich** (Palace of Pomeranian Princes; tel. 34 73 91) overlooks it all from Szczecin's oldest settlement site. The seat of Pomeranian princes until 1630, it later belonged in turn to the Swedes, the Prussians and the Germans. Especially worth seeing are the sarcophagi and the palace tower. The large courtyard is often the site of theater performances and concerts (open daily 10am-6pm; 10,000zł).

POLAND

Behind the palace, on ul. Panieńska, bravely stands the abandoned **Baszta Panieńska Siedmiu Płaszczy** (Maiden's Tower or the Tower of Seven Cloaks), the only one of 37 original towers of the medieval fortifications to survive World War II. The tower was situated only 20m away from the Maiden's Gate, one of the four original gates that led to the city—Brama Młyńska (Mill Gate) from 1268; Brama Św. Ducha (Holy Ghost Gate) from 1306; Brama Panieńska (Maiden Gate) and Brama Passawska from 1307. The medieval city walls were pulled down to be replaced by Prussian fortifications in 1724-1740.

If you head back to the Old Town market square from the palace, you will come upon the old **Ratusz** (Town Hall), built in 1450 in place of the former one from 1425. After World War II, it was rebuilt in the original Gothic style, and since 1975, it houses one of the city's three branches of the **Muzeum Narodowe** (National Museum); this particular branch illustrates Szczecin's history from the Paleolithic to the present. The rest of the museum, chronicling Pomeranian art from the medieval to the modern, is located in the Baroque palace of the Pomeranian Parliament, at ul. Stromłyńska 27/28, north of Castle Hill and 2 blocks west of the St. Peter and Paul Church. (All three branches of the museum open Sat.-Sun. 10am-4pm, Tues. and Thurs. 10am-5pm, Wed. and Fri. 9am-3:30pm. Admission 15,000zł, students 10,000zł. Thurs. free. One ticket gets you into three galleries.)

■ ■ ■ ŚWINOUJŚCIE

A small port and health spa town right on the German border, Świnoujście is a point of departure for cargo ships and passenger ferries to Scandinavia. It is much more, however, than a place to hurry through on your way somewhere else. Świnoujście's shady and mossy emerald parks offer peaceful silence to travelers longing for solitude. The promenade along the sealine (ul. Żeromskiego) is lined with elegant early 20th-century villas that give Świnoujście the appearance and ambience of an old-fashioned resort, where swans play with visitors on the beach.

ORIENTATION AND PRACTICAL INFORMATION

Świnoujście lies on parts of two woody islands, Wolin and Uznam (the latter shared with the German town of Ahlbeck), linked by a ferry on the Świna River. The train and bus stations and the international ferry terminal are all located on the east bank of the Świna River, near the Świnoujście port on Wolin island. The main part of the town is on the west side of the river. You can take the car ferry across the river—it's right next to the bus station. If you arrive in Świnoujście by ferry, it's a five-minute walk from the ferry terminal on ul. Dworcowa, in the northeast direction.

Tourist Offices: ORBIS, ul. Bolesława Chrobrego 9 (tel. 36 67, 48 14, or 44 11), arranges accommodations.

Budget Travel: ALMATUR, ul. Żeromskiego 17 (tel. 58 50), has low rates in private rooms. **PTTK,** ul. Paderewskiego 24 (tel. 26 13), is mainly a travel agency these days, but they are the most willing to help with any other questions (i.e. ferries). This is your chance to purchase a good and inexpensive map of Świnoujście, and to stock up on those hard to find paper goods (padded envelopes, pads). Open Mon.-Tues. and Thurs.-Fri. 7am-3pm, Wed. 9am-5pm.

Currency Exchange: Bank PKO, S.A., ul. Piłsudskiego 4 (tel. 57 33), cashes traveler's checks, exchanges money and does credit card cash advances. Open Mon. and Thurs. 9am-4pm, Tues.-Wed. and Fri. 8am-3pm, Sat. 8am-noon.

Post Office, centrally located at ul. Piłsudskiego (tel. 20 15). Open Mon.-Fri. 8am-8pm, Sat. 8am-1pm. **Photocopier** on the premises. **Postal Code:** 72-600.

Telephone City Code: 9-36

Trains: To: Szczecin (1 per day, 2hr., 48,000zł one way), Prague (1 per day), Warsaw (1 per day) and Kraków (3 per day).

Ferries: For current rates, check with the **Polferries** office, ul. Dworcowa 1 (tel. 30 06), next to the ferries at the main dock. To: Copenhagen (5 per week at

10:30pm, Mon. and Wed. excluded; 9hrs.; 470 Danish kroner round-trip) and Ystad in Sweden (2 per day, 8hrs., 460 Swedish kronor round-trip).

Hydrofoil: In Szczecin, get on the ferry at Przystań, ul. Jana z Kolna 7 (4 tram stops on tram #7 along the river from train station). To Świnoujście (2 per day, 1hr., 130,000zł one way).

Pharmacy: ul. Piłsudskiego 23/25. Open Mon.-Sat. 8am-8pm, Sun. 8am-10pm (the door is locked, but there is always someone on duty inside, so knock).

ACCOMMODATIONS AND CAMPING

If you plan to spend a few nights in Świnoujście, you might want to start the room hunt at the ALMATUR office at ul. Żeromskiego 17 (tel. 58 50). They offer some of the cheapest rates in town and can arrange a stay in a private room for only 125,000zł a night—a great alternative to hotels, which can get pricey. There are no hostels in Świnoujście, so plan ahead if you'll be traveling here in the summer.

Hotel Albatros, ul. Kasprowicza 2 (tel. 23 35). Wake up to the sound of waves in a sunny room. Singles 220,000zł. Doubles 250,000zł, with shower 280,000zł. ("With shower" does not mean with toilet as well!) Triples 390,000zł. Quads 520,000zł. In season, prices go up 50,000zł per person.

Dom Rybaka (The Fisherman's Inn), Wybrzeże Władysława IV 22 (tel. 29 43), faces the port. Primary location for budget prices. Singles 149,800zł. Doubles 214,000zł, with bath and TV 428,000zł. Triples 256,800zł. Quads 286,400zł.

Hotel Bałtyk, ul. Armii Krajowej 5 (tel. 23 91). Centrally located. Singles 220,000zł. Doubles 374,000zł, with bath and TV 495,000zł. Triples 462,000zł. Hotel restaurant serves Polish *kotlet schabowy* and fries starting at 60,000zł.

Hotel Polaris, at ul. Słowackiego 33 (tel. 54 12), is more posh, with thick red carpets, but also more pricey. Singles 385,700zł. Doubles 620,000zł. Triples 738,000zł. All rooms have phones, baths and TVs!

Camping: Camping Relax, ul. Słowackiego 1 (tel. 39 12). Two fees: you pay for each person plus for your tent. Use of camping site 29,000zł/person, students pay 21,750zł. Tents: 9500zł (up to 3 people), 14,000zł (up to 5), 21,000zł (more than 5). 30% off if traveling off-season. Cabins: 3-person cabin—450,000zł in July-Aug., 350,000zł in June, 300,000zł in May and Sept., 200,000zł in Oct. (with fridge 500,000zł in July-Aug.) 4-person cabin with fridge and kitchen—700,000zł in July-Aug., 600,000zł in May-June and Sept.

FOOD

There are **kiosks** by the dozens along ul Żeromskiego. If craving something sweet, try the inexpensive and delicious *gofry*—Belgian waffles with whipped cream and cherries, served hot. **Food stores** include **Kormoran,** ul. Słowackiego 16 (open Mon.-Fri. 7am-7pm, Sat. 7am-5pm). There is another store, by the same name, across the street from the pharmacy, on the corner of ul. Piłsudskiego and ul. Hołdu Pruskiego (open Mon.-Sat. 7am-9pm, Sun. 10am-7pm).

Bar "Neptun," ul. Bema 1, at the beginning of ul. Piłsudskiego across from the post office (tel. 26 43). Quick meal in a Greco-Polish surrounding which includes a blue tub, serving as a fountain, and a fierce plastic, spotted tiger, guarding the bathroom. Run by the charismatic red piranha-wearing Mr. Tomasz Strybel, this self-service place is very affordable: Breakfasts 16,000-43,000zł; pizzas 36,000zł; entrees 25,000-45,000zł. Homemade carrot juice 10,000zł. The sign outside says "We speak a little English," but they speak mainly Italian. Open daily 9am-7pm.

Pizzeria "In Centro," ul. Żeromskiego 12, along the promenade. Delicious Pizza San Francisco, with a curry base and banana and pineapple toppings 33,000zł. 35 varieties of pizza 30,000-70,000zł. Open daily 11am-9pm.

Café Galeria, pl. Słowiański 15. Good coffee, tea and desserts. Full of local high school kids. Open 11am-11pm.

POLAND

■■■ GDYNIA

First mentioned in 1253, Gdynia began as a tiny fishing settlement—major growth came only after World War I, when the town was returned from Germany to Poland by the Treaty of Versailles. Together with the nearby Gdańsk and Sopot, it forms the famous Tri-City metropolitan area, popular with Poles for its seaside piers and beach resorts. Although Gdynia has neither the charm of Sopot or the cultural tradition of Gdańsk, it is of interest to any boat lover.

ORIENTATION AND PRACTICAL INFORMATION

Gdynia is best reached from Gdańsk by the commuter rail, which costs 15,000zł. Gdynia Główna, the main train station, serves as an outreach into other parts of Europe. Both the train and the bus stations are located on the left edge of the town, but it's only a short walk to the center; if you follow ul. 10-go Lutego, it will take you all the way down to the waterfront.

Tourist Offices: IT, at the train station, pl. Konstytucji 1 (tel. 28 53 78; 21 92 25). Very friendly and helpful staff. Maps, referrals to hotels and camping sites, and computerized list of all bus connections from the tri-city area to Western Europe. They also organize trips by hydrofoil—to the resort town of Klapeida in Lithuania (3 days); open Mon.-Fri. 9am-6pm, Sat.-Sun. 9am-4pm. **Sports-Tourist,** ul. Starowiejska 35 (tel. 21 77 34 or 21 91 64, fax 21 99 21), is a member of the International Air Transport Association (IATA). Connected to the LOT Polish Airlines computerized reservation system, it sells air tickets of all major airlines. Multilingual and efficient staff. **ORBIS,** ul. Świętojańska 36 (tel. 20 89 50, 20 28 23, or 20 89 88); open Mon.-Fri. 9am-5pm, Sat. 10am-2pm. **Biuro Zakwaterowań Turystycznych,** ul. Starowiejska 47 (tel. 20 92 87 or 21 82 65), arranges private rooms. Open Mon.-Fri. 8am-6pm, Sat. 10am-6pm. **MART-TUR,** ul. Zamenhofa 17 (tel. 23 02 08), arranges bus connections to Western Europe at the same rates as IT. Open Mon.-Fri. 10am-5pm.

Post Office: ul. 10-go Lutego 10 (tel. 21 87 11). Open Mon.-Fri. 7am-8pm. **Postal Code:** 81-301.

Telephones: at the post office. Open 24 hrs. **City Code:** 0-58.

Ferries: Board at al. Zjednoczenia 2 on Skwer Kościuszki (tel. 20 26 42 or 20 21 54). To: Hel (round-trip 100,000zł, students 70,000zł); Westerplatte (round-trip 100,000zł, students 70,000zł); Sopot (one-way 45,000zł, students 30,000zł); and Gdańsk (one way 100,000zł, students 70,000zł).

Taxis: Radio taxi tel. 91 95, or 91 99 (takes credit cards).

Medical Assistance: In case of emergency, call or stop by ul. Żwirki i Wigury 14 (tel. 20 00 01 or 20 00 02). Private doctors at *Poliklinika EviMed*, ul. Bema 16. (tel. 20 32 35 or 25 07 77). Open 9am-10pm.

ACCOMMODATIONS AND CAMPING

Accommodations in Gdynia are probably the last to fill up in the tri-city area during the summer, a useful thing to keep in mind if you arrive in the Gdańsk area in July or August without a reservation. **Private rooms** can be arranged by the Biuro Zakwaterowań Turystycznych, ul. Starowiejska 47 (tel. 20 92 87 or 21 82 65), opposite the Gdynia Główna train station. Singles 80,000-90,000zł. Doubles 149,000-170,000zł. Triples and quads 60,000zł per person (open Mon.-Fri. 8am-6pm, Sat. 10am-6pm).

Youth Hostel (HI), ul. Morska 108c (tel. 27 00 05). A 5-min. walk from main train station. 132 beds. Polish students 40,000-48,000zł; other Poles and foreigners 52,000-60,000zł. Foreigners must have a valid ID to stay here.

Camping: There's a small camping site (30 places) at ul. Zamenhofa 17 (tel. 23 47 62), next to a soccer field, tennis court, weight room, and sauna. From main train station, take trolley #25, 26, or 30, 7 stops toward Wejherowo (4km, about 12min.), 50,000zł per person. Tent and sleeping bag rental. Tennis courts 40,000zł per hr; weight rooms 15,000zł per hr; sauna 25,000zł per hr.

FOOD

One of the most extensive markets in the tri-city area, **Hala Targowa,** stretches along ul. Jana Radtkego (open Mon.-Fri. 8am-5pm, Sat. 8am-3pm). At the train station, sharpen your sweet tooth at **Wedel** (open daily 6am-10pm) or stock up on drinks and other simple foodstuffs in the food court **Imbis** (open daily 5:30am-midnight). **Chang Cheng,** ul. Dworcowa 1/4 (tel. 20 81 07). A stone's throw from the train station. Extensive menu. Entrees around 100,000zł (open daily 1-10pm).

Bar Ameryka, ul. 10-go Lutego 21 (tel. 21 02 00). Miniature Statue of Liberty above the entrance. Portraits of Lincoln, Reagan, and Nixon adorn the walls. Relatively expensive food. Polish and American entrees 140,000-215,000zł. Open daily 11:30am-1am.

"Róża Wiatrów" Restauracja, al. Zjednoczenia 2 (tel. 20 06 48). Serves tasty duck with apples for only 70,000zł. Wash it down with some gin (60,000zł) or rum (50,000zł). Open daily 1pm-3am.

Bar na kutrze, marooned at Skwer Kościuszki next to the sailboat Dar Pomorza. Serves up fried fish for a mere 8000-14,000zł.

SIGHTS

The **Pier** on Skwer Kościuszki is lined with kiosks which give it a carnival atmosphere. The **warship Błyskawica** is docked here and is open to the public (Tues.-Sun. 1:45am-12:30pm, 1:45-4:30pm; admission 10,000zł, students 5000zł). The **sailboat Dar Pomorza** is also open to the public (ticket window tel. 20 23 71; open Tues.-Sun. 10am-4pm). Built in 1909, this boat served as a school at sea for the Polish navy between 1930 and 1981, and has won several sailing competitions. Also of interest at the pier is the **boat "Bożena,"** which gives tours of the port of Gdynia. (11 per day between 8am and 10pm. Ticket office tel. 51 06 85, ext. 206, after 3pm 57 56 13. Tickets 50,000zł, students 35,000zł for a 1-hr. tour; 35,000zł, students 25,000zł for a 40-min. tour.)

■■■ GDAŃSK

The history of Gdańsk (gda-neesk) is rich in dramatic events. Its strategic location on the Baltic coast and at the mouth of the Wisła River made it a highly desirable site, over which many battles were fought throughout the centuries. Founded by Germans in 1224, it became part of the **Hanseatic League,** a commercial league of North German towns formed in the 13th century to control trade in the Baltic. The city passed into the hands of the Polish kings in 1466, was annexed by Prussia in 1793, and established as a free city by the Treaty of Versailles in 1919. In 1939, the German interference in the dispute between Poland and Gdańsk, then called Danzig, was an immediate cause of World War II, and resulted in many ethnic conflicts. After the war, Gdańsk was fully incorporated into Poland and its population, depleted by the Germans who left, was replenished by refugees from the east. In more recent times, Gdańsk is become known worldwide as the birthplace of *Solidarność* (1980), the first independent workers' union in Eastern Europe, led by Lech Wałęsa, a former electrician at the shipyards.

Today, the city strives to regain its traditional cosmopolitan atmosphere; and the millions of tourists that flock to the city every year attest the success of this policy. Gdańsk is also an outstanding academic and cultural center, home to the Academic Gymnasium originally founded in 1558. Old Gdańsk is associated with such famous names as Hewelius, Fahrenheit, and Shopenhauer.

ORIENTATION AND PRACTICAL INFORMATION

Gdańsk dips its toes in the Baltic Sea, serving as Poland's principal port. From the Gdańsk-Główny train station, the Old Town center lies a few blocks south, across Wały Jagiellońskie, along Motława, tributary of the Wisła River.

POLAND

Tourist Offices: IT, ul. Heweliusza 27 (tel. 31 43 55, fax 31 66 37). The English-speaking staff sells maps, guides, and tickets to major sights. Open Mon.-Fri. 8am-4pm. **ORBIS,** ul. Heweliusza 22 (tel. 31 44 25), sells ferry tickets, international and domestic train tickets, and international bus tickets Call for the ever changing schedules and rates. English spoken. Open Mon.-Fri. 10am-5pm, Sat. 10am-2pm.
Budget Travel: ALMATUR, 2nd floor of Długi Targ 11 (tel. 31 29 31), in the town center. ISICs, bus and train tickets. Open Mon.-Fri. 9am-5pm. **PTTK,** ul. Długa 45 (tel. 31 30 08), and its English-speaking staff will help you arrange a trip to Kaliningrad (where Immanuel Kant lived and taught) from the nearby Elbląg, by hydrofoil (2-hr trip each way; sight-seeing takes 5hrs.; around US$40). For an additional US$40, they will get you a Russian visa. Open daily 9am-6pm.
Consulates: Germany (tel. 41 43 66, or 41 49 80), al. Zwycięstwa 23; **Russia** (tel. 41 10 88), ul. Batorego 15.
Currency Exchange: At hotels, banks, *kantor* desks and certain post offices throughout the city. 24-hr. *kantor* at the train station. **Bank Gdański,** ul. Wały Jagiellońskie 14/16 (tel. 37 92 22), cashes traveler's checks for 1% commission. Visa cash advances without commission. A branch of Bank Gdański is located at the main train station. Open Mon.-Fri. 8am-7pm, "working" Sat. 8am-2pm.
American Express: ORBIS office of Hotel Hewelius. Replaces lost checks; cashes traveler's checks for 3% commission. Holds mail.
Post Office: ul. Długa 22/25 (tel. 38 91 39). Open Mon.-Fri. 8am-8pm, Sat. "free"9am-1pm, "working" 8am-4pm. Kantor and **photocopier** on the premises (1200zł per page). **Fax** bureau. **Postal Code:** 80-800.
Telephones: Open 24 hrs. at ul. Długa 22/25. Ring the bell between 10pm and 6am. **City Code:** 0-58.
Flights: The **airport** is 22km away at Rebiechowo. Buses #110 and B connect it with the train station. The **LOT** office is at ul. Wały Jagiellońskie 2-4 (tel. 31 11 61; open Mon.-Fri. 8am-6pm). All plane tickets also available at **ORBIS.**
Trains: PKP information tel. 31 11 12. To: Warsaw (6 per day, July-Aug. 13 per day, 4hrs.; 144,000zł); Kraków (6 per day, 198,000zł); Prague (1 per day, 15hrs.; 933,000zł plus 300,000zł for optional sleeper), St. Petersburg (1 per day, 36hrs.; 1,350,000zł). For international express trains to Berlin (2 per day; 650,000zł plus 300,000zł for an optional sleeper), take a local commuter train from the Gdańsk Główny station to Gdynia Główna (every 6-12min.). Validate your local ticket by punching it at one of the yellow *kasownik* machines *before* getting on the train.
Buses: PKS information tel. 32 15 32. The bus station is located behind the train station. Enter through the underground passageway. Tickets sold 5:30am-10:20pm. To: Toruń (3 per day, 4hrs.; 106,000zł), Malbork (7 per day; 27,000zł), Vilnius (1 per day, 10hrs.; 300,000zł.)
Ferries: Take the commuter rail to the Nowy Port terminal. To: Oxelösund, near Stockholm (Mon., Wed. and Sun.; off-season only Thurs.; 440kr round-trip); Helsinki (Sun. and Thurs., 260 Finnish markkas one way), Ystad in Sweden (mid-April to mid-Oct. Fri., 360 Swedish kronors round-trip). To book a place, call the **Polferries Travel Office** in Gdańsk (tel. 43 18 87 or or 43 02 12, fax 43 09 75) or the ORBIS travel office.
Taxis: Radio taxi tel. 91 97, 31 59 59, 41 14 11.
Hitchhiking: *Let's Go* does not recommend hitchhiking as a safe means of transportation. Those Warsaw-bound go to ul. Elbląska (near the stadium).
Luggage Storage: at the train station (7000zł per piece per day). Open 24 hrs.
Bookstore: English Books Unlimited, ul. Podmłyńska 10 (tel. 31 33 73). Watch for a black and gold sign and a portrait of Shakespeare. Good selection of books in the English language. Open Mon.-Fri. 10am-6pm, Sat. 10am-5pm.
Pharmacies: 24-hr. **pharmacy** at the train station (one break between 7:30-8am). Pharmacy **Ratuszowa,** ul. Długa 54/55 (tel. 31 51 06); open Mon.-Fri. 8am-8pm, Sat. 9am-2pm.
Medical Assistance: Ambulance service, ul. Nowe Ogrody 1/7 (tel. 41 10 00). Private Doctors are at Podbielańska 17 (tel. 31 51 68). A big blue sign on the building says *Lekarze Specjaliści.* Cost of visit 150,000zł. HIV tests available. Open Mon.-Fri. 7am-5pm.

Central Gdańsk

1 Gdańsk Shipyards Museum
2 Solidarity Monument
3 Old Town Hall
4 Great Mill
5 St. Catherine's Church
6 St. Bridget's Church
7 Ferry to Sopot and Hel
8 Hala Targowa Market
9 Armoury
10 High Gate
11 Golden Gate
12 Church of our Lady
13 Main Town Hall
14 Artus Mansion
15 Neptune Fountain
16 Central Maritime Museum
17 Harbor Crane
18 Holy Ghost Gate
19 Mariacka Gate
20 Chlebnicka Gate
21 Green Gate
22 National Museum
23 Bus Station
24 Gdańsk Główny Railway Station
25 Tourist Office
26 Biuro Zakwaterowań (Private Room Bureau)
27 Almatur

🛈 Police

✉ Post Office

POLAND

Martwa Wisła

STOCZNIA GDAŃSKA

STARE MIASTO

GŁÓWNE MIASTO

OŁOWIANKA

Nowe Ogrody

Hucisko

SPICHLERZE

DŁUGIE OGRODY

BISKUPIA GÓRKA

DOLNE MIASTO

Police

TO TCZEW

Szpital Kliniczny ✚

Emergencies: Emergency doctors, al. Zwycięstwa 49 (tel. 32 39 29 or 32 39 24) or ul. Pilotów 21 in Gdańsk Zaspa (tel. 47 82 51; 56 69 95) are 24-hr. facilities that treat foreigners, but calling ahead is recommended. English spoken. Around 190,000zł per visit. **General Information on Health Emergencies:** tel. 32 39 44. **Drugs hotline:** tel. 41 98 42. **AIDS Information:** tel. 959.

ACCOMMODATIONS AND CAMPING

Gdańsk and the resort town of Sopot up the coast claim Poland's most popular beaches and are commensurately swamped in summer. Reserve well in advance. For help in finding a room, try **Biuro Usług Turystycznych,** at ul. Heweliusza 8 (tel. 31 26 34; 31 17 27), across from the train station. Singles run 165,000zł; doubles 270,000zł (open daily 7:30am-7:30pm). For **private rooms,** try **ORBIS** (tel. 31 21 32; 31 49 44) arranges private rooms in well kept apartments, all centrally located. (Singles 400,000zł. Doubles 600,000zł.) **ALMATUR,** Długi Targ 11 (tel. 31 29 31) directs travelers to student dorms in July-August (doubles 270,000zł). **Mac-Tur,** ul. Beethovena 8 (tel. 32 41 70) also offers private accommodations and can be reached by bus #184. All rooms located near ul. Beethovena. (250,000zł per person on the first day; 220,000zł on following days. Breakfast included.)

Schronisko Młodzieżowe (HI), ul. Wałowa 21 (tel. 31 23 13). Cross the street in front of the train station, head up ul. Heweliusza and turn left at ul. Łagiewniki. Most convenient of the area hostels. Smaller rooms available to escape the kiddie brigade. Kitchen. Showers in basement. Lockout 10am-5pm. Curfew 10pm. 60,000-70,000zł, students under 26 52,000-60,000zł. Sheets 11,000zł. Baggage room 10,000zł.

Schronisko Młodzieżowe (HI), ul. Grunwaldzka 244 (tel. 41 16 60). Take tram #6 or 12 to al. Wojska Polskiego. A long walk even after the endless tram ride. Immaculate and efficiently run. Lockout 10am-5pm. Reception open 5pm-9pm. Curfew 10pm. 48,000-70,000zł per bed. Sheets 10,000zł. Baggage room 10,000zł.

Youth Hostel, ul. Kartuska 245b (tel. 32 60 44). Take bus #161, 167, or 174 from ul. 3-go Maja and get off right at the two-story, cream-colored building surrounded by a brick wall. 1-4-bed rooms. 36,000-70,000zł per bed. Showers. Kitchen.

Camping: Gdańsk-Jelitkowo, ul. Jelitkowska 23 (tel. 53 27 31), opposite the fancy Hotel Marina. From Gdańsk-Główny, take tram #2, 4, or 6 to the last stop. One block from the beach. Use of camping site 32,500zł per person, 22,000zł per tent. Bungalows 80,000zł per person (sleep 3-4). Showers. 10% discount for students. Open May to mid-Sept.

FOOD

From the river walkway, follow the aroma of fresh fish frying. For fresh food of all sorts, try the **Hala Targowa market** on ul. Podmłyńska. (Open Mon.-Fri. and first and last Sat. of the month 9am-6pm.) Appease a late-night craving at the **24-hr. store,** upstairs at Wały Jagiellońskie, across from the train station.

Restaurants

Bar "Neptun," ul. Długa 33/34 (tel. 31 49 88). Hearty, homestyle meat dishes alongside vegetarian entrees. 35,000zł per feed. Open Mon.-Fri. 7am-7pm, Sat. 9am-5pm.

Pizzeria Napoli, ul. Długa 62/63 (tel. 31 41 46). Lives up to the "Best in Town" sign, with its tasty pizza (40,000-80,000zł) and spaghetti (60,000-90,000zł). Take-out and delivery available. Credit cards accepted. Open daily 10am-10pm.

Govinda, ul. Ogarna 107/108, next to Hotel Zaułek. Hare Krishna vegetarian restaurant serving spicy rice (6000zł) with coconut (7000zł) and carrot and beet salads (6000zł). Hindu music a constant. Open daily noon-8pm.

Złoty Kur, ul. Długa 4 (tel. 31 61 63). Clean tables outside. Chicken 45,000zł. *Gołąbki* a must for 35,000zł. Open daily 10am-7pm.

Jadłodajnia u Plastyków, ul. Chlebnicka 13/16 (tel. 31 28 16). In the art students' dorm cafeteria. Homestyle lunches for around 30,000zł. Open Mon.-Sat. 11am-5pm, Sun. 11am-4pm.

"U Szkota" Restaurant, ul. Chlebnicka 9/10 (tel. 31 49 11). This Scottish restaurant with a history serves up Scottish salmon, eel, trout, chicken, duck, and beef for around 100,000zł. Waiters wear kilts. A uniquely red and green plaid experience. Open daily noon-midnight.

"Pod Łososiem" Restaurant (Under the Salmon), ul. Szeroka 54 (tel. 31 76 52). Founded in 1598 by Ambrozy Vermollen; famous for its Goldwasser vodka, containing pieces of gold. Salmon, trout, pike, perch 150,000zł.

Tawerna Restaurant, ul. Powroźnicza 19/20 (tel. 31 41 14), at the end of Długi Targ near the Green Gate. Expensive but delicious, with generous servings. Try the *pstrąg* (trout) for 360,000zł, including side dishes. Veggie plate 157,000zł. House specialty: duck with apples 390,000zł. Open daily 11am-10pm.

Bar Rybny Krewetka, ul. Elżbietańska 10, across from the train station. Cafeteria-style fish bonanza, for less than 20,000zł per meal. Take-out deli section. Fried mackerel, carp, herring, and many other fish for 6700-11,600zł. Open Mon.-Fri. 10am-6pm, Sat. noon-4pm.

Tan-Viet Restaurant, ul. Podmłyńska 1/5 (tel. 31 33 35). Far East meets Eastern Europe at 40,000-290,000zł per entree. Shrimp platters start at 215,000zł. Frog 232,000zł. Open daily 11am-11pm.

Delicje, ul. Rajska 4 (tel. 31 87 35), on the way from the train station to the Old Town. Sparkling new interior. *Bigos* 18,000zł, meat and cabbage *pierogi* 19,000zł. Apple pie 8900zł. Open daily 10am-8pm.

Cafés, Pastry Shops, and Grocery Stores

Palowa, ul. Długa 47 (tel. 31 55 32), in the basement of the town hall. A popular pseudo-medieval café run by the students' union. Tortes from 15,000zł per slice. Coffee 7000-35,000zł. Mixed drinks 40,000-60,000zł. Open daily 10am-midnight.

Kolumbijka, ul. Długa 77/78 (tel. 31 41 20). 11 kinds of coffee 6000-23,000zł. *Barszcz* 5000zł. Scrambled eggs 15,000zł. Open daily 10am-10pm.

Café "Piwnica U Filipa," ul. Długa 45 (tel. 31 08 00). Fashionable pub-like atmosphere promising "muzyka life." Serves salmon (70,000zł), chicken (60,000zł) and margaritas (105,000zł) among other delectables.

Royal, ul. Długa 40/42 (tel. 31 59 24). The ideal pastry shop. Fried apple pastry 7500zł. Open Mon.-Fri. 10am-9pm, Sat. 11am-9pm, Sun. noon-6pm.

Cukiernia Płończak, ul. Na Stoku 46 (tel. 32 349), in the underground passage of the train station. Doughnuts and pastries 3000-5000zł. Open daily 5:15am-7:30pm

SIGHTS

Gdańsk was one of the first Polish cities to undergo an exhaustive postwar facelift. The handsome market square, **Długi Targ,** forms the center of town, where the original 16th-century façade of the **Dwór Artusa** faces out onto the **Fontanna Neptuna** (Neptune Fountain).

Next to the fountain, the 14th-century **Ratusz** (Town Hall) houses the **Muzeum Historii Miasta Gdańska** (Gdańsk Historical Museum); don't miss the fantastic *Red Chamber* with a ceiling covered with allegorical paintings by Baroque masters. A trip up the tower (open July-Aug.) until recently included a series of numbing photographs of Gdańsk just after the war, while the 4th floor exhibited Solidarity printing presses, photographs, and underground journals from 1980-81. (The tower is currently under renovation.) When in the museum, also visit the *White* and the *Winter Chambers,* to read a letter from Oliver Cromwell to the Gdańsk authorities, dated 1656, and written on behalf of English merchants (open Tues.-Sun. 10am-5pm; admission 10,000zł, students 5,000zł).

One block north of Długi Targ is Gdańsk's grandest house of worship, the 14th-century **Kościół Najświętszej Marii Panny** (St. Mary's church). Almost completely rebuilt after its destruction in World War II, the church reigns as Poland's largest brick cathedral. You can climb the 405 steps up the steeple to rise above the din and clatter of the city (open May to mid-Oct. 9am-5:30pm daily. Admission 10000zł. Binoculars at the top of the tower 2,000zł). Enjoy the view—the proud outlines of the Gothic churches seem to float like ships in the sea of brick roofs. In the foreground, you can see the 14th-century **Kościół Św. Katarzyny** (St. Catherine's

POLAND

church) and farther behind, the 15th-century **Kościół Św. Mikołaja** (St. Nicholas's church). The Gdańsk churches were often visited by the Polish monarchs: King Władysław Łokietek supervised court trials in St. Catherine's church, while King Zygmunt III received his electorial diploma in St. Nicholas's church. All monarchs started their stay in Gdańsk with a visit to St. Mary's church. **Ul. Mariacka,** behind the church, is perhaps Gdańsk's most beautiful street. If you follow it through the gate to the Motława River, you will see the huge **Gothic crane** that unloaded medieval freighters.

The narrow street of Długie Pobrzeże along the **Motława River,** lined with cafés and little shops obviously catering to foreigners (check out the prices on some of the silver and amber pieces!), is a popular place with tourists, a nice place for a stroll if you don't mind the crowds. For some more action, visit the 14th-century mill, **Wielki Młyn,** on ul. Wielki Młyn, recently turned into something akin to a mall (open Mon.-Fri. 11am-7pm, Sat. 10am-3pm). The splendid *"Egzotyka"* fruit stand will dazzle you with colorful cherries, tangerines, and papayas for 22,000-38,000zł.

Attend Sunday mass at Lech Wałęsa's parish—the simple brick **Kościół Św. Brygidy** (St. Brigitte's church) at ul. Profesorska 17, just north of the Old Town. Several blocks to the east of the church, on Plac Obrońców Poczty Polskiej, is the **Old Post Office,** which was the rallying point for Polish resistance during the German invasion and since then has become a patriotic symbol. Solidarity flags fly high once again at the **Gdańsk Shipyard** and at the **monument** to the 1970 uprising, north of the center of town, near ul. Jaracza and only one stop from the train station on tram #8. Take a ferry to the island of **Westerplatte,** where you can visit the site of the first shots of World War II. Boats leave from outside the Green Gate at the end of Długi Targ (May-Sept. 9 per day between 9:30am and 6pm, 1hr.; round-trip 70,000zl, students 50,000zł).

The Gdańsk area enjoys more sunshine than any other in the country. To get to **Stogi Beach,** the city's best, take tram #8 or 13 (direction "Stogi") from the train station to the end, or bus #112 or 186 (also direction "Stogi") to the last stop, then follow ul. Nowotna and everyone else, although only the brave (or the foolish) actually venture in the water.

Among Gdańsk's many suburbs, especially worth seeing is **Gdańsk-Oliwa,** with the lush green Park Oliwski on ul. Opata Jacka Rybińskiego (open May-Sept. 5am-11pm, March, April, and Oct. 5am-6pm). Within its gates is the oldest church in Gdańsk, the 12th-century **Katedra Oliwska** (Oliwa Cathedral). You can rest here, while gazing at the golden stars of the high Gothic cross vaults or, if you arrive in August, when the annual Music Festival is held, you can enjoy the sound of the magnificent 18th-century organs.

ENTERTAINMENT

The multi-turreted mansion at ul. Wały Jagiellońskie 1 (tel. 31 61 25) is the home of the student club **Żak,** a center of information on student culture and a most happening place. It has a movie theater (35,000zł, students 30,000zł), a pub downstairs (open Sun.-Thurs. 2pm-midnight, Fri.-Sat. 2pm-2am), and a fashionably downtrodden café upstairs (open Sun.-Thurs. 2pm-2am, Fri.-Sat. 5pm-2am). The café has an "English table' on Tuesdays—beginning at 8pm, only English is spoken. Żak also publishes a magazine (available free of charge), which describes all their events, including weekend live music, usually jazz and rock concerts by both local bands and well-known stars.

For more jazz, head to the **Cotton Club** on ul. Złotnicka 25/29 (tel. 31 88 13) or test your detective skills trying to find the **Yellow Jazz Club,** a ship without an address or a phone number on the Motława River, on ul. Rybackie Pobrzeże. It's worth the hunt. There are three movie theaters, **Neptun, Helikon,** and **Kameralna,** on ul. Długa 57 (tel. 31 53 31).

Every year during the first 2 weeks of August, Gdańsk erupts in the street fair **Jarmark Dominikański.** The **Jantar Jazz Festival,** which visits the city during July and

August, ushers in the September **Polish Film Festival,** held in the NOT building next to the Hotel Hevelius. All tickets are available at ORBIS.

■■■ SOPOT

This little beach resort is the ultimate tourist and recreation spot in Poland. It features miles of white beaches, the longest pier on the Baltic (512m), a horse-racing track, and a spa park. As a health spa, Sopot is renowned in Poland and abroad—every year, thousands of people come here to treat their rheumatic problems with salt and mud baths. Sopot is also an important music center outside Gdańsk, featuring the **Opera and Music Festival** and the **International Song Festival.**

ORIENTATION AND PRACTICAL INFORMATION

Sopot is a suburb of Gdańsk, located 15 minutes away by commuter train (every 12-15min., 10,000zł). It can just as easily be reached by boat from Gdańsk, Gdynia, Westerplatte, or Hel. The train and bus stations are located in the center of the town. Ul. Bohaterów Monte Cassino, the main street in town, is a busy pedestrian mall. It runs perpendicular to the sea and leads to the *molo,* the 512m pier.

Tourist offices: ORBIS, ul. Monte Cassino 49 (tel. 51 41 42), sells train, plane, and ferry tickets, as well as tickets to the Opera Leśna, an outdoor theater built in 1909, where concerts and festivals are held. Open daily 10am-5pm. At the pier, you can buy tickets for boat trips to the Hel peninsula (70min., 150,000zł round-trip, students 120,000zł). **IT,** ul. Dworcowa 4 (tel. 51 26 17), in a little wooden house next to the train station. Arranges budget accommodations in the summer. Also does private accommodations. Open daily 10am-6pm.
Budget Travel: PTTK, ul. Podjazd 1 (tel. 51 06 18). General information and maps. Open Mon.-Wed and Fri. 9:30am-3pm, Thurs. 9:30am-4:30pm.
Currency Exchange: Sopot Bank S.A., pl. Konstytucji 3-go Maja 1 (tel. 51 72 21), opposite the train station. Open Mon.-Fri. 11am-7pm, Sat. 9am-3pm.) **Hotel Grand** changes money 24 hrs. per day, but at lower rates (10%).
Post Office: at ul. Kościuszki 2 (tel. 51 59 51). **Postal Code:** 81-701.
Telephone City Code: The same as in Gdańsk, 0-58.
Ferries: Connect Sopot to: Hel (round-trip 110,000zł, students 80,000zł); Westerplatte (round-trip 80,000zł, students 60,000zł); Gdynia (one way 45,000zł, students 30,000zł). Board at the end of ul. Bohaterów Monte Cassino (tel. 51 12 93).
Taxis: Radio Taxi tel. 51 02 70 or 91 96.
Pharmacy: "Pod Orłem," ul. Bohaterów Monte Cassino 37 (tel. 51 10 18) is the most centrally located. Open Mon.-Fri. 8am-8pm, Sat. 9am-3pm.
Medical Assistance: 24-hr. clinic at ul. Chrobrego 18 (tel. 51 24 55), with entrance on ul. Mieszka I. 190,000zł per visit.

ACCOMMODATIONS AND CAMPING

Sopot *is* one of the most popular resorts in Poland—if traveling in the summer, call ahead and make reservations. Most of the hotels are quite expensive and there are no hostels in the area. Private rooms are often a good alternative; stop by **IT** (see above) for help. Singles run from 77,400-139,000zł, and doubles from 207,300-232,300zł, depending on the category and the location of the room.

Hotel Teodora Dolacińska, pl. Konstytucji 3-go Maja 3 (tel. 51 15 25). Convenient if you can stand the stench coming from the neighboring bar filled with drunks. Singles 165,000zł. Doubles 276,500zł. Triples 334,500zł. Quads 392,000zł.
Hotel Miramar, ul. Zamkowa Góra 25 (tel. 51 80 11), in a wooded area near the beach. Singles with bath 400,000zł. Doubles with bath 560,000-600,000zł. Triples with sink 420,000zł.
Camping: A 100 m from the *Sopot Kamienny Potok* commuter rail station, on ul. Zamkowa Góra, next to Hotel Miramar. Use of camping site 60,000zł per person

per day (plus an extra 35,000zł per day for the tent). Cabins fit up to 3 people (230,00zł, with bath 300,00zł). For more information, tel. 51 80 11.

FOOD

Bar Stefanka, ul. Bohaterów Monte Cassino 41 (tel. 51 45 35). Burgers 14,000-34,000zł. Veggie pizza 30,000zł. Open daily 11am-8pm.

Pod Strzech8, ul. Bohaterów Monte Cassino 42 (tel. 51 24 76). Purple and green lego-land furniture. Specializes in Polish-Jewish food. Lamb and fish 85,000-125,000zł. Salmon 120,000zł. Eel 210,000zł. Open daily 10am-10pm.

Hotel Grand, ul. Powstańców Warszawy 12/14 (tel. 51 00 41). Dine with the rich and famous. Large portions of traditional Polish food for 120,000-220,000zł. Open daily 1pm-midnight.

Kawiarnia Teatralna, ul. Bohaterów Monte Cassino 50 (tel. 51 42 41). Perfect place to enjoy a cup of good coffee. Open daily 10am-10pm.

Minimal, ul. Bohaterów Monte Cassino 67. A mecca for fruit and nut lovers. Various trail mixes as well as domestic and imported fruits. Great for a quick snack between meals. Open daily 9am-midnight.

Pastry shop on the right side of Hotel Grand, ul. Powstańców Warszawy 12/14 (tel. 51 00 41, ext. 294). Satisfy your sweet tooth for affordable prices. *Pączki* only 3500zł. Other pastries start at 4000zł. Open daily 10am-5pm.

Złoty Ul, ul. Bohaterów Monte Cassino 35 (tel. 51 34 79). Choose from 40 kinds of tea and coffee. Entire breakfast for only 30,000zł. Open daily 10am-9pm.

Caffe Bazaar, ul. Bohaterów Monte Cassino 5 (tel. 51 24 37). This self-styled "Kawiarnia Muzyczna" has jazz performers several times a week. Entrees 40,000-90,000zł. Open Sun.-Fri. 10am-midnight, Sat. 10am-2am.

Café Grilland, ul. Bohaterów Monte Cassino 16 (tel. 51 15 44). At the entrance, huge sculptures of a man and a woman carrying the weight of Grilland on their shoulders. Fairly eclectic menu. Gyros 28,000zł, sirloin steak 59,000zł, salads 22,000zł, omelettes 18,000zł. Open daily 11am-9pm.

ENTERTAINMENT

In addition to the aforementioned **Caffe Bazaar,** there is also the **Pub FM** at ul. Monte Cassino 36 (tel. 51 33 59), one of the most popular student beer joints and about the only place in town that seems to be really happening; lots of beer, fun and young people, mostly men. It also serves food; the most notable items on the menu are *pierogi ruskie* (dumplings with potato and cheese filling) for 30,000zł (open daily 12:30pm-2am).

Sopot is truly a music center. The **Opera Leśna** rock and pop music festival dominates the town in mid-August; call ahead for tickets and for other festivals and shows (tel. 51 18 12). Concerts on the pier are held frequently during the summer, on the open air stage. None of them have fixed dates, so watch for street ads to **Amfiteatr na molo** (tickets and information at the pier box office, tel. 51 04 81). Concerts are also organized by the Towarzystwo Przyjaciół Sopotu (Society of Friends of Sopot); call ahead (tel. 51 02 56) or stop by their office at ul. Czyżewskiego 12 for details.

If you're into sports, there are several other places to enjoy the summer fun. At ul. Ceynowy 5/7, **Sopocki Klub Tenisowy** (tel. 51 35 69) rents out its 23 tennis courts. (140,000-150,000zł per hour per court. Open daily 7am-9pm.) The **Sopocki Klub Żeglarski** (Sailing Club), at ul. Bitwy pod Płowcami 67, has boat and windsurfing rentals. The **Stadion Lekkoatletyczny,** at ul. Wybickiego 48 (tel. 51 23 60), has a track and weight room, and a sauna, all of which can be used for 50,000zł per day. West of the Hotel Grand on the Baltic, the recreational complex **Łazienki Północne** (tel. 51 61 51) offers use of a sauna and solarium for a fee, as well as daily rentals of beach chairs.

Stock up on English, French and German newspapers at **Empik** (the Club of International Press and Book), ul. Monte Cassino 51 (tel. 51 10 48), housed in a beautifully revamped building with stained glass Art Nouveau doors (open Mon.-Fri. 10am-6pm, Sat. 10am-2pm). Catch up on recently released American movies at the two cinemas in town: **Kino Polonia,** ul. Monte Cassino 55/57 (tel. 51 03 34), and **Kino Bałtyk,** ul. Monte Cassino 30 (tel. 51 18 56). Tickets 35,000zł.

■■■ HEL

Best known for its beaches these days, the ancient fishing village of Hel once lived off the booty from the boats which became stranded on the Hel peninsula. This arm-like protrusion of land, which shoots out into the Baltic Sea, guards much of the Gdańsk area coast line. Although you can come here from Gdynia by train, the most popular way to get to this windswept village is by boat from Gdańsk or Sopot.

Orientation and Practical Information   There are frequent **train** and **bus** connections between Hel and Gdynia (4 trains per day, 2hrs., 43,000zł; buses every hour, 2hrs., 34,000zł). Hel can also be reached by **boat** from: Gdańsk: (3 per day, 1 per day off-season, 2hrs.; round-trip 150,000zł, students 120,000zł); Sopot (3 per day in season, 70min.; round-trip 110,000zł, students 80,000zł). There is only one **tourist office** in Hel, the **PTTK,** located in a 19th-century fishing hut on ul. Wiejska 78 (tel. 75 06 21, ext. 32 01), which is the main artery of this small fishing village. The entrance to the office is in the back. This non-profit society of Hel fans is staffed by super-friendly volunteers, who try to keep it afloat by running a homey food place, the Bar Turystyczny. Even though their main goal is to organize trips for local youth, they are also willing to help find private accommodations for visitors (open Mon.-Fri. 10am-2pm). The **post office,** ul. Wiejska 55 (tel. 75 05 50), is open Mon.-Fri. 8am-6pm, Sat. 9am-1pm. The **postal code** is 84-150. The **telephone city code** is the same as in Gdańsk, 0-58.

Accommodations   If you want to spend a few days in Hel, stop by the PTTK tourist office; the staff will gladly arrange **private accommodations** for you in the houses of their members (80,000zł per person). If you have no luck with the PTTK office, try to get in touch with the director of Muzeum Rybołóstwa (The Fishing Museum), **Ms. Hanna Bulińska,** who may be able to put you up in her **pensione** at ul. Plażowa 5 (tel. 75 08 48), a large white villa just a few hundred meters west of the museum (70,000zł per person). Another option is the house at ul. Wiejska 82, whose owner, **Mr. M. Michalak** (tel. 75 06 40), can set you up in a double, triple, or quad for 180,000zł per person.

Food   The **Bar Turystyczny,** located in the Wiejska 78 building and run by the PTTK staff, is a tasty and inexpensive choice. The alternate name to this tourist bar is "Jak U Mamusi" ("The Way Mommy Cooks"). This "mommy" away from home serves tomato soup to fight off colds (10,000zł), bean soup (12,000zł), grilled sausage to make you big and strong (12,000zł) and salmon to make you smart (18,000zł). At ul. Wiejska 31, **Bar U Sławka** (tel. 75 06 63), serves up fried salmon (19,000zł), pizza (22,000zł), hot dogs (13,000zł) and fries (10,000zł; open daily 10am-10pm). Farther down the street, at ul. Wiejska 39, **Izdebka**—an old, white and brown hut with a finely crafted street lantern—which feeds its visitors beef stroganoff (30,000zł), tripe (20,000zł) and salmon (18,000zł). This may be one of the few places in the world where salmon is cheaper than tripe (open daily 10am-8pm). At the eastern end of ul. Wiejska are the more fashionable eateries. **"U Maćka" Restaurant,** at ul. Wiejska 82 (tel. 75 06 40), is located in an old sailors' lodge, complete with sheets trapped in nets covering the walls. It serves up salmon for 45,000zł, trout for 19,000zł, and steak for 50,000zł (open daily 9am-midnight).

If you are in the mood for dessert, stop for coffee (10,000zł) and sweets at the coffee house **Maszoperia,** ul. Wiejska 110 (tel. 75 02 97; open daily 10am-10pm), located in a 200-year-old historical hut with a fisherman's traditional half-door. The name of the coffee house means "the Fisherman's House" in the Kashubian dialect—the Kashubs were the initial settlers of the Hel peninsula. Or walk back the way you came to ul. Wiejska 27b, where a huge ice cream cone with green and pur-

POLAND

ple balloons hangs on the side of the building. Inside, the coffee house **"Słoneczna"** ("Sunny") sells the real stuff, which is smaller, less colorful, and tastier, for a mere 3000zł a scoop.

Sights If you arrive by ferry, the first thing you'll see is a red brick building with a wooden tower. This is the **church of St. Peter,** the oldest monument in town (built 1417-1432), which today houses **Muzeum Rybołóstwa** (the Fishing Museum, tel. 75 05 52). The **wooden tower** commands a magnificent view of the town; you will also be able to see Gdynia, Sopot, Gdańsk, and both the military and fishing harbors of Hel. The museum displays nets, canoes, boats, and fishing and boat-building techniques of the last 1000 years. Check out the giant metal "combs" for catching eel, fishermen's ice skates, and needles used for mending nets. The director of the museum, Ms. Hanna Bulińska, will answer all your fish-related questions.

Ul. Wiejska, the main artery of his little town, has retained much of its old atmosphere thanks to a few **19th-century fishermen's houses** (numbers 29, 33, 39 and 110 along the street). These low-set huts with no cellars are made of pine wood and bricks, and face the street sideways. The extension of ul. Wiejska is ul. Kuracyjna; if you continue along this street, you will eventually reach that part of the Hel headland which is closed to visitors. Sight-seeing in this area requires a written permission from the military authorities. This is the location of the **Headland Battery,** which went down in history as the site of the heroic defense of Hel by Polish soldiers at the beginning of World War II. Several concrete firing positions dating from those days still remain on the headland, a tangible proof of the town's valiant past.

■■■ MALBORK

This unassuming little town is known predominantly as the location of Malbork Castle, the main residence of the Teutonic Knights in the 14th century. Today, the castle is one of the largest extant medieval defense systems in Europe.

Orientation and Practical Information Malbork is 40 minutes away from Gdańsk by train, which makes it a perfect destination for a day trip. There are 29 **trains** per day from Gdańsk (49,000zł) and seven **buses** per day. Buses are slightly slower, but also cheaper. (1hr., 27,000zł.) If you need to **exchange currency,** go to the *kantor* at ul. Kościuszki 14 (open Mon.-Fri. 10am-6pm, Sat. 10am-2pm). The **city postal code** is 82-200 and there are several **post offices** in Malbork; one is located opposite the castle ticket window, on ul. Hibnera (tel. 38 38; open Tues.-Sun. 9am-4pm). There is another one next door to the train station at ul. Dworcowa 21. (tel. 26 20 or 25 02; open Mon.-Fri. 8am-8pm, Sat. 9am-1pm.) The **telephone city code** is 0-55.

Accommodations Hotel PKP, ul. Dworcowa 1a (tel. 36 01), is 200m from the train station, on the opposite side of the street. (2-, 3-, 4-bed rooms at 60,000zł per person per night.) Also close to the station is the **Youth Hostel,** ul. Żeromskiego 45 (tel. 25 11), open year-round. To get there, take bus #6, 7, or 8 one stop or bus #1 or 9 two stops to Wielbark. (Polish students 34,000zł, all others 54,000zł. Showers. Kitchen. Reception open 8am-10am and 5-9pm.) The reconstructed **Hotel Zbyszko,** ul Kościuszki 43 (tel. 33 94), is on the right as you head towards the castle. (Singles 193,000zł. Doubles 257,000zł. Triples 322,000zł.) **Hotel Dedal,** at ul. de Gaulle'a 5 (tel. 31 37), originally built for military guests, now welcomes peaceful bed-seekers to its rooms. (Singles with bath 350,000zł. Doubles 400,000zł.) **Hotel Parkowy** (tel. 24 13) doubles as a campsite on the outskirts of town off ul. Portowa; follow the signs from the center. (Singles 200,000zł. Doubles 300,000zł. Triples 360,000zł. Quads 400,000zł. Camping 40,000zł per person; tents 25,000zł. Bungalows 450,000zł.)

Food   There are dozens of **milk bars** on or near ul. Kościuszki, and the winding paths beneath the castle walls along the Nogat River make excellent picnicking grounds. The best of the milk bars on ul. Kościuszki is **Maćko** at no.7 (tel. 25 25), serving cheese-filled naleśniki for 15,000zł, omelette for13,000zł, and meatloaf for 14,000zł (open Mon.-Fri. 8am-5pm, Sat.-Sun. 9am-4pm). Around the castle, ul. Solna, the so-called "Malhattan," ("Mal" for *Mal*bork), is lined with various milk bars and kiosks. Above them all stands the **Bar Pod Wieżą;** gyros 38,000zł, hamburgers 15,000zł, coffee 4000zł (open daily 10am-7pm).

The recently renovated **Café Zamkowa,** located right next to the castle entrance, prepares a regal feast amidst the coats-of-arms that hang on the walls (entrees 110,000-170,000zł; open daily 10am-8pm). Next door, in the Hotel Zamek, the **Sala Bankietowa** is open from noon to midnight and has the same menu. (Disco Fri. and Sat. nights until 3am.) If the long tour of the castle proves to be too tiring, take a break in the **kawiarnia,** located in the basement of the "middle castle," and sip coffee (10,000-15,000zł) or tea (5,000zł) and eat pizza (25,000zł) to regain your vigor.

For a different type of dining experience, go to the busy Italian-style **Pizzeria** at ul. Kościuszki 25 (tel. 39 91), and choose from a variety of tasty pizzas (22,000-55,000zł) or from 5 different kinds of *pierogi*: cheese, *ruskie* (cheese and potatoes), blueberry, meat, or cabbage and mushroom (open daily 11am-9pm).

On your way out of town, stop by the grocery store, **Delikatesy,** ul. Kościuszki 24 (tel. 24 78), and stock up on supplies (open Mon.-Fri. 9am-10pm, Sat. 10am-10pm, Sun. noon-8pm). If, during the day, you were too busy sight-seeing to bother with food, grab a bite to eat at one of the two train station eateries: the **Bufet Non Stop,** open 24 hrs. (with 2 breaks, 7-8am and 7-8pm), and the **café Karolinka,** which serves *bigos* for 14,000zł and pizza for 22,000zł (open Mon.-Sat. 6am-9pm, Sun. 7am-9pm).

Sights   The main sight in Malbork is the **Malbork Castle,** or Marienburg, as it used to be called in its earlier years. To get to the castle, follow ul. Dworcowa from the train station towards the center and take the fork marked "Centrum." Go up the steps to cross the highway, then walk up ul. Kościuszki; you'll see the ruddy castle towers atop the hill. One of the many castles belonging to the Teutonic Knights, Malbork Castle was to become the focal point of the 14th-century power of the Order in Eastern Europe. The Teutonic Knights first came to the region in 1225 at the request of the Polish duke, Conrad of Mazovia. The Order used Conrad's invitation to establish their own state on conquered Prussian soil and in the area of Gdańsk Pomerania; they made Malbork their capital in 1309. The great period of Teutonic castle-building lasted until their crushing defeat at the battle of Grunwald in 1410. Malbork withstood several sieges, until finally in 1457 the Poles defeated their arch enemies under the leadership of King Casimir the Jagiellonian; for the next three hundred years, Malbork served as one of the major arsenals and strongholds in the Kingdom of Poland. After Poland's first partition (1772), Malbork was incorporated into the Prussian state. World War II heavily damaged the fortress, which was used by the Germans as a POW camp (Stalag XXB). With the fall of the Third Reich, Malbork returned to Poland; reconstruction continues to this day.

Like most Teutonic castles, Malbork's layout is rectangular; it was built of brick, on low ground near a river, and it showcases the religious nature and military power of the Order. Despite these similarities, though, it is unique as a complex of three huge castles: the Higher, Middle, and Lower Castles. The construction of the castle began in the mid-1270s with the monastery, later called the **Higher Castle.** It was to contain the main church of the Holy Virgin Mary, the Grand Masters' burial chapel, the chapter-room, the refectory, the brethren's dormitory, the treasury, kitchen premises, a prison cell, and store-rooms. The Higher Castle was surrounded by a fine system of fortifications; between 1335 and 1341 a tower and a bridge over the Nogat River were added. The most splendid additions to the castle were those of the Grand Master Winrich von Kniprode, who had the Rhenish architect Nikolaus Fellenstein design the magnificent **Master's Residence,** located in the so-called **Mid-**

POLAND

dle Castle. Lodgings for guests of the Order were in this part of the castle, along with the biggest and most splendid hall of all, the **Grand Refectory,** where numerous feasts were held. Finally, in the 14th and 15th centuries, an enormous base, called the **Lower Castle,** was developed. It included an armory, chapel, infirmary, servants' lodgings, stables, and storerooms.

After the partition of 1772, the Prussians turned the castle into a military base and a huge storehouse. They repainted the walls in white, covering the characteristic pink and green frescoes; the restoration of the original frescoes is currently under way. In 1961, a **museum** was opened in the castle. Today, it houses collections of medieval sculpture, coins, medals, weapons, ironwork, pottery, tapestries, and amber. (Castle open Tues.-Sun. 8:30am-5pm; Oct.-April 9am-2:30pm. Admission only with guided tour 60,000zł. In English 525,000zł extra).

■■■ FROMBORK

This little town is closely associated with the name and work of Mikołaj Kopernik (Nicholas Copernicus), famous astronomer and scholar, who lived here from 1510 till his death in 1543. It was in this very town that Kopernik conducted most of his observations and research, and composed the masterpiece *De Revolutionibus Orbium Coelestium,* which introduced the revolutionary heliocentric theory that shocked the clergy and greatly influenced the scientific community of that time.

Orientation and Practical Information Frombork is situated on the banks of Zalew Wiślany (Wisła Lagoon), approximately 15km from the Russian border. It is best reached by bus from Gdańsk (5 per day, 2hrs., 42,000-54,000zł). You can also get here by train (49,000zł), but this is more tricky and certainly less direct (you have to change trains in Elbląg) and may easily take up to 4 hours, depending on the connection. Once in Frombork, the **train station** and the **bus stop** are along ul. Dworcowa, with the boat dock right behind them. Return bus tickets must be purchased from the driver, since there is no bus station *per se* in Frombork.

In a parking lot across from the train station stands a wooden hut with the familiar **IT** sign (tel. 75 00). This helpful information office is part of the **"Globus"** chain. (Open daily from 8am until the last customer leaves, sometimes as late as 9pm.) The main office is at ul. Elbląska 2 (tel. 73 54), next to the cathedral in the main town square. The **Czarneckis** (husband and wife team) who run these places, have detailed information on local accommodations, boats to and from Frombork, the cathedral and the Kopernik museum; they also sell brochures and postcards, and arrange **multi-lingual guides** for the major sights (tour in English, German, and French 400,000zł per hr.). Here you can purchase tickets for the **Halex hydrofoil** going to Kaliningrad in Russia (round-trip 450,000zł, under 16: 225,000zł), as well as boat tickets for **excursions off the Frombork coast** (1hr., 45,000zł, students 35,000zł.) In the immaculate whitewashed walls of the mother office at ul. Elbląska 2, you can also have a cup of coffee or a snack, and admire the folk art on display.

There is also another information booth in town, **Interagnus,** located between the cathedral and the PTTK hotel at ul. Katedralna 10 (tel. 73 52). They serve ice cream, but do not have nearly as much info or charm as the Czarneckis! (open daily 9am-4pm). The **post office** is at ul. Pocztowa 1 (tel 71 17), one block from the Rynek (open Mon.-Fri. 8am-6pm, Sat. 9am-1pm); the **postal code** is 14-530. The **telephone city code** is 0-506.

Accommodations and Food If you are stranded in Frombork for the night, try the **Youth Hostel Copernicus** (tel. 74 53), in a quiet wooded area about 400 m from the train station. As you leave the train station, go to the end of ul. Dworcowa and follow the blue and white signs. The rooms in this white cobblestone building are clean and finely decorated for a youth hostel, adorned with plants and pictures of the great astronomer. (121 beds. Poles: 36,000zł, students 24,000zł. Foreigners: juniors 45,000zł, seniors 60,000zł.) For half the price, you can pitch a tent behind the hostel. **Dom Turysty PTTK**, ul. Krasickiego 3 (tel. 72 51 or 72 52), is located next to the cathedral area. (Singles 100,000zł, with bath 150,000zł. Doubles with bath 220,000zł. Triples with bath 300,000zł. Quads 280,000zł.) PTTK also offers dorm-style rooms in three historical buildings in town (60,000zł per person), and a home-style restaurant for travelers (open daily 7am-9pm).

The only real eatery in this little town is **Akcent Restaurant**, at ul. Rybacka 4 (tel. 72 75), off the town square, with entrees for 61,000-73,000zł, and hamburger and fries for 35,000zł (open daily 10am-midnight). The **Hotel Kopernik restaurant** is another option, with *bigos* for 20,000zł, pork chops with swiss cheese for 52,000zł, and a complete breakfast for 60,000zł.

Sights For the main sights, follow the signs from the train station to get to the town square. The Cathedral in the square houses all the major monuments. Enter this massive complex on the south side, facing away from the town. Once you cross the wooden bridge, the *kasa* on the left (tel. 72 18, or 73 96) sells tickets to the **Muzeum Kopernika** (Copernicus Museum) and to the Cathedral. In the museum, you can see copies of *De Revolutionibus Orbium Coelestium* and various documents of Kopernik's life, including a torn piece of paper that served as his Ph.D. diploma, circa 1503. The ground floor of the museum has a fine collection of 14th-century shoes (open Tues.-Sun. 9am-4:30pm; admission 10,000zł, students 6000zł). Next door, in the **Cathedral,** the 17th-century organ has a 7-second echo and is famous for its magnificent sound. There are recitals every Sunday and at various times during the week—the schedule depends on the number of tourist groups on a particular day (admission 14,000zł, students 7000zł.) There is also a **planetarium** in the cathedral square, with frequent shows, but the soundtrack is in Polish only (admission 12,000zł, students 8000zł).

■ ■ ■ OLSZTYN

Olsztyn is the largest town in the Masuria region. Mikołaj Kopernik, the great astronmer, was the town's administrator in the years 1516-1519 and 1520-1521, during which time he continued to defend the town against the Teutonic Knights. In 1772, Olsztyn was annexed by Prussia. After World War I, Olsztyn chose to remain in Prussia—the Poles constituted only one of the four major ethnic groups living in Olsztyn at the time, and they lost the plebiscite to the Germans, Varmians, and Mazurians. After World War II the German population was deported, and ethnic conflicts resulted in a massive emigration of other non-Poles to Germany.

Today, uninteresting Olsztyn's greatest asset is its convenient and lucrative location in the midst of the Mazurian lakes. Every year, thousands of students and other kayak enthusiasts pass through this town on their way to sailing and camping points: Mikołajki, Giżycko, Mrągowo, Ruciane-Nide, Węgorzewo, and Augustów. Of the 6 lakes surrounding Olsztyn, the Jezioro Krzywe (the Crooked Lake) is perhaps the most beautiful, with a beach and miles of trails in the nearby forests.

ORIENTATION AND PRACTICAL INFORMATION

The main train station, Olsztyn Główny, and the bus station are both on pl. Konstytucji 3-go Maja, 15 minutes from the Old Town, where all the main sights are clustered. Follow ul. Partyzantów from the train station to ul. Dąbrowszczaków; turn left and take it all the way to the end. Take a right and you'll find yourself on ul. 22-go Lipca, which leads through the middle of the Old Town.

Tourist Offices: WCIT (Wojewódzkie Centrum Informacji Turystycznej), ul. Staromiejska 1 (tel. 22 27 38) in Wysoka Brama. Maps, general information and directions to hotels. Open Mon.-Fri. 9am-3pm, Sat. 8am-2pm. **ORBIS,** ul. Dąbrowszczaków 1 (tel. 27 45 03; 27 57 93; 27 92 09), does bus, train and plane tickets, and money exchange. Open Mon.-Fri. 8am-5pm, Sat. 8am-4pm. **Travel**

POLAND

Agency Warmia, pl. Konstytucji 3-go Maja 1 (tel. 27 34 92 or 27 64 47), handles bus tickets to Western Europe. Students get a 10% discount on all prices.

Budget Travel: PTTK, ul. Staromiejska 1 (tel. 27 51 56, fax 27 34 42), organizes guides for the Olsztyn area (4-hr. tour in English, French, German, or Russian 400,000zł). They also organize kayak trips (11-day trip about 2,000,000zł, food, kayak, and lodging included. Open Mon.-Fri. 9am-4pm, Sat. 10am-2pm.

Currency Exchange: at the **ORBIS** office, and at various *kantors* in the Old Town, or in the *kantor* next to the bus station, on pl. Konstytucji 3-go Maja 1 (tel. 34 34 80; open Mon.-Fri. 8am-8pm, Sat. 8am-7pm). **Bank Gdański**, ul. Piłsudskiego 11 (tel. 27 22 77), cashes all major brands of traveler's checks for 1% commission. Open Mon.-Fri. 8am-6pm, Sat. 8am-2pm.

Post Office: Main office at ul. Pieniężnego 21 (tel. 27 29 06). Open Mon.-Fri. 8am-8pm, Sat. 9am-3pm. **Postal City Code:** 10-001.

Telephones: at the post office main branch. Open 24 hrs. **City Code:** 0-89.

Trains: PKP Information tel. 33 65 83. To: Warsaw (6 per day, 3hrs.; 115,500zł), Kraków (1 per day, 11hrs.; 192,000zł), Gdańsk (5 per day, 3hrs.; 96,000zł), Toruń (10 per day, 3hrs.; 96,000zł).

Buses: PKS information tel. 33 71 35. To: Warsaw (4 per day, 4½hrs.; 130,000zł); Augustów (1 per day, 4hrs.; 118,000zł); Vilnius (3 per week, 10hrs.; 179,000zł).

Bookstore: "Globooks," pl. Konstytucji 3-go Maja 1 (tel. 34 53 03), above Warmia Travel. Small but adequate selection of English magazines, classics, and dictionaries. Open Mon.-Fri. 10am-6pm, Sat. 10am-3pm.

Pharmacy: At the train station. Open Mon.-Sat. 7:30am-5pm.

Emergencies: Ambulance: tel. 999 or 27 22 22. **Surgery:** tel. 33 77 79, open 4pm-7am. **General Medicine:** tel. 33 77 60, open 5pm-7am. **Dentist:** tel. 33 33 60, open 7pm-7am. **MONAR Drugs Center:** ul. Kajki 3 (tel. 27 22 09), open Mon.-Fri. 10am-4pm.

ACCOMMODATIONS

Hotel Wysoka Brama (High Gate), ul. Staromiejska 1 (tel. 27 36 75). Fresh wood panelling, blankets with stars and the moon to sleep tight. Courteous service; you will be served tea or coffee. Singles 150,000zł. Doubles 200,000zł, with bath 320,000zł. Quads 260,000zł. Single in the tower 390,000zł. Sauna open 24 hrs. (65,000zł/hr).

Youth Hostel, ul. Kopernika 45 (tel. 27 66 50). From the train station, take ul. Partyzantów to pl. Bema, and then take a left onto ul. Kopernika. 30,000-60,000zł per bed. 2- to 12-bed rooms. Lockout 10am-5pm. Open year-round.

Hotel Jantar, ul. Kętrzyńskiego 5 (tel. 33 54 52; 33 54 65). On the square in front of the train station. Used to be a workers' hotel. Singles 90,000zł. Doubles 130,000zł, with bath 170,000zł. Triples 160,000zł.

Hotel Relaks, ul. Żołnierska 13a (tel. 27 75 34). Singles with bath 390,000zł. Doubles with bath 440,000zł. Triples 300,000zł.

Hotel Warmiński, ul. Głowackiego 8 (tel. 33 53 53). Two stops on bus #4 towards the town center from the train station. In the process of being renovated, with higher prices for rooms in the new part. Singles 280,000-420,000zł, with bath 290,000-480,000zł. Doubles 350,000zł, with bath 420,000-700,000zł.

Hotel Garnizonowy, ul. Artyleryjska 15 (tel. 26 93 81). A 15-minute walk from the train station up the hill, along ul. Artyleryjska. Singles 140,000zł, with bath 190,000zł. Doubles with bath 220,000zł.

Hotel Zajazd Lotnisko, ul. Sielska 34 (tel. 27 52 40). 20-minute ride on bus #7 or #13 from the train station towards *Dajtki*. Doubles with sink 240,000zł. Triples with sink 360,000zł. Breakfast, lunch, and dinner included.

Hotel Marko, ul. Jagiellońska 91 (tel. 26 53 48). 20-minute ride on bus #9 from the train station towards *Sanatorium*. Singles 180,000zł. Doubles 350,000zł. Triples 400,000zł.

FOOD

Chicken Bistro, ul. Stare Miasto 3. Packed with young people. Fresh squeezed juices: carrot (8000zł), apple-orange (12,000zł), banana-orange (15,000zł). Fresh salads 10,000-25,000zl. Cheeseburger 17,000zl. Open daily 10am-9pm.

Restaurant Eridu, ul. Prosta 3/4 (tel. 27 94 67). Named after an ancient town in Iraq; serves Middle Eastern dishes. Benjani rice with almonds, raisins, and meat 47,000zł. Open Mon.-Fri. 10am-10pm, Sat.-Sun. noon-10pm.

Dziupla, ul. Stare Miasto 9/10 (tel. 27 50 83). Cherry *pierogi* 14,000zł. Strawberry spaghetti 20,000zł. Open daily 9am-7pm.

Kasztelanka, ul. Prosta 11 (tel. 27 26 68). Traditional Polish food. Pork chop and fries 150,000zł. Open Mon.-Fri. 10am-10pm, Sat.-Sun. 1-10pm.

Jogurcik, ul. 22-go Lipca 5 (tel. 27 50 52). Melt-in-your-mouth milkshakes 8500-17,000zł. Pastries 7000-8000zł. Coffee 6000zł. Open daily 9am-8pm.

Café Staromiejska, ul. Stare Miasto 4/6 (tel. 27 58 83). Live piano music daily noon-2pm and 7-9pm. Coffee 10,000-28,500zł. Pastries 16,500zł. Beer 29,000zł. Open Sun.-Fri. 10am-10pm, Sat. noon-10pm.

Café Sarp, ul. Kołłątaja 14 (tel. 27 33 57). Café of the Polish Architects Society, and the prettiest remodeled granary in Olsztyn. Coffee 10,000zł. Soft drinks 16,000zł. Open daily 10am-10pm.

Ice Cream "Venezia," ul. Kołłątaja 23 (tel. 27 61 88, ext. 206). 1 scoop 2500zł. Open daily 10am-8pm.

SIGHTS AND ENTERTAINMENT

During his sojourn in Olsztyn as administrator of the town, Kopernik lived and conducted his research in the **Gothic castle,** a red hump surrounded by greenery at ul. Zamkowa 2 (tel. 27 95 96; 27 96 97), just steps away from the **Rynek** (main town square). The complex consists of the castle itself, built in the 14th century, and of the defensive walls with dungeons. The exterior wall of the northern castle wing still bears a fragment of an astronomical table, made by Kopernik himself and used by him to study the solar equinox. Today, the castle houses a museum which displays 17th-century Dutch portraits and Art Nouveau works. (Open May 15-Sept. 15 Tues.-Sun. 9am-5pm; off-season, Wed.-Sun. 10am-4pm. Admission 20,000zł; students 10,000zł. Tower 5000zł.)

The other museum, **Dom "Gazety Olsztyńskiej"** (The "Olsztyn Gazette" Press House), is located nearby, on ul. Targ Rybny (tel. 27 95 96 or 27 96 97). It has an exhibit on the history of the Polish Press in Warmia and Mazury from 1718 to 1939. A center of Polish culture under Prussian rule, the "Olsztyn Gazette" has been around since 1886 and has served as an important symbol of Polish presence in the ethnically diversified region (open May 15-Sept. 15 Tues.-Sun. 9am-5pm; off-season,Wed.-Sun. 10am-4pm; admission 10,000zł, students 5000zł).

Through the **Wysoka Brama** (High Gate), you enter the Old Town, which boasts the Gothic **Katedra Św. Jakuba** (Cathedral of St. Jacob), with amazing Baroque chandeliers, and two town halls – the Baroque 16th-century **Stary Ratusz** (Old Town Hall), and the **Nowy Ratusz** (New Town Hall), built in 1912-1915.

When tired of sightseeing, play **tennis** on ul. Lumumby (tel. 26 46 21; 30,000zł per hour until 5pm, 50,000zł per hour after 5pm; open daily 9am-9pm), or go **swimming** in one of the lakes surrounding Olsztyn or in the indoor swimming near Hotel Relaks, ul. Żołnierska 139 (tel. 27 74 02 or 27 75 34), on Lake Krzywe. If interested in **horseback riding,** contact Mr. Janusz Kojrys (a legend in Olsztyn!), at ul. Wędkarska 43 (tel. 27 08 02).

■■■ AUGUSTÓW

Closer to Lithuania than to central Poland, Augustów was named after the Polish King Zygmunt August, who granted it city privileges in 1557. Located on three lakes (Necko, Sajno, and Białe) and in the midst of thick forests, the town sleeps in the winter and wakes up in the summer, when backpackers appear in great numbers to take possession of sailboats and kayaks. The beautiful scenery and the cool, clean air make the region around Augustów a wonderful destination for sojourns away from the noise and pollution of the big cities.

POLAND

ORIENTATION AND PRACTICAL INFORMATION

The train station is a 25-minute walk from Rynek Zygmunta Augusta, which is the center of Augustów. The bus station, on the other hand, is conveniently located on the southwest side of the Rynek. If you arrive by train, the easiest way to reach the center is by bus #1, 2, 4, 6 or 10 from ul. Turystyczna, across from the train station. Hotels in Augustów are scattered all over town.

Tourist Offices: IT, Rynek Zygmunta Augusta (tel. 23 19), provides efficient and friendly service. (Open Mon.-Sat. 9am-5pm.) The travel agency that supports them, **Scirocco,** at ul. Zarzecze 3a (tel. 40 00, fax 22 53), organizes kayak trips (1-2 weeks) on the scenic Czarna Hańcza River. (Kayaks 70,000zł. Cabins 110,000zł. Tent sites in package deals 12,000-24,000zł.) Call ahead for the ever-changing schedules of trips organized in the summer. Open Mon.-Sat. 9am-5pm. **ORBIS,** at Rynek Zygmunta Augusta 13 (tel. 26 13 or 39 13), handles plane, train, and ferry tickets, Wasteels, cashes traveler's checks for 5% commission, and will even set you up on a vacation to EuroDisney! **Agro-Universal,** ul. 3-go Maja 4 (tel. 20 80), sells bus tickets from Białystok, Gdańsk, and Warsaw to any destination in Europe. They also organize trips to *Białowieża,* where European bison still roam; to *Wilczy Szaniec* (Wolf's Lair)—Hitler's hiding place in World War II; and to the Baroque basilica in *Święta Lipka*. Availability of trips depends entirely on the number of people willing to travel to any given destination (the minimum is 15 people per trip).

Currency Exchange: at the ORBIS office and in the *kantors*. The one at ul. Młyń ska 2 (tel. 22 54), next to the Rynek, is open Mon.-Fri. 8am-5pm, Sat. 8am-4pm.

Post Office: Main office at Rynek Zygmunta Augusta 3 (tel. 36 79). Open Mon.-Fri. 8am-8pm. **Postal Code:** 16-300.

Telephones: at the main post office. Open Mon.-Fri. 7am-9pm, Sat. 8am-3pm, Sun. 9am-1pm. **City Code:** 0-119.

Trains: PKP train information tel. 22 77. To: Białystok (5 per day, 2hrs.; 73,500zł) and Warsaw (5 per day, 5hrs.; 169,500zł).

Buses: PKS bus information tel. 36 44. To: Białystok (16 per day, 2hr., 54,000zł), Warsaw (4 per day, 4½hrs.; 142,000zł), and Toruń (1 per day, 10hrs.; 210,000zł).

Ferries: at the dock, ul. 29-go Listopada 7 (tel. 21 52, or 28 81). To: around Augustów (4 per day, 1½hr.; round-trip 50,000zł); Przewięź (2 per day July-Aug. only, 2½hr., round-trip 70,000z); and Białobrzegi (1 per day July-Aug. only, 3hrs.; 80,000zł).

Luggage Storage: at the train station. 7000zł per piece. Open 24 hrs.

Pharmacies: at Rynek Zygmunta Augusta 7 (tel. 34 11). Open Mon.-Sat. 7:30am-9pm, Sun. 9am-4pm.

Medical Assistance: there is an Emergency Hospital at ul. Szpitalna 5 (tel. 34 11).

ACCOMMODATIONS

Hotel Hetman, ul. Sportowa 1 (tel. 453 45). A 20-minute walk north of the center, across the street from the Augustów Port station. A real hotel on the lake shore. Doubles 300,000zł, with bath and TV 650,000zł. Triples with bath 500,000zł. Breakfast 50,000zł.

Ośrodek Żeglarski PTTK, ul. Nadrzeczna 70a (tel. 38 50, or 34 55), in a sailing center on the lake. Doubles 139,000zł. Triples 192,000zł. Quads 256,800zł. Cabins (sleep 5) 321,000zł during the summer. Use of campsite: 4000zł per person in a tent, plus 42,800zł for a double, 64,200zł for a triple, and 85,600zł for a quad.

Dom Nauczyciela, ul. 29-go Listopada 9 (tel. 20 21). Freshly renovated "teacher's house" (on the inside) next to the port and the Augustów canal. Friendly staff. Singles 200,000zł, with shower 200,000zł. Doubles 260,000zł, with shower 300,000zł. Triples with shower 405,000zł.

Motel, ul. Mazurska 4 (tel. 38 96). School-like. A 10-minute walk south of the Rynek on al. Wojska Polskiego. Doubles 264,000zł. Triples 345,000zł.

FOOD

A food store is **Sklep Spożywczy,** Rynek Zygmunta Augusta 36 (tel. 27 77; open Mon.-Sat. 7am-9pm, Sun. 9am-6pm).

Pizzeria Best, ul. Chreptowicza 17 (tel. 478 25). A 10-minute walk from the Rynek, along al. Wojska Polskiego. Ultra modern white-washed inn. Serves New York salad for 30,000zł. Pizza 40,000-98,000zł.

The house of Edwarda and Ryszard Kozłowscy, at ul. Nadrzeczna 100 (tel. 467 57), next to Ośrodek Żeglarski PTTK. Amazing family-style food. All meals at one flat rate: breakfast 35,000zł, lunch 45,000zł, dinner 45,000zł. Call ahead! If you give them advance notice, they may be able to set you up in one of their neighbors' houses for 100,000zł per person. Open June-Sept., 8am-7pm daily.

Restaurant Hetman, at Hotel Hetman, ul. Sportowa 1 (tel. 453 45). Long list of Polish cuisine 80,000-120,000zł. Fried mushrooms and eggs with rice 48,000zł. "Dancing" on the weekends. Open Sun.-Wed. 6am-11pm, Thurs.-Sat. 6am-2am.

Restaurant Albatros, ul. Mostowa 3 (tel. 21 23). For years, the only serious restaurant in town. Chicken 42,500zł. Pork chop 50,800zł. Open Mon. noon-9pm, Tues.-Sun. noon-1am. Disco Tues. and Thurs. 8pm-12:30am (20,000zł). Dancing Fri.-Sat. 8pm-1:30am, Sun. 8pm-12:30am (50,000zł).

Bar Zosieńka, Rynek Zygmunta Augusta 10 (tel. 21 24). Huge polka dot tablecloths. It's like eating on the back of a giant ladybird! Fish 16,000-45,000zł. Potato *naleśniki* 15,000zł. Salads 4000-5000zł. Open daily 9am-5pm.

Bar Relax, Rynek Zygmunta Augusta 15 (tel. 452 37). Lots of beer and young people. Beer 13,00-19,000zł. *Kiełbasa* 12,000zł. Open Mon.-Sat. 9am-7pm.

Grill Bar, Rynek Zygmunta Augusta 30 (tel. 52 80). Pizza 25,000zł. Hamburger 15,000zł. Fishburger 19,000zł. Open Mon.-Fri. 9am-7pm, Sat. 10am-4pm, Sun. 10:30am-5:30pm.

Motel Restaurant, in the Motel, at ul. Mazurska 4 (tel. 28 67). Basic Polish fare. Omelettes 17,000-21,700zł. Pork chop 36,700zł. Open daily 7:30am-10:30pm.

Pracownia Cukiernicza, Rynek Zygmunta Augusta 13 (tel. 36 83). The bakery to end all bakeries! Owned by Polikarp Augustyniak, whose name seems to crop up everywhere. Sells stuff by the kilo (40,000-80,000zł per kg). Open daily 9am-5pm.

SIGHTS AND ENTERTAINMENT

It's hard to believe that the **Augustów Canal** actually links Warsaw with the Baltic Sea. That's exactly why it was built in 1824-1839—to circumvent Prussian bans on Polish trade. You can find out more about its origins at the **Muzeum Historii Kanału Augustowskiego** (Museum of the History of the Augustów Canal), located near the port at ul. 29-go Listopada 5a (tel. 23 60). Another branch of the museum, called **Muzeum Ziemi Augustowskiej** (Museum of the Augustów Region), is located at ul. Hoża 7 (tel. 27 54). Both branches are open Tues.-Sun. 9am-4pm.

The various sports activities and the proximity of lakes and woods are what really make Augustów an attractive place to visit. Just a few steps away from the Hotel Hetman, on Lake Necko, you can rent a kayak or a water bike for 25,000zł per hour, or a boat for 20,000zł per hour. Ask them about their special **windsurfing** and **sailing** opportunities (open daily 9am-dusk). Also, **Ośrodek Żeglarski PTTK** rents out kayaks for 100,000zł per day and sailboats starting at 244,000zł per day. If you decide to lodge here, you automatically get 20% off.

■■■ BIAŁYSTOK

The train station in Białystok hums in Belarusian, Russian, and Polish, or even more frequently, in a mixture of the three. Travelers come here to buy and sell goods, and the city caters to newcomers from the East by printing menus in Russian. Yet, only a small number of foreign visitors seem to be aware that a bloody ghetto uprising took place in Białystok in 1943. There are few signs left today of the once-sizable Jewish population; the ruins of the synagogue on ul. Legionowa are being rebuilt to serve the many new businesses that proliferate in the city.

Nearby villages are predominantly Belarusian. There are, however, two Tatar villages in the Białystok region, Kruszyniany and Bohoniki; as the last centers of Muslim religion and Tatar culture (as well as home to two of the three mosques in the entire country), they stand out in predominantly Catholic Poland.

ORIENTATION AND PRACTICAL INFORMATION

The main street in downtown Białystok is the ul. Lipowa, which is a 10-minute walk from the train and bus stations. From the train station, head to ul. Św. Rocha (on the east side of the station); this street will take you straight to ul. Lipowa.

Tourist Offices: ORBIS has two offices in town. One is centrally located at Rynek Kościuszki 13 (tel. 230 47, 237 25, or 204 54), has a *kantor*, and handles train, bus, and ferry tickets. Open Mon.-Fri. 9am-6pm, Sat. 9am-2pm. **Travel Agency Nowator,** at ul. Skłodowskiej 13, organizes buses to several destinations in Western Europe, and gives out free and friendly information. On the second floor of the bus station, the kiosk **Mapy** (tel. 224 61, ext. 32), gives out free info on the city and has an extensive selection of maps.

Budget Travel: The **ALMATUR** office, at ul. Zwierzyniecka 12 (tel. 289 43), sells ISICs and has info on student travel and accommodations. Open Mon.-Fri. 9am-4pm. **PTTK,** ul. Lipowa 8 (tel. 52 30 05), sells maps, guides, train and bus tickets, and directs to local hotels. They organize trips to the Białowieża reservation of European bison and arrange guides for the city of Białystok: 360,000zł for a 6-hr. tour in Polish, 720,000zł for a 6-hr. tour in English or German. Open Mon.-Fri. 8am-4pm.

Currency Exchange: For cash: *kantors* all along ul. Lipowa. *Kantor* at ul. Lipowa 27 (tel. 240 30; open Mon.-Fri. 10am-6pm, Sat. 10am-3pm). *Kantor Fortuna,* at ul. Lipowa 12, in the Salamander Shoe Store (tel. 238 46; open Mon.-Fri. 10am-6pm, Sat. 10am-3pm). For traveler's checks: **Bank PKO S.A.,** ul. Sienkiewicza 40 (tel. 43 66 26), cashes all major brands for 1.5% commission. Visa/MC advances; no fee. Open Mon.-Fri. 8am-6pm.

Post Office: Main office at ul. Warszawska 10 (tel. 43 59 9; open Mon.-Fri. 8am-8pm, working Sat. 8am-1pm). There is also a post office next to the train station, at ul. Kolejowa 15 (tel. 51 14 41). Open Mon.-Fri. 8am-8pm. **Postal Code:** 15-001.

Telephones: at post offices, open Mon.-Fri. 7am-8pm, Sat. 8am-3pm, Sun. 9am-11pm. **City Code:** 0-85.

Trains: Main train station is on ul. Kolejowa (tel. 910). A rail hub in the east. To: Gdańsk (2 per day, 9hr.; 171,000zł), Warsaw (8 per day, 3hrs.; 96,000zł), Berlin (1 per day, 10hr.; 815,000zł), Vilnius (2 per day, 8hrs.; 380,000zł), and Moscow (1 per day, 25 hrs.; 875,000zł).

Buses: The bus station is next to the train station, on ul. Bohaterów Monte Cassino (tel. 224 61, information 936).

Luggage Storage: at the train station. Open daily 8pm-7am and 8am-7pm.

Pharmacies: *Panacea,* ul. Lipowa 47 (tel. 265 42), is open Mon.-Fri. 8am-7pm, Sat. 8am-3pm. The *Apteka* next door (tel. 233 25) is open Mon.-Fri. 7:30am-9pm, Sat. 11am-6pm, Sun. 10am-5pm.

Medical Assistance: Private Doctors, at **"Eskulap,"** ul. Nowy Świat 11 (tel. 263 42 or 249 11). Private **dentists** at ul. Malmeda 6 (tel. 32 31 52 or 32 56 06).

ACCOMMODATIONS

Hotel Rubin, in a stylish building at ul. Warszawska 7 (tel. 77 23 35). Once part of the Branickich Palace, and still connected by an underground passage. Very affordable, it caters to Eastern European visitors, both price-wise and language-wise. Singles 90,000zł. Doubles 180,000zł. Triples 255,000zł. Quads 340,000zł. Quints 425,000zł. Communal bathrooms. Perks include an on-site currency exchange place, **Warb** (open Mon.-Fri. 9am-5pm, Sat. 10am-2pm), and a dentist, next to the reception (tel. 77 29 35).

Hotel Zwierzyniec, ul. 11-go Listopada 28 (tel. 226 29). Less centrally located, but near a stadium, a huge park, and a zoo. Take bus #10 from the train station to ul. Zwierzyniecka. Doubles 400,000zł, with bath 1,000,000zł. Quads 500,000-560,000zł.

Hotel Cristal, ul. Lipowa 3/5 (tel. 250 61, fax 258 00), is considered the best in town. Singles 350,000zł, with bath 450,000zł. Doubles with bath 500,000zł. 24-hr. money exchange on the premises (with breaks 6-8am and 6-8pm).

POLAND

Hotel Turkus, ul. Zwycięstwa 54 (tel. 77 29 35). Located on the road to Warsaw; take bus #4 from the train station. Singles 300,000zł, with bath and TV 400,000zł. Doubles 400,000zł, with bath and TV 500,000zł.

FOOD

Ulica Lipowa has some of the city's best eateries, ranging from the very cheap and proletarian to the very posh and expensive.

Raj Smakosza (Paradise for Food Lovers), ul. Malmeda 1, on the corner of ul. Malmeda and ul. Lipowa (tel. 260 42). Modern milk bar, with very tasty food; a white-and-green oasis for weary travelers. Fresh green salads 10,000z chicken 39,000zł, *bigos* 17,000zł, and *chłodnik* 13,000zł. Open daily 7am-8pm.

Restaurant Cristal, ul. Lipowa 3/5 (tel. 262 45 or 258 00). Upscale establishment with a sparkling green-and-maroon setting that doesn't quite match the Hotel Cristal's drab looks. An equally impressive menu, with caviar (95,000zł), shrimp cocktail (46,000zł), duck (75,000zł), and pears in red wine for dessert (45,000zł). Open 7am-11am for breakfast, 1pm-3am for lunch and dinner.

Pizzeria Paradiso has two eateries. The bigger one is at ul. Skłodowskiej 19 (tel. 256 06) and is open daily 10am-10pm. The smaller place, at ul. Kilińskiego 13 (tel. 32 82 38), is open daily 10am-9:30pm, and features such attractions as Paul Anka tunes, huge mirrors, and apples in a green neon setting. Both establishments cater mainly to students, and serve up various kinds of pizzas (34,000-50,000zł), including *pizza vegeteriana* with egg, corn, and mozzarella toppings for 45,000zł.

Pizzeria Avanti, ul. Sienkiewicza 3 (tel. 43 59 44). Largest pizzeria in town. Pizzas (44,000-90,000zł), pasta dishes (29,000-44,000zł), lasagna (30,000zł), and salads (36,000-71,000zł). Open daily 10am-10pm.

MacBurger, ul. Kolejowa 16 (tel. 51 39 61), on the square in front of the train station. One of those conveniently located fast-food places, which can save your life if you are stuck at the train or bus station, and don't mind killing your hunger with a quasi-whopper (open Mon.-Fri. 8am-7pm, Sat.-Sun. 11am-7pm). Its clone is at ul. Pałacowa 4 (tel. 32 31 62; open daily 11am-9pm). Both places serve *pizza vegeteriana* (25,000zł) and hamburgers (14,000zł). In addition to the standard fast-food menu, the train station establishment also serves potato pancakes (12,000zł) and *naleśniki* with fruit sauce (16,500zł).

Bar Turystyczny, ul. Lipowa 31 (tel. 233 52), is a good and cheap milk bar, where cheese *naleśniki* cost a mere 4400zł, and potato and mushroom cutlets are even cheaper (3700zł). Open Mon.-Fri. 7am-8pm, Sat.-Sun. 8am-4pm.

Café Ratuszowa, outside the white Town Hall at Rynek Kościuszki 3, prepares fresh sandwiches (10,000-22,000zł), and serves ice cream (18,000-26,000zł) and wine (10,000-26000zł/glass). Jazz and rock musicians give concerts on random dates. (Seating: at a table 40,000zł; on the grass 20,000zł. Open daily 10am-midnight, but only if the weather holds.)

Café Journal, ul. Lipowa 6 (tel. 32 95 65). Burgers 22,000zł. Fries 12,000zł. Large beer selection 15,000-30,000zł. Open daily 10am-midnight.

SIGHTS

Although the interiors of **Pałac Branickich** (Branickich Palace) are closed to tourists, this 18th-century mansion, which once belonged to a powerful aristocratic family, is still worth the visit. It is easily the most impressive building in Białystok, a Baroque reminder of city's once glorious past. Today, it houses the Medical School and bustles with students. The **palace park and gardens** are open to the public (April 1-Sept. 30 daily 6am-10pm, and Oct.1-March 31 daily 6am-8pm). To see them, enter through the main gate on Plac Branickich and walk down a long alley. The park and gardens are behind the palace. Also open to the public is the **art gallery Brama,** at the palace's main entrance, ul. Kilińskiego 1 (tel. 41 64 13), where you can admire works of modern art by Białystok's new talents, and even buy the ones that catch your eye (open Mon.-Fri. 11am-5pm).

A short walk to the west of the Palace takes you to the main square, the Rynek, where you can see the small white **Ratusz** (Town Hall). Originally, it served as a

POLAND

trade center, filled with little shops and booths. In 1940, it was demolished by the Russian occupants, who planned to put a monument to Stalin in its place. This plan never materialized, and the site remained vacant until the present building was constructed in 1958. Today, the Ratusz (tel. 214 73 or 214 40) houses the **Muzeum Okręgowe** (Regional Museum). The ground floor of the museum is the **Gallery of Polish Painting,** with a small but impressive collection of paintings covering the period from the mid-1700s to the 1930s. The gallery is divided into three rooms: the first room displays Classic and Romantic works by such artists as Piotr Michałowski and Jan Matejko; the second room exhibits paintings of the second half of the 19th century by Rosakowski and the Kossak brothers; and the third room boasts a collection of paintings in various styles—Impressionism, Symbolism, Realism—by such famous Polish artists as Chetmoński, Witkacy, Malczewski, and Axentowicz. The lower level of the museum hosts an **archeological exhibit,** "The Ancient History of the Białystok Region," illustrating the history of the region from the time of the first settlers (about 10,000 years ago) to the early Middle Ages. (Open Tues.-Sun. 10am-5pm. Admission 10,000zł, students 5000zł. Free for art students.)

Cerkiew Św. Mikołaja (the Orthodox Church of St. Nicholas), at ul. Lipowa 15, was built in 1846 and serves the city's numerous Orthodox believers. The concrete **Kościół Św. Rocha** (Catholic Church of St. Roch), at ul. Św. Rocha, was built a century later, from 1927 to 1946. Its modernist silhouette is visible from any point in the city.

ENTERTAINMENT

The best puppet theater in Poland is located in this wayward eastern city, at ul. Kalinowskiego 2 (tel. 25 031 or 28 631), and is called **Teatr Lalek.** (Call them for details.) There is also a good theater, called the **Teatr PWST** (Theater of the Acting School), at ul. Sienkiewicza 14. Locals claim that it it's better than the professional theaters in town. If you are interested in seeing one of their shows, call Andrzej Brzeziński, the stage manager (tel. 43 54 53), to find out about their repertoire.

The **Philharmonia** is at ul. Podleśna 2 (tel. 41 73 43). The student club **"Herkules,"** at ul. Mickiewicza 2 (tel. 220 21), has periodic concerts. The student pub **"Bez Lokalu"** (Without a Place), at ul. Skłodowskiej 14 (tel. 204 66), also has occasional concerts and gives out info on local student life.

Go to the **Ośrodek Sportów Wodnych** (Water Sports Center), on ul. Plażowa by the lake Dojlidy (tel. 410 27 71) to jog, swim, or sail. Take bus #15 from the center to Dojlidy, or bus #12 from the train station to the last stop, and then walk southeast for five minutes along ul. Suchowola. (Rentals: kayaks 25,000zł per hour; boats 30,000zł per hour; sailboats 50,000zł per hour; surf boards 50,000zł per hour; and water bikes 30,000zł per hour.)

THE CENTRAL LOWLANDS

The flat lowlands are a picturesque pastiche of fields and woods, gentle hill slopes and lakes. This is where the ancient *Polanie* tribe, to whom Poland owes her name, lived and cultivated their *pola* (fields). Today, both Wielkopolska (Greater Poland) and Mazovia, although not the most fertile lands in Poland, are important agricultural areas. The province of **Wielkopolska** lies in the western part of Poland, on the Warta River; its main urban center is the thousand-year-old-city of Poznań. **Mazovia,** in the east, boasts the capital of Poland, Warsaw.

■■■ POZNAŃ

Poznań has a distinctive flavor that sets it apart from other Polish cities. Its inhabitants are said to be a hardworking, thrifty, conscientious, and patriotic people. They have their own dialect, the result of the 100-year-long cohabitation of Poles and Germans under the Prussian rule. German words were imported freely into the Wielko-polski dialect and modified to fit the different grammatical rules, thus becoming a permanent characteristic of the new "lingo." A typically Poznań-ese word is *pyry*, by which the people of Poznań mean potatoes (called *ziemniaki* in most parts of Poland). Over the years, the word *pyry* acquired a symbolic meaning, and is often used as a pejorative expression in reference to the people of Poznań themselves.

Today, Poznań is the largest city of the Wielopolska region, and since 1925, it has gained world-wide recognition for its International Trade Fairs: in fall and spring, business folk from around the world descend upon the city, filling up hotel rooms and bolstering the local economy. Its location, halfway between Warsaw and Berlin, makes it an important link between the East and West and a major economic center. The city is also a cultural center with old music traditions. Niccolo Paganini in 1829, and Ferenc Liszt in 1843 performed for the Poznań public. Today, many music festivals and competitions are organized here: the **International Festival of Boys' Choirs, Festival of Polish Contemporary Music,** the **Poznańska Wiosna Muzyczna** (Poznań Springtime Music Festival), and the **Henryk Wieniawski International Violin Competition** (Wieniawski (1835-1880), a child prodigy from a musical family, was one of the most celebrated virtuoso performers of the 19th century). One of the best Polish opera companies works and performs in Poznań, together with the world famous Polish Dance Theater, the Poznań Ballet Ensemble, and the "Amadeus" Chamber Orchestra. The city also prides itself on having the best boys' choir in the country, the Poznań Nightingales. The first Polish woman Prime Minister, Hanna Suchocka, was born near here and taught law at the city university.

ORIENTATION AND PRACTICAL INFORMATION

Poznań Główny, the main train station, is in the southwestern corner of the city, a 20-minute walk to the Old Town. To get to the center, take bus #51, 68, or 76 to the end of al. Dworcowa and transfer to any tram headed to the right. The bus station is just 200m down the street from the train station.

Tourist Offices: Biuro Obsługi Cudzoziemców, in the basement of Orbis Hotel Poznań at pl. Gen. Dąbrowskiego 1 (tel. 53 22 05, fax 33 22 11), serves as the local **American Express** representative. Take tram #1 or 2 westward out of the city and get off at the Hotel Orbis stop. Cash traveler's checks, report lost stolen checks, and get in touch with the main office in Warsaw if needed. They will also hold your mail. Open Mon.-Fri. 8am-6pm, Sat. 8am-2pm. **ORBIS,** ul. Marcinkowskiego 21 (tel. 33 09 41), is open Mon.-Sat. 10am-5pm. **Biuro Podróży "Eurostop,"** ul. Fredry 7 (tel. 52 03 44), sells train tickets, often at a discount. Bring your ISIC. Open Mon.-Fri. 9:30am-5pm, Sat. 10am-1pm. **Bon Voyage Business** has two offices: at ul. Towarowa 17/19 (tel. 51 68 02), and at al. Niepodległości 39 (tel. 52 03 33). Bus tickets to Western Europe issued on the spot. Both offices are open Mon.-Fri. 9am-6pm, Sat. 9am-1pm. The bus station office is also open Sun. 2-6pm. **Glob-Tour,** at the train station (tel. 66 06 67 or 69 54 60), arranges private rooms: singles 300,000zł; doubles 400,000-600,000zł. Also a money exchange and tons of **maps.** Open 24 hrs.
Budget Travel: ALMATUR, ul. Fredry 7 (tel. 52 74 44), is always crowded with students, so prepare for a wait, but the staff is quite professional and efficient.
Consulates: U.S. , ul. Chopina 4 (tel. 55 10 88). Phone line always open for emergencies. Open Mon.-Fri. 8:30am-5pm. Stop by their well-stocked library, with over 2000 volumes, and 65 titles of English periodicals (tel. 52 98 74, fax 53 00 53); open Mon.-Fri. 11am-5pm, closed on Polish and American holidays.
Post Office: Main office at ul. Kościuszki 77 (tel. 52 34 53). Open Mon.-Fri. 6:30am-9pm, Sat. 8am-9pm. The post office at the train station (tel. 66 29 50) sells phone cards. Open 24 hrs. **Postal City Code:** 61-743.
DHL International, pl. Wolności 18 (tel. 52 15 74 or 52 15 84). Express packages to over 200 countries in the world.
Flights: All major airlines, including Delta, British Airways, and KLM, are at ul. Gen. Dąbrowskiego 5, down the street from Hotel Orbis. Reservations tel. 48 13 42, 47

POLAND

11 78, 47 11 79 or 47 11 80 (Mon.-Fri. 7am-7pm, Sat. 10am-2pm). **LOT** is at ul. Św. Marcina 69 (tel. 52 28 47).
Trains: PKP tel. 66 12 12 or 69 38 11.
Buses: PKS tel. 53 09 40 (24 hrs.), or 33 12 12; 33 12 28 (7am-7pm).
Public Transportation: trams and buses in Poznań work like the system in Berlin. Tickets correspond to how long they last on the entire system. Maps listing approximate times from one point to another are at each bus and tram stop. The 4800zł ticket is most commonly used. After 11pm the price of a ride doubles.
Taxis: Radio taxi tel. 919, 951, 981, or 51 55 15.
24-Hr. Pharmacies: at ul. 23-go Lutego 18 (tel. 52 26 25) and ul. Głogowska 107/109 (tel. 66 37 01).
Crisis Lines: AIDS hotline: tel. 52 99 18 (open Tues. and Thurs. 3-6pm). **Center of Information for Women:** tel. 52 01 70.
Emergencies: **General Medicine:** ul. Chełmońskiego 20 (tel. 66 37 35). Open Mon.-Sat. 3pm-7am, Sun. 24 hrs. **Chirurgia (surgery):** ul. Kasprzaka 16 (tel. 66 23 55), and ul. Kórnicka 8 (tel. 77 14 42). Open 24hrs. **Dental Emergencies,** at ul Chełmońskiego 20 (tel. 66 00 66 or 66 37 35; open Mon.-Sat. 7pm-6am, Sun. 24hrs.) and at ul. Kórnicka 24 (tel. 77 57 41, ext. 240; open Mon.-Sat. 8pm-7am, Sun. 24hrs.).

ACCOMMODATIONS

There are two youth hostels in Poznań open year-round. For similar prices and better location in the summer, contact ALMATUR (see above), which has the scoop on summer hostels. Poznań hosts several big fairs (March, June, October) and the city fills up very quickly with tourists and businessmen. Getting a decently priced room upon arrival is virtually impossible. Call ahead! For **private rooms,** contact **Przemysław,** ul Głogowska 16 (tel. 66 39 83), or **Biuro Obsługi Cudzoziemców,** pl. Gen. Dąbrowskiego 1 (tel. 53 22 05, 53 17 02, or 33 09 41, fax 33 22 11).

Youth hostel (HI), ul. Berwińskiego 2/3 (tel. 66 36 80). 10-minute walk west of the train station through the Park Wilsona. Very clean, split-level rooms, with two beds on each level. Senior 45,000zł, junior 24,000zł.
Wojewódzkí Ośrodek Metodyczny, the teacher's hostel at ul. Niepodległości 34 (tel. 53 22 51). More spacious, but less centrally located. Take bus #51 from the train station to the Hotel Polonez and walk back one block. 117,000zł per person, students 72,000zł.
Hotel Wielkopolska, ul. Św. Marcina 69 (tel. 52 76 31), near the university in the commercial district. Large and modern with very clean rooms. Singles 360,000zł, with bath 510,000zł. Doubles 620,000zł, with bath 760,000zł.
Hotel Royal, ul. Św. Marcina 71 (tel. 53 78 84). Next door to Hotel Wielkopolska, but much smaller and quieter. If you are tired if the noisy hostel atmosphere, this is a good and not too expensive alternative. Singles 321,000zł. Doubles 428,000zł. Triples 535,000zł.

FOOD

Poznań is the hometown of *pyzy,* a cross between noodles and potato dumplings. These small, round, yeasty rolls are usually served with steak, duck, or other meat as a substitute for boiled potatoes. Poznań's pastries are worth the extra calories—the *rogale świętomarcińskie* (St. Martin's croissants) have various fruit fillings, and are sold by the kilogram on November 11, St. Martin's Day. Every year, over 100 tons of this sweet stuff is sold on just one day!

The tastiest and most accessible restaurants are around the Stary Rynek. The cheapest places get very crowded; both locals and tourists are quick to recognize the "best deal in the square." If there are no places to sit down, try the take-out option and sit somewhere in the Rynek; this is what everyone else seems to do.

24-hr. grocery stores include **Michel Badre,** ul. Libelta 6 (tel. 53 17 93), and **Avon,** ul. Wielka 8 (tel. 53 01 19).

Avanti bistro, Stary Rynek 76 (tel. 66 28 70). Cheap eats. Tasty spaghetti for a mere 14,000-21,000zl. If you are looking for something fast and simple, this may just hit the spot. Open Mon.-Sat. 9am-11pm, Sun. and holidays 11am-10pm.

U Dylla bistro, Stary Rynek 37 (tel. 52 17 76). Regal purple interior. Standard Polish fare. Entrees 8000-12,000zł. Open daily 9am-11pm.

Cara Mia, Stary Rynek 51 (tel. 52 35 81) and **Arezzo,** Stary Rynek 49 (tel. 52 62 53). Enjoy the fresh air and dine outside. Both serve Polish-Italian food. Entrees 24,000-57,000zł. Open Mon.-Sat. 9am-11pm, Sun. and holidays 11am-10pm.

Club Elite, Stary Rynek 2 (tel. 52 62 53), in the Weigh house basement behind the town hall. Some of the best Polish food in town. Dine among three-piece suits. Entrees 85,000-95,000zł. All major credit cards. Open daily noon-10pm.

Snack Bar "U Marcina," Św. Marcina 32 (tel. 52 77 88). Polish food in a pseudo-Greek atmosphere. Check out the daily *polecamy* (recommendations) to get the best food for the least money. Entrees 21,000-42,000zł. Open Mon.-Sat. 10am-8pm, Sun. noon-8pm.

"Adria" Restaurant, ul. Głogowska 14 (tel. 65 83 74), across from the train station. Polish, Ukrainian, Georgian, and Alsatian dishes for 10,000-65,000zł. Open daily 10am-4pm. Dancing Tues., Thurs., and Sun. 9pm-3am, Fri.-Sat. 9pm-5am. Disco daily 11pm-4am. The cafeteria upstairs is open daily 10am-3pm.

SIGHTS

Downtown, in the **Stary Rynek,** opulent 15th-century merchant homes surround the multicolored pearl of Renaissance architecture, the **Ratusz** (Town Hall). The original building was built in the 13th century, and reconstructed after the fires by the architect Giovanni Battista di Quadro in Renaissance style (1550-1560). It is considered to be the finest secular monument of the Renaissance period north of the Alps. Today, it houses the **Muzeum Historii m. Poznania** (town history museum; open Mon.-Tues. and Fri. 10am-4pm, Wed. 10am-6pm, Sun. 10am-3pm; admission 10,000zł, students 6000zł, Fri. free). In front of the Ratusz, where unruly citizens were once flagellated, stands a replica of a **1535 whipping post.** The original, built with the fines paid by maids who dressed too sharply for the tastes of their masters, is on display in the museum.

Behind the Ratusz, on the northeast corner of the Rynek, starts **Ulica Żydowska** (Jewish Street), the center of the prewar Jewish district, with the 1907 synagogue turned in 1940 into a swimming pool. On the opposite side of the Rynek, the **Kościół Farny Marii Magdaleny** (Parish Church), resplendent with frescoes and pink marble, blesses the end of ul. Świętosławska. In the Rynek itself, the **Museum of Historic Musical Instruments,** Stary Rynek 45, stars Chopin's own piano and a collection of instruments from Polynesia and Africa (open Tues. 10am-5pm, Wed. and Fri. 10am-4pm, Sat. 10am-5pm, Sun. 10am-3pm; admission 10,000zł, students 6000zł).

In the oldest part of town, **Ostrów Tumski,** stands the first Polish cathedral, **Katedra Piotra i Pawła** (Cathedral of Sts. Peter and Paul), with a ring of 15 chapels. The original building was constructed in 968, soon after the first Polish bishopric was established in Poznań. Burned down in 1945, towards the end of World War II, it was rebuilt after the war in late-Gothic style. In one chapel, **Kaplica Złota** (Golden Chapel), are the tombs of two famous Piasts: prince Mieszko I (992) and his oldest son, Bolesław Chrobry (the Brave), the first king of Poland (1025).

In 1956, workers protesting high food prices clashed with government troops, and 76 people died. This bloody incident is commemorated in the park on Plac Adama Mickiewicza (next to the university) by two stark crosses knotted together with steel cable and emblazoned with successive dates recalling workers' uprisings across Poland.

ENTERTAINMENT

Pick up a copy of the monthly **Poznański Informator Kulturalny, Sportowy i Turystyczny (IKS)** available at any newsstand. It contains all the information on cultural events in the city and has many useful phone numbers. (It is also translated into English.) All information on the music scene in Poznań can be obtained from Daina Kolbuszewska at the Music Society—**Towarzystwo Muzyczne im. Henryka Wieniawskiego,** across from the Kościół Farny at Świętojańska 7 (tel. 51 64 18). The **Filharmonia,** at ul. Św. Marcina 81 (tel. 52 47 08), has summer concert scenes and attracts some of the best symphonies in Europe.

Jazz Club Żywiec, named after a famous brand of Polish beer, resonates with live jazz and blues Fri. and Sat. nights. Go to ul. Masztelarska (off the Rynek) and turn into the first yard on your left; the club is on your right as you enter the yard. Fencing helmets, Rorschach-type oil paintings make this a compelling hangout for the local youth.
Klub na Żydowskiej, ul. Żydowska 2/3. Definitely worth a visit if you are looking for something more lively. Live rock performances every night of the week.
Stajenka Pegaza (Pegasus' "Little Stable"), located at the corner of Fredry and Wieniawskiego (tel. 51 64 18). Even more "happening." If you like good beer and don't mind spontaneous musical uprisings, drop by and bring your favorite tape; they play it for you. Serious decibels. Open Mon.-Fri. from 11am, Sat. from 1pm, Sun. from 4pm. Till last guest leaves.

For a quick dip in the hot summer months, go to **Jezioro Maltańskie** (Malta Lake), where the **1990 World Kayak Championships** were held. Wooded jogging paths abound. Take trams #1, 4, 6, or 7 from the center and get off at ul. Zamenhofa. There are outdoor swimming pools at os. Piastowskie 106a (tel. 77 23 78), and at ul. Chwiałkowskiego 34 (tel. 33 05 11; open daily 9am-7pm; admission 20,000zł, students 10,000zł; beach chair rental 15,000zł).

■■■ GNIEZNO

Legend has it that the town was built by Lech, the mythological founder of Poland. Archaeological evidence suggests that a stronghold of the *Polanie* tribe existed here in the 8th century. The name of the town is an early form of the Polish word for "nest" (*gniazdo*)—a very appropriate name, considering that, a millennium ago, Gniezno served as the first capital of Poland. In 1000, it also became the capital of the first Roman Catholic archdiocese in Poland, which survived the numerous attacks of the Teutonic Knights in the 14th century, and the Swedish wars and the plague in the 17th. Today, it is a place reigned by nostalgia of the past, but its solemn ambience is livened by groups of tourists, who are continuously reminded of the town's tumultuous past.

Orientation and Practical Information 50km east of Poznan, Gniezno is the perfect destination for a daytrip. The easiest way to get here is by bus (every hour on the hour, 80min., 27,000zł). Gniezno is organized along one main street, ul. Bolesława Chrobrego, which leads from the train and bus stations to the Cathedral. **ORBIS** is at Rynek 7 (tel. 26 48 00, fax 26 37 01); it arranges accommodations and sells train tickets (including Wasteels). For **currency exchange,** stop by one of the many private *kantors* along ul. Chrobrego. There is a 24-hr. grocery store **Jagienka** at ul. Chrobrego 43 (tel. 26 15 97) . The **post office** is at ul. Libelta 3 (tel. 26 52 20); open Mon.-Fri. 8am-6pm. The **postal city code** is 62-200 and the **telephone city code** is 0-66.

Accommodations The **Youth Hostel** at ul. Pocztowa 11 (tel. 26 46 09 or 26 46 00) is connected to the town's elementary school. In 10-bed rooms, 80,000zł per person. In the few 4 and 5-bed rooms, it costs 120,000zł. Kitchen and shower. Lockout 10am-5pm. **Hotel Mieszko,** at ul. Strumykowa 2 (tel. 462 85), overlooks a stadium; it's ideal for joggers. On a side street 10 minutes from the train station, it is one of the few hotels in town. Reservations are recommended. (Singles 230,000zł;

with bath 260,000zł. Doubles with bath 370,000-430,000zł. During the Poznań International Trade Fairs prices go up significantly: singles with bath 410,000-420,000zł; doubles with bath 770,000zł.)

Food At the **Królewska Restaurant,** ul. Chrobrego 3 (tel. 26 14 97, fax 26 46 92), taste the effects of capitalism on the Polish food economy. This pub-like establishment is located in a cellar and boasts sparkling red and white tables, a fireplace, and tuxedoed waitstaff. Pork, beef, and poultry entrees 70,000-100,000zł (restaurant open daily 10am till the last guest leaves; snack bar 9am-10pm, and drink bar 11am-midnight). The **Bar and Café Avanti,** at ul. Łubieńskiego 8 (tel. 26 35 62), on the corner of ul. Chrobrego and ul. Łubieńskiego, serves up spaghetti, hot dogs and burgers for 9,000-18,000zł (open Mon.-Sat. 9:30am-8pm, Sun. 11am-8pm).

Sights At the end of ul. Chrobrego and past the Rynek is the monumental **Cathedral,** dating back to the 14th century. Its walls and foundations, however, conceal a much longer history of pre-Christian presence and at least four earlier churches, the oldest of which was probably constructed in the 9th century. The first Polish king, Bolesław Chrobry (the Brave), was crowned here in 1025, twenty-five years after Gniezno had become the seat of Polish archbishops. Tours descend into the stone building's underworld to explore the various remains of the pre-Christian past, such as the structures used for "pagan" rituals. The Cathedral's bronze 12th-century door presents the life and martyrdom of St. Adalbert (Św. Wojciech) in 18 *bas-relief* scenes with now-illegible Latin inscriptions.

Outside the cathedral, the serene yard leads to the 12th-century **Church of Saint George** and to the **Archdiocesan Museum** (tel. 26 37 78). The exhibits displayed here presumably belonged to the Cathedral in its more active and prosperous days. The 10th-century chalices certainly testify to the good taste of the previous owners; goblet belonged to princess Dobrawa, wife of Mieszko I, the first prince to be baptized in Poland (open Tues. Sun. 10am-4pm; admission 12,000zł, students 6000zł).

If you are interested in more recent history, visit the **Muzeum Początków Państwa Polskiego** (Museum of the Origins of the Polish State), at ul. Kostrzewskiego 1 (tel. 26 48 41), near the lake Jelonek in the western part of the town. Start out by watching the documentary about the Piast dynasty. Once you have familiarized yourself with the origins of Christianity and monarchy in Poland, move on to the two exhibits displayed at the Museum: the paintings of the famous **brothers Kossak** from the turn of the 19th and 20th centuries, mostly of horses and the military; and next, the various **documents** which will tell you all you ever needed to know about the history of the Polish state (open Tues.-Sun. 9am-5pm; admission 15,000zł, students 10,000zł).

■■■ BYDGOSZCZ

Bydgoszcz received city privileges in 1346, and for many years existed as a quiet merchant town. Subjugated by Prussians and Germans between 1772 and 1939, it was then known as **Bromberg.** Today, its infrastructure and organizing spirit are exemplary in the continually changing Poland. Well-positioned between Gdańsk in the north and Poznań in the south, Warsaw in the east and Berlin in the west, it is a popular stopover between any of these destinations. Surrounded by rivers, lakes, and the *Bory Tucholskie,* forests still largely untouched by the industrialization craze, it is a convenient starting point for kayak lovers and backpackers.

ORIENTATION AND PRACTICAL INFORMATION

The main train station, Bydgoszcz Główna, at ul. Zygmunta August 7, is a long walk to the center along ul. Dworcowa, which runs perpendicular to the train station. The bus station is far out in another direction, at ul. Jagiellońska 50/58.

Tourist Offices: IT, ul. Zygmunta Augusta 10 (tel. 22 84 32), opposite the main train station. Maps sold by efficient and friendly staff. Open Mon.-Thurs. 7am-3:30pm, Fri. 7am-3pm. **Voyage Travel Agency,** ul. Gdańska 69 (tel. 28 62 42), arranges buses to Western Europe. Open Mon.-Fri. 10am-4pm. **Sports-Tourist,** at ul. Gdańska 9 (tel. 22 81 11 or 22 81 66, fax 28 69 59), is connected to the LOT reservation system, and sells air tickets of all major airlines. **ORBIS,** ul. Gdańska 42 (tel. 22 96 34), also sells tickets. Open Mon.-Fri. 10am-5pm, Sat. 10am-2pm. **Budget Travel: PTTK,** ul Mostowa 5 (tel. 22 79 10), is on your right just before you hit the Rynek coming from ul. Gdańska. Pick up a free copy of *BIK (Bydgoski Informator Kulturalny)*, published monthly, for all vital information on cultural events in Bydgoszcz.

Currency Exchange: For cash: the *kantor* in the department store Rywal, ul. Gdańska 47 (tel. 22 74 35), is one of the most conveniently located. Open Mon.-Fri. 9:30am-6:30pm, Sat. 9:30am-2pm. For traveler's checks: **Bank PKO,** ul. Gdańska 21 (tel. 22 18 76, ext. 177) accepts all major brands for 1.5% commission. Open Mon.-Fri. 8am-6pm, Sat. 9am-1pm.

Post Office: at ul. Pocztowa 2 (tel. 22 32 51). A smaller office is located at ul. Gdańska 58 (tel. 21 18 11). Open Mon.-Fri. 8am-8pm, Sat. 8am-2pm. **Postal code:** 85-001.

Telephones: at all post offices. **City code:** 0-52.

Trains: Train station tel. 22 06 61 or 22 06 62. To: Toruń (25 per day, 40 min; 40,500zł), Warsaw (3 per day, 4hr.; 135,000zł), Gdańsk (20 per day, 2hr.; 59,000zł), Kraków (2 per day, 8hr.; 162,000zł), Prague (1 per day, 12hr; 762,000zł plus 49,000zł for a reserved seat or 300,000zł for a sleeper). International ticket windows also sell Wasteels and Interrail passes.

Buses: Bus station tel. 22 16 91 or 22 02 68. Local bus #77 links both the bus and train stations.

Taxis: Radio taxi tel. 919.

ACCOMMODATIONS

Szkolne Schronisko Młodzieżowe, ul. Sowińskiego 5 (tel. 22 75 70). A 5-minute walk from the train station. Neat and supremely organized. 95 beds. Singles 150,000zł. Doubles 200,000zł. A bed in 4- to 10-bed room is 42,00050,000zł for Polish students, 42,000zł with HI card. Other Poles pay 80,000zł, with ID 65,000zł. Foreigners: senior 140,000zł, junior 80,000zł. All prices drop by 20,000zł after the first night. Showers. Kitchen. Lockout in July-Aug. only, 11am-5pm.

Hotel Centralny, ul. Dworcowa 85 (tel. 22 88 77). Just a few steps down ul. Dworcowa opposite the train station. Singles 260,000zł. Doubles 450,000zł, with bath 500,000zł. Triples 600,000zł. Quads 720,000zł.

Hotel Torbyd, ul. Chopina 11a (tel. 41 60 25). Across from the bus station. From the train station, take bus #77 to the end; it's the white building next to the hockey rink named "Torbyd." Doubles 270,000zł. Triples 350,000zł.

Hotel Garnizonowy, ul. Sułkowskiego 52 (tel. 71 04 12). If arriving from the east (i.e. Warsaw), get off at the *Bydgoszcz Leśna* station; the hotel is right in front of the station. Otherwise, take bus #77 from the main train station to Rondo Jagiellonów and transfer to bus #52 heading towards *Osiedle Leśne*. Get off at ul. Sułkowskiego and head towards the only tall building in the area. Singles 210,000zł. Doubles 320,000zl. Triples 330,000zł.

FOOD

Bar Bistro, ul. Gdańska 38. Four kinds of *pierogi* 18,000-24,000zł. *Naleśniki* 6500zł. Scrambled eggs 13,000zł. Open daily 9am-7pm.

Bar Wiktor, ul. Gdańska 79 (tel. 21 11 52). Coffee 9000zł. Pizza 23,000-36,000zł. Open Mon.-Sat. 9am-8pm.

Bar Tekla, ul. Gdańska 55 (tel. 21 04 71). Calzone 27,000zł. *Fasolka po bretońsku* (beans in tomato sauce) 15,000zł. *Barszcz* 4000zł. Open Mon.-Fri. 9:30am-8pm, Sat. 10:30am-8pm, Sun. 11:30am-7pm.

U Jędrusia, ul. Gdańska 24 (tel. 27 02 83). Your basic, Polish mother's kitchen. Meatloaf 23,000zł. *Bigos* 23,000zł. Open daily 9:30am-6pm.

Mister Quick, ul. Jagiellońska 2 (tel. 22 71 80). A spotless version of McDonald's. Curry chicken 37,000zł. Pizza 25,000-68,000zł. Burger, fries, and drink 36,000zł.
Savoy, ul. Jagiellońska 2 (tel. 22 94 63). Greek and Polish cuisine. Gyros 64,000-73,000zł. Greek salads 15,000-35,000zł. Sunday "dinosaur" disco 6-10pm; it's either older music or for older people, or both. Comfy red and black 1970s decor, with armchairs that swallow you up! Open Mon.-Sat. noon-4am, Sun. noon-10pm.
Kaskada, ul. Mostowa 2 (tel. 22 85 44), opposite PTTK. Three establishments under the auspices of one. Posh red and white café upstairs and a proletarian milk bar downstairs. The café is open Mon.-Fri. 10am-8pm, Sat.-Sun. noon-8pm. The milk bar serves *krupnik* for 8600zł, *kapuśniak* for 13,700zł, and meat entrees for 22,000-40,000zł. Open Mon.-Fri. 7am-7pm, Sat.-Sun. 9am-4pm. Small 24-hr. grocery store also on the premises.
Hotel Pod Orłem eateries: ul. Gdańska 14 (tel. 22 18 6 or 22 18 62). This freshly renovated hotel, built in 1822, has a restaurant, bar, pastry shop, and a deli. In the **restaurant,** feast on *chateaubriand* for 374,000zł. Most entrees around 200,000zł. Open daily 7am-midnight. The **bar** is open daily 1pm-midnight. Cakes at the **pastry shop** start at 50,000zł per kg. Open Mon.-Sat. 4am-5pm. The **deli** carries many of the dishes served in the gold-dripping restaurant, but at a lower price. Cheese *naleśniki* 50,000zł/kg. *Bigos* 65,000zł/kg. Russian salad 80,000zł/kg. Open Mon.-Fri. 9am-5pm, Sat. 9am-2pm.
Kawiarnia Cristal, ul. Gdańska 35 (tel. 22 02 47). Hip art nouveau *artiste* hangout. Pastries 12,000-17,000zł. Coffee 10,000-28,000zł. Open daily 10am-9pm.
Café Węgliszek, ul. Batorego 1 (tel. 22 66 73), on the Rynek. Beautifully carved wooden interior and exterior. Meeting place for local artists and writers, with occasional live music. Open Tues.-Fri. 11am-midnight, Sun. 4-10pm.
Hala Targowa market place, at ul. Podwale 5, a block from the Rynek. Open Mon.-Fri 6am-7pm, Sat. 7am-7pm, Sun. 9am-1pm.

SIGHTS AND ENTERTAINMENT

One of the most beautiful buildings in Bydgoszcz is the **Hotel Pod Orłem** (Under the Eagle), constructed in 1822 in Classical style, and rebuilt in 1896 by the famous Polish architect Józef Święcicki, who added neo-Baroque elements to the already existing structure. The Hotel got its name from the huge eagle perched on top, spreading outstretched wings. Originally, when the Bydgoszcz region was still under Prussian rule, the eagle wore a Prussian crown. In 1918, when Poland regained her independence, the Prussian crown was replaced with a replica of the Polish monarchs' crown. In 1939, the Germans removed the eagle, and renamed the hotel "Danziger Hoff." It was not until after the war that the eagle was able to return to its rightful roost on the hotel's roof. Reconstruction was undertaken in the early 1980s, and today the hotel has recovered all the splendor of its early days.

The **regional museum,** bearing the name of **Leon Wyczółkowski,** a 20th-century painter, consists of two branches. The museum on ul. Gdańska 4 (tel. 22 75 76, 22 98 14, or 22 16 08) displays around 60 paintings and graphics of Leon Wyczółkowski, as well as 180 works of his students (open Tues.-Wed. 10am-6pm, Thurs.-Sat. 10am-4pm, Sun. and holidays 10am-2pm). The other branch of the museum is in an 18th-century warehouse, **Biały Spichrz,** at ul. Mennica 1 (tel. 27 03 93) on Wyspa Młyńska (Mill Island). It focuses on the history, culture, and craftsmanship of the Bydgoszcz region from the Middle Ages to the early 20th century.

Music lovers can go to the **Opera** to see such all-time favorites as *My Fair Lady* or *Fiddler on the Roof* (*kasa* tel. 21 02 87; open Mon.-Thurs. 3-6:30pm, Sun. 9am-11am), or buy tickets to **Filharmonia Pomorska im. I. Paderewskiego,** ul. Libelta 16 (tel. 21 09 20 or 21 07 52), which has regular series of concerts—all the classics and more. If you are not particularly fond of classical music and prefer a different genre, **Café Węgliszek** at ul. Batorego 1 (tel. 22 66 73) has occasional live performances. There is no real schedule, so call and check with the manager.

If you like to jog or just want to chill out, ease on down the nice paths in the **Park Leśny** in Myślęcinek. Take bus #1 or 2 from ul. Gdańska to the end. There is a **windsurfing school** in Czaplinek on the Drawsko Lake (tel. in Bydgoszcz (052) 61 76 26, or in Czaplinek (0-966) 55 454). They have yachts, tennis courts, and a sauna. You

POLAND

can also take a trip to **Bory Tucholskie,** the forest near Bydgoszcz, or to **Brda River.** Cabins, camp sites, and boat and kayak rentals are available through PTTK (see above). They arrange **kayak trips** down the Brda river (65,000zł per kayak per day plus an extra 250,000zł for maps and transportation of the rented kayaks back to the owners), and they also take care of accommodations.

■■■ TORUŃ

One of the very few cities to escape the World War II bombings and pillaging, the city of Toruń exudes an almost medieval atmosphere; the peace and quiet is interrupted only by the horns of Polish Fiat cars, which are now being steadily replaced by their Western counterparts as Poland continues to pursue its road to capitalism. Situated on the banks of the Wisła River, Toruń was a Slav settlement in the early Middle Ages. In the 13th century, the Teutonic Knights built a town and a fortress on the site. Toruń received city privileges in 1233 and soon afterwards it became a prominent trade center and a member of the Hanseatic League. As a result of the Toruń Peace Treaty in 1466, Toruń was ruled by Polish kings until 1795, when it found itself within Prussian borders. Today, the historic, picturesque town is once again one of Poland's scientific, economic, and cultural centers.

ORIENTATION AND PRACTICAL INFORMATION

Toruń lies 47 km east of Bydgoszcz, halfway between Warsaw and Poznań. There are several train stations in the city; the main one, *Toruń Główny,* is located on the opposite side of the Wisła River. Take bus #22 or 27 across the river. The *Toruń Miasto* station is closer to the Old Town, but not all trains stop here—check train schedules at your point of departure carefully, before you decide to make Toruń Miasto your destination. The bus station is near Toruń Miasto; it's a 10-minute walk north of the Rynek.

Tourist Offices: IT in the town hall on the Rynek. Free information on Toruń and Kopernik. Helpful English-speaking staff. Open Mon. and Sat. 9am-4pm, Tues.-Fri. 9am-6pm, Sun. (May-Aug. only) 9am-1pm. **ORBIS,** ul. Żeglarska 31 in the Old Town (tel. 225 53), sells train and bus tickets. Open Mon.-Fri. 9am-5pm.

Budget Travel: PTTK, pl. Rapackiego 2 (tel. 249 26 or 282 28), sells maps and brochures, handles bus connections to Western Europe, and arranges guides for the city (160,000zł per hour for English, French, German, Russian, and Spanish **tours.** Minimum of 2hr. required). Open Mon.-Fri. 8am-5pm, Sat.-Sun. 9am-1pm.

Currency Exchange: Bank PKO, ul. Kopernika 381 (tel. 109 15 or 102 08) cashes traveler's checks for 1.5% commission. Open Mon.-Fri. 8am-6pm.

Post Office: The two most conveniently located offices are at the train station (open Mon.-Fri. 7am-8pm) and at Rynek Staromiejski 15 (tel. 263 48). Open Mon.-Fri. 8am-8pm, Sat. 8am-1pm. **Postal code:** 87-100.

Telephones: open 24 hrs. at the train station and at Rynek Staromiejski 15. **City Code:** 0-56.

Trains: Information tel. 130 44; ticket office tel. 130 31. The international *kasa* (ticket office) sells Wasteels, Interrail, and international tickets. Open Mon.-Fri. 8am-5pm, Sat.-Sun. 8am-3pm.

Buses: PKS information tel. 228 42.

Taxis: For 24-hr. service tel. 91 93 or 383 73.

Luggage Storage: open 24 hrs. at the train station. (7000zł per piece per day.)

Pharmacy: at Rynek Nowomiejski 13 (tel. 221 76). Open Mon.-Fri. 8am-7pm, Sat. 9am-4pm. Also at ul. Piekary 33 (tel. 107 99), one block from Rynek Staromiejski. Open Mon.-Fri. 8am-7pm, Sat. 8am-3pm.

Medical Assistance: Stomed, ul. Ducha Świętego 14 (tel. 269 01 or 217 17). Doctor's visit 100,000-130,000zł. Open Mon.-Fri. 7:30am-7pm (registration 7:30am-6pm).

AIDS Hotline: tel. 272 56. Hardly a hotline: open Tues. and Thurs. 4-6pm only.

ACCOMMODATIONS AND CAMPING

Hotel Aeroklub Pomorski, ul. Bielańska 66 (tel. 224 74, fax 263 29).Take bus #27 from the train station to pl. Teatralny and change to bus #36 heading towards *Osiedle Bielany* (20 min.) Located next to a small sports airport; fly their hang gliders! Singles 170,000zł. Doubles 200,000zł. A bed in a triple or a quad 60,000zł.
Dom Turysty (Wycieczkowy), ul. Legionów 24 (tel. 238 55). Take bus #22 from the train station to Plac Rapackiego, then bus #10 outside the Old Town gate to the 3rd stop. Singles 160,000zł. Doubles 240,000zł. Triples 330,000zł. Quads 380,000zł.
Hotel Polonia, pl. Teatralny 5 (tel. 230 28), opposite the municipal theater. Large single beds and double rooms with sinks. Singles 170,000zł, with bath 280,000zł. Doubles 240,000zł, with bath 300,000zł.
Hotel Pod Orłem, ul. Mostowa 15 (tel. 250 24). Huge, comfortable rooms. Singles 250,000-300,000zł. Doubles 250,000-300,000zł, with bath 450,000-550,000zł. Triples 400,000zł, with bath 600,000zł.
Hotel Wodnik, Bulwar Filadelfijski 12 (tel. 260 49, fax 251 14). Singles 250,000-270,000zł, with bath 320,000-370,000zł. Doubles with bath 450,000-550,000zł. Triples with bath 500,000zł. Wheelchair access and rooms for the handicapped (grand total of 7): Singles 370,000zł; doubles 550,000zł.
Hotel PCK (Red Cross), ul. Szczecińska 16 (tel. 45 58 85, fax 39 80 78). Bus #22 from the train station to *Działki Kaszownik;* change to bus #21 from in front of Kościół Garnizonowy to ul. Szczecińska. Singles 175,000zł. Doubles 240,000zł. Triples 330,000zł. Quads 400,000zł. A bed in a 6-bed room 100,000zł.
Campground "Tramp," ul. Kujawska 14 (tel. 241 87), across from the train station. 3-person cabins 150,000zł. 4-person bungalows 200,000zł.

FOOD

Grocery stores in town include **Delikatesy,** ul. Szeroka 29 (tel. 105 40; open Mon.-Fri. 7am-8pm, Sat. 7am-7pm, Sun. 9am-3pm) and **Serdelek,** ul. Szeroka 19 (tel. 276 54; open Mon.-Fri. 7am-8pm, Sat. 8am-5pm, Sun. 9am-3pm).

Staromiejska Italian Restaurant, ul. Szczytna 4 (tel. 267 25). Reacquaint your taste buds with oregano and tomato sauce! Entrees 112,000-270,0000zł. Italian *pierogi* (otherwise known as tortellini) 49,000zł. Lasagna 55,000zł. Tiramisu 35,000zł. Open daily 11am-10pm.
Pub "Czarna Oberża" (Black Inn), ul. Rabiańska 9 (tel. 109 63). Serves up tall glasses of Guinness for 46,000zł, Vietnamese entrees 70,000-75,000zł. Chicago-style pizza 38,000zł. Good hangout for English-speaking beer guzzlers. Open Mon.-Thurs. 1-11pm, Fri.-Sat. 1pm-midnight, Sun. 2-11pm.
Palomino, ul. Duże Garbary 18 (tel. 248 95). Tuxedoed waiters in an incredibly elegant green atmosphere. Affordable prices. Soups 20,000-25,000zł. Chinese pork 80,000zł. Shish kebab 80,000zł. Specialty "Bull Provençal" 150,000zł. Open 10am-midnight.
Pizzeria "Bella Italia," Rynek Staromiejski 10 (tel. 274 56). Easy to spot sign in the colors of the Italian flag. Cheap and quick food. Risotto verde 16,000zł. Ravioli 19,000zł. Pinocchio dessert 19,000zł. Open 10am-10pm.
Bar Mleczny, ul. Różana 1 (tel. 224 28). Big ol' bowls of soup for 2800-6900zł. Open Mon.-Fri. 9am-6pm, Sat.-Sun.9am-4pm.
Pizza, ul. Różana 5 (tel. 241 66), offers cheap good pizza for 15,000zł and *barszcz* for 4500zł. Open Mon.-Fri. 9am-7pm, Sat.-Sun. 11am-7pm.
Bar Małgośka, ul. Szczytna 10 (tel. 243 37). Good hearty Polish food. *Gołąbki* for 19,500zł. Meatloaf and potatoes for 24,500zł. Open Mon.-Fri. 7am-6pm, Sat. 7am-4pm, Sun. 8am-4pm.
Lotos, ul. Strumykowa 16 (tel. 104 97). Various Far East specialties; primarily Chinese. Chinese veal 79,000zł. Curried beef 65,000zł. Duck 63,000-75,000zł. Lobster 390,000zł. Fried shrimp 135,000zł. Open daily noon-10pm.
Kawiarnia Pod Atlantem, ul. Św. Ducha 3 (tel. 267 34). Swims in imported alcohol. Milkshake 19,000zł. Iced coffee 12,000zł. Omelettes 19,000-23,000zł. Scrambled eggs 19,000zł. Open daily 10am-10pm.

Kopernik Factory Store, ul. Żeglarska 25 (tel. 237 12). Stock up on Toruń's delicious ginger cookies. Open Mon.-Fri. 10am-6pm, Sat.-Sun. 10am-2pm.
Hortex, ul. Prosta 1. Good place to visit if you are in the mood for ice cream. Milkshakes 8000zł, ice cream 2000zł/scoop. Open daily 9am-7pm.

SIGHTS

An astounding number of attractions are packed into Toruń's medieval ramparts. The **Old Town,** commanding the right bank of the Wisła River, was constructed by the Teutonic Knights in the 13th century, and is the birthplace of renowned astronomer Mikołaj Kopernik (February 19, 1473). Visit his birthplace, **Dom Kopernika,** at ul. Kopernika 15/17 (tel. 267 48). This 14th-century house has been meticulously restored (open Tues.-Sun. 10am-4pm; admission 10,000zł, students 5000zł). The museum also houses a separate exhibit, called **Makieta,** a miniature model of Toruń in 1550. A sound and light show, in five languages, accompanies your visit to this museum (tickets to Makieta 25,000zł, students 15,000zł).

The **Ratusz** (Town Hall), ul. Rynek Staromiejski 1 (tel. 270 38; 240 29, or 211 33), is in the center of the tourist district and sells tickets to most of the sights in town. It is one of the finest examples of monumental burgher architecture in Europe. The original Gothic four-winged building was built in 1391-99; various elements, such as the turrets, were added on throughout the centuries. Renovated in the years 1957-63, the Town Hall houses the **Muzeum Okręgowe** (Regional Museum; open Tues.-Sun. 10am-6pm, admission 15,000zł, students 10,000zł). The exhibits include the famous portrait of Mikołaj Kopernik from the late 16th century, portraits of wealthy and influential citizens of Toruń, and works of modern Polish art. For an additional fee of 20,000zł (students 15,000zł), you can climb the medieval 13th-century tower and survey the whole city. The friendly Ratusz staff is eager to point out the most noteworthy sights to visitors; they direct people to Kamienica Pod Gwiazdą, Dom Eskenów, and to the Teutonic Knights' castle.

Kamienica Pod Gwiazdą (House Under the Star), at Rynek Staromiejski 35 (tel. 211 33), was originally a Gothic building, later redone in Baroque style, with a finely modeled façade decorated with floral and fruit festoons. During the reconstruction of the late 1960s, interesting fragments of Gothic, late Renaissance, and Classical architecture were uncovered. Today, the house exhibits the art crafts of the Far East (open Tues.-Sun. 10am-4pm; admission 10,000zł, students 5000zł). **Dom Eskenów,** at ul. Łazienna 16 (tel. 286 80 or 262 12), houses an exhibition of Polish 20th-century painting, and an array of military uniforms from medieval times to the early 20th century (open Tues.-Sun. 10am-4pm; admission 10,000zł, students 5000zł).

The **ruins of the Teutonic Knights' castle,** on ul. Przedzamcze, are still very impressive. The 13th-century castle was destroyed by Toruń's burghers in 1454. At present, it houses a museum detailing the history of the town and the castle (open in the summer Tues.-Sun. 10am-4pm; admission 10,000zł, students 5000zł). The whole area is dominated by a **toilet tower** from the early 14th century.

Opposite the Ratusz, on ul Podmurna, stands the **Dwór Artusa** (Artus Court), designed in the 1880s by Rudolf Schmidt. This 19th-century house was erected on the site of the original Renaissance building, which had been the seat of patricians belonging to the Hanseatic League, and which was also called Dwór Artusa. The name originated in the legend of King Arthur and his knights, and was meant to emphasize the prestigious status of Toruń's patricians.

Among the tall Gothic churches which crop up everywhere, the **Cathedral of St. John the Baptist and St. John the Evangelist** is the most impressive of its kind. Built in the 13th-15th centuries, it is a mixture of Gothic, Baroque and Rococo elements. The cathedral's tower, built in 1407-33, contains Poland's second-largest bell, cast 1500. The cathedral's chapel witnessed the baptism of Mikołaj Kopernik in 1473. From here, it's a short walk across the Rynek to ul. Panny Marii, where you can stop by **Kościół Sw. Marii** (Church of the Virgin Mary) and appreciate its eerily high aisle and stained glass of geometric designs and pictures. To glimpse other parts of town, stroll along the **Bulwar Filadelfijski,** among fishermen and lingering couples who line the stone steps to the river.

ENTERTAINMENT

Student life revolves around the campus called "Miasteczko Akademickie." You can get here either by bus #11 from pl. Rapackiego or by bus #15 from in front of the NOT building at ul. Odrodzenia 7; get off at ul. Sienkiewicza. The campus **clubs** are **Klub Imperial,** ul. Gagarina 17 (tel. 145 83), **Klub Odnowa,** ul. Gagarina 37 (tel. 282 12), and **Klub Olimp,** ul. Gagarina 33.

There is a **music** scene in the **Stary Browar** (Old Brewery), at ul. Browarna 1, off the Rynek Nowomiejski (tel. 193 20). If you are a classical music fan, attend one of the bimonthly concerts given by the **Toruńska Orkiestra Kameralna** (Toruń Chamber Orchestra) in Dwór Artusa at Rynek Staromiejski 6 (tickets sold at their office, ul. Żeglarska 5, tel. 288 05).

There are eight **tennis courts** at the *Start Wisła Sports Club,* Szosa Chełmińska 3 (tel. 237 59; 35,000zł per hour for a court; open daily 8am-4pm). For **water sports,** visit *Port Drzewny na Wiśle,* ul. Starotoruńska 3 (tel. 271 07 or 262 07), which rents kayaks for 60,000zł per day (open daily 8am-4pm). *"Wodnik" Sports and Recreation Center,* Bulwar Filadelfijski 1 (tel. 260 49 or 282 74), has an outdoor swimming pool. *FSC "Elana,"* ul. Bażyńskich 9/17 (tel. 333 16), has an indoor pool.

Annual **festivals** abound. April brings the **Festival "Pobocza Teatru"** (Side Spaces of Theater), in the MDK (Młodzieżowy Dom Kultury), ul. Przedzamcze 1/3 (tel. 246 37). In May, the Teatr im. W. Horzycy, Plac Teatralny 1 (tel. 250 21) hosts the **International Theater Festival "Kontakt."** In July, students can experience **Music Camping,** Klub Piano, Brodnica, ul. Wodna 3 (tel. (667) 21 21). The **International Grand Knights' Tournament** is held in Golub Dobrzyń (tel. 83 24 55).

THE SOUTHERN UPLANDS AND MOUNTAINS

South of the lowlands lie the uplands of **Śląsk** (Silesia) and **Małopolska** (Little Poland). The old province of Małopolska stretches from the Świętokrzyskie Mountains and the Lublin uplands in the east to Kraków. It is famous for its fertile brown- and black-earth soils, which make it the most important agricultural region in Poland. West of the Kraków agglomeration lies the Śląsk region, rich in valuable minerals, namely coal, iron, and zinc, making it both the industrial heartland of the country and, at the same time, the most polluted area in Poland.

The Polish mountains stretch along the border with the Czech Republic and Slovakia. In the southwest lie the **Sudety Mountains,** and in the southeast, the Karpaty (Carpathian) Mountains embrace a portion of the **Beskidy Mountains** and the **Tatry** (Tatra) Mountains. The Tatras are the highest portion of Polish Carpathians, and reach a maximum elevation of 2499m (8199 ft) at the peak Rysy. At the feet of the Tatras are the most renowned mountain resorts, among them Zakopane. Highlander folklore and skiing facilities attract millions of tourists every year.

■ ■ ■ LUBLIN

As you approach Lublin, you enter a peaceful countryside in the heart of Malopolska, a tranquil patchwork of colorful, geometrically ploughed fields. Occasionally, you'll see horse-drawn carts on the winding, tree-lined roads. But despite its bucolic setting and seemingly slow pace, Lublin is far from being a dull and provincial town. It has a large and lively student population, and is an important cultural center. The city's academic life revolves around the Katolicki Uniwersytet Lubelski (Catholic University of Lublin), known as KUL. Until 1989, KUL was the only private university between Berlin and Vladivostok, and a shelter for free-thinking students.

A town of students, theater, and beautiful parks, Lublin lived through many a grim day during World War II, when the city's Jewish population was mercilessly murdered in Majdanek, one of the largest concentration camps built by the Nazis. The nearby towns of Bełżec (known as Belz during the war) and Sobibór witnessed mass killings as well. Kock and Chełm were pre-war centers of the Hasidim movement, with their famous *yeshivas* (colleges) and powerful *tzaddiks* (religious leaders). Today, Jewish groups from all over the world come to leave their *kvitlehs* (pieces of paper with requests, left on the tzaddiks' graves) on reb Mendel's grave in Kock.

ORIENTATION AND PRACTICAL INFORMATION

Lublin lies 175km southeast of Warsaw, on the historic trade route to Lviv and Ukraine. All principal sights roost on or near **Krakowskie Przedmieście,** which stretches west from the *Stare Miasto* (Old Town), turning into Al. Racławickie before reaching the Ogród Saski (Saxon Gardens) and the Catholic University.

Tourist Offices: IT, ul. Krakowskie Przedmieście 78 (tel. 244 12). Maps (26,000zł). "The traces of Monuments of Jewish Culture in the Lublin Region" by Andrzej Trzciński 13,000zł. Friendly, but no English speakers. Bus tickets to Western Europe. 10% student discount on all prices. Open Mon.-Fri. 9am-5pm, Sat. 10am-2pm. **ORBIS,** ul. Narutowicza 31(tel. 222 56), handles international and domestic train and bus tickets. Open Mon.-Fri. 9am-6pm, Sat. 11am-4pm. **Tourist Agency "Horyzont,"** ul. Gazowa 4 (tel. 226 19, fax 267 12), next to the train station. Its super-friendly and helpful staffs directs travelers to hotels and camping sites in Lublin and throughout Poland. International bus and plane tickets sold. English and German spoken. Open Mon.-Fri. 10am-4pm, Sat. 10am-noon.

Budget Travel: ALMATUR, ul. Langiewicza 10 (tel. 332 38), in the university area. Currency exchange, train tickets, ISICs. Open Mon.-Fri. 9am-4pm, Sat. 10am-2pm.

Currency Exchange: *Kantors* throughout the city have the best rates. Traveler's checks: **Bank PKO S.A.,** ul. Królewska 1 (tel. 210 16), charges 0.5-1.5% commission. Visa/MC cash advances. Open Mon.-Fri. 7:30am-6pm, Sat. 7:30am-2pm. **Bank PKO,** ul. Krakowskie Przedmieście 14/16 (tel. 228 33). Visa traveler's checks only, same commission. Open Mon.-Fri. 7:30am-7pm, Sat. 9am-1pm.

Post Office: ul. Krakowskie Przedmieście 50 (tel. 288 55). Open Mon.-Fri. 7am-9pm, Sat. 8am-2pm. **Fax** bureau (fax 250 61). **Postal Code:** 20-930. There is also a post office next to the train station, at ul. Pocztowa 1 (tel. 363 16), open Mon.-Fri. 8am-8pm, Sat. 8am-2pm.

Telephones: Open 24 hrs. at the Krakowskie Przedmieście post office. Open Mon.-Fri. 7am-9pm, Sat. 7am-3pm at the ul. Pocztowa post office. **City Code:** 0-81.

Flights: LOT Airlines, a one-person desk at the IT office (tel. 269 17).

Trains: tel. 202 19 or 31 56 42, recorded information 933. Main train station, **Lublin Główny,** Pl. Dworcowy 1, south of the Old Town. Take bus #13 to the center. International tickets and Wasteels sold 24 hrs. *Kantor,* open 1am,-6pm. To: Warsaw (11 per day, 2½hrs.; 96,000zł), Kraków (4 per day, 4hrs.; 144,000zł), Zamość (3 per day, 3hrs.; 44,000zł).

Buses: PKS bus station (tel. 77 66 49, recorded information 934, 935, 936), ul. Tysiąclecia 4, near the Old Town. If making a connection from the train station, take bus #1 or 34 (15-20 min.). *Kantor* open Mon.-Fri. 8am-4pm, Sat. 8am-1pm. Buses to: Warsaw (14 per day, 3hrs.; 84,000zł); Zamość (36 per day, 2hrs.; 54,000zł); and Sandomierz (5 per day, 2½hrs.; 64,000zł).

24-hr. Pharmacy: ul. Krakowskie Przedmieście 49 (tel. 224 25; after 8pm, ring the bell, pay 8000zl, and you will be served) and the pharmacy at ul. Bramowa 2/8 (tel. 205 21).

Medical Assistance: ul. Jaczewskiego 1/3 (tel. 77 55 71). Medical Info. 212 11, or 284 67. Open Mon.-Fri. 7am-7pm.

Crisis Lines: AIDS: tel. 248 89 (open Mon.-Fri. 1:30-3pm). **24-hr. psychological service** (Telefon Zaufania): 401 00, toll-free.

ACCOMMODATIONS AND CAMPING

Schronisko Młodzieżowe (HI), ul. Długosza 6a (tel. 306 28), west of the center near the Catholic University. Take bus #13 from the train station to the end of the Saxon Gardens. Old bathrooms, but friendly owners. Kitchen and informal camping facilities. Lockout 10am-5pm. Curfew 10pm. Both flexible. Luggage storage. 2-12-person rooms. Junior 36,000-52,000zł. Senior 40,000-56,000zł. Nonmembers 44,000-60,000zł. Sheets 14,000zł.

ZNP Dom Noclegowy, ul. Akademicka 4 (tel. 382 85). Take bus #13 from the train station just past Ogród Saski. Hostel-esque. Singles 155,000zł. Doubles 190,000zł. 6-person rooms 480,000zł. One shower on each level.

Motel PZM, ul. B. Prusa 8 (tel. 342 32). Follow ul. 3-go Maja from Krakowskie Przedmieście. Courteous service, pleasant atmosphere. Singles 190,000zł, with bath 250,000zł. Doubles 285,000-310,000zł, with bath 400,000-450,000zł.

Hotel Piast, ul. Pocztowa 2 (tel. 216 46). A last resort, convenient if you're stuck at the train station in the middle of the night. Geared to Russian travelers. Singles 160,000zł. Doubles 190,000zł. Triples 240,000zł. Quads 280,000zł. Communal bathrooms.

Hotel PKP, ul. Gazowa 8, just a few steps to the left of the train station (tel. 31 56 62). Doubles 128,400zł. Triples 192,600zł. Quads 256,800zł. Communal bathrooms.

FOOD

Restaurants

Jazz Pizza, in a cellar at ul. Krakowskie Przedmieście 55. Walls adorned with musical instruments and portraits of Dizzy Gillespie. Frequent jazz concerts. English menu: jazzy pizzas 25,000zł plus 8000-17,000zł for extra toppings. Friendly owners give a 10% discount to Canadian citizens, out of love for Canada, as they say. Open Mon.-Sat. 11:30am-10pm, Sun. 3-10pm.

Acerna Pizza, ul. Rynek 2 (tel. 245 31), in a spacious townhouse in the Old Town. 31 kinds of pizzas 27,000-80,000zł. Alcohol served. Home delivery prompt and reliable. Open daily 10am-10pm.

Bar Deli Rood, ul. Krakowskie Przedmieście 21. Modern and agreeable variation on the fast food theme. Choice of healthy salads and soups under 12,000zł. Cafe on the premises. Open Mon.-Sat. 10am-8pm, Sun. 10am-6pm.

Bar Mleczny, ul. Krakowskie Przedmieście 29 (tel. 239 31). The cheapest and drabbest in town. Breakfast foods 8000zł. Cheese *pierogi* 18,000zł. Open Mon.-Sat. 7am-7pm, Sun. 8am-5pm. Closed third Sunday of the month.

Restauracja Unia, in the hotel Unia at al. Racławickie 12 (tel. 320 61). Prepares *boeuf stroganoff* (189,400zł) for those tired of drab milk bars and longing for a change of atmosphere. Their grand piano is yours if you want to play something. Open Sun.-Fri. 1pm-midnight, Sat. 1pm-2am.

Lunch Bar, ul. Królewska 11, outside the Old Town. Despite the English name (an ever-growing trend), it's Polish food on plastic dishes. Soups and salads 8000-20,000zł, entrees 30,000-40,000zł. Open daily 9am-6pm.

U Biesów (At the Devils'), Rynek 18 (tel. 216 48). Shish kebabs 52,000-59,000zł. Solfernus' risotto 38,000zł. Asmodeus' sausage 35,000zł. Open Tues.-Sun. 2pm-midnight. Their sign says: "On Mondays devils sleep."

Cafés

Café and Bar "Zielony Liść" (Green Leaf), ul. Ewangelicka 6 (tel. 279 13). Inexpensive sandwiches and salads under 20,000zł. Take-out and phone orders possible. Open daily 8am-10pm.

Kawiarnia Trzosik, ul. Grodzka 5a. Enter under the "Gardzienice" sign and walk to the end of the dark corridor. Charming courtyard beyond the archway. Delicious desserts 19,000zł. Coffee 7000-14,000zł. Open daily 10am-9pm.

Azzurro, Rynek 18. Both indoor and open-air seating available with a full view of Rynek plaza and the Wedding Palace. Fashionable spot for ice cream (25,000zł) and coffee (12,000zł). Open Tues.-Sun. 11am-9pm.

POLAND

Czarcia Łapa (The Devil's Paw), ul. Bramowa 6 (tel. 203 44). An old café with occasional live music evenings; stop by around 6pm to see what's happening. Pastries 10,000zł. *Fasolka po bretońsku* (hot bean dish) 18,4000zł. Open daily 10am-9pm.

SIGHTS

The 19th-century ochre façades of **Krakowskie Przedmieście,** Lublin's main artery, introduce the more ancient buildings of the medieval *Stare Miasto* (old town). Walk east from **Plac Litewski** and its Tomb of the Unknown Soldier to the1827 **Nowy Ratusz** (New Town Hall), seat of the president of Lublin and other local authorities, on your left. Next door, the Baroque **Kościół Św. Krzyża** (Holy Cross Church) stands on the corner of ul. Krakowskie Przedmieście and Plac Łokietka (Łokietko's Square). To the right of the square starts ul. Królewska with the grand **Katedra Św. Jana Chrzciciela i Jana Ewangelisty** (Cathedral of St. John the Baptist and St. John the Evangelist). Built in 1586-96, it belonged to the Jesuits who also founded a college on the premises; the cathedral's opulent frescoes and gilded altar are well worth the visit. To the left of the square runs ul. Lubartowska, the main artery of the prewar Jewish district in Lublin. Plac Ofiar Getta (Victims of the Ghetto Square) on the left side of the street, is the site of **Pomnik Pomordowanych Żydów** (Monument to the Murdered Jews). At #10 stands **Bożnica,** an early 20th-century synagogue, the only one in Lublin to survive the war. The synagogue also houses **Izba Pamięci Żydów Lublina** (museum commemorating Lublin's Jews). Ul. Krakowskie Przedmieście leads straight through pl. Łokietka to the fortified **Brama Krakowska** (Kraków Gate), which ushers you into the Old Town.

Stare Miasto (Old Town)

Brama Krakowska is one of several gates in the fortification walls once surrounding the Old Town; built in 14th-century Gothic style, it was redone to suit Renaissance tastes in the 16th century. Today, it houses the **Oddział Historyczny Muzeum Lubelskiego** (Historical Division of the Regional Museum). When you cross through the arch and head straight along ul. Bramowa, you will reach the **Rynek Starego Miasta** (Old Town Market Square), lined with early Renaissance houses, the most noteworthy of which are the Klonowice house at #2, the Lubomelskich house at #8, and the Konopniców house at #12. In the middle of the Rynek stands the **Stary Ratusz** (Old Town Hall), seat of the local authorities in the 14th century; redone several times, it now retains its 18th-century Classical style. If you walk past the Lubomelskich house in the northeast corner of the Rynek, and continue along ul. Złota, you will see the **Kościół Dominikanów** (Dominican Church) at the end of the street; this is one of the oldest churches in Lublin. Built in 1342 by King Kazimierz Wielki in Gothic style, the church got a Renaissance facelift in the 17th century.

Zamek Lubelski (Lublin Castle)

A walk along ul. Grodzka , which starts in the northwest corner of the Rynek, across from ul. Bramowa, takes you through the 15th-century **Brama Grodzka** (Grodzka Gate) to ul. Zamkowa, which in turn leads straight to the massive **Zamek Lubelski** (Lublin Castle). The oldest element of the castle is the round tower, dating from the 13th century. Most of the structure was built in the 14th century by King Kazimierz Wielki (Casimir the Great), but was restored in the 19th century with an Arabian Nights theme. Once the court of a feudal kingdom, the castle served as Gestapo headquarters during World War II, and then as a prison until 1954. The fortified walls now house **Muzeum Lubelskie** (Museum of Lublin), featuring archaeological and ethnographic displays (tel. 250 01; open Wed.-Sat. 9am-4pm, Sun. 9am-5pm; admission 12,000zł, students 8000zł, Sun. free). Also on the premises, the Gothic 14th-century **Kościół Św. Trójcy** (Church of the Holy Trinity) once served as the castle's chapel; rebuilt in the 15th century, it was decorated with impressive Byzantine polychromes.

POLAND

Majdanek Concentration Camp

Majdanek can be reached by city bus #28 from the main train station or trolley buses #153 from ul. Krakowskie Przedmieście and #156 from ul. Królewska—they all stop at the huge granite monument marking the entrance to the grounds. The largest concentration camp after Oświęcim (Auschwitz), **Majdanek** was the site of 360,000 murders. The former cell-blocks now house moving exhibits chronicling the operations of this death factory, spread over the 5km Black Road near Lublin's southeastern suburbs. The road takes the visitor to the bath-house, gas chambers, prisoners' barracks, the assembly area, the crematorium, and ends at the **Mausoleum,** where the ashes of murdered prisoners have been deposited. The **State Museum** at Majdanek (tel. 426 47 or 426 48) was founded in 1944 after the liberation of Lublin (open Tues.-Sun. 8am-6pm in the tourist season, Tues.-Sun. 8am-3pm Oct.-April).

ENTERTAINMENT

Pubs and Cafés

Lublin has an impressive number of pubs, many of them run by students.

Bauhaus Café, ul. Świętoduska 20, a block north of Krakowskie Przedmieście, where it reaches the Old Town. Where painters and art students hang out. Wallpapered with Poland's famous daily newspaper, Solidarity's *Gazeta Wyborcza,* this pub is run by a History of Art graduate and her husband. Open Mon.-Thurs. noon-midnight, Fri. noon-2am, Sat. 4pm-2am, Sun. 4pm-midnight.

Old Pub, ul. Grodzka 8 in the Old Town (tel. 201 12), serves Johnny Walker (24,000zł), *wino grzane* (wine "warmed over") with spices (35,000zł), and cappuccino (15,000zł) on antique sewing machine tables. Open daily 11am-10pm.

18 Hester Café, ul. Okopowa 20. Behind the modern entrance to Lublin's Catholic University (**KUL**) on al. Racławickie in an airy courtyard; the entrance to this café in a cellar is in the right wing of the building. Packed with and run by students. Open Mon.-Fri. noon-midnight, Sat.-Sun. 4pm-4am.

Music

UMCS cultural center and the café **Chatka Żaka,** in the Marie Curie University district at ul. Radziszewskiego 8 (tel. 332 01), host concerts and discos. However, both the UMCS and KUL facilities are closed during the summer.

Graffiti, at the theater *Scena Ruchu,* al. Piłsudskiego 13 (tel. 275 42). Rock discos Fri.-Sat. 8pm-3am. Cover Fri. 40,000zł, Sat. 50,000zł. Their pub, bearing the same name, is open Sun.-Thurs. 4-11pm, Fri.-Sat. 4-8pm.

Hades, ul.. Peowiakow 13 (tel. 287 61 or 256 41), rock discos usually on Fri. and Sun. at 8pm. Cover 10,000zł.

The Filharmonia performs classical music concerts. For tickets, contact the booking office at ul. Kapucyńska 7 (tel. 244 21), September-June.

The Fundacja Muzyki Kresów (Foundation for the Music of the Borderlands) sponsors many different folk music concerts and events, and arranges interesting cross-cultural exchanges with Russia, Ukraine, and Belarus. For more information on their latest events, contact Mr. Jan Bernat (tel. 261 35).

The village of Gardzienice attracts theater lovers world-wide; this is where the **Gardzienice experimental theater** lives, performs, and holds workshops for its fans. They travel often, be it to Brazil or Ukraine, but they do find time to play in their home village. Book in advance at their Lublin office, ul. Grodzka 5a (tel. 298 40 or 296 37).

For **sports,** head to **Klub Zdrowia,** ul. Dubieckiego 11 (tel. 54 06 61; open Mon.-Fri. 10am-pm and 4-10pm, Sat. 10am-2pm). **Sport Club,** ul. Kaprysowa 2 (tel. 230 03, ext. 108), features a weightroom and aerobics classes.

POLAND

■■■ KAZIMIERZ DOLNY

Take a day trip to the bewitching town of **Kazimierz Dolny** on the sandy banks of the Wisła River some 45km west of Lublin. The **ruins** of a 14th-century castle overshadow the town, which, as usual, centers around the whitewashed façades of the **Rynek** (market square).

PRACTICAL INFORMATION

Budget Travel: PTTK office, Rynek 27 (tel. 100 46). Sells guides to the town and arranges private rooms. Open Mon.-Fri. 8am-6pm, Sat.-Sun. 10am-5:30pm (April 15-Oct. 15); Mon.-Fri. 8am-3:30pm, Sat.-Sun. 10am-2pm (off-season).

Currency Exchange: at the post office, ul. Tyszkiewicza 2.

Post Office: ul. Tyszkiewicza 2 (tel. 105 15, fax 105 00). One block west of the Rynek. Open Mon.-Fri. 8am-8pm. **Postal Code:** 24-120.

Telephones: at the post office. Open Mon.-Fri. 7am-9pm, Sat. 9am-1pm, Sun. 9am-11pm; between May 1 and Sept. 30 the phones are open from 10am-5pm on Sat. and Sun. **City Code** 0-831.

Buses: Buses to Kazimierz Dolny leave every hour from platform 3 of the Lublin bus station (direction "Puławy," 1½hrs.; 18,000zł), making frequent stops in the countryside.

Pharmacy: at Rynek 17 (tel. 101 20). Open Mon.-Fri. 8am-7pm, Sat. 8am-3pm, Sun. 10am-2pm.

ACCOMMODATIONS

Youth Hostel "Strażnica," ul. Senatorska 23a (tel. 104 27). One block west of the Rynek. 30 beds. Doubles 70,000zł per person, students 50,000zł. Dorm rooms with beds at 50,000zł, students 40,000zł. Lockout 10am-5pm.

PTTK Rynek 27. Arranges accommodations in private rooms. Singles 70,000-125,000zł. Doubles 130,000-210,000zł. Triples 165,000-315,000zł.

Domek Campingowy, ul. Krakowska 35 (tel. 108 14). In this tiny house, Anna Stachyra provides a bathroom, sink, and double room for 60,000zł, garden view included.

Youth Hostel "Pod Wianuszkami," ul. Puławska 64 (tel. 103 277). A 30-minute trek along ul. Puławska from the center. Rooms range from doubles to 10-bed dorms. Junior 36,000-52,000zł, senior 40,000-56,000zł (without ID 44,000-60,000zł). Sheets 15,000zł. Lockout 10am-5pm.

FOOD

Restauracja Staropolska, ul. Nadrzeczna 14 (tel. 102 50), east of the Rynek. Legend of the town. Wander outside to enjoy Polish food at its best in the shade of spruce trees. *Barszcz* 11,000zł. Beefsteak 95,000zł. Open daily 11am-10pm.

Bistro "U Zbyszka," ul. Sadowa 4 (tel. 107 23), is a fun-oriented café and bar with an outdoor swimming pool and mountain bike rental. Dive into the pool (20,000zł per hr.) straight from your dining table (salads 35,000zł, turkey breast 40,000zł, strawberry shakes 10,000zł), or go for a bike ride (3 types of bikes, 20,000-25,000zł per hr., 200,000zł per day, or 250,000-350,000zł per weekend). Open daily 9am-10pm.

Restauracja Łaźnia, ul. Senatorska 21 (tel. 102 49). Polish fare served in the Renaissance interior of an old bathhouse. Soups 15,000-27,000zł. Chicken breast 80,000zł. Cheese *naleśniki* 20,000zł. Open daily 10am-11pm.

Piekarnia Sarzyński, at ul. Nadrzeczna 6, just a few steps from the Rynek, is an old-fashioned bakery with the freshest breads and rolls in Kazimierz. They also bake bread to order, in any shape that you request. Bread roosters and giant hearts 18,000zł. Look for a big rooster sign on a white village hut. Open Mon.-Sat. 6am-7pm, Sun. 8am-7pm.

Café Rynkowa, Rynek 7 (tel. 100 12), is a popular coffee place. Coffee 12,000-15,000zł. Open daily 10am-11pm.

POLAND

SIGHTS AND ENTERTAINMENT

Hike up to the castle tower and pause along the way at the 16th-century Baroque **Kościół Farny Św. Jana Chrzciciela i Św. Bartłomieja** (Farny church of St. John the Baptist and St. Bartholomew) to survey one of Poland's oldest and best-preserved organs, dating from 1620. (Concerts Sat. 7pm. Ruins and tower open daily 9am-5pm. Buy it at the ruins and save on the tower. Admission 4000zł, students 3000zł.)

At Rynek 19 (tel. 102 89), the **Muzeum Sztuki Złotniczej** (Museum of Goldsmithery), displays European jewelry as well as silver and gold religious objects, and a large collection of Jewish silver, dating back to the 15th century (open May1-Sept. 30 Tues.-Sun. 9am-4pm; off-season 10am-3pm). Off the *Rynek*, the **Kamienica Celejowska,** at ul. Senatorska 11/13, houses a collection of paintings inspired by the town's enchanting layout (open Tues.-Sun. 10am-4pm, Oct.-April Tues.-Sun. 10am-5pm; admission 10,000zł, students 7000zł). The **Muzeum Przyrodnicze** (Museum of Natural Science), at ul. Puławska 54 (tel. 103 26 or 103 41), displays fossils and rocks from the Kazimierz region (open Wed.-Mon. 10am-3pm; admission 20,000zł, students 10,000zł). **Kuncewiczówka,** as the house on top of the hill at ul. Małachowskiego 19 is now called (tel. 101 02), was the residence of a famous Polish writer, Maria Kuncewiczowa. Since her death in 1989, a cultural foundation has been keeping it alive by organizing frequent concerts and exhibits. It's a pretty walk up the village road, and once inside, you can admire an old furnace from the Huculszczyzna region (Ukraine) and tapestries from the Caucasus (open Tues.-Sun. 10am-1pm and 3-6pm; free, but donations encouraged).

The 16th-century castle in the nearby village of Janowiec also functions as a museum: the **Muzeum "Zamek w Janowcu"** is open May1-Sept.30 Wed.-Sun. 10am-5pm, and off-season Wed.-Sun. 10am-3pm. You can get to Janowiec by boat; the boat "Wodnik" cruises the Wisła River April15-Oct.15. (open for business around 9am, and leaves the ferry terminal, located at the end of ul. Nadwiślańska, whenever there is a group of at least 15 people; 40min., 30,000zł).

Kazimierz is also famous for its **Ogólnopolski Festiwal Kapel i Śpiewaków Ludowych** (Festival of Folk Groups and Singers), held each year at the end of June. People clad in folk costumes parade all over town; numerous concerts are given.

■■■ ZAMOŚĆ

Designed by the Italian architect Bernardo Morando, Zamość sprang up in the 1580s as a dream come true of a young aristocrat, Jan Zamoyski. Having studied in Padua, Italy, Zamoyski wanted to recreate that beautiful place in his homeland, and succeeded in conjuring up a perfect town with a palace, town hall, opulent houses, churches, and an academy. The town became known as the "Renaissance Pearl" of Poland, the "Padua of the North." Zamoyski encouraged Greeks, Jews, and Armenians to settle in Zamość, and they flocked to the town in large numbers. Today, Armenian houses in the northeast corner of the Rynek and the synagogue at ul. Zamenhoffa still remind visitors of the previous inhabitants of Zamość.

Attractive tourist spot, fashionable hangout for Lublin students, town filled with street performers—Zamość is all of those things. But there is also something surreal about the town; it looks strangely and suddenly deserted, as if someone built an amazing, beautiful little town and simply abandoned it.

Orientation and Practical Information To reach Zamość from Lublin, take the **train** (3 per day, 3hrs.; 49,000zł) or **bus** (36 per day, 2hrs.; 54,000zł).The main train station is at ul. Szczebrzeska 11 (tel. 69 44; information 3401), a short walk southwest of the Old Town. The main bus station is at ul. Reja 2 (tel. 49 86; information 48 32), east of the Old Town, and quite far from the center. Bus "O" links both the train and the bus stations with the Old Town. **IT,** in the Ratusz, at Rynek 13 (tel. 22 92), sells maps and arranges guides to Zamość (300,000zł for a minimum of 4hrs.) and to the neighboring region of Roztocze (460,000zł per day). They also arrange short flights over Zamość for 105,000zł per person (open Mon.-Fri. 7:30am-

POLAND

5pm, Sat. 8am-2pm, Sun. 9am-2pm). **ORBIS,** ul. Grodzka 18 (tel. 57 75 or 30 01), has brochures in English on the town's architecture. You can also **exchange money** and cash your traveler's checks here (open Mon.-Fri. 10am-4:30pm, Sat. 11am-3:30pm). **Bank PKO S.A.,** at ul. Grodzka 2 (tel. 710 57), also cashes traveler's checks. The *kantor* in the bank is open Mon.-Fri. 8am-4pm, Sat. 7:30am-12:30pm. The main **post office** and **telephones** are at ul. Kościuszki 9 (tel. 45 16; open Mon.-Fri. 7am-9pm, Sat. 8am-1pm). The **postal code** is 23-400, and the **telephone city code** is 0-84. For a **radio-taxi** dial 50 50. There is a **24-hr. pharmacy,** Apteka Rektorska, at Rynek 2 (tel. 23 86). In case of **medical emergencies,** go to ul. Kilińskiego (tel. 22 00).

Accommodations   The hostel-like **Hotel Marta,** ul. Zamenhoffa 11 (tel. 26 39), near the synagogue, used to be the PTTK Dom Wycieczkowy. (80,000zł per person regardless of the size of the room.) **Hotel Renesans,** ul. Grecka 6 (tel. 20 01), has a café on the premises. (Singles 250,000zł. Doubles 350,000zł. Communal bathrooms. Café open daily 7am-11pm. Breakfast in the café 50,000zł. Pool table 30,000zł per hour.) **Hotel Sportowy,** ul. Królowej Jadwigi 8 (tel. 60 11), is a 20-minute walk westward from the Rynek, along ul. Pereca and ul. Królowej Jadwigi, past the Zamoyski palace on the left. (Singles 267,000zł. Doubles 329,000zł. Triples 363,000zł. Quads 604,000zł. Outdoor swimming pool 20,000zł. 24-hr. restaurant.) There is also a campsite in Zamosc, at ul. Królowej Jadwigi 14 (tel. 24 99), with 3- and 4-bed bungalows with baths. (50,000zł per person. Tents available at 30,000zł per tent per day.)

Food   **Centralka Restaurant,** ul. Żeromskiego 3 (tel. 23 39) is painfully ugly, with communist frescos on the walls, but it serves up delicious food (carp in sour cream 37,000zł; cabbage *pierogi* 22,000zł; pork chop 33,000zł; grilled sausage 22,000zł). **Ratuszowa Restaurant,** Rynek 13 (tel. 715 57), has good tomato soup at 12,000zł (open daily 10am-11pm). **Café Padwa,** ul. Staszica 23 (tel. 62 56), cooks spaghetti for a mere 28,000zł (open daily 9am-11pm). **Café and Restaurant Muzealna,** ul. Ormiańska 30 (tel. 64 94, ext. 40), offers traditional Polish cuisine (open daily 10am-midnight). The **Cukiernia,** a pastry shop at Rynek 12 (tel. 28 73), serves ice cream (3000zł per scoop) and coffee (5000zł), which you can enjoy at one of their spotless white tables (open daily 10am-6pm).

Sights and Entertainment   The whole town, built in the 1580s, is a monumental sight in itself, with the Renaissance layout, the imposing town hall, the peaceful cobblestone **Rynek,** and the surrounding houses with painted façades. Especially worth seeing are the splendidly preserved **Armenian houses** in the northeast corner of the Rynek, at ul. Ormiańska 22, 24, 26, 28, and 30. The house at #24 is the headquarters of the **Muzeum Okręgowe** (Regional Museum), which displays artifacts from the region—Lusatian jewelry from 1000 BC, 10th-13th-century combs, and other objects of everyday use (open Tues.-Sun. 10am-4pm; admission 10,000zl, students 5000zl).

Don't leave without visiting the **Rotunda** at the end of ul. Męczenników Rotundy. This 19th-century brick fort was converted during World War I to a crematorium and camp (open 9am-6pm, Oct.-April 14 10am-5pm; free).

In the summer, the whole town echoes with life during the annual **Zamojskie Lato Teatralne** (Zamość Theater Summer), when experimental groups perform both in theaters and on the streets. To find out more about the summer schedule, contact **WDK** at ul. Partyzantów 13 (tel. 20 21 or 20 22). In May, jazz musicians from Ukraine and Belarus jam with the Poles during the **Jazz na Kresach Festival** (Jazz of the Borderlands). In September, jazz singers gather here for the **Międzynarodowe Spotkania Wokalistów Jazzowych.** More jazz is available year-round at the Jazz Club Kosz, ul. Zamenhoffa 3 (tel. 60 41). Named after a local jazz pianist, Mieczysław Kosz, this club is a popular concert spot and an artsy hangout (open daily 1pm-1am). **Piwnica Pod Arkadami,** ul. Staszica 25, is worth the steep descent into a "well" with a drink bar and pool tables (open daily noon-midnight).

■ ■ ■ SANDOMIERZ

Another retreat into southeastern Poland's captivating countryside of Małopolska leads to **Sandomierz,** 2½ hours southwest of Lublin. One of the oldest towns in Poland, it was named after Sandomir, the founder of a new settlement on the site of today's Sandomierz. In 1259-60, the settlement was invaded and destroyed by Tatars. It took almost 30 years to rebuild the town; consequently, it was moved to a different location, on a higher, less accessible hill. Under the rule of King Kazimierz Wielki, a castle was built in Sandomierz and the town itself was surrounded by fortifications, of which only the Opatowska Gate remains today. Also around the the 15th century, the wealthy merchants of the town started to build tenement-houses around the Rynek and to construct an underground system of wine cellars, which were later to function as dungeons. Further development of the town was stopped by the Swedish invasion of 1656, and from then on, the status of the town continued to deteriorate. Sandomierz survived the partitions of Poland, the Napoleonic wars, and the two World Wars, only to be hit by the wave of transition to capitalism, when many of the town's neighboring factories were either closed down or forced to operate on much smaller funds.

Sandomierz lies off the beaten track and is often forgotten by tourists. It is worth the visit, since most of its glorious past is kept alive by its monuments. The beautiful Renaissance Rynek seems the perfect set for a historical movie, and the cellars and dungeons tell the story of the merchants and the patriots who fought to save the town. The very existence of those monuments was in question in 1967, when the town started sliding toward the river. Fortunately, the costly but timely restorations sidestepped the catastrophe.

Orientation and Practical Information Sandomierz is connected to most major cities in Poland. Trains run to: Warsaw (3 per day, 4hrs.; 121,500zl), Zamość (1 per day, 2hrs.; 54,000zl), and Przemyśl (2 per day, 3hrs.; 88,500zl). The PKP **train station** is located at ul. Lwowska, on the outskirts of Sandomierz, and on the other side of the Wisła River (tel. 32 23 74). To the center, take bus #3, 8, or 11 from the station. The PKS **bus station** is on ul. 11-go Listopada (tel. 32 23 02), northwest of the Old Town, and a short walk from the center. Buses run to Lublin (5 per day, 2½hrs., 64,000zl). **ORBIS,** at Rynek 27 (tel. 32 30 40), is open Mon.-Sat. 9am-4pm. The budget travel office **PTTK** is right next door, at Rynek 25/26 (tel. 32 23 05, fax 32 26 82). It sells maps and guides, and generally has much more information than ORBIS (open Mon.-Fri. 8am-3pm). **Exchange currency** at *kantors,* post offices, and banks throughout the city. The most centrally located **post office** is on the corner of ul. Bulińskiego and ul. Mariacka (tel. 32 27 23), south of the Rynek (open Mon.-Fri. 10am-3:30pm, 4-5pm). The **postal code** is 27-600. The **telephone city code** is 0-15. All Sandomierz lines have a "3" in front of the old (pre-1993) five-digit numbers. There is a **pharmacy** at Rynek 31 (tel. 32 24 59), open Mon.-Fri. 8am-5pm, Sat. 8am-noon. In case of **medical emergency,** tel. 32 32 03.

Accommodations The town has yet to be hit by a tourist wave large enough to make the hotel business profitable for the local entrepreneurs. As a result, accommodations are still scarce, and of mediocre quality. **Hotel Pod Ciżemką,** Rynek 27 (tel. 32 36 68), has 25 beds and the best location in town. (Doubles 350,000zl. Triples 450,000zl. Quads 600,000zl. Quints 750,000zl. All with bath.) **Hotel Dick,** Mały Rynek 3 (tel. 32 35 91), one block north of the Stary Rynek, used to be called "Flisak." It's cheaper, but lives up to the saying that you get what you pay for—namely mediocre quarters with communal bathrooms. (Singles 150,000zl. Doubles 200,000zl. Triples 250,000zl. Quads 300,000zl.) **Dom Turysty PTTK,** at ul. Krakowska 34 (tel. 32 22 84), is quite a trek from the Old Town. Take bus #6 or 17 from the center and get off when you glimpse the Wisła River (six bus stops). Choose from an array of 156 beds. (Singles with bath 225,000zł. Doubles with shower 180,000zł.)

Food The main eateries in Sandomierz cluster around the Rynek. **Snack Bar,** at Rynek 30 (tel. 32 28 38), offers salads for 20,000zł a bowl and healthy buckwheat for 12,000zł (open daily 10am-9pm). **Pod Ciżemką Restaurant,** at Rynek 27 (tel. 32 36 68), has several specialties: the Sandomierz herring (18,000zł), a spicy soup called *Kociołek zbójnicki* (23,000zł), and the Ciżemka pork chop (71,000zł) are only some of them (open daily 11am-10pm). At the **Cafe Pod Ciżemką,** next to the restaurant, sip cappuccino for 18,000zł, or play pool for 10,000zł per hour (open daily 10am-10pm). **Bar Massimo,** Rynek 28 (tel. 32 20 11), offers strawberry *pierogi* for 23,000zł (open daily 9am-8pm). Take a break from sightseeing at the **Café Zamkowa,** inside the Castle at ul. Zamkowa 14 (tel. 32 38 68), and enjoy coffee for 10,000zł or ice cream for 20,000zł (open Tues.-Sun. 10am-9pm). **Kawiarnia Kasztelanka,** Rynek 14, serves up scrambled eggs for breakfast (12,000zł); pork chops are 32,000zł. For dessert or snack, try their pastry "Napoleonka" for 8000zł (open daily 9am-midnight).

Sights The entrance to the Old Town is marked by the Gothic **Brama Opatowska** (Opatowska Gate), the only remainder of what used to be the town fortifications. You can climb the steep stairs to the top of the gate to get a great view of Sandomierz (open daily 10am-5:30pm; admission 5000zł, students 3000zł). Ul. Opatowska continues past the gate and leads straight to the spacious, sloping, cobblestone **Rynek Starego Miasta** (Old Market Town Square).

A right on ul. Opatowska, just before you reach the Rynek, takes you to ul. Oleśnicka and the entrance to the mysterious **underground tourist route,** stone and brick 14th-century chambers inhabited by Tatar ghosts. Here you will see the cellars in which wealthy merchants stored grain, and wine made from the grapes of the vineyards that covered the sunny slopes surrounding Sandomierz. You will also hear the story of the legendary Halina Krempianka, who sacrificed her life to save her home town from the Tatars. The tour ends, very appropriately, next to a *winiarnia,* where thirsty visitors can stop by for a glass of wine or a swig of the local beer (tours on the half-hour daily 10am-5:30pm; admission 10,000zł, students 6000zł).

In the middle of the Rynek stands the 16th-century Renaissance **Ratusz** (Town Hall), which houses a division of the **Muzeum Okręgowe** (Regional Museum) featuring, among other things, a model of 18th-century Sandomierz (open Tues.-Fri. 9am-4pm, Sat. 9am-3pm, Sun. 10am-2pm; admission 5000zł, students 3000zł). Ul. Mariacka, in the southeast corner of the Rynek, takes you to the grandest monument in Sandomierz, the 14th-century **Katedra** (Cathedral). It has retained its Gothic structure, but its interiors have been redone in Baroque style. Among the Byzantine-style frescoes, there is also a gruesome set of 16 paintings depicting various tortures (open Mon.-Sat. 10am-noon and 2-6pm, Sun. 3-5pm). Ul. Mariacka continues all the way to ul. Zamkowa, from which you can see the **Zamek Kazimerzowski** (Castle of Kazimierz). Built in the 14th century by King Kazimierz Wielki, it was destroyed by the Swedes in the invasion of 1656. Recently restored, it has little to offer the visitor besides its walls and skeleton, which reflect the original layout. The castle also houses another division of the Muzeum Okręgowe, ul. Zamkowa 14 (tel. 32 38 68). The archaeological exhibit includes a chess set from the 11th century (open Tues.-Fri. 9am-4pm, Sat. 9am-3pm, Sun. 10am-2pm; admission 10,000zł, students 5000zł).

■ ■ ■ PRZEMYŚL

Less than a *kupon*'s toss from the Ukrainian border, Przemyśl exhibits an Eastern flair that no other Polish city can match. Southern travelers occupy hotels around the train station and help each other with linguistic matters. Farther out, in the Old

Town, churches stand at every corner, and on Sundays, the city resonates with the sound of Catholic masses flowing from the many loudspeakers placed outside.

ORIENTATION AND PRACTICAL INFORMATION

The train station is at Plac Legionów, a short walk northeast of the Old Town. The bus station is next to the train station, on ul. Czarnieckiego. From either station, head to ul. Mickiewicza, which turns into ul. Grodzka as soon as it crosses ul. Jagiellońska. Ul. Grodzka leads right through the middle of the Old Town.

Tourist Offices: San, ul. Sowińskiego 4 (tel. 40 31), sells international bus tickets. Open Mon.-Fri. 8am-4pm, Sat. 8am-1pm. **ORBIS,** pl. Legionów 1 (tel. 33 66), handles train, ferry, and international bus tickets. Open Mon.-Fri. 8am-6:30pm, Sat. 8am-3pm. **Uni-Tour,** ul. Franciszkańska 22 (tel. 58 11 or 20 74), arranges bus connections to Western Europe. Open Mon.-Fri. 9am-4pm, Sat. 10am-4pm.

Budget Travel: PTTK, ul. Grodzka (tel. 53 74), carries maps and guides, and gives many tips on sightseeing. Open Mon.-Fri. 8am-4pm.

Currency Exchange: at *kantors* throughout the town. The *kantor* in Hotel Przemysław, ul. Sowińskiego 4 (tel. 40 32 or 40 33), is open Mon.-Fri. 10am-6pm. The *kantor* at the train station is open daily 8am-10pm. **Bank PKO S.A.,** ul. Jagiellońska 7 (tel. 34 59), handles traveler's checks and Visa cash advances. Open Mon. and Thurs. 10am-5pm, Tues.-Wed. and Fri. 8am-3pm, Sat. 8am-1pm.

Post Office: Main post office at ul. Mickiewicza 13 (tel. 32 70). Open Mon.-Fri. 7:30am-8pm, Sat. 7:30am-2pm, Sun. 9am-11am. **Postal Code:** 37-700.

Photocopies: at Hotel Przemysław (Mon.-Fri. 8am-4pm, 1000zł per page), and also at the travel agency San.

Telephones: Outside the post office (just a few). **City Code:** 0-10.

Trains: PKP train information tel. 935. To: Warsaw (3 per day, 7hrs.; 162,000zł), Lublin (1 per day, 4hrs.; 115,500zł), Kraków (10 per day, 3hrs.; 121,500zł), Tarnów (11 per day, 2hrs.; 96,000zł). If you want to hop over the border to Ukraine, there are trains to Lviv (2 per day, 5hrs.; 162,600zł), Odessa (1 per day, 18hrs.; 778,500zł), and Kiev (1 per day, 17hrs.; 681,200zł). International ticket window open 7:30am-6pm.

Buses: PKS bus information tel. 54 35. To: Łańcut (via Rzeszów, every ½hr., 44,000zł) and L'viv (13 per day, 3hrs.; 100,000zł). The L'viv buses are always packed with Ukrainian and Polish salespeople. Ticket windows open 24 hrs.

Swimming Pools: Indoor swimming pool at ul. 22-go Stycznia 6 (tel. 64 45). Open daily 8am-10pm.

Tennis Courts: Czuwaj, ul. 22-go Stycznia 6 (tel. 56 82). Open daily 8am-4pm.

Pharmacy: ul. Jagiellońska 6 (tel. 25 06), opposite the Bank PKO. Open Mon.-Sat. 7:30am-8pm, Sun. 9am-6pm.

ACCOMMODATIONS

Youth Hostel Matecznik, ul. Lelewela 6 (tel. 61 45). Take bus #7 from ul. Jagiellońska toward *Żurawica* across the river, and get off at the corner of ul. 3-go Maja and ul. Lelewela. Singles, doubles, and triples 100,000zł per person. 6-bed rooms 90,000zł per person. 13-bed rooms 75,000zł per person. 25% discount with IFYH or PTSM card. Sheets 15,000zł. Lockout 10am-5pm. Open year-round.

Dom Turysty PTTK "Podzamcze," ul. Waygarta 5 (tel. 53 74). In the western part of the Old Town, close to a beach on the San River. Short walk from the station; go down ul. Mickiewicza, then turn right and walk along ul. Jagiellońska and ul. Piłsudskiego; turn left onto ul. Waygarta. One of the PTTK basics, with triples and quads at 60,000zł per person and 20-bed dorms at 50,000zł per person.

Camping, ul. Piłsudskiego 8 (tel. 56 42). Close to a stadium and a beach on the San River. 24,000zł per person per day and 18,000zł per tent per day. Cabins: doubles 125,000zł, with bath 154,000zł; triples 195,000zł, with bath 231,000zł.

Dom Wycieczkowy Przemysław, ul. Sowińskiego 4 (tel. 40 32, or 40 33). Right across from the train station, but plan to wash elsewhere and use the toilet before you arrive. Very friendly staff. Singles 140,000zł. Doubles 185,000zł. Triples 246,000zł. Quads 308,000zł. Quints 385,000zł.

FOOD

There is a **grocery store** at pl. Na Bramie 5 (tel. 35 03; open Mon.-Fri. 7am-9pm, Sat. 7am-8pm, Sun. 8am-12:30pm).

Polonia Restaurant, ul. Franciszkańska 35 (tel 57 77). Delicious blueberry *pierogi* 25,000zł. Swiss pork chop with fries 45,000zł. Open daily 10am-10pm.
Pizzeria Margherita, Rynek 4 (tel. 473 47). 36 kinds of pizza 31,000-60,000zł. Spaghetti 28,000-55,000zł. Open Tues.-Sun. 11am-11pm, Mon. 2-11pm.
Kawiarnia Artystyczna, at the top of the castle hill (tel. 32 97). Stop by on your way to the castle to rehydrate after the hike. Coffee 7000zł. Open Mon.-Thurs. 10am-10pm, Fri.-Sun. 10am-midnight.
Café Pod Arkadami, Rynek 5, serves up scrambled eggs (28,000zł), pork chops (65,000zł), and pastries (15,000zł). Play pool at 10,000zł per hour. Open daily 10am-11pm.
Restauracja Oaza, ul. Mickiewicza 4 (tel. 39 68). Grim dining room, but decent food. Cheese *pierogi* 12,000zł. Fried chicken 35,000zł. *Bigos* 20,000zł. Smoking not allowed—a true oasis for non- smokers! Open daily 9am-9pm.
Bar La Mamma, ul. Sowińskiego 5 (tel. 472 06), opposite the train station. Entrees under 40,000zł and entire breakfasts at 35,000zł. Open Mon.-Fri. 8am-10pm, Sat.-Sun. 10am-10pm.

SIGHTS

It's a slow town. Stroll up twisting cobblestone streets to the **cathedral** on ul. Grodzka and Katedralna; above the Old Town, on ul. Zamkowa, stands the white Renaissance **zamek** (castle), with views of the town and the river below (open 9am-6pm; tower 4000zł, students 2000zł). The **Carmelite Monastery** on ul. Kapitulna boasts Italian-cast bells that ring on the hour.

■ ■ ■ ŁAŃCUT

This tiny town lies 17km east of Rzeszów, near an old trade route that once connected Kraków and Przemyśl. It was founded by King Kazimierz Wielki in the mid-14th century, and its first known owner was Otto Pilecki. Pilecki's wife, Jadwiga of Melsztyn, was the godmother of the famous King Władysław Jagiełło, conqueror of the Teutonic Order at the Battle of Grunwald in 1410. Pilecki's daughter, Elżbieta, was to become the fourth wife of the great king. In 1586, Łańcut passed into the hands of Stanisław Stadnicki, known as the "Devil of Łańcut." In 1610-20, his sons built a fortification on the site of today's palace. In 1629, Stanisław Lubomirski became the new owner of the town. The palace was transformed by Lubomirski's wife, Elżbieta, a princess with French tastes and an eye for fine art.

Orientation and Practical Information The **PKS bus station** is very close to the Rynek, on ul. Kościuszki. Buses to Przemyśl run every 30min. (50min., 44,000zł). The **train station** is located north of the palace, on ul. Kolejowa (tel. 25 23 17). Trains run to Tarnów (10 per day, 2hrs.; 64,500zł), Kraków (9 per day, 2½hrs.; 96,000zł), Warsaw (1 per day, 7hrs.; 153,000zł), and Przemyśl (24 per day, 50min.; 46,500zł). From the train station, it's a a 25-minute walk to the palace; head up ul. Żeromskiego and right on ul. Grodzka, or call a cab (tel. 20 02).

Tickets and guide books to the **palace** can be purchased at the ticket office, ul. Kościuszki 2 (tel. 25 23 38), in the western wing of the palace. Guided tours in English, German, French, and Russian are also an option at 280,000zł for the 2-hr. tour, regardless of the number of people who sign up. At the same entrance as the ticket window, **Trans-Euro-Tours** (tel. 25 30 16) provides tourists with information on Łańcut and on bus connections to Western Europe. *Kantor* and photocopier on the premises (open Mon.-Fri. 9am-5pm, Sat. 9am-1pm).

The **post office,** at ul. Królowej Elżbiety 8 (tel. 25 29 11), is open Mon.-Fri. 7am-8pm, and on working Sat. 9am-1pm. The **postal code** is 37-100. **Telephones** are open Mon.-Fri. 7am-9pm, Sat. 8am-1pm, Sun. 9am-11am. The **telephone code** is 0-

17. When dialing from outside Łańcut, add a "25" in front of all Łańcut phone numbers; when making a local call, use only the four-digit number. There is a **pharmacy** at pl. Sobieskiego 18 (tel. 25 31 03), open Mon.-Fri. 7:30am-7pm, Sun. 9am-4pm.

Accommodations The **Hotel Zamkowy,** in the Łańcut palace, ul. Zamkowa 1 (tel. 25 26 71), has an international population of musicians. Settled in the palace park, it's very quiet at night. (Doubles 130,000zł, with bath 320,000zł. Triples with bath 450,000zł.) **Dom Wycieczkowy PTTK,** at ul. Dominikańska 1 (tel. 25 45 12), is located in the old Dominican church and monastery, and houses mostly Ukrainian workers, but the management is always happy to accommodate tourists. (Doubles 146,000zł. Triples, quads and quints 49,000zł per person. 7-to 11-bed dorms 37,000zł per person.)

Food **Zamkowa Restaurant,** in the palace at ul. Zamkowa 1 (tel. 25 28 05), serves up chicken with mushrooms (81,000zł), as well as breakfast and dessert in two dining rooms, one of which is reserved for non-smokers (open daily 8:15am-9pm). **Bar Quick,** Rynek 3 (tel. 25 24 85), has extra seating outside, and attracts the local youth with a wide choice of hamburgers (under 20,000zł), salads (15,000zł), and pizzas (20,000-40,0000zł), all served in a modern and McDonaldish atmosphere (open daily 9am-10pm). **Café Green Apple,** ul. Danielewicza 4 (tel. 25 27 20), is a modern looking hangout serving a variety of pastries and beverages; try the cheesecake (12,000zł), coffee (8000zł), or strawberry shake (12,000zł). (Open daily 9am-9pm.) **Café and Restaurant Pałacyk,** ul. Paderewskiego 18 (tel. 25 20 43 or 25 43 56), in a cream-colored mansion, serves traditional Polish dishes (dancing Tues., Thurs. Sat. nights; open daily 9am-midnight).

Sights and Entertainment The palace at Łańcut, ul. Zamkowa 1 (tel. 25 20 08, fax 25 20 12), may well be the most splendid building in Poland, with perfectly maintained grounds. (Grounds open 5am-11pm; palace open April 19.-Sept.30. Tues.-Sat. 9am-2:30pm, Sun. 9am-4pm; Feb.1-April 18 and Oct.1-Nov. 30 Tues.-Sun. 10am-2:30pm. Admission 47,000zł, students 32,000zł.) The palace is the site of a May **chamber music festival** and regular concerts. Outside the museum, save your tickets for the **orangery** and **coach museum.** Just outside the palace gates, on the southwestern side, stands a lovely synagogue. Its impressive polychromy has been preserved since the 18th century (open Tues.-Sun. 10am-4pm; admission 5000zł).

■ ■ ■ TARNÓW

Tarnów is truly a patchwork of cultures, religions, and ethnicities. Romany culture still thrives in Tarnów; here visitors can catch a glimpse of Polish Gypsy culture, a way of life little understood by outsiders. Before World War II, Tarnów was 50% Jewish; although the war largely decimated the Jewish population, many signs of the Jewish culture persist here. Meanwhile, the town is also home to a fine collection of Catholic sacred art, housed in a 16th-century cathedral.

ORIENTATION AND PRACTICAL INFORMATION

Tarnów lies 1½ hours east of Kraków by train. Both the train and bus stations are located on Plac Dworcowy, southwest of the Old Town and just a short walk from the center. The main street, ul. Krakowska, leads from the train station to the Rynek Starego Miasta.

Tourist Offices: ORBIS, ul. Krakowska 30 (tel. 21 65 12), is open Mon.-Fri. 9am-5pm, Sat. 9am-1pm. **Gromada** tourist agency, at Rynek 17 (21 19 22), arranges buses to 500 destinations in Western Europe. Open Mon.-Fri. 8am-4pm.
Budget Travel: PTTK Tourist Agency "Lidia," ul. Żydowska 20 (tel. 22 22 00, fax 21 62 29), has a friendly and well-informed staff who shares their knowledge of the city with tourists and arrange English-speaking guides, who can also take you

POLAND

on biking or walking tours of the countryside (700,000zł for 12hrs.). The manager, Ms. Lidia Kłósek, also directs to hotels. Open Mon.-Fri. 9am-4pm.
Currency Exchange: Bank PKO S.A., at pl. Kościuszki 4 (tel. 22 12 53). Cashes traveler's checks for 1% commission, and does VISA/MC cash advances. Open Mon.-Fri. 7:30am-4:30pm, random working Sat. 7:30am-2pm.
Post Office: at pl. Dworcowy 2(tel. 21 36 63), and at ul. Mickiewicza 6 (tel. 21 36 71). Open Mon.-Fri. 8am-8pm and on working Sat. 8am-2pm.
Telephones: Phones at the pl. Dworcowy post office are open 24 hrs. At the ul. Mickiewicza post office, they are open Mon.-Fri. 7am-9pm, Sat. 7am-2pm. **City Code:** 0-14.
Trains: PKP train information tel. 933. To: Łańcut (10 per day, 2hrs.; 64,500zl), Kraków (40 per day, 1hr.; 35,500zł), Warsaw (14 per day, 4hrs.; 162,000zł), Nowy Sącz (15 per day, 2hrs.; 39,000zł), Budapest (1 per day. 10hrs.; 771,000zł).
Buses: PKS bus information tel. 936. To: Kraków (22 per day, 2hrs.; 54,000zł), Zakopane (2 per day, 4hr.; 95,000zł), Nowy Sącz (2 per day, 1½hr., 44,000zł). International bus tickets sold in room #7, 2nd floor (tel./fax 21 41 11).
Pharmacy: ul. Żydowska 6 (tel. 21 59 99). Open Mon.-Fri. 8am-6pm, Sat. 9am-1pm.
Medical Assistance: Emergency Room: ul. Nowodąbrowska 2 (tel. 999).

ACCOMMODATIONS AND CAMPING

Dom Wycieczkowy PTTK, ul. Żydowska 16 (tel. 21 62 29), in the heart of the Old Town. Doubles 220,000zł. Triples 240,000zł. Quads 320,000zł. Quints 350,000zł. Communal bathrooms. The café downstairs is open daily 8am-9pm.
Hotel Polonia, centrally located at ul. Wałowa 21 (tel. 21 33 36), in a newly renovated building. Take bus #2 or 9 from the bus or train station toward the center. Full of foreign students. Singles with bath 210,000zł. Doubles with bath 310,000zł. Triples 330,000zł, with bath 390,000zł.
Hotel Mościce, ul. Kasztanowa 96 (tel. 33 06 36), far from the center in the Mościce district. Take bus #9 from ul. Krakowska toward "Zakłady Azotowe"; get off when you see the Peugeot dealership. Singles with bath 250,000zł. Doubles with bath 340,000zł. Triples with at 450,000zł.
Camping, ul. Piłsudskiego 30 (tel. 21 51 24). Take bus #30 toward *Basen*; get off after a left turn from ul. Romanowicza onto ul. Piłsudskiego. 20,000zł/person per day plus 15,000zł/tent per day. 4- and 6-bed cabins at 45,000zł/bed. Open June-Aug. Swimming pool on the premises (tel. 21 43 92; tickets 24,000zł).

FOOD

Hongkong Restaurant, at ul. Dąbrowskiego 1 (tel. 21 24 01), east of the Rynek. Nicest wait staff in the country and a doting owner. Sweet and sour pork 75,000zł. Carp in moon shadow 105,000zł. Great lemon iced tea 14,000zł. Café and restaurant open daily noon-midnight.
Milk Bar Sam, ul. Lwowska 12 (tel. 21 39 62). Inexpensive food in bleak surroundings. Tomato soup 4750zł. Rice with fruit 8900zł. Open Mon.-Fri. 6am-7pm, Sat. 6am-4pm, Sun. 8am-4pm.
Polonia Restaurant, in the Hotel Polonia, ul. Wałowa 21 (tel. 21 13 30). Separate section on the menu for vegetarians: potato pancakes 42,000zł; soups 10,000-32,000zł.
Bella Italia Restaurant, at Rynek 5 (tel. 22 44 70). Refreshing whitewashed rooms. Spaghetti pesto 46,000zł. Pizzas 39,000-57,000zł. Open daily 11am-10pm.
Bristol Restaurant, ul. Krakowska 9 (tel. 21 22 79). Typically Polish establishment, with starched tablecloths and *kotlety schabowe*. Fried chicken and potatoes 89,000zł. Open Tues.-Sat. 10am-10pm, Sun.-Mon. 10am-8pm.
Cukiernia Kudelski, ul. Krakowska 1 (tel. 22 25 54). Great pastries for 5000zł. Tables for those who want to consume their desserts within the orange-cream mirrored walls of the establishment. Open daily 10am-7pm.
Café Progress, ul. Basztowa 5 (tel. 22 42 05 or 24 09 95), shares the premises with an English bookstore. Have a cup of coffee over a newly acquired English paperback. Cafe and bookstore open Mon.-Fri. 10am-6pm, Sat. 10am-2pm.

SIGHTS

At ul. Krakowska 10, the **Ethnographic Museum** (tel. 22 06 25) traces the history of Polish Gypsies since 1401, when they first came to Kraków. During World War II, 35,000 Gypsies perished in Poland; today, Poland has about 20,000 Gypsies. The museum exhibits a permanent display on their arts and culture, with an outdoor Gypsy camp in summer. Beautifully painted caravans await riders, and the Gypsy flag—a red wheel against a green and blue background—symbolizes the way Gypsies live, wandering under the blue sky. The English brochure by Adam Bartosz *The Gypsies: History and Culture*, gives interesting insights into the subject and is worth the 10,000zł (open Tues., Thurs. 10am-5pm, Wed., Fri. 9am-3pm, Sat.-Sun. 10am-2pm; admission 10,000zł, students 7000zł). In the *Rynek*, the **Town Hall Museum** (tel. 21 47 01) shows off frescoes, furniture, and porcelain (open Tues. and Thurs. 10am-5pm, Wed. and Fri. 9am-3pm, Sat.-Sun. 10am-2pm; admission 10,000zł, students 7000zł). The **Diocesan Museum,** behind the golden 16th-century **cathedral,** holds an enormous collection of sacred and folk art (open Mon.-Fri. 10am-3pm, Sun. 9am-2pm; free, but donations encouraged).

Behind the PTTK hostel on ul. Żydowska, stands the **bimah** (center)—the only remaining part of the 16th-century synagogue that was destroyed in 1939. Today, the *bimah* is fenced off and protected by a roof; its conservation was funded by Ronald Lauder, son of the mascara and eye-shadow magnate, Estée Lauder. The elder Lauder comes from Tarnów, which, no doubt, explains the interest her son takes in the town's synagogue. There is also a **Jewish cemetery** on ul. Nowodąbrowska. Adam Bartosz's brochure, *In the Footsteps of the Jews of Tarnów,* is a handy guide for all those interested in retracing the history of the Jewish population of Tarnów, and is available at the **Muzeum Okręgowe** (Regional Museum), at Rynek 21 (tel. 21 21 49). The museum houses Jewish documents, as well as an exhibit illustrating the role of the Old and New Testament in European art (open Tues, Thurs. 10am-5pm, Wed., Fri. 9am-3pm, Sat.-Sun. 10am-2pm; admission 10,000zł, students 7000zł).

■■■ NOWY SĄCZ

The Carpathian mountains are the home of the last Lemkos (Ruthenians), most of whom were expelled in 1945-47 to Ukraine. Lemko lands stretch from the range of Pieniny to the village of Jaworki in the Bieszczady mountains. The people still speak Lemko, a language close to Ukrainian. Suppressed by the communist government, they strove to preserve their language and their Greek Catholic beliefs. Their most beautiful onion-domed churches are in Klimkówka, Gładyszów, Jastrzębik, and Zyndranowa. Some Lemko icons have also found a home at the museum in Nowy Sącz. The town itself is neatly situated on the banks of the Dunajec River and its tributary, the Kamieniec River. This auspicious site played an important role in the town's prosperous past. Today, the Kamieniec River remains one of the cleanest rivers in Poland.

Orientation and Practical Information Nowy Sącz lies two hours southwest of Tarnów by train (15 per day, 2hrs.; 39,000zł). The **main train station (Nowy Sącz)** is on ul. Kolejowa (tel. 42 30 20), in the southern part of town. There is another station, **Nowy Sącz Miasto,** right in the middle of the Old Town, at ul. Kościuszki 10. Not all trains stop here; double-check your connection before you leave. If you have to get off at the main station, take bus #17 to the center, or prepare for a long walk along al. Batorego, which runs perpendicular to the station, and leads straight to the Old Town. The **bus station** is on pl. Dąbrowskiego (tel. 42 12 02), in the southeastern corner of the Old Town. There are no direct train connections to Zakopane; to get there by train, you have to change in Chabówka. The whole trip may take up four hours. Buses to Zakopane follow a much more direct route (9 per day, 3hrs.; 64,000zł). Unfortunately, they all pass through Nowy Sącz and are crowded; try your luck.

COIT Tourist Information, ul. Jagiellońska 46a (tel. 42 37 24), sells maps and tries to stay afloat (open Mon.-Fri., 8am-3pm). **Artus Tourist,** on the second floor of Hotel Panorama, ul. Romanowskiego 4a (tel./fax 42 27 46), is a much better bet. The staff is energetic, computer literate, and handles plane, ferry, and bus tickets to Western Europe (open Mon.-Fri. 8am-5pm, Sat. 9am-1pm). The Panorama Hotel also houses the **Tourist Agency Poprad** (tel. 42 26 05), which arranges rooms in hotels and private houses in other Carpathian towns, such as Piwniczna and Krynica, for 80,000zł per person (open Mon.-Fri. 7:30am-3:30pm). The budget travel **PTTK** Karpaty office, Rynek 9 (tel./fax 42 08 31), has information on hiking and trips in the area. In the same building, their branch (tel./fax 42 27 23) arranges accommodations in other parts of the Carpathian mountains (open Mon., Wed.-Thurs. 7am-3pm, Tues. and Fri. 11am-7pm).

For **currency exchange,** stop by one of the *kantors* throughout the town. **Bank PKO S.A.,** ul. Jagiellońska 50 (tel. 42 31 29), also cashes traveler's checks and does Visa cash advances (open Mon., Wed. 10:15am-5pm, Tues., Thurs.-Sat. 8am-2:30pm). The main **post office** and **telephones** are at ul. Dylewskiego 10 (tel. 42 00 12; open Mon.-Fri. 7am-9pm, free Sat. 8am-2pm, working Sat. 8am-6pm, Sun. 8am-noon and 3-6pm). The **telephone city code** is 0-18.; the **postal code** is 33-300. There is a **pharmacy** at Rynek 27 (tel. 42 08 02; open Mon.-Fri. 8am-8pm, Sat. 8am-3pm). In case of health **emergencies,** contact ul. Waryńskiego 2 (tel. 999 or 42 22 22).

Accommodations Hotel Panorama, ul. Romanowskiego 4a (tel. 42 00 00 or 42 18 78), lies in a very picturesque spot, and has a restaurant overlooking the Dunajec River. Western-style double beds and MTV. All rooms with baths. (Singles 330,000zł. Doubles 440,000zł. Triples 450,000zł (no TVs). Breakfast in the hotel restaurant 40,000zł.) Strangely enough, the reception of Panorama is the place to ask for a **private room** in Nowy Sącz. Rooms run at 50,000zł per person, but the hotel crew loyally warns that they are not very comfortable. **Dom Wycieczkowy PTTK,** ul. Jamnicka 2 (tel. 42 50 12), is also located on the bank of the Dunajec River. Take bus #6 from the train station and get off on the first stop on the other side of the river. Hostel-like rooms. (Doubles 240,000zł. Triples 300,000zł. Quads 350,000zł. Use of camping site: 30,000zł per person per day; 10,000zł per tent per day.) **Hotel Zajazd Sądecki,** ul. Królowej Jadwigi 67 (tel. 42 26 05), also on the river, is far from the city center. Take bus #23 from the train station, and get off at the church, just before the bridge. (Doubles 250,000zł. Triples 330,000zł. All rooms with bath.) The **Youth Hostel,** at ul. Batorego 72 (tel. 42 32 41), is located in a gray-blue building next to a school. (6-10-bed rooms at 25,000-35,000zł per person. 25% off with hostel ID. Open year-round.)

Food Piwnica Pod Ślepowronem, ul. Jagiellońska 2 (tel. 42 00 21), is a candle-lit cellar filled by a trendy crowd. (Shish kebabs 49,000zl, wine by the glass 10,000-30,000zł; open daily 11am-11pm). **Mandaryn Restaurant,** ul. Lwowska 1 (tel. 42 32 50), in the southeastern part of the Rynek, offers typical Chinese cuisine: vegetarian fried rice (33,000zł), lemon chicken (47,000zł), and egg rolls (28,000zł). (Open daily 10am-9pm.) The **Café and Restaurant Imperial,** ul. Jagiellońska 14 (tel. 42 29 06), serves all sorts of Polish fare: ham and cheese omelette (39,000zł), dinner entrees (40,000-70,000zł). (Café open daily 9am-10pm; restaurant open daily 11am-until last guest leaves.)† **Bona Restaurant,** at Rynek 28 (tel. 42 11 02), occupies a pleasant white and blue hall decorated with paintings of horses. (Turkey 92,000zł. Spaghetti carbonara 69,000zł. Cabbage *naleśniki* in mushroom sauce 33,800zł. Open daily 9am-10pm.)

Sights The **museum** at ul. Lwowska 3 (tel. 42 07 49) exhibits primitives by Nikifor, a famous artist from nearby Krynica, and old Orthodox icons (open Tues.-Thurs. 10am-2:30pm, Fri. 10am-5:30pm, Sat.-Sun. 9am-2:30pm; admission 10,000zł, students 7000zł, guide 35,000zł). North of the Rynek, the 18th-century **synagogue**, at ul. Berka Joselewicza 12, is a museum of Jewish culture (open Wed.-Thurs. 10am-

2pm, Fri. 10am-5:30pm, Sat.-Sun. 9am-2:30pm). For a scenic and relaxing walk along the Dunajec River, head down ul. Romanowskiego. Mr. Paweł Stefanowski, an ethnographer who organized the Lemko political party "Hospodar" in 1990, will soon exhibit his rich collection of Lemkoisms in the village of Bielanka at house #4.

■ NEAR NOWY SĄCZ: STARY SĄCZ

The tiny town of Stary Sącz is set like a jewel amid hills and fields of gold, on the banks of the Dunajec and Poprad Rivers. The entire region of Sącz was given by King Bolesław Śmiały to his wife, Kinga, a Hungarian princess. In 1273, as Queen of Poland, she founded the **Convent of St. Clara** on the site of what became known in the 14th century as Stary Sącz. After her husband's death, Kinga joined the convent and became its first Abbess.

To get there from the Rynek, walk along ul. Kopernika and watch for the convent's gate at ul. Bandurskiego. Inside, there is a Baroque church and a treasury, where Kinga's ring and her agate spoon are kept. At Rynek 6, the historic **Dom na Dołkach** (tel. 46 00 94) functions as the **Regional Museum,** which houses a collection of folk sculpture and pottery, and an exhibit of the town's history and famous citizens, including Ada Sari, the most honorable citizen of Stary Sącz (open Tues.-Sun. 10am-1pm; admission 10,000zł, students 5000zł).

Stary Sącz is a base for trips into the mountains of Beskidy, or down the postcard-pretty Dunajec River through the Pieniny Range. The range stretches southwest of Stary Sącz, along the border with Slovakia. Highlanders pick up tourists at the village of Sromowce and float their rafts 14.5km down Dunajec to Szczawnica.

Located 8km southwest of Nowy Sącz, Stary Sącz is easily accesible by train or bus, and is the ideal destination for a daytrip, if you plan to stay in Nowy Sącz longer than a day. Bus #24 (4400zł) from the Nowy Sącz Rynek will take you directly to Stary Sącz; it's a 25-minute ride. The **tourist agency Kinga** is located at Rynek 21 (tel. 46 05 53 or 46 00 21). In a room adorned with folk sculptures and a painted furnace, the owners organize rafting trips on the Dunajec River (departs from the village of Sromowce, 3hrs., 150,000zł, May-Oct. only), campfires, accommodations, and distribute free brochures on the area, also available in English (open Mon.-Fri. 8am-3pm). The **postal code** is 33-340 and the **telephone city code** is 0-24.

The **Zajazd Szałas,** at ul. Jana Pawła II 79 (tel. 46 00 77), stands on the edge of the forest and is surrounded by trees. These peaceful, somewhat isolated quarters consist of two doubles, one triple, and one quad. A bed in any of the rooms costs 107,000zł for the first night and 74,000zł for each additional night. The restaurant on the premises serves traditional Polish dishes (open daily 9am-10pm). The **campsite** at the same location charges 15,000zł per person per day and 10,000-15,000zł per tent per day, depending on the size of the tent.

In the town proper, the **Marysieńka Restaurant,** in a white house with red window panes at Rynek 12 (tel. 46 00 72), has a breezy terrace, and serves breakfast for 15,000-26,000zł, chicken for 18,000-40,000zł and 4 kinds of *pierogi for* 25,000zł (open daily 9am-10pm). At the **Staromiejska Restaurant,** Rynek 18 (tel. 46 00 71), you won't get a bird's-eye view of the Rynek, but fresh trout (25,700zł) may be worth paying a visit (open daily 9am-10pm). On a hot day, cool down with delicious ice cream at **Lody tradycyjne,** Rynek 22. A family-run establishment, it uses recipes perfected by the ancient Carpathian folk (open Mon.-Fri. 10am-4pm, Sat. 10am-2pm).

■ ■ ■ KRAKÓW

Capital of Poland until the 16th century, **Kraków** is a gem among European cities. Unlike most of Poland, the city miraculously escaped the obliteration of World War II; instead, the Nazis desecrated Wawel Castle, using Kraków's most precious landmark as their headquarters. Many of its beguiling buildings now bear instead the scars of severe air pollution from the smokestacks of industrial Nowa Huta,

Kraków's "model" socialist suburb to the east. Nevertheless, a stroll through Kraków's cobblestone alleys punctuated with baroque cupolas and church spires transports you to a more innocent century.

ORIENTATION AND PRACTICAL INFORMATION

The city fans outward in roughly concentric circles from the large Renaissance **Rynek Główny** (main market square), at the heart of the **Stare Miasto** (old town). The refreshingly green belt of the **Planty** gardens rings the Stare Miasto, and the **Wisła River** skims the southwest corner and **Wawel Hill.** For maps, try **ORBIS** or **COIT,** near the train station.

Tourist Offices: There are 3 **ORBIS** offices in Kraków. The one at Rynek 41 (tel. 22 40 35) sells ferry, plane, international bus and train tickets, including Wasteels, and arranges tours to Wieliczka and Oświęcim. Open Mon.-Fri. 8am-7pm, Sat. 9am-1pm. The branch at al. Focha 1, in the Hotel Cracovia (tel. 21 98 80 or 22 46 32), houses the **American Express** office and is open Mon.-Fri. 8am-8pm, Sat. 8am-3pm. There is also an office on Plac Szczepański 2 (tel. 22 61 47) that handles foreign trips. **Point Tour** has its main office at the Ibis Hotel, ul. Przy Rondzie 1 (tel. 21 84 33), and organizes sightseeing tours in English (Kraków, Wieliczka, Oświęcim). Open Mon.-Sat. 8am-8pm, Sun. 8am-4pm. **INT Express Travel Agency,** ul. Św. Marka 25 (tel/fax 21 79 06), is a registered KLM, Lufthansa, Delta, Swissair, and LOT agent. English-speaking staff. Open Mon.-Fri. 8am-8pm, Sat. 8am-3pm. **Fregata,** ul. Szpitalna 32 (tel. 22 41 44 or 22 49 12), arranges English-speaking city guides for 860,000zł. Open Mon.-Fri. 8am-6pm, Sat. 9am-2pm.
Budget Travel: ALMATUR, Rynek Główny 7/8 (tel. 22 63 52), in the courtyard in back. Eurotrain tickets, bus tickets to Western Europe, and ISICs. Open Mon.-Fri. 9am-5pm. **PTTK,** ul Westerplatte 15 (tel. 22 20 94), provides a city guide service; they'll show you the city in 5 hours, in Polish (400,000zł), or English, German, French (600,000zł per trip). Open Mon.-Fri. 9am-3pm.
Consulates and Cultural Centers: most of these institutions are located in the *Stare Miasto,* which is also Kraków's center.
    Austria, ul. Krupnicza 42 (tel. 21 99 00 or 21 97 66). **Austrian Commerce Office,** ul. Grodzka 1 (tel. 21 10 00).
    Germany, ul. Stolarska 7 (tel. 21 84 73, 21 89 80, or 21 83 78). The Goethe Institute is at Rynek 20 (tel. 22 69 46).
    Hungary, ul. Józefa 12.
    Russia, ul. Westerplatte 11 (tel. 22 83 88 or 22 90 55).
    Vilnius (Lithuanian) Cultural Center, ul. Św. Krzyża 1 (tel. 22 11 00).
    U.S., ul. Stolarska 9 (office tel. 22 12 94; Consular Dept. tel. 22 97 64; Visa Dept. 22 14 00). Library open Mon.-Fri. noon-4:45pm.
Currency Exchange: At *kantor* booths all over the city, ORBIS offices, and hotels. **Bank PKO S.A.,** Rynek 31 (tel. 22 60 22), cashes traveler's checks and does Visa/MC cash advances. Open Mon.-Fri. 7:30am-7pm, Sat. 7:30m-1:45pm.
American Express: at **ORBIS** on al. Focha (see above). Lost checks replaced, but no wired money accepted nor traveler's checks sold. AmEx traveler's checks cashed for a bargain 1% commission. Mail held for US$1 per piece.
Post Office: main office at Westerplatte 20 (tel. 22 48 11; 22 26 48, fax 22 36 06), is open Mon.-Fri. 7:30am-8:30pm, Sat. 8am-2pm. **Poste Restante** at window #7. Sun. 9-11am. **Postal Code:** 31-045.
Postal Services: DHL, ul. Racławicka 56 (tel. 33 80 96). **Express Mail Service** (EMS), at pl. Kolejowy 5 (tel. 22 40 26, open daily 8am-8pm, except on free Sat. 8am-1pm), and ul. Westerplatte 20 (tel. 22 66 96), open Sun.-Mon. 7:30am-9pm, working Sat. 9am-3pm, free Sat. 8am-2pm.
Telephones: 24-hr. phones at the main post office, and also at the office opposite the train station, ul. Lubicz 4 (tel. 22 14 85 or 22 86 35). **City Code:** 0-12.
Photocopies: available Mon.-Fri. 8am-6pm, Sat. 9am-2pm (650zł per page) at the main post office, and Mon.-Fri. 8am-7pm, Sat. 8am-4pm at the Lubicz office (900zł per page). Also at **Copy Felix,** ul. Floriańska 43 (tel. 21 76 44). 1000zł per page. Open Mon.-Fri. 9am-7pm, Sat. 10am-2pm.

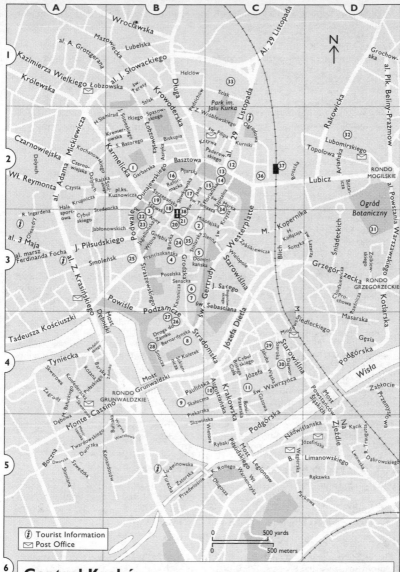

Central Kraków

Flights: The **airport** is 11km west of Kraków, in Balice (tel. 11 19 55). From the train station, take bus #208 (40min.). The downtown **LOT** office, at ul. Basztowa 15 (tel. 22 50 76 or 22 70 78), is open Mon.-Fri. 8am-7pm, Sat. 8am-3pm.
Trains: Alight at **Kraków Główny** (tel. 22 41 82 or 22 22 48) on pl. Kolejowy, an easy 10-minute walk northeast from the center of town. To: Warsaw (16 per day, 3½hrs.; 180,000zł); Zakopane (9 per day, 2½hrs.; 88,500zł); Gdańsk (6 per day, 6-9hrs.; 18,000-216,000zł); Tarnów (40 per day, 1½hrs.; 52,500zł), Wrocław (13 per day, 4hrs.; 127,500zł). International destinations: L'viv (1 per day, 12 hrs.; 40,000zł); Vienna (1 per day, 8hr., 795,000zł plus couchette 341,000zł); Kiev (1 per day, 23 hrs.; 990,000zł); Bratislava (2 per day, 7hrs.; 640,000zł); Budapest (1 per day, 840,000zł plus couchette 260,000zł). There are no direct connections to Prague; all trains to Prague depart from Katowice (1 per day, 10hrs.; 840,000zł plus couchette 260,000zł). Some trains to southeastern Polish cities leave from **Kraków Płaszów,** south of the city center. Tickets sold at stations or at ORBIS.
Buses: The **PKS station** (tel. 936), on ul. Worcella, faces the train station. To: Oświęcim (8 per day, 1hr. 40min., 44,000zł); Nowy Sącz (14 per day, 3hrs.; 64,000zł); Zakopane (30 per day, 2hrs. 20min., 64,000zł). International tickets to cities in Western Europe can be arranged by the travel agent **Sindbad,** located in the main hall of the bus station (tel. 22 12 38), open Mon.-Fri. 8am-6pm.
Car Rental: Budget, at Airport Balice (tel. 11 19 55, ext. 289), and at pl. Szczepań ski 8 (tel. 22 37 45); open daily 9am-5pm. **Avis,** tel. 21 10 66. **Hertz,** in the Hotel Cracovia, al. Focha 1 (tel. 37 11 20, fax 22 29 39); open Mon.-Sat. 8am-6pm
Luggage Storage: at the train station (7000zł per piece per day). Open 24 hrs.
Bookstore: PTTK's bookstore **"Pod Wierchami,"** ul. Jagiellońska 6/6a (tel. 22 28 40, fax 21 21 13), carries maps and guides, very handy if you plan to go hiking in the Tatras. They also give you plenty of advice on planning your itinerary. Open Mon.-Fri. 11am-7am, Sat. 10am-3pm. At Rynek 17, the bookstore **Księgarnia Hetmańska** (tel. 22 14 13) features many books in English, and is open daily 9am-9pm. The French bookstore **"Edukator"** (tel. 22 09 82), is next to the Institut Français de Cracovie at ul. Św. Jana 15. Open Mon.-Fri. 11am-6pm, Sat. 11am-2pm. The Jewish bookstore **Jordan,** at ul. Szeroka 2 (tel. 21 71 66) in the Kazimierz district, sells books on Jewish culture, maps, guides, and tapes with Jewish music. Open Mon.-Fri. 10am-6pm, Sat.-Sun. 10am-4pm.
Pharmacy: There are pharmacies *everywhere*. The one at Rynek 13 (tel. 22 41 90) is open Mon.-Fri. 8am-8pm, Sat. 8am-3pm. If it's after hours, check the signs on the door; all places post lists of the closest pharmacies still on duty.
Medical Assistance: Private doctors are at **Profimed,** Rynek 6 (tel. 21 79 97), and ul. Grodzka 26 (tel. 22 64 53). Open Mon.-Fri. 8am-8apm, Sat. 9am-1pm.
Emergencies: Police tel. 21 00 20 or 10 71 15.

ACCOMMODATIONS AND CAMPING

Friendly neighborhood room-retrievers **Wawel Tourist** (tel. 22 19 21, fax 22 16 40) reside next to the tourist office at ul. Pawia 8 (open Mon.-Fri. 8am-9pm, Sat. 8am-3pm. Singles 170,000-200,000zł. Doubles 250,000-320,000zł). Reservations are vital in summer. **ALMATUR, IT,** or **PTTK** can call ahead for you.

Near the Train Station

Hotel Europejski, ul. Lubicz 5 (tel. 22 09 11, fax 22 89 25) is the nicest establishment in this area. Singles 375,000zł, with bath 445,000zł. Doubles 480,000zł, with bath 695,000zł. Triples with bath 810,000zł.
Hotel Polonia, ul. Basztowa 25 (tel. 22 12 81), next to the Hotel Warszawski. Cosmopolitan but noisy. Singles 375,000zł, with bath 450,000zł. Doubles 450,000zł, with bath 695,000zł. Triples 540,000zł, with bath 810,000zł.
Hotel Warszawski, on ul. Pawia (tel. 22 06 22); slightly cheaper than the Europejski and Polonia, but so noisy. Singles 290,000zł, with bath 350,000zł. Doubles 410,000zł, with bath 510,000zł. Triples 510,000zł. with bath 620,000zł.

Old Town and Vicinity

PTTK Dom Turysty, ul. Westerplatte 15/16 (tel. 22 95 66), near the central post office. Big, brown, and efficient. Dandy location on park and near Rynek Główny. 8-bed dorms 120,000zł per person. Reception open noon-10pm.

Hotel Saski, ul. Sławkowska 3 (tel. 21 42 22, fax 21 48 30). Half a block from the Rynek and the night life! Full of international students. Singles 390,000zł, with bath 510,000zł. Doubles 600,000zł, with bath 780,000zł. Triples 680,000zł, with bath 890,000zł.

Hotel Pollera, ul. Szpitalna 30 (tel. 22 10 44; 22 11 28, fax 22 13 89). Yet another architectural gem in the Old Town, it slows down the price race: singles 425,000zł, with bath 475,000zł; doubles 550,000zł, with bath 795,000zł; triples with bath 960,000zł.

Outside the City Center

Schronisko Młodzieżowe (HI), ul. Oleandry 4 (tel. 33 82 22). Take tram #15 or 18 from the train station; or walk (15min. from the *Stare Miasto*). Flexible lockout 10am-5pm. Curfew 11pm. Nonmembers welcome. The doubles are clean and pleasant (100,000zł). 4-5-bed rooms 90,000zł per person. 6-16 bed rooms 80,000zł per person. 25% off with hostel ID.

Schronisko Młodzieżowe (HI), ul. Kościuszki 88 (tel. 22 19 51), inside the convent gate. Take tram #2 from Westerplatte. Run by nuns in a heavenly setting—a Renaissance courtyard tucked away behind the high convent walls. Reception open Mon.-Fri. 8am-3pm and 5-11pm, Sat. 8am-2pm and 5-11pm, Sun. 8-10am and 5-11pm. Curfew 11pm. 6-16-bed rooms 80,000zł per person. 25% off with hostel ID. Sheets 11,000zł.

Summer Hotel AWF, ul. Jana Pawła II 82 (tel. 48 02 07, fax 48 29 277), in student dorms. Tak tram #4,5,10; or 44 from the train station toward Nowa Huta, and get off after you see a park on your right, next to a stadium. Singles 200,000zł. Doubles 300,000zł. All rooms with bath. With hostel ID only 100,00zł per person per night. Open June27-Sept.24.

Summer Hotel Piast, ul. Piastowska 47 (tel. 37 49 33). Popular with foreigners who come every year to Kraków to learn Polish. Singles 160,000zł. Doubles 240,000zł. One bathroom serves two rooms. Open July-Sept.

Camping: Camping Krak, ul. Radzikowskiego 99 (tel. 37 21 22 or 37 58 40). Take tram #4, 8, 12, or 44 to *Fizyków* and walk north. (50,000zł per person per day. Open May 15-Sept. 15.) **Camping Krakowianka,** ul. Żywiecka 4 (tel. 66 41 91), in the *Borek Fałęcki* area. Quite a long ride by tram #19 from the train station to *Borek Fałęcki*; get off when you see a post office and a park on your right. Turn right onto ul. Kościuszkowców, then left onto ul. Żywiecka. 6-person bungalows 385,200zł. Tents 42,800zł per person per day.

FOOD

There are several **24-hr. grocery stores** in town: **Delicje,** ul. Basztowa 12, on the north side of the Old Town; **Społem,** on pl. Kolejowy, across from the train station; and **Non Stop,** ul. Szewska 10, west of the Rynek. *Obwarzanki* (soft pretzels with poppy seeds) are Kraków's street-stand specialty. All the eateries listed below are within a few blocks of the Rynek Główny.

Polish Cuisine

Hawełka Restaurant, at Rynek 34 (tel. 22 47 53). Occupies an airy, white and green dining hall in the heart of Old Town. Traditional Polish cuisine in an informal environment. Delicious blueberry *pierogi* 45,000zł. Open daily 10am-10pm.

Bar Mleczny Uniwersytecki, ul. Piłsudskiego 1 (tel. 22 32 47), across from the Jagiellonian University. A last bastion of proletarian dining—a full meal is under 20,000zł. Egg-salad sandwich 3800zł. Cheese *naleśniki* 11,200zł. Open Mon.-Fri. 6am-8pm, Sat. 7am-4pm, Sun. 7am-3pm.

Jadłodajnia Pani Stasi, ul. Mikołajska 16. A one-person operation—Pani Stasia is in charge. Definitely low-budget, but actually quite famous for its traditional Polish food. *Pierogi* with cheese 14,000zł; with meat 21,000zł. Open Mon.-Fri. 12:45pm till the food runs out.

POLAND

Wierzynek, at Rynek 15 (tel. 22 98 96). The legendary Wierzynek, where kings have dined since the 14th century, has a café downstairs and a ceremonious dining hall upstairs. Breakfasts in the café: scrambled eggs 35,500zł; cheesecake 21,300zł; delicious blueberry milkshakes 23,500zł. Restaurant entrees 150,000-250,000zł. Café open daily 8am-10pm; restaurant noon-11pm.

Bistro Piccolo, ul. Szczepańska 4 (tel. 22 17 39), one block northeast of the Rynek. Specializes in grilled chicken (30,000-40,000zł, depending on the size of your bird). Home delivery. Open daily 9am-10pm.

Ethnic Cuisine

Akropolis, ul. Grodzka 9 (tel. 21 77 55). Greek grill in the southern part of the Rynek. Gyros 45,000zł. Greek salad 30,000zł. Open Sun.-Thurs. 10am-midnight, Fri.-Sat. 10am-2am.

Chiński Pałac Restaurant (Chinese Palace), in the elegant hotel Saski, ul. Sławkowska 3 (tel. 21 35 42). Permanently invaded by Chinese tourists. Curry chicken 95,000zł. Egg rolls 25,000zł. Take-out available. Open daily 7am-11pm.

Balaton, ul. Grodzka 37 (tel. 22 04 69). Its divine Hungarian cuisine always attracts crowds. Entrees 40,000-150,000zł. Try the *placki ziemniaczane po węgiersku* (potato pancakes, 65,000zł). Open daily 9am-10pm.

Ariel Restaurant, ul. Szeroka 17 (tel. 21 38 70), in the old Jewish district of Kazimierz. Elegant interior with antique-style furniture, fresh roses on tables, and beautiful paintings. Calls itself the "Jewish Artistic Café," and hosts concerts of Jewish, Russian and Gypsy music daily at 8pm. Jewish-style carp 50,000zł. Gefilte fish 95,000zł. Purim cake for dessert 6000zł. Open daily 10am-midnight.

Andalous Restaurant, pl. Dominikański 6 (tel. 22 52 27). Middle Eastern/Spanish food. Tunesian rice with chicken 70,000zł. Paella 94,000zł. Veggie couscous 75,000zł. Open daily 10am-midnight.

Salad Bars

Różowy Słoń, ul. Straszewskiego 24. Pop art decor and delicious salads. Good-looking guys serve food... big bowls of salad around 30,000zł; otherwise 11,000zł/10dkg. Open Mon.-Sat. 9am-9pm, Sun 11am-9pm.

Pychotka, ul. Stradomska 12 (tel. 21 25 12). Great place for vegetarians. Big salads 15,000zł. Small salads 12,000zł. *Pierogi* 10,000-18,000zł. Open daily 9am-8pm.

Natural Foods Store and Bar Meus, ul. Św. Jana 3, next to the Św. Jana church, off the Rynek. Large selection of whole grain breads. Bean sprouts, cauliflowers, and fruit salads 10,000zł/10dkg. Less healthy but delicious torte Marcello 15,000zł.

Cafés

Café Ariel, ul. Szeroka 18 (tel. 21 79 21), next to the Ariel Restaurant; similar decor. Swarms of German and American tourists drop by for a glass of Coke. Open daily 10am till last guest leaves.

Café Malma, at Rynek 25 (tel. 21 98 94). Popular spot, always crowded. American, London, or Kraków-style breakfast 70,000zł. Tortes 19,000-21,000zł. Open daily 10am-11pm. (Lunch and dinner in the cellar daily noon-8pm.)

Café Maska, ul. Jagiellońska 1 (tel. 22 85 66, ext. 131), in the basement of the Teatr Stary. The theater curtains may still remember the famous actress Helena Modrzejewska, who charmed the American public as Modjeska. Cheese plate 25,000zł. Ice cream 30,000zł. Coffee 13,000zł. Open daily 9am-3am.

Kawiarnia u Zalipianek, ul. Szewska 24 (tel. 22 29 50). An entertaining outdoor café on the *Planty,* garnished with local folk art. Tortes 10,300-16,800zł per slice. Open daily 9am-10pm.

SIGHTS

Unlike Warsaw, Kraków was fortunate enough to be spared the destructions of World War II, but pollution from the postwar factory Nowa Huta wreaked considerable havoc nevertheless. Throughout the last four decades or so, Kraków's magnificent monuments were eroded by the deathly fumes. Only recently did the city obtain fundings from UNESCO that enabled it to save many of its dilapidated buildings. Today, Kraków is the site of ongoing restoration works, and is slowly regaining its previous beauty and character.

Stare Miasto (Old Town)

Entering the Stare Miasto from ul. Basztowa, you pass by the **Barbican** and through the **Brama Floriańska** (Gate), remnants of the town fortifications. A left onto ul. Pijarska from ul. Florianska takes you to the **Muzeum Czartoryskich,** at ul. Św. Jana 19 (tel. 22 55 66). The museum shelters paintings from the Renaissance to the 18th century, including the famous "Lady with Ermine" by Leonardo da Vinci (open Mon.-Tues. and Sat.-Sun. 10am-3:30pm, Fri. noon-5:30pm; admission 30,000zł, students 15,000zł). A few blocks southwest of the museum stands the **Kamienica Szołayskich,** at pl. Szczepański 9 (tel. 22 70 21). This tiny museum houses religious art from the 15th-18th centuries (open Mon. and Fri.-Sun. 10am-3:30pm, Tues. noon-5:30pm; admission 20,000zł, students 10,000zł).

At the center of the old town is the **Rynek Główny,** one of the largest and most distinctive market squares in Europe. In its northeastern corner rise the red towers of the **Kościół Mariacki,** a richly decorated cathedral with a 500-year-old carved-wood altarpiece by Wit Stwosz. The invading Nazis dismantled it and stashed it away; Allied forces discovered the buried pieces in Germany at war's end. Reassembled, it is ceremoniously unveiled at noon each day (Mon.-Sat. noon-6pm, Sun. 2-6pm. 5000zł). Diagonally across the square stands the lonely **Ratusz** (Town Hall) **Tower,** spared when the rest of the building was torn down in 1820 (open Wed. and Fri.-Sun. 9am-4pm, Thurs. 11am-6pm; admission 7000zł). Dividing the square in half, the Italianate **Sukiennice** (Cloth Hall) is as mercantile now as it was in guild times; the ground floor is an enormous souvenir shop. Upstairs, the **Muzeum Narodowe** (National Museum; tel. 22 11 66) houses a gallery of 18th- and 19th-century Polish classics (open Wed. and Fri.-Sun. 10am-3:30pm, Thurs. noon-5:30pm; admission 30,000zł, students 15,000zł, Thurs. free). During the academic year, Polish students cruise the area around the statue of Adam Mickiewicz, Poland's most celebrated Romantic poet.

Kraków's **Jagiellonian University,** over 600 years old, is the second-oldest in Eastern Europe after Prague's. Astronomer Mikołaj Kopernik and drama scholar Agnieszka Marszałek are among its distinguished alumni. The university's oldest building is the 15th-century **Collegium Maius,** southwest of the Rynek on ul. Jagiellońska 15 (tel. 22 05 49), with a bewitching Gothic courtyard and vaulted walkway (open Mon.-Fri. 11am-2:30pm, Sat. 11:30am-1:30pm to groups only—join or form one; admission 20,000zł, students 10,000zł).

Wawel (The Royal Castle)

The **Zamek Wawelski** (Wawel Castle) is one of the finest surviving pieces of Renaissance architecture in Poland. Begun in the 10th century, the castle has 71 chambers, a magnificent sequence of 16th-century tapestries commissioned by the royal family, and a series of 8 tapestries from Arras depicting the story of Noah's Ark. The castle is undergoing renovation—not all the chambers are open to the public. At the entrance to the castle, there is a guide office (tel. 22 09 04, fax 37 48 37), where you can purchase an English guidebook. A 3½-hour tour in English is 375,000zł. (Office open Mon.-Sat. 8am-3pm, Sun. 10am-3pm. Wawel open Mon.-Thurs., and Sat. 9:30am-4:45pm, Sun. 10am-3pm. 30,000zł, students 15,000zł. Wed. free. Treasury free.) To see **Wawel's Oriental Collection,** including the embroidered Turkish tent, you have to buy a separate ticket at the general Wawel ticket window (open Mon.-Sat. 9:45am-2:45pm, Sun. 10am-3pm; admission 20,000zł, students 10,000zł).

Next door is Kraków's **Katedra** (Cathedral), where Poland's kings were crowned and buried. Its former archbishop, Karol Cardinal Wojtyła, is now Pope John Paul II. (Open Mon.-Sat. 9am-5pm, Sun. 12:15-5pm. Ticket window for graves and the *dzwon Zygmunta* (Zygmunt's bell) open Mon.-Fri. 9am-5:15pm, Sat. 9am-4:45pm, Sun. 12:15-5:15pm. Admission 20,000zł, students 10,000zł.) Outside, look for the statue of Tadeusz Kościuszko, the Polish patriot who joined the American Revolution and died fighting Russian invaders in the late 18th century. Beneath Wawel hill is the **Smocza Jama** (Dragon's Den), the dungeon which in legend is home to Kraków's fire-breathing mascot.

Kazimierz (The Old Jewish District)

South of the old town center lies **Kazimierz**, the 400-year-old Jewish quarter. Take tram #6, 8, 10, 18, or 19 from the center or walk down ul. Stradomska from the Castle. You can still see remnants of what was once a large and vital community; the beautiful **R'emuh Cemetery** near ul. Szeroka, and the two operating synagogues of Kraków. The synagogue at the intersection of ul. Podbrzezie and ul. Miodowa, known as **Templ**, was founded by progressive Jews in 1860-62; it features a polychromed ceiling and 36 splendid stained-glass windows. Poland's oldest synagogue, the **Stara Synagoga** at Szeroka 24, now houses the **Muzeum Judaistyczne** (tel. 22 09 62), depicting the history and culture of Kraków's Jews (open Wed.-Thurs. 9am-3:30pm, Fri. 11am-6pm, Sat.-Sun. 9am-3pm; admission 20,000zł, students 10,000zł). Close to the synagogue, the **Jewish bookstore Jordan**, at ul. Szeroka 2 (tel. 21 71 66), organizes tours of Kazimierz (open Mon.-Fri. 10am-6pm, Sat.-Sun. 10am-4pm). Tours depart from the the bookstore and trace the sites named in *Schindler's List* (2hrs., 170,000zł, in English and other languages).

ENTERTAINMENT

Classical music buffs will appreciate the **Filharmonia Krakowska** (tel. 22 09 58 or 22 94 77) playing regularly in its hall at ul. Zwierzyniecka 2.

Clubs

Student clubs romp from about 8pm to midnight or 1am, and charge a minimal cover. The **Rotunda**, at ul. Oleandry 1 (tel. 33 35 38), has information on student events and concerts; it's the "official" student cultural center.

Pod Jaszczurami, Rynek Główny 7 (tel. 22 09 02), features quality jazz (Mon. 6-10pm and Tues. 8pm-1:30am) and a popular disco (Wed.-Thurs. and Sun. 8pm-2am, Fri.-Sat. 8pm-4am).

Jazz Club "U Muniaka," ul. Floriańska 3 (tel. 22 15 61). Café run by a well-known Polish jazzman, who often invites his friends for music sessions. Concerts Thurs.-Sat. at 9:30pm. Open daily 3pm "to the end."

Stańczyk, in the cellar under the Town Hall (tel. 21 13 26). Americans crowd this café. Jazz Fri.-Sat. at 10pm. Open 10am-1am, except for the performance nights.

Cabarets

Jama Michalika, ul. Floriańska 45 (tel. 22 15 61). Kraków's best-known café. Home of the Green Balloon cabaret, it's festooned with political caricatures and eclectic, plush decor. Ice cream 23,000-42,000zł. Open daily 9am-10pm.

Piwnica pod Baranami (Cellar Under the Rams), Rynek 27 (tel. 22 32 65). The longest running cabaret in Kraków. Changes gears in the summer, and instead of the intellectual ballads, features "Summer Dances." Open daily 9pm-3am. Mon.-Fri. free, Sat.-Sun. 30,000zł.

Pubs

Pub Pod Papugami (Under the Parrots), ul. Św. Jana 18. Cellars frequented by a cosmopolitan crowd of students. Open Mon.-Fri. noon-2am, Sat.-Sun. 4pm-2am.

Free Pub, ul. Sławkowska 4. Popular with international students. When are they open? Who knows with these free souls. They seem to be there every evening.

John Bull Pub, ul. Mikołajska 2. A little England in the heart of Poland; everything inside was allegedly imported from Britain. Besides British beer, also serves juices, coffee, and snacks. Open 11am till last customer leaves.

Galleries

Andrzej Mleczko Gallery, ul. Św. Jana 14 (tel. 21 71 04). Exhibits the works of the famous cartoonist and sells hilarious T-shirts and mugs.

Krzysztofory, ul. Szczepańska 2 (tel. 22 93 60), in the cellars of the Krzysztofory House. Modern art gallery and a café, it also hosts avant-garde theater performances. Open Thurs. 11am-6pm, Wed., Fri.-Sun. 9am-3:30pm. (Closed on second Sat. and Sun. of each month.)

BWA Gallery, Plac Szczepański 3a (tel. 22 10 52). Site of provocative exhibits such as the recent "Theatrical Spaces." Tickets 30,000zł, students 20,000zł, Thurs. free. Open Tues.-Sun. 11am-6pm.

Cricot 2, an avant-garde group once led by the late Tadeusz Kantor, has a museum of its works at ul. Kanonicza 5 (tel. 22 83 32). Open Mon.-Fri. 10am-2pm.

Sports

Fitness Clubs: Studio Maśka, ul. Grodzka 4 (tel. 22 25 74), south of the Rynek. Step and aerobics classes; weightroom. Open daily 10am-9pm. **Sauna** and **jacuzzi** at ul. Krupnicza 29 (tel. 34 02 43, ext. 17), open Mon.-Sat. 11am-11pm, Sun. 2-9pm.

Swimming Pools: Indoor swimming pool *Wisła* at ul. Reymonta 22 (tel. 10 15 29), open daily 10am-6pm (admission 30,000zł, students 20,000zł). Outdoor swimming pool *Cracovia* on al. 3-go Maja open daily 10am-6pm (admission 25,000zł, students 20,000zł).

Tennis: 24-hr. courts at Hotel Piast, ul. Radzikowskiego 72 (tel. 36 46 00). Dawn-1pm 30,000zł; 1pm-dusk 50,000zł; dusk-dawn 75,000zł.

Horseback Riding: Contact the *Krakowski Klub Jazdy Konnej* (Horseriding Club) at ul. Niezapominajek 1 (tel. 39 95 48), or the club *Krakus*, in the village of Swoszowice (5km from Kraków), ul. Kąpielowa 51 (tel. 66 00 88, ext. 484).

Kayaking: Rent kayaks at the club *Nadwiślan*, ul. Kościuszki 16 (tel. 22 32 69).

Skiing: A popular sport in this area, since Kraków is situated close to the Beskidy mountains and Poland's best-known winter resorts, Zakopane, Krynica, Nowy Targ, Szczyrk, and Korbielów.

■■■ NEAR KRAKÓW

OSWIĘCIM (AUSCHWITZ)

The Nazi concentration camps at **Auschwitz** (Oświęcim) and **Birkenau** (Brzezinka) are places of unspeakable horror, debris of an apocalypse that many have tragically begun to forget. Millions were murdered here; thousands more suffered in devastating ways at Nazi hands. The camps are in the town of **Oświęcim; buses** leave from the central Dworzec PKS across from Kraków Główny (8 per day, 1½hrs.; 44,000zł). **Trains** leave from Kraków Główny to reach the site (4 per day, 1¾hrs.; 31,000zł). An alternate way of reaching Oświęcim, is to take a half-day trip, organized by either Point Tour or ORBIS. Both agencies charge the same prices: 340,000zł, students 250,000zł (5hrs.). For details contact **ORBIS** at al. Focha 1 (tel. 22 46 32, fax 22 28 85), or **Point Tour** offices: in the Holiday Inn Hotel at ul. Armii Krajowej 11 (tel. 37 50 44), or in the Hotel Ibis at ul. Przy Rondzie1 (tel. 21 84 33). Tickets are also sold on the bus; the ORBIS bus leaves daily at 9:05am from pl. Szczepański 6, and the Point bus leaves daily at 9:15am from the same place.

Prisoners were originally kept at the smaller **Konzentrazionlager Auschwitz I,** within the city limits. By foot, turn right as you exit the train station, go 1 block and turn left; the camp driveway is 1.6km down on your right. Or catch bus #2, 3, 4, or 5; all will drop you near the kiosks outside the driveway. The camp itself is now a museum; barracks and crematoria hold displays detailing Nazi atrocities. An excellent English guidebook is available at the entrance. Begin your visit with the utterly terrifying film shot here by the Soviet Army on January 27, 1945. (Camp open 24 hrs. Museum areas open daily 8am-7pm; May and Sept. 8am-6pm; April and Oct. 8am-5pm; March and Nov.-Dec. 15 8am-4pm; Dec. 15-Feb. 8am-3pm. Free.) You must not leave Oświęcim without visiting the starker and vaster **Konzentra-tionlager Auschwitz II-Birkenau.** In the countryside, 3km from the original camp and a good half-hour's walk west of the train station, Birkenau was constructed later in the war. There are only endless rows of barracks and watchtowers and the untouched, collapsing remains of gas chambers and crematoria. In the right corner of the camp is a pond still gray from the ashes deposited there half a century ago.

WIELICZKA

Thirteen km southeast of Kraków is the 1000-year-old salt mine at **Wieliczka,** where pious Poles have carved an immense 20-chapel complex in salt 100m underground. The most spectacular one is **St. Kinga's Chapel.** Kinga, daughter of the Hungarian King Bela, was married to prince Bolesław Śmiały (the Bold), at that time ruler of Kraków, Sandomierz and Lublin, and later king of Poland. According to the legend, the princess wanted her dowry to be a present not just to Bolesław, but to all the people of Poland; upon questioning the delegates of the prince, she discovered that Poland had no salt. That night she heard a mysterious voice in her dream, which told her what to do. The following day, she asked her father to give her whatever her ring would touch, after she threw it across the mountain barrier separating Poland and Hungary. He agreed, and Kinga hurled the ring over the mountains. Upon arriving in Poland, she ordered workers to start digging in the spot where the ring had supposedly fallen—after days of digging, the men came upon a remarkable deposit of salt, and Kinga's ring in one of the salt crystals. Thus, salt followed Kinga across the mountains and came to Poland. Today, the Wieliczka salt mine has been declared by UNESCO as one of the 12 most priceless monuments in the world. (Open daily 8am-6pm; Oct.15-April 15 8am-4pm. Obligatory guided tours; last leaves 1½hr. before closing. Admission 90,000zł, students 50,000zł.)

Get to Wieliczka by signing up for one of the trips organized by **ORBIS** or **Point Tour** (3hrs., 340,000zl). The ORBIS bus to Wieliczka leaves daily at 3:10pm from pl. Szczepański 6, and the Point bus leaves daily at 3:20pm from the same place. Or choose the budget option: **trains** travel from Kraków (hourly, 25min.; 10,000zł); **private buses** leave from the PKS bus station (every ½hr., 15,000zl). Once in Wieliczka, follow the tracks' former path and then the *do kopalni* (to the mine) signs. A guidebook in English is available at local kiosks.

■■■ ZAKOPANE

Directly south of Kraków, the placid Polish landscape shoots up 2500m to form the Tatry Mountains. Zakopane is the crowded center of the region. Set in a valley surrounded by jagged peaks and soul-stirring alpine meadows, the town is Poland's premier ski and hiking resort.

ORIENTATION AND PRACTICAL INFORMATION

Bus and (slower) **rail** lines link Zakopane to Katowice, Kraków, and Warsaw; a direct train connects to Budapest (Mon., Thurs., and Sat.). For Slovakia border crossing information, tel. 662 65.

> **Tourist Offices:** The main tourist office in town is ORBIS, which does absolutely everything. There are a number of other tourist agencies in Zakopane, but none of them cater to travelers' needs quite as extensively as ORBIS.
> **ORBIS,** ul. Krupówki 22 (tel./fax 122 38). Gives out tourist information, in English; cashes traveler's checks at 5% commission; does VISA/MC cash advances at 3% commission (tel. 146 09); sells plane, ferry, and bus tickets (tel. 639 77); organizes trips to Morskie Oko (8hrs., 65,000zł), rafting on the Dunajec River (7hr., 260,000zł), trips to Vienna (2 days, 450,000zł) and Slovakia (1 day, 130,000zł). *Kantor* on the premises. Open Mon.-Fri. 8am-8pm, Sat. 8am-noon.
> **Biuro Przewodnickie PTTK,** at ul. Krupówki 12 (tel. 124 79), and the **Centrum Przewodnictwa Tatrzańskiego,** at ul. Chałubińskiego 42 (tel. 637 99), hire professional guides who know the Tatras like the back of their hands. (4-hr. tour of Zakopane in English 480,000zł; 8-hr. tour 720,000zł. 1-day hiking trip in English 800,000-1,650,000zł, depending on the height of the peaks.)
> **Tourist Information,** ul. Kościuszki 23 (tel. 122 11), close to the train and bus stations. Open 8am-8pm April-May and Nov., otherwise 24 hrs.

Trip, ul Zamoyskiego 1 (tel. 159 47), arranges bus connections to Western Europe. Open Mon.-Fri. 9am-5pm, Sat. 9am-1pm.

Gromada, in the hotel Gazda, ul. Zaruskiego 2 (tel. 158 42), carries useful maps, and helps plan itineraries. Open Mon.-Fri. 8am-4pm, Sat. 8am-2pm.

Tatry, next to the train station at ul. Chramcówki 35 (tel./fax 143 43), has a *kantor* and gives out info on vacant rooms. Open Mon.-Fri. 8:30am-6pm.

Currency Exchange: *Kantor* at the main post office, ul. Krupówki 20. Open Mon.-Fri. 9am-2pm and 3-6pm, Sat. 9am-3pm. **Bank PKO S.A.,** ul. Gimnazjalna 1 (tel. 685 05), cashes traveler's checks for 0.5-1.5% commission, plus Visa cash advances. Open Mon. and Wed. 10:15am-5pm, Tues. and Thurs.-Sat. 7:45am-2:30pm.

Post Office: the main office is at ul. Krupówki 20 (tel. 129 90). Open Mon.-Fri. 8am-8pm, Sat. 8am-2pm, Sun. 9am-11am. **Postal City Code:** 34-500.

Telephones: around the corner at ul. Zaruskiego 1. Open Mon.-Fri. 7am-9pm, free Sat. 7am-2pm, Sun. 8am-noon. **City Code:** 0–165.

Trains: the train station is at ul. Chramcówki 35. PKP information tel. 145 04. To: Kraków (16 per day, 2½-4hrs.; 51,000-118,000zł), Warsaw (4 per day, 7-10hrs.; 170,000zł plus 290,000zł for a sleeper).

Buses: across from the train station, at ul. Kościuszki 25. PKS information tel. 146 03. To: Kraków (22 per day, 2½hrs.; 64,000zł), Lublin (2 per day, 9hrs.; 224,000zł), Vienna (7 per week, 10hrs.; 480,000zł), Budapest (2 per week, 9hrs.; 374,000zł), Poprad in Slovakia (7 per week, 2hrs.; 44,000zł).

Taxis: Radio taxi tel. 142 32.

Bike Rental: Rent a mountain bike at the **Bzyk Sport** sporting goods store at ul. Krupówki 37 (tel. 147 07). 30,000zł per hour, or 200,000zł per day. Open Mon. 10am-4pm, Tues.-Sun. 10am-6pm. They have seven bike rental points in the area. The *Informator Zakopiański,* with a map of bike paths in the Tatra National Park, is available at any tourist office for 25,000zł.

Luggage Storage: Open 24 hrs. at the train station (7000zł per piece per day). At the bus station, open daily 8am-7pm (large pieces 8000zł, smaller ones 5000zł).

Late-Night Store: Baca at ul. Krupówki 32 (tel. 17 32). Open daily 2:30pm-7am.

Pharmacy: at ul. Krupówki 30 (tel. 633 31). Open Mon.-Sat. 8am-8pm.

Medical Assistance: ul. Kamieniec 10 (tel. 144 09).

ACCOMMODATIONS AND CAMPING

Since Zakopane is at the summit of mountain tourism in Poland, it gets very crowded in the summer (July-Sept.) and in the winter, especially around Christmas and during the winter break in February. Prices skyrocket in season. Serious hikers may want to stay far out in the mountains where no car can interfere with their solitude—call ahead in the summer to avoid being stranded in the middle of nowhere, with no roof over your head. **IT** at ul. Kościuszki 23 (tel. 122 11) is a popular source of private rooms for 150,000zł per person.

Youth hostel (HI), ul. Nowotarska 45 (tel. 662 03); walk down ul. Kościuszki toward the town, then take the second right onto ul. Sienkiewicza and walk 2 blocks. Lockout 10am-5pm. Curfew 11pm. Doubles 264,000zł, students 208,000zł. Dorm rooms 43,000-75,000zł (Poles) and 75,000zł (foreigners).

PTTK Dom Wycieczkowy, ul. Zaruskiego 5 (tel. 632 81). Large traditional chalet in the very center of the town. Singles with bath 220,000zł. Doubles with bath 320,000zł. Triples with bath 600,000zł. 6-8-bed rooms 70,000zł per person. 12-28-bed rooms 60,000zł per person.

Student Hotel "Żak," ul. Marusarzówny 15 (tel. 157 06), in the southern part of town on the Biały Potok River. Close to all hiking trails. 30-minute walk from the train and bus stations along ul. Kościuszki, Krupówki and Grunwaldzka. Quads 60,000zł/bed. Bigger rooms 50,000zł/bed.

Hostel Morskie Oko, by the Morskie Oko lake (tel. 776 09). Ideal location, if you plane to visit the scenic lake. Triples and large dorm rooms at 120,000zł per person. Reservations a must.

Camping Pod Krokwią, ul. Żeromskiego (tel. 122 56), across the street from the base of the ski jump. 25,000zł per person, 25,000zł per tent. Open May-Aug.
Camping Za Strugiem, ul. Za Strugiem 39 (tel. 145 66). Far from the center—catch a cab or walk along ul. Kościuszki, right onto ul. Krupówki, left onto ul. Kościeliska and left again onto ul. Za Strugiem (25 min.). Location makes up for the long hike: 35,000zł per tent per day and 35,000zł per person. 2- to 4-bed cabins 73,000zł per person. 10% off for stays longer than three days.

FOOD
The local specialty is *oscypek* (goat cheese) made by the Highlanders. Because of its strong and salty flavor, it can only be eaten in small quantities at a time.

Restaurant Świarna, ul. Kościuszki 4 (tel. 138 71). Tasty breakfast 25,000zł. Trout 39,000zł. Regional *Janosik* pork chop 62,000zl, named after the legendary highlander, who robbed the rich to give to the poor. Open daily 8am-10pm.
Kawiarnia, at the Hotel Orbis Giewont, ul. Kościuszki 1 (tel. 120 11). Breakfast 30,000zł. Strawberry or blueberry *naleśniki* 30,000zł. Open daily 8am-8pm.
Karczma Redykołka, ul. Kościeliska 1 (tel. 663 32). Irresistible tourist haunt fashioned after the traditional *chaty góralskie* (mountain huts). Food served by waitresses in regional costumes. Veal 55,000zł. *Oscypek* 10,000zł. Open 10am-9pm.
Karczma Obrochtówka, off the beaten path at ul. Kraszewskiego 10a (tel. 639 87). Worth the search for its fabulous kitchen and charming folk atmosphere. Open Tues.-Sun. noon-10pm.
Pizzeria Grace, ul. Krupówki 2 (tel. 138 54). Modern self-service place. Pizza Campaniola 51,000zł. Open daily 10am-10pm.
Morskie Oko, ul. Krupówki 30. Polish fast food center. Meatloaf 25,000zł. Blueberry *pierogi* 30,000zł. Fries 15,000zł. Open daily 9am-10pm.
Steak House, ul. Krupówki 28. Restaurant with salad bar. T-bone steak 90,000zł. Salad 20,000zł. Open noon-midnight.
Zbyrcok Restaurant, ul. Krupówki 29 (tel. 132 10). Regional yuppie place. Large selection of fish entrees, 100,000-145,000zł. Open daily noon-11pm.
Kolorowa, ul. Krupówki 26 (tel. 123 19). Delicious *pierogi* for 45,000zł. Open daily 11am-midnight.
Restaurant Gubałówka, on the Gubałówka mountain (tel. 636 30). Sweet cheese *naleśniki* 30,000zł. Open daily 10am-6pm.
Café Samanta, ul. Krupówki 4a. Best ice cream in town. Open in season Tues.-Sun. 10am-8pm, off-season 10am-6pm.

SIGHTS AND ENTERTAINMENT
Short mountain hikes are a specialty of the region, which is part of the **Tatrzański Park Narodowy** (National Park). The park entrance, at the end of ul. Strążyska, is a starting point for hikes of 2½-6 hours (admission 8000zł, students 5000zł). **Giewont** (1090m) is 4½ hours away. The mountain lake of **Morskie Oko** dazzles herds of tourists; take a bus (9 per day, 45 min., 10,000zł) from Zakopane to Polana Palenica, then hike 10km (6hr.). For a more dramatic vista, catch a bus to **Kuźnice,** 20 minutes south of central Zakopane, and hop on the **Kasprowy Wierch** chairlift (open daily 7:30am-8:10pm, Dec.-Feb. 8am-4pm, March-May and Oct. 7:30am-5:40pm, June 7:30am-6:10pm; 115,000zł round-trip). Go up a cable car to the **Gubałówka** mountain (20,000zł, students 10,000zł) and hike down (easy 25 min.), or walk to the **Butorowy Wierch** peak and take a chairlift down, to get a beautiful view of Zakopane and the slopes of Gubałówka (15,000zł).
    Dive into the hot springs of the **Antałówka Sports Center** on ul. Jagiellońska (tel. 639 34; open daily 6am-10pm). Visit the **Władysław Hasior Gallery** at ul. Jagielloń

ska 186 (tel. 668 71), where the works of the famous Polish sculptor are on display (open Wed.-Sat. 11am-6pm, Sun. 9am-3pm). Or stop by the **Old Cemetery at Pęksowy Brzyzek,** ul. Kościeliska, next to an old wooden church. The first burial ground of Zakopane, it is the resting place of many Tatra climbers, and writers and artists, who had been affiliated with the region.

Zakopane was well loved by the composer Karol Szymanowski, who spent most of his life here, in the house called **Atma,** at ul. Kasprusie 19. Today, Zakopane is the site of several music festivals. July brings the **Days of Karol Szymanowski's Music,** and August is the month of the **Festival of Highlanders' Folk Music.**

■■■ CZĘSTOCHOWA

Częstochowa is the Catholic Mecca of Poland. Every year hundreds of thousands of natives and foreigners make the pilgrimage to the most sacred of Polish icons, the **Black Madonna** in the towering monastery of **Jasna Góra,** to take part in the feast days of Our Lady known as the Great Festivals: on May 3 (the Feast of Our Lady Queen of Poland), August 15 (the Feast of the Assumption), and August 26 (the Feast of Our Lady of Częstochowa). The neo-Renaissance tower is visible from afar. The Paulite monastery itself resembles a Baroque fortress; it was founded in 1382 by Duke Władysław Opolczyk, who also donated the miraculous painting of the Blessed Mother and the Child in 1384. The church tower is perhaps the only visible sign of the spiritual life of the city; the old communist government seems to have done all it could to make the city gray, bleak, and incovenient for the faithful who walk, bike, and drive here.

ORIENTATION AND PRACTICAL INFORMATION

Częstochowa lies two hours northwest of Kraków by train. Both the main train and bus stations are located close to the town center and linked with the Jasna Góra monastery by the Aleja Najświętszej Marii Panny (Avenue of Our Lady), a 20-minute walk up the hill. All main offices and eateries are located along the avenue.

Tourist Offices: WCIT, al. NMP 65 (tel. 24 13 60, fax 24 34 12), is extremely organized and has detailed information on the town's hotels, but does not direct to private rooms. Well-stocked traveler's bookstore on the premises. Open Mon.-Fri. 9am-6pm, Sat.-Sun. 10am-4pm. **Travel Agency Zawadzkie,** al. NMP 39/41 (tel. 65 35 02; 65 35 10), handles bus connections to Western Europe. Open Mon.-Fri. 10am-6pm, Sat. 10am-noon. **ORBIS,** al. NMP 40/42, sells train, ferry, plane, and international bus tickets, and has a *kantor.* Open Mon.-Tues., and Thurs.-Fri. 8am-4pm, Wed. 9am-5pm. Also, there is a huge white and blue board in front of the PKS bus station at al. Wolności 45/49, with addresses and phone numbers of all hotels, youth hostels, swimming pools, and tennis courts in the area, as well as a tourist map of Częstochowa.

Budget Travel: PTTK, al. NMP 39/41 (tel. 24 67 55 or 24 31 34), gives helpful hints, arranges city guides in English, French or German (700,000zł for 4hrs.), organizes walks and hiking trips around the city, and 3-day trips to Prague (1,070,000zł including hotels). Open Mon.-Fri. 9am-4pm. **ALMATUR,** al. NMP 37 (tel. 24 43 68; 24 443 78, fax 24 43 78), sells ISICs and directs to summer student hostels. Open Mon.-Fri. 9am-5pm, Sat. 10am-2pm.

Currency Exchange: at *kantors* throughout the city. **Bank PKO S.A.,** at ul. Kopernika 17/19 (tel. 65 50 60), cashes traveler's checks for 1% commission and does Visa/MC cash advances. Open Mon.-Fri. 8am-6pm.

Post Office: main office is between bus and train stations, at ul. Orzechowskiego 7 (tel. 24 13 42). Open Mon.-Fri. 7am-9pm. **Postal Code:** 42-200.

Telephones: at the post office, open Mon.-Fri. 24 hrs, Sat.-Sun. 7am-9pm. **City Code:** 0-34.

Trains: PKP train information tel. 24 13 37. The main train station is on ul. Pilsudskiego, south of al. NMP. Get to Częstochowa by train from: Kraków (6 per day, 2hr., 81,000zł), Warsaw (7 per day, 3hrs., 115,500zł), or Wrocław (3 per day,

POLAND

3½hrs.; 103,000zł), but enquire about where you should get off—some trains stop at the Częstochowa Główna station (main), others at Częstochowa-Stradom. From Stradom, take bus #15 or a cab (50,000zł) to the center. International tickets and Wasteels window at Częstochowa Główna open 24 hrs.

Buses: main bus station at al. Wolności 45/49 (tel. 24 66 16). To: Warsaw (night express 11 per day, 4hrs.; 130,000zł), Kraków (3 per day, 3hrs.; 84,000zł), Wrocław (3 per day, 4hrs.; 95,000zł). Information on international routes, mainly to Germany, at windows 6 and 7.

Taxis: Echo Taxi (tel. 61 19 19) has 24-hr. service.

Luggage Storage: at both the train and bus stations (7000zł per piece). 24 hrs.

Pharmacy: al. NMP 50 (tel. 24 62 74). Open Mon.-Fri. 8am-9pm.

Medical Assistance: Private doctors at *Medyk*, al. Wolnosci 22 (tel. 65 46 66), open Mon.-Fri. 7am-7pm. Also, the monastery at Jasna Góra has a **first aid center**; look for their "first aid" sign in English. Open daily 6am-6pm.

ACCOMMODATIONS AND CAMPING

Dom Pielgrzyma (The Pilgrims' House), behind the monastery on Jasna Góra, at ul. Wyszyńskiego 1/31 (tel. 24 70 11; 65 66 68, ext. 315). Hostel-like building. Singles with bath 300,000zł. Doubles with bath 300,000zł. Quads 200,000zł.

Hotel Miły, (used to be called Mały), ul. Katedralna 18 (tel. 24 33 91), behind the train station. Look for the cheerful yellow and green signs. Modest but acceptable. Singles 120,000zł. Doubles 160,000zł. Triples 210,000zł. Quads 240,000zł.

Hotel Ha-Ga, ul. Katedralna 9 (tel. 24 61 73). Central location. Singles 140,000zł, with bath 210,000zł. Doubles 170,000zł, with bath 260,000zł. Triples 210,000zł, with bath 330,000zł. Quads 250,000zł, with bath 360,000zł. Quints 310,000zł.

Dom Rekolekcyjny, ul. Św. Barbary (tel. 24 11 77), close to the monastery, on the southern slope of Jasna Góra. Run by nuns, and primarily for pilgrims, but you may get lucky. Singles 50,000zł. Doubles 100,000zł. Dorm rooms 40,000zł/bed. Communal bathrooms.

Youth Hostel Internat TZN (high school dorm), ul. Jasnogórska 84/96. 4-, 5-, and 6-bed rooms at 20,000zł per bed. 25% off with hostel ID. Communal bathrooms. Open July1-Aug.31.

Camping Oleńka, ul. Oleńki 10/30 (tel. 24 74 95; 65 57 99, fax 25 14 79), behind the monastery and near *Dom Pielgrzyma*. Tents 30,000zł/person per day. Bungalows: singles with bath 80,000zł; doubles with baths 160,000zł; triples with bath 270,000zł; quads with bath 360,000zł; quints with bath 450,000zł. Open year-round.

FOOD

Dom Pielgrzyma, at the Dom Pielgrzyma hotel, ul. Wyszyńskiego 1/31 (tel. 24 70 11). Simple self-service entrees dished up in a modern dining hall; additional seating outside. Salads 6000zł. Entrees 35,000zł. Open daily 7am-8pm.

Bar Yuppie, ul. Piłsudskiego 13 (tel. 65 54 00), opposite the train station. It's not what it sounds like. Extensive menu including *bigos* (20,000zł), veal breast (75,000zł), and continental breakfast (50,000zł). Open 24 hrs.

Restauracja Polonia, on the first floor of Hotel Polonia, at ul. Piłsudskiego 9 (tel. 244 23 88). Chicken breast 87,000zł. Steamed veggies and fried eggs plate 37,000zł. Open Tues.-Sun. 7am-1am, Mon. 7am-10:30pm.

La Croissanterie Leury Michon, al. NMP 53 (tel. 24 78 21). Croissants 3500zł. Vegetarian pizza 25,800zł. Open Mon.-Sat. 7am-9pm, Sun. 10am-8pm.

Family Burger, al. NMP 63/65 (tel. 24 06 80; 24 83 20). Besides the usual hamburger menu, this fast food place offers Polish dishes such as *barszcz* (12,000zł).

Vecchia Milano, al. NMP 57/59 (tel. 65 49 29). Dozens of ice cream flavors. Try the tiramisu flavor at 5000zł per scoop. Outdoor tables.

Astoria, al. NMP 46 (tel. 24 13 11). Metal roosters give the dining room a quasi-folk character. Pork chops (40,000-50,000zł). Open daily 10am-10pm.

SIGHTS

The **Paulite monastery** on top of Jasna Góra is *the* sight in town. Everyone wants to catch a glimpse of the miraculous **icon of the Blessed Mother and the Child**. Created toward the end of the 14th century in Italy, and donated to the Paulite monastery by Duke Władysław Opolczyk in 1384, the icon was desecrated in 1430 by Hussites, and later renovated on the same surface. Two scars on the Madonna's cheek were left, however, as a reminder of the sacrilegious conduct of the Hussites and as proof to the faithful that the miraculous icon could not be destroyed. The beautiful and ornate **Basilica**, with the **Kaplica Matki Bożej** (Chapel of Our Lady) housing the icon, was built in the 15th century. Today, countless crutches, medallions, and rosaries strung upon the chapel walls attest to the icon's miraculous powers. (Chapel open daily 5am-9:30pm. The icon is revealed daily 6am-noon, 3-4:40pm, 6:30-7:15pm, and 9-9:15pm.)

The monastery also houses the largest **treasury** in Poland, which contains invaluable works of art, many of them donations of previous pilgrims: monstrances, chalices, crosses, candelabra, liturgical vestments, jewelry. (Open in summer Mon.-Sat. 9am-11:30am and 3:30-5:30pm, Sun. 8am-1pm and 3-5:30pm; in winter Mon.-Sat. 9am-10:30am and 3:30-4:30pm, Sun. 9am-12:30pm and 3:30-5pm. Donations encouraged.) The **Arsenał** (Arsenal), located nearby, exhibits weapons, military insignia, medals and orders, including those from World War II. (open Mon.-Sat. 9am-noon and 2:30-6pm, also Sun. 9am-noon and 1-6pm in summer). The **Muzeum Sześćsetlecia**, commemorating the 600th anniversary of the founding of the church and monastery on Jasna Góra, contains an impressive collection of musical instruments from the 17th-19th centuries (open daily 11am-4:30pm, 11:30am-4:30pm in winter). Also worth seeing is the **tower** on the western side of the Basilica and the fortifications surrounding the monastery (open daily 8am-4pm).

■■■ WROCŁAW

Wrocław is the active capital of Lower Silesia (Śląsk Dolny), straddling the Odra River. Under Prussian and German rule between 1741 and 1945, the city's elaborate postwar reconstruction is another example of the fiery Polish spirit. Only old photographs recall the city's destruction in World War II, when it became Festung Breslau, one of the last battling grounds on the route to Berlin. Still known to many as Breslau, Wrocław charms with its many bridges and lush parks and gardens. The 19th-century buildings give this vast, yet graceful city an antique feel.

PRACTICAL INFORMATION
Tourist Offices: The well-stocked, brand new **IT**, at Rynek 14 (tel. 44 31 11), will answer all your questions and supply you with handy maps. Open Mon.-Fri. 9am-5pm, Sat. 10am-2pm. **ORBIS**, ul. Piłsudskiego 62 (tel. 44 44 08), sells train, plane, ferry, and international bus tickets, organizes trips to various parts of Poland. Open Mon.-Fri. 9am-5pm, Sat. 10am-2pm. Another branch is at Rynek 29 (tel. 44 77 51); open Mon.-Fri. 10am-5pm, Sat. 10am-2pm.
Budget Travel: ALMATUR, ul. Kościuszki 34 (tel. 44 39 51), in the student center "Pałacyk." Look up their info on concerts, while buying ISICs or international bus tickets. Open Mon. and Fri. 9am-4pm, Tues.-Thurs. 9am-5pm, Sat. 10am-2pm. **PTTK**, in the town hall at Rynek 11/12 (tel. 303 44), organizes multilingual tours of the city (5hr., 1, 075,000zł). Open Mon.-Fri. 9am-5pm. The **Haisig and Knabe** travel agency, Rynek 45 (tel. 44 47 99 or 44 17 28), is the best spot in town to purchase plane and international bus tickets, and to make sightseeing plans: a half-day tour of Wrocław in any foreign language costs 300,000zł. Free brochures of the *Welcome To Wrocław* magazine. Open Mon.-Sat. 8am-7pm, Sun. 10am-4pm.
Consulates: Germany, ul. Podwale 76 (tel/fax 44 20 06).
Currency Exchange: at the *kantors* throughout the city. **Bank PKO S.A.,** pl. Solny 16 (tel. 30 96 43), cashes traveler's checks and does Visa/MC cash advances. Open Mon.-Fri. 8am-5pm.
Post Office: to the right of the train station at ul. Małachowskiego 1 (tel. 44 62 61, fax 44 41 19). Open Mon.-Fri. 7am-8pm, free Sat. 9am-3pm. **Postal Code:** 50-415.
Courier Services: DHL, ul. Powstańców Śląskich 95 (tel. 60 53 14, fax 60 58 15).
Telephones: open 24 hrs. at the post office. **Telephone city code:** 0-71.

Flights: The LOT office is at ul. Piłsudskiego 36 (tel. 390 31; 390 32). Open Mon.-Fri. 8am-6pm, Sat. 8am-3pm.
Trains: The main train station is on ul. Piłsudskiego (tel. 36 02 31; 36 60 32), a true traveler's center with a 24-hr. money exchange booth, pharmacy, and many eateries. To: Warsaw (9 per day, 5-7hrs.; 162,000zł), Kraków (13 per day, 4hrs.; 127,500zł), Częstochowa (3 per day, 3½hrs.; 103,000zł), Prague (2 per day, 7hrs.; 600,000zł plus couchette 300,000zł), Budapest (1 per day, 12hrs.; 1,008,000zł). Also plentiful connections to Germany.
Buses: The main bus station is behind the train station, at ul. Sucha 2 (tel. 61 81 22 or 61 22 99). To: Warsaw (3 per day, 8hrs.; 242,000zł), Kraków (1 per day, 7hrs.; 165,000zł). Also connects to Western Europe; inquire at **Almabus,** ul. Kościuszki 34 (tel./fax 44 77 13) for fares with a 10% student discount.
Taxis: Radio taxi at 919, 63 37 37, or 21 03 03.
Luggage Storage: At the train station. 5700zł per piece per day. 24 hrs.
24-hr. Pharmacy: At ul. Kościuszki 53 (tel. 44 30 32)
Medical Assistance: Private doctors at ul. Krasickiego 17a (tel. 48 18 19; 57 76 43; 51 91 18). Open 24 hrs.

ACCOMMODATIONS

Youth Hostel, ul. Kołłątaja 2 (tel. 338 56), directly opposite the train station. Doubles 39,000-66,000zł per person. 6-7-bed rooms 36,000-63,000zł per person. 8-bed rooms 40,000-49,500zł per person. 22-bed rooms 22,500-49,500zł per person. The higher price includes sheets. Lockout 10am-5pm.
Private Rooms: Biuro Usług Turystycznych (Tourist Services Center), ul. Piłsudskiego 98 (tel. 44 78 85; 44 41 01). Singles 170,000zł. Doubles 300,000zł. Open Mon.-Fri. 8:30am-4pm, Sat. 9am-2pm.
Hotel Piast, ul. Piłsudskiego 98 (tel. 300 33). Near the train station. Singles with sink 140,000zł. Doubles 260,000zł, with bath 340,000zł. Triples with sink 360,000zł. Quads with sink 440,000zł.
Hotel Grand, ul. Piłsudskiego 102 (tel. 360 71; 339 83). Near the train station. Singles 250,000zł, with bath 300,000zł. Doubles 380,000zł, with bath 480,000zł. Triples with bath 510,000zł.

FOOD

There are **24-hr. grocery stores** in town. **"U Pana Jana,"** pl. Solny 8/9 (tel. 356 85), is close to the Rynek. **Lokomotywka,** ul. Piłsudskiego 103a (tel. 331 56), is close to the train station.

Train Station Eateries: The **restaurant Książęca,** open daily noon-1am, tempts with Chinese chicken (42,000zł). The 24-hr. **bar Książęcy** offers sandwiches at 12,000zł. The 24-hr. **restaurant Micha** specializes in escargots (8000zł/piece). The 24-hr. **Golden Café** offers breakfasts at 30,000zł.
Bar Vega, at Rynek 27a (tel. 44 39 34), is modern and spiffy. Vegetarian entrees—full meal under 30,000zł. Open Mon.-Fri. 8am-7pm, Sat.-Sun. 9am-5pm.
Bar Miś, ul. Kuźnicza 48 (tel. 349 63). Cafeteria-style meal for under 20,000zł. Rice with blueberries 7900zł. Open Mon.-Fri. 6:30am-6pm, Sat. 8am-5pm.
Café Herbowa, Rynek 19 (tel. 44 38 11). Murals depict the city's merchants. Delicious *herbata po muzułmańsku* (tea the Muslim way), with milk, dates, raisins and nuts (14,000zł). Breakfast 16,000zł. Dinner entrees 30,000zł. Open daily 9am-until the last guest staggers home.
Café Uni, pl. Uniwersytecki 9/13 (tel. 40 28 36). Run by Wrocław University students. Coffee 7600-38,000zł. Banana in chocolate 21,4000zł. Open daily 11am-midnight.
Café Witaminka, at Rynek 52 (tel. 315 24). Recently renovated, shiny interior. Milkshakes 10,000zł. Poppy seed tortes 8000ł. Open daily 11am-11pm.
Dwór Wazów, at Rynek 5 (tel. 44 16 33), very fancy restaurant and café. Additional summertime café seating in the yard. Gypsy pork chop 160,000zł. Ice cream 24,000-53,000zł. Restaurant open daily 1pm-midnight; café 10am-10pm.

Spiż, restaurant and beer cellar located in the Ratusz (tel. 44 72 25; 44 52 67). Beer lovers appreciate this cool shelter on hot summer evenings. Restaurant open daily noon-11:30pm; beer cellar noon-2am.

Tutti-Frutti, Plac Kościuszki 1/4 (tel. 44 43 06). Endless list of ice cream desserts 18,000-113,00zł. Milkshakes 15,000-24,000zł. Tortes 30,000-39,000zł. Open daily 10am-10pm.

SIGHTS AND ENTERTAINMENT

The oldest neigborhood of Wrocław, **Ostrów Tumski** (Cathedral Island), ages gracefully across the river from the center of town, next to the **Botanical Gardens.** The stately **Katedra Św. Jana Chrzciciela** (Cathedral of St. John the Baptist) gives this section its dignified character. Inside the cathedral, a nun shows you the amazing marble Chapel of St. Elizabeth (donations suggested).

On your way to the populous bank of Wrocław, stop by the main University building at pl. Uniwersytecki 1 in the northern part of the *Stare Miasto*, to ogle the **Aula Leopoldina,** an 18th-century lecture hall with magnificent ceiling frescos. (Open Thurs.-Tues. 10am-3:30pm. 10,000zł, students 5000zł.) In the heart of the Stare Miasto, the Renaissance and Gothic **Ratusz** (town hall) on the *Rynek Główny* (main market square) contains the **city museum** (open Wed.-Fri. 10am-4pm, Sat. 11am-5pm, Sun. 10am-6pm; admission 20,000zł, students 10,000zł, Wed. free). East of the Old Town, the **Panorama Racławicka Museum,** at ul. Purkyniego 11 (tel. 44 23 44), houses a 120m mural, which circles the inside of the round building and recounts the peasant insurrection led by Kościuszko after Poland lost its independence in the 18th century (open Tues.-Sun. 8am-7pm; admission 60,000zł, students 30,000zł).

The **Jewish cemetery,** located in a park at ul. Ślężna 37/39, has only recently been opened to the public. Pay your respects to famous citizens such as Ferdinand Lasalle and the family of Thomas Mann's wife (open only Sun. at noon May-Oct.; admission 30,000zł).

At night, day-time denizens of the *Rynek* are replaced by a younger, hipper crowd. The student clubs **Studnia,** ul. Szewska 19 (tel. 315 13) and **Pałacyk,** ul. Kościuszki 34 (tel. 380 94), and the jazz club **Rura,** ul. Łazienna 4 (tel. 44 24 10), are *the* places to go for concerts.

In the theater building at ul. Kuźnicza 29 (tel. 44 75 28) in the university area, the art nouveau **Café "Pod Kalamburem"** is an artists' corner. Piano concerts are held here every Thursday and Saturday. Pick up a free copy of the *Wrocławski Informator Kuturalny* to find out more about the city's cultural events (open Mon.-Sat. 10am-until the last guest leaves, Sun. 4pm-until the last guest leaves).

In the southern area of the city, the **Operetka,** the **Teatr Polski,** and the **Filharmonia** are all on the same stretch of ul. Piłsudskiego. The month of June brings the international **Jazz nad Odrą** festival to Wrocław. Tickets are available at clubs Pałacyk and Rura.

In the northeastern part of the city, the **Morskie Oko beach** at ul. Chopina 27 (tel. 48 63 94), has kayaks, tennis courts, volley ball fields, and a weight room (open daily 9am-7pm; tickets 15,000zł). Three indoor **swimming pools** are located in a pre-war building at ul. Teatralna 10 (tel. 44 16 56), in the center of the town (tickets 30,000zł). You can also visit the relaxing **Park Szczytnicki** in the eastern part of the city, with the Japanese house on water, or the old **Park Południowy** in the southern part of the city (take tram #6, 7, 8, or 17 from the center toward *Krzyki*).

ROMANIA

US$1	= 1650lei (ROL)		1000lei =	US$0.61
CDN$1	= 1200lei		1000lei =	CDN$0.83
UK£1	= 2590lei		1000lei =	UK£0.39
IR£1	= 2540lei		1000lei =	IR£0.39
AUS$1	= 1230lei		1000lei =	AUS$0.81
NZ$1	= 900lei		1000lei =	NZ$1.11
SAR1	= 460lei		1000lei =	SAR2.15
DM1	= 1070lei		1000lei =	DM0.93

Country Code: 40   International Dialing Prefixes: EU: 00; USA: 011

Ensconced within the mysterious Carpathian Mountains, the fortified towns of Transylvania still look like an array of medieval woodcuts, and the green hills of Moldova remain as serene as the frescoes on their monastery walls. Here, rural Romanians preserve folk traditions which the rest of Europe has discarded centuries ago. The country's stains—ruined, soot-blackened towns and decades of forced resettlement in urban industrial nightmares like Bucharest—date from the days when Romania was the poorest and most totalitarian country in the Soviet bloc. Romania is no longer Communist, but many of its tragedies and leaders remain; for the tourist, Romania is still untamed and unexplored.

Romania is roughly one-third mountains, one-third hills, and one-third plains. The Carpathian mountains cross the country from the north to its center, turn west in a strange arch, then cross the Danube to connect with the Balkan Range; a secondary branch turns north into the Apuseni ("western") mountains. Hill regions border the mountains then descend into the vast plains of the Campia Romana in the south and the Campia de Vest in the west. Transylvania and northern Moldova are mostly hilly; Dobrogea, the region between the Danube and the Black Sea, is dry and rocky. The Danube flows along the Serbian and Bulgarian border, then heads north and east into the delta and the Black Sea.

ROMANIA ESSENTIALS

Citizens of the U.S., Canada, the U.K., Ireland, Australia, New Zealand, and South Africa all need visas to enter Romania; single-entry (US$31) and multiple-entry (US$68) visas allow a six-month stay; a transit visa (US$21) is valid for 72hrs. You can obtain a visa at a Romanian embassy (see Essentials: Embassies and Consulates, page 3) or at the border with a US$6 surcharge.

GETTING THERE

By **train,** the best access points into Romania are Sofia, Belgrade, and Budapest; other trains run from Poland, Slovakia, Russia, and Ukraine. Six trains per day head to Budapest from Bucharest (one on its way to Vienna and another to Munich). There are also direct trains to and from Prague, Warsaw, Sofia, Moscow, Belgrade, and Kishinev, Moldova. To buy **international tickets** in Romania, go to the **CFR** (CHE-FE-RE; in Bucharest, appears as SNCFR) office in larger towns and be prepared to wait a while. Budapest-bound trains may exit Romania through either Arad or Oradea; when you buy your ticket, you'll need to specify which town you want to exit though. In southern Romania, it is customary to give your smaller change to the desk officer after purchasing your ticket. It is now possible, but complicated, to pay for international train tickets with lei—at the counter you may be given a special receipt saying how much you have to pay. If this happens you must change money at a nearby bank or bureau and then return with the validated receipt. An ISIC entitles you to discounts on tickets throughout Eastern Europe, and if you're lucky, a 50% discount on domestic tickets (try flashing your ID at the counter, but the discount may only be available to Romanian students).

You can **fly** into Bucharest on Delta, TAROM, Swissair, Lufthansa, Air France, Alitalia, or AUA. **TAROM** (Romanian Airlines) is currently trying to renew its aging fleet. So far, a few Airbus and Boeings have been acquired, and TAROM flies direct from Bucharest to New York and Chicago (sometimes with a stop in Timişoara or elsewhere in Europe). Bucharest-New York runs about US$600 round-trip, sometimes discounted and usually a couple of hours late. TAROM also flies to most major European cities. The recent renovation of the Otopeni International Airport has improved the notoriously bad ground services, but the airport is still far from ideal.

Buses connect Bucharest and Constanta to Varna, İstanbul, and Athens.

GETTING AROUND ROMANIA

Trains

Agentie de Voiaj CFR (CHE-FE-RE; in Bucharest, appears as SNCFR) sells domestic and international train tickets. At train stations there is always an information desk (staffers will not necessarily speak English) where you can inquire about which counter sells tickets to your destination. Knowing the number of the train you want is crucial; get a copy of the train timetable *(Mersul Trenurilor;* 650 lei, US$0.30; instructions in English, Romanian, French, and German). Tickets can be purchased at CFR offices up to 24 hrs. before the train departs; after that, the train station will only sell tickets. **Interrail** is accepted.

There are three types of trains: *rapid* or *expres* (indicated in green on timetables and at train stations), *accelerat* (red), and *persoane* (black or blue). *Rapid* trains have 2-digit codes and are the fastest; *accelerat* have 3-digit codes and are slightly slower; and *persoane* have 4-digit codes, are slow and dirty, and stop at almost all stations. Even slower trains, called *cursă*, are also indicated by 4-digit codes and stop at every single stop. When going from one major city to another, avoid *persoane* or *cursă;* take them only to get to stations where faster trains won't stop. Only the shortest rides on *persoane* trains are bearable. The difference in price between first class *(clasa-întîi,* wagons marked by a yellow stripe on the side, 6 people per compartment) and second class (8 people per compartment) is minimal by Western standards, while the comfort and security difference is significant (even in first class, however, there will be no curtains and most likely no lights.) If you want to take an overnight train, opt for first class in a sleeping carriage *(vagon de dormit).* During holiday periods, it's a good idea to purchase tickets for *rapid* trains at least five days in advance. Lock your compartment, stay with your belongings at all times, and don't fall asleep unless you trust the people around you.

Flights

Old, rickety aircraft make domestic flying quite an experience. Domestic flights use Soviet-made Antonov-24 airplanes, which soar at low altitudes (with great views on sunny days). Although domestic flights tend to be noisy and bumpy, TAROM's safety record is pretty good, with no major accidents in the past few years. Domestic flights connect Bucharest (Băneasa Airport, closer to downtown than Otopeni) to all major cities around the country. Fares are much higher than for trains; foreigners are charged four times the price of Romanians (even though everyone pays the same fares on trains). Fares are still lower than in Western Europe, and planes are much quicker than trains (Bucharest-Satu Mare is 1hr. by plane, 12hrs. by train).

Buses and Hitching

Use the extensive local **bus** system only when trains are not available; though they cost about the same as trains, they are usually packed and poorly ventilated. Look for the signs for the bus station *(autogară)* in each town. **Hitchhiking,** though risky, remains popular throughout the country. *Let's Go* does not recommend hitchhiking as a safe means of transportation. Hitchers report that it works best in the mountains and Transylvania. A wave of the hand, rather than a thumb, is the recognized sign. Drivers may expect a payment of 50-100% of the equivalent bus fare for giving you a lift. Women traveling alone should find another means of transport.

TOURIST SERVICES

ONT (National Tourist Office) used to be one of the most hated and corrupt government agencies in Romania; it was customary to bribe its employees for any service they performed. The times are now a-changing, but slowly; ONT still doesn't always give reliable info about the price and availability of cheap rooms. Branches in expensive hotels are often more useful than the main offices. **CTT,** the youth travel agency, is designed for organized groups and will be utterly befuddled by your presence. In addition to the hostility of some tourist officials, another problem is the chaos that reigns in the Romanian tourist industry; nobody knows what belongs to whom, and prices change at dizzying speeds. Some ONT branches have closed, and some have been replaced by private bureaus (which aren't always helpful either, since they're run by the same people who used to run the ONT). Hotels and restaurants open and close all the time; it's a good idea to double-check all important data.

Be wary of weekend **business hours.** Under Ceauşescu, weekends meant shorter work days for Romanians, not days off. The new government immediately gave everyone weekends off but has since had second thoughts. Many banks and important businesses may be closed on Friday afternoons. Tourist and CFR bureaus are usually open Mon-Fri. 8am to 8pm. They may be open on Saturday mornings as well, but almost everything is closed on Sundays. Many shops (even privatized ones) tend to close by 6pm. 24-hr. cafés and food stores can be found in some cities. **National holidays** include New Year's Day (stores closed Jan. 1-3), 3-4 days for Orthodox Easter (a week later than Roman Catholic Easter), May Day (May 1), Union Day (Dec. 1), and Christmas (some businesses may be closed Dec. 25-31). Romania is in the same time zone as Bulgaria, one hour ahead of Western Europe.

MONEY

The most common banknotes in Romania are 500, 1000, and 5000 **lei.** Bills worth 100 lei are still in circulation, but are nearly worthless and looked at with suspicion; the new 10,000 lei bills are less widely used. You can pay for almost anything except plane tickets in lei; due to currency fluctuations, however, *Let's Go* lists many prices in U.S. dollars. It's a good idea to keep all receipts for money exchanged and folk art purchased in Romania. Private exchange bureaus can be found throughout the country now; there's little variation among their rates and commissions. Avoid changing money on the street, and make sure you know the going rates and commissions before exchanging. U.S. dollars and Deutschemarks are preferred, though most Western currencies can be exchanged somewhere. Avoid traveler's checks; they can be a hassle, and you may be charged higher commissions.

Although unofficial currency exchange is still illegal, it's not much of a bargain, and getting jailed is now less of a risk than getting cheated; train stations demand special wariness. An exchanger may take your large American bills, hand you back US$1 bills, and run away claiming that the police are coming. Never hand over your money before you get your lei, and *always* count it.

Try befriending English-speaking Romanian students; they'll help you find better lodgings and can assist in restaurants where you might otherwise be overcharged. It is customary to give inexact change, especially if it is under 100-200 lei. **Prices listed below are at US$1=1650 lei.**

COMMUNICATION

You can now dial abroad directly; the **international prefix** is 00. Orange phones take phone cards; blue phones take coins. Unless you like the idea of carrying around a pound of coins, use a phone card, available at post and telephone offices in 5000, 10,000, and 20,000 lei denominations. Rates per minute run around US$0.10 (142 lei) to the Republic of Moldova, US$0.50 (870 lei) to other neighboring countries, US$0.75 (1230 lei) to most of Europe, and US$1.75 (2970 lei) to the U.S. To reach the **AT&T USADirect operator,** dial 018 00 42 88; to reach the **Sprint Express operator,** dial 018 00 08 77; to reach the **Canada Direct operator,** dial 018 00 50 00; to reach the **BT Direct operator** (U.K.) dial 018 00 44 44. Many hotels and companies have international direct-dial phones; in Bucharest, these numbers start with 2, 3, or 4 (most people have numbers that start with 6 or 7, which means they may not dial directly abroad, but they can still dial Direct-type services). Local calls cost 20 lei and can be made from any phone; intercity calls can be made from the new digital phones (orange and blue) or from old phones marked *telefon interurban.* City codes are three digits (first digit 0) followed by the 6-digit local number; Bucharest has only two digits (01) and local numbers have seven digits.

It's also possible to make intercity or international phone calls from some post or telephone offices. It's no easy task, but it may be the only option in small cities. At the phone office, write down where you want to call, how long you want to talk, and the telephone number. Operators shout your telephone destination in the most incoherent way possible, so stay nearby. Pay up front and always ask for the rate per minute. Better wait for a digital phone to call back home.

ROMANIA

LANGUAGE

Romanian is a Romance language; travelers familiar with French, Italian, Spanish, or Portuguese can usually decipher public signs. In Transylvania, German and Hungarian are widely spoken. Throughout the country, French is the second language for the older generation, English for the younger. Spoken Romanian, however, is a trial for the average visitor. The biggest problem is caused by the two additional vowels: "ă" (like the e in hammer) and "â" or "î" (like the last vowel sound in "roses"). The other two characters peculiar to the Romanian alphabet are "ş" (pronounced sh) and ţ (pronounced ts or tz). Also, ci and ce are pronounced "chi" and "che," while chi and che are pronounced "ki" and "ke," as in Italian. In many words ending in i, the i is very soft (almost unnoticed).

Yes	*da*	DAH
No	*nu*	NOO
Hello	*bună ziua*	BOO-nah zee wah
Good morning	*bună dimineaţa*	BOO-nih dee-mee-NYAH-tsah
Good evening	*bună seara*	BOO-nih SYAH-rah
Goodbye	*la revedere*	lah reh-veh-DEH-reh
Excuse me	*mă scuzaţi*	mah skoo-ZAH-tz
Sorry	*lertaţi-mă*	ler-TAH-tzee mih
Please/You're welcome	*vă rog*	vih rohg
Thank you very much	*mulţumesc frumos*	muhl-tzoo-MESK froo-MOHZ
When?	*cînd?*	KIHND?
Where?	*unde?*	UN-deh?
How much is this?	*Cît costă?*	kiht KOH-stih?
How do I get to...?	*Cum se ajunge la...?*	koom-se ahzhun jeh-la..?
Do you speak English?	*Vorbiti englezeste?*	vohr-BEE-tee ehng-leh-ZEHS-teh
My name is ...	*Mă cheamă ...*	mah-kyama
I don't understand	*Nu înţeleg*	noo un-TZEH-lehg
Leave me alone; get lost!	*Lasă-mă în pace!*	lah-seh meh-un-pah-cheh
Help!	*Ajoutor!*	AH-zhootor

1—unu (OO-noo); 2—doi (DOy); 3—trei (TRAY); 4—patru (PAH-truh); 5—cinci (CHEEN-ch); 6—şase (SHAH-seh); 7—şapte (SHAHP-teh); 8—opt (AWPT); 9—nouă (NOAH); 10—zece (ZEH-che); 20—douăzeci (doh-wah-ZECH); 30—treizeci (tray-ZECH); 40—patruzeci (pah-truh-ZECH); 50—cincizeci (chin-ZECH); 60—şaizeci (shay-ZECH); 70—şaptezeci (shahp-teh-ZECH); 80—optzeci (awpt-ZECH); 90—nouăzeci (noah-ZECH); 100—o sută (oh SOO-teh); 1000—o mie (oh MEE-eh).

HEALTH AND SAFETY

Public hygiene in Romania may challenge some Westerners. Most public restrooms lack soap, towels, and toilet paper. Even "privatized" public bathrooms that charge 50-100 lei may give you only a shred of toilet paper. However, you can find bathrooms at most restaurants, which you can use for free even if you're not a patron. Feminine hygiene products are sometimes available, but always expensive. Stash basic medicines in your backpack also; drug stores *(farmacie)* may not have what you need. If you do buy medicines in Romania, know what you're purchasing: they use *antinevralgic* for headaches, *aspirină* or *piramidon* for colds and the flu, and *saprosan* for diarrhea.

The hospitality of the Romanian people will surely be a high point of your visit; though many do not speak English, most will make an effort to understand you. Be aware, though, that due to the extreme difficulty of life here, some Romanians might befriend you in the hopes of receiving an invitation to your country (which facilitates their visa process). Westerners are walking gold mines to Romanians:

US$55 is a month's wages here. Beware of gaggles of children trying to distract you long enough to steal your belongings or wallet. Be alert, but not paranoid; register with your embassy and watch your wallet at all times.

Weather is generally more temperate in Transylvania than in the south. Summers are hot but relatively dry. Typical summer temperatures are about 30°C in Bucharest (up to 38°C on hot days) and slightly less in the north. Winters can be harsh, sometimes with heavy snowfalls (they're slightly milder and shorter than Boston winters). Spring comes as early as March and is beautiful, but the weather is still unstable. Fall starts around the end of September and is usually rainy. The weather is, of course, harsher in the mountains. The typical Black Sea swimming season is June-September.

ACCOMMODATIONS AND CAMPING

Hotels in Romania charge foreigners two to four times the Romanian price. Hotels are still less expensive than in the West, but don't expect the same quality. As a loose rule, 1-star hotels are iffy, 2-star are almost decent, and 3-star are decent but expensive. The inscrutable relationship between hotels and the ONT leads to occasional paradoxes; in some places, if you go to the ONT office (often called *Dispecerat Cazare*) and ask for a room, you may get a price up to 50% lower than that quoted directly at the hotel.

Private accommodations are generally the way to go, but hosts rarely speak English and travelers should be aware that renting a room "together" means sharing the same bed. Through ONT, rooms run about US$12 per person, breakfast included. Always fix a price before you accept anything. Freelance housing offers normally run under US$6. Your hosts may also expect you to change money with them at an unfavorable rate. Many towns reserve **university dorms** for foreign students at insanely low prices. Ask at the local university rectorate; the ONT *may* be able to help you. Prices at 2-star hotels start at US$12 for singles and US$24 for doubles (showers cost US$4-5 more). **Campgrounds** are crowded, and their bathrooms redefine the word "foul." Bungalows are relatively cheap, but are often full in summer (US$5-10). The tourist map *Popasuri Turistice* (in French) lists most sites.

LIFE AND TIMES

HISTORY

The **Greeks** had heavily settled the Black Sea of what is now Romania coast by the 6th century BC, trading with the more primitive peoples up the Danube. The interior was inhabited by a variety of peoples since the Stone Age, though most of the area was invaded by the **Celts** in the 3rd century BC. The **Dacian** tribe of Eastern Romania were warriors bold enough to cross the Danube and attack the powerful **Roman Empire.** After several bloody battles between 101 and 106 AD, Emperor Trajan managed to conquer the Dacians, and Roman colonization followed. The Roman administration of Dacia retired in 271 AD in face of the barbarian attacks from the east, but the colonists stayed, and the Daco-Roman population faced successive waves of Goths, Huns, and Slavs. Roman influence can still be traced in the Romanian language and culture.

Throughout the Middle Ages, there were three Romanian kingdoms: **Moldova** in the east, **Transylvania** in the northwest, and **Vallachia** (a.k.a Muntenia or Tsara Romaneasca) in the south. All were often at the mercy of their more powerful neighbors despite short periods of glory under national kings. Vallachia fell quickly under **Bulgarian** rule (c. 650 AD), Transylvania, briefly the independent **Gepid Kingdom,** went to the **Hungarians** (c. 900 AD), along with much of Moldova. Invasions by Asiatic Patzinaks and Cumans kept Moldova and Vallachia in flux until both were conquered by the **Ottoman Turks** between 1451 and 1566. Ruler of the Ottoman Vassal state of Transylvania, King **Mihai Viteazul** (Michael the Brave) succeeded in unifying the three provinces in 1600, but the union didn't endure after his death one year later. Surrounded by the Austrian Empire to the west, the Polish to the north, the Russian to the east, and the Turkish to the south, Romania was a battleground for the eastern superpowers until the 19th century, when a surprising **national revival** took place, paralleled by declines and/or upheavals in the three eastern empires. Moldova and Vallachia unified in 1859 and became independent from Turkey in 1877. Transylvania was added in 1918, after the end of World War I.

Between the world wars, things were looking up for Romania: rich oil fields (the only oil fields in Europe at the time) brought foreign investors and economic development into the country. They also brought Hitler who, cut off from overseas supplies during **World War II,** needed Romanian oil. Squeezed between the Stalinist Soviet Union and Nazi Germany, Romania chose the latter. When Soviet troops marched into the country in 1944, **King Michael** orchestrated a coup, herded up over 50,000 German troops, and denounced the Nazis. But within several years, the Soviets had infiltrated the government, arrested hundreds of citizens, and forced the king into exile.

Opposition was violently suppressed throughout the **post-war era.** More than 200,000 Romanians died in jails or workcamps during the Stalinist-style purges of the 1950s. Farmers were forcibly collectivized. In 1965, the infamous **Nicolae Ceau7escu** became the leader of the Communist Party. Though he played an independence game from Moscow in his foreign policy—which earned him the praise of the West—he pursued ruthless domestic policies. As his power grew, so did his megalomania. His industrialization plans, intended to make Romania into an economic power, created useless and polluting industrial giants. To cover the resulting foreign debt, he exported basic products such as food, creating chronic domestic shortages. The average Romanian lacked food or heat in winter, and electric power was randomly cut off for "energy savings." In the 1980s, Ceaușescu began to "systematize" Romania's villages by demolishing them and forcibly transplanting the population into concrete-block nightmares. The ultimate monument to his despotism is Ceaușescu's immense palace in Bucharest, ironically called *Casa Poporului* ("People's House").

In 1989, the country finally erupted in a **revolution** as ruthless as the man it pulled down. The revolt started as a minor event in the western city of Timișoara, when the dreaded *Securitate* (secret police) arrested a Hungarian priest. Riots ripped across city, then around the country. Clashes with security forces in Bucharest on December 21-22 brought hundreds of thousands of protesters into the streets, and Ceaușescu fled the angry crowds. He and his wife were quickly arrested, summarily tried, and executed on Christmas Day. Meanwhile, protesters and the army battled Securitate "terrorists" for control of the national television system. The chronology of those days is still unclear; many claim the revolution was actually a carefully prepared coup.

The immense enthusiasm that followed those December days didn't last, as power was seized by **Ion Iliescu's National Salvation Front,** accused by many to be only a continuation of the Communist party. Iliescu was himself a high-ranking Communist official, but Ceaușescu pushed him into minor positions because of his pro-Russian leanings (Iliescu had attended college in Moscow, and was apparently a classmate of Mikhail Gorbachev). Despite these accusations of Communism, Iliescu won the 1990 presidential elections with an astonishing 70% of the vote, and his government began to reform the system (albeit slowly, and many say half-heartedly). In June 1990, Iliescu garnered international condemnation after he called detachments of miners to repress student demonstrations in Bucharest; for three days, the miners terrorized the city, beating anyone resembling a protester.

ROMANIA TODAY

As the Romanian economy worsens and unemployment climbs, the initial enthusiasm for democracy is turning into apathy and even disgust. Nevertheless, President Iliescu economic reforms have earned the praise and money of the World Bank and the IMF, and the country is moving slowly towards capitalism. Romanians now enjoy free speech, a free(r) press, and freedom to travel. Romania is now a democracy, but dire living standards make the downtrodden long for the "good old days" of Ceauşescu, when at least they had a job and bread on their tables. Hope may like in increased trade with the West. The U.S. recently extended favorable trading status to Romania, and currently invests about US$110 million in the country, mostly in Coca-Cola and Colgate-Palmolive manufacturing plants. But prosperity is far away; ragged beggars in front of flashy shop windows remind visitors that Romania has a long and painful climb ahead.

FOOD AND DRINK

Finding food in Romania is no longer such a problem; marketplaces are excellent sources of inexpensive food. It's a good idea to carry a water bottle. There are taps—often actual wells—in train stations and at regular intervals along major roads, although it's always a safer bet to buy bottled water. Wines of the Murfatlar region, near the Black Sea, are world-famous and wonderfully inexpensive (US$3-5/bottle). A good, cheap local drink is *ţuică* (ts-WI-ca, plum brandy). Three or four shots should be enough to dull your hunger pangs.

With the current exchange rate, even some of the most expensive restaurants are affordable (full meals US$10-12). But double-check your bill and politely ask for an explanation if the amount appears incorrect. Many restaurants list prices per serving of 100 grams, so be sure both you and your waiter understand how much you plan to spend. Except in the more expensive establishments, you are expected to seat yourself wherever there is space available, including at a partially occupied table. Restaurants are generally open from 7am to 10pm but stop serving an hour before closing. Tip by rounding the bill to the nearest 500 or 1000 lei. Don't expect to pay with anything other than cash—only the *most* expensive places take credit cards.

Romanian food is pretty mainstream European, with a bit of Balkan and French influence. If you stay in the countryside, look for homemade food; home-cooked pies or *cîrnaţi* (sausages) will probably be better than those in any restaurant. In the mountains, shepherds are often willing to sell you fresh cheese, sometimes in exchange for a pack of cigarettes. Bread (*pîine*) can be great or awful, depending on where you buy it and whether it's fresh; try a privatized bakery. Milk (*lapte*) is rather fatty; powdered milk is available in many shops.

Lunch usually starts with a soup, called *supă* or *ciorbă* (the latter is saltier and usually better), followed by a main dish (usually grilled pork, beef, or chicken) and dessert. Pork comes in several varieties, of which *muşchi* and *cotlet* are the best quality; beware of restaurants trying to pass off random pieces of meat as either of these. Fish can be an alternative to beef or pork; vegetarians will probably want to stick to salads, which are usually pretty good and cheaper than meat anyway. Soups can be very tasty; try *ciorbă de perişoare* (with vegetables and ground meatballs), *ciorbă de văcuţă* (with vegetables and beef), *ciorbă de fasole* (bean soup), or the local favorite, *ciorbă de burtă*. For dessert, *clătite* (crepes) or *papanaşi* (donuts with jam and/or sour cream) can both be great if they're fresh. Other local specialties include *mămăligă* (corn stew, unappealing unless eaten with butter, cheese, and sour cream) and *sarmale* (ground meat wrapped in grape or cabbage leaves).

CUSTOMS AND ETIQUETTE

For many Romanians, America (or even Western Europe) is a dreamland; most will be very excited to meet a Westerner, and eager to help and make friends. People may be incredibly hospitable, offering to show you a town or inviting you to their homes even though they may be facing extreme poverty. Others may just try to rip you off, because they assume that all Westerners have money. Don't let yourself be intimidated and follow your (sensible) instincts. Keep in mind that many Romanians hold conservative attitudes towards sexuality. Unfortunately, these attitudes may translate into harassment of gay, lesbian, and bisexual travelers.

ROMANIA

■ Bucharest (Bucureşti)

Polluted, bad-mannered, and anarchic, Bucharest bears the scars of Romania's struggles. First mentioned in a document dated 1459 and signed Vlad Ţepeş (a.k.a. Count Dracula), Bucharest spent centuries as just another stop on the road from the Balkans to Central Europe. Made the capital of a unified Romania in 1859, the city was dubbed "Little Paris" and "Pearl of the Balkans" for its beautiful boulevards, parks, and fine neo-Classical architecture. Only a vivid imagination can re-create this vision today; relatively untouched by war, this city has been destroyed in times of peace. Ceauşescu's government demolished historic neighborhoods, replacing them with concrete-box housing projects. Though the streets that saw the gore of Romania's bloody revolution are now cleaner (some even have trash cans) and new shops and restaurants are shyly cropping up, Bucharest remains a grimy, jaded Gotham that can wipe the smile off even the most determined traveler's face.

ORIENTATION AND PRACTICAL INFORMATION

Some 60km from the Danube in southern Romania, Bucharest is built on a radial plan, with the main streets diverging from the center. Direct trains connect Bucharest with most Eastern European capitals. From the train station, head east on **Calea Grivitei** and take a right onto **Calea Victoriei,** which leads to most sights and tourist spots. Or walk down another four blocks on Strada Biserica Amzei, the continuation of Grivitei, to **Bulevardul Magheru** (which becomes Bd. Bălcescu and Bd. Brătianu), the main artery in Bucharest. Or take the metro or trolley #79 from the station to Piata Romană, where Bd. Magheru starts.

Tourist Offices: The **ONT** office at the Gara de Nord is apparently just for show. Open Mon.-Fri. 7:30am-8pm, Sat. 7:30am-3pm, Sun. 7:30am-2pm. For reliable help, go to the main office, Bd. Magheru 7 (tel. 614 11 38; fax 312 25 94) next to the *Magazinul Eva* (EVA store), for **maps** (1000 lei, US$0.60) and information on sights, accommodations, and camping throughout the country. Private rooms US$12 per person, showers and breakfast included; ask for a central location. Open Mon.-Thurs. 8am-4pm, Fri. 8am-2pm. Most major hotels also have ONT desks or newly privatized tourist offices.

Embassies: U.S., Str. Tudor Arghezi 7-9, one block behind Hotel Intercontinental. For services, go to the adjacent consulate on Str. Snagov 25 (tel. 10 40 40). Open Mon.-Fri. 8am-5pm. **Canada,** Str. Nicolae Iorga 36 (tel. 50 61 40), near Piata Romană. Open Mon.-Fri. 9am-5pm. **U.K.,** Str. Jules Michelet 24 (tel. 12 03 03). Open Mon.-Thurs. 8:30am-5pm, Fri. 8am-1pm. Citizens of **Australia** and **New Zealand** should contact the British embassy. **Bulgaria,** Str. Rabat 5 (tel. 33 21 50). Open Mon.-Fri. 8:30am-12:30pm and 2-5pm. **Hungary,** Str. Jean-Louis Calderon 63 (tel. 614 66 21, 614 66 22, or 614 66 23). Open Mon.-Thurs. 8am-4:30pm, Fri. 8am-3:30pm. **Russia,** Şoseaua Kiseleff 46 (tel. 617 23 22). Open Mon., Wed., and Fri. 9am-1pm.

Currency Exchange: Avoid changing money on the street; there are plenty of currency exchange offices. Banks will usually be slower, and rates aren't that different; many of them are listed in the newspapers. For traveler's checks, try the reception at Hotel Minerva (3% commission, and you can only cash them into lei).

American Express: At Hotel Minerva on Bd. Ana Tpătescu (tel. 312 39 69; fax 312 27 38). Go up to the second floor and turn left; AmEx is the last door on the left. Replaces lost cards and checks, but won't accept wired money and doesn't cash traveler's checks. Mail held; address it to Minerva International S.A., 2-4 Gh. Manu Str., Bucharest 1, Romania.

Post Offices: There are lots; main office is at Str. Matei Millo 10 (tel. 614 40 54), off Calea Victoriei. Open Mon.-Fri. 7:30am-8pm, Sat. 7:30am-2pm. **Poste Restante** down the street next to the Hotel Carpati. **Postal Code:** 70154.

ROMANIA

Bucharest

1 Village Museum
2 Russian Embassy
3 Ministry of Foreign Affairs
4 Geological Museum
5 Romanian Peasant Museum
6 Museum of Natural History
7 Government of Romania
8 Dynamo Stadium
9 Emergency Hospital
10 Bucharest Circus
11 North Railway Station
12 Art Collections Museum

13 Goethe Institute
14 Canadian Embassy
15 British Council
16 French Library
17 Romanian Development Agency
18 Romanian Atheneum
19 State Ownership Fund
20 National Military Museum
21 Opera House
22 National Art Gallery
23 Great Palace Hall
24 Senate

25 Natl. Agcy. for Privatization
26 National Theatre
27 American Library
28 Italian Library
29 Palas
30 Ministry of Justice
31 City Hall
32 National History Museum
33 Caritas
34 Jewish Theatre
35 Progresul Arena
36 Casa Republicii

Telephones: Orange card phones allowing international calls are located throughout the city center, in the train station, and near the telephone company at Calea Victoriei 37; there you can also order collect or operator-assisted calls. Calls to the US average US$1.50 per min; to Europe less than US$1 per min. For directory assistance, tel. 11 51 50. Wait for the English-speaking operator. Other useful numbers include: 951 (general inquiries), 971 (international phone calls), and 991 (intercity phone calls). **City Code:** 01.

E-Mail: Connections exist at the Politechnic Institute, the Physics Institute (IFA), and the Computer Science Institute (ICI); none is very easy for an outsider to access. Not many students have e-mail, but try to befriend students at the politechnic; you might get lucky. Telnet to the US is currently very slow.

Photocopying: Everywhere. Look for "XEROX" signs. Many copy shops and some post offices also offer fax services. Copies should be less than US$0.05 per page.

Flights: Otopeni Airport (tel. 633 66 02, info 633 31 37), 16km out of the city, handles international traffic. Buses to Otopeni (#783) leave from Piaţa Unirii every 1-2hrs.; buy tickets on board. Coming from Otopeni, buses let you off near the Hotel Intercontinental on Bd. Magheru. **Băneasa Airport,** connected with Piata Romană by bus #131, handles domestic flights. Buy international tickets at Str. Brezoianu 10 (tel. 646 33 46; see directions under Trains below); domestic tickets at the **TAROM** office, Piata Victoriei (tel. 659 41 85 or 659 41 25). Both offices are open Mon.-Fri. 7:30am-7pm.

Trains: Gara de Nord (tel. 952) is the principal station. **Domestic tickets** can be purchased in advance (though not in English) at the **Agence de Voyage, CFR,** which has two offices: Calea Grivitei 139 (tel. 650 72 47), two blocks down from the train station, and Str. Brezoianu 10, 1st floor (tel. 613 26 44), two blocks south of Bd. Mihail Kogălniceanu between Calea Victoriei and Cişmigiu Park (use the TAROM entrance). Learn the phrase *Un bilet pentru...* ("One ticket to..."). To: Constanta (class I, 4320 lei, US$2.70); Braşov (class I, 2560 lei, US$1.60); Cluj-Napoca (class I, 7200 lei, US$4.50). **International tickets** must be bought at the CFR office in Piata Unirii (tel. 613 40 08). All offices open Mon.-Fri. 7:30am-7pm, Sat. 7:30am-noon.

Buses: Three stations serve Bucharest. **Filaret,** Piata Gării Filaret 1 (tel. 641 06 92), and **Rahova,** Şos. Alexandriei 164 (tel. 776 47 95), are both in the southern suburbs; **Băneasa,** Str. I. Ionescu de la Brad 5 (tel. 779 56 45), is to the north. All are virtual madhouses. Scores of buses to İstanbul via Bulgaria leave from the main train station (17hrs., US$15; outside and to the right, one company charges US$10). Each representative will *claim* that their bus is air-conditioned. Suspicious dealings with customs officials are common. For buses to Athens, inquire at Hotel Majestic or at the office in room 129 in Hotel Union, Str. I Cîmpineanu (tel. 613 26 40). Generally, trains are a better mode of transportation out of Bucharest.

Public Transportation: Buses, trolleys, and trams all cost 100 lei. Tickets available at kiosks near most stops or on the buses. Buses are packed to the gills on busy routes—people literally hang out the doors. Hold on to your valuables. The metro offers reliable service to all major points in Bucharest for 100 lei (open 5am-midnight). Punch your ticket when you get on the bus, or ask your neighbor to do it for you. If caught without a punched ticket you'll have to pay a hefty fine. It's better to buy tickets before you get on—not all buses sell tickets on board. There are also express buses, which cost about twice the price; pay the driver directly.

Taxis: tel. 9053. Expect to pay 240 lei per km. Try to hail "state taxis" with the number 053 on the rear passenger door. Arrange the price *(pretul)* before you accept a ride (*bine* means "good").

Car Rental: At ONT or the car rental office nearby, the lowest price is US$26 per day plus US$0.22 per km, or US$72 per day for unlimited mileage, for a Dacia (a Romanian made car); a Citroen costs slightly more. Some other agencies you can try: **Sebastian,** Calea Victoriei 135 (tel. 659 30 14); **Touring ACR,** Str. Chioschi 1 (tel. 650 70 76); or **Jet Turist,** Bd. Cantemir 2 (tel. 614 80 82).

Hitchhiking: *Let's Go* does not recommend hitchhiking as a safe means of transportation. Those hitching north take bus #149 (or the TAROM shuttle) to the airport. Those heading to the Black Sea and Constanta take tram #13 east; to Giurgiu and Bulgaria, tram #12; to Piteşti and western Romania, tram #13 west.

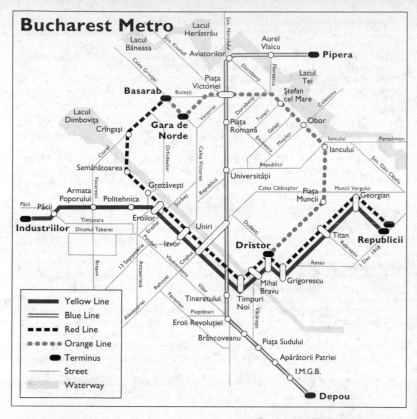

Bucharest Metro

- ▬▬▬ Yellow Line
- ═══ Blue Line
- ■ ■ ■ Red Line
- ● ● ● ● Orange Line
- ● Terminus
- ⋯⋯ Street
- ▒ Waterway

Luggage Storage: Gara de Nord has one check for foreigners and one for locals.
Pharmacies: At Bd. Magheru 18 (tel. 659 61 15) across from the ONT office and in the train station (tel. 618 20 55). Open 24 hrs. Ring the bell at night. Open at night. **Info:** tel. 065.
Medical Assistance: Clinica Batiştei, Str. Tudor Arghezi 28, behind Hotel Intercontinental. Or the emergency room of most hospitals.
Emergencies: Police: tel. 955, non-emergency 055. **Ambulance:** tel. 961 or 679 43 10. Also call your consulate.

ACCOMMODATIONS

The ONT office on Bd. Magheru can arrange private rooms or accommodations in hotels. You're better off avoiding offers for private rooms by individuals at the train station. During the school year (early Sept.-late June), Romanian students will often share their rather drab rooms. Try the dormitories of the **Polytechnic Institute** near the Semănătoarea Metro stop.

The hotel situation is unrosy. Even rat-holes cost more than they should, and it's hard to find nice rooms under US$30 per person. 1-star hotels are the cheapest. Most of the rooms in these hotels are identical; the difference lurks in price and location. Check the signboard posted outside the ONT office in the train station for more information.

Hotel Dunărea, Calea Griviteí 140 (tel 617 32 20), across from the Gara de Nord train station. Among the cheapest in Bucharest. Rooms are bearable for short layovers, and it's only 15min. from downtown. Singles US$15, doubles US$24.

Hotel Munteniea, Str. Academiei 21 (tel. 614 60 10). Behind the Bucharest University, 1min. away from Piata Universitatii. Very central location. Singles US$20. Doubles US$40.
Hotel Carpati, Str. Matei Millo 16. On a quiet street near the central post office. Singles US$25. Doubles US$38. No phone reservations.
Hotel Minerva, Bd. Ana Ipătescu, same location as American Express (tel. 311 15 50). Newly renovated, nice location. Singles US$46. Doubles US$60.

FOOD

Try one of the **open-air markets, either** Piaţa Amzei (between Calea Victoriei and Bd. Magheru, close to Piaţa Romanâ), Piaţa Matache (5min. from the train station towards downtown), or Piaţa Unirii. All should have a decent selection of fruits and vegetables. **Unic,** on Bd. Magheru near the University, has a decent food selection (they also sell Kodak film). Try the Greek-owned **food store** ("la Fourmi") in Piaţa 1 Mai (four stops on bus #300 outbound from Piaţa Romanâ). For excellent bread, try one of the plentiful Turkish bakeries or the **Ana** bakery on Calea Dorobanţilor; they also sell *croissants au chocolat.* Kiosks sell inexpensive snacks, soft drinks, and ice cream on the streets.

Velvet, Str. Ştubei-Vodă across from the Palace (tel. 615 92 41), is considered the most *chic* place in Bucharest, the place to go if you have money to spare.
Restaurant Elegant-Efes, Bd. Magheru 24A (tel. 659 54 30), across from the main ONT office. Opened in the summer of 1993, it quickly gained a following for its *pui* (roasted ½-chicken, US$4) and *crenwurst* (pork sausages, US$1). Wash the meal down with a pint of cold draft beer imported from Turkey. Open until late.
Hanul Lui Manuc, Bd. Iuliu Maniu 30 (tel. 615 33 00), near the southern end of Calea Victoriei. Traditional cuisine in a beautifully restored 17th-century manor that's also a pricey hotel. Restaurant inside, day bar in courtyard, café in cellar. Meals US$6-12 (make sure waiters don't overcharge you). Restaurant open daily 7am-midnight. *Crama* (cellar) open Mon.-Fri. 11am-11pm, Sat.-Sun. 10am-midnight. *Bar de Zi* (day bar) open Mon.-Fri. 10am-10pm, Sat.-Sun. 10am-11pm.
Restaurant Dunărea, Bd. Nicolae Bălescu 315 (tel. 615 40 13), across from the Hotel Intercontinental. Excellent view from its outdoor terrace over Piaţa Unirii. Soft drinks an astounding US$1.50 per can, but pizza is a delicious bargain at US$1. Open daily 10am-11pm.
Restaurant Capşa, Calea Victoriei 36 (tel. 615 61 01), near the University. A Bucharest legend, it used to be popular with writers, artists, and intellectuals. Fair quality. You can enjoy excellent ice cream at the *brasserie* next door.
Restaurant Mercur, Pasajul Victoriei. Turn right from Calea Victoriei, across from the Telephone Palace. Not your dream lunch, but you can sit and people-watch through the passage. Entrees US$2-3.
Restaurant Doina, Şos. Kiseleff 4 (tel. 616 67 15); a 10-min. walk from Piaţa Victoriei. Before 1992, high-school kids from the nearby Liceul de Informaticá used to come here to smoke, sip coffee, and cut class. It was then renovated into a rather pricey restaurant. Entrees around US$10.
Spring Time, in Piaţa Victoriei. This fast-food place has an outstanding view of the government building. Hamburgers go for US$1 and are more sophisticated than McDonald's patties. Also available are cheeseburgers, eggburgers, and french fries *(cartofi prăjiţi).* Delicious ice cream (four scoops of your choice) costs only US$2; order it to go and eat it in the Herăstrău Park.
Pizza Julia, on Bd. Nicolae Titulescu, a 10-min. walk from Piaţa Victoriei. One of the best pizza places in town. Slice US$2-4. Popular with students.

SIGHTS

In the heart of downtown is **Piaţa Universităţii,** home to the high-rise luxury hotel **Intercontinental** and the nearby **National Theater.** Demonstrators fought Ceauşescu's forces here on Dec. 21, 1989, one day before his fall, and the confrontations left several casualties among the bare-handed crowd. In the spring of 1990, students protesting the new ex-communist leaders occupied the square and declared it a "communist-free zone"; for almost two months they had daily meetings, gathering tens of thousands of people, with many of Romania's top intellectuals speaking from the balcony of the University. President Iliescu called the protesters *golani* (hooligans), and this instantly became a word of pride; every day the crowd sang *Imnul Golanilor* ("Hymn of the Hooligans"). The demonstrations were smothered in June 1990 by the brutal three-day intervention of several thousand miners, brought in by the government. Signs of the of turmoil can still be seen on the walls of the university and the nearby Architecture Institute.

Heading south on Bd. Brătianu towards **Piaţa Unirii,** the banking district is on your right. A few hundred meters from Piaţa Universităţii is the famous **Str. Lipscani,** named after the Leipzig merchants who used to do business here. They have been replaced by Gypsies and Turks selling everything imaginable. The street is worth a look for its buildings and its kitschy Balkan atmosphere, but watch your wallet carefully. Turn right onto Str. Lipscani to walk to Calea Victoriei, or continue on Bd. Brătianu up to **Piaţa Unirii,** home of communist Romania's biggest supermarket, now converted into a weird shopping mall. The nearby marketplace was empty before 1989; locals called it **Circul Foamei** (Circle of Hunger).

Ceauşescu drastically rearranged the square, but he spared **Dealul Mitropoliei,** the small hill on the south-western side. On the hill are the **Parliament building** and the headquarters of the Romanian Orthodox Church in one of the largest **cathedrals** in the country. Down the hill west from the square stretches Bd. Unirii, formerly called "Victory of Socialism"; at its end rises the world's second largest building (after the Pentagon), **Casa Poporului** (People's House). Ceauşescu demolished several historical neighborhoods and spent billions of dollars on a private palace he called the country's "civic center"; the new government is not sure what to do with it. In the spring of 1994, Casa Poporului was renovated and hosted a business forum and Israeli-Palestinian peace talks.

Ceauşescu also renovated the shores of **Dîmboviţa,** but couldn't make the river any bigger. The most interesting *quai,* Splaiul Independenţei, runs along the river west from Piaţa Unirii; the imposing **Palace of Justice** stands on the southern shore. Twenty minutes away from Piaţa Unirii is Piaţa Operei, with the **Opera House.** From the opera, continue west on Bd. Eroilor Sanitari to the **Cotroceni Palace,** residence of the president of Romania. Part of the palace is a museum that can be toured. Turn right, then left on Şos. Cotroceni; across from the palace are the **Botanical Gardens,** and a few hundred yards west is the green campus of the **Politechnical Institute,** swarming with students during the school year (Oct.-June).

The oldest buildings in Bucharest are northwest of Piaţa Unirii, in the triangle between the river, Bd. Brătianu, and Bd. Kogálniceanu. Near Piaţa Unirii are the ruins of the old princely court. Near Calea Victoriei is the **Stavropoleos church,** and a few yards up is the **History Museum of Romania** (tel. 615 70 55). Bd. Mihail Kogálniceanu bears the name of Romania's first foreign affairs minister; today, it has a few shops and a bunch of dirty cinemas. Ten minutes from Piaţa Universitaţii, on the right are the **Cişmigiu Gardens,** the oldest park in Bucharest. Alleys curve elegantly around a small lake; you can rent a **boat** and row through the dark tunnel.

North of Piaţa Universitaţii, the avenue connecting it to Piaţa Romană (named Bd. N. Bălcescu, then Bd. Magheru) becomes the less-elegant Bucharest equivalent of Champs-Elysées. Turn left on any of the several streets connecting it to the parallel **Calea Victoriei;** it too was a beautiful street in the good old days. In **Piaţa Revoluţiei** (also called Piaţa Palatului) is the imposing **Royal Palace,** former residence of Romania's kings and its communist dictator, now the **National Art Museum.** The Western European painting collection is small, but there are some nice Italian and Dutch works (including a Rembrandt). It might still be closed for renovation in 1995; the building was badly damaged in December 1989 when a meeting of several hundred thousand people celebrating the fall of communism was interrupted by gunfire from Securitate forces. Bullet holes are still visible in the wall.

Across the square is the elegant **Ateneul Român,** Romania's premier classical music hall, built in the late 18th century according to the plans of a French architect. In 1994, Placido Domingo sang here. Near the Ateneu, the third big building in the square has served several functions; before 1989 it was the headquarters of the Communist party. The **Muzeul Colecţülor de Artă** (#111; tel. 650 61 32), is north on Calea Victoriei, grouping several private collections of Romanian painting. A 10-min. walk from the museum is **Piaţa Victoriei,** where the massive marble government building was the site of several turbulent demonstrations in 1990. On the northern side of the square is the **Antipa Museum of Natural History** (tel. 650 47 10).

Several avenues diverge from Piaţa Victoriei. Bd. Ana Ipătescu leads back to Piaţa Romană, while Şos. Kiseleff and Bd. Aviatorilor lead north. These are the most fashionable streets in Bucharest, with many fancy houses and foreign embassies. A 20-min. walk north is the beautiful **Herăstrău Park.** Take the subway to Piaţa Aviatorilor. The park has a big lake (with rental rowboats and windsurfing), a rose exhibition (May-June), a small amusement park, several restaurants, and tennis courts. For **boat rental,** lake tours, and lake crossings, head left (west) around the lake. For surf rentals, turn right. Across the lake, peacocks occasionally venture on the paths, and a ferris wheel offers a panorama of the park. Bucharest is replete with parks, compensating in part for its urban wastescape. Well-groomed central **Cişmigiu Park,** a few blocks west of Calea Victoriei, along with Herăstrău Park is a focal point for much of the city's social life. Elderly pensioners, young couples, soccer players, and chess whizzes are everywhere. The bars in Herăstrău Park provide ample opportunity to rub elbows with the locals. Join the crowds at **Parcul Studentilor** (Student Park) on Lacul Tei; swim or play volleyball, basketball, tennis, or ping pong. Take trolley #86 to the end or bus #282 and follow the signs.

Near the park, on Şos. Kiseleff, is the **Triumphal Arch,** built to celebrate Romania's independence from Turkey in 1877. Ten minutes north rises **Casa Presei** (Press House), built in the '50s in Stalinist style as a copy of the Moscow University; many newspapers have their offices here. Although it is no substitute for traveling through the countryside of Moldova or Maramureş to discover Romanian folklore, the open-air **Village Museum** (tel. 617 17 32) recreates peasant dwellings from all regions of Romania. The museum is in the park, along Şos. Kiseleff (open Tues.-Sun. 9am-8pm, Mon. 9am-5pm). Enter from the park on the northern side, or take bus #131, 331, 282, or 205 to the Triumphal Arch, then walk along Şos. Kiseleff.

From Piaţa Aviatorilor, Calea Dorobanţilor runs south; a few yards from the square, the **TV building** played a major role in the events of 1989. Rebels broadcast from here under fire from the Securitate forces. Entrance is forbidden, but the bullet-scarred buildings in the vicinity attest to the power of the press in modern society. Continue south to reach Piaţa Dorobanţilor; in the middle of the small park lies Bucharest's copy of the Roman Lupus Capitolinus.

ENTERTAINMENT

Bucharest hosts some of the biggest **rock festivals** in Eastern Europe, that include indie groups like Phoenix and Compact as well as stars like Michael Jackson. Tickets are much cheaper than in the west. Inquire at the tourist office.

Cinemas show mostly American movies, some less than six months old; the vast majority are in English with Romanian subtitles. You may want to avoid cinemas in the periphery; they are often dirty and uncomfortable, and rats are rumored to await in the dark (or fall onto your head from the balcony). Concentrate on the establishments on Bd. Magheru: **Patria** (#12, tel. 611 86 25) and **Scala** (#2, tel. 611 03 72) show new movies first (tickets around US$0.50). **Studio** (tel. 659 53 15), near Piaţa Romană, is also an option. **Luceafărul** (tel. 615 87 67), one block from Piaţa Universităţii on Bd. Brătianu, has been specializing lately in sex and violence (on screen).

Many of the theaters are very good, and tickets are extremely cheap; however, most shows are in Romanian. Huge banners hang from the **National Theater** in Piaţa Universităţii, announcing the season's plays (tel. 615 47 46). In the same building is the **Eugene O'Neill Romanian-American Theater** (tel. 615 82 15). Also famous are the **Nottara,** Bd. Magheru 20 (tel. 659 52 60) and **Bulandra** theaters, while near Piaţa Amzei is the privately-owned **Masca** theater, Str. Biserica Amzei 5 (tel. 659 42 80). Tickets are usually sold starting on Saturday for the following week's performances at each theater's box office. Bucharest also has the only **Jewish State Theater** *(Teatru Evreesc)* in Europe, at Str. Iuliu Baraş 15; performances are staged throughout the summer. The shows are in Yiddish, though simultaneous headphone translations into Romanian should make everything clear. The **Atheneum** in Piaţa Revoluţiei (tel. 615 81 42) often holds excellent concerts at incredibly low prices; the magnificent concert hall includes an organ. Also check out the **Opera House** (tel. 614 69 80) and the **Operetta** near the National Theater (tel. 613 63 48). Tickets sell quickly, so buy well in advance.

Bucharest's seemingly random selection of stores does not include a department store in the Western sense. **Unirea,** in Piaţa Unirii and **Bucur Obor,** Piaţa Obor are the biggest general stores in town. **Coleus** has an underground store in the Piaţa Obor subway station.

NIGHTLIFE

Whatever you do in the evening, pack a map and cab fare; the streets are very poorly lit and buses are unreliable. Bars and nightclubs crawl with *nouveaux riches* and foreign businessmen; they're are too expensive for most Romanian youth. A big hit was scored with the 1991 opening of **Sexy Club,** whose raunchy shows quickly made it one of the trendiest nightspots in Bucharest. Now, there are many bars around, and most luxury hotels have their own. Try **007** at Bd. Bălcescu 4 (tel. 613 70 40) or **Salon Spaniol,** Calea Victoriei 116 (tel. 659 53 45; open until 4am).

Martin, at the intersection of Calea Dorobanţilor and Bd. Iancu de Hunedoara (tel. 679 71 26), is the best disco in town. They've started to invite popular Romanian rock and pop singers for evening jams (open 10pm-5am).

Casa de Culture Studentilor, Calea Plevnei 61, near the Eroilor metro stop behind the opera. Nicknamed *Preoteasa* ("Priestess"), it grinds with Romanian students, many of whom speak English. The service is not spectacular. Open Thurs.-Sun. 7:30pm-midnight.

Vox Maris is a name shared by two fancier nightspots: one at Bd. M. Kogálniceanu 2-4 under the Cercul Militar Naţional (tel. 615 50 30; open 10pm-4am), and the other recently opened in Piaţa Victoriei, across from the Tarom office, which draws soccer stars to its posh dance floor.

■ NEAR BUCHAREST

If Bucharest drives you mad, take a daytrip to **Snagov,** a tiny village half an hour north of Bucharest by car or train. Many people hitch. *Let's Go* does not recommend hitchhiking as a safe means of transportation. In summer, hordes descend upon **Snagov Park,** 5km west of Snagov village, where you can swim in the brownish lake or rent a rowboat and navigate to **Snagov Monastery** (30min.). Here lies the grave of the infamous Vlad Ţepeş. The so-called **Count Dracula** earned his reputation by defying the Ottomans and impaling the heads of the Turkish police (and lots of other people) on spikes, setting them around the walls of his capital. Women may desire to do the same to the monastery keepers: only men may enter.

Another option for an escape is a daytrip to the mountains. **Sinaia** is only 1¾ hours by train on the route to Braşov. Here looms the 19th-century summer castle of King Carol I, the first King of Romania. Be sure also to visit the **Sinaia Monastery,** built in the 17th century and used as a refuge during the Russo-Turkish War. Predeal and Braşov are also near. (See the Prahova Valley, below.)

ROMANIAN MOLDOVA

Not be confused with the neighboring Republic of Moldova (called Bessarabia by most Romanians), this eastern province of Romania extends from the Carpathian mountains to the river Prut. Its early history is foggy; legends tell of a king coming from Transylvania across the mountains with his dog, Molda. During a hunt, the mutt drowned in a river, giving a name to both the river and the region. The kingdom saw glory in the 15th century under the rule of **Ştefan cel Mare** (Stephen the Great; 1457-1504) who created a flourishing economy, built beautiful monasteries, and defended the country from foreign invaders. He defeated the Ottoman Empire several times; finally, however, the Turks won the upper hand and forced Moldova to pay tribute in exchange for peace. Ştefan repulsed several Tartar invasions and fought Poland, Hungary, and other Romanian kingdoms in small border conflicts. In 1993, the Romanian Orthodox Church canonized Ştefan as a saint for his defense of Christianity against the Turks and Tartars. Some were upset by the move, recalling his numerous girlfriends and drinking parties.

After Ştefan's death, the kingdom decayed as Turkish influences grew stronger. Moldova was a battlefield between Russia and Turkey in the 18th century. Finally, the 1848 revolutions shook it from its lethargy, and in 1859 it unified with Muntenia. Today, the region is considered rather backward, though many people here are friendlier than in the south. The south is flat and rather dull, but as you go north, the landscape becomes more varied, rolling into beautiful, gentle-sloping, green hills. The north also has some of the most beautiful churches and villages in Romania.

The city of **Iaşi** (pronounced "Yash"; Frenchified "Jassy") was the 19th-century capital and remains rich with culture and monuments. Further north towards the mountains is the region of **Bucovina,** whose major city is **Suceava.** This region is perhaps the most beautiful part of Moldova, due to the landscape, amazing painted monasteries, unspoiled villages, and traditional festivals. During the 19th century, Bucovina was part of the Austro-Hungarian Empire; some German influences are still evident. Iaşi and Suceava are easily accessible by direct trains (6hrs. from Bucharest) or by Tarom flights. Suceava is the starting point for tours of Bucovina; though they can be done by train or bus, a car is much more convenient. Iaşi is the best starting place for a short stroll into the neighboring Republic of Moldova.

■■■ IAŞI

Located in northern Moldova, Iaşi is the Romanian city richest in monuments and churches. In the second half of the 19th century, Iaşi was Romania's second administrative and first cultural center. Its spiritual life revolved around the Junimea society, founded by some of Romania's top writers, nobles, and intellectuals (many of them educated abroad). They opened the country to European culture, and filled the city with neo-Classical homes and palaces.

Orientation and Practical Information Iaşi is the biggest city in Moldova, a six-hour train ride northeast of Bucharest. There's a largely unhelpful **tourist office** on Str. Anastasie Panu, near Hotel Moldova. The **CFR agency** is in Piaţa Unirii (tel. 14 76 73). The **telephone city code** is 032. From the train station, take tram #3, 6, 9, or 16 (buy tickets on the tram for 100 lei) or walk 20-30min. following the tram tracks to reach Piaţa Unirii downtown. There starts the main street, Str. Ştefan cel Mare. The **bus station** (tel. 11 38 87) is one tram stop up from the train station.

Accommodations For **private rooms,** try to look confused in front of Hotel Traian, or have a Romanian friend call Mrs. Dincă, Str. Cuza-Vodă 6, Bl. Plomba, et.1, apt 5 (tel. 11 57 67); she has a room only a few minutes away from downtown (full board available). Receptionists at Hotel Traian or Hotel Continental may have a few other addresses, but probably won't admit it unless their hotel is full. **Hotel Continental,** P-ţa Cuza Voda (tel. 11 43 20), near Piaţa Unirii, is the cheapest hotel in town, but it's one-star quality. (Singles US$14, with bath US$16. Doubles US$20, with bath US$24. Triples US$26.) **Hotel Traian,** Piaţa Unirii (tel. 143 33 00), is in a beautiful, but aging building with big but not perfectly clean rooms. There are two categories: ask for the best since the price is almost the same. (Singles US$20. Doubles US$32. Triples US$45. Breakfast included.) **Hotel Moldova,** Str. Anastasie Banu 32 (tel. 14 22 25), is in Piaţa Ştefan cel Mare, near the palace. The pleasant rooms could be bigger, but they have cable TV and digital phones. Ask for a room on the palace side for a great view. (Singles US$37, doubles US$59.) **Hotel Unirea,** Piaţa Unirii (tel. 14 21 10) offers the same quality and prices as Hotel Moldova and is more central, but the view is less attractive and the area noisier.

Food   For groceries try **UNIC** on Piaţa Unirii or one of the two "supermarkets": **Moldova,** in Piaţa Ştefan cel Mare, and **Copou,** on Bd. Copou opposite the park. **Restaurant Bolta Rece** (Cold Ceiling), Str. Rece 10 (tel. 11 31 67) was founded in 1799. Go down into the basement for real cellar ambiance. Many great writers got drunk here. The service is friendly; the food is good and cheap (full meals US$3-5).

Sights   Monuments line both sides of Bd. Ştefan cel Mare, which runs from Piaţa Unirii to Piaţa Ştefan cel Mare. Piaţa Ştefan cel Mare, with the king's statue, is dominated by the massive neo-Gothic **Palace of Culture** dating from 1906. It was damaged by a 1977 earthquake, but the clocktower still plays the song of the 1859 union of Moldova and Vallachia—*Hora Unirii* (Dance of the Union). In the Palace are four museums: the **Museum of History of Moldova,** the **Ethnographic Museum of Moldova,** the **Art Museum** (opened in 1860, it's the country's oldest), and the **Polytechnical Museum.** The last is most interesting. Nearby, at Str. Anastasia Panu 65, is the **St. Nicholas Church** *(Stăntu Nicolae-Domnesc),* built in 1491 by Ştefan cel Mare.

A few meters up Str. Ştefan cel Mare on the left rises the beautiful **Trei Ierarhi** church, whose exterior walls are carved in elaborate geometrical models with delicate frescoes of Christ and the Virgin Mary above the entrances. The interior is worth a look, though you won't be able to get in if wearing shorts. The church was built between 1637 and 1642 by Prince Vasile Lupu, and in 1642 became the site of the first printing press in Moldova. In 1821, the flag of the Eteria (the secret organization for the liberation of Greece from Turkey) was sanctified here.

Further up on the right, past the **City Hall** and **National Theater,** is the statue of the theater's founder, Vasile Alecsandri. Educated in France, Alecsandri was one of the most progressive nobles in 19th-century Moldova and a leader of the 1848 revolution. From exile, he actively fought for the union of Moldova and Vallachia. He later became a member of several governments and was one of the founders of modern Romanian literature and drama. Across the street on the left rises the eclectic **Sfântu Gheorghe Church**. Nearby is the **Mitropolie** (the Orthodox equivalent of a bishopric), with paintings by the famous Romanian painter Gheorghe Tattarescu.

From Piaţa Unirii, a short walk up Str. Cuza Vodă takes you to the **Golia Monastery,** an imposing monument of medieval architecture (1650-1660). The façade is in late Renaissance style and the main building is surrounded by thick defensive walls and capped with a 30m high tower. The exterior gates lock at 7:30pm; make sure you're not trapped inside. About 10 min. from Golia and a few steps down to the right is the famous **Bojdeuca** (hut) where writer Ion Creangă lived his last years. Creangă was born a peasant and became a priest until he was expelled for shooting crows in the churchyard with his gun. He then turned to writing and became famous in the "Junimea" circle for his story-telling. Besides his tales, his most important work is *Memories from Childhood* in which he depicts his native village.

From the Bojdeuca, walk a few yards uphill, then turn left on Str. Ralet and continue on Str. Berthelot. On the right, you will pass the house of **Gen. Berthelot** who was sent by the French government to help the Romanian army in World War I. The government had moved to Iaşi while Bucharest was occupied by Germans. Food shortages and disease terrorized the population. Romania lost major battles against Germany in 1916, but managed to defend northern Moldova. Eventually, Germany collapsed on the western front and Romania got everything back, plus Transylvania and Basarabia (only to lose it again later).

At the end of St. Berthelot, turn right on Bd. Copou. The beautiful neo-Classical **Alexandre Ioan Cuza University** on the left was built between 1893 and 1897 on the plans of French architect Le Blanc. Prince Cuza unified Moldova and Vallachia in 1859. The building today houses only a few of the university's departments, most of which are scattered around the city. Uphill on Bd. Copou, the French Cultural Center, is on the right; a bit farther up is **Copou park.** The park, arranged by king Mihail Sturza in 1836, is famous for the **linden of Eminescu,** the tree which shaded Mihail Eminescu, Romania's greatest poet, as he wrote. Eminescu was born in Bucovina, which at the time belonged to Austria. He studied in Vienna and Berlin but returned to Iaşi for a few years before moving to Bucharest. The nearby promenade has statues of several writers and satirists, including Creangă, Eminescu, Veronica Micle (possibly Eminescu's girlfriend). Near the park are the **Botanical Gardens.**

If you have time, take a stroll down to the River **Bahlui** (10 min. south of the Palace of Culture; you can't miss it). On summer night, frogs give loud concerts along its shores. The river is small but has three bridges: the stone bridge, the wood bridge, and the red bridge (after a particularly bloody battle, it is said, the water beneath it became red).

■ NEAR IAŞI

The **Cetăţuia Monastery** perches on a hill 4km south of the city. Built between 1669 and 1672 by Prince Duca, it has thick walls and great views of the city.

Cucuteni is the site of a 5000 year-old Neolithic settlement. Head first to Târgu Frumos, 46km west of Iaşi, then take a bus for the 10km ride to Cucuteni.

Iaşi is the best starting point to enter the neighboring **Republic of Moldova.** All Bucureşti-Chişinău trains stop for border control in the Nicolina station in Iaşi (not the main station), though most trains also stop at the main station. Most trains leave at night, making for an unpleasant journey.

■■■ SUCEAVA

Though Suceava proffers some monuments of its own, it is most useful as a base for exploring the Bucovina painted monasteries. The capital of Moldova in the time of Ştefan cel Mare, it was a powerful citadel that the Turks tried in vain to conquer. Between 1775 and 1918, Suceava (together with the whole of Bucovina) belonged to Austria. It was returned to Romania after World War I, but Stalin annexed northern Bucovina in1940, and it is now a part of Ukraine.

The ruins of the **Suceava Royal Fortress** *(cetatea de Scaun)* are in **Parcul Cetăţii,** east from Piaţa 22 Dec. Head north on Bd. Ana Ipătescu, then turn right on Str. Cetăţii. The fortress was built in 1388 when the prince of Moldova moved the capital to Suceava. Ştefan cel Mare erected four meter-thick walls that resisted the siege of Sultan Mahomed II, the conqueror of Constantinople. The park itself is huge and provides wonderful strolling gardens. It also has a huge equestrian statue of Ştefan (22m high, of which the statue itself is 8m). More medieval ruins lie farther from the center, in the neighboring hills. **Cetatea Scheia** is to the north of the city (follow the road to Rădăuti) while the **Zamca Medieval Complex** lies in the northwest (from the main square, head west on Str. N. Bălcescu, then on Str. Dragoş Vodă; turn right on Str. G. Enescu, then left on Str. Zamcii). Back in the center, check out the **Sfântu Ioan cel Nou Monastery.** From the main square, turn south on Str. Ana Ipătescu, then left on Str. Ioan Vodă cel Viteaz. Thousands of people come from all around Bucovina for the **city festival** on June 24, a celebration of the local St. John the New *(Sf. Ioan cel Nou).*

The **tourist office** is in the main square, Piaţa 22 Decembrie, str. N. Bălcescu 2 (tel. 22 12 97). They have some of the nicest staffers in Romania, ready to help or chat with you about the region's history and folklore, or their own problems and low wages. They have **maps, exchange currency,** organize **tours** of Bucovina, and **rent cars** (but only with drivers; US$0.40 per km). The main industrial areas lie a few kilometers from the center, as do the two **train stations: Suceava,** Str. N. Iorga 7, Cart. Burdujeni (tel. 21 38 97) and **Suceava Nord,** Str. Gării 4 Cart. Iţcani (tel. 21

00 37). Buses run from the stations to the center. The **bus station** is at Str. Vasile Alecsandri 2 (tel. 21 62 39), not far from the center. **TAROM** flies from Bucharest to the airport in the village Salcea (tel. 21 48 85); the **ticket agency** is at Str. N. Bălcescu 8 (tel. 21 46 86). The **CFR agency** is next door (tel. 21 43 35).

The tourist office can find you a **private room** if you ask nicely, or, if the mood strikes them, they'll arrange for a hotel room at a discounted price. **Hotel Suceava,** Str. N. Bălcescu 2 (tel. 21 30 47 or 22 24 97), is in the main square with clean rooms. (Singles US$26, doubles US$34.) **Hotel Bucovina,** Bd. Ana Ipătescu 5 (tel. 21 70 48), is reachable from the east side of P-ţa 22 Dec.; turn right on Bd. Ana Ipătescu and walk about five minutes. It offers about the same quality as Hotel Suceava, but it's slightly farther from the center (singles US$24, doubles US$39).

■■■ BUCOVINIAN MONASTERIES

Bucovina's painted monasteries have napped away the centuries among green hills and forests, near villages in which time seemingly stands still. Built 500 years ago by Ştefan cel Mare and his successors, the tiny structures serenely mix Moldovan and Byzantine architecture, and Romanian soul with Christian dogma. Most of the monasteries are small, with stone walls and wooden roofs, surrounded by living quarters for monks or nuns and heavy stone walls which never managed to keep looters out.

Their unique **frescoes** were originally executed for a very practical reason—to explain the Bible to the illiterate. Since the small churches could not fit many people, paintings were done on the exterior walls. Many of the frescoes are of remarkable beauty, even though their style is strikingly different from that of Western cathedrals; they were painted by local artists in the tradition of Byzantine religious painting and have somehow survived 500 years of wind and rain. Some have been recently restored, while others are badly in need of attention.

The monasteries are scattered throughout Bucovina. The most convenient way to visit them is by car, though many are accessible by train or bus from Suceava. Since most are in very rural settings, there's not much to see besides the building itself and beautiful scenery; it takes one-two hours to see one monastery. You can either make day trips from Suceava, or do a multi-day tour and sleep in a different place every night. There are several hotels or motels around the region. Some monasteries provide lodging at affordable prices. Ask to speak to the Mother Superior (*Maica Stareţă*) where appropriate and don't wear shorts or short-sleeve shirts when visiting. Most are open from 7 or 8am until sunset.

VORONET AND HUMOR

Voroneţ is the most famous of the monasteries, with well preserved, monumental frescoes. Though the tourist pamphlet description of a "Sistine Chapel of the East" may be a bit much, the *Last Judgement* mural is a masterpiece. Christ sits on the judgement throne, surrounded by prophets and martyrs; sinners, Turks, and Tatars are agonizing in the fire of Hell, while the blessed wait in a huge traffic-jam at the gates of Heaven. Wild animals hand back the body parts of humans dismembered by beasts, in a variation of the Biblical text. Many other allusions are obscure unless you're an expert in the history of Moldova. Jesse's Tree, on the southern wall displays a genealogy of Jesus, while the northern wall (in rather poor condition) depicts the Genesis and a legend about Adam's pact with the Devil. The frescoes are in a color unique to the monastery, called Voroneţ blue. Despite chemical analysis, its derivation is unknown. To get there from Suceava, take the train to Gura Humorului (about 1 hour), then an infrequent bus for Voroneţ from near the train station, take a cab, or walk (Voroneţ is about 5km from the station).

Not far from Voroneţ is **Humor,** 6km north of Gura Humorului; the two can be visited during the same day trip. It was founded in 1530 by Petru Rareş, son of Ştefan cel Mare. A fresco represents the Virgin Mary saving Constantinople from a Persian attack in 626, based on a poem written by the patriarch of Constantinople. The painter substituted the Persians for Turks. Another fresco depicts the return of the prodigal son, with a Moldovan-style *hora* (round dance).

MOLDOVIŢA AND SUCEVIŢA

Suceviţa and Moldaviţa are both on road 17A, connecting Rădăuţi (about 50km northwest of Suceava) to Câmpulung Moldovenesc. If you drive, a circuit through Suceava-Rădăuţi-Suceviţa-Moldoviţa-Voroneţ-Humor-Suceava is both scenic and practical; the roads are decent and you can take detours to see other monasteries. If you don't have a car, you can reach Moldoviţa by train (the station is in Vatra Moldoviţei, 2km away; make sure you don't miss the last train). Suceviţa, however, is problematic. It's 29km north of Moldoviţa and 20km southwest of Rădăuţi. Buses run there from both towns, but schedules are erratic. There's a train station in Rădăuţi, on the Suceava-Putra line. Ask there for connecting bus to Suceviţa.

Moldoviţa is the largest of the painted monasteries. It was built in 1532 and painted in 1537. There's another *Last Judgement*, another *Jesse's Tree*, and a monumental *Siege of Constantinople*. The museum has the original throne of prince Petru Rareş. The frescoes are among the best preserved in the area.

Suceviţa is beautifully set in fortified hills where its white walls shine on sunny days, making it look more like a citadel than a monastery. The frescoed southern wall has another *Geneaology of Jesus* and a *Procession of Philosophers* that represents Pythagoras, Socrates, Plato, Aristotle, and Solon in Byzantine cloaks. Plato is carrying a small coffin with bones. On the northern wall, *The Scale of Virtues* depicts the Last Judgement. The western wall remains unpainted—supposedly the artist who was painting it fell from the scaffolding and died; some say his ghost still haunts the place. Another legend tells about a woman who carried stone for the construction in her ox-wagon for 30 years. Her head is carved in black stone under an arch.

Three kilometers south of Suceviţa on the road to Moldoviţa, excellent lodging can be found at the private **Popasul Turistic Bucovina,** the former villa of Communist party-boss Emil Bodăraş. Set on a beautiful hill, a few meters off the national road, the rooms are clean, small, and rather spartan—it may get cold at night. (Singles US$25-30; doubles in wooden bungalows, US$6. Try to reserve in advance; call the Suceviţa central, and ask for ext.165. Open March-Dec.) The menu is excellent, though limited. Try a *muşchi de porc* (pork steak). Dinner US$3, breakfast US$1.50. In sunny weather, breakfast is served on the porch to the chirping of swallows.

PUTNA, ARBORE, AND DRAGOMIRNA

Putna has less spectacular frescoes than the other monasteries, but it's well-kept, easy to access, and has the tomb of Ştefan cel Mare (among others) and an interesting museum. Catch direct trains from Suceava for the scenic ride to Putna (about 75km northwest of Suceava). The monastery is 2km from the station.

The tiny church of **Arbore** has some of the most beautiful frescoes in the region, though they are badly in need of restoration. No monks or nuns live here and its small, quiet courtyard is off a secondary road rarely trod by visitors. The dominant color is green, in five different shades. It's easy to get here by car: from Suceava head north to Rădăuţi, and turn left at the village of Milişăuţi, on the road to Solca. Bus travel is also possible; inquire at the station in Suceava.

Dragomirna is the closest monastery to Suceava. No exterior frescoes here, but the building is rather interesting. The fortified walls are imposing, and its setting on a lake at the edge of a forest is beautiful. Not very many visitors come here. The monastery was built between 1602 and 1627. In 1653 it was looted by the Ukrainian troops of Chunielnicki. Access by car is easy, and a local bus also makes the trip; ask at the bus station in Suceava or at the tourist office.

BLACK SEA COAST

Dobrogea, the land between the Danube and the Black Sea, has had a troubled history. Conquered by the Turks in the 14th century, it remained part of the Ottoman Empire until 1877, when it was granted to Romania as a compensation for losing southern Moldavia to Russia. Since then, there have been several border disputes with Bulgaria. Its population is now mostly Romanian, with a small Turkish minority. Its biggest city is Constanţa; south of it, beautiful beaches are the site of a large tourist industry. The coast north of Constanţa is much less developed; further to the north lies the exotic Danube Delta. The interior, a land of dry valleys and rocky hills, has Roman ruins and some of Romania's best wines. The coast used to be jam-packed in summer, but prices are rising too high for many Romanians. Finding a place is easier, but July and August are still crowded. As a foreigner, you'll always be charged more in hotels; there's nothing you can do about it.

Dobrogea is a dry land, with almost no running water except the Danube. In the south, construction of the Danube-Black Sea channel was initiated by communists in the 1950s, as an ideal way to eliminate opponents: hundreds of thousands of political prisoners died while digging rock with sledgehammers. But this accomplished nothing (in terms of water), and the project was abandoned; it was resurrected by Ceauşescu in the 80s and completed with an enormous waste of resources. The channel starts at Cernavodă on the Danube, near Romania's soon-to-be-inaugurated nuclear power plant, and ends in the Black Sea, 15km south of Constanţa. Some areas are now using water from the Danube or from the channel, some (like the Black Sea resorts) still use their own wells, and some places, particularly in the north-east of Dobrogea, still have to bring their drinking water from far away. The channel also shortens ships' way to the Black Sea, but few use it.

For a map of the Black Sea Coast area see page 129 in the Bulgaria chapter.

■■■ COSTANŢA

A Greek harbor known as Tomis 2500 years ago, Constanţa is now named for the daughter of Emperor Constantine. Some residents still playfully regard Constantinople as "the fatherland." Ceauşescu's megalomania made the Constanţa port one the biggest in Europe, though much of it sits unused. Nevertheless, Constanţa is the best place to catch buses to resorts along the Black Sea coast.

Escape the innumerable gray apartment blocks that stifle the city by exploring the Old Town. The **archeology museum** in Piaţa Ovidiu has several items from the Roman past (open 9am-8pm; admission US$0.60). Nearby, there are excavations of a **Roman palace** with an interesting floor mosaic. Several walls remain along with a collection of amphorae and iron anchors. Explanations are only in Romanian, French, and German (admission US$0.60—1000 lei).

In the middle of Piaţa Ovidiu the **Statue of Ovid** commemorates the Roman writer who wrote his most famous poems while exiled here by Emperor Augustus, ostensibly for writing his *Art of Love* (though the real reason was his affair with the emperor's daughter). Ovid hated Constanţa and in his letters from exile, he complains about having to live in the midst of the barbarians (but maybe he was just making it up to be allowed to return). The epitaph on the statue, written by Ovid himself, asks you to pray for him to have a tranquil sleep.

The **mosque** on Str. Muzeelor is one of the few reminders of Turkish domination and has one of the largest oriental carpets in Europe, made in the 18th century on the island Ada-Kaleh on the Danube (the island has been flooded by an electrical power plant project and no longer exists). The doors are constructed of black Italian marble and banners bearing the name of the prophet hang from the walls. The tower is 50m high (140 steps) and offers a bird's eye view of the town; it is currently under renovation, but you can still climb it (open 9am-5pm; admission 100 lei).

Further toward the sea is the **orthodox cathedral** and a beautiful statue-lined waterfront promenade. On its southern end, engineer Anghel Saligny (the designer of Romania's first bridge over the Danube) looks thoughtfully toward the industrial port. Below is the small pub **Vraja Mării** (Charm of the Sea), affectionately nick-named *Javra Mării* (*javră* means scurvy dog). A few yards to the north is the elegant **Casino.** Across from it is the **Aquarium** (open 9am-8pm; admission 500 lei). Further up, the statue of the poet Mihai Eminescu looks dreamily toward the sea. At the other end of the promenade, sailors procrastinate in the small passenger port. Ferry routes to Mangalia have been suspended, but you can bargain a yacht trip for a few hours. It's cheaper for large groups; talk directly with the owners.

Near Bd. Tomis, across from Hotel Continental, is an archeological, but dirty, **park** featuring several rocks, amphorae, and the remains of the ancient defense wall. The ugly green wall lists all antique settlements in Dobrogea, from 5000 BC onward. Near Lacul Tăbăcáriei, close to Mamaia, are a **planetarium** and a **delfinarium.**

The **train station** and the main **bus station** are near each other; northbound buses leave from a different station, **Autogara Tomis Nord** (from the train station, take tram #100 for five stops.) To get to downtown from the train station, take trolley #40 or 43 and get off where Bd. Tomis intersects Bd. Republicu (about five stops). A short walk down on Bd. Republicu is **Piața Ovidiu,** in the middle of the old city. The **ONT office,** Bd. Tomis 66 (tel. 61 48 00), can help arrange **private accommodations** and provides useful information about the coast. **Traveler's checks** can be cashed at Continental for a hefty 10% fee. You can make international **telephone** calls in the building a few meters off Bd. Tomis on the left, a few meters down from the tourist office (open 7am-9pm). Nearby, Bd. Tomis narrows down; there's a restaurant, "Pescarul" ("the Fisherman"), in front of which **taxis** hang out. The **telephone city code** is 041.

Hotel Tineretului, Bd. Tomis 20-26 (tel. 61 88 55), has average-sized and semi-clean rooms with TVs (singles US$25, doubles US$33). **Hotel Continental,** further up on Bd. Tomis has singles for as little as US$17. There are plenty of fast-food and pizza places in Constanța. For some ambience, try **Casa cu Lei** (House with Lions), a few yards up from Hotel Intim. Chicken goes for about US$1, beef and pork US$2-4. At **Piața Unirii** next to Bd. Republicii, there's a large **food store** and a **fruit and vegetable market.**

■ SOUTH OF CONSTANȚA

The coast south of Constanța is lined with sandy beaches and 1970s-revival tourist resorts. Buses run south from Constanța about every half-hour in the direction of Mangalia (40km, 500 lei); private buses are cheaper than the state-run service. The first resorts to the south are **Eforie Nord** and **Eforie Sud,** reknowned for the mud baths near **Lake Techirghiol.** The water of the lake is rumored to be so salty that you can't drown, but don't try it (drowning, that is).

Farther along is **Costinești,** the coolest place on the coast that gets unbearably crowded with young people. You can hike the 3km from the bus stop; hitchers say it's easy to get a ride. *Let's Go* does not recommend hitchhiking as a safe means of transportation. The **telephone city code** is 041. Try to call ahead for accommodations at **Biroul de Cazare** (tel. 74 29 77), **Hotel Forum** (tel. 74 16 77), or **Hotel Amiral** (tel. 74 16 34), where bungalows (US$6 per person) and less desirable rooms (US$3 per person) abound. **Hotel Azur** (tel. 74 28 50, ext. 112) has small and unclean but bearable rooms (singles US$15, doubles US$18). **Hotel Forum** also has brighter and larger rooms, with TV and sea views but unclean bathrooms (doubles US$30). Reservations are recommended. Both hotels have hot water for only a few hours per day. Across from Hotel Forum, the disco-club **Vox Maris** is the choicest in town, though there are plenty of others. Ice cream booths and pizza places abound;

there's also a **cafeteria** selling cakes with a less-than-confidence-inspiring sign *"Prǎ jituri foarte proaspete. Serviți cu încredere."* ("Very fresh cakes. Eat confidently.")

Continuing farther south, you'll pass through the intergalactic resorts **Neptun, Jupiter, Venus,** and **Saturn.** Neptun and its northern affiliate, Olimp, have some of the best beaches, but tend to be more expensive. The **tourist office** in Neptun, Dispecerat de Cazare (tel. (041) 73 13 10) can help you find rooms; their prices are 50% lower than those at hotels. One-star hotels run about US$6 per person, and two-star about US$12 (prices rise in July-August). **Hotels Craiova, Slatina,** and **Arad** cluster to the north of the resort. They're not great, but they're close to nice beaches. Two-star rooms (US$12) are small and not very clean. Most restaurants have only a few dishes, and some are open only July-August. **Restaurants Amfiteatru** and **Flamingo,** both on a terrace, have similar prices (chicken US$1, pork US$2-3).

The **gulf** between Venus and Saturn has one of the best beaches on the coast, as does the military port and railway terminus of **Mangalia.** Three kilometers south of Mangalia is **2 Mai,** the village least spoiled by the heavy tourist industry. There are no hotels, so bring a tent or arrange private accommodations with the villagers (set the price before you move in). Most young people camp at the southern end of the village, on the beach, and every night set up campfires and play guitar. The village is popular among intellectuals, artists, and free-spirited students. From here you can walk to Bulgaria (4km away), and then take a bus to Varna.

■ NORTH OF CONSTANȚA

A kilometer north of Constanța lies **Mamaia's** lovely 4km-long beach, sadly infested by aging hotels. Normally a good alternative for cheap accommodations, the town is invaded by masses of Constanțans on weekends. Most hotels are sandwiched between the sea and the highway. Left of the highway is **Lake Siutghiol.** Rumor has it that because of the channel built by Ceaușescu to link the lake and the sea, the whole resort is slowly sinking.

A 10-minute walk from the southern end of Mamaia, **Hotel Victoria** has mediocre doubles for US$18. Better nests await nearby at **Hotel Albatross** (tel. 83 10 47; doubles US$40) and **Hotel Condor** (doubles US$30). Prices rise up to 50% in July and August. For a reprieve from Mars ice cream, head to **Restaurant Hotel Rex** (former Internațional) on the beach, 10-15 minutes from Albatros. Though the hotel is expensive, the restaurant is affordable and one of the best in the resort. A full meal from the varied menu costs US$6-8. Great views of the sea are free.

■ ■ ■ DOBROGEA

Romania's most famous wines are made in the hills of .**Murfatlar** in the heart of Dobrogea. ONT organizes trips with wine tastings. Transportation in Dobrogea, as elsewhere in Romania, can be a hassle. Without a car, the only option is a slow and crowded bus. Smaller sights in the region include the village of **Adamclisi,** south of Constanta, which is the site of **Tropaeum Traiani,** a monument raised by Emperor Traian to commemorate his victory against the Dacs. Buses come from the main Constanța station. **Jurilovca** is one of the few fishing villages left; it's hard to access (60km north from Constanța on secondary roads), and there is no tourist infrastructure. If you're somehow beamed down here, try the fish soup and sign language; the locals are completely incomprehensible.

HISTRIA

A Hellenic colony mentioned by Greek historian Strabo in the 5th century BC, Histria was rediscovered in the early 20th century by Romanian archeologist Vasile Pârvan. The excavations are about 30km north of Constanța, on the shore of Lake Sinoe (a lagoon separated from the sea by a thread of sand). Buses leave from the Tomis Nord station in Constanța, but drop you off 7km from the site.

The **museum** and **excavations** follow the city's 14 centuries of recorded history, from the 7th century BC to the 7th century AD. Most explanations are in Romanian, French, and German. The city is named after the Danube *(Istros* in Greek), which ultimately caused its decay by blocking the city harbor with its mud. So much for gratitude. Excavations trace the town's glory and ruin, until its collapse under the attacks of migrant tribes. Several walls and a few columns still stand, and the museum has carved stones, fragments of statues, and amphorae (some have been claimed by swallows). The ruins are surrounded by stork-infested wilderness (museum open until 5pm; admission 1000 lei, Romanians 400 lei). Near the museum, a small **pub** sells Coke (500 lei per bottle), snacks, and even full meals (starting in July). No running water.

PORTIŢA

You'll have to brave hunger, thirst, and mosquitoes to revel in the pristine beaches of **Portiţa** ("little gate," denoting the small patch of sand that separates the lagoons of Razelm, Goloviţa, and Sinoe from the sea), 50km north of Constanţa. Only part of the road is drivable; the rest of the way is a walk in the wilderness. In theory there's camping, but water is a problem. Lagoon water is not drinkable; bring your own.

DANUBE DELTA

The Danube Delta, with the only pelican colony in Europe, occupies the northern half of the coast. The terrain between the three arms of the Danube from Tulcea to the Black Sea is a world of natural and artificial canals cutting their way through kilometers of roads—a paradise for anglers, birdwatchers, and adventurers armed with small boats. This huge ecosystem changes perceptibly within a single lifetime; 40m of land are created every year. **Tulcea** is the main gateway, five hours from Bucharest by fast train via Medgidia, and four hours from Constanţa by slow train.

Because of poor infrastructure, the region is hard to access—but this also makes for its charm. Expect *tons* of mosquitoes, and water and food shortages. Organized **tours** are a way to avoid these hassles, but there's a risk you won't see anything but channels and marshlands. Renting a **motorboat** in Tulcea costs about US$12 per hour and you can bargain for longer periods with owners on the docks. The best way to explore the Delta is to rent a **rowboat** (engines scare wildlife); though hard to do in Tulcea, it's easy in **Crişan**, on the Tulcea-Sulina ferry route. Try to hire one of the rowers hanging around the docks.

There's nothing to do in Tulcea itself but to fraternize with the mosquitoes on the waterfront. Tulcea's **train station** and **bus station** are both on the waterfront; walk east toward downtown along the river until you see the ugly red building with square columns *(Casa de Cultură a Sindicatelor).* The **tourist office** Eurodelta offers boat trips to the Delta and the Ukrainian city of Izmail, and the **Tarom** agency offers flights to Constanţa and Bucharest. A **post office** and **marketplace** are on Str. Păcii. **Ferry tickets** to Sulina and Galati are sold in the same building as the bus station; there are slow and fast ferries, neither is very expensive. Turn right at the *Casa de Cultură a Sindicatelor* for the ultra-cheap, three-star **Hotel Trei Stele** (tel. 51 67 64); cross Str. Isaccea and the hotel is a short walk up hill at Str. Carpaţi 16. No English spoken. Small, dark doubles are only US$2, and triples are US$3.

TRANSYLVANIA

Though the name evokes a dark, evil land of black magic and vampires, Transylvania *(Ardeal)* is a beautiful, peaceful region of green hills, descending gently from the Carpathians toward the Hungarian Plains. Conquered by the Romans around 100 AD, by the Hungarians in the 9th century, settled by Germans in the 12th century, conquered by the Turks in the 16th century, and shortly afterwards by the Austrians, Transylvania finally became a part of Romania in 1918. Evidence remains—villages built around fortified churches and citadel ruins stand on nearly every hill.

While economic hardship has driven many Germans back to Germany, Transylvania has a large Hungarian minority which recalls persecution under Ceaușescu and demands minority rights. Meanwhile, Romanians fear any threat to Romanian control, remembering centuries of Hungarian rule.

Transylvania is the most westernized part of Romania, due to geography and the influence of Austrian rule and its minorities. Cities are cleaner, services are better, and waiters friendlier than elsewhere in Romania. Even the speech is slower, more musical, with a few regional expressions such as *"Servus!"* ("hello") and *"fain"* ("good, fine, nice, or cool"). You can also hear Hungarian, and occasionally German. Until the 19th century, Romanians weren't allowed to settle in cities, but they kept their traditions and pride in their Latin origin and in being *Ardeleni*. From this followed a mentality of self-sufficiency and of doing things slowly and well, with a certain feeling of superiority over those south of the mountains. Nonetheless, the *Ardeleni* believe in a unified Romania: "The sun rises in Bucharest" was a popular 19th-century saying. Unfortunately, the friendly feeling was not entirely mutual and jokes often portray Transylvanians as slow and stupid. (A Transylvanian shepherd sitting on the grass was asked if he was sitting and thinking. He replied, "No, I'm only sitting.")

The beautiful medieval centers of Transylvanian towns escaped the bulldozers as Communist planners contented themselves with building eyesores on the outskirts. The cities of Brașov, Sibiu, Sighișoara, Cluj-Napoca, and Timișoara are all worth a visit. All have reasonably good access by train. The Bucharest-Budapest railroad heads north to Brașov, after which it ramifies: most trains go slightly north through Sighișoara, but there is also a southern route through Sibiu. The two join again west of Sibiu. Then there is another bifurcation: west to Arad and Budapest, or northwest to Cluj-Napoca, Oradea and Budapest. Timișoara is about 30km south of Arad. Reasonably quick direct trains connect all those cities together and with Bucharest; TAROM also flies to Sibiu, Cluj, and Timișoara.

Venturing outside cities may be a hassle because of poor transportation, but may well be the most beautiful part of your trip. The Carpathians are almost always within reach: from Sibiu you can climb the **Făgăraș mountains,** and from Cluj you can explore the **Apuseni.** The northern **Maramureș** preserves traditions centuries old and untouched villages. The depression of **Hațeg** has a beautiful castle, old churches, and ruins 2000 years old. In many places, scenic passes over the mountains will take you to Moldova or Muntenia; and, if you get tired of it all, direct trains will take you to Vienna in no time.

■■■ BRAȘOV

Brașov, rising from the foot of Mt. Timpa, is one of the most beautifully restored cities in Romania and a good base for excursions to the Carpathian mountains. Like many other Transylvanian cities, Brașov was founded by Saxons in the 13th century; throughout the Middle Ages it was an important commercial center because of its location overlooking the main pass south across the mountains. Now it is a transportation hub between Bucharest and the west. Communism spared its center, but birthed industrial mammoths on the periphery. Riots broke out in Brașov in 1987 demanding the resignation of Ceaușescu; quickly and brutally repressed, they erupted again in 1989 along with the rest of the country. Now, as Brașov looks toward capitalism, spiffy shops and expensive cars are appearing on its tired streets

Orientation and Practical Information From the train station, ride bus #4 for 10 minutes. On Bd. Eroilor, the Hotel Aro Palace is on the left facing a park; the ONT **tourist office** (tel. 14 16 48) in its lobby has **maps** and information on hotel accommodations (open daily 8am-8pm). To walk from the station (2km), head straight on Bd. Victoriei, follow the road to the right around the civic center, then turn right on Bd. 15 Noiembrie which becomes Bd. Eroilor after Piata Teatrului. Two of the city's biggest hotels, Aro Palace and Capitol, are on Bd. 15 Noiembbrie. To reach the main square, Piata Sfatului, turn right on Str. Republicui after the Hotel Capitol. The **CFR** office is on Str. Republicii 53. (Open Mon.-Fri. 7am-7:30pm. The **telephone office** is also on Bd. 15 Noiembrie. The **telephone city code** is 029. The city is Transylvania's major **train** hub, 2½-3 hours from Bucharest; all Budapest-Bucharest trains stop here. The **bus station** is near Hotel Aro Palace.

Accommodations Your best bet might be **private rooms.** Offers at the train station tend to be more reliable than in Bucharest. Just act confused in front of Hotel Capitol or Hotel Aro Sport where locals roam around in search of lodgers (US$6-10 per person, but you can bargain). The jovial and energetic **Mr. Babes Aurel** offers rooms in his house for US$5. He and his wife (who speaks French) go out of their way to make you feel at home (Str. Cerbului 32; tel. (29) 14 05 17). **EXO,** Str. Post-ăvarului 6 near the central square (tel. 14 45 91), is an agency that offers private rooms at US$17 per person. As you face Hotel Aro Palace, walk 350m left and then make a right onto Str. Republicii. Turn left at the first crossing, walk for a block, and turn right onto Str. Postăvarului. (open Mon.-Fri. 11am-8pm, Sun. 11am-2pm). The cheapest hotel in town in **Hotel Aro Sport,** Str. Sf.Ioan 3 (tel. 14 28 40), at the back of the Hotel Aro Palace. Ask for the Aro Sport reception. Spartan but clean rooms with communal bathrooms (singles US$22, doubles US$36). Rooms may be available in the **dormitory** complex off Str. Memorandumului from July to September.

Food In the main square, **Restaurant Gustări** offers traditional Romanian meals for US$2 (open daily 8:30am-10pm). For dessert, head across the square and take a right onto Str. Muresenilor to the **Mamamia,** where banana splits, milkshakes, and sundaes are expensive (about US$3) but well worth it. Riding up the **Mount Tîmpa** cable car gets you both a transfixing view and a reasonably priced restaurant, the **Panoramic** (tel. 11 98 51). One of the best restaurants in town is in **Hotel Aro Palace** where a full meal costs US$7-10. Try the fish or *papanaşi*, but beware of the bread; on bad days it could be used to fill holes in the Braşov-Gheorgheni highway.

Sights Piata Sfatului, in the center of the old town, and the nearby Str. Republicii, provide splendid strolling ground and give a sad glimpse of the beauty Romania lost when the housing projects took over. The fairy-tale-esque **Orthodox Cathedral** in the square was built in 1858 of marble and delicate gold. The **History Museum,** in the middle of the square, was formerly a courthouse; legend holds that the condemned had to jump from the tower to their deaths (closed for restorations in summer 1994). Uphill from the square along Str. Gh. Baritiu looms the **Black Church,** the most celebrated Gothic building in the country; it received its name after being charred in a fire in 1689. The church was built by the Saxons that settled here in 1221; it was finished only in 1480, and rebuilding after the fire took more than 80 years. Magnificent organ concerts are offered during the summer several times a week (open Mon.-Sat. 10am-6pm; admission 100lei).

Poarta Schei is a city gate built in 1828 to separate the old German citadel from the Romanian *Schei,* a quiet area of picturesque houses. The **Ethnographic Museum** on Bd. Eroilor between Hotel Aro Palace and Hotel Capitol exhibits Transylvanian folk costumes and ceramics (open Tues.-Sun. 10am-6pm; students 50 lei). A few doors down at no. 21, the **Muzeul de Arta** (National Art Museum), shows the work of Romania's newest talent (open Tues.-Sun. 10am-6pm; students 25 lei). In early September, the city hosts the international music festival, **"The Golden Stag"** ("Cerbul de Aur"), in the beautiful central square. Inquire at the tourist office.

■ NEAR BRAŞOV

The popular mountain resort **of Poiana Braşov** is only 10km from Braşov (buses leave from in front of the main building of the university on Bd. Eroilor; 2 per hour,

200 lei). Ask for *"maşina de Poiana."* The beautifully green, open area among the mountains, perfect for hiking or skiing, is crammed with restaurants and one-star hotels. **Mount Postăvaru** has great views and is easy to climb (1½hrs. from the center of the resort, or take the cable car). Beware of crowds in August and December to January.

Bran, 23km southwest of Braşov, is a picturesque town housing the famed **Castle of Vlad Tepeş.** Ostensibly home to the count who inspired Bram Stoker's novel *Dracula,* the castle still poses majestically, though not very mysteriously, on a hill (open Tues.-Sun. 9am-4pm). Although Count Dracula had nothing at all to do with this castle, Bram Stoker traveled in Transylvania and was impressed enough with it to base the castle in his novel on this model. The castle used to guard the important commercial route between Vallachia and Transylvania along the Rucăr-Bran pass. A drive along the pass is still very scenic and the castle merits a look, even if it won't leave its mark (or two) on you. The locals try to keep it interesting with the **Muzeul Vama Bran,** which contains old photos and relics from the place, and with an **ethnographic museum** of Transylvania (both open Tues.-Sun. 10am-4pm; admission 75 lei, students 25 lei). To get to Bran from Braşov, take the **bus** marked "Bran" from the station on Bd. Eroilor (hourly, 200 lei).

■■■ PRAHOVA VALLEY (VALEA PRAHOVEI)

About 20km south of Braşov, the road and railway to Bucharest cross the Predeal (1100m), the highest point in the Carpathian mountains. From here, a valley follows the small river Prahova, slowly descending into the plains. On these plains lies the city of Bucharest, flanked by beautiful mountains on both sides. The wilderness elsewhere in Romania is more pristine, but the valley's infrastructure is good and several day-hikes can be done from Braşov or even Bucharest (it you catch a 2hr. morning train.) Both Sinaia and Predeal have good **skiing** facilities; the season usually lasts until April. Beware that heating may be a problem in some hotels.

Orientation and Practical Information From south to north, the major resorts are **Sinaia, Buşteni,** and **Predeal,** followed by a steep descent into Transylvania by Timişul de Sus, Timişul de Jos, and Braşov. Express **trains** take about 1 hour to reach Sinaia from Braşov, and stop only in Predeal (the Bucureşti-Sinaia run is 1¾ hours with one stop at Ploieşti). Trains, local and express, are frequent. The main route is the one north of Predeal. Sinaia and Predeal tend to be fancier and more expensive. The major mountains are **Bucegi,** west of the valley and parallel to it, stretching from Sinaia to Predeal, with a wide plateau at a height of about 2000m. North of Predeal and east of the valley (north of Bucegi) is the **Postăvaru mountain.** Across from it is **Poiana Braşov.**

Accommodations Owners will often wait for tourists in the train station with offers of inexpensive private rooms. There are cabins in the mountains, but they tend to be dirty. Call ahead in the summer, especially in July and August. In **Predeal, Hotel Carmen** (tel (068) 25 65 17) is near the station on the main road. Unimpressive singles are US$22. Doubles US$40. In **Sinaia, Hotel Montana** (tel (044) 31 27 51) has decent rooms 2min. from the cable car. Singles US$26. Doubles US$42. Triples US$50. 30% increase July 15-Aug. 31.

Sights A small valley near Sinaia is home to three wonderful castles. The **Peleş Castle,** built for King Carol I around 1900 using Austrian motifs, is splendidly set on a wooded hill. A bit upstream is the queen's castle, **Pelişor,** and at the end of a valley rise the round red towers of **Foişor.** Up from the valley on the left is the **Sinaia Monastery,** built in the 17th century and a refuge during the Russo-Turkish war. All these sights are within a day trip from Bucharest.

In **Predeal,** several easy walks can be made around the Cioplea hill, east of the railroad. Watch for **Ceaşescu's summer villa.** He moved to Sinaia after he was told that Predeal's high altitude might damage his health. Only 5km away from Predeal is the **Trei Brazi** (Three Fir Trees) cabin, surrounded by lovely meadows.

Hikes The following trips should be done only during the summer (July -Sept.). Listen to the weather forecast and take the proper equipment before setting out.

The **Bucegi plateau** is easily accessible from Sinaia or Buşteni by cable car. Hiking up is easy from Sinaia and takes about three hours. From Buşteni, the three to five hour climb is steep and dangerous in bad weather. Once on the plateau, there are many possible routes. The most popular is from **Cota 2000** (above Sinaia) to **Babele** (above Buşteni); it takes about two hours, and it takes two hours more to reach the highest peak in Bucegi, **Omu** (2508m). From Omu it's possible to go down directly to Buşteni through **Valea Cerbului** (Stag Valley, 4-5 hrs. heading down) or continue north down to **Cabana Mălăieşti,** where you can spend the night and get to Pîrîul Rece and Predeal the next day. On the way is the **Caraiman Cross,** 45 minutes from Babele, with an incredible view of the valley. It was raised in the memory of those killed fighting Germany in World War I. Several cabins are on the ridge, such as Cabana Piaţa Arsă and Cabana Babele. The rocks near the latter are supposed to represent two old women *(babe),* hence the name.

An easy day-hike from Braşor or Bucharest could be Sinaia to Cota 2000 to Babele to Buşteni. The last portion is very steep. You may prefer to go down through Sinaia again. You can even take a stroll to the cross, if you have time. Mt. Omu can be done in a long day-hike, but you absolutely need good weather. Possible routes are Sinaia-Cota 2000-Babele-Omu-Valea Cerbului-Buşteni, or Buşteni-Babele-Omu-Valea Cerbului-Buşteni. You need to start early. There's a cabin on Mt. Omu if you need help in an emergency. The **Piatra Mare** mountain can also make a great day-hike. You can go up through Predeal (the trail starts on top of the Cioplea hill) and go down through Dîmbul Morii; from here you can walk to Braşov. Don't miss the impressive **Şapte Scări** (seven stairways) canyon. Watch your feet; many steps are missing.

■■■ SIBIU

Built by German colonists in the 12th century, Sibiu is one of the oldest cities in Romania, and has some of the finest medieval monuments in the country. The center was overlooked by Ceauşescu's "systematizing." The Făgăraş mountains, visible on sunny days, are only one hour away by train. Lately, an exotic touch was added by the coronations of two rival "rulers of all Gypsies," king Cioabă and emperor Iulian. Still, Sibiu remains one of the most Westernized cities in Romania and retains a German and a Hungarian minority.

Orientation and Practical Information Direct **trains** connect Sibiu to Bucharest and many cities in Transylvania. Otherwise, change trains in Braşov for Bucharest and in **Copşa Mică** for Cluj. (Copşa Mică is famous as one of the most polluted places in Europe.) TAROM also flies from Bucharest to Sibiu. From the train station, take trolleys #1 or 2 (100 lei) to the center, or just walk 10-15 minutes up Str. General Magheru. The huge central square was divided into two by the construction of the **Catholic Cathedral** in the 18th century. The two parts are now called **Piaţa Mare** and **Piaţa Mică** (big and small squares). From Piaţa Mare (also called Piaţa Republicii) walk up Str. Nicolae Bălcescu to get to Piaţa Unirii. Most interesting sights are in this area. Str. N. Bălcescu has many official buildings like the **CFR agency** (#6), the **TAROM** agency (#10), **DHL Worldwide Express** (near TAROM), and the **telephone office** (across from TAROM). Nearby the **Humanitas** bookstore also sells books in foreign languages.

Accommodations and Food **Hotel Parc** is a10-min. walk from Piaţa Unirii (tel. 42 44 55); take Str. Someşului, then Str. Şcoala de Înot. Decent rooms at one of the lowest prices in town. Those with rooms on the side of the soccer stadium can watch the matches of local team Inter for free (Sept.-May, usually every second Sunday). Singles US$18. Doubles US$31. Suites US$46. Breakfast included. The **Hotel Bulevard,** Piaţa Unirii 2-4 (tel. 41 21 40, fax 41 57 06), is liveable and has a very friendly staff. (Singles US$27. Doubles US$39. Breakfast included. Discounts for groups.) **Hotel Continental,** also on Piaţa Unirii (tel. 41 69 10) is of about the same quality as Bulevard. Currently it's undergoing renovation, though rooms are still available; they promise to become much better (and expensive; singles US$24, doubles US$39). The best cafeterias are **Perla** (in Piaţa Mare) and **Eugen** (nearby, on Str. Avram Ianau). In Paiţa Unirii you'll find the **Dumbrava supermarket** (open Mon.-Fri. 8am-8pm, Sat. 9am-2pm).

Sights and Entertainment Piaţa Mare is dominated by the massive Catholic Cathedral built by the Austrians after they conquered Transylvania, but they didn't succeed in converting the Saxons back to Catholicism. In front of it is an ugly statue of Gheorghe Lazăr, founder of Romanian schools. In the nearby Piaţa Mică are the **Museum of Pharmacy,** more interesting than its sounds (open Tues.-Sun. 9am-5pm), and the **Liar's Bridge.** The Protestant Church (open 9am-1pm) is one of the biggest in Romania and holds organ concerts during the summer (Wednesdays at 6pm). Nearby **Brukenthal High School** is the oldest school in southeastern Europe (over 600 years young). Don't miss the 1588 **Turnul Sfatului** (Council Tower), where the German city council once met, and the 13th-century **Turnul Scărilor** (tower of the stairs). The **History Museum** is housed in the Gothic Old City Hall (open Tues.-Sun. 9am-5pm). Nearby, on Str. Avran Lancu, is the oldest inhabited house in the town, a Gothic 14th century construction.

The **Brukenthal Museum** in Piaţa Mare is still interesting, despite the fact that some of its finest paintings were stolen in the 1960s and others were moved to Bucharest by Ceauşescu. Baron Samuel von Brukenthal was the governor of Transylvania and a passionate art collector. The gallery on the second floor has strong Dutch and Italian painting collections. On the first floor, a collection of Transylvanian paintings is worth a visit. The interior of this former baron's palace is highly decorated (open Tues.-Sun. 10am-5pm). Moving towards Piaţa Unirii on Str. N. Bălcescu, an **Orthodox church** will be on your right on a parallel street. The second largest in Romania, it was built as a copy of the St. Sophia in Istanbul on a 1:4 scale. The nearby **Snack Annabelle** is popular with high schoolers.

From Piaţa Unirii, continue south on Str. Someşului, then onto Str. Şcoala de Înot. At the end of it is the **soccer stadium** and the **park Sub Arini,** a favorite hangout for a mostly young crowd. On your way you'll pass along the **Museum of Hunting Trophies** featuring Romanian and Exotic exponates (open Tues.-Sun. 10am-6pm). The **Sub Arini park** has tennis courts and outdoor and indoor swimming pools (admission US$1). The Student Bar is nicknamed **Budibar** since it used to be a public toilet (*budă* means toilet—please, no Budapest jokes). Turn left and walk a few yards to get to **Birtul Radului** (Radu's Pub) for cheap Romanian drinks. The nearby **Grădina de vară Bolta Rece** ("Cold Ceiling Summer Gardens") sells either Coke or the cheap local beer *Trei Stejari* ("Three Oaks") for US$0.25. Experts say it's better than Bud. Back in town, the city warms up in May-June for its annual jazz festival, the biggest in Romania. For an American movie, try **Cinema Pacea** across the street from the Humanitas bookstore.

■ NEAR SIBIU

A few kilometers south of Sibiu is **Dumbrava.** Locals go here on weekends to walk in the forest or just hang out. Take trolleys #1 or 4 from downtown, or walk along **Calea Dumbrăvii** (30-45min.). There is **camping,** a **forest,** a **zoo,** and an interesting **Museum of Folk Civilization.** When coming from Sibiu, turn right and walk down to the lake. The museum is on the left, the zoo on the right. The museum has hundreds of buildings scattered around meadows and forest: you can see the entry of a

ROMANIA

gold mine, miner's tools and dwellings, and a 19th century bowling alley (open Tues.-Sun. 10am-6pm; invest US$0.60 for an English guide, or you won't understand anything; student discounts available).

Cisnădie, 8km from Sibiu, likes to party and has one of the oldest clock towers in Transylvania. Up in the mountains of Cindrel, the town of **Păltiniş,** 35km from Sibiu, is the highest mountain resort in Romania (1440m). Beautiful location, fresh air, and numerous hiking opportunities made the place a favorite both to Nicu Ceauşescu, son of the former dictator and Sibiu party-boss, as well as to many of Romania's modern philosophers who gathered around Constantin Noica, now buried here.

■■■ THE FĂGĂRAŞ MOUNTAINS

The Făgăraş ridge, the longest, highest, and most spectacular in Romania, extends over 60km from the Olt Valley in the west to the Piatra Craiului mountains in the east. Touring the ridge is one of the most popular hikes for Romanian mountain lovers. Beautiful meadows, majestic summits, and the view of the Vallachian plains and the Transylvanian hills cure any fatigue. It's never packed, although many tourists attempt the climb during the summer. If you're looking for loneliness there are places to go. Whatever you do, you'll need a **map.** You can procure one in Sibiu or at one of the *cabans.* June is usually too early to go; the normal hiking season is July-mid September. Prepare for harsh weather; it can snow up there as late as July, and make sure you have all the proper equipment.

The ridge can be traversed in seven days. It's usually hiked from west to east, but there are several entry and exit points along the way in case you don't have enough time or just get tired. Most access points are from Transylvania; it's harder to get on the ridge from the south. You can either camp or sleep in one of the *cabans,* usually for less than US$5. There are also a few isolated huts on the ridge where you can stay for free. Most *cabans* have electricity and running water nearby, but don't expect luxuries. They tend to get packed during the weekends, and the surroundings are usually very dirty. You may want to avoid them and stay on the ridge. Most *cabans* are 30-60 minutes down from the ridge. Tents can usually be set slightly under the ridge or in the worst case, near a *caban.* Camping is legal everywhere, but there are not so many spots where you can actually set up a tent and feel safe in it, so keep your eyes open. Fire wood is scarce. Water is said it's safe, but its always better to disinfect it. In August and September, the valleys under the ridge fill with raspberries, blueberries, and blackberries. Watch out for potential bear competitors.

Once on the ridge, plan your schedule according to time, weather, and level of fatigue. Many hikers plan their daily schedule as Puha-Bălea or Capra-Podragu-Sîmbăta, a good route if you're up to it. No schedule is wrong if you *don't exceed your abilities.* There are countless variations on the itinerary; if you don't have a tent, it's possible to plan so that you always end up at a *caban* for the night.

The ridge path is marked by a red band bordered by white bands. It starts in the Olt Valley on the railroad from Sibiu to the south, but most hikers dismiss the first portion as uninteresting and enter the ridge at the **Avrig Lake** or the **Puha Saddle** *(Şaua Puha).* For any of these, take a train to **Avrig** (on the Braşov-Sibiu line), and follow the signs starting at the station. The first 10km or so is rather dull, on a flat and dusty road. The usual route goes from Avrig to the Poiana Neamţului *caban* and then climbs for about two hours to Cabana Bărcaciu, from which the ridge is three to four hours away. You should always allow one full day for getting near the ridge.

There are a few landmarks on the ridge that should not be missed. From west to east, the first is **Custura Sărăţii** (one hour east of Şaua Puha), the most spectacular and difficult portion of the ridge trail. For about two hours, you'll be hanging from rocks on a path which is sometimes less than one foot wide, surrounded by cliffs on both sides. For the less ambitious, an alternate path leaves the ridge, to join it again under Negoiu. From Negoiu, the ridge goes down to an alpine lake, then continues for a few hours until **Lake Capra** (goat), a wonderful place to spend the night. Less than one hour under the ridge from Capra is **Lake Bâlea,** the largest and, once, the most beautiful alpine lake in Fāgāraş. Now it has been spoiled by the construction of the **Transfăgărăşan,** a highway that crosses the mountains from the south to Transylvania. The lake and its surroundings are very dirty, but still merit a look (you can see it from the edge as well), and you might be able to get some food here.

East of Lake Capra, the ridge trail is a bit dull at first, but becomes very beautiful after you pass **Fereastra Zmeilor** (The Dragon's Window), a strange opening in the rock wall. The trail gets very narrow in places, and one spot is named **La Trei Paşi de Moarte** (Three Steps from Death), but it's not quite that bad. The ridge continues among various valleys and summits, and most hikers end the day by going down to the **Podragu lake and hut** (30 min. down from the ridge). The lake is gorgeous but dirty, so if you find a place for the tent it may be better to stay on the ridge. Less than 3hrs. east of Podragu is Romania's highest summit, **Mount Moldoveanu** (2544m). A 15-minute path connects it to the main ridge. East of Moldoveanu, the ridge gradually mellows and many hikers leave it and go down into the **Sîmbăta Valley.** Others follow the ridge to its end and finish their hike at Cabana Plaiul Foii near the Piaţra Craiului mountains, about 30km from Braşov.

If you go down through **Sîmbăta,** it will take almost a whole day to reach the town of **Făgăraş,** with frequent trains to Sibiu and Braşov. On your way down, don't miss the beautiful **Sîmbăta Orthodox Monastery.** Razed by the cannons of the Austrian army during the forced conversion to Catholicism of the 17th century, it was rebuilt after 1918, renovated after 1989, and inaugurated in a big ceremony in 1993. If you wear shorts they might not let you in. From the monastery, about four buses per day go to Făgăraş, and the last one is insanely crowded as hikers fight for a ride home. The **bus station** is on the main road.

■■■ SIGHIŞOARA (SEGESVÁR/SCHÄSSBURG)

Of all the medieval towns in Transylvania, **Sighişoara** is perhaps the least spoiled and most enchanting. Surrounded by mountains and crowning a green hill on the railroad line between Cluj and Braşov, its gilded towers, old clock tower, steeples, and irregular tile roofs are almost entirely unobstructed by modern buildings. The old walled town is preserved as a museum, and visitors can wander into the surrounding hilly farmland. Though beautiful and relaxing, the city is small and probably won't keep you busy for more than one day.

Sighşoara was founded by Saxon colonists in 1191, and people still live in its well-preserved, fortified hill. Enter the **Old Town** through the **old clock tower,** a few meters down from Hotel Steaua to P-ţa Hermann Oberth, then uphill. The tower is 64m high and was built in 1556. A **History Museum** inside offers glimpses into the city's past as well as an outstanding panorama of the surrounding area (tel. 77 11 08; open Tues.-Sun. 9am-6:30pm). The ground-level rooms were used as torture chambers. Watch the clock figures move every hour: they represent Peace and Justice. Nearby is the **Museum of Medieval Armory,** whose three rooms display cannonballs, Middle-Eastern-style swords *(iatagan),* and other weapons of Dark-Age domination (open Tues.-Sun. 10am-3:30pm). Check out the old Saxon **church** (closed for renovations in the summer of 1994) and graveyard. The church, built between the 14th and 16th centuries, has a 175-step **covered wooden staircase** (built 1662). Below the church is the oldest high school in town. The lower town has itself some interesting sights. Take a stroll along the river and visit the **Orthodox Cathedral** (built around 1800). Or, head up for a walk on any of the surrounding hills.

Almost all **trains** on the Bucharest-Budapest and Bucharest-Cluj routes stop on Sighişoara (1½hrs. from Braşov, 4½hrs. from Bucharest, 2½hrs. from Cluj). From the train station, take a right, then a quick left, and follow the main street until it crosses the river. Then take a right onto Str. 1 Decembrie to reach the town's **tourist office** (tel. 77 10 72; open Mon.-Fri. 8am-3:15pm, Sat. 10am-1pm) and only hotel. Alternately, you can cross the river on the bridge by the orthodox church, then take a left to reach Str. 1 Decembrie. The reception at **Hotel Steaua** can also provide information and maps of the city in Romanian, English, and German. The **CFR office** is nearby (tel. 77 18 20; open Mon.-Fri., 7am-8pm). Farther down on the main street is the **post office** (open Mon.-Fri. 7:30am-noon and 5-7pm) and the **telephone office** (open daily 7am-10pm, international calls available). The **telephone city code** is 065. The **bus station** (tel. 77 12 60) is near the train station.

A few steps from the tourist office, **Hotel Steaua** ("Star"; tel. 77 19 30, fax 77 19 32) is not nearly as luminous as its name suggests, though the rooms are fairly big. (Singles US$14, with bath US$17. Doubles US$25, with bath US$31. Triples with bath US$35. Breakfast included.) For a **private room,** try the tourist office; you might be offered one by somebody if you look confused in front of the hotel. **Dealul Gàrii** offers camping on the north side of the rail tracks (tel. 77 10 46). From the station, turn left, then left again across the railway, then head up Str. Dealul Gàrii. It also has a non-stop restaurant.

In the Old Town, you can have an excellent meal of local delicacies. Try the corner house on the second side street on your left, after entering through the clock tower. The **Restaurant Cetate,** P-ta Muzeului 5 (tel. 77 15 96), here is run by a company called Dracula SRL; Vlad Dracul, father of Vlad "Count Dracula" Țepeș lived in this house between 1431-1436. Service is friendly, though a bit slow, and the food is delicious, served amidst massive wooden chairs. Full meals less than US$5. Try the dungeon-like *berărie* (bar) downstairs, if there's anybody there; a lack of tourists kept the place empty in the summer of 1994. Other options are at **Hotel Steaua,** or one of the pizza places nearby. If you take the first side street after the clock tower and walk toward the Lutheran church atop the hill, you'll come to the small square where **Cofetarie Boema** is located. This cozy café offers magnificent cakes with aromatic coffee (open daily 9am-9pm)

■■■ CLUJ-NAPOCA

Cluj, on the river Someșul Mic below the gentle sloping hills of Feleac and Făgeti, is Transylvania's unofficial capital and largest student center. Romans called it Napoca, Germans called it Klausenburg and Hungarians, Kölosvar. Over 70% of the population is now Romanian, but the city has a vocal Hungarian minority and ethnic tension has increased with the election of an ultra-nationalist mayor. "*Pe dealul Feleacului/Trec carele Iancului*" goes an old folk song: "On the hill of Feleac/Iancu's chariots/They don't go like chariots/They shine like the sun." Even this verse is a reminder of ethnic strife: Avram Iancu was the leader of the Romanian resistance against the Hungarian army in the 1848 revolution.

In 1993, Cluj became famous as the location for the headquarters of the "Caritas" get-rich-quick pyramid scheme. Depositors were paid back eight times their deposit in an interval of only three months. Huge lines waited outside their offices as people from all over the country rushed to Cluj, dreaming of fabulous wealth. The scheme collapsed after one year, sucking in the savings of two million Romanians and prompting a front-page article in the *New York Times*.

ORIENTATION AND PRACTICAL INFORMATION

To get to the city center from the train station, take either bus #3 or 4 or head straight down the Str. Horea, which changes its name to Str. Gheorghe Doja after crossing the river. Adjacent to Str. Horea you may notice Str. Cloșca and Str. Crișan. These are the three leaders of the 1784 Romanian peasant rebellion, who were eventually caught, tortured, and put to death. The same fate was suffered by Gheorghe Doja, the local leader of the 1514 peasant revolt. Legend says he was crowned—with red-hot iron. At the end of Str. Gheorghe Doja is Piața Unirii, the city's central square (20 min. from the train station).

Tourist Office: KmO is located at Piața Unirii 10 (tel. 19 65 57); open Mon.-Fri. 9am-6pm, Sat. 9am-1pm. **Feleacul** is on Str. Memorandumului, a few meters from

the main square. There's a city map in front. Open Mon.-Fri. 8am-4pm, Sat. 9am-noon. Check with either for a **map, tours** around Cluj, or currency exchange. If you're lucky they might be able to get you a **private room** or a university dorm. **Budget Travel:** Next to KmO is the **CFR agency** (tel. 11 24 75). For domestic tickets go to P-ța Mihai Vitearul (tel. 11 22 12).
Currency Exchange: Shaker on Str. Memorandumului 9, around the corner from KmO. Open Mon.-Fri. 9am-5pm, Sat. 9am-1pm.
Post Office: Str. Gh. Doja 33. Open daily 7am-10pm. A **general store** is nearby.
Telephones: The office on the central square is chaotic. You're better off going to the one on Str. G. Barițiu, only five minutes away; open 7am-10pm.
Flights: The **TAROM** agency is in P-ța Mihai Viteazul (tel. 13 02 34). A ticket to Bucharest is US$44 one way (3 per day). Open Mon.-Fri. 7am-7pm, Sat. 7am-1pm.
Trains: Frequent trains connect Cluj to all major cities in Transylvania. To: Bucharest (7hrs.), Budapest (6hrs.), Brașov (4hrs.).

ACCOMMODATIONS AND CAMPING

Check the accommodations board at the train station for directions to the hotels in Cluj-Napoca.

Hotel Continental has a great location in Piața Unirii (tel. 19 54 05). A beautiful façade, and decent rooms. Singles US$20, with bath US$30. Doubles US$32, with bath US$50. Suites US$60-75
Hotel Vlădeasă, Str. Gh. Doja 20 (tel. 11 84 91). Singles US$16. Doubles US$25. Triples US$37.
Hotel Astoria, Str. Horea 3 (tel. 13 01 66), is farther from town; the yellow edifice's rooms are spacious but bland. Singles US$17, with bath US$21. Doubles US$25, with bath US$29. Triples US$40, with bath US$43.
Camping Făget, 8km from the city towards Bucharest (tel. 11 62 34). US$4 for 1 person, US$5 for 2 people, US$6 for 3 people. Open May-Oct. 15.

FOOD AND ENTERTAINMENT

There are a few cafeterias in Cluj, but none of the food is fabulous. Try **Croco** in P-ța Păcii, or **Carpati** in P-ța Unirii. The local specialty cake **Doboș Cluj** sells for US$0.50. Cluj has a rapid turnover of establishments, with many opening and closing overnight. Local students may give you some useful hints. There's a big **market** on Piața Mihai Viteazu (covered section open Tues.-Sat. 8am-4pm).

Restaurant Belvedere, on the Cetătuia hill, with a great view of the town. Also expensive. Disco-bar and night club (sometimes with strip-tease).
Restaurant Casino has a quiet location inside the central park, and a terrace with shade and trees. Everybody in Cluj drinks beer here during the summer.
Pizzeria New Croco is up Str. Pasteur from P-ța Păcii, a student hang-out with a cheerful crocodile mascot. They sell good pizza, or just sip a drink on the terrace.
Flipper, past Pizzeria New Croco; turn right on Str. Hașdeu, then right on Str. Piezișa. You'll find a mainly hippy clientele.
Restaurant Spaghetti, across from Flipper serves students beer from barrels.
Cofetăria Tineretului (nicknamed Arizona), across from Hotel Continental. Where college kids cut class to smoke and drink coffee. Open Mon.-Fri. 8am-8pm, Sat. 9am-5pm.

The hottest night spot in town is the **Bianco e Nero** disco club, Str. Universitătü 7-9, with a high tech sound and light system to keep you moving. Or try **Disco Sun** (bus #28 from the center). If you have some money to throw away, try your luck at **Salto Casino** near Hotel Continental.

SIGHTS

Most strolls start in **Piața Unirii,** where the Gothic steeple of the Catholic **Church of St. Michael** rises majestically. The tower is 80m high and has a magnificent view of the city, but is almost always closed. The church was built in 1350-1480; when you enter, watch for the skewed portal, the result of a change in proportions after the construction had begun. Near the cathedral stands what is probably the most disputed statue in all Eastern Europe, the **equestrian statue of Mathias Rex** *(Matei Corvin)*, the Cluj-born king of Hungary from 1458 to 1490. Commissioned in 1896 to mark the millennium of the Magyar arrival in Europe, and erected in 1902 when Transylvania was still Hungarian, the statue has come to symbolize ethnic tensions between Transylvanians and the local Hungarian minority. In 1933, Romanian historian Nicolae Iorga added an inscription to the pedestal which denied that King Mathias had ever conquered Transylvania. The Hungarians deleted the inscription after taking over in 1940. When the Communists took charge in 1945, they diplomatically labelled the monument in Latin, simply "Matthias Rex." In 1992, Cluj elected Gheorghe Funar, a nationalist mayor described as "Romania's Zhirinovsky," who had Iorga's words reinscribed. Funar also set about constructing buildings in Cluj that soon overshadowed the town's Hungarian monuments. While digging the foundations to one of these, remains of a Roman workshop were stumbled upon. Funar wanted them to be excavated (and the statue removed). This incurred the anger of Hungarians both in Romania and in Hungary, who consider Mathias one of their greatest kings. (Romanians don't agree; the king kept local boy Count Dracula in prison for 15 years). For now, Funar has relented and the statue remains, but the quarrel rages on in headlines in both Romania and Hungary.

Around the square rise several palaces, most of them built by Hungarian nobles in the 17th-19th centuries. The fanciest is **Bánffy Palace** P-ța Unirii 30 (tel. 11 69 53), now home of the **Art Museum.** Nearby is the **Museum of Pharmacy,** at #28. Across from the cathedral entrance is a blue house with a plaque commemorating the visit of Austrian Emperor Joseph II. In the opposite corner is the new **Monument of the Memorandum,** topped by a bell. The Memorandum was a petition sent to the emperor in 1891 by Romanians claiming national rights; many of its writers were sued by the Hungarian authorities. From Piața Unirii, head to **Piața Avram Iancu,** along either Str. 21 Dec. 1989 (commemorating the victims of the 1989 revolution) or Bd. Eroilor (formerly Corso). In the square rises the **Orthodox Cathedral,** built in a beautiful Byzantine-Romanian style. In front of it is the newly-built **statue of Avram Iancu,** one of Mayor Funar's favorite projects. The long pipes below Iancu's feet are a traditional musical instrument called a *tulnic.* The other major building in the square is the **National Theater.**

North of Piața Unirii, a short walk down Str. Gh. Doja will take you to Piața Mihai Viteazul, named after the king of Muntenia who unified the three Romanian kingdoms in 1600; his equestrian statue dominates the square. Some say that no horse could really assume that position. Walk east on str. G. Baritiu, cross the river to the right, and climb **Cetățuie hill;** a great view awaits at the top. Down the hill, back across the river, lies the long and narrow **Central Park.**

Backtracking to Piața Unirii, look to the northwest corner for Str. Matei Corvin, where Gypsies once traded gold. A few steps up the street is the **inn** where King Mathias was born in 1443; a plaque in Hungarian commemorates the event. Nearby in P-ța Muzeului is a 13th-century Franciscan **monastery**, now home to the Music High School. Close to P-ța Unirii is also the **Ethnographic Museum** of Transylvania at Str. Momeorandumului 21 (tel. 11 23 44; open Tues.-Sun. 9am-5pm).

South of the main square, head on Str. Universității to enter the student area of the town. Turn left on Str. Mikhail Kogălniceanu for the main university building. Further up is a 15th-century **Protestant Church** which often holds organ concerts. In front of it is a replica of the famous **statue of St. George** slaying a dragon; the original statue is in Prague and was executed in 1373 by sculptors from Cluj. Some say that the statue here is the original, and the one in Prague is a copy. A few steps up is **Bastionul Croitorilor** (Taylor's Bastion), one of the few remnants of the medieval defense wall; rock-climbing is sometimes possible. In front of the bastion is a statue of Baba Novac, a general in the army of Mihai Viteazul, slain here in 1601. A legend tells about his Houdini-esque escape from a Turkish prison.

For another piece of history, visit the small but beautiful **Orthodox Church** nearby; from P-ța Unirii, walk down Str. Universității, turn right on Str. Avram Iancu, and then left on Str. Bisericii Orthodoxe and walk a few steps uphill. The Ottomans did not permit the Romanians to build an orthodox church of stone until 1795, and then only outside the city walls.

The **Botanical Garden** is perhaps the most relaxing and beautiful in Romania. From P-ța Unirii take Str. Napoca to Piața Pacii, then head up Str. Gheorge Bilașcu (also called Republicii). There's a Japanese garden with a pond and bridge, a Roman garden, greenhouses with waterlilies and palm trees, and an ivy-clad tower; vegetation obscures the view of the city. Don't walk on the grass or you'll be fined.

■ NEAR CLUJ

The nearby **Apuseni Mountains** are a wonderful hiking area, and have numerous caves that attract international spelunkers as well as an underground glacier at **Scărișoara.** The fanciest resort is **Beliș-Fântânele,** but there are many remote villages which preserve old folk tradition of the gold-mining region.

Two hours by train on the way to Budapest, the city of **Oradea** has some interesting monuments. One hour east of Satu Mare is the twin city of **Baia Mare,** although (in)famous for its pollution, it has some nice sights and is a gateway to **Maramureș,** a beautiful land of hills and mountains; villages here preserve old architecture, folk songs, and festivals. In the **Cimitrul Vesel** (Jolly Cemetery), in the village of **Săpînța** on the Satu Mare-Sighet road, the crosses that mark the gravesites are brightly colored and include funny poems about the deceased (but you'll need a Romanian-speaking companion; guides are available). From here you can cross the mountains into Moldova.

ROMANIA

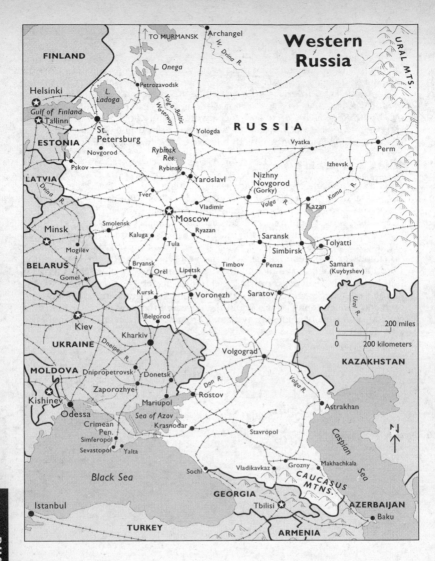

Western Russia

RUSSIA (РОССИЯ)

US$1	= 2250R (Rubles)	1000R =	US$0.44
CDN$1	= 1650R	1000R =	CDN$0.61
UK£1	= 3530R	1000R =	UK£0.28
IR£1	= 3470R	1000R =	IR£0.29
AUS$1	= 1680R	1000R =	AUS$0.60
NZ$1	= 1220R	1000R =	NZ$0.82
SAR1	= 630R	1000R =	SAR1.58
DM1	= 1460R	1000R =	DM0.68

Country Code: 7

In Russia's unstable economy, expect prices to have changed dramatically. As of July 1994, inflation of ruble prices was 10-15% a month, and the exchange rate was going up by 3 rubles to the dollar every day.

It is a riddle wrapped in a mystery inside an enigma.
—Winston Churchill, in 1939 on Russia

Immense changes have occurred in Russia in just the past 5 years, and Churchill is as right today as he was 55 years ago. Russia and the processes it is going through are mindboggling and incomprehensible. Though considered a world superpower, Russia is much more a chaotic eastern bazaar with its own ever-changing rules and frustrations. The collapse of the Soviet Union has allowed the vast patchwork of autonomous regions and minority nationalities that make up Russia to tear apart, or at least fray—it sometimes seems that every street corner has declared itself an autonomous republic.

Russia is now redefining itself as a country of nationalities as opposed to ideology and has metamorphosed from the world's largest bastion of socialist power into an enormous, sprawling yard sale. Red banners are visible only in souvenir shops, *babushki* (elderly women) peddle the contents of their *dachas* (summer cottages), and enterprising young capitalists buy and sell Western goods on street corners. Russians manage to endure with unique resourcefulness and a heavy dose of black humor, saving, bartering, growing vegetables on their windowsills, and taking refuge around the kitchen table with homemade pickles and a pot of tea.

RUSSIA ESSENTIALS

Russian visas require an invitation stating itinerary and dates of travel and thus are inherently difficult to get without a contact in Russia. Fortunately, the following organizations specialize in supplying invitations and/or visas for individual tourists:

Travellers Guest House, 50 Bolshaya Pereyaslavskaya 10th fl., Moscow, Russia 129401 (tel. (095) 971 40 59, fax 280 76 86 (Moscow); e-mail tgh@glas.apc.org). In **Hong Kong:** Global Union Espress (H.K.) Ltd. Rm 22-23 New Henry House, 10 Ice House St., Central, Hong Kong (tel. 868 32 31, fax 845 50 78). They arrange visa invitations, will register you once you arrive in Russia, make reservations, and get train tickets.

Russia House, in U.S. 1800 Connecticut Ave. NW, Washington DC 20009, attn: Chris Poor (tel. (202) 986-6010, fax 667-4244). In **Russia,** 17 Leningradsky Prospect, Moscow, Russia 125040 (tel. (095) 250 01 43, fax 250 25 03). Russia House provides a visa, reservations, train tickets, etc.

Red Bear Tours, 320B Glenferrie Rd., Malvern, Melbourne, Victoria 3144, Australia (tel. (3) 824 71 83, fax 822 39 56; toll free (008) 33 70 31). For those in Australia, Red Bear also provide rail tickets across Russia and assorted tours. Their newsletter has the most recent information on their services.

Russian Youth Hostels, in **U.S.:** 409 N Pacific Coast Highway, Building 106, Suite 390, Redondo Beach, CA 90277 (tel. (310) 379-4136, fax. 379-8420; e-mail 71573.2010@compuserve.com). In **U.K.:** YHA Travel Store, 14 Southhampton St., London, WC2E 7HY (tel. (0171) 836 10 36); in **Finland:** urohostel, Linnankatu 9, SF-00160 Helsinki (tel. (90) 66 44 52); in **Germany:** DJH (German YHA), Templehofer Ufer 32, D 1000 Berlin 61 (tel. (030) 264 95 20); and in **Estonia:** Karol Travel Agency, Lembitu 4, EE0001, Tallin (tel. (2) 45 49 00).

IBV Bed & Breakfast Systems, 13113 Ideal Drive, Silver Spring, MD 20906 (tel. (301) 942-3770, fax 933-0024), provide varied services for those going to Russia.

RUSSIA

Host Families Association, HOFA. In Russia, tel./fax (812) 275 19 92; e-mail alexei@hofak.stu.spb.su); in **U.S.**, tel. (202) 333-9343; in **U.K.**, tel. (01295) 71 06 48; in **Australia** (03) 725 85 55.
Home & Host International, 2445 Park Ave., Minneapolis, MN 55404 (tel. (612) 871-0596, fax 871-8853).

If you have received just an invitation, the actual visa must be applied for at the Russian Embassy or Consulate. For addresses see Essentials: Embassies and Consulates, page 3. Send a photocopy of your invitation, a photocopy of the front pages of your passport, a completed application (contact the embassy or a travel agent for blanks), 3 photographs, a cover letter with your name, dates of arrival and departure, date of birth, and passport number, and the visa fee (most recently US$20 for two-week processing, US$30 for one-week service, US$100 for same-day service) to the embassy or consulate. Include a return envelope with postage.

Most organizations will register your visa for you on arrival, but if this service is not included, go down to the central OVIR (ОВИР) office (in Moscow, at ul. Chernyshevskaya 42 and called УВИР) to register; many people ignore this step, but it's the law. This is also where you should attempt to extend your visa, a beaurocratic hassle, better to get a long enough one before you come. Officially, you can freely travel anywhere that isn't off-limits to foreigners (such as military bases and power plants), but local administration may give you a hard time if the city is not on your visa. It's OK to enter Russia through a city not specifically listed on your visa.

Many organizations in the U.S. run special educational tours to Russia. Try contacting **CIEE** (tel. (212) 661-1414; see the addresses in Essentials: Travel Organizations) or the **American Council of Teachers of Russian** (ACTR), 1776 Massachusetts Ave. NW, Suite 300, Washington, DC 20036 (tel. (202) 833-7522). **Volunteers For Peace,** 43 Tiffany Rd., Belmont, VT 05730 (tel. (802) 259-2759), has innovative workcamps and language programs across the former Soviet Union which run about US$300-700; group airfare to Russia for the programs runs US$950 round-trip. Visa-free Cruises are available with many of the major Scandanavian lines, but their prices are prohibitive and not really fit for the budget traveler.

GETTING THERE
Flying on British Airways to St. Petersburg or Moscow is the most direct way to reach the former Soviet Union; they have student fares all the way to Russia. **Rail travel** from Helsinki and other European capitals to Moscow and St. Petersburg is a cheaper way to enter Russia., if you have the time. If you are coming from Warsaw, check to see if you are going through Belarus, for which you need a transit visa. Get it (US$25) at the Belarusian consulate in Warsaw, see page 384,or at another capital. If you wait until the border, it may be more expensive and you risk not getting back on your train in time. **Buses** run by **Finnord** leave for St. Petersburg four times per day from Lahti, Finland, and are even cheaper than the trains.

Customs
Customs enforcement is arbitrary and unpredictable. There's not much you can do except be polite; one day they'll tear your pack apart, the next they'll just nod and dismiss you. If you fly in—especially with a group—your baggage will probably not be inspected. You may encounter more difficulty if you arrive by train or car. If you have doubts about anything, bring a lot of documentation or check with the Russian embassy before you go. Politely answer the questions the border officials ask, but *do not* offer any information that they don't specifically ask about.

You cannot bring rubles into or out of the country, not that you would ever want to. At the border, you will be given a **Customs Declaration Form** on which to declare all your valuables and foreign currency. Don't lose it. Everything listed on the customs form must be on your person when you leave the country.

You may not export works of art, icons, old *samovars* (not the electric kind), and antique books—technically, anything published before 1945. Military items such as

army belts and flags are nominally contraband, but authorities hardly ever bother with them anymore.

GETTING AROUND RUSSIA

Be flexible. Expect airport delays, tour cancellations, hotel changes, cold showers, and bathrooms *sans* toilet paper. The rules have chnaged so often no one really knows what they are anymore. As a result, an authority figure can choose whatever version suits him or her the best. Argument is usually futile.

Travel in Russia requires ample preparation. Pack carefully; bring your sense of humor and any Western goods you will need. Most toiletries and other items are available in Mosow and St. Petersburg, but for higher prices. Ziploc bags and pocket packs of kleenex are indispensable. Roach traps can be a godsend if you are staying in a dormitory.

Restrictions (Tickets)

Foreigners are now allowed free movement in Russia. You are officially required to buy internal plane and train tickets at inflated Intourist prices, but this is only enforced in Moscow and St. Petersburg. Elsewhere, you buy your train tickets at the station like everyone else—and run the risk of only being able to get a 3rd-class seat, as trains are often crowded. You cannot buy train tickets originating in a different city, so it is best to use Moscow or St. Petersburg as a base and make a series of round-trip journeys from there.

Planes, Trains, and Buses

Russia boasts an extensive rail and bus network and a vast, not-so-reliable air system monopolized by **Aeroflot**. The Aeroflot fleet is aging and has recently had numerous disasters. In the summer of 1994, the U.S. Consulate in Russia warned its employies to avoid using the airline if possible. **Train** cars are divided into three classes: luxury 2-bed "L" (Л) compartments, 4-bed cozy "coupés" (К) and *platskarti* (open-car couchettes; П). *Elektrichka* (commuter rail, marked on train station signs as пригородные поезда ; *prigorodnye poezda*) have their own platforms at each train station; buy tickets from the *kassa* (касса; ticket counter). These trains are often packed, especially on weekends; you may have to stand for an hour or more. **Buses** are slightly more expensive and terefore less crowded than trains; they are a good option for shorter distances. Buy seats on *myakki* (мягкий; "soft") buses only and you will get a seat assignment in a fairly comfy reclining chair. You can usually store your luggage in the undercarriage of the bus for about 100R.

Public Transportation and Taxis

Within Russian cities, overcrowded **buses, trams,** and (in major metropoli) unbelievably efficient **Metro** systems ferry citizens for 50-150R per ride. In the Metro, you buy tokens (*zhetoni*) at the *kassa* which you then drop into machines that let you onto escalators. Buy bus tickets at newsstands or from the *babushki* at Metro stations. For longer stays, ask at a ticket window for a *yediny bilet*, a pass valid on all forms of public transport for one calendar month. On the bus you must validate your ticket in one of the little hole-punchers. Since it's often bone-crushingly crowded, riders often ask their neighbors to pass tickets up to be punched. The same goes for purchasing tickets, which can sometimes be done from the driver. Don't try to ride for free; the system is very energetic in searching out joyriders, especially in the last week of the month, and fines are punitive (5000R). It is customary for passengers to tap each other on the shoulder and ask if they are getting off at the next stop (Вы выходите?—sounds like "Vee vee-HOAD-it-yeh") so that everyone can push their way to an exit. Metro stations are labeled only in Cyrillic; if you don't read Russian, you can usually recognize stations by memorizing the first and last letters. When two lines intersect, there is often a different station name for each line. You'll want to know the words *vkhod* (вход; "entrance"), *vykhod* (выход; "exit"), *vykhod v gorod* (выход в город; "exit to the city"), and *perekhod* (переход; "passage to another line"). Metro stations are marked above ground by a fluorescent red *M*. Try to acquire the newest city map possible, for stations and street names have been changing wildly in recent years as tastes in politics have spun. However, in Moscow and St. Petersburg, maps and street signs have all caught up with the times.

Hailing a **taxi** is indistinguishable from hitchhiking, and should be treated as such. Almost all of those who stop will be private citizens, taking passengers to make a little extra cash. Those seeking a ride stand off the curb and hold out a hand; when a car stops, riders tell the driver the destination before getting in. He will either refuse the destination and speed off, or nod his head, at which point haggling about the price begins. Meters are non-operational. Non-Russian speakers will get ripped off, and are lucky to get away for less than 10,000R.

SHOPPING

Russia can be a user-unfriendly society: state shops are crowded, with frustrating inefficiency and long lines. A three-line process is the rule in stores. In the first line, ogle the products and find out their prices. Then stand in line to tell the cashier their departments and prices; pay and take the receipt. In the third line, present the receipt to the salesperson and pick up your purchase—unless the store has already run out. This process will only work in Russian; if you're linguistically challenged, have a local friend show you the ropes. If there are two of you, one can stand in the cashier line while the other gets the prices; this expedites the process considerably.

In Moscow and St. Petersburg there is a whole new crop of small Western-style supermarkets selling food, toiletries, and household supplies, often for hard currency or credit cards. If you are wary of Russian meat and dairy products, these sell recognizable brands, and they have fancy food gifts like chocolates or liqueur.

For souvenirs, look for enterprising Russians selling pins, dolls, and military gear outside major tourist attractions. The old state-run hard currency souvenir stores are slowly being converted to private ventures; look for *beriozhka* (берёжка) signs.

Because of the recent influx of Western goods, token packs of cigarettes and ballpoint pens are no longer accepted as currency, and don't make very good gifts for Russians. When visiting friends, it is better to bring flowers or cookies or candy. Sweatshirts and t-shirts with city of college logos make good larger presents, as do cassettes of Western pop music. A bottle of imported wine is a very special present.

MONEY

Changing money in Russia is now easy as one-two-three. You will have no problem changing unspent rubles back at the end of your trip, but the exchange rate is so unstable, it's best not to change large sums of money at a time. **Step 1.** Find an *Obmen Valyuty* (Обмен Валюты; "currency exchange") sign. **Step 2.** Give them your U.S. dollars. Many places will change Deutschmarks, and some Francs and British Pounds, but few will change traveler's checks, and you are best off with greenbacks. **Step 3.** Receive your rubles. These are now convertible, honest-to-god real currency, with a published exchange rate (that often rises daily).

COMMUNICATION

Mail, Telegrams, Faxes, and E-Mail

There is neither rhyme nor reason to the former Soviet Union's **mail service.** Delivery can take anywhere from two weeks to eternity. *Let's Go* does not recommend using the Russian postal service for international mail, inwards or outwards. Domestic mail will usually reach its destination; send letters to Russian recipients via friends who are traveling there (and do the same to get mail out). **American Express** card- and traveler's check-holders can receive letters at the AmEx travel service bureaus in Moscow and St. Petersburg; this strategy is usually more reliable than Russian mail (see the addresses in the specific cities). They will hold your mail for 30 days. **DHL** has offices in Moscow, St. Petersburg, and Nizhny Novgorod; their services are expensive but reliable.

Telegrams (sent from telegraph (телеграф) offices, usually connected to post offices) are relatively cheap (650R per word to the U.S.). Look for a stack of blanks (the international forms say Международная Телеграмма), fill one out in Roman characters, and bring it to the window. Central post offices are also now equipped to send and receive **faxes.** Sending them costs 10,800R per page to the U.S.; receiving is a mere 500R per page. The international **electronic mail** (e-mail) network offers an instant and free connection to selected universities and institutes inside the country; ask student friends about setting up a trans-oceanic connection home.

Telephones

Local telephones in Moscow take special tokens, sold at Metro station *kassas* for 100R; in St. Petersburg they take Metro tokens. In most small towns, payphones are free for local calls. You can make intercity calls from private homes, telegraph offices, your hotel room, or special phone booths (marked междугородные) in each city. Have patience; it will take a while, but you will almost always get through, although calls from small towns are not always possible. Dial 8, wait for the tone, then dial the city code.

Direct international calls can be made from from telegraph offices and hotel rooms: Dial 8, wait for the tone, then dial 10 and the country code. You cannot call collect. To make calls from the telephone office, you can either buy tokens and use the *mezhdugorodny aftomat* telephones (междугородный афтомат; "intercity phones"); be sure to press the *otvet* (ответ) button when your party answers, or you will not be heard. If there are no automatic phones, you must pay for your call at the counter and dial it youself (your money will be returned if you do not get through) or have it dialed for you by the operator. Calls to North America cost 2000-5000R per minute with a 3-minute minimum; calls to Western Europe are 1500-3000R per minute. Several hotels in Moscow now have direct-dial booths operated by a special card or credit card. The cost is astronomical (at least US$6 per min. to the U.S.). To reach **AT&T USADirect,** dial 155 50 42 in Moscow. To reach the **Sprint Express** operator, dial 155 61 33 in Moscow. Dial 095 first when calling from another city; you will pay for the phone call to Moscow in addition to the international connection. To reach the **Canada Direct** operator, dial 810 80 04 97 72 33. To reach the **BT Direct** operator (U.K.), dial 810 80 04 97 72 66. Calling into the country can be equally frustrating. The U.S. and Canada as well as most European countries have direct dial to Moscow and St. Petersburg. For other cities, go through the international operator. It may take 30 tries, giving you ample opportunity to chomp into *War and Peace.*

Media

After a week or so in Russia, you may begin to feel hopelessly out of touch with the outside world. Most hotels stock recent issues of *Time, Newsweek,* and the *International Herald Tribune* (US$2). If you plan on being in Russia for an extended period of time, a short-wave radio is invaluable. The BBC World Service comes in at around 1508MHz.

In Moscow, the *Moscow Tribune* and the more widely read *Moscow Times* are both good English-language dailies with news of Moscow; they are distributed Tues.-Sat. in major hotels as well as Western restaurants and grocery stores—and they're free. In St. Petersburg, the same is true of the weekly *St. Petersburg Press.*

LANGUAGE

Though more and more people speak English in the Russia, take some time to familiarize yourself with the Cyrillic alphabet. It's not as difficult as it looks and will make getting around and getting by immeasurably easier. The "r" in Russian is trilled.

Cyrillic	English	Pronunciation	Cyrillic	English	Pronunciation
А, а	a	D*a*cha	Р, р	r	B*r*ad
Б, б	b	*B*altimore	С, с	s	*S*arala

В, в	v	The *V*illage People	Т, т	t	*T*homas
Г, г	g	*G*alina	У, у	u	Kit 'n' cab*oo*dle
Д, д	d	*D*avid	Ф, ф	f	*F*riend
Е, е	ye	*Ye*llowtail	Х, х	xh	*Ch*utzpah (*hkh*)
Ё, ё	yo	*Yaw*n	Ц, ц	ts	Le*t's* Go
Ж, ж	zh	*Zh*irinovsky	Ч, ч	ch	*Ch*icken tender
З, з	z	*Z*ack	Ш, ш	sh	*Ch*arlotte
И, и	i	*W*eevil	Щ, щ	shch	Khru*shch*ev
Й, й	y or j	(no sound)	Ъ, ъ	(hard)	(no sound)
К, к	*k*	*C*orrigan	Ы, ы	y	Glottal "i"
Л, л	l	*L*anguid	Ь, ь	(soft)	(no sound)
М, м	m	*M*oscow	Э, э	eh	*A*lexander
Н, н	n	*N*atasha	Ю, ю	yoo	*You*
О, о	o	*L*a*w*	Я, я	yah	*Ya*hoo!
П, п	p	*P*uffin			

Yes	Да	Dah
No	Нет	N-yet
Today	Севодня	se-VOhd-nya
Tomorrow	Завтра	zav-trah
Hello	Добрый день	doh-bree-DEN
Good morning	Доброе утра	doh-bro-OOtra
Good evening	Добрый вечир	doh-bree-VECH-eer
Goodbye	До свидания	Dus-vee-DAHn-ia
Excuse me	Извините	eez-vee-NEET-yeh
OK	хорошо	hkhor-a-SHOW
Please	пожалуйста	pa-ZHOW-a-sta
Thank you	Спасибо	spa-SEE-bah
When?	Когда?	kahg-DAh?
Where?	Где?	gdyeh?
How much does it cost?	Сколька стоит?	SKOAL-ka stow-it?
My name is ...	Меня зовут ...	menYA-za-Voot ...
Do you speak English?	Вы говорите по англиськи?	Vih-hoVORihte po anglihs-kih?
I don't understand	я не понимаю	Ya nee pa-nee-MY-you
Help!	Поможит!	Pah-mah-ZHEET!

1—один (ah-DEEN); 2—дба (d-VAH); 3—три (t-RIh); 4—четыре (che-tIH-Rih); 5—пять p-yAh-T); 6—шесть (SHAY-st); 7—семь (s-YIM); 8—босемь (VOH-sem); 9—дебять (dyEV-yat); 10—десять (dyES-et); 20—двадцать (dVAd-tset); 30—тридшать (TRIH-dtset); 40—сорок (SOR-ok); 50—пятьдесят (pyat-deSyAHT); 60—шестьдесят (shay-st-d-yeSyAHT); 70—семьдесят (SIM-d-yeset); 80—восемьдесят (VᴐSim-deset); 90—девяносто (devya-NOsta); 100—сто (stOH); 1000—тысяча (TIH-sᴇ cheh).

In the Slavic world, plurals of words are usually formed by adding the letter "ы" or "и" to the end, so the plural of *matryoshka* is *matryoshki*. Note that улица (*ulitsa;* abbreviated ул.) means "street"; проспект (*prospect;* пр.) means "avenue"; площадь (*ploschad;* пл.) means "square"; and бульвар (*bulvar;* бул.) is "boulevard." Once you get the hang of recognizing the letters, you can pronounce just about any Russian word—give it a try.

HEALTH AND SAFETY

The water in Russia is generally suspect. It is potable in small doses in much of Russia. However, in Moscow the water should be filtered or boiled, and in St. Petersburg it's a stomach-pounder; the water's infected with a bacteria called **giardia** that comes with the swampy territory. It is easily curable with U.S. medicine (buy it in advance). Without such treatment, a bout with giardia will make you feel like your intestines have declared independence and eliminated all visa requirements. Water purification (iodine) tablets, sold at camping stores, and boiling (at least10 minutes) will kill giardia. Talk to a physician before going, as contact with contaminated water is unavoidable. Preferably, drink foreign bottled water. A gamma globulin shot will lower your risk of hepatitis.

Reports of crime against foreigners are on the rise. These are largely exaggerated, but it is important to remember that as a foreigner, you are a walking target—more so in Moscow and St. Petersburg than in small towns less used to tourists. Try to be as inconspicuous as possible; if you can't look Russian, at least look poor. Your trip will be that much more pleasant if you never have to file a crime report with the local *militsia*, who will definitely not speak English and will most likely not help you. Reports of mafia warfare are scaring off tourists; unless you bring a kiosk for them to blow up, you are unlikely to be a target. However, street crime is a problem; be especially wary of groups of children, who can quickly separate a foreigner from his or her belongings.

If traveling independently, leave a copy of your itinerary with your embassy, along with your name, address, date and place of birth, and passport number. If your passport and/or visa are stolen, go to your ebassy or consulate; otherwise, you have no legal recourse.

For medical emergencies, get to St. Petersburg of Moscow immediately, and go to a clinic for foreigners (if possible, get out of the country completely). Local ambulance drivers will speak no English, and may have to be bribed to come get you. Be sure you have traveler's health insurance before you leave (ISICs, for example, provides some coverage); you can then more easily use one of the foreign clinics here, or even be evacuated if necessary.

Women should bring their own feminine hygiene supplies; although they are often available, you can never be sure. Women traveling alone will face at least the same risks and difficulties as elsewhere. If you are hassled, keep you head down and keep walking. You will probably encounter drunk men on the Metro at one time or another; they are usually irksome but harmless.

ACCOMMODATIONS AND CAMPING

Western-style **youth hostels** have begun to appear in Russia. The **Moscow Traveler's Guest House** and its affiliate, the **Holiday Hostel,** as well as the **St. Petersburg International Hostel** provide comfortable facilities in the two Russian capitals. Both arrange visas for your stay. Especially during summer, reserve well in advance. Hotels offer several classes of rooms: A "Lux," usually a two-room double with TV, phone, fridge, and bath, is the most expensive. "Pol-lux" is a one-room single or double with TV, phone, and bath. Rooms with bath and no TV, if they exist, are cheaper. The lowest price rooms are *bezudobstv* (безудобств), which means one room with a sink. Many hotels have restaurants on the ground floor, often the best eatery in town; all have at least a buffet or cafeteria—probably the worst food in town. In Russia, hot water gets turned off during part of the summer for pipe repairs, so you may have to make do with cold showers.

Another cheap option can be staying a **university** or institute dorm; many will take in foreign students for US$10 per night. The rooms are liveable, but don't expect sparkling bathrooms or reliable hot water. Make arrangements with an institute from the West.

LIFE AND TIMES

HISTORY

The Eastern Slavs, ancestors of the Russians, started migrating from central and eastern Europe to present-day Russia around the 6th century AD. They converted to

Christianity in the 9th and 10th centuries, a lengthy process which had been initi-ated by the missionaries Cyril and Methodius, who also introduced the Cyrillic alphabet. The Slavic tribes established strong trade relations with the Byzantine Empire in the south, and the Vikings in the North. Well aware of the abundance of natural resources and cheap labor that the Slavs had to offer, the Vikings set out to conquer their lands. In 862, Rurik of Jutland founded Novgorod (southeast of mod-ern Moscow) after having unified the areas under his control; this was the beginning of the Rurikid dynasty and of the Russian state. After Rurik's death, Kiev emerged as the dominant power and became the seat of the Russian Orthodox church in 988; the entire region became known as Kievan Rus ("Rus" was probably derived from the name of a powerful Kievan clan).

Kiev's Golden Age lasted several centuries. In the early 12th century, Vladimir Monomakh founded the city of Vladimir in the fertile region of Rostov-Suzdal, to the north of Kiev and Novgorod. In 1169, he moved the capital from Kiev to Vladimir, which was then the main center of economic activity. Following a general lapse in trade, the Mongol invasion of the 13th century, though brutal, restored the trading lines and brought some wealth to the region. Ivan the Great set out to make Mos-cow a dominant power; he conquered Novgorod and other neighboring principali-ties. **Ivan the Terrible** was the first ruler to have himself formally called "tsar." He conquered the neighboring Kazan, expanding his empire into the European sphere, but also alienated his generals, suffered severe skeletal deformation all his life, and killed his oldest son and heir with his own hands. A deft move that clipped the con-tinuity Russia always fell short of enjoying—Ivan's second son, **Fyodor I,** was too weak to rule the empire. His brother-in-law, **Boris Godunov,** was the actual ruler; when Fyodor died childless in 1598, Boris became tsar of Russia, thus putting an end to the Rurik dynasty. Conspiring against Godunov, the Russian *boyars* (nobles) brought forward a pretender to the throne named Dmitry, claiming that he was the son of the deceased Fyodor I. After Godunov's mysterious death, the *boyars* suc-ceeded in making **"False Dmitry"** tsar of Russia. What followed was a decade of unprecedented instability and chaos, with the boyars continually striving for more power and control over the numerous tsars. Finally, in 1613, **Mikhail Romanov** was elected tsar, thus starting the Romanov dynasty that ruled until the Bolshevik Revo-lution of 1917.

Peter the Great was the Romanov who dragged Russia into Europe. Tsar from 1682, he became known as the "Westernizer of Russia", although he was not intent on Westernization *per se*, but simply sought to ridicule and destroy those in power. He created his own elite and built a trading capital on the Baltic—he killed innumer-able workers in the process, hung the opposition, traipsed around Europe causing more damage than the average *Let's Go* traveler, killed his own son in anger, and in general precipitated a permanent crisis of cultural identity. He died in 1725, without leaving a male successor to the throne. His daughter Elizabeth reigned from 1741-61, until the advent of **Catherine the Great.** Daughter of an impoverished Prussian aristocrat, Catherine came to Russia to marry Elizabeth's nephew, Peter III. Shortly after Peter became tsar, Catherine managed to overthrow him in a coup and took over as tsarina. She raised Russia to a place equal among to European monarchies—and incited the building of the Potemkin villages (two dimensional town façades) because she wanted to see what Russia was *really* like.

Serfdom persisted in Russia up to 1861; in the late 1800s, famine, peasant unrest, and a wave of strikes culminated in the failed **1905 revolution.** Although the unfor-tunate tsar **Nicholas II** established a progressive congressional body, the *Duma*, and made attempts to address the demands of the people, World War I toppled his authority, forcing his abrupt abdication. The organizational genius of one **V. I. Lenin** then led the bloodless "coup" of October 1917: a combination of a few well placed words to **Alexander Kerensky** and the provisional government and a harmless shot from the old Aurora naval ship.

Then began the great failed experiment. After the Bolshevik revolution came the **Civil War;** the White Army backed by foreign powers struggled with Bolshevik troops. A period of social liberation followed the Red Army's victory. 1922 witnessed the birth of the **Union of Soviet Socialist Republics (USSR).** Lenin died in 1924 without naming a successor. **Joseph Stalin** succeeded in eliminating his rivals, Trotsky, Zinoviev, and Kamenev, and in 1929 became the sole leader of the Communist Party. The first wave of political executions and socialist realism (read: intellectual stifling) began soon after. The five-year economic plans, forced collectivization of Russia's farms, and the institution of Siberian labor camps formed the basis of the massive totalitarian regime headed by Joseph Stalin. Priority was given to national defense and heavy industry, which led to severe shortages of consumer goods. The numerous purges resulted in millions of casualties. The people lived in constant fear of offending the regime or the dictator. In a society full of spies and informers, there could be no trust, no lasting alliances or friendships; to survive, everyone had to live in semi-isolation.

In 1949, the Soviet Union formed the **COMECON** (Council of Mutual Economic Assistance), which incorporated all the Eastern European countries, reducing them to satellite states and linking them even closer to the Party's headquarters in Moscow. After Stalin's death in 1953, **Nikita Krushchev** emerged as the new leader of the Soviet Union with all its satellite states. In his famous "secret speech" (1956), he denounced the terrors of the Stalinist period—a political and cultural "thaw" followed in the early 1960s. In 1964, Krushchev was ousted by **Brezhnev**, who stayed in power until 1983, overseeing a period of monstrous political repression. **Yuri Andropov** and **Konstantin Chernyenko** followed him in humorously quick succession. The geriatric government finally gave way to the much younger (56-year-old) and more dynamic **Mikhail Gorbachev** in 1985. As the shedding of the aging elite consumed the political circle in Moscow, the "proletariat" (read: army) was becoming frustrated with their losses in the Afghanistan War. Gorbachev reflected this anxiety and desire to improve the deteriorating life in Russia. His political and economic reforms were aimed at helping Russia regain the status of a Super Power nation. The reforms began with the slow steps of *glasnost* (openness) and *perestroika* (rebuilding), and the state gradually turned into a bewildering hodge-podge of semi-anarchy, deepening economic crisis, and cynicism. Ironically, Gorbachev was the architect of his own demise. Despite his great popularity in the West (and the 1990 Nobel Peace Prize to show for it), discontent with his reforms and a failed right-wing coup in August 1991 led to his resignation, the dissolution of the union, and Boris **Yeltsin's** election as President of (now-sovereign) Russia. Fragments of the union have remained together under the **C.I.S.** (*Commonwealth of Independent States*) under threat of increased trade tarrifs with Russia, but other areas have gone their own way.

RUSSIA TODAY

Russia's future is uncertain. Yeltsin, while trying to construct a new Russian economy, is continually engaged in a power struggle with the Russian Parliament, which includes such figures as the right-wing nationalist Vladimir Zhirinovsky. At the same time, in the name of democracy, Yeltsin has at times assumed (or tried to assume) near-dictatorial powers. The power struggle turned violent in October 1993, when the Parliament staged a coup from inside the White House (the Parliament building in Moscow), which Yeltsin then had bombarded with tank fire. That Parliament was dissolved, and Yeltsin is once more on top, but it is almost anyone's guess what will happen next. Come and see for yourself.

FOOD AND DRINK

Although Moscow and St. Petersburg are now sprinkled with Western restaurants and Georgian cooperatives offering all kinds of delicious food options, in the smaller towns and cities, while there is plenty to eat, little of it is actually tasty. Russians look upon food for its principle value—nourishment—and are not concerned with taste. The standard hotel **dinner menu** includes *salat* (салат; salad), usually cucumbers or beets and potatoes with mayonnaise and sour cream; soup (суп), either meat or cabbage; and *kuritsa* (курица; chicken) or *myaso* (мясо; meat), often called *kutlyeti* (кутлеты; cutlets) or beefsteaks (бифштекс), a distant relative of hamburger. Dessert is *morozhenoye* (мороженое; ice cream) and coffee (кофе) or *chai* (чай; tea). Russian **cafés** (кафе) offer similar-quality food for lower prices; often the tables have no chairs. *Stolovayas* (столовая; cafeterias) are often unsanitary and should be viewed suspiciously. After a few such meals, you may want to cook for yourself.

There are essentially three ways to buy food in Russia: on the street, from a store, and at a farmer's market (where prices are high but produce fresh). The stores are subdivided into **dietas** (Диета), which sell goods for people on special diets (such as diabetics); **produkty** (Продукты), which specialize in one good or another and tend to be small; **gastronome** (Гастроном), which carry sorry-looking meat, fish, and dairy products; and **universam** (Универсам), which sell packaged goods and fruits and vegetables.

The **market** (рынок; *rynok*) in every town has abundant fruits and vegetables, butter, honey, and cheese. Wash everything before you eat it—Russian farmers use pesticides with a liberal hand. Be sure to bring all the containers you need—bags for carrying food and pots for honey; these are not provided. **Bakeries** (булочная; *bulochnaya*) have fresh black and white bread daily, and sometimes will also have tasty sweet rolls, cakes, and cookies. **Ice cream** is for sale everywhere, even in winter; in most towns you can choose between the cheap and ultra-creamy Russian variety and more expensive imported cones and bars.

If worse comes to worst, the ubiquitous **kiosks** in every town are mini-convenience stores, selling soda, juice, candy bars, and cookies; all you have to do is point at what you want. They also often sell alcohol; imported cans of beer are safe (though warm), but be wary of Russian beer and vodka labels—you have no way of knowing what's really in those bottles. Buy your booze in a Western gocery store. *Zolotoye koltso, Russkaya,* and *Zubrovka* are the best vodkas; *Stolichnaya* and *Moskovskaya* are known names, and generic brands get the job done.

Travelers are generally advised not drink the **water** in Russia. While often potable in limited doses, water cleanliness is on the decrease. It is recommended that you boil water for at least 10 minutes; for more information on water in Moscow and St. Petersburg see Health and Safety above. A final word of advice: take Pepto-Bismol and snack foods such as peanut butter, instant soup, and granola to tide you over on those days when you can't face another sour cream salad. Bon appetit!

CUSTOMS AND ETIQUETTE

With luck you will be invited into a Russian home—which, unlike the streets, are very clean; you will usually be asked to take off you shoes and will be provided with a pair of slippers (which will probably fit you better than museum *tapachki*). Russians save up all their friendliness and hospitality for home use; the people who scream at you on the street (or at least people who *would* scream at you on the street) will smile warmly and stuff you with food in their homes. Russians do not usually shake hands when greeting people; if they already know you, they may kiss you on the cheek.

██ Moscow (Москва)

Moscow is huge, apocalyptic, and compelling. Home to one in fifteen Russians (and more every day), the city throbs with energy and noise. You may not love it (you may even hate it), but you will not regret you came.

The Moscow of today is a result of the combined despotic forces of Ivan the Terrible and Uncle Joe Stalin; there is a noticeable gap of influence on the city's politics and architecture when the capital was moved to St. Petersburg. Brezhnev's faceless high-rises plow past gold-domed churches valiantly standing against the architectural onslaught of the Soviet era.

But behind the anonymous gray walls the city has a soul. The same Russians who can make riding the Metro feel like trench warfare will offer you all the food in their kitchens when you visit them at home. Russian apartments are a cultural landmark; spotless and full of books and knick-knacks; they are like pools of light at the end of the dank and filthy hallways in Moscow's crumbling buildings.

Out on the street, Moscow is exhausting and exhilarating. Haphazard and anarchic, the city is really a sprawling conglomerate of peasant villages onto which an illusion of order has been imposed. The city feels like one huge bazaar, where *mafiosi* selling Japanese televisions out of the back of a truck stand next to grandmothers offering up the potatoes and dill they've been growing at their *dachas* for the past 30 years. In Moscow, anything and everything is possible; after enough time here, the contradictions begin to seem normal. Moscow is now the world's third most expensive city and the casino capital of the world; nightclub entrance fees can be upwards of US$50. At the same time, the average pensioner earns the ruble equivalent of US$40 per month and can't afford to buy a banana. Moscow is made by contrast; Stalinist edifices make a gray backdrop to churches' and monasteries' splashes of color. And some beauty is not so hard to find; cool and peaceful parks line the eight-lane avenues where it's easy to forget you're in a city of 10 million.

Founded by Yuri Dolgoruki in 1147, Moscow was burned to the ground at least three times in its history—once by Genghis Kahn's grandson and most recently by the Russians themselves after Napoleon reached the Kremlin. Its early peak was in 1571, when it had over 100,000 citizens and was probably one of the largest cities in the world. (Unfortunately, the Crimean Tatars burnt it that same year.)

Moscow was the capital of the Russian state until 1714, when Peter the Great moved it to his newly-built "Window on the West". The city originally built up by Ivans the Great and Terrible in the 16th century did not regain its political role until 1917, when the Bolsheviks moved the capital back. Since then, it has been the focus of 50 years of foreign policy in the U.S. and NATO, and the site of some of the most theatrical political maneuvering of the 20th century.

Today free enterprise—and the Russian Mafia—are eating away at Stalin's massive Socialist carcass. Moscow is the center of change in Russia, and as such provides the visitor with a dizzying view of the country's possibilities.

ORIENTATION AND PRACTICAL INFORMATION

Moscow is laid out in a series of concentric rings, emanating from the Kremlin. The outermost "ring road" forms the city boundary, but most sights of interest to visitors lie within the inner "garden ring." **Red Square** (Красная Площадь; *Krasnaya Ploschad*) and the **Kremlin** (Кремль) mark the city center; nearby starts Moscow's popular shopping streets, **Novi Arbat** (Новый Арбат, formerly Prospect Kalinina), running west parallel to the Metro's blue lines, and **ulitsa Tverskaya** (улица Тверская), which goes north along the green line. Ul. Tverskaya was formerly called ulitsa Gorkovo; the upper half, which leads to the **Garden Ring** (Садовое Кольцо), the original limit of 19th-century Moscow, is now known as ulitsa Pervaya Tverskaya-Yamskaya. Learn Cyrillic, orient yourself by the **Metro**, and you can never get really lost. All buses and trams eventually stop at one of the stations, marked by a red neon **M**. An extensive map of Moscow, including all public transportation routes and a street index, is sold at many kiosks for less than a dollar.

See **colored insert** in this book for a map of Moscow and its Metro.

Agencies

Tourist Offices: Even in the capital city of Moscow, tourist office are mainly excursion bureaus—to find a free map of the city, a free Metro map, and a free business telephone directory, head to one of the major hotels (like the second floor of the Radisson-Slavyanka Hotel, next to M: Kievskaya) instead. **Intourservice Central Excursion Bureau,** ul. Belinskovo 4A (ул. Белинского; tel. 203 80 16 or 203 82 71, fax 200 12 43), is around the corner from the Intourist Hotel and two blocks from Red Square. A good resource center if you feel like spending lots of Western currency, but they'll be reluctant to tell you about anything payable in rubles. If you don't speak Russian, you may have to buy your out-of-town excursions here. Credit cards accepted; open daily 9am-6pm. A smaller branch is located in the Intourist Hotel. The **Moscow Excursion Bureau,** ul. Rozhdestvenka 5 (ул. Рождественка; tel. 923 89 53), behind Detski Mir. If you speak some Russian, it is your best bet for out-of-town excursions, walking tours, etc. Historic tours of Moscow plus daytrips to Vladimir and Suzdal, all for rubles. Open daily 10am-2pm and 3-6pm. Other tourist offices for hard currency include **Novoye Vremya,** Avtozavodskaya ul. 17, korpus 1 (Автозаводская ул.; tel. 274 46 94); **Panoramatour,** Okhotny Ryad 2, M: Teatralnaya (tel. 292 64 66); **Moscow Tours Limited,** Bolshoy Starodanilovdky Per. 5, #535A (tel. 954 04 31); or **VAO Tourist,** ul. Mokovaya 13 (ул. Моковая; tel. 292 12 78). **Aerotourservice Travel Company,** ul. Stroiteley 8/1 (ул. Строителей; tel. 118 23 09), offers tours to and from St. Petersburg, Zagash, Suzdal, and central Moscow, as well as transportation by car or bus. Open Mon.-Fri. 9am-6pm.

Embassies: U.S., Novinski bul. 19/23 (formerly ulitsa Tchaikovskovo; tel. 252 24 51 through 252 24 59). M: Баррикадная (Barikadnaya). Open Mon.-Fri. 9am-6pm. **Canada,** Starokonyusheni per. 23 (tel. 241 50 13 or 241 11 11). Open Mon.-Fri. 8:30am-1pm and 2-5pm. **U.K.,** nab. Sofiskaya 14 (formerly nab. Morisa Toreza; tel. 230 63 33, fax 233 35 63). Open Mon.-Fri. 9am-12:30pm and 2:30-6pm. **Australia,** Kropotkinski per. 13 (tel. 246 50 12 through 246 50 16). Open Mon.-Fri. 9am-12:30pm and 1:30-5pm. **New Zealand,** ul. Povarskaya 44 (formerly ul. Vorovskovo; tel. 290 12 77 or 290 34 85). Open Mon.-Fri. 8:30am-12:30pm and 1:30-5pm; Sept.-May 9am-12:30pm and 1:30-5:30pm. **Czech Republic,** ul. Yuliusa Fuchika 12/14 (tel. 251 05 40). Open Mon.-Fri. 8:30am-5pm. **Finland,** Kropotkinsky per. 15/17 (tel. 246 40 27). Open Mon.-Fri. 9am-1pm, 2-4pm. **Hungary,** ul. Mosfilmovskayu 62 (tel. 143 86 11 through 15). Open Mon.-Fri. 8:30am-4:30pm. **Ireland,** Grokholsky per. 5 (tel. 288 41 01). **Poland,** ul. Klimashinka 4 (tel. 255 00 17). Open Mon.-Fri. 9am-5pm.

Currency Exchange: Currency exchange (обмен валюты) places are all over Moscow. There are banks at almost every corner and ads in every English-language newspaper. The pamphlet *Moscow Express Directory*, updated every two weeks and available free in most luxury hotels, gives a list of addresses and phone numbers of many of these banks, as well as places to buy and cash traveler's checks. **Sberbank** (Сбербанк) will cash Visa, AmEx, and Thomas Cook traveler's checks, but for a commission. **Credo Bank,** main office Leantyersky Per. 10 (tel. 925 80 83), also cashes traveler's checks and deals with international money orders.

American Express: ul. Sadovaya-Kudrinskaya 21a (ул. Садовая-Кудринская; tel. 956 90 00 or 956 90 05). M: Mayakovskaya (Маяковская). Take a left out of the metro onto ul. Sadovaya-Bolshaya (ул. Садовая-Большая), which becomes ul. Sadovaya-Kudrinskaya. Travel services assistance and all banking services for cardmembers. Mail service for card and traveler's check holders. **Automatic teller machine** in lobby dispenses dollars 24hrs. Office open Mon.-Fri. 9am-5pm. **ATM express machine** also at Hotel Mezhdunarodnaya, Krasnopresnenskaya nab. 12.

Western Union: Appropriately located next to the former Marx and Engels Museum, inside the bank Vostok (Восток), ul. Marksa Engelsa 5 (ул. Маркса Энгелса), just behind the Pushkin Museum of Fine Arts. Go through the courtyard until you see Western Union signs (15 min.). On the second floor, room #213 (tel. 203 32 21 or 291 85 63). No English spoken, but filling out the usual forms is all that's necessary. Open Mon.-Fri. 9am-4pm. Also one at **Russian Credit Bank** (Российски Кредит), M: Sportivnaya. Exit to the right and it is down on the right.

United Card Service: Grafsky Per. 10/12, bldg. 2 (tel. 216 68 71 or 216 76 39). For Visa, Diner's Club, Eurocard, MC, and JCB International cardholders.

Post Offices: The main national post office is at Chistoprudnyi Bulvar 2, M: Turgenevskaya. Open Mon.-Fri. 8am-8pm, Sat. 8am-7pm, Sun. 9am-7pm. **Moscow**

Central Telegraph, ul. Tverskaya 7, a few blocks from the Kremlin, has everything needed. Look for the globe and the digital clock out front. M: Okhotny Ryad. **Poste Restante:** 103009. **International mail** there is open Mon.-Fri. 8am-2pm and 3-9pm, Sat. 8am-2pm and 3-7pm, Sun. 9am-2pm and 3-7pm. For higher prices but better guarantees, try one of the private mail services, like **Post International, Inc.,** located in the Novoe Vremya magazine building, M: Pushkinskaya (tel. 209 01 21), **DMS Mail Service** at Michurinsky Pr. 1 (tel. 939 24 73), or **DHL Express Mail** (listed below). **RGW Express,** another courier service, is located at Pogodinkaya ul.14/16, #53 (tel. 245 62 31). The **International Post Office** is located at Varshavskoye Chaussée 37a (tel. 114 46 48). A less crowded branch at **Novi Arbat 22,** near Dom Knigi. Express Mail Service 9am-noon, 1-4:30pm. Open Mon.-Fri. 8am-8pm, Sat. 8am-6pm, Sun. 10am-6pm. Poste Restante also at the **Intourist Hotel Post Office,** ul. Tverskaya 3/5. Address mail to Bострeбо-вания *(Do Vostrebovania),* K-600, Intourist Hotel, ul. Tverskaya 3/5, Moscow, Post Office at ul. Myasnitskaya 26. To mail **packages,** especially books, bring them unwrapped to the Intourist Hotel Post Office or to Moscow Central Telegraph; they will be wrapped and mailed while you wait. Open Mon.-Fri. 9am-1pm and 2-5pm, Sat. 9am-1pm and 2-4pm. But an easier and faster way to receive mail may be by fax (500R per fax received). Simply deposit 500R in order to get the fax number and come by to check.

DHL Express: Radisson-Slavyanskaya Hotel, Berezhovskaya nab 2.; M: Kievskaya (tel. 941 86 21), or at Olympic Penta Hotel, Olympisky pr. 18/1 (tel. 971 61 01) or at Mezhdunarodnaya Hotel, entrance 3, #902, Nab. Krasnopresnenskaya 12 (tel. 253 11 94 or 253 12 95), or at **Intergraphics** (see *Fax and Photocopy Services* below). **DHL Worldwide Express:** main office at Chernyshevskovo per. 3, M: Novoslobodnaya (tel. 956 10 00, fax 971 22 18). Open Mon.-Fri. 8am-5pm.

Telephones: Calling from Moscow is getting progressively easier. At **Moscow Central Telegraph** you must prepay at the counter for how long you expect to talk. You will then be given a stall number from which to dial directly, it may take 5-10 tries to get through. In order to collect your money if you do not reach your party, you must stand in line again at the same counter. Depending on the time of day, calls to the U.S. range from 2000-6000R per min. If you have an AT&T calling card, though, the procedure is much simpler. Use any local phone, tel. 155 50 42, and you will be connected to an AT&T operator. **AT&T USADirect** is available all over Russia, but you will be charged for the call to Moscow. (Traveller's Guest House should be installing satellite phones by 1995, which will also make the connection clearer.) **Telegrams** at windows 7-9. (650R per word). **Faxes** 10,800R per page. Open daily 8am-8pm. Branch office at 22 is less crowded. **International telephone cabinets** (международный телефон; *mezhdunarodni telefon)* at M: Boykovskaya (Бойковская) are much less of a wait. Major hotels have direct-dial international phone booths at exorbitant prices (1min. to the U.S. US$6-15!). International calls can also be placed from private homes (direct dial: 8+10+country code+phone number). **Local calls** require either a metal *zheton* (жетон) or a one-ruble coin: these are sold at some (not all) metro stations or kiosks for 150R. **City Code:** 095.

Fax and Photocopy Services: These are appearing all over Moscow. For a complete list, pick up a copy of *Moscow Business Telephone Guide,* free in most luxury hotels, and check under copy services listing. **Intergraphics** (Интерграфикс), ul. primeraya Tverskaya -Yamskaya 22 (1-ая Тверская-Ямская), M: Mayakovskaya or Belorusskaya (tel. 251 12 15 or 251 12 08, fax 230 22 07). Every possible business convenience all in the same place. Stamps, passport photos, color photocopies, color laser printing, and even **DHL express.** Regular photocopies for 500R per page, but price decreases for large orders. English-speaking staff. Open Mon.-Fri. 9am-6pm. AmEx, MC, Visa, EuroCard accepted. **American Print Production Store** in the Raddison-Slavyanskaya Hotel, Berezhkovskaya nab. 2, M: Kievskaya, turn right, walk past the Kievski Vokzal and the hotel is in front of you (tel. 941 87 39 or 941 87 40). Test out new Macintosh products here, or photocopy or print in every possible way, with quality results. Black & white copying 25¢ per page for 1-49 pages, 15¢ per page for 50 or more. Color copying US$4. Open daily 10am-9pm. AmEx, MC, Visa, Diners welcomed. Payment in rubles also accepted.

Transportation

Flights: Moscow has three main airports, all outside the city limits. International flights arrive at **Sheremetyevo-2** (Шереметьево-2) to the north (tel. 578 91 01, 578 71 79, or 578 56 14). The **Central Airport Station** (Центральный Аэровокзал) is located between M: Aeroport and M: Dinamo. A special airport express (экспресс) bus leaves approximately every two hours (5000R). The schedule is written up at the station. A cheaper but longer way is to take the green line to the last stop Rechnoy Vokzal (Речной Вокзал) and take the same express bus to Sheremetyevo, two terminals (1200R), no stops (20min.). Bus #511 also goes to the airport (but with stops, 1hr., 150R). Taxis will rip you off like you've never experienced, up to 100,000R, but you have no choice. This is the one reason to arrive in St. Petersburg and go to Moscow second. Most domestic flights originate at **Vnukovo** (Внуково; tel. 436 22 81), **Domodedovo** (Домодедово; tel. 323 86 56), or **Sheremetyevo-I** (tel.578 62 20). Buses link all three airports; commuter rail goes to Vnukovo and Domodedovo.

Foreign Airline Representatives:

Air France, Korovy Val 7 (tel. 237 23 25, at Sheremetievo-2 578 27 57). Open Mon.-Fri. 9am-1pm, 2-6pm.

Austrian Airlines, Krasnopresnenskaya nab. 12, 18th floor, office 1805 (tel. 253 82 68). Open Mon.-Fri. 9am-5:30pm, Sat. 9am-1pm.

British Airways, Krasnopresnenskaya nab. 12, 19th floor, office 1905 (tel. 253 24 92). Open Mon.-Fri. 9am-5:30pm. Airport office (tel. 578 29 23) open daily 10:30am-7pm.

Czechoslovak Airlines, ul. 2-Bestskaya 21/27 (tel. 250 45 71). Open Mon.-Fri. 9am-1pm, 2-5pm, Sat. 9am-noon.

Delta, Krasnopresnenskaya nab. 12, 11th floor, office 1102A (tel. 253 26 58-60). Open Mon.-Fri. 9am-5:30pm.

Finnair, Kamergersky per. 6 (tel. 292 87 88, at Sheremetiero-2 578 27 18). Open Mon.-Fri. 9am-5pm.

Lufthansa, Olimpiysky pr. 18/1, in Hotel Olympic Penta (tel. 975 25 01). Open Mon.-Fri. 9am-5:30pm, Sat.-Sun. 9am-5pm. Sheremetiero-2 (tel. 578 31 51). Open daily 11am-7:30pm, 9pm-7am.

Malev, Kamergersky Per. 6 (tel. 292 14 34). Open Mon.-Thurs. 9am-1pm, 2-5:30pm, Fri. 9am-1pm, 2-5pm.

SAS, Krasnopresnenskaya nab. 12, 20th floor, office 20 03 (tel. 253 89 88 or at Sheremetiero-2 578 27 40). Open Mon.-Fri. 8:30am-noon and 1-5:30pm, Sat. 9am-2pm.

Trains: Moscow has eight main stations, most clustered around the Metro's Ring Line. Trains to St. Petersburg and some to Estonia depart from **Leningradski vokzal** (Ленинградский Вокзал; "Leningrad station"). M: Komsomolskaya (Комсомолская). Across the street are **Kazanski vokzal** (Казанский Вокзал; "Kazan station") and **Yaroslavski vokzal** (Ярославский Вокзал; "Yaroslav station"), where the Trans-Siberian leaves (3 per week, US$250). Other stations are served by similarly named Metro stops: **Paveletski vokzal** (Павелетский Вокзал) and **Kurski vokzal** (Курский Вокзал) serve the south. **Rizhski vokzal** (Рижский Вокзал) serves Rīga, Latvia (3 per day, 16hrs.) and Estonia. Trains from Warsaw (2 per day, 22hrs.), Vilnius, Lithuania (2 per day, 18hrs.), and Prague (1 per day) arrive at **Belorusski vokzal** (Белорусский Вокзал). Trains to Ukraine, the Czech Republic, Slovakia, Bulgaria, and Romania use **Kievski vokzal** (Киевский Вокзал). **Train info:** tel. 266 90 00 through 266 90 09, or: Belorussky 251 60 93, Kazanski 264 65 56, Kievski 240 11 15, Kurski 924 57 67, Leningradski 262 91 43, Paveletski 235 68 07, Rizhski 971 15 88, Savelovski 285 58 91, Yaroslavski 221 59 14. **Intourist general info:** 262 33 42.

Public Transportation: The **Metro** is large, fast, and efficient—a work of art in urban planning. It will get you within a 15min. walk of wherever you want to be. It will be a continual reminder that indeed, 10 million people *do* live in Moscow and all 10 million of them are *always* riding the Metro. It will also impress upon you the importance of learning the Cyrillic alphabet. Remember: Вход means "entrance", Выход "exit", Выход в город "exit to the street", and Переход "passage to a different line" and often to a new station: a station which serves more than one line will generally have different names. Trains run 6am-1am (fare 150R). Rush hour is later in Russia, 9-10am and 5-6pm. Buses and trolleys cost 150R per ride; tickets available in metro station *kassi* (кассы) and sometimes from the driver. Be sure to punch your ticket when you get on, especially in the last week of the month when ticket cops are out in full force. The fine for not doing so is 10,000R. *Yedinye bilyeti* (единые билеты; "month-passes") let you ride on any form of transportation (16,500R). Buy them in the first few days of the month. Monthly metro passes (for the Metro only) are more cost-effective (9000R). Purchase either from the *kassi*. Metro maps are on the wall inside the entrance to every station. Otherwise metro maps are included on the back of the Moscow map (free in hotels) or buy one at any kiosk.

Taxis: Tel. 927 00 00, for Kutozovsky, Gruzinsky, Sadovaya, and center tel. 137 00 40, for hard currency only tel. 457 90 05. If you don't speak Russian, it's nearly impossible to get anyone to take you for rubles. Ask around for the going rate before you get in a cab, and be sure to agree on a price before you set off. Either way, you're likely to get ripped off. Taxi stands are indicated by a round sign with a green "T." Meters are purely ornamental. Many people just flag down any car and agree to a price from the start. Of course, it's a risk and requires knowledge of exact directions to the destination.

Train and Airplane Tickets: Intourtrans Main Office, ul. Griboyedova 8, bldg. 6. Turn right off Myasnitzkaya. M: Turgenevskaya. Left building is international tickets and right building is national (which *includes* Riga and Kiev, for example). Purchase tickets as far as 10 days in advance. Cheaper student rates available. Open Mon.-Fri. 9am-8pm, Sat.-Sun. 9am-7pm (usually no line on Saturday). Other offices include one on ul. Petrovka 15/13 (tel. 927 11 81, fax 921 19 96), to the right of the Bolshoi Theater. In the courtyard of building #15; enter under the archway on ul. Petrovka or in the Intourist Hotel. Same hours as main office. These offices only have limited tickets, however. Purchase same-day tickets at the appropriate train station, but be warned: there is usually a long line. Foreigners are required to purchase tickets from Intourist, but the lesser hassle and shorter lines also make buying tickets at the main office a preferable option. If you speak Russian or have a friend who does and don't mind waiting two hours, you can purchase your tickets for the cheaper Russian price at the train station. Be warned that conductors are adept at spotting foreigners and if you're caught with a non-Intourist ticket, you will likely have to pay a bribe or be otherwise harassed.

Lost Property: tel. 222 20 85 (for the Metro) and 923 87 53 (for trolleys, trams, and buses).

Other Practical Information

Media: Although one in nine Russians lives in Moscow, a statistic which makes the visitor feel greatly outnumbered, there is a large and growing foreign community. To cater to this audience are two free daily English-language newspapers easy to find in hotels and restaurants across the city. *The Moscow Times*, most widely distributed and read, and *The Moscow Tribune;* both have foreign and national articles, sports news, and the like for news-starved travelers, but more importantly they both have weekend sections (Sat. during the year, Fri. during the summer) which list exhibitions, theatrical events, and English-language movies of note. The *Moscow Business Telephone Guide* and *What and Where in Moscow*, both free, are excellent informational resources if you don't want to shell out US$25 for *Information Moscow* (useful only if you are actually living here), published quarterly. For housing and job opportunities the two free dailies are most useful. Foreign magazines like *Time* and *Newsweek* or *The International Herald Tribune* (US$2) are available in Western supermarkets and major hotels. To get week- or two-week-old magazines for a cheaper ruble rate, check at some of the stands at the bottom of Tverskaya near the Kremlin.

Laundromat: Unless you want to shell out megabucks for a dry cleaner, there are no laundromats in Moscow. **Traveller's Guest House** will do your laundry for 6000R per load. Otherwise, your bathtub is the only option. Bring your own detergent, buy it for a high price at a Western goods supermarket, or happen upon the random kiosk which stocks Tide for a reasonable 3000R. In summer 1994, a kiosk in front of Delhi Restaurant (see page 522) had a large stock.

Medical Assistance: European Medical Center, Gruzinski per. 3, korpus 2 (tel. 253 07 03 or 229 65 36). French joint venture offering walk-in medical care for hard currency (US$76 per visit, students US$61). Open Mon.-Fri. 9am-6pm. **Euro-medical Club/Athens Medical Center** provides emergency medical assistance. Michurinsky pr. 6 (tel. 143 23 87 or 143 25 03). The **American Medical Center** (tel. 256 82 12 or 256 33 66) also has a well-stocked pharmacy and provides 24-hr. emergency assistance. Located at Shchmitovsky Proezd 3. M: Ulitsa 1905 goda, walk down ul. 1905 goda then turn right on Shchmitovsky; the AML entrance is in an alley on the left.

Dental: Beiker Dental Clinic, Kuznetsky Most 9 (tel. 923 53 22), open Mon.-Fri. 8am-6pm, is for hard currency and rubles. The **Tourist's Clinic** (tel. 254 43 96) is located at Gruzinsky Proezd 2. **Intermedservice** provides dental care. Located in the Hotel Intourist, ul. Tuerskaya 3/5, 20th floor #2030-2031 (tel. 203 86 31).

24-Hour Pharmacies: ul. Krasnaya Presnya 4 (tel. 252 35 84), pr. Mira 71 (tel. 281 11 24), or Leningradsky Pr. 74 (151 28 81). With hard currency, go to **Vita,** ul. Poklonnaya 6 (tel. 249 78 18), or in Hotel Pulman Iris, Korovinskoye Chaussée 10 (tel. 488 82 65).

Emergencies: Don't have one. **Ambulance:** tel. 03. **Fire:** tel. 01. **Police:** tel. 02. There is little legal recourse if you have an emergency. Try the above centers for medical emergencies; call your embassy for passport and visa problems; give up on legal retaliation: there is a number to report offenses *by* the police (tel. 299 11 80, no coins needed from pay phones). Also try the **U.S. Embassy's emergency number** (tel. 252 24 51). **International SOS:** tel. 120 52 51; to trace people in hospitals (free) tel. 255 00 06; **lost children** tel. 232 07 22. The **Medical Evacuation** (with *Delta Consulting*) number is 299 65 36.

ACCOMMODATIONS

Moscow is a unique city. Interested in the dusty furniture of long-dead writers? Many styles are available for viewing. Want an American candy bar? Take seven steps to the next kiosk. A loaf of bread? Mere pennies for the asking. Ah, a place to live, you say? Cheap, comfortable lodgings for a few nights? Let's see, there's that one place near Prospect Mira...

Suffice it to say that the concept of budget accommodations for student travelers has yet to arrive in Moscow—nor does it appear to be on the horizon. There are good accommodations to be had, but options are slim, so in summer, reservations are a must. And if you don't speak any Russian, well...

Traveller's Guest House, Bolshaya Pereyaslavskaya 50 (Большая Переяславская; tel. 971 40 59, fax 280 76 86, e-mail tgh@glas.apc.org). M: Prospect Mira, walk north along pr. Mira and go right on Banny Pereulok (Банный Переулок), the third right turn and left at the end of the street. The Guest House is the white, 12-story building across the street; take the elevator to the 10th floor. If you are arriving in Moscow speaking no Russian and knowing no Muscovites, the TGH will be all you'll ever need. And even if you do have some connections, the Guest House is a great place to meet other travelers, get tips, and find companions (and buy tickets) for that Trans-Siberian Railroad trip you might make. There is also a full-service travel agency, providing visa support, train, and plane tickets both within Russia and to other destinations in Eastern Europe, and tourist info for guests and anyone who stops by. The English-speaking staff is helpful and enthusiastic. The Guest House has kitchen facilities, a laundry service, and a common room with TV and phone. Dorm beds US$15 per night. Singles US$30. Doubles US$35. Reservations are a must, especially in the summer (reservations can also be made in Hong Kong, see Russia Essentials page 505 for the address).

Prakash Guesthouse, ul. Profsoyuznaya 83 (ул. Провсоюзная; tel. 334 25 98). M: Belyaovo (Беляюго), several stops beyond Oktyabrskaya (Октябрьская) on the orange line. From the center, take the exit nearest the first car of the train, and then go all the way to the left, exiting on the left side of the *perehod*. The guest-house is one block up on the right (they can meet you at the Metro). Run by Indians, this guesthouse is a renovated dormitory and is the only place in Moscow for Indian food. Singles US$30 (payable in dollars or rubles). Doubles US$40. Both with shower and toilet. Telephone for local calls in each room. Breakfast US$5, dinner US$10. Movies—Indian and American—every night. Open 7am-11pm; call ahead if you are arriving later or earlier.

Tsentralnaya Gostinitsa (Центральная Гостиница; "Central Hotel"), ul. Tverskaya 10 (tel. 229 89 57). M: Okhotny Ryad (Охотный Ряд), then walk up Tverskaya. Right next door to Pizza Hut, this hotel has as yet escaped renovation and so is still charging Soviet-era prices. Ideally located, it's your standard Russian hotel, with floor women to keep your key and a guard downstairs. Reception open 24 hrs. All rooms have a sink, but no bath or toilet; these are in the hallway. Rooms are clean and well-lit, with phone and TV. Singles the ruble equivalent of US$30. Doubles US$45.

FOOD

Eating out in Moscow is a luxury mainly enjoyed by wealthy foreigners and the new Russian elite. Meals are outrageously expensive and quality is no better than in the provinces; the capital's *bifsteaki* certainly would never have lured Chekhov's three sisters. There are, of course, a few exceptions, but everybody knows them so reservations are a must—simply make a round of calls at noon to secure a table for that evening. Alternately, adopt an early eating schedule; Russians tend to come later and linger until closing making a meal an extended social outing, although this is becoming somewhat less common as the concept of business meals enters into Russian life. Restaurants with prices listed in dollars usually accept either credit cards or rubles; dollars are no longer legal tender for such transactions. This same law also decrees that rubles must be acceptable everywhere, opening Western-goods supermarkets to anyone who can afford them. If you're going for ethnic fare, Georgian is usually best—both tasty and cheap. Furthermore many of these restaurants were cooperatives from the beginning, which means service is usually efficient. If you do go Russian, make sure that you're getting a *chisti stol* (clean table—without a large assortment of appetizers for which you will pay dearly). **Cafés**, which are substantially cheaper than restaurants, often serve even better food—offering one or two well-prepared dishes rather than a selection of mediocre ones; they are also much faster, less dark, and less formal. **Fast food stands** selling hot dogs, hot pizza, and Pepsi guard almost every street corner—some are quite good, others may not be so kind to your stomach. And then, of course, there is always ice cream, rain or shine, summer or winter. So don't despair at the dingy local joint and its "cutlet"; you didn't come here for the food anyhow.

Foreign Restaurants

Patio Pizza, ul. Volkhonka 13a (ул. Волхонка; tel. 201 50 00), directly opposite the Pushkin Museum of Fine Arts. M: Kropotkinskaya. This place rocks, and everybody know it—come early (before 7pm, when there's a line). Spacious and light and the service is impeccably fast. Checkered red and white tablecloths go well with the international clientele, but it's not the buzzing atmosphere that brings everyone here—it's the food and prices. Delicious thin crust pizzas and a scrumptious array of desserts will fill your tummy and please your taste buds, but without lightening your wallet excessively. Well-stocked all-you-can-eat salad bar (at last) US$6. 28cm pizzas US$5-15 (most are US$6). Lasagna US$6. Italian wines from US$7. Chocolate mousse or sinful chocolate nutcake US$4. Open daily noon-midnight. AmEx, Visa, and MC accepted.

Santa Fe, ul. Mantulinskaya 5/1 (ул. Мантулинская; tel. 256 14 87). M: Ulitsa 1905 goda. A hefty walk—exit onto ulitsa 1905 goda from Metro and follow it straight to the Mezhdunarodny, where you will turn right. The restaurant is on your left. Packed nightly, this large restaurant is one of the only places to get good American food for prices you'd pay in the States. The adobe colored New Mexican decor and bustling foreignness of this place make it a yummy oasis even for the budget traveler—splurge for your one night out. Fast service with a smile. Reservations a must. Black bean soup US$4. Cajun burger US$10. Vegetable pasta US$10. Large desserts US$6-10. Open noon-midnight.

American Bar and Grill, Sadovaya Triumfalnaya ul. (tel. 250 95 25 or 250 79 99), directly opposite M: Mayakovskaya. This place is almost always packed, and because no reservations are allowed, the wait can be as long as two hours. It's worth it. Despite the low-ceilinged *faux*-American decor (cowboy hats hang from the ceiling), the menu and prices are truly American. A good place for large groups and noisy fun, and if you have to wait, the bar at the entrance is a scene itself. New England clam chowder US$4. Chips and salsa US$3. BBQ baby back ribs US$12. NY style cheesecake US$6. Bud US$3. Real American breakfast served daily 4am-11am. French toast with maple syrup US$5. Open 24 hrs.

Trenmos Bistro Bar, ul. Ostozhenka 1/9 (ул. Остоженка; tel. 202 57 22). Across the street from M: Kropotkinskaya. A more affordable, less frequented second location to the main TRENMOS restaurant at Komsomolsky pr. 21 (tel. 245 12 16). Although this pleasant bistro has a French chef, the name (which stands for Trenton (New Jersey/Moscow) and the founders are all-American, as is the menu. Juicy cheeseburger US$7, spaghetti marinara US$5, spinach lasagna US$6, mushroom and ham pizza US$7. Come here for a relaxing, elegant evening meal and then head for the more hectic Trenmos bar next door. Weekly bar events concocted by "crazy Zeegy" can lower beer prices—if you've got the right name on the right day. Restaurant open noon-11pm. Bar open 5pm-1am.

Delhi (Дели), ul. Krasnaya Presnya 23-b (tel. 255 17 66). M: ul. 1905 goda (ул. 1905 года). Turn left as you exit the station, heading toward the Stalinist tower at the end of the avenue. Next to the Olimp (Олимп) sports store, in the blond-brick block of stores. Gracious service, tasty meats, and iced drinks make this a luxurious oasis. A refreshing number of vegetarian options. Menu in Russian, Urdu, and English. Show up at noon for lunch or reserve for dinner; specify that you want to eat in the ruble room, to the right when you enter. Both rooms have the same menus with vastly differing prices. Chicken Landoori US$18 or 7500R. Spicy chick peas US$4 or 5000R. Lamb curry US$11 or 7900R. Open noon-5pm, 7-11pm. Credit cards accepted in the dollar room only.

Restaurant Praga, corner of ul. Arbat and ul. Novi Arbat. M: Arbatskaya. This mammoth, labyrinthine building could lose you fast—the restaurant is on the fourth floor. An elegant dining experience, this restaurant allegedly serves Czech nourishment, but the menu resembles most Russian ones. Chicken kiev 13,904R. Beef stroganoff 12,474R. But it's not the main course the budget traveler will crave; creator of the infamous "Praga" chocolate tort sold all over Moscow, the bakery to the right of the restaurant sells scrumptious goodies for a few rubles. A stand out front offers delicious chocolate eclairs daily for a mere 600R. Eat one on your way down the Arbat and take a few home. Restaurant open 11am-11pm.

Baku-Liban (Баку Ливан), ul. Tverskaya 24. M: Mayakovskaya. Wait in line for *schwarma* (2500R) and other middle eastern delicacies for deliciously low prices at the stand-up café on the right side. On the left, upstairs, is an elegantly set restaurant of the same name (tel. 299 85 06) which serves *tabborleh* (US$6), *hummus* (US$7), falafel (US$6), and pricier plates entitled "With love from Lebanon." Open daily 11am-5pm and 6-11pm. Credit cards accepted at the restaurant.

Aztec, in the Hotel Intourist, ul. Tverskaya 3/5, 20th floor (tel. 956 84 89). M: Okhotny Ryad. If the super-friendly service and good Latin American food don't entice you, the superb view will. The one large window of this tiny two-story restaurant looks out over Moscow—count the Stalinist buildings to rate the view. Upstairs has the view and romantic music, downstairs is good for a quick snack or a margarita. Nachos US$7. Chicken burrito US$15. Cheese enchilada US$13. Sunday brunch with complimentary cocktail 10am-3pm. Restaurant open 2-4hrs.

Rocky's (Рокки'с), Kuznetski Most 7 (Кузнетский Мост; tel. 921 25 29). Yet another oasis for homesick Americans—this one's a bar/bar 'n' grill, complete with posters of Stallone and loud American pop music. Some of the waitstaff speaks English. Fish and chips US$11. *Chile con carne* US$10. Deluxe burgers US$8. Pint of beer US$5, half-pint US$3. Open daily 11am-midnight. Come hang out with expats—and a healthy dose of seeming Russian *mafiosi*.

Moscow Bombay, ul. Nemirovicha-Danchenko 3 (Немировича-Данченко). Just off ul. Tverskaya. M: Pushkinskaya or Okhotny Ryad (tel. 292 97 31). The red carpeting, small tables, and plants should be familiar. Menu in English reveals vegetarian options in this well-advertised establishment. Veggie samosa US$7. Tandoori chicken US$8. *Naan* US$2. Open daily 12:30-3:30pm and 6-11pm. Reservations recommended.

La Cantina (Ла Кантина; tel. 292 53 88) ul. Tverskaya on the right of the Intourist Hotel. M: Okhotny Ryad. The small booths, long bar, and especially the mural of the "Moscow honky-tonk" all spell a carefully designed Mexican restaurant with a Russian flavor. Popular with tourists, who can check the bulletin board for upcoming events. Nachos and chili US$6. Large chicken enchiladas a whopping US$12. Open 11am-11pm.

Spanish Bar, Hotel Moskva, Manezhnaya Ploschad. Two rooms; one on the first floor, one on the second. Real Spanish food at American prices (pay in dollars or with credit card). Appetizers US$2-5. Omelette US$5. *Paella* for two US$28. Downstairs open noon-5pm, upstairs open 5pm-midnight. Visa, MC, and AmEx.

Italian Bar, ul. Arbat 49. Although the restaurant itself serves pricey fare, you can have a seat at the snack bar outside and watch the hordes tramp past as you enjoy a cappuccino and sandwich in the shade. Beer US$4. Cappuccino US$4. Sandwich US$4. Open 11am-11pm. Credit cards accepted.

Restaurant San Marco, ul. Arbat 28 (tel. 291 70 89). A calm, neatly decorated restaurant which seems an oasis compared to the bustling street it's on. Yummy pizzas described in English, Italian, and Russian are devoured hungrily by a mostly touristy crowd. Pizza margherita US$6. Pizza with sausage US$8. *Rigatoni* with ham US$10. Credit cards accepted. Open daily noon-11pm.

Foreign Cafés and Fast Food

McDonald's (Макдоналдс, not that you need the Cyrillic to recognize it), ul. Bolshaya Bronnaya 29, on Pushkin Square. M: Pushkinskaya. You can't miss the golden arches. This centrally-located fast-food machine is a model of American efficiency—even so, it's always packed mostly with Russians lining up for a hamburger and *kartofel fri* that taste just like they do back home, wherever home is. Caution: filling is hot here too. Big Mac 3600R, large fries (Большая порция картофеля-фри) 2500R. Cheeseburger 200R. Less crowded but missing the unique ambience of the central location, two other McDs are at ul. Arbat 50/52 (M: Smolenskaya) and Gaznetny per. 17/9, near Central Telegraph (M: Okhotny Ryad). There is relative calm until 2pm, when Russians tend to eat.

Kombi's, with locations at 46-48 Prospect Mira near the Traveller's Guest House, Tverskaya ul. 4, M: Teatralnaya, and ul. Tverskaya-Yamskaya 2 off ul. Tverskaya at M: Mayakovskaya. A clean Western-style sandwich shop with subs (3500-5000R), salads (1500-2800R), milkshakes (2100R). English menu. Open daily 10am-10pm.

Rostik's (Ростик'с), second floor of GUM department store, at the end nearest Kazan Cathedral. Moscow's answer to Kentucky Fried Chicken, only here the birds are roasted. Cheaper than McDonald's, and no sour cream or *Geets* in sight. Two pieces of chicken with roll 3200R. Three pieces 6000R. Sixteen chicken pieces 26,000R. Fries 1000R, shakes 1400R. The menu is in Russian and English; order and pay at one of the *kassas* and then go get your food. Takeout, too. Open 10am-8pm.

Pinguin, ul. Arbat 36, as well as Okhotny Ryad 2, Nikolskaya 4/5, Novi Arbat 13 and 28, and Leninsky pr. 37. A Soviet-Swiss joint ice cream venture which arrived as one of the first to start up in Moscow. Remarkably low prices for exotic flavors such as kiwi and orange. One scoop 500R. Open daily 10am-8pm.

Pizza Hut (Пицца Хат), Kutuzorsky pr. 17 (M: Pushkinskaya or Okhotny Ryad). Except for the two guards outside the door and the upscale interior, Pizza Hut is comfortingly similar, complete with requisite salad bar and American customers. The riff-raff grab a slice at the slice bar on the street but the folks over here aren't quite so adept at keeping the slices fresh and warm. One slice 3000R, glass of Pepsi 1000R. Inside, a small cheese is US$4.50, a medium veggie US$10.50, and a slice of good ol' apple pie US$1.50. Open 11am-10pm. Slice bar open 11am-8pm. Credit cards accepted.

RUSSIA

Art Café Cappuccino (Арт Кафе Капучино; tel. 290 14 98), 12 Suvorovsky bul. M: Arbatskaya. One of the true European cafés in Moscow, appropriately situated off one of the city's oldest leafy boulevards. This light café, bedecked with interesting art for sale, serves cheap pizzas, superb Italian ice cream and, of course, cappuccinos. Very hip. Pizza *al prosciutto* US$5. Pizza "Sofia Loren" US$6. Cappuccino US$2.

Grill Chicken (Курия Гриль), Sadko Arcade. M: Ulitsa 1905 goda and then a 45min. walk to the river and right along the embankment. Designed as a true American mall, this arcade, which apart from this lone chicken is lined with expensive foreign restaurants and Swiss bakeries, can really only be reached by car. If you are in this post-apocalyptic what-is-Moscow-coming-to land, this is the one place you can easily afford, and it's really good. Neon yellow booths and foursomes of teenagers create the appropriate backdrop to this fast-food place that knows what fast food is. One half of a juicy, large grilled chicken only 6000R. Fries 1800R. Swiss roll 400R. Half-liter of light beer only 1200R.

Baskin Robbins, all over Moscow—on the Arbat, at the Hotel Rossiya, and in bright pink kiosks dotting the city. The not-always-thirty-one flavors are losing their appeal here, due mostly to the high prices and influx of other Western ice cream. But the familiar BR taste is still there, and darn good. One tiny scoop is a whopping 2000R. Open daily 10am-9pm.

Gyros Express (Джайро Экспресс), ul. Gertsena 15 (ул. Герцена). This stand-up café serves its namesake dish and tasty croissant sandwiches (5000R). A gyro sandwich 7500R. A very cold cake (a serious rarity) 1300R. Open Mon.-Sat. 10am-10pm. Sun. 11am-10pm.

Burger Queen (Бургер Квин), Suvorovsky bul. 25 (now Nikitsky bul., Суворовский Бульвар; tel. 291 32 62). A small fast-food joint with lower prices than McDs, this chain is mostly frequented by Russians. Hamburger 1300R. Fries 1600R. Double cheeseburger 2500R. Open daily 10am-10pm.

Italian Dream, on the first floor of GUM. This is a small, by-the-slice pizza joint with a few stand-up tables. The pizza isn't exactly what you'd find in Naples, but it's more authentic than what's sold on the streets. Plain slice 2900R. With ham 3500R. Small Coke 1500R. Open daily 8am-8pm.

Copacabana Café, second floor of GUM. It calls itself Brazilian, but the food is standard quasi-foreign café fare: hot sandwiches, some salads, all 3500-4500R. Ice cream sundaes 2800R. Notable for its breakfast fare. Open 8am-8pm.

Café Kitaiskoy Kykhnoy (Кафе Китайской Кухной; "Café of Chinese Cooking"), ul. Krasnaya Presnya 34. M: Ulitsa 1905 goda. Turn left from the Metro; it's on the left, marked by yellow lettering that lights up at night. A small, dark café that looks just like so many across the city. The difference is that it serves Chinese food, very cheap. Your best bet for the menu (only some of it is translated into English) is to look at what the Russian customers get and point. Fried emperor's chicken 6000R. Boiled rice 500R. Dumplings 5500R. Open daily 10am-10pm.

Georgian Restaurants

Guria, pr. Komsomolski 7 (tel. 246 03 78). M: Park Kultury. Walk down Komsomolski pr.; the café is located at the corner of ul. Timura Frunze and Komsomolski pr. opposite the Church of St. Nicholas of the Weavers. Walk through a courtyard to the left of the building to enter this homey restaurant that serves delicious Georgian fare for some of the lowest prices in the city. As a result, it's one of the hottest eateries for both locals and foreigners in the know. A vegetarian meal of *lobio* (beans), *khachapuri,* salad, and Georgian yogurt comes to 10,000R. *Satsivi* (turkey in walnut sauce) 6000R. *Khachapuri* 2000R. Menu in English. Bring your own drinks. Open daily 11am-11pm.

U Pirosmani (У Пиросмани), pr. Novodevichi 4 (tel. 247 19 26), across from the Novodevichi Convent (giving it one of Moscow's best view). M: Sportivnaya (Спортивная), turn left out of the Metro and walk straight until you see the pond on the left; the restaurant will be on your left. Specializing in delicately spiced Georgian cuisine, a cooperative above the rest for its flavorful dishes served with panache. Menu on a chalkboard at the entrance; ask the waiter to decipher. *Lobio* US$3. *Khachapuri* US$1. *Baklazhany* US$4. A bottle of Georgian wine US$12.

Open daily noon-4:30pm, 6-10:30pm. Dinner reservations a must: this is the place most foreign Moscow inhabitants in search of good Georgian food come to.

Mziuri, Arbat 42 (tel. 241 96 51). Downstairs inside the Georgian cultural center; tasty meals in an elegant setting. Despite its dark, fancy interior and prime tourist location, a meal here won't break your budget. Red *lobio* 5000R. *Khachapuri* 8000R. Veal *shashik* 6900R. *Lavah* 500R. Open 11am-11pm.

Uzbekistan (Узбекистан), ul. Neglinnaya 29 (tel. 924 60 53). M: Tsvetnoi Bulvar (Цветной Бульвар) or Kuznetski Most (Кузнецкий Мост). A hangout for homesick Uzbeks, Kazakhs, and Tadzhiks; also popular with tourists. Authentic Uzbek decor—enough to pretend you've left Moscow for the evening. Salads 6000-8000R. *Lagman,* a meat and vegetable soup, 5800R. *Plov* (pilav) 8500R. Try *tkhumdulma* (boiled egg with a fried meat patty), followed by *shashlyk* ("shish kebab") Uzbek-style (18,000R). Try the Uzbek bread, baked on the premises. Open daily noon-11pm. Last entry 11:30pm. Reservations necessary at dinner time. Women may not feel comfortable alone in this area at night.

Aragvi (Арагви), ul. Tverskaya 6 (tel. 229 37 62 noon-7pm). M: Okhotni Ryad (Охотный Ряд). Entrance on pl. Sovetskaya; turn right off Tverskaya. Georgian cuisine; specialities include *satsivi* (cold chicken in walnut sauce, 7000R), *kharcho* (spicy soup), and caviar. Russian singers in the evenings give the mosaic-covered restaurant even *more* ambience. A full meal will lighten your wallet considerably. Small menu. Open daily noon-11pm.

Russian Restaurants

Café Margarita (Кафе Маргарита), ul. Malaya Bronnaya 28 at the corner of Maly Kosikhinski (Малый Козихинский; tel. 299 65 34). The door is carefully and artistically painted. Super-trendy café opposite the Patriarch's Ponds, where Bulgakov's *The Master and Margarita* begins. Enjoy the speciality of the house, tomatoes stuffed with garlic and cheese, or just sip a cup of tea and watch the artsy crowd gossip and smoke away the afternoon. Live piano music nightly (cover 3000R). *Lobio* 5000R, *blini* with mushrooms 7000R. Open daily 2-5pm and 6pm-midnight.

Mkhat (Мхат), Kamergersky proezd 3, just off ul. Tverskaya, entrance 3, second floor (tel. 229 91 06). M: Okhotny Ryad (Охотный Ряд). Similarly named to the well-known theater, this tastefully decorated restaurant serves decent Russian food at correspondingly higher prices. Carefully prepared Chicken Kiev costs 16,000R. The well-stocked bar is open late. Beer (330gr.) 5000R. Open noon-3am.

Café Romance (Кафе Романс), ul. Krasnya Presnya 36 (tel. 255 59 11). M: Ulitsa 1905 goda. A tiny, intimate restaurant with elegantly set tables for two—a decor designed to go with the name. A slightly larger menu than usual but for reasonable prices. Spaghetti with mushroom sauce 5000R. Chicken Kiev only 6000R. Open 11am-11pm.

Zaydi i Poprobuy (Зайди и Попробуй), pr. Mira 124 (tel. 286 75 03 or 286 81 65). M: Alekseyevskaya (Алексеевская), then take the trolley bus a couple of stops north. Entrance on ul. Malaya Moskovskaya (Малая Московская). The name of this establishment means "Drop In & Try," and drop in you do, since the restaurant is below street level, through a very dim entrance hall. The interior is pleasant with bright tablecloths and a mural on the walls. The food is your favorite Russian cuisine, well-prepared. *Borscht* 1150R, entrees 10,000R. Open daily 1-11pm.

Hotel Moskva (Москва), Manezhnaya pl., next to Red Square. Restaurant on the third floor. *Shvedski stol* ("buffet smorgasbord") especially popular with the bureaucrats across the street at Gosplan. All the *borscht,* beet salad, fried potatoes, and *cutlyeti* you can eat for 10,000R. Open daily for breakfast (5000R, 8-10:30am) and lunch (noon-4pm). There is also a regular á la carte menu at lunchtime. *Borscht* 2000R. *Shashlik* 8000R. Chicken *cutlyeti* 3000R.

Russian Cafés

Café Russkaya Kykhnya (Кафе Русская Кухня). On the second floor of GUM department store, at the St. Basil's end. The name means "Russian kitchen", and that's definitely what this is. But the café is one of the nicest serving Russian food you'll find—clean and bright, with marble floors and fake ivy on the walls. Good food at good prices, too. *Borscht* 755R, pizza 1200R, mushroom omelette 2000R. Open 8am-8pm.

Blinchiki (Блинчики). Not a café, but a stand off Tverskaya on Strasnoy Bulvar (Страстной Бульвар) across from the Kinoteatr Rossiya (Кинотеатр Россия) and diagonally opposite McDonald's. Scrumptious apricot-filled *blini* ("Russian crêpes") 400R. There's a long line at midday, but that means this is the real thing. Open daily 10am-8pm.

Pizza (Пицца). Right next to Blinchiki, this also has long lunch lines, and cheap *authentic* pizza, baked on the premises. Slice 1200R. Whole pie 5300R. Open daily 11am-7pm.

Café Oladi (Оладьи), ul. Pushkinskaya 15, just past the Tchaikovsky Conservatory. The namesake dish are small, sweet pancakes (400R). They come with jam or sour cream. Order at the counter and then stand at one of the tall tables to eat. Yum. Open daily 9am-7pm.

Blini (Блины), ul. Myasnitskaya 14/12 (ул. Мясницкая), two blocks north of Lubyanka Ploschad. An unassuming little Russian café; look for the vertical "Блины" sign outside. Pancakes with chocolate, vanilla, or raspberry sauce (or fairly good imitations thereof) 350R. Open Mon.-Sat. 10am-6pm.

Aist (Аист), ul. Malaya Bronnaya 1/8 (tel. 291 66 92). M: Pushkinskaya. Hearty soups and appetizers make this a cozy spot to sample solid Russian food. Wraparound red velvet decor simulates a '70s opium den and large secluded booths make this better for large groups. *Lobio* (лобио) 9000R. *Plov* (плов) 8800R. Open daily noon-10pm. Credit cards accepted.

Bistro (Бистро), ul. Rozhdistvenka (ул. Пождиственка) right next to the Savoy Hotel. A clean, bright Russian eatery. Cafeteria-style layout. *Borscht* 1800R. *Pelmeni* 1800R. Pork chops 3500R. Open daily 10am-8pm.

Krisis Genre, corner of per. Ostrovskovo (пер. Островского) and Bolshaya Vesinaya per. 22/4 (Большая Весиная пер.; tel. 243 86 05). M: Kropotkinskaya. Walk through the courtyard—it's the third door on the right. A small European-style café near the Arbat catering to pensive, artsy types—bring your *Crime and Punishment*. Bloody Mary 3000R. American coffee 1000R. Open Tues.-Sun. noon-1am.

Markets

Cheaper than the Western supermarkets, in summer these are the best bets for fresh fruit and vegetables, as Georgians, Armenians, Uzbeks, and peasants from all over cart their finest produce to Moscow. There is lots of fresh produce for sale right on the street, but a visit to a market is worth it for the visual experience—sides of beef, piles of tomatoes, peaches, and grapes, jars of glowing honey, and huge pots of flowers all crowded together.

Unfortunately, the **Central Market,** next to the Old Circus, is closed for reconstruction for the next two years. But enterprising Russians are hawking their wares on the street nearby. M: Tsvetnoi Bulvar (Цветной Бульвар) and turn right.

The alternative is the **Rizhski Market** at M: Rizhskaya (Рижская). Exit the Metro and keep turning left until you see it. Otherwise, impromptu markets spring up around Metro stations; some of the best are at M: Turgenevskaya (Тургеневская), Kuznetski Most (Кузнетский Мость), Aeroport (Аэропорт), and Baumanskaya (Бауманская). In general people appear with their goods around 10am, and leave by 8pm, though a few stragglers stick around until 10ish.

Supermarkets

The number of Western-style supermarkets is expanding monthly as the need to use them decreases. Many of the goods sold here can be found in kiosks and in even smaller combination markets selling Russian and Western foods, but little beats the convenience of knowing you can find everything you need all at the same place. All of these supermarkets accept rubles, dollars, and credit cards, but since the exchange rate is usually less than favorable, it is often more convenient to pay in hard currency. Listed below are a few of the largest—there is likely a small formerly named "dollar store" in your neighborhood.

RUSSIA

Sadko Arcade, behind Krasnya Presnya park along the river. M: Ulitsa 1905 goda. A 45-min. walk from the Metro, this massive supermarket is convenient only if you have a car. Surprisingly, some of the best prices in town and certainly one of the largest selections. Open 10am-8pm.

The Arbat Irish House, 11 Novi Arbat, M: Arbatskaya, is a supermarket clothing electronics store with an Irish Bar to boot. A well-stocked Russian supermarket, **Novoarbatski Gastronom,** flanks the Irish House on the left. Irish House open Mon.-Sat. 9am-9pm and Sun. 10am-8pm.

Garden Ring Supermarket, ul. Bolshaya Sadovaya 1 (tel. 209 15 73), Leninsky Pr. 113/1, and ul. Serafimovicha. Stocks foreign publications from *Playboy* to *Rolling Stone* to *Newsweek,* with a lot in between. Video rental also. Open 9am-8pm.

Global USA Supershop, ul. Usacheva 35 (Усачева). M: Sportivnaya (Спортивная). Stocks electronics and clothing, but some food too. Open daily 10am-10pm.

Stockmann, M: Paveletskaya (Павелетская), is a Finnish grocery emporium for credit cards only. Prices are in dollars. Get out on the side of the street opposite the metro station and walk left two blocks; past the *blini* (блины) stand on your left and behind the white curtains is the glassed-in store. Moscow Information available here (US$25). Open daily 10am-8pm.

Colognia, Bolshaya-Sadovaya 5/1. Part of the Peking Hotel. Open daily 10am-8pm.

Sweet, Sweet Way, ul. Tverskaya between Gastronom #1 and Pizza Hut. M: Okhotny Ryad or Pushkinskaya. A sweet, sweet tooth's delight. Filled with candies of every sort, sold by weight. Gummy bears 17,460R per kilo. Open Mon.-Sat. 10am-2pm, 3-9pm, Sun. 10am-2pm, 3-7pm.

Gastronom #1, ul. Tverskaya 14, is Moscow's most famous grocery store, which tends to reflect the economic situation of the times. These days the shelves are packed with foreign goods but the lines are long as the prices are lower than in the hard currency supermarkets. Even if you don't buy anything, this landmark is worth a long gaze inside; remodeled in 1901, it is endowed with stained glass, high ceilings, and chandeliers. Open Mon.-Fri. 8am-8pm, Sat. 8am-7pm.

SIGHTS

Although Moscow proper is enormous, the city's sights are concentrated in its oldest region, which is surrounded by the Garden Ring Road. Here are most of Moscow's art and history museums, as well as its prettiest parks and neighborhoods. However, the city's strange history is reflected in its sights: the visitor may choose among many 16th-century churches and monasteries or among Soviet-era museums, but little in between. And recent political upheaval has taken its toll on the latter; museums such as the **Lenin Museum** and the **Marx and Engels Museum** are closed indefinitely while their historical significance is reassessed.

Although Moscow is the current center of political and cultural activity in Russia, its sights suffer from the 200 years during which St. Petersburg was the capital. Moscow has no grand palaces, fewer great art museums, and not as many artists and writers it can claim as native sons. Still, there is plenty to do and see, and, with a little grit and a lot of humor, much to enjoy.

Red Square (Красная Площадь; Krasnaya Ploschad)

There is nothing red about it; *krasnaya* meant "beautiful" long before the Communists co-opted it. It is a 700-meter long lesson in Russian history and culture: on one side the **Kremlin,** at once the historical and religious center of Russia and the seat of the Communist Party for 70-odd years; on the other, **GUM** department store, once a market, then the world's largest purveyor of the grim consumer goods of the Soviet economy, now a bona fide shopping mall. At one end, **St. Basil's Cathedral** with its crazy-quilt onion domes, the second oldest building in the square; at the other, the **History** and **Lenin Museums,** both of which are now closed for physical and ideological repair. Indeed, Lenin's historical legacy has finally come into question, and his name and face are coming down all over Moscow. The Party, so to speak, is finally over. But his mausoleum still stands in front of the Kremlin—dejected and patrolled by a lone, grinning cop.

Red Square has been the site of everything from a giant farmer's market to public hangings to political demonstrations to a renegade Cessna's landing. Begin your Moscow visit here; tradition has it that first-time comers must enter with their eyes closed so as to get the full effect. Remember, the first time only happens once.

Kremlin (Кремль)

Like a spider in her web, the Kremlin sits geographically and historically in the center of Moscow. Here Ivan the Terrible reigned with his iron fist; here Stalin ruled the lands behind the Iron Curtain. Napoleon was here while Moscow burned, and here the Congress of People's Deputies dissolved itself in 1991, ending the Soviet Union and, at least for now, totalitarianism in Russia. If any buck has done stopping anywhere in Russia, this is the place it happened. Despite the tremendous political history of the one-time fortress, the things to see here are largely churches. Buy tickets at the *kassa* in **Aleksandrovsky Sad** on the west side of the Kremlin and enter through Borovitskaya gate tower in the southwest corner. Shorts and large bags are not allowed; there is a check-room.

Much of the Kremlin is still government offices; watchful policemen will blow whistles if you stray into a forbidden zone. Your best bet is to follow the people with cameras, and you will soon come to **Cathedral Square,** where the most famous gold domes in Russia rise. All the churches are now museums; buy tickets to each at the door or an all-for-one ticket at the main *kassa.*

The first church to your left is the **Annunciation Cathedral.** It holds the loveliest iconostasis in Russia, with luminous icons by Andrei Rublyev and Theophanes the Greek. Originally only a three-domed church, it was elaborated and gilded by Ivan the Terrible. The second, southeast entrance is also his work; four marriages made him ineligible to use the main entrance.

Across the way is the square **Archangel Cathedral,** also with very vivid icons and frescoes. But this church has a more morbid attraction; it is the final resting place for many Tsars prior to Peter the Great. Ivans the Great and Terrible (III and IV) are behind the south end of the iconostasis; Mikhail Romanov is in front of it.

The center of Cathedral Square in **Assumption Cathedral,** where Ivan the Terrible's throne still stands by the south wall. The icons on the west wall are 15th-century; the others are from the 1640s. Napoleon, securing his excellent reputation with the Russians, used the place as a stable in 1812. To the east of the Assumption Cathedral is the **Ivan the Great Belltower,** which is not, we repeat, not named for Ivan the Great. Its tower is visible from 30km thanks to Boris Gudonov (the one pre-Peter tsar not buried in the Kremlin—he's in Sergievsky Posad, formerly Zagorsk) who raised the tower's height to 81m. The ground floor has exhibits from the Kremlin's collection. Behind Assumption Cathedral is **Patriarch's Palace,** site of the Museum of 17th-Century Russian Applied Art and Life and the **Church of the Twelve Apostles,** built by Patriarch Nikon in the 17th century as revenge against Ivan the Terrible's extravagant St. Basil's Cathedral.

Behind the Archangel Cathedral is the **Tsar Bell,** the world's largest. It has never rung and never will: a 11½-ton piece cracked off after a fire in 1737. Also open to visitors is the **Armory Museum,** just to the left as you enter. All the riches of the Russian Church, and those of the State that are not in the Hermitage can be found in these nine rooms. Room three (on the second floor) holds the legendary Fabergé eggs—each opens to reveal an impossibly intricate jewelled miniature. Room six holds thrones and other royal necessities: crowns and dresses (the Empress Elizabeth is said to have had 15,000 gowns, of which one is on display). Room nine holds royal coaches and sleds—Elizabeth's sled was pulled by 23 horses at a time (not one for understatement, that Elizabeth). **The Diamond Fund,** an annex of the Armory, has still more glitter, including a 190-carat diamond given to Catherine the Great by Gregory Onov (a "special friend" of hers). That's all of the Kremlin you can actually go into, except for the **Kremlin Palace of Congresses,** the square white monster built by Krushchev in 1961 for Communist Party Congresses. It's also a theater, one of the few open in the summer for concerts and ballets. (The Kremlin, and every-

Kremlin

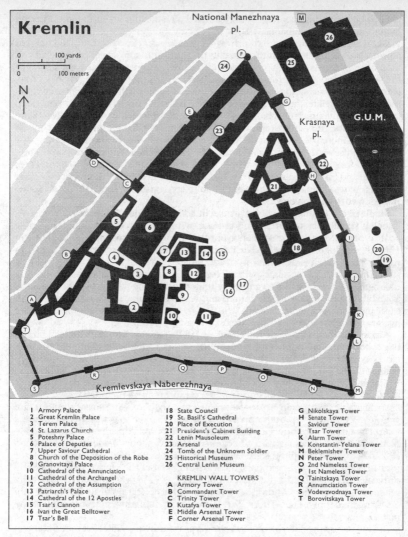

National Manezhnaya pl.

| 0 | 100 yards |
| 0 | 100 meters |

N↑

Krasnaya pl.

G.U.M.

Kremlevskaya Naberezhnaya

I	Armory Palace	18	State Council	G	Nikolskaya Tower
2	Great Kremlin Palace	19	St. Basil's Cathedral	H	Senate Tower
3	Terem Palace	20	Place of Execution	I	Saviour Tower
4	St. Lazarus Church	21	President's Cabinet Building	J	Tsar Tower
5	Poteshny Palace	22	Lenin Mausoleum	K	Alarm Tower
6	Palace of Deputies	23	Arsenal	L	Konstantin-Yelana Tower
7	Upper Saviour Cathedral	24	Tomb of the Unknown Soldier	M	Beklemishev Tower
8	Church of the Deposition of the Robe	25	Historical Museum	N	Peter Tower
9	Granovitaya Palace	26	Central Lenin Museum	O	2nd Nameless Tower
10	Cathedral of the Annunciation			P	1st Nameless Tower
11	Cathedral of the Archangel		KREMLIN WALL TOWERS	Q	Tainitskaya Tower
12	Cathedral of the Assumption	A	Armory Tower	R	Annunciation Tower
13	Patriarch's Palace	B	Commandant Tower	S	Vodevzvodnaya Tower
14	Cathedral of the 12 Apostles	C	Trinity Tower	T	Borovitskaya Tower
15	Tsar's Cannon	D	Kutafya Tower		
16	Ivan the Great Belltower	E	Middle Arsenal Tower		
17	Tsar's Bell	F	Corner Arsenal Tower		

thing in it, is open Fri.-Wed. 10am-4:30pm. An entrance ticket, *Vkhodni bilyet* (вхог-ный биллет), is 200R. Entrance to each cathedral is 5000R, students 2500R. Entrance to all cathedrals is 20,000R, students 10,000R. The Armory and Diamond Fund are US$10, students US$5, payable in rubles. Patriarch's Palace is 5000R, students 2500R. The exhibit in the Belltower is the same price.)

Near the Kremlin

Alexander Gardens (Александровский Сад; Aleksandrovsky Sad). More than just the place to buy your Kremlin tickets, this is a pleasant garden and a cool green respite from the carbon monoxide fumes of central Moscow. At the north end is the **Tomb of the Unknown Soldier** where, like those in every city in Russia, an eternal flame burns in memory of the catastrophic losses the country suffered in World War II, called in Russia the Great Patriotic War. Twelve urns containing soil from the country's "hero cities" which withstood especially heavy casualties stand there as well. It used to be the trendy spot to get your picture taken on your wedding day—that and Lenin's mausoleum. Romantic, eh?

GUM (ГУМ), the *Gosudarstveny Universalny Magazin* ("State Department Store"), built in the 19th century, used to be a great place to come and be glad you didn't live in Russia. It is built to hold 1000 stores, and resembles a train station of the last century with its wrought iron and arched glass roofs. But during Soviet rule, it was a depressing shopping experience; there's not much grimmer than a thousand stores all selling the same goods. These days, it has been completely renovated and is a shopping mall of which any American town would be proud. Most of the stores sell goods for hard currency—most have lines outside the doors, too. The second floor is more basic Russian dry goods, and there is also a **Kodak Express,** a copy center, and several decent restaurants. (See the *Practical Information* and *Food* sections for more on these. The whole place is open daily from 8am to 8pm. Enter from the end by the History Museum and leave your credit card at home; especially after a few weeks in Russia, the sight of so many consumer goods might do something funny to your brain.)

St. Basil's Cathedral (Собор Василия Блажного; *Sobor Vasiliya Blazhnovo*). Nothing says Russia more than this church, whose multicolored domes get a new coat of paint every couple of years to preserve their...uh, vividness. Completed in 1561, it was built by Ivan the Terrible to celebrate his victory over the Tatars in Kazan. The church is best seen from the outside; after all that color, the inside is anticlimactic. There are some pretty frescoes, but all are restorations, and the central, highest chapel was still completely under scaffolding in July '94. Downstairs is an exhibit on the history of the church and Ivan's campaign against the Tatars, all in Russian. (Cathedral is open Wed.-Mon. 10am-5pm. Buy tickets (4000R) from the *Kassa* outside the entrance; they are on sale until 4:30pm.)

Kazan's Cathedral is on the opposite end of the square. This pink and gold birthday cake church has just been reopened for services after being completely demolished in 1936 to make way for May Day parades. The interior is new and much plainer than most Russian churches; this iconostasis is free from any gold Baroque madness. There is a healthy mix of tourists and worshippers, so you won't feel out of place (services daily at 8am and 5pm; men must remove their hats).

In the glory days, **Lenin's Mausoleum,** a squat red tomb in front of the Kremlin, was guarded by fierce goose-stepping guards, and the line to get in was three hours long. The guards have now been replaced by one bored cop, and the line has completely vanished—getting in is a cinch, except that the hours the mausoleum is actually open are few. No photos are allowed of Vlad's embalmed remains—is it he or isn't it?—and backpacks and bags must be checked at the cloakroom in Aleksandrovsky Sad. Entrance to the Mausoleum also gives access to the **Kremlin wall** where Stalin, Brezhnev, Andropov, Gagarin, and American John Reed, among others, are buried (open Tues.-Thurs., Sat. 10am-1pm, Sun. 10am-2pm; admission to the mausoleum and the wall are free).

As you admire the mausoleum on your stroll around Red Square, note the balcony on top where Russia's leaders stood during May Day and November 7 parades. Rumor has it that the plushest bathroom in Moscow is hidden somewhere in the back. Unfortunately, it has not yet been opened to the public.

Art Museums

The **Pushkin Museum of Fine Arts** at ul. Volkhonka 12, M: Kropotkinskaya (Кропоткинская) is becoming better organized, with new buildings to house its large and very respectable collection of European Renaissance, Egyptian, and Classical art. The freshly painted aqua-building to the left of the main entrance opened with great fanfare in 1994. The completely renovated, modern interior is thoughtfully designed to house the **Museum of Private Collections,** displayed on three floors leading off a main staircase. These private collections come from more than fifteen sources and include a wide range of mostly 19th- and 20th-century famous foreign and Russian art. They were founded in part by Ilya Siberstein, one of Russia's leading collectors who gave his collection to the state. The artwork was put in this building, which in the late 19th century has served as a hotel, the Prince Yard Hotel, frequented by such prominent Russian figures as Ilya Repin and Maxim Gorky. The exhibits do not move chronologically but focus on the private individual collector—a sign that even museums here are changing. Part of Sergei Tredyakov's fabulous collection may still be housed here in 1995. Although the quality of the works varies, it is definitely worth a lengthy visit (and the separate entrance fee, 8000R, Russian 600R. Open Wed.-Sun. 10am-4pm, ticket office until 3pm.) On the right, with a garden in front, is the more imposing main entrance to the **Pushkin Museum of Fine Arts,** Russia's second most famous European art museum after the Hermitage in St. Petersburg. It was founded in 1912 by famous Russian poetess Marina Tsvetaeva's father, who wanted his art students to have the possibility of seeing classical art in the original. It gained the majority of its impressive collection after the revolution made sure that *every* museum would no longer be a museum of private collections. The Egyptian exhibit on the first floor and the French impressionists (mainly Monets) are understandably two major pilgrimage areas, but as the museum frequently rotates its large collection, spending time in each section is probably more advisable. Although not as daunting as most museums of its caliber, this museum still requires a few hours visit. The floor plan on each floor is quite detailed, but you can buy an excursion Walkman which lasts one hour (4000R) to walk you through the museum. (Open Tues.-Sun. 10am-7pm, ticket booth to 6pm. Admission 8000R, Russians 600R.)

Located in the picturesque inner south section of Moscow, with its numerous churches and 18th-century manor houses, it is one of Russia's premier art galleries, the **Tretyakov Art Gallery,** Lavrushensky per. 10 (Лаврушенский пер.), M: Tretyak-ovskaya (Третьяковская); straight out of the Metro turn left, cross the first street and continue straight until you see the large red building. Undergoing major renovation in summer of 1994, the building is due for completion in September. This means that visitors in 1995 will have the great fortune to see most of the Tretyakov's superb Russian works hung in style. The Tretyakov gallery was, unlike most museums in Russia, founded as a private collection before it was nationalized by the state after the revolution. It holds some of the most important Russian works, both paintings and sculptures, including a magnificent collection of icons. The icons have come under some debate recently as many of the churches from which they were taken wish to reclaim them. One way in which the museum hopes to resolve this problem is by hanging some of the icons in the Tretyakov churches, two churches which were destroyed after the revolution and have recently been reconstructed. Although the art of interest goes up to the present day (including Malevich's infamous *Black Square*), the Mona Lisa equivalent here is the 12th-century Vladimir icon *God and Mother,* taken from Constantinople, which hung for centuries in the Uspensky Sobor in the Moscow Kremlin and allegedly saved Moscow from the Poles. (Open Tues.-Sun. 10am-8pm.)

There are numerous other museums of artistic note in Moscow; many of the more renowned are listed below:

Manege (Манеж) is located on Manezhnaya Ploschad, west of the Kremlin. This one-time riding school for the military (hence the French name) is now the Central Exhibition Hall and often has interesting modern Russian exhibits. Enter from the north end, on the square. Open Wed.-Mon. 11am-8pm; ticket window closes one hour before exhibitions. Admission 1000R, students 500R.

New Tretyakar Art Gallery (Государственная Третьяковская Галерея), ul. Krymsky Val 10 (tel. 230 77 88). M: Oktyabrskaya. Directly opposite the Gorky Park entrance, on the right side. This museum, built to house newer works and exhibitions of Russian art, shares a building with the **Central House of Artists;** the Tretyakov is the building in back, with an entrance to the right side. This is the place to come for comprehensive exhibits on a particular Russian artist: the ground floor usually hosts contemporary art (in 1994 it showed Marina Romanovskaya's sculptures) and the second floor, a 19th-century artist's life-work (in 1994 it showed a well-hung exhibit of Polenova's etchings and paintings). The top floor contains the permanent exhibit, a huge retrospective of Russian art from the 1910s to the 30s, which intelligently shows the development of socialist realism over time. The permanent exhibit alone is worth an hour, although the fine depictions of the Russian body-ethic can be passed quickly. Open Tues.-Sun. 10am-8pm. Admission 7500R, students 3500R, Russian adults 700R, Russian students 200R. Behind the gallery to the right is one of the strangest sights in Moscow, a makeshift graveyard for **fallen statues.** These huge black ghosts stand disorderly staring off into the distance. Stalin himself, nose broken, lies uncomfortably on his elbow and the unfortunate Krushchev's head rolls on the grass.

Central House of Artists (Центральный Дом Художника), at ul. Krymsky Val 10. M: Oktyabrskaya. The only large museum which does not charge separate prices for foreigners, it houses numerous small and mostly interesting exhibitions—some of which are for sale. Come here for cutting edge Russian art, as well as progressive historical exhibits which come and go quickly. Summer 1994 boasted well-attended exhibits on the history of Jews in the USSR, architecture from Jerusalem, and Moscow paintings from 1948-1970. Check *The Moscow Times* for exhibit info or go to the auction hall and start your own private collection (for a price, of course; admission 500R, students 300R). Open Tues.-Sun. 11am-7pm.

Moscow Metro is worth a tour of its own. All the stations are unique, and those inside the ring line are quite elaborate, with mosaics, sculptures, and crazy chandeliers. It's only 150R—and with trains coming every two minutes, you can stay as short or long as you like, with no *babushka* in the corner to yell at you. Stations Kievskaya (Киевская), Mayakovskaya (Маяковская), and Ploschad Revolutsii (Площадь Революции) are particularly good, as are Novoslobodskaya (Новослободская) and Mendeleevskaya (Менделеевская). Note the atomic-model light fixtures in the Mendeleevskaya station—they're for the chemist Gregory Mendeleev.

All-Russia Museum of Decorative and Applied Folk Art (Все-российский Музей Декоративно-Прикладного) at Delegatsaya ul. 3 (ул. Делегация), just north of the Garden Ring. M: Tsvetnoi Bulvar (Цветной Бульвар). This is what the junk they sell on the Arbat is supposed to look like. The museum has two buildings. The first, where you buy your tickets, has rooms of contemporary painted and lacquered wood, very fine quality, and 17th- and 18th-century textiles. Also a whole room of samovars. The second building, #5 ul. Delegatsaya, is more interesting. The first room has traditional Russian peasant costumes of the last century, juxtaposed against what the St. Petersburg glitterati were wearing in the same period. There is also more contemporary work—pottery, wood carving, and incredibly intricate lacquered boxes. Open Mon., Wed., Sun. 10am-6pm, Tues., Thurs. 12:30-8pm; ticket booth closes an hour before museum. Admission 3000R, students 1500R.

Museum of Folk Art (Музей Народного Искусства), on ul. Stanislavsky Museum (tel. 290 52 22). M: Pushkinskaya. The sign for the museum is not on the door, but the large black doors are the entrance to this one-room museum. The exhibit changes continually, with the right half of the room simply for display and the left half for sale; there are often interesting pieces to buy. Open Sun.-Tues. 11am-6pm. Admission 250R, prices of art upwards from 5000R.

Oriental Art Museum, at Nikitsky (formerly Suvurovsky) Bulvar 12a (Никитский Бульвар; tel. 291 96 14). M: Arbatskaya, Pushkinskaya. A tiny museum looking more like a gallery with very knowledgeable curators, this often has excellent exhibits. In summer 1994 it showed a fascinating (and ultimately extended) exhibition of "The Art of Central Asia and the Caucasus." The permanent exhibit includes, as the name would suggest, art from the Far East, with somewhat mystical Russian explanations. Open Tues.-Sun. 11am-8pm. Admission 1000R, Russians 500R.

Historic Sights

The White House, M: Krasnopresnenskaya (Краснопресненская). You can't visit this symbol of recent political upheaval. But since you've probably seen it already on TV, you could always stroll by and see what it's like in times of relative peace. Yeltsin climbed atop a tank here, brandishing the flag of the Russian Federation and declared himself the only legitimate ruler of the country. Not long after, Yeltsin switched positions when he bombarded an anti-reformist Parliament with cannon fire during the October 1993 coup. The building has since been renovated, but if you look closely you can still see bullet-holes in the fence.

Museum of the Revolution (Музей Революции), ul. Tverskaya 21 (tel. 299 67 24). M: Pushkinskaya (Пушкинская). This fascinating museum housed in a beautiful mansion which was ironically the former Moscow English club could easily be called a history of Russia in the 20th century, as it covers everything *since* the revolution, although it often has exhibits from previous centuries. Amazingly, this Soviet archive has moved with the times, adding statistics on the ill-effects of socialism (in 1989, 40% of pensioners earned less than 60 rubles per month) as well as eclectic documents such as those on 80s rock bands in the later rooms. The museum usually has at least one interesting and unique exhibit; in summer 1994, it was paintings by children from all over Russia and other parts of the world. And even their beat-up trolleybus has a recent story to tell: it was the one damaged in the August 1991 coup that clinched Yeltsin's support, another example of a Russian pseudo-revolution. But it is the museum shop on the first floor that reflects a revolutionizing Russia. One of the best places to buy Soviet medals, this store also stocks old posters and T-shirts with slogans like "The Party is Over" or "Хард Рок Кафе." Museum open Tues.-Sat. 10am-6pm, Sun. 10am-5pm. Admission 1500R, Russians 300R, Russian students 100R.

Museum of the History of Moscow, Noraya Ploschad 12 (Новая Площадь). M: Kitai-Gorod. This is one of those Soviet-era museums, where they turn the lights on as you go through the rooms, and the collection is anything old enough and pretty enough to display. The ground floor is the most interesting; it has archaeological finds from the area, and a very interesting collection of old maps and plans of Moscow showing how the city expanded from the Kremlin. Upstairs is Lev Tolstoy's desk chair and things from the 19th century. Open Tues., Thurs., Sat., Sun. 10am-6pm, Wed., Fri. 11am-7pm. Admission 600R, students 300R.

Central Museum of the Armed Forces of the USSR (Центральный Музей Вооруженных Сил СССР). M: Novoslobodskaya (Новослободская), then walk down ul. Seleznebskaya (ул. Селезнебская) to the square and go left. It's about a block down on the right. Largely military paraphernalia from World War II, the most interesting item in the museum's collection is the milepost 41 marker from the Moscow-Leningrad highway, the closest the Nazis got to Moscow. Otherwise, lots of tanks and guns and propaganda posters. The museum's guests seem to be largely 8-year-old boys and World War II vets. Open Tues.-Sun. 10am-5pm; closed Mon. and the 2nd Tues. and last week of each month. Admission 2000R, Russians 400R.

Borodino, M: Kutozovskaya and then a ten-minute walk to the right down Kutozovsky prospect to #38. A giant statue of Commander Kutuzov stands in front of the large cicular building that houses the **Borodino** panorama and museum. Commemorating the bloody battle with Napoleon in August 1812, the 360 degree painting and accompanying exhibitions usually require you to wait in line, along with the others eager to enter this bizarre memorial. Closed in summer 1994, it should reopen in full glory by Dec. 1994.

Monasteries and Churches

When you can't take the grime and bedlam any more, escape to one of Moscow's hidden parks or monasteries. Among the most famous is the **Novodevichi Monastir** (Новодевичи Монастырь; convent), near M: Sportivnaya (Спортивная). Take the exit out of the Metro that *doesn't* go to the stadium, then take a right on that street. The convent is several blocks down on the left. You can't miss the high brick walls, golden domes, and tourist buses. Tsars and nobles kept the coffers filled by exiling their well-dowried wives and daughters here when they grew tired of them. Buried within the monastery's walls are some well-known 16th-century Russians, such as the philosopher Solovyov, but all the truly famous folks are entombed at the cemetery next door. Wandering around the grounds is rewarding on a pleasant day, but a few of the buildings are also open. The **Smolenski cathedral,** in the center of the convent, is stunning inside; it contains an interesting exhibit of Russian icons. Unfortunately, due to staff shortages it is closed in rainy weather, when only the museum, housed in a white building to the left, is open—on sunny days, the museum is closed (you figure out what's open when it's cloudy). Other buildings of interest include the **Assumption Cathedral** to the right of Smolenski, and a small three-room **exhibit hall** at the far end of the grounds, which in summer 1994 was entitled "Images of Russia." Entrance to the grounds is free; to buy tickets to the other buildings, stop by the white *kassa* on the left once you enter through the gate (tel. 246 85 26; open Wed.-Mon. 10am-5pm; admission 1500R, Russians 600R). Avoid visiting the convent on Sundays when tour buses hog the place.

Turning right and down the street, the convent's **cemetery** cradles the graves of Gogol, Chekhov, Stanislavsky, Khrushchev, Shostakovich, Mayakovsky, Bulgakov, and other luminaries. The gravestones are often highly creative representations—visual or symbolic—of the deceased. Originally closed to prevent too many from flocking to Krushchev's strange black and white tomb straight through the entrance at the back of the cemetery, it is now open to the public. The famous writers are conveniently clustered near each other. A story surrounds Bulgakov's interestingly shaped stone. Apparently Bulgakov's wife saw the stone and knew immediately this would be the gravestone for her deceased husband. Upon buying it, she learned it had originally been considered for Gogol, whom Bulgakov greatly admired; she was then even more convinced she had made the right choice. Buy tickets to the cemetery at the small kiosk across the street from the entrance; a useful map of the cemetery is sold there too if you can read Cyrillic (500R; open daily 10am-6pm; admission 1500R, children 800R).

Danilovsky Monastery, M: Tulskaya (Тулская), is gaining importance each day, as it is home to the head of the Russian Orthodox Church, the Patriarch. Although the grounds and building are stunning, there is little but the exterior to see. A map on the left side of the entrance explains the different buildings, and it is worth a visit simply to see the long-robed Orthodox monks scurrying about their business. The Patriarch's office is hard to miss, due to an enormous mosaic of a stern-looking man watching over the visitors to his domain. Many of these buildings, with their hot, ornate, incense-filled interiors were renovated in 1988 and as a result appear in even greater glory than many of Moscow's other churches. Nonetheless, the churches, built between the 17th and 19th centuries, lack the gold chandeliers of elsewhere. The monastery itself is a pastel montage, with buildings freshly painted in soft pinks, yellows, and blues. Entrance is free; simply turn right from the metro and you can't miss the whitewashed walls and turrets.

Donskov Monastery, M: Shabolevskaya (Шаболевская; tel. 954 48 57), the least famous of Moscow's monasteries, is as a result the most authentic; those who stroll along its leafy paths believe in the serenity of this place. Even in the cemetery next door, the graves show the faces of Muscovites who passed away only in the last five or ten years. Walk straight down Shabolovka until the second street, turn left, and you will see the tall red brick walls of the monastery. Since the fall of communism, Donskov Monastery has gained a congregation, but not quite the prestige it had when it was built in 1591. Still, on Easter and the other Russian Orthodox holidays, the monastery teems with life, and on other days it sits peacefully in the golden sunlight. The church straight ahead from the entrance is cased in the traditional clearly painted frescoes while the smaller church to the right is also operational, but due to its greater age, less ornate (open daily 7am-7pm).

Large and airy and lovely, **Moscow Synagogue,** ul. Arkhipova (ул. Архипова), is very different from the feeling Russia's churches give you. Go to M: Kitai-Gorod (Китай-Город), then walk up Arkhipova two blocks; it's the yellow building with white columns on the right with the Hebrew over the door. Under the Russian system, Judaism is a race—if you are Jewish, you are not Russian. Services are held daily, morning and evening, during which time women are not allowed downstairs and men must cover their heads. Otherwise, it's open to the public.

If the old **Tretyakov Museum** is still closed in 1995, go to the **Andrey Rublyov Museum** (Музей имени Андрея Рублёва), M: Ploschad Ilicha (Площадь Ильича). Take ul. Sergei Radonezhskovo (ул. Радонежского) to pl. Pryanikova (пл. Пряникого) and make a sharp right. The museum is in the **Andronipov Monastery** across the street in the park. It has a large, lovely icon collection from the 13th and 14th centuries, as well as an applied art collection and a museum of recent acquisitions (open Thurs.-Tues. 11am-6pm, closed last Fri. of the month; admission to each 2000R, all museums free on the last Thurs. of the month).

To get an understanding of Russian spiritual life, attend an Orthodox service. One 17th-century jewel is the **Church of St. Nicholas** at Komsomolski pr. and ul. Frunze (M: Frunzenskaya). Daily services are at 8am and 6pm; women must cover their heads. Another ecclesiastic gem is the 18th-century **Church of Ionna Voina,** on ul. Dimitrova, M: Oktyabrskaya (Октябрьская), named after the patron saint of the tsar's musketeers (services daily 8am and 6pm). The inner south region in general is speckled with numerous, sometimes boarded-up churches; simply walk around the neighborhood to find one you like. The **Yelokhovski Cathedral,** ul. Spartakovskaya 15 (M: Baumanskaya; Бауманская), is Moscow's largest and perhaps most beautiful operational church. Built in 1845, the brilliant turquoise exterior is outshone only by the gilded interior. The cathedral has the grand honor of being one of the main administrative locations of the ever-growing Russian Orthodox Church (services Mon. and Sat. 8am and 6pm, Sun. and holidays 7am and 10am).

One non-working church which survives as a museum is **Fili,** set in a large grassy field. Take M: Fili, exit left and walk until you see the red brick stairs and the church. Buy your ticket at the *kassa* to the right before walking up the two flights of stairs to the entrance. One high-ceilinged room showcases a magnificent iconostasis. The church seems to have mystical powers this far out, in a flat wasteland (admission 2000R, Russians 500R, Russian students 200R, Russian children 100R.)

The **Church of St. Nicholas of the Weavers** is one of Moscow's better known churches, mainly because it's very hard to miss. Located at the corner of Komsomolsky pr. and ul. Timura Frunze across from the very popular Café Guria (M: Park Kultury), it looks like a church Hansel and Gretel's witch would have designed—whitewashed with deliciously artificial green and orange trimming. Enter off ul. Timura Frunze around the back of this functioning church to witness the low-ceilings and colorful interior for yourself (evening service daily 6pm).

Regions for Walking

Several blocks away, at M: Arbatskaya, the **Arbat,** a pedestrian shopping arcade, was once a showpiece of *glasnost,* a haven for political radicals, Hare Krishnas, street poets, and *metallisti* (heavy metal rockers). Now, however, it boasts a McDonald's, a Baskin Robbins, and the United Colors of Benetton. With these forerunners of capitalism, this formerly infamous street has lost much of its political significance and life. You can still buy Russian souvenirs from amber to *matroshka* dolls, but the commercial aspect once so unique has spread across the city. Midway up, on a sidestreet, is a graffiti wall dedicated to the memory of rocker Victor Tsoi of the Soviet group Kino, who served as an idol to many young Russians before his death in a car crash three years ago. Moscow youths still hang out and smoke here, but the graffiti and memory are fading.

Intersecting but almost parallel with the Arbat is **Novy Arbat,** a wide thoroughfare lined with western businesses like the Arbat Irish House and Sports Bar, and massive Russian stores like the famous **Dom Knigi,** a giant bookstore, and **Melodiya,** one of the top record stores. Halfway up ul. Tverskaya from Red Square, **Pushkin Square** (M: Pushkinskaya) is Moscow's favorite rendezvous spot. Amateur politicians gather here to argue and hand out petitions, while missionary groups try to attract followers. All the major Russian news organizations are located in this region, perhaps one of the reasons the square is the center of free speech—though as eight-story **Izvestia,** the formerly communist-controlled newspaper, looks disapprovingly at Moscow's golden arches nearby, the changes are not so easy to read. Everything on the square is large—from the McDs to the **Cinema Rossiy,** Moscow's largest, which has brought *The Terminator* to the masses. Follow ul. Bolshaya Bronnaya, next to McDonald's, down to the bottom of the hill, turn right and follow ul. Malaya

Bronnaya to the **Patriarch's Ponds,** where the action of Mikhail Bulgakov's novel *The Master and Margarita* begins. This region, known as the Margarita, is popular with artsy students and old men playing dominoes by the shaded pond.

Ulitsa Razina (Улица Разина), a nice walking street, is one left turn past St. Basil's. Here Soviet and Old Russian architecture have their showdown: the on- and off-ramps of the **Rossiya,** the world's largest hotel (closed recently due to the world's most publicized rodent problem), snakes around a series of lovely churches. Most churches were closed for renovation in 1994, but the museum **House of the Boyars Romanov,** a 17th-century house built by the grandfather of Tsar Mikhail, the first Romanov, may open in 1995.

Turn right out of GUM down **Nikolskaya Ulitsa** (ул. Никольская); this is a nice walking street that leads you to **Lubyanka Ploschad** (пл. Лубянка), currently site of the headquarters of the KGB and formerly of a huge statue of Fyodor Derzhinsky, the organization's founder. Previously called Ploschad Derzhinskovo, it has now been named Lubyanka—after the name of the KGB prison.

On the northeast corner of the square is the **Mayakovsky Museum** (Государственный Музей В.В. Маяковского), a fascinating achievement in Futurist museum design. Look for the bust of Mayakovsky surrounded by huge red metal shards; the museum is in the building behind it. Here the avant-garde poet and artist lived in a communal apartment from 1919. His room is preserved at the top of the building, the eye in a the storm of steel girders and shards of glass chronicling his initial love affair with the revolution and his travels abroad. Mayakovsky shot himself here in 1930, for reasons still unknown. The museum makes that chapter less clear than the others. (Open Fri.-Tues. 10am-6pm, Thurs. 1-9pm. *Kassa* closes 1hr. earlier than the museum. Closed Wed., last Fri. of the month. Admission 500R, guided tours 1500R in Russian, 2000R in English, French, German, or Spanish.) The tour is well worth it: the museum is well laid-out, very funky, and somewhat incomprehensible.

The **Moscow State University** (known as МГУ; EM-GEH-OO) a hefty walk from M: Universitet (Университет), lies within a single Stalinist edifice. To fully appreciate its size, you must go inside, which means persuading a student-friend to take you. If you're desparate for foreign company, hang out in the neighborhood: you're bound to run into some of the many foreigners who come to study here. Near Moscow State University, in the **Lenin Hills** (a leafy enclave overlooking the city center), is a one of the city's best viewing areas from which you can see the **Luzhniki Sports Complex,** the **Lenin Stadium** (sites of the infamous 1980 Olympics), and all of Moscow behind it. Considered a highly romantic spot, this could be a Russian make-out point, except for the camera-toting tourists and the not-so-picturesque view. Most of the golden splashes are lost in the sea of gray.

Authors' Houses

Russians take immense pride in their formidable literary history, preserving authors' houses in their original state down to the half-empty teacups on the mantelpiece. Each is guarded by a team of *babushki* fiercely loyal to their master's memory.

Lev Tolstoy Estate, ul. Lva Tolstova 21 (ул. Лва Толстого), M: Park Kultury. A hefty walk down Komsomolsky pr. toward the colorful Church of St. Nicholas of the Weavers; turn right at the corner on ul. Lva Tolstova. The estate is up three blocks on the left. The famous author lived here between 1882 and 1901 in the winters. The summers he spent at Yasnaya Polyana (a beautiful daytrip only reachable by car), which may explain why he kept the large garden overgrown and wild; the current curators have left the lush dark green foliage as unkempt as in Tolstoy's day. The house itself is one of the most perfectly preserved house-museums in Moscow—one might imagine that the author and his family have just run into the garden, leaving the elegantly furnished wooden house exactly as it appears. Tolstoy was apparently a very precise man; he always drank barley or acorn coffee, dined at 6pm every evening, and wrote *The Resurrection* in the study here between 9am and 3pm exactly. But the personalities of Tolstoy's children, many of whom died young, are present in the house too, providing a more comprehensive understanding of the author as a father than as a writer. Helpful explanations of each of the rooms are written in English on the doors. See the bicycle Papa Tolstoy learned to ride at the age of 60. The *kassa* is to the right of the entrance gate, or if that is closed, in the yellow house down a path to the left inside the entrance. Open Tues.-Sun. 10am-6pm, off-season 10am-3pm, closed last Fri. of the month. Admission 2000R, students 500R, Russian adults 500R, Russian students 200R.

Dostoevsky Flat Museum (Музей Квартира Ф.М. Достоевского), M: Novoslobodskaya (Новослободская), ul. Dostoevskovo 2 (ул. Достоевского) just off Ploschad Kommuny (Площадь Коммуны). Dostoevsky was born here—it is located on the grounds of the hospital where his father was a doctor. It is all preserved, and many of the contents are original. Each room is labeled (in Russian and English) with an excerpt from the memoirs of Fyodor's brother, Aleksandr, describing the room and what went on in it. The women working here revere the house's former resident and will gladly talk about him if you speak Russian. They even have the pen Dostoevsky used to write *The Brothers Karamazov*. Open Thurs., Sat., Sun. 11am-6pm, Wed., Fri. 2-9pm, closed last day of the month. Admission 1000R.

Tropinin Museum, 10 Shchetininsky per. (tel. 231 17 99), M: Polyanka. Housed in a superb 19th-century building owned by the serf Tropinin, this museum is chock full of paintings by Russian artists. In summer 1994, the exhibition "Romana Dynasty: Three Centuries of Russian Culture" was well-received; it is often the setting for exhibits on Russian 19th century life. Open Thurs.-Mon. noon-7pm, Sat. 10am-5pm. Admission 2000R, students 1000R, Russians 500R.

Bakhrushin Theater Museum, ul. Bakhrushina 31 (ул. Бахрушина), M: Paveletskaya (Павелетская) and turn left (across the street from the station). One of the surprisingly numerous theater museums in Moscow, this one is certainly superb. It celebrates one of Russia's great art forms with a chronologically arranged permanent exhibit of costumes, dressers, programs, stunning photos, and other intricately crafted artistic creations all pertaining to the theater. The pamphlet at the ticket desk for 100R will tell you, in English, all you need to know about the museum. Open Mon., Thurs., Sat., Sun. noon-7pm, Fri. 1-8pm, *kassa* closes 1hr. before museum. Admission 500R, Russians 300R, students 150.

Gorky's Flat Museum, ul. Kachalova 6/2, off ul. Sadovaya-Kudrinskaya just north of ul. Gertsena, M: Pushkinskaya, is a pilgrimage site for Americans and other tourists more for its architectural interest than for its collection of Maxim Gorky's possessions. Designed by Shekhtel in 1906, this house is one of the best examples of Art Nouveau you'll find. The main staircase is designed to project the feeling and movement of waves on the sea. Open Wed. and Fri. noon-7pm, Thurs., Sat., Sun. 10am-5pm; closed the last Thurs. of the month. Free.

Chekhov's House Museum, at ul. Sadovaya-Kudrinskaya 6, M: Barikadnaya (Баррикадная) is where Chekhov lived from 1886-1890. It was here he wrote and received patients—while you can see some of his possessions, you won't really get a feel for the author/doctor who understood the Russian psyche so well. Open Tues., Thurs., and Sat.-Sun. 11am-6pm, Wed. and Fri. 2-8pm. *Kassa* closes an hour before. Closed last day of the month. Admission 1000R.

Shalyapin House-Museum (Дом-музей Шаляпин), ul. Sadovaya-Kudrinskaya, M:Varrikadnaya (Варрикадная). The home to opera singer Shalyapin from 1910 to 1922, this tastefully furnished house was donated by the musician's son as a museum; it is better known as a frequent concert hall for often superb, small performances. Open Tues.-Sun. 11am-6pm. Admission 1000R, Russians 500R, students 300R.

Stanislavsky Museum (Музей-Дом Станиславского), ul. Stanislavskovo 6 (tel. 229 28 55), M: Pushkinskaya. Walk down Tverskaya, and take a right on ul. Stanislavskovo. The much respected theater director held lessons in his home here, whose rooms have different themes. More interesting than his upstairs apartment, however, even with the explanations written in English, are the collections of costumes in the basement used for such famous productions as Gogol's *Government Inspector* and Shakespeare's *Othello*. The *babushkas* will proudly explain the director's importance and point out the vase offered to Stanislovsky by Isadora Duncan. Open Thurs., Sat.-Sun. 11am-6pm, Wed., Fri. 2-9pm, closed last Thurs. of the month.

Pushkin Literary Museum (Литературный Музей Пушкина), on the corner of Prechisterka ul. (formerly Kropotkinskaya ul.) and Khrushevsky per. (Хрушевский пер.), M: Kropotkinskaya. In case you haven't yet experienced Pushkin-worship first-hand, this carefully tended-to museum will convince you that indeed Pushkin is much beloved. If the first editions Pushkin owned don't thrill you, his doodles should amuse. Unfortunately, plans are to renovate this museum over five years; it will likely not be open in 1995. Open Wed.-Sun. 10am-6pm, closed last Fri. of the month. Admission 1000R, Russians 400R, Russian students 100R.

A. I. Hertzen Museum (Музей А. И. Герцена), Sivtsev Vrazhek 27, on a side street parallel to Arbat. Take a left off Arbat one street before the graffiti wall coming from M: Arbatskaya, then turn right at the first street. The museum where the famous Russian philosopher Hertsen lived from 1843-46 is on the left hand side. A fairly typical and well-reconstructed 19th-century mansion with much of Hertzen's furniture and unique portraits, this museum was only opened in 1976. Alexander wrote the novels *The Thieving Magpie, Doctor Krovpov,* and *Who Is to Blame*—all in the mere three years he lived here. Open Tues., Thurs., Sat.-Sun. 11am-6pm, Wed., Fri. 1-6pm. Admission 1000R, Russians 300R, Russian students 100R.

Gogol Museum (Музей Гоголя), Suvorovsky (or Gogolevsky) bul. 7 (tel. 291 12 40), M: Arbatskaya. Gogol spent his last months here; you could spend your last days trying to find the museum. Actually only two small rooms inside a library, the good thing about this museum is that you can imagine the difficult end to this brilliant 19th-century writer's life and look at his few meager possessions without spending a ruble. Open Mon., Wed., Thurs. 1-7:30pm, Sa.-Sun. noon-5:45pm.

Lermontov House-Museum (Дом-Музей Лермонтова), ul. Malaya Molchanovka 2 (Малая Молчановка), off of ul. Novi Arbat, M: Arbatskaya. One of Russia's much loved and well-respected poets lived in this small house—appropriately well-preserved and closely guarded by *babushkas*. Enter through the white gate to see another example of fairly well-to-do 19th-century life. Open Tues., Thurs., Sat.-Sun. 11am-5pm, Wed., Fri. 2-5pm. Admission 1000R, Russians 500R.

Art Galleries

House of the Union of Artists (Дом Союза Художника), Kuzuetski Most 10 (Кузнетский Мость), M: Kuznetski Most, then turn left. Not to be confused with the much larger **House of Artists** across from Gorky Park, this is a gallery of contemporary—interesting and *real*—art, and unlike most museums, offers a picture of Russian cultural achievement that hasn't been spoiled by some state planner—it is what people are doing here, *now*. The gallery itself is large, and works include sculpture, prints, lithographs, and paintings. Many are for sale. On the way out is an art supply store—stop in and stock up on cheap acrylics. Tickets 500R, a bargain for a crash course in the latest in Russian art. Open Mon.-Fri. noon-6:30pm, Sat. noon-5:30pm.

Exhibition Hall of the Union of Artists (Выставочный Зал Союза Художников), Kuznetski Most 20 (Кузнетский Мость), M: Kuznetski Most, and turn right. This smaller gallery shows a more bite-sized array of contemporary Russian art—some good, some bad, much interesting. Four good-sized room, informally hung with the latest stuff. Open Mon.-Fri. noon-7pm, Sat. noon-6pm. Admission 500R.

Union of Soviet Artists, ul. Prechistenka 21/12. M: Kropotkinskaya, near the Pushkin Literary Museum. A well-visited exhibit hall which displays the life work of a popular (even *trendy*) artist—including artists from the Soviet period. Exhibits are changed periodically. Open Wed.-Fri. noon-7pm, Sat.-Sun. 10am-5pm. Free.

MARS Gallery, ul. Malaya Filyovskaya 32 (ул. Малая Филевская; tel. 146 20 29), M: Pionerskaya (Пионерская). Probably the most widely known gallery for contemporary art (and the avant garde). In summer 1994, it collaborated with the Stanbet gallery, produce a large and well-attended exhibit on contemporary Russian art. Check *The Moscow Times* for exhibits. Open Tues.-Sun. noon-8pm.

International Slavonic Cultural Center, Chernigovsky per. 9/13, M: Tretyakovskaya. Exhibits of varying interest, but of good quality. Summer 1994 showed

"Russian society of the 18th and 19th centuries as viewed by foreign masters," mostly portraits from the Tropinin Museum. Open Tues.-Sat. noon-6pm, Sun. noon-5pm.

Photocenter, Gogolevsky Bul. 8 (Гоголевский Бульвар), M: Kropotkinskaya or Arbatskaya. Widely varying exhibits of photography. Check *The Moscow Times* to see if there's anything of interest. In summer 1994 it displayed a popular and talked-about exhibit of Heidi Hollinger's portraits of the political opposition, such as Vladimir Zhirinovsky in "non-political" poses. Open Wed.-Sun. noon-7pm.

DAR Gallery of the Contemporary Art Center, ul. Bolshaya Yakimanka 2/6 (Большая Якиманка; tel. 238 24 54). M: Polyanka (Полянка). On the second floor, enter through an archway on the embankment. A small gallery showing older Russian art such as nave paintings. Open Tues., Fri.-Sat. 2-6pm or by appointment.

Rosizo Gallery, ul. Petrovka 28/2. M: Pushkinskaya (tel. 928 14 45). One of the more centrally located galleries, it usually has small, eclectic exhibits. In summer 1994, it hosted the first public display of artwork confiscated by Soviet customs during the 1970s—intriguing for the curious. Open Tues.-Sat. noon-7pm.

State Institute of Glass, Chernigovsky per. 4 (Черниговский пер.; tel. 253 10 13), M: Novokuznetskaya. Tired of paintings and furniture? This gallery exhibits crafted glass from all over the former USSR. Open Mon.-Fri. 10am-6pm.

ENTERTAINMENT AND NIGHTLIFE

Moscow is a large and fast-paced city, and it has the entertainment options to show it. The only problem here is that the scene moves so fast it is impossible to keep on top of what's in and what's out.

Theater

If you are here in the summer, you came at the wrong season for theater. Those companies not on vacation are on tour, and the only thing playing in Moscow is other touring companies that come here. This being the capital, many do come, but the productions are of erratic quality. However, starting September 1 and running well into June, Moscow boasts very good theater, ballet, and opera, as well as excellent orchestras. If you buy your tickets far enough in advance and/or don't demand front row center, you can go very cheaply. Just purchase them at the *kassa* in the theater, usually open from noon to 7pm, when performances start. All theaters have a labeled model in the lobby so you can identify your seats when you buy.

Tickets to performances at the Bolshoi and the Tchaikovsky Concert Hall are often snatched up by Intourist and scalpers; if you have no luck at the box office, hang out outside the theater and look foreign. This is especially true at the Old Circus. Try not to look too rich, though: speak some Russian, and you may well get your price, probably US$5-10.

Bolshoi Theater (Большой Театр), M: Teatralnaya Ploschad (Театральная Площадь). Literally called "the Big Theater," the Bolshoi was unfortunately closed for renovation in 1994. If it is open in 1995, it is worth a trip; both the opera and ballet companies are still good, despite multiple defections to the West, and the theater itself is pure pre-Revolutionary elegance. Champagne and caviar at intermission under crystal chandeliers—pretend you're Vronsky, Anna Karenina's lover.

The Maly Theater (Малый Театр), just north of the Bolshoi on Teatralnaya Ploschad. The "Small Theater," as its name literally means, shows drama—a different production every night. Difficult for non-Russian speakers, it is fun if you can understand the language. The *kassa* is open daily 12:30-3pm, 4-7:30pm.

Vakhtangav Theater, ul. Arbat 26 (tel. 241 07 28), M: Arbatskaya. An actor's theater, formerly one of the most popular (helped partially by its prime location), and it remains good.

Conservatory Big-Small Halls, ul. Gertsena 13 (tel. 229 81 83), M: Pushkinskaya. Centrally located and big. Even the small one is big.

Luzhniki Sports Palace, Luzhnetskaya nab. 24 (tel. 201 09 55), M: Sportivnaya. Simply huge. Mostly rock concerts are held here.

Scriabin Memeorial Museum, ul. Gertsena 19 (tel. 201 64 08), M: Pushkinskaya. Holds small, classical concerts. Check the dailies for performance listings.

Tschaikovsky Concert Hall, Triumphalnaya Square 4/31 (tel. 299 03 78), M: Mayakovskaya. Well-known and as a result hard to get tickets, except from scalpers. A better bet is the **Tschaikovsky Conservatory,** ul. Gertsena 19 which gives stunning albeit erratic productions for next to nothing.

Leninsky Komsomol or LENKOM, ul. Chelchova 6 (tel. 299 96 68), M: Pushkinskaya. The director of this theater is well-known in Russia and attracts crowds.

Mossoviet Theater, Bolshaya Sadovaya 16 (tel. 200 59 43), M: Mayakovskaya. Quite popular, depending on the performance. Usually possible to get tickets.

Satire Theater, Triumfalnaya Square 2 (tel. 299 63 05), M: Mayakovskaya. One of the best, but probably over your head if you aren't fluent in Russian.

Stanislovsky Theater, ul. Tverskaya 23 (tel. 299 72 24), M: Tverskaya. Named for the famous director. Avant garde productions, mostly.

Students' Theater of Moscow State University, ul. Gertsena 1 (tel. 203 68 76). Performances range, but prices are usually low.

Children's Musical Theater, Prospect Vernadskovo 5 (tel. 930 70 21), M: Univesitet. Popular with the kiddies, and you'd be able to understand it too.

Chekhov Moscow Art Theater (МХАТ, *MKhAT*; pronounced EM-KHAT), Kamergevsky per. 3 (tel. 229 87 60 or 290 52 18), M: Teatralnaya. A more academically oriented theater, this formerly hip place has lost much of its public.

Estrada Theater, Bersenevskaya nab. 20/2 (tel. 230 04 44), M: Polyanka. Classical plays in a medium-sized theater.

Hermitage Theater, Karetny Ryad 3, Hermitage Garden (tel. 209 67 43), M: Chekhovskaya. Most popular among intellectuals, this theater still has an avid public.

Chekhov Theater, ul. Kuznetski Most 3 (ул. Кузнетский Мость), M: Kuznetski Most, then turn right. This drama theater, where Chekhov's *The Seagull* opened successfully after failure in St. Petersburg, has traditionally had more avant garde productions, and annoyed the Soviet government to no end. *Kassa* open daily noon-3pm and 4-7pm—when there's a performance, the *kassa* opens at 11:30am.

Old Circus (Старый Цирк), M: Tsvetnoi Bulvar (Цветной Бульвар). Turn right out of the metro and walk half a block; it's on the right, newly renovated. Traditionally better than the new circus near MGU, it usually has animal acts in the first half and a glittery acrobatic performance in the second. Perfect for non-Russian speakers. *Kassa* open 11am-2pm, 3-7pm. There are also approx. 137 eager scalpers outside the building, so you can comparison shop.

Taganka Theater (tel. 915 12 17), M: Taganka (Таганка), directly across the street from the ring line exit. Also an avant garde theater, it's the only excuse to come to this oppressive square on the Garden Ring Road; the intersection of several 6-lane roads make it loud and dusty. The theater is closed in summer. *Kassa* open daily 1-3pm and 5-7pm. Tickets 1000-6000R.

Nightclubs and Bars

Moscow isn't Barcelona, Buenos Aires, New York, or Paris. But sometimes it thinks it is. While Moscow may be the casino capital of the world, you won't be able to afford most of the exorbitant cover charges (more than US$25, usually), which leaves finding advertised free nights your best option. Clubs really do change all the time (the two consistent favorites are Hermitage and Manhattan Express) and even *techno* is out, but the Irish bars which pack out on weekend evenings have been around for a while. Check the weekend editions of the **Moscow Times** or **Moscow Tribune** for music festival listings (the annual jazz festival thrills Moscow every summer) and club ads; these daily newspapers are very comprehensive. The **Moscow Revue** found free at the Traveller's Guest House and sprinkled around the city also has good up-to-date listings of what's happening in the city.

Sports Bar, 10 Novy Arbat (tel. 290 42 11), M: Arbatskaya. Next to Melodiye and across from the Irish Bar. The 2 floors fill up fast for big games; otherwise the second floor is the place to be. A true paradise for lovers of Eurosport: 8 TVs at the bar alone and a large screen will let you see the sport of the season from every possible angle. Cute bus boys to boot. By 1995, the disco, once one of the city's most popular, should have started up again. Bottle of beer 6300R. Glass of beer 9450R. Hamburger and fries 12,600R. Menu in English. Open 9:30am-midnight.

Arbat Irish Bar, Novy Arbat 13 (tel. 291 76 41), M: Arbatskaya. A total scene on weekend nights, this place packs out with large groups of Americans, Irish, and Russians, many of them exhaling cigarette smoke. Chicken wings US$3. Bud 6000R. Guiness 8000R. Open 11am-midnight.

Rosie O'Grady's, ul. Znamenko 9/12 (ул. Знаменко; tel. 203 90 87), M: Borovitskaya (Боровитская), go right out of the metro, then right on Znamenko. Rosie's is on the left at the corner of ul. Marksa-Engelsa. A genuine Irish pub in the middle of Moscow, with friendly Irish staff and largely ex-pat clientele. Loud and cheerful and distinctly un-Russian. Pub food and drink, all somewhat pricey. Pint of Guiness 9000R. Salads and sandwiches 8000R. Open daily noon-1am.

Club 011, gets going around midnight, behind AmEx at ul. Sadavaya-Kudrinskaya 19. Open Thurs.-Sat. 10pm until everyone leaves. Cover.

Manhattan Express (tel. 298 53 54), on the northwest corner of the Hotel Rossiya, M: Kitai Gorod (Китай Город). One of the hippest clubs in town, this self-proclaimed New York supper club creates weekly extravaganzas—fashion shows, strip shows, and performances by top Russian bands. Cover is US$20-25 every night except Thursday, when foreigners get in free with one guest and proof of passport before 1am. This restaurant/bar doesn't even start discoing until 11:30pm, so make sure you can get a ride home. Happy 2hrs. and no cover charge 7-9pm. Open nightly until the wee hrs. (5am).

Hermitage, ul. Karetny Ryad 3 (ул. Каретний Ряд; tel. 229 11 60), just south of the Garden Ring between M: Mayakovsky and M: Tsvetnoi Bulvar. A real Western-style dance club with occasional live music. Cover 20,000R. Open 10pm-5am.

Pepela (Пепела), Arbat 42. On the well-known pedestrian thoroughfare, this nightclub is mostly frequented by tourists and others with money. But no cover until 9pm, 9-11pm cover only US$5. Disco starts around 11:30pm. Cover US$10 after 11pm when there is a "show." Half-liter beer US$5. Open 3pm-6am.

RUSS (Русс Бар), Golotvinski per 2a (Голутвинский пер.). M: Oktyabrskaya. In the inner south region, this sleepy bar is a small local hangout—for foreigners in the neighborhood. Hamburger US$4. Beer 0.5L US$3. Credit cards. Open 1pm-4am.

Parks and Baths

From M: Park Kultury (Парк Културы), cross the **Krimski Most** bridge to **Gorky Park,** or from M: Oktyabrskaya (Октябрьская) enter through the main flag-flanked gate on Krymski Val. This is Moscow's amusement park, where droves of out-of-towners and young Muscovites promenade and relax, smiling and munching on some sweet delicacy sold at the numerous kiosks in the park. Huge outdoor speakers blare energetic tunes day in and day out, and in winter the paths are flooded to create a park-wide ice rink. A ride on the large **ferris wheel** (8min.) in the center of the park affords a 360 degree look at the tallest (and ugliest) of Moscow's architectural landmarks: all the Stalinist sister buildings can be seen from the top. (Park is open daily 9am-10pm; admission Mon.-Thurs. 1000R, kids 500R; Fri.-Sun. 2000R, kids 1000R. Most rides cost 2000R. Ferris wheel is 2000R, under 12 1000R.) Come on cloudy days to avoid the lines.

Izmailovsky Park (Измайловский Парк), M: Izmailovsky Park. The main reason to come this far out from the center is not the park but the weekend market, which is colossal. (Go left out of the Metro and follow the hordes.) The best time to come is late Sunday afternoon, when people want to go home and are willing to make a deal. Use you're Russian and you're less likely to get ripped off. And comparison shop, too—the first painted box you see will not be the last, guaranteed. If you're not buying, this is a window-shopper's paradise. Everything is on sale here, from carpets and samovars to military uniforms, pins, and old Soviet money. There is jewelry, shawls, scarves, old books, T-shirts tacky and cool, and Russia's favorite form of folk art: variations on the theme of painted wood. Boxes, eggs, spoons, cutting boards, all decorated with designs and flowers. And of course, the ubiquitous *matryoshkas*—nesting dolls that used to be painted with pretty girls' faces, but now come in other themes; past Soviet premieres, the seven dwarfs, and the Chicago Bulls. Some stalls even take orders, delivery in a week (bazaar open Sat.-Sun. 10am-4pm; small entrance fee (200R in July 1994)).

Another relatively untouristed respite from Moscow's chaos is the tsars' **Kolomenskoye Summer Residence,** on a wooded rise above the Moskva River at M: Kolomenskaya (Коломенская). Follow the signs "к музею Коломенское" exiting the Metro. Walk about 400m south on ul. Novinka (ул. Новинка) past the *Kinoteatr* (Кинотеатр; "movie theater") and go right just before the long fence. Peter the Great's 1702 log cabin and Bratsk Prison, where the persecuted Archpriest Avvakum wrote his celebrated autobiography, have been moved here from Arkhangelsk and Siberia respectively. Also here is **Kazan Church,** to the left after you enter, which is still in use. At the edge of the complex, overlooking the river, is the 16th-century **Ascension Church,** the first example of a brick church built like a traditional wooden building. (St. Basil's is a more famous example of the same style.) Note the gold double-headed eagle at the top of the entrance gate: this emblem of the Romanovs, made of plastic, was installed in 1994. (Grounds open daily 7am-10pm. Free. Museums open Tues.-Sun. 11am-6pm. Admission 4000R.)

Serebryany Bor (Серебряный Бор) is the cheapest and fastest way to get into the countryside and relax, if you haven't been invited to a friend's *dacha*. Take trolley-bus #20, which starts at M: Okhotny Ryad and stops at Pushkinskaya ploshad (in front of Izvestia) and Mayakovskaya Ploshad on its way straight up Tverskaya to the very last stop (50min.). Join the groups of Russians heading to this gorgeous natural park and island. Literally translated as "silver pine forest," the 2.5 square km it encompasses are crisscrossed with paths, making it possible to explore the countryside before taking your picnic down to the riverside and sunbathing. It is understandably one of Muscovites' favorite weekend afternoon recreation spots— *shashlik* stands and other signs of civilization cater to the frolicking urbanites. A region much loved by the Tsars, it now belongs to the masses in their bathing suits.

The **Moscow Zoo** (ЗооПарк), located on both sides of ul. Bolshaya Gruzinskaya (ул. Большая Грузинская; tel. 255 53 75), M: Barrikadnaya or Krasnopresnenskaya, is a depressing lesson for both the kids and you, that while the zoo of the world's largest nation may be centrally located, it does not mean it is well kept. If you can stand the circus, you can survive this, still a favorite outing for young Muscovites. Buy fuzzy hand-made monkeys for 1000R (open 9am-7pm; admission 100R, children, students, and pensioners 10R).

Although Moscow is filled with serene green areas, one of the largest and most popular with small children is **Krasnay Presnya** (M: Ulitsa 1905 goda) where the restaurant Santa Fe is located. Simply walk down ul. 1905 goda until the Mezhdunarodny and turn right for the leafy oasis, scattered with small playgrounds.

An exit from the Kropotkinskaya Metro still reads "Бассейн Москва", or **Moscow swimming pool,** but like many unfortunate Soviet creations, this former landmark is no more. It lies empty, a gaping reminder, waiting to be bulldozed into a public garden. The tale of this site is a long and strange one, filled with appropriate amounts of Soviet planning, Russian superstition, and hot air. Originally a glorious cathedral twice the height of the Statue of Liberty stood here, but Stalin tore it down, intending to erect a palace of Soviets to rival the church in size (though not in beauty). The ground proved too soft for any edifice, leading many to mutter about a curse, but Stalin, undaunted, built an enormous outdoor heated swimming pool—one of his stranger creations. The steam from the pool, however, which fogged the air for quite a distance in the winter, also had the undesirable effect of harming the precious paintings in the nearby Pushkin Museum. As a result, the pool has been closed. As of summer 1994, plans were to build a small church on a nearby site and create a square where the pool had been. Due to lack of interest and funds, however, it seems unlikely much will be done in the near future. Instead, all that can be seen is a small, wooden makeshift prayer hut where a few devout believers can be seen praying by a giant, blue crater.

Sandunovsky Baths (Бани Сандуновского). Just east of ul. Neglinnaya (ул. Неглинная), between the first and second Neglinny Pereulok, stands a restored green-and-white building bearing a sign that reads "Бани." If the sometimes confusing, always exhausting life of a tourist in Russia has driven you to the edge, come here for a break, and simultaneously one of the best windows on Russian culture. Saunas are Russia's chicken soup; taken regularly, they will make you live forever—at least, so say the *babushkas*. Certainly the experience of sitting in oppressive, magnificent heat (perhaps while flogging yourself with birch branches) followed by intense cold is life-changing, if not life-lengthening. Russians love the public bathhouse, too—they will stay here for hours, gossiping and (for the men) drinking. And visitors are welcome to join them (baths are open daily 8am-10pm; tickets are 10,000R, super-fancy baths 25,000R). Men enter at the corner, women at the side of the building.

VDNKh (ВДНХ). M: VDNKh. Go left out of the metro towards the pavilions. The **Vystavka Dostizhenii Navognovo Khozyaistra,** or "Exhibition of Soviet Economic Achievements," has, well, changed since its original conception. Now that it has been fairly conclusively shown that there were no Soviet economic achievements, this World's Fair-esque park with its multiple pavilions (each in a more garish architectural style than the last) has become a large department store with many people exiting the park carry televisions and microwaves. On nice days, it's a fun place for a midday walk; lots of kiosks selling *shashlik* and pizza make it a good picnic spot, and the central fountain, proving that Russia truly does have the world's largest stash of gold, is worth a look. At the far end is the **Cosmos Pavilion,** where you can see a couple of Aeroflot jets and the rocket that launched Sputnik (admission to the park is free). None of the shops open before 10am, and visitors leave by dark.

SHOPPING

You can now buy anything in Moscow, from exercise machines to French perfume, but most Western-produced goods will take all you've got. The only goods whose prices haven't gone through the roof (and the stratosphere) are books and records; in addition to the shopping possibilities listed elsewhere, a number are listed below. Typical tourist presents to take home, like *matroshka* dolls and amber, are most easily found at the large markets like Izmailovsky Park (see Parks and Baths above). The hidden treasures on the other hand are usually buried in local gift shops where Russians buy cheap but often beautifully crafted traditional birthday presents for their friends. At the **Melodiya** record store, Novi Arbat 40, you can find hard-to-get Russian classics and records by popular Russian and Western artists, often cheaper than in the U.S. Records run 1500R (chamber music) to 10,000R (Run DMC); CDs cost 20,000-35,000R (open Mon.-Sat. 9am-8pm). **Dom Knigi** (Дом Книги), Novi Arbat 26, is a towering landmark, worth visiting for an understanding of the Russian love of books. Tourists and Russians alike scour the shelves for a wide variety of books (open Mon.-Sat. 10am-7pm). The **Book Beryozka**, ul. Prechistenka 31 (formerly Kropotkinskaya), M: Kropotkinskaya, sells Russian classics in the original and art books in English. Pick up your photo guide to the Moscow metro here (open Mon.-Sat. 10am-6pm). Just north of Lubyanka Ploschad, **Torgovi Dom Biblio-Globus** (Торговы Дом Библио-Глобус), Nitskaya ul. 6 (Нитская ул.), is a privatized bookstore also selling imported office supplies and electronic equipment. Here you can find very nice art books and Russian literature, ancient and classical, at excellent prices (open Mon.-Fri. 10am-2pm and 3-7pm, Sat. 10am-6pm).

■ NEAR MOSCOW

PEREDELKINO (ПЕРЕДЕЛКИНО)

An easy trip out of the city and into peaceful, green *dacha* territory is to Peredelkino (Переделкино), where Nobel Prize-winning writer and poet Boris Pasternak had a *dacha*. The area remained a kind of dissident writers' colony well after Pasternak's death in 1960, and even when it was dangerous to do so, hundreds of visitors came to his grave here every year.

The village of Peredelkino is a 25-minute *elektrichka* ride from Moscow's Kiev Station; buy a ticket from the *prigorodnye kassi* (пригородные кассы) to the left as you exit M: Kievskaya. To get to the cemetery, walk away from Moscow on the Peredelkino platform and turn left on the first road. When that dead-ends, take a left; the cemetery will be on your right just before a sharp bend in the road. Pasternak is at the back of the graveyard; keep to the right up a slight rise, towards two pine trees. The gravestone is unremarkable and reads Пастернак.

SERGIEVSKY POSAD (СЕРГИЕВСКИЙ ПОСАД)

Sergievsky Posad (Сергиевский Посад), more commonly known by its former Soviet name, Zagorsk (Загорск), is possibly Russia's most famous pilgrimage point trekked to by Orthodox believers who wish to pray in the many churches inside the small town's main sight—the **Troitske-Sergieva Lavra** (the "Trinity Monastery of St. Sergius"). Approximately 70km from Moscow, Sergieva Posad, the Golden Ring town closest to Moscow, is on the road to Yaroslavl but is often considered one of the capital's outermost sights because of its ease as a daytrip. The stunning monastery, founded in 1340, is again a religious center—the paths between the colorful collection of churches are now dotted with monks in flowing robes. The entire complex, the complete and mystical view of which can be seen in full glory from a distance, contains within its walls a number of different sights.

Although entrance into the *lavra* (the name for the highest order of monastery) and each of the many colorful churches is free; it costs separate fees for the wall's ramparts, the folk art exhibit, the art museum, and the historical museum. Although each of the churches is exquisite in its unique way and each is worth a peek inside, the pinnacle of the opulence of Russian Orthodoxy is visible inside the **Trinity Cathedral,** to the back of the enclosure and to the left, where the numerous covered heads and quickly crossing hands almost entrance the visitor as much as the gilded Andrei Rublyov icons. The **Chapel-at-the-well** has an appropriately superstitious history—inside a tiny chapel in the middle of the Monastery, a spring allegedly appeared out of nowhere one day and is said to contain magical healing powers—old women can still be seen coming here with empty bottles to carry this holy water home. The **art museum,** at the back of the museum, contains many magnificent icons—but many have also been returned to the interiors of the churches themselves (admission 10,775R, Russians 600R, students 200R). The historical museum next door includes artifacts from the surrounding region (admission 6105R, Russians 400R, students 150R). The wall ramparts afford a pretty view of the surrounding wooden houses through the small slits—it's quiet and peaceful here, well worth a stroll (admission 500R, Russians 100R, students 50R). All the above sights are open Tues.-Sun. 10am-5pm. The churches are closed to the public on weekends, however. To get to Sergievsky Posad, take the *elektrichka* (2hrs.) to Сергиефский Посад (last stop) from Yaroslavl station. Trains leave every 40min., more on weekends. (For round-trip, just say "too-DAH ee oh-BRAHT-na"; 1000R.)

THE GOLDEN RING (ЗОЛОТОЕ КОЛЬЦО)

To the north and west of Moscow lie a series of towns known as the Golden Ring,. Their ancient churches and kremlins are widely considered Russia's most beautiful. These towns gained importance in the 12th century as Kiev weakened and power shifted to the north. Vladimir and Sudzal were capitals of Russia and are now the main attractions on any Ring tour. Yaroslavl and Zagorsk were the capitals of their own principalities in the 13th century. After Alexander Nevsky liberated Moscow from the Mongol Tatars in 1252, the entire region fell under Moscow's control.

Today, the Golden Ring towns are worth a visit for their architectural monuments and slower pace of life.

■■■ YAROSLAVL (ЯРОСЛАВЛЬ)

Considered by many to be the most Russian of cities, Yarloslavl is reputed to be an example of what this country is all about. Located a mere 300km from the capital, Yaroslavl has had continued contact with the outside world, making it more a picturesque Moscow satellite than a dull backwater. A sister city to towns in the U.S., it is crowded in summer with tour groups and missionaries. In the 16th and 17th centuries the city built its wealth from trade with the Middle East and the West. Only in its founding days did it reject outside influence; when Prince Yaroslav the Wise considered founding a town on this spot, local inhabitants kindly set a bear on him; the undaunted prince killed the bear and founded the town anyway. Yaroslavl today sleeps peacefully at the intersection of two rivers; its attractive central region, dotted with merchants, churches, parks, and essentially free of Soviet monstrosities, can easily be strolled in one day.

ORIENTATION AND PRACTICAL INFORMATION

Yaroslavl lies on the west bank of the Volga River, 280km northeast of Moscow. It straddles the **Kotorosl river**, but most of its sights and churches lie on the north side. Many bus lines originate from **Ploschad Volkova** (Площадь Волкова); it is a good orientating point. Ulitsa Kirova (Улица Кирова) runs east to the river, and Ulitsa Komsomolskaya (Комсомолская) and Pervomayskaya (Первомайская) lead south to **Moskovski Prospect** (Московский Проспект) and Moskovski Vokzal ("Moscow Station"). South of pl. Volkova is **Ploschad Podbelskovo** (Площадь Подбельсково); from here, Bolshaya Oktyabskaya Ulitsa (Большая Октябрьская Улица) leads to Yaroslavski Vokzal ("Yaroslavl Station").

Tourist Office: The **Excursion Bureau of Monastery of the Transfiguration of the Savior,** inside the entrance to the left (tel. 22 00 69), will help with sightseeing in Yaroslavl, but nothing else. The eager, helpful staff can arrange tours of the monastery's many museums or of individual churches and the city itself. Although the young Yaroslavians don't speak English, they can find you a guide who does. Tours of the city cost 12,000R per group, of the famous church of Elijah the Prophet 3000R per group. Open Tues.-Sun. 8:30am-5:30pm. **Intourist,** in the Hotel Yubilenaya (Гостиница Юбиленая), on Kotoroslnaya Naberezhnaya, a 1-min. walk from pl. Podbelskovo (tel. 22 16 13, fax. 22 19 20). They speak English, can arrange pricey **tours** of the city, they can get train tickets (for higher prices than at the station) for any towns more than 24hrs. in advance. Excursions to Tolga Monastery and Rostov. No maps. No help with accommodations. Open Mon.-Fri. 9am-1pm and 2-5pm.

Post and Telephone Office: Podbelskovo pl. (Подбелсково пл.). Pay at the counter, get a booth, then collect what you haven't used after you make the call. The three tone sound simply means the call has yet to go through. Be sure to press the "ответ" (*otvet*) button on the phone once your party answers. Open 24 hrs. Another telephone/telegraph office (and post office) is on Moskovski pr. one stop beyond the bridge over the Kotorosl R. It's open 8am-10pm; the post office is on the ground floor and telephones are upstairs. Buy tokens for local and intercity call and use the phones labelled "между городный автомат." **City Code:** 0852.

Trains: Passenger trains leave daily for Moscow, St. Petersburg, and Nizhny Novgorod (formerly Gorky; Горький) from **Moskovski Vokzal** (Московский Вокзал; "Moscow Station") on Moskovski Prospect across the Kotorosl R. (Take autobus #5 or 9 from just below pl. Volkova). *Kassa* #4 is open 24 hrs., and there you can buy tickets on trains leaving that day. You are best off, though, if you buy a round-trip ticket from Moscow. **Yaroslavski Vokzal** (Ярославский Вокзал), at the end of ul. Sovietskaya (ул. Совиетская)—take autobus #1 from pl. Volkova—has daily fast trains to Moscow and St. Petersburg. Try here first before going to the other station.

Buses: Yaroslavl's local transportation system is excellent, with trolley and autobuses stopping every 2 min. Trolleybus #5 and 9 go up and down Moskovski pr. through the center of town (pl. Volkova) to Leninsky pr. Trolleybus #1 travels from the Yaroslaski Vokzal to the center. Buy tickets (60R) at the kiosks at the Moskovski Vokzal stop, the pl. Volkova stop, or elsewhere.

Ferries: To the north on the river on Volzhskaya Naberezhnaya (Волжская наб.). Here you can buy hydrofoil tickets to Golden Ring towns Kostroma and Rostov and sleeper berths to Moscow, Volgograd, and Kazan.

ACCOMMODATIONS

Yaroslavl has always been a popular tourist town for Russians as well as foreigners. As a result, the visitor has more budget accommodations here than in either Moscow or St. Petersburg. Hotel Yuta and Hotel Tourist formerly catered only to Russians; their prices are correspondingly lower. The rest were large Intourist hotels pre-*perestroika;* consequently the staff is more likely to speak English but accommodations will not be better, simply more expensive.

Hotel Yuta (Гостиница Юта), ul. Respublikanskaya (ул. Республиканская) (tel. 21 22 43). From pl. Volkova, walk down ul. Svobody (ул. Свободы) and turn left on ul. Respublikanskaya; it's the huge red building in front of you. The wide range of rooms lets you choose your comfort and price—and makes this the best place to stay in Yaroslavl as a result. Centrally located, this tall hotel also has unbelievable views of the town and region. The rooms they'll give you are on the 9th-12th floors. The 10th and 11th floors have singles and doubles with private showers and toilets (called *pol-lux*), carefully tended by the friendly *dejurnaya.* Singles with toilet 20,000R, with toilet and shower 24,000R. Doubles 28,000R, with shower 35,000R. Adding TV and telephone ups the price by 10,000R and 25,000R.

Hotel Yubilenaya (Гостиница Юбиленая), Kotoroslnaya nab. 16 (tel. 22 15 05; or call Intourist 22 16 13), from pl. Volkova walk down Komolskaya ul. to pl. Podbelskova down past the Church of the Epiphany (on your left) and turn right—the hotel is on the corner. Intourist's first choice and thus home to the tour groups which traipse through this pretty city, this large (7 floors) hotel is nonetheless a comfortable place to stay. English spoken. Single and doubles have private showers, mini-tubs, and toilet. Although front rooms face the river for an attractive view, they're incredibly hot; ask for a room on the back side. Singles 53,200R. Doubles 81,000R.

Hotel Volga (Гостиница Волга), ul. Kirova 10 (ул. Кирова; tel. 22 19 51 or 22 91 31). Ideally located just off pl. Volkova, this is a fairly small Soviet-era hotel. Singles without bath 22,000R. Doubles 34,000R. Doubles with bath and sitting room (*pol-lux*) 79,000R. Bring your own toilet paper. Rooms on the fourth floor are cheaper, but are above the restaurant and can be noisy. Russian speaking staff. There are lockers in the lobby where you can store your bags.

Hotel Yaroslavl (Гостиница Ярославль), pl. Volkova 2 (пл. Волкова; tel. 22 12 75). Huge and centrally located, the Yaroslavl offers serviceable rooms at the end of long, sometimes dire corridors. Rooms without bath often at one end, the toilet and shower are at the other. Singles 45,000R. Doubles 74,000R. Triples 81,000R. Doubles with bath and sitting room (*pol-lux*) 91,000R. You're better off at the Volga down the street—similar accommodations, better rates.

Hotel Tourist (Гостиница Турист), pr. Lenina 2a (пр. Ленина). Take trolleybus #3 from pl. Volkhova directly to the "Turist" stop, or the more frequent trolley bus #9 to "Leninsky Prospect" stop. Turn left down Leninsky pr. and the hotel is two blocks down on the left (tel. 22 15 76 or 22 28 15). No English spoken in this modest hotel which rarely sees foreigners. But they will take you if you explain patiently what you want—they will probably even give you one of the best rooms—ask for one on the back side where its cooler. Although getting yourself installed will test your communication skills, it's worth it for the cheaper price you pay for the same basic accommodations you get elsewhere in the center of the town. Two bare but well-cared for, clean doubles (One with four beds, the other with two) share a shower, mini bathtubs, sink, and toilet 50,000R. *Lux* double (two rooms with a single bed in each) 90,000R. Bar and restaurant in the hotel, open 8am-10pm.

FOOD

Yaroslavl is not Moscow or St. Petersburg—there is no McDonald's here, not even a Georgian restaurant. Your best bet is to buy fruits and vegetables at the **market** on Moskovski pr. just across the Kotorosl R., bread in a bakery, and supplement them with kiosk candy bars. The restaurant in the **Hotel Yubileynaya** and the **Restaurant Medved** have acceptable Russian fare, too.

Restaurant Medved (Ресторан Медведь), ul. Svobody near pl. Volkhov (tel. 22 36 28). Medved means "bear" in Russin and you can recognize this standard restaurant by the big wooden bear sign hanging out front. An old-style, characteristically undecorated eatery, Medved serves edible Russian food in a central location for surprisingly reasonable prices. *Bifsteak* 1939R. *Mintay* fish 1734R. Omelet with onions 708R. Tea 41R. Open 10am-9pm.

"Yubileynaya" Restaurant (Юбиленая Ресторан), in the hotel of the same name (see Accommodations listing for directions). Most tourists, which means tour groups, eat here for breakfast, lunch, and dinner. Low prices for well-prepared Russian food. *Bifsteak* 2000R. *Blini* 1215R. Omelette 500R. *Mintay* fish 1915R. Open daily 8am-11pm.

Restaurant Staroye Mesto (Ресторан Старое Место), ul. Komsomolskaya 3 (ул. Комсомольская), just off pl. Volkhova. Nice atmosphere—enter through a beaded curtain, down a flight of stairs, and sit in high carved chairs in the nooks of this whitewashed cellar room. Then choose another Russian meal for yourself from the short menu. Vegetable salad 4000R. Beef cutlet 6800R. Mushrooms in sour cream 6000R. Open daily noon-10pm.

Restaurant Volga (Ресторан Волга), on Volzhskaya Naberezhnaya (Волжская наб.) right by the river station. This is a café in the daytime, a restaurant in the evening (at midnight, it changes into a pumpkin). Café open 10am-6pm, restaurant 7-12pm. Well-prepared Russian food and elaborate pastries on the banks of the Volga. Café entrees 1000-2000R, restaurant entrees 3000-6000R.

Café Lira (Кафе Лира), Volzhskaya nab. 43 (Волжская наб.). One block south of the river station, this café distinguishes itself by offering decent salami pizza for 6000R a serving. Grilled chicken 1800R. Sangria 12000R. Open daily noon-11pm.

SIGHTS

Monastery of the Transfiguration of the Savior (Спасо-Преображенский), on pl. Podbelskovo (пл. Подбелского) is Yaroslavl's principal sight, crowded with tour groups in summer. Holding fort on the banks of the Kotorosl River since the 12th century, the high white walls of what Yaroslavians call their *Kremlin* surround a number of buildings and exhibitions, which frustratingly all have separate entrance fees.

The **bell tower** located in the rear entrance is the most popular attraction, the top of its long flight of stairs affords a spectacular panorama of the town. The 15th-century church in the center, on the other hand, is usually passed over by visitors who head left to **Medveditsa Masha**, a six-year old Russian bear found as a baby and installed in the monastery after a plea to the citizens of Yaroslavl yielded success. The bear more than pays for its supper though, as it delights tourists by posing for cameras. A litter of wolf cubs was held in the grounds before, until they became too big and wild to control; this bear from the nearby Taiga looks cuddly, despite being kept in an iron cage little more than six times her size.

A larger but stuffed bear also inhabits the monastery—in the *Otdel Prirody,* or **Museum of Natural History,** housed alongside the more popular **History Museum,** that focuses on local history, especially of the monastery itself. The temporary exhibits are occasionally of interest—summer 1994 showed "My Angel, My Genius, My Friend," an historical retrospective on Russian women and children over the past 100 years—a topic not so easily covered in the few rooms. Entrance to the monastery grounds is on the side facing the river. Grounds and monuments (памятники спасского монастыря; *pamyatniki spasskovo monastyrya*) 600R. Exhibitions (выставка; *vystavka*) 600R each. History Museum (Исторический Отдел; *Istoricheski Otdel*) and Natural History Museum (Отдел Природы; *Otdel Prirody*) 600R each. Local art exhibit, also popular (Древнерусское и народно прикладое йскусство) 2500R. Panorama from the belfry (Звонища; *Zvonitsa*) 2500R. Open Tues.- Sun. 10am-5pm.

Yaroslavl was a town long dominated by the Russian Orthodox Church and it shows. Many characteristic churches dot the city. Although some are closed, unlike in Pskov most stand proudly with no renovation scars in sight.

Churches

Church of the Epiphany (Церковь Богоявления; *Tserkov Bogoyavlenia*), pl. Podbelskovo (пл. Подбельского) across from the monastery. This large red brick church has an entrance fee, but is worth it to see the one frescoed room and the small exhibition of fragments of frescoes taken from destroyed Yaroslavl churches. The main room has a simple, wooden 17th-century iconostasis and wooden benches; concerts are often held here at 6pm—ask at the Monastery. The three other rooms allow you to examine the frescoes up close. Church open Wed.-Mon. 10am-1pm and 2-5pm. 1500R, children 600R, Russians 300R, students 200R, children 100R.

Church of Elijah the Prophet (Церковь Илья Пророка; *Tserkov Ilya Proroka*), on Sovietskaya pl. (Советская пл.) at the end of ul. Kirova. Widely considered Yaroslavl's most beautiful church, it is replete with glowing original frescoes (the iconostasis is a partial restoration, though). Services every Sun. 9-11am; otherwise, the museum is open Thurs.-Tues. 10am-1pm and 2-6pm. Tickets 2500R, photos 5000R. A map of the city is available at the *kassa*.

Church of the Archangel Michael, across the park from the bottom right hand corner of the monastery when facing its entrance. Similar to the more famous Church of the Epiphany with its red brick and green domes, but it is operational and old women pray before the mostly bare, wooden iconostasis.

Church of the Savior On-The-City and Garden (Церковь Спаса на Городу; *Tserkov spasa na gorodu*), continue along the same road which overlooks the Kotorosl R. Built in 1672, the church is closed but its exterior is worth a brief stop. Continuing along the same road is the *strelka*, where the Volga and Kotorosl rivers meet. The view is spectacular and a garden has been built at the spot; bring a picnic lunch and enjoy it on one of the benches.

Museums

Museum of Metropolity Palaty (Музей Метрополиты Палаты, or Живопись Ярославля), Volzhskaya nab. 1 (and at 23). Housed in an attractive 19th-century mansion, this museum displays the best of Yaroslavl's icons from the 13th to 16th centuries—and that's it, so you'd better appreciate icons. Most of the large museum was under renovation in summer 1994, perhaps by 1995 there will be more to see, such as the collection of sculpture and metal work. Open Sat.-Thurs. 10am-5:30pm. *Kassa* closes at 4:30pm. 3000R, Russians 600R, students 300R. Another branch at #23 displays 18th-century Russian paintings.

Museum of the City of Yaroslavl (Музей Историй Города Ярославля), corner of Volzhskaya nab. and ul. Sovietskaya (ул. Советская). This 11-room museum proudly displays the architectural and culture of Yaroslavians before the revolution in one of the 19th century houses the exhibition highlights. Open Thurs.-Mon. 10am-6pm. Adults 300R, students 100R. No special price for foreigners.

Museum of Music and Time (Музей Музыки и Время), Volzhskaya nab. 33 (Волжская наб.). This tiny, charming museum in a restored 19th-century brick house has a friendly staff and a cheerful collection of old clocks, musical instruments, and a few icons. Definitely not your typical museum. Tickets 2000R, students 800R. Open Tues.-Sun. 10am-6pm. Join an organized tour.

■■■ VLADIMIR (ВЛАДИМИР)

Once the capital of all Russia and the headquarters of the Russian Orthodox Church, Vladimir suffered at the hands of the Tatars in the 13th century and eventually fell to

Moscow's dominance in the early 1300s. Until that time, it was a city to rival Kiev in size and splendor; now it is a smallish Russian town—a good base for exploring Suzdal and the proud possessor of the Golden Ring's most attractive churches. It's an easy 3½-hr. trip from Moscow's Kursky Station (Курский Вокзал), worth a half-day stopover before going on to Suzdal.

ORIENTATION AND PRACTICAL INFORMATION

Everything of interest to the tourist in Vladimir is along Ulitsa III Internationala (Улица III-ого Интернационала), a 5-min. walk uphill from the train station. **Maps** can be purchases at the Golden Gate Museum at the west end of town (see Sights).

Tourist Office: (Экскурсионное Бюро), ul. III Internationala 43 (tel. 242 63). Associated with the main Vladimir history museum across the street. Helpful staff can arrange restaurant and hotel reservations and English-language **tours** of Vladimir and Suzdal (Vladimir and Suzdal 35,200R, Vladimir 8000R). Arranged restaurant meals around 19,000R per person. No maps here; buy them at the Crystal Exhibit behind the Golden Gates (see Sights).

Currency Exchange: Any of the Обмен Валюты (*Obmen Valyuty*) places on the ul. III Internationala.

Telephones: 24-hr. office in the train station for intercity (but not international) calls.

Trains: Station on Vokzalnaya Ulitsa (Вокзальная Улица).

Buses: Station across from the train station; buses to Sudzal every 40min.

Pharmacy: Hotel Zarya-1 has a **medical center** on the second floor (tel. 916 60); if you can't get back to Moscow for **medical assistance,** try here.

ACCOMMODATIONS

Although Vladimir is not nearly as atmospheric a place to stay as Suzdal, its prices are not prohibitive to the budget traveler and it is a more convenient place to get a train back to Moscow. The tourist office will house visitors in a 19th-century home, with only 11 rooms but all conveniences (doubles 160,000R). Called **Likhansky Dom,** this hotel can be called directly (tel. 219 01).

Hotel Vladimir (Гостиница Владимир), ul. III-International 74 (tel. 230 42), is about a 10-min. walk from the train station and the cheapest option. Singles 21,000R, with bath 40,000R. Doubles 38,000R, with bath 60,000R.

Hotel Zarya (Гостиница Заря), Pushkina ul. 36a (Пушкина ул.), (tel. 252 81). Take trolleybus #5 from the station or walk past the Golden Gates around to the left; the hotel will be immediately on your right. Pricey and far from the center, this need be an option only if the Vladimir is full. There are two buildings with differing prices and options. Zarya-2 has bathtubs, Zarya-1 does not; Zarya-1 has more rooms with toilets (без удобств; biez udobstv). It is well kept; a typical, clean, upscale Soviet joint. In Zarya-1: Singles 17,000R, with toilet 53,000R. Doubles 40,000R, with toilet 84,000R. You're better off in Zarya-1 only if you don't want a toilet or shower. Zarya-2, to the left of Zarya-1: Singles 51,000R. Doubles 70,000R. Triples 93,000R.

FOOD

Café Blinchiki (Кафе Блинчики), ul. III Internationala, directly opposite the trading arcades in a large square—you can't miss it. Simply to die for! Delicious, steaming-hot *blini* with lots of fillings and toppings—eat here for breakfast, lunch, and dinner, and you may still hunger for more. *Blinchiki* stuffed with meat 391R, with egg 297R. Topped with butter 317R, honey 507R. Open 9am-3pm and 4-8pm.

Café Yaipki (Кафе Яипики). This small café, situated at the bottom of the park which leads up to Vladimir's Assumption Cathedral and Dmitrievsky Sobor, serves yummy, greasy fried dough for 270R. Pizza 1320R. No smoking here—only one health hazard at a time, please. Open 8:30am-8pm.

Bar Diana (Бар Диана), ul. III Internationala 80 (tel. 254 47). What Vladimir's hip hangout would be, if there were one. Colorfully and elaborately painted murals give this intimate café character. The Bohemian decor extends to the tables and a mini dance floor. Coffee 130R. Open 11am-11pm.

Restaurant Vladimir (Ресторан Владимир), ul. III Internationala 74 (tel. 247 41). In the Hotel Vladimir, around to the right. Well-prepared and reasonably priced Russian dishes in a long wooden hall with the emblem of Vladimir (a lion) prominently displayed. *Pelmeni* (meat pies) 1493R. *Borscht* 1179R. Grilled chicken 3492R. Tea 45R. Open 7-10am, 11am-4pm, and 5-11pm.

Restaurant "At the Golden Gate" (Ресторан "У Золотых Корот"), ul. III Internationala 17. Well-priced Russian food in a dim, wood-panelled room on the second floor. Caviar 6500R. *Pelmeni* (meat dumplings) in boullion 700R. Meat and chicken cutlet entrees 3500-4000R. Open daily noon-11pm.

Restaurant Stari Gorod (Старый Город), ul. III Internationala 70. An elegant restaurant with a dimly lit interior. This is a place for dining, not snacking, and the staff may look at you suspiciously if you're not attired for the occasion. Nonetheless, prices are much lower than in Moscow. Beef with mushrooms (говашина) 5255R. Soup 1293R. Open noon-midnight.

Restaurant Zarya (Ресторан Заря), (tel. 916 70). In the Hotel Zarya at the west end of town, this is convenient only if you are staying in the hotel—the same food can be had for better prices elsewhere. Salads 1500R. *Schi* (spicy cabbage soup) 1400R. *Pelmeni* in boullion 1300R. *Blini* with butter 2000R. Open daily noon-5pm and 6-11pm.

SIGHTS

The **Cathedral of St. Dmitry** (Дмитриевский Собор; *Dmitrievski Sobor*), built in 1197, is the only surviving building of the palace of Prince Vsevelod III of Vladimir. Its exterior, especially the upper walls, are covered with all kinds of stone carvings, from King David soothing the beasts with music (north, south, and west walls) to Alexander the Great ascending to heaven (south wall) to the labors of Hercules (west wall). The interior holds lovely original 12th-century frescoes, probably Byzantine.

Vladimir's **Assumption Cathedral,** to the right of Dmitrievsky Sobor, is more famous for what it once held than what it holds now. The cathedral once housed the famous Mother of God icon, now in Moscow's Tretyalkov Gallery (see Moscow Sights) but still named the Vladimir Icon. However, its interior, which includes some frescoes by the famous artists Andrei Rublyov and Daniil Chiorny, is still stunning. Looming large and white at the top of a small hill, the cathedral is a combination of different styles and architects. Begun in 1158, four more domes and two more aisles were added in 1189, making the cathedral the majestic structure it is today. The church may only be seen in fine weather—on other days it is closed (open Tues.-Sun. 10am-5pm).

The **Museum of the History of Vladimir** (Музей История Владимирского Края), ul. III Internationala 64, is next door to the newly re-opened **Nativity Monastery** (Рождественский Монастырь), former burial site of Alexander Nevsky. The poor guy's remains were moved to St. Petersburg by Peter I; his original coffin is now on display at the museum (open Tues., Thurs.-Sun. 10am-4:30pm, Wed. 10am-3:30pm; admission 2000R). You can also get tickets to tours of **Assumption Cathedral** here.

The **Zolotiye Vorota** (Golden Gates) stand triumphantly in the center of Ulitsa III Internationala, creating a barrier between the city center and the rest of town. For 1000R you can climb the short way to the top (pay upstairs), and get a view of Vladimir's central street through one of the low windows. The ostensible reason to make the climb is for the small exhibit on Vladimir's heroes, men and women who have stood the city well through such wars as the one against the Turks and World War II. There is even a large model of the Tartar Mongol invasion of 1238. But the appeal really comes from the fact that you are climbing a fortification of ancient Russia, built from 1158-64 (open Mon.-Wed. 10am-4pm, Thurs.-Sun. 10am-5pm; closed last Fri. of the month).

In the red brick building behind the golden gates is the crystal, lacquer exhibit (Выставка Христаль Лаковая Миниатюра и Вышивки), one large room filled with gorgeous crafts form the surrounding region. Buy maps of the city here (open Wed.-Sun. 11am-6pm, Mon. 11am-5pm; closed last Fri. of the month). Continuing further along the street as it slopes around to the left is the exhibit of **Clocks and Time**, also part of the Golden Gates complex of exhibits but somewhat far away. **The Exhibit of Old Vladimir** (Выставка Старого Владимира; *Vystavka Starovo Vladimira*) is in an old brick watertower just south of the golden gate. It has a collection of archaeological finds of the last few centuries (open Wed.-Thurs. 10am-4pm, Fri.-Sun. 10am-5pm; 2000R).

Down the hill to the right of the exhibit is a strange monument, familiar to most Americans, but bizarrely out of place in this Golden Ring Town. Yes, the weirdly familiar low fence, encircling lawn, and attached garage is, indeed an **"Amerikansky Dom,"** ("American House") built to demonstrate what can be done with U.S. investments in Russia. Only to be admired from the outside, you can imagine a Boris and Natasha "Go get moose and squirrel" Cleaver living inside.

■■■ SUZDAL (СУЗДАЛЬ)

Set in green countryside with slow moving streams and dirt roads, the miracle of Suzdal is that it looks much as it always has. The colorfully painted wooden houses and churches on every corner boast distinct charm, and the friendly village itself moves at the same slow pace of its streams, have hardly changed through the ages. Just as the village (pop. 10,000) withstood 70 years of communist rule to emerge free of the usual gray monstrosities that destroyed the beauty of nearby Vladimir; it stands strong as a historically protected landmark against the current tourist hordes. Despite the daily stares of French and American tour groups, villagers smile as they work in the fields. Suzdal offers the visitor a beauty and serenity which are hard to believe exist a mere five hours from Moscow.

Suzdal was the capital of the Rostov-Suzdal principality until the 12th century, when Andrei Bogolyuboz made Vladimir the capital. Suzdal continued to grow due to its fertile territory; in the 16th century Ivan the Terrible established the monasteries that still operate today. The town's many churches did not adorn the streets until the 17th and 18th centuries, when rich merchants donated the funds to build these monuments to the Russian Orthodox Church. Most are now closed, but they add to the almost mystic montage that is Suzdal today. If possible, spend at least a night in this less commercialized, more authentic Russo-Williamsburg.

ORIENTATION AND PRACTICAL INFORMATION

Suzdal's main axis is the anachronistically-dubbed **Ulista Lenina** (Улица Ленина), running north-south down the center of the town. Most of the pretty churches and monasteries are on or near the central 1.5km stretch. The **Trading Arcades** (Торговые Ряды) are on the west side of ul. Lenina, roughly in the center of town. Across from them, **Vasilevskaya Ulista** (Василевская Улица) runs east to the bus station. The **Main Tourist Complex** and **Intercession Complex** are a 15-minute walk from the center: go north on ul. Lenina to the Monastery of the Deposition, recognizable by its 70-meter yellow belltower, and go left. Cross the Kamenka (Каменка) River, to take the footpath to the right along the river and up the hill to the monastery. From there, go north one block and pick up the footpath again; it will recross the river and lead you to the Main Tourist Complex. The entrance is around to the right. Bus #3 runs from there to the bus station via the town center; from town, bus #2 will take you to the station.

Tourist Office: Intourist, in the Main Tourist Complex, **Glavny Turistsky Komplex** (ГТК). Go to the left inside the GTK hotel. Possibly the most helpful tourist office in Russia. They have maps of Suzdai (100R) and the friendly staff will patiently explain anything you want to know about the village, from cheap restaurants to bus stops. Open Mon.-Fri. 9am-5pm.

RUSSIA

Currency Exchange: in the GTK (see Accommodations). Also takes AmEx traveler's checks, Visa, and MC. Open 9am-noon and 1:30-7pm.

Telephone and Telegraph Office: On ul. Lenina (ул. Ленина), directly across from the Monastery of the Deposition's yellow belltower. Only intercity calls; there is an international credit card phone with exorbitant rates in the lobby of the Main Tourist Complex—wait until you get back to Moscow. Open 2pm-1pm (that is, 24 hrs. with a lunch break).

ACCOMMODATIONS

Although Suzdal's accommodations are among the best in Russia, they're not cheap. One night in a log cabin on the grounds of a gorgeous **monastery** (US$40) may be a unique experience, but it's not exactly budget travel. Travelers wishing to save money should stay in nearby Vladimir. Other than the two accommodations listed here, it is possible to stay in a 19th century home (US$40 per person), arranged by the Vladimir tourist office (see Vladimir Practical Information and Accommodations). The **Hotel Sokol,** in the central square of the trading arcades and the Rizonolozhenski Monastery, is cheaper but only houses Russians. Perhaps this will have changed by 1995, but, in the words of the eight-ball, "outlook not good."

Intercession Convent (Покрофский Монастырь). Thirty rooms in little log cabins on the grounds of a working convent at the northwest end of town (a 20-min. walk from where the bus lets you off on ul. Vasilyevskaya; tel. 208 09). Perhaps the nicest place to stay in all of Russia. The staff is friendly and helpful, and the setting couldn't be lovelier. Open 24 hrs. Rooms all have private bath. The rates are steep but worth the splurge. Doubles 166,000R. Triples 249,000R. No singles.

Glavni Turistski Komplex Hotel (Главный Туристский Комплекс). From the bus station, bus #2 goes to the hotel, or from the Intercession Convent on Pokrovskaya ul. walk straight along the foot path that crosses a wooden bridge (tel. 209 08 or 215 91). An upscale modern hotel with clean rooms and full tourist facilities. Only slightly cheaper than the more desirable Pokrovsky Monastery, unless you stuff two people in a single. Cafés, a 25m swimming pool, and sauna facilities (in 15-min. seances), tourist office, and currency exchange. Singles with bed and wide divan 108,000R. Doubles 155,000R.

GTK Motel, next door to and run by the Glavni Turistski Komplex Hotel. A little house including a single, double, bathroom, and garage 207,000R.

FOOD

Long used to annual inundations of foreign tourists, Suzdal has more upscale Russian restaurants than many cities ten times its size. However, reservations, especially in the evening, are a must, particularly at hotel restaurants; call ahead or stop by earlier in the day. You might be better off having your main meal in the middle of the day and picnicking in the evening. Bring supplies from Moscow, or go to the bakery in the trading arcade or the impromptu market at the north end where you can get cucumbers and tomatoes in summer.

Traktir (Трактир), Vasilevskaya ul. (tel. 211 91), a 10-min. walk from the arcades heading to the bus station. This would be the place to eat in town, if it were quite in town. Located next to St. Basil's church, this one-room restaurant looks over the rolling green countryside. Prettily decorated with white and red embroidered curtains, Traktir serves freshly prepared Russian delicacies for reasonable prices. *Blini* with caviar 2000R. Fish 1192R. Cutlet of beef 2073R. Open 10am-10pm.

GTK Café, inside the GTK complex (see Accommodations) down a long hallway to the right. A cafeteria-style joint, this is one of the cheapest places to eat in Suzdal. Choices such as fried squash and *blini* stuffed with meat and sweet rolls, prepared with more than the usual care. Arrive early to get the freshest items. Entrees 100-600R. Open 8am-10am, noon-3pm, and 6-8pm.

Restaurant Pogrebok (Погребок), Kremlyovskay ul., directly opposite Gostiny Dvor in the trading arcades. Suzdal specialties served in a long, light hall resembling a school cafeteria (due to the Russian tour groups who, intelligently, eat here). Centrally located just off the town's main square and a 1-min. walk from the Kremlin, this is the place to experience Suzdal's tourist industry—and some reasonably priced, good food. *Blini* with caviar 4746R. Vegetable plate 1971R. Mushrooms and sour cream 1500R.

Restaurant Trapeznaya (Ресторан Трапезная), (tel. 216 39). This restaurant stands out for its location—it's on the grounds of the Intercession Convent. Prices are good, too, although the staff is less than effusive in their manner. *Schi* (spicy cabbage soup) 1500R. *Blini* with caviar 11,000R. Omelette 2300R. Open 9-11am, 1-4pm and 7-8pm. Reservations are definitely a good idea.

Restaurant Suzdal, (Ресторан Суздаль), (tel. 209 50), on the second floor of the Main Tourist Complex. Food, even Russian food, is tastier and better prepared in Suzdal where they have long been used to hordes of tourists, and the Restaurant Suzdal is no exception. Mushrooms in sour cream 3300R. *Blini* with caviar 11,000R. Meat entrees 5000R. Reservations recommended in the evenings (speak Russian or do it through the hotel). Open daily noon-6pm and 7-11pm.

Gostini Dvor (Гостиний Двор), at the south end of the trading arcade. Enter around back on the lower level; the restaurant is upstairs. More expensive than many of your other options in Suzdal; you're probably better off in the café across the street, especially for lunch. The menu is fairly limited and very basic. *Borsch* 1700R. Meat entrees 3500-5000R. Open daily noon-10pm.

SIGHTS

Suzdal's **Kremlin,** founded in the 11th century, is less striking than counterparts in other Golden Ring towns only because of the beauty of the surrounding countryside and the smaller size of the earth ramparts. Nonetheless, the easily visible **Rozhdestvensky Church,** with its golden star-studded bright blue domes, and three history and art exhibits should draw you here. The early 13th century church is even more gorgeous on the inside; they are still in the process of renovating the frescoed interior, whose icon covers and doors glisten in lavish contrast to the dull colors of the 13th- and 17th-century frescoes. The **Krestovaya Palata** is a large room with an impressive archway; the **art exhibit,** consisting primarily of icons from later periods; and the **history exhibit,** which includes nine rooms of clothing and weapons from the past seven centuries, each charge separate entrance fees. When the weather is good, a 15-minute Troika ride is available around the ramparts. (US$3 per person; museums 100R each, students 200R. Open Wed.-Thurs., Sat.-Sun. 10am-5pm, Mon., Fri., 10am-4pm; closed last Fri. of the month.)

The **Savior Monastery of St. Euthymius** (Спасо-Евфилмиевский Монастырь; *Spaso Evfilmievski Monastyr*) is located just north of the Intercession Convent. This is Suzdal's largest monastery, thanks to heavy 16th-century fundraising drives by Ivan the Terrible, among others. It is still operational—try to be here when the hours strike to see the bell-ringer. Inside are the 16th-century **Cathedral of the Transfiguration** and the **Museum of Russian Decorative and Applied Art of the 11th-20th Centuries.** The former, though built in the 1590s, reflects the 12th-century style of the rest of Vladimir's and Suzdal's churches. The upper frescoes are restorations, but the lower level is original and the church is vivid with color. In the ante-chamber is a small photo exhibit on the restoration project. The art museum is also definitely worth a look. It's at the north end of the monastery, next to the old prison for religious dissidents; the collection itself is housed in the former hospital of the monastery. The heavy white walls and cool, low-ceilinged rooms are the setting for the 8th century jewelry, old textiles, and church art, including some beautiful icons with haunting mellow colors. (Complex open Tues. 10am-5pm, Wed.-Thurs. 10am-4pm, Fri.-Sun. 10am-5pm; closed the last Thurs. of the month. Admission 1000R, cathedral and museum are each an additional 1000R at the *kassa* at the entrance.)

The **Museum of Wooden Architecture and Peasant Life** (Музей Деревянного Зодчества и Крестьянского Быта) is just south of the Kremlin, across the river. It's a collection of 18th-century wooden houses and churches, most brought in from nearby villages, and a display of tools and craftwork. The churches, especially the **Transfiguration Church** (Приображенская Церковь; *Priobrazhenskaya Tserkov*), built in 1756, and the **Resurrection Church** (Воскресенская Церковь; *Voskresen-skayq Tserkov*), built in 1776, are the most interesting (open May-September Wed.-Mon. 10am-5pm; admission 2000R).

Smaller sights in Suzdal include a white stone **17th-century house,** directly opposite Our Lady of Smolensk Church and St. Euthymius Monastery, furnished in period style (open Tues., Fri.-Sun. 10am-5pm, Wed.-Thurs. 10am-4pm; closed the last Thursday of the month). The 17th-century **Alexandrovsky Convent,** on ul. Gasteva off ul. Engelsa, near the Monastery of the Deposition, is a working monastery open to visitors. It was built on the site of a large 13th century church built by the infamous Alexander Nevsky. Today the neighborhood is quiet and deserted (open Tues.-Sun. 10am-6pm).

VOLGA-DON REGION

■■■ NIZHNY NOVGOROD (GORKY, НИЖНИЙ НОВГОРОД)

Once on the edge of the Russian state but now the center of privatization (other than Moscow and St. Petersburg), Nizhny Novgorod is entrenched in all three eras of Russian history. Monuments to Lenin and privatized grocery stores share blocks with Baroque 18th-century architecture. Nizhny Novgorod was opened to foreigners only in late 1990. Before then it was called Gorky (Горький), after the writer Maxim Gorky, born here in 1868 and never happy about having a city named for him. It was then most famous for being where the physicist and Nobel laureate Andrei Sakharov "lived" (continuously monitored and not allowed to leave the country—the Soviets called it "internal exile").

These days, Nizhny Novgorod is still shrugging off the heavy blanket under which it was stifled during Soviet rule. Major steps have already been taken to make the town more welcome to tourists; Intourist has opened an office here and there are plans to build a new hotel. But people will sometimes still stare at foreigners the way they would at a zebra walking down the street; locals will occasionally corral you into conversation, asking endless questions about what life is like in the West.

This city of two million is Russia's third largest, and as such is quite lively, especially around the center. Its citizens, many of whom voted for Zhirinovsky's ultra-nationalist party in the last elections, are nonetheless (or consequently) energetic and industrious, seeming more optimistic about their future than most Russians.

ORIENTATION AND PRACTICAL INFORMATION

Nizhny Novgorod is clearly laid out, but it's bigger than most Russian towns; you'd be well off to use the public transportation systems (one-day pass 200R). Most of the places you'll need a bus to get to are clearly marked as destinations on the front of buses. Any bus or trolley bus labeled Московский Вокзал (*Moskovski Vokzal*) goes across the river to the station and stops at the river station and the Centralny Hotel. Any bus or tram, with #1 **Muhuha** (Ploschad Minina) on the side goes to the center of town, the Kremlin; it is on the upper bank of the river and all roads lead to it.

Central Nizhny has two levels—the lower, smaller one includes the river station and **Ulista Mayakovskaya** which has some cafés, but the upper, larger level includes the Gorky museums, the Kremlin, the art museums, and the main walking street of Nizhny—**Ulista Bolshaya Pekrovskayay** (ул. Большая Пекровская), formerly Ulista Sverdlova (Улица Свердлова), which runs from the Kremlin to Ploschad Gorkovo (Площадь Горького). It is a pedestrian street lined with stores, restaurants and outdoor cafés. **Verlchny-Volzhskaya nab.** (Верхне-Волжская наб.) starts near the Kremlin and is perfect for strolling as it runs along the top of a cliff which overlooks the river and the land around. Buy **maps** outside the train station.

Volga-Don Region

Tourist Office: Intourist is located at Centralny Hotel (see Accommodations). Open Mon.-Fri. 9am-5pm.

Currency Exchange: If you have cash (but only U.S. dollars or Deutschmarks), there are exchange offices in the center, especially along Bolshaya Pokrovskaya. Just look for the Обмен Валюты (*Obmyen Valyuti*) signs. If you have a credit card or traveler's checks, go to the **Hotel Oktyabrskaya** (Гостиница Октябрьская) on Verhknye-Yolzhskaya Naberezhnaya (Верхне-Волжская), about 1km from the Kremlin along the river. Open daily 8:30am-1pm and 2-6:30pm.

Post and Telephone Office: Bolshaya Pokrovskaya 56 (Большая Покровская) on pl. Gorkovo (Площадь Горького). International calls and fax are in the room on the left; intercity calls are straight ahead. For international calls, you must book your call and wait for the operator to put you through, but there is usually no line. Do the same for intercity calls or buy tokens (600R) and use the *avtomat* (автомат) phones. Pay phones for local calls are free. Open 24 hrs. **City Code:** 8312.

Photo and Film Developing: Kodak Express, Bolshaya Pokrovskaya 48 on the second floor. Development in one or three days on Kodak paper; you are charged extra for negatives. 10x15cm photos 1000R per print for same-day development, 800R for three-day developing. 15x21.5cm photos 2250R per print for same-day, 1500R for three-day. Negatives 3000R. Open daily 9am-6pm.

Trains: Moskovski Vokzal, across the river from the Kremlin. Buses run to and from the Kremlin every two minutes. Trains to Moscow, 5 per day, 8hrs. 18,000R; Yaroslavl, 1 per day, 7hrs. 18,000R; Vladimir, any Moscow-bound train, 4hrs.; 6000R; St. Petersburg, 1 per day, 19hrs; and Odessa, Lvov, and Riga, each 1 per day. The *kassas* are inside the station and to the right (open 6:30am-1pm, 2-5pm, and 6-5:30pm).

Buses: the **station** (Автостанция) is to the right of the train station around a bend. It's crowded, and much less desirable then catching a train. To Vladimir, 1 per day, 5hrs., 7180R and Moscow, 5 per day, 9hrs., 1255R. Open 6am-10pm.

Ferries: the **river station** on Nizhnye-Volzhskaya Naberezhnaya (Нижние-Волжская наб.); take any bus from the center going to Moskovski Vokzal (Московский Вокзал) and get off at the Rechnoi Vokzal (Речной Вокзал; "river station"). Daily runs to Moscow, Rostrov, Kostroma, Kazan, and Yaroslavl (first-class ticket to Yaroslavl 67,000R, second-class 51,000R). Ticket booths open daily 7am-6pm.

Emergencies: Best to wait until you get back to Moscow, or, better yet, out of Russia. There is, however, a **private polyclinic** with walk-in-and-pay services, ul. Gryzinskaya 5 (ул. Грузинская), off ul. Bolshaya Pokrovskaya through a courtyard. Open Mon.-Sat. 8am-8pm. Russian emergencies: **Police:** tel. 02. **Fire:** tel. 01. **Ambulance:** tel. 03.

ACCOMMODATIONS

Nizhny Novgorod still hasn't forgotten the days when it was Gorky. Although Intourist has installed itself in the Centralny Hotel and both the Hotel Rossiya and Hotel Oktyabrskaya take foreigners, the latter is well beyond your price range and the many other cheaper establishments will have nothing to do with imperialist infiltrators. So, as of yet, there are no budget choices in Nizhny (but as for many things in Russia, who knows what will happen soon?). If you arrive during weekday office hours, you could try one of the many dormitories—for a small payment to the right person, it is reputed that they may let you stay there.

Centralny Hotel (Центральная Гостиница), pl. Lenina (пл. Ленина). A ten-minute walk to the left from the station or one stop on any bus going from the station (#43 stops in front). Lenin points directly at the hotel, as if ordering Intourist to set up here (tel. 44 46 92 or 49 98 73). Designed for tourists, it is in a depressing neighborhood but offers 24-hr. room service and has a 24-hr. café on every floor. Peeling wallpaper but otherwise clean rooms. Singles with toilet, shower, and bathtub 60,900R. Doubles 89,700R. Triples 99,000R. 24-hr. luggage storage. Currency exchange and free copies of the local English-language 4-page Nizhny newspaper in the lobby.

Hotel Rossiya (Гостиница Россия), Verkhne-Volzhskaya nab. 8 (Верхне-Волжская наб.), (tel. 39 19 17, fax. 36 38 94). Walk towards the right when facing the Kremlin and turn right at the river. Expensive, but it's one of the only two games in town. A standard large Soviet-style hotel in a quiet neighborhood, this beats the Centralny for convenience to the center but it's farther from the train station and doesn't have 24-hr. room service. Singles with no shower (bee-YEZ oo-DOBE-stv) 51,000R, with bathroom 60,000R. Doubles with no shower 122,000R, with bathroom 130,000R.

FOOD

The recent explosion in private enterprises has benefitted the tourist by plentiful new cafés and quick lunch stops. Ul. Bolshaya Pokrovskaya boasts numerous pizza stands as well as sit-down cafés. Do-it-yourselfers should go to the **Dmutrievski grocery store** (Дмитриевский) off Bolshaya Pokrovskaya on ul. Piskunova (ул. Пискунова); this privatized shop sells cheese, salami, juice, yogurt, bottled water, and alcohol (open daily 8am-8pm). Next door at **ul. Bolshaya Pokrovskaya** 74 is a small bakery to make your dinner complete (open Mon.-Sat. 8am-1pm and 2-8pm, Sun. 8am-6pm). The **Mytnny Rynok** (Мытный Рынок) between #2 and 4 on ul. Bolshaya Pokrovskaya has good fruits and vegetables in the summer, and there are also lots of vendors on the street.

For eating out, this is still a soviet-era town in many ways, but a few new restaurants have also cropped up (without Soviet-era low prices, alas) and more may soon follow.

Gardinia (Гардиния), Verkhnye-Volzhskaya nab. (Верхне-Волжская наб.), across from the art museum, a 5-min. walk along the cliff. You can't miss this large outdoor

Central Nizhny Novgorod

1 Tsentralny market
2 Train station
3 Bus Station
4 River boat station
5 Kremlin
6 Art Museum
7 Café Gardinia
8 Apartment of A. M. Gorkovo

Volga R.→

Nizhne-Volzhskaya nab.

Verkhne-Vozhskaya nab.
ul. Minina
Bolshaya Pechorskaya ul.
ul. Ulyanova
ul. Semashko
ul. Varvarskaya
ul. Osharskaya
ul. Piskunova
ul. Alekseyevskaya
ul. Pokrovskaya
ul. Gruzinskaya
ul. Bolshaya
ul. Krasnoflotskaya
ul. Gogolya
ul. Maslyakova
ul. Maksima Gorkovo
ul. Belinskovo

Park
im.
Kulibina

Sad
im.
Pushkina

PL.
GORKOVO

ul. Matakovskovo

Kanavinski Most

Oka R. ←

Grebnevskie Kanal

Grebnevskie Peski

ul. Dolzhanskaya

PL.
LENINA

ul. Sovyetskaya

ul. Litvinova

ul. Chkalova

HOTELS
1 Centralny Hotel
2 Hotel Rossiya

RUSSIA

restaurant with flowered umbrellas and a large model airplane. Started by an American, this fast-food joint is frequented by wealthy Russians who can afford a taste of America. Fried chicken 7500R. Chili 7500R. Pizza 5000R. Also fried potatoes, onion soups, spaghetti, and rice. Take away fudge and Cuban cigars are kept in large fridges. Open daily 11am-9pm.

Ptitsa (Птица), Bolshaya Pokrovskaya ul. 15. Whole, grilled chicken for the road 2000R. Open Mon.-Fri. 9am-8pm, Sat. 9am-5pm.

Restaurant Kolizei (Ресторан Колизей), at Bolshaya Pokrovskaya 32. One of the 1001 operations run by the private firm "Russki Club," this is both a restaurant and an outdoor café—the atmosphere makes up for the prices. Fish soup 2000R. *Pelmeni* (meat dumplings) in boullion 3500R. Chicken entrees 5000R, Beef filet 9000R. Cake 350R. Imported beers 4000R. Open daily 10am-4pm and 6-11pm.

Russkiye Pelmeni (Русские Пельмени), Bolshaya Pokrovskaya 24. *Pelmeni,* Russian meat-filled dumplings, served in boullion or with cheese, sour cream, or butter— all for less than 1000R. They also have *blini* (yummy Russian pancakes) served with butter, jam, or sour cream for around 500R. Open daily 10am-8pm.

Kafe Lykova Damba (Кафе Лыкова Дамба), on corner of Bolshaya Pokrovskaya and Lykova Damba ul. Large outdoor terrace and mirrored interior crowded with locals gossiping. Small menu of drinks, sandwiches, and cigarettes (1000-3000R). Open daily 10-am-8pm.

Restaurant and Café Vitalich (Ресторан Виталич), ul. Bolshaya Pokrovskaya on the right hand side, ¾ of the way up to pl. Gorkovo (tel. 34 37 14). The restaurant, set with folded cloth napkins, is fairly pricey; the café outside is extremely popular. *Blini* with sour cream 2300R. Assorted vegetables 3234R. Kiev Chicken 8348R. The extensive menu includes 10 different kinds of fruit. Outside the café sells hot dogs and exotic ice cream with fruit (1000R). Open noon-11pm. Another café branch is just to the left of the Kremlin.

Restaurant U Shakhovskovo (Ресторан У Шаховского) in the *Dom Aktyora* (Дом Актёра) on ul. Piskunova (ул. Пискунова), one block off Bolshaya Pokrovskaya. This is a fancy restaurant/jazz bar with prices to match. The management requires evening dress after 6pm to match the gleaming black and white decor. There are jazz performances in the evenings. Crab salad appetizer 6000R. *Shashlik* 8000R. Chicken Kiev 11,000R. Ice cream 1500R. Imported beers 3000-4000R. Cover 5000R. AmEx accepted. Open noon-4pm and 6-11pm.

Restaurant Rossiya (Ресторан Россия), in the Hotel Rossiya on Verkhnye-Volzhskaya Naberezhnaya (Верхне-Волжская наб.). Oh-so-Soviet, with heavy, carved-wood walls *and* ceiling. The menu is more extensive than most restaurants of this type. Caviar on bread 5000R. *Pelmeni* (meat dumplings) in boullion 4000R. Meat entrees 4000-5000R. Chicken 6000R. Open daily noon-4pm and 5pm-midnight.

SIGHTS AND ENTERTAINMENT

Nizhny Novgorod's importance as a border town is most visible in the view from the kremlin, which stands atop one of Russia's few hills and looks out over a vast expanse of Russia, making the town a perfect guard against the hordes of Genghis Khan and his descendents. The kremlin's walls are eight meters thick, and even today are utilized for a defensive purpose: the main tower now houses a bank.

Like most Russian kremlins, this one houses the local governor's and mayor's offices as well as a cathedral—in this case the 1631 **Archangel Cathedral** (Архангельское Собор; *Arkhangelskoe Sobor*), now a museum of the history of the kremlin and the city (open daily 10am-4pm, admission 2000R). The courtyard boasts an impressive collection of World War II-era tanks and other military vehicles. All can be climbed on, if you like that sort of thing. The governor's office was the site of an unwelcome visit from ultra-nationalist Vladimir Zhirinovsky in spring 1994; the governor cleverly arranged to be out of the city all day while Zhirinovsky sat in his office twiddling his thumbs.

The Nizhny Novgorod **Art Museum** (Художественный Музей) is currently housed in the kremlin while its home on Verkhnye-Volshkaya Naberezhnaya (Верхне-Волжская наб.) is being renovated. The museum holds Russian art from the 15th-20th centuries—some good and some painfully bad. Ignore the glares of the women guarding every room and look at the paintings and icons you like. The works from before the 17th century, largely icon and other church art, are labelled in English as well as Russian and are also the most interesting. Art from the 18th-19th centuries here is largely portraits of Tsars and other Russian VIPs, although there are a few paintings by the Russian artist Repin, including a vivid sketch of Ivan IV embracing the son to whom he has just given a fatal blow. There are also some good images of Russian peasants and country life. The 20th century paintings just aren't worth your time (open Thurs.-Mon. 10am-5pm, Wed. noon-7pm; admission 2000R).

The best part of the **Gorky Library Museum** (Литературной Музей им. А.М. Горький), ul. Minia 26 (ул. Минина) (tel. 36 65 83) is the building its housed in—an old 19th century mansion complete with large tacky mirrors, cherubs, velvet wallpaper, and rooms of carved dark wood. The inside supposedly shows the literary and cultural achievements of Gorky's contemporaries, with a sprinkling of his handwriting specimens, etc. A photo of 19th-century Nizhny lends some historical perspective (open Wed.-Sun. 9am-5pm). The **Museum-Apartment A.M. Gorkovo** (Квартира А.М. Горького), ul. Semashko 19 (ул. Семашко; tel. 36 16 51). It's on a street perpendicular to Verkhe-Volzhskaya nab.—turn right one street after the Hotel Oktyabrskaya and keep walking for a couple of blocks; the museum is on the right. Gorky lived here for a whole two years (1902-04), hence the museum. The large rooms do look comfortable and the kitchen is clean (open Fri.-Wed. 9am-1pm and 2-5pm; admission 300R, Russians 100R, children 50R).

The **Sakharov Museum** (Музей Сахарова; *Muzey Sakharova*), Prospect Gagarina 214 (Проспект Гагарина; tel. 66 86 23) is reachable by bus #43 down pr. Gagarina to the Sakharov Museum stop (about 30 min. from pl. Gorkovo). Cross the street and it is a little to the right. The Nobel Laureate and physicist Andrei Dimitievich Sakharov lived on the first floor of this typical Soviet apartment building while in internal exile. Guards watched him every moment; he was even forbidden to speak to people on the street. He is now honored with this museum (open Sat.-Thurs. 9am-6pm).

There are two monasteries in Nizhny. The **Blagoveshensku Monastery** (Благовещенский Мужской Монастырь) is located up the hill a short distance from where ul. Mayakovskaya ends and the bridge over the river begins, is currently operational. Black-robed monks lead daily services in the small, renovated Rozhdestrovskaya Church (1719). The church's walls are white-washed and the iconostasis is fresh wood. Come here only if you love monasteries, though; the architecture is charming, but there's little reason to make the trek (services 9am and 4:30pm). The **Pechari Monastery** is on the lower banks of the Volga is closed, but if you're willing to climb down and back up again, the crumbling building and overgrown foliage is peaceful and picturesque. Take any bus #2 or 17 labeled В. Печори.

Nizhny Novgorod Synagogue, ul. Gruzinskaya Ба (ул. Грузинская), is to the right off ul. Bolshaya Pokrovskaya—there is a sign to the synagogue. For approximately fifteen years Lipa Gruzman held secret services in his home. In 1989, he petitioned the state to be allowed to open a synagogue in this building, a 19th-century synagogue (during the Soviet era it became a furniture factory). His dream was fulfilled in 1990. To the surprise of many visitors, Nizhny Novgorod has an estimated Jewish population of 25,000, of which 6000 acknowledge their identity and 150 attend Shabbat services regularly. Despite lacking both a Rabbi and a true center, this one-room temple has the feeling of a religious community. An Orthodox temple, women stand behind a line of two pillars, but anyone is allowed in when services are in progress if they wish to pray. There are Hebrew lessons and a Sunday school.

Literally translated as **Museum-Preserve** (Музей-Заповедник) but closed for renovation in summer 1994, this museum usually displays recreations of pre-revolutionary Nizhny Novgorod apartments, including furniture and clothing, all housed in an attractive white stone building with statues carved into the façade (open Mon., Wed., Sat., Sun., 10am-5pm and Tues. 10am-10:30pm).

Museum-Dobrolyubova (Музей на Добролюбова), (tel. 34 22 49) is part museum, but mostly an antique salon. You can check out the antiques every Sat. at 11am or admire the icons, porcelain, old money, and books in the shop/museum itself (open Fri.-Wed. 9am-5pm).

The **Katameran Otdykh-I** (Катамаран Отдых-1), docked along the river, is a "boat for rest." It's safer during the day when you can relax on deck and have a drink from the café or bar. Cover 11am-5pm 4000R, 10pm-5am 15,000R, "with cabin" 25,000R. There's a disco from 6:30-9:30pm.

■■■ KAZAN (КАЗАНЬ)

The Khanate of Kazan held out against Ivan the Terrible's army for so long that the Tsar had his top generals executed. Eventually the city succumbed, and in the following 400 years the Tatar city was thoroughly Russified, becoming more famous for its university than for its dwindling Muslim population. Today the city is so typically Soviet that, except for the bilingual street signs, you would scarcely believe that Kazan is the capital of the sovereign Republic of Tatarstan, one of the more fractious regions of the Russian Federation. The predominantly Russian population is more concerned with surviving economic changes than their leaders' separatist rhetoric.

ORIENTATION AND PRACTICAL INFORMATION

Kazan, a city of a little more than a million inhabitants, lies on the east bank of the **Volga** (Волга) at the point where the river turns from east to south. Moscow is 700km to the west, Ulyanovsk 172km to the south. The city straddles the **Kazanka** (Казанка) **River** as it feeds into the Volga from the northeast. The streets of the old city on the south bank of the Kazanka splay outwards from the 16th century Kremlin. **Ul. Baumana** (ул. Баумана), the main shopping street, links the Kremlin with **pl. Kuibysheva** (пл. Куйбышева), the city's commercial center—and the only place where you can buy a **map** of the city (in the lobby of Hotel Tatarstan for an extortionate 8000R). Be wary of its accuracy. To reach the center from the train station, catch tram #2 or 4 in front of the main building. From the river station (речной вокзал), take trolley #2.

> **Tourist Office: Intourist,** 9 ul. Baumana, is no friend of the budget traveler. Straightforward questions—in Russian—can be answered (for a small fee) at the **Gorspravki** booth in pl. Kuibysheva opposite the Univermag (Универмаг) department store
>
> **Currency Exchange:** U.S. dollars and D-marks can be exchanged at any *obmen valiuty* (обмен валюты). Rates do not vary greatly and there is generally no commission. **Sberbank** is a safe choice.
>
> **Post Office:** 8 ul. Lenina (ул. Ленина). *Poste Restante* and photocopying. Open Mon-Fri 8am-7pm, Sat-Sun 9am-6pm.
>
> **Telephones:** *Mezhdugorodny telefon* (Междугородный телефон), 17 ul. Kuibysheva. International calls must be ordered in advance. Open 24 hours. When cruise ships are in port, the **International Phone Center** in the river station offers direct international calls for $3 per minute to Europe and Turkey and $4 per minute to the rest of the world.
>
> **Telephone City Code:** 8432
>
> **Flights:** The airport is to the southeast of the city (tel. 37 98 07).
>
> **Trains:** The station is on ul. Said-Galeeva (Саид-Галиева) (tel. 39 23 00). Daily connections to most cities in Russia; several trains daily to Moscow, Nizhny Novgorod, and Volgograd.
>
> **Public Transportation: Trams, trolleys,** and **buses** are cheap and frequent although often very crowded. Tickets are 100R and can be purchased in strips of ten from the driver or from kiosks at the stations and pl. Kuibysheva. Tickets are sometimes collected as you exit. There are billboard maps of the tram and trolley routes posted at the river station and in pl. Kuibysheva. The tourist map available at the Hotel Tatarstan also contains a small transport guide. There are also mysterious *marshrutnye taksi* (route taxis) but no one seems to know much about

them. The best way to find one's way is to ask. The locals all seem to know the tram and trolley routes.

Ferries: The river station *(rechnoi vokzal)* is at ul. Portovaya (Портовая) (tel. 37 97 00). River boats *(teplokhody)* leave for Moscow and all points along the Volga several times per week. Cheaper and faster **hydrofoils** *(rakety* and *meteory)* cover shorter routes at least once per day. Departures are often early in the morning. Tram #7 links the river station with the train station.

Luggage Storage: Lockers in station cost 1300 rubles for the first 24 hrs. (1900R for larger bags) and 2500R for each additional 24 hrs. Open daily midnight-7:45am, 8am-1pm, 2-6.45pm and 7-11pm.

Emergency: Fire: tel. 01. **Police:** tel. 02. **Ambulance:** tel. 03.

Police: The **MVD** headquarters is at 19 ul. Dzerzhinskovo (ул. Дзержинского) (tel. 02). The **passport office** (OVIR) is around the corner on ul. Gorodetskovo. Registration is required for stays of longer than two days.

ACCOMMODATIONS

The Tatarstan authorities have directed that foreigners pay roughly 150% more than "Soviet" citizens for hotel rooms. Don't take it personally: hoteliers will reassure you that Latvians, Lithuanians, Estonians, and Moldovans suffer the same fate. With a struggle, foreign students studying at Russian universities can pay the Soviet rate. Bring your student card and a letter from your institution.

Gostinitsa (Гостиница), rechnoi vokzal. In the main building of the river station, on your left as you face the river. The only hotel in town that ignores the markup for foreigners. No showers or hot water and only basic toilet facilities, but the rooms are clean. Curfew 11pm. One bed in a double with basin 6000R. It's 1/6 the price of the next-cheapest hotel. The only drawbacks are sharing a room with a Muscovite whose snores echo across the Volga, and the water is turned off late at night, making toilet-flushing rather difficult.

Hotel Kazan (Казань), 9/15 ul. Baumana (tel. 32 17 87). It's a 15-minute walk from pl. Kuibysheva and an equal distance from the train station along ul. Chernyshevskogo. This pre-revolutionary relic has seen better days. The lobby is ornately decorated but the rooms are crumbling. Keep your door locked. Showers are on the first floor (when the city has hot water). Singles with TV and toilet 30,000R. Doubles with TV and toilet 45,000R. Two-room double with shower 82,000R.

Hotel Tatarstan (Татарстан), 2 ul. Kuibysheva (tel. 39 04 92). The usual destination for foreign tourists and the best of Kazan's large hotels. Even here no one speaks English. Rooms are clean and bland. Singles 31780R. Doubles 51900R, with shower, TV, and refrigerator 86400R.

Gostinitsa molodezhnogo tsentra (Молодежный Центр), 1 ul. Dekabristov (ул. Декабристов) (tel. 32 79 54), across the dam from the Kremlin. The youth center hotel should not be confused with a youth hostel. Doubles with shower, TV and refrigerator 80,400R. Don't let them send you to the far more expensive private hotel on the fifth floor ($40 per person in a double—but they speak English).

Hotel Duslyk (Дуслык), 49 Pravo-Bulachnaya ul. (Право-Булачная) (tel. 32 53 20). Turn left with your back to the Hotel Tatarstan and right when you reach the Bulak canal. Adequate but overpriced rooms. Singles 50000R. Doubles 87600R, with second room, shower, TV, and refrigerator 131400R.

FOOD

Tatars are red-meat eaters, so the health-conscious must either resign themselves to the standard Soviet *salaty* of fresh vegetables or visit the kolkhozny rynok near the train station. Bread, cheese, and basic groceries can be found on ul. Baumana near pl. Kuibysheva ...and Snickers, Twix, Coke and Pepsi in kiosks on every corner.

Dom chaya, 64 ul. Baumana. Booths around the central samovar are lined with flowery cows, velvet cats, and outrageous tapestries of peasant life. Local specialties. A several course meal costs under 6000R. Open daily 9am-3pm and 4-9pm.

Restoran Kazan, 9 ul. Baumana. Black-faced lions with gold manes guard the entrance and set the tone. Moderately priced Soviet cuisine (entrees under 5000R) and a loud band in the evening. Open daily 11am-5pm and 6-11pm.

Café Bliny (Кафе Блины), 47 ul. Baumana. A vegetarian outpost. Bliny with butter, honey or *smetana* for well under 1000R, as well as fresh vegetable *salaty*. Open daily 7am-3pm and 4-8pm.

There is also a **farmers' market** *(kolkhozny rynok) at* Gabdully Tukaya ul. (Габдуллы Тукая), one tram stop (#2, 4 or 7) from the end of the line at the train station or three tram stops (#2 or 4) from pl. Kuibysheva in the direction of the train station. Covers all major food groups, including ketchup. Arrive early and don't forget to haggle. Open Mon., Wed., Fri. and Sun. 6am-2pm, Tues., Thurs. and Sat. 6am-5pm.

SIGHTS AND ENTERTAINMENT

The white-washed **Kremlin fortress,** presiding over the Kazanka, was built by Ivan the Terrible to celebrate the destruction of the previous Kremlin. It made sense to him. The main entrance is at the end of ul. Lenina. The buildings inside currently house government offices and are not open to the public. The **Tower of Syuyubike** can be admired from a short distance; the **Blagoveshchensky Cathedral,** designed by Pskov masters in 1561, now holds state archives. There are unconfirmed rumors of tours around the eight remaining towers of the Kremlin wall (daily 10am-5pm, beginning in the courtyard of the government buildings). Across the square from the entrance to the Kremlin is the **Tatar State Museum.** Destroyed by fire in 1989, it is currently under reconstruction. Meanwhile, it displays an exhibit on the early history of Kazan, as well as local arts and crafts. Look out for the winking Satan against the back wall (open Sun.-Fri. 9am-4:30pm).

One block down ul. Lenina and downhill to the right is the 18th century **Sobor Petra i Pavla** (Peter and Paul Cathedral), built to commemorate Peter the Great's visit to Kazan in 1722. Its Baroque octagonal central tower looks all the more colorful against the spare white walls of the nearby Kremlin. The interior, featuring a 25m tall iconostasis, somehow survived decades of Bolshevik despoliation, including a brief stint as a pool hall, before being returned to the Orthodox Church in 1989. Pick up your copy of *"Popery and its Struggle against Orthodoxy"* on your way out. During repairs in the late 1980s, someone stole its multi-ton bell that had been left in the courtyard. They tracked down the thieves half way across Ukraine. A short walk further down ul. Lenina brings you to the campus of **Kazan State University**. A rare beardless statue of Lenin, easily recognizable by his trademark pout, honors the university's favorite expellee. Nearby stands a 3-dimensional solid representation of Nikolai Ivanovich Lobachevsky, inventor of non-Euclidean geometry and immortalized for non-mathematicians by the songs of Tom Lehrer.

Turning right on ul. Kuibysheva at the end of ul. Lenina leads to pl. Svobody. At one end is the pillared **Tatarstan State Academic Theater of Opera and Ballet** (box office open Tues.-Sat. 10am-7:30pm, Sun.-Mon. 10am-2pm and 3-7:30pm); at the other end is the economic of Tatarstan. Next to the theater is another classical building, the **Officers' House,** where the pre-revolutionary gentry assembled; the composer Rakhmaninov performed here from 1910-1916. On the first floor is a kiosk selling Red Army surplus jackets; on the second, next to the concert hall, is a gallery of local contemporary art. The gallery's flier declares that it was founded "not only for commercial reasons, but also for aesthetic ones" (open daily 10am-6pm).

Elsewhere in the city are two 200 year-old **mosques** on the banks of the first of three Kaban lakes (ul. Kayuma Nasyri), and an exhibit of weapons and war photographs in the **Dom Kultury** at 26 ul. Karla Marksa. (Why an art gallery in the officers' house and a gun exhibit in the house of culture? We don't know.) A large **park** sits to the northeast on the shore of the Kazanka. The tall red-brick tower on ul. Baumana near pl. Kuibysheva, currently occupied by a knitting store, an engraver, and an eyeglass repair shop, is the tower of **Tserkov Bogoyavleniya**. Local believers are struggling to reclaim it from the city government.

■■■ ULYANOVSK (УЛЬЯНОВСК)

On April 22, 1995, Ulyanovsk will somewhat awkwardly commemorate the 125th birthday of its most famous resident and namesake, Vladimir Ilich Ulyanov—better known as Lenin. Twenty-five years ago, the Soviet authorities threw their hearts and bulldozers into the construction of a memorial zone encompassing much of the center of town and the riverfront. They were already making plans for 1995 when the events of 1991 brought Soviet rule to an abrupt end. Today, few visitors make the pilgrimage to this Bethlehem of Bolshevism, and those that do come to make business deals rather than to pay homage. Local women, who used to lay flowers at Lenin's feet every April 22, now take their bouquets to the local war memorial. Inside the various museums, however, elderly guides faithfully preserve the cult of Lenin, reciting their encomia without a hint of irony, as if oblivious to the changes of the past few years.

ORIENTATION AND PRACTICAL INFORMATION

Ulyanovsk, formerly the Tsarist outpost of Simbirsk, flanks the Volga River 170km south of Kazan and 900km north of Volgograd. The city center sits on a hill above the west bank of the **Volga**, bounded to the west by the smaller **Sviyaga River** (Свияга). **Ul. Goncharova** (ул. Гончарова), the main shopping street and transport hub, runs parallel to the Volga. A short walk east from ul. Goncharova down any cross-street takes you to the main tourist sights overlooking the river. A short walk west along **ul. Lenina** (ул. Ленина) takes you to *Ulyanovskturist* at Dom Lenina, the only place in town that always has tourist **maps**. From the train and river stations, take tram #4 to ul. Goncharova. From the airport, take bus #6.

Tourist offices: Ulyanovskturist (Ульяновсктурист), 78 ul. Lenina (tel. 32 64 12). From the central train station, take tram #4 towards park Pobedy (Победы) and get off at Dom Lenina. From the river station, take tram #1 or 4 towards the park. Ulyanovskturist designed the tourist map of the city, but do not necessarily always have copies to give away. Only Russian spoken.

Budget Travel: Rosintour, 38 ul. Lva Tolstovo (ул. Льва Толстого), room 310 (tel. 31 46 98, fax 32 08 94). Tram: *Dom Lenina*, entrance on ul. Zheleznoi Divizii (ул. Железной Дивизии). Hotel and transport reservations, as well as city tours. Open Mon.-Fri. 9am-1pm and 2-6pm. If you're planning ahead, their Moscow office (and hotel) is at ul. Bakhrushina 15 (ул. Бахрушина), (tel. 235 60 65, 235 11 02 or 235 81 41). **Intourist,** 19 Sovietskaya ul., room 306 (tel. 39 48 12, fax 31 97 35), in the Hotel Venets. From the train and river stations, take tram #4 towards park Pobedy as far as Gostinitsa Venets. Reduced rates with the city's major hotels. Open Mon-Fri 9am-5pm. Neither budget travel office's staff speaks English, but they have access to expensive interpreters.

Currency Exchange: Banks on ul. Goncharova have poor rates but do not charge a commission. A better bet is the **Sberkassa** at 50 ul. Goncharova.

Post Office: 56 ul. Goncharova.

Telephones: Intercity and international calls can be made at the train station 24 hrs. per day, and during working hours at the river station. **City Code:** 8442.

Flights: The airport is to the west of the city, 40 minutes from the center, (tel. 36 54 55). Bus #6 from ul. Goncharova. Ticket office 38 ul. Minayeva (tel. 31 44 42). Several flights per week to Moscow; 2 flights per week to Volgograd during the summer, 1 per week during the winter. Both routes around $90 for foreigners.

Trains: Ulyanovsk-tsentralny, 30 minutes southwest of the center on tram #4 (tel. 37 07 07 or 32 37 39). Several trains daily to Moscow (17 hours, *coupé* 35000R), Volgograd (22 hours, *coupé* 20000R), and other Russian cities.

Buses: Avtovokzal, ul Polbina 48 (tel. 36 57 31). Hourly buses to Kazan during the day (5 hrs).

Public Transportation: Trams serve the center of the city. Tickets cost 20R and can be bought at ticket kiosks but *not* from the driver. Buses and trolleys link the center with the other regions, including across the river. The driver sells tickets in strips of 5, 6 and 10 for 50R per ticket. The tourist map indicates transport routes with colored lines. Route-taxis ironically no longer follow their routes.
Ferries: Rechnoi vokzal (речной вокзал), just south of the center off ul. Kirova (tel. 39 64 31 or 31 85 32). Take tram #1 or 4 from the center to rechnoi vokzal and walk down a lot of steps. Fast and inexpensive **hydrofoils** make daily trips as far as Kazan in the north and Samara in the south. They usually leave between 7 and 8am; buy tickets at least the day before. Cruise boats pass through several times a week on their way north to Nizhny Novgorod and Moscow and south to Volgo-grad and Astrakhan or Rostov, making many stops along the way. The 36-hour sail from Ulyanovsk to Volgograd includes what are reputed to be the most beautiful stretches of the Volga. The trip to Moscow takes five days.
Luggage Storage *(kamera khraneniya):* Office and lockers open 24 hrs. except 6:30-7am, 1-2pm, and 6:30-7pm. Small bags 1300R for the first 24 hrs. Large bags 1900R for the first 24 hrs. Both sizes 2500R per additional 24 hrs.
Public Market: Tsentralny rynok, ul. Shevchenko. Outdoor market open May-Sept. Mon. 7am-2pm, Tues.-Sun. 7am-4pm. Indoor market open Apr.-Oct. Mon. 7am-noon, Tues.-Thurs., Sat.-Sun. 7am-7pm, Fri. 7am-5pm.; Nov.-Mar. Mon. 8am-noon, Tues.-Thurs., Sat.-Sun. 8am-6pm, Fri. 8am-5pm.
Laundramat: 23 ul. Goncharova (tel. 31 88 91).
Emergencies: Fire: tel. 01. **Police:** tel. 02. **Ambulance:** tel. 03.
Police: 32 ul. Karla Marksa (tel. 31 23 60). **Passport office** (tel. 32 85 94). Registra-tion is not usually required.

ACCOMMODATIONS

The regional government has instituted a "desiatikratny tarif" (900% mark-up) for for-eigners staying in state-owned *(kommunalnye)* hotels. There are two ways to avoid the mark-up. The first is to stay in a *vedomstvennaya* hotel owned by a local enter-prise. The second is to plan ahead and make reservations through Intourist or Rosin-tour. **Intourist** offers rooms in the city's main tourist hotel, the Hotel Venets, for US$25 per person, US$28 with breakfast; they can be persuaded to negotiate cheaper rooms in other hotels and college dormitories. **Rosintour,** an upstart rival to Intourist, can find inexpensive rooms in hotels far from the center of town. Both need at least two days notice. A third possibility for confident Russian-speakers, is to negotiate directly with one of the local institutes. The Pedagogical Institute's dormi-tory borders the memorial zone. If it's not still under construction, call Anatoly Ale-kseyevich Khovryn, the prorector (tel. 31 42 63).

Tsentr grazhdanskoi aviatsii, 5 ul. Ostrovskogo (ул. Островского) (tel. 34 35 54 or 39 94 72). Take tram #4 to ul. Ryleyeva or #1 to ul. Orlova. The rooms are far from immaculate, and there are no toilet seats, but the hotel does have a pool table and kitchen facilities. Singles with shower 47240R, with telephone 63000R. Doubles with shower and telephone 54600R. Triples with shower and telephone 77100R. Add small surcharges for optional towels, TV, use of refrigerator and kitchen equipment, etc., and then a 23% tax. Review the price list and bill thoroughly.
Gostinitsa, rechnoi vokzal (речной вокзал). Talk to the dezhurnyi administrator on the first floor of the river station. Rudimentary bathroom facilities at best. The hotel's sink does have a reliable flow of clear cold water, but the same cannot be said of its only (seatless) toilet. A night in a 4-bed room is 3750R.

FOOD

Lenin believed that no-one should go hungry, but did not promise that the food would be good. In Ulyanovsk, the capitalist **farmers' market** might be the best option. There are several **cafés** along ul. Goncharova and ul. Karla Marksa, some serving ice cream and Turkish coffee *(kofe turetskii* or *vostochnii),* others Russian staples such as *bliny, shashlyki,* and *pelmeni.* **Café Uyut,** 5 ul. Karla Marksa, serves *pelmeni* and pizza to local trendies for around 1000R (open daily 11am-7pm). **Café**

Sport (Кафе Спорт), 25 ul. Engelsa, offers *salaty, borsch,* and "goulash" (meat and potatoes) to an older crowd for under 4000R (open Mon.-Sat. 10am-6pm). The restaurant in the Venets, 19 ul. Sovietskaya, has typical Soviet cuisine and decor (including a band after 8pm) at above average prices (a four-course meal costs around 15000R).

SIGHTS AND ENTERTAINMENT

If you have no interest in the minute details of the early life of the founder of Bolshevism, you've come to the wrong town. Otherwise, the challenge is to read between the party lines to learn about Lenin the man. The first stop for Ulyanophiles is the **Dom-musei Lenina,** 68 ul. Lenina (tel. 31 22 22), next door to *Ulyanovskturist.* The Ulyanov family lived here (quite comfortably) from 1878 to 1887. You will be asked to put on leather overshoes so as not to soil the holy ground. The carefully restored house contains a grand piano, icons in the corners, and other bourgeois touches (open Sun.-Mon., Wed.-Fri. 9am-4:30pm; admission 100R).

Less interesting are the houses in the pl. 100-letiya so dnya rozhdeniya V.I. Lenina (the **100th Anniversary of Lenin's Birth Square),** where Vladimir Ulyanov was actually born and spent his first five years. The **birthplace,** a more modest abode than the house on ul. Lenina, contains furniture typical of the period, including a large Russian *pech* (oven); the **kvartira-muzei** is just a collection of family photographs. Look for the nearby statue of mother-and-child-with-receding-hairline. The concrete **Lenin Memorial** building (tel. 39 49 41) surrounding the museums holds a **concert hall** and, tucked in one side, a rich collection of Bolshevik memorabilia. The exhibit culminates in a glittering shrine to Ilich himself (open Tues.-Thurs., Sat.-Sun. 9am-5pm, Fri. 9am-4pm; admission 400R).

At the south end of the 100th Anniversary Square is the **Classical Gymnasium** (high school), where Vladimir Ulyanov, son of the regional school superintendant, finished top of his class. Note the glowing recommendation letter written by the director of the school, whose son, Aleksandr Kerensky, went on to lead the Provisional Government that was deposed by Lenin in October 1917 (open Tues.-Sat. 9am-5pm, Sun. 9am-4pm). Sloping down to the Volga from the 100th Anniversary Square is the **Friendship of the Peoples Park**, constructed for the centenary celebration by teams from each of the 15 Soviet Republics. Much of the park is in poor condition and the cable car down to the embankment hangs idle, a suitable monument to the friendship of the peoples.

For those who have seen one Ulyanov family snapshot too many, the city offers few reprieves. The **Dom-musei Goncharova,** 20 ul. Goncharova on the corner of ul. Lenina, chronicles the unremarkable life of the 19th century writer Ivan Goncharov. He wrote his most famous novel, *Oblomov,* in seven weeks at stenographic speed (open Wed.-Sun. 10am-6pm, Tues. 10am-4pm; admission 100R). An interesting late Tsarist building at 3 bul. Novy Venets houses the **Krayevedchesky Museum** (Regional Studies); stuffed vultures and mounted insects galore. Upstairs sits a modest collection of European art (open Wed.-Sun. 10am-6pm, Tues. 10am-4pm; admission to each 300R). Rickety wooden houses of indeterminate age line the sidestreets near the center, giving a glimpse of how the genuinely poor lived (and live) in provincial Russia.

■■■ VOLGOGRAD (ВОЛГОГРАД)

On January 31, 1943, General-Field Marshal Friedrich von Paulus and the remains of the Nazi Sixth Army surrendered to Soviet troops in Stalingrad, as this city was then known—bringing to an end one of the bloodiest battles in history and handing Hitler his first major defeat. In the course of the 200-day Battle of Stalingrad, German bombardment destroyed 91% of the city's buildings, and each side had suffered an estimated 1.5 million casualties. After the war, the Soviet authorities rebuilt the center of Stalingrad with uncharacteristic good taste, clearing broad and colorful avenues out of the ruins of the pre-war city. Numerous monuments and plaques mark

RUSSIA

the sites of wartime exploits, the most famous of which is the colossal statue on Mamayev Kurgan. Today locals are keen to point out that the history of this sunny southern city did not begin with the "Great Patriotic War": nearby is the Medieval capital of the mysterious Khazar Empire (now submerged under a Soviet-era reservoir), a Cossack settlement, and a 200-year-old German colony. The population of modern Volgograd is diverse and cosmopolitan, with a regular flow of foreign students and businesspeople. The city's heavy industry is struggling to survive in the new economic environment, but the huge Red October metallurgical factory, now in private hands, is already making deals with customers in the West.

ORIENTATION AND PRACTICAL INFORMATION

Volgograd is a crescent-shaped city that stretches 80km around a bend in the Volga, 900km south of Ulyanovsk and 900km southeast of Moscow. The **Volga-Don Canal,** which begins in the southernmost region of the city, links Volgograd with Rostov-on-Don, 500km to the west, and with the Asov and Black Seas beyond. The streets of the city's midsection form a grid parallel to the river, with **pr. Lenina** the main north-south thoroughfare. The broad **alleya Geroyev** (Alley of Heroes) leads from the river port across pr. Lenina to the **pl. Pavshikh Bortsov** (Square of Fallen Fighters), which itself lies immediately southeast of the train station and contains the Intourist and Volgograd Hotels. North of the center along the waterfront sprawls a vast region of metallurgical, turbine, and tractor factories, the strategic objective of the Nazi attack on Stalingrad. Mamayev Kurgan—102m tall according to military maps—overlooks the factories and the city center. The newer southern regions of the city are primarily agricultural and residential. A kiosk in the basement of the train station is one of a very few places that sell city maps

Tourist Office: Volgograd Turist, Kommunisticheskaya ul. 23 (tel. 34 00 05, 34 82 66, or 34 69 67), a 10-minute walk from the alleya Geroyev along Kommunisticheskaya ul. The Russian-speaking staff cannot help with budget accommodations but can arrange excursions. Open daily 7am-noon and 1-7pm; staff on duty Mon.-Fri. 8am-noon and 1-5pm. The **Hotel Intourist** has a service bureau (tel. 36 14 68) with English-speaking staff, city maps, and glossy brochures.

Currency/Exchange: Banks on pr. Lenina and kiosks around the train station buy U.S. dollars and *Deutschemarks* for no commission.

Post Office: Pochtamt, pl. Pavshikh Bortsov, opposite the Intourist Hotel. Open Mon.-Fri. 8am-8pm, Sat.-Sun. 8am-6pm. Postcards show that a sign above used to read "The ideas of V.I.Lenin are alive and will triumph." **Postal Code:** 400066.

Telephones: Payphones take tokens *("zhetony"),* sold at the *Pochtamt* for 100R. Long distance calls and faxes can be ordered at the **Mezhdugorodny telefon,** ul. Mira 16 (tel. 33 55 01), next door to the Intourist Hotel. Open 24 hours. **City Code:** 8422.

Flights: The airport is 35 minutes west of the center (tel. 31 73 78). **Aeroflot** ticket office: alleya Geroyev 5 (tel. 33 59 66). Three flights daily to Moscow ($108 one way), three flights per week to Rostov-on-Don ($78 one way), and regular flights to other Russian cities. Open 8am-1pm and 2-7pm. Express buses between the airport and the Aeroflot office leave every 15-30 minutes (tickets 600R).

Trains: Volgograd-1, northwest of pl. Pavshikh Bortsov (tel. 005). Three trains daily to Moscow (23-29 hours, *coupé* 40,000R (US$20)), two daily to Rostov-on-Don (13 hours, *coupé* 17,000R).

Buses: Tsentralny avtovokzal, ul. Mikhaila Balonina 11, behind the train station (tel. 37 83 38). Nowhere of any real interest is within bus range.

Public Transportation: The **"metrotram,"** a hybrid said to have been devised when the city did not have enough money to finish its metro, runs north from the center along pr. Lenina. It travels underground in the center, but otherwise resembles Russian trams. Tickets are sold individually at kiosks by the overground stops and at ticket counters underground (100R). The stop closest to the alleya Geroyev is one block north on the corner of Komsomolskaya ul. **Buses** link the train station with the southern and western regions of the city. Pay the conduc-

Central Volgograd

1 Ferry terminal
2 Movie Theater Salyut
3 Central Market
4 Train station
5 Movie Theater Rodina

N
↑

Park Pobedy

Mamayev Kurgan

prosp. Lenina

ul. Bakinskaya

ul. 7-ya Gvargeyskaya

ul. Mikhaila Balonina

Kommunisticheskaya

pr. IstoricheskI

ul. V. I. Chukova

2

PL. LENINA

Park Pobedy

ul. P. Osipenko

ul. Ladozhskaya

ul. Medvediskaya

ul. Parkhomenko

ul. Mira

ul. Gagarina

Naberezhnaya Armii

5

4

3

Krasnoznamenskaya ul.

ul. Angarskaya

PL. PAVSHIKH BORTSOV

ul. Sovyetskaya

alleya Geroyev

1

Tsaritsa R.

ul. Cherepovetskaya

ul. Azizbekova

ul. Vokzalnaya

ul. Raboche-Krestyanskaya

Volga River

tor, if there is one, or else the driver (100R). Transport runs 7am-11pm. A map of the transit routes hangs at the river station. For information tel. 75 35 82.

Ferries: Rechnoi vokzal, Naberezhnaya 62-armii (наб. 62-армии) (tel. 44 52 09), near the foot of the steps at the end of alleya Geroyev. Cruise boats on their way to Moscow pass through every other day. The journey takes a week, and costs between 42,000R (US$20; hard class) and 235,000R (US$120; first class). Hard class gets you a space in a quad on lower deck; second class abunk-bed double on middle deck; first class a double with a basin, and shower off the hall on the upper deck. There are also outrageously priced deluxe cabins. Boats to Rostov-on-Don via the Volga-Don Canal pass every four days. The journey takes 36 hours and costs between 15,000R (hard class) and 85,000R (first class). Ticket office open 8am-5pm, 6-10pm. Hour-long boat-rides (1200R) leave from near the river station on summer afternoons. On weekends, annoy local fishermen on a two-hour disco cruise (3000R).

Luggage Storage: kamera khraneniya in the basement of the train station. Small bags 1300R until midnight, 1300R per day thereafter; large bags 2500R until midnight, 2500R per day thereafter Open 8am-6:30pm, 7pm-7:30a. Also in the basement of **river station.** Small bags 900R up to 48 hours, 1200R per day thereafter; large bags 1200R up to 48 hours, 2100R per day thereafter. Open Tues.-Sat. 8am-1pm and 2-5pm After hours, you can retrieve your bags by pestering the duty administrator in room 107.

Market: Tsentralny rynok, ul. Sovietskaya 17. Entrances on Komsomolskaya ul. and pr. Lenina behind the Central Bank. Open summer Mon. 7am-4pm, Tues.-Sat. 7am-7pm, Sun 7am-5pm; winter Mon. 7am-4pm, Tues.-Sat. 7am-6pm, Sun 7am-5pm. Fishing rods available for hunter-gatherer types.

Emergencies: Fire: tel. 01. **Police:** tel. 02. **Ambulance:** tel. 03.

Police: Passport Office (OVIR): Registration is supposedly required for stays of longer than 3 days, but enforcement is spotty; the Intourist Hotel automatically registers you.

ACCOMMODATIONS

Most of Volgograd's hotels either refuse to take foreigners or charge a mark-up that pushes them well beyond the price-range of the budget traveler.

Volgograd State University: Their dormitory, ul. Vtoraya Prodolnaya 30 (vtaRAya praDOLnaya) is by far the best deal for students. The International Contacts Division needs to know the number and sex of the travelers and the length of their stay at least 2 days in advance. Call Irina Anatolyevna Dudina (tel. 43 37 86 or 43 12 02) and mention *Let's Go* (she speaks English). The drawbacks are that the university is a 40min. bus ride from the train station and that it insists on registering visitors with OVIR (often a painful experience). Comfortable if sparsely furnished suites with bathrooms and showers for US$5 per person.

Intourist Hotel, ul. Mira 14 (tel. 36 45 53, fax 33 91 75), in the pl. Pavshikh Bortsov. An unusually worthwhile Intourist hotel. The management of this grand 1958-vintage hotel has fended off several hostile take-over bids—including one by an American company—since it was sold to its employees in 1993, but it fully intends to bring the service up to world standards. The rooms are clean, the staff polite, and the hot water almost reliable. MTV is currently being installed. When the hotel is not crowded, a place in a double (MESTa vdvookh-MESTnom NOMer'e) can effectively be a half-price single. Singles US$40, with shower US$65. Doubles with toilet, TV, and telephone US$47, with shower US$80 The difference between rooms with and without showers is substantial. Accepts Visa, MC, and American Express.

Gostinitsa, Rechnoi vokzal, on the fourth floor of the river station. Extremely reluctant to host foreigners, but does not charge a mark-up. Hot water is sporadic, but the six-legged locals that may share your bathroom don' t seem to mind. A bed in a double with shower 12,000R ($6).

Hotel Volgograd, pl. Pavshikh Bortsov (tel. 36 33 47, fax 33 99 24) Unlike the Intourist Hotel across the street, the Volgograd remains in state hands, and the difference is apparent: rooms are clean but very Soviet. Singles with shower, Russian cable, TV, and fridge 94,000R. Doubles with shower, Russian cable, TV, and fridge 112,600R.

FOOD

Cafés serving ice-cream, coffee, and alcohol abound near the alleya Geroyev on pr. Lenina and ul. Chuikova. Fish is the local specialty, but most restaurants serve only meat and potatoes.

Dyadya Misha, on the waterfront just north of the river station. This outdoor Caucasian restaurant may look like a streetside café, but some locals hold their wedding banquets here. Pork lulia kebabs are the house specialty. A meal without alcohol costs under 10,000R.

U drakona, pr. Lenina 12, squeezed between a joint-venture café and a casino near the alleya Geroyev. The restaurant's original chef has long since returned to China, but it continues to serve almost recognizable Chinese food. The challenge, however, is to decipher the Russian menu. A band plays distinctly un-Chinese music in the evening. Amaze the waitress and fellow diners by asking for chopsticks *(Palochki)*. A several-course meal costs 10,000-15,000R. Open noon-4pm and 6pm-midnight.

Kafe Mayak, ul. Chuikova, south of the river station in a short but conspicuous lighthouse. The café is beautifully situated, but for some unknown reason only the kitchen has a view of the Volga. The interior is elegantly decorated, but the menu is limited. A band plays after 8pm every Tues.-Sun. evening. *Salat* and entree for around 5000R. Open noon-midnight.

Restoran Neptun, ul. Kalinina 4, south of the center near the pl. Chekistov. Above a bar, casino, and fish store. Thanks to industrious Soviet dam-construction, the Roman God of the Sea has taken up residence in parts of the Volga. Seafood entrees for 3000-4000R. Open daily noon-5pm and 6-11:30pm.

Restoran Druzhba, pr. Lenina 15. Typically Russian decor, typically Soviet menu. Entrees under 5000R. Open 11am-3pm and 4-10pm.

SIGHTS

War memorials around Volgograd fall roughly into two categories: those commemorating the tragedy of the destruction of Stalingrad, and those celebrating the glorious triumph of the Soviet forces. Polar opposites in this respect are the city's two most famous sights, the Mamayev Kurgan memorial complex, a short ride from the center on the metrotram, and the Museum-Panorama of the Battle of Stalingrad.

The strategic peak of **Mamayev Kurgan** changed hands 13 times in the course of the battle, and the earth was so clogged with shrapnel that for two years afterwards nothing would grow on the mound. Today, the slopes are covered with trees, many dedicated to individual soldiers and still tended to by elderly loved-ones. A poplar-lined path leads to the memorial complex around the peak. The complex itself is a moving tribute to the horror of the battle, an example of socialist realism at its most effective. Grim heads protrude from crumbling walls, and magnified graffiti affirm the soldiers' resolve to stand until death, as somber martial songs flow from unseen speakers. Communist slogans are remarkably inconspicuous: patriotism is the overwhelming theme, culminating in the 52m-tall sword-wielding **Motherland,** her face contorted in an anguished battle-cry.

In contrast to the memorial complex, the **Museum-Panorama,** ul. Chuikova 2 (tel. 34 67 23), on the riverfront behind pl. Lenina, is pure Soviet kitsch. The museum presents a chronological blow-by-blow account of the Soviet counterattack, including numerous photographs, uniforms, guns, and Communist Party membership cards retrieved from the dead. The **Panorama** above the museum—entitled "The Route of the German-Fascist Troops Around Stalingrad"—dramatizes various heroic moments in the final recapture of Mamayev Kurgan. As the tour-guides make clear, the exhibition is an extended polemic against Western historians who have tried to downplay the Soviet Army's role in the defeat of Nazism (open Tues.-Sun. 10am-5pm, closed last Fri. of each month; tours available in English). Next to the museum-panorama stand the gutted ruins of a mill, preserved as an example of the wartime destruction. Across the street is the rear of the **Dom Pavlova,** the house where Sergeant Yakov Pavlov and 23 soldiers held out for 58 days against continuous German attacks. Murals celebrate the feat on the front and back of the house.

Southwest of the center lies **Lysaya Gora** (Лысая гора; Bald Hill), a site of particularly fierce fighting where construction workers, collectors, and local children to this day find unexploded shells and mines. Further south is Sarepta, a colony of Germans that dates back to the time of Catherine the Great. The **Museum of Old Sarepta** chronicles the history of the local German community. Near the southern edge of the city is the mouth of the Volga-Don Canal, guarded by a dapper Lenin on one side and a bare pedestal where Stalin once stood on the other. Near the triumphal arch of the canal's first lock, local teenagers jeer and spit at passing cruise ships. For those nostalgic for Five Year Plans, the city's industrial megaliths can be admired from the river on hour-long **boat rides,** which also include a close-up view of the massive hydroelectric power plant just north of the city. For card-carrying Stalinists, the metallurgical, tractor, and turbine factories also have **museums** celebrating their war experiences and industrial achievements.

The city also has the inevitable **fine arts museum** (tel. 36 39 06; open Thurs.-Tues. 10am-5:30pm); a **railroad museum;** a **krayevedchesky museum** of flora and fauna (tel. 33 81 45); and a **museum of musical instruments** (tel. 42 10 56). Two hours by bus from the city center is a **Cossack Museum** at Stanitsa Ilovlya, open by request. The trip can best be arranged through a tourist office.

ENTERTAINMENT AND NIGHTLIFE

Volgograd teenagers hang out on summer evenings in the café-bars of alleya Geroyev and along the waterfront near the river port. A trendier crowd—including many foreigners—head for the **Argo club** in the side of the Pobeda movie theater, Kommunisticheskaya ul. 1 (tel. 36 22- 49). Dancing and occasional live bands. Their ban on sweatsuits sends a clear message that local body-building thugs are not welcome. Cover 10,000R for men, 5000R for women (open daily 8pm-4am).

The New Experimental Theater (NET), pl. Pavshikh Bortsov. An internationally-known troop whose repertoire includes interpretations of Romeo and Juliet, A Streetcar Named Desire, and Don Juan. Box office open Tues.-Sun. 2-7pm.

Planetarium, ul. Gagarina 14 (tel. 36 34 83). The marble-pillared planetarium has astronomy for children and astrology for adults, as well as films on the reconstruction of Stalingrad. Shows Sat.-Thurs. 10am, noon, 2pm and 4pm. The observatory is open Tues.-Sat. 10am-2pm, and at night only by special arrangement.

Kazachya Volya, A popular Cossack folk ensemble, it gives private concerts arranged through the tourist bureaus.

Puppet Theater, pr. lenina 15. Performances at 11am and 1pm. Box office open Tues.-Fri. 11:30am-2pm and 3-6pm, Sat.-Sun. 10am-2pm and 3-5pm

There's also a circus, as well as countless movie theaters showing dubbed American movies, all too-often (depending on your outlook) pornographic.

■■■ ROSTOV-ON-DON
(РОСТОВ-НА-ДОНУ)

Rostov-on-Don, Russia's "Gateway to the Caucasus," is a flourishing and polluted commercial and industrial city of over a million people; its streets are clogged with foreign cars and its shops filled with imported consumer goods. For several millennia, European merchants travelled to the mouth of the Don to trade with the tribes of the south Russian plains. In 1749, the Tsarist government decided to cash in on this trade by establishing a customs post on the site of modern Rostov. Commerce and agriculture have attracted communities of Armenians, Greeks, and, most recently, Koreans to the area. In contrast to thriving Rostov, however, the peasants and Cossacks who cultivate the fertile black-earth soil of the Don valley barely subsist on their earnings, thanks to the enduring legacy of Soviet collective farming.

ORIENTATION AND PRACTICAL INFORMATION

Rostov-na-Donu rises over the north bank of the Don, 1000km south of Moscow and 400km southwest of Volgograd. Thirty-five kilometers west of the Rostov, the Don feeds into Taganrog Bay and the Asov Sea. Rostovskaya Oblast shares a long border with Ukraine, whose eastern edge is directly north of the city of Rostov. The main street of the city's central grid is **ul. Bolshaya Sadovaya** (Большая Садовая; formerly ul. Engelsa), which runs parallel to the river from the suburban train station to the Park of the October Revolution. The quieter eastern region of Rostov was until 1928 the separate Armenian city of Nakhichevan-on-Don, and still has a large Armenian community and several active Armenian Orthodox churches. **Budennovsky pr.** (Буденновский пр.) climbs from the River Port, past the Central Market and across Bolshaya Sadovaya. Buses and trolleys link the airport in the east of the city with Bolshaya Sadovaya and the train station.

Tourist Offices: A.O. Rostovturist, Budennovsky pr. 21, on the corner of Bolshaya Sadovaya (tel. 62 32 59). This semi-private successor of the Soviet trade union travel bureau can arrange excursions in and around Rostov, as well as accommodations in the Hotel Turist. They have glossy brochures but are reluctant to part with city maps. Some English spoken. Open Mon.-Fri. The service bureau of the **Intourist Hotel,** Bolshaya Sadovaya 115 (tel. 65 90 66 or 65 90 82) is willing to serve tourists not staying in the hotel. English-speaking staff are on duty 8am-8pm to take orders for train- and plane-tickets (US$1 commission) and to organize group and individual **tours** (major credit cards accepted). Plenty of brochures, but no city maps. The International Contacts Division of **Rostov State University** at Bolshaya Sadovaya 115, room 507 (tel. 65 32 36, fax 64 52 55, e-mail rec@rsu.rnd.su) usually deals with student exchanges, but can also help young tourists with excursions and has a miraculous supply of city **maps.** Open Mon.-Fri. 10am-5pm.
Passport Office (OVIR): ul. Serafimovicha 28 (tel. 39 42 52). Receives foreigners on Wednesdays and Fridays, 11am-noon. Arrive early and take a place in the line. The passport officials do not speak any English, so take a Russian with you if at all possible. Registration in Rostov is not compulsory if you have already registered elsewhere in Russia, but some hotels appear to be unaware of this fact.
Currency Exchange: Donkombank operates a 24-hr. currency exchange with good rates and no commission in the Telegraph, Budennovsky pr. 50. **Yugmebel'bank,** ul. Sholokhova 31 A (tel. 51 17 66 or 53 97 85), opposite the old bus station, can give you dollars in cash from your Visa card for a 2% commission. Open Mon.-Fri. 9:30am-12:30pm.
Post Office: Pochtamt, Soborny per. 24 (tel. 66 72 09). **Postal Code:** 344007.
Telephones: Payphones take 10-ruble coins, which, as a result, are in desperately short supply. International calls can be made from the **Mezhdugorodny telefon** adjacent to the Hotel Turist in pl. Lenina, and domestic long-distance calls from token-operated phones in the train station (open daily 8-11am, 11:30am-5pm, 5:30-7:30pm and 8pm-7:30am) and at Voroshilovsky pr. 77. **City Code:** 8632.
Electronic Mail: The **Telegraph** at Budennovsky pr. 50 sends e-mail for US$1.20 per page (tel. 66 27 59); open 24 hrs.
Flights: The airport is east of the center. Conspicuously invisible on Soviet tourist maps, it's the large empty space next to the Aeroflot Hotel (tel. 54 88 01). **Aeroflot** flies to: Moscow-Vnuknovo (3 per day, US$108 one way); Volgograd (several per week, $78 one way); and in summer to Sochi, Odessa, and Simferopol. From the train station and ul. Bolshaya Sadovaya take bus #7, express bus #62 or 93, or trolley #9. The Aeroflot **ticket office,** Sotsialisticheskaya ul. 146 (tel. 65 71 15), is open for foreigners Mon.-Sat. 8am-1pm and 2-5pm.
Trains: Glavny zheleznodorozhny vokzal (main railroad station), pl. Pervoi Russkoi Revoliutsii 1905 goda 1/2 (tel. 66 21 03). From the Central Market, take tram #1 to the end of the line (heading right as you face the market). Many trains daily make the 25-29-hour trip to Moscow (*coupe* 24,000R), but make sure to get

on one passing through Voronezh, in Russia, rather than Kharkiv, in Ukraine, because border officials will gladly relieve you of your hard currency (or send you back to Rostov) if you do not have a transit visa. Also to: Sochi (4 per day, 13hrs.; *coupe* 18,000R); Volgograd (2 per day, 13hrs.; *coupe* 17,000R); as well as several per day to Kiev. **Prigorodny vokzal** ("suburban station") is a short walk or one stop on tram #1 from the main station (tel. 38 36 00 or 38 36 49). The information bureau is on the second floor. *Elektrichki* ("commuter trains") costing a few hundred rubles leave almost every hour for Novocherkassk (1hr. 20min.) and Taganrog-2 (2hrs., or 1½hrs. on the twice daily *"skorostnoi"* express), and slightly less frequently for Asov (1½-2hrs.). Tanais is 50 minutes away on the Taganrog line.

Buses: Glavny avtovokzal (a.k.a. *Novy avtovokzal*), pr. Siversa 1, opposite the train stations. Buses to Asov leave every 20-25 minutes, and there are frequent departures to Novocherkassk (40min.), Taganrog (1½hr.) and Starocherkassk. Three buses daily head to Veshenskaya (9hrs., 8000R) and Volgograd (11hrs., 13,000R). Buses tend to be crowded, bumpy, and much more expensive than commuter trains, but they leave more often and are sometimes marginally faster.

Public Transportation: Rostov's trams, trolleys, buses, and express buses run from roughly 5am-1am. The center of town gets congested during rush hour (around noon), so it is often quicker to cover shorter distances on foot. The comfortable and slightly more expensive express buses were imported from Germany and Sweden, complete with advertisements in the respective languages; the Rostov transport authority has not yet managed to replace the Hanover regional bus maps with a local equivalent.

Boats: Rechnoi vokzal, Beregovaya ul. 10 (Береговая ул.) (tel. 66 52 76), at the foot of Budennovsky pr. Cruise ships bound for Volgorad (38hrs.) and Moscow (9 days) via the Volga-Don Canal leave every four days. Hydrofoils to Asov (40min., 1300R), Starocherkassk (40min., 1200R), and Taganrog leave every 2-3 hours during the day. In summer, a small ferry near the Voroshilovsky pr. bridge carries pedestrians across the river to the beaches on the south shore every 10-15 min.

Luggage storage: In the train station, a small bag costs 800R, a large bag 1900R for the first calender day and 1300R or 2500R thereafter. Open 10am-1:35pm, 2-6:50pm, 7pm-1:10am, 2-6:50am, and 7-9:35am Luggage storage in the bus station open 7:30-10am, 10:30am-4pm, 4:30pm-1am, and 3-7:15am.

Weather: tel. 51 46 10 (Russian of course).

Pharmacy Information: tel. 003

Emergency: Police: tel. 02. **Fire:** tel. 01. **Ambulance:** tel. 03.

ACCOMMODATIONS AND CAMPING

Rostov State University can put up foreigners in its **dormitory,** ul. Zorga 28 corp. 4b, for marginally less than the tourist hotels in the center, but they need at least a month's notice and, if possible, an official-looking written request. Russians and students from developing countries live in far cheaper and more primitive rooms, but the university is reluctant to house Westerners in them. Contact Nikolai Pelikhov, pro-rector for international relations (tel. 22 68 36 or 65 32 36, fax 24 43 11, e-mail rec@rsu.rostov-na-donu.su, attn: international relations division). Doubles and triples, with TV, fridge, basic bathroom facilities, and use of a washing machine around US$15 per person.

Hotel Turist, pr. Oktyabrya 19 (tel. 32 43 09). Tram #6 or 16 from the central market, or any trolley north along Voroshilovsky pr. from Bolshaya Sadovaya. Rooms are Soviet but clean, and bathrooms are adequate. The hotel has an excursion bureau, a good but overpriced restaurant (which lost most of its business when the reputed mafia was driven out), a modest buffet, and English-speaking floor ladies. Singles with shower 50,000R, doubles with shower 80,000R, triples with shower 75,000R plus a small charge for "insurance." One bed in a double 40,000R, in a triple 25,000R. TV, phone, and fridge extra. Foreigners must have Rostov listed as a destination on their visas or a registration stamp from the city passport office.

Hotel Intourist, ul. Bolshaya Sadovaya 115 (tel. 65 90 02 or 65 90 82). The best hotel in town; not exactly five-star but its hot water is reliable. English-speaking service bureau. The Coke machine in the lobby also sells Pepsi. Singles and doubles with shower, TV, fridge, and telephone US$40.

Aldan, ul. Beregovaya 29 (tel. 66 58 38). This cruise ship spends most of its time tied to the Rostov embankment, serving as a floating hotel, restaurant and bar. Toilets and decrepit showers on each deck, but with reliable hot water. Single cabins with sink 25,000R. Doubles 10,000R, with sink 24,000R, with bunk-beds 22,000R. Triples 15,000R. Quads 20,000R. Don't be too alarmed if the hotel disappears for an hour or two during the day with your belongings on board.

Prigorodny vokzal, in an out-of-service train near the suburban train station. A hotel of last resort. The car has four bunk-bed doubles, a quad, and a sextet. All beds cost 4000r, available on a first-come, first-serve basis. There are sinks, but the nearest toilet is 100 meters away in the station building. It is seemingly vulnerable to all the safety dangers of stations *and* overnight trains. Open 5pm-8am.

Numerous **turbazy** (tour bases) across the river and slightly downstream of the center offer wooden huts for 2-3 people and basic bathroom facilities. There is also a campground in the northwest of the city near the zoo (campers were classified as wild animals by the Soviet regime). Locals with cars pitch their tents along the picturesque banks of the Don upstream of Rostov.

FOOD

Rostov is at the center of Russia's wheat-growing region, so it is worth tasting the local bread and especially the pastries on sale at street stands along Bolshaya Sadovaya. Regional wines are available at **Solntse v bokale** ("sun in a wineglass"), Budennovsky pr. 25, on the corner of Bolshaya Sadovaya (open Mon.-Sat. 9am-1pm and 2-6pm). There are numerous cafés along Bolshaya Sadovaya and Pushkinsky bul., of varying quality and life-expectancy. The public market, **Tsentralny rynok,** Budennovsky pr. 18, is at the corner of ul. Stanislavskogo. The usual staples, plus Korean noodles and fresh fish (open April-Sept. Mon. 6am-1pm, Tues.-Sat. 6am-8pm, Sun. 6am-5pm; Oct.-March Mon. 7am-1pm, Tues.-Sat. 7am-7pm, Sun. 7am-5pm).

Kafe Alisa, in the park on the corner of ul. Gorkovo and Kirovsky pr., near the "Krepostnoi" trolley stop on Bolshaya Sadovaya. Remarkably good food and pleasant service, a favorite of young Rostovchiki. A full meal for roughly 7000R. Open daily 11am-10pm. Closed on the 30th of each month.

Lilia, ul. Mechnikova 75A, off Budennovsky pr., four tram stops north of Bolshaya Sadovaya. An emotional experience for those who have forgotten the taste of seasoned food. Courteous if slow service. Entrees 5000-10000R. Open Mon-Fri noon-4pm and 5-11pm, Sat-Sun. 4-11pm.

Pitstsa pai, ul. Krasnoarmeiskaya 66, near Budennovsky pr. The pizzas have a thin crispy crust with cheese, toppings, and just a hint of ketchup. Interesting decor and background music. Individual pan pizzas 2500-5500R.

Zolotaya rybka, on the main path through Gorky park, tel. 66-90-89. The restaurant is operating outside while the interior is renovated, and in spite of its name has no fish on the menu. Excellent barbecue shashlyk kebabs 2000-5000R. Open Tues.-Sun. 1-11pm.

Rus/Volgadon, ul. Beregovaya 31, a few minutes walk from the river port. In theory, an outdoor restaurant on the waterfront should have a perfect view of the river. In theory. During the day the restaurant plays cassettes at deafening volumes, but the flies are undeterred. Small sturgeon kebabs with herbs 10000R, other entrees cheaper. Open 9am-9pm.

SIGHTS AND ENTERTAINMENT

Rostov itself does not have a lot to offer the visitor. The **Cathedral of the Birth of the Holy Mother of God** next to the Central Market on ul. Stanislavskogo was built in 1860 and now holds regular services. **Surb-Khach,** an Armenian Orthodox church on ul. Myasnikyana in the north of the city, contains a **museum of Russian-Armenian friendship** (take bus #25 from the Central Market to the Northern Market). The blocklike statue complex in Zmiyevskaya Balka ("Snake Hollow") in the

RUSSIA

north-west of the city is a **memorial to the Red Guards** (and parenthetically to the Jews) massacred in 1942 during the Nazi occupation. Schoolchildren used to compete for the honor of standing guard at the monument; now, the hollow is overgrown and the small museum is boarded up. Take bus #6 from the Central Market. The **Krayevedchesky museum** (regional studies), Bolshaya Sadovaya 79, has unremarkable exhibits on the local flora and fauna, stone-age settlements in the region, Rostov's war years, and the city's merchants of the last century. Allegedly, the museum also contains a "Gold Room" of the most valuable finds from regional archeological excavations. There is also an **art museum** at Pushkinsky bul. 115 and several exhibition halls around the city.

Locals stroll and play chess in Gorky Park, on Bolshaya Sadovaya near Budennovsky pr. On summer evenings there are free open-air jazz and classical **concerts** from 5-8pm, followed by a nightly **disco**. Billboards by the entrance to the park list coming attractions.

■ NEAR ROSTOV

STAROCHERKASSK (СТАРОЧЕРКАССК)

Cherkassk—now **Starocherkassk** (40 minutes by hydrofoil, 1180R one way)—was the capital of the Don Cossacks from 1644 to 1806, during which time it played a role in nearly all of Tsarist Russia's major peasant uprisings. Now a picturesque farming village *(stanitsa)* on an island in the Don, its center has been preserved as a **museum** of Cossack life and history (open daily 9am-5pm; tel. (250) 297 49 in advance for an English-speaking guide). The village was flooded for over a month in the spring of 1994, so it is worth checking on the weather conditions before you make the trip. Bring your own lunch.

The older houses are constructed in typical Cossack style, with high cellars to protect the residents from the annual floods and meter-thick walls to defend against slightly less frequent human attacks. The active nine-cupola **Resurrection Cathedral** *(Voskresnii sobor)* dates to 1706, and contains unique biblical frescoes and a six-level iconostasis. By its doors hang the chains in which the legendary **Stepan Razin**, most famous of Russia's Cossack rebels, was dragged to Moscow to be executed in 1671. After the suppression of Razin's revolt, the previously independent Cossacks were made to pay homage to the Tsar (open Thurs.-Tues.). In front of the cathedral lie the gateposts and weighing scales from the marketplace of Asov, trophies of the Cossack occupation from 1637 to 1644. Nearby stands the house where **Kondratii Bulavin,** another well-known rebel leader, was murdered by treacherous Cossacks in 1708. His body—minus head and hands—was subsequently displayed in Asov as a warning to would-be revolutionaries. Seven kilometers from the center are the ruins of a star-shaped **Petrine** fort. In summer on the last Sunday of every month the village holds a **festival** of Cossack songs and dances.

NOVOCHERKASSK (НОВОЧЕРКАССК)

Novocherkassk (40 minutes by bus or twice as long by commuter train from Rostov—sit on the right side of the train for a view of the Don steppe) became the Cossacks' capital in 1806, after they gave up attempts to protect Cherkassk from flooding. The city is strategically located on a hill between the Aksai and Tuzlov Rivers, overlooking the surrounding steppe, and continues to house a large contingent of Russian troops. Soviet propaganda, including the classic novel *And Quiet Flows the Don* by Mikhail Sholokhov, portrayed the Cossacks as active supporters of the Bolshevik Revolution, but in fact Novocherkassk was one of the centers of White counterrevolutionary opposition during the Civil War. During World War II, the Nazi occupiers treated the city well, a show of gratitude to anti-Soviet Cossack collaborators. The **Ascension Cathedral** *(Voznesenskii cafedralnii sobor)* in the cobblestone pl. Yermaka (bus #1 from the train and bus stations; pay the conductor) is the third largest cathedral in Russia. Envisioned by the ataman Matvei Platov as a Russian version of St. Peter's in Rome, the cathedral ended up taking a century to build because the cupolas kept on falling down. Inside the cathedral are monuments to Cossack heroes in the defeat of Napoleon. Next to the cathedral in pl. Yermaka is a statue of **Yermak Timofeevich,** who conquered Siberia for the Tsar in the late 16th century. The original design of the monument had a Tsarist two-headed eagle at Yermak's feet, but the authorities in St. Petersburg worried that the Cossacks might get the wrong idea and ordered the eagle removed.

Down pr. Platovskii from pl. Yermaka, at the corner of ul. Sovietskaya, is the **Museum of the History of the Don Cossacks. It** contains a large collection of Cossack artifacts, including ceremonial weapons, portraits, medals, and a bronze statue of Stepan Razin, as well as important archeological finds from Tanais and other ancient sites in the region. The second floor, which chronicled Cossack history in Soviet times, has been closed for ideological renovations (open Tues.-Sun. 10am-5pm; admission 2000r, group tours in English 20000R).

TANAIS (ТАНАИС)

Tanais (50 minutes by commuter train from Rostov—sit on the left on the way there for an impressive view of the Don delta) is a museum and archeological dig at the site of a two-thousand-year-old Greek colony. Founded in the 3rd century BC, the colony grew into a major trading center between Greeks and the nomadic tribes of the steppe. In return for olive oil, wine, cloth, and pottery from the Mediterranean, the Greeks would buy fish, wheat, cattle, wool, and slaves. The city was destroyed and rebuilt several times before it was finally abandoned in the 4th century AD.

Archaeologists took interest in the ruins over 170 years ago, initially sending most of their important finds to museums in Moscow and St. Petersburg. Systematic excavations began in 1955; every summer since, groups of students from Moscow and Vladimir have come to work on the dig, enduring the scorching sun and neolithic living conditions. So far, only a fraction of the city has been uncovered, but archeologists have already learned much about life and commerce in the city from the wealth of inscriptions, pottery, ornaments, and human remains that they have unearthed. Recently, teams from Germany and Poland have reinvigorated the excavations using modern scanning equipment in their search for the city's agora. The on-site **museum** displays finds from the last 40 years, including elegant amphorae from the Mediterranean, miniature statuettes of Greek gods, bronze oil-lamps, glass vials, and even a pair of ancient hand-cuffs. A couple of the ancient buildings have been reconstructed to aid the imagination, but otherwise the original walls and foundations speak for themselves (open April 25-Nov. 25 Mon. 9am-2pm, Wed.-Sun. 9am-1pm and 2-5pm; tours of the excavations and museum in English 6000R, students 4000R).

TAGNAROG (ТАГАНРОГ)

Taganrog (1 hour by hydrofoil or 2 hours by bus or commuter train) is the birthplace of playwright and story-writer Anton Chekhov, and several museums celebrate the town's favorite son. The **Literary Museum,** ul. Oktyabrskaya 9 (tel. 636 97), in the Gymnasium where Chekhov studied, contains reconstructed classrooms and a large collection of manuscripts, letters, journals, and early editions of Chekhov's works, interspersed with choice quotes from Lenin and Marx (open Tues.-Sun. 10am-6pm). The house where Chekhov was born in 1860 has been preserved as the **Domik Chekhova,** ul. Chekhova 69 (tel 622 76; open Tues.-Sun. 9am-5pm). The Lavka Chekovykh at ul. Sverlova 100 (tel. 627 82) was the Chekhovs' home and shop from 1869 to 1874. The front-room grocery store—which illicitly doubled as a pharmacy—has been restored (with emblematic food items). The rest of the house has been reconstructed on the basis of Chekhov's reminiscences, and includes paintings by Anton's brother and furniture of the period (open Tues.-Sun. 10am-6pm).

ASOV (АЗОВ)

Asov, (a scenic 40 minutes by hydrofoil), has the longest and most complicated history of any city in the region, but, except for a small section of 18th-century battlements, that history is buried under Soviet concrete. Tana, a Genoese and Venetian trading post, arose in the late 12th century, and was later absorbed into the Mongol-Tatar city of Azak. The Turks took over in the 15th century, and gave the city its current name. The Cossacks then invaded in 1637, and made the city their capital for seven years until the Tsar ordered them to give it back to the Turks. Before leaving, they razed it to the ground. Next, Peter the Great held the city for 15 years, but again gave it back to the Turks. The city definitively became part of the Russian Empire after the Russo-Turkish War of 1768-1774.

The excellent Regional **Studies Museum,** ul. Moskovskaya 38/40 (tel. 303 71), on the corner of Petrovskii pr., is probably the only reason a tourist would ever want to come to this industrial town, although the exhibits are all in Russian and the museum no longer employs English-speaking guides. In addition to perfunctory displays on Cossack life and local wildlife, the museum narrates the region's history from the prehistoric "pit" and "catacomb" cultures through the Cossack invasion, with cameo appearances by Huns, Polovtsi, Sarmatians, Alani, Khazars, and many others. The narrative is richly illustrated by the museum's collection of tools, pottery, weapons and documents, including a 600,000-year-old proto-mammoth skeleton and a 1361 decree in Latin ordering Genoese and Venetian merchants to stop squabbling. There are also exhibits on Russian and Soviet money and on World War II (open Tues.-Sun. 10am-5pm). Affiliated with the museum is the **Gunpowder Magazine** *(Porokhovoi pogreb)* of an 18th-century fort at ul. Lermontova 6 (tel. 311 09). The underground building now contains a one-room exhibition on Peter the Great's siege of Asov, with portraits, maps, cannonballs, and a diorama (open Tues.-Sun. 10am-6pm).

■■■ SOCHI (СОЧИ)

In an earlier era, admirers dubbed Russia's Black Sea coast the "Caucasian Riviera," but Sochi now aspires to be the next Miami. The warm, opaque waters of the Black Sea, the subtropical climate, and the pebble beaches marred only by the occasional concrete slab make this purpose-built resort city a perpetual favorite among Russian vacationers. If beaches in the West are the preserve of the young and healthy, in Russia they attract an older and more sickly crowd, who come to feel young and regain their health in one of the region's numerous sanitoria and spas. But perhaps more striking than Sochi's beaches are the densely forested Caucasus mountains that descend right to the coast, clear-cut in places to make way for tea plantations and ski runs.

The 1992-3 civil war in neighboring Abkhazia did not spill over into Russia, but wary tourists steered clear of the region and the local economy was devastated. Now the vacationers have returned, but many of the most beautiful mountain hikes and coastal cruises remain off-limits.

ORIENTATION AND PRACTICAL INFORMATION

Greater Sochi extends 145km along the Caucasian coast of the Black Sea from Tuapse to the border of Abkhazia. The city center is roughly 1400km south of Moscow on the same latitude as Marseilles, France, and Buffalo, New York. North of the center are the resort towns of Lazarevskoye and Dagomys; south are Khosta and Adler. The central section of the city, draped around several hills, bears little relationship to the two-dimensional grid shown on tourist maps. **Ul. Gorkovo** (ул. Горького) links the train and bus stations with the seashore; **Kurortny pr.** (Курортный пр.) runs along the coast from the **Park Riviera** towards the airport in Adler, crossing ul. Gorkogo at the Hotel Moskva and passing most of Sochi's major sanatoria. **Maps,** for what they are worth, are available from kiosks and street bookstalls.

Tourist Offices: The city **tourist bureau,** ul. Navaginskaya 14 (ул. Навагинская) (tel. 92 37 79, 92 40 03, or 92 05 54), organizes group daytrips to the region's tourist attractions with Russian-speaking guides, but has little to offer independent or English-speaking travelers (open Mon.-Fri. 9am-1pm and 2-5pm). There are service bureaus in the **Zhemchuzhina,** ul. Chernomorskaya (tel. 92 60 84, fax 92 87 97), and **Olimpiiskaya,** Dagomys (tel. 32 22 94). Hotels have helpful English-speaking staff who can help nonresidents with transport reservations and can arrange moderately expensive individual and group tours. Check with the **Tourist Club** at ul. Voikova 19 (tel. 92 02 18) to see if they have hiking maps and guides. **City Inquiries: tel.** 92 06 16

Tourist Police: A single Russian and Turkish speaking official deals with crimes against foreigners (tel. 99 68 07).

Passport Office (OVIR): ul. Severnaya 16 (tel. 99 97 69). Registration in Sochi is "desirable" but not "compulsory" if you have a valid registration elsewhere in Russia. Open Mon.-Fri. 8am-1pm and 2-5pm

Currency Exchange: The city abounds with exchange offices, most offering competitive rates. The reception desk in the **Radisson Lazurnaya Hotel,** Kurortny pr. 103, offers cash advances in dollars from Visa for a 5% commission and cashes American Express travelers' checks.

Post Office: Pochtamt, ul. Vorovskogo 1 on the corner of Kurortny pr. Sends **faxes,** makes **photocopies,** and claims to get packages to the U.S. in 72 hours. Open 24 hours. **Postal Code:** 35400.

Telephones: Local public phones, believe it or not, are both free and *reliable*. Long-distance calls can be made from the **Mezhdugorodny telefon,** ul. Vorovskogo 6, across the street from the Pochtamt; from there you can dial Moscow without even using a city code.

Flights: The airport is in Adler, a few kilometers northwest of the Abkhazian border (tel. 44 00 55 or 44 00 88), just under an hour by bus #4e or 84e from the bus station. During the summer, **Transaero** flies to Moscow (4 per week, US$130). **Aeroflot** flies to Moscow (3 per day, 1 per day in winter, US$128); St. Petersburg (2 per day, US$155); Volgograd (1 per day, US$97); Simferopol (4 per week, US$84); Odessa (1 per week, US$104); and Lviv (1 per week, US$133). Charter companies fly irregularly (in all senses) to Turkey and Eastern Europe. Transaero and Aeroflot tickets can be purchased in Sochi at the Aeroflot office, ul. Navaginskaya 12 (tel. 92 29 36). Foreigners must use the plush "international hall," even to buy tickets on domestic flights.

Trains: Zheleznodorozhny vokzal, ul. Gorkovo, tel. 92 30 44, 99 12 58, advance reservations tel. 92 31 17. Several trains daily travel to Moscow in 36-39 hours (42000R coupe), but make sure to choose one via Voronezh in Russia rather than Kharkiv in Ukraine, or else you risk falling into the clutches of dollar-hungry border officials. Four trains daily to Rostov (13 hours, 18000R coupe). Less frequent service to St. Petersburg (56000R coupe), Kiev (42000R coupe), Minsk (70000R coupe), Lviv (49000R coupe) and Riga (69000R coupe). Local trains (*elektrichki*) travel up the coast as far as Tuapse. Luggage storage open 24 hours, lockers 1300r, small (large) bags 800R (1900R) until midnight, 1300R (2500R) each additional day.

Buses: Avtovokzal, ul. Gorkovo next to the train station (tel. 99 63 53). The #4e and 84e expresses leave every 10-15 minutes for Adler from 7am-7pm. Buses also go to Dagomys and other resorts along the coast. Buy tickets in the bus station or pay the driver.

Ferries: The picturesque Sea Port is under reconstruction, but there is still a daily hydrofoil up the coast to Novorossiisk via Tuapse (4hrs., 16500R), and occasional cruises to Turkey. **Ticket office** open daily 8am-7pm (tel. 996 62 03).

Public Transportation: Buses converge on the central bus station; the local and long-range systems are not entirely distinct. Fares within the Sochi are flat, but rise in proportion to distance out of town. Pay the driver or conductor—punching tickets is not usually necessary. Some tourist maps include bus routes.

Weather: 99 70 41, **water temperature:** 92 05 69.

ACCOMMODATIONS

Passengers arriving in Sochi by train are accosted on the platform by elderly women and young entrepreneurs offering apartments or rooms in apartments for US$5-30 per night, depending on size, location, and time of year. Rules of common sense apply, but in general such arrangements are safe and almost legal. Brokers ask a finder's fee of around US$15, and may be reluctant to show you a room before you agree to take it. Expect to pay up front on arrival at the apartment. Elderly landladies are often happy to prepare meals and do laundry at mutually agreeable rates.

The over 80 sanatoria and "pansionaty" in Sochi offer varying degrees of luxury and service, ranging from US$90 per night at the Radisson Lazurnaya to more affordable hotels primarily aimed at Russians. Foreigners are usually charged extra. Down a notch from the sanatoria are "turbazy" and "kempingi"—little more than wooden huts for 2-3 people, usually further from the center of town but with access to a beach. The **Kemping Mamaika,** ul. Krymskaya 60 on the way to Dagomys (tel. 93 56 29), has dirty bathrooms and communal showers for US$5 per night.

Availability of rooms fluctuates from year to year and from month to month. August is the peak month, followed by July. During the war in Abkhazia, space was plentiful as vacationers avoided the region altogether. In the summer of 1994, the crowds were beginning to return, but most hotels still had vacancies.

Hotel Olympiskaya, Dagomys (tel. 32 22 94 or 32 11 94). The round hotel with semicircular balconies Clean Soviet-style rooms with English-speaking service bureau, tennis courts and miniature golf. Noon checkout. Singles with TV, telephone, breakfast, beach and pool access US$36, doubles with same US$50.

Hotel Zhemchuzhina, ul. Chernomorskaya 3 (tel. 92 60 84). This 20-year-old luxury hotel near the center of Sochi has numerous restaurants, bars, and discos as well as a private beach, pool and tennis courts. Clean rooms with view. Singles with bath, cable TV, and fridge US$60, offseason US$40; doubles with shower, cable TV, and fridge US$80, offseason US$60. Breakfast included.

Sputnik International Tourist Center, Novorossiiskoye shosse 17/1 (tel./fax 97 58 28 or 97 52 16). Offers a fixed two-week package of activities—sea sports, sightseeing, concerts, nightly disco—aimed primarily at Russian parents with young children. The woody surroundings partially mitigate the sheer ugliness of the concrete buildings and highway bridge. Clean private beach and sports facilities. Depending on the month and the size of room, places cost US$20-$45 per night. Breakfast included.

FOOD

There is a public market at the corner of ul. Moskovskaya and ul. Konstitutsii SSSR. Try the ready-to-eat Caucasian delicacies at your own risk. Excellent Georgian bread and fresh fruits. The density of cafés increases dramatically as you approach the beach. Most are little more than bars; some serve more or less edible food. Each of the hotel complexes contains several restaurants. In theory, spicy Caucasian food is the local specialty, but most restaurants serve standard Russian fare.

Kavkazski aul, off the road to Adler (tel. 97 08 17). Get there by taxi, or bus #4 to Sputnik and then a 20-minute walk inland. In a secluded grove by a sulphurous stream, this Caucasian restaurant and bar is well worth the expedition, if only for the atmosphere. There is no menu—tell them how much you can pay and they will feed you accordingly. The *lobio* (beans) and *baklazhan* (eggplant) are excellent. 10000-15000R buys a several course meal with Georgian wine. At night, the road back is very dark (open 11am-midnight).

Kubanski khutor, on the road to Dagomys at the turnoff to Mamaika (tel. 90 25 05). Three restaurants in one, with a view of the hills. The **Varenichnaya Khata** is the best bet, specializing in dumplings with savory vegetable *zakuski* (open 10am-8pm). The **Traktir** and **Brazhny Pogreb** are open later into the evening, but offer more conventional Russian cuisine.

RUSSIA

SIGHTS AND ENTERTAINMENT

The city's remarkable **arboretum,** Dendrarii, Kurortny pr. 74 (tel. 92 36 02), contains 1600 types of plant from around the world (open 9am-12:45pm and 1:45-5pm). A cable car (1000R) takes visitors from Kurortny pr. up to an observation post at the top of the park, from which you walk back down through the park. The **Park Riviera** at ul. Yegorova 1 is just a typical Soviet "park of culture and rest." The observation tower at the peak of Gora Akhun, an 8km walk (or taxi ride) up from Sputnik on the road to Adler, affords a panoramic view of Sochi, Khosta, Adler, the foothills of the Caucasus, and, of course, the Black Sea (open Wed.-Mon. 10am-5pm). The **Shashlychnaya Akhun Café** at the base of the tower prepares Georgian-style spicy vegetable salads and barbecue kebabs that by themselves merit the trip (a substantial meal for 10000R). Do not count on finding transportation back down.

The **tea plantations** of Dagomys—the northernmost in the world—display their samovar collection and offer tea-tasting feasts to tour groups at Tea Huts *(Chainiye domiki).* The huts open only when groups are expected, so make arrangements through one of the hotel's service bureaus. For rainy days, Sochi boasts a **Museum of the History of the Resort-City,** ul. Ordzhonikidze 29 (tel. 92 23 49), an **art museum,** Kurortny pr. 51 (tel. 92 45 73; open Tues.-Sun. 10am-5:30pm), and a squalid **terrarium-aquarium,** ul. Konstitutsii SSSR 26, with (barely) live snakes, turtles, toads and fish (open Tues.-Fri. noon-6pm, Sat.-Sun. noon-7pm).

The city has a flourishing cultural life, with a major annual independent film festival in June and an art festival in September. During the peak tourist season in July and August, theater troops, orchestras and rock bands come from all over Russia to play for the vacationing elite. The astoundingly hideous **Winter Theater** *(Zimnii teatr),* ul. Teatralnaya 2 (tel. 99 77 06), holds frequent concerts and shows, among them by the Philharmonia (tel. 99 77 51). There are also several outdoor **Summer Theaters** *(Letniye teatry),* among them one in the Frunze Park at ul Chernomorskaya 2 (tel. 99 77 72). The weekly "Sochi" newspaper, available at kiosks, lists some coming attractions, or call Galina Korneyeva, Deputy Head of the city's Department of Culture and Tourism (tel. 92 43 17); her husband, Sasha Korneyev, is a local impresario. Zhemchuzhina, the up-and-coming local **soccer** team, plays at the Central Stadium on Kurortny pr.

The cleanest and most pleasant beaches tend to be the private ones of the fancier hotels and sanatoria. Many allow in nonresidents for an fee (the Zhemchuzhina, for example, charges 4000R). Half of the main city beach south of the Sea Port has been leased by a private firm which dreams of creating a second Miami. Along the beachfront are cafés, saunas, and weight rooms. Changing rooms and showers are available. (Admission 1500R; umbrella and recliner 5000R per day, peddle boats and surf board rentals 3000R per hour, waterskiing 15000R per hour, jetskis US$2 per minute. Open from mid-May to mid-October.) The other half of the beach is free and more crowded. Mamaika beach on the way to Dagomys (take bus #7 to the end) is not developed and attracts mainly local residents who want to avoid the risk of being mown down in the water by reckless jetskiers.

■ NEAR SOCHI: KRASNAYA POLYANA

Boris Yeltsin recently put forward Sochi as Russia's bid for the 2002 Winter Olympics. Although few would bet on its chances against the likes of Salt Lake City, Sochi has resolved to develop its ski resort, **Krasnaya Polyana,** at the moment little more than an idyllic mountain village. From Adler's central market, bus #135 makes the terrifyingly scenic 57km journey hourly, speeding round bends in the narrow mountain road and blistering the hands of standing passengers (in the days when oil was effectively free in the Soviet Union, a helicopter used to make the trip for 2 rubles). In summer, many treks into the **Caucasus Preserve** begin in Krasnaya Polyana; in winter, extreme skiers helicopter-ski on the surrounding untracked slopes, while average skiers use the few existing lifts. Telephone lines to the outside world have

RUSSIA

been down for over a year (the reconnection of the village is promised in late 1994) so reservations must be made by mail or telegram.

The **Hotel Krasnaya Polyana** (better known as the Tsarskii Domik), 4-5km from the bus stop, has clean rooms and a restaurant with an amazing view. Doubles with shower, fridge and TV 28000R, deluxe doubles 42000R. For dedicated skiers, there is a heated cabin with bunk beds, an outdoor toilet, and a sauna right at the bottom of the first ski-lift—bring your own food and equipment (ski rental roughly 25000R per day, but quantity and quality are limited). Contact Sergei Chorny through Sergei Blynski in Sochi (tel. 99 67 30 or 99 16 15) at least two weeks in advance in summer or two months in advance in winter. The **Gorny Vozdukh turbaza** has modern dormitory-style accommodations with showers on every floor, a dining hall and sauna. It also rents out skis and camping equipment, and provides guides for treks into the Caucasus Preserve. Room and board 20000R. Contact Pavel Fedin by mail or telegram at 354594 Sochi-A, poselok Krasnaya Polyana, Turbaza Gorny vozdukh. The Radisson Lazurnaya is currently building a luxury ski-lodge, which will probably make skiing here both easier and far more expensive.

■ St. Petersburg (Санкт-Петербург)

The brainchild of Peter the Great, St. Petersburg has been heavily shaped and molded by its creator and numerous subsequent adopted parents. It was here that westward-looking tsars tried to drag Russia out of Byzantium, and it was here that Lenin and Trotsky formed the Bolshevik Party that ended the rule of the Romanovs and ushered in a new breed of tsar. A city of contradictions, it is a gateway to the West on a seaport that is ice-locked five months of the year and a graceful European capital of palaces and canals on the edge of the Russian steppe. A city of change; Russia's history is written in its name, which has changed to Petrograd and Leningrad and back again in the last 100 years.

Founded by Peter I in 1703, Russia's new capital was built according to the Tsar's strict plan. He forced his friends to build their palaces on the canals he dug to drain the swamp on the Gulf of Finland, and drove his laborers so hard that untold thousands died in the city's construction. The result was a distinctly European metropolis with Baroque and Neoclassical mansions, and a new cultural life that produced Pushkin, Dostoevsky, Tchaikovsky, and others.

In 1917 the battleship *Aurora* fired a blank shot over the Winter Palace, scaring Kerensky's provisional government into turning over power to Lenin and the Bolsheviks. After Lenin's death in 1924, the city which had been Petrograd (changed from the German-sounding *Sankt Peterburg* during the war) was officially renamed Leningrad. During World War II, Leningrad suffered more than most cities. Under siege by the Nazis for 900 days, it lost close to a million people. The population did not recover until the 1960s; even today, almost every family can claim victims.

Three quarters of a century of communist rule have left an indelible mark on St. Petersburg. As in other cities of the former Soviet Union, long lines snake around generic "Bread" and "Meat" stores punched into the crumbling façades of former mansions. Yet here and there a bit of the old glitter remains: St. Petersburg boasts some of the world's finest art museums, gorgeous Imperial palaces in the suburbs, and some of the finest ballet in the world.

Today, the newly-renamed St. Petersburg is trying (with Western help and dollars) to restore itself to its former glory. Have a little patience as you negotiate the mad and sometimes maddening crowds on the streets, and you will be impressed by the old glamor and opulence of the palaces and by the pride of the people.

ORIENTATION AND PRACTICAL INFORMATION

St. Petersburg is in northwestern Russia, just a six-hour train ride east of Helsinki, Finland, and nine hours northwest of Moscow. It sits on a former swamp at the mouth of the **Neva River** (Нева), on the **Gulf of Finland** (Финский Залив, *Finsky Zalif*). Several canals run roughly parallel to the river, and the main thoroughfare is **Nevsky Prospect** (Невский Проспект), which runs from the **Admiralty** (Адмиральтество, *Admiraltestvo*) on the river to **Uprising Square** (Площадь Восстания, *Ploschad Vosstaniya*) and **Moscow train station** (Московский Вокзал; *Moskovsky Vokzal*) before veering south to Alexander Nevsky Cemetery. Across the river and to the north of the Admiralty is the **Fortress of Peter and Paul**, the historic heart of the city. The Metro is a semi-convenient way to get around the center; better are **trolleybuses #5** and **7,** which go up and down Nevsky pr. Walking is easy, as most major sights are close to one another, and the city is lovely—you'll never find a seat in the Metro anyway.

Tourist Offices: As of June 1994, your best bet is the **Russian Youth Hostel** on 3rd Sovetskaya ul. M: Ploschad Vosstaniya (Площадь Восстания). They sell maps, offer advice, get train tickets, and procure visas. There is a **tourist office** opening soon, and should be in operation by summer 1995, to be located directly across from the Grand Hotel Europe on Nevsky Prospect, M: Gostiny Dvor (Гостиный Двор). Intourist, now the **St. Petersburg Travel Company**, has offices in the Hotel Astoria, right across from St. Isaac's Cathedral (tel. 210 50 46). M: Gostiny Dvor, then walk left down ul. Gertsena (ул. Герцена) to the square and take a right. They offer **tours** and excursions (20,000-30,000R) and sell maps, but aren't very useful for the budget traveler.

Consulates: U.S., ul. Furshtadtskaya 15 (ул. Фурштадтская, formerly Petra Lavrova; tel. 275 17 01). M: Chernyshevskaya (Чернышевская). Open Mon.-Fri. 9:15am-1pm and 2pm-5:30pm. Provides emergency passports and help with stolen credit cards, notarials, tax info, and voting. **U.K.,** pl. Proletarskoy Diktatury 5 (пл. Пролетарской Диктатуры; tel. 119 60 36). Open Mon.-Fri. 9:30am-5:30pm. **Bulgaria,** ul. Ryleeva 27 (ул. Рылеева; tel. 273 73 47). Open Mon.-Fri. 2-4 pm. **Czech and Slovak,** ul. Tverskaya 5 (ул. Тверской; tel. 271 04 59). Open Mon.-Fri. 9:30am-12:30. **Finland,** ul. Chaikovshovo 71 (ул. Чайковского; tel. 273 73 21). Open Mon.-Fri. 9am-5pm. **Hungary,** ul. Marata 15 (ул. Марата; tel. 312 67 53). Open Tues.-Wed., Fri. 10am-noon. **South Africa,** nab. Reki Moyki 11 (наб. Р. Мойки). Open Mon.-Fri. 9:30-noon.

Currency Exchange: Look for the Обмен Валюты (*Obmen Valyuty*) signs everywhere. Changing money is easy now, since there is no more illegal on-the-street exchanging—the *kassa* you go to will often even have a calculator. A decent rate for your dollars and traveler's checks can always be had at the **Central Exchange Office,** ul. Mikhailovskaya 4 (ул. Михайловская), formerly ul. Brodskovo (ул. Бродского), off Nevsky pr. and across from the Grand Hotel Europe. M: Gostiny Dvor (Гостиный Двор). Credit cards accepted with 5% commission. Traveler's checks with 3% commission. Open 10:30am-7:30pm. Expect a long wait (if you can risk it, cash is more convenient here, or AmEx traveler's checks, for which the wait is shorter). There is no need to keep all your exchange receipts, *unless* you plan to re-exchange rubles back into dollars when you leave.

American Express: ul. Mikhailovskaya 1/7 (ул. Михайловская, formerly ul. Brodskovo; tel. 119 60 09, fax 119 60 11), in the Grand Hotel Europe. Provides travel service including domestic and international flights, replaces lost and stolen AmEx cards, refunds and sells traveler's checks. Mail held for cardholders, no packages. Send mail to: c/o American Express, P.O. Box 87. SF-53501, Lappeenranta, Finland. Open Mon.-Fri. 9am-5pm.

Post Office: ul. Pochtamskaya 9 (ул. Почтамская). From Nevsky Prospect, go west on ul. Gogolya (ул. Гоголя), which becomes Pochtamskaya. It's about 2 blocks past St. Isaac's Cathedral on the right, just before an overhanging arch. Open

A   B   C

1

Morskoy Prospect
Primorski Park Pobedy

← PETERHOF
25 km.
← KRONSTADT
20 km.

Malaya Nevka

Bolshaya Zelenina ul.

PETRO
ST

PET

2

Malaya Neva

Bolshoy Prospect

Uralskaya ul.

Korablestroiteley ul.

Krony

PRIMORSKAYA

Ⓜ

*Lyuteranskoe
Cemetery*

Tuchkov most

Malaya Neva

Birzhevoy most

3

Novosmolenskaya nab.

Smolenka canal

**VASILEVSKI
OSTROV**

*Smolenskoe
Cemetery*

Maly Prospect

Ⓜ

VASILEOSTROVSKAYA

St. Petersburg
State University ■

Nakhimova ul.

Universitetskaya nab.

Most.

④

Nalichnaya ul.

Sredni Prospect

Bolshoy Prospect

Lyteynfä
Shmidta

④

②

4

Bolshaya Neva

Mayka canal

Glinki ul.

Dekabristov.

①

**OKTYABRSKI
RAYON**

St. Nicholas
Cathedral ■

Passenger Sea Terminal ■

Pryazhka canal

Lermontovski Pr.

5

N
↑

Sadovaya
ul.

TE

Staro-Petergofski
Pr.

**LENINSKI
RAYON**

TE

6

Obvodnyy canal
Obvodnovo   Canala   Naberezhnaya
BALTIYSKAYA

Ⓜ

**Baltic
Station** ■

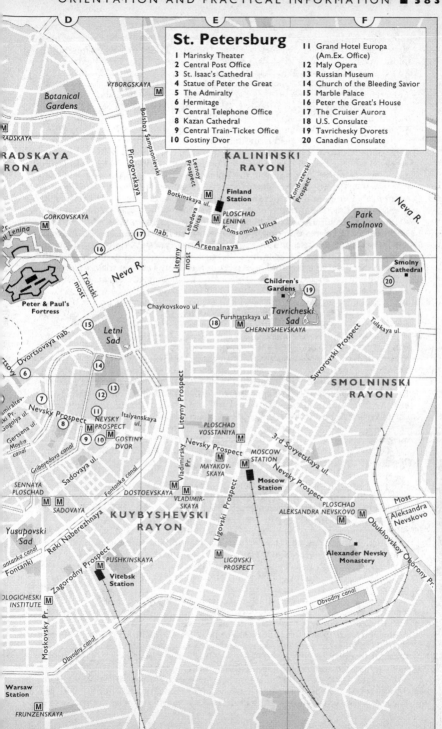

St. Petersburg

1 Marinsky Theater
2 Central Post Office
3 St. Isaac's Cathedral
4 Statue of Peter the Great
5 The Admiralty
6 Hermitage
7 Central Telephone Office
8 Kazan Cathedral
9 Central Train-Ticket Office
10 Gostiny Dvor
11 Grand Hotel Europa
   (Am.Ex. Office)
12 Maly Opera
13 Russian Museum
14 Church of the Bleeding Savior
15 Marble Palace
16 Peter the Great's House
17 The Cruiser Aurora
18 U.S. Consulate
19 Tavrichesky Dvorets
20 Canadian Consulate

RUSSIA

Mon.-Sat. 9am-8pm, Sun. 10am-6pm. The postal system in Russia is utterly unreliable; those needing to send mail should use DHL, or do without. Come here to change money or make inter-city or international calls. However, the system is impossible to negotiate if you don't speak some Russian.

DHL: Canal Griboyedova 5 (Канала Грибоедова) office #325, second floor (tel. 311 26 49, 311 85 57, 210 75 75, or 210 76 54, fax 314 64 73). DHL will ship packages and letters to the U.S. in 3 business days, and will also hold mail and packages. A 15-page document to the U.S. costs US$52. Open Mon.-Fri. 9am-6pm. There is a **branch office** in the Nevsky Palace Hotel, Nevsky pr. 57 (tel. 119 61 00 or 119 61 17, fax 119 61 16). They have advertisements in the weekly *St. Petersburg Press,* available for free at both hostels and most hotels.

Telephones: Central Telephone and Telegraph, ul. Gertsena 3-5 (ул. Герцена), off Nevsky pr. near Palace Square. Buy a phone card from the *kassa* in the third hall, then use any of the phones in the front room. **AT&T USADirect** is in Moscow: tel. 095 155 50 42. You will be charged for calling Moscow for the duration of your call, but it's still cheaper than dialing direct. When your party answers, be sure to push the little round button bearing an arrow for a few seconds; it's the all-important volume control (there are good pictograms on the phones, too). **Local calls** can be made from any phone booth on the street; use Metro tokens. For **intercity calls,** use one of the *mezhdugorodni* (междугородный) phone booths at the Central Telephone office; they take special grooved zhetoni (жетоны, "coins") that are sold across from the booths. When making long-distance calls, dial 8 and wait for the tone before proceeding. **Telegrams** and **faxes** can also be sent. Open 24 hrs., except 12:30-1pm. **City Code:** 812.

Photocopies: Shvedski per. 2 (Шведский пер.) parallel to Nevsky pr. off Bolshaya Konnyushenaya pl. (Большая Конюшенная пл.; tel. 311 18 10 or 210 76 69). You can't miss the huge Xerox sign outside the building. Basic services, including large photocopies, color copies, and business cards. One page 250R. Color photocopies US$2.40. Discounts on large orders. Open Mon.-Fri. 11am-5pm. Branch store, **Xerox,** ul. Sablinskaya 7 (ул. Саблинская). M: Vasileostrovskaya (tel. 233 30 08). One page 250R. No color copier. Can receive and send faxes (fax 233 88 95).

Flights: The main **airport** is Pulkovo (Пулково). There are two terminals: Pulkovo-1 for domestic flights and Pulkovo-2 for international flights. For Pulkovo-2 take bus #13 from M: Moskovskaya (Московская), or the youth hostels can arrange for you to be taken (or met) by taxi for US$15. There is also a bus that leaves from the Aeroflot (Аэрофлот) building at Nevsky and ul. Gertsena and takes about 45 minutes. Buy tickets on the bus. **Foreign airlines: British Airways,** ul. Gertsena 36 (ул. Герцена). Mon.-Fri. 9am-5pm, closed 1-2pm (tel. 311 58 20). **Bulgarian Airlines** (direct flights to Sofia), ul. Gertsena 36 (tel. 315 50 30). **Delta Airlines,** ul. Gertsena 36. Mon.-Fri. 9am-5pm, closed 1-2pm (tel. 311 58 20 or 311 58 19). **Finnair** (daily flights to Helsinki and the Baltics), ul. Gogolya 19 (ул. Гоголя). Mon.-Sat. 9am-5pm (tel. 104 34 39). **Lufthansa** (direct flights to Frankfurt), Voznesensky pr. 7 (Вознесенский пр.; tel. 314 49 79 or 314 59 17). **SAS (Swissair),** Nevsky pr. 57 (in the Nevsky Palace Hotel; tel. 314 50 86).

Trains: St. Petersburg has four main railway stations, all accessible by Metro. Trains to Estonia (Tallinn 28,000R), Lithuania, Latvia, and Poland leave from the **Varshavski Vokzal** (Варшавский вокзал), M: Baltiskaya (Балтийская). To: Ukraine (Kiev 61,000R) and Belarus from the **Vitebski Vokzal** (Витебский вокзал), M: Pushkinskaya (Пушкинская). To Moscow (15 per day, 9hrs.; 37,000R) and all other points in Russia from the **Moskovski Vokzal** (Московский вокзал), M: pl. Vosstaniya (пл. Восстания). To Helsinki (2 per day, 6hrs.; 113,700R) from the **Finlyandski Vokzal** (Финляндский вокзал), M: pl. Lenina (пл. Ленина). The **Central Ticket Office** for rail travel (Центральны Железнодорожные Кассы, *Centralny Zheleznodorozhny Kassy*) is at Canal Griboyedova 24 (канал Грибоедева). Open Mon.-Sat. 8am-8pm, Sun. 8am-4pm. Foreign tourists must purchase tickets at the special **Intourist** department inside the ticket office (windows 100-104 on second floor, inside and to the right, up the Intourist stairs); they also handle international tickets (windows 90-99. If you simply want information on prices, go to ticket window 89, inside the station to the left). Open daily 8am-noon and 1-7pm. There are also Intourist offices at each train station. If you miss your train, you

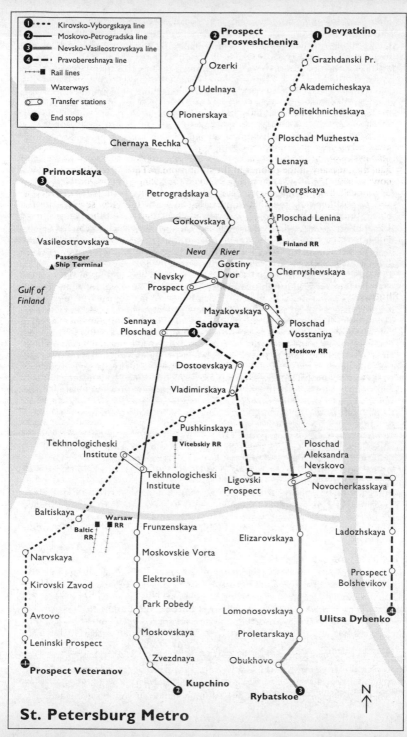

St. Petersburg Metro

Legend:
1 ···· Kirovsko-Vyborgskaya line
2 —— Moskovo-Petrogradska line
3 ═══ Nevsko-Vasileostrovskaya line
4 ─ ─ Pravobereshnaya line
╟──■ Rail lines
     Waterways
⊙─⊙ Transfer stations
●   End stops

2 Prospect Prosveshcheniya
1 Devyatkino
Ozerki
Grazhdanski Pr.
Udelnaya
Akademicheskaya
Pionerskaya
Politekhnicheskaya
Chernaya Rechka
Ploschad Muzhestva
Primorskaya
Lesnaya
3
Viborgskaya
Petrogradskaya
Ploschad Lenina
Gorkovskaya
Finland RR
Vasileostrovskaya
Passenger
Ship Terminal
Neva River
Gostiny Dvor
Nevsky Prospect
Chernyshevskaya
Gulf of Finland
Mayakovskaya
Sennaya Ploschad
Sadovaya
4
Ploschad Vosstaniya
Dostoevskaya
Moskow RR
Vladimirskaya
Pushkinskaya
Vitebskiy RR
Ploschad Aleksandra Nevskovo
Tekhnologicheski Institute
Tekhnologicheski Institute
Ligovski Prospect
Novocherkasskaya
Baltiskaya
Warsaw RR
Baltic RR
Frunzenskaya
Elizarovskaya
Ladozhskaya
Narvskaya
Moskovskie Vorta
Kirovski Zavod
Elektrosila
Prospect Bolshevikov
Avtovo
Park Pobedy
Lomonosovskaya
Ulitsa Dybenko
4
Leninski Prospect
Moskovskaya
Proletarskaya
Prospect Veteranov
1
Zvezdnaya
Obukhovo
Kupchino
2
Rybatskoe
3

N

RUSSIA

must go to the *Dejurnaya Kassa* (Дежурная Касса) within 3 hours of missing your train and you will pay only a 6% surcharge for a new ticket. The *kassa* is open 24 hours; if you do not do this you will pay full price—no arguments, dears.

Buses: These are often cheaper and more comfortable than trains if you are travelling during the day, but prices are high enough for Russians that they aren't too crowded. The **Main Bus Terminal** is on Canal Obvognovo (Канала Обводного); take tram #19, 25, 44 or 49 from Moscow train station 10-15 minutes until just after you cross the canal. Walk east two blocks along the canal, and the station is on your right, set back from the road (enter from the side). Buy tickets on the day you leave; advance tickets can be purchased from the *Predvaritelnaya Kassa* (Предварительная Касса) next to the exchange booth. You can only buy one-way tickets. The station is open daily 6am-1pm and 2-11pm (advance ticket booth open 8am-2pm and 3-8pm).

Public Transportation: The one thing the Soviets did supremely well has disintegrated into a confusing mess. **Buses** (Автобус), **tramvayas** (Трамвая), which run on tracks, and **trolleybuses** (Троллейбус), which connect to electrical wires, run infrequently and irregularly, and often change routes. Asking the locals will not necessarily help; most will admit to being as confused as you are. Read the list of stops posted on the outside of the bus. Two important trolleybuses are #5 and 7, which both go from Uprising Square down to the bottom of Nevsky Prospect, near the Hermitage. It will be a rough ride, however; the buses are often packed to overflowing, which may even mean jumping off and on again at every stop to let people out. The *Traveller's Yellow Pages* map shows all the buslines on its city plan—marked with thin black lines. The **Metro**, so beautifully efficient in Moscow, is rather meager here (open 6am-1am). To get anywhere, a change of line is usually required and the stops are few and far between; getting getting to almost every sight necessitates a significant walk. Tickets 150R; buy them at each metro station. The announcements for metro stops are also confusing; the conductor announces the following stop as you are arriving, not the stop at which you are actually arriving at. Bus tickets also cost 150R. Buy them in groups of ten from the driver at the front of the bus (when it stops). The exchange is made easier if you give the driver the exact amount. Be sure to punch your ticket; although many citizens do not, the fine is 5000R (not to mention great humiliation), and they *do* check. An 8000R *yedini billet* (Единый Билет) pays for all public transportation (metro, bus, trolley, tram) for a calendar month; buy them at metro stations during the first few days of the month.

Laundromat: The **Russian Youth Hostel** has a washing machine but no dryer, and will wash your clothes for US$1 (this is not offered at the Holiday Hostel). Otherwise, use the sink, and bring your own detergent or buy a Western brand.

Medical Assistance: Use **Polyclinic No. 2** (tel. 110 11 02) or **Hospital No. 20** (tel. 108 48 08), which are for foreigners.

Emergencies: Try not to have one. Police and ambulance drivers do not speak English. If you are a victim of a crime, report it *immediately* to the local police station—bring a Russian-speaker—and to your consulate. The U.S. consulate has a 24-hr. emergency number: tel. 274 86 92. **Fire:** tel. 01. **Police:** tel. 02. **Ambulance:** tel. 03.

ACCOMMODATIONS

Nowhere is Russia's constantly changing political and economic situation more visible to the tourist than the accommodations scene. Where once travelers were assigned a hotel by Intourist, now they can choose among deluxe new joint ventures, such as St. Petersburg's **Grand Hotel Europe,** old Intourist dinosaurs like **Moskva** and **Leningradskaya, hostels,** and **Russian apartments**. For the budget traveler, the last two are really the best options. However, do some research: if you are planning to stay in Petersburg for longer than a few days, you may find more options. The *St. Petersburg Press* lists apartments for rent, both long- and short-term; pick up a free copy in the Grand Hotel Europe or at one of the hostels. The International Hostel also sells a guide called *The Traveller's Yellow Pages* that has current listings of accommodation options.

Travelers who speak Russian may want to consider a **homestay** in an apartment with a Russian family. This can be arranged through the **Traveller's Guest House** in Moscow (tel. (095) 971 40 59, fax 280 76 86.), either from Moscow or from St. Petersburg. If arranged from Moscow, the family will meet you at the train. Most homes are not in the center, but they are guaranteed convenient to a Metro or tram line. The Guest House cannot, however, guarantee an English-speaking family member (US$10 per night). Another option for arranging homestays is the **Host Families Association** (HOFA; tel./fax 275 19 92 or 395 13 38), based at the St. Petersburg Technical University. They can provide bed and breakfast in apartments less than 1km from a Metro station, with a family guaranteed to have one English-speaking member. But be warned—what may seem like basic Russian hospitality on the part of the host family (meeting you at the station, serving dinner, etc.) will show up as additional charges on your bill. They can also provide transit to and from trains or airports, tours, and theater tickets. Given 2-3 weeks notice, the association will find you a bed in any city in the Commonwealth of Independent States. (Singles US$30. Doubles US$50. Students US$25 and US$40, respectively. Discounts for non-central locations and families with poor English.)

There are two hostels in St. Petersburg which, together with the Traveller's Guest House in Moscow and establishments in Novgorod and Irkutsk, form the California-based **Russian Youth Hostels** organization. Both hostels in St. Petersburg accept reservations by phone, and offer services such as providing visas, booking train tickets, and providing rides to the airport. They are, at this writing, the closest thing to a tourist office in St. Petersburg, selling maps, guidebooks, and bottled water.

International Youth Hostel (HI). In a restored 5-story building near M: pl. Vosstaniya (пл. Восстания) on 3rd ul. Sovyetskaya 28 (третая ул. Советская; tel. 277 05 69 or 329 80 18, fax. 277 51 02 or 329 80 19). The first hostel in Russia (it opened in June 1992), and the only one of the five here to be a member of Hostelling International (as of June 1994). The neighborhood is quiet and pleasant; the hostel itself is clean and modern, even by Western standards. Rooms have 2, 3, or 4 beds (50 beds total). There is a kitchen on the third floor. Single sex floors. Reception open 8am-noon and 3pm-midnight. Check in by 9:30pm. Check-out 11am. Lockout 1-7am. US$15 includes sheets and breakfast. Reservations can be made from all over the world; from the U.S. and Canada contact the California office (tel. (310) 379-4316, fax 379-8420). Only paid reservations will be honored if the hostel is full. Visa and MC accepted.

Hostel "Holiday," ul. Mikhailova #1 (ул. Михайлова; 542 73 64, fax 277 51 02). M: Ploschad Lenina (пл. Ленина). Exit at Finlandsky Vokzal (Финландский Вокзал) and turn left on ul. Komsomola (ул. Комсомола), then right on Mikhailova. Just before the river, turn left into a courtyard, then right. There is a "YH" on the wall ahead of you. The door is locked (there is a code for guests); ring the bell. The hostel is next to a prison, and the prisoners' relatives are in the courtyard all day, shouting messages to the inmates. The entrance to the hostel is on the third floor; the hostel itself occupies 3 stories. The staff here is younger and friendlier than at their big brother hostel down the street. Provides all the same services as the International Youth Hostel (it is also part of Russian Youth Hostels), but as of June 1994 was not a member of Hostelling International. Similar accommodations, though a little shabbier. Has its own bar on the premises, with an incredible view of the Neva R. and Peter and Paul's cathedral. Open 24 hrs. Check-out at 11am. US$15 per night, breakfast and sheets included. Dinner US$5. They will celebrate your birthday for you (if you're there for it). Reservations accepted.

Oktyabrskaya Hotel (Гостиница Октябрьская) is near the Moscow Train Station, on Ligovsky pr. 10 (пр. Лиговский)—go left from the train station and it's down the street. There is a second building of the same hotel on the other side of the square. Both offer spacious clean rooms with bath at reasonable prices. Like other Intourist dinosaurs, these hotels are not really a dependable option for the budget traveler: most of them already have high prices, and many are slated for conversion to luxury hotels. This is a Russian hotel, of course, so you can't count on English being spoken. Reception open 24 hrs. in the building across the square from the station. Each floor is guarded by a key-keeper, to whom you must surrender you key whenever you go out. They accept phone reservations (tel. 277 63 30) but unless you are comfortable speaking Russian, it's best just to walk in—there's no way this behemoth will ever be filled. Singles 47,000R. Doubles 80,000R. This hotel may have become a Holiday Inn by the time you read this; it may, however, still be a good budget option.

FOOD

Tap water is not safe to drink in St. Petersburg and Russian bottled water can be putrid. Boil or filter your own or buy large foreign **bottled water** (the delicious Finnish kind is quite cheap) at any of the neighborhood supermarkets or those listed above for under a dollar. It's best to avoid unpackaged **snacks** on the street, but you won't go hungry walking around St. Petersburg—every ten meters there is someone selling imported, packaged food. Check the expiration date before you buy. In summer, ice cream and fruit will keep you going. In fact, eating **ice cream** is a national pastime; the whole year through you and your *morozhenoe* (мороженое; "ice cream") will fit right in with the Russians of all ages licking their cones.

The first advice any Russian will give you is that prices (and places) change every day. While this is true, successful restaurants do stay in business; some are flourishing in the new capitalist era, others have been around practically since the revolution. Most Russians cannot afford to eat out; prices are high and the food in their homes is much better. If you are invited to a home-cooked meal, prepare for a feast—and for multiple insistencies that the raw fat you've been purposefully avoiding is indeed necessary to your survival. If you do eat out, it is advisable to save up for one good meal rather than partake of three grimy ones. St. Petersburg may have once been "the window to the west," but today it's barely even a porthole, with most of the good joint-ventures establishing themselves in Moscow. There's no McDonald's or Pizza Hut, and the other Western venues are both overpriced and only reminiscent of the food they're trying to replicate, or otherwise well beyond a *Let's Go* budget.

Russian menus vary about as much as Stalinist architecture, but preparation can make a big difference. Restaurants along Nevsky are likely to have better food, as they are more aware of tourists' sensitive palates, but prices will be correspondingly higher. Food at local places is almost always inedible and no one will speak English; even in restaurants in highly-touristed regions, menus are often only in handwritten Cyrillic. But because of the favorable exchange rate, elegant Russian restaurants are often a good deal for foreigners—far better than a mediocre place serving cheap Western food for hard currency. Your best bet is probably "ethnic" cuisine, including not only Indian and Chinese, but cuisine from other regions of the former Soviet Union such as Georgia and Armenia, which is often both delicious and cheap. Because of the small number of really good restaurants and the small size of most of these establishments, the top restaurants fill up fast; make reservations (usually on the same day) by phone or in person; be aware that the telephone will not be convenient unless you speak Russian and are patient. Since the Metro stops are few and far between and trams are unreliable, getting to restaurants often requires a good walk; make sure you know how to get there before you set off or you may arrive very hungry. Breakfast and late night snacks are difficult to find—most places are open 11am-11pm; hotels, supermarkets, and bakeries are off hours options.

For more information on restaurants and cafés, check the *St. Petersburg Press*, or ask at the hostels, which keep running travelers' notebooks. The *Traveler's Yellow Pages* has an up-to-date list of restaurants, but without descriptions.

Restaurants

Tbilisi, ul. Sytninskaya 10 (ул. Сытнинская; tel. 232 93 91). M: Gorkovskaya (Горьковская), follow the iron-wrought fence that wraps around the park until you see the Sytny (Сытный) market. Tbilisi is just around the corner. Or, take a left off Kronverkskaya ul. (Кронверкская ул.). A wide selection of sumptuous Georgian appetizers (*satsivi*—chicken in walnut sauce 4500R) and hot dishes (*tolma*—

meat wrapped in grape leaves 4500R). A good option for vegetarians. Menu in Russian, English, and Finnish. A cooperative that, despite a partly tourist clientele, has maintained its atmosphere. Excellent Georgian wine, but pricey; if you do splurge, order by the glass. Open daily 11am-11pm.

The Restaurant (Ресторан), ul. Sadovaya 22 (ул. Садовая). Off Nevsky, near Gostiny Dvor. Don't be intimidated by the grand staircase and huge dining hall; this place has seen better days. Opened in 1864, it became a restaurant for Party officials; now, it has waiters in tuxes longing for business. Good Russian food for reasonable prices and a hall that will make you feel like a king. Orchestra in the evenings and a floor for dancing, under an out-of place disco ball. Caviar 7105R. Baked chicken 1660R. Beefsteak with egg 3430R. Open daily noon-midnight.

House of Architects, ul. Gertsena 52 (tel. 311 59 00), off Nevsky pr. Located in an elegant building in central Petersburg. Above-average Russian fare, attentive service, and elegant. A full meal 18,000R. Open daily noon-midnight.

Tandoor, ul. Voznesensky (ул. Вознесенский; tel. 312 38 86), on the corner of Admiralteysky, 2-block walk left from the bottom of Nevsky pr. For an affordable treat, head here, if only to see adorable Russian boys in Indian costume, complete with gold shoes. The unfamiliar odor of good food wafting onto the street should entice you in if this description doesn't. A tidy, tasteful restaurant whose red carpeting and mournful music give it a homey feel. Tandoor is frequented by elegantly dressed groups of Russians as well as foreigners. Although the service would like you to linger before your meal, the food (and prices) make up for the wait. Tandoori chicken US$5. *Nan* bread US$.50. Open daily noon-11pm.

Assemblaya (Ассемблая), ul. Bolshaya Konyushenaya 13 (ул. Большая Конюшенная; tel. 314 15 37), off Nevsky pr. A beautifully decorated restaurant with pricey but satisfying courses. Each table is caged in with white trellising and ivy, giving a secluded, romantic effect. A little over the *Let's Go* budget, but not a bad place to bring your Russian lover. Menu in English and Russian. Tongue 5700R. Omelet 1200R. Filet mignon 12,400R. Musical program 5000R; to avoid the charge, leave before 8pm. Open 24 hrs.

Le Café, Nevsky pr. 142 (tel. 271 28 11), convenient to the Russian Youth Hostel. An oasis for Westerners, this modern, immaculate café/restaurant sells foreign fashion magazines and newspapers, including the previous day's *Herald Tribune* as well as German biscuits for reasonable prices. A guitar-accordian duet adds a Russian flavor to this otherwise Western establishment. With the kitchen in full view it may be one of the few places you feel sure about what you're eating. Prices to match the security, though. *Borscht* US$4.70. Cheeseburger with fries US$7.85. Apple pie US$3.15. Open 11am-11pm. AmEx, MC, and Visa accepted.

Koryeiski Domik (Корейский Домик, Korea House), nab. Reki Fontanki 20 (наб. Реки Фонтанки; tel. 275 72 03), through an archway from the canal. Closest to M: Chernushevskaya (Чернышевская), take a left off ul. Pestelya (ул. Пестеля), but also two very long blocks from Nevsky pr. Korean-style meat cooked before you. Mmmm.... Also serves soup, rice, noodles, and dumplings. Finally a haven for a vegetarian—plenty of veggies, and they'll even prepare the bouillon and noodles without meat. Korean cabbage soup 3000R. Pickled radishes with crab 2500R. Menu in Korean, English, and Russian. Call for reservations (either the day of or the day before). They will ask if you want a low Korean table, where you sit on cushions or a "European" table. Open 1-10pm.

Demyanova Ukha (Демьянова Уха), pr. Kronverski 53 (tel. 232 80 90), at M: Gorkovskaya (Горьковская) in a building under complete overhaul in summer 1994. Entrance around to the right. Fresh-fish dishes in a jovial, hectic atmosphere. The staff works industriously to keep the good food coming. Assorted fish 14,350R but tea only 60R. Menu changes daily. Open noon-9pm. Reservations needed even for lunch; call in the morning.

Chebey (Хлебей), on Bolshoy pr. 61 (пр. Большой; tel. 233 20 46). M: Petrogradskaya (Петроградская). Down the street from Café Tet-a-Tet. One of the few places which play pleasant music over the stereo, this modest restaurant serves yummy Chinese and Russian fare for appropriate prices. Lazy Susans and round tables make this good for large groups. A full meal for 20,000R. Sweet and sour fish 12,850R. Chicken Gumbo 2510R. Open daily 11am-7pm.

RUSSIA

Kroonk (Крунк), Solyanoy per. 14 (Соляной пер.; tel. 273 16 91). M: Chernyshevskaya (Чернышевская), one block away from the Fontanka up by the summer garden. Frequented by well-dressed Russians in the know, this small restaurant downstairs from the street serves well-prepared Armenian cuisine. Salad 3000R. *Tolma* "Yerevanskaya" 9000R. Open daily noon-10pm.

Petrostar (Петростар), ul. Bolshaya Pushkarskaya (ул. Большая Пушкарская; tel. 232 40 07), two blocks from Tbilisi and not nearly as good, serving Russian and Ukrainian specialities. Come here to gain an understanding of new-found capitalism. Filled with Russian biznessmen at bizness lunches, this could be the equivalent of a men's club with similar secluded high-backed booths. Rabbit 8000R. Salad 3400R. *Lavash* (Georgian bread) 100R. Open daily 1pm-midnight.

Victory Restaurant on Kamennostrovsky pr. 24 (Каменностровский пр.; tel. 232 41 43 or 232 30 55). A 10-minute walk right from M: Petrogradskaya (Петроградская). Near the Kirov Museum, this Russo-German joint venture provides an extensive menu in rubles. Typical markings of a joint venture, complete with modern (but *kitsch*) furniture and fresh flowers on each table. Dominated by the well-stacked bar. Menu typed beautifully in German, English. Vodka 2500R. Pizza 9000R. Roast chicken with vegetables 14,000R.

Petrovsky (Петровский), on a ship docked at corner of Kronverkskaya pr. (Кронверкская пр.; tel. 238 47 93) and the eastern bridge across to Zayachy ostrov, M: Gorkovskaya. On the second floor of the shabby ship the restaurant, first opened in 1925, is none-the-less neatly set-up, with tables on the deck in summer. Enjoy the tasty but high-priced Russian specialities, with a view on the river and across to the Winter Palace. This Venice-imitation is clearly designed for foreign tourists, but prices are still in rubles and thus affordable. Salad Petrovski 4576R. Beef Stroganoff 9126R. *Blini* 404R. Open 7pm-midnight. Call for reservations.

Hotel Mockva, M: pl. Aleksander Nevskovo. Come out of the Metro and you're there (tel. 274 02 67). Downstairs serves dinner only, but upstairs offers pricey Russian snacks all day. The menu changes daily, but the English-speaking staff will give you the run-down. Like the hotel and, well, Russia in general, this place is large, with the atmosphere to match. Bifsteak 12,000R. Open daily 8:30am-11pm.

Chaika (Чайка), Kanal Griboyedeva 14 (Канала Грибоедова; tel. 312 46 31), off Nevsky pr. near Dom Knigi. German fare, hard liquor, caviar, and cheesecake for hard currency. Wooden, boat-oriented decor will make you forget you're in Russia. As will the food and prices. Mostly foreign crowd especially in the evenings, enticed perhaps by the exceptionally large selection of alcohol and food. Chaika is run on a card system, so you pay at the end. Don't lose the card—it costs you 120,000R. Main dishes run DM5.50-30. Open daily 11am-3pm. MC, Visa, AmEx.

Café Tet-a-Tet (Кафе Тет-а-Тет, spelled Мет-а-Мет on the sign), pr. Bolshoi 65 (пр. Большой; tel. 232 10 35). M: Petrogradskaya (Петроградская) on Petrogradskaya side. Turn left from the Metro onto Bolshoi pr. (Большой пр.) An elegant, intimate restaurant; live music on grand piano and tables for two—bring a date. Standard Russian fare with a number of fish dishes, entrees approximately 10,000R. Open 1pm-midnight. Menu in Russian and English. Make reservations; it gets crowded.

Balkany (Балканы), Nevsky pr. 27 (tel. 315 47 48), between the Kazan Cathedral and Gostiny Dvor. Standard Russian fare; just pick a table, sit down, and ask for a menu. Neatly set and clean, complete with plastic ketchup and mustard containers on each table. Main courses 2100-2600R. Open daily 11am-10pm.

Shanghai, ul. Sadovaya 12 (ул. Садовая; tel. 311 27 51). M: Gostiny Dvor, off Nevsky pr. First floor serves Russian food for cheaper ruble prices in addition to the more expensive Chinese menu in dollars. Despite its prices, the first floor has an orchestra and is dimly lit with prettily arranged white cloth napkins. Second floor offers Chinese fare all day. Second floor menus in Chinese, Russian, and English with large round tables for big groups (or families). There are several vegetarian main dishes. Spicy asparagus US$2. Fried frog legs US$10. Deep fried fish in soy sauce US$2.50. Blini with caviar US$2.50. Open daily noon-11pm.

Daddy's Steak House, Moskovsky pr. 73 (Московская пр.; tel. 298 95 52), M: Frinzhenskaya (Фрижженская). If your willing to shell out the bucks for a few tastes of home, this Finno-Russian joint venture is the place to do it. Juicy steaks and the large check delivered to your table with a smile. Open noon-11pm. Pizza Express located next door.

Literaturnoye Café (Литературное Кафе), Nevsky pr. 18 (tel. 312 60 57). A famous 19th-century chat spot for writers and artists, gracefully restored to its original elegance. Pushkin had his last meal here before departing for his fatal duel. Pricey, but unbeatable for champagne and sweets in the afternoon. *Prix fixe* meal includes caviar, fish, *borscht* and other Russian delicacies, but no alcohol (40,000R). Cover 2500R. Orchestra plays Russian songs. Reservations by phone or in person highly recommended. Open daily noon-5pm and 7-10pm.

Café Druzhba (Кафе Дружба), Nevsky pr. 15. Across the street from the Literaturnoye. Pricey but carefully prepared Russian food for primarily Russian customers. The two large rooms are somewhat dark, but the atmosphere is lively. At night a small, all-red disco opens between the rooms. Caviar (Икра) 2940R. Pork—Russian style (Свиня) 6185R. Open daily 11am-11pm. The same people own the café around the corner at ul. Gertzina 14 (ул. Герцина).

Fortetsiya (Фортеция), ul. Kuybysheva (ул. Куйбышева; tel. 233 94 68). M: Gorkovskaya (Горьковская), off Kronvertsky pr., a little beyond the Russian Political History Museum. The bilingual menu, red plush walls, and copies of St. Petersburg Press suggest this place is reaching out to foreigners. Maybe it's just movin' with the times. Ah, capitalism! Cold *borscht* (for the frustrated vegetarian) 4500R. *Kartofel fri* (french fries) 100R. Open daily noon-5pm and 7pm-midnight.

Restaurant Metropol (Ресторан Метрополь), ul. Dumskaya (ул. Думская), right from M: Gostiny Dvor. A dingy place interesting to enter for the true experience. *Piroshki* (pies) with unidentifiable meat are dirt-cheap, which explains the long line of older women and the smell of grease and meat. Nonetheless, you can get an open-faced salmon sandwich for 960R. Lots of watery *napitok* (literally, drink). Banquet room advertised for large parties. Open Mon.-Sat. 8am-3pm and 4-8pm, Sun. 11am-3pm, 4-6pm.

Cafés

Baghdad (Багдад), ul. Furshtadtskaya 35 (tel. 272 23 55) M: Chernyshevskaya (Чернышевская). Turn right from the metro and then right again. Serving delicious Uzbek and Russian cuisine, this small, colorful café located downstairs from the street serves a hearty bowl of fatty *lagman* (soup with meat) and a recommended rice *plov,* 4000R. Very popular, and with good reason. Open noon-11pm.

Café Diasto (Кафе Диастро), Nevsky pr. 44. A sunny, informal café with a cool grey and pink décor, this bright spot offers sweet pastries and hamburger-equivalents (1200R) for decent prices. Enjoy a chocolate brownie (730R) on the run. Standing room only. Open Mon.-Sat. 9am-9pm, Sun. 9am-7pm.

Café Primyera (Кафе Примьера), ul. Dekabristov 36 (ул. Декабристов). M: Sadovya (Садовая). Not worth a trek out there, but if you're near St. Nicholas Cathedral or the Marinsky Theatre, it's a sure place for a decent snack, of which there are few in the area. A modest, local joint that makes fairly successful attempt at Western cuisine. Pizza 7300R. Bifsteak *po-hamburgersky* 6600R. Open 11am-11pm.

Café Morozhenoe (Кафе Мороженое), Nevsky pr. 24, opposite the Kavkazki (tel. 311 80 11). St. Petersburg's premier ice cream parlor. Faded elegance and pastel green walls, green chairs, green carpet. Room in front is cheaper and more informal, while the large room in back has the grandeur of a well-loved piece of furniture. Homemade ice cream of various mixed flavors. Large ice cream 4000R. Turkish coffee 1500R. In front, single ice cream 1050R. Open daily 11am-10pm.

Café Margarita (Кафе Маргарита), Liteyni pr. 64 (Литейный пр.). A rare find, just off Nevsky. Standing room only, but light and roomy, with delicious sandwiches (not the open-faced kind!) and pastries. Lemon meringue pie 550R. Cucumber and egg sandwiches 600R. Open Mon.-Sat. 9am-7pm, Sun. 9am-5pm.

St. Petersburg Café, Canal Griboyedova (Канала Грибоедова), directly opposite the Church of the Spilled Blood (*Spasi na Krave*). Tiny but packed, with a healthy mix of Russians and tourists. Order scrumptious apricot tarts and carrot pies at the counter, then sit down; a table will probably have cleared by the time it is your turn. Full meal 4000R. Take-out available. Open noon-11pm.

Baskin Robbins 31 Flavors, Nevsky pr. 79. M: Ploschad Vosstaniya (Площадь Восстания). Next to the Metro. As always, pretty in pink, just not quite so well-lit as the usual. Exceptionally artificial colors adorn the familiar array of ice-cream cakes and a rather bizarre assortment of smiling pigs. No Dunkin' Donuts in sight. Menu in Russian and English. Sundae 5100R. Single cone 1700R. Open daily 10am-10pm. Also in stands all over the city; another store in Park Lenina, M: Gorkovskaya (Горьковская).

Gino Ginelli, on Canal Griboyedova (Канала Грибоедова), just off Nevsky pr. near Dom Knigi. Next to Chaika. DM5.50-7.50 buys pizza or cheeseburgers for homesick Westerners in a tiny Western-style café to boot. Ice cream DM2 per scoop. Cheeseburger DM5. Open 10am-1am.

Metekhi (Метехи), ul. Belinskovo 3 (ул. Белинского; tel. 272 33 61), just off the Fontanka canal and parallel to Nevsky pr. This tiny Georgian cooperative café with stained glass windows and six tables ladles out a terrific bowl of *kharcho* soup and *lobio* (vegetarian chili) for about 2000R each. *Lavash* (лаваш, very Georgian) 1000R. *Shashlik* (шашлык) 5000R. Open 11am-8pm.

Dessert Hall (Десерт Хол), next door to Metekhi, but farther down Belinskovo. Great place for a cheap snack and hanging out with friends. Mostly a young, local crowd who wait for the doors to open after the one-hour afternoon break. Salad, open sandwiches, and pastries all under 2000R. Open 11am-3pm and 4-10pm.

Vody Lagidze (Воды Лагидзе), also next door to Metekhi. Standing room only. Come here for a quick snack in winter to get out of the cold. Cheesy *khachapuri* (хачапури; a Georgian national treasure). Eastern coffee 200R. Open 11am-3pm and 4-10pm.

Volkhov (Волхов) right off Canal Griboyedeva (Канала Грибоедова) on Inzhenernaya ul. (Инженерная ул.; tel. 273 00 55). Generic Russian food although somewhat more upscale than the typical neighborhood joint because of its proximity to Nevsky. Quite a number of large tables and musical accompaniment in the evenings. Assorted fish (рыба, *ryba*) 6150R. Fried pork 3770R. The *solyanka* (солянка) is homemade. Open daily 11am-11pm.

Novy Vek Café, ul. Galernaya 33. Good vegetarian food. Meals under 5000R.

Café Aurora (Кафе Аврора), on Nevsky pr. near M: Gostiny Dvor (Гостиный Двор). The strange penguin-bird you see on ice cream everywhere? Well, they serve it here too. Tiled with appropriate white and blue mosaic (this bird's glorious colors), this café is pleasant and clean. The tasty and cheap ice cream is even weighed to determine price. Wouldn't want to pay a ruble more, certainly. If you're missing the latest top-40 song, this place is likely to be blaring it, but so is the radio in you train compartment. One portion 700R. Champagne 550R.

Café Veronika (Кафе Вероника), a 2-minute walk from the Russian Youth Hostel on the corner of Nevsky pr. and Suvorovsky pr. A convenient place to watch the locals gather. Nothing out of the ordinary except its location and hours. A chocolate soufflé is a marshmallow coated in hard chocolate. Holsten beer 2500R. Bifsteak 3500R. Open 24 hrs.

Café Vityaz (Витязь), Stroganoff Palace, across from Nevsky pr. 20. and the 1-hr. photo shop. Situated in the crumbling courtyard of a previously magnificent palace, this romantic café is open only in the summer. Covered by a makeshift white awning, tables with yellow parasols surround a gurgling fountain. On a warm summer evening, enjoy the late setting sun as you are served tea in red plastic cups by waiters in tuxes. Beer 2438R. Tea 335R. Open late May-Sept. 11am-11pm.

Beer Garden, Nevsky pr. directly across from Nevsky Palace Hotel, to the right of the Afrodite Restaurant through an archway into a large courtyard. A 15-min. walk from the Russian Youth Hostel. This outdoor café looks like you've stepped into another world. The lawn is covered with tables, parasols, and a barbecue grill cooks up tasty meat-treats. Live music on weekends. Menu in English. Beer US$3.50. Barbecued chicken US$5. Open daily noon-4am (lunch noon-4pm, grill 6pm-4am). The Afrodite next door has delicious seafood but will kill your budget.

Kabachok Flint (Кабачок Флинт), just to the west of the Fortress of Peter and Paul is this little tavern, located on a boat docked by the bridge. Offers standard café fare and lots of mixed drinks. A great place if your idea of a good time is getting drunk on a slightly rocking boat. Sandwiches 1500R. Beer 3200R. Gin and Tonic 2800R. Open daily noon-4am.

Supermarkets

Beyond the standard range of Russian food stores, St. Petersburg also has supermarkets which charge slightly more for imported products. All offer prices in rubles, and if they do not are required by law to take them according to the exchange rate the supermarket states. Most open at 11am and take a 1-2pm break for lunch, closing again at 8 or 9pm. One possible **dieta** is on Nevsky 30 (open Mon.-Sat. 8am-1pm, 2pm-7:30pm). A few 24-hr. supermarkets also exist. The advantage to these stores is that they offer you quality produce you're used, all in one place. But they are *much* more expensive.

Surprise, on Nevsky pr. 113, and **Tauras**, Kondratevskiy pr. 34 (break from 2-3pm) are most convenient. More upscale places charge high prices but the luxury of walking into a well-stocked, clean store is often well-worth it.

Antenta Supermarket, on Tuchkov per. 1115, M: Vasileostrovskaya (Василеостровская). Open noon-10pm.

Express Market, Nevsky pr. 113 and ul. Kharkovskaya 1 (ул. Харьковская). Imported Finnish goods. Open 10am-10pm.

Babylon Super, Maly pr. 54/56 (Малый пр.), off Bolshoy pr., M: Petrogradskaya (Петроградская). Open Mon.-Sat. 10am-9pm, Sun. noon-8pm.

Stockmann, Finlandsky pr. 1 (Финляндский пр.), M: Ploschad Lenina (Площадь Ленина). Open daily 10am-9pm, MC, Visa, and AmEx accepted.

A number of hotels also contain stores—such as the **Neva Star** in the Hotel Moskva and the **Baltic Star** in Hotel Pribaltiskaya. For the curious and the wary, there is a radioactivity testing service which checks your food: just one block from the hostel, it's called **Radioactivity Tests for Food,** Sovetskaya L.S. 4-a (tel. 277 52 92).

Markets

Markets (Рыноки) stock fresh produce, meat, cheese, honey, and occasionally a prepared dish or two, but they are comparatively more expensive than state-owned stores. Markets are a Russian experience themselves and require energy on the part of all involved. Foreigners are easy to spot, and the ingenious seller *will* try to cheat you; watch out for fingers on the scales or money behind the table. If you are not satisfied, simply walk away; indeed a simple "nyet" will do wonders to bring the price down and bargaining is what these places are all about; these are bazaars, not *Safeways*, after all. Don't forget to bring bags and an odd jar. The **covered market** at Kuznechni per. 3 (Кузнечный пер.), just around the corner from M: Vladimirskaya (Владимирская; closed second Tues. of the month), and the **Patent Cooperative Trade Center** (Maltsevski Rynok), ul. Nekrasova 52 (ул. Некрасова), at the top of Ligovski pr. (Лиговский пр.), M: Ploshad Vosstaniya (open Tues.-Mon. 8am-7pm, Sun. 8am-4pm), are the biggest and most exciting. **Krondratevsky Rynok,** Polyustrovsky pr. 45 (Полюстровский пр.), M: Ploshad Lenina, bus #138, is a pet market on weekends (closed third Tues.of the month).

SIGHTS

St. Petersburg is a city obsessed with its glorious past. Citizens speak of "before the Revolution" as though it were the 1970s and of dear old Peter and Catherine as though they were their cousins—the ones who made it, of course. As a result, the museums scattered throughout the city are rich in historical significance, and visiting them reveals as much about the city's present inhabitants as about its past lives.

There are essentially four kinds of museums in St. Petersburg: The big, famous ones; the very Soviet ones (though these are fast disappearing); the recreated homes of cultural figures; and the churches, monasteries, and cemeteries. The first are a must for all, despite the large tour groups and high prices for foreigners. The second appeal largely to history buffs and lovers of the absurd, though they are beautifully

RUSSIA

organized and usually (unintentionally, at times) humorous. The third are mostly pilgrimage sights where you can see (and say you saw) this or that famous author's pen and toothbrush, but are less revealing if you don't read Russian. The fourth are less museums than monuments and memorials to the dead of World War II.

Although most museums are in central St. Petersburg, they are often far from a Metro station and trams can be unreliable. It is best, if you have the time, to pick an area of the city to explore. You will also thus get a better feel for the neighborhood.

Negotiating Museums: Almost all museums list two sets of prices, one for Russians and one for foreigners. Some, but not all, museums offer a student discount to foreigners with an ISIC card. Otherwise, you are stuck paying the much higher (usually by ten times) foreigner price—some try to hand the old woman at the ticket-booth (Касса; *Kassa*) the exact amount of rubles for a Russian ticket and don't say anything.

After purchasing your ticket (sometimes before) you will often be required to check your bag in the cloakroom (Гардеръоб). This sometimes costs a small amount (50R or thereabouts).

Russian museums can be very confusing—whole sections are sometimes closed for no apparent reason. "Начала Осмотра" marks the beginning of the exhibition, or follow the arrows labelled "Выставкаэ."

Rather than cover the floors, many museums provide you with *tapachki*, giant slippers which fit over your shoes and transform the gallery into a skating rink. Make sure you get ones which fit well, especially if you have small feet, or you will drag yourself around the museum only to kill yourself on the stone stairs.

Finally, look carefully at everything in the museum, or risk the wrath of the elderly ladies who watch fiercely over each room.

The Hermitage (Эрмитаж)

Housed in four opulent buildings, the State Hermitage Museum is the world's largest, and one of the world's finest art collections. Begun as 25 paintings belonging to Catherine the Great, the Hermitage now rivals the Louvre and the Prado in Architectural, historical, and artistic magnificence. It cannot disappoint.

Nor can the whole museum be absorbed in one visit—indeed, only 15-20% of the collection is on display at any one time. Rather than attempting a survey of the world's artistic achievements, pick a building, a time period, or a floor, and focus on it. There is no equivalent of the *Mona Lisa* or Michelangelo's *David* here that everyone must see; you get to pick your own. One Austrian writer was led through the museum with his eyes closed until he reached the Rembrandts, so as not to be distracted by the rest of the glitter.

Lines can be long, so come early or in the middle of the week. Allow for 3-4 hours to see the museum. It's easy to latch onto a tour group, especially if you understand Russian. (Open Tues.-Sun. 10:30am-6pm. Tickets sold until 5pm; the upper floors start closing an hour early. Admission 16,000R, under 18 9000R. Russians 300R, Russian students 200R. Cameras 6000R, videocameras 14,000R.)

The museum actually consists of four buildings: The **Winter Palace,** the **Little Hermitage,** the **Large Hermitage,** and the **Hermitage Theater** (which is often closed). There are floor plans in English on each level, and you can buy your own plan near the ticket booth for 500R. The rooms are numbered. The museum is organized chronologically by floor, starting with **Egyptian, Greek** and **Roman** art on the ground floor of the Little and Large Hermitages, and **prehistoric artifacts** in the Winter Palace. On the second floors of the Hermitages are collections of **French, Italian,** and **Dutch** art of the 17th and 18th centuries. **Rembrandt** is in the Large Hermitage, rooms 249-254. **Titian** is in rooms 218-19. In rooms 226-27 is an exact copy of **Raphael's Laggia** in the Vatican, commissioned by Catherine the Great.

The second floor of the Winter Palace is spectacular: Room 189 is the famous **Malachite Hall**, containing six tons of malachite in the form of columns, boxes and urns. If you wondered why there was a revolution, the extravagance of this home is explanatory. On the third floor of the Winter Palace (the only building with three floors) is **impressionism, post-impressionism,** and 20th-century European and American art. Try not to miss these rooms; if you're running late, visit them first—the museum closes starting at the top.

Some historical background: The **Winter Palace** was commissioned from Rastrelli by Elizabeth in 1754. Catherine the Great remodelled it in 1837, and it was restored in the same style after a huge fire in the same year. It made a cozy home for the Tsars until 1917. The **Small Hermitage** was built by Nicholas II as a museum, and was opened to the public in 1852. Catherine built the **Large Hermitage** to house her ever-expanding art collection in the 1830s. The collection was shown by special appointment and today the museum publishes some of the rules for her visitors:

> —One shall speak with moderation and quietly so that others do not get a headache.
> —One shall be joyful, but shall not try to damage, break or gnaw at anything.
> —One shall eat with pleasure, but drink with moderation, so that each can leave the room unassisted.

Try to do the same while you are here.

Russian Museum, Summer Gardens, Palace and Mars Field

The Russian Museum (Русский Музей; *Russki Muzey*), is reachable by M: Gostiny Dvor. Go down ul. Mikhailova (ул. Михайлова) past the Grand Hotel Europe; on the other side of Pushkin's monument is the museum, a grand yellow palace. It houses the largest collection of Russian art outside the Tretyakov Gallery in Moscow. Unfortunately, most of the 20th-century collection is either in storage or out of the country on tour. Nevertheless, the museum is an excellent introduction to the breadth of Russian art history, and a reminder of how much has been going on here culturally for the past few centuries. While the building is being restored, enter through the basement in the right corner of the courtyard; go downstairs and turn left.

The collection, begun by Alexander III, is housed in the Mikhailovsky Palace, originally built for the son of Paul I. Nicholas II bought the palace and opened a museum here in 1898, the first public museum of Russian art in the country. The palace rooms themselves are works of art, with inlaid wood floors and gorgeously gaudy ceilings. The collection is now arranged chronologically, starting on the first floor. If you are at the top of the main staircase, head left and begin with the icons from the 14th to 17th centuries in the first two rooms. Then continue to 18th-century paintings and sculpture; downstairs are paintings and sculptures from the 19th century. Don't miss the room devoted entirely to Repin's painting of the Ceremonial Meeting of the State Council (May 7, 1901) showing Tsar Nicholas II and his councilors at work. There is also a large collection of Russian folk-art on the first floor, including delicate ivory carvings and an absurd group of ceramic teapots.

From the ground floor, you can also reach the Benois Wing—go up the staircase by the giant bronze soldier. It is currently under repair; only the third floor galleries are open. But the most modern paintings (both the worst and the most interesting art) are here, and are worth a look. There is a gift shop by the staircase on the ground floor—prices are steep and listed in dollars. (Open Wed.-Mon. 10am-6pm. Ticket office closes one hour before museum. Admission 9500R, students 4700R. Children under 7 free. Russians 600R, Russian students 300R.)

The **Summer Gardens and Palace** are behind the Russian Museum and directly across the river from Peter and Paul's Fortress. They are a lovely place to rest and cool off. They can be entered from the north or south end only, and have long paths lined with marble busts of famous Russians. These days the grounds aren't kept very well, but green is green, and in summer they are pretty. In the northeast corner of the gardens is Peter's **Summer Palace**, a small building that was once part of a larger complex. Individuals must join tours given in Russian—after you buy your ticket, wait outside until they invite you in. Peter lived downstairs, surrounded by heavy German furniture and lots of clocks, while upstairs resided his children and wife Catherine, who upon his death became Russia's first Tsarina. (Gardens open 8am-10pm, winter 8am-7pm. Free. Palace open Wed.-Mon. 10:30am-6pm. Closed the last Mon. of the month. Admission US$2, students US$1—payable in rubles only. Russians 600R, Russian students 300R.)

Mars Field (Марсого Поль; *Marsovo Pol*) is right next to the Summer Gardens, so named because military parades were held here in the 19th century. The park, open and broad, is now a memorial to the hundreds of thousands of people who died in Leningrad in World War II. There is a monument in the center with an eternal flame. Don't walk on the grass; you'd be treading on a massive common grave.

St. Isaac's Cathedral and Environs

For an awe-inspiring view of the city's rooftops, climb to the dome of **St. Isaac's Cathedral** (Исаакиевский Собор; *Isaakievski Sobor*), on Isaakievskaya pl., a massive example of 19th-century civic-religious architecture designed by Frenchie Auguste de Montferrand. The long climb to the top is suitable for all ages, as the steps are shallow despite their vast number (272). The dome of the cathedral is coated with almost 100kg of pure gold, which in sunlight glints from miles away. Gold was never cheap, and the cost of building this opulent cathedral was well over five times what it cost to build the Winter Palace. The cost to human life was severe as well, including 60 laborers who died from inhaling mercury fumes during the gilding process. It took forty years to finish, in part due to a superstition (those mystics again!) that the Romanov dynasty would fall with the cathedral's completion. The cathedral was completed in 1858, the Romanovs fell in 1917, and while we're about it, Rasputin was probably a charlatan, but that's all water under the mystic bridge anyway.

Although the interior is simply breathtaking for the first few minutes upon entering, once one is more accustomed to the beauty and grandeur of this religious place it is worthwhile to walk around the walls, looking carefully at the details. The murals and mosaics inside are the works of some of Russia's greatest artists, such as the intricate carvings of saintly scenes by sculptor I. Vitali on the huge wooden doors. The chips in the marble columns appear courtesy of German artillery fire during the siege of Leningrad.Because the cathedral is technically a museum, the paintings have their titles explained in English; but the cathedral still holds religious services and is packed with *babushkas* at Easter. The cathedral is dedicated to St. Isaac, the saint with the great fortune to have his fall on Peter the Great's birthday (May 30th—Peter was a Gemini; ask any Russian astrologer what they think about that. (Museum open Thurs.-Tues. 10am-6pm. Colonnade (the climb to the top) open 10am-5pm. To the right side of the cathedral is a *Kassa*. The price of admission there for the museum is 400R, students 300R; for the colonnade 500R, students 200R. They will give you a ticket to show at the door. Or, you can go straight to the main door in front—where foreigners are charged an absurd 15,000R just to enter the cathedral.)

Despite the fact that the cathedral was the Nazi air force's "reference point number one" during World War II, the starving citizens of Leningrad planted cabbages in the square directly in front; once these ran out they ate the square's rats. Photographs of the cabbage-field can be seen at the **State Museum of the History of St. Petersburg,** not to be confused with the **Museum of the History of Leningrad** (Государственный Музей Историй Ленинграда), nab. Krasnaya Flota 44 (наб. Красная Флота), along the embankment, a five-minute walk from the Admiralty heading away from the Hermitage (the other museum is on Peter and Paul Island, see below). This museum covers the history of the city after the revolution—or so it purports. What it covers for now is the 1941 blockade, while the other periods are reinterpreted for democratic digestion. Every St. Petersburg inhabitant will tell you to go here; if you don't understand the devastating effect World War II had on this town, you absolutely should. (Open Mon., Thurs.-Sun. 11am-6pm, Tues. 11am-4pm;

admission US$1, students US$0.50 (or ruble equivalent), Russian adults 300R, Russian students 200R.)

Nevsky Prospect (Невский Проспект) and environs

The Prospect begins at the **Admiralty** (Адмиралтество, *Admiraltestvo*), whose golden spire, painted black during WWII to disguise it from German artillery bombers, towers over the Admiralty gardens and Palace Square. Originally a wooden shipyard, this Admiralty was built in the early 1820s. Supposedly, the tower's height allowed the Tsar to supervise the continued construction of St. Petersburg and ascertain that everything was going to plan. The gardens surrounding the building now hold the statues of important Russian literary figures; the space was initially designed to allow for a wider firing range when defending the shipyard.

On the river side of the Admiralty is the unforgettable **Bronze Horseman,** Etienne Falconet's sculpture that has become the symbol of the city and it's birth as a child of Peter the Great's massive will. The statue was commissioned by Catherine the Great as a "gift" to Peter I in 1782; the stone reads "To Peter I from Catherine II" in Russian and Latin. It shows Peter the Great mounted on a rearing horse that is crushing a snake (symbolizing evil) below its hind hooves. Peter himself is pointing out at the Neva, and looks ready to build another capital city. The rock the horse is standing on is from a site outside of St. Petersburg, said to be where Peter stood when he surveyed the city.

Palace Square (Дворцовая Площадь; *Dvortsovaya Ploschad*), the huge windswept expanse in front of the Winter Palace, has been the site of many turning points in Russia's history. Here Catherine was hailed as Tsarina after she overthrew her husband, Tsar Peter III; on "Bloody Sunday" in 1905 Nicholas II's guards here fired into a crowd of peaceful demonstrators, the beginning of the end for the Romanovs; and here was the quasi-mythical storming of the Winter Palace in the Revolution of 1917, when Lenin's Bolsheviks seized power from Kerensky's provisional government. Today you can here buy an ice cream cone, get your portrait drawn, and ponder all the things the angel at the top of the **Alexander Column** has seen. The column is a monument to the Russian defeat of Napoleon in 1812. The inscription on the Hermitage side reads "To Alexander I from a grateful Russia"; the angel is said to have the Tsar's face. The column itself weighs 700 metric tons and took two years to cut from a cliff in Karelia, and another year to bring to St. Petersburg. However, with the help of 2000 war veterans and a complex pulley system, it was raised in just 40 minutes—and today sits on its pedestal without any mortar, held there only by its massive weight. But don't lean on it too hard.

The Pushkin Museum (Пушкин Музей), nab. Reki Moiki 12 (наб. Реки Мойки) is just off Palace Square on the canal, the yellow building on the right. Alexander Pushkin holds a place in the hearts of Russians unequaled by any other native son. They worship and fear Papa Tolstoy; they *adore* Pushkin. Most Russians consider him as good as or greater than Shakespeare, and any Russian with more than a year of schooling can recite some of his verses. He's a politically correct hero, too; his great-grandfather was an Ethiopian who served Peter I and was educated by the Tsar. Pushkin's early and tragic death gave him martyr status in Russia; this museum is not only the apartment where he lived, but the place in which he died. He was killed in a duel with a French officer who had insulted him by courting Pushkin's beautiful wife Natalya (it is widely thought that the whole affair was a put-up job by Tsar Nicholas I, who did not approve of Pushkin's poetics). Pushkin was fatally wounded in the duel and died here several days later, in his beloved library. The clock there is stopped at 2:45, the time of his death.

Most of the museum is now empty, containing only prints from the early 19th century and items such as Natalya Pushkin's ballet slippers and many examples of the poet's drafts and sketches (Pushkin loved to sketch profiles of funny-looking people; he was said to be rather ugly himself, actually, perhaps indicating why his wife slept around on him). Downstairs is the original front door of the apartment, with "Pushkin" scrawled across the upper panel, as well as the original notices posted by Pushkin's doctor about the poet's condition (an enormous crowd gathered outside the house when they heard the news). The books in the library are exact replicas; the furniture is original. Whether you are a Pushkin lover, or just wish a little more insight into the nation's greatest obsession, this small and elegant museum is an hour well spent. You must wear "tapachki" in the museum—enormous slipper-like footwear that protect the floors from your shoes and make it possible to skate through the exhibits. There is also a souvenir shop. Enter through the courtyard; the ticket-booth (Касса) and museum entrance are on the left (open Wed.-Mon. 10:30am-6pm, closed the last Friday of each month; admission 4000R, Russians 700R, cameras 2000R).

Dom Knigi, Nevsky pr. 28. This landmark art deco building was the Russian headquarters of the Singer Sewing Machine company before the revolution, and the globe at the top is that company's emblem. The store has lost most of its former glory—only the first two floors are open—but it's worth investigating. It is still organized the way it was during Soviet times—annoy the clerk at the fiction desk by asking if they have *Dr. Zhivago*. The West has invaded the ground floor, and there you can buy Microsoft Word and expensive office supplies. The poster collection is hardly worth looking at these days—just cute fluffy animals (open daily 9am-8pm). Farther down Nevsky towards the Admiralty, at #14, there is a blue and white sign that's been kept up for 50 years beyond its time. It reads, in translation, "Citizens! During artillery bombardments this side of the street is more dangerous."

The colossal edifice across the street from Dom Knigi, modeled after St. Peter's in Rome but designed and built by Russian architects (and left to decay by the Soviets) is the **Kazan Cathedral** (Казанский Собор; *Kazanski Sobor*), which used to be the **Museum of the History of Religion and Atheism,** but now is the **Museum of the History of the Russian Orthodox Church**—its gold cross was restored just this year. The cathedral was originally created for the purpose of housing **Our Lady of Kazan**, a sacred icon now lost; today the exhibition, while interesting, is nothing to revere. It combines morning religious services in the front with an eclectic collection of Russian religious artifacts in the back. While the Museum of Atheism used to show pictures of monks and nuns fornicating, today's mother-of-pearl carvings are comparatively tame. The few icons, priests robes and bibles, are displayed in glass cases, dwarfed by the interior of the cathedral—the real reason to pay the museum entrance fee. As one last attraction, Marshal Kutuzov is buried here. As it would be contrary to the perverse "Russian Rule of Appearances" (the more dilapidated the outside, the more you will appreciate the inside) to enter through either the main entrance (to the right side of the cathedral) or the front door, a small door around to the left is actually the museum entrance (open Mon.-Tues. Thurs.-Fri. 11am-6pm, Sat.-Sun. 12:30pm-6pm. *Kassa* closes at 5pm; admission 5500R, student 2500R, Russian 500R, Russian student 200R).

The plaza between the cathedral's wings has been the center of St. Petersburg's political and religious activity since Plekhanov, an early revolutionary, spoke out here in 1876. New political parties deliver speeches from the east wing; discussion circles gather starting about 8pm. Stop to admire the monarchists, anarchists, fascists, hypnotists, Christian fundamentalist missionaries, and Hare Krishnas—and meet Russians ravenous for contact with the West. There are even a few vocal Communists left. The plaza, once an open square, was allegedly covered with lawn and turned into a garden to hinder large demonstrations—as if there aren't other large, open spaces for revolutionaries to congregate in this city. Women should not wander around this area alone in the evening; the wings of the cathedral are reportedly a favorite meeting spot for prostitutes and their customers.

The colorful church on the Griboyedov canal (канал Грибоедова), the **Church of the Bleeding Savior** (Спас На Крови; *Spas Na Krovi*; a.k.a. the Church on the Spilled Blood) sits on the site of Tsar Alexander II's (bloody) 1881 assassination. Though the cathedral has been under repair for the past 20 years and remains closed to the public, the minutely detailed mosaics on the exterior merit a close look. It does indeed look suspiciously like St. Basil's—would the folks back home really notice? Farther down Nevsky pr. at no. 35 stands the pale yellow **Gostiny Dvor** (Гостиный Двор), St. Petersburg's largest department store. Under renovation in summer 1994, it might return to its former glory as souvenir haven within a year. Then again, it might not. In any case, its scaffolding and crumbling walls still bustle with shoppers; this is a major Nevsky pr. landmark and was one even in the 18th century (open Mon.-Sat. 10am-8pm). Beware the shady (read: presumed mafia) folk in the neighborhood.

The **Sheremetyev Museum** (Дворец Шереметевий), nad. Fontanki Reki 34 (над. Реки Фонтанки), is one block from Nevsky pr. This former mansion of the Sheremetyev family was still in the process of being restored (although two rooms were already open) in summer 1994; by 1995 it should be beautiful. This could be a very unique museum—a tribute to the pre-revolutionary nobility in central St. Petersburg (Sheremetyev was one of Peter the Great's Marshalls), very different from the many recreated apartments (open Wed.-Sat. 2-6pm; admission 2000R, Russians 300R).

The **Theatre Museum** (Музей Театрального и Музыкального Ускуства), pl. Ostrovskovo 6, third floor, is just off Nevsky, a minute from M: Gostiny Dvor. It's next to the formerly named **Alex and Rinsky Theatre**, the oldest theater in Russia; the first production of Nikolai Gogol's *The Government Inspector* was staged here in 1836. This chock-full museum is covered with posters, programs, and set designs, making it a colorful visit. Elaborate costumes from such classics as Romeo and Juliet also on display. The last room contains magnificent costumes from the actor Shalyapin, who died in Paris. (Museum open Mon.-Sun. 11am-6pm, Wed. 1-7pm. Admission 2000R, Russian 300R. Tickets to concerts and lectures which take place here in a small concert room may also be bought at the entrance and range 500-2000R.) In this same square is also the Vaganova School of Choreography, out of which came Vasily Nyinsky, Anna Pavlova, Rudolf Nureyev, and Mikhail Baryshnikov.

The **Anna Akhmatova Museum** (Музей Анны Ахматовы) is housed at Fontanka 34 (Фонтанка), but the entrance is actually at Liteyny pr. 51 (Линтейный пр.). Go through an archway into a large, green courtyard and keep to the left, following the signs to the museum. Looking over this poetic park, the museum houses the famous poetess' personal possessions. Akhmatova, whose poetry spoke for many who suffered through the Soviet years, is now a national heroine. Her most famous poem, *Requiem*, was not written down for 25 years but passed on orally. She lived here during some of her most difficult years (1944-54 as well as in 1933 and 1941). Akhmatova had many profiles painted of her, perhaps because her nose was so distinctive. (open Tues.-Sun. 10:30am-6:30pm, *kassa* closes at 5:30pm; admission 3000R, students 1500R, Russians 400R, Russian students 200R).

The **Dostoevsky Museum** (Достоевский Музей) is in the writer's apartment at Kuznechny per. 5/2 (Кузнечный пер.), around the corner to the right from M: Vladimirskaya (Владимирская). The neighborhood is more like Dostoevsky's St. Petersburg, with tall narrow buildings like the one Raskolnikov lived in. There are expensive tours of the neighborhood; inquire at the museum which, for once, is well-labeled in both Russian and English. The apartment itself is very orderly, which, they will tell you, is thanks to his secretary/wife, Anna. *The Brothers Karamazov* was penned here. On display are the writer's notes for various novels, as well as his wife's bills. Dostoevsky's study is preserved as it was when he died, and the clock on the table points to the exact hour of his death—8:38pm, January 28, 1881; obviously the author was not very lucky with eights. Screening of film versions of Dostoevsky's novels once a week here. (Open Tues.-Sun. 10:30am-6:30pm, *kassa* closes 5:30pm, closed last Wed. of month; admission 3000R, students 1500R.)

The **Arctic and Antarctic Museum,** on the corner of Kuzneshny per. (Кузнечный пер.) and ul. Marata (ул. Марата), M: Mayakovskaya, is one block from the Dostoyevsky Museum. An exhaustive collection of model ships, nautical instruments, and anything these expeditions could possibly have used, are housed under a dome. Not for animal lovers—rows of fox-furs and stuffed wolves snarl menacingly, and the museum glorifies the invasion of humankind into the wild; the environmental disasters in the region are not on display. (Open Wed.-Sun. 10am-6pm, closed last Sat. in month; admission 2000R, Russian 200R.)

Uprising Square (Площадь Восстанияь; *Ploshad Vosstaniya*) is the halfway point of Nevsky Prospect, marked by the Moscow train station. Here took place some of the bloodiest confrontations of the February Revolution, and it is here the Cossacks turned on the police during a demonstration—hence the name. The obelisk in the center was only erected in 1985, replacing a statue of Tsar Alexander III that was removed in 1937. Across from the train station is a pale green building bearing the words "Город-герой Ленинград" which mean "Leningrad, the hero city," in reference to and remembrance of the crippling losses suffered during the German siege.

Alexander Nevsky Monastery

At the far end of Nevsky Prospect, directly opposite the M: Ploschad Aleksandrer Nevskovo, is the **Alexander Nevsky Monastery** (Лавра Александра Невского; *Lavra Aleksandra Nevskovo*), a peaceful spot for a stroll, as well as a major pilgrimage destination. The monastery got its name and fame from Prince Alexander of Novgorod, whose body was moved here by Peter the Great in 1724. It was not until 1797 that it received the highest monastic title of "lavra," bestowed on only four monasteries in the whole Orthodox tradition. Placement of the dead is important in the Russian Orthodox faith; not only are cemeteries of major importance and grave-stones carefully sculpted, but the most desired place to be buried was under the entrance to the church (for it was considered that the more people who walked over your grave, the less your soul suffered in purgatory). This belief was apparently no longer in vogue by the time Alexander Nevsky Monastery was established, for many of the tombs in the two cemeteries which lie in the monastery's grounds are quite imposingly large and therefore virtually impossible to walk over. A cobble-stone path, lined with souvenir-sellers and beggars, connects the monastery's cathedral and two cemeteries. The graveyard on the left is the small **Lazarus Cemetery,** the oldest in the city, established in 1716. If you keep going around the edge of the cemetery to the left, you will come upon the explain black tomb of **Natalya Lan-skaya,** the wife of Russia's poet-hero Alexander Pushkin. Smack in the middle of this tiny cemetery are the graves of two famous St. Petersburg architects, **Andrei Voronokhin,** who designed the Kazan Cathedral which is depicted on his tomb, and **Adrian Zakharov,** architect of the Admiralty. In a surprising concession to non-Russian speaking tourists, most of the graves have plaques next to them with the deceased's name and profession in English.

Across the way, on the right side as you walk in, the **Tikhuin Cemetery** is not as old but larger, and its ground holds more famous names. The most important is **Feyodor Dostoyevsky** (who could not afford to be buried here but thanks to the Russian Orthodox Church was anyway). The grave can be found around to the right, fairly near the entrance. His benevolent but stern stare is easily recognizable and his tomb is often strewn with fresh flowers—the benefits of fame. Continuing along the right edge of the cemetery, you arrive at the cluster of famous musicians. **Mikhail Glinka,** composer of the first Russian opera and a contemporary of Pushkin's, has a simple tomb. **Mikhail Balakurev,** next to Glinka on the left, was a teacher of **Rimsky Korsakov** and instrumental in gathering this group of musicians together in life. Balakurev's famous pupil's grave is easily recognized by its unfriendly angels and white marble Orthodox cross. But it is Borodin's grave that many stop in front of, drawn to the gold mosaic of a composition sheet from his famous *Prince Igor.* **Mussorgsky, Rubinshtein,** and **Tschaikovsky** are in magnificent tombs next to Borodin. Tschaikovsky was buried here, despite the scandal associated with his death. Once Tschaikovsky's homosexuality was discovered—and widely publicized—the conservative Conservatory deemed it more appropriate that the unfortunate musician commit suicide and end his brilliant career than disgrace their hallowed halls. Whether the composer truly complied or was murdered is, like most of Russian history, still unclear (but black angels watch over his tomb). Evidently, it would not have been hard for Tschaikovsky to kill himself, however; drinking a glass of St. Petersburg water would have done it—there was a deadly plague loose at the time far worse than today's *Giardia.* The tomb to the left of the entrance is that of **Stravinsky.**

The **Church of Annunciation** further along the cobblestone path on the left was the original burial place of the Romanovs, who were then moved to Peter and Paul Cathedral (exhumation is possibly the only Russian government activity as popular as rewriting history). The church currently under renovation; it used to house the **Museum of Urban Sculpture,** but now belongs, once again, to the monastery. The Trinity Cathedral, at the end of the path is still functioning and therefore teems with Russian workmen crossing themselves and Orthodox priests in flowing black robes. The interior of the cathedral is large, with many different altars and a select few paintings by artists such as Rubens and Van Dyck. Strangely, the clock over the door looks exactly like the clocks in the Metro (or vice versa).

As the monastery is a major tourist site, it is often possible to join English-speaking tours; while the herd mentality may annoy you, the guides are often very knowledgable. Pay at the entrance to *each* of the cemeteries. (Cathedral open 9am-noon, and 5-7pm. Free. Check board for service times. Cemeteries open Fri.-Wed. 11am-5pm. Admission 1000R, students 500R.)

Smolny Institute and Cathedral

Smolny Institute/Cathedral (Смольный), M: Chernyshevskaya (Чернышевская) then autobus #136 or 46 from the stop across the street from the Metro. The **Smolny Institute** was once a prestigious school for aristocratic girls, but in 1917 it earned its place in history when Trotsky and Lenin set up the headquarters of the Bolshevik Central Committee here and planned the Revolution from behind its yellow walls. Now it is the municipal office of St. Petersburg and closed to the public, but a worthwhile stop on the tour of any history buff. The gate buildings at the end of the drive read, from left to right, "first Soviet of the dictatorship of the proletariat," and "proletarians of all nations, unite!" Farther down the walk, again from left to right, are busts of Engels and Marx (one wonders if their position in the garden has political significance). Next door is the blue-and-white **Smolny Cathedral,** notable for combining European Baroque and traditional Orthodox Russian architectural styles. The church is now a concert hall and only open during performances (twice per week), but you can also climb to the top and survey Lenin's—er, Peter's—city (open Fri.-Tues. 11am-6pm, Wed. 11am-5pm, tickets sold until 45min. before closing; admission 3000R, Russians 1000R).

Peter and Paul Fortress (Петропавловская Крепость)

Across the river from the Hermitage, the **Peter and Paul Fortress's** spreading walls and golden spire beckon. Take the Metro to M: Gorkovskaya (Горьковская) and turn right exiting the station. Go right on Kamennostrovsky pr. (Каменностровский пр.), the main street in front of you (there is no street sign). Follow the street to the river, and cross the wooden bridge to the fortress on an island. Check out the Russians enjoying the water—in the summer they sunbathe standing up, and in the winter they swim in holes cut through the ice.

The construction of the fortress was begun in May 1703, a date now considered the birthday of St. Petersburg. It was actually built as a defense against the Swedes, but Peter I defeated them before the fortress was finished. It was also the last stronghold of the Provisional government in 1917. The fortress now houses a gold-spired cathedral that gives the complex and several other museums its name. Purchase a single ticket to all the buildings at the *kassa* (Касса) on the right just as you enter. (Open Thurs.-Mon. 11-5pm, Tues. 11-4pm. Closed the last Tuesday of the month. Admission US$2.50, students US$1.25, payable in rubles only. Convince them you're a Russian student and pay only 230R.)

Inside is the **Peter and Paul Cathedral.** The icons are currently under restoration, but you can see the graves of every Tsar since Peter the Great (whose coffin still bears fresh flowers) with the exception of Peter II, Ivan IV and Nicholas II. Just outside the church is Mikhail Shemyakin's controversial rendering of Peter the Great in bronze, which at once fascinates and offends Russian visitors (open Thurs.-Mon. 10am-5:40pm, Tues. 10am-4:40pm). **The State Museum of the History of St.**

RUSSIA

Petersburg is just to the left of Shemyakin's statue, housing paintings and clothing from the late 19th century, as well as posters, serving machines, phonographs, and telephones from the same era. It gives a nice feel for the grand old place this town once was (open Thurs.-Mon. 11am-6pm, Tues. 11am-5pm; closed the last Tues. of the month).

Nevsky Gate (Невские Ворота; *Nievsky Vorota*) is beyond the museum to the left. Here prisoners were sent to their executions. On the wall are plaques marking the water level of the city's worst floods. The **Trubetskoy Bastion** (Трубетской Бастион) in the southwest corner of the fortress is a reconstruction of the prison where Peter the Great imprisoned and tortured his first son, Aleksei. Dostoevsky, Gorky, Trotsky, and Lenin's older brother also spent time there (same hours as museum).

Elsewhere in the Petrogradski Rayon (Петроградский Район)

Peter's Cabin, as you exit the fortress, is right along the river. From M: Gorkovskaya (Горьковская), walk to the river and turn right. After two blocks the cabin is a small brick building set back from the road in a small park on the left. The brick building actually houses a log cabin, the first building constructed in St. Petersburg. It was the home of Peter I while he supervised the construction of the city; it is rather like a shrine, with all the furniture still there and Peter's compass on his desk. (Open daily 10am-6pm. Closed the last Monday of each month. Admission 3000R (US$1.50), students 1500R (US$0.75). Russians 400R, Russian students 200R. Cameras 2000R (US$1), videocameras 3000R (US$1.50).)

The Cruiser Aurora (Аврора). Continue along the river past Peter's Cabin to this warship, initially used in the Russo-Japanese war, that later played a critical role in the 1917 Revolution by firing a blank round by the Winter Palace and scared the pants off Kerensky and his Provisional government. Inside are exhibits on revolutionary and military history (open Tues.-Thurs. Sat.-Sun. 10:30am-6pm; free). The **Artillery Museum** (Артиллерпейский Музей), M: Gorkovskaya, is directly across from the Fortress of Peter and Paul. This is one of the oldest museums in the city—it was opened in 1756, and moved to its present site in 1868. The building was initially a fortress built to protect the Peter and Paul Fortress (hmm...) from the Swedes, and as a result the walls are almost 1m thick. The museums' collection is heavily oriented towards cannons; there is even the toy cannon Peter the Great played with as a boy. There are examples of early rifles, including a Winchester, and the third floor is devoted to World War II, with a special Normandy exhibit. The 28,000 sq. m courtyard is full of tanks you can climb on—this museum is a great break if you have had enough art and architecture of the 18th century. (Open Wed.-Sun. 11am-6pm, tickets sold until 5pm; admission 3000R, Russians 150R.)

Russian Political History Museum and **Wax Museum** (Музей Политической Историй Россий), ul. Kuybysheva 4 (Куйбышева), M: Gorkovskaya (Горьковская), are right down Kronverksky pr. toward the **Mosque** (covered in scaffolding in summer 1994), then a left turn onto ul. Kuybysheva. Both museums (with separate entrance fees, of course) are housed in the mansion of Matilda Kshesinskaya, once the Marinsky Theatre's prima-ballerina and Nicholas II's lover. Soviet propaganda still pervades the **Political History Museum,** which focuses primarily on the 1905 and 1917 revolutions, and then rushes past Stalin to end with a menacing photo of everybody's favorite nationalist, Vladimir Zhirinovsky. Even if you don't read Russian, the photos and relics are more interesting than most Petersburg museums. An old printing press, revolutionary uniforms, and other such artifacts are carefully displayed. On the left side of the entrance (use the same ticket) are a couple of rooms containing the ballerina's possessions—portraits, programs, costumes, and the like—but little evidence of her tryst with the last Tsar (open Fri.-Wed. 10am-6pm; admission 5000R, Russians 1500R). Also in the same building (but for a high price) is the **Wax Museum.** Go downstairs to the measly few rooms depicting illustrious Soviets in wax. Lenin looks like a nice man and Papa Stalin is as benevolent as ever, but Krushchev looks deathly and Gorbachev nothing like himself. They're not doing anything of interest (same hours; admission 5000R, Russians 1500R).

The **Kirov Museum** (Музей Кирова), Kamennostrovsky pr. 20, fifth floor, M: Petrogradskaya (Петроградская), is to the right of the exit and a 10-minute walk. A quite perverse but fascinating little museum; a Bolshevik hero and probable Stalin victim, Kirov liked to hunt and it shows (he didn't just like to "hunt" animals, so who knows when the next historians will decide to close this museum). Two huge bear rugs and other stuffed unfortunates populate his recreated home. A major stop on the tourist route, this is probably the most magnificent apartment-museum in St. Petersburg; after all, Kirov was a politician, not a writer. The lower floor contains, ironically, rooms filled with Stalins—Stalin in dyed wool, on a carved wooden plate, on a porcelain vase, embroidered, etc., most donated by the executioner himself. The upper floor contains his belongings (open Thurs.-Tues. 11am-4pm; admission 100R, students 70R).

Vasilevsky Island (Остров Василевское)

The **Museum of Anthropology and Ethnography** (Музей Антропологий и Этнографий) faces the Admiralty from across the river. Not for the squeamish, this is a natural history museum with a ghoulish twist. Most of the galleries are exhibits of the "lives and habits" of the world's indigenous peoples—Native Americans, Inuits, African tribes, Pacific Islanders, etc. In a central gallery, though, is Peter's anatomical collection, bought from a professor at a surgical school in Amsterdam. It is ostensibly an exhibit of the then-modern art of organ preservation (by sticking them in jars of formaldehyde). Among the "organs" preserved are two severed heads and many deformed fetuses, including several siamese twins. There is also a sizeable collection of pulled teeth. On the top floor is another inexplicable gallery—the **Lomonosov Museum.** Lomonosov was the founder of Moscow University and a well-known scientist, but you'd hardly know it from this gallery. It contains, among other things, Peter I's dining room table, busts of Benjamin Franklin and Voltaire, and portraits of Catherine and Peter the Great—the latter done in mosaic. You must exit the museum the way you came, so if you missed the Navajo sand paintings the first time, you can catch 'em on the rebound (open Sat.-Wed. 11am-6pm; admission 7000R). You must check your bag for a small fee (45R in summer 1994).

Menshikov Palace, Universitetskaya nab. 15 (Университетская наб.), is reachable by M: Vasileostrovskaya (Василеостровская), but you're better off crossing the bridge north of the Admiralty and walking left; the palace is a yellow building with a small courtyard, well-labeled. Alexander Menshikov was a good friend of Peter I and governor of Petersburg under the Tsar. Peter entertained here before he built the Summer Palace, and his second wife Catherine, who became Tsarina and ruled Russia after his death, was originally a serving-girl of Menshikov's. There was even a rumor floating around that Menshekov and the Tsar himself were lovers. The museum shows the palace as it looked when Menshikov lived there—come see how the better half lived, and why the revolution started here. (Open Tues.-Sun. 10:30am-4:30pm, tickets go on sale at 10:15am. Admission 8000R, students 5000R, Russians 800R. Because the palace rooms are small, they send you through in groups of fifteen or so with a Russian-speaking guide.)

Oktyabrski Rayon (Октябрьский Район)

The **Oktyabrski Rayon** is a poetic region of Petersburg, where the canal Griboyedova narrows and meanders through quiet neighborhoods with leafy parks. On the outer borders of the rayon is **Yusupovsky Sad,** a large park with an island and a peaceful spot for a picnic lunch. Named after the infamous prince who succeeded in killing Rasputin only after poisoning, shooting, and ultimately drowning the resilient monk, the park is far from tumultuous today. In the center of the Rayon is the Nikolsky Cathedral and, easily visible from there, the **Theatre Square** on which the large aqua Marinsky Theater, formerly the Kirov, stands (see Entertainment).

The **Blok Museum** (Музей Блока), ul. Dekabristov 57 (ул. Декабристов), is accessible by M: Sadovaya (Садовая), but only because there is *nothing* closer; it can be a nightmare to get to. Tram #31 and 33 will take you to the corner of Makina pr. Or, if you're visiting the nearby synagogue, it's only a three-block walk. Of interest mainly to Russian poetry lovers, Blok wrote during the late 19th and early 20th centuries but still is greatly read and recited today. Married to the daughter of the famous scientist Mendeleev, Blok lived in this house, wrote poetry, and got depressed. As any good museum *babushka* will tell you, he loved his mother too. Reason enough to give him a museum. The house is left mostly intact, with many of Blok's paintings and personal possessions all here—the weirdest room is the one where he died, containing only a plaster bust of his head—his death mask. (Open Thurs.-Tues. 11am-6pm; admission 100R, students 75R.)

The **Large Choral Synagogue of St. Petersburg**, St. Petersburg's only functioning synagogue and the second-largest synagogue in Europe, is located at Lermontovsky pr. 2 (tel. 114 11 53; morning and evening services daily—call for times). Although the grounds are not well-kept, once you enter (not through the original main door, but to the left) you may find an English-speaking guide. The synagogue, which celebrated its 100th anniversary on Dec. 8, 1993, has approximately only 70 regular members. In 1893, it had 5000, the decline being a sign of the persecution and/or emigration of much of the Russian Jewish population. The guides are very knowledgable; make sure they show you the separate hall for weddings (open daily 9am-9pm).

Nikolsky Cathedral is a magnificent blue-and-gold structure, a striking example of 18th-century Baroque, and thus is easy to find. Turn right off ul. Sadovaya across the canal onto ul. Rimskovo-Korsakovo (Римского-Корсакого), near the Marinsky Theater and Conservatory. The entrance is directly across from the spectacular bell tower, whose bells are supposed to have special mystic powers. Inside, the smell of burning wax is particularly potent because the church was built to house two levels; the ceilings are therefore very low (services daily at 10am and 6pm).

The **Central Museum for Railway Transport** (Центральный Музей Телезнофрожного Транспорта), ul. Sadovaya 50 (ул. Садовая), M: Sadovaya, is a few blocks down toward Nikolsky Cathedral, next to a big, beautiful park (Yusupovskiy Sad). This is persuasive socialist propaganda at its best, and a perfect place to take children (although not for that reason). The first few rooms show the development of trains in the Soviet era, with plenty of pictures of joyous rail workers; of interest to those who delight in old paperwork are their diplomas and posters. The last rooms are by far the most exciting. Model trains and stations curve around the entire room; you must wait for the guide to press all the exciting buttons. In the final room you may walk through a section of an old "soft class" sleeper with plush upholstery and beautiful fixtures, nothing like the trains you take today (open Sun.-Thurs. 11am-5:30pm; admission 200R, students 100R, pre-school 50R).

Leninski Rayon (Ленинский Район)

Near M: Pushkinskaya (Пушкинская) are very few museums, but a number of sights of historical significance and no aesthetic value. **Vitebski Vokzal** (Витебский Вокзал), the oldest train station in Russia and the one you leave from to reach Pushkin and Pavlovsk, is immediately to the left. It still contains a replica of a 19th century steam engine (in a glass case). Nearby Gorokhovay ul. 64 (Гороховая ул.) was home to Russia's infamous sex-machine, **Gregory Rasputin.** Although today the site is nothing of interest, Rasputin reputedly hosted fabulous orgies here until his untimely (and extremely difficult) demise. In the long and noble tradition of bloodshed and gore that so marks the Russian past, the **Semyonovsky Barracks** were the site of Dostoevsky's aborted execution in 1849. It wasn't a great neighborhood back then either.

Kalininski Rayon (Калининский Район)

Piskarovskoye Memorial Cemetery (Пискаровское Мемörальное Кладбище). To truly understand St. Petersburg's obsession with World War II, come to this remote and chilling memorial. During the 900 days that the city was under siege by the Germans, close to a million people died. This cemetery is their grave. The park is nothing but mounds of grass-covered earth, marked with the year. There is an eternal flame and a monument, and both still bear flowers. The place is nearly empty, yet the emotion is palpable—this is the grave of the hero city. The monument reads, "No one is forgotten; nothing is forgotten." Stop at M: Ploschad Muzhestva (Площадь Мужества) and go left to the street. Walk left to the corner, cross the street in front of you (Непокоренных пр.; *Nepokorennikh pr.*) and catch bus #123 from the shelter. Ride about six stops, 7-10 minutes. On your right will be a large flower shop, on your left the cemetery, recognizable by a low granite wall and two large square stone gate buildings, each with four columns. The bus stops almost automatically.

ENTERTAINMENT

St. Petersburg's famed White Nights lend the night sky a pale, bewitching glow from mid-June to early July. Unfortunately, most activities in St. Petersburg draw to a close by 11pm, so there's diddly to do but wander about and watch the drawbridges go up at about 1:30am. This can be quite romantic, but remember to do it from the *same* side of the bridge your hotel is on: the bridges don't go back down again until 3am.

Classical Music, Opera, and Ballet

While St. Petersburg does not have the options of Prague or Vienna, it is much easier to get cheap tickets to impressive performances here, such as by the Marinsky Ballet, one of the best in the world. Sprinkled across the city are a few large concert halls, seating more than 1000; depending on the day, you can often hear world-class performers for a mere US$0.50. During the third week in June, when the sun barely touches the horizon, the city holds a series of outdoor evening concerts as a part of the **White Nights Festival.** Check kiosks and posters for more information. The theater season comes to an end around the time of this festival and begins again in early September, but check for summer performances at ticket offices (tickets 1500R and up at Nevsky pr. 42, across from Gostiny Dvor, or from kiosks and tables near St. Isaac's Cathedral and along Nevsky pr., but it is often more fruitful to go to the *kassa* of the theatre where your desired performance will be held). A monthly program is usually posted on kiosks throughout the city.

In general, theaters start selling tickets 20 days before the performance; good seats sell out fast but there are almost always cheap seats left the day of the performance. A three-dimensional model of the theater is always displayed, so you can see where you will be sitting. Three *yarus* (ярус) are the cheapest seats. Intourist keeps many of the better seats, but charges exorbitantly high prices. Getting to the performance more than fifteen minutes early is usually unnecessary; performances usually start a few minutes late, enough time for the hundreds of culture-loving Russians (and German tour groups) to get seated. Dress ranges from black tie to jeans; both are perfectly acceptable. In St. Petersburg, people come for the performers, not the audience; the days of *War and Peace* have long past. But, since Russians do dress up for such occasions, it is much more respectful to put on your evening best.

Marinsky Theater (Мариинский Театр), Teatralnaya pl. 1 (Театральная пл; tel. 114 12 11). M: Sadovaya (Садовая). A 10-minute walk along the Canal Griboyedova and then right onto the square. This imposing aqua building, formerly the Kirov Opera and Ballet, is one of the most famous theaters for ballet in the world. Pavlova, Nureyev, Nijinsky and Baryshnikov all started here and it was here that Tschaikovsky's *Nutcracker* and *Sleeping Beauty* premiered. Although the ballet, still outstanding, goes on tour for two months in the summer, and good seats are mostly sold out, it's worth a try anyway. For two weeks in June, the theater hosts White Nights Festival, for which tickets are easier to get. If you can go, do. Tickets start selling 10 days before the performance from 1000R upwards. *Kassa* open Wed.-Sun. 11am-3pm and 4pm-7pm.

Maly Theater (Малый Театр), pl. Iskusstv 1 (пл. Искусств; tel. 314 37 58), near the Russian Museum. Second to the Marinsky for opera and ballet, but has the advantage of being open in July and August when the Marinsky is closed. Similarly impressive concert hall, however, and certain ballets can be well-performed.

Kassa open daily 11am-3pm and 4pm-8pm. Tickets sold 20 days before performances.

Shostakovich Philharmonic Hall (Шостакович), Mikhailovskaya ul. 2 (Михайловская ул; tel. 311 73 33), opposite the Grand Hotel Europe. M: Gostiny Dvor (Гостиный Двор). Large concert hall with both classical and modern concerts. Acoustics are not exactly perfect, due to its former use as a hall for Boyar Council meetings, which had no need for such subtleties.

Akademicheskaya Kapella (Академическая капелла), nab. Reki Moiki 20 (наб. р. Мойки; tel. 233 02 43). M: Nevsky Prospect. Small concert hall for choirs and solos (as well as smaller orchestras). Concerts begin at 7pm. Prices upwards from 1500R. *Kassa* open daily noon-3pm, 4-7pm.

Glinka Maly Zal (Hall), Nevsky pr. 30 (tel. 312 45 85), part of the Shostakovich Philharmonic Hall, but the acoustics are better than in the main hall, which is across from the Hotel Europe.

Conservatorium (Консерватория), across from Marinsky Theater, Teatralnaya pl. 3 (Театральная пл.; tel. 312 25 19), M: Sadovaya. Student ballets and operas performed here; often excellent. *Kassa* open daily noon-6pm.

Oktyabrskaya Concert Hall (Концертный зал Октябрьский), Ligovsky pr. 6 (Лиговский пр.), a 5-min. walk from M: Ploschad Vosstaniya (Площадь Восстания; tel. 277 69 80). St. Petersburg's large and modern concert hall for orchestras, ballets, and rock concerts. In June 1994 there were performances by Run DMC, Falco, a-ha, and Lane Davis. Tickets from 1500R. *Kassa* open daily 11am-8pm.

Yubileyni Sports Palace, pr. Dobrolyubova 18 (пр. Добролюбова; tel. 238 40 49), equally far from M: Vasileostrovkaya (Василеостровская) and Gorkovskaya (Горьковская). Sports Palace, as the name would suggest. Graceful ballet-on-ice shows in winter—this is no Disney-on-ice.

Theater, Musicals, Puppets, and Circuses

Theater is really only accessible to those fairly fluent in the language; other options, such as mime, marionettes or the circus, are likely to be more entertaining. The Russian theatrical style contains subtleties which the Russian audience will understand better than you will and make you feel like you're sitting in on a national inside - joke. The costumes and sets (for which Russian, and in particular St. Petersburg, theater was famous) vary greatly—from obviously under-budgeted productions to clear artistic talent. If you hear of a good performance, it will be worth it for the experience, even if you don't understand what's going on—if possible, pick a classic you known in English already. St. Petersburg is the place to see this stuff, as it prides itself on being the cultural capital of Russia; as a result the theaters will be packed with the city's residents.

Pushkin Dramatic Theater (Академический Театр Драмы им А.С. Пушкина), pl. Ostrovskovo 2 (пл. Островского; tel. 311 12 12). M: Gostiny Dvor. Right on Nevsky, then right at small park. Ballet and theater—mostly classics like Hamlet and Cyrano de Bergerac. Beautiful theater built by Rossi in 1832. Summer ballet season starts July 25. Morning performance 11am, evening 7pm. Tickets 700R-10,000R. *Kassa* open 11am-7pm. Tickets available 20 days before performance.

Bolshoy Dramatichesky Theater, nab. Reki Fontanki 65 (tel. 310 92 42), M: Gostiny Dvo. Like its name, this theater is big and very classical—nothing particularly off-beat about it. Conservative productions of Russian classics, and very good at what it does. *Kassa* open daily 11am-6pm.

Marionette Theater (Театр Марионетой), Nevsky pr. 52 (tel. 311 21 56). Puppet and marionette shows, playing on irregular days. Closed July-Aug. *Kassa* open Tues.-Wed., Fri-Sun. 10:30am-4pm.

Circus (Цирк), pl. Belinskovo (пл. Белинского; tel. 210 44 11), near the Russian Museum. M: Gostiny Dvor. The oldest circus in all of Russia, but with the exception of a pretty cool live orchestra, it has the requisite exploited animals and other trappings of a good Russian circus—and they are a breed to themselves. Closed July-Sept. *Kassa* open 11am-4pm.

Music Hall, in park Lenina, M: Gorkovskaya (tel. 233 02 43). A fully decked out (plumes and all) Russian cabaret. A cheezy experience. Cheap tickets—between 1000-3000R. *Kassa* open daily noon-3pm and 4-7pm.

Nightclubs

During the pre-Gorbachev era, Petersburg was always the heart of the underground music scene, and this is still evident today in the quantity of interesting clubs in the city. There are plenty of dance clubs for Russian "business men," too, but better evening fare can be found. Be careful going home late at night, especially if you've been drinking—loud, drunk foreigners might as well be carrying neon signs saying "rob me!" Clubs come and go like the Top 40 groups here; both hostels can recommend the newest places. Or check the *St. Petersburg Press* for ads.

St. Petersburg Rock Club (Рок Клуб), ul. Rubinshteina 13 (ул. Рубинштайна; tel. 314 96 29), M: Dostoevskaya (Достоевская), in the courtyard and through the right door on the far wall. Soviet rock superstars like Kino and Igry got their starts in this dingy old building. Tickets can be hard to get. Cover 3000R.

Rock around the Clock, in the "Saturn" movie theater, Sadovaya ul. 27 (Садовая ул.). M: Sennaya Ploschad (Сенная пл.). Fairly high cover and expensive drinks, but the music is good. Open 9pm-6am (tel. 310 02 37).

Tunnel, located in an old bomb shelter, is the place to come for techno and dancing. No address—it's a bomb shelter after all. Located on Lyubansky per. (Любянский пер.) between ul. Blokina (Блокина) and Zverinskaya (Зверинская). M: Gorkhovskaya (Горковская). Open Thurs.-Sat. midnight-4am. No phone (that bomb shelter thing again).

Joy, Canal Griboyedovo 28 (Канала Грибоедого; tel. 331 35 40), 2 blocks south off Nevsky Prospect. Your basic nightclub, catering to tourists and businessmen. Fairly good, recent music from the U.S. Cover 30,000R, including one drink. Open daily 10am-5am.

Jazz Philharmonic Hall (formerly *Jazz Club*), Zagorodny pr. 27 (Загородный пр.; tel. 164 85 65 or 113 53 31), M: Vladimirskaya (Владимирская). Nightly concerts at 8pm; jam sessions every Friday and Saturday night until midnight. Open 8pm-until people leave. Tickets sold 2-8pm.

Art Café, ul. Gertsena 58, not far from Marinsky Theater, is a small, informal jazz club in a back room. Cover 1000R. Open Fri.-Sat. 7pm-11.

Movies

Blockbuster American films are often showing, if you are desperate for celluloid images of home. Russia still lacks the funds to subtitle foreign films; they are all dubbed by a single male voice, with the English often still audible underneath. The **Barrikada** (Баррикада), at Nevsky Pr. 15 and **Kalizey** (Кализей) at Nevsky Pr. 100, show only dubbed American films (tickets 3000R).

SHOPPING

These days, most Western convenience-oriented goods are available in St. Petersburg—for a price. It's best to bring enough into Russia with you, but if emergency strikes, don't panic—you *can* buy Finesse Conditioner for damaged hair. As for souvenirs, the best place to go is on Nevsky Prospect, just beyond Gostiny Dvor towards the Admiralty. If you speak any Russian, use it—you're less likely to get ripped off. Comparative shopping is a good idea, too—know what price you should get—even the black market has fixed prices. Or you may want to shop in actual stores, where there are posted price tags so you know you aren't paying the sucker foreigner rate.

Pharmacies/Drugstores: Most Western toiletry items are widely available now. The 24-hr. **supermarket** at Ploschad Vosstaniya (see Food) sells shampoo, Kleenex, and toothpaste, as well as tampons and pads (Tampax 8000R). On Nevsky prospect, just before the Admiralty on the South side (left as you face the

Admiralty) is a pharmacy selling German lotions, cosmetics, and tampons. Prices are higher here, though. Open Mon.-Fri. 9am-8pm, Sat.-Sun. 10am-5pm.

Film: Best found at the 1-hr. photo processing store on Nevsky at the corner of Narodny Most (Народный Мость). Open Mon.-Sat. 10am-8pm.

Souvenirs: The outdoor markets on either side of Nevsky just beyond Gostiny Dvor have the widest selection of both classical and tacky Russian souvenirs (for example, *matryoshka* dolls painted with characters from *Aladdin* and *The Little Mermaid*). Prices are fairly reasonable, and you can often bargain them down if you speak Russian. The stands usually open at around 11am, and close just after 8pm. Watch your moneybelt here, and keep an eye out for thieves—this is where the foreigners are, and they know it. There are also a few **souvenir shops** where more interesting items can be found, often for better prices—though books tend to cost more than in the U.S. Museum gift shops are a good place to find things, too—often they stock a small selection of lacquer boxes and amber jewelry.

Crafts and Antiques: There's a limited selection of craft art you can buy here—largely variations on the theme of painted wood. Here is a nice little antique store at Kamennostrovsky pr. 17 (Каменностровский пр.), called the **"Antikvariat Rus"**(Антиквариат Русь). It sells silver candlesticks, *samovars,* old books, paintings, and silver tea-glass holders for reasonable prices. Walk four blocks north of Kamennostrovsky out of M: Gorkovskaya. Open Mon.-Sat. 11am-2pm and 3-7pm.

Bookstores: Dom Knigi (Дом Книги; open daily 9am-8pm) and **Dom Voyennoy Knigi** (Дом Военной Книги; open Sun.-Fri. 10am-7pm, Sat. 10am-6pm) on Nevsky pr. 22 sell books and office supples. The **"Isskustva"** (Искуство) bookstore on ul. Gertsen at Nevsky also offers art books and jewelry as well as an eclectic assortment of CDs (US$8-15); open daily 10am-2pm, 3-7pm.

■ NEAR ST. PETERSBURG

Ride the suburban *Electrichka* trains any spring or summer weekend day and you will witness the Russian love of the countryside. Most Russians own or share a *dacha* outside the city and go there every weekend, and on the trains you will find crowds of families loaded down with fresh milk, potatoes, live chickens, a new puppy, and perhaps some lumber for a new construction project. The Tsars were no different; they, too, built country houses, and several of these palaces have been restored for tourists. They make particularly good day-trips from St. Petersburg when one more stroll along Nevsky turns the stomach. All three—Peterhof, Tsarskoe Selo and Pavlovsk—are easily reached by suburban train, and there are hydrofoils that leave regularly for Peterhof from the front of the Winter Palace. Hydrofoil ticket prices are high, however (10,000R one way). All three museums are equipped with cafés that serve fairly good food at tourist-level prices; avoid getting overcharged by bringing lunch. And wear a jacket if your destination is Peterhof—the grounds abut the Gulf of Finland and the garden can get quite windy.

The three palaces stand on what was German territory during the siege of Leningrad in 1942-44. Tragically, all were burned to the ground during the Nazis' retreat, but in one of the great paradoxes of the Soviet regime, Stalin provided the staggering sums of money necessary to completely rebuild these symbols of the tsars during the postwar reconstruction of the Soviet Union.

PETERHOF (ПЕТЕРГОФ)

Also known as Petrodvoretz (Петродворец), it is the most thoroughly restored of the palaces, and in fact work there is still progressing. As of June 1994, the main fountains descending from the Grand Palace to the Gulf of Finland were still in their Nazi-induced state, but that will hopefully have changed by the time you read this. The entire complex at Peterhof is 300 years old, and many of the Tsars added to it or expanded existing palaces.

Orientation and Practical Information Hydrofoils leave for Peterhof twice an hour from the dock in front of the Hermitage (10,000R one way). It's also an easy trip by *electrichka* from Baltisky Station, M: Baltiskaya (Балтийская). Buy tickets (800R) round-trip from the ticket office (Биллетные Кассы) in the courtyard—ask for "No-VEE Pehter-GOAF, too-DAh ee oh-BRAHT-nah" ("there and back again"). **Trains** leave every 15 minutes or so—find Novi Petergof (Новый Петергоф) on the map in the center of the courtyard, and pick a train going beyond it. Then find the track with your train on it, and get on—keep your ticket for the ride home. The ride is about 40 minutes—look for the sign on the platform. Then catch bus #350, 351, 353, or 356 to the "Fontain" (Фонтаны; *Fontany*)—about a 10-minute ride. Get off at the stop just after the cathedral. The best time to go is on the weekend, since everything is open, but the crowds are also the heaviest then.

Parks open daily 9am-9:30pm. Fountains flow May-Sept. 11am-8pm (9pm on Sun.). All museums open 10:30am-6pm. The Grand Palace is closed Mon. and the last Tuesday of the month. Monplaisir and the Hermitage are closed Wed. and the last Thurs. of the month. The Catherine building is closed Thurs. and the last Fri. of the month. Got it?

Food   At the bottom of the park is a **Café** selling soda and sandwiches as well as beer, wine, coffee and caviar. There is also an outside grill offering pork *shashlik* (шашлик), yummy Georgian shish kebab. The food is good, but prices are rather high—8000R for *shashlik*, 2500R for beer, 2000R for caviar on bread.

Sights   **The Grand Palace** (Большой Дворец) was Peter's first residence here, but was later greatly expanded and remodelled, first by his daughter, Empress Elizabeth, and then by Catherine the Great. The rooms have been almost completely returned to their previous gaudiness—er, glory—and a tour of the palace is worthwhile.

Enter up the ceremonial staircase, marvelling at the golden cherubs, and enter the the palace. Just before the throne room, recognizable for the throne at one end and for being larger than most comfortable single-family homes, there is the bizarre **Chesma Gallery,** full of nothing but paintings depicting the Russian victory over the Turks at Chesma Bay in 1770. Alexander Orov supposedly arranged for a frigate to be exploded in front of the painter to ensure the authenticity of the images. Farther along are two Chinese studies flanking a weird picture gallery that contains 360 portraits of the same eight women, all by the Italian Pietro Rotari. Apparently his widow, strapped for cash, sold the whole lot to Catherine the Great.

The last room on the tour is the nicest, and a rest for the eyes after all the glittering "frou-frou." It's **Peter's study** (clearly he was the Tsar with the best taste) and is lined with elegantly carved wood panels. Much of the room inexplicably survived the Nazi invasion—the lighter panels are reconstructions, some of which took 1½ years to complete. (Palace admission 9800R, students 4900R. Cameras 3900R, videocameras 9800R. You must check any and all handbags 50R.)

From the Grand Palace, descend to the **Lower Gardens,** less well-kept but much more extensive than the Upper Gardens (to the right is a **Wax Museum,** containing figures of the residents of Peterhof; open daily 9am-5pm). The fountains are still being restored, but work is progressing on them more quickly than any other construction project in Russia, and they may be finished by summer 1995. The view up the cascade from the Gulf of Finland, with the Grand Palace as a backdrop, is stunning (admission to the Lower Gardens 2000R, students 1000R).

To the left of the café is the **Hermitage Dining Room,** notable for having a table on the second floor that could be lowered to the first floor, where servants would then perform their magic (admission 5700R, students 2850R; cameras 2000R, videocameras 4000R). Then follow the sound of children's shrieks and giggles to the **"joke fountains,"** which, activated by one misstep, suddenly splash their unwitting victims. (Watch the man behind the curtain; these fountains are no joke!)

On the other side of the garden is **Monplaisir,** the house Peter actually lived in (the big palace was only for special occasions). Smaller and less ostentatious than its neighbors (remember, he was the Tsar with good taste), it is graceful and elegant and even small. Long, marble-floored galleries flank the main wing, and the place is peaceful even on the busiest Saturdays (admission 9500R, students 4750R). Next

RUSSIA

door is the **Catherine Building,** where Catherine the Great lay low while her husband was (on her orders) being overthrown (admission 5700R, students 2850R).

TSARSKOYE SELO (ЦАРСКОЕ СЕЛО)

Twenty-five kilometers south of the city, Tsarskoye Selo ("Tsar's Village"), harbors Catherine the Great's summer residence, a gorgeous azure, white, and gold baroque palace overlooking sprawling, English-style parks. The area was renamed "Pushkin" during the Soviet era—most Russians and train conductors still use that name.

Orientation, Practical Information, and Food   Although Pushkin and Pavlovsk can be combined in one day, a leisurely visit is more enjoyable. Take any *electrichka* from Vitebski Vokzal (Витебский Вокзал; M: Pushkinskaya), leaving from Platforms 1, 2, or 3. To buy your ticket, go around to the right of the station to a gray bunker-like building. Ask for "Detskye Selo" or "Pushkin" (300R one way). Ask for "Tuda i obratna" if you want a ticket for the way home as well. Do not be worried that none of the signs say Pushkin; take the next *electrichka* that leaves. It is the sixth stop on the line, recognizable both by the number of people who get off and because it is the first platform which looks like a station. The conductor should mumble "Pushkin" at some point before you arrive there. Once at the station it is a 15-minute walk or 10-minute bus ride (you're less likely to get lost with the bus). Take bus #371or 382 almost to the end. There will be a yellow building on your left and the palace barely visible through the trees on your right. Ask someone for the "dvorets" if you get confused. Although there are decent cafés at the Tsarskoye Selo, the ones near the palace are overpriced and cater to tourists. As a result though, the food is usually good.

Sights   Built in 1756 by the architect Rastrelli for Empress Elizabeth, before he went to work on the Winter Palace, the opulent palace was remodeled by Charles Cameron under the orders of Catherine the Great; among other qualities, she had the good taste to remove the gilding from the façade, desiring a modest, little palace where she could relax. The Baroque Palace, named **Yekaterinsky Dvorets** (Catherine's Palace, after Elizabeth's mom, Catherine I) was largely destroyed by the Nazis during World War II; each room exhibits a photograph of it in a war-torn condition. The **Amber room** suffered the most; its walls were stripped and probably lost forever (one rumor places the hidden furnishings somewhere in Paraguay). The room now boasts a sign that reads "Ruin of the amber room is loss of all of mankind. You sacrifice us—we atone for our common duty to the world culture." While the English leaves much to be desired, the idea is clear—even the exorbitant foreign entrance fees can't pay to completely repair these mansions. Despite this, many of the rooms, especially the huge, glittering **Grand Hall** ballroom, have been magnificently restored. Elizabeth used to hold costume parties in the large hall; today there is ample space for you to waltz around—even in *tapichki*. North of the main staircase are the rest of the mostly bare, amazing rooms—with few pieces of furniture in their proper places, the largely empty palace poses a stark contrast to the clutter of most Russian homes. Included in the collection are a number of exquisite artifacts from East Asia, another sign of Catherine's far-reaching artistic taste. Tag along with one of the many English-speaking tours to learn more about the palace; guidebooks are available but absurdly expensive (palace open Wed.-Mon. 11am-5pm; admission 9800R, students 5900R, Russians 1500R, Russian students 800R, cameras 5900R).

Although Catherine's Palace alone is worth the trip, it is more fun to take a picnic and make a day of it, taking the time to wander through the nearby parks (open 9am-8pm; admission 1500R, students 800R, Russians 400R, children 50R). Alexander I's palace, though closed to the public, stands guard over a wild forest, and the rest of the 1400-acre **Catherine Park** is a gardener's paradise—a mixture of English, French, and Italian styles. The **Great Pond** is the centerpiece of the English park; it is possible to **rent rowboats** here in summer. To the east lies the Italian-landscaped park, where Catherine would ramble with her dogs, who were buried by the **Pyramid.** Muffy and Fido (or the Russian equivalent) were well-loved and respected, possibly more so than her children. Also in the park are numerous other architectural curiosities (wander around for a look) such as the **Ruined Tower,** built already ruined (saving later invaders the trouble, it may be supposed). Next to Catherine's Palace is one other museum, the **lycée,** where the much-beloved Pushkin studied (open Wed.-Mon. 10:30am-4:30pm; admission 900R, students 800R, Russians 500R, Russian students 300R). Pushkin, then twelve, was one of the first students here and his cubbyhole can still be seen, along with the classrooms, laboratory, and music rooms. The dorms, on the top floor, are neatly set-up and appear to be more comfortable than Russian hotels.

PAVLOVSK (ПАВЛОВСК)

Twenty-nine kilometers south of St. Petersburg and an easy bus ride from Tsarskoye Selo, Pavlovsk is a modest and Classical contrast to both Pushkin or Peterhof. Given to Paul I by his frightening mother, Catherine the Great, on the birth of her grandson (the future Tsar Alexander I), Pavlovsk was one of the last imperial palaces to be built. Originally only a three-story domed square with wings curving halfway around the courtyard, Paul I expanded it to its present size and lived here with his wife Maria Fyodorovna, whose face can be admired in numerus paintings in the place. Paul I and his imperious mother did not get along well; and as soon as Catherine died, Paul moved here.

If you are combining Pushkin and Pavlovsk in one trip, it is best to go on a weekend when both palaces are completely open and more *electrichkies* run. From Petersburg, take an *electrichka* from Vitesbski Vokzal (Витебский Вокзал; M: Pushkinskaya) to Pavlovsk (800R one way). Any of the trains on Platforms 1,2, and 3 are fine; the longest wait is less than two hours. Get off at one stop past Pushkin (which makes seven stops from Petersburg). The conductor will say "Pavlovsk". Take bus #370 or 383 to the palace; it is the fifth stop and the palace is on the left. Bus #370 and 383 also go all the way to Pushkin. There is no place to eat at Pavlovsk; bring a picnic lunch. (Park open 10am-5pm. Admission 1000R, Russian adults 200R, children 50R. Closed first Mon. of month. Palace open Sat.-Thurs. (state rooms only on Thurs.) 11am-5pm; admission 11,500R, students 5850R.)

Paul I's taste was more restrained than his mother's (it wasn't hard) and resulted in a more tailored French approach, which Cameron's assistant Vincenzo Brena designed. This restrained look, though popular today, does not draw crowds of tourists, so Pavlovsk is peaceful most of the time. One of the largest landscaped **parks** in the world, speckled with the usual colonnades and temples, is still its biggest draw. Although life at Pavlovsk was deathly dull in Paul's day (mostly because he was obsessed with training his troops), it later spiced up with the completion of Russia's first rail-line to Pavlovsk. Leo Tolstoy, who made the trip, wrote of Pavlovsk: "Went to Pavlovsk. Disgusting. Girls, silly music, girls, mechanical nightingale, girls, girls, heat, cigarette smoke, girls, vodka, cheese, screams and shouts, girls, girls, girls!" He obviously had a good time. Completely destroyed during World War II the palace was restored to perfection; nonetheless, in the gardens lies a grave for the soldiers who died clearing Pavlovsk of mines. But while you won't find the above there today, you can row a boat out on the lake, or stroll into the beautiful landscape. You may come across such pavilions as the circular **Temple of Friendship,** built to symbolize a partial reconciliation between Maria and her fierce mother-in-law. Maria got along well with others though; while her husband was obsessed with war, she liked peace, and she befriended Marie Antoinette in Paris; Marie gave her the toilet that is on display in the palace. (While the palace was being built, Paul and Maria took a tour through Europe worthy of a *Let's Go* itinerary—although they weren't exactly on a budget—they sat in a carriage for 190 of the days they traveled!)

■■■ NOVGOROD (НОВГОРОД)

Novgorod is a particularly proud city, in large part because it fended off the Mongol Tatars that weaker Moscow could not. The surrounding lakes and swampland helped. But a few centuries later, under the rule of Ivan III and then Ivan the Terrible, Moscow brought this once powerful town under its yoke and residents have been grumbling about it ever since.

Founded in the 9th century by Prince Rurik, Novgorod ("New Town") grew throughout the Middle Ages, at one point having almost double its current population. Much of Novgorod's glorious past still stands due to energetic restoration efforts. Novgorod's Kremlin, the oldest in Russia, was the first architectural landmark to be restored after World War II; photographs of this proud moment may be seen in the Kremlin Museum.

Novgorod is a religious town, within its borders at least 230 churches were built between 1100 and 1500. Many of these architectural monuments still stand; some are still functioning, but most are closed to the public. One legend tells of how the town was saved from the Suzdal army (in those days, warring princes were as common as mosquitoes in summer, and about as pesky and annoying) by hanging an icon on the town's gates. When the Virgin's likeness began to cry, the besieging army fled in terror. Easily explored in a day (a good daytrip from Moscow or St. Petersburg via the night train), Novgorod is yet bigger and more thoroughly restored than Pskov; it makes a good introduction to the Russia of the 12th-15th centuries.

ORIENTATION AND PRACTICAL INFORMATION

In theory, Novgorod has two centers—the **Kremlin** on the west side of the river, and **Yaroslav's Court** on the east. There are some hotels on the east side, notably the Rossiya and the Sadko, but the **train station, bus station, telephone office,** and **hostel** are all on the west side. The west is laid out like a spiderweb, with the Kremlin in the center. Prospect Karla Marxa (пр. Карла Маркса), runs from the train station to the earth walls that surround old Novgorod; turn left here for the hostel. There are usually good fruit stands on this corner. From the halls, ul. Sovietskaya, now ul. Oktyabrskaya (ул. Советская, now ул. Октябрьская) runs to Ploschad Pobedi (пл. Победи) and the Kremlin. Along Sovietskaya are **grocery stores** and the **telephone** office. **Maps** can be purchased at Hotel Intourist, from the kiosk at the east side of the Kremlin, or in the St. Petersburg youth hostel. As of the summer of 1994, all maps still have the old street names, street signs have both the old and new names, and everyone uses the old names. Be prepared for confusion.

Tourist Offices: ul. Nikolskaya (ул. Никольская), (tel. 353 32). South of Yaroslavl's Court on the east side of the river. Pass through an archway into a courtyard; there is a plaque reading "Новгородское Бюро." Open daily 9am-5pm. **Group tours** of Novgorod, the Kremlin, the Church of St. Sophia, among other places. Offered in French, German, and English, and priced according to the size of the group. No maps, no brochures. **Intourist Hotel,** ul. Dmitriyevskaya 16 (ул. Дмитриешевская), (tel. 750 89 or 942 90). Bus #4 and 20 from the station go within 500m at the Univermag (Универмаг) stop, or walk along the street next to the earth wall, left from the station for five long blocks until you reach the river; the hotel is directly in front. Designed mainly to serve groups. Does provide guided **tours** of the city in English (US$15 for 2). **Maps** sold in lobby. You're better off getting train or bus tickets directly from the station. Open 24hrs.

Currency Exchange: At the Telephone and Telegraph Office; open daily 10am-1pm and 2-5pm. Or Hotel Intourist, second floor; open Mon.-Fri. 9am-1pm and 2-8pm, Sat.-Sun. 9am-7pm.

Post Office: Hotel Intourist, second floor (see Tourist Offices for directions), or at 9 Bolshaya Sankt Peterburgskaya (Большая Санкт Петербургская), formerly Leningradskaya (Ленинградская). Open Mon.-Fri. 9am-2pm and 3-8pm, Sat. 9am-7pm. **Postal Code:** 173001.

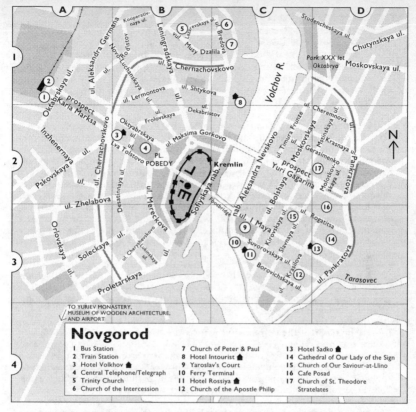

Novgorod

1 Bus Station
2 Train Station
3 Hotel Volkhov ♠
4 Central Telephone/Telegraph
5 Trinity Church
6 Church of the Intercession
7 Church of Peter & Paul
8 Hotel Intourist ♠
9 Yaroslav's Court
10 Ferry Terminal
11 Hotel Rossiya ♠
12 Church of the Apostle Philip
13 Hotel Sadko ♠
14 Cathedral of Our Lady of the Sign
15 Church of Our Saviour-at-Llino
16 Cafe Posad
17 Church of St. Theodore Stratelates

Telephone and Telegraph Office: Ploschad Pobedy (Площадь Победы), at the corner of ul. Gorkhovo (ул. Горхого) and Sovietskaya (Советская; now Oktyabrskaya, ул. Октябрьская). Open 24hrs. On the left are several phones that dial direct to Moscow. Buy a token (*zhetoni*; 400R) from the *kassa* in the room on the right for use here or in any "междугородный автомат" telephone (large gray phones with the funky slide for your token); it will provide you a minute to Moscow. Otherwise, book your call in one of the other booths at the same *kassa*—pay in advance per minute. Book international calls in advance in the *kassa* in the room on the left; your best bet is to call AT&T USADirect in Moscow or a similar service as the wait for international calls can be several hours. **City Code:** 8160.

Trains: Straight ahead at the end of ul. Karla Marxa. To: St. Petersburg (2 per day, 7:20am and 5:40pm, third train on Sun., 4-6hrs.); Moscow (1 per day, 9:40pm, 8hrs., *Lux* 57,000R, *kupé* 18,000R). More expensive than the bus, but a lot more comfortable. For regular tickets more than 24 hrs. in advance go to *kassa* #5 or 6. Open daily 9am-noon and 1-8pm. For *lux* (люкс) or same-day tickets, go to the *sutochnaya* (суточная) *kassa* #3, open daily 8am-1pm and 2-7pm.

Buses: At the end of pr. Karla Marxa (пр. Карла Маркса), to the right as you face the train station. It's a small white building labelled "Автостанция." Daily buses to: Moscow (26,00R), St. Petersburg (9600R), and Pskov (11,000R; one leaves in the early morning and arrives at midday, perfect for a daytrip). The departure listings are somewhat confusing. To the right of destination listings are departure times (отправление из Новгорода). To the left are the times buses arrive in Novgorod from that place (прибытие в Новгород). Station open 5am-10pm.

Luggage Storage: To the left as you enter the bus station (400R).

Pharmacy (Аптека): Bolshaya Sankt Peterburgskaya 14. Open 11am-10pm.

RUSSIA

ACCOMMODATIONS

The one area where privatization and joint-ventures are readily visible, Novgorod's accommodations provide a wide variety of comforts and prices. The hostel, actually a Russian dorm-turned-cheap hotel, is the most viable option for budget travelers, but a few other old hotels offer reasonable rates. The Hotel Intourist, affordable in '94, is to become a four-star complex by '95; the Bereska Palace is already well out of reach. Both provide perfect examples of what *perestroika* has done for these old Golden Ring towns.

Novgorod Hostel, 27a ul. Komsomolskaya, now ul. Novo-Luchanskaya (ул. Комсомольская, now ул. Ново-Лучанская), (tel. 720 33). From the station, go down pr. Karla Marxa (пр. Карла Маркса), take the first left (banked by an earth wall), and follow the curving road almost to the first main intersection (with ul. Komsomolskaya). The big red building on the right side is the hostel. An oasis for the budget traveler tired of musty, old Intourist hotels, this converted dorm has shabby but clean, bright, and airy rooms with firm beds. The staff doesn't speak English, but is helpful and friendly. Reception open 24 hrs. Full use of large kitchen with two stoves and four sinks; teapot, casserole bowl, plates, and silverware provided. Private or semi-private baths with working shower, sink, and toilet. Singles with private bath 36,000R. Doubles with bath shared with a triple 31,200R. Doubles with private bath 80,000R.

Hotel Sadko (Гостиница Садко), Prospect Yuri Gagarin 16 (пр. Юри Гагарина) (tel. 753 66). Reception open 24 hrs. The corridors are well lit, and the rooms include a proper shower as well as TV and phone. Singles 30,000R. Doubles 48,000R. Triples 62,000R. Reservations recommended. Currency exchange in the lobby, open Mon.-Fri. 9am-noon, 2-6pm.

Hotel Rossiya (Гостиница Россия), Naberezhnaya Alexander Nevskovo (наб. Александра Невского) at the corner of ul. Bolshaya Moskovskaya (ул. Большая Московская, was pr. Lenina, пр. Ленина) (tel. 341 85). Reception open 24 hrs. The hallways are dark and nest-colored decor. Rooms are clean and spacious, but the beds a little soft. Each room has a toilet and "shower" (a spray fixture attached to the wall.) No singles. Doubles 48,000R. Triples 67,5000R. Baggage check available. Reservations not necessary for small groups.

Hotel Volkhov (Гостиница Волхов), ul. Frolovskaya 24, formerly ul. Nekrasova (ул. Фроловская, formerly ул. Некрасова), (tel. 759 39). From the train station walk straight down pr. Karla Marxa and ul. Sovetskaya (ул. Советская, now Октябрьская), one block and turn right on ul. Frolovskaya. Centrally located between the train station and Kremlin. Reception open 24 hrs. It has the basics—long dark hallways, dim rooms, and institutional wooden beds—for slightly more than the prices charged by other old warhorses due to its prime location. Spend the extra money on the private bathroom. Singles with private shower and toilet 45,000R. Doubles 30,000R. Doubles with private shower and toilet 72,000R.

FOOD

The few eateries with any kind of ambience cater primarily to tourists—and raise their prices accordingly. *Shashliki* (шашлыки) and *sloiki* (слойки, a delicious pastry with jam) are available at a stand outside the Kremlin; if it's a sunny day, you're best off taking a picnic and sitting on a bench or by a lake.

Restaurant Detinets (Детинец), in a stone tower of the Kremlin; follow the signs (tel. 746 24). Tables set artisically into the walls of the bar are designed to appeal to the tour groups who fill the place. Reservations recommended. A double-sided wooden staircase leads to the restaurant on the second floor which serves tasty Russian specialties such as mushrooms and sour cream (2700R) and *schi* (cabbage soup, 1396R). Fish of the Tsar 4332R. Open daily 11am-11pm.

Pri Dvore (При Дворе), ul. Sovetskaya 3 (ул. Совемская). Within 5min. of the Kremlin and the hostel. Wide umbrellas shelter the large outdoor courtyard. Yummy *shashliki* (1500R) grilled outside, extensive Russian menu indoors. Courtyard bar open noon-11pm. Restaurant open daily noon-4pm and 6-11pm.

Bar Pallada (Бар Паллада), ul. Shtykova 22, now ul. Yakovleva (ул. Штыкова, now ул. Яковлева), (tel. 722 27). To the left going down Leningradskaya to the Kremlin. Go downstairs and through a hallway. High-backed black leather seats and metal railings make this new bar a perfect battle zone for late-night poker wars (and a morning-after caffeine fix). Large coffee 400R. Beer 750R per liter. Open 24hrs.

Restaurant Rossiya (Ресторан Россия), nab. Alexander Nevskovo (наб. Александра Невского) in the Hotel Rossiya. Unlike in most Russian restaurants, they actually open the curtains—to a lovely view of the river and the Kremlin. The menu changes daily, but you can bet it's variations on the same old theme: "meat" *borscht* 700R. Beef cutlets 2500R. Open daily 8am-11pm; kitchen closes at 10pm.

Restaurant Sadko (Ресторан Садко), pr. Yuri Gagarin 16 (пр. Юри Гагарина), in the Hotel Sadko. Finally, a cheerful Russian restaurant—a funky marine mural is complemented by red plush Star Trek chairs, and the room is light and airy. Standard Russian cuisine, well-prepared. And cloth napkins to boot! Salads 1000-1400R. Pork shops 3500R. Chicken Kiev 3600R. Open daily 11am-5pm, 6-11pm.

Café Posad (Кафе Посад), ul. Bolshevikov 14 (ул. Большевиков), now (sometimes) called ul. Rogatitsa (ул. Рогатица). Down the steps from street level, this warmly lit café serves up Russian standards for less than the hotel restaurants. *Borscht* 990R. Beef stroganoff 2700R. Chicken fillet 2800R. Open Mon.-Sat. noon-midnight.

SIGHTS AND ENTERTAINMENT

Entering the **Kremlin** from the lake side is most impressive, affording a panoramic view of the huge red brick walls, the **Novgorod horseman** (a statue commemorating the city's survival through the ages), and, not quite so appealing, the sandy lakeside spotted in summer with sunbathing Russians. The walls of the Kremlin, punctuated by towers, were first built in the 11th century, when according to legend it was still custom to lay the first stone on the body of a still (for a moment) living child. Wandering through the oldest Kremlin in Russia is free, as are most of the interesting sights. To the immediate right of the lakeside entrance is the **belfry,** outside which stand huge examples of the sort that used to ring forth from here. No bats, though. Continuing to the right past the abysmal sounds of the music school (no young Rostropoviches in there) walk straight to the **St. Sophia Cathedral** (Софийский собор; *Sofiysky Sobor*), the religious pinnacle of any trip to Novgorod. The oldest stone building in Russia, this 11th century Byzantine cathedral is most imposing from the outside, where the Swedish west doors depict intricately carved scenes from the Bible. Inside, only a few icons remain (most are in the museum) and, with the exception of the inside of the dome, all the frescoes were painted fresh in the 19th century. The dark interior and heavy iron chandelier make the cathedral oppressively gloomy (open daily 8am-8pm; services 10am and 6pm; free).

Behind the cathedral are the **clock tower** (часозвоня; *chasozvonya*) and the **Chamber of Facets** (Грановитая Палата; *Granovitaya Palata*). The striking tower's bell used to call citizens to meetings of the *veche* (city council)—a partially democratic government. Both the bell and the *veche* were quickly done away with by the Ivans. The chamber, next door, contains many precious religious artifacts; but you require a guide to enter—buy your ticket at the museum and wait for a group to gather or arrive (open Wed.-Mon. 10am-6pm, closed last Friday of the month). Returning to the center of the park, don't miss walking around the **Millenium of Russia Monument** (Тысячелетие России; *Tusuacheletie*). Taking one minute to encircle this bronze depiction of all Russian history is bound to be less painful than it was to go through it—as shown by the numbers of fallen men holding daggers sculpted onto this black ball. The old favorites, Rurik, Prince Vladimir of Kiev, and Peter the Great are all there—as well as the hordes of others being smushed by a gleeful Dmitry Donskoy.

Directly behind the monument stands the town's **museum,** a large building conveying the full duration of Novgorod's history. Starting on the ground floor with thin arrowheads and birchbark inscriptions from the 12th century, move on through delicately carved combs and amulets from the 14th century. The rubles from the period were long and heavy metal rods—serious-looking things that look like they could improve the Russian economy today. Also on the ground floor are recreations of Novgorodian life through the centuries—with the requisite red rooms on the Soviet period. The second floor holds the famous icons, -including the one which supposedly saved the town from the Suzdal army. Go slowly through the first rooms, admiring the craftsmanship; the 20th-century art is not much to look at anyway (open Mon.-Wed. 10am-1pm and 1:30pm-5:20pm; admission 2500R, students 1250R, Russians 200R, Russian students 100R).

Directly across the footbridge from the Kremlin and to the right, **Yaroslav's Court** is the old market center of Novgorod, and the original site of the palace of the Novgorod princes. There are remains of the 17th-century waterfront arcade, several churches from the 13th-16th centuries, and the market gatehouse which is now a museum where you can see some of the old frescoes that were in the other buildings (open Wed.-Sun. 10:30am-7:30pm; closed the last Thurs. of the month). Everything else is closed to the public.

The **Yuriev Monastery** and the **Museum of Wooden Architecture** is the last of over 20 that once surrounded Novgorod; it is striking for its location, in the middle of broad and windy marshes, but little else. Take bus #7 from pl. Pobedy (пл. Победи) for about 20 minutes. You can then walk to the museum. The church has been heavily reconstructed, and most buildings are closed to the public (open Wed.-Mon. 10am-4pm). One kilometer west of the monastery is a **Museum of Wooden Architecture,** a collection of houses and churches from surrounding towns, some dating from the 16th century (open Thurs.-Tues. 10am-6pm).

Churches abound in the northern area of the town; many up beyond the Hotel Intourist are picturesque and still functioning. A stroll in that area will lead you to any number of them—if you get lost, simply look for the next dome.

Look for posters advertising the disco bar and laser-show called **Baccara** (Баккара) (tel. 745 04) on Fridays and Saturdays at 11pm. Visit the **Pushkin Theater** next to the Hotel Intourist, or perhaps catch a performance at the **Concert Hall** in the Kremlin (*kassa* open Mon.-Fri. 2-7pm, Sat. noon-5pm).

■ ■ ■ PSKOV (ПСКОВ)

From its founding sometime early in the 10th century until 1721, when Peter the Great took Estonia and Livonia from Sweden, Pskov was an important border town and still has the fortress walls to prove it. These 18-foot thick limestone monsters have withstood 26 sieges; thanks to energetic restoration they are still in good shape in many parts of this small city, ready to withstand tourists. Pskov was also the site of Nicholas II's abdication in March 1917 and was Lenin's home for a short time before the revolution.

Pskov's long history is still palpable. Unlike in Russia's larger cities where the tumultuous changes of recent decades have created amnesiac metropolises with no sense of what came before, Pskov has integrity. The ancient Kremlin is still quiet, its courtyard empty, green, and windy. The Trinity Cathedral in the center is one of Russia's loveliest. Walk along the river by the walls, and imagine you are a knight on guard in the 14th century. Then walk into town, and into Kruschev's Russia: Lenin stands proudly in front of the Pedagogical Institute, and the central market still feels like an Eastern bazaar rather than the racketeering rip-off most have become in Moscow and St. Petersburg. Peaceful and barely noticing the world changing around it, Pskov is the place to find old Russia—several old Russias.

ORIENTATION AND PRACTICAL INFORMATION

Pskov's main axis is Oktyabrskaya Prospect (Октябрьская пр.), with the Hotel Oktyabrskaya, telephone office, post office, and number one café all located within a five-minute walk of each other on this street. It runs into the main square, Oktyabrskaya Ploschad, where it intersects with ul. Sovetskaya (ул. Советская) which itself runs up to the Kremlin in the northern end of the town. The Velikaya (Великая) and

Pskova (Псков) rivers intersect just north of the Kremlin. Across the Velikaya river along Rizhsky Prospect (Рижский пр.) is the Rizhskaya Hotel. The outer town walls run along the river and along ul. Sverdlova (ул. Свердлова) by Pskov's two big parks.

Tourist Offices: The ever-faithful, newly-democratized **Intourist** is in Hotel Rizhskaya, 25 Rizhsky pr. second floor #207-216 (Рижский пр.), a 10-min. walk from Oktyabrskaya pl. over the bridge. Or take bus #17. No maps, brochures, etc.; just **tours** for a high price. Also **exchanges money.** Open Mon.-Fri. 9am-6pm. A **tourist bureau** is at the entrance to the Kremlin on the right. No maps here either; it seems the Pskovians fear another German invasion. Expensive group **tours** (you provide the group, they provide the English-speaking guide) to Pechori, Stariy Izborsk, around the city, and around the Kremlin. Open Mon.-Fri. 8am-1pm and 2-6pm, Sat.-Sun. 8am-5pm.

Post Office: On the north side of pl. Oktyabrskaya. It's very musty. Hold your breath, buy your stamps, and pray. Open Mon.-Fri. 8am-8pm, Sat.-Sun. 8am-1pm and 2-5pm.

Telephones: Oktyabrskaya pr. (Октябрьская пр.), in a large grey building opposite the proud statue of Kirov between ul. Nekrasova (ул. Некрасова) and ul. Gogolya (ул. Гоголя). Telegram to U.S. 650R per word. International calls must be ordered (takes up to 1hr.). **Faxes** available. Operator for international calls open 7:30am-10:30pm. Office open 24 hrs. **City Code:** 81122.

Trains: Buses #2, 11, and 17 all end their routes at the train station (вокзал; *vokzal*). There are daily trains to Moscow (12 hrs., 2nd class 70,000R), St. Petersburg (7 hrs., 2nd class 29,000R), and Tallinn. Buy advance tickets at the booth in the waiting room, open 8am-7pm. Ticket office open 24 hrs.

Buses: The bus is the best way to get in and out of Pskov, unless you're going to Moscow. Novgorod (2 per day, 4hrs., making Pskov a good day trip; 11,200R); St. Petersburg (2 per day, 6hrs.; 17,100R); Pechori (1 per day in summer, 1½hrs.; 1200R). Buy tickets to Novgorod and St. Petersburg at *kassa* #6, inside the station. Buy tickets to Pechori at Spravochnoye bureau (Справочное Бюро). *Kassa* open 8am-1pm and 2-7pm. Station open 5am-10pm.

Public Transportation: Bus #11 and 17 leave from in front of the train station, turn to the right from the autobus station, and go through the center of the town. Bus #17 stops in front of Hotel Rizhskaya. #11 stops near Hotel Oktyabrskaya. Buy 10 tickets from the bus conductor for 600R.

Gay and Lesbian Hotline: C'mon, you're in Pskov.

ACCOMMODATIONS

Options are slim in Pskov. The old Intourist Hotel Rizhskaya and Oktyabrskaya, a former Sputnik hotel, fall within the *Let's Go* traveler's budget. For a bit more, **HOFA** (see St. Petersburg Accommodations) provides homestays (US$20 per night). A large hotel is being built along the river, but it has been under construction for the past four years and shows no signs of nearing completion.

Rizhskaya Hotel (Гостиница Рижская), Rizhsky pr. 25 (Рижский пр.), (tel. 623 01), a 10-min. walk from the bridge near Oktyabrskaya pl., or bus #17 from the station. Huge and very Intourist: clean well-kept rooms with squishy beds and soft blankets. Large windows make the medium-sized rooms cheerfully light. Reception open 7am-1am. You can buy tea, soap, and other necessities from the hall guardian. English spoken. Small bathtub, shower, and toilet in each room. Singles 28,800-36,000R. Doubles 54,000-62,400R. TV, phone, and fridge extra.

Oktyabrskaya Hotel (Гостиница Октябрьская), Oktyabrskaya pr. 36 (tel. 399 12), a 5-min. walk from Oktyabrskaya pl. past a park on the left side, or bus #11 from the station. Not equipped to deal with foreigners, it offers the barest essentials for a correspondingly low price. No English spoken. Reception open 24 hrs. Small, musty rooms but firm beds and clean sheets. Couch, TV, sink, and telephone included. The one toilet for the long hallway is clean but may be malodorous; the one shower is a good 2-min. walk at the opposite end of a dark hallway. But if you don't want to wash, it's adequate. Singles 30,000R. Doubles 40,000R. Triples 52,500-70,000R.

FOOD

If you eat solely at the Russian restaurants here, you will "enjoy" a salty, fatty, potato-oriented diet. The Western foodstuffs available in kiosks consist of mostly cookies and candy bars. Your best bet is to mix and match, supplementing everything with fruit or cucumbers bought at the **Central Market** or on the street; in summer, fresh bananas and oranges are widely available, as well as honey, cheese, meat, salami, and other fruits and vegetables. There is also a buffet (буфет) with a small variety of pastries. The market is off Prospect Karla Marxa (Проспект Карла Маркса) down a dirty, narrow street about 50m past a church that's being renovated. Behind a fence, it's the large building labelled "РЫНОК" in huge letters (opens 8am).

Cafe Cheburechnaya (Кафе Чебуречная), Octyabrskaya Prospect 10 (Октябрьская Проспект). The café is in a yellow clapboard building; enter from the back. This Georgian cooperative is your best bet for food in Pskov. Cheerful and well-lit, its specialty are "chebureki," somewhat greasy, though tasty meat pies in yummy dough 1000R. They also have dumplings (4 for 1600R) and shish kebabs (1900R). *Real* Turkish coffee 500R. Open 11am-6pm.

Restaurant "Riga" (Ресторан "Рига"), in the Hotel Rizhskaya, Rizhki pr. 25 (Рижский пр.). Very standard Russian—heavy orange curtains lend a strange color to your dinner partner. *Borscht* 1000R, "beefsteak" 2000R, mushrooms in sour cream 3000R. Cloth napkins on the tables are a welcome break from the shreds of tissue paper most places call napkins. Open noon-5pm and 6-11pm.

Restaurant Aurora (Ресторан Аврора), Oktyabrskaya pr. 36 (Октябрьская пр.), next to the Hotel Oktyabrskaya. The restaurant is on the second floor (which means you may be able to just walk in and use the bathrooms downstairs). Lighter curtains make this restaurant less oppressive than most; otherwise, it's your basic Russian joint. Entrees 3000-3500R. Open 1-5:30pm, 6:30pm-12:30am.

Café Zolotaya Rybka (Кафе Золотая Рыбка), Sovetskaya ul. 35 (Советская ул.). You could tour Pskov's retaurants and remember which was which by the curtains— here they're heavy maroon and velvet. The room is hot and smells. The menu is heavily beverage-oriented and the food is expensive. Entrees 4500-5000R. Open Mon.-Fri. 11am-11pm, Sat.-Sun. 5-11pm.

Movie Theater Café (Пицца; *pizza*). On the left side of the Oktyabr movie theater (Октябрь кино) on Lenin Square is a little window selling ice cream, drinks, and "pizza" (Пицца; actually Russian bread with onions, cheese, and salami, which is quite tasty). Open noon-6pm.

SIGHTS

Although many of Pskov's later walls and towers (15th-16th century) can be seen along the river and ul. Sverdlova, the oldest (13th century) are in north, around the **Kremlin** (Кремль) and Dovment Town. It is the small area which also encompasses the magnificent Holy Trinity Cathedral (Тройцкий Собор; *Troitsky Sobor),* the places which tourists—many from other parts of Russia—come to see.

In **Dovment Town** (Довмонтов Город; *Dovmontov Gorod),* the foundations of nine churches, all built between the 12th and 15th century, can still be seen—the ruins are not much to look at, but the thought of the once-thriving religious center is impressive (Kremlin area open 24 hrs.). Through an archway, past the beggars which line the cobblestoned path, is the pinnacle of Pskov's many churches. The **Holy Trinity Cathedral,** founded in the 10th century by Saint Olga (the first Russian woman to adopt Christianity and thus the Sarah of all *babushkas*) on her way to nearby Novgorod, is actually the fourth cathedral to stand on this spot. The current structure was built in the 12th century and is covered with frescoes from the same time (those closest to the ceiling are the oldest and most valuable). The center gilded dome can be seen for kilometers. The colorful interior and collection of icons make this one of the most beautiful old churches in Russia, but it is the feeling of being in another time that is so awe-inspiring; from the beggars to the bearded priests to the windy courtyard to the man sweeping the tiles of the church for hours, this sacred place is closer to 1795 than 1995. Walking back out into the green courtyard, it is possible to walk through an archway to a spot overlooking the intersection of the Velikaya and Pskova rivers (near the Kremlin, you can rent **boats** to take out on the river July-Aug.). Looking out over the wide, quiet rivers, high grass, and yellow flowers, this village appears for the moment to have survived every effort to invade it, including Stalin's. (Church open 9am-end of evening service. Public services held daily 9-11am and 6pm-'til late, presided over by bearded priests in flowing gold and blue robes. Free, but donation appreciated.)

The **Pogankin Palace and Museum** (Поганкины Палаты и Музей; *Pogankiny Palaty*) is on Komsomolskaya Pereulok (Комсомолская Переулок) at the corner of Sovietskaya ul. (Советская ул.). Enter through the new wing—quickly walk past Soviet art and history and the glares of the guards, through the courtyard to the main house. Originally the home of a wealthy 17th-century merchant, it holds an exhibit on the history of Pskov, including the Dovmont sword that was passed on to each new prince. (Open Tues.-Sun. noon-7pm. Closed the last Tues. of each month. Admission 3000R, Russians 500R, Russian students 200R.)

Mirozhsky Monastery (Мирожский Монастыре) is along the Velikaya River, across the southernmost bridge and to the right. Still under restoration, the monastery is nonetheless open to visitors; its spectacular 12th century frescoes are typical of the Pskov region and will remind you of those found in the Russian art books you see displayed on the streets of Moscow and St. Petersburg. Certainly worth a quick visit, if only to impress your Russian friends, who are understandably in great admiration of this place (open Tues.-Sun. noon-6pm; free, but donations appreciated here too). Pskov has more **churches** than restaurants and hotels combined; unfortunately most are in desperate need of repair and closed to the public. One, across the Velikaya on the way to the Rizhskaya Hotel, is being repaired and is open to the public to encourage donations. A couple of old churches, including the 16th-century **St. Nikolas-on-Usokha** (Никольна-Усохе), are scattered around the main Oktyabrskaya Ploschad. To see the interior of a typical Pskov church, head to Pechory Monastery.

■ NEAR PSKOV: PECHORY MONASTERY

If you happen to be in Pskov overnight, Pechory Monastery is a good excursion for the second day; you can go in the morning and be back in time for the night train to Moscow or St. Petersburg or the afternoon bus to Novgorod. Buy a ticket to Pechory at the bus station (1100R) and then one back again to Pskov as soon as you arrive, about an hour later. The monastery is to the right at the end of Yurevskaya ul. (Юревская ул.). Go left out of the station, then make your first right. It was founded in 1473 and is still in operation—about 70 monks live here. The buildings and caves (where monks are buried) are closed to the public—be sure to obey the "хода нет" ("do not enter") signs. The rest is a lovely place to walk in, though; well kept grounds and beautifully colored churches are an amazing rest for the eyes after Stalin's urban architecture. Women must be in skirts and may not wear t-shirts (wear a jacket); men may not wear hats. Photography is forbidden. There are two churches outside the monastery's gates that are open to the public; women should wear head scarves when entering these. A tourist booth sells some brochures in Russian. (Open 9am-1pm and 2-6pm. Monastery free, but donation for its upkeep requested; 100R or so is fine.)

■■■ SMOLENSK (СМОЛЕНСК)

Smolensk (pop. 350,000) may be near the border, but its heart and soul are firmly planted in Russia. On the rail route between Moscow and major Eastern European capitals, Smolensk has nonetheless not benefitted from trade; it looks much like any other Soviet city—impressive ramparts and a glorious cathedral (almost alone worth the trip), but with few cafés or restaurants and little change to be seen. In fact, despite Smolensk's attractiveness from afar (all of the picturesque churches and the

Kremlin stand on hills, and the town is situated on the wide and meandering Dniepr River) it has mostly suffered—through invasion upon invasion upon invasion.

Since its origins in 863, the Tatars have sacked it, Moscow and Lithuania fought over it (for a few centuries, no less), Poland snatched it (for a mere 45 years though), Napoleon stormed it, the Nazis reached it, and the Soviet state demoralized it. Now it is only slowly recovering. In the West, the town is known best for one of the Soviet Union's most infamous wartime crimes—the Kahyn massacre. Only in 1990 did the authorities admit to killing 4000 Polish officers in nearby Kahyn Forest in 1940, officers who had surrendered to the occupying Soviet troops; the Soviets had until then always blamed the Nazis for their deaths. Despite this series of disasters, Smolensk might be worth a half-day foray, and tickets from Moscow on the overnight train are cheap, so if you need a place to sleep. . .

ORIENTATION AND PRACTICAL INFORMATION

Smolensk is one of the few hilly towns in Russia thanks to eons of work by the Dniepr River on whose banks the city stands. The old **city walls** surround the center on the south bank of the river where all the sights and hotels are located. The **train station** (with daily trains to Prague, Frankfurt, Warsaw, Minsk, and Vilnius) is north of the center, across the river. Also across the river is **Kolkhoznaya Ploschad** (Колхозная Площадь), site of the farmer's market. Ulitsa Bolshaya Sovietskaya (Улица Большая Советская) leads from the square to the center, up the hill past **Assumption Cathedral**. Tram #3 runs from the train station to Kolkhoznaya pl. and then to the Hotel Rossiya; trams #1 and 4 run from Kolkhoznaya pl. up ul. Bolshaya Sovietskaya to the cathedral and the center.

Smolensk's branch of **Intourist** is all but defunct. The office is at ul. Konyonkova 3 (Конёнкова), near the Tsentralnaya Hotel, but it cannot even offer maps of the city. However, the staff is friendly; stop by if you are desperate for tourist-type guidance (speak Russian; open daily 9am-1pm and 2-6pm).

ACCOMMODATIONS

One of Smolensk's three centrally-located hotels should do you well. All double their rates for foreigners, but the prices are comparable. The Hotel Rossiya is less well-located than the others, but its rooms come with breakfast. As for comparative quality, well... these are Soviet-era hotels, and there was no such thing as comparison shopping when Brezhnev ruled the land. Just say eenie-meenie-minie-moe.

Tsentralnaya Gostinitsa (Центральная Гостиница), ul. Lenina 2/1 (ул. Ленина; tel. 338 04). True to its name this hotel is well-located right near Glinka Garden and about a 10-min. walk from Assumption Cathedral. Reception open 24 hrs. The hotel is old and has not been renovated in a while, but the bathrooms are clean and serviceable, though lack toilet paper. Foreign prices are fairly steep, but if you call ahead and explain (in Russian) that you are a group or students (or both), you may be able to stay for Russian prices. For foreigners, single with bath (in a two-room double suite) 60,000R, double (same setup) 120,000R. One-room singles 36,000R, with bath 44,000R. Doubles 60,000, with bath 80,000R. For Russians the prices are reduced by 50%. The hotel has a parking lot, a currency exchange (open Mon.-Sat. 2:30-4pm) and a sauna (open 8am-10pm; 8000R).

Hotel Rossiya (Гостиница Россия), ul. Dzerzhinskovo 23/2 (ул. Дзержинского; tel. 336 70). Take tram #3 from the station and get off at the Spartak Stadium stop. Huge Soviet-style monster of a hotel with all the conveniences. Standard rooms with standard bathrooms—bath, shower (with high water pressure), and plastic toilet—for standard prices. The one extra is that breakfast is included in the room price, consisting of bread, cheese, macaroni, beef stroganoff, and tea. Singles 44,000R. Doubles 80,000R. Quadruples 120,000R. Breakfast served 7:30-10am.

Hotel Smolensk (Гостиница Смоленск). On the corner of ul. Glinka (ул. Глинка; tel. 995 66), just off Bolshaya Sovietskaya (Большая Советская) north of Ploschad Smirnova (Площадь Смирнова). Run by the same people as the Tsentralnaya it has the same rates and facilities, minus the parking lot. Also, it mostly has rooms without bath and fewer luxury suites. Reception open 24 hrs.

FOOD

There are plenty of little, dark Russian cafés in Smolensk, most squatting sternly on ul. Bolshaya Sovietskaya (Большая Советская) and ul. Lenina (ул. Ленина), but there is nothing out of the ordinary. However, since this is a southern town on the border with another country (Poland), there is plenty of produce—your best bet is the large **market** (Заднепровский Рынок; *Zadneprovski Rynok*) on ul. Belyaeva, across the river and directly downhill from the Assumption Cathedral (trams #1 and 4 roll by here on their way to the cathedral). Inside the covered market is mostly meat and butter, but the outdoor market behind sells lots of fruits and veggies.

Bar "Holstein 777," on ul. Bolshaya Sovietskaya (ул. Большая Советская), just south of ul. Lenina (ул. Ленина); look for the Holstein Beer sign and enter the courtyard. This private venture café—seemingly the only one of its kind in Smolensk—has cheesy decor, American music, foreign beer, and fairly high prices, but better food than the hotel restaurants. Vegetable soup 4000R. Cutlet of beef with potatoes and mushrooms 9600R. Coffee 1000R. Holstein beer 5000R.

Russian Tea (Русский Чай), ul. Bolshaya Sovietskaya, near the corner of ul. Lenina. The wooden sign indicating the restaurant is difficult to read. A cozy, wooden café with small tables and a low ceiling, this is a good place for a rainy day. Pizza 2730R. Ice cream with chocolate sauce 500R. Open daily 11am-11pm.

Blinnaya (Блинная), right next door to Holstein 777 on ul. Bolshaya Sovietskaya. *Blini*, Russia's (some would argue better) answer to crêpes, served all day, everyday. With sour cream 240R. With butter 280R. With honey 360R. Stuffed with meat 720R. Open daily 8am-5pm.

Kulinaria (Кулинария), ul. Lenina (ул. Ленина), to the left of the Chess Federation. Your basic stand-up shop/café (note the name—meaning essentially a place where you can get food) but serving very tasty, fresh *bulki* (бульки), sweet rolls with raisins and icing for 125R. Café of same name next door is also popular with locals. Open daily 10am-2pm and 3-7pm.

Café Zarya (Кафе Заря), corner of ul. Lenina and ul. Konyonkova (ул. Ленина and ул. Конюнкова). To the right is the informal café, with only a few meager food options. To the left is the main restaurant with fresh flowers on the tables and music in the evenings. Entrees are good and reasonably priced. Chicken 3590R. *Blini* with caviar 5070R. Salad 694R. Coffee 132R. Open daily noon-5pm, 6-11pm.

Restaurant Rossiya (Ресторан Россия) in the Hotel Rossiya on ul. Dzerzhinskovo (ул. Дзержинского). Your basic hotel restaurant, though lighter than most and with cloth napkins and flowers on the table. Quite reasonably priced, except there's a 1000R cover at dinner for the live music—which you may be better off avoiding anyway. Crab salad 2700R. *Pelmeni* 800R. Chicken entrees 6-7000R. Hot breakfast 3000R. Open daily 7:30-10am, noon-5pm, and 7pm-midnight.

Restaurant Dnepr (Ресторан Днепр), ul. Glinka (ул. Глинка) to the left of the Hotel Smolensk. The huge, chandeliered restaurant is on the second floor. The peeling pink paint is evidence of a very faded but nonetheless still visible elegance. Lots of pork dishes (швинина; *shvinina*) for 3-4000R. Fries 182R. Beef stroganoff 2141R. Open daily noon-4pm and 5pm-midnight.

Restaurant Tsentralnaya, in the Hotel Tsentralnaya. One dim room serving usual Russian fare—mushrooms with sour cream (грибы; *griby*) 3756R. Salad 1500R. Tea 45R. Open daily noon-4pm and 5-11pm.

SIGHTS AND ENTERTAINMENT

Assumption Cathedral (Успенский Собор) can hardly be missed; this spectacular green-and-white cathedral rises from the highest hill in Smolensk. It is approached by a flight of steps from ul. Bolshaya Sovietskaya, and the east end of the cathedral terrace affords an incredible view. There has been a cathedral standing here since 1101; this latest model was completed in the early 18th century, and is said to have so impressed Napoleon that he had it guarded from the pillaging of his own men. The interior is indeed magnificent; it is one of Russia's largest churches and is spectacularly gilded inside. It is still in use (although women may enter bareheaded); to the right as you enter, up a flight of steps, is a supposedly miracle-working icon of the Virgin and Child. It's actually a 16th-century copy of the original, which was said to be by St. Luke and was stolen in 1923 after being here since 1103. Even today, it is surrounded by candles and worshippers (open daily 10am-6pm).

Apart from the Assumption Cathedral, far and away (indeed from far away) the most striking architectural landmarks are the 6-km long 15m-high walls of the **Smolensk Kremlin,** which stand as a reminder of the many wars this town has withstood, from the Tatars to Moscow to Poland to Napoleon to the Nazis. While the walls can be seen from numerous places in the city, the one spot you can actually climb a tower is just off ul. Oktyabrskoy Revolutsii (ул. Октябрьской Революции) to the left. The **Gromovaya Tower** (Громовая Башня) may be climbed daily between 10am-5pm (admission 100R, students 70R). You can hear the delighted shouts of young boys on the ramparts from a block away.

The **History Museum** (Исторический Музей) is on ul. Lenina (ул. Ленина) 100m west of Glinka Garden. As of July 1994, only the second- and third-floor exhibitions were open. The second floor is basic town-history fare: archaeological finds from the area, including some 13th-century graffiti; 15th- and 16th-century icons; local textiles and handicrafts. These last are unusually pretty—Smolensk is a huge flax-growing region, and as a result it was home to many skilled weavers and embroiderers (for more on the long and glorious history of flax in Smolensk, head to the Smolensk Flax Exhibition). The third floor has three rooms: the first, bearing the title "Peter I: A Time of Reform," has maps and other political paraphernalia from the time of Peter the Great. The second room, called "1812: In the Memory of the People," is largely portraits and photographs of the Russians who fought against Napoleon, whose army occupied Smolensk. The last room is a history of peasant life in Smolensk, and contains pottery, household tools, and more linen clothing (open Tues.-Sun. 10am-6pm; admission 100R, students 70R).

The **Smolensk Flax Exhibition** (Выставка Смоленский Лён) is on ul. Bolshaya Sovietskaya (ул. Большая Советская) in the Trotsky Monastery, a pink building on the left side of the street after a two-minute walk uphill from the Assumption Cathedral. This three-storied exhibit displays every aspect of Smolensk's main trade in full detail, with a Soviet touch. Two lower floors have photographs and models of linen-producing equipment of earlier times with the results—peasant women's folk dresses—hanging in the final room. Many of the examples of lace and other material craftsmanship are from the last three years, when such individual talent has been encouraged. The top floor, however, seems like a strange anomaly, with glass exhibits of cooperative #2031's model worker #3567 supposedly illustrating the brilliant success of mass-produced Soviet clothing; no final clothing display is needed for this—you can see it on the not-so fashions of old women on the street (open Tues.-Sun. 10am-6pm; admission 100R, students 75R).

Take the footbridge over the tram tracks to get to the **Church of SS Peter and Paul** (Петропавловская Церковь), at the intersection of ul. Kasnena and ul. Dzerzhinskovo. This 12th-century red brick church is built in the Kiev-style; restored to its former glory thirty years ago, it is currently a functioning church, but the plain whitewashed interior is not of the lavish sort that many tourists expect. (Open daily 8am-9pm. Services daily 9am and 5pm, Sun. 11am. Enter on the left side.) On the left of the simple church is **St. Barbara's Convent,** still standing in its original form but currently housing a shop for repairing imported electronic equipment—yet another of this country's strange contradictions.

The **World War II Museum** (Музей Великой Отечественной Войны), ul. Dzerzhinskovo (ул. Дзержинского), is to the right just after pl. Smirnova (пл. Смирнова). Walk past the busts of Soviet war heroes flanking the path to the main museum—yet another proof of the devastation WWII wreaked on this country. The German army reached Smolensk and the personal possessions of Nazi soldiers are included here alongside photographs of Smolensk boys who died in the Great Patriotic War. The sign over one exhibit reads "the war still hasn't ended" (Ещё не кончилась Война), which although referring to the situation at the time, could just as easily make a statement about Russia's attitude toward the war today. Come here only if you're a hard-core WWII buff; you'll be firmly directed to the high point of the exhibit—a collection of tanks, cannons, and a lone airplane sitting in the backyard of the museum (open Tues.-Sun. 10am-6pm; admission 100R, students 70R).

Central House of Artists (Центральный Дом Художника) ul. Bolshaya Sovietskaya 21 (ул. Большая Советская), is a contemporary art museum with monthly exhibits—check the poster outside to see if anything good is hanging (open Wed.-Sun. 10am-6pm; free).

Club "Discovery" is in the Dom Mologozhy (Дом Молодёжи), ul. Communist-icheskaya 4 (ул. Коммунистическая) at the corner of ul. Oktayalorskoi Revolutsii (ул. Октябрьской Революции); enter from the courtyard. Meet and greet local Russian youths at the bar or on the dance floor (open Wed.-Sun. from 10pm). Flyers in all the hotels with a map and directions (in Russian).

NORTH RUSSIA AND KARELIA

Karelia, one of the sovereign republics of the Russian Federation, is an enormous region between St. Petersburg and the Arctic Circle, largely consisting of forest and lakes—60,000 lakes, the two largest of which, Ladoga and Onega, are the largest in Europe and second in Russia only to the great Baikal. The Karelians are descendents of the Finns and consider themselves autonomous from, and more civilized than and cultured than the Russians. Signs are often in both Russian and Finnish, and the capital city, Petrozavodsk, has a distinctly Scandinavian feel.

The region is easily accessible by a night train from St. Petersburg, and its clean air and pristine beaches and waters will lure the city-weary traveler from Peter's gateay. Besides Petrozavodsk, Karelia boasts Kizhi Island, a restored village with some of the oldest wooden churches in Russa, an easy ferry ride from Petrozavodsk. The whole region makes for a nice one- or two-day excursion from St. Petersburg when the smog and cigarette smoke are threatening to give you premature emphysema.

■■■ PETROZAVODSK
(ПЕТРОЗАВОДСК)

With its clean(er) air, small, quiet streets, and (relatively) well-kept buildings, Petrozavodsk is Russia's answer to a New England town—down to the Ben & Jerry's store in the center. Founded in 1703—the same year as St. Petersburg—Petroza-vodsk ("Peter's Factory") was originally a foundry and armaments plant for the Tsar. Later, it was used as a place to exile misbehaving intellectuals and disfavored politi-cians by both the Tsars and the Bolsheviks. Now, it is mostly a stopping-off point for an ice-cream cone, some R&R, and a quiet stroll on Kizhi Island. There is also a **Fine Arts Museum** with a good collection of icons from the churches in Kizhi, as well as an eclectic array of 19th- and 20th-century paintings from the region (open Tues.-Sun. 11am-6pm).

ORIENTATION AND PRACTICAL INFORMATION

As of June 1994, Petrozavodsk had not undergone the frenzy of street name-chang-ing that makes Moscow and St. Petersburg lessons in Russian pre-revolutionary his-tory. However, this may have changed by 1995; be alert in obtaining a map.

Tourist Office: Intourist, in the Hotel Severnaya (Гостиница Северная) on Ploschad Lenina. The place to **exchange currency** as well as purchase train tickets from a *kupé* wagon if the *kassas* by the station are out (which they probably will be). One way to Petersburg around US$20. Also offers guides to the city (US$4) and **tours** (min. 15 people) to **Martsialyne Vody,** Russia's first mineral spa, and a nature reserve and waterfall at **Kivach.** Open daily 10am-6pm.

Telephones: ul. Sverdlova 31(ул. Свердлова). Keep going on pr. Lenina past the Hotel Severnaya, take the next right on ul. Andropova (ул. Андропова), then left on Sverdlova. Buy 300R tokens for intercity calls. Open daily 6am-2am. Try making international call from the Severnaya Hotel—Intourist sells cards. "Pay" phones on the street are free. **City Code:** 814.

Post Office: ul. Sverdlova 29 (ул. Свердлова). Open daily 10am-2pm and 3-5pm.

Trains: The train station stands at the head of pr. Lenina (пр. Ленина), which runs into pl. Lenina. From there, take pr. Marxa (пр. Маркса) to the ferry dock to get to Kizhi. If you can't get return tickets in St. Petersburg (which is often), try the tourist office (see above), rather than here; the station usually just has third class seats available, which are unsafe.

ACCOMMODATIONS

Hostel "Nicely" ("Ники"), ul. Titova 3 (ул. Титова), (tel. 144 88). Take trolleybus #3 from the train station to Titova, or walk down pr. Lenina to ul. Kuibisheva (ул. Куйбишева) and take a right; then go left at Titova. The building is in the middle of the block; enter through the front door and follow the "Nicky" (Ники) signs. Two rooms and a kitchen in the basement, with room for eight. No shower. US$8-15, depending on what's included. US$10 with breakfast. Reservations required. Nicki, the proprietor, speaks English.

Hotel Severnaya (Северная), pl. Lenina (пл. Ленина), (tel. 749 67). Russian standard issue hospital-green corridors, and a large number of old women cleaning everything with wet rags. No English spoken. Reception open 24 hrs. Rooms are clean and airy and come with TV, phone, showers, and toilet. A few singles 49,000R. Mostly doubles 66,000R. Call for reservations.

Hotel Karelia (Карелия), nab. Gyullinga 2 (наб. Гюллинга) (tel. 588 97), a 5-min. walk from the ferry dock. Head down Prospect Marxa from Ploschad Lenina, turn right on ul. Lunacharskovo, pass the fountain, and take the first left directly overlooking the water. A pink 10-story building with spectacular views. Reception open 24 hrs. Small rooms with TV and telephone. Primitive bathrooms, but the shower, sink and toilet all work. Singles 52,500R. Doubles 70,000R. Triples 94,500R. Sauna and breakfast included.

Hotel Sovmin, ul. Sverdlova 10 (ул. Свердлова), (tel. 756 61). From pr. Lenina, right on Andropova, then the first left onto Sverdlova and down two blocks. Renovated in March '94, this Finnish hotel is a sign of a changing Russia. Tastefully decorated large rooms with modern TV and telephone. Absolutely spotless white bathrooms (no carpeting and immaculate floors). Cleanliness is next to godliness but also close to unaffordable. Singles 73,000R, subsequent nights 49,200R. Doubles 129,150R, subsequent nights 86,100R.

FOOD

Petrozavodsk has the usual collection of grimly basic (and basically grim) Russian restaurants, the shining, glorious exception being Ben & Jerry's, where you can get Vermont's Finest for rubles. Don't tell your mom we said this, but if you eat anywhere else, you're being silly. **The Central Market** (Центральный Рынок) is on ul. Antikaynena (ул. Антикайнена), a left turn off pr. Lenina two blocks from the train station. In the summer, you can find a good assortment of fruits and veggies—cherries, bananas, tomatoes, etc. Good for picnic supplements, or some vitamins to go with your ice cream (open daily 8am-6pm; closed the second Mon. of the month).

Ben and Jerry's, Krasnaya ul. (Красная ул.), on the corner of ul. Andropova (ул. Андропова). From the train station, go left on Krasnoarmeyskaya ul. (Красноармейская ул.) and take the first right (Krasnaya ul.) and walk five blocks. Housed in a former Pioneer (boy and girl scouts) Palace, but you'll recognize the painted cows. Just the basics: chocolate, cappucino, mint, blackberry, but sooooo good and very cheap. The ice-cream and waffle cones are made on the premises. There's even a "No Smoking. It affects the flavor of our ice cream." sign. Small cone 550R. Double in waffle cone 800R (about US$0.40). They're less expensive than the Mars and Snickers ice cream bars you can get everywhere on the street for 1500R. T-shirt 8000R. Open Tues.-Sun. 11am-8pm.

Petrovsky Restaurant (Ресторан Петровский). Just off pr. Marxa on Andropov street; take a left as you face the ferry dock. Traditional Karelian cuisine (which doesn't seem that much different from the Russian stuff). Entrees 2000-5000R. There's also a dance floor. Popular among locals. Open noon-5pm and 7pm-2am.

Severnaya Hotel Restaurant, at the Hotel Severnaya. Serves breakfast for 3000-5000R, with seatings at 8 and 9am. Dinner is standard Russian fare—sausages, mayonnaise-oriented salads, etc. Entrees 2000-3000R. Open noon-5pm and 7pm-2am.

Hotel Karelia Restaurant, at the Hotel Karelia. Entrance off the street, to the right of the lobby entrance. Cheaper than the Severnaya, but colder and more industrial atmosphere. Entrees 2000-3000R. Open 1-5pm, 7pm-1am.

■ NEAR PETROZAVODSK: KIZHI ISLAND (КИЖИ)

Kizhi, a small undisturbed island serving as an outdoor museum of 18th century wooden architecture, is the main reason to go to Petrozavodsk. An ancient pagan ritual site which drew Russian Orthodox colonizers in the 12th century, the five-kilometer-long island still shimmers with mysticism. Covered in tall grass and Queen Anne's lace, Kizhi is essentially a nature reserve, where while strolling over the green hills or along the banks of the placid lake you'll see only the occasional wooden hut, church, or windmill, all part of the museum's display.

The southern part of this hushed island is dotted with wooden buildings, most of them moved here from the Medvezhye region around Lake Onega; you must pay to enter this "museum," but once on the premises, you are free to explore both the architecture and the natural beauty of what the Karelians call "our Greece." The most striking church, **Preobrazhensky Sobor** (Cathedral of the Transfiguration) and its 22 domes, all of unpainted wood, are visible from afar. Unfortunately, entry is prohibited; it must be left in peace so it will (unfortunately) decay slowly. Despite UNESCO protection, not one expert has figured out how to restore the church, built in 1714 (allegedly) without nails. Another church, the child-size 14th-century **Church of the Resurrection of Lazans,** was moved here from the former Murom monastery and may be the oldest wooden building in all of Russia—reason enough to stare in awe. Although most of the other buildings—a windmill, sauna, barn, etc.—are closed to inspection, three **peasant houses,** directly out of a Yiddish fairytale, are filled with peasant possessions.

The house of **"Wealthy Peasant Osheuner"** is a traditional "koshel" home. It is quite dark inside. Be careful of banging your head on the doorways; Wealthy Peasant Osheuner and his less wealthy neighbors were obviously very short. The houses of **"Average Peasant Yelizarov"** and **"Poor Peasant Shchepin"** look strikingly similar to Osheuner's—but note well, there are differences. A leisurely walk, including a relaxing picnic in the grass (beware of snakes) or on a dock should take about three hours—exactly the amount of time between when a ferry arrives and departs (open noon-5pm and 7pm-2am; admission 4000R, Russians 800R, students 100R).

In **Petrozavodsk,** to get to the ferry walk all the way down Prospect Marxa (пр. Маркса) to the lake. You can take a short cut through the amusement park playground, complete with ferris-wheel and mini-rollercoaster. Buy tickets in the big white building on the right. The schedules are confusing; walk up to the ticket booth and read the signs behind it (you want the one that reads КИЖИ). Although Velikaya Guba indicates that it goes to Kizhi, you don't want that one. Once on the island, the "museum" is a two-minute walk; follow the other passengers—there is only one way to go (ferries run mid-May-mid-November at a frequency determined by the whim of some higher power; 90min., round-trip 7800R).

KALININGRAD (КАЛИНИНГРАД)

Fate and a naval base have conspired to leave the region of Kaliningrad a part of Russia, yet estranged from the rest of the country by 150km of Lithuania. This separation anxiety is not new for the region; between the two World Wars, East Prussia remained part of Germany yet separated from the rest of the country by Poland's corridor to the sea. The aptness of this enclave smacks of socialist surrealism.

■ ■ ■ KALININGRAD (КАЛИНИНГРАД)

Originally in the driver's seat of the German state of Prussia, Kaliningrad was appropriately called Königsberg (King's City) from the 13th century until 1945. In World War II, British bombs, followed by a Red Army invasion, leveled the once-beautiful city. After the war, Stalin, in a rare display of gratitude, renamed the city after his faithful henchman, Kalinin, and then annexed it to Russia. Very little remains today from seven centuries of German rule; the few buildings that weren't destroyed in the war were torn down. Even the Germans who once lived here have disappeared, either killed in the war, deported to West Germany in 1948, or exiled to Siberia. Today Kaliningrad is a very Russian city, and nothing like the Teutonic town that gave rise to Kant. It was only opened to tourists in 1991, and for good reason (by Soviet standards): Kaliningrad, once home to over 500,000 Russian troops and the Baltic Sea Fleet, was one of the most heavily militarized cities in the world during the Cold War, and today the Russians and their base remain.

ORIENTATION AND PRACTICAL INFORMATION

The only way you'll make it around Kaliningrad is to take along a compass and a native. The two currently available maps are as useless as the red string in a Band-Aid wrapper. The orange-colored "Туристская Схема Кёнигсберг Калининград" (*Turistskaya Skhema Kyonigsberg Kaliningrad*; 700R) is marginally better, but be warned that the cartographers for both have loose definitions of left and right. The bus and southern train stations sit at the south end of **Leninski Prospect** (Ленинский Проспект), which runs north across the river and the island with the old cathedral; it continues through **Tsentralnaya Ploschad** (Центральная Площадь) and past the hideous House of Soviets, ending at **Ploschad Pobedy** (Площадь Победы), the central square graced by a statue of Lenin and the northern train station. From this square, **Prospect Mira** (Проспект Мира) runs west past the zoo, while **Ulitsa Chernyakhovskovo** (Улица Черняховского) runs east past the market to the amber museum.

Tourist Office: Given all the German tourists here, you'd expect there to be one. Try the desk workers in the **Hotel Kaliningrad,** on the north end of Tsentralnaya pl. (Центральная пл.); they can often answer basic questions.

Currency Exchange: The best rates are in the booth (somewhat hidden) at the central market, on the left as you go in. Other booths are scarce, but there's one in the Hotel Kaliningrad, just north of the Leninski pr. (Ленинский пр.) bridge.

Post Office: Ul. Leonova 22 (ул. Леонова), in a residential, out-of-the-way spot. Take tram #1 past the zoo one stop, then hike north. Open Mon.-Fri. 9am-8pm, Sat.-Sun. 10am-6pm. No stamps sold on Sundays. **Postal Code:** 236006.

Telephones and Telegraph: The central telephone/telegraph office is through the back entrance of the post office on ul. Leonova. Open 24hrs. **City Code:** 0112.

Flights: The airport is located 20km north of the city; take the special "Аэропорт" (*Aeroport*) bus from the main bus station for 1500R. SAS and Lufthansa are scheduled to begin flights to Kaliningrad in the fall of 1994, but for the moment, only Aeroflot (tel. 44 66 66) comes here. To: Moscow (usually 2 per day, depending on fuel, demand, availability of sober pilots, and such; US$150).

Trains: Two stations in K-grad. **Cheverny Vokzal** (Чеверный Вокзал; north station), just north of pl. Pobedy, behind the big pink building, is almost exclusively for

trains going to the Baltic coast. To: Svetlogorsk (480R); Zelenogradsk (400R).
Uzhny Vokzal (Ужный Вокзал; south station), on the south side of pl. Kalinina,
handles most international arrivals/departures. For train information, tel. 005. To:
Rīga (1 every other day, 12hrs.; 16,000R); Berlin (1 per day, 12hrs.; 170,000R);
Moscow (5 per day, 19hrs.; 60,000R); Minsk (4 per day; 10hrs.; 32,000R).
Buses: The bus station is east of the Uzhny Vokzal on pl. Kalinina. For station info,
tel. 004. To: Grodno (1 per day, 10hrs.; 11,400R); Vilnius (1 per day, 8hrs.;
12,100R); Klaipeda (4 per day, 4hrs.; 5800R). Most buses to Klaipeda travel via
Sovietsk, but 1 per day goes up the Curonian Spit, via Neringa. Tickets for buses
to Poland only at window 11, from the firm **Kyonig-afto** (Кёниг-авто) (tel. 46 03
16). Window open daily 6am-4:30pm and 6:30-10pm. To: Gdansk (2 per day,
7hrs.; 12,000R); Warsaw (1 per day, 8½hrs.; 18,500R).
Ferries: Mercuri Co., has a boat to Kiel, Germany (dep. Fri. midnight, dep. Kiel
Thurs. 2pm; 14hrs.; 300DM each way).
Public Transportation: Trams and buses roam the streets in obscure, arcane patterns, charging 100R per ride (buy blocks of ten tickets on the bus or at some
kiosks). Tram #10 runs through most of the city, from the bus station up past the
Central Market; tram #1 runs east-west from past the zoo towards the market.
Taxi: Taxis stand at every major square, especially around the train stations, the
zoo, and pl. Pobedy. A cross-city ride at night in the rain when the driver knows
you're a foreigner still shouldn't cost more than US$5.
Pharmacy: Apteka (Аптека), Leninski pr. 63/67. Rather modern compared to
other stores in Kaliningrad. Open Mon.-Sat. 8am-8pm, Sun. 10am-7pm.
Emergencies: Fire: tel. 01; **Police:** tel. 02; **Ambulance:** tel. 03.

ACCOMMODATIONS

Hotels in K-grad play a simple zero sum game; the owner will always win and you'll
always lose. Hotels have quickly realized that foreigners (read: suckers) will pay
US$100 per night for (sub)standard Soviet rooms.

The same company that organizes buses to Poland from Kaliningrad is taking a
run at the hotel business. The **Hotel Kyonigavto** (Кёнигавто) opened in late 1994 at
Moskovski pr. 184 (tel. 46 76 52). No information on rates was available at press
time. If none of the options listed below appeal to you, hop a train to Svetlogorsk, a
sea-side holiday town just 30 minutes north of the city. Hotels and sanatoria abound
there, some of which are willing to take foreigners.

Hotel Moskva (Гостиница Москва; *Gostinitsa Moskva*), pr. Mira 19 (tel. 27 20 89).
   Strangely, the Moskva has yet to raise prices for foreigners, making this the obvious choice for the budget traveler. Dreary, somewhat musty rooms are brightened by a TV. Located not far off pl. Pobedy, a short walk from most sites. Singles
   with shared bath 15,000R, with private bath 27,000R. Doubles with shared bath
   30,000R, with private bath 54,000R.
Hotellschiff Hansa, Naberezhnaya Bagramyana 6 (наб. Баграмянь tel. 43 37 37). The
   hotel is an old Volga River cruise ship that mysteriously ended up moored just
   west of the Leninski pr. bridge. Hordes of German tourists all eager to pay DM90
   for cramped singles with teensy bath/shower. More cramped doubles DM160.
   For "luxury" rooms (an extra three cubic meters of space), add DM30. Great location and buffet breakfast (costs extra).
Hotelschiff Baltcompany, nab. Bargamyana 10 (tel. 46 16 04). One kilometer
   downriver from the Hansa, the rooms are identical on this sister ship, but you
   don't need Deutschmarks to stay here. Singles 98,100R. Doubles 125,500R.
Hotel Patriot (Гостиница Патриот; *Gostinitsa Patriot*), ul. Ozernaya 25-a (ул. Озер-
   ная; tel. 27 50 23). Far from the center, but a definite second choice if the *Moskva*
   is full. Take tram #6 or 10 from pl. Pobedy north along ul. Gorkovo until you cross
   the bridge over the railroad tracks. Ozernaya is the first street back from the tram
   stop—walk about 200m and turn right at house #25. The hotel is just past the gun
   club. Shared showers and toilets. Singles 35,000R. Doubles 50,000R.

FOOD

Pickings are a bit slim in K-grad. Luckily there's the **central market** (Центральный Рынок; *Tsentralny Rynok)* up on ul. Chernyakhovskovo, at the intersection with ul. Gorkovo (open 9am-6pm daily). The huge halls of this market were built for a 1930s trade exhibition, but are now crammed with merchants from Baku and their fruits. The **Universam** (Универсам) grocery store does a reasonable impersonation of a supermarket at ul. Moskovski 63, just north of the river (open daily 9am-9pm).

Restoran Belarus (Ресторан Беларусь), ul. Zhitomirskaya 44 (ул. Житомирская), to the west of Tsentralnaya pl. A throwback to the Evil Empire, this place serves up some of the meanest *stroganoff* and *salat* around. Main courses 4000-9000R, soups and salads about 2000R. Don't miss the *solyanka,* flavored with olives, lemon, peppers, and other influences from the Georgian chef (1550R, and worth every kopeck). Live music most nights, MTV otherwise. Open daily noon-11pm.

Stadthaus Club, on the side of the History/Art Museum facing ul. Shevchenko. We think the combo of *Schnitzel* (4000R) and *borscht* (1700R) symbolizes Königsberg coming to terms with Kaliningrad, or maybe it's just to make the German tourists feel a little more at home. A dark, underground atmosphere. Main courses are pseudo-German, but the rest are solidly Russified. Open daily noon-6am.

Italy Bar, Leninski pr. 27/31, just south of the Mother Russia statue. An upscale pizzeria with Russian staples (e.g. fried potatoes, fried pork, black bread, and cabbage) and western prices. Pizza 5500R, bouillon 3500R, Pepsi 2000R. Immensely popular, especially with the Baltic Sea Fleet officers who come here daily to pinch the waitresses. Open daily 10am-midnight.

Restorans Moskva, in Hotel Moskva. The cheapest place in town for a solid meal: soup, two salads, juice, coffee, bread & butter, and beef stroganoff runs about 4800R. Goofy fake stained-glass windows make the setting pleasant enough. Open daily noon-5pm and 6-11pm.

Pinguin, Leninski pr. 95, on the south side of the bridge. Ice cream 2000R. Coffee 300R. Vodka 1000R. Open daily 10am-10pm.

SIGHTS

Kaliningrad's once-pretty *prima donna* is the old **cathedral,** located on the large island in the Pregolya River at the city center. Its scarred, burnt-out shell stands as both a reminder of Königsberg's German heritage, and as a monument to the Russian conquest of the city. Plans to perform plastic surgery (currently in progress) may lend the old church a third metaphor, the reflection of the heavy flow of German tourist money into the city. First built in the mid-14th century, a fire in the 1540s left the city without the funds for complete restoration; only one of the two towers on the west facade was rebuilt, leaving the cathedral with a definite "personality." Tombs line the walls of the cathedral, but many have been vandalized or eroded over time. One grave that has been immaculately kept is that of **Immanuel Kant,** the famous 18th-century German philosopher who lived his whole life in Königsberg. Kant's tomb was originally a much less gaudy affair, but since World War II it has been surrounded by several pink marble colonnades, making the tomb eerily evocative of Lenin's Tomb in Moscow.

Just north of the cathedral, Leninski pr. widens out into **Tsentralnaya pl.,** another spot endowed with a Soviet symbolism. Since 1255, when the Teutonic knights first arrived in this area, a castle had stood on the hill just east of the square. Following the Russian conquest in 1945, a concerted effort was made to turn Königsberg into a truly Soviet city. At the height of this orgy of Sovietization, the 700-year old Königsberg Castle was blown up in 1962 to make way for the Kaliningrad's **House of Soviets,** an H-shaped monstrosity that, after 30 years, still hasn't been completed and likely never will be. Be sure to save a photo (but be careful not to crack your lens) of this poured-concrete paean to soulless Soviet architecture.

Ul. Shevchenko runs along the north side of the House of Soviets, hugging the eastern rim of **Prud Nizhni** (Пруд Нижний), the smaller of two lakes famous in German times as the cultural center of the city. About halfway up the length of the lake is the **Museum of History and Art** (Историко-Художественный Музей; *Istoriko-Khu-dozhestvenny Muzey);* the second floor is devoted to the glorious Soviet army and its heroic conquest of the depraved German city of Königsberg in 1945. There is also a newer, less bombastic display on the recent war in Afghanistan. Rotating exhibits of modern Russian/former-Soviet-Union artists make up the third floor (open Tues.-Sun. 11am-6pm; admission 1200R, Russians 300R). Further north, ul. Shevchenko ends right across the street from where the **Amber Museum** (Музей Янтаря; *Muzey Yantarya)* encases thousands and thousands of gleaming pieces of amber, the bulk of which is modern jewelry but includes some typically Soviet sculptures from the Amber-mining Collective of the Kaliningrad Oblast. More than 90% of the world's amber is gleaned every year here in a process explained in the museum. Magnifying glasses line the walls, allowing a closer look at insects and other specimens—just like in *Jurassic Park* (open Tues.-Sun. 10am-6pm; admission 1200R, locals 300R). The museum is housed in one of the seven remaining **City Gates** of old Königsberg; the other six are all different in style, and are worth seeing only if you're a fan of Gothic brick monuments badly in need of repair.

Off Leninski pr., on the first street north of Tsentralnaya pl., a courtyard garden in front of the University of Kaliningrad stands in front of the **Bunker Museum** (Музей Блиндаж; *Muzey Blindazh),* the network of rooms from which the German command directed the defense of Königsberg in 1945. The museum presents the conquest of the city in great detail; unlucky Room 13 has been left exactly as it was when the German commander of the city signed the surrender to the Red Army (open daily 10am-5:30pm; admission 1200R, Russians 300R). The Kaliningrad City **Zoo** is on pr. Mira, across from the Gostinitsa Moskva. See well-fed **lions** here (but don't put your arms into the cage; open daily 9am-8pm; admission 300R).

ENTERTAINMENT AND NIGHTLIFE

There are several theaters in town. The **Puppet Theater** (Театр Кукол; *Teatr Kukol)* in the Kalinin Park of Culture and Rest (ПКиО) is two stops past the zoo on tram #1 or 4. The turn-of-the-century Luise Church caters to the kindergarten crowd (box office open Mon.-Fri. 10am-5pm; tickets 500R). **Organ concerts** are frequently given in the large brick church at ul. В. Khmelnitskovo 63-а (ул. Б. Хмельницкого), just a couple blocks east and north of the south train station. Prices and times vary; check posters for information. There's also the **Russian Drama Theater** (Драматический Театр; *Dramaticheski Teatr),* at pr. Mira 4, in the Weimar-era theater, behind the statue to Schiller, just east of the zoo. Performances are only in Russian; check at the box office for times and prices (open Mon.-Fri. 10am-5pm).

Nightlife in good ol' Königsberg was a lot livelier (it was depraved, remember?) than it is in modern Kaliningrad. That said, there are still a few good discos in town.

Diskoteka Vagonstra (Дискотека Вагонстра), on ul. Radischeva (ул. Радищева), is currently the favored hangout for the *glitterati* of the oblast. In a cavernous, unmarked grey building that could at one time have been a movie theater, church, or elementary school. Presumed mafiosi rub shoulders with students and soldiers and shimmy to the Pet Shop Boys until dawn. Take tram #1 or 4 five stops west past the zoo, and go down ul. Vagonstroitelnaya (Вагонстроительная), the street immediately behind the tram as you get off. The first street on the right is ul. Radischeva. Cover Sun.-Wed. 5000R, Thurs.-Sat. 7000R; women pay less. Open Sun.-Wed. 10pm-5am, Thurs.-Sat. 8pm-whenever.

Penta Club (Пента Клуб), in the old sky-blue stock exchange at the foot of the Leninski pr. bridge. Chiefly a hangout for the under-20 set, but foreigners make for popular dance partners there. Cover 2000R. Open Fri.-Sat. 6-10pm.

■ NEAR KALININGRAD

ZELENOGRADSK

The Baltic shore north of Kaliningrad is dramatic; high hills run right up to the sea, where pine trees and salt air smell like Glade room freshener. Zelenogradsk (Зеленоградск) sits 30km north of Kaliningrad at the base of the Curonian Spit (Куршская Коса), the 2-km wide, 100-km long peninsula of sand that stretches up into Lithuania. Known as Cranz when this region was still part of German East Prussia, from the mid-1960s Zelenogradsk was one of the most popular holiday destinations in the Soviet Union. Even now it is still the most popular spot for Kaliningraders to go to the beach; on weekends, it can be hard to find a spot on the wide, soft sand. Still, the loss of tourism to the city has been dramatic since the breakup of the Soviet Union, and the beautiful beach is somewhat marred by a backdrop of abandoned and half-completed buildings along the boardwalk. There is no denying, though, that this is the spot in the oblast to come to for a good day of sun and surf.

Take one of the approximately 25 trains per day (320R) from Kaliningrad's North Station (Северный Вокзал); some of these originate at the South Station (400R). Just north of the station is the town **bus** stop, where you can catch a bus up the Curonian Spit towards Lithuania, but only as far as "Дюни" (*Dyuni*), about 6km south of the Lithuanian border town of Nida (2 per day, 2hrs.; 500R; see Lithuania page 353 for info. on the Lithuanian section of the Spit). The Zelenogradsk **market** is right behind the station; walk through and pick up supplies before heading to the beach. On the other side of the market, the **post office** licks 'em and sticks 'em in a nondescript grey concrete building (open Mon.-Sat. 9am-5pm). **Store luggage** at the train station in Zelenogradsk in lockers (300R, or two 15-kopeck coins if you have them). Turn left at the post office and follow the street north through a small square and you'll reach the beach right at the central part of the **boardwalk,** next to the **Restoran Priboy** (Ресторан Прибой), which has an inexpensive cafeteria downstairs and a café on the upstairs balcony. The beach to the right on the boardwalk is better; if you go far enough past the end, you'll arrive at the **nude bathing** area.

SVETLOGORSK

Svetlogorsk (Светлогорск) was known as **Rauschen** (disturbance) in German times for good reason; it was *the* premier resort for fashionable Königsbergers. The town somehow escaped the heavy hand of Soviet architecture, and still retains much of its old German flavor, with tree-lined streets and *fin-de-siècle* villas set on high coast-hugging dunes. Buses from Kaliningrad are rare, but **trains** arrive every 20 minutes from North Station (400R). There are two train stations in Svetlogorsk, but they're only a kilometer apart; Svetlogorsk II is closer to the beach. From Svetlogorsk II, there's a chairlift to the left down to the sand (200R). From Svetlogorsk I, wander down the forested path just past the station to pr. Kaliningradski, in front of the GAI (traffic police) station. Another road, ul. Gagarina, leads steeply uphill from behind the small gas station just west of the GAI. Where ul. Gagarina meets ul. Oktyabrskaya, you'll find the town **telephone office** (open daily 10am-5pm); the **telephone city code** is 253. Behind it is the **post office,** at ul. Octrovskovo 3 (open Mon.-Fri. 8:30am-5pm, Sat. 8:30am-2pm). Walking down ul. Oktyabrskaya will lead you through the central district of the city, and eventually to the beach.

If you find yourself smitten with a desire to stay in Svetlogorsk, there are good-sized, airy rooms available in the **Pansionat Kaliningradskovo Morskovo Torgovovo Porta** (Пансионат Калининградского Морского Торгового Порта), ul. Lenina 48-а (tel. 35 27), west of Svetlogorsk II station, a one-time sailors' sanatorium. (Doubles 22,000R, with bath 30,000R.)

To the right of Svetlogorsk II is the **Restoran Yantar** (Ресторан Янтарь), where you can get some excellent *shashlik* (4800R) at their outdoor café (open daily noon-6pm and 7pm-2am). The town **market** (open daily 8am-3pm) is right behind the town **Pinguin,** ul. Oktyabrhskaya 18 (ice cream 500R; open daily 8:30-am-9pm). There's an inexpensive eatery just past Pinguin, attached to a place known simply as the **Bar** (Бар). Pancakes with butter, a soda, and some boullion comes to about 534R (open daily 10am-6pm). Across the street, the old *Jugendstil* town water tower and bathhouse stand out as symbols of the Kaliningrad region.

SLOVAKIA (SLOVENSKO)

US$1 = 31.35SK (Koruny)	10SK = US$0.32
CDN$1= 22.94SK	10SK = CDN$0.44
UK£1 = 49.18SK	10SK = UK£0.20
IR£1 = 48.26SK	10SK = IR£0.21
AUS$1 = 23.35SK	10SK = AUS$0.43
NZ$1 = 17.04SK	10SK = NZ$0.59
SAR1 = 8.83SK	10SK = SAR1.13
DM1 = 20.39SK	10SK = DM0.49
Country Code: 42	International Dialing Prefix: 00

Survivor of centuries of nomadic invasions, Hungarian domination, and Soviet industrialization, Slovakia has emerged triumphant as an independent country. Natural wonders cover the map: the mountainous and forested north slopes into the gorgeous landscapes of central Slovakia. Hiking and skiing are national pastimes. The countryside is dotted with castle ruins, relics of the defense against Tartars and Turks. In the smaller towns, even suburban factories have not destroyed the old-time atmosphere. Take a deep draught of Slovak wine, put on the hiking boots, and enjoy the freedom.

SLOVAKIA ESSENTIALS

Citizens of the U.S. and Ireland can visit Slovakia visa-free for up to 90 days, and citizens of the U.K. for up to 180 days. Citizens of Australia, Canada, New Zealand and South Africa need visas (US$20 for single-entry; US$47 for multiple-entry; payable money order; cash or personal check accepted if applying in person). Apply by mail, in person or at the border (additional fee involved). See Essentials: Embassies and Consulates, page 3.

GETTING THERE AND GETTING AROUND

The main Slovak **railway** starts in Košice and ends in Bratislava; international links to Hungary, Austria, and Poland (but not the Czech Republic) are 35% cheaper for students. EastRail is valid in the Slovak Republic; Eurail is not. **ŽSR** is the national train company; every information desk has a copy of **Cestovný poriadok** (58SK), the master schedule. *Odchody* (departures) and *príchody* (arrivals) are on the left and right sides respectively, of schedules and posters, but be sure to check revolving timetables, as the train platform (*nástupište*) often changes from the one listed. A reservation (*miestenka*, 6-7SK) is required for international voyages (including the Czech Republic), *expresný* trains, and first-class seats, but not for domestic *rychlík* (fast), *spešný* (semi-fast), or *osobný* (local) trains. Buy a reservation at the boxed-R counter before you buy a ticket. The Czechoslovak **bus** company, **ČSAD,** still operates and publishes a master schedule; it's generally easier to let the information desk decipher it. **Bicycling** is popular; **hitchhiking** is legal, but Let's Go does not recommend it as a safe means of transportation.

TOURIST SERVICES

The former Czechoslovak travel bureau **ČEDOK** is rapidly disappearing in Slovakia and is being replaced with various professional travel companies, often with **Satur.** The former Czechoslovak travel bureau for youth CKM has been renamed **CKM Slovakia** and still operates in most areas. Many small private travel agencies (*cestovná kancelária*) have emerged, among which is **Slovakoturist,** but it dedicates more effort into arranging package tours to Italy and Croatia for wealthy Slovaks than into helping foreign budget travelers.

Everything closes on New Year's Day, Easter Sunday and Monday, Cyril and Methodius Day (July 4), October 28, and Christmas (Dec. 25-26). If a holiday falls on a Sunday, the next day becomes a holiday. The week between Christmas and New Year's is almost void of commerce and public transport.

MONEY

The unit of currency is the **koruna.** The old Czechoslovak and the modern Czech coins and bills are not valid in Slovakia; you must use the shiny new coins and the ugly, hastily-designed Slovak bills. Telephones and ticket machines accept only Slovak coins. You cannot buy Western currency or Czech crowns in Slovakia without a Slovak passport; find a Slovak friend to change your extra koruny back into dollars, deutschmarks, or pounds.

COMMUNICATION AND LANGUAGE

The **mail** service in the Slovak Republic is quite modern; **Poste Restante** mail with a "1" after the city name will arrive at the main post office. Local **telephone** calls cost 2SK; drop the coin in after you've been connected. To reach the **AT&T USA-Direct operator** dial 00 42 00 01 01. To reach the **MCI WorldPhone operator** dial 00 42 00 01 12. To reach the **Canada Direct operator** dial 00 42 00 01 51. To reach the **BT Direct operator** (U.K.) dial 00 42 00 44 01.

The Slovak **language** can be divided into three major dialect groups: Eastern, Central and Western. The Eastern and Western dialects are closer to one another than to the Central dialect. The Eastern dialects have some similarities with Polish (long vowels), while the Western dialects are closer to the Moravian dialects of the Czech language. There are no sharp linguistic frontiers between the dialects of Slovak and Czech—they are all mutually comprehensible. Many Slovaks know German, and English and French are common in Bratislava. The diligent tourist can turn heads with a phrase or two in Slovak:

Word or Phrase	Spelling	Pronunciation
Yes	*Áno*	AH-noh
No	*Nie*	NYEH

Hello	*Ăhoj, Nazdar*	AH-hoy, NAHZ-daar
Today	*Dnes*	dnyehs
Tomorrow	*Zajtra*	ZAY-trah
Good morning	*Dobrý deň!*	DOH-bree den
Good night	*Dobrú noc*	doh-BROO notz
Goodbye	*Do videnia*	DOH vee-dane-yah
Excuse me	*Prepačte mi*	preh-PAHCH-tyeh me
Please	*Prosím*	proh-SEEM
Thank you	*Ďakujem*	DYAK-oo-yem
When?	*Kedy?*	KEH-dih?
Where?	*Kde?*	gdyeh?
Help!	*Pomoc!*	POH-motz!
How much is this?	*Koľko to stojí?*	KOHL-koh toh stoy-eeh?
How do I get to...?	*Ako sa dostanem...?*	ah-koh sah doh-stah-nyem?
My name is ...	*Volám sa...*	Voh-LAHM sah
Do you speak English?	*Hovoríte po anglicky?*	hoh-voh-REE-tyeh poh ahn-GLEETZ-kee?
I don't understand	*Nerozumiem*	nyeh-roh-zoo-myem
Leave me alone; get lost!	*Daj mi pokoj; Zmizni*	day meee poh-koy; zmee-znee

1 — jeden (YEH-den); **2** — dva (dvah); **3** — tri (tree); **4** — štyri (shti-REE); **5** — päť (pehtsh); **6** — šesť (shehstsh); **7** — sedem (SEH-dyem); **8** — osem (OH-sehm; **9** — deväť (DYEH-vyehtsh); **10** — desäť (DYEH-sehtsh); **20** — dvadsať (DVAH-tzatsh); **30** — trridsať(TREE-tzatsh); **40** — štyridsať (SHTI-ree-tzatsh); **50** — päť'desiat (pehtsh-dyeh-syaht); **60** — šesť'desiat (shestch-dyeh-syaht); **70** — sedemdesiat (seh-dyem-dyeh-syaht); **80** — osemdesiat (oh-sehm-dyeh-syaht); **90** — devät'desiat (dyeh-vyehtsh-dyeh-syaht); **100** — sto (stoh); **1000** — tisíc (tee-seetz).

HEALTH AND SAFETY

Visitors are advised not to drink tap water, which is chlorinated and may cause abdominal discomfort. Bottled water is available in grocery stores. Citizens of the U.K. will be glad to know that there is a reciprocal Health Agreement between Slovakia and the U.K. If you are in possession of a U.K. passport, you are entitled to free medical care while traveling in Slovakia (prescribed medication is *not* free of charge, but is fairly inexpensive). The **emergency phone number** is 158.

ACCOMMODATIONS AND CAMPING

In Bratislava, **summertime hostels** open when university students leave; get info at CKM. **Juniorhotels (HI),** though uncommon, are a step above the usual brand of hostel. In the mountains, **chaty** (chalets) range from plush quarters for 400SK per night to a friendly bunk and outhouse for 100SK. **Hotels** in the boonies provide comparable service to those in cities but are much cheaper. **Campgrounds** abound near the country's five national parks but are often open only in summer. A campground map is intermittently available at CKM offices.

LIFE AND TIMES

HISTORY

The Slovaks, like the Croats, were never very powerful but have a distinct history. Slovakia was settled by **Slavs** in the 6th and 7th centuries AD. The Slovaks were incorporated into the Greater Moravian Empire in the 870s, with Bohemia, southern Poland, and what is now western Hungary. The empire converted to Catholicism in 880 but fell to invading Magyars in 906. Slovakia was soon assimilated by the **King-**

dom of Hungary. In the 12th century, a Hungarian king invited German **Saxons** from the Rhineland to help develop the area of the Hungarian kingdom inhabited by the Slovaks. The Saxons founded several *Spiš* towns, including Poprad and Levoča. Though the Hungarians were defeated by the Mongols in 1241, and local rulers, the Csáks, came to rule Slovakia, the Hungarian monarchy regained control in 1308 and ruled Slovakia for another two centuries.

After the Ottomans defeated Hungary at the 1526 **Battle of Mohács,** Slovakia became a bulwark of the West against the Turks. The **Habsburg** emperors, who ruled Hungarian Slovakia between 1526 and 1918, eventually freed all of Hungary from Turkish occupation and by 1700 began to redevelop the region. **Lutheranism** and **Calvinism** had become popular among the German, Slovak and Magyar communities of Slovakia, particularly in the East. The Habsburgs proceeded to restore Roman Catholicism in the lands, leading to Slovakian religious wars of 1603 and 1669-71.

In the 19th century, various national movements emerged in the Kingdom of Hungary. Led by L'udovít Štúr and Jozef Šafárik, the Slovak movement voiced its concerns at **Liptovský Svätý Mikuláš** during the tumultuous **Revolution of 1848,** which brought little change to Slovakia and disaster to their Hungarian overlords. After the Austro-Hungarian *Ausgleich* (Compromise) of 1867, Hungary was proclaimed a political equal of Austria within the Habsburg lands, and resumed control over Slovakia. Slovakia remained one of the most submerged nationalities in the polyglot Austro-Hungarian Empire; without even their own province, they lived under direct Hungarian rule. Ignoring the wise advice of Hungarian intellectuals, the Hungarian government, particularly under Tisza from 1875-90, launched the process of Magyarization, forcing many Slovaks to leave their homeland and alienating those who stayed behind. The Slovak national movement blossomed in this period, but the "Czecho-Slovak National Committee," which had been meeting in Pittsburgh during the war, opted for a joint Czecho-Slovak state. On October 28, 1918, six days before Austria-Hungary sued for peace, Czechoslovakia was proclaimed an independent state, giving Slovakia the greatest degree of self-rule it had known after a millenium of Hungarian rule. At the end of WWI, Slovakia was attached to Bohemia, Moravia, and Sub-Carpathian Ruthenia to form chain-like **Czechoslovakia,** a new state in the heart of Europe, with a federal capital at Prague and regional capital at Bratislava. The state made a good start, repelling an invasion of Slovakia by the Hungarian communist Bela Kun in 1919 and securing withdrawal of Romanian troops from Ruthenia. It became a **liberal democracy** on an American model and one of the world's wealthier nations, and was the sole state in Central or Eastern Europe that did not descend into fascist, authoritarian, or communist rule. Though the policies of the Czechs toward the German and Slovak minorities were relatively liberal, they were often not liberal enough for Slovak nationalist parties. Many Slovaks came to resent what they regarded as Czech domination.

Czechoslovakia was, after Germany, the strongest country in the area, and Hitler had to make it an early target. Abandoned by the British and French at Munich and with Poland and Romania unwilling to permit Soviet assistance, the democratic state could not fight, buckling under German pressure in March 1938. By October 1938, Slovakia proclaimed an autonomous unit within a federal Czecho-Slovak state. After German troops invaded Bohemia and Moravia in March 1939, Slovakia emerged as a nominally independent state under the leadership of **Monseignor Tiso;** in fact it was a collaborative Nazi puppet regime. Authoritarian Hungary took advantage of the difficult position of the formerly prosperous, democratic state; in 1938 Hungary helped itself to about a third of Slovakia. Resentment against the Nazis caused a two-month **uprising** in the summer of 1944.

After the Second World War, Slovakia joined the reconstituted, democratic Czechoslovakia, which the communists were only barely able to subvert, with massive Soviet support, in February 1948. In theory, the 1960 constitution guaranteed Slovakia equal rights, but ever since the communists gained power, many Slovaks felt oppressed by a Czech-dominated government. Post-war Czechoslovakia expelled members of Slovakia's Hungarian and Saxon communities and was forced to cede Ruthenia to the Soviet Union. The Stalinist regime that emerged in Czechoslovakia remained subservient to Moscow until Slovak **Alexander Dubček** introduced his **"Prague Spring"** reforms in 1968. Soviet tanks crushed Dubček's allegedly disloyal government and the country returned to totalitarianism in 1969. With the defeat of the reformist regime, Slovakia acquired increased autonomy and Bratislava was made a "capital city" in 1969. Rural Slovakia underwent heavy industrial development. After the Soviet invasion, the Communists remained in power in Czechoslovakia until the Velvet Revolution of 1989. Václav Havel was appointed President and set about introducing a pluralistic political system and a market economy. In this atmosphere of increased freedom, Slovak nationalism began to gain ground and ultimately triumphed in the 1993 **Declaration of Independence.** Less than four years after Czechoslovakia played a crucial role in burying the Soviet empire, the state ceased to exist, making an independent Slovakia a reality for the first time.

SLOVAKIA TODAY

Today some Slovaks are having second thoughts about independence, but there seems to be no turning back the clock in the fast-paced post-Communist world. In order to cope with a substantial national debt and a largely obsolete heavy-industry, Slovakia has introduced limited privatization methods, but the economy still lags behind that of the Czech Republic.

FOOD AND DRINK

Many **Slovak dishes** resemble those of neighboring Hungary, Austria, and Moravia in the Czech Republic, including the ever-popular *guláš*. A similar dish is the *perkelt,* except it has no cream in the gravy. Viennese-style *Nockerln* (very small fried pieces of dough) or *knedla* (like the Bohemian *knedlík* or Austrian *knödel*) often accompany meat entrees. Native to the mountain regions of Slovakia is *halušky* (potato pasta) with *bryndza*, a ewe's milk cheese. *Viedeňský rezeň* (Wiener schnitzel) is a pork scallopini cutlet fried in a light batter; *lečo* is a spicy but very tasty vegetable concoction. Also popular is Serbian-style pork, which consists of a skewer of spiced pork pieces.

Serve yourself to a cafeteria-style meal at a *bufet, samoobsluha,* or *občerstvenie.* It's fast, but you must eat while standing up. A *kaviarň* serves coffee, tea, and often desserts. *Mliečný* (milk) and *denný* ("day") bars serve Slovak-type fast food; the *denný* bars also serve alcohol and are open during the day, as opposed to *nočný* (night) bars. At a restaurant, always check the bill to make sure you were not overcharged. All grocery stores are closed between Saturday noon and Monday morning. *Potraviny* (grocery stores) and *ovocie zelenina* (greengrocers) pop up on every other corner. Almost every major city has a vegetarian restaurant.

Fine white **wines** are produced in the Small Carpathians to the northeast of Bratislava, especially around the town of Pezinok. *Riesling* and *Müller-Thurgau* grapes are typically used and quality varies greatly. *Tokaj* type of wines are produced in the region to the south of Košice. You can enjoy any of these wines at a local *vináreň* (wine hall). Slovakia also brews some good **beers.** Especially successful are *Stein Danubius* of Bratislava and *Topvar* of Topol'čany—light, flavorful, and well-balanced—as good as a Czech or German beer. A delicious Slovak specialty is *Martiner Porter,* an excellent dark beer. Beers from inner Slovakia, however, are usually rough around the edges and not as easy to drink. Beers such as *Corgoň* from Nitra and *Sitňan* tend to be mediocre; *Zlatý Bažant* is a mass-produced average product. Beer is served at a *pivnica* or at a *piváreň* (beer hall). Lovers of hard drinks and spirits will not be disappointed in Slovakia. The aromatic *marhulovica* is an apricot brandy; *borovička* is a juniper-berry brandy that is distinctly Slovak. Typically Central European *slivovica* (plum brandy) is very good in Slovakia too.

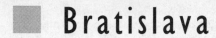

Bratislava

Though giddy with excitement over its recaptured role as cultural center, the debu-tante capital is quickly sobering up to face the country's grown-up economic and political challenges. The streets of the old town are turbulent with reconstruction and renewal and the city's highways and concrete towers defy the sleepy agricul-tural surroundings. But on peaceful Castle Hill, the traffic is distant and the staid cas-tle peers down sternly on the urban roar bellow. In the early 19th century, Bratislava was inhabited by German-speaking Swabians who called the city Pressburg. Later in the century, the city acquired a Hungarian character and was called Pozsony, Prešporok by the Slovaks. Only in 1918 was it christened Bratislava. The city has always loved beer and according to local chronicler Paul Ballus, in 1823 it had over three times as many beer halls per citizen than did neighboring Vienna. Two entire districts of the city once dedicated themselves to the noble art of brewing beer, but they have since been replaced by highways.

ORIENTATION AND PRACTICAL INFORMATION

Bratislava lies on the banks of the Danube, a proverbial stone's throw from the Aus-trian and Hungarian borders. Trains and buses connect the city with Budapest and Vienna; hydrofoils also serve Vienna. Traveling by rail to Prague sometimes requires a change at Brno. Avoid debarking at the *Nové Mesto* train station, which is much farther from the center than Bratislava's *Hlavná stanica* (main station).

The Danube runs west-to-east across Bratislava. The Old Town, with its cluster of tourist offices and restaurants, sits just north of the river bank, bordered by the **Staromestská** highway to the west, **námestie SNP** to the north, **Štúrova** to the east, and **Hviezdoslavovo námestie** to the south. From the train station, take tram #1. Buy tickets (5SK) for the tram from the orange automat machines (near major tram stops). Maps of Bratislava range in price 10-50SK. Make sure to buy a new one that has the accurate post-communist street-names. Lenin, Klement Gottwald, and the Red Army are out of fashion.

Tourist Offices: BIS (*Bratislavská Informačná Service*), Panská 18 (tel. 33 37 15 or 33 43 25). Oodles of information, pamphlets, and **maps** of Bratislava. Open Mon.-Fri. 8am-6pm, Sat. 8am-1pm. **Slovakoturist,** Panská 13 (tel. 33 57 22 or 33 34 66). Colorful glossy pamphlets on Slovakia, few on Bratislava. Open Mon.-Fri. 9am-5pm. **Satur,** Jesenského 9-11 (tel. 36 76 24 or 36 84 06) is a former Čedok office with useful brochures and maps. Open Mon.-Fri. 9am-6pm, Sat. 9am-noon.
Consulates: Czech Republic, Panenská 33, to the northwest of the Old Town. **Hungary,** Palisády 54 (tel. 33 56 01), near Hodžovo námestie. **Poland,** Hum-melova 4 (tel. 31 52 22 or 31 52 20). **Romania,** Fraňa Krála 11 (tel. 49 16 65). **U.S.,** Hviezdoslavovo nám. 4 (tel. 33 33 38), open Mon.-Fri. 8:30am-noon and 2-4pm for regular services. **Austria,** Holubyho 11 (tel. 31 11 03).
Currency Exchange: VÚB Všeobecná Úverová Banka, Poštová at Obchodná; cashes American Express traveler's checks. Open Mon.-Thurs. 8am-5pm, Fri. 8am-noon. Branch in the *Hlavná* train station open daily 7:30am-6pm. **L'udová Banka,** nám SNP 15; cashes AmEx traveler's checks for a reasonable 1% commis-sion. Open Mon.-Fri. 8am-5pm. **Tatra Banka,** Štefánikova 22 (tel./fax 49 53 51) and many other locations in Bratislava. Cashes Thomas Cook traveler's checks at reasonable rates. Open Mon.-Thurs. 8am-noon and 1-3pm, Fri. 8am-1pm.
Post Office: Main office at nám. SNP 35. **Poste Restante** counter #6. Open Mon.-Fri. 7am-8pm, Sat. 7am-6pm, Sun. 9am-2pm. **Postal Code:** 81000 Bratislava 1.
Telephones: The second floor from the *"Telefón Telegram"* entrance of the post office building, nám. SNP 35. Open Mon.-Fri. 7am-8pm, Sat. 7am-6pm, Sun. 9am-2pm. For 24 hr. service, visit the phone office at Kolárska 12. **City Code:** 07.
Trains: The main **train station** *Bratislava Hlavná stanica* is located north of the town at the end of Štefánikova (tel. 469 45). International connections to Vienna

(5 per day), Budapest (4 per day), and Prague (5 per day). International tickets at counter #13, 14 or 15.

Buses: The main **bus station** *autobusová stanica* is located along Mlynské nivy, east of the Old Town at the end of Dunajská (tel. 632 13 or 21 22 22). Connections to Vienna (6 per day), Budapest (2 per day), and Prague (8 per day). Check ticket for bus number (*č. aut.*); several different buses may depart simultaneously.

Taxis: A large private taxi company can be reached at tel. 31 13 11.

Hydrofoils: An interesting way to travel to Vienna or Budapest. The station is next to Slovak National Museum at Fajnorovo náb.

Hitchhiking: *Let's Go* does not recommend hitchhiking as a safe means of transportation. Those hitching to Vienna cross the SNP bridge and walk down Viedenská cesta. The same road takes them to Hungary via Győr, though fewer cars head in that direction. Those headed to Prague take bus #104 from the center up Pražská to the Patronka stop.

24-Hr. Pharmacy: *Lekáreň* at Špitálska 3 (tel. 51 01 14).

Emergencies: Ambulance: tel. 155. **Fire:** tel. 150. **Police:** tel. 158. The station at Mestská sprava VB, Špitálska 14 (non-emergency tel. 593 41 or 531 71).

ACCOMMODATIONS AND CAMPING

Bratislava revels in student accommodations, largely due to the Vienna-bound crowds in the summer. Since the city sprawls along the Danube and penetrates the Small Carpathians, some places are quite far from the Old Town. Most accommodations agencies are helpful and efficient. **Satur Cestovná Kancelária** is at Jesenského 9-11 (see above). Its professional and friendly English-speaking staff arranges rooms in the center for 300SK per person. **CKM Slovakia,** Hviezdoslavovo 16 (tel. 33 16 07 or 33 41 14; fax 33 56 44), arranges accommodations at hostels for 170SK per person. English spoken. (Open Mon.-Fri. 8:30am-5pm.) **BIS Bratislavská Informačná Služba,** Panská 18 (see above), provides several options, including private rooms (singles 500SK, doubles 700SK) located well outside the center and pensions (singles 600SK, doubles 1080SK, triples 1320SK, shower and breakfast included).

Pension Gremium, Gorého 11 (tel. 32 18 18, fax 33 06 53). New in the heart of the Old Town. Reception on 2nd floor open until 2am. German spoken. Singles 640SK, doubles 990SK. Shower and breakfast included. Restaurant and café.

American House, Kremnická 7 (tel. 83 88 90). On the other side of the Danube; take bus #40, 50, 23, or 47 three stops from the center. English spoken. Rooms 300-600SK, breakfast included.

Bernolák Youth Hostel, Bernolákova 1 (tel. 49 77 21). Take trolleybus #210 to Račianské mýto and turn right near a lovely monument. A high-rise student dorm. English spoken. Doubles 234SK, with ISIC 204SK. Call in advance. Open July-Aug.

YMCA na Slovenska, Karpatská 2 (tel. 49 80 05). Old terraced building two blocks down Šancová from the train station. German spoken. Reception open 8am-11pm. Doubles, triples, quints 150SK per person. Open mid-July to mid-Aug.

Mladá Garda, Račianska 103 (tel. 25 31 36). Cheap rooms in the suburbs. Take tram #3 to the Mladá Garda stop. English spoken. Singles 180SK. Doubles 240SK. Open mid-July to mid-August.

Juniorhotel Sputnik CKM (HI), ul. Drienová 14 (tel. 29 41 67 or 23 43 40). Take bus #22 to the seventh stop or tram #8 from train station to the eighth or ninth stop and look for a small lake on your left: across it lies the hotel. Deluxe student lodging. English spoken. Disco, café, and restaurant. Singles 1100SK. Doubles 1700SK. Members and ISIC-holders 450SK. Reservations recommended.

Camping: Motel Zlaté Piesky, ul. Vajnorská (tel. 633 06), in suburban Trnávka. Take tram #2 or 4 to last stop or bus #110 from Trnavské mýto to last stop. Campground and bungalows down by the lakeside, way out of town. Camping 150SK per person. 4-person bungalow 550SK.

FOOD

Bratislavans enjoy stewed meats and superb Slovak wine. Ubiquitous *Denný* bars offer salads, sandwiches, and other ready-to-eat foods. Most eateries in Bratislava fall

SLOVAKIA

into one of two categories—expensive and eager to trap the tourist or very cheap self-serve joints. **AS Potraviny,** at Obchodná 14, is a sizeable grocery store with baked goods, meats, and beer, and some of the most flexible hours in Bratislava (open Mon.-Fri. 6am-7pm, Sat.-Sun. 6:30am-5pm). Fruit stands nearby.

Restaurant Gremium, Gorého 11, second floor (tel. 32 18 18, fax 33 06 53). Expensive, but exquisite. The *guláš* here is sumptuous. Entrees 50-150SK. Open Mon.-Sat. 11am-8pm.

Občerstvenie Polom, Obchodná 8. Cheap but edible self-serve food. Bottles of *Topvar* beer 12 SK. Open daily 8am-6pm.

Zelený Dvor, nám SNP 30 (tel. 36 45 86). An outdoor eatery with sausages, *guláš,* and daily specials from 40-140SK. A half-liter of *Zuzana* dark beer 20SK. Open daily 10am-11pm.

Piváreň U Corgoňa, Mickiewiczova 8. Inexpensive Slovak dishes (40-50SK) in a pub to the east of Old Town. *Corgoň* drafts 13SK. Open Mon.-Sat. 11am-11pm.

Bufet Centrum, Špitálská 9. Outdoor fast-food. Satisfy your hunger pangs for 40SK and wash it all down with a half-liter of *Topvar* (13SK). Open Mon.-Fri. 9am-7pm.

Veľkí Františkání, Františkánske nám 10. Expensive but good. Try the *lečo* or the *Wiener schnitzel*. Entrees 70-170SK, draft *Topvar* 25SK. Open daily 10am-1am.

Piváreň U Eda, Biela 5. Traditional Slovak fare in a beer-pub atmosphere. Meals 40-120SK. *Pilsner Urquell* on tap. Open daily 9am-10pm.

SIGHTS

Bratislava is a mixture of the exquisitely beautiful and the tragically ugly. The **Old Town** is an ensemble of late medieval churches, aristocratic palaces, and burghers' houses. Recently restored and refurbished, it's a pleasure to wander through during the day and crackles with life at night. Outside the Old Town, Bratislava is less impressive. The former Communist regime razed **Schlossberg,** Bratislava's old Jewish quarter, and replaced it with an out-of-place freeway.

The Old Town

Hlavné námestie is the main square of the Old Town. The **Old City Hall** *(Stará radnica)* is a complex of several buildings, the oldest of which are in Gothic style. The distinctive yellow tower is a hallmark of Bratislava; on warm summer evenings, brass bands play popular tunes on its balcony. The courtyard is in particularly good condition; from here you can enter the **Bratislava Municipal Museum** with its fascinating collections of Gothic sculpture, aristocratic furniture, bourgeois mugs, old Slovak books, and 19th-century pub signs. At a reasonable pace, it can be covered in just under an hour (open Tues.-Sun. 10am-4:30pm; admission 10SK, students 3SK).

On the other side of the Old Town Hall is the **Primate's Square** *(Primaciálné námestie),* surrounded by several restored buildings. The most impressive is the Neoclassical **Primate's Palace** *(Primaciálny palác),* where the victorious Napoleon and the temporarily vanquished Austrian Emperor Franz I signed the Peace of Pressburg (1805). Also adjacent to Primate's Square is the **Johann Nepomuk Hummel Museum** *(Múzeum Johanna Nepomuka Hummela)* at Klobučnicka 2, in the house where the composer was born in 1778. A Hungarian-Swabian by birth, Hummel left his native Bratislava for the excitement of Stuttgart and Weimar. The museum houses several displays of Hummel memorabilia that successfully convey what life in Bratislava was like in the 19th century. (Open Tues.-Sun. 10am-5pm; admission 5SK, students 2SK.)

South of Hlavné námestie is the long and wooded **Hviezdoslavovo námestie.** The square is really a park surrounded by pretty 19th-century buildings. Particularly striking is the **Slovak National Theater** *(Slovenské národné divadlo),* a beautifully restored neo-Renaissance building that has hosted performances for over a century. South of Hviezdoslavovo námestie along Mostová is the **Reduta,** an eclectic but grand 19th-century building. Mostová ends at **námestie Štúra,** with its clumsy monument to the namesake of the square. To the east of námestie Štúra is the **Slovak National Museum** *(Slovenské národné múzeum).* It houses archaeological and geological collections illustrating the history of the region, and an exhibit on the Great Moravian Empire. (Open Tues.-Sun. 9am-5pm; admission 6SK, students 3SK.) A walk down Panská from Hlavné námestie leads to **St. Martin's Cathedral** *(Dóm svätého Martina)*, the Gothic church, where Hungarian kings were crowned for three centuries. The locked doors render the church treasures inaccessible to tourists. Across Panská is the **Salvator Pharmacy** *(Lekáreň Gyógyszertár Apotheke Salvator)*, a wonderfully maintained 19th-century building. Next to St. Martin's runs a noisy freeway which separates the Old Town from the castle; it was built by the Communist regime on the ruins of **Schlossberg**, Bratislava's old Jewish district. The freeway crosses the Danube on a modern suspension bridge with a tower that looms over the city.

North of Hlavné námestie is the **Franciscan Church** with a pretty Gothic tower from the 13th century and a more recent interior. The church has a powerful organ that is sometimes heard from the square. From the church, Zámočnícka leads to **Michalská,** the busiest pedestrian street in Bratislava's Old Town. At the north end of the street is the **Michael Tower** *(Michalská brána)* a beautiful and tall Baroque structure that once served as a watchtower.

North of the Michael Tower is **Hodžovo námestie,** a noisy nightmare of traffic and congestion. Down Staromestská on the Konventná side is the former **Evangelical Lyceum,** which has played a significant role in Bratislava's intellectual life and produced several renowned figures in Central European history. Among its students were Slovak leaders Štúr, Kollár, and Šafárik, Swabian writers Eduard Glatz and T. G. Schröer, Hungarian poets Petöfi and Jókai, and Czech historian František Palacký. On the north side of Hodžovo námestie is the **Grassalkovich Palace** *(Grassalkovičov palác),* the grandest of the residences that Hungarian aristocrats maintained in this city. The harmony of the white late-Baroque façade is broken by frequent street lamps and an ugly modern fountain. Behind the castle linger the **Grassalkovich Gardens,** offering escape from the noisy chaos of Hodžovo námestie.

Bratislava Castle (Hrad)

From the banks of the Danube to the historic squares of the Old Town, the four-towered **Castle of Bratislava** remains a visible landmark. Of strategic importance for over a millennium, the castle burned down in 1811, and for many years was nothing more than a romantic ruin. In 1953 it was restored to its 15th-century appearance and housed the leaders of the Slovak Socialist Republic. Today it serves as the meeting place of the Slovak National Assembly and is home to several collections of the **Municipal Museum** *(Mestské Múzeum)* whose rich displays chronicle Slovak history, art, and culture. (Open Tues.-Fri. 9am-5pm, Sat.-Sun. 10am-6pm; admission 40SK, students 12SK.)

ENTERTAINMENT AND NIGHTLIFE

For concert and theater schedules, pick up a copy of *Kám* at BIS. Although not in English, the information is easy enough to decipher. The **Slovak Philharmonic** plays regularly on ul. Palackého; buy tickets at the Reduta office behind the concert hall up to one hour before performances. **National Theatre** tickets are also sold here; the theatre is on Komenského nam. Also look for performances by the internationally-known **Bohdan Warchal Quartet,** based in Bratislava in summer.

Bratislavans prefer the conversation and carousing of a wine pub, beer hall, or café to the flash of a dance club.

Smíchovský Dvor, Mariánska at Heydukova. A popular local beer garden with draft *Staropramen* from Prague (½-liter 18SK). Open Mon.-Sat. 10am-10pm.
Stará Sladovňa, Cintorínska 32. One of Europe's largest beer-halls, housed in a 19th century malthouse. Open daily 10am-11pm.
Vel'kí Františkáni, Františkánske nám 10. A wine-pub in the heart of the Old Town with a Medieval terrace. A ½-liter of *Topvar* 25SK. Open daily 10am-1am.

Záhrada, Obchodná 45. A local beer garden that serves Bratislava's very own *Stein* beer. Open daily until 9pm.

Zelený Dvor, nám SNP 30. Literally the "green court." An outdoor complex that serves beer, wines, spirits, and coffee. Very popular before and after dark. Bottles *Zuzana, Pilsner Urquell,* and *Gemer* beers. Open daily 10am-11pm.

Piváreň U Eda, Biela 5. A beer pub in the Old Town serving *Pilsner Urquell.* Indulge in a few drafts. Open daily until 10pm.

Piváreň U. Corgoňa, Mickiewiczova 8. A local beer hall well outside the Old Town (hence inexpensive!). Corgoň drafts 13SK. Open Mon.–Sat. until 11pm.

■ NEAR BRATISLAVA: DEVÍN CASTLE

The banks of the Danube between Vienna, Bratislava, and Budapest are studded with ruins, castles, and fortresses. A short distance to the west of Bratislava is **Devín Castle (Hrad Devín),** a partly ruined stronghold that continues to overlook the mighty Danube. The village of Devín now resembles a suburb of Bratislava, but the castle remains in its original green entourage. Walks along the Danube provide mighty views of the Castle and are a peaceful alternative to the busy streets of Bratislava. The landscape across the Danube is Austrian. From the Danube just below Bratislava Castle, take bus #29 to the village of Devín. To reach the castle, walk down either Slovanské nábrežie, Hradná, or Brigádnická and cross the greenspace.

■ ■ ■ NOVÉ ZÁMKY

If you are planing a grand tour of Central Europe, chances are you will pass through Nové Zámky. In the east-west direction, the Bratislava-Budapest railway line passes through Nové Zámky, as do trains that connect Berlin and Prague with Bucharest, Arad, and Braşov in Romania. In the north-south direction, Nové Zámky lies on the main railway line that links Budapest to Warsaw, Katowice, and Szczecin in Poland. A brief stop-over en route is enough time to see the sights of Nové Zámky.

An army of apartment blocks now encircles the small historic Old Town, formerly guarded by a six-sided Habsburg fortress. A large Hungarian community calls the city *Éreskujvár,* and many street signs are bilingual. Nové Zámky developed quickly after the Austrian Army liberated it from Turkish rule in the 17th century. Juraj György Széchenyi, the influential bishop of Esztergom, granted Nové Zámky special privileges in 1691 and remains a celebrated figure today. The Habsburg fortress **Neuhäusel** eventually became obsolete and Nové Zámky emerged as an important market town.

ORIENTATION AND PRACTICAL INFORMATION

The city has fewer than 50,000 inhabitants and can easily be covered on foot. To reach the Old Town from the train station, turn left and pass the post office. Turn right on Štefánika and follow it for 5-10 minutes.

Tourist Offices: Satur, Štefánika 2 (tel. 277 36 or 228 28, fax 223 31). The helpful staff offers free **maps** of Nové Zámky and information about the region. German spoken. Open Mon.-Fri. 9am-4pm. **Slovakoturist,** Kukučínova 2 (tel. 262 44, fax 250 98). The Slovak-speaking staff will grudgingly provide a **map** if you're persistent; don't expect further help. Open Mon.-Fri. 8:30am-4:30pm.

Currency Exchange: VÚB Všeobecná Úverová Banka, Hlavné námestie Fötér 5, is the best place in town to change traveler's checks or plain cash. The adjacent *Bankomat* (ATM) is linked to Mastercard and the Cirrus network. Bank open Mon.-Thurs. 8am-noon and 1:30-5pm, Fri. 8am-noon.

Post Office: A convenient *Slovenská Pošta* is next to the train station on Námestie Republiky, open Mon.-Fri. 7am-7pm, Sat. 7am-noon. In the heart of Old Town is another office on Hlavné námestie Fötér, open Mon.-Fri. 7am-7pm, Sat. 7am-1pm.

Telephone City Code: 817.

Trains: The **Žel. stanica** is at námestie Republiky along Bratislavská cesta between Masaryka and Štefánika, a 7-min. walk from the Old Town.
Buses: The **Autobusová stanica** is one block down from the train station along Štúra. Do not be deceived by the old bus platforms near the post office.
Taxis: This town can be covered on foot, but a taxi can be hailed at tel. 266 66. Remember to set a price in advance or risk getting ripped off.
Pharmacy: A **Lekáreň** is on the main square Hlavné námestie Fötér next to the large bank. Open Mon.-Fri. 7:30am-5pm, Sat. 7:30am-noon.
Police: Main building at Bratov Baldigarovcov 7. You can't miss the dozen police vehicles parked in front.

ACCOMMODATIONS

Finding a place to stay in Nové Zámky is neither difficult nor expensive. A one-hour commute from Bratislava, Nové Zámky is a good place to avoid the crowds and scams of Bratislava while remaining close to Slovakia's fine capital city. **Satur,** Štefánika 2 (tel. 277 36 or 228 28, fax 223 31) can fill you in on the latest in inexpensive accommodations in Nové Zámky. German spoken (open Mon.-Fri. 9am-4pm).

Hotel Stardust, Komárňanská Komáromi 3 (tel. 289 56 or 289 89). Reception open 24 hrs. Brand new rooms with toilet, shower, TV, A/C, radio, and telephone. Singles 90SK. Doubles 180SK. Breakfast included.
Hotel Astra, Štefánika 73 (tel 220 70). Small, old, simple rooms at low prices. Reception open 24 hrs. Communal toilets and showers. Singles 130SK. Doubles 230SK. Triples 320SK. Quadruples 400SK. Restaurant on the ground floor.
Hotel Korzo, Rákócziho 12 (tel. 248 45 or 221 62, fax 265 02) in the Old Town. Old. Reception open 24 hrs. Singles 370SK. Doubles 470SK. Breakfast 40SK.

FOOD

Restaurant Mladost, Björnsonova at Bratov Baldigarocov. Inexpensive Slovak and Hungarian dishes under 30SK. Bottled *Topvar* beer 9SK. Open daily 7am-2:30pm.
Stardust Restaurant, Komárňanská Komáromi 3 (tel. 279 84). Classy European entrees, including Swiss *schnitzel* for 52SK. Delicious salads 15SK. Beer at 40SK. Menu in Slovak, Hungarian, German, and French. Open daily 9am-midnight.
Restaurant Astra, Štefánika 73 (tel. 220 70). Inexpensive daily specials under 50SK, usually Czech, Slovak, or Hungarian dishes. Beer 13SK. Open Mon.-Thurs. 8am-8pm and Fri.-Sun. 8am-9pm.

SIGHTS

The main square in Nové Zámky called **Hlavné námestie Fötér** bears witness to the trials that have afflicted this small city. Though most buildings on the square are charmless products of the communist period, the **Parish Church** (*Farský Kostol Plébánia Templom*) rescues the east side of the square with its great tower. Built in 1787 after local hero and powerful bishop Széchenyi gave the green light, the church has a very simple but tasteful interior that is open to inspection. The trees and benches in front are the most popular meeting place in town. Down from the church along M. Flenger is a small monument to the famous local resident of the previous century Anton Bernolák, who helped to standardize the Slovak language. At the end of M. Flenger at Česká is the 19th-century **Synagogue** (*Synagóga*). It's closed to the public, but the exterior bears Hebrew inscriptions above the main door and on a free-standing stone tablet on the roof.

One block west of Hlavné námestie Föter along Petöfiho is the **Franciscan Square** (*námestie Františkanov Ferencesek tere*). On the east side stands the **Local Museum** (*Vlastivedné Honismereti Múzeum*). In a matter of 20 minutes, you get to see a depressing collection of black-and-white sketches from the 1950s and 60s and, in grand contrast, a fascinating exhibit on local folklore, including old porcelain and glass mugs and wine barrels, as well as other curious relics from previous centuries (open Tues.-Fri. 9am-5pm, Sat.-Sun. 9am-noon; admission 6SK, students 3SK).

SLOVAKIA

A two -minute walk down either Petöfiho or Turecko takes you to **Bernolákovo námestie** (the city park). With abundant trees and long grass, the sprawling park on the western part of the Old Town is an excellent place to walk, jog, down a cold drink or simply watch the world go by. At the northeast corner of Bernolákovo námestie is T. G. Masaryka, which leads through a jungle of apartment blocks to Nové Zámky's final attraction: the lonely **Kuczmann Chapel** *(Kuczmannova Kaplnka)*, at the corner of Masaryka and Doracka. When residents erected the building just before the outbreak of World War I to honor a community member, the site was at some distance from the city proper. Times have certainly changed; the adorable little chapel is now steeped in urban concrete.

ENTERTAINMENT

Lighten up by heading to Nové Zámky's beloved **Thermal Baths** *(termálne kúpalisko Štrand)*, situated on a great green island on the Nitra River. Cross the train tracks on Štefánika, which becomes Šurianska, and turn right on Bezručová until you reach number 21. In addition to several thermal swimming pools, the complex features tennis courts, miniature golf, and a large park.

Scattered in and out of the Old Town are beer halls, wine pubs, and bars. For live entertainment, check out the **amphitheater** *(amfiteáter)* whose entrance is on Turecká near Ernestova bašta. Things start happening there after dark.

Panda Piváreň, Ernestova Bašta 3. A friendly neighborhood beer hall serving *Topvar* drafts for 9SK. Open Mon.-Sat. 10am-11pm.

Piváreň Slovan, Masaryka at SNP. An older beer pub with light and dark *Zlatý* Bažant on tap. A half-liter for 10SK. Open Mon.-Sat. 9am-10pm.

Bar Piccolo, Bratov Baldigarovcov 16. A new and friendly bar in the Old Town. Open Mon.-Fri. 10am-10pm, Sat.-Sun. 5-10pm.

Cukráreň Horoskop Cukrászda, námestie Františkánov Ferencesek tere in the narrow alley next to the museum. A much-frequented café with plenty of coffee and other beverages. Open daily 9am-7pm.

■■■ KOŠICE

Košice has handled a mixture of old and new very well. While thousands of gray apartment blocks suffocate the suburbs, the Old Town is well-preserved and boasts a gorgeous Gothic cathedral. In the late Middle Ages, Košice knew wealth and prosperity as a center for gold and silver markets. One of the largest cities in Central Europe, its population consisted of Saxons who referred to it as **Kaschau.** At the end of the 1800s, the city was taken by the Ottoman Turks and entered into a period of decline. After the Austrian liberation, Košice emerged as a cosmopolitan city of Slovaks, Hungarians, and Germans; the Hungarian majority called it **Kassa.** After World War II, many Hungarians were expelled and the city was repopulated with Slovaks and Gypsies. Today Košice has a Hungarian minority and strong Gypsy flavor.

ORIENTATION AND PRACTICAL INFORMATION

Tourist Offices: Tatratour, Alžbetina 4 near the cathedral. Maps and information on Košice and Eastern Slovakia. They're the local **American Express** representative, so bring your traveler's checks here. Open Mon.-Fri. 9am-noon and 1-5pm, Sat. 9am-noon. **CKM Slovakia,** Alžbetina 11, down the street from the cathedral. The former Czechoslovak youth tourist bureau also offers maps and answers questions. Open Mon.-Fri. 8:30am-5:30pm.

Currency Exchange: VÚB (Všeobencá Uverová Banka), one of the largest banks in Slovakia, offers quick service and decent rates. Open Mon.-Fri. 8am-noon and 1:30-5pm, Sat. 8am-noon. At this location there is also a *Bankomat* (ATM) linked to the Mastercard and Cirrus networks, as there also are at Hlavná 8 and at Hlavná 81. **Slovenská Sporitel'ňa,** Hlavná 96-98. Another large Slovak bank with acceptable rates. Visa welcome. Open Mon.-Fri. 7:30am-7pm and Sat. 8am-noon.

Post Office: There are strangely few post offices in Košice. The *Slovenská Pošta* is relatively central, at Palackého and Mojmírova behind the department store across the street from Hotel Slovan (open Mon.-Fri. 8am-7pm and Sat. 8am-noon).
Telephone City Code: 95.
Trains: The main **train station**, *Košice Hlavná Stanica*, is east of the Old Town. Walk down Mlynská from the Cathedral and cross the park. Košice is also an important rail center. To the west, trains to Prague (9hrs.) and Bratislava (6hrs.) are fairly frequent. Eastbound trains to Lviv (8hrs.) and Kiev (17hrs.) run at least once a day; they often continue all the way to Moscow. Trains from Hungary pass through to Nowy Sącz and Kraków in Poland. In the opposite direction, trains from Poland head either to Budapest and Miskolc in Hungary or Oradea and Arad in Romania. Some connections to Budapest require a change at Miskolc. Slovak destinations from Košice include Poprad (1½-2hrs.) and Žilina (2-2½hrs.). Also nearby are Prešov (30min.) and Rožňava (1hr.).
Buses: The **Košice Autobusová Stanica** is located next door to the train station.
Taxis: Slovan Taxi (tel. 62 21 11) or another private taxi firm at tel. 622 22 44.
Pharmacy: The **Lekáreň Sv. Alžbety** is at Hlavná 10 near the cathedral. Open Mon.-Fri. 8am-6pm and Sat. 8am-noon.
Emergencies: Police: tel. 158. **Fire:** tel. 150. **Ambulance:** tel. 155.

ACCOMMODATIONS

Several organizations offer accommodations for budget travelers and the hotels in Košice are also affordable. **Satur,** Hlavná at Rooseveltova (in the Slovan Hotel; formerly ČEDOK) arranges accommodations at a pension in the suburbs for 150SK per person, breakfast included. **Tatratour,** Alžbetina 4 (see above) can arrange a night at an affiliated pension for 200SK per person. **CKM Slovakia,** Alžbetina 11 (see above) offers inexpensive hostel-type accommodations.

Hotel Európa, Štefánikova 4 (tel. 622 38 97), across the park in front of the train station. An old 19th-century hotel in reasonably good condition. Reception open 24 hrs. Communal showers and toilets. Singles 210SK. Doubles 360SK. Triples 480SK. Breakfast 20SK.
Pension Rozália, Orvaská 14 (tel. 397 14). Take bus #13 from námestie Maratónu Mieru to the Krupinská stop. A large house in the suburbs now serving as a pension. Shared toilets and communal showers with plenty of hot water. German spoken. Small but clean rooms 150SK per person. Warm breakfast included. Beware that offers of "free" chauffeuring to the city center will actually cost 100SK. Call before making the trek.
Hotel Coral, Kasárenské námestie 5 (tel. 260 95 or 268 19, fax 211 56). Reception open 24 hrs. Shared toilets and showers. Singles 340SK. Doubles 670SK.

FOOD

There appear to be many places to eat in Košice, but this is only an illusion. People go to restaurants to drink coffee, beer, or wine and skip food altogether. To find people actually *eating* at a restaurant usually means that the food is worthwhile.

Reštaurácia Grand, Kováčska 65 (tel./fax 622 79 64). The food is quite good and the prices are reasonable. Try the *Hovädzie na korení,* a rather mild *guláš,* for 40SK. Efficient service. Open Mon.-Sat. 10am-10pm, Sun. 3-10pm.
Tatraburger, Hlavná 74. The Slovak version of American fast food. Decent burgers for 20SK. Ketchup 3SK. Drinks 20SK. Open Mon.-Fri. 9am-9pm, Sat. 8am-2pm, Sun. 2-8pm.
Potraviny Lahôdky, Hlavná 2. Across from the Slovan Hotel. A self-service food and drink area on the ground floor and a **grocery store** in the basement. Open Mon.-Fri. 7am-7pm, Sat. 7am-1pm.
Grill Veverička, Hlavná 95 (tel. 622 33 60). Allegedly serves fast food, but most people come here to drink. Open Mon.-Sat. 9am-9pm and Sun. 11am-8pm.
Caffé U Františkánov, Kováčska 44. A nice quiet café that also serves sweets and simple meals. Open Mon.-Fri. 9am-10pm, Sat.-Sun. 11am-8pm.

SLOVAKIA

Reštauracia Ajvega, Orlia 10 (tel. 204 52). Košice's only vegetarian restaurant. Open daily 10am-11pm.

SIGHTS

Wide **Hlavná** street is the heart of the Old Town. At the widest point is the glorious Gothic **Cathedral of St. Elizabeth** *(Dom sv. Alžbety)*, designed in the 14th century by the French architect Villars d'Honnecourt on request of the Hungarian King Lajos I. The golden **High Altar** inside was created by German sculptor Wohlgemuth. The cathedral also has an elaborate organ and pure Gothic pulpit.

To the south of the cathedral is the small and closed to public **Chapel of St. Michael** *(Kaplnka sv. Michala)*, frozen on its way from Romanesque to Gothic. To the north of the cathedral is the **Urban Tower** *(Urbanova veža)*. The exterior arcade has interesting tombstones placed in its walls, but the puddles and the stench betray its use as a giant urinal. The tower houses a **Metallurgical Museum,** with cast iron bells, pewter doorknockers, and golden candlesticks (open Tues.-Sat. 9am-5pm, Sun. 9am-noon; admission 10SK, students 5SK).

Mlynská is lined with 19th-century buildings; a **Secessionist Building** *(Secesný dom)* stands at the corner of Hrnčiarska, and the grand neo-Gothic **Jakab Palace** *(Jakabov palác)* rests at the corner of Mlynská and Štefánikova. Backtrack down Mlynská and turn left onto Puškinova, to find the **Synagogue** *(Synagoga)*, currently closed to the public.

At the end of Unverzitná at Hlavná is the grim and gray **Jesuit Church** *(Jezuitský kostol)*. Its somber façade contrasts with the joyful aristocratic palaces in this part of Hlavná. At the corner of Hlavná and Poštová is the **Dessewffy Palace** *(Dessewffyho palác)*, a neo-Classical edifice that houses parts of the Museum of East Slovakia (see below). Across the street, at the corner of Hlavná and Biela is the **Andrássy Palace** *(Andrássyho palác)*, a neo-Baroque residence of the Andrássy family transformed by the Communist regime into a poorly-stocked grocery store. At the corner of Hlavná and Františkanská stands the Baroque **Franciscan Church** *(Františkánsky kostol)*. As the third oldest church in Košice, it was originally Gothic but acquired a primarily Baroque character in the 1720s.

As Hlavná becomes narrower, it loses its majesty and eventually ends at Hviezdoslavova. At the corner of Hviezdoslavova and Komenského is the **Museum of East Slovakia,** noted for its exhibits on archaeology and prehistory, and particularly for its collection of 3000 gold coins (open Tues.-Sat. 9am-5pm and Sun. 9am-1pm; admission 20SK, students 10SK). Farther down Hviezdoslavova at Moyzesova is a bulky **Municipal Building** *(Budova obvodného úradu)*. An overbearing and awkward construction from the early 20th century, it marks the border between Košice's Old Town and the endless rows of concrete apartment blocks erected after 1948. Cross this border only if you must.

ENTERTAINMENT

Along with traditional beer-halls and wine-pubs, Košice has several dance clubs.

Piváreň Herňa, Alžbetina 21. A new and popular beer hall with *Zlatý Bažant* (light and dark) on tap. Open daily 10am-10pm.

Tokaj Vináreň, Poštova 3. A small and intimate wine pub with several varieties of Slovak wine available. Simple meals served as well. Open daily 9am-10pm.

Piváreň Smädný Mních, Hlavná 80. Loosely translated as the "thirsty monk," this centrally-located beer garden is very popular among the locals. Clientele is diverse in all ways except gender: females are in the minority. A half-liter of draft *Smädný Mních* from Veľký Šariš is a mere 15SK. Open daily until 10pm.

Disco Vináreň U Bocatia, Hlavná 59. A wine pub by day and a disco by night. Mixed drinks, Slovak wine, and *Gemer* beer (12SK per half-liter). Wine pub open Mon.-Thurs. 10am-11pm, Fri. 10am-2am. Disco open Fri.-Sat. 9pm-2am.

Hacienda Disco Night Club, at the corner of Hlavná on the second floor of Levoča House. Couldn't have described it better ourselves. Open daily 9pm-3am.

A Club, Hlavná 22. Not only is it popular, but it's open later than most other beer gardens in Košice. Open daily 10am-1am.
Piváreň, Hlavná 97. A smaller watering hole serving imported Czech *Pilsner Urquell* and Budweiser *Budvar.* Open daily 10am-midnight.
Caffé U Františkánov, Kovačska 44. A quiet café away from the main drag. Simple meals served as well. Open Mon.-Fri. 9am-10pm, Sat.-Sun. 11am-8pm.

■■■ PREŠOV

Prešov has as many obscure languages as it has bricks. In 1374 the city's Saxon population succeeded in making medieval **Preschau** a privileged Royal Town. By the end of the 19th century, Hungarian-speaking Jews were one of the largest communities in the city, then known as **Eperjes.** The Saxons and Jews disappeared after fascist persecutions and post-war expulsions. Today the largest minority community are the Rusins, a Slavic people who speak a language that resembles Ukrainian. They are emphatically *not* Russian, although their language is written in Cyrillic. Prešov's Rusin community has its own churches and cultural institutions, including a theater and a newspaper. Another piece in Prešov's great cultural mosaic are its Gypsies. The genuine and unpretentious atmosphere of the Old Town make this little town one of Slovakia's best kept secrets.

ORIENTATION AND PRACTICAL INFORMATION

Tourist Offices: Tatratour, Hlavná 129 (tel. 343 00 or 339 62, fax 343 01). Friendly and patient staff offer information on Prešov and Šariš county. German spoken. Open Mon.-Fri. 8am-5pm. **Slovrast,** Hlavná 135 (tel. 517 23). Recognize it by the loud music booming from the inside. **Maps** and information on Prešov and surroundings. Open Mon.-Fri. 9am-6pm. **Satur,** Hlavná 1 (tel. 240 42, fax 240 40). Unfriendly and uncooperative English-speaking staff offer an expensive but detailed **map** of Prešov for 31SK. Open Mon.-Fri. 9am-5pm.
Currency Exchange: VÚB Všeobecná Úverová Banka, Hlavná 133 in the courtyard. One of the largest banks in Slovakia. Cashes American Express traveler's checks. Open Mon.-Thurs. 8am-noon and 1:30-4pm, Fri. 8am-noon. **Investičná Rozvojová Banka,** Hlavná 80. A smaller banking company with more flexible hours. Open Mon.-Fri. 8am-4pm. **24-hr. Currency Exchange,** Hlavná 24. Let the wonders of technology turn your home currency into crowns for fair rates.
Post Office: *Slovenská Pošta* is slightly south of the Old Town at the corner of Masaryková 2 and Nálepkova. Open Mon.-Fri. 8am-7pm and Sat. 8am-1pm.
Telephones: Several new, gray public telephones are located outside the post office building. The **telephone city code** is 91.
Trains: *Prešov Žel. Stanica* is located 10 min. to the south of the Old Town down Hlavná, which becomes Masaryková. Most northbound trolley buses from the station head towards the Old Town, so cross under Masaryková in the new subterranean passage and purchase a ticket from the orange automats for 4SK.
Buses: *Prešov Autobusová Stanica* is located on Masaryková across from the train station. To reach the Old Town, turn right and walk north along Masaryková for 10 min. or take a trolley-bus.
Public Toilets: Underground facilities for a fee at the corner of Masaryková and Nálepkova. Open Mon.-Fri. 6am-10pm.
Taxis: 'Round the clock (tel. 244 11 or 332 22).
Pharmacy: Lekáreň Salvator is at Hlavná 20. Open Mon.-Fri. 8am-4pm.

ACCOMMODATIONS

Prešov has several decent and relatively inexpensive hotels which are almost invariably available. Otherwise, **Tatratour,** Hlavná 129 (see above) has friendly and professional travel agents. **Satur,** Hlavná 1 (see above), the former Club ČEDOK, does not offer private rooms but grudgingly arranges reservations at hotels and pensions.

Mestská hala, Pod Kamennou (tel. 345 72). From Masaryková, north of the main train station, turn left on Škultétyho and cross the river. Simple but decent accommodations outside the Old Town. Doubles only for 360SK. Call in advance.

Hotel Dukla, námestie Legionárov 2 (tel. 227 41, fax 321 34), at the corner of Halvná and Grešova just south of the Old Town. Merry English-speaking reception open 24 hrs. Newly renovated rooms, with shower and toilet. Singles 835SK. Doubles 1522SK. Breakfast included. Also in the hotel are a restaurant, bar, café, and a *Bankomat* linked to Mastercard and Cirrus.

Hotel Šariš, Sabinovská 1 (tel. 463 51 or 463 52), north of Old Town. Reception open 24 hrs. All the rooms in this older hotel include toilet and shower. Singles 690SK. Doubles 1380SK. Breakfast included.

Penzion ZPA, Budovateľská 1 (tel. 232 06), south of Maybaumova near the main train station. Doubles only with toilet and bath for 300SK. Not close to the Old Town, but convenient to the train station. Call in advance.

FOOD

Slovenská Reštaurácia, Hlavná 11. A very popular restaurant with inexpensive exquisite food. The soups are first-rate. Try the *rezeň (schnitzel)* or the *Tokajská mäsová zmes* (assorted pan-fried veal and pork cutlets) for 70SK. Good *Šariš* beer on tap for 12SK. Open daily 9am-10pm.

Eckhaus Bufet, Hlavná 21. An impressive selection of salads and cold cuts. Quick and inexpensive. Open Mon.-Fri. 6am-8pm, Sat. 7am-1pm, Sun. 8am-2pm.

Reštaurácia U Richtára, Hlavná 71 (tel. 232 36). In the cellar of the Town Hall. Delicious entrees 90-200SK. Open Mon.-Fri. 11am-11pm, Sat.-Sun. noon-11pm.

Občerstvenie, Floriánova at Jarkova. Fast and inexpensive self-serve fare. Wash down the eats with a draft of lager. Open Mon.-Fri. 6am-6pm, Sat.-Sun. 8am-2pm.

SIGHTS

The yellow and orange facades of the elegant 19th-century buildings along Hlavná are being enthusiastically restored. The church with the tall tower under reconstruction is **St. John's Cathedral** *(Katedrálny chrám sv. Jána Krstiteľa)*. As Hlavná splits into two main streets, the tower of **St. Nicholas** *(Kostol sv. Mikuláša)* captures the visitor's attention. The proportions and the distinctive turrets of the Gothic church are reminiscent of Saxon churches in Transylvania and attest to Saxon influence in Prešov during the late Middle Ages. The interior of the church has a tremendous **High Altar** that literally reaches the ceiling. The organ is also very large and features an unusual variance in the size of each pipe.

On the eastern side of Hlavná is the **City Museum** *(Vlastivedné múzeum)*, featuring displays on the rich history of Prešov (open Tues.-Fri. 10am-5pm, Sat.-Sun. 11am-3pm; admission 10SK, students 5SK). Farther down the street, at no. 62, is the **Clubhouse of the Rusins** *(Ruský Klub)*, another 19th-century edifice. An office on the second floor sells books on Rusin history and culture, as well as the local Rusin newspaper. Two blocks east of Hlavná on Kováčska is a remnant of Prešov's medieval **Bastion** *(Bašta)* that now houses private businesses.

West of Hlavná, down the alley Švermova, is the **Synagogue** *(Synagóga)*. The exterior is undergoing repair, but the ornate and well-maintained late 19th-century interior is open to the public. Constructed in 1897 by Kollacsek and Wirth, the synagogue was the religious center of Prešov's Jewish community until World War II. A **monument** erected in 1991 commemorates the six thousand Jews of Prešov who fell victim to the Nazis and the regime of Tiso. Part of the synagogue houses the **Museum of Judaica** *(Múzeum Judaík;* open Tues.-Wed. 11am-4pm, Thurs. 3-6pm).

From the west side of Hlavná extends a narrow medieval street called **Floriánova.** At the corner of Floriánova and Jarkova stands a curious **medieval building** with small windows and Gothic features. It resembles Gothic slaughter houses in Plzeň and České Budějovice *(Budweis)* in the Czech Republic. At the end of Floriánova is **St. Florian's Gate** *(Brána sv. Floriána)*, a remnant of an early Renaissance fortification. South of Floriánova along Hlavná is the **Šariš Gallery** *(Šarišská galéria)*, housed in a Gothic building. The gallery features a collection of art from the local Šariš region (open Tues.-Fri. 8:30am-4pm; admission 6SK, students 2SK).

ENTERTAINMENT

Beer gardens, clubs, and bars fill the courts of the Old Town.

Lord Club, Slovenská 54. A large beer garden with popular music and inexpensive drafts. A half-liter of *Zlatý Bažant* costs a mere 10SK. Open Mon.-Fri. 10am-9pm.
Piváreň Smädný Mních, Hlavná 41. A centrally-located beer pub with drafts of the fine beer brewed in nearby Veľký Šariš. Open daily 11am-11pm.
Nightbar Corso, Hlavná 72 (tel. 248 62). A new dance club swimming in hard liquor. Open Mon.-Fri. 11am-3am, Sat.-Sun. 5pm-3am.
Admiral Disco, Slovenská at the corner of Kováčska. The grim, gray walls conceal a grinding dance club and a casino. Open daily until 4am.

THE HIGH TATRAS

Slovaks take great pride in the **High Tatras** *(Vysoké Tatry),* a mountainous mecca for hikers, skiers, campers, and nature-lovers. Far taller than the **Little Tatras** *(Malá Fatra)* to the west, the **Low Tatras** *(Nízké Tatry)* to the south, and the **Matras** in Hungary, the High Tatras form a natural barrier between Slovakia and Poland. The entire range, a mere 26km long, is one of the most compact mountain ranges in the world. The majestic peaks and the plethora of glacial lakes *(pleso)* make for memorable scenery, as do the deer, bears, and edelweiss that thrive in the forest.

The key transport center in the Tatra region is **Poprad,** a good starting point for hiking trips; a **map** of the Vysoké Tatry is indispensable (15-50SK). To the north of Poprad lie the ski resorts of **Starý Smokovec** and **Tatranská Lomnica.** Tatranská Lomnica is also a springboard for trips to the Polish Tatras. To the west of Poprad lies the well-endowed hiking and skiing center of **Štrbské Pleso.** To the south of Poprad and on the other side of the Low Tatras lies the **Slovenský Raj National Park,** a paradise of stately pines and untamed wilds. The park also contains several breathtaking caves. The **Dobšinská Jadova Jaskyňa** (Dobšiná Ice Caves) are the most accessible. From the Dobšinská bus stop, head uphill along the blue and yellow path for 20 min. (The caves are inaccessible during winter.) The more extensive caves at **Ochtina** are easier to reach from Rožnava, the end of the bus line from Poprad.

Also close to Poprad are several lovely medieval **Spiš** towns. The wealthiest mining centers in 15th-century Europe, they were jealously contested by Hungarian and Polish kings. Their inhabitants were **Saxons** from Western Europe, primarily Belgium, recruited by Hungarian kings to work in the mines. The ornate Gothic and early Renaissance architecture of the Spiš towns is indeed reminiscent of Western Europe. **Levoča,** the former capital of the Spiš region and the most impressive of the Spiš towns, is difficult to reach from Poprad. **Kežmarok,** on the other hand, is a mere half-hour away and has a gorgeous medieval center.

■■■ POPRAD

With its international airport and excellent train and bus connections to Slovak and international destinations, Poprad is the "gateway to the High Tatras"; it is also a convenient access point to the **Low Tatras** to the south and to the **Slovak Paradise** *(Slovenský raj)* to the southeast. A wealth of affordable accommodations make Poprad *the* budget alternative to the overpriced surprises sinisterly nestled in the valleys of the Tatras.

Communist Czechoslovakia transformed the once-sleepy village of Poprad into a large city. Today's Greater Poprad includes not only Old Poprad but also the formerly independent villages of **Spišska Sobota, Stráže,** and **Veľká.** The center of

Poprad consists mostly of post-World War II architecture, yet the city scores well on atmosphere. Thousand of tourists mill down the long main square and visit the impressive selection of shops, boutiques, and restaurants. Local rumor has it that Poprad will compete to be the site of the 2002 Winter Olympic Games.

ORIENTATION AND PRACTICAL INFORMATION

Tourist Offices: Poprad Information Agency *(Popradská Informačná Agentúra)*, námestie sv. Egídia 2950 (tel. 636 36). The helpful English-speaking staff sells maps of Poprad and Eastern Slovakia and can handle almost any inquiry. Open Mon.-Fri. 8:30am-7pm, Sat. 9am-1pm, Sun. 2-6pm. **Tatratour,** námestie sv. Egídia 9 (tel. 637 12 or 229 83, fax 638 09). One of the most professional and efficient travel offices in Slovakia. Plenty of maps and information. Cashes **American Express** traveler's checks. Open Mon.-Fri. 8am-6pm, Sat. 8am-noon. **Satur,** námestie sv. Egídia 2950 (tel. 234 30, fax 636 19). The staff is not particularly enthusiastic, but offers maps and information on Poprad and the High Tatras. Open Mon.-Fri. 9am-noon and 1-6pm, Sat. 9am-noon.

Currency Exchange: Všeobecná Úverová Banka, Mnoheľova 9 (tel. 325 11). Open Mon.-Fri. 8am-noon and 1:30-5pm, Sat. 8am-noon. There's a *Bankomat* (ATM) connected to Cirrus and Mastercard around the corner. **Slovenská Sporiteľňa,** námestie sv. Egídia 95 (tel. 611 35 or 612 45, fax 656 63). On the main square in the center of town. Open Mon.-Fri. 7:30am-5pm, Sat. 8am-noon.

Post Office: Descend the stairs from the train station and turn left on Wolkerova; *Slovenská Pošta* is next door. Open Mon.-Fri. 6:30-11:30am and noon-8pm, Sat. 7am-2pm. Closer to the center of town is the post office at Mnoheľova 11. Open Mon.-Fri. 7am-8pm, Sat. 8am-noon and 2:30-7:30pm.

Telephone City Code: 092.

Trains: *Poprad-Tatry Železničná Stanica* (tel. 312 44) is located to the north of the main square námestie sv. Egídia on Wolkerova. To reach the center, walk down either Alžbetina, Mnohelova, Hatalova, or 1. mája and cross the Poprad River. Then head for the crowds along námestie sv. Egídia.

Buses: *Poprad Autobusová Stanica* (tel. 233 90) is located near the train station at the corner of Wolkerova and Alžbetina. Look for the communist-era building with oft-filthy windows.

Flights: Poprad International Airport *(Letisko Poprad)* is located 3km to the northwest of town in the direction of Gerlachov (tel. 229 77). Bus #12 connects the airport with the city.

Taxis: One firm operates from the train station (tel. 633 33).

Pharmacy: Centrally located at námestie sv. Egídia 33 is the relatively new **Lekáreň Tatra Apotheke.** Open Mon.-Fri. 7:30am-5pm, Sat. 9am-noon.

Police (polícia): tel. 156.

ACCOMMODATIONS

The city's accommodations agencies are among the most efficient and least expensive in Slovakia. **Satur** (see above) arranges the cheapest private rooms for a mere 150SK per person. **Poprad Information Agency** (see above) offers private rooms for 200SK per person. **Tatratour** (see above) arranges private rooms right on the main square, námesties sv. Egídia, with private toilet and shower for 250SK.

Hotel Európa, Wolkerova 3 (tel. 327 44 or 237 53). Next to the train station, with old but clean rooms. Reception sells beer and snacks and is open 24 hrs. Communal toilets and baths. Singles 220SK. Doubles 350SK. Decent restaurant inside.

Hotel Gerlach, Hviezdoslavova 2 (tel. 337 59, fax 636 63). Clean rooms in a Communist-era building. Reception open 24 hrs. All rooms with private toilets, some with bath. Singles 410SK. Doubles 790SK.

Hotel Satel, Mnoheľova 5 (tel. 471 111, fax 620 75). Clean, modern rooms have private toilet and shower. Singles 1220SK. Doubles 1890SK. Breakfast included.

FOOD

Poprad's eateries range from very good sit-down establishments to inexpensive bistros and cheap stand-up sausage kitchens.

Slovenská Reštaurácia, 1 mája 9 (tel. 228 70). Authentic Slovak cuisine in a folkloric atmosphere. Plows and sickles make for creative wall ornaments. Delicious *halušky* with *bryndza* 30SK. Daily specials, often including fried chicken, 50SK. Live Gypsy music nightly. Bottled *Tatran* beer 17SK. Open daily 10am-11pm.
Gastrocentrum, námestie sv. Egídia 21. Cheap, stand-up fare for under 40SK. The sausages are popular. *Tatran* beer is a bargain for 10SK per bottle. Open Mon.-Fri. 8am-6pm, Sat. 7am-noon.
Pasta & Basta, 1 máje 5 (tel./fax 234 80). Locals come here to buy bulk pasta and eat the inexpensive food. Fried cheese 30SK. The *rezeň (schnitzel)* is fresh but somewhat tough (50SK). Bottled *Tatran* beer 12SK. Open Mon.-Sat. 11am-10pm.
Bistro Pod Vežou, námestie sv. Egídia 25. Cheap fast-food eats on an outdoor patio. Hamburger 16SK. Inexpensive coffee and non-alcoholic beverages. Open Mon.-Sat. 10am-9pm, Sun. 4-9pm.

SIGHTS

Námestie sv. Egídia, a long pedestrian street, is the place to find drugstore supplies, hiking equipment, a quick meal, beer, or coffee. Don't expect many architectural delights unless gray concrete turns you on. The **main square,** however, boasts a few medieval buildings: the most eye-catching is the fortified **Roman Catholic Church** (*Rímskókatolický Kostol*) elevated by Saxons in the Middle Ages. The seemingly impenetrable wall surrounding the church was meant to protect it from Mongol and Tartar raids, but today it only serves to keep tourists off the church premises. Next door stands a rather dilapidated Renaissance **Watchtower** (*Zvonica*), a typical structure found in every Saxon village in the Spiš region. The only other noteworthy edifice in central Poprad is the **Church of St. Aegidius** (*Kostol sv Egídia*), after which the square is named. Unfortunately, it is also closed to visitors.

A 15-minute walk down Štefánikova and then left on unmarked Kežmarská, or a three-minute ride on bus # 2 or 3 in the same direction, leads to **Spišská Sobota,** a historic village that is now a district of Poprad. After 45 years of unprecedented neglect under the Communist regime, the whole village has been declared historic and is currently the site of ongoing restoration.

Spišská Sobota centers around **Sobotské námestie.** All major sights lie on this square. **St. George's Church** (*Kostol sv. Juraja*), built by Saxons in the late medieval times, gave the village its original name of **Georgensberg.** Next to the church fortifications stands a poorly-maintained Renaissance-style **Watchtower** (*Zvonica*). On the north side of the square, which becomes **Matejovská,** there are some restored **folk dwellings.** Their dark wooden triangular roofs are characteristic of the Spiš region, as are their jolly shades of yellow, orange, and blue.

Back on Sobotské námestie, the **Tatra Museum** (*Podtatranské Múzeum*), features collections on the history of the village and its Hungarian and Saxon inhabitants until their expulsion in 1945, as well as on Slovak culture and folklore in the Spiš region (open Mon.-Sat. 9am-4pm; admission 10SK, students 5SK).

ENTERTAINMENT

Discos, wine pubs, and beer halls center around námestie sv. Egídia. Although the name of **Vináreň Zlatý Kalich,** námestie sv. Egídia 36, suggests a wine pub, it proudly focuses on inexpensive 10SK drafts of *Tatran,* Poprad's very own beer (open Mon.-Fri. 9am-10pm, Sat. 3-10pm). **Globus Club Disco,** námestie sv. Egídia 11, is a centrally located dance club with restaurant (open Sun.-Thurs. until 11pm, Fri.-Sat. until 4am). **Piváreň,** námestie sv. Egídia 49, is one of the few beer pubs in Poprad and stays open later than most other establishments (open Mon.-Sat. 9am-11pm, Sun. 2-11pm).

SLOVAKIA

■■■ KEŽMAROK

At the feet of the High Tatras in the east lies the tidily preserved medieval town of Kežmarok. Although today the town is peripherally connected to Poprad by a slow train, it was once one of the most important economic, cultural, and military centers in the Kingdom of Hungary. Like other towns in the Spiš region of the Tatras, Kežmarok once had large Saxon and Hungarian communities. During the revolutionary chaos of 1918 a **"Spiš Republic"** was proclaimed in Kežmarok, but the fledgling state became part of Czechoslovakia. Although life is quieter in Kežmarok nowadays, the town remains an excellent base for day-trips to the Tatras.

ORIENTATION AND PRACTICAL INFORMATION

Only 30 minutes by train from Poprad, Kežmarok is well worth the trip. With its medieval center and spruce-clad environs, Kežmarok is best seen on foot.

Tourist Office: Satur, Hlavné námestie 63 (tel./fax 31 22). Helpful and friendly staff. German spoken. A new map of Kežmarok was in preparation during the summer of 1994. Open Mon.-Fri. 9am-noon and 1-5pm, Sat. 8am-noon.

Currency Exchange: VÚB Všeobecná Úverová Banka, Garbiarska 61, inside the Hotel Lipa. Also a *Bankomat* (ATM) linked to Cirrus and Mastercard networks. Open Mon.-Fri. 8am-4pm. **Slovenská Sporiteľňa,** Garbiarska 30, across the street from Hotel Lipa. Visa is welcome here. Open Mon.-Fri. 7:30am-3:30pm.

Trains: Kežmarok Železničná Stanica is located to the northwest of the Old Town at the end of Alexandra Street. It seems rather over-sized for a town of this size, but its 19th century decor is interesting, although in dilapidated condition.

Buses: Odchody Autobusov ČSAD, the main stop, is located outside the door of the train station. The lot desperately needs to be paved. Frequent service to virtually every hamlet in the Tatras.

Post Office: The local *Slovenská Pošta* is inconveniently located beyond the wooden old Evangelical Church at the corner of Hviezdoslavova and Nálepku.

Telephone City Code: 0968.

Pharmacy: Lekáreň Pharmacie is on the main square at Hlavné námestie 58. Open Mon.-Fri. 7:30am-4pm.

Police (mestská Polícia): In the Town Hall building at the end of Hlavné námestie. Open for non-emergencies Mon.-Fri. 10am-12:15pm and 12:45-3pm.

ACCOMMODATIONS

While not especially numerous, Kežmarok's hotels and accommodations agencies are of a good caliber. **Satur** arranges private rooms for 200SK per person and hotel reservations at 300SK per person.

Hotel Lipa, Garbiarska 61 (tel 20 37 or 20 38, fax 20 39). Reception open 24 hrs. A Communist-era hotel with clean rooms, each with private toilet and shower. Conveniently located near the main train station. Singles 370SK. Doubles 570SK.

Hotel Club, MUDr. Alexandra 24 (tel. 40 51, fax 40 53). A new hotel one block from the famous Renaissance watchtower in the heart of the Old Town. Reception open 24 hrs. All rooms with shower and toilet. Free sauna. Satellite TV 100SK. Singles 600SK. Doubles 1100SK. Breakfast included.

FOOD

Club Restaurant, MUDr. Alexandra (tel. 40 52). Excellent Slovak cuisine in the Old Town. *Halušky* 30SK, *guláš* 50SK, roast beef 90SK. Tatran beer overpriced at 25SK. Open daily 7am-10pm.

Pekáreň, Hlavné námestie 82. A wonderful bakery with fresh treats. The cinnamon rolls (4SK) are especially good. Open Mon.-Fri. 7am-6pm, Sat. 7am-noon.

Espresso Andjele, MUDr. alexandra 36. A new café serving various dessert items, most under 10SK. Coffee 7SK. Open daily 9am-9pm.

Piváreň Zlatý Bažant, Topotcerova near the entrance to the cemetery. Simple and inexpensive Slovak dishes in a Communist-era building. Open daily 6am-10pm.

SIGHTS

Wide cobblestone streets and narrow alleys connect the sights in the Old Town; no modern buildings disturb the medieval surroundings. Kežmarok is famous for its **Renaissance buildings,** which include a castle that belonged in turn to the Habsburgs, the Thurzos, and the Thökölys. Unlike Poprad, Kežmarok has succeeded in preserving its rich past; almost every building tells a story about life in the former **Kesmárk** of the Hungarian Kingdom.

In the middle of the Old Town, **Námestie Požiarnikov** is dominated by the **Church of the Holy Cross** *(Kostol sv. Kríža),* a late Gothic Catholic hall church. Open at seemingly random hours, the interior boasts several 15th-century Gothic altars, two organs, and the tomb of the aristocratic Thököly family who resided in Kežmarok Castle in the 16th century. Next to the church is the **watchtower** *(Zvonica),* the most famous landmark in Kežmarok. Typical of Spiš Saxon towns, this watchtower was built in 1591 in Renaissance style by Ulrich Materer. Although some of the plaster is falling off, much of the Renaissance *graffito* remains.

Down Nová street is the **Kežmarok Castle** *(Kežmarský hrad)* on Hradné námestie. The huge towers are Gothic, but the walls are topped with Renaissance decor. The gate to the impressive courtyard dates back to the 16th century, when the Thököly family owned the castle. Today, the castle houses the **Kežmarok Museum** in its well-preserved interior. Kežmarok politics, medieval weapons, and portraits of Austrian emperors all merit a moment of your time, but the 19th-century newspaper clippings, posters and books that convey the town's former importance are the most interesting part of the exhibit. The Baroque **Chapel of St. Elizabeth** is a product of local artistic talent. (A guided tour in Slovak or German lasts roughly an hour. Museum open Tues.-Sun. 9am-4pm; admission 28SK, students 14SK.)

Hradné námestie eventually becomes **Hlavné námestie,** the attractive main square of the Old Town. The Baroque tower of the **Town Hall** *(Radnica)* is visible even from the countryside surrounding Kežmarok. Although the original building burned down in 1922, its replacement is a unique synthesis of Gothic, Baroque, Renaissance, and Neoclassical elements. The huge arcaded Neoclassical building north of the Town Hall on MUDr. Alexandra is the **Reduta,** the center of Kežmarok's social life in the 19th century. As the Grandhotel Schwarz, the Reduta once housed elegant balls and posh restaurants.

Down Hviezcloslavova is the eclectic pink **New Evangelical Church** *(Nový evanjelický kostol),* built by Danish architect Theofil Hansen in 1894. Next to this garish construction is the humble wooden **Old Evangelical Church** *(Drevený atikulámy kostol),* a rustic Baroque structure with an entirely wooden interior built by Poprad architect George Müttermann in 1717. In this same area is the **Lyceum** *(Lýceum),* founded in 1774 and attended by many famous Slovaks, Hungarians, and Saxons. Those who remained in Kežmarok after long after their studies ended found a resting place in the **Historic Cemetery** *(Historický cintorín)* north of the churches on Toporcerova. The tombs and monuments to Slovak, Hungarian, and Saxon burghers, professors, and aristocrats are tangible reminders of Kežmarok's multicultural past (open daily until 6pm).

ENTERTAINMENT

Kežmarok is a quiet mountain town; the main scene here is peace and solitude.

Piváreň Zlatý Bažant, Toporcerova near the entrance to the cemetery. Cheap draft beer in an ugly Communist-era building. Open daily 6am-10pm.

Espresso Andjele, MUDr. Alexandra 32. A popular new café in the Old Town. Coffee 7SK, desserts under 10SK. Open daily 9am-9pm.

Castellan Club Disco, Hradné námestie. Shake down the castle to *Ace of Bass,* if you can stand it. Open daily 9pm-3am.

■■■ STARÝ SMOKOVEC

Kafka-esque with a rustic mountain twist, **Starý Smokovec** is situated on a gentle incline; simply by walking through you scale the Tatras. Founded in the late 18th century, the oldest resort town in the region is also the most international. Most businesses are trilingual (Slovak, German, English), and hikers from all over the world come to take on the Tatras; the tree- and flower-lined streets buzz with Dutch, Polish, Hungarian, German, and Québécois. Beware the thousands of wasps awaiting in the mountains.

ORIENTATION AND PRACTICAL INFORMATION

Starý Smokovec is easily reached from Poprad's train station, Poprad-Tatry. The narrow-gauge **Tatra Electric Railway** (TEŽ) trains depart from the upper-level platform (every ½-hour during the day; less frequently after dark; under 20SK). While Starý Smokovec is a small place, the lack of street names, signs or a good map makes getting around a real challenge.

Tourist Offices: Satur is up a short path from the train station (tel. 27 10, fax 32 15). Formerly ČEDOK, Satur has English-speaking staff that provide information, pamphlets, and **maps.** Average currency exchange rates. Open Mon.-Fri. 8am-6pm, Sat. 8am-12:30pm. **Tatranská Informačná Kancelária,** in the Slovenská Sporiteľňa building west of the post office (tel. 34 40). Friendly and professional staff offer several brochures and maps of the region. Open daily 8am-7pm.

Currency Exchange: Slovenská Sporiteľňa, west of the post office and the train station. Visa traveler's checks cashed. Excellent rates and no commission. Open Mon.-Fri. 7:30am-3pm, Sat. 8am-noon. 24-hr. currency exchange machine on the premises. **Poštová Banka,** in the post office building west of the train station. Mediocre rates. Open Mon.-Fri. 8am-3:30pm.

Post Office: The local *Slovenská Pošta* is west of the train station. Pass several fast-food stands to reach the entrance. Open Mon.-Fri. 8am-4:30pm, Sat. 8am-10am.

Telephone City Code: 0969.

Trains: Starý Smokovec Železničná Stanica is at the lowest point of town south of the Hotel Grand. The Tatra Electric Railway (*Tatranská Elektrická Železnica* or TEŽ) provides frequent service to Poprad and Lomnica (every 30-60min.) and smaller hamlets in the Tatras.

Buses: Starý Smokovec Autobusová Stanica is east of the main train station along the road to Horný Smokovec. Good connections to other Tatra resorts.

Public Toilets: West of the train station near the post office by the fast food stands. Here's the shocker: they're free.

Pharmacy: The only one in town is the **Lekáreň U Zlatej Sovy Apotheke,** on the second floor of the Slovenská sporiteľňa building west of the post office. Open Mon.-Fri. 7:30am-5pm, Sat. 8am-noon.

Police (Polícia): West of the Hotel Grand at the same altitude. Look for the sign.

ACCOMMODATIONS AND CAMPING

Satur, located above the train station up a short path (see above) can arrange accommodations in many of the hotels, chalets, and campgrounds listed below, most of which are within reach of Starý Smokovec by the Tatra Electric Railway.

Bilíkova Chata, atop Hrebienok up the funicular (tel. 24 39, fax 22 67). A mountain chalet at an altitude of 1255m originally built by Hungarian singer Rózsa Graefl-Györffy in the 19th century. Reception open daily 7am-8pm or book through Satur. All rooms with bath and toilet. 740SK per person.

CKM Juniorhotel Vysoké Tatry, in Horný Smokovec two stops on TEZ towards Tatranská Lomnica (tel. 26 61). Among the cheapest rooms in the Tatras: 140SK per night for ISIC or HI cardholders (nonmembers 200SK). Call in advance.

Hotel Bellevue, in Horný Smokovec two stops on TEZ towards Tatranská Lomnica. Many decent rooms. Reception open 24 hrs. or book through Satur. Singles with shower 900SK. Doubles with shower 1400SK. Rooms with private toilet are much more expensive. Breakfast included.

Hotel Šport, in Horný Smokovec two stops on TEZ towards Tatranská Lomnica. Reception 24hrs. or book through Satur. Doubles 940SK, breakfast included.

Chata Kpt. Morávku, in the woods at Popradské pleso near Štrbské pleso, a 15-min. trip by TEZ from Starý Smokovec. Simple rooms 350SK per person. Reserve in advance through Satur in Starý Smokovec.

Ternocamp, down the road or railway to Poprad about 3km from Starý Smokovec (tel. 24 06). Great new chalets. All rooms include private toilet and bath. Singles 570SK. Doubles 1080SK. Breakfast included. Call in advance.

Camping: Eurocamp, 2km from Tatranská Lomnica (15min from Starý Smokovec on TEZ; direction: "Veľká Lomnica"). Bargain 4-bed chalets with private bath and toilet 1500SK. Reserve in advance through Satur in Starý Smokovec.

FOOD

Most people eat "on-the-go" in Starý Smokovec. Dozens of stand-up buffets offer hamburgers (13-23SK) and corn on the cob (4SK). The town's main restaurant is mediocre, but Starý Smokovec has a first-rate grocery store: **Potraviny,** across from the Hotel Grand next door to Satur, or a 3-min. walk from the train station. A great selection of bread, pastries, meat, candies, beer, and liquor; outdoor terrace for consuming your groceries (open Mon.-Sat. 6am-8pm, Sat. 10am-6pm).

The **Reštaurácia Taverna** in the Hotel Grand has a good selection of entrees, but the portions are unsatisfyingly small. *Guláš* 50SK, *schnitzel* 60SK, roast beef 70SK, omelette 30SK. Drafts of *Tatran* beer 15SK (open Mon.-Sat. 10am-10pm).

HIKING

The convenient funicular (every 30min. 6am-7pm; 10SK) to **Hrebienok** takes you to the heart of hiking country. The 2km ride ends at an altitude of 1285m above sea level, and an easy 20-minute hike from Hrebienok leads to the foaming **Cold Waterfall** *(Studenovodské vodopády)*. The truly ambitious can climb the **Slavkovský Štít,** whose stony face overlooks Starý Smokovec. With a peak at 2450m, Slavkovský Štít is one of the highest peaks in the Tatras. For advanced hikers, the trek to and from Slavkovský Štít originating in Hrebienok lasts roughly eight hours.

To descend the Tatras less strenuously, take the **blue trail** through the towering pines to **Tatranská Lomnica,** a 90-minute journey. In the opposite direction, the westward **red trail** leads after several hours to **Popradské Pleso** and ultimately Štrbské Pleso. Particularly challenging is the 6km trek along the blue trail through the **Veľká Studená Dolina** (literally the "Big Cold Valley") that, in three hours, leads to the **Zbojnicka Chatka**. If the **Malá Studená Dolina** ("Little Cold Valley") sounds more appealing, take the green trail through the eerily barren landscape to the **Téryho Chatka,** a convenient little chalet; this is a four-hour journey.

SLOVAKIA

SLOVENIA (SLOVENIJA)

US$1 = 129SIT		100SIT =	US$0.78
CDN$1= 93SIT		100SIT =	CAD$1.08
UK£1 = 196SIT		100SIT =	UK£0.51
IR£1 = 197SIT		100SIT =	IR£0.50
AUS$1 = 95SIT		100SIT =	AUS$1.05
NZ$1 = 69SIT		100SIT =	NZ$1.43
SAR1 = 36SIT		100SIT =	SAR2.76
DM1 = 83SIT		100SIT =	DM1.20
Country Code: 386		**International Dialing Prefix: 00**	

Slovenia wants you to forget that it was ever part of Yugoslavia. Worlds away from the conflict in Bosnia, the most prosperous of the breakaway republics is relishing its independence, rapidly modernizing, and turning a hungry eye toward the West. Half the size of Switzerland, Slovenia is extraordinarily diverse: in the space of a day, you can breakfast in the Alpine peaks, lunch under the Mediterranean sun, and dine in the vineyards of the Pannonian plains.

On the "sunny side of the Alps," Slovenia borders Italy to the west, Austria to the north, Hungary to the northeast, and Croatia to the east and south. Though the Italian port-city of Trieste takes a bite out of its coastline, Slovenia has a small window onto the Adriatic. In the northwest, the Julian Alps offer fabulous hiking before gradually descending into gentle hills near the Hungarian plains in the northwest. The river Sava originates in the Alps, circles around Ljubljana, then descends toward the Danube River; its valley is marked by beautiful hills scattered with castles, manors, monasteries, and churches with tall and slender towers.

SLOVENIA ESSENTIALS

Citizens of the U.S., Australia, Canada, and New Zealand can visit Slovenia visa-free for up to 90 days. Citizens of the U.K., Ireland, and South Africa need visas (US$32 for single-entry and transit; US$64 for multiple-entry; payable by check or money order). Apply by mail, in person, or at the border. See Essentials: Embassies and Consulates, page 3.

GETTING THERE AND GETTING AROUND

Altogether, there are 63 international border crossings in Slovenia. The country is easily accessible by car, train, or plane. Ljubljana is 100km from Trieste, 500km from Milan, 80km from Klagenfurt, and 500km from Budapest, and has frequent and uncrowded international train connections. **Trains** are cheap, clean, and reliable. Second class is a good option for the budget traveler. You can usually find a seat on local trains, although it's best to avoid peak commuting hours in and out of Ljubljana. Discounts are available for travelers under 26; check at the Ljubljana station (look for the BIJ-Wasteels logo). Round-trip tickets are 20% cheaper than two one-way tickets. Most stations have luggage storage. *"Vlak"* is the word for train; *"prihodi vlakov"* means arrivals; *"odhodi vlakov"* means departures. Schedules usually list trains by their direction.

  Buses are more expensive and usually slower, but reach some otherwise inaccessible places. Tickets are sold at the station or on board; bring your luggage with you in the passenger compartment if its not too crowded. *Let's Go* does not recommend hitchhiking as a safe means of transportation. However, hitchers report some success in the countryside, although they suggest to beware the busy tourist season.

  There are three international **airports** in Slovenia: the Ljubljana Airport in Brnik, 25km from the city center, with a regular bus service for incoming and outgoing flights; the Maribor Airport in the east; and the much smaller Portorož Airport on the coast. The modernized national carrier **Adria Airways** flies direct to Munich, London, Paris, Vienna, Moscow, Tel Aviv, Rome, and Frankfurt.

  There is a regular **hydrofoil** service between Venice and Portorož.

TOURIST SERVICES AND MONEY

Tourist offices are located in most major cities and tourist spots; the staff are generally friendly, speak English, give general information, and can help you find accommodations. Most businesses are open Mon.-Fri. 8am-7pm, and Sat. 8am-1pm or 7am-noon. Services are generally closed on Sundays, but many restaurants stay open. **Holidays** of the newly independent state in 1995 include: Jan. 1, 2 (New Year); Feb. 8 *(Prešeren* Day); Easter Sunday and Monday; April 27 (Day of Uprising Against World War II Occupation); May 1, 2 (Labour Day); May 22 (Whit Sunday); June 25 (National Day); August 15 (Assumption Day); Oct. 31 (Reformation Day); Nov. 1 (All Saints' Day); Dec. 25 (Christmas); and Dec. 26 (Independence Day).

  The national **currency** is the Slovenian **Tolar** (1SIT), divided into 100 **stotins** which you'll probably never need; most shops round up bills to the nearest tolar. Inflation, though much lower than in other Eastern European countries, is still a problem. Prices in hard currency tend to be stable but are usually set in Deutschmarks (DM) rather than in U.S. dollars, though most establishments accept payments in any hard currency, and exchange offices are plentiful. The exchange rate for deutschmarks is slightly better than for U.S. dollars. Banks and exchange offices are usually open Mon.-Fri. 7:30am-6pm, Sat. 7:30am-noon. There is little variation among their rates and most charge no commission (which is reflected in the rates). All major credit cards are accepted, including Eurocard, Visa, Mastercard, Diner's Club, American Express; the most widely accepted credit card is Mastercard/Eurocard, followed by Visa. For purchases of at least 9000SIT you can get a 13% value-added tax refund at the border (ask the store salesperson for a tax-free check).

COMMUNICATION

Postal facilities and services are reliable. **Post offices** in Slovenia are usually open Monday through Friday 8am to 6pm, and Saturday 8am to 2pm (in larger cities, there is also a night service). When at the post office, stock up on **phone tokens** or purchase a **magnetic phone card** (440SIT). There are two kinds of tokens: "A" for local calls and "B" for long-distance calls. To call Slovenia, dial the appropriate international dialing prefix, the **country code** for Slovenia (386), followed by the city code and the local number. To call abroad from Slovenia, dial 00, followed by the country code (1 for the U.S.) and the city code/area code and local number as appropriate. AT&T USADirect and similar services are not yet available. For operator assistance in connecting calls, dial 90 in Ljubljana, Kranj, Maribor, and Nova Gorica and 900 in other Slovene cities. Calling the U.S. is expensive (almost US$3/min); you can try calling home from a neighboring western country.

Foreign newspapers and magazines are available in all larger cities. Slovenia also receives **satellite programs** in English, French, German and Italian. Every evening during tourist season, local TV programs broadcast news for foreign visitors in English and in German. Also, **Radio Ljubljana** broadcasts daily news, weather, and traffic information in English, German, Italian, and French.

LANGUAGE

If you speak any other Slavic language, you'll be able to decipher many Slovene words. The Roman alphabet is used for writing. Most young people speak at least some English, but the older generation is more likely to speak German (in the north) or Italian (along the Adriatic). Many cities along the Italian border are officially bilingual. The tourist industry is generally geared toward German speakers, though most tourist office employees speak English.

Word or Phrase	Spelling	
Yes	*Da*	da
No	*Ne*	neh
Today	*Danes*	da-nes
Tomorrow	*Jutri*	yoo-tree
Hello	*Idravo*	ee-drah-voh
Good morning	*Dobro jutro!*	doh-broh yoo-troh
Good afternoon	*Dober dan!*	doh-ber dan
Good evening	*Dober večer!*	doh-ber vey-tcher
Good night	*Lahko noč!*	lah-koh notch
Goodbye	*Na svidenje!*	nah svee-den-yeh
Excuse me	*Oprostite!*	oh-proh-stee-teh
Please	*Prosim!*	proh-seem
Thank you	*Hvala!*	hvah-lah
You're welcome	*Dobro dosli*	doh-broh doh-slee
When?	*Kdaj?*	kuh-day
Where?	*Kje?*	k-yeh
How much does it cost?	*Koliko to stane?*	koh-lee-koh toh stah-neh
How do I get to ...?	*Kako pridem do ...?*	kah-koh pree-dem doh
My name is ...?	*Ime me je...*	ee-meh meh-yeh
Do you speak English?	*Ali govorite*	ah-lee goh-voh-ree-teh
I don't understand	*Ne razumem*	neh rah-zoo-mehm
Leave me alone; get lost!	*Pusti me na miru!*	pooh-stee meh nah mee-roo
Help!	*Na pomoc!*	nah poh-mots

SLOVENIA

HEALTH AND SAFETY

Come prepared for the weather. Climate varies with the region of the country: mediterranean near the Adriatic, alpine in the mountains, moderate continental in the eastern plains, and pleasant everywhere during the summer. It can snow as late as June in the Alps. A Slovene proverb says that if it *doesn't* rain on May 15, it *will* rain on each day for 40 days afterward, but don't take it as a truth or reason to avoid visiting Slovenia in May or June.

In case of emergencies, you can contact one of the following departments: the **police** (tel. 92), the **fire** department (tel. 93), the **ambulance** service (tel. 94).

ACCOMMODATIONS AND CAMPING

At the height of tourist season, prices go up, services are slower, sights are crowded, and rooms are hard to find. The seaside tends to become packed as early as June, and is very crowded in July and August. In the mountains, the high season tends to be only during July and August. Student rooms are commonly available in the mountains during summer vacation (late June-early Sept.) Early August may be the most pleasant time to visit the Alps, when the weather is usually fair. **Hotels** are classified into five categories (L (deluxe), A, B, C, D) and tend to be expensive. **Youth hostels** are cheap, but they're generally open only during the summer. The same is true for student dormitories. Usually, the best option is to rent **private rooms;** prices depend on the location, but they are rarely above US$20, and the rooms are usually a delight. In some places, you can find rooms advertised on the streets ("*sobe*" or "*zimmer*" is "room"), or ask at the local tourist offices for help.

LIFE AND TIMES

HISTORY

The area now known as Slovenia was important as a trade route from the Baltic to the Adriatic as early as the 2nd millenium BC. Settled by Bronze Age **Celts** after 1300 BC, the territory weathered assaults from Cimmerians, Thracians, and Illyrians before being vanquished by the **Romans** in the early 2nd century BC. The Romano-Celts enjoyed over 500 years of peace before the Empire fell, opening the area to Germanic and Slavic invaders. Modern **Slovenes** are descendants of the west Slavic tribes who migrated through Moravia into the Eastern Alps in the 6th century AD.

Ostrogoths, Lombards, and Carolingian Franks shared the territory between the 6th and 10th centuries. In the 9th century, Slav Prince Kocely of **Carniola,** as the area was called, introduced Christian worship in the Slavic language and script. By the 980s Carniola had been annexed by the Holy Roman Emperor Otto II and remained under foreign rule for the next millennium. Divided into various fiefs and duchies, the Slovenes were ruled by German Emperors, Czech Kings, and Venetian Oligarchs through the Middle Ages. The 1300s saw Carniola slowly swallowed by the **Austrian Habsburgs,** under whose rule most Slovenes remained until the 20th century.

During World War I, Slovene politicians pressed for an independent state of South Slavs, which was to consist of present Slovenia, Croatia, and Bosnia and Herzegovina. In 1918, **Yugoslavia** (Land of the South Slavs) was officially created, with its capital in Zagreb, and Slovenia ceased to be a part of the Austro-Hungarian empire. The new Kingdom of Yugoslavia was too weak, however, to withstand the attacks of Hitler's armed forces during World War II. When Yugoslavia fell in 1941, Slovenia was partitioned among Germany, Italy, and Hungary. The Germans took the region north of Ljubljana and the Sava, the Italians got Ljubljana and the areas south of the city, and the Hungarians received the plains in the west. The Germans then proceeded to Germanize the lands under their occupation, while the Italians initially left more freedom to the Slovenes. After the German attack on the Soviet Union in the summer of 1941, Slovene Communists, Christian Socialists, and other left-wing groups joined the Yugoslav partisan army of Josip Broz Tito. Led by the Communist party, the army was eventually recognized by the British and Americans as an ally against Hitler, and as such, was supplied with arms to continue the fight.

In 1945, the partisans liberated the territories that had belonged to Yugoslavia, and once again the state came into being, this time with Tito in command and with headquarters in Belgrade. This was the beginning of the **Communist** era, which was to last until 1990. After the rift between Tito and Stalin in 1948, Yugoslavia opened up to the West and began to introduce certain features of market economy. Slovenia was soon acknowledged as its most Western and economically viable republic. Tito died in 1980, and with his death, confusion invaded the scene of what was seemingly a peaceful and stable country. The long-suppressed ethnic conflicts reemerged and threatened to shake the foundations of the entire state. Unlike most European nations, which are usually built around a single set of ideas and a single ethnicity, Yugoslavia comprised several large ethnic groups who had little in common, beside the fact that they were all descendants of Slavic tribes and happened to occupy neighboring territories. The efforts of the Communist party to find a strong and reliable leader to replace Tito failed. Without the fear of a strong hand in Belgrade, opposition speedily emerged in Slovenia, as well as in the other republics.

The Slovenes took their first step toward independence in 1989, when the Slovene Assembly adopted an amendment to the republican constitution. In December 1990, the plebiscite on a sovereign state resulted in over 80% of the voters opting for independence. Six months later, in June 1991, the Assembly proclaimed Slovene independence and sovereignty and the annulment of the Yugoslav constitution. At first, the Yugoslav army responded with force, but after 10 days of violent clashes, it gave up the fight (July 7); Serbia, the driving force behind Yugoslavia and the conflict, had no border claims against the Slovenes, and no large Serbian minority lives in Slovenia (as opposed to Bosnia). The final step toward full independence was the new Slovene constitution, adopted in December 1991, one year after the plebiscite.

SLOVENIA TODAY

Slovenia's cities and shops look more Austrian than Yugoslav, most of its government and commercial services are as reliable as in Western Europe, and the country is quickly moving toward integration into European structures. Only recently (1993), Slovenia completed an agreement with the European Union on Trade and Economic Cooperation. The process of economic reform is far from over, but the pains of the transition have so far been easier to bear here than in many parts of Eastern Europe; in recent years, per capita GNP fell from US$8000 to US$6000, but is still far ahead of most Eastern European countries. Today, Slovenia attracts around three million tourists per year, outnumbering the members of its own population (two million).

FOOD AND DRINK

Self-serve fast food places have mushroomed in Slovenia, especially in the larger, more touristed cities. Although a convenient and inexpensive option for the budget traveler, they are not necessarily the most exciting or original choices of food. Traditional Slovene cuisine, however, is becoming increasingly hard to find; private family homes are often the last bastions of mouth-watering, home-style cookery. If you can get your hands on a good menu, try the national dish *jota*, a potato, bean, and cabbage soup, which is said to have originated in the region of Goriška Brda. Potatoes are so well liked that they have earned the Slovenes the nickname of "potato-eaters." The cabbage used to make *jota* is sauerkraut rather than fresh cabbage; it adds a tangy flavor to the soup that would otherwise be quite bland. There are many variations on the *jota*, depending on which region you are currently visiting. Browned onions, bacon, garlic, parsley, sage, and bay leaves are often added to the three essential components; less often, tomatoes or sour turnips will also become part of the tasty mixture. *Jota* is supposed to be thick, but not too heavy (easy on those explosive beans!), and it should never be too sour. Slovenes also have good pastries; one of their favorite cakes is *potica*, consisting of a sheet of pastry, spread with a rich filling, and rolled up. The most common and popular of all fillings is the one made from walnut kernels (walnut *potica).*

The **wine** tradition of the country dates from antiquity; monks and feudal lords preserved it in the Middle Ages. Slovenia lies in the center of the so-called European wine zone, at almost the same latitude as Burgundy in France. Better Slovene labels are *Merlot, Cabernet* and *Tokay* among the red wines and *Muscat, Malvazjia, Pinot Blanc,* and *Sauvignon* among the whites. Locals claim that the less familiar *Dolenjski Cviček* has curative properties in addition to its pleasant sourish taste.

Slovenia has three distinct wine regions. The **Podravje region** stretches on the Pannonian plains in the northeastern part of the country. Thanks to the warm continental climate, winegrowers are able to leave grapes on the vine for a longer period of time and thus obtain late vintage wines. The region is known for the finest quality white wines, fresh, aromatic, and mellow. The most famous wines come from Lutomer in the center of Podravje. The *Ljutomer Riesling* is medium-sweet, while *Ljutomer Traminer* provides a pleasant, spicy edge to the medium-sweet style. *Ljutomer Sauvignon Blanc* is crisp and fruity and should be imbibed as young as possible. Another specialty of the region is ice wine, produced from frozen grapes. South of Podravje stretches the **Posavje region,** which boasts younger white wines and rose and red wines with higher acidity and lower alcohol content than in the north. Finally, the **Primorje (Coastal) region** along the Adriatic coast is the sunniest part of Slovenia. Endowed with a mild mediterranean climate, this region produces full-bodied and aromatic wines, close in flavor to the wines of Italy, of which the best known is the ruby-colored *Kraški Teran.*

■ Ljubljana

Legend has it that Jason the Argonaut, Golden Fleece in tow, fled across the Black Sea, up the Danube to the Sava and Ljubljanica Rivers in order to to escape King Aietes. Trapped by the Barje marshlands, Jason is said to have founded a city on the banks of the Ljubljanica. In the 1st century AD, Roman soldiers returning from campaigns settled along the same river. Their stronghold evolved into the fortified town of *Colonia Iulia Aemona,* frequently plundered by barbaric warriors. In the Middle Ages, Slavic tribes settled the city they named Ljubljana.

A transportation hub since the 19th century, when its railroads first linked Vienna with the more remote parts of the Austro-Hungarian Empire, Ljubljana is Slovenia's commercial and cultural center. The Old Town charms visitors with its colorful Renaissance, Baroque, and Secession façades.

ORIENTATION AND PRACTICAL INFORMATION

Situated just 40km from the Austrian border, Ljubljana is a major junction between the main north-south and east-west rail lines in the region. It is easily accessible from the neighboring Italy, Austria and Hungary. The **train** and **bus stations** stand side-by-side near the center of town. From either one, turn right on Masarykova cesta, then left at Miklošičeva cesta, which will lead you directly into the central square, **Prešernov Trg.** Beyond this square lies the **Triple Bridge;** cross it, and you'll find yourself in the **Old Town,** at the base of the castle hill.

Trieste, Italy, is an easy day trip from Ljubljana; refer to Gateway Cities, page 745

Tourist Office: TIC-Tourist Information Center, Slovenska 35 (tel. 22 42 22, fax 22 21 15), offers excellent brochures. (Open Mon.-Fri. 8am-7pm, Sat.-Sun. 8am-noon and 4-7pm.) **Slovenÿaturist,** Slovenska 58 (tel. 31 18 51).

Budget Travel: Mladiturist, Celovska 49 (tel. 32 18 97, tel./fax 31 21 85). Take bus #1 or 3 from Slovenska. Information for young travelers. ISIC and HI cards.
Embassies: U.S., Pražakova 4, 61000 Ljubljana (tel. 30 14 85, fax 30 14 01); **U.K.,** Trg Republike 3, 61000 Ljubljana (tel. 125 71 91, fax 125 01 74), open Mon.-Fri. 9:30am-noon and 1-4pm; **Albania,** Ob Ljubljanici 12, 61000 Ljubljana (tel. 132 23 24, fax 132 31 29); **Austria,** Štrekljeva 5, 61000 Ljubljana (tel. 21 34 36; fax 22 17 17); **Croatia,** Grubarjevo nabrežje 6, 61000 Ljubljana (tel. 21 16 35, fax 125 81 06); **Czech Republic,** Kolarjeva 30, 61000 Ljubljana (tel. 132 80 35, fax 31 84 23); **Germany,** Robova 18, VI, 61000 Ljubljana (tel. 173 44 31, fax 173 44 42); **Hungary,** Dunajska 22, 61000 Ljubljana (tel. 131 51 68, fax 131 71 43); **Italy,** Snežniška 8, 61000 Ljubljana (tel. 126 21 94, fax 125 33 02); **Macedonia,** Kardeljeva ploščad 1/I, 61000 Ljubljana (tel. 168 44 54, fax 168 41 81); **Romania,** Nanoška 8, 61000 Ljubljana (tel. 26 87 02); **Russia,** Cesta II #7, 61000 Ljubljana (tel. 26 22 50, fax 15 41 41).
Currency Exchange: At most hotels, travel agencies, and banks. Little variation and few charge commissions. **Slovenÿaturist** at the train station open 24 hrs.
American Express: Atlas, Mestni Trg (tel. 22 27 11), in old city one block from river. Holds mail, but does not cash traveler's checks or wire money. Agency open Mon.-Fri. 9am-5pm, Sat. 9am-noon. AmEx rep. Mon.-Fri. 9am-3pm.
Post Offices: Cigaletova 15 (tel. 31 45 73), 3 blocks right of train station. Tall yellow building; enter at back. Open 24hrs. Also office at Slovenska 32 (tel. 21 07 40) by tourist office; open Mon.-Fri. 7am-8pm, Sat. 7am-1pm. **Postal Code:** 61000.
Telephones: Buy tokens or phonecards at any post office. **City Code:** 061.
Flights: Airport is in Brnik, 26km away (tel. (064) 22 27 00, fax 22 12 20). Buses leave from the central bus station. **Airline Offices: Adria Airways,** Gosposvetsta 6 (tel. 31 33 12); **Austrian Airlines,** Dunajska 107 (tel. 37 17 47); **Lufthansa,** Slovenska 54 (tel. 32 66 62); **Swissair,** Hotel Lev, Vošnjakova 1 (tel. 31 76 47).
Trains: Trg OF *(Osvobodielne Fronte;* tel. 131 51 67 or 31 67 68). Trains to: Venezia (3 per day, 6hrs.); Trieste (4 per day, 3hrs.); Vienna (1 per day, 6hrs.); Zagreb (10 per day, 2½hrs.); Budapest (2 per day, 10hrs.); Salzburg (3 per day, 4½hrs.); Munich (2 per day, 6hrs.). Student discounts make Budapest accessible for US$25 and Zagreb for US$7, among others.
Buses: The station neighbors the train station (tel. 133 61 36). Buses to all major destinations: Bled and Postojna 1hr., Adriatic coast 3hr.
Public Transportation: Buses run until midnight. The fare is 60SIT (drop exact change in the box next to the driver) or you can buy tokens for 43SIT at post offices and newsstands. One-day, weekly, and monthly passes available at *Ljubljanski potniški promet,* Celovška 160 (tel. 159 41 14).
Hitchhiking: *Let's Go* does not recommend hitchhiking as a safe means of transportation. Hitchers to Bled take bus #1 to the last stop. Hitchers to the coast take bus #6 to the last stop or walk out of town along Tržaška cesta.
Laundromat: Kam on university campus, Building C, Kardeljeva ploščad 14 (tel. 34 00 49), open Mon.-Fri. 8am-noon and 2-6pm, Sat. 8am-3pm. **Tič,** Building 9, Cesta 27 aprila 31 (tel. 126 32 33), Mon.-Fri. 9am-7pm, Sat. 9am-2pm and 4-7pm.
Pharmacies: Prešernov Trg 5 (tel. 133 50 44), open Mon.-Fri. 8am-7pm, Sat. 8am-1pm. Or go to Miklošičeva 24 (tel. 31 45 58), open Mon.-Sat. 8am-8pm.
Medical Assistance: In case of emergency, call **Bohoričeva Medical Centre** (tel. 32 30 60) or **Klinični center,** Zaloška 2 (tel. 131 43 44).
Emergencies: Police: tel. 92. **Fire:** tel. 93. **Ambulance:** 94. **General info:** 981.

ACCOMMODATIONS AND CAMPING

In the summer reserve rooms. **Private rooms** are available through tourist offices (scarce singles US$10). July-August ask about student **dorm rooms** (US$10/person) in **Dom Učencev Tabor,** Vidovdanska cesta 7 (tel. 32 10 67) or **Dijaški Dom Ivana Cankarja,** Poljanska cesta 26-28 (tel. 133 52 74). To reach the latter from the train station, take bus #11 or walk down Resljeva cesta to Poljanska cesta and turn left; follow the path between 24 and 26 to the end and turn left.

Park Hotel, Tabor 9 (tel. 133 13 06, fax 32 13 52), near youth hostel. Cheapest in town. Depressing building from the outside, but only 10min. from downtown.

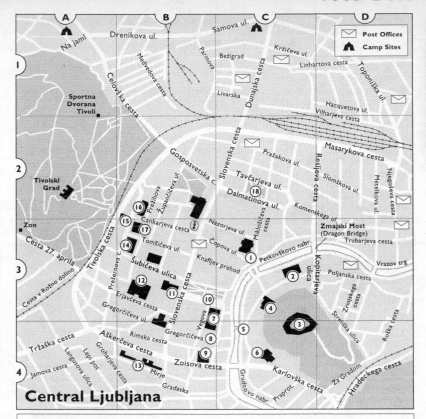

Central Ljubljana

1 Prešernov Trg (Prešeren Square)
2 Stolnica (Cathedral), Škofijski Dvorec (Bishop's Palace) Semenišče (Seminary)
3 Ljubljanski Grad (Castle)
4 Rotovž (Town Hall)
5 Mestni Trg and Stari Trg (Town Square and Old Square)
6 Levstikov Trg (Levstik Square)
7 SAZU (Slovene Academy of Arts and Sciences)
8 NUK- National and University Library
9 Trg Francoske Revolucije (French Revolution Square)
10 Kongresni Trg (Congress Square)
11 Uršulinska Cerkev (Ursuline Church)
12 Trg Republike (Republic Square and Parliament Building)
13 Roman Wall
14 Narodni Muzej (National Museum)
15 Moderna Galerija (Museum of Modern Art)
16 Narodna Galerija (National Gallery)
17 Opera
18 Miklošič Park

Clean but very spartan rooms; get one that isn't missing a light bulb. Singles US$21, with shower US$27.

Pri Mraku, Rimska 4 (tel. 22 34 12, fax 30 11 97). A pension with cozier rooms. Singles US$23, with shower US$33. Doubles US$33, with shower US$48. Reservations recommended.

Camping: Autocamp Ježica, Dunajska 270 (tel./fax 37 13 82). Near the river; take bus #6 or 8. US$7 per person. Open May-Sept.

FOOD

For a supermarket, head to **Maximarket,** across from the Parliament building. Anything you need at Western prices. MasterCard accepted (open Mon.-Fri. 9am-8pm, Sat. 8am-7pm). The Old Town hosts a large **outdoor market** (open Mon.-Sat. until 2pm). Face the old city and the three bridges, take a right, and you'll find bargain riverfront restaurants. The popular cafés line Mestni Trg and Stari Trg.

Zlata Ladjica, Jurčičev Trg 1, south along the river. Enjoy pizzas and pasta in a grotto with stained-glass windows.

Gostilna Sestica, Slovenska 40 (tel. 21 95 75) is Ljubljana's oldest restaurant, with a formidable selection of entrees.

Triglav, Mikosičeva 12, is an inexpensive self-serve restaurant north of the river, 200m from the train station.

Pizzeria Romeo, on the wharf on the castle side of the river. Inexpensive pizza and ice cream (meals US$7). Nice views of the river.

If it's fast food you crave, try the **Dairy Queen** on Slovenska near the tourist office (open Mon.-Thurs. 9am-11pm, Fri.-Sat. 9am-midnight, Sun. 4-10pm). Or prostrate yourself to Western decadence and grab a tasty burger at **McDonald's,** Copova 14 near Presernov Trg. Hamburgers 110SIT, Big Mac 220SIT, small french fries 70SIT (open Mon.-Sat. 9am-11pm, Sun. 10am-11pm).

SIGHTS AND ENTERTAINMENT

While a few buildings in Ljubljana were designed on a gigantic socialist scale, the city also has many older monuments, in styles ranging from Renaissance to Secession. After a disastrous earthquake in 1895, the destroyed buildings were rebuilt in neo-Baroque style, adding to the multitude of styles represented in the Old Town.

Prešernov Trg and Environs

On the train station side of the river is the main square, **Prešernov Trg,** named after the great Slav poet France Prešeren. From either the bus or train stations, walk along Resljeva cesta, which runs perpendicular to Trg Osvobodilne fronte and the stations; tturn right onto Komenskego ulica, and then left on Dalmatinova ulica. Another left, from Dalmatinova onto Miklošičeva cesta, takes you straight to Prešernov Trg. The square's **Franciscan Church** was built in the 17th century in neo-Classical style; the altar inside the church is the work of the native sculptor, Francesco Robba (1736). Another prominent feature of the square is **Triple Bridge** (*Tripmostovje*); in the 1930s, the old *Špitalski* Bridge was modernized by the revered Slovene architect Jože Plečnik, who added two footbridges to the former stone bridge, transforming it into one of Ljubljana's most admired architectural jewels. Plečnik also arranged many parks and squares in town and designed the National and University Library, the open market by the Ljubljanica, the Žale cemetery, and St. Michael's Church.

To the left of the Triple Bridge, when facing the Ljubljanica River, is the **Dragon Bridge** (*Zmajski most*), built in 1901 in place of the former wooden "Butcher's Bridge." The bridge was named after the Emperor Franz Joseph, but the name was never adopted in practice. Instead, locals call it the Dragon Bridge, because it is decorated with dragons, the symbol and coat-of-arms of Ljubljana.

East of the Ljubljanica River

Cross either the Triple Bridge or the Dragon Bridge to get to the **Cathedral** (*Stolnica*), built on the site of an old Romanesque church that had been dedicated by the boatmen and fishermen of Ljubljana to their patron St. Nicholas. The original church was later rebuilt many times, and today's cathedral dates from the early 18th century; few original works of art remain, but visitors can still admire a well-preserved 15th-century Gothic Pietà. Narrow streets on both sides of the river provide strolling grounds. The shores were arranged by the same Jože Plečnik who built the Triple Bridge. Watch the lazy waters from under the shade of the trees; most benches are occupied by young couples.

From the Cathedral, follow Ciril-Metodov Trg to the Baroque **Mestni Trg** (Town Square). Don't miss the **City Hall** (*Rotovž*) on Mestni Trg, close to the Triple Bridge, erected in 1484, and then rebuilt in 1718. In front of the hall stands an impressive fountain (1751), yet another work of the great local master Francesco Robba, embellished with allegorical sculptures of three rivers: the Ljubljanica, Sava and Krka.

From the City Hall, the **Ljubljana Castle** (*Ljubljanski Grad*) is a few steps away. Walk up the hill for a beautiful panorama of the city and the Alps. Archeological evidence indicates that the hill was fortified as early as the 9th century, but the castle itself is mentioned only in 1144. Rebuilt after the earthquake of 1511, it housed a prison in later centuries. The castle and the courtyard are currently being renovated (tower open daily 10am-dusk).

Around the Trg Francoske Revolucije

The French Revolution Square (*Trg Francoske Revolucije*) and its immediate surroundings were once occupied by the Teutonic Knights; the neighborhood is still called **Križanke.** The Knights built their monastery in the square; demolished in the 18th century, the complex was restored under Plečnik's guidance, and now hosts musical, theatrical and dance performances of the **Ljubljana International Summer Festival** (mid-July to end of Sept.). North of the French Revolution Square stands the National and University Library (*Narodna in Univerzitetna Knjižnica*), designed in the 1930s by Jože Plečnik; its rich collections include medieval documents, Renaissance editions, and an interesting **exhibit of resistance literature** printed in occupied Ljubljana between 1941 and 1945.

North of the Library and the **Slovene Academy of Arts and Sciences** (*Slovenska Akademija Znanosti in Umetnosti*) lies the Baroque **Congress Square** (*Kongresni Trg*), named after the Congress of the Holy Alliance, signed by the Austrian Emperor, the Russian Tsar, and the Neapolitan King in 1821. South of the square stands the **University of Ljubljana.** Westward, across Slovenska cesta, is the **Ursuline church** (*Uršulinska Cerkev*), one of the most beautiful Baroque buildings in Ljubljana, also known as the Holy Trinity church because of the Holy Trinity monument out front. The original wooden monument (1693), a symbol of Ljubljana's gratitude for having survived the plague, was later replaced with a stone replica (the original is in the City Museum in French Revolution Square).

Museums and Music Centers

Ljubljana's museums cluster around the Slovene **Parliament** buildings, near Trg Republike (Republic Square) on the train station side of the river. From Prešernov Trg, walk east on either Nazorieva, Čopova, or Knafljev ulica to Slovenska cesta, one of the main arteries of Ljubljana. The Parliament buildings are on the other side, two blocks away from Slovenska. Museums are open Tues.-Sat. 10am-6pm, Sun. 10am-1pm. The **National Museum** (*Narodni Muzej*), at Muzejska 1 (tel. 21 88 86), exhibits archaeological, ethnological, cultural, and historical collections. The nearby **Museum of Modern Art** (*Moderna Galerija*) displays works of 20th-century Slovene artists. Every odd year, it also hosts the **International Biennial of Graphic Art,** the largest exhibition of its kind in the world. To the left of the Modern Art Museum, stands the **National Gallery** (*Narodna Galerija*), Cankarjeva 20 (tel. 21 97 16); it exhibits works by Slovene artists from the Middle Ages to the present. Near the museums, across from Tivolska cesta, is the **Tivoli park,** with some of the prettiest strolling grounds in Ljubljana and excellent paths for jogging. The park also features a castle and a zoo. The **Tivoli Castle** (*Tivolski Grad*) was built in the 17th century by Jesuits, and now houses the International Center of Graphic Art.

The **Slovene Symphony Orchestra** performs regularly at **Cankarjev Dom,** across from the Parliament buildings. Various events, from violin concerts to grunge music, are held throughout the year; pick up the *Where To?* brochure at tourist offices for listings of the month's cultural events. The most popular disco in town is **Babilon,** at Kongresni Trg 2 (tel. 21 43 36; open Tues.-Sat. 10pm-4am). For a more underground scene, try **K-4** at Kersinkova 4 (tel. 131 32 82) or the **Acapulco** and **Eldorado.**

THE JULIAN ALPS (JULIJSKE ALPE)

The southern Alps are not as high as their Austrian or Swiss counterparts, but they are no less beautiful. The mountains cover the northwest of Slovenia, peaking at 2864 meters on **Mt. Triglav** in the heart of the **Triglav National Park.** *"Triglav"* means "three heads," and the summit is indeed flanked by two smaller peaks. It is a sacred mountain; the ancient Slavs believed that it was the god of the Sun. Even today some say that you are not truly Slovene until you climb Mt. Triglav.

Mt. Triglav is hardly the only attraction of the Julian Alps. East of Triglav is **Bled,** a world famous resort. The more peaceful **Bohinj,** southwest of Bled, is the place to get information about climbing Mt. Triglav. A railroad crosses the mountains connecting Jesenice, Bled, Bohinj, and Most na Soči; scenic train rides in antique cars are offered throughout the spring and summer. The **Soča Valley** stretches up from **Most na Soči;** some claim that it's the most beautiful place in the world. It was here that an Italian offensive was stopped by the Germans during World War I; more than a million people died in three weeks. A museum in **Kobarid,** northwest of Most na Soči, is dedicated to the history of this tragic event. Not far away is a hotel owned by an American with nightly jazz music.

The Julian Alps are also the source of one of the region's largest rivers, the **Sava.** The Sava Dolinka originates north of Triglav, and the Sava Bohinjka starts its flow from the Bohinj Lake, south of Triglav; these two rivers meet not far from Bled, and form the wider Sava. Close to the source of Sava Dolinka is the resort of **Kranjska Gora,** with some of the best skiing facilities in Slovenia. A little farther to the north, on the Austrian border, stretch the **Karavanke mountains,** with the idyllic village of **Planina pod Golico**.

The Julian Alps are easily accessible by train or bus. From the northeast, the gateway city of Bled is at most one hour from Ljubljana, and Bohinj only 1½ hours. Jesienice and Bled can also be reached from Austria, while **Nova Gorica** *(Gorizia)*, in the southern part of the region, is only one hour away from Trieste in Italy.

■ ■ ■ BLED

"This place is so beautiful, I couldn't help but win."
—Bobby Fischer, chess prodigy

In a pleasant valley with a gorgeous view of the Alps, Bled has been a world-class resort for more than a century, and its lake has hosted the world rowing championships three times. Bled is an excellent base for trips into the mountains and to nearby ski centers of Straža, Zatrnik, and Pokljuka, on the Pokljuka plateau.

Orientation and Practical Information Trains stop in **Lesce,** 5km away from Bled on the Ljubljana-Salzburg-Munich line (310SIT; 50min.). You can also get here by **bus** (hourly from Ljubljana; 90min.). If you take the train from Ljubljana, catch one of the frequent buses going from Lesce to Bled, or consider taking a taxi (the 900SIT may be bearable if you pool with someone else).   Buses from Lesce stop on Ljubljanska, the main street of Bled, just a few steps from the tourist office. You can get off here and head straight to the tourist office for more information, or you can stay on the bus until it reaches the main bus station, which is closer to the castle and the youth hostel.

Bled is scattered around the lake, but most buildings lie on the east side, clustered along the shore and the main street, which leads straight to the lake. The **tourist office** is by the lake, at Ljubljanska 4 (tel. 772 35 or 772 45, fax 781 81; open Mon.-Sat. 8am-6pm, Sun. noon-6pm); pick up a copy of the *Bled Tourist News* for the latest information on hiking and skiing. The tourist agencies **Kompas Bled,** at Ljubljanska 7 (tel. 781 82 or 775 75, fax 781 81), and **Globtour,** at C. svobode 9 (tel. 779 09 or 777 90, fax 781 85), both close at 7pm. To **exchange currency** at a good rate with no commissions, go to **General Turist** by the lake. The **post office** is also on the main street (tel. 772 00; open Mon.-Fri. 7am-7pm, Sat. 7am-noon). The **telephone city code** is 064.

> **Warning:** Bled's phone numbers are in the process of being converted to six-digit numbers. The numbers listed below may change. Check the 1995 *Bled Tourist News* for updates.

Accommodations The best option is a **private room;** rates are reasonable and the rooms are often lovely. Both **Kompas** and **Globtour** can help you find a room; the latter's rates tend to be better. Off-season (Sept. and March-June), singles run around are US$14, doubles US$21; otherwise US$16 and US$26 respectively. Breakfast runs around US$3 per person. You can also book directly; look for signs advertising *"sobe."* For about US$28 you can stay on a **farm;** you get a room and a home-cooked breakfast and dinner. The drawback is location: around 30 minutes from the center. Book at a tourist office or check the *Bled Tourist News*.

The **youth hostel,** 17 Grajska C. (tel. 782 30), is in a quiet location, not central but close to the castle. From the bus station, head uphill; turn right at the first fork and left at the second one. The hostel is on top of the hill (5min.). It has small but clean rooms; crowded during the summer, it is virtually deserted in the off-season. (DM15 per person, with breakfast DM20. HI membership required. Open most of the year; call ahead.) **Camping Zaka, C.** svobode 13 (tel. 779 32 or 773 25), is on the opposite shore of the lake, 2km from the center. It has a private beach and charges DM12 per person (open May-Sept.).

Food Restaurants in Bled are becoming increasingly expensive, but most are still affordable. For cheap food, check out the **Market Bled** near the *Kompas* office; it also carries postcards and souvenirs (open Mon.-Sat. 7am-8pm, Sun. 9am-noon). There is also a small market by the bus station. Among the restaurants, **Blejski Grad** in the castle (tel. 770 13) boasts a candle-lit interior with medieval Italian murals. Arrive early to snag a table with a view of the lake. The menu is in Italian: fish, meat, and pasta specialties (entrees 800-1400SIT).

The **Park Restaurant** sits across from the Park Hotel near the main street on the lake shore (tel. 779 45). It's on the expensive side (entrees 1200-1700SIT), but the beautiful view of the lake may be worth it. The airy interior with large windows is filled with plants. (MasterCard/Eurocard accepted.) From the main street, a 5-minute walk along the shore toward the castle takes you to a stylish **restaurant** shy about its name, offering a quiet and discreet ambience. The rich and tasty menu is worth the extra walk: spaghetti around US$5 (500-700SIT), other entrees US$7-14 (900-1700SIT). Take someone here on a first date (open noon-10pm).

Pizzeria Gallus is by the main street close to the lake, across from the hotel park. It's a very informal place; the main attraction is a terrace with a nice view of the lake and castle—but beware the mosquitoes. Pizzas 500-800SIT (open 11am-midnight). **Okarina,** at Riklijeva 9 (tel. 74 14 58; fax 74 18 30), is close to the bus station and the youth hostel. Its soft music and friendly staff make you feel at home. There is a wide selection of standard, traditional and vegetarian dishes: carnivores will pay 1000-1600SIT for an entree, while veggie lovers will preserve their money and the environment by spending only 500-800SIT.

Sights The **Bled Castle** (*Blejski Grad*) is on top of a hill 10 minutes from the center of the resort. Climb one of the steep paths, or follow the mellower road. The castle has a wide terrace, from which spreads an incredible view of Bled and its surroundings. The castle itself is an appealing combination of red-tile roofs and ivy-covered stone walls. (Museum open daily 8am-7pm; admission 200SIT, ages 3-10 100SIT, or free with a deposit of 500SIT toward a meal.) Down from the castle, small palm trees guard the Gothic entrance to the tiny **church;** its red tower contains a working clock. Near the church is the town **cinema,** with all the latest American mind-fodder.

Sculls, ducks, and swans float on the clear waters of **Bled Lake.** The waterfront promenade has frog-shaped trash cans and a moss-covered fountain, where you may end up if you're unlucky at the nearby magical **casino** (open Mon.-Sat. at 7pm, Sun. 5pm). Rent a **boat** for 600SIT per hour to test your navigational skills. The water is surprisingly warm for a mountain lake. If you walk or jog about 1km to the left of the resort along the lake, past the campground and boat rental facility, you'll reach the best place to cross to the island in the center. If you're a good swimmer, you can try to reach the **island** in the middle of the lake (a 5-25min. swim, depending on your skills). Don't try it if you're not absolutely sure you can handle all the exercise; the island is farther than it seems. The island houses a beautiful old **church,** once a destination for pilgrims. They took a boat; there's no shame in your doing so, too.

■■■ RIBČEV LAZ

Ribčev Laz is one of the resort centers of the scenic Bohinj region lying in the heart of the Julian Alps. Though not as large as Bohinjska Bistrica, it boasts a more beautiful location on the southeastern edge of the Bohinj Lake. Legend has it that the fabulous *Zlatorog* ("goat with golden horns") lived in the Alps somewhere near the lake. With his miraculous powers, *Zlatorog* built himself a wonderful garden in the mountains, filled with gold and jewels. One day, a jealous man attacked and slew *Zlatorog*. From his blood grew a plant that brought him back to life. In his blind rage, the *Zlatorog* killed the man and all his mountain gardens, then disappeared forever. What's left today is a legend, a Hotel Zlatorog by the Bohinj Lake, and a popular brand of beer (surprise—*Zlatorog).* But even without the legendary gardens the Alps remain a beautiful spot to visit.

The Bohinj area is as beautiful as Bled's environs, but more isolated and less touristed, though it can get crowded in July and August. In June it is almost sure to be wonderful, quiet, and inexpensive. There are no direct bus connections to Ribčev Laz, but the resort is only 5km west of Bohinjska Bistrica, and buses run every hour from Bled to Bistrica (20km, 260SIT); they stop near the tourist office in Bistrica. To get to Ribčev Laz, catch the local bus on the main road in front of the post office (110SIT). Bohinjska Bistrica can also be reached by train; all trains on the Bled-Most na Soči line stop here (101SIT to Bled, 377SIT to Nova Gorica, 470SIT to Ljubljana; 8 trains per day in each direction).

Most of the interesting walks and hikes start in Ribčev Laz, so you might as well come here instead of staying in Bohinjska Bistrica. Once in Ribčev, stop by the **tourist office,** located near the main road; the staff is friendly but the office often closes before 6pm. There is also a **post office** and a reasonably-priced **supermarket** nearby. Remember to pick up a walking/hiking map from the Ribčev tourist office. Hiking trips include a visit to the **Savica waterfall.** Bohinj is also a starting point for climbing Mt. Triglav; alternate starting points are in the north in the Sava Valley. When you're ready to leave the area and if you have a tent, you can consider hiking farther west to Krn and into the Soča Valley. Otherwise, return to Bohinjska Bistrica and head on to Bled or Most na Soči and Nova Gorica; from the latter, you can take a bus or train to Postojna, to the coastal resorts of Slovenia, or into Italy.

Private rooms are generally excellent and inexpensive. Singles run about US$10, breakfast US$4. Ask the tourist office for a room with a Triglav-view. Farther along the lake, there is a **youth hostel** that keeps changing its name (in 1994 it was the Hotel Apollon; inquire at the tourist office). You can feed yourself at any of the hotel restaurants, but also try **Restaurant Triglav,** 15 minutes away in Stara Fužina, north of Ribčev Laz. Turn right 50m down from the tourist office and cross the bridge. Then follow the main road; admire the picturesque church by the lake on the way. It's a bit expensive (full meals US$10-15), but worth the hike for the excellent food and great views from the terrace; don't forget to ask about national specialties.

■ NEAR BOHINJ: MOUNT TRIGLAV

You don't need to spend US$8 on the fancy *How to Climb Mt. Triglav* brochure in order to make the climb. Be aware, however, that it is a difficult enterprise. Doing it in one day from Bohinj takes about 14 hours (round-trip); it's more realistic to do it in two days and spend a night in a hut. Snow can make the hike difficult and the last portion dangerous as late as June. Don't try it unless you have the proper equipment.

Starting from **Bohinj Lake,** cross the bridge and go past the monastery. Follow the main road into **Stara Fužina** for 10-15 minutes. A narrower road branches off to the left, with a sign reading *Voje.* Follow the road out of the village and into the **Triglav National Park.** Continue for about one hour. It's an easy and pleasant walk among fields of flowers and patches of forest, with a dreamy view of the Alps on the horizon. It's even better on the way back—if you have the energy to enjoy it.

A path branches left with a sign reading *Velo Polje, 3½hrs.* It's an easy walk at first, but the path quickly becomes narrower and eventually starts climbing steeply through the forest. The dark green of the conifers mixes with the lighter foliage of the beech trees—but keep your eyes on the trail. After about one hour, the path enters a large clearing. Fill your empty water bottles here. From the clearing, the trail continues to climb steeply, at first through forest and then a rocky valley. After 2-3 hours you'll finally reach **Vodnikov dom** (cabin; open July-August), offering a great view of Mt. Triglav and the whole ridge from an elevation of 1805m. There is a spring nearby with crystal-clear and very, very cold water.

Here the trail divides again, this time into three branches. Continue on the middle path (marked *Triglav).* As you emerge above the treeline, the weather can be harsh. Use common sense; turn back if you discover that the weather conditions are worsening. About 45 minutes later, you will reach a small plateau, where the path splits again. Both branches lead to huts about the same distance from the top, **Dom Planika** (2408m; usually open July-Sept.; check back in town first!) and **Kredarica/Triglavski Dom** (2545m); each hut is about 1½ hours from the plateau. Kredarica is always open; you can get water or tea at the meteorological station located nearby (they will let you stay the night for 1000SIT—just think of it as the world's most inconvenient hostel).

Once you've reached one of the huts, the peak is one hour away. This is the toughest part! The trail as you've known it ends; from now on, you will be literally hanging on a stone wall. At many points, a single wrong step could lead to serious injury or death. *Don't attempt the climb to the peak unless you have sufficient mountaineering experience.* If there is still snow cover, an ice-axe is essential; you *may* be able to borrow one at Kredarica. From either hut, the trail is incredibly steep; after about 20 minutes, they join to form a single path that continues to the twin summit. **Triglav,** the main summit, is 30 minutes away, after an endless walk on a narrow ridge and a final vertical climb. Take your time to rest and enjoy the amazing view from 2864m—but remember to leave sufficient time to get back.

The first part of the descent can be even more dangerous than the ascent; watch every step. If you plan to return via a specific hut, make sure you don't miss the point where the paths separate. Once back at one of the huts, the rest will seem almost a trifle. You can make it back to Bohinj in half the time. Don't rush, however, since you'll probably be tired (and don't forget about the view of the Alps on the horizon). And watch for the *Zlatorog.*

■■■ PLANINA POD GOLICO

Planina pod Golico (Planina below Golica) is an idyllic village in the Karavanke mountains, famous for its daffodils. When they blossom in May, the mountain meadows turn white and the air is filled with their fragrance. By mid-June, the daffodils disappear, but an unspoiled spot of nature remains with hiking trails and amazing views of the Julian Alps. To reach Planina, first go to **Jesenice** (1 hour north of Ljubljana by train on the Salzburg route or by bus from Bled). Jesenice itself is an industrial city in the east of the Upper Sava Valley and an access point to the Kranjska Gora ski resort. The steel factory is now less of a polluter than it was once, and its employees wait eagerly for their shifts to end so they can take off for the mountains; some of the best climbers in Slovenia live in Jesenice.

Orientation and Practical Information   Most buses in Jesenice stop in front of the railway station. Don't be misled; the few buses per day to Planina stop across the street. Check the schedules, but unless you're lucky, you'll have to walk. Follow the main road west, opposite the direction to Ljubljana, or walk on a quieter parallel side street. After 10-15 minutes, the road to Planina branches off to the right. From here, it's a 4km walk; hitchers report success on this stretch of road, although they note that drivers may find it hard to stop on the slope. *Let's Go* does not recommend hitchhiking as a safe means of transportation. If you walk, the **supermarket** on the road near the branch is a good place to refuel; food may be harder to buy higher up toward Planina.

If you were lucky enough to catch a bus, get off at the last bus stop on the main road of Planina, near a small market. Follow the road to reach the **tourist office,** located at 39 Planina pod Golico (tel. 835 47). They arrange private rooms for 1200SIT and stay open late in the evening, but you may need to knock. The **telephone city code** is 064.

Accommodations and Food   From the bus stop, walk along the main road to #32 on your left; if the cabin **Dom pod Golico** is open, you may be able to find a bed here. Farther down the road, past a bridge and the tourist office, is **Pri Fencu.** They will put you up for the night, if the place isn't already crammed with schoolchildren. The final, and possibly the best (although not in terms of comfort), option is the **Golica caban** (*koča*). This small hut is slightly above the treeline (1500m) at the end of a steep but relatively easy climb (45-60 minutes from *Pri Fencu*). Crowded but clean, it offers an impressive view of the Julian Alps. It's packed on weekends and during the summer. (40 beds. A night in a four-bed room is 900SIT, in the dorm-style attic 700SIT. Modest but nourishing meals available; delicious and fragrant mountain herb tea 60SIT. Open May-Sept.)

Hiking near Planina   The Karavanke mountains run from west to east, separated from the Julian Alps by the Upper Sava Valley. The border between Austria and Slovenia runs along this thin ridge. The *Golica caban* (see below) is a few hundred meters below the summit of **Golica** (1836m), right on the border. Notice the signs that read *Pozor! Državna Meja* ("Attention! State Border") on the ridge. Armed soldiers once guarded this border; most controls are now gone, but bring your passport just in case you run into a patrol. Write your name down in the notebook hidden under the stone at top, then enjoy the panorama: the Julian Alps with Mt. Triglav to the south and Austria's Drava Valley to the north. The river Drava flows through Austria, Slovenia, Croatia, and Serbia before it joins the Danube in its run to the Black Sea. On the left is the city of **Villach;** on the right **Klagenfurt.** They look impressive; find out for yourself with your *Let's Go: Austria and Switzerland.*

Walks on the ridge are a delight if the wind isn't blowing too hard; the trail is easy and the views are great. Even after the daffodils are gone, the meadows are filled with flowers of all colors of the rainbow. **Kepa** (2143m) is three hours west of Golica on the ridge and **Stol** (2236m) is 4 hours east. The path to Stol starts under the *caban*. Walk a few meters on the trail to Planina and turn left at the first intersection. The path goes under the ridge, running parallel, and eventually joins it. The path is relatively easy, winding over the border several times. Again, take your passport. Remember that Alpine weather can be treacherous; bring appropriate gear.

THE SLOVENIAN RIVIERA

Slovenia has only 40km of the Adriatic coast, but this stretch of green bays, little seaside towns, and beaches with myriad recreational facilities, is well worth visiting. The towns of Koper, Izola, and Piran are an attractive blend of Slovene and Italian. The main tourist center is the summer and spa resort of Portorož.

■■■ PORTOROŽ (PORTOROSE)

Built in a Mediterranean style, the town's terraces and houses with red-tiled roofs march down to the sea. The higher you climb, the less touristy the town gets. The waterfront is extremely commercialized, with hotels, restaurants, and souvenir shops. The resort doesn't have real beaches, but most of the shore has been arranged with sand leading up to the water behind concrete barriers. Every summer the sea lures thousands of Austrians and South Germans, filling the air with Teutonic *"oh, ja!"*s. In high season (July-August) accommodations will be scarce and expensive. June and Sept. are also crowded; spring may be the best time to see Portorož.

Frequent **buses** run from Ljubljana and Postojna to Portorož; you can also take a bus to Koper, and from there a local bus to Portorož. Thomas Mann once said that Venice should be entered only by sea. And indeed, a **ship** named "Prince of Venice" makes the Portorož-Venice trip Fri.-Sun. from April to mid-Oct. (departs Portorož 8am, arrives Venice 10:30am; departs Venice 5:30pm, arrives Portorož 8pm). It's hard to get lost in town; most streets start from Obala, the waterfront boulevard, and head uphill. The bus station is just meters from the sea; across from it is the main **tourist office,** Obala 16 (tel. 763 72, fax 730 54; open Mon.-Sat. 8am-noon and 4-7pm, Sun. 8am-noon). For the **Slovenia Turist Office,** face the sea and turn left. It's about 100m down Obala (open Mon.-Sat. 8am-7pm, Sun. 9am-3pm). There's no shortage of other agencies, a few open for your Deutschmarks after 7-8pm. The **telephone city code** is 066.

As a rule, hotels are expensive, although prices go down drastically in the off-season months. There are a number of **pensions** that offer reasonable rates, but they're frequently packed; check directly or with the tourist office. **Private accommodations** remain the least expensive option, at around DM25 per night. However, stays of less than three nights accrue a beastly 50% surcharge. Breakfast costs around DM8. Singles are hard to find, doubles somewhat less so; most owners are oriented toward renting apartments (for 4 or more people). If you look for lodging on your own, the key word to spot is *"sobe."* There are two **campgrounds** in Portorož: **Lucija** (tel. 710 27) and **Strunjan** (tel. 786 38). Rates run DM8-12 per day. For alternative accommodations, try any of the nearby towns: Izola, Strunjan, Piran (see below), or Koper. There is a **youth hostel** in Koper.

Most restaurants are on the waterfront. **FENIKS,** near the tourist office, has fresh fish (entrees 600-1300SIT). **Rest Grill** is 100m to the left of the tourist office, when you face the sea. (Spaghetti 500SIT, other entrees 600-1200SIT.) Farther down, **FANCY** has a nice terrace and a menu in English. At night, its lights reflect beautifully on the water; beware the mosquitos as you wait for service. (Pizzas 400-700SIT; small Italian-style smoked ham 700SIT; meat entrees 900-1600SIT.) Visit one of the **supermarkets** near the train station to save money: **Jestvina** (open Mon.-Fri. 7am-8pm, Sat. 7am-7pm, Sun. 8am-noon) or **Degro** (open Mon.-Fri. 7am-8pm, Sat. 7am-6pm, Sun. 8am-11pm).

■ NEAR PORTOROŽ: PIRAN

Only 3km from Portorož, tiny Piran is just as touristed, but proffers considerably more charm. Built on a peninsula by Venetians, the narrow stone-tiled streets and crowded houses feel like a little slice of Italy. Buses run frequently from Portorož to Piran; take the ordinary bus (60SIT) or the casino mini-van (70SIT).

Once there, follow the wharf to the central square. The square is dominated by a **statue** of the famous violinist and composer Giuseppe Tartini, born in Piran. The narrow streets near the center are worth a look. A short walk uphill is the Baroque-Renaissance **Church of San Giorgio** (built ca. 600 AD, rebuilt in the 14th century), the most prominent church in Piran. Take a break from the midday sun to admire its cool and quiet neo-Classical interior. The tower is closed, but the terraces have an amazing view of the sea, with seagulls hovering overhead. Climb up to the ruins of the castle for an even better view.

Back by the sea, walk along the quay to the oddly-combined old small church and lighthouse at the end of the peninsula. There is no real beach, but you can enjoy a meal in one of the waterfront restaurants. **Pavel** (tel. 736 19) has entrees at 700-1400SIT. To book a room or for more information on Piran and its environs, visit the **tourist office** in the main square (tel. 74 60 95, fax 74 61 01). Singles are DM13-19; doubles DM19-31. Expect a 50% increase in prices in July-August as well as a 50% surcharge for stays of less than three nights. The **telephone city code** is 066.

UKRAINE (УКРАЇНА)

US$1	= 45,000Krb (Kupony or coupons)	10,000Krb = US$0.22
CDN$1	= 33,000Krb	10,000Krb = CDN$0.30
UK£1	= 70,700Krb	10,000Krb = UK£0.14
IR£1	= 69,300Krb	10,000Krb = IR£0.14
AUS$1	= 33,600Krb	10,000Krb = AUS$0.30
NZ$1	= 24,500Krb	10,000Krb = NZ$0.40
SAR1	= 12,700Krb	10,000Krb = SAR0.79
DM1	= 29,300Krb	10,000Krb = DM0.34
Country Code: 7		International Dialing Prefix: 810

As of July 1994, Ukrainian currency was continuing to experience hyperinfla-
tion. 45,000 Kupons (*Karbonovets*) equalled US$1. In 1993 the rate was 9000
Kupons per US$1; in 1992 they were exchanged at 230 Kupons per US$1. Prices
listed reflect the cost in July 1994; drastic fluctuations can be expected.

Ukraine: the word meant borderland in the East-Slavic languages, a massive stretch
of rolling farmland (*steppe*) naturally unforested and fertile, spilling into the beautiful Black Sea. It is the second largest country in Europe, bested only by Russia—an
expanse that attracted nomadic horsemen, Polish gentry, Russian Tsars, Hitler's

armies, and the Bolsheviks. Today Ukraine is struggling to resurrect its cultural identity, once repressed by neighboring states. Unable to recover from severe economic and political backwardness, it remains a nation of great beauty, but one with a troubled soul. With patience and a positive attitude, the traveler to Ukraine will glimpse not only the landscapes and rich cultural heritage of this land, but also of the extraordinary process that is now redefining life in Ukraine.

Ukraine is a nation of big cities and a vast countryside. The cities have many lovely neighborhoods, but skylines often reflect the zealous Soviet effort to provide compact housing for all, humanity be damned. The periphery of each population center is crammed with rows of highrises, all seemingly from the same blueprint, that disappear suddenly to make way for enormous collective farms. The gently rolling plain goes on forever; hundreds of thousands of acres are covered with a golden carpet of wheat, barley, and oats. Only in the western half of the country will you find a few of the tiny, almost primitive villages which once characterized this terrain.

Eastern Ukraine is mostly industrial, and sports an urban style that belies the country's agricultural foundations. To the south, plopped in the middle of the Black Sea, the Crimean Peninsula lures vacationers and sun-seekers. This peninsula, only very shakily a part of Ukraine, looks across at the cosmopolitan Black Sea coast. In the west, the center of the independence movement, business is carried on with an eye towards Europe, and with a culturally-inherited Polish bent. In the center of the country, where the Dniepr River flows towards the Black Sea, Kiev stands solemn and beautiful, not yet destroyed by wave after wave of foreign invaders.

UKRAINE ESSENTIALS

Foreign travelers arriving in Ukraine must have a **visa,** which requires an **invitation** from a citizen, official organization, or a tourist voucher from a travel agency. Regular visa processing at an embassy—with invitation in hand—takes up to two weeks and costs US$50. Priority processing (less than 7 days) is US$60, while express (same-day service) costs US$100; prices do not include cost of postage or express mail. See Essentials: Embassies and Consulates, page 3. **Transit** and short term (72-hr.) visas are available at the larger border crossings and airports; prices vary, but are still exorbitant.

If you are in Moscow, the **Travellers Guest House** can get you a full visa in 10 days. Otherwise, the following **private organizations** can arrange visas (as well as homestays, tickets, etc.) for a fee:

Home & Host International, in the U.S. dial (800) SOVIET-U or (612) 871-0596; fax (612) 871-8853.

IBV Bed & Breakfast Systems, 13113 Ideal Dr., Silver Spring, MD 20907 (tel. (301) 942-3770; fax 933-0024).

Kobasniuk Travel, Inc., 157 Second Ave., New York, NY 10003 (tel. (212) 254-8779; fax 454-4005).

Russia House, 1800 Connecticut Ave., NW Washington, D.C. 20009 (tel. (202) 986-6010; fax 667-4244). In **Russia:** Leningradsky Prospect, Moscow, Russia 125040 (tel. (095) 250 01 43; fax 250 25 03 17).

If you arrive in the **Kiev airport** without a visa, you can buy a tourist voucher at window #8 (1-5 days US$5; 6-10 days US$10, etc.) for up to a month, which will serve as an invitation; then go to the window just at the entrance to buy your visa (transit visa US$15, short-term visa US$50). This will allow you to go through customs: you must declare all valuables and foreign currency in order to settle your tab when leaving the country. Expect the process to take several hours. Visas can also be obtained in the airport if you have a telegram confirming the urgency of your travel. Anyone working in Ukraine must have an additional letter stating the content and purpose of the work; the letter must come from an official Ukrainian agency, even if you will be working for a foreign company. A copy of your invitation and your letters of introduction should be carried on your person at all times, lest you be harrassed by bored police officers.

Upon arrival in Ukraine you must check into a hotel or register with the **Office of Visas and Registration** (OVIR), in Kiev at bul. Tarasa Shevchenka 34 (бул. Тараса Шевченка; tel. 225 13 54) or in police stations of smaller cities, within the first three working days (US$10); visas may also be extended here. Your visa not only lets you into the country but also allows you to leave; DON'T LOSE IT. Once you leave Ukraine, your visa becomes invalid. If you have a double-entry visa you will be given a re-entry slip upon your first arrival (въезд). Keep this with you—it is your ticket back into the country.

GETTING THERE

One of the easiest ways to get to Ukraine is by air. **Air Ukraine International** (tel. (202) 833-4648) flies from a number of European capitals (as well as Chicago, New York, and Washingon, DC) to Kiev and near Lviv (Ivano-Frankivsk). Swiss Air, Air France, ČSA, Lufthansa, LOT, Malev, and SAS also fly to Kiev, generally 1-2 times per week. Offices are located in Kiev.

More economical **international trains** run to Ukraine from Warsaw, Prague, Sofia, Kishinev, and Moscow; a weekly train runs from Berlin but tickets must be reserved a significant amount of time in advance. Crossing the border may be easier for those coming from Brest, where trains run daily to Kiev and Simferopol.

International buses are rare, but some exist; the bus from Przemyśl, Poland, to Lviv is cheaper than the train, and private companies are beginning to form routes such as the one from Sofia to Odessa. Routes to Poland from Lviv are common.

Relying on any water transport is risky. **Ferries** across the Black Sea have now been reduced to a few routes between Odessa, Yalta and Istanbul. However, several companies run **ships** from İstanbul for US$97; you can be pretty sure of getting a place if you reserve a week in advance. **River transport** is also infrequent, but some routes do exist; the port agents know more than the Intourist offices, which feign absolute ignorance of the existence of boats.

GETTING AROUND IN UKRAINE

Public transportation is cheap. To the uninitiated, the sheer number of people who use it is astounding. For long-distance transport, it is *essential* to buy tickets in advance. Well in advance. For trains, this means two to three days; for buses, at least the night before.

Trains go everywhere, are dirt cheap, and are reasonably comfortable. The bad news is that getting **tickets** can drive people to tears. Officially, foreigners are not allowed to travel without the proper **Intourist covers** on their tickets, which can only be obtained through an official Intourist ticket-window. In large cities these are often found within the train station itself, frequently at the same window where citizens buy international tickets. The rules keep changing, and cashiers know this; some overcharge foreigners and demand US$25 for a ticket that really costs US$10. If this happens, you can delare "Снимайте!" (Snee-MY-tyeh, "Withdraw the ticket request") and take the bus; arguing rarely works. If you've planned ahead, you can come back later and pin your hopes on the next cashier. Often a cashier will declare that there are no more places when in fact only the two upper classes are full—try the other classes as well. You may be told to come back at 8am, 2pm, or 8pm (when tickets are redistributed) to see if there is space.

If you positively need a ticket that day, try the **scalpers** in the main ticket hall in front of the large posted schedules, asking, "Вам нужни билет?" (Vahm nuzh-NEE bihlyeht, "Do you need a ticket?"). They charge US$10-20 for overnight trips and do not bargain. The tickets they offer are usually valid—you can check by showing it to a cashier and asking "When does the train arrive?" There are no Intourist covers on these tickets, however. Most towns also have a **central ticket bureau** which may also have an Intourist window. The lines here are just as long and the cashiers just as unpredictable, but they are usually closer to the center.

Your **ticket** is labeled across the top with the train number, the date and time of departure, the car number and type ("л" for "Люкс", "к" for "Купейний", etc.). A few lines down you can find your place (место; *myesta*). If you've planned far enough ahead to have a choice of **class**, there are four to choose from. At the top is *lyuks* (люкс), or *2-myagky* (мягкий; 2-person soft), a 2-bunk cabin in the same car as 2nd-class *kupeyny* (купейний) which has 4 bunks. Both classes have the same type of beds: sort of cushioned, almost comfortable with the roll-up mattress and pillow. The next class down is *platskartny* (плацкартний), an open car with 52 bunks. The bunks are shorter (about 3m long) and harder. Places 1-37 are most stable; if you get an odd-numbered bunk among them you can store your belongings in the compartment underneath your bunk and sleep soundly, knowing that anyone who wants to rob you will have to wake you up first. Women traveling alone can try to buy out a *lyuks* compartment to avoid nasty drunks, or can travel *platskartny* with the regular folk and depend on the crowds to shame would-be harrassers into silence.

In the upper classes, the car monitor will come by to rent out **sheets** for US$0.50; in *platskartny* you must go to the end of the car to pick them up yourself. Most car monitors do not care if you bring your own sheets and use the roll-up mattress, but some grumpy ones will not let you use the mattress unless you've paid for sheets. Occasionally, hot **tea** is sold for US$0.10.

Except in Kiev where **platform** numbers are posted on the electronic board, the only way to figure out which platform your train is on is usually to listen to the distorted loudspeaker announcement. In large cities, trains arrive some time before they are scheduled to depart, so you'll have a few minutes to show your ticket to fellow passengers, look helpless, and say "платформа?" (plaht-FORM-ah?). Regional hubs have a separate section of the station devoted to **local trains** (примиський, *primiski*). The ticket-windows are separate from the long-distance ticket-windows and the system is a bit different as well; foreigners will do well to stick to the Intourist window and the buses. However, local trains do stop at a number of rural destinations not covered by buses.

Buses are a bit more expensive but less-crowded and the best way to travel short distances. In large cities, buy tickets at least the night before at the regular ticket-windows with everyone else. The **platform** numbers of arriving buses are announced over the loudspeaker and each platform has its buses posted. If you did not buy a ticket in advance, you can occasionally get on the bus once the driver arrives by paying him for a standing spot.

Local **public transportation** goes everywhere in a hurry but is unbelievably crowded. Buy **tickets** for trams, trolleybuses, and local buses at kiosks for next to nothing; punch them on board (large baggage requires an extra ticket). A ticket that says "5Krb" cost 100Krb in summer 1994—don't worry, inflation often outruns the printing presses. Tickets must be bought within a given city to be valid there. However, the monthly pass available at kiosks at the beginning of the month is valid all over the country. A *kontroler* occasionally shows up with a контролер medallion and exacts US$0.05-0.10 fines from those without tickets. Buy **metro** tokens at the *kassa* in any station and drop them in the slot before going through the turnstile. On **buses**, pay the conductor on board or the driver as you get off. Don't be afraid to push your way on board crowded buses or trams. To get off, ask the person in front of you, "Вы сходите сейчас?" (Vih skhah-DEE-tyeh s-chass; "Are you getting off now?") and he or she will move out of the way. Likewise, if asked, you are expected to move aside quickly. In Western Ukraine, the expression is "Ви зараз виходите?" (vih ZAH-rahz vih-KHOH-dih-teh). Transport runs from 6am-1am.

Taxis often overcharge foreigners; agree on a price before getting in. State taxis (recognizable by their checkered signs) wait for passengers at taxi stands throughout cities. Unregulated "private transport" can be hailed by holding the hand at a downward salute. Pay the driver and face the same risks that are associated with hitchhiking. *Let's Go* does not recommend such private transport as a safe means of transportation.

TOURIST SERVICES AND MONEY

The breakup of the Soviet Union brought about the demise of the official state travel agency, **Intourist,** which was responsible for foreigners traveling to Ukraine. **Private tourist offices** are emerging, and are useful places to get maps or hard-to-find train tickets. They are used to dealing with groups, not individual travelers, however, so be sure to smile a lot, speak slowly, and be persistent. Making friends in any travel office can work wonders for your travels throughout Ukraine.

The currency of Ukraine is the **karbovanets** (Крб; Krb), usually referred to as "kupon." Inflation is endemic; expect all prices *Let's Go* lists to change considerably. Hotels usually ask for kupons in payment, and only occasionally for dollars. Bus tickets are usually sold for kupons. As of July 1994, all domestic train tickets are sold for kupons, but international tickets are sold only for dollars. **Dollar-stores,** or "*Kashtans*" (Каштан) sell foreign merchandise only for dollars. Prices marked "т" or "m" simply means "thousand." **Exchanging** dollars and Deutschmarks is fairly simple, and can be done at Обмін Валют (*obmin valyut*) kiosks. Bring a large stash of US$1-bills; hotels and dollar-stores do not give change in dollars. Exchange of other currencies is difficult, and **traveler's checks** are rarely accepted. There is a national phobia of old, wrinkled, or torn bills, both in kupons and other currencies. They are never accepted and must be traded in at banks. The easiest places to exchange money and sometimes traveler's checks (for a 2.5% commission) is the lobbies of the expensive hotels that cater to a Western clientele. Go early in the morning (they sometimes run out of money) and bring your passport. Exchange with individuals is illegal but quite common. Black-market exchangers offer a rate slightly above the daily rate. Fraud is common; an exchanger may ask to see your money, then take it and run.

COMMUNICATION

Telephones are struggling out of the dark ages. Order your international call at the post office for the cheapest rate; when the call is ready, 5-25 minutes later, you'll be pointed to the right booth. In Kiev, *Utel* (Ukraine telephone) has started producing electronic **phonecards** but the phones with which they can be used are still scarce. You can take advantage of Utel's new technology to make **collect calls** from some phones. Dial 27 10 36 and ask for an ITNT operator. **AT&T USADirect** is available from some phones in some cities; the number is 81 00 11. From private or Utel phones, the international dialing prefix is 810. For intercity calls, order at the post office and pay up front; in Western Ukraine, payphones marked "Мижміський" (*mizhmiskiy*) work with tokens. At some post offices you will be handed a **plug** when you pay for the first three minutes; insert it into the upper left corner of the front of the phone to get a dial tone, then dial (city code plus number). **Local calls** have been free in most cities from any gray payphone, ever since the 15-kopeck coin was abandoned. In Lviv, buy **tokens** at the post office or at kiosks.

Mail is cheap but slow; allow a minimum of 2-3 weeks from Kiev to any foreign destination. From other cities and mailboxes off the beaten track, it may never arrive or even be picked up. In principle, you can drop pre-stamped mail in any Пошта (*pochta*) box, with twice-daily pick-ups, but post offices are usually a better bet. The easiest way to mail letters is to buy pre-stamped envelopes at the post office. The international courier service **DHL** is available in Kiev and Odessa, and pick ups can be arranged in Lviv on Thursdays through the Kiev office.

LANGUAGE

Your trip will go more smoothly if you can throw around a few words of Ukrainian or Russian (see Russia Essentials, page 509). In Crimea and most of Eastern Ukraine, Russian (spoken with a Ukrainian accent) is more common than Ukrainian; even in

Kiev most people speak Russian on the streets. The common language of Western Ukraine is Ukrainian, and Polish is frequently spoken and understood.

The Ukrainian alphabet looks similar to Russian; however it has important differences in characters and pronunciation. The most noteable addition is the і (*ee* sound) and the ї (*yee* sound)—the и is closest to "s*i*t." The г (hard "g") has been reintroduced since independence and is not yet widely used. The alphabet is not as difficult as it looks, and learning it will make getting around immeasurably easier. Note: the "r" is rolled, though not flamboyantly.

Cyrillic	English	Pronunciation	Cyrillic	English	Pronunciation
А, а	a	M*o*xie	Н, н	n	*N*ancy
Б, б	b	*B*uh-bye	О, о	o	Sc*o*re
В, в	v	*V*oom *V*oom	П, п	p	*P*uffin
Г, г	g	Ida*h*o potatoes	Р, р	r	*R*um *R*aisin
Ґ, ґ	h	Jerry *G*arcia	С, с	s	*S*arala
Д, д	d	Dr. *D*oolittle	Т, т	t	*Th*omas
Е, е	ye	B*e*t	У, у	u	kit 'n' cab*oo*dle
Э, э	*ye*	*Ye*p	Ф, ф	f	*F*antastic
Ж, ж	zh	Bre*zh*nev	Х, х	xh	*ch*utzpah
З, з	z	*Z*arf	Ц, ц	ts	*ts*ar
И, и	i	s*i*t	Ч, ч	ch	*ch*imichanga
І, і	ee	*I*ce cr*ea*m	Ш, ш	sh	*sh*toopa
Ї, ї	yee	*y*east	Щ, щ	shch	lu*sh ch*erries
Й, й	*y*—	*y*ippy (not ippy)	Ю, ю	yoo	*you*
К, к	*k*	*K*errigan	Я, я	yah	*Ya*hoo!
Л, л	l	*L*oopy	Ь, ь	—	(soft sign)
М, м	m	*M*oist			

Yes	Так	tak
No	Ні	nee
Today	Сьогодні	syo-HOhd-nee
Tomorrow	Завтра	zav-tra
Hello	Добрий день	doh-bree-DEN
Good morning	Доброго ранку	DOh-broho RAhn-koo
Good evening	Добрий вечір	doh-bree-VECH-eer
Goodbye	До побачення	Doh poh-BAH-chen-nya
Excuse me	Вибачте	VIH-bach-te)
Please	Прошу	PRO-shoo
Thank you	Дякую	DYA-kou-yoo
When?	Коли?	KOh-lih?
Where?	Де?	Deh?
How much does it cost?	Скільки коштує?	SKEEL-kih kahsh-tOOye?
How do I get to ...?	Як туди дістатися?	YaktuDIH dihsTAHTeesya
My name is ...	Мене звуть...	Mene zvoot
Do you speak English?	Ви говорите по-англиськи?	Vih-ho-VOR-ihte poh-an-hlihskih?
I don't understand	Я не розумію	Ya ne roh-zoo-meee-yu
Leave me alone; get lost!	Дайте мені спокій!	DAyte menee spah-kee!
Help!	Поможіт!	Pah-mah-ZHEET!

1—одін (ah-DEEN); 2—два (dVAh); 3—три (tREE); 4—чотири (cho-TIH-rih); 5—п'ять (P-yaht); 6—шість (shEEst); 7—сім (SEEm); 8—вісім (VEE-sihm); 9—дев'ять (d-YEV-yet); 10—десять (d-YES-yet); 20—двадцять (d-VAHd-tsyet); 30—тридцять (tRIHdtsyet); 40—сорок (SOAR-uk); 50—п'ятдесят (p-yet-des-YAHT); 60—шістдесят (sheest-des-

УАНТ); **70**—сімдесят (seem-des-YAHT); **80**—вісімдесят (veeseem-des-YAHT); **90**— дев'ятдесят (dev-yaht-des-YAHT); **100**—сто (STOH); **1000**—тисяча (Tih-se-cheh)

HEALTH AND SAFETY

Anyone recognizable as a Westerner is an instant target of **theft.** Laws are minimally observed of late, and the best way to protect yourself is to act as understated as possible. Con-artists abound, in offical postions as well as unofficial ones; it is a good idea to keep your guard up every minute of every day.

Alcoholism is an ongoing problem in Ukraine. While not all drunk men (and women) are dangerous, they abound at all times of day, in trams, on buses, and on the streets. Fistfights are common here and more frequent when alcohol is involved.

Traveling in Ukraine may be even more difficult for racial minorities. While there is no official **discrimination,** international students from Africa and East Asia claim to have been subject to closed doors at hotels, harrassment, and even violence. They advise bringing dollar bills, packs of cigarettes, and other "gifts" for unwilling authorities; many resident African students profess a willingness to help out those from abroad.

Women traveling alone are often harassed. Women never go to restaurants alone and may be significantly threatened if they do, even at midday. Small cafés and cafeterias are safer options; even hotel restaurants may be dangerous. Feigned deafness, sitting motionless, and staring at the ground will do a world of good that no reaction will ever achieve. If need be, turn to an older woman for help in an uncomfortable situation; her stern rebukes will usually be enough to embarrass the most persistent jerks. Looking like a native involves wearing a generous amount of make-up, always wearing flats or heels, and very rarely donning shorts or t-shirts.

Most citizens agree that drinking large amounts of tap water is unhealthy, although a glass or two won't hurt. Authorities recommend boiling tap water for 7 minutes before drinking. Buying fruits and vegetables at open markets is generally safe, although storage conditions and pesticides render thorough washing absolutely necessary. Any meats bought at public markets should be checked very carefully and cooked quite thoroughly; refrigeration is a foreign concept and insect life thrives. Embassy officials declare that Chernobyl-related **radiation** provides only a minimal risk to short-term travelers, but the region should be given a wide berth.

Pharmacies and pharmacy kiosks are quite common, and prescription medications prescribed by local doctors are usually available. Aspirin is usually the only painkiller available and *Tampax* the only brand of sanitary supplies, but plenty of cold remedies and bandages are always at hand. In large hotels, Western medications may be available for hard currency. For sanitary napkins (гігієнічні пакети; gee-gee-eh-NEE-chnee pah-kYET-ih) or condoms (презервативи; prey-zer-vah-tIHV-ih), consult everyday kiosks; they are intermittently available, usually imported from Poland.

It's a wise idea to register with your embassy once you arrive in Ukraine. Besides making the process of recovering lost passports much quicker, the embassy staff may be able to offer important information on travel or the situation in Ukraine.

ACCOMMODATIONS AND CAMPING

Formerly, only one Intourist hotel accepted foreigners in each town; now, some hotels accept foreigners even without a specific invitation, but always for many times what a citizen would pay. Hotels fall into two categories, **"hotels"** and **"tourist bases"** called "Турбаза" (TOOR-bah-zah) which usually form part of a complex targeted at motoring tourists, but are otherwise nearly indistinguishable from hotels.

Though hotel prices in Kiev are astronomical, singles run US$2-25 per night throughout the rest of the country. Places in communal rooms cost less, but no one can predict who your roommates will be. Prices drop when you ask for rooms without television, telephone, etc.—receptionists will be stunned that a rich foreigner like you would want a room without a refrigerator. Make sure everything on the bill is really in the room. The phrase "самое дешёвое место" (SAHM-ah-yih dih-SHOHV-ah-yih MYEST-ah) means "the cheapest place." Approaching cautiously, smiling, looking innocent, and not interrupting the receptionists' conversation can also lower your price.

Tourism is slow, so hotels usually have room. If not, a window sign declares "мест нет" ("No places"). Still, it's worth approaching the receptionist with a careful, "У вас есть места?" (oo vas YEHST myehst-ah; *Do you have any places?*). Make inquiries and hand your passport over to the **administrator** (администратор), who will ask for your last name ("фамилия," fah-MEEL-ee-yah), where you arrived in the country, and how long you are staying. Pay the **cashier** (кассир). Your passport may be kept for the duration of your stay. You will be given a **hotel card** (визитка; vee-zEET-kah) to show to the administrator or hall-monitor (дежурная or черtoвa) to get your key. You must give up your key to leave the building. Check-out time is often noon.

Conditions are usually adequate, although you will need your own **toilet paper** (buy it at kiosks or markets). Hot water is a godsend when you find it. Valuables should never be left in the room unattended; the administrator usually has a **safe** where you can leave them if absolutely necessary.

Most cities have a **campground** on the edge of town. The old Soviet complexes can be quite posh, with saunas and restaurants, but are never new. Space in an electrified bungalow runs US$7-10 per night; tent space and use of facilities runs US$3-8. Free camping is illegal and enforcement will be merciless if that's what the person responsible decides to do that day. **Private rooms** are available through overseas agencies and bargaining at the train station. Prices run US$1-2 per person but conditions are quite variable.

LIFE AND TIMES

HISTORY

Ukraine has developed at the confluence of four major cultures and has been heavily influenced by each: Byzantium lay to the south; nomadic horsemen (and Islam) to the east; Russia (Moscow in particular) to the north; and Poland (and the rest of Europe) to the west. No one empire could control the region for long before another displaced it from the *steppe*. In this manner, Western Ukraine developed a heavily Polish culture, and Eastern Ukraine a Russian one.

The **Scythians** plied the *steppe* during the time of the Ancient Greeks, replacing the pre-Indo-European, battle-axe wielding peoples who came before them. The Scythians terrorized their neighbors with brilliant archery and horsemanship, as well as frightening their own wives and servants, who were killed to accompany princes in burial mounds, or *kurgans,* which still dot the Ukrainian countryside. While the Crimea and the Black Sea coast were extensively settled by **Greeks** and **Romans,** the Scythians of the steppe were succeeded by Sarmatians, Heruls, and **Ostrogoths,** the latter occupying the entire area from 250 AD. The **Huns** rode out of Mongolia in the 370s AD, settling in southern Ukraine for 300 years. Recorded Ukrainian history, however, did not begin until the **Kievan Rus** dynasty sprang from the infiltrations of Viking and Baltic fur traders into the Dniepr River region in 882. They grew wealthy from the newly opened north-south fur trade between Constantinople, Novgorod, and the Baltic trading organizations, superseding the Judaic Khazars operating on the Volga. Though the Kievan aristocracy were Varangian Swedes, they created the first Slavic state and, more importantly, the first Slavic culture. They adopted and modernized Cyril and Methodius' alphabet and searched for a religion suitable for a young, aspiring dynasty. Prince Vladimir chose **Christianity,** welcoming missionaries from Constantinople, and was baptized in 988. With the conversion came an influx of Byzantine ideas and culture, so enrapturing the Kievan Rus that they attempted to conquer their southern neighbors three times. After a few centuries of prosperity, the empire splintered as succession problems, meddling Byzantines, and slowing trade depleted its coffers.

Following the collapse of the Kievan Rus, the Ukraine was divided between nomadic Cumans and Patzinaks and leftover Varangian parcels. The "Golden Horde," a fictitious term for the **Mongol** army formed by Ghengis Khan, moved in the 1230s, establishing khanates which became the power bases in the area. **Batu,** Ghengis Kahn's grandson, conquered Kiev in 1240 and continued to extend his rule into Europe until his death, which halted the otherwise seemingly inevitable penetration of Europe and allowed the khanates to splinter.

Ukraine soon became the center of numerous power plays. The Cossacks, armed bands on horseback, became the indigenous power structure. They supported themselves by renting their services to the **Polish** and **Lithuanian** kings, who occupied parts of the Ukraine and had the native Cossacks ward off excursions from Constantinople and **Muscovite Russia.** The fiercely independent Cossacks revolted, however, in response to Polish expansion into their territory, rejecting their newly acquired place in the Polish nobility. The famous rebellion led by the *hetman* **Bogdan Khmelnitsky** defeated a Polish force and reclaimed Kiev and Lviv. An agreement with Moscow helped ward off Polish domination, and the Cossacks led the Muscovite expansion into Siberia. A treaty of 1667, however, divided Ukraine between Russia and Poland. The indigenous population, along with its language and Cossack culture, was strongly suppressed by both powers.

Ukrainian nationalism resurfaced in the 19th century, led by the poet Taras Shevchenko, who sought to revitalize the Ukrainian language and safeguard it from Polish and Russian cultural imperialism. The movement culminated in a *rada* (council) in Kiev declaring Ukrainian independence in 1917, taking advantage of the tsar's political weakness. The **Bolsheviks** set up a rival government in Kharkiv and seized complete power during the "Russian" Civil War in 1920. They solidified power after repulsing a Polish invasion, and thus "defending" the Ukrainian State.

Under Communist rule, Ukraine was fully incorporated into the **Soviet Union,** answerable in all realms to Moscow. However, the nationalist movement endured, drawing strength from Soviet mismanagement and collectivization, Stalin's forced famine of 1931 (a genocide which claimed 7 million lives), hatred of Nazi invaders and Russian settlers, the long-standing ban on the teaching of Ukrainian in Soviet schools, and the Chernobyl disaster of 1986.

UKRAINE TODAY

Caught for years in a love-hate relationship with Russia, Ukraine finally pulled out of the Soviet Union on December 1, 1991, following an overwhelming vote by 95% of its population for complete independence. Ukrainian currency and visas have since appeared. Ironically, Ukraine was a member of the United Nations for 46 years before it truly gained its independence. In 1945, Stalin had insisted that each Soviet Republic was an independent entity worthy of membership; the West compromised by granting seats in the General Assembly to Belarus and Ukraine. Ukraine has also become the beneficiary of a sizeable nuclear arsenal and a still-disputed portion of the Soviet Black Sea fleet. Yet some will tell you that little has really changed. Ukraine is a gigantic territory where change can come about only very slowly. New rules and ideas have not yet been instituted to replace the old ones, and people fall back into their old ways in the absence of new direction. It is not yet a free country.

Although conditions are improving, travel is still quite difficult in Ukraine; many travel restrictions have not yet been lifted. A trip takes significant preparation, careful planning, and a total disregard for comfort. Still, you'll be able to tell your grandchildren "I was there back when..."

FOOD AND DRINK

Unless you eat in someone's home, getting a decent meal is difficult. **Restaurants** (Ресторан) have a different purpose here than in the West—people go to eat, yes, but also to drink, dance, and party. The food is usually not superb and the atmosphere a bit rough. Cheaper and tastier options are **cafés,** where you order from the menu posted on the bar. **Tipping** is optional in principle but expected from foreigners. If you don't round up the bill up, it may be done for you. Bread is always served, and you'll always be charged for it. Little **cafeteria**-style cafés ("Кафе") offer one main dish, soup, a few vegetable side dishes, and tea or milk. Pick up the side dishes on your tray and ask the server for the main dish; when you have paid the cashier you are expected to put the tray back. Meals rarely run over US$1. **Vegetarians** can usually fill up here, although cucumbers, tomatoes and carrots get tiresome. Regular restaurateurs' reactions to vegetarians are positively hostile, and the menu rarely offers anything other than mushrooms (грибы, *gribi*).

Produce is sold by the kilogram in jam-packed **markets** that fill enormous warehouses. Bring your own bags or buy them at nearby kiosks. You can have a free meal by sampling a bit of everything. Ask "Можно попробовать?" (MOHZH-nah pa-PRO-bah-vaht?; "May I taste?"). You can touch most things as long as you ask. Markets are open daily, usually by 7am, and close no earlier than 5pm.

State food stores are classified by content. Гастроном *(gastronom)* sells everything but concentrates on packaged goods. Молоко *(moloko)* sells milk-products. Овочі-Фрукти *(ovochi-frukti)* sells fruits and vegetables, often preserved in large jars. Мясо *(meso)* sells meat, Хліб *(hlib)* bread, Ковбаси *(kovbasi)* sausage, and Риба *(riba)* fish. You must usually pay the cashier for the item you want (just tell her the price), point out the counter where you're going to obtain the merchandise, retrieve a receipt, and only then trade the receipt for the item (this also goes for the state department stores, Универмаг, *univermag*). In the suburbs, there is one store per designated region, labeled simply "Магазин" (mag-ah-ZIN; "store").

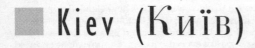

Kiev (Київ)

"...Most often of all I soothe my aged imagination with pictures of gold-domed, garden-cloaked and poplar-crowned Kiev."
—Taras Shevchenko (from exile)

Kiev once ruled Kievan Rus, the first Slavic empire that stretched from the Black Sea to the Danube. Today, the capital of the second largest country in Europe still stands largely undiscovered by the West. Life here, everyone admits, can be difficult for residents and travelers alike. But it is all worth it to see the "Mother of All Rus," laced with all that is splendid, glorious, and grandiose.

There is almost too much to see in Kiev. Stepping away from the main streets, you can spend a whole day wandering, savoring the façades. Beautiful buildings of no particular fame line the central streets among green gardens and parks. Kiev is a city filled with every kind of history, where remnants of golden and dark pasts still stand.

ORIENTATION AND PRACTICAL INFORMATION

Situated on the lush, steep banks of the Dniepr (Дніпро) River, Kiev is a busy port serving ships headed south to the Black Sea and north to Russia. The city itself is divided into two parts: upper Kiev clings to the hills, while lower Kiev skirts the river banks. **Khreshchatik** (Хрещатик), the city's main boulevard, is lined with theaters, shops, and cafés. Running parallel, **vulitsya Volodimirska** (вулиця Володимирська) hosts a variety of historical sights. Keep your eyes open for a free copy of the **Kiev Times,** an English-language newspaper which provides excellent coverage of both local and national events.

Tourist Office: No central office yet. On vul. Hospitalna 12 (вул. Госпітальна), just behind the Respublikanski Stadion, **Intourist Kiev** arranges domestic and international flights as well as train tickets, but little else (domestic flights tel. 224 10 45, international 224 29 50, train tickets 224 25 59). Expect to pay up to a 2000% commission (in which case it's probably better to go to the source). Down the hill at no. 9 is the **Hotel Rus** (tel. 220 42 55 or 220 52 33) where you can pick up a city **map.** They also organize **tours** of the city for US$10 per hour. Open daily 8am-8pm. **Balkantour Travel Company,** vul. Bogdana Khmelnikovo 10 (вул. Богдана Хмельникого; tel. 229 04 67) offers similar services. Maps are also available at **Hotel Mir** (Гостиница "Мир").

Embassies: U.S., vul. Kotsyubinskovo 6 (вул. Кошюбинского; tel. 244 73 49, after-hours emergencies 244 73 45, 24-hr. answering machine 244 73 44). Entrance at right for American citizen services. Open Mon.-Fri. 9am-6pm. **Canada:** vul. Yaroslaviv val 31 (вул. Ярославів Вал; tel. 212 02 12). **U.K.:** vul. Desyatinna 9 (вул. Десятинна; tel. 288 05 04). **Australians** and **Irish** should contact the British Embassy. The closest New Zealand and S. Africa embassy are in Moscow. **Russia:** pr. Kutuzova 8, (tel. 294 67 01). Open Mon., Wed., and Fri. 9am-noon. Processes visas for Armenia, Azerbaijan, Belarus, Kyrgyzstan, Russia, and Turkmenistan. Visas to Uzbekistan are only obtainable at the embassy in your home country. For other bordering countries, visas are obtainable at points of entry. **Hungary:** vul. Rejtarska 33 (вул. Рейтапська; tel. 225 02 98). **Czech Republic:** vul. Yaroslaviv Val (вул. Ярославів Вал; tel 212 02 10) processes visas for Slovakia. **Poland:** vul. Yaroslaviv Val (вул. Ярославів Вал;tel. 225 51 14). **Estonia:** vul. Kutuzova 8 (vul7 Kutuzova; tel. 296 28 86).

Currency Exchange: Traveler's checks can be cashed at **Hotel Intourist** on vul. Gospitalna 12 (вул. Госпитална) behind the Respublikanski Stadion (Республиканськи Стадион) metro stop for 2.5% commission. Open Mon.-Fri. 8am-noon and 1-7:30pm, Sat.-Sun. 8am-5pm. **Cash** is much easier to change. Old, wrinkled bills and those of high denominations are regarded suspiciously and often refused. Kiosks marked *Obmin-Balyut* (Обмін-Балют) typically do not change kupons to hard currency, and deal only in dollars, Deutschmarks, and one or two other currencies. Most major currencies can be changed at poor rates in major **hotels** such as Hotel Dnipro (Готель Днипро) at vul. Khreshchatik ½(вул. Хрещатик), Hotel Moskva (Готель Москва) at Majdan Nezalezhnosti (Незалежності), or Hotel Khreshchatik (Готель Хрещатик) at vul. Khreshchatik 16 (вул. Хрещатик). The lobby of the department store has an orange exchange kiosk. Private moneychangers flourish in front of the **department store,** Универмаг, on Plosha Peremohi (пл. Перемоги), and at the train station. It's illegal, but little is done to stop it.

Post Office: vul. Khreshchatik 24 (Хрещатик), next to Majdan Nezalezhnosti (Майдан Незалежності). **Poste Restante** at counters 26-28. The easiest way to send international letters is by pre-stamped airmail envelope (8000Krb) at counter #10 or #14; drop them in any box marked "Пошта" (*pochta*). Otherwise, use the servants' entrance behind the fountain to get your letter weighed and stamped. Information: counter #10 (no English spoken). Packages: counter #42.

Courier Service: DHL is available at Sport Palace, Sportivnaya pl.1 (Спортивная пл; tel. 221 50 95).

Telephones: Credit card calls can be made from the service bureau of Hotel Rus at Gospitalna 9 (Госпиталн), open daily 8am-8pm. **Utel phonecards** are available at the post office in denominations of US$10 or US$20 for international calls at Utel phones, located in the post office, large hotels, and the Dim Ukraincki (Дім Український) cultural center across from Hotel Dnipro. **International calls** can also be made from any post office; give your order to the clerk and pay for 3min. up front. The call will be ready here in up to an hour, and you will be pointed to the appropriate booth. Return after you have finished to settle up the bill. **Local calls** are free from any gray telephone in the street. International calls can be dialed directly from private phones; for international calls dial 810. **City Code:** 044.

Flights: Kiev-Borispol takes incoming flights from most Western European cities. A **bus** leaves the bus stop in the parking lot every 30min. and drops you off at the Livoberezha (Лівобережа) metro stop, across the river from most of Kiev (60,000Krb). **Taxis** charge foreigners outrageous prices (up to US$70). **Airplane tickets** are sold at airline offices in the city. **Air Ukraine** is at the Intourist office on Gospitalna (Госпитална) 12. **Swissair, SAS,** and **Austrian Airlines** are inside the blue-fence "Makulon" area at the corner of vul. Khreshchatik (вул. Хрещатик) and bul. Shevchenko (бул. Шевченко). Inside the Hotel Khreshchatik on vul.

UKRAINE

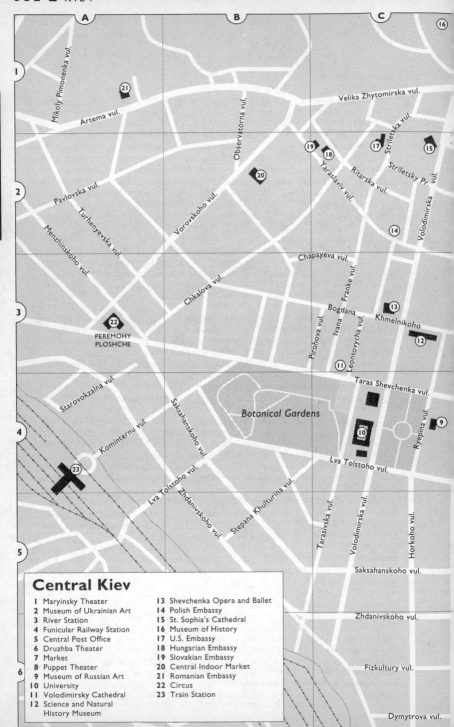

Central Kiev

1 Maryinsky Theater
2 Museum of Ukrainian Art
3 River Station
4 Funicular Railway Station
5 Central Post Office
6 Druzhba Theater
7 Market
8 Puppet Theater
9 Museum of Russian Art
10 University
11 Volodimirsky Cathedral
12 Science and Natural
   History Museum
13 Shevchenka Opera and Ballet
14 Polish Embassy
15 St. Sophia's Cathedral
16 Museum of History
17 U.S. Embassy
18 Hungarian Embassy
19 Slovakian Embassy
20 Central Indoor Market
21 Romanian Embassy
22 Circus
23 Train Station

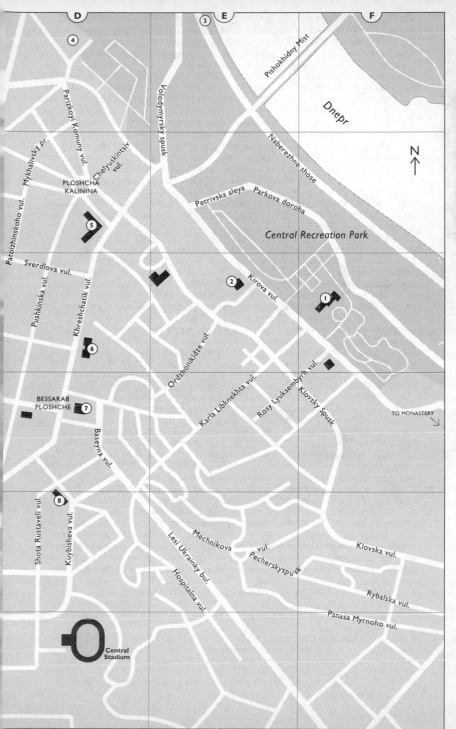

UKRAINE

D

4

3

E

F

Pishokhidny Mist

Dnepr

N
↑

Parizkoyi Komuny vul.

Mykhalivsky pr.

Volodymyrsky spusk

Naberezhne shose

Chelyuskintsiv vul.

PLOSHCHA KALININA

Patoizhinskoho vul.

Petrivska aleya   Parkova doroha

5

Central Recreation Park

Sverdlova vul.

Pushkinska vul.

Khreshchatik vul.

2   Kirova vul.

1

Ordzhonikidze vul.

6

Rosy Lyuksembyrh vul.

Klovsky Spusk

BESSARAB PLOSHCHE

7

Karla Libknekhta vul.

TO MONASTERY
↘

Baseyna vul.

8

Shota Rustaveli vul.

Kuybisheva vul.

Mechnikova

vul.

Klovska vul.

Lesi Ukrainky bul.

Pecherskyspusk

Hospitalna vul.

Rybalska vul.

Panasa Myrnoho vul.

Central Stadium

Khreshchatik 16 are: **LOT**, open Mon.-Fri. 9am-5pm, Sat. 10am-2pm; **Air France** (tel. 229 13 95), open Mon.-Fri. 9am-5pm; **Lufthansa** (tel. 229 62 97), open Mon.-Fri. 9am-5:30pm); **KSG** (tel. 229 62 97), open Mon.-Fri. 9am-1pm and 2-6pm; **ČSA**, open Mon.-Fri. 9am-5pm. **Balkan** is at vul. Bogdana Khmelnikovo 12 (вул. Богдана Хмельникого), open Mon.-Fri. 10am-1pm and 2-5pm. **Malev** is at vul Volodimircka 20 (вул. Володимирська; tel. 229 36 61), open Mon.-Fri. 10am-5pm.

Trains: Kiev-Passazhirski (Київ-Пассажирський), M: Vokzalna (Вокзальна) or tram #2. **Tickets** can be purchased at the Intourist window on the second floor of the station, window #42, open 8am-1pm, 2-7pm, and 8pm-7am. Your passport is normally demanded and the transaction takes time. Be wary of any clerk who demands payment in dollars at an unreasonable price. There are also potential ticket-buying intermediaries on the main floor. Officially, you may be kicked off the train if you do not have the proper Intourist travel documents, though this is entirely at the discretion of the conductor. Buy tickets at least one day in advance; spaces fill fast and every train is booked to capacity. Standing-room space is sometimes possible to obtain by paying (bribing) the conductor at the door to the train. **Schedules** are posted on the main floor; check which **track** you will leave on by spotting the "Колія" (*kolia*) entry on the electric board near the stairs. To: Kharkiv: (12hrs., US$3); Odessa: (11hrs., US$5); Lviv: (12hrs., US$4). Direct connections: Vienna, Berlin, Moscow, Warsaw, Bratislava, Chelm, and Brest.

Buses: Most long-distance buses leave from the central **Avtovokzal** (Автовокзал) at pl. Dzerzhinskovo (пл. Дзержинського). Buses to Dnipropetrovsk leave from the Darnica station at pr. Yiruya Gagarina (пр. Юрія Гагаріна). Regional buses to points north leave from Polese at pl. Tarasa Shevchenka, to points south from Juzhnaya at pr. Akademika Glushkova 3 (Академика Глушкова) and Podol at vul. Nizhnij Val 15a (Нижній Вал). Regional buses to points east leave from Dachnaya at pr. Peremogi 142 (пр. Перемоги).

Ferries: M: pl. Poshmova (пл. Пошмова). When there's fuel, boats and hydrofoils run to Cherkasi (Черкаси), Peremtsy (Перемцы) and Kremenchuk (Кременчук), all for under US$5. Buy tickets one level below the main entrance.

Public Transportation: Kiev's **metro** system is clean, efficient and abnormally deep. Buy tokens at the "Касса" (*kassa*) for 150Krb or a monthly pass from a numbered kiosk for US$0.75. Drop the token in the slot and wait for the light to change before going through. If you buy a pass, slide it through the slot on top of the turnstile to enter. Guards watch all the time; you won't get away with anything. Check the map before you go down the escalator; there are only lists of names at the bottom. "Перехід" (*Perekhid*) indicates a walkway to another station, "вихід у місто" (*vikhid u misto*) an exit onto the street, and "вихід" (*vikhid*) an entrance to the metro. Tickets for **trams, trolleybuses,** and **buses** are sold at numbered kiosks for 100Krb and must be punched on board. Beware trolleybuses and buses with identical numbers; they sometimes have very different routes. Monthly passes are good on all forms of public transportation.

Taxis: A trip for a foreigner will cost a bundle; avoid taxis if you can. Otherwise, give the driver a nearby address rather than a hotel address; the driver won't assume so quickly that you're a foreign businessperson on an expense account. **State taxis** are more consistently priced and are identifiable by the checkered sign on top. **Private cars** that function like taxis cost about 10,000Krb per km in the city; agree on a price before getting in—and use your judgement. *Let's Go* does not recommend such private transport as a safe means of transportation.

Luggage Storage: Located at hotels and the train station. Hotels will often charge less, but they only keep luggage if they think you have a room there.

Library: America House at vul. Parkhomenko 1/2 (вул. Пархоменко), has a library of Western literature. Take tram #16 or18 from Maydan Nezalezhnosti (Майдан Незалежності) to the vul. Parkhomenko stop.

Pharmacy: Apteka (Аптека) #1 on vul. Bogdana Khmelnikovo (Богдана Хмельникого) across from the opera house, has one of almost everything (but not necessarily in your favorite brand) and is centrally located. Open daily 8am-8pm. **Apteka #7 vnochi** (Аптека #7 вночі) at vul. Artyoma 10 (вул. Артёма) is open 24 hrs. Hard-currency pharmacies in the lobbies of **Hotel Intourist** and **Hotel Rus** have many Western products.

Kiev Metro

Geroev Dnepra
Minskaya
Obolon
Petrovka
Tarasa Shevchenko
Kontraktovaya ploschad
Pochtovaya ploschad
Dnepr River
Pionerskaya
Komsomolskaya
Darnitsa
Levoberezhnaya
Gidropark
Dnepr
Arsenal-nayo
Maydan Nezalezhnosti
Kreschatik
Bortnichi
Svyatoshino
Lvovskaya ploschad
Nivki
Zhovtnevaya
Zavod Bolshevik
Politekhnicheski
Vokzalnaya
Universitet
Zolotye vorota
Ploschad Lva Tolstovo
Dvorets sporta
Mechnikova
Pecherskaya
Druzhby Narodov
Vydubichi
Slavutich
Poznyaki
Osokorki
Respublikanski stadion
Krasnoarmeyskaya
Dzerzhinskaya

- Red line
- Blue line
- Under construction
- Transfer station

N

Medical Assistance: Polyklinik #1, vul. Verkhna 5 (вул. Верхна; tel. 296 66 68), accepts foreign patients in room 355 for hard currency, though the service is not the same as at home. English spoken.

Emergencies: Fire: tel. 01. **Police:** tel. 02. **Medical:** tel. 03 (a Ukrainian service intended for Ukrainians). In case of emergency, contact your **embassy.**

ACCOMMODATIONS AND CAMPING

Kiev's tourist industry is aimed at rich foreign businesspeople. Hotel prices will make budget travelers cringe. During July and August it is possible to stay in the **dormitories** of the several institutes and universities. Many residents know of unofficial places to stay. Check ex-pat hangouts, such as **America House** (see above), for info.

Institute of Foreign Languages, vul. Chervnoarmiska 73 (вул. Червноармійска; tel. 269 93 08, fax 227 67 88), rents dorm beds (US$3-7) July 1-Aug. 25. English spoken. Call Margarita Dvorzhetskaya. Open Mon.-Fri. 10am-1pm and 2-5pm.

Hotel Mir (Готел Мир), 40-leji Oktyabrya 70 (40-лейі Октября; tel. 264 96 46), near Goloceyevskaya pl. (Голосеевская пл.). Take the metro to Libidska (Либіська) and tram #4 to *magazin knigi "Yuvilejnij"* (магазин книги "Ювілейний"), then walk 0.5km or so. Sputnik's attempt at low-income lodging is a fascinating study of the long-term effects of a lack of maintenance on concrete high-rises. The view from the fifteenth floor isn't half-bad. The plunger in the toilets must be manually lifted—but at least there are toilets. Doubles US$36 in kupons. Exchange counter, café, restaurant, and casino.

Motel-Camping "Prolisok," pr. Peremogi 179, (tel. 444 12 93) From M: Svyatoshno (Святошно) take trolleybus #7 to the "Автостанция Дача" (Avtostantsiya

Dachna); stop and walk down the highway 2km. Dim but comfortable doubles US$65 in the motel. Bungalows with kitchen and shower US$17.50 per person. Tent space US$7. The restaurant, sauna, and casino at the motel attract foreign tractor trailer drivers.

Hotel Libid (Готель Лыбидь; tel. 274 00 63), pl. Peremogi. Take tram #2 one stop from the train station. Another big block full of identical boxes, but this time closer to town. The elevator leaves much to be desired. Singles with bath US$53.

FOOD

Kiev **restaurants** are dress-up-and-celebrate establishments, not places to sit back and fill up. **Cafés** generally serve some substantial fare along with coffee and liquor; some better ones are on Andriyivsky uzviz (Андріївський узвіз) and vul. Karla Marksa (вул. Карла Маркса). **Markets** are well-stocked in summer and many serve ready-to-eat dishes along with their wide variety of bulk foods.

Restaurants and Cafés

Spadishchina (Спадшина), vul. Spask 8 (вул. Спаськ; tel. 417 03 58). M: Kontraktova pl. (Контрактова пл.). Quiet and traditionally Ukrainian by day; hip and fancy by night when young mafiosos in suits and slinky dresses dance and down vodka. Small portions. Full meal US$5, mostly meat. Open daily noon-11pm.

Bistro Maksim (Бистро Максимь), vul. Bogdana Khmelnikovo 21 (вул. Богдана Хмелникого; tel. 224 70 21), across from the opera house. This crowded undergroud meeting-place serves up soup and salad, meat and potatoes to an international crowd, all for under US$3. Open Mon.-Sat. noon-midnight.

Restaurant Khreshchatik, vul. Khreshchatik 16 (вул. Хрещатик), in the Hotel Khreshchatik. The best of the hotel restaurants, it is elegant, rather empty, clean, and safe-feeling. The lunchtime menu is vastly superior to the dinner menu. Full meal US$5-6. Open daily 8am-11pm.

Café Virmenia (Вирмения), Andriyivsky uzviz 11 (Андріївський узвіз; tel. 416 42 79), down from St. Andrew's Cathedral. Mouth-watering grilled lamb *shashlyk* loaded with vegetables and french fries, all served on the terrace. Full meal US$5.

Slavuta, vul. Gorkovo 12 (вул. Горково; tel. 227 03 91). Fosters a thriving nightlife but is also an excellent place to tuck your napkin under your chin, grab a fork and knife and gobble down a hearty lunch full of pork, potatoes and *pelmeni* (dumplings). Large, well-cooked portions. Open daily noon-midnight.

Cafe-theatre Koleso (Кафе-Театр Колесо), Andriyivski Uzviz 8 (Андріївський Узвіз), serves a decent dinner with the show. Tickets available at 5:30pm. Closed Thurs.

Pizza Fantasy, in the Bessarabskiy Rynok (Бессарабський Ринок). Serves you there or sends you away with a hot pie. Plain pizza US$4. Open Mon.-Sat. 11am-7pm.

Vesuvio Pizza, vul. Reytarska 25 (вул. Рейтарська; tel. 216 74 60). Mediocre slices served in square boxes. Restaurant, take-out, and even delivery daily noon-10pm.

Markets

Bessarabski Rynok (Бессарабський Ринок), vul. Khreshchatik (вул. Хрещатик), and vul. Taras Shevchenko (вул. Тарас Шевченко). Big. Real Big. So busy in summer that vendors spill out of the gigantic building into the neighboring streets. An enormous variety of vegetable products from domestic and foreign sources. Open Tues.-Sun. 7am-7pm, Mon. 7am-5pm.

Kolhospniy Rynok (Колгоспний Ринок) at vul. Vorovskovo (вул. Воровського) and vul. Observatorna (вул. Обсерваторьна). A pretty good selection of foods, with fewer people and lower prices than Bessarabski. It also has row of kiosks upstairs where bargains and everyday bizarre items can be found. Open daily 10am-7pm.

Livoberezhniy (.Ливобережний) Rynok, at M: Livoberezhna (Ливобережна), coming from the city center take a right off the platform and look for the entrance to the market behind the café. Slightly less expensive, but further from the center.

NIKA, across from the Bessarabski Rynok on vul. Taras Shevchenko 3 (вул. Тарас Шевченко). Pay in dollars for not-so-fresh Western foods; if your total is not an exact number, they'll throw in a can of Coke or some penny-candy as change. Uniformed security guards make sure you don't run away with that package of Teddy Grahams. Open Mon.-Sat. 10am-8pm, Sun 10am-6pm.

SIGHTS

Vul. Khreshchatik

The center of downtown Kiev lies on vul. Khreshchatik (вул. Хрещатик), the historical nucleus as well as the contemporary heart of the city. From the street's inception at the intersection with bul. Tarasa Sherchenka (бул. Тараса Шевченка) it is lined with shops, bookstores, cafés, and *people*. At bul. Tarasa Shevshenka, **Lenin** gazes serenely into the future, with inspirational sayings carved on the side—one of Kiev's rare Communist monuments that has not been desecrated. Across the street, the blue-fenced **Makulon** complex was once the residence of top party officials; now it's *the* place to live for foreign businessmen and ambassadors. On the opposite corner, the **Bessarabian market** (Бессарабский Ринок) is one of the most ornate of its kind. Walking along Khreshchatik, you can check out the central **department store** ЦУМ (TSUM), where everything is sold in a terrifically confusing jumble of counters (open Mon.-Sat. 9am-8pm). A few more steps bring you to the corner of vul. Bogdana Khmelnitskoho (вул. Богдана Хмельницького). Take a stroll up the street to the **Literature Museum** (Музей Літератури України) on the left at #52 (open Thurs.-Tues. 9am-6pm), and the **opera house** on the right at #50. English-speaking guides for the museum are available only through Intourist for an exorbitant rate, but the museum staff will happily explain everything in Ukrainian or Russian, and they will smile as if you're understanding everything. Next door to the literature museum, the **drama theater** shows Ukrainian productions nightly.

Back on Khreshchatik, you can spot the **archway** to vul. Engelsa (вул. Енгелса), which leads to a quiet, residential neighborhood along a street filled with pretty stone façades. Suddenly, you arrive at **Maydan Nezalezhnosti** (Майдан Незалежності), or "Independence Square" (formerly "October Revolution Square"). This is the very center of town; the terrace surrounding the large fountains is filled with people-watchers and political discussion. It was the site of the execution of Nazi war criminals and of the 1905 uprising. Today large posters affixed to the **post office** walls declare political opinions and throw out provocative topics. Men and women gather to debate away the evening over a few tankards of beer or *kvas*. Right-wing, left-wing, and tourist **propaganda** is sold along the fountain walls, and the occasional **street performer** pleases crowds. The metro stop underneath is a haven for the nascent **street musician** clique as well.

Continuing along Khreshchatik brings you to the **Ukrainski Dim** (Український Дім), the "Ukrainian House" on the left, just across from the Hotel Dnipro. Formerly the Lenin Museum, this weird example of Communist architecture now houses commercial and cultural exhibitions and a carnival of kiosks. Just ahead is the Khreschatiy park. The huge silver croquet wicket that towers over the park is the **arch of brotherhood,** a monument to Russian-Ukrainian union. Locals refer to it as "the yoke." Also inside the park is the **monument to brave soccer players.** As the story goes, invading Nazis discovered that one of their prisoners was a member of the Kiev Dynamo soccer team; they rounded up the other players and arranged a "death match" against the German army's Luftwaffe team. Despite their weakened condition and a referee dressed in a Gestapo uniform, the Dynamo team won the match 5 to 3. They were immediately thrown into a concentration camp, where all but one perished in front of a firing squad.

Old Kiev

Up the hill from the opera house on vul. Volodimirska (вул. Володимирська) are the **Golden Gates** (Золотой Ворота), which are not actually made of gold but wood and stone. They have stood here since 1037, marking the entrance to the city and separating it from the wilds outside. A museum is now housed inside the gates (open Fri.-Tues. 10am-5pm, Wed. 10am-4:30pm). They stand in front of the enormous, elaborate **St. Sophia Monastery Complex** at vul. Volodimirska 24. This is what tourists come to Kiev to see: the golden onion domes, decorated façades, and exquisite Byzantine icons from the 11th century. The monastery was the cultural center of

Kievan Rus and the site of the first library in Rus. Act Ukrainian when you buy the entrance ticket; otherwise you may be charged US$3, the foreigner fee, instead of US$0.03, the "real" price. As you exit the complex, walk onto **pl. Bogdono Khmelnitskoho,** a square of gorgeous 18th- and 19th-century façades surrounding the **monument to Bogdan Khmelnits'kiy,** another national hero, frozen while checking his horse in mid-gallop. Across the square at vul. Volodimirska 2, the **Museum of Ukrainian History** (Націоналъний Музей Історії; tel. 228 48 64) contains exhibits from the Stone Age to the present. Out front are the very foundations of the old city, preserved under glass. Tours are available in Ukrainian or German (open Thurs.-Tues. 10am-6pm).

At the end of vul. Volodimirska, an ancient, winding road leads into the oldest section of Kiev. This is **Andriyivskiy uzviz** (Андрїївський узвіз), now a modern artists' colony, lined with cafés, souvenir shops, and galleries. Look for signs saying "Виставка" (exhibition). Independent galleries show the newest and boldest work Ukrainian visual artists have to offer, but a great number just sell touristy paintings of the street's eponymous cathedral. **St. Andrew's Cathedral,** the edifice in question, proudly looks down on its street; you can learn about it and the street below at the **Andriyivskiy Uzviz Museum** (tel. 416 03 98; open Mon.-Fri. 9am-5pm). Once the scaffolding comes down, you'll be able to get an excellent view from the **steps to castle hill** on the other side of the street. The steps, built by the Committee for the Restoration of Kiev, don't lead anywhere, but are an easier way to climb the hill than scrambling through weedy gardens. Back on level ground, you can stop by the **Museum of Kiev History** at #3 (open daily 11am-7pm). Take a stroll downhill on Andriyivsky uzviz away from St. Andrew's and into lower Kiev and the historic **Podol** district. Halfway down, at no. 13, is **Bulgakov's House** (open Tues.-Sun.). If your legs can still handle it, take a stroll down vul. Petra Sahaydachnoho (Петра Сагайдачного) toward the scenic **funicular,** across from the **river station** on pl. Poshtova (пл. Поштова). This little set of cars is one of the oldest of its kind in the former Soviet Union, and will give you a trip back to upper Kiev for the price of a metro ticket (open daily 6:30am-11pm; Sundays free). At the top you can spot a **monument to King Volodymyr** peeking through the trees of his namesake park.

Bul. Tarasa Shevchenka

A walk past Lenin's metal figure takes you up one of the most pleasant, shady streets in the city. It is dedicated to the poet Taras Shevchenko, the father of Ukrainian nationalism who fought against serfdom in the mid-19th century. Banished in 1847, he never returned to Kiev. On the left side of the street, inside one of Kiev's many glorious parks, a **monument** to the hero stands at least 1½ times the size of Lenin's paltry form. His namesake **university,** on the other side of the park, still leads independent thought in the Ukraine. Farther up bul. Taras Shevchenko at #20 stands the many-domed ochre **Vladimirska Cathedral,** built to commemorate 900 years of Christianity in Kiev. The spectacular interior blends Byzantine styles with art nouveau. At #12 stands the **Taras Shevchenko Museum,** one of the largest and most beautiful literary museums in the former Soviet Union; the museum is well-kept for good reason. Exhibits are labeled in Ukrainian and Russian, but an English-speaking guide is under US$1 (open Tues.-Sun. 10am-5pm; closed on last Fri. of the month).

Kiev Outskirts

A few major points of interest lie outside the city's main district. The **Monument to Mother Ukraine** towers over the city skyline and houses a World War II museum in its base. Plans are underway to tear down this iron lady and replace her with a memorial to the victims of Chernobyl, so be sure to snap a photo while it still stands. Trolleybus #20 takes you along this route, also passing by the **Park of Eternal Glory** (Парк Вічної Слави) with its enormous **obelisk** commemorating those who fell in World War II. Down the road on vul. Sichnevovo Povstanya is the fascinating **Pech-erska Lavra monastery** (Печерска Лавра Софіївський собор), founded in 1051 and considered one of the holiest places in Ukraine. The museums established on the monastery grounds during the Soviet period are gradually being returned to the Orthodox Church. Although the view from the bell tower is a highlight of the visit, the most memorable part of the grounds are the **catacombs,** caves in which monks lived and were buried during the Middle Ages. Women must cover their heads when visiting the caves (no shorts or short skirts either). Take a cab or trolleybus #20 from the Dnipro Hotel downtown to the last stop (open Wed.-Mon. 10am-5pm; cameras US$1, guide US$5).

Farther along the outskirts of Kiev is the moving World War II monument at **Babi Yar** (Бабий Яр). A large group of carved figures commemorates the place where victims of the Nazis were buried starting in September of 1941. Although the plaques state that 100,000 Kievans died here, current estimates double that figure. Many of the victims, most of them Jews, were buried alive. Take trolleybus #27 eight stops from the Petrivka (Петрівка) metro stop or the #16 trolleybus from Maydan Nezalezhnosti. The monument stands in the park, near the TV tower.

ENTERTAINMENT

In the summer, locals café-hop up and down Kreshchatik and gather to talk at the fountains of Maydan Nezalezhnosti, which are lit up at night. If you desire more spirited company, **Slavuta,** vul. Horkoho 12 (вул. Горкого; tel. 227 03 91), is open until midnight and has beer on tap (US$3 per half-liter). Take trolleybus #16 or 18 from Maydan Nexalezhnosti toward **pl. Lvivska** (пл. Львівська), another café-hopping relay track, for a closer look at the less touristed sections of town. Late-nighters in Kiev gravitate to the **24hr. mini-bar** on vul. Chervonoarmeiska just across the street from Respublikanski Stadion.

The local arts scene thrives at a number of **theaters;** some of the more interesting ones are the small independent companies that line Andriyevski uviz, including the **Koleso theater-café** at #8 (tel. 416 05 27; ticket office open Thurs.-Tues. 5:30-7pm). Also try the **Theater Studio "Na Podoli"** (tel. 416 01 94) and the tiny, recently established **Life-Art Cabaret,** in the Academia at #34, which often hosts folk singers. Most of them close down in the summer. A seat at the national **Opera and Ballet Theater** costs about US$0.25 if you buy a ticket there at vul. Volodymyrska 50 (ticket office open Tues.-Sat. noon-2pm and 4-7:30pm, Sun. 11am-1:30pm; shows daily at noon and 7pm). The **National Drama Theater** across the street (M: Teatralna; Театральна) is just as good a bargain (ticket office open Thurs.-Tues. noon-2:45pm and 4-7pm; Wed. noon-2:45pm and 4-6pm; shows daily at 7pm). For all tickets to the opera, **philharmonic,** and other performances, check with the ticket office (Театральна каса), vul. Bogdana Khmelnitskoho (вул. Богдана Хмельницького; open Tues.-Sun. 9am-5pm). If you're in Kiev during **soccer** (football) season (late spring to mid-autumn), see a **Dynamo Kiev** game. Kievans go bonkers with good reason: their team is one of the best on the planet. Buy tickets at the stadium on vul. Chervonoarmeiska (M: Respublikanski Stadion; Республиканский Стадион).

On hot summer days, Kievans hang out at **Gidropark** (Гідропарк), where you'll find an **amusement park** and **beach** on an island in the Dnieper. Tucked in a corner near the bridge is the **Venice Beach of Ukraine,** where young Kievan men lift spare automobile parts to keep in shape. The beach has showers, toilets, and changing booths, yet no one seems to charge admission. **Boat rentals** are available. This is also a hot pick-up spot for the college-age crowd, for which there is also no charge.

Pick up Ukrainian ceramics, baskets, and embroidered goods for koupons at the **Ukrainian Souvenir** (Український Сувенір) store, vul. Chervonoarmeiska (open Mon.-Fri. 10am-2pm and 3-7pm, Sat. 10am-6pm). The daily and weekend **bazaars** in the summer time in Respublikanski Stadion are an experience in themselves even if you don't buy anything from the myriad goods hauled here from all over Eastern Europe and the former Soviet Union. Try to come to Kiev on **Ukraine Sovereignty Day** (July 16), when the city becomes a moveable feast.

■■■ LVIV (ЛЬВІВ)

Lviv, alternately called Lvov (by the Russians), Lwów (by the Poles), and Lemberg (by the Germans), dates back to 1256, when the city's first fortress arose in a valley at the confluence of Eastern European trade routes in an area called Galicia. From the start an integral part of Eastern-Central Europe rather than the Russian empire, its narrow cobblestone alleys and magnificent Gothic and Baroque cathedrals are reminiscent of such former Austro-Hungarian jewels as Prague and Kraków. The Polish empire acquired Galicia in the 14th century, and remained until repartitioned by the Habsburg empire in the 18th century. Lviv became the center of the Uniate church that arose in Galicia, which recognized both the Pope *and* Orthodox tradition. After World War I and a stint at independence which created the state of Ruthenia (Eastern Galicia), the Polish Empire reclaimed the area until 1939 when Western Ukraine was annexed to the rest of the Ukrainian Soviet Socialist Republic. Lviv's Uniate church and nationalist population fled, scarlet banners were hung, and decades of Sovietization ensued.

In the post-Soviet age, Lviv has become the center of Ukrainian national revival. Lviv's many Greek Orthodox churches are being handed back to their congregations after decades of closure, and the Uniate church is coming back with vigor. The yellow and blue Ukrainian flag flies over the headquarters of the democratically elected city council, and *Rukh,* the Ukrainian popular front, maintains its headquarters here. Nonetheless, life goes on quietly in the city's medieval squares and coffeehouses as locals contemplate a way out of the drab, crumbling Soviet legacy.

ORIENTATION AND PRACTICAL INFORMATION

The center of the old town is **pl. Rynok** (пл. Ринок), the old market square. Around it a grid of streets forms the Old Town, and along the western side **prosp. Svobody** (пр. Свободи) runs from the Opera House to **pl. Mitskievicha** (пл. Мішкевича). Tram #1 runs from the northwest train station to the center of the old town, tram #6 to the north end of prosp. Svobody. Tram #9 goes back the way tram #1 came.

Tourist Offices: Grand Hotel (Гранд-Готель), prosp. Svobody 13 (пр. Свободи; tel. 76 90 60), is neither a tourist office nor does it have a separate service bureau. However, the reception desk of this Ukrainian-American joint venture understands the meaning of "customer service"; everyone speaks perfect English, **maps** are given out free, and questions are answered with a smile. Obtains **train and bus tickets,** but only for a US$10 service charge. The cheapest **fax** in town, open 24 hrs. The **Hotel George** (Готель Жорж) **service bureau** plans guided **tours** and possesses a lot of information about the city, but only reluctantly lets you have it. This used to be the Intourist office; how did you guess? Open Mon.-Fri. 9am-5pm. The **travel bureau** across the hall is the definitive place to get **train tickets** or schedule **flights.** Open daily 9am-6pm.

Currency Exchange: Traveler's checks accepted for 2.5% commission at the **Hotel George** exchange bureau. Open Mon.-Sat. 9am-5pm, Sun. 9am-3pm. Many Western currencies exchanged, including Australian and Canadian dollars, at **Dendi Exchange,** ul. Kopernika 16, open daily 8am-8pm. Dollars and Deutschmarks exchanged at Обмін-Валют *(Odmin-Valyut)* kiosks; those that accept Polish złoty are also marked кантор *(kantor).*

Post Office: vul. Slovatskovo 1 (вул. Словацькови), one block from park Ivan Franko, to the right as you face the university. **Poste Restante** here. Open Mon.-Fri. 8am-8pm, Sat. 8am-6pm, Sun. and holidays 8am-2pm. **Postal Code:** 290000.

Telephones: Doroshenka 39 (Дорошенка), around the corner from the post office. Order your call at window #3; at night, use window #1. Open 24 hrs. Payphones take **special coins** which can be bought at the telephone office for 30krb each. For local and intercity calls, buy **tokens** (жетон, *zheton*) at the telephone office or at kiosks. Insert the coin, pick up the phone, and wait for the dial tone. Intercity calls can be made only from the telephone office or from telephones that say "Міжміські" (meezh-MEEs-kee; *intercity*). US$7.50 to send **faxes;** 10,000krb to receive (fax 76 15 85). Fax office open Mon.-Fri. 8am-10pm. **City Code:** 0322.

UKRAINE

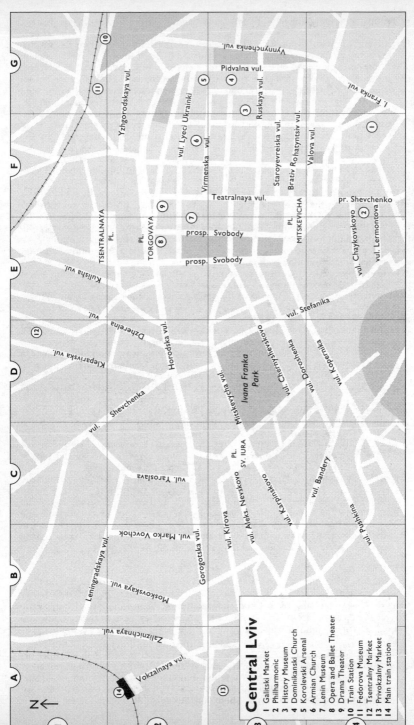

Central Lviv

1 Galitski Market
2 Philharmonic
3 History Museum
4 Dominikanski Church
5 Korolevski Arsenal
6 Armian Church
7 Lenin Museum
8 Opera and Ballet Theater
9 Drama Theater
10 Train Station
11 Fedorova Museum
12 Tsentralny Market
13 Privokzalny Market
14 Main train station

Vynnynchenka vul.

Pidvalna vul.

Yzhgorodskaya vul.

Ruskaya vul.

I. Franka vul.

vul. Lyeci Ukrainki

Staroyevreiska vul.

Brativ Rohatyntsiv vul.

Valova vul.

Virmenska vul.

Teatralnaya vul.

pr. Shevchenko

TSENTRALNAYA PL.

PL. TORGOVAYA

prosp. Svobody

prosp. Svobody

PL. MITSKEVICHA

vul. Chaykovskoyo

vul. Lermontova

Kulisha vul.

vul.

vul. Stefanika

vul. Dzherelna

Horodska vul.

Ivana Franka Park

vul. Chernyshevskovo

vul. Doroshenka

vul. Kopernika

Kleparivska vul.

vul. Shevchenka

Mitskevycha vul.

PL. SV. IURA

vul. Yaroslava

vul. Kirova

vul. Aleks. Nevskovo

vul. Kapitskovo

vul. Bandery

vul. Pushkina

Leningradskaya vul.

vul. Marko Vovchok

Gorogotska vul.

Moskovskaya vul.

Zaliznichnaya vul.

Vokzalnaya vul.

N

Trains: Train station on pl. Voksalna (пл. Вокзальна) at the end of vul. Vokzalna (вул. Вокзальна). Trams #1 and 6 take you near the city center; #6 drops you off near the end of prosp. Svobodi (просп. Свободи). From the city, take tram #9. Bus #18 takes you to the bus station. **Tickets** available at windows #23-25 on the second floor, or at the travel bureau of the Hotel George. Buy tickets well in advance; international tickets should be reserved in the morning and bought 2hrs. before scheduled departure. The travel bureau will be a much bigger help than the train station. Direct trains daily to: Sofia, Budapest, Prague, Bratislava, and Belgrade; twice daily to Przemyśl, Poland; trains on odd days only to Warsaw.

Buses: The station on the outskirts of town at vul. Striycka (вул. Стрийська). From the station, bus #18 takes you to the train station where trams into town are frequent. Extensive regional service; for long-distance destinations, buy tickets a day in advance. Almost hourly service to Przemyśl, Poland (4hrs.; пермишл); daily to Lublin (Люблін), Warsaw (Варшава), and Krakow (Краків). Buy tickets for Polish destinations at window #1 in advance, or take a same-day risk at window #2.

Public Transportation: Buy tickets for **trams, trolleybuses** and **buses** at kiosks; punch on board. Controllers are especially vigilant and ready to slap you with that US$0.10 fine if you should dare ride without paying. A recent public transit **map** is available at some kiosks. Tram lines are marked in brown, trolleybuses in red, and buses in blue; it's worth the US$0.13 for the lists of new street names.

Library: On vul. Mularska (вул. Муларська) behind the Mir (Мир) movie theater. Stocks foreign and Ukrainian works.

Laundromat: Hotel George will take in wash for its guests; others can ask at their service bureau about the Майоровка (Mah-yer-ovka) washers.

Pharmacy: Apteka #1 (Аптека), vul. Kopernika 8 (вул. Коперника). Open 24 hrs.

ACCOMMODATIONS

Hotel Georges (Готель Жорж), pl. Mickiewicza 1 (пл. Міцкевича; tel. 79 90 11). Take tram #1 from the train station to Дорошенка. Brand-spanking-newly restored and simply posh, but somehow the elevator doesn't always work, the mirrors in the hallways are a bit cracked, and the staff is only grudgingly friendly. Singles US$9, with bath US$14. Doubles US$17, with bath US$22.

Hotel Sputnik (Готель Спутник), vul. Knyahini Olgi 116 (бул. Княгині Ольги; tel. 64 58 220). A 15-min. ride from the city center (tram #3 to the last stop); or trolleybus #5 from the bus station to the seventh stop, then backtrack and take a left onto Knyahini Olgi. Though you may suffer from culture shock shuttling between here and the old part of town, the facilities are wonderfully modern. Plus, it's practically next door to the concrete Универмаг *(Univermag)* **department store,** an architectural "wonder" of its time. All rooms with bath. Singles US$15. Doubles US$16, with "*lyuks*" facilities US$27. Breakfast included.

Hotel Lviv (Готель Львів), vul. 700r. Lvova 3 (вул. 700р. Львова), just behind the opera house. Take tram #6 from the train station to the Оперний Театр *(Operni Teatr)* stop; backtrack about 50m and take a left; the hotel is on the right. The facilities are not as pretty as in the newer hotels but the beds are comfortable, the location is central, and the staff doesn't have that know-it-all attitude about tourists. Singles US$7, with bath US$9.50. Doubles US$11, with bath US$16. Asking for rooms without television and refrigerator may lower the price.

FOOD

Pl. Rynok is the center of restaurants and cafés; the most central **market** is on Prospect Shevchenko, a block past Hotel George, though it's not as big as **Rynok Noviy** (Ринок Новий), reachable by bus #18. **Halytski Rynok** (Галицький Ринок), behind the flower stands across from the Church of St. Andrew, has fresh berries, honey, and vegetables (open summer 7am-6pm).

Restaurants

Stari Royal (Старий Рояль), at vul. Stavropitivska Dnestr (вул. Ставропітівська Днестр), next to the pharmacy museum. The city's first cooperative welcomes guests to the soft strains of its namesake piano. Full meal with *borsch, vareniki,* and pork cutlet just under US$2. Open daily noon-11pm.

Pid Lyevom (Пид Левом; "Under the Lion"), pl. Rinok 20, behind the gate with the brass lion's head. Large hall at street level supplemented by atmospheric brick cellar. Full meal US$4. Open daily noon-5pm and 6pm-midnight.

Restaurant Festival (Фестивальний), vul. Sichovich Strilsti 12 (tel. 72 20 59), behind the main university building. Traditional Ukrainian fare under US$3. Music and cabaret show 7:30-8:30pm. Open daily noon-11pm.

Restaurant Lyuks (Люкс), Kopernika 6/7, across from the Mickiewicz column. Step upstairs past the hall of mirrors to the turn-of-the-century dining room; the food and service have not kept up with the stylish decor, but you can have the standard cucumbers, meat, and potatoes. Open daily noon-5pm and 6-11pm.

Café Bilya Fontana (Café White Fountain), prospect Svobody, across from Lyuks. Inexpensive and quite popular place where the menu hangs unceremoniously on the wall. Open daily 9am-8pm.

Pizza Pronto on vul. Gorodska 61, down the street from the circus. A busy little restaurant serving hot pizza; by the slice or whole (US$2). Open daily 10am-9pm.

Litali (Літалі), bul. Katedralna 4 (вул. Катедрална). A cheap and charming pizzeria, café, and bar frequented by locals in search of a change from sausage and potatoes. Open daily 9am-noon and 1-10pm.

Cafés

Reflecting its Polish and Austro-Hungarian heritage, Lviv is a city of coffee and cafés. Although few elegant coffeehouses remain, there are a couple of spots to sit down and have a cup with friends. If you're greeted with the Ukrainian *"kavy nemaye"* (no coffee), walk on down to the next place.

Kofeynya (Кофейня), vul. Virmenska 19 (вул. Вірменська). Pastries for pennies and coffee for less. A family hangout in the early afternoon, but when the little kids leave, the way-friendly owners turn up the rock 'n' roll and troubled, idle urban youths drift in. Open daily 9am-3pm and 4-8pm.

Pingvin (Пінгвін), prosp. Svobodi 43 (пр. Свободи). An extremely popular ice cream parlor, and with good reason—it has some of the best in town. Open Mon.-Sat. 9am-2pm, 3-9pm; Sun. 9am-2pm and 3-8pm.

Korona (Корона), prosp. Svobody (пр. свободи), next to the Hotel Ukraina. Summertime sherbets make this another crowd-pleasing ice cream parlor. Pastries too. Open daily 9am-3pm and 4-8pm.

SIGHTS AND ENTERTAINMENT

Lviv's historical center is compact and best seen on foot. Start your walk on **prospect Svobodi,** next to the ornate neoclassical **Opera and Ballet Theater** (Театр Опери та Балету). The dazzlingly complicated exterior is surpassed only by the interior, complete with gilded sculpture. The opera opens onto a pedestrian mall that runs down the middle of the boulevard, splitting it in two. As you face the center, with your back to the opera, walk on the right side of pr. Svobodi to get a look at the city's principal shops and hotels, lodged in the ochre façades of old Polish apartments. On the left, the **Lviv National Museum** and **civic buildings** command attention if only for their impressive fronts. Part of the town's original **city walls and gates** still stand next to the museum. A third of the way up pr. Svobodi at #15 (at the intersection with vul. Hnatyuka) is the **Ethnographic Museum** (Музей Етнографії). The museum harbors an exhibit of Ukrainian dress, archeological artifacts, painted eggs, and embroidery; it's worth a look inside, if only just for the fabulous marble staircase and lofty decorated ceilings (open Wed.-Sun. 10am-6pm). Turn off onto vul. Hnatyuka and you will come to a fork in the road; head left to the **park of Ivan Franko,** fronting on **Lviv University.** The monument to Franko looks kindly down on the students; the ones who can muster the energy to walk all the way uphill through the park will be rewarded by the sight of the beauteous, ochre-walled, gold-studded **St. Yura Cathedral** to the right; this 18th-century wonder remains youthful through the hundreds of baptisms it sees yearly (open daily 7am-1pm and 3-8pm).

Back on pr. Svobody, you eventually reach the **Mickiewicz column,** honoring the Polish poet and patriot. This is the site of concerts, crowded political discussions, and the occasional Hare Krishna singalong. Turn left at the Ukraine movie theater and head toward the stone-gray façade of the former 17th-century Bernardine Monastery, now the Greek Catholic **Church of St. Andrew.** The church boasts a cavernous interior covered in frescoes, and a massive gilt altar of rich gold and black granite. To reach the very heart of the old city, make a sharp left here and take one of the narrow streets leading up to **pl. Rynok,** the historic market square, presenting a collage of 4-story, richly decorated merchant homes dating from the 16th-18th centuries. More Polish than Poland; the square gazes up at the *Ratusz* (Ратуша; town hall), a 19th-century addition, whose corners are guarded by statues of Adonis, Diana, Amphitrite, and Neptune.

There are enough museums around the square to help you with cocktail party banter for the next year. Try the **Historical Museum** at pl. Rinok 4 (open Thurs.-Tues. 10am-6pm) and the adjoining **Italian Courtyard** at pl. Rinok 6. The **Pharmacy Museum** (Аптека Музей) is housed in Lviv's oldest drugstore and sells small bottles of iron-fortified "wine" designed to cure all your ills; ask for the *vino* (open Mon.-Sat. 9am-7pm, Sun. 10am-5pm). Before going out with the artsy crowd, prepare to stun them with knowledge gleaned at the **Museum of Furniture and Porcelain** (Музей Меблів і Порцеляни) at #24 (open Thurs.-Tues. 10am-6pm).

Up above the old city, where the television tower now stands, rises **High Castle Hill** (Високий Замок; *Vysoki Zamok*), from whose top a stunning panorama of Lviv unfolds. Continuing farther east, take tram #2 or walk along vul. Lichakivska to vul. Krupyarska (Крупярська). Walk up the street on the left to the outdoor **Museum of Architecture,** also known as the **Shevchenskivski Hai** (Шевченьківський Гай). Lying on a vast park, the museum harbors a collection of authentic wooden houses brought here from around western Ukraine (open Tues.-Fri. and Sun. 10am-6pm, Sat. 11am-7pm). Back on Lichakivska, head down vul. Mechnikova to the whitewashed chapel and the **Lichakivski Cemetery** (Личаківський Цвинтар). On the terrain of Lviv's most famous necropolis are the graves of Polish and American nobles beside the simple graves of local residents from throughout the centuries. Tram #2 takes you from the cemetery back to town; from downtown, take #4.) **Striski Park** (Стрийський парк) is a splendidly manicured park with swans and a greenhouse.

Lviv is jam-packed with beautiful examples of ecclesiastic art and architecture; if you're going to get churched-out anywhere, this is the town for it. Just beyond Neptune's gaze is pl. Katedralna, where the main attraction is the Polish **Roman Catholic Cathedral** (open Mon.-Sat. 6am-noon and 6-8pm, Sun. and holidays 6am-3pm and 5:30-8pm). Next door stands a small Renaissance chapel, **Boimi's Chapel** (Каплиця Боїмів), whose portal displays a frieze of delicately sculpted stone. At the east end of the square (between Adonis and Diana) are the massive **Assumption Church** (next to the 60m Korniak belltower) and the Baroque cupola of the **Museum of Religion,** formerly a Dominican monastery and church, whose masterfully carved wooden figures are worth a look (open Fri.-Sun. 11am-6pm). Behind it at the end of vul. Staroivreiskka (бул. Староіврейська), curators at the **Arsenal Museum** have preserved iron and steel examples of the many things humans have used to kill each other (open Thurs.-Tues. 10am-5:45pm, cashier closes ½-hr. earlier; admission will be really cheap, whatever it is when you're there, with students half-price). Keep going north past the pharmacy museum to the **Armenian Cathedral,** now closed to the public but worth a look; it seems so out of place you'd never guess it has been there since the 14th century. Take a quick left on to vul. Lesi Ukrainky (вул. Лесі Українки) and the **Transfiguration Church** (Преображенська церква) is one block away on vul. Krakivska (вул. Краківська), remarkable for the vivid iconic paintings that grace every interior pillar. Turn left as you exit the church, walk a few blocks, and take a right at the park to **St. John the Baptist Church,** probably the most *darling* brick and stucco structure you'll ever see. Carefully preserved since the 13th century, it's one of the best postcard scenes in the city (open Tues.-Sun. noon-6pm).

At night, Lviv offers comparatively little. Near the arsenal on vul. Vinnichenka is **Pid Veshayu** (Під Вежею; *Under the Tower*), a popular, rowdy beer hall. Coffee is served upstairs, draft beer in the smoky grotto basement. Part of Lviv's original city wall (c. 1256) is visible downstairs near the bar (open daily 9am-3pm and 4-8pm; the beer sleeps late and is on tap only after 10am). Catch a performance at the **Opera** or the **Symphony**, vul. Chaikovskoho 7. The ticket windows (*teatralni kasi*; театральни каси) are at pr. Svobodi 37 (open Mon.-Sat. 11am-2pm and 4-7pm).

■ NEAR LVIV

A few hours west and south by car, bus, or train rise the pine-covered **Carpathian Mountains**, steep valleys carpeted with wildflowers and chalets that overlook crystal streams. Rock-climbing and hiking are popular at the **Chorna Skala cliffs** (Чорна Скала). Take tram #2 to the end of the line (near the medical institute); just before the terminus the tram takes a right turn. Walk in the direction the tram *was* going to reach a bus that will take you there. **Boats** are rented on the nearby lake.

■ ■ ■ LUTSK (ЛУЦЬК)

Lutsk has seen more foreign rulers in its 909 years than most cities have cross-streets. When the Golden Horde had finally given it a rest and the Polish nobility had taken the day off, it was the Russians, Lithuanians, or occasionally Swedish invaders who tried to take advantage of the city's key location and the region's fertile ground. Lutsk has held up pretty well and is even recovering gracefully from Soviet rule. People speak polite Ukrainian to each other in the streets and are almost completely untouched by the xenophobia that characterizes so many of the larger cities. The Old Town does not have a coherent atmosphere but does sport an impressive number of architectural treasures; it's all quite picturesque and worth a visit for a lazy summer day.

ORIENTATION AND PRACTICAL INFORMATION

A **map** of the city was published a few years ago. Not only have all the copies been sold, but all the street names have since changed. Even Intourist doesn't have a map of its own. The central region of the city fits nicely into a curve of the Styr River; **Ploshcha Teatralna** (площа Театральна) is the center of town, reachable by trolley-bus #7 from the train station, recognizable by the Hotel Ukraina and the statue of Lesya Ukrainka. The main commercial street, **prosp. Voli** (пр. Волі) runs east from the square, and the all-pedestrian **vul. Lesi Ukrainky** (вул. Лесі Українки) runs south-west toward the old town from the other side of the statue, crossing vul. Kafedralna (вул. Кафедральна) and becoming vul. D. Halytskoho (вул. Д. Галицького). Stores in Lutsk typically close from 2-3pm.

Tourist Office: Intourist, inside the Hotel Ukraina. English spoken, train and plane tickets sold, directions given. No maps, some free Intourist brochures which have grown more humorous with age. Open Mon.-Fri. 9am-5pm.

Currency Exchange: Difficult in Lutsk. It is not possible to change currency on weekends or to exchange anything but dollars or Deutschmarks. The **INKO** банк (bank) on the second floor of vul. Lesi Ukrainky 52 (вул. Лесі Українки) is centrally located and does occasionally change Canadian dollars also. Open Mon.-Fri. 9am-1pm and 2-6pm.

Post Office: Kryviy Val 19 (Кривий Вал); turn right from vul. Lesi Ukrainky. Open daily 8am-8pm.

Telephones: At the post office, open 24 hrs. (international calls daily 7am-11pm only); or at prosp. Voli 14 (пр. Волі), open 24 hrs.

Flights: Krupa airport, accessible by shuttle bus from the train station every 30min. All flights handled by Air Ukraine, in the "Аэрофлот" building at vul. Slovatsky 62 (вул. Словацки); tickets also available through the Intourist office.

Trains: Station at pl. Vokzalna (пл. Вокзальна), at the northern end of the #7 trolley-bus line. Officially, foreigners can only buy tickets in the Intourist office, but they don't seem to mind if you buy long-distance tickets 2-30 days in advance at window #7, or for local destinations (such as Lviv) a few hours in advance at window

#2; late at night, use window #1. To: Kiev (3 per day, 11hrs); Lviv: (2 per day, 5hrs.). Direct connections to Brest, St. Petersburg, and Moscow.

Buses: *Avtostantsia* (Автостанція) #1, Lvivska vul. 148 (Львівська вул.); trolleybus #5 and bus #6 run from the station to the central Универмаг stop. Ticket windows open 5am-9pm. To: Lviv (8 per day, 5hrs.); Kiev: (5 per day, 9hrs.). Covers some regional destinations as well.

Public Transportation: Buy tickets for trolleybuses and buses at numbered kiosks and punch them on board. Trolleybuses #1 and 6 head to the Old Town from pl. Teatralna (пл. Театральна), and #7 and 2 run along prosp. Voli (пр. Волі) and #7 goes to the train station.

Taxis: Stands are throughout the city (tel. 058).

Luggage Storage: At the train station and airport.

Pharmacy: Apteka (Аптека) #65, prosp. Voli 3 (пр. Волі). Open daily 8am-8pm; prescriptions filled 24 hrs.

Medical Assistance: At prosp. Hrushevskoho 5 (пр. Грушевського), near the train station; foreigners are accepted for hard currency. Better not to try, though.

Emergencies: Police: tel. 01. **Fire:** tel. 02. **Ambulance:** tel. 03.

ACCOMMODATIONS

Hotel Ukraina (Готель Україна), right on pl. Teatralna (пл. Театральна) at Slovatski 2 (Словацькі; tel. 433 51), offers Intourist's best. All rooms with telephone, television, and bathroom. Singles US$5. Doubles US$9.

Hotel Svityaz (Готель Світязь), vul. Naberezhna 4 (Набережна; tel. 441 72 or 434 81). Nine cement stories close to the Old Town. From the right side of pl. Teatralna (пл. Театральна; with your back to Hotel Intourist), take trolleybus #1 or 6 one stop; backtrack 50m and take the first left through the parking lot. If you don't mind clashing colors, the hotel is a good deal and perfectly modern. Singles (on the fourth-floor) US$3.50-4.50, with telephone and television (and less elevation) US$9. Doubles US$5 per person. Triples US$3.50 per person, with television US$4.35 per person. All rooms have bath; individual travelers can buy one space in a larger room and risk spending the night with strange roommates.

FOOD

Most of the better **cafés** and state **grocery stores** lie along the pedestrian zone of vul. Lesi Ukrainky (вул. Лесі Українки). Fresh veggies are sold by the kilo in the **Tsentralniy Rynok** (Центральний Ринок) at the corner of vul. Kafedralna (вул. Кафедральна) and vul. Molodizhna (вул. Молодижна), reachable by trolleybus #1 or 6. Summertime vendors sell produce to travelers at the huge **Vokzalni Rynok** (Вокзальний Ринок) next to bus station #1.

Café Stariy Zamok (Кафе Старий Замок), vul. Lesi Uraïnky 24 (вул. леси Українки), is a subterranean grotto simmering with atmosphere and better food. On the left, the "dessert room" serves excellent pastries for US$0.50-0.75. Open daily 11am-8pm.

Restaurant Teatralniy (Ресторан Театральний), vul. Lesi Ukrainky 67 off the square, serves big portions of good chow for relatively low prices. You'll be told what's available that day.; take it or leave it. Open Fri.-Wed. 1-5pm and 6-10pm, Thurs. 1-5pm and 6-8pm.

SIGHTS AND ENTERTAINMENT

A **statue of Lesya Ukrainka** stands at pl. Teatralna (пл. Театральна), as if just struck by inspiration. The revered poetess grew up in the region in the late 19th century and put Volnya on the map. Next to her, the **Holy Trinity Cathedral** (Святотроїцьки Кафедра) stands serenely behind iron gates (open daily 8am-6pm). Strolling down vul. Ukrainky you'll pass understated but elegant 19th-century houses which add warmth to the brick streets. At the end of the road, the **Khrestodvyzhenska Church** (Хрестодвиженська; Elevation of the Holy Cross) effuses a majesty which almost seems out of place in this humble city. The **Jesuit and Basilisian monastery** has stood within the complex since the 17th century. The Ukrainian folk-art influences make the whole complex more appealing than the usual cold, impressive churches of the West. A left on vul. Kafedralna (вул. Кафедральна) brings you to the **Brigittine Convent** at #16, dating from 1624 but endlessly rebuilt; in summer 1994 it was undergoing extensive renovation.

Further down on vul. Kafedralna stand the three towers and castle walls of **Lutsk Castle,** also being restored. One tower has been converted into a **bell museum.** From the top you can see the nearby park, which drips with willows and poplars. It's a good place to write a novel. The hall on the right as you enter shows rotating exhibitions. Try to convince someone to let you see the **vaults** underneath the street. (Castle open Tues.-Sun. 10am-6pm. Admission US$0.10, children US$0.03. Guidebook in Ukrainian US$0.02.) Backtrack on to vul. D. Halylskoho (вул. Д. Галицького); a little farther down is the **Pokrovska Church** (Покровська, *Protection of the Blessed Virgin Mary*) at #12. The church's treasured Volynian Blessed Virgin Mary icon hangs in its 13th-century glory at the Ukrainian Art Museum in Kiev. Down the road at #33, the former **synagogue** stands as the lone testament to a Jewish population that was persecuted, deported, and executed over the centuries. The **river** just beyond is quiet and lazy, and makes for good resting.

For **entertainment** in Lutsk, head to the cafés around pl. Teatralna (пл. Театральна) where young folk while the night away. Check out the **puppet theater** (Областной Театр Кукол) on vul. Bogdana Khmelnikoho (вул. Богдана Хмельникого) for daytime shows (ticket windows open daily 10am-5pm).

■■■ KHARKIV (ХАРКІВ)

A few years ago, CIA agents must have foamed at the mouth to get to Kharkiv, the bastion of Soviet arms manufacture. The Manhattan Project of the USSR progressed in one of the underground laboratories. Now that the area is open to Westerners, it seems strangely calm. There is no sign on the broad avenues or in the quiet parks of the world's second-largest prison (it's underground), or the enormous nuclear arms factory (also underground). It will be some time before you're even allowed to officially know if any of it exists.

Russia has always held a certain fascination with this industrial town without apparent industry. Founded in 1654 as a Tsarist outpost, the Tsars again made it the administrative center of Ukraine in the 18th century. In 1920, the Bolsheviks formed their rival Ukrainian government here. Unhappily, its stint as administrative center under the communists has left Kharkiv bursting with Lenin's administrative architecture. For now, you can take advantage of the large and thriving community of international students and the happening nightlife that accompanies the daytime academic world. And listen for the bugle.

Orientation and Practical Information A map of the town is difficult to come by, but the city's **metro,** swift and military, is good enough by itself. The center of town is the vast, tree-lined **Ploshad Svobodi** (Площадь Свободи) at the **Universityet metro stop** (Университет). Think what might be going on below. Now stop; you're here to enjoy yourself. There's no official **tourist office;** the lobby of the Hotel Kharkiv (Готель Харків) on Ploshad Svobodi may sometimes have a **map** and helps purchase opera tickets, and the Hotel Intourist (Готель Интурист) at Lenina 21 (Ленинс) plans to start running tours of the city. For **currency Exchange,** head to large hotels or "Обмін-Валют" kiosks. No traveler's checks. Send mail (no packages) and receive Poste Restante at the **post office** on the opposite end of the pl. Svobodi from the metro station, at #5; the entrance, difficult to find, is around the corner from the telephones and up a tiny staircase (open daily 8am-6pm). The **postal code** is 310022. **Telephones** are at pl. Svobodi 5 (пл. Свободи), under the "Междугородные Автоматы" sign. Expect very long lines (open 24 hrs.; international calls daily 7am-10pm).

The main **train** station is M: Vokzalna (Вокзальна) at vul. Slavyanska (вул. Славянська). Intourist counters are down the street half a block on the right at counters #7 and 8 (open 9am-7:30pm). Look for the "кассы" sign. To: Kiev (12hrs.,

130,000Krb); Donetsk (8hrs., 8600Krb). The delightful **metro** system takes plastic tokens (150Krb) in a brilliant shade of orange, and is a little less crowded than its big brother in Kiev. **Trams** and **buses** cover the rest of the city. Buy tickets (100Krb) from any numbered kiosk and punch them on board if you can possibly fit into the door. If you can't reach the punch, pass your ticket on to someone who can. There's **luggage storage** at the train station. Look for the suitcase and key symbol.

Accommodations and Food With this many dormitories, you'd think there would be some system of renting them out to travelers. Head to the "student village" on vul. Otakara Yarasha (вул. Отакара Яраша) just beyond the Hotel Mir and chat with one the hosts of English-speaking international students. Or, in a dorm, ask for the *kommandant* (коммандант) and speak sweetly in Russian or Ukrainian. **Hotel Mir** is at Prospect Lenina 27a (Проспект Ленина; tel. 30 55 43). Take the #8 or 38 bus from Universityet (Университет). Rooms are spacious, with bath, telephone, TV, toilets that flush, and good views (singles US$30, doubles US$50). **Hotel Intourist,** pr. Lenina 21 (пр. Ленина; tel. 32 05 08) is big and stuffy, but one of the only three acts in town (singles US$40, doubles US$74). Pickings are slim when it comes to food. Try the **market** that forms in front of Universityet (Университет) for groceries. The **cafeteria** in the student village is also a possibility in the early afternoon for a cheap meal. **Café Bolonya** (Кафе Болонья), is on vul. Pushkinska (вул. Пушкінська) just past the Post Office. M: Pushkinska (Пушскінська). Good atmosphere and a young, cheery crowd; meals are appetizing (open daily noon-11pm). **Restaurant Kharkov,** pl. Svobodi, part of Hotel Kharkov, is cheap but serves the same stuff as everywhere else (open daily 9am-11pm).

Sights and Entertainment By day, Kharkiv is calm and dull, but you can find ways to amuse yourself. Try the **historical museum** at M: Muzey (Музей; open Wed.-Mon. 10am-5pm). Animal lovers should stay away from the **zoo** in the park near pl. Svobodi (open Wed.-Mon. 8:30am-8pm, cashier closes at 7:30pm; admission 6000Krb). You can take a dip at the **public swimming pool** on Pushkinski (Пушкінськи), a five-minute walk from the metro stop in the sports complex.

By night, check out the scene around the **fountain** in the park next to pl. Svobodi (music and dancing until 1am, Fri. and Sat. until 2am). International students hang out at the **Meridian Club** on Alesirka vul. (Алесирка вул.); at the **Zmina café** (Змина кафе) and the **Karlova café** (Карлова кафе), dancing goes on until all hours. Both are on vul. Otakara Yarasha (вул. Отакара Яраша) in the student's village. **African night** is on Saturdays at Zmina and on Fridays at Karlova. The **opera house** on pl. Svobodi has shows almost daily and tickets are cheap (US$0.25); chill here in the early evening (shows start at 7pm) and emerge saying, "the night is young, yet."

■ ■ ■ DNIPROPETROVSK (ДНІПРОПЕТРОВСЬК)

There's an eclectic charm to this city that belies the fact that Dnipropetrovsk is the third largest city in all of Ukraine and a major river and rail shipping center. Originally called Yekaterinoslav, in honor of Catherine II who founded it in 1784, "Dnepro" (or "dne-sk") has been open to individual foreign travelers only since 1990. Bear left as you leave the train station and take tram #1 to get to the main boulevard, Prospect Karla Marksa (Проспект Карла Маркса), divided by trees and filled with weird, sometimes ornately beautiful and sometimes outlandish, structures. Look for the **National Library** on the left and **Hotel Ukraine** on the right, both historic landmarks. This may not be a bar- and café-hoppers' paradise, but it's the best one in *Dnepro*. Wear the best clothes your backpack affords if you want to fit in, or buy new ones at the well-stocked Univermag (Универмаг) **department store** at #70. The smaller **Samara** (Самара) **River** flows into the Dniepr here, making this a center for river sports. Tram #9 takes you close to the river. **Kayaking** and **rowing** competitions begin as soon as the ice melts.

The **post office** and **telephones** are at pr. Karla Marksa 62 (open Mon.-Sat. 8am-8pm, Sun 8am-7pm). **Trains** to Dnipropetrovsk run daily from Kiev, Donetsk and Simferopol. The **river station**, ul. Gorkovo 19 (ул. Горького) was inactive in summer 1994 but check to see if boats and hydrofoils are running to Kiev and Odessa. If you spend the night, **Hotel Astoria** (Гостиница Астория), pr. Karla Marksa 66, (tel. 44 23 04), has snazzy doubles (US$13 in kupons) and a friendly young staff. Down the road at #50, **Hotel Tsentralnaya** (Гостиница Центральная; tel. 45 03 47), offers simple but airy singles for US$7 in kupons. If you speak Ukrainian or Russian, try **Workers' Dormitory #1**(Общежитие), ul. Koksovaya 12a, (ул. Коксовая; tel. 59 31 12). Take tram #8 or 15 from the right side of the train station to the "Kievskaya" (Киевская) stop; backtrack down the left fork; follow the train tracks and it's on the right. A bed and use of the kitchen and showers costs US$0.45 if you ask nicely.

Although the pastries and snacks here are delicious, more substantial fare is mostly limited to the realm of hotel restaurants. Try the **Tsentralnaya** (Центральная) at Karla Marksa 50 (open daily 8am-11pm). The **Cafeteria** (Кафетерий) at 7 Shmidt (Шмидт) serves up hot meals for a pittance (open Tues.-Sun. 8am-1pm and 2-6pm). Take bus А or Б from the train station. The **central market** is on the way over.

■ ■ ■ DONETSK (ДОНЕЦЬК)

A model Soviet city, Donetsk is straight out of a manual. The surreal coal-mining town has perfectly oriented perpendicular streets with a mathematically-determined number of strategically-placed parks. The buildings are set back from the straight, level avenues and the sidewalks are spacious and perfectly centered. There is a feeling of dead calm. It is a perfect image of Camoazotz in Madeleine L'Engle's *A Wrinkle in Time,* except twenty years have passed and the Brain has atrophied. The natives will tell you—things were better before.

A visit to the city's **regional history museum** (Областной Краеведческий Музей) will tell you anything you could possibly want to know about the Donetsk region and more. The museum is located at ul. Chelyuskintsev 189 (ул. Челюскинцев; open Tues.-Sun. 10am-4pm). Or try the **planetarium** on ul. Artema 145 (shows hourly 11am-4pm). Otherwise, just sit back and enjoy the exactness of it all.

The intersections of two sets of three main roads form the center of town. Prosp. Mira (пр. Мира), bul. Shevchenko (бул. Шевченко), and pr. Grinkevicha (пр. Гринкевича) run east-west; ul. Chelyuskintsev (ул. Челюскинцев), ul. Artema (ул. Артема), and Universitetskaya ul. (Университецкая ул.) run north-south. Trolleybus #2 services ul. Artema; bus #9 takes care of Universitetskaya ul. The central **Intourist** office is in the Hotel Druzhba at Universitetskaya ul. 48 and will let you look at their map even though they have none to sell (open Mon.-Fri. 9am-1pm and 2-5pm).

The **train station** dominates Tovarnaya ul. (ул. Товарная) at the end of the #2 trolleybus line, where people also (illegally) change currency. The station's **ticket office** is on the second floor (open daily 8am-1pm and 2-7pm). To: Kharkiv (overnight, US$2); Dnipropetrovsk (5 hrs., US$1.50). The **bus station** is at the end of the #9 bus line, with frequent connections to Kharkiv, Dnipropetrovsk and Izyum. From Kharkiv, any bus going to Lugansk will stop in Izyum, and buses run from Izyum to Donetsk almost hourly. The trip costs about US$2.50. The **regional bus station** with connections to the Azov Coast is in the university district at the corner of ul. 50-letiya SSSR (50-летия СССР) and pr. Mira. The **airport** is reachable by trolleybus from ul. Artema. The Air Ukraine office is in the former Aeroflot building, ul. Artema 167.

Prices are a bit steep for foreigners since the usual visitors are industrialists or politicians. Check with the commandant in the **dormitories** on ul. Chelyuskintsev (ул. Челюскинцев); he may be able to strike you a deal. Otherwise, standard doubles with bath go for 604,000Krb in the **Hotel Tourist** (Гостиница "Турист"), Blvd. Shevchenko 20 (tel. 93 91 14), and singles with bath, television, refrigerator, and radio run 714,000Krb at the **Hotel Druzhba** (Гостиница "Дружба"), Universitetskaya ul. 48 (tel. 91 19 68).

For groceries, try the **Central Market** (Центральный Рынок) at the corner of ul. Chelyuskintsev and blvd. Shevchenko, or the spontaneous **market** at Universitetskaya ul. and prosp. Mira. **Restaurant Druzhba** inside the Hotel Druzhba has surprisingly good food and friendly service. Entrees US$1-2 (open daily 8am-9pm). A decent cup of coffee and some jocular companions can be found at the **Café Express** (Кафе Экспресс) at the corner of prosp. Mira and ul. Artema (open daily 11am-4pm and 6pm-midnight).

■■■ ODESSA (ОДЕСА)

In a cosmopolitan port-town mélange of Russian, Ukrainian, Jewish and Turkish influences, Odessa is full of everyman's markets, quick-changing roadside business, dour but impressive monuments, and sunny, sandy beaches. You can feel the activity the minute you step off the train—people-watching is gratifying and exhausting. From auto parts to Nikes, it's all about buying and selling, and most of it goes on in public.

The city came through World War II with relatively little damage compared with other Ukrainian cities, especially Kiev; it was not the Germans who occupied most of Odessa, but the comparatively less destructive Romanians. As a result, most of the city's 19th-century French-style buildings reminiscent of St. Petersburg survived, allowing you to have the strange pleasure of being dwarfed before them.

The sea is always in the background, a little wilder here than at other Black Sea ports, and affects city life. Shipments of foreign goods coming in over the docks causes one item to become suddenly popular, and then to lose favor just as suddenly, overshadowed by a newer shipment. Vacationers in search of swimming and sunlight add a little variety and a lot of holiday good will to the city's atmosphere.

ORIENTATION AND PRACTICAL INFORMATION

Odessa lies in a long strip along the coastline; the central section is bounded by the train station to the south and the port to the north. All streets are labeled in both Ukrainian and in Russian. The main street in Odessa is **vul. Deribasovskaya** (вул. Дерибасовская), closed in part to traffic to allow pedestrians to enjoy its many shops and cafés. The northern end of Deribasovskaya intersects **vul. Sovetskoi Armii** (вул. Советськоі Арміі); in the opposite direction, heading towards the sea, it comes across **vul. Pushkinskaya** (вул. Пушкинская). A right onto Pushkinskaya from Deribasovskaya leads to the train station, and a left ushers you onto **Primorski Boulevard** (Приморский бул.) a tree-lined premenade favored for its panoramic views of the sea. **Maps** are intermittently available at kiosks for US$0.50. Check at the train station, hotel kiosks, and the post office.

Tourist Office: For train, plane or bus tickets, go to **Intourist,** ul. Pushkinskaya 17 (ул. Пушкинская), in the lobby of the Hotel Krasnaya (Гостиница Красная). Trolley-bus #1 or 4 takes you there from the train station. Open Mon.-Fri. 9am-6pm. The **service bureau** upstairs is less hectic and has plenty of advice on Odessa's sights—if you can find a common language (French and German sometimes spoken). Open daily 9am-1pm and 2-5pm. Buy a **map** in the downstairs lobby. Just as friendly and a little more likely to speak English, the **service bureau** in the **Hotel Chornoye Morye** (Готель Чёрное Море), ul. Lenina 59, runs **tours** of the city (US$10 per hr.), offers English-speaking guides for museums, and the usual Intourist *schtick*. There are also places around the city that claim to be "travel bureaus"—mostly they set up package tours to the Canary Islands or Greece.

Currency Exchange: Most major European currencies are exchanged at **Dendi Exchange,** ul. Pushkinskaya 54 (ул. Пушкинская), open daily 8am-8pm. Take trolleybus #1 or 4 from the train station. **Traveler's checks** are accepted at the exchange bureau of the **Hotel Krasnaya** (Гостиница Красная), ul. Pushkinskaya 17, for a 2.5% commission. Take trolleybus #4 from the train station. Arrive early;

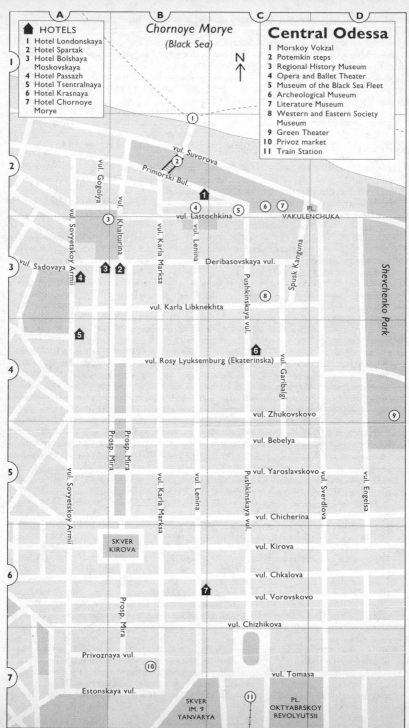

UKRAINE

HOTELS
1 Hotel Londonskaya
2 Hotel Spartak
3 Hotel Bolshaya Moskovskaya
4 Hotel Passazh
5 Hotel Tsentralnaya
6 Hotel Krasnaya
7 Hotel Chornoye Morye

Chornoye Morye (Black Sea)

N

Central Odessa
1 Morskoy Vokzal
2 Potemkin steps
3 Regional History Museum
4 Opera and Ballet Theater
5 Museum of the Black Sea Fleet
6 Archeological Museum
7 Literature Museum
8 Western and Eastern Society Museum
9 Green Theater
10 Privoz market
11 Train Station

vul. Suvorova

Primorski Bul.

vul. Gogolya

vul. Khalturina

vul. Sovyetskoy Armii

vul. Karla Marksa

vul. Lenina

vul. Lastochkina

PL. VAKULENCHUKA

vul. Sadovaya

Deribasovskaya vul.

Pushkinskaya vul.

Spusk Kanguna

vul. Karla Libknekhta

vul. Rosy Lyuksemburg (Ekaterinska)

vul. Garibaldi

Shevchenko Park

vul. Zhukovskovo

Prosp. Mira

vul. Bebelya

vul. Yaroslavskovo

vul. Sverdlova

vul. Engelsa

vul. Karla Marksa

vul. Lenina

Pushkinskaya vul.

vul. Chicherina

SKVER KIROVA

vul. Kirova

vul. Chkalova

vul. Vorovskovo

Prosp. Mira

vul. Chizhikova

Privoznaya vul.

vul. Tomasa

Estonskaya vul.

SKVER IM. 9 YANVARYA

PL. OKTYABRSKOY REVOLYUTSII

they frequently run out of money. Open Mon.-Fri. 9am-5pm, Sat. 10am-1pm.
Major European currencies also accepted in the exchange bureau of the **Hotel
Londonsakaya** (Гостиница Лондонская) on Primorski bul. 11 (Приморськи бул.).
Open Mon.-Fri. 8am-6pm. You can also exchange dollars and deutschmarks at any
"Обмен—Валют" kiosk and in many dollar stores.

Post Office: ul. Sadovaqa 8 (ул. Садовая). **Poste Restante** at counter #8; pre-
stamped airmail envelopes at counter #9 (8000Krb). Post cards also at counter #9.
Exchange kiosk too. Open daily 8am-8pm.

Courier Service: DHL is at vul. Lenina 27 (вул. Ленина; tel. (048) 224 42 69).

Telephones: At the post office. Order international calls at the large wooden booth
in the back, intercity calls up front. Announce at the beginning how many minutes your call will be; pay when the call is over. They are accustomed to dealing
with foreigners. Open 24 hrs. For hard currency, the **telephone bureau** on ul.
Lenina 19 (ул. Ленина) is a bit cheaper. To: Western Europe: US$1.50 per min;
U.S.: US$2.50 per min.; Australia: US$4 per min. Open 8am-8pm. Local calls are
free from any phone that works. **City Code:** 048.

Photo and Film Developing: AGFA Photo at the intersection of ul. Rishe-
liyevskaya (former ul. Lenina) and ul. Rozy Luxemburg. **Kodak** is in the middle of
ul. Sadovay a (walking towards the post office, it is on the right side).

Trains: Zh. D. Vokzal (Ж. Д. Вокзал; station) on Privokzalnaya pl. (Привокзальная
пл.) at the southern end of ul. Pushkinskaya (ул. Пушкинская). Trolleybus #1 or 4
takes you close to the city center via the eastern section; tram #3 or 12 takes you
along vul. Sovetskoi Armii (вул. Совєтської Армії) to the northern end of ul. Deribasovskaya (ул. Дерибасовская). Buy tickets well in advance at window #18 in the
International Room (Міжнародни Зал; *Mizhnarodni Zal*—the same booth where
you buy international tickets), to the left as you enter the building. If you're feeling lucky, you can try to get a ticket for same-day travel at window #20. **Scalpers**
hang out in the main hall to the right asking "*Vam nuzhni bilyet?*" Check that the
tickets are valid. To: Kiev (10hrs.); Kharkiv (17 hrs.); L'viv (12hrs); Simferopol
(13hrs.). Direct connections to Warsaw, Moscow, and Riga. **Platform** numbers
of arriving trains are announced over the loudspeaker; fellow passengers can
interpret. **Schedules** are posted in the main hall. Tickets also available at the
Central Ticket Bureau on ul. Srednefontanskaya (ул. Среднефонтанская). Take
bus #146 or 136 and look for the large sign "Центральные Железнодорожные кассы."
Also try the **Intourist office** in the Hotel Krasnaya (Гостиница Красная).

Buses: The main bus station is on ul. Dzerzhinskovo 58 (ул. Дзержинского). Tram
#5 goes to the train station; #15 leads downtown. Buy tickets inside the station at
least the night before, or get on the bus as it's about to depart and buy a standing-
room ticket from the driver. To: Kiev: (11hrs., US$7). **Tinra** (Тинра), 26 ul. Zhuk-
ovskovo (ул. Жыковсокого) services Varna, Bulgaria (Tues. 7am, 24hr.; US$34).

Flights: Air fare to Moscow now depends on the plane owner. Expect US$90 for a
Russian plane, US$30 for a Ukrainian plane. Several airlines now offer direct con-
nections to European cities; check their offices in the airport for current prices.
Austrian Airlines flights to Vienna are Mon. and Fri. at 3pm (US$240). **Aeroflot
offices** are at the airport, at ul. Karl Marx 17 (tel. 22 23 00). Take bus #101. To:
Moscow (US$125); Kiev (US$78). Open daily 8am-6pm.

Ferries: Schedules are unpredictable. Inquire at the booking office of **Black Sea
Steamship Line** on Potemkin pl. at the top of the stairs by the same name. (Open
Mon.-Thurs. 8am-12:30pm and 1-5pm, Fri. 8am-12:30pm and 1-4pm, Sat.-Sun.
10am-12:30pm and 1-2pm.) İstanbul US$97. Piraeus US$180. **Morskoi Vokzal**
(Морской Вокзал), down the bottom of the Potemkin stairs at ul. Suvorova 6 (ул.
Суворова), also has a window in the main terminal. To the left of the main dock
depart ferries that run to beaches surrounding Odessa. Buy tickets for irregular
Crimean routes inside the station; tickets for ferries are also sold on board—if one
is running that day.

Public Transportation: The train station is the center of the system; the main terminus is at Gretska pl. (Грецька площа). Trams and trolleybuses leave from the
south side of the station if they are heading south, the west side if they are heading west, etc. Starting in September 1994, the government plans to make all trams
and trolleybuses **free.** It is uncertain how long such a policy will be maintained.

In any case, tickets are normally only 100Krb. Buses are less frequent but cover more territory. Pay the driver on board (3000Krb). Information is available (no English spoken) for 1000Krb from the booth just inside the train station doors.
Pharmacy: Apteka #1, ul. Sadovaya 5 (ул. Садовая). It still looks like an old-fashioned Apothecary where they sell marvelous elixirs. Tampax tampons. No condoms, but these are found with the street vendors who are usually around this store. Open daily 8am-8pm; prescriptions filled 'round the clock.
Medical Assistance: Polyklinik, Sudostroitelnaya ul. 21 (Судостроительная ул.), accepts foreign patients for hard currency.
Emergencies: Fire: tel. 01, **Police:** tel. 02, **Ambulance:** tel. 03.

ACCOMMODATIONS AND CAMPING

There are a few choices in Odessa. You can camp or hole up in a **bungalow** at the campground on the edge of town; you can check in to one of the **downtown hotels,** crumbling remnants of a glorious marble past; you can empty your purse to stay in one of the hotels in the Arkadia district; or, you can stay in someone's **apartment.** The last is by far the cheapest (US$1-2 per person), but you'll be lucky to get anything near the center of town. Train-station hawkers are recognizable by their signs, usually some variation on "Сдаю комнату." Ask "Скілько?" (SKIHL-koh, "how much?") You will then be asked how many of you there are—usually they do not take individuals, but even if you buy the other 2 or 3 places it will probably still be cost-efficient. Don't pay until you see the room, or risk the ubiquitous port-town con-artist. The cost will jump if you seem Western—fix a price before letting on where you're from. Collateral often required for keys.

Prices are nebulous in the downtown **hotels** as well—make sure a ghost television or refigerator isn't added into your bill. Usually you can ask for one place in a triple or quad, if you don't mind spending the night with strangers to save some money. Prices range widely, depending whether you have a sink, toilet, shower, etc. Truly budget-minded travelers ask for "самое дешёвое место" (SAM-mah-yeh dih-SHOV-ah-yeh MYEH-stoh, "the cheapest place"). Take tram #3 or 12 from the train station to reach the downtown hotels; they are all located very close to each other.

Hotel Tsentralnaya (Гостиница "Центральная"), vul. Sovetskoi Armii 40 (вул. Советскоі Арміі; tel. 26 84 06). The tall marble staircase and elegant lobby complement the fine location. The rooms are spacious and bright, but aging. Singles US$21, with bath US$28. Doubles US$13 per person, with sink US$18 per person, with bath US$26 per person. Triples US$11 per person, with bath US$15 per person. Showers US$0.25, on the first floor.

Hotel Passazh (Гостиница "Пассаж"), vul. Sovetskoi Armii 34 (tel. 22 48 49). Skanky businessmen aside, this one has a fair amount of charm, and is next to the real "Пассаж." Pleasant, boxy little rooms. Singles with or without bath US$24 (go for "with"). Doubles with sitting room US$71, with bath US$106.

Hotel Bolshaya Moskovskaya (Гостиница Большая Московская), ul. Deribasovskaya 29 (ул. Дерибасовская; tel. 22 40 16). Grand sweeping staircases; an ornate exterior; high ceilings; long mirrors with carved frames; and tired, mediocre little rooms. Prices go down after the first night. Singles US$19-35. Doubles US$16-27 per person. Larger rooms (4-6 beds) US$12-20 per person. For showers, pay on the fourth floor, get your ticket, and shower on the second floor.

Hotel Spartak (Гостиница Спартак), ul. Deribasovskaya 25, (tel. 26 89 24). Quite friendly receptionists; bright rooms with colorful wallpaper. You make your own bed. Singles US$21-29. Doubles US$47-71.

Camping: Dolphin Camping (Кемпинг "Дельфин"), dor. Kotovskovo 307 (дор. Котовского; tel. 55 50 52, or 55 00 66). From the train station, take trolleybus #4 or 10 to the terminus (a small loop in the road) and transfer to tram #7; get off 20min. later at the "Лузановка" stop and continue for 0.5km. Distant even as campgrounds go, but the staff is very friendly and the bungalows attract young German backpackers. No kitchen facilities, but the surprisingly elegant and cheap restaurant, the sauna, the bar, and the private beach might make up for it. Bungalows US$7 per person, wooden cottages US$5 per person, tents US$3 per person.

FOOD

Odessa is blessed with a few good restaurants, an amazing market, and one or two cafés that go beyond "hip" into the realm of "meta-hip." Curiously, Odessan restaurants have a thing for subterranean settings—indoor restaurants are often underground. Good options line **vul. Sovetskoi Armii** (вул. Советької Армії) south of ul. Deribasovskaya (ул. Дерибасовская). The **Privoz** (Привоз) **market** on Privoznaya ul. (Привозная ул.) will provide any food that Odessa port handles, and more.

Galaxy Restaurant, vul. Sovetskoi Armii 23, below the street. A real shining star in the bitter night of Ukrainian restaurants, with superior, delicately-prepared food and soberly polite service. Some vegetarian entrees. Menu in English, with, surprisingly, everything available as listed. Two rooms, one with live music nightly beginning at 8pm. Full meal US$5-7. Open daily noon-midnight.

Café na Gretseskoe (Кафе на Грецеское), vul. Gretska 11 (вул. Грецька), downstairs form the street. An eclectic mix of styles, from Italian baroque to seventies-kitsch, where the hyper-cool sip foreign liquors and discuss where to shop, while looking disdainfully across the room at the regular folk, who are enjoying juicy cutlets for US$2. Open daily noon-11pm.

Restaurant Stanbul (Ресторан Стамбул), ul. Vorovskovo 113 (ул. Воровського), is actually around the corner, underground on ul. Sovetskoi Armii—the sign outside says "Турецкая Кухня." Inside they serve up a fairly good Turkish/Ukrainian mix of dishes in a pseudo-Near-East setting. Full meal US$3-4. Open daily 11am-11pm.

Restaurant Zhanetta (Ресторан Жанетта), vul. Gretska 23 (вул. Грецька). Below street-level (surprise!), decent food, not too formal, warm service, and full meal; US$3-5. Open daily 11am-11pm.

Café (Кафе), ul. Karla Marksa 12 (ул. Карла Маркса). The cheapest meal in town. One or two dishes available. Open daily 8am-8pm.

Pizza Spaghetti, ul. Lenina 6 (ул. Ленина). If you're interested in a traditional Italian-Ukrainian cuisine, here it is. Pizza: two slices for US$0.75. Open daily.

Pecheskato Café (Печеcatól Кафе), on one edge of the small city park on ul. Deribasovskaya (ул. Дерибасовская), features a delicious menu of grilled hamburgers, chicken, and *shashlik* for US$2. If you can't find a table in this extremely popular eatery, order directly with the chef and take your meal into the nearby park, where the atmosphere is just as pleasant. Open daily 11am-8pm.

Restaurant Fav (Фав), ul. Tracheskaya 50 (ул. Траческая), serves traditional Ukrainian and Russia specialties in an old theater; the restaurant still makes good use of the stage with nightly cabaret performances. Dinner and show around US$6. Open daily 6pm-4am.

Café Old Odessa (Старая Одесса). At the end of Primorski bul. (Приморски бул.; bordering on Vorontsov's Palace) offers strictly outdoor eating. You can munch sandwiches, order *shashlik*, and wash it down with a cup of Turkish coffee or a cocktail while gazing at the magnificent view of the harbor, all for only US$3. On weekends, an endless stream of newly-weds parades by the café to have their pictures taken at the nearby bridge.

SIGHTS

The vehicle-free **ul. Deribasovskaya** is not just the center of town. It's also a center of street culture, with street-musicians playing good jazz, mimes who will tailor their performances to the wishes of the most generous donor, open-air cafés that attract the young, fashionable element, and dozens of artists who will draw your portrait (or your caricature) for the price of a chocolate bar. From the western end of Deribasovskaya, you can cross vul. Sovetskoi Armii to see the **statue of Mikhail Vorontsov,** the rich and powerful governor of Odessa in the 1820s. Although the statue is quite cleverly constructed, it's a poor substitute for the cathedral that used to stand here, destroyed in an effort to quell the ecclesiastic-political forces that threatened Soviet rule. The square is still called Sobornaya pl., referring to the cathedral; you can see pictures of it in the **regional history museum** (Историко-краеведческий музей) on ul. Khalturina 4 (ул. Халтурина; open Wed.-Sat. 10am-4pm).

One block to the left grows the superbly aromatic **flower market**, where old women advise young men on the choice of flowers they should bring to their sweethearts. At the other end of the Deribasovskaya pedestrian zone, turn left on ul. Lenina to find the **Opera and Ballet Theatre**, an imposing edifice which towers over the surrounding gardens, and another wedding-photo hot-spot. The nearby **Museum of the Black Sea Fleet** (Музей морского флота) at ul. Lastochkina 6 (ул. Ласточкина) is, alas, undergoing reconstruction. If it has reopened, you can see exhibits recounting the history of Odessa as a vital naval port. At #4 on the same street, you can check out the **Archeological Museum of Odessa** (Археологичний Музей) that houses artifacts found in the Black Sea region, dating back to ancient Greece and Rome. Especially worth a look is the **collection of gold coins** stored in a basement vault (open Tues.-Sun. 10am-5pm). The façade is graced by a small sculpture of classical figures; don't forget to look at the **garden**, too. At #2, the **Literature Museum** (Литератруний Музей), housed in an 18th century palace, offers a fascinating account of the city's history through its many books, prints and photographs. Consider hiring an English-speaking guide (US$0.25), since the museum's exhibits are labeled only in Russian (open Tues.-Sun. 10am-5pm).

From here you can descend the stairs to pl. Vakulenchuka (пл. Вакуленчука) and check out the **memorial to the port-workers** killed in World War II, or you can retrace your steps and take a right at the Archeological Museum onto the shady, tree-lined **Primorski Boulevard**, the most popular spot in Odessa to stroll and people-watch. The statue of the great Russian writer **Alexander Pushkin** (c. 1881) has his back unceremoniously turned to city hall, since the local government refused to help fund its construction. On either side of city hall are the figures of **Fortuna**, goddess of fate, and **Mercury**, god of trade, the two symbols of the city of Odessa. Strolling down Primorski bul. you'll come upon the statue of **Duc de Richelieu**, whose concrete stare looks down toward the **Potemkin stairs** and the more distant **Morskoi Vokzal**. Director Serga Eisenstein used these stairs in his epic 1925 film *Battleship Potemkin*, originating the oft imitated visual cliche of a baby carriage loose on an incline, and since then the name has stuck. If you are too tired to climb back up the stairs, an **escalator** (150Krb) will bring you back.

A left at this point will bring you to a **monument** commemorating the actual mutiny of that famous ship. Continue farther along to the end of Primorski to the **Palace of Vorontsov** (c. 1826), now a club for schoolchildren, and you'll understand why this early governor of Odessa had his home built at this spot. The view is spectacular and gets better as the sun sinks, casting its final rays over the city and the ships in the harbor below. To your left is the long, white **Mother-in-Law Bridge**, built, they say, so an elderly lady could more easily visit her son-in-law, a high ranking official in the local Communist party. It sways and creaks with each sea breeze (the bridge, not the party). A few blocks away the **state university** at vul. Petra Velikovo1/3 (вул. Петра Великого) is the place to find student culture, the cafés, and the bookstores.

On the other side of town, at Pushkinskaya ul. 9 (Пушкинская ул.), you can drop in at the **Western and Eastern Society Museum**, more for the 1856 exterior than for the collection. Further along at #13, the **Pushkin Museum** (Литературно-мемориальный музей А. С. Пушкина) commemorates the writer and his works. The building was built in 1821, and is often noted for its grand façade, which faces away from the sea to avoid salt air damage. Finally, at the intersection of Pushkinskaya and vul. Ekaterinska (вул. Екатеринська and П. Люксембург on maps), the **Regional Philharmonic**, built in 1894-99, looks out sternly from the street corner. A short walk past the Philharmonic, a right and a quick left will bring you to **Shevchenko Park**, a vast stretch of greenery which separates the city from the sea; at the entrance stands the monument to the poet Shevchenko himself, gazing pensively along the path to the sea, turned away from the bustle of the city.

Far from the busy commercial center of Odessa lies one of the more entertaining World War II monuments, the **Memorial Complex of the 411th Battalion** (Мемориальный комплекс на месте огневой позиции 411-й батареи береговой обороны).

Spread out over a large park, all of the typical armaments of the Soviet forces are here in their colorful glory. You'll think the guns and torpedoes are impressive until you get to the other end of the park and see the tanks (even the turrets move), the bomber, and yes, the battleship, carried here in pieces by tractor trailer. The best part is that they're all free for you to climb on, in, and around. The adjoining **museum** tells you the whole story if you can read Russian, but isn't very interesting if you can't (open Tues.-Sun. 10am-5pm; admission 1000Krb). The **rocky coast** is also a short walk away, and worth a visit to see the cliffs which surround this area. At high tide the sea provides a rather brilliant, violent spectacle. The complex is on ul. Amundsena (ул. Амундсена), reachable from the train station by bus #127 or tram #26, a half-hour trip.

ENTERTAINMENT

Afternoon **people-watching** is best done on Primorski bul. (Приморский бул.) or on ul. Deribasovskaya (ул. Дерибасовская); Saturdays afford a better catalogue of wedding-dresses than any fashion mag, as newlyweds have their pictures taken. **Portrait-painters** on Deribasovskaya also make for a fascinating picture of artists-in-action. The **Opera and Ballet Theater** at the end of ul. Lenina (ул. Ленина) has shows nightly and tickets go for a song—US$0.15-0.35. It's worth a visit just to see the ornate golden interior. Audiences are enthusiastic and a bit more irreverent than Western European crowds—bring flowers to cast upon the principal dancers from your velvet-cushioned box. Saturday and Sunday matinees begin at 1pm, evening performances at 6pm. Buy tickets a day in advance, or at least that morning, from the ticket office on the right side of the theater (open daily 8am-8pm). For **theater tickets,** consult the Central Ticket Office at vul. Sovetskoi Armii 28 (вул. Советскоі Арміі). In the Shevchenko Park on summer weekends at 6pm, a **Green Theater** (Зелёный Театр) performs.

Odessa has enough **bars** to equip a zoo; many are tiny grottoes under bright signs (look for "Бар" on signs). One of the more youthful options is **Bar Vuldai** (Бар Валдай), vul. Potemkintsev 3 (вул. Потемкинцев), next to guess-whose stairs. There is no way you are cool enough to go here, but it's probably worth a shot if you've packed enough black clothes (open daily noon-midnight). For teeny-bopper-free dancing, try the **"13th station of the Fountain,"** on the beach out of reach of public transportation. Take a cab and say "Treeh-nahd-tsah-tah-ya fon-tah-na, vneezk stoh-yan-keh" ("13th of the Fountain, down to the parking lot"). They play good music (occasionally live) and you can come as early as 7pm, though the program doesn't start until 9pm. Average age is 25-27. For a younger crowd (average 21) try the **Gulfstream** at the yacht-club. It is called a restaurant—indeed you can eat here, but it is really a dance-club with top 40 music. Caution should be taken going to both of these places. Both are in poorly lit areas with no taxi service—go in a large group or arrange to have a car pick you up. The risk-taker can take *his* chances at any of the numerous **casinos** along the eastern end of ul. Deribasovskaya (ул. Дерибасовская). Women should steer clear; they're not good bets.

BEACHES

Most of Odessa's sandy shore is reachable by public transportation. Tram #5 stops at **Lanzheron** (Ланжерон) **beach,** the closest to central Odessa, at **Vidrada** (Видрада) **beach,** with its pleasant sheltered **forest road** leading into town through Shevchenko Park, at **Delfin** (Дельфин) **beach,** also on the edge of the park, and at **Arkadia** (Аркадия), the most popular beach in town because of its wide stretches of sand. Arkadia is also reachable by trolleybus #5 and bus #129. To the south, the **Golden Shore** (Золотой Беріг) is farther away but boasts the most impressive sea and surf. Trams #17 and 18 stop here, as well as at **Chayka** (Чайка) and **Kurortniy** (Курортний) beaches. The beach of the proletariat is just outside the high-rise monstrosity of a neighborhood, **Chornomorka** (Черноморка). Take tram #29 to the terminus and keep going. Real people swim here, not just tourists. Campground-dwellers can take advantage of their own beach as well as **Luzanovka** (Лузановка), just down the street, where there is also an amusement park. Tram #7 goes right there.

SHOPPING

Commerce is what port towns are all about. Odessa is no exception. First and foremost is the fabulous **Privoz** (Привоз) **market,** just left of the train station on ul. Privoznaya (ул. Привозная). Several acres large, the market supplies just about everything you can picture as salable. Roughly speaking, fruit and vegetables are in the middle, milk products are in the building on the northeast corner, hardware and clothes around the edges. Once you're inside it's tough to get out because of the crowds. This is not a good place to change money—snatch-and-run theft is rampant (open daily 8am-6pm). Odessa's **Tsentralniy Universalniy Magazin** (ЦУМ), the central department store on Pushkinskaya ul., is another shopping haven (open daily 9:30am-7:30pm). Along ul. Lenina the **state department stores** sell everything from cloth to radios; cassette tapes are good bargains here. From Deribasovskaya ul.'s collection of stores, you'd think you were in the West—until you see the armed security forces with attack dogs. Along ul. Sadovaya (ул. Садовая) cluster the city's fanciest **boutiques.** Look for "Магазин" and an English word or woman's name—the best ones are below street level. Many require payment in dollars and most are closed on Sundays. Also try the **"Passage"** (Пассаж) next to the Passazh Hotel, a baroque passageway leading from vul. Sovetskoi Armii to vul. Deribasovskaya; it's filled with expensive shops and fashion-conscious shoppers.

THE CRIMEAN PENINSULA (КРИМ)

The Crimean peninsula has been inhabited since antiquity, and only more recently by Russians. Now tsars' palaces stand alongside the sanitoria and resorts built in the past half-century for the ailing proletariat of colder climates. Meanwhile, farther in the hills, there are plush estates formerly maintained by powerful Party bosses. The peninsula has drawn people to its shores throughout history for a simple reason—it is a beautiful place to live.

In the fifth century BC Herodotus recorded that Scythians and Greeks were dwelling in the Crimea, the former in the plains and the latter along the southern coast—and these were surely not the first. Since then new invaders constantly made their way across the marshy Perekop Isthmus and invariably became part of the indigenous population. The Sarmatians (of Amazon myth) followed the Scythians in the 4th century, who were subsequently followed by the Romans, then by the Germanic Ostrogoths, Mongolian Huns, Slavs (of Pripet Marsh origin), Judaic Khazars, and Scandinavian Varangians. The peninsula fell under the strong influence of Byzantium until the great Batu Khan (grandson of Gengis Khan) and his nomadic troops established themselves as the local power in the 13th century, opening the Crimea to north-south trade. Pleased with the land (as most were), many settled and became the indigenous Crimean Tatar population; the Khan built his palace in Bakhchisaray near the Byzantine "cave monasteries."

The Crimea remained autonomous, with some Ottoman influence, until its annexation in 1783 by Russia when it became the expanding edge of the Russian Empire and summer resort extraordinaire for the rich and powerful. During the Crimean War, in 1854, France and Britain clashed with Russia over the city of Sevastopol, memorialized by bloodshed, the work of Florence Nightingale, balaclava, and the inspired poem of Alfred Lord Tennyson, "The Charge of the Light Brigade" honoring the deadly misdirected English boys: Theirs not to reason why/Theirs not to make reply/Theirs but to do and die (an infectious idea). Tennyson also penned the slightly less famous poem "The Charge of the Heavy Brigade" in honor of the same clash. This typical meeting of empires ended with mutual defeat, and mutual bloodshed, forcing each to retreat and allowing the Tatars to assume more self-rule—and

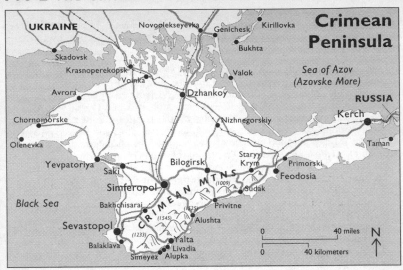

to revive their national heritage, language, and culture. In the power vacuum of 1917, the Tatars put together a *Kurultay*—a Tatar National Constituent Assembly—which essentially declared their autonomy, a word the Bolsheviks could not assimilate. The Russians quickly regained control, opening the beaches to the proletariate, and even paid Russians to settle. Recognizing their enmity with the Tatars, they erased its cultural elites; and on the night of May 18, 1944 Stalin had the *entire* Crimean Tatar population loaded into train cars (lacking on the front but deemed crucial for this task) and shipped to Uzbekistan.

Crimea was officially made part of Ukraine in 1954 as a "gift" from Khrushchev. But the Ukrainians have always been wary of the large Russian presence; Russians grew up with full access to the Crimea; welcomed and catered to—it was always their first choice for summer vacation. Now, they are thinking twice before relinquishing this prime vacation spot. Indeed, Sevastopol, home to the Russian part of the Black Sea Fleet, has recently voted to remain a Russian city, a small step, but leaving the peninsula in a tenuous political situation. Adding to this confusion is the returning Tatar population demanding land and preferring an independent Crimea.

Today vacationers pour in by the trainload to the main port of entry, **Simferopol,** also reachable by bus and plane. Who they are and where they are coming from is often unclear—but the new Eastern European elites are sure to be among them. From Simferopol, the world's longest trolleybus line, and perhaps the Soviet Union's one effort at conservation, runs southwest to **Alushta** and **Yalta.** From Yalta, regional buses cover the rest of the western half of the south shore. The eastern half is also most easily reached from Simferopol. Buses run to **Feodosia** and **Kerch** from the main Simferopol bus station. Crimean time is one hour ahead of Kiev time.

A rail line and road connect the peninsula to the north. Ferries are known to dock at Yalta and one crosses the straits of Kerch. Most of Crimea is *steppe* except for the Crimean Mountains at the southern lip, which build to over 1500 meters before falling to a narrow strip of land dotted with Black Sea resort towns. With an average 290 days of sunlight yearly, summer daily temperatures reaching 36°C, abundant fruit, mountains, beaches, and palaces from centuries of royal vacationers and sanatoria for ill proletariate, this is the place to ruminate on the hardships of life—but careful, you may never want to leave.

■■■ SIMFEROPOL (СИМФЕРОПОЛЬ)

Simferopol is the city where all Crimean roads meet. Originally the site of the Scythian town of Neapolis and a subsequent Tatar town, it is still the crossroads of the Crimea—busy, very Soviet, startlingly varied, and probably only a stop on your way somewhere else. With the decrease in ferry traffic on the Black Sea, Simferopol's importance as a point of arrival has increased. From Simferopol, visitors disseminate in all directions, but most end up on the southern Black Sea coast.

ORIENTATION AND PRACTICAL INFORMATION

The center of town is located two kilometers to the south-east of the train station down **ul. Karla Marksa** (ул. Карла Маркса; which runs parallel to ul. R. Lyuksemburg), where it crosses **pr. Kirova** (пр. Кирова).

Tourist Office: Intourist is in the Hotel Ukraina at ul. R. Lyuksemburg 9 (ул. Р. Люксембург); they take a lengthy perusal of your visa before offering you over-priced guided **tours;** look for "Экскурбюро" (*Ekskursbiuro*) kiosks if guided excursions are your aim.

Currency Exchange: Plenty of "Обмын-Валют" kiosks and trucks cluster around the train station, along with the omnipresent private exchangers.

Post Office: Next to the Hotel Ukraina at ul. R. Lyuksemburg 11 (ул. Р. Люксембург). Open daily 8am-8pm. A second is at the train station, open 24 hrs. Think twice before putting much effort into postcards.

Telephones: At the post offices.

Trains: ul. Gagarina (ул. Гагарина), reachable by city buses #2, 4, 5, and 6. The Intourist ticket window is just to the left as you enter the main courtyard, in Zal (Зал) 2, *kassa* #5. Open Mon.-Sat. 7am-5pm, Sun. 10am-5pm. To: Kiev (19hrs., US$4); Odessa (12hrs., US$3); Moscow (22hrs); Warsaw via Brest (once per week, 36hrs.). Trains are often crowded during the summer get your ticket early.

Buses: The station is reachable by local trolleybus #2 or 6, 20min. from the train station. Buy tickets at least one day in advance or argue with the driver for stand-ing-space. To: Feodosia (2½hrs., US$1); Kerch (3½hrs., US$1.75). Closer destinations are reached via the regional station next to the train station. Buy tickets at the windows closest to the road.

Public Transportation: The trolleybus is the best way to Alushta (#51) and Yalta (#52), departing next to the train and regional bus station (every 10min. 5:30am-11pm). Tickets windows 50m to the left after you leave the main courtyard of the train station, where the trolleybuses stop—just look for the long lines: window #1 and 2 for Yalta, #3 and 4 for Alushta. Buy return tickets in advance; before noon it is usually possible to get a ticket for within the next hour or two, but after that spots fill quickly. It is not possible to buy standing-room space but "extra" tickets are occasionally sold for relatively high prices by people standing nearby.

Taxis: Stands are all over town, and private drivers hawk rides to Yalta, Feodosia and Kerch. Fares multiply like lightning if they learn you're a Westerner.

Luggage Storage: At the end of the first train platform. Pay whatever the going rate is for a 15-kopek coin, choose a locker, and drop the coin in the slot. Set your private combination inside. To retrieve it, set the combination outside. Max. 24 hrs. without significant hassle.

Emergencies: Fire: tel. 01. **Police:** tel. 02. **Medical:** tel. 03.

ACCOMMODATIONS

Turbaza Tavaria (Турбаза "Тавария"), ul. Bespalova 21 (ул. Беспалова; tel. 23 20 24); take trolleybus #2 from the right side of ul. Karla Marksa (ул. Карла Маркса) leading away from the train station to the "Тавария" (*Tavaria*) stop, two stops after the bus station. Walk uphill to the complex; the reception desk is on the far right. Small endurable rooms. Singles US$9. Doubles US$14. **Hotel Ukraina** (Гостиница "Украйна") ul. R. Lyuksemburg 9 (ул. Р. Люксембург); take trolleybus #2 from the train station to the third stop. Nice courtyard. Rooms have working televisions on which you can watch Moscow game shows. Singles US$16, with bath US$19. Doubles with bath US$38. Hall showers US$0.20, hot water 8am-11pm only.

FOOD

The **central market** at the intersection of prosp. Kirova and ul. Kozlova (просп. Кирова and ул. Козлова) is the place to stock up on foodstuffs and a good way to see the city at work. Another more reachable **market** opens outside the train station and sells the local specialties. Among the delicacies are a small shrimp that is eaten like sunflower seeds from a piece of newspaper rolled into a cone. These should only be eaten only if fresh (and can be sold legally only with a permit to guarantee that they are). The market thrives off of bulk sales to travelers returning to higher latitudes who invariably fill their train berths with fruit. The **Hotel Ukraina restaurant** is calm but still a good place to grab a meal (open daily 9am-4pm and 6-11pm).

SIGHTS AND ENTERTAINMENT

Most travelers only know Simferopol as a pit stop on the way to the coast, but there are a few possibilities for daytime visits if you take the time. The main site of historical interest is the **Neapolis archaeological site** (Скифский Неаполь; *Skifski Neapol*), reachable by bus #4 from the train station, a vast excavation of the former Crimea region capital. Most of the Neapolis' loot, however, is contained in the **regional history museum** (Крымский краеведческий музей) at ul. Pushkina 8 (ул. Пушкина; open Thurs.-Mon. 10am-7pm, Wed. 11am-8pm; admission 1000Krb). The city's **parks** are a joy, well-maintained and full of people. Try the central parks near ul. Pushkina or the Children's Park (Детский Парк) on ul. Shmidta (ул. Шмидта), via trolleybus #2 or 4, with its mammoth concrete jungle gyms.

■■■ YALTA (ЯЛТА)

Yalta is the resort town for everyone—the wrinkled and the nubbly, the pallid and the bronzed, the muscled and the sanitorium patient. It is the most popular resort in Crimea and has much to offer; but underlying it all is the sun and the Black Sea. The Black Sea is smooth, beautiful, and clean, providing a stark contrast to the beaches that, though clean, are pebbly, badly wrought, and over-crowded. The sun shines just about all the time, and never with the merciless furor that it does over the Mediterranean. Yalta itself is locked on the coast by the Crimean mountains, providing alternative excursions and respite from the crowds.

Yalta was frequented by Tolstoy, Chekhov (*"Lady and a Lapdog"* begins in Yalta and his last works were written there), and Tsar Alexander II, who built a huge residence nearby. Along with the Tsars came many aristocratic families who built magnificent estates, turning Yalta into an upscale resort. That architectural and cultural mood has served the resort well, allowing it to pass through the Soviet building frenzy with unheard-of style and grace. However, its location on the Black Sea and natural resources are tempting entrepreneurs—which may be more difficult to weather than central planning.

ORIENTATION AND PRACTICAL INFORMATION

Yalta lies in a strip along the coastline; **naberezhnaya Lenina** (набережная Ленина) runs nearly from one end of town to the other and is mostly closed to all traffic but pedestrians and ice-cream venders. The road to the bus and trolleybus stations is **ul. Moskovskaya** (ул. Московская), which meets nab. Lenina at **pl. Lenina** (пл. Ленина). Along **nab. Lenina,** the kitsch runs hot and heavy. Trolleybuses #1 and 3 run frequently up and down Moskovskaya. From pl. Lenina, turning left off of Moskovskaya takes you to the older part of town, whose main street is **Rooseyelta ul.** (Рузвельта ул.). Off Moskovskaya to the right is Sovetskaya pl., a main telephone site and bus stop. Buy **maps** from kiosks.

Tourist Office: The main **Intourist** bureau is in the **Hotel Yalta** at ul. Drazhin-skava 50 (ул. Дражинская). For short **tours** look for *Ekskursbyuro* (Экскурсбюро) kiosks along nab. Lenina; their rates are far cheaper than Intourist's, but are all in Russian. Excursions to Livadia, Alushta and Feodosia.

Currency Exchange: Traveler's checks accepted for no commission at the **State Import-Export Bank of the Ukraine,** nab. Lenina 3. Open Mon.-Fri. 8:30am-1pm and 2-5:45pm. Checks also accepted at the **Hotel Oreanda,** nab. Lenina 35/2, for a 10% commission; open daily 9am-1pm and 4-10pm. At **Xchange Points,** near Hotel Yuzhniya at ul. Roosevelta 8, most major currencies are changeable; open daily 8am-8pm. The best rates for dollars may be found among the (illegal) private exchangers in the rear corner of the market, at the intersection of Mosk-ovskaya ul. and ul. Karla Marksa (ул. Карла Маркса), but it can be a costly experi-ence. The rates at the kiosk in **Hotel Yalta** are the next best.

Post Office: next to the port on pl. Lenina (пл. Ленина). Open daily 8am-8pm. **Postal Code:** 33 42 00. **DHL** service available at **Xchange Points,** Roosevelta 8.

Telephones: International calls are most easily made with hard currency at the **Hotel Oreanda** at 35/2 Lenina. To U.S.: US$2.50 per min. Telephone bureau open daily 9am-4am. Phonecards allow 24-hr. direct dialing within the hotel (US$30). **Telefonnaya Stantiya** (Телефонная Станцияя), ul. Moskovskaya 10 (ул. Московская), has cheaper rates but lines. Open daily 8am-10pm. **City Code:** 0654

Film and Photo Developing: If the Polaroid-wielders and their various scenes are too much for you, try the **Foto-Avtomat** shop at 25 Lenin. Photos 5000Krb. Open Mon.-Sat. 8am-7pm.

Buses: The bus station is at Moskovskaya ul. 57, and is connected to the trolleybus station across the street. Trolleybuses leave every 10min. for Simferopol, Simfer-opol airport, and Alushta. Buses cover coastal points such as Alupka, Nikitsky Botanical Gardens and Simeiz. Tickets for buses can be purchased on board; tick-ets for trolleybuses must be purchased in advance.

Public Transportation: Buses cover Yalta and environs; **trolleybuses** run within the city. Buy tickets for trolleybuses at kiosks and punch on board (100Krb).

Ferries: Although all of Greater Yalta was once covered by frequent waterbus ser-vice, fuel and funding shortages have brought the service to a trickle. Ferries still run to Istanbul twice per week and the **water shuttle** to Alupka, Feodosia and Alushta still leaves from piers 7 and 8. Buy tickets at the port at Roosevelta 5.

Bookstore: Maps are available at the bookstore at Roosevelta 4 (Рузвельта), open daily 9am-8pm.

Luggage Storage (Камера Хранения); is at the port and the trolley station (6000Krb).

Pharmacy: Dezhurnaya Apteka #26 (Дежурная Аптека), located at ul. Botkin-skaya 3 (ул. Боткинская), has a varying supply of goods. Open 24 hrs.

ACCOMMODATIONS AND CAMPING

In the height of the summer, there are serious crowds, political unrest or no politi-cal unrest, in search of serious tans. It's wise to book ahead. Otherwise, the **Service Bureau** (Бюро Обслуживанния, byoo-roh ob-sluzh-ee-VAH-nyah) at Roosevelta ul. 6 (tel. 32 78 73) will guide you to hotel rooms for a US$3 fee. Sometimes it's only pos-sible to book rooms in the Hotel Krym and Hotel Yuzhniya through this agency. The more affordable options of the hotels usually come without showers or baths (agency open daily 9am-1pm and 2-10pm).

Hotel Otdykh (Гостиница Отдых), Drazhinskovo 14 (Дражинского; tel. 35 30 79), in the old town above the Massandrovskiy beach. Friendly, helpful service. Often full. Doubles and triples with bath US$4.25 per person.

Hotel Volna (Гостиница Волна), ul. Sadovaya 4 (ул. Садовая; tel. 32 39 40). Take trolleybus #1 from the trolleybus station or from Sovetskaya pl. to the "Кинопрокат" (*Kinoprokat*) stop and backtrack 150m. Once elegant but aging. Relaxed garden setting on a lovely hillside alleyway. With bath, US$5 per person.

Hotel Krym (Гостиница "Крым"), Moskovskaya ul. 1/6 (tel. 32 60 01). Unbeatable central location, but odd color scheme. All rooms have high ceilings and comfortable beds; some have balconies. No showers available for cheaper rooms. Singles US$7.50, with bath US$10. Doubles US$11, with bath US$18.

Hotel Yuzhinya (Гостиница "Юбнпая"), ul. Roosevelt 10 (tel. 32 78 73). Rooms vary widely, from small and harmless to luxurious. US$5.60 per person. Singles with bath US$10-25. Doubles with bath US$22-39. Reservations only through the Service Bureau.

Motel-Camping Polyana Skazok (Поляна Сказок), ul. Kirova 167 (ул. Кирова; tel. 39 52 19). Take bus #26, 27, or 11 from the upper platform of the bus station to the *Polyana Skazok* (Поляна Сказок) stop; it's about a 20-min. walk uphill from there through wild blackberry-lined, winding roads. (Bus #8 runs every 40min. from the Kinoteatr Spartak stop in town, a main stop on the #1 line.) A real class-act campground in a charming high-altitude setting, with showers, kitchen facilities, and sauna, as well as a café and restaurant. Tents US$1 per person. Cute bungalows in the style of Old Russian houses US$3 per person. Motel singles with bath US$14, with balcony US$19. Doubles with bath US$19, with balcony US$24. Hot water only in mornings and evenings. Campground open June 1-Oct. 31.

FOOD

Probably the easiest way to keep your stomach happy in Yalta is to pick and choose from the numerous kiosks and snack stands that litter the street and beaches. *Shashlyk* is readily available for a pittance, as well as various pastries and corn on the cob.

For a state store, the **Gastronom** (Гастроном) market on nab. Lenina 4 is surprisingly well-stocked with foreign products. But if that isn't good enough, the **Ay-Petry market** on Morskaya ul. 5 (Морская ул.) sells Western foods for dollars (open daily 8am-8pm). If you're satisfied with local foodstuffs, there is a **general market** at the corner of Moskovskaya ul. and ul. Karla Marksa (open daily 8am-6pm).

Restaurants

Restaurant Gurman (Ресторан "Гурман"), nab. Lenina, in the alleyway to the left of the Casino Diana building. Wonderfully cooperative service and excellent meaty food in this dimly-lit co-op restaurant. Entrees US$1.50-3. Open daily noon-11pm.

Restaurant Vanda (Ресторан "Ванда") nab. Lenina 11. Eager waiters and loud rock music make this an exciting place to have dinner, but the food is fine and reasonably priced. Open daily noon-11pm.

Cafés

Café Krym (Кафе "Крым"), Moskovskaya ul. 1/2. A good selection and fresher than usual entrees can fill you up for less than US$1. Open daily 8am-8pm.

Café Russkiy Chay (Кафе Русский Чай), ul. Lenina, next to Casino Diana building. Busier and more central than the others, but pretty much the same idea. Open daily 9am-2pm and 3-9pm.

Café Siren (Кафе "Сирень"), Roosevelta 6. Even cheaper than Café Krym. One of everything still runs about US$2.50. Open daily 8am-4pm, 5-7pm.

Café (Кафе), Korskaya 8. So cheap they couldn't afford a name, or perhaps the name is Кафе "Café"—who knows? Open daily 8am-7pm.

SIGHTS AND ENTERTAINMENT

Yalta is a resort town, and most of the entertainment leaps out at you. Strolling along the promenade is a favorite pastime after a hard day of sun-bathing. Museums are common and serve as a needed break from the sun. The beaches themselves are an institution, and people-watching *never* gets better. Just remember, crowds are fun.

Museums and Galleries

Chekhov called Yalta home for the last five years of his life, and from the wealth of monuments and plaques, you can practically trace his path. On nab. Lenina at the entrance of the present-day Restaurant Gurman you can see where he slept, in a hotel that used to be there. On ul. Litkensa (ул. Литкенса) is the **school** where he once taught. On Pushkinskaya ul. 5a (ул. Пушкинская) you can drop in at the Yalta **historical-literary museum** if it has reopened (admission 1000Krb). Finally, at ul.

Kirova 112 (ул. Кирова), you can visit the **house** he built with his own hands, see the garden he planted, and visit the museum dedicated to him by his sister. Bus #8 takes you there every 40 minutes from the Кинотеатр Спартак stop on ul. Pushkinska.

The old **Soviet Gallery** is at ul. Gogolya 1 (ул. Гоголя) next to the Hotel Oreanda (open Tues.-Sun. 9am-5pm; admission 2000Krb), and there is an **art gallery** across the street at Pushkinskaya ul. 5, (open Wed.-Sun. 10am-6pm). Having sufficiently refined your taste, you can now stop at **Crimea Wines,** on nab. Lenina underneath the "Marino" sign in the Casino Diana building (wine tastings hourly 11am-5pm).

Beaches

The beaches in Yalta proper are covered with grey, smooth pebbles and can be a bit disheartening at first sight. But the cobalt waters of the Black Sea reach 25°C (77°F) in summer and the beaches here are mercifully free of any of the nasty ocean evils. There are no stinging jellyfish, no overbearing surfers, and no sticky sand. Although there are a few spots along nab. Lenina where you can bathe for free, one 15,000Krb **ticket** will give you access to any public beach all day. Showers, toilets, lifeguards, changing booths, and wooden sunbathing planks come with the ticket. Officially it is forbidden to smoke, dive, or use inflatable rafts, but visitors don't care. **Delfin** beach at the western end of town is a little sandier and a little less crowded than the east-end **Massandtovskiy,** but has fewer vendors. **Sanatoria** and **hotel beaches** are also open for a fee, usually not much more than the public beach fee. **Campground** guests have free use of the Hotel Oreanda and Hotel Yalta beaches.

Outdoors

By day, Yalta's parks are among the most luxuriant the peninsula has to offer; in the **Gagarin Primorsky Park** at the west end of nab. Lenina you can find an **exotic fish aquarium** (open Tues.-Sun. 9am-5pm) and an **open-air mime theatre** as well. Shhh. On Moskovskaya ul., about a ten-minute walk from town, the **circus** puts on a nightly show (Tues.-Sun. May 28-Oct. 28; ticket windows open Tue.-Sun. 10am-6pm). If you aren't feeling childish enough yet, the **Polyana Skazok** (Полина Сказок) children's park next to the campground takes characters from Russian and Ukrainian fairy tales and immortalizes them in larger-than-life figures (open daily 8am-8pm). A number of **hiking trails** begin in Yalta, reaching the **Uchan-Su waterfall** and other natural wonders. Consult the campground staff for advice. Lazier visitors can use the **chairlift** to get to a high-altitude **lookout point.** It lifts you from behind the Casino Diana building (June-Oct. daily 10am-2pm and 4-9pm; 10,000Krb).

■ NEAR YALTA

LIVADIA

A 45-minute walk or a 10-minute bus ride away, the town of Livadia (Ливадия) was the site of the ultimate government junket, the Yalta Conference. Roosevelt, Churchill, and Stalin met in 1945 in Nicholas II's summer palace (built in 1911) to finalize their post-war territorial claims, and to commit the Russians to enter the war against Japan after the defeat of Germany. The #5 bus from Kinoteatr Spartak (Кинотеатр Спартак) in Yalta drops you off every 40-50 minutes across the park from the **White Palace** (Белы Ливадийский Дворец) where it all happened. The second floor has been converted into an exhibition hall and Nicholas II museum, but the rest has been preserved in memory of the conference. The surrounding grounds and park are also a splendid example of what a good gardener can do. A series of elevators takes you down the side of the mountain to the beach, a slightly less-crowded version of Yalta's beaches. Show your beach-ticket to get back to the top. From the park it is possible to walk nearly to the next town on the ridge path known as **Sunny Path.** Beyond this lies **Golden Beach** (Золотой Пляж), also directly reachable four times per day by bus #34 from Kinoteatr Spartak (Кинотеатр Спартак) in Yalta, and the **Swallow's Nest castle** (Ластоукино гнездо) via bus #26 from the Yalta station.

ALUSHTA

Although this town is still officially closed to individual travelers, Alushta (Алушта) is an excellent alternative daytrip to Yalta if you're not enthusiastic about the 2½-hour Simferopol-Yalta trek. From Simferopol, trolleybuses #51 and 52 take an hour to reach Alushta's pebbled **beaches** (be sure to buy a return ticket before you leave, or risk getting stuck in a region whose hotels only accept natives or Intourist groups). The **house-museum of architect A. N. Beckett,** built in 1896, stands at ul. Komsomolskaya (ул. Комсомольская); take bus #2 or 3 from the trolleybus station (open Tues.-Sat 8am-5pm). Right on the shore at ul. Lenina 8 (ул. Ленина) is the **regional history museum** with fascinating ethnographic displays (open Wed.-Mon. 10am-6pm). The town's layout reflects its shoreward orientation; almost everything lies on ul. Lenina. But if you take any perpendicular from there, you will reach the town's central **market,** one of the region's best.

FEODOSIA

Two-and-a-half hours east of Yalta the pebbly beaches end. Outside the ancient slave-trading town of Feodosia (Феодосія), a ten-mile stretch of bronzed sand speckled with tiny, smooth bits of seashell creates a variegated shoreline that has attracted vacationers from Roman times until the present. The sea floor slopes gently down from the shore into waters slightly cooler than those in the west. **Buses** run to Feodosia from Simferopol 14 times per day from the main bus station; the trip take about 2½ hours and tickets *must* be bought in advance, particularly for the return trip. Buses to Feodosia usually have Kerch (Керч) as their final destination. To spend the night, inquire at the **Hotel Astoriya** (Гостиница "Астория"). From the bus station, **city buses** #2 and 4 head into town, where the main hotels await along with a few Roman ruins. But if you are only there for the day, you don't have to leave the general area of the bus station—head out the front door and cross the street and the train tracks to reach the sea (beach tickets 5000Krb).

conduit between the industrial democracies of Western Europe and the fledgling market economies of the east.

For deeper understanding, pick up a copy of *Let's Go: Austria and Switzerland.*

GETTING THERE AND GETTING AROUND

Rail travel in Austria is extraordinarily reliable and efficient, but can be expensive. **Eurail** is valid. The **Rabbit Card** gives four days of unlimited travel over a 10-day period (second class 1130AS; juniors (under 27) 700AS). The **Bundes-Netzkarte** provides unlimited travel on Austrian trains for one month and a 50% discount on railway-operated boats and Danube steamers (second class 3600AS). Seniors (men over 65, women over 60) are entitled to **half-price tickets** *(Umweltticket für Senioren)* on trains, long-distance buses, Danube steamers, and many cable cars; you must show an official **Reduction Card** *(Ermässigungsausweis),* valid for one year (240AS). All cards are available at major post offices and train stations.

The Austrian **bus** system consists of orange **Bundes Buses** and yellow **Post buses.** Both are efficient and cover mountain areas inaccessible by train. They usually cost a bit more than trains, and railpasses are not valid. Tickets are sold on-board, and at tabak stands. **Hydrofoils** follow the Danube to Budapest. Austria is a **hitchhiker's** nightmare—Austrians rarely pick up, and many mountain roads are all but deserted. *Let's Go* does not recommend hitchhiking as a safe means of transportation. Hitchhikers stand on highway Knoten (on-ramps) and wait. The thumb signal is recognized, but signs with a destination and the word *bitte* (please) are common. The **Mitfahrzentrale** ride-share office charges roughly half the going rail fare to connect travelers with somebody traveling by car in the same direction.

Bikes can be rented at train stations for 90AS per day—half-price if you have a train ticket *to* the station from which you are renting and have arrived on the day of rental. Look for signs with a bicycle and the word *Verleih.* Pick up a list *(Fahrrad am Bahnhof)* of participating stations at any station. Tourist offices provide regional bike route maps. 30AS will get your bike aboard a train; look for the *Gepäckbeforderung* symbol on departure schedules to see if bikes are permitted. All Austrian train stations offer luggage storage (up to several months) for 20AS per piece; many offer lockers as well (10-20AS, depending on size).

LANGUAGE

English is the most common second language. Any effort, however incompetent, to use the mother tongue will win you loads of fans; *Grüß Gott* (God bless) is the typical Austrian greeting.

> Austria's **telephone** network is becoming digitized, and telephone numbers may change without notice. If a listed number has changed, consult a tourist office.

ORIENTATION AND PRACTICAL INFORMATION

In eastern Austria, 40km from the Hungarian, Czech, and Slovakian borders, Vienna is divided into 23 **districts** *(Bezirke)*; the oldest area, *die Innere Stadt,* is the first. The **Ringstraße** separates the first district from the second through ninth. The districts spiral around the center. Street signs indicate the district number in either Roman or Arabic numerals (e.g. "XIII, Auhofstr. 26" is in the 13th district) and postal codes reflect the district (1010 represents the first, 1020 the second, etc.). *Let's Go* lists the district number where possible. The intersection of the **Opernring, Kärntner Ring,** and **Kärntner Straße,** is home to the Opera House, tourist office, and the **Karlsplatz** U-Bahn stop. After dark, avoid the beautiful Karlsplatz, and its pushers and junkies. Pickpockets work the parks and **Kärntner Straße,** where hordes of tourists make tempting targets; the avenue leads to **Stephansplatz** and the **Stephansdom,** the center of the city and its *Fußgängerzone.*

Tourist Offices: I, Kärntner Str. 38, behind the Opera House. A small bureau dispensing many brochures. Free city **map.** The brochure *Youth Scene* provides a

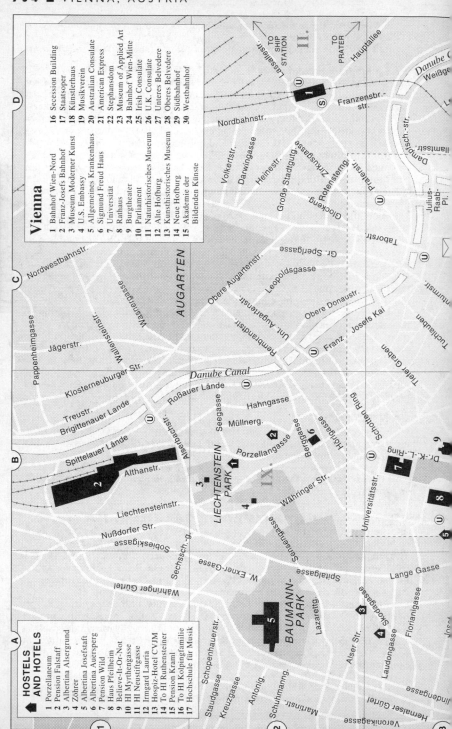

GATEWAY CITIES

Vienna

1 Bahnhof Wien-Nord
2 Franz-Josefs Bahnhof
3 Museum Moderner Kunst
4 U.S. Embassy
5 Allgemeines Krankenhaus
6 Sigmund Freud Haus
7 Universität
8 Haus Pfeilheim
9 Rathaus
10 Parliament
11 Naturhistorisches Museum
12 Alte Hofburg
13 Kunsthistorisches Museum
14 Neue Hofburg
15 Akademie der Bildenden Künste
16 Secession Building
17 Staatsoper
18 Künstlerhaus
19 Musikverein
20 Australian Consulate
21 American Express
22 Stephansdom
23 Museum of Applied Art
24 Bahnhof Wien-Mitte
25 Irish Consulate
26 U.K. Consulate
27 Unteres Belvedere
28 Oberes Belvedere
29 Südbahnhof
30 Westbahnhof

HOSTELS AND HOTELS

1 Porzellaneum
2 Pension Falstaff
3 Albertina Alsergrund
4 Zöhrer
5 Albertina Josefstaft
6 Albertina Auersperg
7 Pension Wild
8 Haus Pfeilheim
9 Believe-It-Or-Not
10 HI Myrthengasse
11 HI Neustiftgasse
12 Irmgard Lauria
13 Hospiz-Hotel CVJM
14 To HI Ruthensteiner
15 Pension Kraml
16 To HI Kolpingfamilie
17 Hochschule für Musik

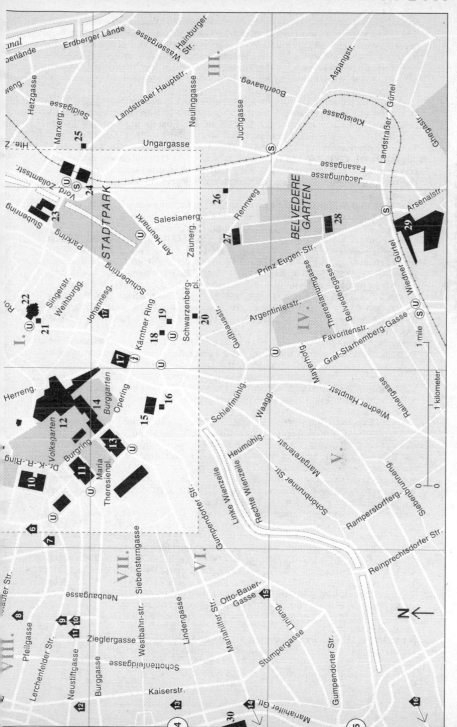

•   wealth of vital information for travelers of all ages. The restaurant and club sections are particularly useful. Books rooms (350-400AS) for a 35AS fee and the first night's room deposit. Open 9am-7pm. Other offices at **Westbahnhof** (open 6:15am-11pm), **Sudbahnhof** (open 6:30am-10pm, Nov.-April until 9pm), the **airport** (open 8:30am-11pm; Oct.-May until 10pm), and at the **Richtung Zentrum** exit off the A1 Westautobahn. **Jugend-Info Wien** (Youth Information Service), Bellariapassage (tel. 526 46 37), in the underground passage at the Bellaria intersection. Entrance at the Dr.-Karl-Renner-Ring/Bellaria tram stop (lines 1, 2, 46, 49, D, and J). additional entrance from the Volkstheater U-Bahn station. Info on cultural events. Hip and knowledgeable. Pick up the hostels and pensions list, as well as cheap rock concert tickets. Open Mon.-Fri. noon-7pm, Sat. 10am-7pm. **Tourist Information:** tel. 211 14 54 or 211 14 27. Patience is rewarded.

Budget Travel: ÖKISTA, IX, Türkenstr. 6 (tel. 40 14 80), will book sharply-discounted flight and train tickets. Young staff understands budget traveling and English. Open Mon.-Fri. 9:30am-5:30pm. **Branch** office, IV, Karlsgasse 3 (tel. 505 01 28), same hours.

Consulates and Embassies: U.S. Embassy, IX, Boltzmangasse 16, off Währingerstr. **U.S. Consulate** I, Gartenbaupromenade 2, off Parkring (tel. 313 39). Open Mon.-Fri. 8:30am-noon and 1-5pm. **Canada,** Laurenzerburg 2 (tel. 533 36 91). Open Mon.-Fri. 8:30am-12:30pm and 1:30-3:30pm. **U.K.,** III, Jauresgasse 10, near Schloß Belvedere (tel. 714 61 17). Open Mon.-Fri. 9:15am-noon, for British citizens 9:15am-noon and 2-4pm. **Ireland,** III, Hilton Center, 16th floor, Landstraßer Hauptstr. 2 (tel. 715 42 46 0). **Australia,** IV, Mattiellistr. 2-4 behind the Karlskirche (tel. 51 28 58 01 64). Open Mon.-Fri. 8:45am-1pm and 2-5pm. **New Zealand,** I, Lugeck 1 (tel. 52 66 36). Open Mon.-Fri. 8:30am-5pm. **South Africa,** XIX, Sandgasse 33 (tel. 326 49 30). **Czech Republic,** XIV, Penzingerstr. 11-13, in Hütteldorf (tel. 894 37 41 or 894 62 36). Open Mon.-Fri. 9-11am. **Hungary,** I, Bankgasse 4-6 (tel. 533 26 31). Open Mon.-Fri. 8:30am-12:30pm.

Currency Exchange: Banks open Mon.-Wed. and Fri. 8am-3pm, Thurs. 8am-5:30pm. Bank and airport exchanges use same official rates (min. commission 65AS for traveler's checks, 10AS for cash). Longer hours (Mon.-Fri.) and lighter commission at train stations: Opernpassage 9am-7pm, Westbahnhof 4am-10pm, Südbahnhof 6:30am-10pm, the Air Terminal 8am-12:30pm and 2-6pm, and Schwechat airport 6am-11pm. Cash advances with Visa at numerous banks. Most ATMs in the inner city accept Cirrus and MC.

American Express: I, Kärntnerstr. 21-23 (tel. 515 40; 24-hr. refund service toll-free 066 02 79), down from Stephansplatz. Holds mail. 40AS min. to exchange traveler's checks, 15AS min. for cash. Open Mon.-Fri. 9am-5:30pm, Sat. 9am-noon.

Post Office: I, Fleischmarkt 19. Also has currency exchange (60AS per traveler's check, no charge for cash). Open 24 hrs., as are branches at Westbahnhof, Südbahnhof, and Franz-Josefs Bahnhof. All these change currency. Address **Poste Restante** to *Postlagernde Briefe,* 1 Fleischmarkt 19, A-1010 Wien. **Postal Codes:** in the first district 1010, in the second 1020, etc.

Telephones: I, Börseplatz 1, near the Schottenring. Open daily 6am-midnight. Also at main post offices. **City Code:** in Austria, 0222; from abroad, 1. Buy telephone cards (*werkarten*) at post offices and train stations (48AS and 95AS). Push red button on older pay phones to connect. 1AS and up for local calls, 9AS for long-distance. For AT&T's **USADirect,** tel. 022 90 30 11; for MCI's **WorldPhone,** 022 90 30 12; for **Sprint Express,** 022 90 30 14; for **Canada Direct,** 022 90 30 13; for **BT Direct,** 022 90 30 44; for **Ireland Direct,** 02 29 03 03 53; and for **New Zealand Direct,** 022 90 30 64. Note that the use of any of these services is considered a local call, so you have to keep dropping shillings into the phone or have an Austrian phone card. For assistance calling abroad, tel. 08. For directory assistance, tel. 16 11.

Flights: Wien Schwechat airport (tel. 711 10 22 33), 18km from the city center, is linked by bus (60AS) to Westbahnhof, Südbahnhof, and the City Air Terminal (next to the Hilton in district III; take U-3 or U-4 to Landstr. or train to Wien-Mitte). *Schnell-Bahn* metro railway also runs there hourly from Wien Mitte or Wien Nord stations (30AS, Eurail and Vienna public transport passes valid).

Trains: tel. 17 17, 24hrs. English spoken. There are three principal stations in Vienna. **Wien-Mitte,** in the center, handles commuter trains. **Franz-Josefs-Bahnhof** handles local trains and trains to Berlin via Prague; tram D "Südbahnhof" runs to the Ring. **Westbahnhof** services France, western Germany, Switzerland, the Netherlands, Belgium, the U.K., Bulgaria, Romania, Hungary, and western Austria; take U-6 then U-4 to Karlsplatz or take tram #52 or 58 to the Ring. **Südbahnhof** has trains to Italy, Greece, Czech Republic, Slovakia, Poland, and (June-Sept.) Bulgaria and Hungary; take tram D "Nußdorf" to the Ring. To: Prague (5-6hrs., 410AS); Berlin (1hr., via Prague 790AS, via Munich 1314AS); Budapest (4-5hrs., 372AS plus 80AS InterCity supplement). Showers and baths available in the Westbahnhof at **Friseursalon Navratil,** on the ground floor. 48AS per 30min. shower; 60AS per 30min. bath. 10AS extra on Sun. Open Mon.-Sat. 10am-8pm, Sun. 8am-1pm.

Buses: City bus terminal at **Wien-Mitte** rail station. Post and Bundesbahn buses across Austria; private international buses. Currency exchange and lockers available. Domestic ticket desk open 6:15am-6pm; international private lines maintain travel agencies in the station. **Information:** tel. 711 01 (open 6am-9pm).

Public Transportation: Excellent **U-Bahn** (subway), bus, and tram systems. Single fare is 20AS, 17AS if purchased in advance at ticket office or tobacco shop; a 24-hr. pass is 50AS, and a 72-hr. pass is 130AS. The 7-day pass (142AS) requires a passport-sized photo, and is valid from Mon. at 9am to the next Mon (i.e. if you buy it Sat. you only have two days left). An 8-day ticket costs 265AS; it must be stamped for each ride. With this card, 4 people can ride for 2 days, 8 for 1, etc. All passes allow unlimited travel on the system, except on special night buses. To validate a ticket, **punch the ticket immediately** upon entering the bus, tram, etc. in the orange machine; if you possess a ticket that is not stamped, it is invalid, and plain-clothes inspectors may fine you up to 500AS. Tickets can be purchased from Tabak kiosks or automaten in major U-Bahn stations. Most of the system closes shortly before midnight. Special **night buses** run Fri.-Sat. 12:30-4am between the city center, Schwedenplatz, and various outlying districts (25AS, day-transport passes not valid). Night bus stops are designated by "N" signs. Streetcar lines and U-Bahn stops are listed on a free city map, available at the tourist office. There is a **information** number (tel. 587 31 86, **English-speaking operator** available upon request) that will give you directions to any point in the city by public transportation; open Mon.-Fri. 7am-6pm, Sat.-Sun. 8:30am-4pm.

Ferries: Cruise with **DDSG Donaureisen** to Budapest for 750AS, round-trip 1100AS (daily April 24-Sept. 18). Buy tickets at tourist offices. Boats dock at the Reichsbrücke on the New Danube. Take U-1 to Reichsbrücke.

Taxis: tel. 313 00, 401 00, 601 60, or 910 11. Base charge 22AS. 12AS surcharge for taxis called by radiophone; 10AS for trips 11pm-6am and on Sun. and holidays; 12AS for luggage over 20kg; and 24AS surcharge for luggage over 50kg.

Bike Rental: Best bargain at **Wien Nord** and **Westbahnhof** train stations. 90AS per day, with train ticket 45AS from day of arrival. Elsewhere in the city rental averages 30AS per hr. Pick up the Vienna By Bike brochure at tourist office.

Hitchhiking: *Let's Go* does not recommend hitchhiking as a safe means of transportation. Those who hitch to Salzburg take the tram to the end of the line at Hütteldorf station and walk over to the beginning of the Autobahn. Those hitching south try the traffic circle near Laaerberg (tram 67 to the last stop).

Mitfahrzentrale: Mitfahrzentrale Wien, III, Invalidenstr. 15 (tel. 715 00 66), pairs drivers and riders (Salzburg 230AS, Innsbruck 280AS). Open Mon.-Fri. 9am-6pm, Sat. 10am-2pm.

Luggage Storage: Lockers at all train stations (24hrs. 30AS). Adequate for sizable backpacks. Checked luggage 20AS. Open 4am-1:15am.

Lost Property: Central Lost Property Office, IX, Wasagasse 22 (tel. 313 44 91 11). Open Mon.-Fri. 8am-noon. For objects lost on public transport system, tel. 50 13 00 within three days.

English Bookstores: Shakespeare & Company, I, Sterngasse 2 (tel. 353 50 53). Open Mon.-Fri. 9am-6pm, Sat. 9am-noon. **British Bookshop,** I, Weihburggasse 8. Stocks *Let's Go.* Open Mon.-Fri. 9am-6pm, Sat. 9am-noon.

GATEWAY CITIES

Gay and Lesbian Information: Rosa Lila Villa, VI, Linke Wienzeile 102 (tel. 586 81 50). A favored resource for Viennese homosexuals and visiting tourists. Lending library available. Open Mon.-Fri. 5-8pm.

Laundromat: Münzwäscherei Kalksburger & Co., III, Schlachthausgasse 19 (tel. 78 81 91). Wash 90AS per 6kg, dry 10AS. Soap 10AS. Open Mon.-Fri. 7:30am-6:30pm, Sat. 7:30am-1pm. **Münzwäscherei Margaretenstraße,** IV, Margaretenstr. 52 (tel. 587 04 73). Wash 85AS per 6kg, dry 10AS. Soap included. Open Mon.-Fri. 7am-6pm, Sat. 8am-noon.

Crisis Lines: House for Threatened and Battered Women, emergency hotline tel. 545 48 00 or 408 38 80. Open 24 hrs. **Rape Crisis Hotline,** tel. 93 22 22. Open Mon. 10am-1pm, Tues., Thurs. 6-9pm. **English-language Suicide Hotline,** tel. 713 33 74.

Medical Assistance: Allgemeines Krankenhaus, IX, Währinger Gürtel 18-20 (tel. 404 00). Your embassy can provide a list of English-speaking physicians.

Emergencies: Police: tel. 133. **Ambulance:** tel. 144. **Fire:** tel. 122.

ACCOMMODATIONS AND CAMPING

The only unpleasant aspect of Vienna is the hunt for cheap rooms. The June crunch abates slightly from July to September, when university dorms metamorphose into hostels. Write ahead or call the day before for reservations, and pick up the lists of hostels and hotels from the tourist office. Beware of offers of closet-sized *Studentenzimmer* (student rooms). **Tourist offices** handle private homes (3-day min. stay) in the 180-250AS range, but many of these are in the 'burbs. **ÖKISTA** (see Budget Travel, above) finds cheaper rooms and charges no commission. The office is at IX, Türkenstr. 4-6 #314 (tel. 40 14 80), adjacent to the budget travel office (open Mon.-Wed. and Fri. 9:30am-4pm, Thurs. 9:30am-5:30pm). In summer, the **Mitwohnzentrale** at Laudongasse 7 (tel. 402 60 61) finds rooms from 200AS per day (commission included); for stays of a month or longer, rooms start at 2500AS (book four weeks in advance). Bring your passport (open Mon.-Fri. 10am-2pm and 3-6pm).

Hostels

Myrthengasse (HI), VII, Myrthengasse 7 (tel. 523 94 29 or 523 63 16, fax 523 58 49). From Westbahnhof, take U-6 to Burggasse, then bus 48A to Neubaugasse; walk back on Burggasse about a block, and take the first right. About 15min. by bus to city center or Westbahnhof. Sparkling modern rooms with 2-6 beds, washroom, and big lockers. Enthusiastic management, game room. Reception open 7:30am-1am. Lockout 9am-2pm. Curfew 1am. 140AS. Breakfast (7-8:30am) and sheets included. Reservations recommended. Wheelchair access.

Believe-It-Or-Not, VII, Myrthengasse 10, #14 (tel. 526 46 58). Across from Myrthengasse hostel (above). Cramped but sociable quarters. Fully equipped kitchen, sheets, down quilts, hot water, and thoughtful owner. Believe it. Or not. Lockout 10:30am-12:30pm. 160AS per person; Nov.-Easter 110AS. Call ahead.

Gästehaus Ruthensteiner (HI), XV, Robert-Hamerlinggasse 24 (tel. 893 42 02 or 893 27 96). From Westbahnhof, walk down Mariahilferstr., take first left at Palmgasse, then first right (3min.). Small, sunny rooms. Courtyard and kitchen. Reception open 24 hrs. Dorm bed (bring sheets or sleeping bag) 129AS. Singles and doubles 209AS per person. Breakfast 25AS. Lockers and kitchen facilities. Reservations recommended.

Neustiftgasse (HI), VII, Neustiftgasse 85 (tel. 523 74 62, fax 523 58 49). Around the corner from Myrthengasse hostel (above) and managed by the same folks. Reception open 7:30am-1am. Lockout 9am-noon. Curfew 1am. Members only. 140AS. Breakfast and sheets included. Laundry 50AS per load. Reservations recommended. Wheelchair access.

Jugendgästehaus Wien Brigittenau (HI), XX, Friedrich-Engels-Platz 24 (tel. 33 28 29 40, fax 330 83 74). U-1 or U-4: Schwedenplatz and then tram N to Floridsdorfer Brücke/Friedrich-Engels-Platz. Efficient and helpful management oversees brigades of high-school kids. 334 beds. Reception open 24hrs. Lockout 9am-3pm. Curfew 1am. Members only. 140AS. Breakfast included. 3-night max. stay.

Kolpingfamilie Wien-Meidling (HI), XIII, Bendlgasse 10-12 (tel. 83 54 87, fax 812 21 30). U-4 or U-6: Niederhofstr. Head right on Niedgerhofstr. and take the third right onto Bendlgasse. Well-lit and modern rooms with 4, 6, and 8 beds are 140AS, 125AS, and 95AS per person respectively. Doubles 405AS. Sheet rental 65AS. Breakfast 42AS. Reception open 6am-midnight. Curfew midnight. Doors locked midnight-4am. No daytime lockout. Check-out by 9am.

Hostel Zöhrer, VIII, Skodagasse 26 (tel. 43 07 30, fax 408 04 09). From the Westbahnhof, take U-6: Alserstr., then take tram 43 "Dr. Karl Lueger Ring" two stops to Skodagasse. From the Südbahnhof, take bus 13A to Alserstr./Skodagasse. About 10min. from the city center. Crowded but comfortable, in a good location. Dorm beds, singles, 4-, 6-, or 7-bed rooms, each with showers, all 160AS per person. Laundry 70AS. Kitchen facilities. Reception open 7:30am-10pm. Checkout 9am. No curfew, no lockout. Front door/locker key deposit 50AS. Breakfast (7:30-9:30am), sheets, and kitchen facilities included.

Jugendgästehaus Hütteldorf-Hacking (HI), XIII, Schloßberggasse 8 (tel. 877 02 63, fax 877 026 32). From Karlsplatz, take U-4 to the end station Hütteldorf; walk over the footbridge and follow the signs (10min.). From the Westbahnhof, take S-50 (Eurail valid, last train 10:15pm) to Hütteldorf. Often packed with student groups, but there are two separate buildings for individual travelers to escape from the little monsters. Midnight curfew is not enforced in these buildings. 139AS. Laundry 70AS per load. Large closets without locks—it's *much* wiser to use the safes available at reception (10AS per day). Reception open 7am-11:45pm. Curfew 11:45pm, but it can be loud for an hour or two. Lockout 9am-4pm. Breakfast and showers included.

Schloßherberge am Wilhelminenberg (HI), XVI, Savoyenstr. 2 (tel. 458 50 37 00). From Westbahnhof, take U-6 "Friedensbrücke" to tram 46 to Maroltingerstraße and then bus 46B or 146B to Schloß Wilhelminenberg. On a hill, abutting a beautiful palace. 164 beds in comfortable quads, all with shower and toilet. Reception open 7am-11:45pm. 205AS. Breakfast included. Open March-Oct. Wheelchair access.

Dormitories

Mass-produced university cubicles become summer hostels from July to September.

Porzellaneum der Wiener Universität, IX, Porzellangasse 30 (tel. 34 72 82). From the Südbahnhof, take streetcar D "Nußdorf" and get off at Fürstengasse. From the Westbahnhof, take streetcar 5 to the Franz-Josefs Bahnhof, then streetcar D "Südbahnhof" to Fürstengasse (20min.). The Crazy Eddie of hotels. Reception open 24 hrs. Singles and doubles 160AS per person, with some triples and quads. Sheets and showers included. Reservations recommended.

Rudolfinum, IV, Mayerhofgasse 3 (tel. 505 53 84). Just a few yards down Mayerhofg. from U-1: Taubstummeng. Reception open 24hrs. Rock on dude! Buy a beer at the reception and veg in front of MTV. Great location. Singles 250AS. Doubles 420AS. Triples 540AS. Sheets, showers, and breakfast included.

Katholisches Studentenhaus, XIX, Peter-Jordanstr. 29 (tel. 34 92 64). From the Westbahnhof, take U-6 "Heiligenstadt" to Nußdorferstr., then streetcar 38 to Hardtgasse, and turn left onto Peter-Jordanstr. From the Südbahnhof, take streetcar D to Schottentor, then streetcar 38 to Hardtgasse. Unexciting rooms, but the price is right. Reception on second floor. Singles 220AS. Doubles 166AS per person. Showers and sheets included. Call ahead.

Gästehaus Pfeilgasse, IV, Pfeilgasse 6 (tel. 408 34 45). U-2: Lerchenfelderstr. Head right on Lerchenfelderstr., first right on Lange Gasse, and first left on Pfeilgasse. The homesick will be reminded of their freshman dorm. Singles 250AS. Doubles 420AS. Triples 540AS. Showers and breakfast included. Reception open 24 hrs.

Hotels and Pensions

Irmgard Lauria, VII, Kaiserstr. 77, #8 (tel. 522 25 55). U-6: Burggasse-Stadthalle, then take a right onto Burggasse, and then the second left onto Kaiserstr. About 15min. from center. Eclectically decorated but attractive rooms with murals ranging from the African plains to a crazily-pastelled forest. Dorms 160AS. Doubles 530AS. No curfew. Coed rooming possible. Reservations strongly recommended but require a 2-day-min. stay.

Pension Falstaff, IX, Müllnergsse 5 (tel. 317 91 27, fax 349 18 64). U-6: Roßauer Lände, cross Roßauer Lände and head down Grünentorgasse, taking the third left onto Müllnergasse. Much quieter than its boisterous namesake. Singles 345-465AS. Doubles 565-680AS. Triples 680AS. Extra bed 200AS. Breakfast included.

Pension Kraml, VI, Brauergasse 5 (tel. 587 85 88, fax 586 75 73), off Gumpendorferstr. From the Westbahnhof, walk across the Gürtel and up Mariahilferstr., and take the third right onto Otto-Bauerstr.; make the first left on Königseggasse, then the first right (15min.). About 10min. from the city center. Tidy, comfortable, new, and run by a cordial family. Singles 260AS. Doubles 530-660AS. Triples 720-930AS. Quads 1120AS. Continental breakfast included. Call ahead.

Hedwig Gally, XXV, Arnsteingasse 25 (tel. 892 90 73, fax 833 10 28). By the Westbahnhof, but the U-3 to the city center is a short walk away. Singles 250-300AS. Doubles 400-460AS. Triples 540-600AS. Quads 720-760AS. Breakfast 50AS.

Hospiz-Hotel CVJM, VII, Kenyongasse 15 (tel. 93 13 04). From the Westbahnhof, cross the Gürtel, walk 1 block down Stallgasse and turn left on Kenyongasse (3 min.). This large old building, part of the Austrian YMCA, provides a quiet location close to the station. Singles 350-380AS. Doubles 620-680AS. Triples 870-990AS. Quads 1120-1280AS. 40AS surcharge for one-night stay. Ample parking. Key to entrance and room provided.

Camping

Wien-West I (tel. 94 14 49) and **II** (tel. 94 23 14), at Hüttelbergstr. 40 and 80, respectively, are the most convenient campgrounds; both lie in the 14th *Bezirk* about 8km from the city center. For either, take U-4 to the end station at Hütteldorf, then switch to bus #52B "Campingpl. Wien West". 58AS per person, children 33AS; 53AS per tent; 53AS per car. Both offer laundry machines, grocery stores, and cooking facilities. I is open July 15-Aug. 28; II year-round.

FOOD

Viennese cuisine reflect the patchwork empire of the Habsburgs. *Serbische Bohnensuppe* (Serbian bean soup) and *Ungärische Gulaschsuppe* (spicy Hungarian beef stew) are examples of eastern European influence. *Knödel,* bread dumpling found in most side dishes, originated in the Czech lands. Even the famed *Wiener Schnitzel* (fried and breaded veal cutlets) was first cooked in Milan. The *gastehaus* and the *beisel* serve inexpensive rib-sticking meals that are best washed down with much beer. *Würstelstands,* found on almost every corner, provide a quick, cheap lunch. Vienna's sublime desserts and chocolates are unbelievably rich, but priced for patrons who are likewise blessed. *Sacher Torte, Imperial Torte,* and even *Apfelstrudel* cost up to 40AS, the Viennese swear that they are worth every *Groschen.*

Imbibing in Austria is easy—beer is sold more commonly than soda, and anyone old enough to see over the counter can buy it (although those under 18 will have trouble purchasing liquor and getting into nightclubs). Eastern Austria is famous for its white wine. Grüner Veltliner's *Klosterneuburger* is both reasonably priced and dry. Austrian beers are outstanding; try *Stiegl Bier,* a Salzburg brew, *Zipfer Bier* from upper Austria, and *Gösser Bier* from Graz. Austria imports lots of Budweiser beer, a.k.a. *Budwar*—the Czech original, not the watery American imitation. For a more potent potable, try the whopping 180 proof *Ströh Rum.*

Restaurants in the touristy **Kärntnerstraße** area are generally overpriced. Budget *Gaststätten, Kneipen* (bars), and restaurants are easy to find north of the university where **Universitätsstraße** and **Währingerstraße** meet. The **Naschmarkt** is open-air relief for vegetarians in an otherwise carnivorous city (U-4 to Kettenbrückengasse; open Mon.-Fri. 7am-6pm, Sat. 7am-1pm). For discount supermarket fare, try the **Billa, Konsum,** or **Hoffer.** Except at train stations, grocery stores close from Saturday afternoon to Monday morning. Beat the summer heat at **Gelateria Hoher Markt,** 1010, Hoher Markt just off Rotenturmstr (open March-Oct. 9am-11pm).

Restaurants

Most restaurants expect you to seat yourself; a small tip (usually rounding up the bill) is customary. The server won't bring your check without first being asked. Say *zahlen, bitte* (TSAH-len BIT-uh) to settle up.

Trzesniewski, I, Dorotheergasse 1, three blocks down the Graben from the Stephansdom. A famous stand-up restaurant, this unpronounceable establishment has been serving petite open-faced sandwiches for more than 80 years. 7AS per *Brötchen.* Open Mon.-Fri. 9am-7:30pm, Sat. 9am-1pm.

Maschu, I, Rabenstr. From U-1 or U-4: Schwedenpl. Facing away from the canal, head right on Franz-Josefs-Kai, then left. Surrounded by five bars, smack in the middle of the Triangle, this stand-up restaurant is ideal for a bite before, during, or after the night's revels. Succulent *Schwarma* (38AS) and delicious falafel (55AS). Open 10am-2am.

Bizi Pizza, I, Rotenturmstr. 4 (tel. 513 37 05), on the corner of Stephanspl. This self-service restaurant boasts a deliciously fresh salad bar (small plate 30AS, large plate 50AS) and huge individual pizzas (60-75AS, slices 27AS). Open 11am-11pm. Branch with the same hours at Franz-Josefs-Kai (tel. 535 79 13).

Fischerbräu, XIX, Billrothstr. 17 (tel. 319 62 64). From U-2: Universität or U-2 or 4: Schottentor, take tram 38 to Hardtgasse, and walk back 50m. Popular spot for youngish locals. The leafy courtyard, accompanied by jazz music, makes this an ideal spot to consume the home-brewed beer (large glass 38AS) and delicious food. The veal sausage (56AS) is excellent, and the chicken salad (78AS) has made more than one New Yorker squeal with glee. Open Mon.-Sat. 4pm-1am, Sun. 11am-1am.

Tunnel, VIII, Florianigasse 39 (tel. 42 34 65). U-2: Rathaus, and with your back to City Hall, head right on Landesgerichtstr., then left on Florianigasse. Dark and smoky, with funky paintings and the occasional divan instead of chairs. Cheap eats featuring Italian, Austrian, and Middle-Eastern dishes. Vegetarian options. The best affordable breakfast in Vienna—29AS buys anything from a Spanish omelette to an "Arabian" selection. Entrees 35-120AS. Open 9am-2am.

Schnitzelwirt Schmidt, VII, Neubaugasse 52 (tel. 93 37 71). From the Burgring, take bus 49 to the end station at Neubaugasse (5min.). Every kind of Schnitzel imaginable (56AS). Huge portions and low, low prices will sate your most carnivorous desires and spare your budget. Open Mon.-Fri. 11am-11pm, Sat. 11am-2:30pm and 5-11pm.

Cafés and Konditoreien

One of life's great enigmas is how a country with such unremarkable cuisine can produce such heavenly desserts. In mid-afternoon, Austrians flock to *Café-Konditoreien* to nurse the national sweet tooth with *Kaffe und Kuchen* (coffee and cake). Try *Sachertorte,* a rich chocolate pastry layered with marmalade, or *Linzertorte,* a nutty pastry with raspberry filling. Choose cake at the counter before sitting down; often you'll pay for it immediately, give your receipt to the server when you order drinks, and wait for it to be brought to you. Coffee can be ordered *schwarzer* (black), *brauner* (a little milk), *melange* (light), and *mazagron* (iced with rum).

Demel, I, Kohlmarkt 14. Walk 5min. from the Stephansdom down Graben. *The* Viennese coffee shop. The atmosphere is near-worshipful in this legendary fin-de-siècle cathedral of sweets. Waitresses in convent-black serve divine confections (35-48AS). Don't miss the *créme-du-jour.* Open 10am-6pm.

Hotel Sacher, I, Philharmonikerstr. 4 (tel. 512 14 87), around the corner from the main tourist information office. This historic sight has been serving the world-famous *Sacher Torte* (45AS) in red velvet opulence for years. Exceedingly elegant; most everyone is refined and bejeweled. Open 6:30am-midnight.

Café Central, I, at the corner of Herrengasse and Strauchgasse, inside Palais Ferstel. Former patrons include Leon Trotsky, Theodor Herzl, Sigmund Freud—the list goes on. And they serve coffee. Open Mon.-Sat. 9am-8pm.

Café Hawelka, I, Dorotheergasse 6, three blocks west from the Stephansdom. Incredible *buchteln* (sweet dumplings filed with preserves, 25AS, served only after 10pm). Coffee 30-40AS. Open Mon., Wed.-Sat. 8am-2am, Sun. 4pm-2am.

Café Drechsler, VI, Linke Wienzeille 22 (tel. 587 85 80). By Karlspl., where Operngasse meets Linke Wienzeille. *The* place to be the morning after the night before. Early birds and night owls roost over pungent cups of *mokka*. Open Mon.-Sat. 4am-8pm.

Café Willendorf, VI, Linke Wienzeile 102, in the Rosa Lila Villa (tel. 587 17 89). A café, bar, and restaurant with an outdoor terrace that attracts a mainly gay and lesbian clientele. Open 7pm-2am.

SIGHTS

Vienna from A to Z (30AS from the tourist office, more in bookstores) gives all you need for a self-created tour. The free *Museums* brochure from the tourist office lists all opening hours and admission prices. Individual museum tickets usually cost 15AS; 150AS will buy you a book of 14.

Ecclesiastic and Imperial Vienna

Start your odyssey at the Gothic **Stephansdom** (U-1 or U-3: Stephansplatz). The smoothly tapering stone lace spire of this magnificent cathedral has become Vienna's emblem, appearing on every second postcard. (Tours in English Mon.-Sat. 10:30am and 3pm, Sun. and holidays 3pm; 30AS. June-Aug. spectacular evening tour Sat. 7pm; 100AS.) View Vienna from the **Nordturm** (North Tower; open 9am-5:30pm; elevator ride 30AS).

The enormous Hofburg rising southeast of the **Michaelerplatz** was home to the Habsburg emperors until 1918, and is currently the Austrian president's office. Wander through the *Burggarten* (Gardens of the Imperial Palace), *Schweizerhof* (Swiss Courtyard), the *Schatzkammer* (treasuries), the *Burgkapelle* (chapel, where the Vienna Boys' Choir sings Mass on Sun. and religious holidays), the *Neue Burg* (New Palace, now the *Kunsthistorisches Museum*—see Museums, below), built from 1881-1913, and the *Schauräume* (state rooms; open Mon.-Sat. 8:30am-noon and 12:30-4pm, tours 40AS, students 20AS.) Between Josefsplatz and Michaelerplatz, the Palace Stables *(Stallburg)* are home to the Royal Lipizzaner stallions of the **Spanische Reitschule** (Spanish Riding School). Performances (April-June and Sept. Sun. at 10:45am and Wed. at 7pm; March and Nov. to mid-Dec. Sun. at 10:45am) are always sold out; you must reserve tickets six months in advance. Write to Spanische Reitschule, Hofburg, A-1010 Wien. Write only for reservations; don't send money (tickets 200-600AS, standing-room 150AS). Watching the horses train is much cheaper. (March-June and Nov. to mid-Dec. Tues.-Sat. 10am-noon; Feb. Mon.-Sat. 10am-noon, except when the horses tour. Tickets sold at door at Josefsplatz, Gate 2, from about 8:30am. 50AS, children 15AS. No reservations.)

Fin-de-Siècle, Cosmopolitan Vienna, Outside the Ring

Hofburg's Heldenplatz gate presides over the northeastern side of the Burgring segment of the **Ringstraße.** In 1857, Emperor Franz Josef commissioned this 187-foot-wide and 2½-mile-long boulevard to replace the city walls that separated Vienna's center from the suburban districts. Follow Burgring west through the **Volksgarten's** ocean of roses to reach the neoclassical, sculpture-adorned **Parliament** building. Just up Dr.-Karl-Renner-Ring is the **Rathaus,** a remnant of late 19th-century neo-Gothic with Victorian mansard roofs and red geraniums in the windows. The **Burgtheater** opposite contains frescoes by Klimt. Immediately to the north on Dr.-Karl-Lueger-Ring is the **Universität.** The surrounding side streets gush cafés, bookstores, and bars.

Kärntner Straße connects Stephansdom to the **Staatsoper** (State Opera House). During the summer, street music fills the air with everything from Peruvian folk to Bob Dylan to Schubert. If you miss the shows (standing-room tickets 15-20AS) at the Opera House, tour the glittering gold, crystal, and red velvet interior (featured in the movie *Amadeus* and once home to Mahler's skilled conducting; tours 11am-3pm on the hour; Sept.-June on request; 40AS, students 25AS). Alfred Hrdlicka's poignant 1988 sculpture **Mahnmal Gegen Krieg und Faschismus** (Memorial Against War and Fascism), behind the opera in the Albertinapl., memorializes the suffering of Austria's people—especially its Jews—during World War II.

Music lovers trek out to the **Zentralfriedhof** (Central Cemetery), XI, Simmeringer Hauptstr. 234, where Beethoven, Wolf, the Strausses, and Schönberg are buried. Take tram #71 (open May-July 7am-7pm; Sept.-Oct. and March-April 7am-6pm; Nov.-Feb. 8am-5pm). One of the more unforgettable buildings in Vienna is the **Hundert-wasser Haus,** at the corner of Löwenstr. and Kegelgasse in the third district, a municipal housing project named for the artist who designed it in 1983. The structure is a wild fantasia of pastel colors, ceramic mosaics, and tilted tile columns.

The **Schloß Schönbrunn** and surrounding gardens encompass 1.6 sq. km of glorious space. The former Habsburg summer residence holds the **Wagenburg** (coach collection), displaying the coronation carriage and imperial hearse. Inside, the **Bergl** rooms have frescoes of peacocks perched on rose bushes. (Apartments open 8:30am-5:30pm; Nov.-March 8:30am-5pm; admission 80AS, tours available in English. Wagenburg open 9am-6pm, April and Oct. 9am-5pm, Nov.-March 10am-4pm; admission 30AS.)

MUSEUMS

On the Burgring in what used to be the *Neue Hofburg* is **Kunsthistorisches Museum,** home to one of the world's best art collections, including entire rooms of prime Brueghels, Vermeer's *Allegory of Painting,* and numerous works by Rembrandt, Rubens, Titian, Dürer, and Velázquez. Cellini's famous golden salt cellar is here, along with a superb collection of ancient art and a transplanted Egyptian burial chamber. Gustav Klimt decorated the lobby. (Picture gallery open Tues.-Wed., Fri.-Sun. 10am-6pm, Thurs. 10am-9pm. Egyptian and Near-Eastern, Greek and Roman, and sculpture collections open Tues.-Sun. 10am-6pm. 95 AS students 45AS.) Fans of Klimt and his fellow radicals, Egon Schiele and the always colorful Oskar Kokoschka, should visit the **Austrian Gallery,** in the **Belvedere Palace,** entrance at Prinz-Eugen-Str. 27. Check out the *Biedermeier* paintings and the view of the city from the upper floors (open Tues.-Sun. 10am-5pm; admission 60AS, students 30AS).

Kunst Haus Wien, III, Untere Weißgerberstr. 13, built for the works of Hundert-wasser, is one of his greatest works in and of itself. The crazily-pastiched building also hosts international contemporary exhibits (open 10am-7pm; hundertwasser exhibition 60AS, students 44AS). **Historisches Museum der Stadt Vienna** (Historical Museum of the City of Vienna), IV, Karlspl. 5, to the left of the Karlskirche houses collection of historical artifacts and paintings that document the city's evolution from the Roman Vindobona encampment through 640 years of Habsburg rule to the present (open Tues.-Sun. 9am-4:30pm; 30AS).

The greatest monument of *fin-de-siècle* Vienna is the **Secession Building,** I, Friedrichstr. 12, built by Wagner's pupil Josef Maria Olbrich to accommodate the artists, led by Gustav Klimt, who scorned historical style and broke with the Viennese art establishment. Olbrich's ivory-and-gold reaction against the overblown neoclassicism of the Ring museums now exhibits contemporary art, including Klimt's 30m *Beethoven Frieze.* Inscribed above the door: *Der Zeit, ihre Kunst, der Kunst, ihre Freiheit* (to the age, its art; to art, its freedom; open Tues.-Fri. 10am-6pm, Sat.-Sun. 10am-4pm; admission 30AS, students 15AS). The **Künstlerhaus,** from which the Secession seceded, is to the east at Karlsplatz 5. The entrance to Vienna's conservative museum is guarded by statues of Old Masters.

For more of the art nouveau movement, visit the **Österreichisches Museum für Angewandte Kunst** (Museum of Applied Art), I, Stubenring 5, the oldest museum of applied arts in Europe. Otto Wagner furniture and Klimt sketches pose amid crystal, china, furniture, and rugs from the Middle Ages to now (open Tues.-Wed. and Fri.-Sun. 10am-6pm, Thurs. 10am-9pm; admission 90AS, students 45AS). Unmissable creations are Otto Wagner's **Pavilion** at Karlsplatz, the major U-Bahn station, his

Kirche am Steinhof, 1140 Baumgartner Höhe 1 (take bus #48a to the end of the line), and his **Postsparkassenamt** (post office savings bank), on the Postgasse.

ENTERTAINMENT

Music and Theater

You can enjoy Viennese opera in the imperial splendor of the **Staatsoper** (State Opera House) for a mere 15-35AS. Queue up on the west side about 3:30-4pm for standing room (*Stehplätze*, sold only on day of performance, 15AS balcony, 20AS orchestra). Get tickets for the center; you see nothing standing at the side. Bring a scarf to tie on the rail to save your place during the show. Costlier advance tickets (100-850AS) are on sale at the **Bundestheaterkassen,** I, Goethegasse (tel. 514 44 22 18; open Mon.-Fri. 8am-6pm, Sat. 9am-2pm, Sun. 9am-noon). Students with ID (not ISIC) can buy unsold seats ½hr. before curtain. They also sell tickets for Vienna's other public theaters: the **Volksoper, Burgtheater,** and **Akademietheater.** Discount tickets for these go at the door an hour before performances (50-400AS). The **Wiener Philharmoniker** (Vienna Philharmonic Orchestra) is world-renowned, performing in the **Musikverein,** I, Dumbastr. 3, on the northeast side of Karlsplatz.

Even the most musical of cities wanes somewhat in summer; the **Staatsoper** and the **Wiener Sängerknaben** (Vienna Boys' Choir) vacation during July and August. During the rest of the year, the pre-pubescent prodigies sing 9:15am mass each Sunday at the **Burgkapelle** (Royal Chapel) of the Hofburg. Reserve tickets (50-250AS) at least two months in advance from Verwaltung der Hofmusikkapelle, Hofburg, Schweizerhof, A-1010 Wien. Do not enclose money. Unreserved seats are sold starting at 5pm on the preceding Friday. Standing room is free. Heavenly choral or organ music accompanies Sunday High Masses in major churches (Augustinerkirche, Michaelerkirche, Stephansdom).

The **Theater an der Wien,** VI, Linke Wienzeile 6 (tel. 58 03 02 65), opens with musicals in July (performances 7:30pm; 100-990AS), and the **Wiener Kammeroper** (Chamber Opera) performs during the summer in Schönbrunner Schloßpark (tickets 50-350AS). Consult the monthly *Programm* at the tourist office.

English-language drama is offered at **Vienna's English Theatre,** VIII, Josefsgasse 12 (tel. 402 12 60 or 42 82 84; box office open Mon.-Sat. 10am-6pm, evening box office opens at 7pm; tickets 150-420AS, students 100AS on night of performance). If you still yearn to hear more English, head to the **International Theater,** IX Porzellangasse 8 (tel. 31 62 72; tickets 220AS, students under 26 120AS).

Heurigen

Uniquely Viennese, *Heurigen* (outside seating at picnic tables, with mugs of wine hung over the door) began when Emperor Joseph II, in a fit of largesse, allowed the local wine-growers to sell and serve their wine in their homes at certain times of year. The worn picnic benches and old shade trees provide an ideal spot to contemplate, converse, or listen to *schrammelmusik* (sentimental, wine-lubricated folk songs played by the aged musicians of the *Heurige*). Once upon a time, patrons brought picnics with them. Today's *Heurige* serves simple, inexpensive buffets of grilled chicken, salads, and pretzels. In mid-summer, sweet but potent *Stürm* (cloudy, unpasteurized wine) is available. The word for "dry" is *trocken*. After the Feast of the Martins on November 11, wine from last year's crop becomes "old wine," no longer proper to serve in the *heurigen*; the Viennese do their best to spare it this fate by consuming Herculean quantities before time's up.

Heurigen freckle the northern, western, and southern suburbs, where grapes are grown. **Grinzing** is the largest *Heurigen* area, but atmosphere and prices are better in **Nußdorf** (tram D from the Ring), in **Sievering, Neustift am Wald** and in **Stammersdorf.** Hidden from tourists and beloved by locals, **Buschenschank Heinrich Niersche,** XIX, Strehlgasse 21, overlooks the field of Grinzing. (Take bus #41A from the U-6: Währingerstraße/Volksoper to Pötzleindorfer Höhe; walk one block and turn left on Strehlgasse. Open Thurs.-Mon. 3pm-midnight.) The tourist office has a list of *Heurigen*. Most are open 4pm to midnight; wine costs about 30AS per mug.

NIGHTLIFE

Rock me, Amadeus. The city parties until dawn, though public transportation closes at midnight. An extensive club scene every night; the door game is minimal, and the cover charges reasonable. *Falter* has opera schedules and club theme nights. Revellers lose themselves in the notorious **Bermuda Dreieck** (Triangle), a collection of about thirty bars crammed into an area northwest of Stephanspl. bordered by Rotenturmstr. and Wipplingerstr. The action moves indoors at 10pm, until 2am or even 4am. The area around the U-3: Stubentor station is another stomping ground of the hip, as is the region surrounding **Bäckerstraße** behind the Stephansdom and the **8th District** behind the university.

Zwölf Apostellenkeller, I, Sonnenfelsgasse 3, behind the *Stephansdom* (tel. 52 62 77). Walk into the archway, take a right, go down the long staircase, and discover grottoes that date back to 1561. One of the best *Weinkeller* in Vienna, the underground tavern is a must for catacomb fans. The lowest level is the liveliest. Beer 34AS. *Viertel* of wine starts at 25AS. Open Aug.-June 4:30pm-midnight.

Santo Spirito, I, Kampfgasse 7 (tel. 512 99 98). From Stephanspl., walk down Singerstr. and turn left onto Kumpfgasse (5min.). The stereo pumps out Rachmaninoff while excited patrons co-conduct. Open 6pm until people leave.

Jazzland, I, Franz-Josefs-Kai 29 (tel. 533 25 75). U-1, U-4: Schwedenplatz. Jazz music—Austrian style. Excellent live music filters into soothingly cool grottoes. Hefty cover 120-200AS. Open Tues.-Sat. 7pm-2am. Music 9pm-1am.

Fischerbräu, XIX, Billrothstr. 17 (tel. 31 962 64). A rare Viennese beer garden. Stained and lacquered hardwood interior and the leafy garden outside. Open Mon.-Sat. 4pm-1am, Sun. 11am-1am.

Tunnel, VIII, Florianigasse 39 (tel. 42 34 65). Frequented by students for the bohemian, Euro-chic atmosphere, and live music in the cellar (from 8:30pm, cover 30-100AS, Mon. free). Upper level holds a regular bar/restaurant. Open 9am-2am.

P1, I, Rotgasse 9, (tel. 535 99 95). From the Stephansdom, head down Rotenturm, left on Fleischmarkt, and left on Rotgasse. A younger crowd dances the night away to assortments of house, hip-hop, and acid jazz. Cover 50-100AS. Open Sun.-Thurs. 9pm-4am, Fri.-Sat. 9pm-6am.

Volksgarten, I, Burgring/Heldenpl. (tel. 63 05 18). Nestled on the edge of the Volksgarten Park, near the Hofburg. Wallflowers watch the Viennese shake their *hinter* from comfy red couches. Open-air bar after midnight. Students enter free and nosh the free buffet on Tues. Cover 70AS, students 60AS. Open 10pm-5am.

Café Berg, IX, Berggasse 8 (tel. 319 57 20). A mixed gay café/bar at night. Casual hang-out by day. Open 10am-1am.

■ Trieste, Italy

US$1	= L1587 (lire)	L1000 =	US$0.63
CDN$1	= L1161	L1000 =	CDN$0.86
UK£1	= L2490	L1000 =	UK£0.40
IR£1	= L2444	L1000 =	IR£0.41
AUS$1	= L1182	L1000 =	AUS$0.85
NZ$1	= L863	L1000 =	NZ$1.16
SAR1	= L447	L1000 =	SAR2.24
DM1	= L1033	10AS =	DM0.97
Country Code: 39		**International Dialing Prefix: 00**	

GATEWAY CITIES

The unofficial capital of Friuli-Venezia Giulia lies at the end of a narrow strip of land sandwiched between Slovenia and the Adriatic. Given its strategically placed harbor and proximity to Austrian and former Yugoslavian borders, Trieste has been a bone of contention over the centuries. Even as an independent city from the 9th to 15th centuries, and Venice's main rival in the Adriatic until La Serenissima overtook it, Trieste was always coveted by the Habsburgs. Austria finally got its crack at a real Adriatic port in the post-Napoleonic real estate market, and proceeded to rip the medieval heart from Trieste, replacing it with neo-Classical bombast.

The mix of political intrigue and coffee-culture elegance brought by the Austro-Hungarian Empire attracted various intellectuals to turn-of-the-century Friuli: James Joyce lived in Trieste for 12 years, during which he wrote the bulk of *Ulysses;* Ernest Hemingway's *A Farewell to Arms* draws part of its plot from the region's role in World War I; Freud and Rilke both worked and wrote here. The mixture of Slovenian, Friulian, and Italian peoples has produced an indigenous literary tradition of its own, which includes Italo Svevo and the poet Umberto Saba.

The heavy-handed style of government brought by the Habsburgs succeeded in turning the mostly Italian population into fervent *irredentisti* clamoring for the return of the vaguely Italian province to Italy. They emerged victorious in 1918 when Italian troops occupied the Friuli, but unification only brought more trouble: Mussolini's thicket of fascist statuary provided appropriate counterpoint to the Austro-Hungarian architecture, while his policies of cultural chauvinism offended anyone not already alienated by the Habsburg rulers.

Today, evidence of Trieste's multinational history lingers in the numerous buildings and monuments of Habsburg origin and the Slavic nuances in the local cuisine. The city's Italian identity, on the other hand, is vehemently asserted by the persistence of fascist and anti-Slav parties, and more tangibly in the formidable **Piazza Unità d'Italia**, the largest piazza in Italy.

To venture deeper into the country, snag a copy of *Let's Go: Italy.*

GETTING THERE AND GETTING AROUND

The **Ferrovie dello Stato (FS),** the Italian State Railway, runs on time, more or less, and its network is comprehensive. A *locale* stops at nearly every station; the *diretto* is more direct, while the *espresso* stops only at major stations. The *rapido* zips along but costs a bit more (Eurailpass and BTLC holders exempt). The *Biglietto Chilometrico* (Kilometric Ticket) is good for 20 trips or 3000km, whichever comes first, and can be used for two months by up to five people. (first class US$264, second class US$156, plus US$10 per pass.) If you have no railpass and are under 26, the **cartaverde** (L40,000, good for 3 years) entitles you to a 20% discount on rail tickets.

Intercity **buses** are often more convenient for shorter hauls off the main rail lines, and they serve countryside points inaccessible by train. The relatively uncrowded *autostrade* (super-highways) are gorgeous celebrations of engineering, but gas and tolls are prohibitive, and Italian drivers tend to be crazed speed demons. **Bicycling** is a popular national sport but bike trails are rare, drivers often reckless, and, except in the Po Valley, the terrain challenges even the fittest. **Women traveling alone should never hitchhike.** Italian men have earned their sullied reputation. Even for men, *Let's Go* does not recommend hitchhiking as a safe means of transportation.

LANGUAGE

Any knowledge of Spanish, French, Portuguese, or Latin will help you understand Italian. Most tourist office staff speak at least some English. If your conversation partner speaks Italian too quickly, ask her or him to *rallenta* (rah-LEN-ta; "slow down"). Useful phrases include: *Quanto costa* (KWAN-toe CO-stah; "How much does it cost?"); *Dov'è* (doh-VAY; "Where is...?"); *Che ore sono* (Kay oreh SO-no; "What time is it?"); *Non capisco* (non cah-PEE-sko; "I don't understand"); *Grazie* (GRAHT-zeeyeh; "Thank you") and *Il conto, per favore* (ill KON-to pehr fah-VO-reh; "The bill, please").

GATEWAY CITIES

ORIENTATION AND PRACTICAL INFORMATION

Trieste is a direct train ride from Venice or Udine, and several trains and buses cross over daily to neighboring Slovenia and Croatia. Less frequent ferry service runs the length of the Istrian Peninsula. The gray, industrialized quays catering to ferries and fishermen taper off into Trieste's equivalent of a beach—a stretch of tiered concrete, populated with bronzed bodies, which runs 7km from the edge of town out to the castle at Miramare. Moving inland one encounters **Piazza Oberdan,** which opens onto the ever-busy **Via Carducci.** Shopping sprees are common on the fashion-oriented streets that intersect with this central artery near P. Goldoni. The artistically inclined can head to the pride and glory of Trieste, **Piazza Unità d'Italia,** which looks out to the harbor. Public transportation runs throughout the city, and most buses stop in the immediate vicinity of the train station.

Tourist Office: In the train station (tel. 42 01 82), to the right before exiting the station. Copious information on Trieste including a list of *manifestazioni* (cultural events) occasionally encompassing international programs as well. For cheap accommodations also ask about staying at private homes. English spoken. Open Mon.-Fri. 9am-7pm, Sat. 8:30am-1:30pm. Another branch is located in the **Castello di San Giusto** (tel. 30 92 98).

Budget Travel: CTS, P. Dalmazia, 3 (tel. 36 18 79). Agency for air and train tickets plus a variety of other vacation information. Open Mon.-Fri. 9am-1pm and 1:30-7pm. **Aurora Viaggia,** Via Milano, 20 (tel. 63 02 61), one block from Via Carducci. Information on transportation and lodging in former Yugoslavian territory. Open Mon.-Fri. 9am-12:30pm and 4-7pm, Sat. 9am-noon.

Consulates: The **U.S.** no longer has a consulate here, but it does have an honorary representative at Via Roma, 15 (tel. 66 01 77). Ask for Sig. Bearz. Otherwise try the consulate in Milan. **U.K.,** Vicolo delle Ville, 16 (tel. 30 28 84), available Tues. and Fri. 9am-12:30pm. The closest **Canadian** and **Australian** consulates are in Milan. **New Zealand, Irish,** and **South African** citizens should contact their embassy in Rome. To check on the current state of visa requirements for travel east, contact **Slovenia,** Via Carducci, 29, (tel. 63 61 61), or **Croatia** in Rome, Via Santi Cosma e Damiano, 26 (tel. (06) 33 25 02 42).

Currency Exchange: Banca d'America e d'Italia, Via Roma, 7 (tel. 63 19 25). Cash advances on Visa cards. Open Mon.-Fri. 8:20am-1:20pm and 2:35-3:50pm. Also try **Assomar Cambio** in the bus station in P. della Libertà (tel. 42 53 07). Open daily 7:30am-8pm. No commission.

Post Office: P. Vittorio Veneto, 1 (tel. 36 67 42), from the train station, take the second right off Via Ghega onto Via Roma. **Poste Restante** (*Fermo Posta*) at counter #21, stamps at #30. **Fax** downstairs. Open Mon.-Sat. 8am-7:30pm. **Postal Code:** 34100.

Telephones: SIP, Viale XX Settembre, 5. Open Mon.-Sun. 7:50am-8pm. Another office at P. Oberdan. Open Mon.-Fri. 8:30am-noon and 2-3:50pm. **ASST,** Via Pascoli, 9, off P. Garibaldi. Open 24 hrs. **City Code:** 040. For **directory assistance,** tel. 12. There are three types of phones in Italy. Dark-age phones take only tokens (*gettoni*), available for L200 from machines in bus and train stations. (One *gettone* per 5min.) *Scatti* calls are made from a phone run by an operator. A meter records the cost of the call, and you pay when you finish. Check first for a service fee. The most common type of phone accepts either coins or **phone cards** (L5000 or L10,000 from machines). For **AT&T USADirect,** use your phone card or deposit L200 (which will be returned), then tel. 172 10 11; **MCI WorldPhone** 172 10 12; **Sprint Express** 172 18 77; **Canada Direct** 172 10 01; **BT Direct** (U.K.) 172 00 44; **Ireland Direct** 172 03 53; **Australia Direct** 172 10 61; **New Zealand Direct** 172 10 64; **SA Direct** (South Africa) 172 10 27.

Trains: P. della Libertà (tel. 41 82 07), down Via Cavour from the quays. Train info open daily 8:30am-12:30pm and 3:30-6:30pm. To: Udine (15 per day, 1½hrs.; L6700); Venice (16 per day, 2hrs.; L12,700); Milan (1 per day, 5½-7½hrs.; L31,200); Ljubljana (6 per day, 3½hrs.; L15,000); Budapest (1 or more per day, L71,000).

Buses: Corso Cavour (tel. 336 03 00), in the fringe of P. della Libertà near the train station. To: Udine (8 per day, L6200); Rijeka/Fiume (2 per day, L11,400). There are also several smaller lines that run throughout the region. Check at the station.

Public Transportation: ACT, Via d'Alviano, 15 (tel. 779 51). Open Mon.-Fri. 9am-1pm.

Ferries: Agemar Viaggi, P. Duca degli Abruzzi, 1/A (tel. 36 37 37; fax 777 23), by the waterfront next to the canal. Will arrange trips with **Adriatica di Navigazione** and provide the latest visa requirements for entering the former Yugoslavia. To: Grado (15min., L9500); Lignano (1¼hrs., L11,000); Rovigno (3hrs. 10min., L31,500); Pirano (1½hrs., L14,500); Umago (2½hrs., L22,500). Office open Mon.-Fri. 8:30am-1pm and 3-7:30pm.

Taxis: tel. 545 33 or 30 77 30.

Car Rental: Hertz, in the bus station, P. della Libertà (tel. 42 21 22; fax 41 89 46). Open Mon.-Fri. 8:30am-12:30pm and 3-6:30pm, Sat. 8:30am-12:30pm. Another office at the airport (tel. 77 70 25). **Avis,** also in the bus station (tel. 77 70 85). Open Mon.-Fri. 8am-12:30pm and 3:30-7pm, Sat. 8am-noon. Rates at all around L150,000 per day.

Luggage Storage: In the bus and train stations (L1500). Train station office open daily 5am-midnight; bus station office open daily 6:20am-8pm.

Bookstore: Libreria Cappeli, Corso Italia, 12B (tel. 63 04 14). English books (in the back right corner) and travel guides. Open Tues.-Sat. 8:30am-12:30pm and 3:30-7:30pm. AmEx, Diner's Club, Visa.

Laundromat: Via Ginnastica, 36 (tel. 36 74 14). Coin-operated. Open Tues.-Fri. 8am-1pm and 3:30-7pm, Sat. 8am-1pm.

Swimming Pool: Piscina Communale "Bruno Bianchi," Riva Gulli, 3 (tel. 30 60 24), along the waterfront. Indoor. Open Oct.-July, Mon.-Sat. noon-3pm, Sun. 9am-1pm. L5000. Lockers L1500.

Late-Night Pharmacies: tel. 192. Insert three telephone tokens.

Emergencies: tel. 113. **Police:** Via del Teatro Romano (tel. 379 01), off Corso Italia. **Hospital: Ospedale Maggiore,** P. dell'Ospedale (tel. 77 61), up Via Tarabocchia from Via Carducci. **Ambulance:** tel. 118.

ACCOMMODATIONS AND CAMPING

Associazione Italiana Alberghi per la Gioventù (AIG), the Italian **hostel** federation, operates youth hostels *(ostelli Italiani)* across the country, especially in the north. A complete list is available from most EPT and CTS offices and from many hostels.

The **hotel** industry is rigorously controlled in Italy; prices are set not by owners but by the state. Under Italian law all guests must be registered by passport on a special form; check the room *first,* and then don't be afraid to hand the passport over for a while (usually overnight), but ask for it as soon as you think you will need it. By law, the price must be posted on the door of each room; if it isn't, get it in writing from the management. It's illegal to charge more than what's posted. Always check to see if tax (IVA), breakfast, and shower privileges are included and/or mandatory. For doubles, specify *doppia* (two beds) or a *letto matrimoniale* (double bed).

Watch out for weekdays, when companies often fill up the smaller *pensioni* with workers. Consult the tourist office, which leaves a helpful list of Trieste's hotels and *pensioni* taped to the door for those who arrive after hours.

Ostello Tegeste (HI), Viale Miramare, 331 (tel. 22 41 02). From station take bus #36 (L1200). You'll find the bus stop #36 on Viale Miramare, the street to the left of the station. The hostel is located on the seaside, just down from the castle Miramare, about 6km from the city center. Get off of the bus just before it starts heading up the hill. Also look out for signs to the castle. There is a popular garden bar at the hostel and the view over the sea back towards town is terrific. Live bands play here periodically; other times loud recorded American music fills the air. Average of 4 bunks per room. Personal lockers with locks provided free of charge after 6pm. HI members only. Reception open noon-11:30pm. Checkout 9:30am. Lockout 9:30am-noon. Curfew 11:30pm. L17,000 includes hot showers and

breakfast. Also serves lunch and dinner *(menù* L13,000, though you can eat 1 or
2 courses for less). Call or write ahead to reserve a bed during suntanning season.

Centrale, Via Ponchielli, 1 (tel. 63 94 82). Located centrally, as the name suggests,
right off the canal. Large yet standard 1-star hotel rooms. Clean, no frills. Singles
L30,000, with bath L45,000. Doubles L50,000, with shower L54,000, with bath
L65,000. Triples L73,000. Showers L3000.

Julia, Via XXX Ottobre, 5 (tel. 37 00 45), up two flights. Big, well-lit rooms with
shower, sink and toilet. Singles L29,000. Doubles with bath L46,000.

Centro, Via Roma, 13 (tel. 63 44 08 or 37 11 16). Downtown. Small rooms with
high ceilings. Singles L30,000. Doubles L55,000. Triples L73,000.

Camping: Camping Marepineta (tel. 29 92 64), along the coast, SS #14, provides
beachside luxury. L5000-9500 per person, L8500-19,000 per tent and L5000 per
car (or any sort of camper). Hot water, electricity, and a bar included. Open May-
Sept. Located in Sistiana; buses leave for Sistiana from the terminal every hour
(L2500). Alongside the campground is a charming 2km trail billed as the **Rilke
Sentiere** after the poet Rilke, who lived in **Duino,** the village at the other end of
the trail. Duino presides over the haunting ruins of the **Duino castle** (open by
reservation only; tel. 20 81 20).

Camping: Camping Obelisco, Strada Nuova Opicina, SS #58 (tel. 21 16 55), is
7km from Trieste in Opicina, a suburb on the rocky *carso*—a beautiful place to
camp for those not umbilically attached to the beach. Fewer facilities than Marepineta, and lower prices. L4000-5500 per person, L7000-10,000 per tent, light
L1500. Trains leave frequently from the station (L2800), or take the tram from P.
Oberdan (L1500).

FOOD

"Mangia, mangia!" The production, preparation, and loving consumption of food
are all close to the core of Italian culture. A full meal consists of an *antipasto* (appetizer), a *primo piatto* (pasta or soup), a *secondo piatto,* meat or fish with a vegetable *(contorno),* and usually salad, fruit, and/or cheese. Coffee is another focus of
Italian life. *Espresso* is meant to be quaffed quickly. *Cappuccino,* a mixture of
espresso and hot, frothy milk, is the normal breakfast beverage. *Caffè macchiato*
("spotted") is *espresso* with a touch of milk, while *latte macchiato* is milk with a
splash of coffee. *Caffè corretto* ("corrected"), is *espresso* spiked with liqueur.

Starting with the delicate white *Asti Spumante* from Piedmont and *Soave* from
Verona, Italian local wines get rougher and earthier as you proceed south, although
there are several exceptions. Italian beer leaves something to be desired. Drink *Per-
oni* or *Würher* only if there are no imports in sight. Try *grappa,* the gut-wrenching
liqueur of the Veneto flavored with various fruits, and Roman *sambuca,* a sweet
anise concoction served flaming, with coffee beans floating on top. Sitting down at
a table in bars doubles the price of anything you order.

Italy's greatest contribution to civilization is *gelato* (ice cream). Look for the
produzione propria (homemade) sign. Also delicious on hot summer days are
granite ("Italian ices") and *frullati* (cool fruit shakes), both guaranteed to please.

Many dishes in Trieste's restaurants have Eastern European overtones (usually
Hungarian) and are often loaded with paprika. The city is renowned for its fish; try
sardoni in savor (large sardines marinated in oil and garlic). Monday is a non-day in
Trieste: many shops and restaurants close. Sit-down establishments charge *pane e
coperto* (a bread and cover charge), with luck not much more than L1500-2500.
Check whether service is included *(servizio compreso).*

To fend for yourself, visit one of the several **alimentari** on Via Carducci or try
Supercoop on Via Palestrina, 3, at Via Francesco (open Mon. and Wed. 8am-1pm,
Tues. and Thurs.-Sat. 8am-1pm and 5-7:30pm). If you're near the waterfront, go to
Supermercato Despar across from the public pool (open Mon.-Fri. 8:30am-1:30pm
and Tues. and Thurs.-Fri. 4:30-7:30pm, Sat. 8:30am-7:30pm). While in town, sample
a bottle of **Terrano del Carso,** a dry red wine with a low alcohol content that has
been valued for its therapeutic properties since the days of ancient Rome. To pur-

chase grapes in their unadulterated form, stroll through the open-air **market** in P. Ponterosso, by the canal (open Tues.-Sat. 8am-5:30pm).

Paninoteca Da Livio, Via della Ginnastica, 3/B (tel. 63 64 46), inland off Via Carducci. Small, smoky shop boasts monster *panini* (L2500-7000) and dozens of brands of beer. Usually crowded with customers. Open Mon.-Sat. 9am-3pm and 5-10pm. Closed last week of June and first week of July.

Pizzeria Barattolo, P. Sant'Antonio, 2 (tel. 64 14 80), along the canal. Amazing pizza (L6000-13,000). Also bar and *tavola calda* offerings. Open Tues.-Sun. 8am-1am. AmEx, Diner's Club, Eurocard, MC, Visa.

Brek, Via San Francesco, 10 (tel. 73 26 51). Self-service restaurant. Economical, efficient and tasty. Everything is *alla carta* so pick and choose between fresh fruit, wine, pasta and more. *Primi* L3600-4100, *secondi* L9500. Open Sat.-Thurs. 11:30am-2:30pm and 6:30-10:30pm.

SIGHTS

In honor of the Habsburg empress, 19th-century Viennese urban planners carved out a large chunk of Trieste to create Borgo Teresiano, a district of straight avenues bordering the waterfront and the canal. Facing the canal from the south is the district's one beautiful church, the Serbian Orthodox **San Spiridione.** Unfortunately, the church is surrounded by a steel barricade, so you'll have to admire it from afar. The **Municipio** at the head of **Piazza dell'Unità d'Italia,** a monument to the limits of ambition, sags under the weight of its heavy ornamentation and oversized tower. In the corner of the piazza stands an allegorical fountain with statues representing four continents. The surreal effect is completed by the stone warehouses rotting slowly along the waterfront.

The 15th-century Venetian **Castle of San Giusto** presides over **Capitoline Hill,** the city's historic center. You can take bus #24 (L1100) from the station to the last stop at the fortress, and ascend the hill via the daunting **Scala dei Giganti** (Steps of the Giants—all 265 of them) rising from P. Goldoni. It offers a great view of the sea and downtown Trieste, and is a prime sunset-watching spot, if the bora winds don't blow you away. Within the walls is a huge outdoor theater where film festivals are held in July and August (pick up a copy of *Trieste '95, Eventi Luglio-Agosto* at the tourist office). Directly below are the remains of the old Roman city center, and across the street is the restored **Cathedral of San Giusto.** Its irregular plan is due to its origin as two churches built simultaneously from the 5th through 11th centuries, one dedicated to San Giusto, the other to Santa Maria Assunta. Inside are two splendid mosaics in the chapels directly to the left and right of the altar. Walk around the ramparts of the castle (open daily 8am-7pm), or peek into the **museum,** which has temporary exhibits in addition to a permanent collection of weaponry (tel. 31 36 36; open Tues.-Sun. 9am-1pm; admission L2000).

Down the other side of the hill, past the *duomo,* lies the eclectic **Museo di Storia de Arte** and **Orto Lapidario** (Museum of History and Art and Rock Garden), Via Cattedrale 15 (tel. 37 05 00 or 30 86 86), in P. Cattedrale. The museum provides archaeological documentation of the history of Trieste during and preceding its Roman years, and boasts a growing collection of Egyptian art and artifacts from southern Italy (open Tues.-Sun. 9am-1pm; admission L3000, students L1500). Descending the hill towards the ruins of the *Teatro Romano* you end up only a few short blocks from P. Unità d'Italia. The Teatro Romano on Via del Teatro Romano off Corso Italia was built under the auspices of Trajan (1st century BC). Gladiatorial contests were held here; later, spectators enjoyed more killing in the form of Greek tragedies.

An excellent collection of drawings and a less impressive selection of paintings by Tiepolo, Veneziano, and others has been moved from the Capitoline Hill to an elegant 18th-century villa at Largo Papa Giovanni XXIII, 1, which is now the **Museo Sartorio** (tel. 30 14 79). The museum is easily reached by walking a short distance from the center along the quays (open Tues.-Sun. 9am-1pm; admission L3000). Back in the thick of things, stop at the **Museo del Risorgimento,** Via XXIV Maggio, 4 (tel. 36 16 75), in a *palazzo* by Umberto Nordio off P. Oberdan. The museum contains the cell of Guglielmo Oberdan, the 19th-century Irredentist who met his death at the hands of the Austrians in 1882 and posthumously gave his name to the piazza (open Tues.-Sun. 9am-1pm; admission L3000).

ENTERTAINMENT

The regular opera season of the **Teatro Verdi** runs November to May, but a six-week operetta season is held in June and July. Purchase tickets or phone for reservations at P. Verdi, 1 (tel. 36 78 16; open Tues.-Sun. 9am-noon and 4-7pm; seats from L10,000). Inquire at the tourist office about other performances in the **castle** or **Teatro Romano.**

    Caffè Tommaseo, in P. Tommaseo along the canal (closed on Mon.), and **Caffè San Marco,** on Via Battisti, preserve the city's turn-of-the-century coffee culture (the latter frequently offers live music; open Thurs.-Tues. 7am-2am). Coffee in Trieste is an art form, thanks to the influence of the Viennese. It comes to you on a silver platter, with a glass of water and frequently a few sweet pastries (typically L4000-6000). The liveliest *passeggiata* takes place along Viale XX Settembre, a cool and largely traffic-free and *caffé*-lined avenue—a good place to relax in the shade.

■ NEAR TRIESTE

West of Trieste you can sunbathe along the rocky coast and visit the **Castello Miramare** (tel. 22 41 43), the 19th-century Disneyesque castle of Archduke Maximilian of Austria. It was rumored that anyone spending the night here would come to a bad end, a belief helped along by the decision of Archduke Ferdinand to spend the night here on the way to his assassination at Sarajevo. Poised on a high promontory over the gulf, Miramare's white turrets are easily visible from the Capitoline Hill in Trieste or from the train on the journey through the *carso;* its extensive parks are open to the public at no cost. To reach Miramare, take bus #36 (30min., L1200), get off at the hostel stop (see above), and walk along the water. Fortunately, each room has a description and history provided in English. (Castle museum open daily 9am-6pm. Admission L6500, L8000 with tour in Italian. English tours L22,000.) In July and August, a series of **sound and light shows** transforms Miramare into a high-tech playground. (Shows Tues., Thurs., and Sat. at 9:30pm and 10:45pm. The show is in English. Admission L9000. Call the tourist office for more info.)

    Near the castle, a **marine park** (tel. 22 41 47) sponsored by the World Wildlife Fund conducts programs throughout the year, including guided introductions to the coast's marine life. The park is marked by buoys off shore surrounding Castle Miramare. Swimming is not allowed without a guide. Guided water tours (snorkeling and scuba) are offered. (Open Wed. and Fri. Admission L29,000, children L18,000. In Italian only. Reservations required. Office open Mon.-Fri. 9am-7pm, Sat. 9am-5pm. You can also rent snorkel, fins and mask together for L27,000 or separately.)

    About 15km from Trieste in Opicina, you'll find the **Grotta Gigante** (tel. 32 73 12), the world's largest accessible cave. Staircases wind around the 90m-high interior, which the brochure claims could hold the whole of St. Peter's. (Open Tues.-Sat. 9am-noon and 2-7pm, Nov.-Feb. 10am-noon and 2:30-4:30pm. Transportation from P. Oberdan and admission L9000. You can also take bus#45; 5 per day, L1600.)

Index

★ FREE T-SHIRT ★

JUST ANSWER THE QUESTIONS ON THE FOLLOWING PAGES AND MAIL TO:

Attn: Let's Go Survey
St. Martin's Press
175 Fifth Avenue
New York, NY 10010

WE'LL SEND THE FIRST 1,500 RESPONDENTS A LET'S GO T-SHIRT!

(Make sure we can read your address.)

■ LET'S GO 1995 READER ■ QUESTIONNAIRE

1) Name _____

2) Address _____

3) Are you: female   male

4) How old are you?   under 17   17-23   24-30   31-40   41-55   over 55

5) Are you (circle all that apply):   in high school   in college   in grad school
employed   retired   between jobs

6) What is your personal yearly income?
Under $15,000 $15,000 - $25,000 $26,000 - $35,000 $36,000 - $50,000
$51,000 - $75,000 $76,000 - $100,000   over $100,000   not applicable

7) How often do you normally travel
with a guidebook?
This is my first trip
Less than once a year
Once a year
Twice a year
Three times a year or more

8) Which *Let's Go* guide(s) did you buy
for your trip?
_____
_____

9) Have you used *Let's Go* before?
Yes   No

10) How did you first hear about
Let's Go? (Choose one)
Friend or fellow traveler
Recommended by store clerk
Display in bookstore
Ad in newspaper/magazine
Review or article in newspaper/
magazine
Radio

11) Why did you choose *Let's Go*?
(Choose up to three)
Updated every year
Reputation
Easier to find in stores
Better price
"Budget" focus
Writing style
Attitude
Better organization
More comprehensive
Reliability
Better Design/Layout
Candor
Other _____
_____
_____

12) Which of the following guides have
you used, if any?
Frommer's $-a-Day
Fodor's Affordable Guides
Rough Guides/Real Guides
Berkeley Guides/On the Loose
Lonely Planet
None of the above

13) Is *Let's Go* the best guidebook?
Yes
No (which is?) _____
Haven't used other guides

14) When did you buy this book?
Jan   Feb   Mar   Apr   May   Jun
Jul   Aug   Sep   Oct   Nov   Dec

15) When did you travel with this
book? (Circle all that apply)
Jan   Feb   Mar   Apr   May   Jun
Jul   Aug   Sep   Oct   Nov   Dec

16) How long was your trip?
1 week   2 weeks
3 weeks   1 month
2 months   over 2 months

17) Where did you spend most of your
time on this trip? (Circle one)
cities   small towns   rural areas

18) How many travel companions did
you have?   0 1 2 3 4 over 4

19) Roughly how much did you spend
per day on the road?
$0-15 $51-70
$16-30 $71-100
$31-50 $101-150
over $150

20) What was the purpose of your trip?
(Circle all that apply)

Pleasure	Business
Study	Volunteer
Work/internship	

21) What were the main attractions of your trip? (Circle top three)
Sightseeing
New culture
Learning Language
Meeting locals
Camping/Hiking
Sports/Recreation
Nightlife/Entertainment
Meeting other travelers
Hanging Out
Food
Shopping
Adventure/Getting off the beaten path

22) How reliable/useful are the following features of *Let's Go*?
v = very, u = usually, s = sometimes
n = never, ? = didn't use

Accommodations	v u s n ?
Camping	v u s n ?
Food	v u s n ?
Entertainment	v u s n ?
Sights	v u s n ?
Maps	v u s n ?
Practical Info	v u s n ?
Directions	v u s n ?
"Essentials"	v u s n ?
Cultural Intros	v u s n ?

23) On the list above, please circle the top 3 features you used the most.

24) Would you use *Let's Go* again?
Yes
No (why not?) _____
_____

25) Do you generally buy a phrasebook when you visit a foreign destination?
Yes   No

26) Do you generally buy a separate map when you visit a foreign city?
Yes   No

27) Which of the following destinations are you planning to visit as a tourist in the next five years?
(Circle all that apply)

Australia	Hong Kong
New Zealand	Vietnam
Indonesia	Malaysia
Japan	Singapore
China	India

Nepal	U.S. Nat'l Parks
Middle East	Rocky Mtns.
Israel	The South
Egypt	New Orleans
Africa	Florida
Turkey	Mid-Atlantic
Greece	States
Scandinavia	Boston/New
Portugal	England
Spain	The Midwest
Switzerland	Chicago
Austria	The Southwest
Berlin	Texas
Russia	Arizona
Poland	Colorado
Czech/Slovak	Los Angeles
Rep.	San Francisco
Hungary	Seattle
Baltic States	Hawaii
Caribbean	Alaska
Central America	Canada
Costa Rica	British Columbia
South America	Montreal/Que-
Ecuador	bec
Brazil	Maritime Prov-
Venezuela	inces
Colombia	

28) Please circle the destinations you visited on your trip:

Albania	Belarus	Berlin
Bulgaria	Croatia	Estonia
Czech Rep.	Hungary	Latvia
Lithuania	Macedonia	Moldova
Poland	Romania	Russia
Slovakia	Slovenia	Trieste
Ukraine	Vienna	

29) What other countries did you visit on your trip? _____
_____

30) How did you get around on your trip?

Car	Train	Plane
Bus	Ferry	Hitching
Bicycle	Motorcycle	

31) Which of these do you own?
(Circle all that apply)

| Computer | CD-ROM |
| Modem | On-line Service |

Mail this to:
Attn: Let's Go Survey
St. Martin's Press
175 Fifth Avenue
New York, NY 10010

Thanks For Your Help!

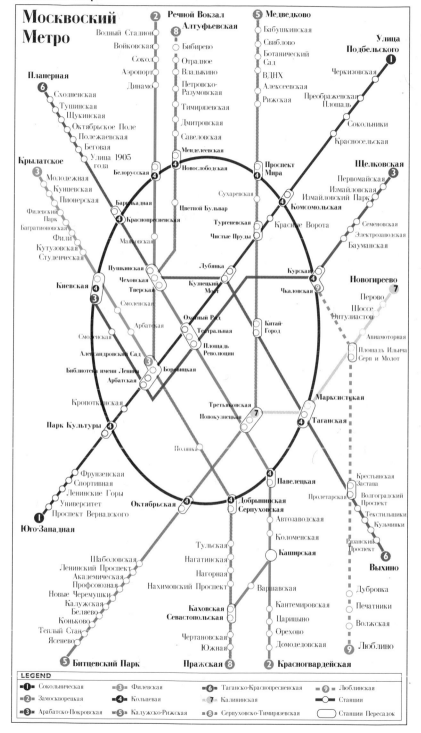

Москвоский Метро

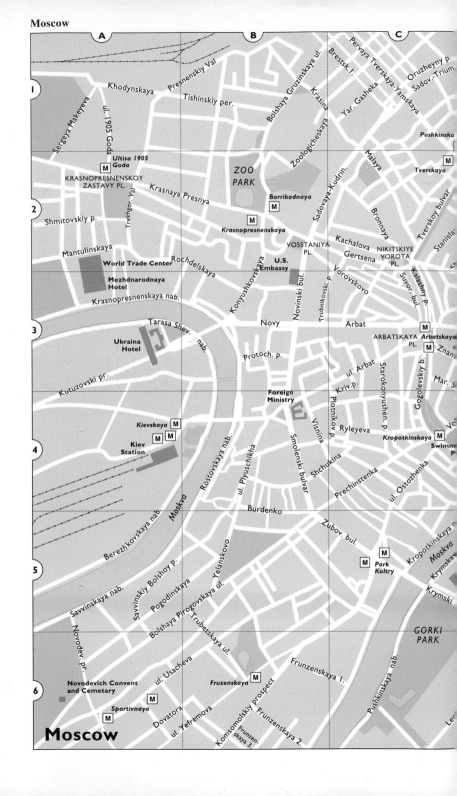

Moscow

D E F

OTECHNAYA PL.

Garden Ring

Sadovaya-Sukh.

TO LENINGRADSKI STATION

Komsomolskaya

Kazan Station

Karetny Ryad

Tsvetnoy bul.

Trubnaya

Sukharevskaya

Sadovaya-Spasskaya

Novokirovskaya

Kalanchevskaya

as. bul.

Petrovsky bul.

Tsvetnoy Bulvar

Rozh. bul.

Ulanskiy p.

Krasny Vorota

Sad Cher.

Petrovka

TRUBNAYA PL.

Sret. bul.

Myasnitskaya

khovskaya

Neglinnaya

Turgenevskaya

Chistye Prudy

Christopud. bul.

Chernyshevskovo

Zemlyanoi Val

Pushkin.

Kuznetskiy Most

B. Lubyanka

Lubyan. M.

Myasnitskaya

Krivoko p.

erskaya

Bolshoy

Lubyanka

Pokrovskiy bul.

Kurskaya

Teatralnaya Pl.

Okhotny Ryad

Maroseika

pr. Serova

Kursk Station

Belinskovo

Okhotny Ryad

Pl. Revolyutsii

Arkhipova

Podkolokiny p.

Obukha

Mokhov.

GUM

Ilyinka

STARAYA PL.

ksandrovski Sad

RED SQUARE

St. Basil's

Varvarka

Kitai-Gorod

Yauz bul.

Biblioteka im. Lenina

KREMLIN

Rossia Hotel

Ustin pr.

Serebryaniches. nab.

Bernikovsk. nab.

skaya

Kremlevskaya nab.

Moskvoretskaya nab.

Ulyanovskaya

Zemlyanoi Val

nab. Morisa Tor.

Raushkaya nab.

Serafim.

Labaznaya

Osipenko

nab. Maksima Gorkovo

Kadashevsk. nab.

Ovchinnikov nab.

Kotelnicheskaya nab.

TAGANSKAYA PL.

erseney-naby.

Ordynka Bolshaya

Taganskaya

Bolotnaya nab.

Staromonetnyy per.

Tretyakovskaya

Osipenko

Marksistskaya

Yakiman.nab.

Polyanka Bol.

Novokuznetskaya

Zemlyachki

Gonch. pr.

Taganskaya

Ostrovskovo A.N.

Novokuznetskaya

Ozerovskaya nab.

Vorontsovskaya

Polyanka

Tatarskaya

Bakhrushina

Kras. Ni.

Art Gallery Central House tists

Oktyabrskaya

Zatsep. Val

Shlyuzov. nab.

Lenin ument

Zhitnaya

Valovaya

Paveletskaya

Kozhevnicheskaya

yabrskaya

Dobryninskaya

Dobryninskaya

Serpukhovskaya

Paveletski Station

Shabolovka

Mytnaya

Lyusinovskaya

Serpukhovsk. Bol.

Dublininskaya

Krutitskaya nab.

Moscow Metro

Moscow Metro

Rechnoi Vokzal
Medvedkovo
Babushkinskaya
Vodny Stadion
Altufevskaya
Sviblovo
Ulitsa Podbelskovo
Voikovskaya
Bibirevo
Botanicheski Sad
Sokol
Otradnoye
VDNKh
Cherkizovskaya
Aeroport
Vladykino
Preobrazhenskaya Ploschad
Planernaya
Dinamo
Petrovsko-Razumovskaya
Alekseyevskaya
Skhodnenskaya
Timiryazevskaya
Rizhskaya
Sokolniki
Tushinskaya
Dmitrovskaya
Krasnoselskaya
Schukinskaya
Savelovskaya
Oktyabrskoye Pole
Mendeleyevskaya
Polezhayevskaya
Prospect Mira
Schelkovskaya
Begovaya
Ulitsa 1905 goda
Novoslobodskaya
Pervomaiskaya
Krylatskoye
Belorusskaya
Izmailovskaya
Molodezhnaya
Izmailovski Park
Kuntsevskaya
Sukharevskaya
Komsomolskaya
Pionerskaya
Barrikadnaya
Tsvetnoi Bulvar
Semenovskaya
Filevski Park
Krasnopresnenskaya
Turgenevskaya
Krasnye Vorota
Elektrozavodskaya
Bagrationovskaya
Mayakovskaya
Chistye Prudy
Baumanskaya
Fili
Kutuzovskaya
Studencheskaya
Lubyanka
Pushkinskaya
Kurskaya
Novogireyevo
Kievskaya
Chekhovskaya
Kuznetski Most
Chkalovskaya
Perovo
Tverskaya
Shosse Entuziastov
Smolenskaya
Okhotny Ryad
Kitai-Gorod
Aviamotornaya
Arbatskaya
Teatralnaya
Ploschad Ilicha
Smolenskaya
Ploschad Revolyutsii
Serpi i Molot
Aleksandrovski Sad
Biblioteka imena Lenina
Borovitskaya
Arbatskaya
Marksistskaya
Tretyakovskaya
Kropotkinskaya
Novokuznetskaya
Taganskaya
Park Kultury
Polyanka
Paveletskaya
Krestyanskaya Zastava
Frunzenskaya
Proletarskaya
Volgogradski Prospect
Sportivnaya
Dobryninskaya
Leninskiye Gory
Oktyabrskaya
Serpukhovskaya
Tekstilshiki
Universitat
Avtozavodskaya
Kuzminki
Prospekt Bernadskovo
Kolomenskaya
Pyazanski Prospect
Yugo-Zapadnaya
Tulskaya
Kashirskaya
Vykhino
Shabolovskaya
Nagatinskaya
Leninski Prospect
Nagornaya
Dubrovka
Akademicheskaya
Nakhimovski Prospect
Varshavskaya
Profsoyuznaya
Pechatniki
Novye Cheremushki
Kaluzhskaya
Kakhovskaya
Kantemirovskaya
Volzhskaya
Belyayevo
Sevastopolskaya
Tsaritsyno
Konkovo
Chertanovskaya
Orekhovo
Tyoply Stan
Yuzhnaya
Domodedovskaya
Lyublino
Yasenevo
Bitterski Park
Prazhskaya
Krasnogvardeiskaya

LEGEND

1 Sokolnicheskaya	**3** Filevskaya	**6** Tagansko-Krasnopresnenskaya	**9** Lyublinskaya
2 Zamoskvoretskaya	**4** Koltsevaya	**7** Kalininskaya	Station
3 Arbatsko-Pokrovskaya	**5** Kaluzhsko-Rizhskaya	**8** Serpukhovsko-Timiryazevskaya	Transfer station